BUSINESS LAW, LEGAL ENVIRONMENT, TRANSACTIONS, AND REGULATION

SIXTH EDITION

George D. Cameron III
Graduate School of Business Administration
The University of Michigan

Phillip J. Scaletta, Jr.
Krannert Graduate School of Management
Purdue University

2000

DAME
Thomson Learning™

Australia • Canada • Denmark • Japan • Mexico • New Zealand • Philippines
Puerto Rico • Singapore • South Africa • Spain • United Kingdom • United States

Business Law: Legal Environment, Transactions, and Regulation—Sixth Edition,
by George D. Cameron III/Phillip J. Scaletta, Jr.
Desktop Publishing: Jan Tiefel
Cover Design: Andrea P. Leggett
Cover Photos: © Corel Professional Photos. Images may have been combined and/or modified to
          produce final cover art.
Printer: R.R. Donnelley

Printed in the United States of America
1 2 3 4 5 02 01 00 99

For more information contact Thomson Learning Custom Publishing, 5101 Madison Road,
Cincinnati, Ohio, 45227, 1-800-355-9983 or find us on the Internet at
http://www.custom.thomsonlearning.com

For permission to use material from this text or product, contact us by:
• telephone: 1-800-730-2214
• fax: 1-800-730-2215
• web: http://www.thomsonrights.com

Library of Congress Cataloging-in-Publication Data: 98-74476

ISBN 0-87393-835-6

This book is printed on acid-free paper.

To Julie and Helen

Preface

CHANGE AND CONTINUITY

As the old proverb has it, "the more things change, the more they remain the same."

We continue to make changes, edition by edition, in the text's format and content. For this edition, we have restructured several chapters, particularly in Parts Six and Seven. We have added a new chapter on Intellectual Property, including some great new cases and problems (Amistad, Spa'am, O.J., and others). Reflecting business schools' increased concern for coverage of ethical and international dimensions, we have significantly re-worked Part I. Chapter 1 more explicitly highlights "Justice" as the intersection of Law and Ethics, and explains how each of the three distinguishing characteristics of Anglo-American common law contributes to the search for Justice. Our coverage of International Law now appears in Chapter 2, together with an overview of Comparative Law. The students are thus presented immediately with the basic features of our legal system, the major alternative legal systems, and the international legal rules. This enhanced coverage should provide a solid basis for further reflection on these ethical and international dimensions as the student proceeds through the various substantive law topics.

We have also added about forty new cases (some 25% of the total in the book), even though we had 100 new cases in the last edition. Again, we have tried to use 1990s cases wherever possible, to give the book a more current flavor. Some of the old favorite cases were, however, inserted as end-of-chapter problems. Two of these new cases are worthy of specific mention; both have to do with the legal status of Hong Kong and its citizens and corporation. One case appears in Chapter 2—a Hong Kong criminal prosecution for a common law crime, begun prior to the change of sovereignty. The question being raised was whether there was still a chargeable offense after the turnover. The other case (appearing in Chapter 4) arises in the context of a civil suit by a Hong Kong corporation in a U.S. District Court, with jurisdiction based on diversity of citizenship. Judge Kimba Wood's ruling (sustained on appeal) is a bit startling, to say the least. Our new cases on sexual harassment (Ellerth) and directors' responsibilities (Caremark) are also worth examining.

So we have made some significant changes in content and format. But, in line with the quote, what we have not changed is perhaps even more significant.

We have not changed our commitment to the core values of completeness, accuracy, and readability. We still believe strongly that students need to read real cases' language, not just watered-down editorial summaries. Without the courts' own words, our customers might well ask: "Where's the beef?"

There are indeed legal rules which substantially impact nearly all business functions and operations. We see our job as communicating those rules to our students, who will be the future managers of businesses and other organizations. We are dedicated to doing that in an effective—and enjoyable—way. We invite users of this new edition, both professors and students, to send us their reactions and suggestions.

2000   *George D. Cameron III*
                                                          Phillip J. Scaletta, Jr.

Brief Contents

Part One

Legal Environment

Part Two

Contract Law

Part Three

Sales of Goods

Part Four

Creditors and Debtors

Part Five

Commercial Paper

Part Six

Property

Part Seven

Business Associates

Part Eight

Government Regulation

Table of Contents

Part One

Legal Environment

5   Criminal Law and Procedure 101

6   Tort Law 123

7   Liability of Accountants and Other Professionals 151

Part Two

Contract Law

8 Contracts and Agreements 175

9 Consideration and Unconscionability 201

10 Statute of Frauds and Parol Evidence Rule 221

11 Reality of Consent 243

Part Three

Sales of Goods

Part Four

Creditors and Debtors

19 Perfection, Priorities, and Remedies 429

Part Five

Commercial Paper

20 Types of Instruments, Requirements of Negotiability 457

Part Six

Property

24 Forms of Co-Ownership; Personal Property 541

25 Intellectual Property 563

Part Seven

Business Associations

Part Eight

Government Regulation

Business Law:
Legal Environment,
Transactions, and
Regulation

Sixth Edition

Part One

Legal Environment

Part One is an introduction to the legal environment of business. It covers the definition of law, ethics and the law, civil procedure, court systems, the regulation of business by administrative agencies and the constitutional guarantees and limitations on such regulation, the international legal implications in trade outside the United States, criminal law and tort law, and professionals' legal responsibility.

These topics are all related to the general legal framework within which all of us function, in both business and private capacities. Nearly all the topics in the remaining sections of the book will focus more specifically on business relationships.

Chapter 1

Ethics and the Common Law

This chapter discusses Society's need for rules of human conduct, and the relationship between ethical "rules" and legal rules. Our main focus is on the workings of a common law system, using the U.S. legal system as our primary example. We show how the three main distinguishing features of the common law system try to promote the ethical values of Truthfulness and Fairness in human relationships. We also identify the sources of law in the United States, and define the major categories of legal rules.

SOCIETY'S RULES OF CONDUCT

Nearly all of us live and work in close proximity to others, and interact with them daily. For most of us, most of the time, these relationships are probably positive—or at least not negative enough to lead us to demand sanctions against the person guilty of the offensive conduct. Many of the problems that do arise are resolved through informal discussions, with a little good will and understanding on both sides. Rarely does a neighbor's loud playing of radios and televisions reach the level of interference at which we feel forced to go to court for a remedy—but the courts are there for those exceptional cases.

There are, in other words, informal rules (and sanctions) as well as society's formal rules and sanctions, found in its legal system. Simpler, smaller, more homogeneous societies can function quite well without many formal legal rules. Acceptable conduct is learned by observing others, especially the society's elder members. Customs for the sharing of land, water, and other resources are established through long usage. At some point, however, social relationships become so complex and diverse that customary, informal rules no longer provide the needed guidance. Nations trying to function effectively in the terribly complex world of the second millennium will surely need sophisticated legal systems, to provide rules and sanctions for today's much more complicated social relationships.

Ethics. How *should* we treat each other? What duties do we owe one another? What is the proper relationship between the citizen and the nation? What is "*Justice*"? These are the kinds of questions usually discussed under the heading of "Ethics." Philosophers have pondered over these questions since earliest historical times. Indeed, some of the best studies of these issues were done by the ancient Chinese scholar Confucius and by the early Greek writers Plato and Aristotle. In the intervening centuries, many others—Thomas Aquinas, Kant, Locke—made important contributions to the discussion. In modern times, such authors as Morris Cohen and John Rawls have continued to expand our understanding of these difficult and profound problems.

Law. When a society reaches that developmental stage in which the informal, customary rules evolve into mandatory forms of behavior, with governmental sanctions for noncompliance, it is appropriate to say that "Law" has arrived. Private revenge ("an eye for an eye") is replaced by a criminal prosecution, with the government prosecuting the offender, and often also by a private lawsuit, asking for monetary compensation for the harm caused to the victim of the offense.

In the broadest sense, the difference between "Law" and "Ethics" is the difference between "must" and "ought." Law tells us what we must do, and provides governmentally imposed sanctions if we fail to do it. Ethics tells us what we should do, but there are no sanctions for purely ethical violations—other than our own consciences, and public disapproval if our unethical conduct comes to light.

Law is a rough synonym for the noun *rule*. A law is a rule of conduct. In the physical sciences, one studies the "law of gravity" and other similar rules regarding the behavior of physical objects. We are concerned here with the rules for human and organizational conduct for which governmental sanctions are provided. As defined by the famous English jurist, William Blackstone, law is the expression of the nation's sovereign, "commanding what is right and prohibiting what is wrong." In the United States, law is promulgated by the sovereign people, acting through our selected representatives. The people as a whole, through these constitutionally chosen "agents," prescribe the rules of conduct for individuals and organizations.

Writing in the late 1800s, the great jurist Oliver Wendell Holmes, Jr., provided another famous definition of law: "The prophecies of what the courts will do in fact, and nothing more pretentious, are what I mean by the law." At the time, the courts were clearly the dominant legal institution in this country. Congress and the state legislatures were generally not inclined to interfere in individuals' private conduct or business affairs. There were very few regulatory agencies. Today, by contrast, the legal scene is much changed. Our legislatures have created hundreds of national, state, and local regulatory agencies that have the power to issue regulations, to decide disputes on matters falling under their jurisdiction, or to do both. Our legislatures continue to pass more and more laws to tax and to regulate businesses and individuals. Clearly, today, the courts are only one source of law, although they still do set the ground rules for the operation of our legal system as a whole.

Justice—The Intersection of Law and Ethics. There is, of course, considerable (but not complete) overlap between Ethics and Law. In their operations, legal systems generally try to achieve "Justice," which is itself an ethical concept. Some criminal laws prohibit actions which would be seen by most if not all people as wrongful in an ethical/moral sense—murder, rape, libel, arson. These crimes are often referred to as "malum in se," that is, wrong in and of themselves. Other criminal statutes create offenses simply because society needs to have everyone operating under the same set of assumptions, such as which side of the road is the proper place for driving one's motor vehicle. In some nations it is the right-hand side of the road; in other, the left-hand side. There is no ethical/moral superiority in either rule, but each nation must have a set of such auto operation rules, if chaos is to be avoided.

Out of the many ethical principles developed over the centuries, two—Truthfulness and Fairness—seem particularly relevant to legal relationships. Both are also principles of long standing, dating back at least to Aristotle's great work, *Nicomachean Ethics*.

Truthfulness is required in commercial transactions, and indeed in all human interactions, because we communicate with each other. We exchange information, and then act, at least in part, on the basis of that information. Lying to the other party, in the hopes of gaining a commercial advantage, would generally be defined as unethical conduct. For Aristotle, the truth-teller was "worthy of praise."

> [T]he man who loves truth, and is truthful where nothing is at stake, will be more truthful where something is at stake; he will avoid falsehood as something base, seeing that he avoided it even for its own sake; and such a man is worthy of praise.

Fairness, in the context of commercial transactions, implies an exchange of values of approximate equality. At least as of the time of the exchange, each party believes he or she is receiving value for value given. It is of course often true that our expectations are not fulfilled. Some of the things we receive turn out not to be as useful or as pleasurable as we imagined they would be. To a great extent, that is simply the nature of things. We often desire something intensely, only to be severely disappointed by the post-acquisition actuality. Fairness in the ethical sense does not imply the "complete satisfaction" which is used in so many advertisements. Fairness does mean that each party receive the thing bargained for, and that the thing have a real value. Aristotle also discussed fairness, in the context of what is just:

> Both the lawless man and the grasping and unfair man are thought to be unjust, so that evidently both the law-abiding and the fair man will be just. The just, then, is the lawful and the fair, the unjust, the unlawful and the unfair.

The idea of dealing fairly and justly with other persons is "the greatest of virtues." "It is complete [virtue] because he who possesses it can exercise his virtue not only in himself but towards his neighbor also; for many men can exercise virtue in their own affairs, but not in their relations to their neighbor."

How, then, does our modern legal system try to implement these two great ethical principles? There are three distinguishing features of an Anglo-American legal system—the separate court of equity, the doctrine of precedent, and the trial by jury. Each of the three operates to help ensure Truthfulness and Fairness in our legal system.

ANGLO-AMERICAN COMMON LAW

Equity. Appropriately enough it is also Aristotle who best explains a legal system's need for equity. Equity's flexibility is required to supplement the rigidity of the general legal rules, to provide for the exceptional case.

> Our next subject is equity and the equitable, ... and their respective relations to justice and the just....
>
> What creates the problem is that the equitable is just, but not the legally just but a correction of legal justice. The reason is that all law is universal but about some things it is not possible to make a universal statement which shall be correct. In those cases, then, in which it is necessary to speak universally, but not possible to do so correctly, the law takes the usual case, though it is not ignorant of the possibility of error.... When the law speaks universally, then, and a case arises on it which is not covered by the universal statement, then it is right, where the legislator fails us and has erred by over-simplicity, to correct the omission—to say what the legislator himself would have said had he been present, and would have put into his law if he had known.

The English legal system responded to its need for equity by developing a second set of courts, using different judges (the chancellors) to administer these supplementary principles. According to Plucknett, however, "many rules which have since become distinctive of chancery make their first appearance in the common law courts." (Plucknett, *A Concise History of the Common Law*, Fifth Edition, Boston: Little, Brown & Company, 1956; page 677.) Further, he says, "[t]here was, therefore, no fundamental inconsistency between equity and common law; the one was not alien to the other." The new Chancery Court "did not originate English Equity, for it simply carried on the work of the older courts by developing in greater fullness and with a different machinery the equity inherent in royal justice" (Plucknett, 679).

There was no logical necessity for using different courts to administer the principles of equity. Plucknett remarks on "the abandonment by the common law judges of their ancient powers of discretion." Why this happened remains somewhat unclear. Political factors—fear of giving too much power and independence to the common law judges—probably played a part. Philosophically, most common law lawyers and judges preferred the law's certainty to equity's flexibility. Plucknett notes that "the common law was essentially the law of land." Land titles and land transactions required certainty, not creativity. "The [common law] lawyers had a maxim that they would tolerate a 'mischief' (a failure of substantial justice in a particular case) rather than an 'inconvenience' (a breach of legal principle)" (Plucknett, 680).

The chancellors, acting in the king's name, developed a set of equitable remedies for situations where the normal remedies of the common law did not provide complete justice. The injunction was the equity remedy to prevent a continuing wrong. The equity court ordered the offender to cease and desist, in the king's name. Failure to comply with the court order could result in a fine and/or imprisonment. Specific performance was the remedy to require performance of a contract for land or for unique goods. Money damages, the usual common law remedy, would not provide adequate relief in such cases, since the plaintiff would still not have the thing bargained for. The chancellors also developed an assortment of other remedies to deal with special situations, including reformation, rescission, restitution, and redemption. They recognized rights created by assignments and trusts. In sum, it was the chancery courts, applying the principles of equity, which provided the rules required by a developing English society.

Many aspects of the English legal system were transplanted to the American colonies. Blackstone's *Commentaries on the Laws of England*, first published in 1765, were widely read and widely used in America. "The Commentaries had a tremendous sale there, for not only did they contain some very useful matter on public law, but also served as the principal means of the colonists' information as to the state of English law in general" (Plucknett, 287).

After independence, guarantees of the right to trial by jury were written into the national Constitution and the constitutions of most, if not all, states. The Seventh Amendment to the U.S. Constitution preserves the right to a trial by jury in civil cases at common law involving $20 or more. The key phrase "at common law" thus excludes equity cases, and freezes the law/equity distinction into the Constitution. Later, when most states and the national courts combined legal procedure with equity procedure, these constitutional provisions meant that the statutory combination could not be complete. The law/equity distinction still has to be made to determine whether the parties are entitled to a trial by jury.

England reunited Law and Equity, by statute, in 1875. Similar recombination has taken place in the U.S. courts and in most states. Judges in these "combined" courts have all the powers of the common law judges and all the powers of the equity chancellors. A few states still maintain separate equity courts, most notably Delaware, where many corporate litigations are heard by the Chancery Court.

Whether administered by a separate court or not, the function of Equity remains essentially what has been for centuries—providing special remedies to do more complete justice between the parties. In this sense, then, Equity continues to serve as "the keepers of the King's [Queen's] conscience." The "maxims" of Equity developed by the chancellors retain their force and utility: "Equity acts on the conscience;" "Equity looks to the intent rather than to the form;" "He who seeks equity must do equity." Perhaps the greatest and most basic equitable principle of all is stated as: "Equity will not suffer a wrong to be without a remedy." Even though no longer separate and independent, Equity operates within our modern legal system as a built-in guarantor of the ethical principle of Fairness.

Criminal Law	Civil Law				
	Common Law Writs (forms of action)				Equity
	Assumpsit	Trespass	Replevin	Ejectment	
	contract dollar damages	tort dollar damages	return of personal property	return of real property	
JURY	*JURY*				*NO JURY*

English Legal System
(1350—1873)

Doctrine of Precedent. The doctrine of precedent is the second distinguishing feature of an Anglo-American, or "common-law," system. The key to a common-law system is the courts' decisions in actual cases that have been litigated in the past. Current cases are decided on the basis of the rules announced in prior ones. To produce fairness and predictability, the rule used yesterday to decide the case between Jones and Smith should also be used to decide the similar case which is now before the court between Green and Harris. The working presumption of the system is summed up in the Latin phrase *stare decisis*: "Let the decision stand."

Once a particular rule has been announced for a particular kind of case, that rule should generally be followed in future cases involving the same problem, unless there are compelling reasons for changing the rule. Confronted with a new problem that demands a solution, the judges try to reason by analogy from the older rules to develop the new rule for the new situation.

The **doctrine of precedent** operates in three different ways, or at three different levels: the effect of the decisions of a higher court on lower courts within the same system, the effect of prior decisions of the same court on a current case, and the effect of prior decisions in other states or countries on a current case. Where there is a clearly applicable precedent case, a lower court in the same jurisdiction should follow the precedent and apply the rule it establishes. In practice, the rule is not quite that simple because trial judges may try to avoid the precedent if they disagree with the result it produces in the case at hand. When that happens, the trial court will, of course, be reversed on appeal, unless the higher court wishes to change its mind and reverse or modify its own precedent.

Typically, when judges, lawyers, and commentators speak of the doctrine of precedent they are referring to its second level of operation; that is, the relationship between prior decisions of the same court and the case which is to be decided now. What impact should these prior decisions in similar cases have on the case at hand? Most courts will follow their established precedent cases most of the time, particularly in the commercial law areas emphasized in this book. Societal changes since the precedent-setting decision may determine whether or not the court will follow a particular precedent. In 1954, in *Brown v. Board of Education*, the U.S. Supreme Court was unanimous in overruling the clearly incorrect precedent established in the 1896 *Plessy* case, which permitted racially-segregated public facilities. On the other hand, the Supreme Court has repeatedly refused to overrule its 1922 baseball precedent, as seen in the *Flood* case.

FLOOD v. KUHN
407 U.S. 258 (1972)

FACTS: Curtis C. Flood began his major league career in 1956 when he signed a contract with the Cincinnati Reds. He had no attorney or agent to advise him on that occasion. He was traded to the St. Louis Cardinals before the 1958 season. Flood rose to fame as a center fielder with the Cardinals during the years 1958-1969.

In October 1969, Flood was traded to the Philadelphia Phillies of the National League in a multiplayer transaction. He was not consulted about the trade. He was informed by telephone and received formal notice only after the deal had been consummated. In December, his request to the commissioner of baseball to be made a free agent was denied.

Flood then instituted an antitrust suit in U.S. District Court. The complaint charged violations of the U.S. antitrust laws and civil rights statutes, violation of state statutes and the common law, and the imposition of a form of peonage and involuntary service contrary to the 13th Amendment. Flood sought declaratory and injunctive relief and treble damages.

The District Court judge denied the request for an injunction. Trial was held in 1970. The judge held that the cases of *Federal Baseball Club v. National League*, 259 U.S. 200 (1922), and *Toolson v. New York Yankees, Inc.* 346 U.S. 356 (1953), were controlling. Judgment was entered for the defendants.

The U.S. Second Circuit Court of Appeals affirmed the District Court opinion. The case was accepted for review by the U.S. Supreme Court.

 JUSTICE BLACKMUN:

For the third time in fifty years the Court is asked specifically to rule that professional baseball's reserve system is within the reach of the federal antitrust laws. Collateral issues of state law and of federal labor policy are also advanced.

Federal Baseball Club v. National League ... was a suit for treble damages instituted by a member of the Federal League (Baltimore) against the National and American Leagues and others....

Mr. Justice Holmes, in speaking succinctly for a unanimous Court said:

> The business is giving exhibitions of baseball, which are purely state affairs.... But the fact that in order to give the exhibitions, the Leagues must induce free persons to cross state lines and must arrange and pay for their doing so is not enough to change the character of the business.... The transport is a mere incident, not the essential thing. That to which it is incident, the exhibition, although made for money would not be called a trade or commerce in the commonly accepted use of those words. As it is put by the defendant, personal effort, not related to production, is not a subject of commerce. That which in its consummation is not commerce does not become commerce among the states because the transportation that we have mentioned takes place....

In the years that followed, baseball continued to be subject to intermittent antitrust attack. The courts, however, rejected these challenges on the authority of *Federal Baseball*. In some cases, stress was laid, although unsuccessfully, on new factors such as the development of radio and television with their substantial additional revenues to baseball. For the most part, however, the Holmes opinion was generally and necessarily accepted as controlling authority....

The Court ... in the *Toolson, Kowalski*, and *Corbett* cases ... affirmed the judgments of the respective courts of appeals in those three cases.... *Federal Baseball* was cited as holding that the business of providing public baseball games for profit between clubs of professional baseball players was not within the scope of the federal antitrust laws, and:

> Congress has had the ruling under consideration but has not seen fit to bring such business under these laws by legislation having prospective effect. The business has thus been left for thirty years to develop, on the understanding that it was not subject to existing antitrust legislation. The present cases ask us to overrule the prior decision, and with retrospective

effect, hold the legislation applicable. We think that if there are evils in this field which now warrant application to it of the antitrust laws it should be by legislation. Without reexamination of the underlying issues, the judgments below are affirmed on the authority of *Federal Baseball Club of Baltimore v. National League of Professional Baseball Clubs*, supra, so far as that decision determines that Congress had no intention of including the business of baseball within the scope of the federal antitrust laws....

This series of decisions understandably spawned extensive commentary, some of it mildly critical and much of it not; nearly all of it looked to Congress for any remedy that might be deemed essential.

Legislative proposals have been numerous and persistent. Since *Toolson*, more than fifty bills have been introduced in Congress relative to the applicability or nonapplicability of the antitrust laws to baseball....

In view of all this, it seems appropriate now to say that:

1. Professional baseball is a business and it is engaged in interstate commerce.

2. With its reserve system enjoying exemption from the antitrust laws, baseball is, in a very distinct sense, an exception and an anomaly. *Federal Baseball* and *Toolson* have become an aberration confined to baseball.

3. Even though others might regard this as unrealistic, inconsistent, or illogical, see *Radovich*, ... the aberration is an established one, and one that has been recognized not only in *Federal Baseball* and *Toolson* but in *Shubert*, *International Boxing*, and *Radovich*, as well, a total of five consecutive cases in this Court. It is an aberration that has been with us now for half a century, one heretofore deemed fully entitled to the benefit of *stare decisis*, and one that has survived the Court's expanding concept of interstate commerce. It rests on a recognition and an acceptance of baseball's unique characteristics and needs.

4. Other professional sports operating interstate—football, boxing, basketball, and presumably hockey and golf—are not so exempt.

5. The advent of radio and television, with their consequent increased coverage and additional revenues, has not occasioned an overruling of *Federal Baseball* and *Toolson*.

6. The Court has emphasized that since 1922 baseball, with full and continuing congressional awareness, has been allowed to develop and to expand unhindered by federal legislative action. Remedial legislation has been introduced repeatedly in Congress, but none has ever been enacted. The Court, accordingly, has concluded that Congress as yet has had no intention to subject baseball's reserve system to the reach of the antitrust statutes. This, obviously, has been deemed to be something other than mere congressional silence and passivity....

7. The Court has expressed concern about the confusion and the retroactivity problems that inevitably would result with a judicial overturning of *Federal Baseball*. It has voiced a preference that if any change is made, it come by legislative action that, by its nature, is only prospective in operation....

This emphasis and this concern are still with us. We continue to be loathe, fifty years after *Federal Baseball* and almost two decades after *Toolson*, to overturn those cases judicially when Congress, by its positive inaction, has allowed those decisions to stand for so long and far beyond mere inference and implication, has clearly evinced a desire not to disapprove them legislatively.

> Accordingly, we adhere once again to *Federal Baseball* and *Toolson* and to their application to professional baseball. We adhere also to *International Boxing* and *Radovich* and to their respective applications to professional boxing and professional football. If there is any inconsistency or illogic in all this, it is an inconsistency and illogic of long standing that is to be remedied by the Congress and not by this Court. If we were to act otherwise, we would be withdrawing from the conclusion as to congressional intent made in *Toolson* and from the concerns as to retrospectivity therein expressed. Under these circumstances, there is merit in consistency even though some might claim that beneath that consistency is a layer of inconsistency....
>
> [W]hat the court said in *Federal Baseball* in 1922 and what is said in *Toolson* in 1953, we say again here in 1972; the remedy, if any is indicated, is for congressional, and not judicial, action.

The *Flood* decision has at long last been partially corrected by Congress. On October 27, 1998, President Clinton signed the "Curt Flood Act of 1998," which removes baseball's unique antitrust exemption as to as to employment matters. Only baseball's employment decisions are now subject to the Sherman Act, however; organized baseball's decisions as to team relocation, league expansion and the like remain exempt. After 76 years, Justice Holmes has been partially overruled.

Courts are generally more willing to reexamine points of constitutional, criminal, and tort law than they are to upset established rules in contract and commercial law where parties have based business relationships on existing rules. In many cases, a court may not want to reverse its previous decision, as in the *Brown* case, because doing so might upset many other contracts and relationships; however, the court still may not want to follow its precedent. In such cases, a court may use one of several devices to avoid the precedent. Occasionally, a court will simply ignore one of its own precedents, although this is hard to do if one of the lawyers has cited the precedent case in his or her legal brief or argument. The most common avoidance tactic is called distinguishing the precedent on the facts, meaning that the court shows how the precedent case really involved facts which were sufficiently different to justify a different decision. That process was at work in the *Radovich* case, in 1957, in which the Supreme Court "distinguished" football from baseball.

In the years since *Radovich*, the Court has continued to uphold the baseball exemption from antitrust, while at the same time subjecting other professional sports to antitrust regulation.

Another mechanism for avoiding an undesirable precedent is to distinguish the precedent on the law. The precedent is a precedent only for the rule of law that was actually necessary to the decision in the case. The judge writing the opinion of the court may have said a lot of things, but not everything in the opinion is necessarily a binding rule for future cases. These nonbinding "extra" statements in opinions are called *obiter dicta*, or just *dicta*, meaning that the court is saying things that are not actually necessary to decide the case. Perhaps the most famous example of such *dicta* is Chief Justice Marshall's 1803 opinion in *Marbury v. Madison*. None of his comments on the validity of Marbury's claim are "the Law," since the Supreme Court actually decided it could not, constitutionally, hear the case.

In the more recent *State Oil* case, the Supreme Court not only overruled an antitrust precedent, it also distinguished *Flood* and *Toolson*, the baseball precedents.

STATE OIL CO. v. KHAN
118 S.CT. 275 (1997)

FACTS: Respondents, Barkat U. Khan and his corporation, entered into an agreement with petitioner, State Oil Company, to lease and operate a gas station and convenience store owned by State Oil. The agreement provided that respondents would obtain the station's gasoline supply from State Oil at a price equal to a suggested retail price set by State Oil, less a margin of 3.25 cents per gallon. Under the agreement, respondents could charge any amount for gasoline sold to the station's customers, but if the price charged was higher than State Oil's suggested retail price, the excess was to be rebated to State Oil. Respondents could sell gasoline for less that State Oil's suggested retail price, but any such decrease would reduce their 3.25 cents-per-gallon margin.

About a year after respondents began operating the gas station, they fell behind in lease payments. State Oil then gave notice of its intent to terminate the agreement and commenced a state court proceeding to evict respondents. At State Oil's request, the state court appointed a receiver to operate the gas station. The receiver operated the station for several months without being subject to the price restraints in respondents' agreement with State Oil. According to respondents, the receiver obtained an overall profit margin in excess of 3.25 cents per gallon by lowering the price of regular-grade gasoline and raising the price of premium grades.

Respondents sued State Oil in the United Stated District Court of the Northern District of Illinois, alleging in part that State Oil had engaged in price fixing in violation of S.1 of the Sherman Act by preventing respondents from raising or lowering retail gas prices. According to the complaint, but for the agreement with State Oil, respondents could have charged different prices based on the grades of gasoline, in the same way that the receiver had, thereby achieving increased sales and profits.

The District Court found that the allegations in the complaint did not state a *per se* violation of the Sherman Act because they did not establish the sort of "manifestly anti-competitive implications or pernicious effect on competition" that would justify *per se* prohibition of State Oil's conduct. Accordingly, the District Court entered summary judgment for State Oil on respondents' Sherman Act claim.

The Court of Appeals for the Seventh Circuit reversed.

 JUSTICE O'CONNOR:

Under S.1 of the Sherman Act,... "[e]very contract, combination..., or conspiracy, in restraint of trade" is illegal. In *Albrecht v. Herald Co.*, ... this Court held that vertical maximum price fixing is a *per se* violation of that statute. In this case, we are asked to reconsider that decision in light of subsequent decisions of this Court. We conclude that *Albrecht* should be overruled....

Although the Sherman Act, by its terms, prohibits every agreement "in restraint of trade," this Court has long recognized that Congress intended to outlaw only unreasonable restraints.... As a consequence, most antitrust claims are analyzed under a "rule of reason," according to which the finder of fact must decide whether the questioned practice imposes an unreasonable restraint on competition, taking into account a variety of factors, including specific information about the relevant business, its condition before and after the restraint was imposed, and the restraint's history, nature, and effect....

Some types of restraints, however, have such predictable and pernicious anti-competitive effect, and such limited potential for procompetitive benefit, that they are deemed unlawful *per se*.... *Per se* treatment is appropriate "[o]nce experience with a particular kind of restraint enables the Court to predict with confidence that the rule of reason will condemn it." ... Thus, we have expressed reluctance to adopt *per se* rules with regard to "restraints imposed in the context of business relationships where the economic impact of certain practices is not immediately obvious."...

Albrecht ... involved a newspaper publisher who had granted exclusive territories to independent carriers subject to their adherence to a maximum price on resale of the newspapers to the public. Influenced by its decisions in *Socony-Vacuum*, *Kiefer-Stewart*, and *Schwinn*, the Court concluded that it was *per se* unlawful for the publisher to fix the maximum resale price of its newspapers.... The Court acknowledged that "[m]aximum and minimum price fixing may have different consequences in many situations," but nonetheless condemned maximum price fixing for "substituting the perhaps erroneous judgment of a seller for the forces of the competitive market." ...

Albrecht was animated in part by the fear that vertical maximum price fixing could allow suppliers to discriminate against certain dealers, restrict the services that dealers could afford to offer customers or disguise minimum price fixing schemes.... The Court rejected the notion (both on the record of that case and in the abstract) that, because the newspaper publisher "granted exclusive territories, a price ceiling was necessary to protect the public from price gouging by dealers who had monopoly power in their own territories." ...

After reconsidering *Albrecht's* rationale and the substantial criticism the decision has received, however, we conclude that there is insufficient economic justification for *per se* invalidation of vertical maximum price fixing. That is so not only because it is difficult to accept the assumptions underlying *Albrecht*, but also because *Albrecht* has little or no relevance to ongoing enforcement of the Sherman Act.... Moreover, neither the parties nor any of the *amici curiae* have called our attention to any cases in which enforcement efforts have been directed solely against the conduct encompassed by *Albrecht's per se* rule.

Respondents argue that reconsideration of *Albrecht* should require "persuasive, expert testimony establishing that the *per se* rule has distorted the market." ... Their reasoning ignores the fact the *Albrecht* itself relied solely upon hypothetical effects of vertical maximum price fixing. Further, *Albrecht's* dire predictions have not been borne out, even though manufacturers and suppliers appear to have fashioned schemes to get around the *per se* rule against vertical maximum price fixing. In these circumstances, it is the retention of the rule of *Albrecht*, and not, as respondents would have it, the rule's elimination, that lacks adequate justification....

Respondents' reliance on *Toolson v. New York Yankees, Inc.* ... and *Flood v. Kuhn* ... is similarly misplaced, because those decisions are clearly inapposite, having to do with the antitrust exemption for professional baseball, which this

Court has described as "an aberration ... rest[ing] on a recognition and an acceptance of baseball's unique characteristics and needs." ... In the context of this case, we infer little meaning from the fact that Congress has not reacted legislatively to *Albrecht*. In any event, the history of various legislative proposals regarding price fixing seems neither clearly to support nor to denounce the *per se* rule of *Albrecht*. Respondents are of course free to seek legislative protection from gasoline suppliers of the sort embodied in the Petroleum Marketing Practices Act.... For the reasons we have noted, however, the remedy for respondents' dispute with State Oil should not come in the form of a *per se* rule affecting the conduct of the entire marketplace.

Despite what Chief Judge Posner aptly described as *Albrecht's* "infirmities, [and] its increasingly wobbly, moth-eaten foundation," ... there remains the question whether Albrecht deserves continuing respect under the doctrine of *stare decisis*. The Court of Appeals was correct in applying that principle despite disagreement with *Albrecht*, for it is this Court's prerogative alone to overrule one of its precedents.

We approach the reconsideration of decisions of this Court with the utmost caution. *Stare decisis* reflects "a policy judgment that 'in most matters it is more important that the applicable rule of law be settled than that it be settled right.'" ... It "is the preferred course because it promotes the evenhanded, predictable, and consistent development of legal principles, fosters reliance on judicial decisions, and contributes to the actual and perceived integrity of the judicial process." ... This Court has expressed its reluctance to overrule decisions involving statutory interpretation, ... and has acknowledged that *stare decisis* concerns are at their acme in cases involving property and contract rights.... Both of those concerns are arguably relevant in this case.

But "*[s]tare decisis* is not an inexorable command." ... In the area of antitrust law, there is a competing interest, well-represented in this Court's decisions, in recognizing and adapting to changed circumstances and the lessons of accumulated experience. Thus, the general presumption that legislative changes should be left to Congress has less force with respect to the Sherman Act in light of the accepted view that Congress "expected the courts to give shape to the statute's broad mandate by drawing on common-law tradition." ... As we have explained, the term "restraint of trade," as used in S.1, also "invokes the common law itself, and not merely the static content that the common law had assigned to the term in 1890." ... Accordingly, this Court has reconsidered its decisions construing the Sherman Act when the theoretical underpinnings of those decisions are called into serious question....

Although the rule of *Albrecht* has been in effect for some time, the inquiry we must undertake requires considering "the effect of the antitrust laws upon vertical distributional restraints in the American economy today." ... As the Court noted in *ARCO*, ... there has not been another case since *Albrecht* in which this Court has "confronted an unadulterated vertical, maximum-price-fixing arrangement." Now that we confront *Albrecht* directly, we find its conceptual foundations gravely weakened.

"In overruling *Albrecht*, we of course do not hold that all vertical maximum price fixing is *per se* lawful. Instead, vertical maximum price fixing, like the majority of commercial arrangements subject to the antitrust laws, should be evaluated under the rule of reason. In our view, rule-of-reason analysis will effectively identify those situations in which vertical maximum price fixing amounts to anti-competitive conduct.

There remains the question whether respondents are entitled to recover damages based on State Oil's conduct. Although the Court of Appeals noted that "the district judge was right to conclude that if the rule of reason is applicable, Khan loses," ... its consideration of this case was necessarily premised on *Albrecht's per se* rule. Under the circumstance, the matter should be reviewed by the Court of Appeals in the first instance. We therefore vacate the judgment of the Court of Appeals and remand the case for further proceedings consistent with this opinion.

Finally, the doctrine of precedent operates in a third way. Suppose that the case which has to be decided today is unprecedented, that is, no decided cases in the state have ever dealt with the problem. The court can respond in two ways. One approach is simply to dismiss the complaint for failure to state a cause of action; this usually occurs where the plaintiff wants the court to recognize a new right or a new theory of liability. Where the underlying theory of liability has been recognized but there is simply no case applying it to the given situation, the courts will use precedents in a third way—by borrowing precedents from other states, or even from other countries, particularly from countries with similar legal systems. However, it is important to note that one state's decisions are not binding rules in a second state unless and until courts in the second state accept them as precedents in cases decided there.

Trial by Jury. The trial by jury is a third distinguishing feature of an Anglo-American legal system. While early Greek law used a vote of all assembled freemen to decide some trials (you may recall that Socrates was condemned to drink poisonous hemlock), and while other systems have used and do use some form of the jury, it has a very special place in the historical development and the current operation of the Anglo-American legal system.

Historically, the jury developed as an important check against the arbitrary exercise of governmental power, both in England and in the United States. Particularly in criminal cases, this function continues to be exercised by the jury today. In civil cases, the jury injects into the legal system the "conscience of the community" on such matters as the standard of care expected of an ordinary reasonable person.

In no other legal system does the jury have the power to hear such a wide range of cases. All but the most minor criminal violations are triable to a jury. Many regulatory violations are also subject to trial by jury. It is true that a litigant seeking a special equitable remedy will not have the right to a jury in most states, but that exception still leaves most ordinary civil cases subject to a trial by jury. The ordinary civil lawsuit for money damages for tort or for breach of contract is required to be tried to a jury if either litigant demands one. (Many states, however, do not use a jury in their small claims courts, where only a limited dollar recovery is permitted, usually $1,000 or less.)

Likewise, in no other system is the jury given as much discretion in arriving at its verdict, or is the verdict given the same finality, as in an Anglo-American system. If the plaintiff alleges facts which state a valid legal claim, and then at the trial introduces some minimal evidence in support of those allegations, the result in that civil case is up to the jury. The trial judge will instruct jurors as to what the law is and what their options are, and in some states may even comment on the weight of the evidence presented, but the jury will decide the outcome. There are some procedural safeguards against obviously incorrect verdicts, but in the vast majority of cases the judgment will be entered based on the verdict of the trial jury.

Judicial Review. There are, of course, differences from country to country within the Anglo-American legal family. Again, England no longer uses the distinction between law and equity. It also rarely uses the trial by jury for civil cases, in contrast to the United States. Perhaps the most significant difference, however, is that Great Britain does not recognize **judicial review**: the power of the courts to declare legislative acts unconstitutional. As in most parliamentary systems, the legislature is the final source of political power (other than the people as a whole); the courts are subordinate to the legislature.

Under the separation of powers doctrine, U.S. courts have the power to invalidate legislative as well as administrative acts found to be in conflict with the Constitution. State courts have similar power under their state constitutions. Moreover, the issue of constitutionality may be raised by any litigant in any sort of case. A debtor whose car is repossessed because monthly payments were not being made may ask a state or national court to declare that the repossession procedure provided by state law violates the due process clause of the U.S. Constitution, for example. While a few countries have so-called constitutional courts, their jurisdiction can be invoked only in a special, limited procedure. Judicial review as it is practiced in the United States is still a unique institution.

The *J.E.B.* case reviews a state's system for selecting jurors.

J.E.B. v. ALABAMA EX REL. T.B.
114 S.Ct. 1419 (U.S., 1994)

FACTS: On behalf of T.B., the mother of a minor child, the State of Alabama filed a complaint for paternity and child support against petitioner J.E.B. in the District Court of Jackson County, Alabama. On October 21, 1991, the matter was called for trial and jury selection began. The trial court assembled a panel of thirty-six potential jurors, twelve males and twenty-four females. After the court excused three jurors for cause, only ten of the remaining thirty-three jurors were male. The State then used nine of its ten peremptory strikes to remove male jurors; petitioner used all but one of his strikes to remove female jurors. The selected twelve jurors were all female.

Before the jury was empaneled, petitioner objected to the State's peremptory challenges on the ground that they were exercised against male jurors solely on the basis of gender, in violation of the Equal Protection Clause of the Fourteenth Amendment. Petitioner argued that the logic and reasoning of *Batson v. Kentucky*, which prohibits peremptory strikes solely on the basis of race, similarly forbids intentional discrimination on the basis of gender. The court rejected petitioner's claim and empaneled the all-female jury. The jury found petitioner to be the father of the child and the court entered an order directing him to pay child support. On post-judgment motion, the court reaffirmed its ruling that *Batson* does not extend to gender-based peremptory challenges. The Alabama Court of Civil Appeals affirmed.

The Supreme Court of Alabama denied certiorari. The U.S. Supreme Court then heard the case on certiorari.

 JUSTICE BLACKMUN:

Discrimination on the basis of gender in the exercise of peremptory challenges is a relatively recent phenomenon. Gender-based peremptory strikes were hardly practicable for most of our country's existence, since, until the 19th century, women were completely excluded from jury service. So well-entrenched was this exclusion of women that in 1880 this Court, while finding that the exclusion of African American men from juries violated the Fourteenth Amendment, expressed no doubt that a State "may confine the selection [of jurors] to males...."

Many states continued to exclude women from jury service well into the present century, despite the fact that women attained suffrage upon ratification of the Nineteenth Amendment in 1920. States that did permit women to serve on juries often erected other barriers, such as registration requirements and automatic exemptions, designed to deter women from exercising their right to jury service....

The prohibition of women on juries was derived from the English common law which, according to Blackstone, rightfully excluded women from juries under the doctrine of *propter defectum sexus*, literally, the "defect of sex" ... in this country, supporters of the exclusion of women from juries tended to couch their objections in terms of the ostensible need to protect women from the ugliness and depravity of trials. Women were thought to be too fragile and virginal to withstand the polluted courtroom atmosphere.... "Criminal court trials often involve testimony of the foulest kind, and they sometimes require consideration of indecent conduct, the use of filthy and loathsome words, references to intimate sex relationships, and other elements that would prove humiliating, embarrassing, and degrading to a lady.... The civil law, as well as nature herself, has always recognized a wide difference in the respective spheres and destinies of man and woman. Man is, or should be, woman's protector and defender. The natural and proper timidity and delicacy which belongs to the female sex evidently unfits it for many of the occupations of civil life.... The paramount destiny and mission of woman are to fulfill the noble and benign offices of wife and mother. This is the law of the creator...."

[T]he only question is whether discrimination on the basis of gender in jury selection substantially furthers the State's legitimate interest in achieving a fair and impartial trial. In making this assessment, we do not weigh the value of peremptory challenges as an institution against our asserted commitment to eradicate invidious discrimination from the courtroom. Instead, we consider whether peremptory challenges based on gender stereotypes provide substantial aid to a litigant's effort to secure a fair and impartial jury....

Discrimination in jury selection, whether based on race or on gender, causes harm to the litigants, the community, and the individual jurors who are wrongfully excluded from participation in the judicial process. The litigants are harmed by the risk that the prejudice which motivated the discriminatory selection of the jury will infect the entire proceedings.... The community is harmed by the State's participation in the perpetuation of invidious group stereotypes and the inevitable loss of confidence in our judicial system that state-sanctioned discrimination in the court room engenders.

When state actors exercise peremptory challenges in reliance on gender stereo-types, they ratify and reinforce prejudicial views of the relative abilities of men and women. Because these stereotypes have wreaked injustice in so many other spheres of our country's public life, active discrimination by litigants on the basis of gender during jury selection "invites cynicism respecting the jury's neutrality and its obligation to adhere to the law...." The potential for cynicism is particularly acute in cases where gender-related issues are prominent, such as cases involving rape, sexual harassment, or paternity. Discriminatory use of peremptory challenges may create the impression that the judicial system has acquiesced in suppressing full participation by one gender or that the "deck has been stacked" in favor of one side....

Our conclusion that litigants may not strike potential jurors solely on the basis of gender does not imply the elimination of all peremptory challenges. Neither does it conflict with a State's legitimate interest in using such challenges in its effort to secure a fair and impartial jury. Parties still may remove jurors whom they feel might be less acceptable than others on the panel; gender simply may not serve as a proxy for bias. Parties may also exercise their peremptory challenges to remove from the venire any group or class of individuals normally subject to "rational basis" review.... Even strikes based on characteristics that are disportionately associated with one gender could be appropriate, absent a showing of pretext.

If conducted properly, *voir dire* can inform litigants about potential jurors, making reliance upon stereotypical and pejorative notions about a particular gender or race both unnecessary and unwise. *Voir dire* provides a means of discovering actual or implied bias and a firmer basis upon which the parties may exercise their peremptory challenges intelligently....

The experience in the many jurisdictions that have barred gender-based chal-lenges belies the claim that litigants and trial courts are incapable of complying with a rule barring strikes based on gender.... As with race-based *Batson* claims, a party alleging gender discrimination must make a prima facie showing of intentional dis-crimination before the party exercising the challenge is required to explain the basis for the strike.... When an explanation is required, it need not rise to the level of a "for cause" challenge; rather, it merely must be based on a juror characteristic other than gender, and the proffered explanation may not be pretextual....

Failing to provide jurors the same protection against gender discrimination as race discrimination could frustrate the purpose of *Batson* itself. Because gender and race are overlapping categories, gender can be used as a pretext for racial dis-crimination. Allowing parties to remove racial minorities from the jury not because of their race, but because of their gender, contravenes well-established equal pro-tection principles and could insulate effectively racial discrimination from judicial scrutiny.

Equal opportunity to participate in the fair administration of justice is fundamen-tal to our democratic system. It not only furthers the goals of the jury system. It reaffirms the promise of equality under the law—that all citizens, regardless of race, ethnicity, or gender, have the chance to take part directly in our democracy.... When persons are excluded from participation in our democratic processes solely because of race or gender, this promise of equality dims, and the integrity of our judicial system is jeopardized.

In view of these concerns, the Equal Protection Clause prohibits discrimination in jury selection on the basis of gender, or on the assumption that an individual will be biased in a particular case for no reason other than the fact that the person happens to be a woman or happens to be a man. As with race, the "core guarantee of equal protection, ensuring citizens that their State will not discriminate, ... would be meaningless were we to approve the exclusion of jurors on the basis of such assumptions, which arise solely from the jurors' [gender]."

CLASSIFICATIONS OF LAW

Public versus Private Law. Most legal systems recognize two broad categories of legal rules: public law and private law. Private law is concerned with the legal relationships between individuals. The role of the government is limited to setting and enforcing the ground rules of the game; the decision on whether to "play" or not, with whom, about what, and on what terms, is left to the individuals and organizations involved. For example, no one (as yet) orders you to buy a new TV: if you think you might want one, you decide on the make and model and then negotiate with one or more retailers to try to get the best price and terms. The role of the government in this private law transaction is limited to specifying the requirements for an enforceable contract and the remedies available in the event of a breach by one of the parties.

Public law areas, by contrast, involve the government acting in its sovereign capacity in some way—either as a contending party, or by forcing action or inaction, or by specifying the terms of a relationship. Criminal law, constitutional law, and administrative law are major public law areas. **Criminal law** involves the government as the prosecutor, claiming that a wrong has been done against society as a whole. **Constitutional law** provides the basic framework for the functioning of the government, as well as guarantees of rights and prohibitions against certain government actions. **Administrative law** covers all the areas of governmental regulation through administrative agencies. In the field of labor law, for example, the National Labor Relations Board (NLRB) polices union-management relations and the Equal Employment Opportunity Commission (EEOC) tries to prevent discrimination in employment. Although commercial law was (and perhaps still is) primarily a private law topic, there are now many important public law aspects in this field. We will examine most of these, as well as the more traditional public law areas such as labor law, antitrust law, and securities law. These public law rules are sometimes called the "legal environment" of business.

Criminal Law and Civil Law. Criminal law encompasses national and state statutes that make the commission or omission of certain acts punishable by fine or imprisonment. In criminal cases, the state or national government prosecutes the person who disobeyed the criminal law.

For example, Harry Horrible mugged a woman, took her pocketbook, and ran. The police arrested him and he was prosecuted for assault and battery and theft, found guilty, and sentenced to jail. The woman lost her purse and several dollars, missed several days of work at her job, and still has unpaid doctor and hospital bills because of her injuries. The criminal law does not give her the right to have her bills paid, to be compensated for her pain and suffering, or to be reimbursed for the cost of a new purse. Criminal law only attempts to fine or imprison the wrongdoer. The wrong being punished is a wrong against society.

Civil law provides for compensation for personal injury, loss of property, and breach of contract. This is the body of statutory and case law that sets out the rights and duties between individuals in society. For example, in the previous situation, the state may put Harry Horrible in jail under criminal law, but who is going to pay the bills and reimburse the victim for her loss? Under civil law, more specifically tort law, the woman could sue Harry Horrible for monetary damages. This would be a separate lawsuit.

Substantive and Procedural Law. Law is also classified as substantive law and procedural law. **Substantive law** defines the rights and duties of individuals and institutions in their mutual relationships. In a jury trial, for example, after the jurors have heard the evidence, the judge instructs them on "the law." The judge is giving them the substantive law of the case. In the same trial, **procedural law** governs the admission of evidence, the sequence of the lawsuit, and possible appeal. Procedural law can be defined as the law that governs the enforcement of substantive law. It is essentially concerned with the rules of the game, not necessarily the outcome. Procedural law will be discussed further in Chapter 4 when we review the court system and its procedure.

National Law and State Law. A final generalized distinction needs to be made—between national law and state law. As we will discuss in more detail in Chapter 3, ours is a federal system of government, meaning that we have both a national government and the several state governments. Both levels of government have law-making powers. Most of the topics which we cover in this book are private-law topics, within the states' jurisdiction. There are, however, many significant national regulations which impact on business operations (and our personal activities). In addition, it is the national Supreme Court that is the final "umpire" within the system, at least until a constitutional amendment is passed which changes the Supreme Court's interpretation of the Constitution.

SOURCES OF U.S. LAW

It is often said that the source of American law is English law. True, the early settlers of our country were primarily of English origin, and their legal traditions influenced the American legal system. Our legal system is not entirely independent of its English counterpart. However, the framers of the U.S. Constitution had lived under the English legal system and had fought and won a revolution to free themselves of some of its features. Thus, the U.S. legal system differs from the English legal system in many ways.

Constitution of the United States. The Constitution of the United States is the "supreme law of the land." This means no statute enacted by the U.S. Congress or a state legislative body, no decision of any court, and no state constitution can be contrary to the U.S. Constitution. Any enactment or decision found to be contrary to the Constitution will be declared null and void by the courts.

The Constitution provides for additional sources of law in Articles I, II, and III. Article I establishes Congress as the legislative branch of government and specifies congressional powers and the limitations on those powers. Article II establishes the office of the President and the executive branch of government and defines the scope of the executive's power. Article III provides that the judicial power of the United States shall be vested in one supreme court and such other courts as the Congress may establish.

Thus, these three articles of the Constitution established the three branches of our national government—the legislative branch to create law, the executive branch to administer and enforce the law, and the judicial branch to interpret the law and to act as guardian of the Constitution.

Treaties. Article II, Section 2, of the Constitution, also gave the President the power to make treaties; however, all treaties must be made with the advice and consent of the Senate of the United States. This source of law is increasingly important in our relationships with foreign nations, as treaties affect both military matters and our trade relationships with the other nations of the world. With today's satellite communication and computer networks interwoven across the globe, we need new international legal agreement on rules for conducting international business. Treaty power is an important way to meet those needs.

The treaty power of the United States is a source of law not only for international affairs but also for internal affairs. A treaty, once approved by the Senate, has the same force and effect as laws enacted by the U.S. Congress. Thus, a treaty concerning U.S. internal affairs is superior to any state law or any state constitution.

The *Stovall* case shows how courts apply treaties to disputes arising in the United States between U.S. parties.

STOVALL v. NORTHWEST AIRLINES, INC.
595 N.E.2d 330 (MA App.Ct., 1992)

FACTS: This appeal concerns the scope of an international air carrier's liability under Art. 17 of the Warsaw Convention, as amended by the Montreal Agreement, which provides that an airline is strictly liable in an amount up to $75,000 for injuries sustained by a passenger on an international flight during "the operations of embarking or disembarking." The defendant, Northwest Airlines, Inc. (Northwest), filed a motion for summary judgment claiming that, for purposes of the Warsaw Convention, neither the plaintiff, Dawn J. Stovall, nor her mother, Esther A. Shaleen, was in flight or in the course of embarking or disembarking when their accident occurred. The trial judge denied Northwest's motion and ordered summary judgment in favor of the plaintiff.

The material facts are undisputed. In the spring of 1983, Stovall and Shaleen purchased roundtrip coach tickets for Northwest flights between Minneapolis and London. Although the tickets provided for round trip transportation between Minneapolis and London, the flight in each direction was scheduled to stop in Boston with a change of airplanes. On November 9, 1983, Stovall and Shaleen began their return flight. The airplane landed at Logan Airport in Boston, and passengers were processed through immigration and customs in the international terminal. When Stovall and Shaleen completed that process, their baggage was taken by Northwest personnel, and they were given vouchers for a public Massachusetts Port Authority bus which was to take them to the domestic air terminal where they were to board a different plane to continue their flight. The bus, to which Northwest personnel escorted Stovall and Shaleen, was crowded. Although they believed they were required to take the bus to continue their trip, nothing was said or done to prevent them from making alternative arrangements for reaching the domestic terminal. As the bus rounded a curve, the rear doors opened, and Stovall and Shaleen fell from the stairway where they were standing. Stovall was injured, and her mother, Shaleen, was killed.

 JUSTICE FINE:

Neither the text of the convention, nor its history, clearly defines the scope of liability for accidents in and around an airport terminal.

Some courts, looking only to the passenger's location at the time of the accident, have defined the scope of liability narrowly. Thus, a passenger who fell in the baggage area of an airport was deemed to have disembarked from "the time [he] ha[d] descended from the plane by the use of whatever mechanical means ha[d] been supplied and ha[d] reached a safe point inside of the terminal, even though he may [have] remain[ed] in the status of a passenger of the carrier while inside the building...." With the advent of airport terrorism, a growing risk of air travel, courts have been called upon to extend the protection of the treaty to passengers within airport terminals.... [C]ourts have held that coverage would depend upon the particular facts analyzed on the basis of a number of factors: (1) the activity in which the passenger was engaged at the time of the accident, (2) the degree of control the airline had over the passenger at the time, (3) the physical proximity of the passenger to the aircraft, and (4) the closeness of the time of the accident to the passenger's entering or leaving the airplane....

Even under the more expansive ... test, which is now routinely applied whether the issue raised relates to embarkation or debarkation, the plaintiff in this case may not prevail. The accident occurred while the two women were engaged in the activity of traveling on a public bus from one terminal to another. True, they were required to travel between terminals to continue their flight, but the activity in which they were engaged presented none of the dangers generally associated with air travel with which the Warsaw Convention was concerned.... Airline personnel exerted some restrictions and control over Stovall and Shaleen's activities by providing them with vouchers and escorting them to the Massachusetts Port Authority bus. The airline did not tell them they were required to take that particular bus, however, and they were free to proceed by any means of transportation to the domestic terminal.... If any agency was directly in control of the two women at the time of the accident, it was the Massachusetts Port Authority, operating the bus, rather than Northwest. With regard to the relative proximity of the accident scene to the aircraft, the accident occurred a considerable distance from the airplane, the tarmac, or even the type of secure passenger waiting area on occasion found to be covered.... Finally, with regard to the time factor, more than an hour had elapsed since the flight from London had landed and the Minneapolis flight was not scheduled to depart for yet another two and a one-half hours....

The plaintiff emphasizes the facts, different in some respects from those in the numerous cases cited by Northwest in which no liability was found, that at the time of the accident Stovall and Shaleen remained passengers on the Northwest flight from London to Minneapolis, they were in possession of their boarding cards, their baggage was in custody of the airline, and Northwest had made arrangements for their transportation between terminals. The plaintiff contends, therefore, that the women were on one continuous journey to their final destination. The entire duration of a stop-over in the course of such a journey, however, is not necessarily included within "the operations of embarking or disembarking" as that phrase is used in the Warsaw Convention.... Where an accident occurs, as this one did, outside any airport terminal building while the passengers are on a public bus, substantially removed both in time and space from their flight, we think the uniform result in courts throughout this country would be that the accident is not covered by the Warsaw Convention. The risk that materialized was not a risk of aviation.

Statutes. Congress creates new law and changes prior law by passing legislation, often referred to as "Acts of Congress." Each House of Congress must pass the same bill, and the President must sign it, before it becomes a law. If the President refuses to sign a bill, Congress can override the veto by re-passing the bill by a two-thirds vote in each House.

Administrative Agencies. Another large body of law is created by the various regulations and pronouncements of administrative agencies, both national and state. On the national level we have agencies such as the National Labor Relations Board (NLRB), the Federal Trade Commission (FTC), and the Equal Employment Opportunity Commission (EEOC). On the state level, we have agencies such as the Public Utilities Commission (PUC), the Workers' Compensation Board, and various consumer commissions.

Administrative agencies are created by national or state legislatures, which delegate specific tasks and functions to the agency. The legislature may later limit the agency's authority or dispose of the agency entirely. We will discuss constitutional law and administrative agencies in more detail in Chapter 3.

State Legal Systems. The Tenth Amendment to the Constitution provides that the powers not delegated to the United States by the Constitution or prohibited by it to the states are reserved to the states, respectively, or to the people. This amendment is often called the states' rights amendment. It allows the states to govern themselves in all areas where the Constitution does not specify national regulation.

Each state thus has its own constitution, and its own governor, legislature, and courts. State court systems will be discussed in Chapter 4.

Uniform Laws and Restatements. Since much business is done across state lines, there is a need to minimize conflicts among state laws. The National Conference of Commissioners on Uniform State Laws was created in 1891. Representatives from each of the states, the District of Columbia, and Puerto Rico gathered to promote uniformity in state laws. The conferees reviewed the various state laws and judicial decisions and, in cooperation with the American Law Institute, drafted model statutes governing various areas. They then suggested that the states adopt these new model laws and repeal their previous laws. The ultimate goal was uniform state business laws throughout the country. The most notable accomplishment of the Commissioners is the Uniform Commercial Code, which has been adopted in forty-nine states. Louisiana is the only state that has not adopted the entire Uniform Commercial Code. Other uniform laws deal with such topics as partnerships and decedents' estates.

The task of systematizing case law has been undertaken by a private agency, the American Law Institute. The ALI is a group of law professors and practitioners. It has published treatises called Restatements of the Law covering many business related areas, such as torts, property, trusts, and agency. The American Law Institute's writers have attempted to review the vast volume of case law and to set out in organized, encyclopedia-like form the generally accepted rules of law on specific topics. These Restatements are not like the statutes of a state. They are only for reference and are periodically revised and updated. They serve a very useful purpose by allowing lawyers and judges to quickly see what the generally accepted rule of law is on a specific legal point. Judges often adopt the rules set out in the Restatements, thus making those rules part of the actual law.

SIGNIFICANCE OF THIS CHAPTER

Before beginning to study and learn specific rules of law, a student must first establish a general foundation upon which to build further blocks of knowledge. In establishing such a foundation, it is necessary for the student to be able to define law, to understand the need for law in our society, to know the sources of our law, and to have a general understanding of how our legal system operates.

PROBLEMS FOR DISCUSSION

1. Alumsports, Inc., a manufacturer of baseball bats, sued Batoff Company for alleged patent infringement. Alumsports said that it had the patent on a certain design for aluminum baseball bats and that Batoff was making the same product. Batoff argues that the patent is invalid since baseball is not commerce and Congress lacks the power to regulate it. Thus the congressionally established patent system cannot be applied to baseball equipment.
    What result, and why?

2. Uysserv advertised and sold "Trust Forms," which he claimed would eliminate the user's personal income tax liability by transferring all income to the "trust" and deducting all personal living expenses as "trust operations." The State Attorney General brought a court action to enjoin Uysserv from further sales, to force him to repay all money collected from sales to his customers, and to assess him a fine and attorney fees (for the State's attorneys). The statute authorizing such lawsuits on behalf of consumers did not provide for a jury trial. Uysserv demanded a jury trial but did not get one. The trial court judge found him guilty of "deceptive consumer practices," and gave the State all the remedies it requested. Uysserv appeals, alleging that the statute is unconstitutional, since it deprives him of his constitutional right to a trial by jury.
    How should the appeals court rule? Explain.

3. Bropp was convicted of possession of burglar tools after police had stopped his car, searched it without a warrant, and found the burglar tools. He was convicted in 1990. At that time, a state could permit the use of improperly seized evidence in a criminal trial if it wished to do so. In 1991, the U.S. Supreme Court reversed its earlier precedent case, and held that a state could not use any illegally seized evidence in a criminal trial. Bropp now appeals his conviction, on the basis of the new ruling by the U.S. Supreme Court.

    How should the state appeals court rule? Explain.

4. Harold owns and operates a traveling dog and pony show. He gives exhibitions in several states. The U.S. Secretary of Agriculture attempted to impose regulations on Harold as to the care and feeding of his animals, pursuant to authority granted under the Animal Welfare Act. Harold says that his exhibitions are not interstate commerce and that he is, therefore, not subject to congressional regulation under the authority of the Federal Baseball case.

    How should the court rule, and why? Would there be a different result if Harold had a permanent location and gave exhibitions only in that one place?

5. The Crow Indian Tribe is established on a large reservation in the State of Montana. Valuable coal deposits underlie a large part of the reservation. In 1975, the tribe leased coal mining rights to Moreland Resources, which quickly began operations. In 1985, Montana enacted a coal mining tax, imposed at the rate of 30 percent of market value, on all coal producers in the state. Between 1985 and 1998, Moreland paid over $60,000,000 in coal taxes to Montana. In 1998, the Crow Indian Tribe enacted its own coal tax of 25 percent. Moreland doesn't want to pay both coal taxes.

    What arguments can it make in a lawsuit?

6. Richard Alan Rothchild became engaged to be married to Carol Sue Cohen. Both were over 21 years of age. Richard gave Carol a diamond "engagement" ring which was valued at $1,000. Shortly before the wedding date, Richard was killed in an automobile accident, and his estate sued to recover the ring.

    The state has no statute or court decision that provides a rule for this sort of case. The court must decide this case, since one way or another, someone will end up with the ring.

    How should the trial court judge proceed in making his or her decision? Explain.

Chapter 2
Comparative Law
and
International Law

Today most large U.S. corporations and many smaller U.S. firms are engaged in international trade. Nearly all of our businesses and workers are subject to foreign competition, and to the effects of international financial and economic operations. Many of our large companies derive over half of their income from overseas operations; in that sense, they are truly "multinationals." Nearly all of our largest corporations fall into this category.

Thus, the international stakes are very high. While our economy is not yet as dependent on foreign trade as many others, we are not immune from international economic trends. The global economy is not fully integrated, but there are substantial connections—enough so that serious problems in one nation do tend to spread to others. If nothing else, a particular nation's economic problems will surely impact U.S. companies' operations in that nation. Doing business in other nations therefore requires an understanding of those nations' economic, political, *and legal* systems. Since the doing of business *by definition* involves the establishing of legal relations, international managers simply must be aware of the possibility that different legal rules will apply to their international transactions.

Added legal complications arise in different ways when business is transacted across national borders. Nearly always, questions may be raised about which nation's law applies to the cross-border transaction. These "conflict-of-laws" problems are similar to those that arise within the U.S. in many interstate transactions, but in the international context are much more complex, due to the much greater differences between the legal systems involved. We thus begin this chapter with a brief overview of the major types of national legal systems, and compare them to our own Common Law System.

There is also a separate body of International Law that may be applicable to particular commercial transactions. There is now a treaty that provides many of the legal rules for international sales of goods, for example. International Law rules are also very important in commercial dealings with other governments as buyers of goods and services, and in protecting investors in other nations. International Law also plays a role in sorting out where lawsuits can occur, and which nation's law applies to international disputes.

Most recently, regional groupings of nations, most especially the European Community, have created supranational legal institutions. There are EC courts and administrative agencies that have the power to create and to administer binding legal rules for the nations who are EC members, and for businesses operating within the EC. Since the EC is the world's largest trading unit, these rules are very important to all the world's businesses.

COMPARATIVE LAW

There are several other types of legal systems existing today, in addition to the Common Law System used by the U.S., the U.K., Canada, Australia, New Zealand, and other nations. Of course, even within this Common Law "family," there are differences from nation to nation. Most countries in this group do not permit their courts to declare acts of the national legislature "unconstitutional," as the U.S. does. Some have unified, written constitutional documents; others do not. In some, jury trials are generally available, even in ordinary civil cases; other nations use the trial jury much more sparingly. All, however, recognize the doctrine of precedent, as discussed in Chapter 1. "The Law" is in the cases: prior judicial decisions are the sources of rules that are used to decide present cases. There is no comprehensive legislatively-produced "Code;" statutes tend rather to be specific solutions for specific problems. It is the reliance on case law which primarily distinguishes the common law nations from those using the various other types of systems.

Civil-Law Systems. The major alternative system that developed under Western civilization is called the civil-law system, or the code-law system. There is some ambiguity in either term. All legal systems hear and decide civil-law cases, in the sense of disputes between individuals, and many countries refer to their statutes dealing with particular topics as "codes." A civil-law or code-law system, however, is one in which the body of the legal rules is contained in one or a few comprehensive legislative enactments. All the law is brought together at one time in a systematized statement of the applicable legal rules. In France, for example, the process occurred in the early 1800s, under Napoleon's reign. National legal codes for the whole of France were adopted, covering civil law, civil procedure, criminal law, criminal procedure, and commercial law. The civil code is still the basic law in France today; the same rules would be applied to work out much the same results in ordinary cases of tort and contract.

Court cases in such a system are not considered to be an authoritative source of the legal rules, as they are in an Anglo-American system. The fact that a particular court interpreted a particular provision of the civil code in a particular way does not mean that future courts are bound to interpret that provision in the same way. They may or may not do so. The law is in the code, not in the cases. Where several cases all have interpreted a provision in a particular way, the French courts may feel bound to reach the same result in future cases, under the doctrine of *jurisprudence constante*. The major agency for growth and change, however, is the legislature, not the courts.

Civil-law systems are used by most of the countries of Europe, and Central and South America. Many of the countries of Asia and Africa adopted civil and commercial codes patterned on those of Europe to facilitate business transactions and commercial development. Many countries which were colonies have residues of the codes that were imposed on them during their colonial period.

Roman-Dutch Systems. As the result of another historical combination of circumstances, a very few countries today operate under what is called a Roman-Dutch System. These are former Dutch colonies, which were under Dutch rule at a time when the Netherlands had not yet adopted its modern civil code. (It did so in 1823.) The Dutch system at the time was based on the Roman law, as explained and developed by Dutch commentators. Several centuries of Roman legal developments had been summarized and systematized under the Emperor Justinian in the *Corpus Juris Civilis*, published from 529 to 534 A.D. The Dutch scholars then wrote comments explaining how the various Roman law rules applied in their country. Under this system, the "law-giver" is the professor, not the judge and not the legislator. The judges should be guided by the authoritative textbook statements as to what the law is and how it is to be applied. The legislature, of course, has the power to change the law by enacting statutes, but until it does so, the law is in the textbooks.

This rather strange system exists, at least in residual form, in the former Dutch colonies of South Africa and Sri Lanka (Ceylon) and, perhaps, in Guyana.

Communist (Soviet) Legal Systems. While Communist theory initially emphasized a future society in which there would be no need for law and the other organs of state power, the reality of governing a large and diverse empire forced some rather dramatic doctrinal and operational changes. Prior to the Bolshevik Revolution in 1917, Russia had been slowly developing as a civil-law system. Tsarist Russia was an autocracy of the most extreme sort for most of its history, but some substantial progress toward the development of an independent Bench and Bar had been made with the reforms of 1861 and 1864. Presumably, further progress along these lines would have been made under the non-Bolshevik revolutionaries.

During most of its history, the Bolshevik regime had wavered between the ideological purity expressed in the idea that the law would "wither away" after the Revolution, and the practical necessities involved in ruling the Soviet Union. Stalin decided in the 1930s that he needed a stronger state apparatus, rather than a "withered" one, and the concept of "socialist legality" was emphasized. Communist law was to be developed as law of a "new type," not based on the exploitation of one class by another, as were all "bourgeois" legal systems. This new legal system was to function in the interim period between the Revolution and the achievement of the stage of full Communism. Officially, the law was still supposed to "wither away" at some future date, but the time frame became rather indefinite. The practicalities of governance prevailed over ideological purity.

How, then, does Communist law differ from other systems? First, of course, its theoretical underpinnings are quite different. Justice is a bourgeois abstraction. Soviet judges should be guided instead by their revolutionary legal consciousness. Second, all governmental agencies and institutions are really sources of legal rules; the decree or order of a lower level agency stands as the rule to be obeyed, unless and until it is superseded by a rule from a higher authority. Third, and perhaps most significant, the government and the party are above the law, rather than the other way around. One would find it hard to imagine, for instance, that any Soviet court could have ordered Gorbachev to produce documents that he wished to keep secret, as happened to President Nixon. Fourth, as a corollary, the Bench and Bar in the USSR were not fully independent of governmental and political control. While Soviet lawyers had some considerable latitude in handling ordinary contract, tort, and property cases, they could not function as the fearless champions of civil rights. As a result, there is a fifth dissimilarity from Western systems: civil rights were granted or withheld by a Soviet-style regime to suit its own political and economic purposes; they may be exercised or..y in accordance with the wishes of the regime.

The Soviet-type system does have codes that have been adopted by the legislative bodies (although they may not be organized in quite so comprehensive a fashion as those in most civil-law countries). It does have courts, judges, and lawyers. In recent years, the regime had seemed to give the legal experts more freedom to operate. None of these surface similarities, however, should be allowed to obscure the fundamental differences that remained. The USSR itself, of course, no longer exists. Remnants of this system survive in China, North Korea, Viet Nam, and Cuba.

Religious and Customary Systems.

For hundreds of millions of people, a religious or customary legal system provides the rules for their personal rights and behavior. Such topics as parent-child and husband-wife relationships, inheritance and other property rights, charitable transfers, and an individual's relationship with a religious organization are likely to be covered under these systems. A religious or customary system typically does not cover the legal topics involved in modern commerce and industry—business organizations, commercial contracts, patents and copyrights, and the like.

Customary tribal law still governs the personal lives of many Africans. In the Moslem countries of North Africa, the Middle East, and the rest of Asia, the Koran provides an authoritative source of legal rules for the topics which it covers. In India, Hindu law applies to the vast majority of the population. Jewish law contains provisions for marriage, divorce, and charitable giving which many of that faith feel are binding legal rules. Tribal law is still applied in many cases involving the personal or property rights of American Indians.

In the following case, the defendant is attempting to introduce Jewish law rather than the law of the state of Michigan as the controlling law concerning the transaction between the parties.

CONGREGATION B'NAI SHOLOM v. MARTIN
173 N.W.2d 504 (MI, 1969)

FACTS: In January 1959, defendant Morris Martin became chairman of the Synagogue Building Committee. On April 22, 1959, plaintiff contracted Ira J. Miller, a professional fund raiser, to assist in raising funds to build a new synagogue. On or about June 1, 1959, Morris Martin delivered to plaintiff's campaign office four pledge cards. The first three were signed, respectively, by Irving Martin, Jack Martin, and Morris Martin. The fourth was signed by Morris Martin in the name of Bessie Martin Steinberg. The four pledge cards were not filled out as to amount. Morris Martin wrote the words, "Total Donation $25,000.00" on an attached scrap of paper. Later in the year 1959, disputes arose between Morris Martin, Chairman of the

Synagogue Building Committee, and other members of the Congregation. On October 29, 1959, and again on November 8, 1959, Morris Martin attempted to withdraw the pledge.

On December 20, 1962, plaintiff, a nonprofit corporation, brought suit against Morris Martin, Irving Martin, Jack Martin, and Bessie Martin Steinberg. On November 17, 1965, the defendants filed a motion to amend their answer, which the trial judge denied. On August 24, 1966, the trial judge issued an opinion in which he granted judgment in favor of plaintiff against defendant Morris Martin for the sum of $25,000, plus interest at 5 percent from June 30, 1964; Morris Martin was granted the right within thirty days to introduce a third party action for contribution from defendants Jack Martin and Irving Martin. Appeal was taken from the judgment in favor of plaintiff and against Morris Martin to the Court of Appeals, which affirmed the trial judge. The case was then appealed to the Michigan Supreme Court.

 JUSTICE ADAMS:

The trial judge erred in denying defendants' motions for leave to amend for the reason that the affidavit of Dr. Rabbi Bernard B. Perlow raised a question of fact as to Jewish custom which may be controlling upon the parties....

The proposed amendment would have added an affirmative defense to the effect that:

> ... Jewish religious law and the custom and usage of Plaintiff synagogue prohibits the institution of a law suit in a nonreligious court before resort is had to Beth Din, or religious courts. There has been no effort on the part of Plaintiff to seek relief in a Beth Din. Whether or not the cards on which Plaintiff relies would otherwise form a legally binding contract, it was the intent of the parties that the Jewish law should govern the transaction. Since the Jewish law prohibits the institution of this suit, the parties did not intend to enter into a contract which is legally enforceable under Michigan law.

The defendants' motions to amend were supported by the affidavit of a Dr. Rabbi Bernard D. Perlow, a rabbi and a scholar. After stating his qualifications as an expert witness, he included the following points in his opinion:

> 5. That the religious customs, practices, and laws binding on all Jews are codified in the work known as the Shulchan Aruch; that this code is generally regarded as binding as a matter of religious faith by both orthodox and Conservative Jews....
>
> 6. That in the opinion of this deponent, the Shulchan Aruch, as well as the custom and tradition for more than a thousand years, prohibits the bringing of a suit in the civil courts of any state by a synagogue against any of its members or vice versa and is contrary to Jewish law and is prohibited; that any such civil controversy must be first brought before the Jewish religion court known as the Beth Din (a Jewish rabbinical court); that under Jewish law, matters of charity to the synagogue go to the heart of the Jewish religion; that a charitable contribution to a synagogue is considered a religious matter by and between the synagogue and the member; that for a synagogue to file a suit against one of its members upon an alleged charitable contribution without submitting it to a Beth Din is what is known in Jewish law as a "Chillul Hashem" which is a profanation of God's

name and such action is such a grave sin in Jewish law, that it warrants excommunication....

7. That it is expressly stated in Hyman E. Goldin's translation of Rabbi Solomon Ganzfried's Code of Jewish Law, Kidzur Schulchan Aruch published in New York City by the Hebrew Publishing Company in 1961, volume 4, page 67, that it is forbidden to bring a suit in the civil courts even if their decision would be in accordance with the law of Israel; that even if the two litigants are willing to try the case before such a court, it is forbidden; that even if they make an oral or a written agreement to that effect, it is of no avail; that whoever takes a case against another Jew involving religious matters, is a Godless person and he has violated and defiled the law of Moses....

Nothing appears in the record before us in this case to warrant the trial judge's denial of the motion. When the rights of the parties are being tested on motions for summary judgment filed, not at the election of the parties themselves but at the behest of the trial judge, a defendant should most certainly be allowed to amend to assert any defense he may have before the court has ruled....

Reversed and remanded for further proceedings in accordance with this opinion.

Mixed Systems. Because of the worldwide dispersal of legal, political, economic, and social ideas, many countries today have what might be best described as a "mixed" legal system. After the Dutch had imposed their Roman-Dutch legal system on the island of Ceylon, for example, the island became an English colony. English commercial statutes like the sales of goods act were adopted for Ceylon by the new colonial power. Both of these colonial legal systems continued to coexist with several earlier customary systems that predated the Dutch. The English commercial statutes were also adopted for India during its colonial period; since independence, India has patterned many of its constitutional law concepts on those of the U.S. Supreme Court. Iraq patterned its commercial code after that of France. And so it goes.

One of the most interesting legal "mixtures" ever was created on July 1, 1997, when the British Crown Colony of Hong Kong was returned to the People's Republic of China, as a "Special Administrative Region." Under the UK/PRC treaty providing for this change of sovereignty, and under the PRC's "Basic Law" for the Hong Kong S.A.R., Hong Kong was to retain its British-derived common law (except where it conflicted with the Basic Law) for fifty years after the transfer. This attempt to maintain a common-law island in a communist sea raises any number of very interesting questions, which the courts are only beginning to decide. The following case is one early interpretation of how these unmatched pieces are going to be fitted together.

HONG KONG S.A.R. v. MA WAI KWAN & ORS.
1997-2 HKC 315 (H.K. Court of Appeal, 1997)

FACTS: Three persons were on trial in Hong Kong for the crime of "conspiracy to pervert the course of public justice," when the U.K. returned the colony to the P.R.C. (on July 1, 1997). On July 3, the defendants suggested to the trial court that the common law (i.e., non-statutory) crime with which they were charged was no longer part of the law in the H.K.S.A.R. For an authoritative interpretation of that legal issue, the prosecution asked the Court of Appeal for a ruling. A three-judge panel (Chan, Nazareth, and Mortimer) heard the arguments and made the ruling.

 CHIEF JUDGE CHAN:

On 19 December 1984, the Joint Declaration was signed between the Government of the People's Republic of China (PRC) and the Government of the United Kingdom. By this Joint Declaration, Hong Kong was to be restored to China with effect from 1 July 1997. Under art. 3 of the Joint Declaration, China declared certain basic policies regarding Hong Kong. There was to be established the HKSAR, which would enjoy a high degree of autonomy. Under art. 3(12), these basic policies would be stipulated in a Basic Law to be promulgated by the NPC [National People's Congress], and would remain unchanged for fifty years from 1 July 1997. These policies were further elaborated in Annex I to the Joint Declaration. The Basic Law for the HKSAR was drafted by the Drafting Committee of the Basic Laws, which consisted of members from China and Hong Kong. It took many years to complete. It was promulgated on 4 April 1990, and was to take effect from 1 July 1997.

The Basic Law is not only a brainchild of an international treaty, the Joint Declaration. It is also a national law of the PRC and the constitution of the HKSAR. It translates the basic policies enshrined in the Joint Declaration into more practical terms. The essence of these policies is that the current social, economic, and legal systems in Hong Kong will remain unchanged for fifty years. The purpose of the Basic Law is to ensure that these basic policies are implemented and that there can be continued stability and prosperity for the HKSAR. Continuity after the change of sovereignty is therefore of vital importance....

The Basic Law is a unique document. It reflects a treaty made between two nations. It deals with the relationship between the Sovereign and an autonomous region which practices a different system. It stipulates the organizations and functions of the different branches of government. It sets out the rights and obligations of the citizens. Hence, it has at least three dimensions: international, domestic and constitutional. It must also be borne in mind that it was not drafted by common law lawyers. It was drafted in the Chinese language with an official English version, but the Chinese version takes precedence in case of discrepancies. That being the background and features of the Basic Law, it is obvious that there will be difficulties in the interpretation of the various provisions.... In my view, the generous and purposive approach may not be applicable in interpreting every article of the Basic Law.

However, in the context of the present case which involves the constitutional aspects of the Basic Law, I agree that this approach is more appropriate....

In my view, the intent of the Basic Law is clear. There is to be no change in our laws and legal system (except those which contravene the Basic Law). These are the very fabric of our society. Continuity is the key to stability. Any disruption will be disastrous. Even one moment of legal vacuum may lead to chaos. Everything relating to the laws and the legal system except those provisions which contravene the Basic Law has to continue to be in force. The existing system must already be in place on 1 July 1997. That must be the intent of the Basic Law....

The wording is equally clear. The Basic Law is the constitution of the HKSAR. It is the most important piece of law in the land. It states clearly what the position is as from 1 July 1997. In my view, the word "shall" in these provisions can only be used in the mandatory and declaratory sense. The meaning of these provisions is this. On 1 July 1997, when the HKSAR comes into existence and the Basic Law comes into effect, these are to be the laws and legal system in force and the principles applicable in place. There is no express or implied requirement in any of these provisions that the laws previously in force or the legal system previously in place need to be formally adopted before they can continue to be applicable after the change of sovereignty. On the contrary, the use of the terms "shall be maintained," "shall continue" and "shall be" leaves absolutely no doubt in my mind that there can be no question of any need for an act of adoption. These terms are totally inconsistent with such a requirement....

The respondents' argument is based mainly on Article 160, which uses the words "shall be adopted." It is suggested that "shall" in this term is used in the future tense. In my view, that provision cannot be read in isolation but must be considered in the light of the rest of the Basic Law, including in particular the articles to which I have referred above. It cannot be construed to have a meaning which is inconsistent with the other articles relating to the adoption of the existing laws and legal system....

For the reasons which I have set out above, I have come to the conclusion that upon a true construction and interpretation of the relevant provisions of the Basic Law, the laws previously in force in Hong Kong, including the common law, have been adopted and became the laws of HKSAR on 1 July 1997, the judicial system together with the principles applicable to court proceedings have continued, and indictments and pending court proceedings have continued to be valid.

The answers to the questions reserved for this court are that the common law has survived the change of sovereignty, and the three respondents are liable to answer to and be tried under the amended indictment.

While this first major decision on Hong Kong's new status is thus very encouraging, the jury is still out as to how long this special situation will be able to exist. The serious financial crisis which spread through much of Asia in late 1997 and early 1998 may force some painful adjustments in Hong Kong's unique economic and financial arrangements. Whatever occurs, the SAR's economic importance within the world trading system will make developments there closely watched by global businesses.

INTERNATIONAL LAW

History. International trade is of course nothing new. Neither are international relations, or treaties between sovereign states. Almost from earliest recorded times, customs developed for the proper handling of international affairs and the problems which inevitably arose. Much of early international law was concerned with the law of the sea—freedom of passage, rights of ships in foreign ports, salvage and fishing rights, and the like—and with the rules covering foreign diplomatic personnel. City-states and nations which were important commercial and trading centers often published collections of the customs that governed international trade. There is evidence that the Egyptians had such international law practices as early as 1400 B.C. Rhodes, the largest of the Dodecanese Islands, in the Aegean Sea, had a "code" of international law by 700 B.C. The Greek city-states also adopted certain practices for dealing with diplomatic personnel and trading disputes. Roman law developed the *ius gentium*, which dealt with relations between non-citizens, as an alternative to the *ius civile*, which applied only to citizens. Because of its adoption of more universally-applicable legal principles, the *ius gentium* eventually came to dominate the great Roman legal system. Important collections of international legal practices were published by Visby, Sweden, one of the most important members of the Hanseatic League in the 11th century, and by Louis IX of France (the Code of Oleron) in the mid-13th century. Legal historians generally date modern international law from the adoption of the Treaty of Westphalia in 1648.

These rules were originally labelled the "Law of Nations," indicating that they were applicable primarily (or exclusively) to the relations between nations. With the increasing recognition of the international rights of public and private organizations—and of individuals, the phrase "international law" came into general use. The terms "supranational law" and "transnational law" are also applied to these rules which transcend national boundaries.

Sources. International law is drawn from the widest variety of sources; custom, treaties, judicial precedents, and textbooks have all played a part in its development. Hugo Grotius, a Dutch lawyer, is usually called "the father of international law" because of his great work, *De Jure Bellis ac Pacis*, published in 1625. In it he spoke of international law as being based on natural law, which was common to all nations—the "dictate of right reason." This was in marked contrast to the "positivists," who derived international law from the customs of nations in their dealings with each other. In fact, both of these elements have played a part, along with specific treaties governing the international relations of two or more countries, and decisions of arbitrators and national and international courts.

The Covenant of the League of Nations established the World Court in the Hague after World War I. A similar body, the International Court of Justice, functions there today under the United Nations Charter. Not all nations have fully accepted the jurisdiction of the ICJ in all matters, and many very important matters remain to be resolved by specific treaties. One of the major unresolved international law problems relates to the use of the seabed of the world's oceans, and the right to the enormous quantities of mineral nodules that are to be found there. The Communist nations and the "have-nots" generally favor some sort of world ownership, through the UN. The United States and most of the developed countries favor an arrangement which will leave substantial room for free enterprise mining of the ocean floor. The economic and political stakes in this one question are enormous.

By definition, customs take time to develop. This is especially true in the international area, with the many different forms of political, economic, and social arrangements—in over 100 sovereign nations. The relationships which are occurring in our modern world at lightning speed won't wait for "custom" to develop over decades, or centuries. International sales, financing, investment, communication, franchising, and other transactions are happening, whether the legal rules are there or not. Increasingly, to meet the demands of modern trade and commerce, nations have turned to treaties. The U.N. Convention on Contracts for the International Sale of Goods is perhaps the most notable example of this sort of international legislation. There are many others, on topics such as the international carriage of goods, the use of letters of credit and negotiable instruments, and the taking of evidence in other countries. Within the European Community, massive new bodies of laws and regulations are being generated by the legal institutions set up under the 1958 Treaty of Rome.

Treaties also take time to draft and to adopt, but much less time than the development of customs. Once properly adopted by a nation according to its constitutional procedures, the treaty becomes law for that nation. There is generally no question as to when and how this happens. The treaty will still need to be interpreted and applied by the various courts to specific situations, but there is usually no argument over what "the law" is—it's the treaty, as written.

INTERNATIONAL COURTS

Since nations have been very reluctant to give up any of their ultimate sovereign power to international bodies, the use of truly international courts has, historically, been quite limited. National governments do not want to have their own decisions reviewed by a multinational body which may represent very different political and ideological views than their own. As a result, most cases involving international law are in fact litigated in national courts, including, in the United States, the state courts. The *Stovall* case in Chapter 1 illustrates this point, as do many other examples. Two international courts are worth noting. Additionally, arbitration has been a popular method of resolving international disputes, both those arising between private parties, and those involving governments or their agencies.

International Court of Justice. The ICJ was established as the successor to the Permanent Court of International Justice, to hear disputes between nations. The ICJ was authorized by Chapter XIV of the Charter of the United Nations, and an annexed statute. This statute is a comprehensive statement of the ICJ's organization, jurisdiction, and procedure.

The statute provides that the ICJ shall consist of fifteen judges and that no more than two of them shall be citizens of the same nation. They must be persons of high moral character, and they must have the same qualifications as would be required in their respective countries for appointment to the highest judicial offices in those countries, or they must be "jurisconsults" of recognized competence in international law. The judges are elected by the General Assembly and by the Security Council of the United Nations from a list of nominations submitted by nominating bodies from the various member nations. Their term of office is nine years, with five members of the court being reelected or replaced every three years.

The General Assembly and the Security Council must hold their elections independently of each other. If a person's name appears on the list of successful candidates of both the General Assembly and the Security Council, that person is elected. If there are no successful candidates after the first meeting and ballot, then two more meetings may be held and ballots cast. If there is still no agreement, then a deadlock procedure must be followed. Three members of the Security

Council and three members of the General Assembly will then meet and make the final selection of the persons to fill the vacancies.

The International Court of Justice was not set up to hear disputes between private citizens concerning international contract or property disputes. Since only nations may be parties in cases which are brought before the International Court of Justice, the court's decisions are of less significance to international business operations than are the decisions of national courts which apply international law.

European Community Courts. As noted above, the EC has a number of legal bodies which are empowered to establish rules binding across national borders. Originally, there was only one court—the European Court of Justice. To help with the greatly increased workload of interpreting all the many new EC regulations, the Court of First Instance was set up in 1987.

These courts hear cases involving EC law and regulations, which supersede national laws to the extent of any conflict. Each nation's courts are supposed to follow EC law, but if one party feels they did not, an appeal can be taken to the EC courts. While these EC court decisions are binding only with the Community, they may be used as evidence of customary international law. As a result of the activity of these EC courts, therefore, international law is growing rapidly.

Thus far, no other regional economic grouping has set up a supranational court system of this kind.

International Arbitration. It is very common for international business contracts to contain an arbitration clause whereby the parties agree to submit any controversy relating to the contract to an arbitrator or an arbitration panel, rather than to go to court. In any business contract dispute, arbitration will almost certainly save time and legal expense, and the parties can select an arbitrator with expertise in the substantive area involved. These same advantages hold at the international level, but there are additional procedural reasons for including such a clause in the international contract. With an international dispute, there are always potential questions as to which court in what country would have jurisdiction, how service of process can be effected across international boundaries, and which country's law applies. These problems can be minimized with an arbitration clause that specifies the law to be applied, the method of selecting the arbitrator, the procedures to be followed, and the allocation of expenses between the parties. While it is true that arbitrators' awards are sometimes not paid voluntarily, they will generally be enforced by the courts of most nations if a lawsuit is necessary.

CONFLICTS OF LAWS

Much of Private International Law (the rules covering international disputes between private parties) has to do with the conflicts which inevitably arise as to which nation's law should apply. This is also described as the "choice of law" problem. Much the same set of problems, albeit on a smaller scale, exists between state legal systems within the United States.

Whose Law Should Apply? An elaborate set of rules, or at least presumptions, has been worked out for international disputes. Questions as to the validity of a contract are generally decided according to the law of the nation where the contract was made. Issues arising out of the performance of a contract are usually resolved by the law of the nation where performance occurs.

If there are questions as to the internal management or organization of a business, those are decided according to the law of the nation where the firm was organized. For tort cases, the court may use the law of the place where the tort was committed, or the law of the nation which has the greatest interest in the case, all facts considered. Each of these rather simplistic "rules" is of course subject to interpretation and to various exceptions.

There is also a clear rule that the court hearing the case uses its own procedure. However, there may still be sharp differences in interpretation as to what is "procedure" and what is "substantive law."

Due to the uncertainties surrounding this choice of law problem, the parties to an international contract may very well want to include their own "choice" clause in their contract. Within limits, courts will generally recognize and enforce such contract clauses. This latter point was at issue in the *Spink* case.

SPINK & SON, LTD. v. GENERAL ATLANTIC CORPORATION
637 N.Y.S.2d 921 (1996)

FACTS: In June 1991, defendant Edwin Cohen, chairman of defendant General Atlantic Corporation, attended an antiques fair in London, England. While there, Cohen spoke with an employee of plaintiff about the possibility of purchasing six pieces of the exhibited art. Although Cohen admits that he looked into the possible purchase of the art, he denies that he made a commitment to make an acquisition. It is undisputed that defendants never took possession of any art or signed a writing with respect thereto.

After returning to New York, defendants received an invoice requesting payment of $33,968 for the purchase of works of art, to which they did not respond. On June 25, 1993, after notice to the defendants, plaintiff sold one of the pieces and reduced the amount allegedly owing to $32,768.

The complaint asserts causes of action under both New York and English law. The motion before the court seeks a dismissal of the causes of action under New York law as barred by the Statute of Frauds, and the cause of action under English law for failure to adequately allege such law. Plaintiff cross-moved to amend its complaint to plead the necessary foreign law. At oral argument, that application was granted on consent and the branch of defendants' motion to dismiss for failure to adequately plead the foreign law was withdrawn. Thereafter, both parties submitted memoranda as to the appropriate law to be applied, with plaintiff maintaining that English law governs and defendants urging the law of the forum.

 JUDGE LEHNER:

The central issue on this motion by defendants for summary judgment is whether New York or English law is applicable to determine the enforceability of an alleged oral contract for the purchase of artwork made in England between a New York resident and an English art gallery....

In determining the law applicable to matters bearing upon the execution, interpretation, validity, and performance of a contract, the modern approach is to apply the law of the jurisdiction having the greatest interest in the litigation.... [T]he theory of "grouping of contacts," "instead of regarding as conclusive the parties' intention or the place of making or performance, lays emphasis rather upon the law of the place 'which has the most significant contacts with the matter in dispute.'... The merit of (this) approach is that it gives to the place 'having the most interest in the problem' paramount control over the legal issues arising out of a particular factual context, thus allowing the forum to apply the policy of the jurisdiction 'most intimately concerned with the outcome of [the] particular litigation'."...

[W]hen determining choice of law, the "five generally significant contacts in a contract case [are]: the places of contracting, negotiation, and performance; the location of the subject matter of the contract; and the domicile of the contracting parties."

Applying these criteria, it appears that, on balance, England has a greater interest in this matter. While defendants are New York residents, the place of the alleged negotiation and contracting is England, and the art is located in there as is plaintiff's place of incorporation and place of business. Cohen traveled there to attend the antiques fair, and England has an interest in enforcing contracts made there by its citizens doing business in the country. When a person travels abroad, it is not unfair that they subject themselves to the laws of the land to which they visit.

While the court finds that England has a greater interest in the subject of this litigation, defendants assert that such law (which allegedly does not require a writing for the enforcement of the subject contract) should not be applied in light of the public policy of New York in requiring a writing in order to enforce a contract for the sale of goods for a price in excess of $500....

It is recognized that notwithstanding that a proper application of conflict of laws principles suggests the application of foreign law, New York law may still be applied if the foreign law violates a strong public policy of this State. With respect to the Statute of Frauds, in [a] 1969 decision..., our Court of Appeals wrote: "Whether or not a contract, valid and enforceable in the jurisdiction where made, is subject to the Statute of Frauds of a jurisdiction where an action is brought upon the contract is a question not yet settled in this State." In that case ... the Court criticized the test of examining whether the foreign Statute of Frauds was substantive or procedural, finding that such characterization "does little more than restate the problem and has even less relevance to our modern approach to the conflict of laws."... There the Court traced the legislative history of the statute and, noting that it "is common knowledge that New York is a national and international center for the purchase and sale of businesses and interests therein," concluded that the statute contributed to New York's economic development, which it opined constituted a strong State interest. In that case, however, most of the negotiations took place in New York and the Court ruled that "[t]hese contacts give New York a substantial interest in applying its own law in view of the policy underlying the applicable provision of our Statute of Frauds to protect principals in business transactions from unfounded claims and thereby encourage use of New York as a national and international business center."...

"In search of the public policy of the State, courts of course are not free to indulge in mere individual notions of expediency and fairness but must look to the law as expressed in statute and judicial decisions."... [I]t was recently stated that "if New York statutes ... were routinely read to express fundamental policy, choice of law principles would be meaningless." The Court concluded that in "view of modern choice of law doctrine, resort to the public policy exception should be reserved for those foreign laws that are truly obnoxious."...

With respect to ... (the Statute of Frauds provision requiring a writing for an enforceable guarantee), in *Finnish Fur Sales Co. v. Juliette Shulof Furs*..., it was ruled that the section would not be a bar to a purchase of personal property at auction in Finland in that its requirements "do not constitute a 'fundamental policy' for the purpose of choice of law analysis."...

The Court concludes that the UCC provision pertaining to the enforcement of a contract for the sale of goods does not represent such a strong public policy that the courts of this State should deny enforcement of an oral contract that is enforceable where made. There is nothing, per se, "obnoxious" in granting enforcement of an oral, agreement.... Hence, since it cannot be said that the policy underlying our law on sales outweighs the interest of England in enforcing oral contracts made in that country by merchants doing business there, English law will determine the enforceability of the oral contract sued upon herein.

Accordingly, defendants' motion is granted solely to the extent of dismissing the causes of action asserted under New York law, and this action shall proceed applying the substantive law of England.

Where Can the Case Be Tried? An equally difficult problem arises in choosing the place where the case is to be heard. Usually, a defendant will want the trial in its home nation, where it has a kind of "home-court advantage," due to logistics and its familiarity with the system. The plaintiff will have to weigh the costs of travel and local counsel into the equation, in deciding whether to pursue the case in another nation which could be some distance away. Plaintiff's lawyer will try to find a forum where there is a good chance of winning the case, *and* a good chance of recovering substantial damages. It is this last point that motivates the plaintiffs in the next case.

DOW CHEMICAL CO. v. CASTRO ALFARO
786 S.W.2d 674 (TX, 1990)

FACTS: Domingo Castro Alfaro worked for Standard Fruit Company on its banana plantation in Costa Rica. He and eighty-one other employees claim they suffered personal injuries, including sterility, from being exposed to a pesticide which was manufactured by Dow and by Shell Oil and then sold by those companies to Standard Fruit. The eighty-two employees and their wives filed a lawsuit against Dow and Shell in Houston, Texas, in state court. Both defendants are incorporated in Delaware. However, Shell has its corporate world headquarters in Houston, and Dow operates the largest chemical plant in the United States' in Freeport, Texas, about sixty miles from Houston.

Dow and Shell asked the Texas court to dismiss the case as being brought in an "inconvenient" location, since the injuries occurred in Costa Rica, to Costa Rica citizens. (The legal doctrine which permits courts to dismiss lawsuits on such grounds is called *forum non conveniens*). A Texas statute says that personal injury actions "may be enforced" in Texas courts even though the injury occurred in another country. The pesticide at issue, dibromachloropropane (DBCP), was banned for use in the United States in 1977. Dow and Shell, both before and after the U.S. ban, shipped hundreds of thousands of gallons of DBCP to Standard Fruit in Costa Rica for use there. The estimated maximum recovery per worker for the injuries claimed here would be $1,080 in Costa Rica.

The Texas trial court did dismiss the case, on the basis of *forum non conveniens*. The Texas Court of Appeals reversed that decision, and sent the case back to the trial court for a trial on the merits of the plaintiffs' claims. Dow and Shell then filed a further appeal with the Texas Supreme Court.

 JUSTICE RAY:

The doctrine of *forum non conveniens* arose from [a similar rule] in Scottish cases.... The Scottish courts recognized that the [rule] applied when to hear the case was not expedient for the administration of justice.... By the end of the nineteenth century, English courts had accepted the doctrine....

Texas courts applied the doctrine ... in several cases prior to the enactment of Article 4678 in 1913 [the section on which the current Texas statute was based]....

Our interpretation of the [current statute] is controlled by ... *Allen v. Bass*.... In *Allen*, the court of civil appeals conferred an absolute right to maintain a properly brought suit in Texas courts....

We conclude that the legislature has statutorily abolished the doctrine of *forum non conveniens* in suits brought under [this statute]....

 CONCUR—JUSTICE DOGGETT:

The [dissenting judges] are insistent that a jury of Texans be denied the opportunity to evaluate the conduct of a Texas corporation concerning decisions it made in Texas because the only ones allegedly hurt are foreigners. Fortunately, Texans are not so provincial and narrow-minded as these dissenters presume. Our citizenry recognizes that a wrong does not fade away because its immediate consequences are first felt far away rather than close to home. Never have we been required to forfeit our membership in the human race in order to maintain our proud heritage as citizens of Texas.

The dissenters argue that it is inconvenient and unfair for farmworkers allegedly suffering permanent physical and mental injuries, including irreversible sterility, to seek redress by suing a multinational corporation in a court three blocks away from its world headquarters and another corporation, which operates in Texas this country's largest chemical plant.... [T]he "doctrine" they advocate has nothing to do with fairness and convenience and everything to do with immunizing multinational corporations from accountability for their alleged torts causing injury abroad....

The banana plantation workers allegedly injured by DBCP were employed by an American company on American-owned land and grew Dole bananas for export solely to American tables. The chemical allegedly rendering the workers sterile was researched, formulated, tested, manufactured, labeled, and shipped; by an American company in the United States to another American company. The decision to manufacture DBCP for distribution and use in the third world was made by these two American companies in their corporate offices in the United States. Yet now Shell and Dow argue that the one part of this equation that should not be American is the legal consequences of their actions....

A *forum non conveniens* dismissal is often, in reality, a complete victory for the defendant.... "In some instances ... invocation of the doctrine will send the case to a jurisdiction which has imposed such severe monetary limitations on recovery as to eliminate the likelihood that the case will be tried. When it is obvious that this will occur, discussion of the convenience of witnesses takes on a Kafkaesque quality-everyone knows that no witnesses ever will be called to testify...." Empirical data available demonstrate that less than 4 percent of cases dismissed under the doctrine ... ever reach trial in a foreign court....

The abolition of *forum non conveniens* will further important public policy considerations by providing a check on the conduct of multinational corporations.... The misconduct oi even a few multinational corporations can affect untold millions around the world. For example, after the United States imposed a domestic ban on the sale of cancer-producing ... children's sleepwear, American companies exported approximately 2.4 million pieces to Africa, Asia, and South America. A similar pattern occurred when a ban was proposed for baby pacifiers that had been linked to choking deaths in infants.... These examples of indifference by some corporations towards children abroad are not unusual.

Where Can a Company Be Taxed? Equally important to the bottom line (or perhaps even more so) is the question of where a company can be taxed—and for what. In general, the rules for international taxation are similar to those applicable among the states, within the U.S.

A company's sales can be taxed by the nation where those sales are made. This rule may cause litigation over sales made on the internet, but the probable interpretation is that the "net" sale is made in the country where the customer's order is accepted by the seller. If such out-of-nation sales are exempt from sales tax there, the customer company may have to pay a so-called "use" tax to its government, for the privilege of using the goods in that nation. In many nations, property owners are required to pay annual taxes. This is a simple enough calculation for real estate, which by definition is immovable. For personal property, however, there can be very complex apportionment issues when the property is used in more than one nation. Which country gets to tax how much of an airline's airplane fleet which is being used in many nations over the course of a year? The problem is complicated by the fact that nations are not required to use the same formula to do the apportioning, and by the fact that there is no international court to set the ground rules, as there is in the U.S. A company owes an income tax (if there is one) to any nation where it is earning income. For multinationals, some income may in fact be taxed twice, if nations are using different apportionment formulas for calculating their appropriate taxable shares of the multinational's income. The company will of course have to pay fees and charges to its home nation for the privilege of organizing as a firm, and may have to pay annual fees for the privilege of doing business as such in any nation where it has operations.

In addition to the complexities involved in the above rules, there are some additional constitutional problems in the United States, with respect to the taxation of international business operations. State and local governments may not be able to impose personal property taxes on planes and ships which are being fully taxed by their home country. The Constitution prohibits states from imposing tariffs on exports or imports, and the national government from taxing exports. Various national government programs also limit taxation in "duty-free" zones and locations. Similar restrictions doubtless exist in most nations, so that the job of keeping a multinational company in tax compliance, in all its locations, is probably having a significant impact on the bottom line.

Extraterritoriality. Conflict of laws is virtually inevitable any time one nation attempts to enforce its laws with respect to persons and things outside its geographical territory. While there is a general presumption against the validity of such extraterritorial enforcement, nations are increasingly trying to justify it under one theory or another. The United States has been one of the most aggressive "legal imperialists," to the point of causing the serious alienation of some of our strongest allies.

Antitrust law is the oldest, and perhaps still the most controversial area in which the U.S. applies its law to activities overseas. In the 1945 *Alcoa* case, the U.S. Second Circuit ruled that acts in other nations which were intended to have, and in fact did have, significant "effects" within the U.S. market could be prosecuted under the Sherman Act. Since that time, a considerable body of international law has developed in support of this "effects" doctrine. Other nations have also used this argument as a basis for applying their laws to conduct outside their geographical borders.

In response to discovery orders from U.S. courts directed against their businesses, the U.K. and several other nations have passed so-called "blocking" statutes. These laws order the nation's businesses *not* to comply with the U.S. courts' discovery orders. In addition, the U.K. also has "clawback" statutes which permit its businesses to sue U.S. companies (that are subject to the U.K. courts' jurisdiction), to recover the punitive parts of treble damages awarded in U.S. antitrust cases. Nation-to-nation negotiations have thus far been unable to resolve these serious conflict of laws issues.

If antitrust is the most controversial area of international application of national laws, the U.S. Foreign Corrupt Practices Act of 1977 is surely a close second. The FCPA prohibits payments by U.S. companies to foreign government officials to influence those persons' decisions on purchases of goods and services for the government. The FCPA applies even if such payments are customary, and expected, in that other nation. Such payments are permitted by the FCPA only if they are expressly permitted by statute in the other nation. The FCPA does permit the reimbursement of a foreign official's reasonable expenses, incurred during contract negotiations. It also allows payments of small sums to minor officials as a kind of "tip" ("grease payment") for doing their (nondiscretionary) duties swiftly and effectively. It would thus be illegal to make a payment to a foreign official to get her to decide to buy your goods rather than a competitor's, but it would be permissible to pay a few dollars to the local customs inspector to have him expedite the processing of your incoming goods. What is illegal is bribery of an official to influence that person's discretionary decision.

Serious criminal penalties are provided for illegal bribes. Individuals are subject to up to five years in prison, plus fines up to $100,000, for each willful violation of the Act. Companies may be fined up to $2,000,000 for each offense. Companies are not permitted to reimburse their employees for fines paid for such violations.

Other nations have accused the U.S. of "cultural imperialism" in applying its business standards to transactions in their country. Our jurisdictional justification for the FCPA is that we are merely regulating the conduct of *our* businesses, including their conduct overseas. We are not attempting to tell French firms what they can do in France, only telling U.S. firms what they can do in France. Nonetheless, there is certainly an extraterritoriality problem with the FCPA. More recently, the U.S. has led efforts to get some international standards for trade practices, especially through such organizations as the Organization for Economic Cooperation and Development. The OECD nations include most of Western Europe, Japan, Australia, New Zealand, and Canada, in addition to the U.S. Adoption of a multinational standard by most of the world's developed nations would go a long way towards easing the conflicts of laws related to business practices.

The OECD has also been very active in developing rules to protect the environment. Here, too, such multinational agreement would minimize the potential conflicts among the very different national environmental standards. Multi-nation treaties on this subject have also been proposed. In the absence of international standards, companies clearly have a legal duty to comply with the environmental rules where their facilities are located. The more difficult questions relate to whether they also have a duty to consider the rules in other nations, where their operations may inflict environmental damage. Cutting down the Brazilian rain forest has world-wide environmental (and other) implications. Is it sufficient merely to comply with Brazil's environmental laws? If there is such a further obligation, by whose standards is it to be judged? Who protects the "global commons"—space, the oceans, Antarctica? In a 1993 case, the U.S. Court of Appeals for the District of Columbia Circuit decided that the activities of U.S. agencies in Antarctica were subject to U.S. environmental laws. Since the agency which had made the decision was located in D.C., and directing its own personnel in Antarctica, the decision required the filing of an environmental impact statement, in accordance with U.S. law.

Sovereign Immunity and Act of State Doctrines. Two recognized rules of international law limit the ability of courts in one nation to review the acts of other nations' governments. The sovereign immunity doctrine says that a government cannot be sued without its consent—not only in its own courts, but also in the courts of other nations. Some nations claim this immunity extends to all governmental activities, of whatever nature, including the actions of a government as the operator of nationalized/socialized industries. Other nations (including the United States) limit the sovereign's immunity from suit to more traditional governmental operations, and do not extend it to a government's "business" activities. The U.S. Foreign Sovereign Immunities Act of 1976 codifies this more limited immunity rule, for lawsuits in U.S. courts.

While only a government may claim "sovereign immunity," the act of state doctrine may be raised by private litigants as well as governments. This rule says that the validity of the actions of a government within its own nation cannot be reviewed by the courts of other nations. Thus, in the famous *Sabbatino* case, the U.S. Supreme Court decided that our courts could not judge the legality of Cuba's nationalization of certain business assets. And despite the very unfriendly relations between the U.S. and Cuba, our State Department actually filed an *amicus curiae* brief in support of the Cuban government's position!

SIGNIFICANCE OF THIS CHAPTER

As business operations have become increasingly global, it has become more and more important for managers to have some appreciation of other nations' legal systems. Dealing across national boundaries inevitably involves questions of whose law will apply to the transaction. To the extent that contracting parties have some choice in deciding this question for themselves, it is important for them to know something about what the choices are, and how particular choices may impact on the transaction. Hence, comparative law and international law have become essential parts of the modern manager's tool package.

PROBLEMS FOR DISCUSSION

1. Mitsubishi Motors made an agreement to distribute automobiles manufactured by Mitsubishi to Chrysler dealers outside the United States. Soler Chrysler-Plymouth is such a dealer in Puerto Rico. The sales agreement provided for arbitration of all disputes arising out of the agreement or a breach of the agreement. There were disputes and the parties couldn't work them out so Mitsubishi filed a suit in U.S. District Court to compel arbitration of the disputes. Soler Chrysler-Plymouth responded with allegations of antitrust violations. The district court ordered arbitration of the disputes, including the antitrust issues. The appellate court reversed the trial court insofar as the arbitration of the antitrust issues, as it felt antitrust matters should be decided by courts, not arbitrators. The case was later heard by the U.S. Supreme Court.

    Should the parties' mutual agreement to arbitrate all disputes be restricted to only non-antitrust disputes? Why or why not?

2. In response to certain U.S. foreign policy actions with which it violently disagreed, the government of Bwana nationalized all assets owned by American nationals within its jurisdiction. At that point, a large freighter loaded with bauxite ore belonging to Metallics, Inc. was preparing to leave Bwana's main port. The ship and its cargo were subjected to the seizure order and were later sold by the Bwana government to Ivan Rushoff. Ivan then brought the ship and cargo to New York, to try to resell them at a profit. Metallics has learned what's happening and has filed an appropriate action in New York, asking for immediate possession of the ship and cargo which were illegally seized by Bwana.

    How should the court rule in this case? Explain.

3. The International Association of Machinists (a U.S.-based labor union) was disturbed by the high price of oil and petroleum-derived products in the United States. They believed the actions of the Organization of the Petroleum Exporting Countries, popularly known as OPEC, were the cause of this burden on the American public. Accordingly, IAM sued OPEC and its member nations, alleging that their price-setting activities violated United States antitrust laws. IAM sought injunctive relief and damages. The District Court entered a final judgment in favor of the defendants, holding that it lacked jurisdiction and that IAM had no valid antitrust claim.

   The OPEC nations produce and export oil either through government-owned companies or through government participation in private companies. Prior to the formation of OPEC, these diverse and sometimes antagonistic countries were plagued with fluctuating oil prices. Without coordination among them, oil was often in oversupply on the world market, resulting in low prices.

   OPEC achieves its goals by a system of production limits and royalties which its members unanimously adopt. There is no enforcement arm of OPEC. The force behind OPEC decrees is the collective self-interest of the thirteen nations.

   After formation of OPEC it is alleged, the price of crude oil increased tenfold and more. How should this lawsuit be decided?

4. Sumitomo Shoji America, Inc. is a New York corporation and wholly owned subsidiary of Sumitomo Shoji Kabushiki Kaisha, a Japanese general trading company. Plaintiffs are past and present female secretarial employees of Sumitomo. All but one of the plaintiffs are U.S. citizens; that one exception is a Japanese citizen living in the United States. Plaintiffs brought this suit as a class action claiming that Sumitomo's alleged practice of hiring only male Japanese citizens to fill executive, managerial, and sales positions violated Title VII of the Civil Rights Act of 1964. Respondents sought both injunctive relief and damages.

   Sumitomo asked the court to dismiss the complaint as it was exempt from coverage of the civil rights laws as a result of the Friendship, Commerce, and Navigation Treaty between the United States and Japan. The FCN Treaty permits companies of each country to follow that country's rules in selecting executives and managers. The District Court refused to dismiss. The Court of Appeals reversed, saying Sumitomo was exempt under the provisions of the treaty.

   On review, how should the U.S. Supreme Court rule, and why?

5. Fishing is very important to the economy of the small nation of Portos. Traditionally it had claimed exclusive fishing rights, or at least the right to regulate fishing by citizens of other nations, only out to a distance of twelve miles from its coastline. As Russia and Japan modernized their fishing fleets, however, it became apparent that they were having a substantial impact on Portos' fishing industry. The government of Portos then declared that henceforth it would claim exclusive fishing rights, or the right to regulate catches by foreigners, out to a distance of 200 miles. Japan and Russia challenge this claim before the International Court of Justice.

   Does the International Court of Justice have jurisdiction over this type of case? What do you feel the decision should be, and why?

Chapter 3
Constitutional Law and Administrative Regulation

The United States Constitution provides the framework within which the three branches of the national government, the state governments, and all of society must operate. It provides the legal rules for deciding disputes between government agencies and between government agencies and private persons, including business organizations. We previously referenced this constitutional structure in Chapter 1. Constitutional issues will appear in various contexts throughout the rest of the book, since our system permits private litigants to raise constitutional arguments in any ordinary lawsuit. Because it is so frequently involved in our example cases, the Constitution is reprinted in full as Appendix A.

In this chapter, we will discuss the primary constitutional limitations on the regulation of business. Protection exists against improper actions by both national and state governments. Similar protections are found in state constitutions against arbitrary or unfair actions by the states and their agencies. A business affected by such arbitrary state action may thus challenge such action under applicable provisions of that state's constitution, as well as under the appropriate clauses of the U.S. Constitution.

Since much business regulation results from action taken by national and state administrative agencies, this chapter also outlines their origin, functions, and procedures.

U.S. CONSTITUTIONAL FRAMEWORK

Most readers of this text are probably already familiar with the basic provisions of our Constitution, but these legal concepts are so important that they are worthy restating briefly. The two basic structural rules are *separation of powers* and *federalism*. Each of these basic rules has significant consequences for business regulation by the national and state governments.

Separation of Powers.
The Founding Fathers were well aware of the dangers involved when governmental powers were concentrated in one person or one agency. They had been subjected to various acts of tyranny during the colonial period, and had fought a five-year revolution to establish an independent nation. They did not want to replace "a foreign tyrant with a domestic one."

They did see the need for a national government, but it had to be controllable. The answer was to divide governmental authority among three branches—legislative, executive, and judicial. Each would have only *some* powers and authority, and each would operate to check the others. This is known as the system of "checks and balances." To take just one example, the Supreme Court decides what actions by the other two branches (and by the states) are constitutional. But their decision can be overridden by a constitutional amendment. Likewise, the Court's decision on the meaning of an act of Congress can be overridden by Congress's passing of an amendment, or a whole new statute. (The Curt Flood Act of 1998 did this to the 1922 baseball precedent, as noted in Chapter 1.)

This "separation" is reinforced by having each of the three branches selected by a different method. The President is elected by popular vote, state by state, with the plurality vote-getter in each state receiving all of that state's electoral votes. The candidate receiving a majority of the electoral votes nationally is elected for a four-year term. Senators are elected by popular vote, on a state-wide basis, for six-year terms, but only one-third of them are elected each two years. Members of the House of Representatives are elected for two-year terms, from local districts within a state; each state has at least one member, with additional members being apportioned on the basis of population. Justices of the Supreme Court are appointed for life ("on good behavior"), after nomination by the President and confirmation by the Senate. Thus, each part of the government has a different constituency, and a different term of office.

Federalism.
The second structural device by which the Constitution limits government power is *federalism*, that is, a system in which there are two levels of government, each level operating independently within its own sphere of authority. (This contrasts with the *unitary system* of government found in France, Japan, the U.K., and other nations. Other federal systems include Canada, Australia, Germany, and Switzerland.)

The Constitution delegates certain powers to the national government; all other powers are reserved to the States, or to the People. These grants of national power are very broad, but not unlimited. If any branch or agency of the national government acts outside its delegated powers, that action can be challenged in court, and declared unconstitutional. There are several examples of such challenges in this chapter, and throughout the book.

The *Green* case, which follows, discusses the national/state relationship in a specific context.

GREEN v. INDUSTRIAL HELICOPTERS, INC.
593 So.2d 634 (LA, 1992)

FACTS: Plaintiff Michael J. Green was employed as an offshore oil meter technician for Southern Petroleum Labs ("Southern"). Southern contracted with Industrial Helicopters, Inc. ("Industrial") to carry workers from Louisiana shore sites to offshore platforms. Doug Wright was employed by Industrial as a helicopter pilot. There occurred an emergency helicopter landing on the high seas approximately 150 miles off the Louisiana coast. Plaintiff's lawsuit, filed in the Fifteenth Judicial District Court, State of Louisiana, named as defendants the pilot of the aircraft, Wright, and the pilot's employer, Industrial.

Wright picked up the plaintiff in Milton, Louisiana. From there plaintiff was to be taken to his worksite in the Gulf of Mexico from which he was later to be returned to Milton. Enroute to the worksite, the pilot refueled at an Exxon platform located 140 miles off the coast of the State of Louisiana. After refueling and soon after taking off from the Exxon platform, mechanical failure caused the pilot to make an emergency landing in the Gulf. The helicopter's governor had malfunctioned. Workers on the nearby Exxon platform assisted in the rescue of plaintiff and the pilot. Plaintiff suffered injuries in the emergency landing and in the rescue.

 CHIEF JUSTICE CALOGERO:

Generally, federal maritime jurisdiction is invoked whenever an accident occurs on the high seas and in furtherance of an activity bearing a significant relationship to a traditional maritime activity.... The United States Supreme Court has stated that although a helicopter is not a "traditional maritime conveyance," when it is used to ferry passengers from an island to the shore or vice versa it is engaged in a function traditionally performed by waterborne vessels....

The United States Constitution grants to federal district courts jurisdiction in all "cases of admiralty and maritime jurisdiction...." State courts, however, have concurrent jurisdiction by virtue of the "savings to suitors" clause of the Judiciary Act of 1789. This case, although within the federal admiralty jurisdiction, is brought in state court pursuant to the savings clause.

It is well settled that by virtue of the savings clause "a state having concurrent jurisdiction, is free to adopt such remedies, and to attach to them such incidents as it sees fit, so long as it does not attempt to make changes in the substantive maritime law...." As a general proposition, "a maritime claim brought in the common law state courts ... is governed by the same principles as govern actions brought in admiralty (i.e., by federal maritime law)...." Since the general maritime law is not a "complete or all inclusive system," a federal court may adopt state statutory law and common law principles as the federal admiralty rule.... State law and regulations may also supplement federal maritime law when "there is no conflict between the two systems of law and the need for uniformity of decision does not bar state action...."

Louisiana has a strong interest in applying its own law in this case: Plaintiff is a Louisiana resident, Industrial a Louisiana corporation, the pilot a Louisiana resident, and the helicopter was stored in a Louisiana hangar. The contract of carriage between plaintiff's employer and defendants was confected in Louisiana. The mission started in Louisiana and was to end in Louisiana. Plaintiff and defendants, more likely than not, expected to be governed by Louisiana law.

Moreover, LA C.C. Art. 2317 embodies a strong social policy to place liability with the owner or custodian of an injury causing thing. This type of liability is not imposed exclusively on helicopter or aircraft owners. Article 2317 liability is imposed on owners and custodians of any thing which, because of an unreasonably dangerous condition, causes injury to another. Also, in the personal injury area, states have much freedom to provide redress for their citizens....

Accordingly, a Louisiana state court should respect Louisiana law unless there is some federal impediment to application of that law contained in federal legislation or a clearly applicable rule in the general maritime law. We have found no such impediment or contrary general maritime rule. Rather, the general maritime law *authorizes* application of state law as a supplement to the general maritime law....

Generally, where maritime contracts are involved, the federal interest is at its "zenith" ... while in maritime tort cases the interest in uniformity is minimal because of the "fortuitous nature of accidental injuries and the strong state interest in providing redress for injuries...." The uniformity requirement is also tempered with a recognition that in some matters local concerns outweigh the federal need for a uniform admiralty rule. To this end, the "maritime but local" doctrine emerged from U.S. Supreme Court decisions....

Underlying the "maritime but local" doctrine is the rationale that "[i]f it [can] be said that the work activities of the injured employee [have] no direct concern with navigation or commerce, it [is] local and therefore the State laws [are] applicable...."

An offshore worker's employment activities have no "direct concern" with maritime shipping or commerce.... The U.S. Supreme Court has stated that work related to offshore oil and gas exploration is not "maritime employment."... Therefore, the tangential relationship of offshore drilling to traditional maritime activities along with the strong Louisiana interest in a case of this nature bring this case within the "maritime but local" doctrine....

In summary, we conclude that there is no applicable contrary federal legislation and that LA C.C. Art. 2317 neither prejudices the characteristic features of the general maritime law nor interferes impermissibly with any required uniformity in such law.

Article 2317 applies in this case. The Court of Appeal panel, in its opinion of April 18, 1990, is correct. The more recent opinion of the Court of Appeal sitting en banc is incorrect.

U.S. CONSTITUTIONAL LIMITATIONS

Limits on National Government Regulations. The general prohibition against unfair or arbitrary action by the national government and its agencies is the **due process clause** contained in the Fifth Amendment: "nor shall any person ... be deprived of life, liberty, or property, without due process of law." This clause is one of the greatest legal statements ever made, an important step in the development of Anglo-American common law. The clause has both procedural and substantive content. Procedurally, it means that actions of the national government that affect specific individuals can only be taken by following certain required steps, and that, overall, the government's decision must be reached through a process that is "fundamentally fair" to those affected. Fairness in the constitutional sense usually requires a hearing before an impartial decision maker, adequate notice of the proposed action, the right to be represented by counsel, the right to confront and cross-examine adverse witnesses, the right to present one's own witnesses and arguments, and the right to court review of the initial decision.

Substantively, the due process clause means that there are some things that the government simply may not do, even if it follows an established procedure. This clause is thus an important protection against the possible tyranny of a majority. Even if a bill is passed by Congress and signed by the President, the statute may still be challenged as being unconstitutional. It may be ruled unconstitutional because it violates one of the specific provisions of the Constitution, such as freedom of speech, or because it violates the division of power established between national and state governments or among the three branches of the national government. Statutes may also be invalidated where they attempt to regulate matters that are none of the government's concern. In 1970, for example, the U.S. Supreme Court overturned a state law prohibiting the distribution of birth control information to married adults (*Griswold v. Connecticut*). Presumably, a similar national statute would also be unconstitutional. There is a constitutional "right to privacy" even though it is not expressly stated anywhere in the Constitution. The Ninth Amendment specifically states that the list of rights in the other amendments is not exclusive.

Violations of Specific Bill of Rights Sections. Even though proper legislative procedure was followed in passing a statute, and even though the enforcement agency is proceeding in accordance with the statute's provisions, such action by the government cannot violate any of the specific protection found in the Bill of Rights. These include all the specific criminal procedures requirements that will be discussed in Chapter 5; the First Amendment freedoms of speech, press, assembly, and religion; the prohibition against taking private property unless just compensation is paid; the protection against warrantless searches and seizures provided by the Fourth Amendment; and others. Not all of these provisions have always been vigorously enforced, especially when businesses are being affected rather than individuals. The privilege against being forced to testify against oneself in a criminal case is generally not applicable to corporations.

Outer Limits of the Commerce Clause. Congress is given full power to regulate interstate commerce, foreign trade, and commerce with the Indian tribes. On these topics, the Supreme Court has said several times that the power of Congress is as complete as if there were only a national government and is subject only to the restrictions contained in other sections of the Constitution. Congress clearly has the power under the commerce clause to pass OSHA, for example, but it could not provide for warrantless searches of private property.

So long as it acts within constitutional limits, however, Congress has a free hand as to the extent and type of regulation it places on interstate commerce. It may outlaw practices that are harmful to the public, and it may restrict or prohibit interstate shipments of dangerous products. It may itself specify illegalities in some detail, or it may choose to legislate only broad guidelines and to delegate to an administrative agency the power to make the detailed rules of practice. It may adopt national legislation which preempts state laws, or it may delegate most of its power to regulate a particular area to the states.

If it wishes, Congress may also regulate intrastate commerce which has an impact on interstate commerce. The rationale for this auxiliary power is that it is necessary, or may be necessary, to effectually regulate interstate commerce. In the famous case of *Wickard v. Filburn* (1942), the Supreme Court upheld, under the commerce clause, regulations of agricultural production which reached all the way to a farmer who was growing grain for use on his own farm. If that analysis is valid, it's hard to imagine very many activities that could not be subjected to the commerce power if Congress wished to do so. Of course, if a particular statute says that it applies only to those activities "in" commerce, rather than to any which "affect" commerce, Congress is indicating that the statute is not to apply to purely intrastate matters.

Limits on State Government Regulation. As units of government which are sovereign within their own area, the states retain, under the U.S. Constitution, their "police power." The police power of a government is its power to regulate activities under its jurisdiction to promote the public health, safety, and welfare. The states' powers in this regard are limited, however, by general and specific provisions in the Constitution. Some of these limitations are prohibitions against particular types of state action, such as the Contracts Clause. Article I, Section 10 reads in part as follows: "No State shall pass ... any ... Law impairing the obligation of Contracts...." Originally, the provision was intended to prevent state legislatures from passing laws that would prevent the enforcement of valid contracts and the collection of debts. For a period of some fifty years after the Civil War, the contracts clause was one of the major legal arguments used to invalidate government regulations of business. Rejected as an argument in 1934 in the *Blaisdell* case, the Contracts Clause fell into disuse until 1978, when it was revived in the *Allied Structural* case.

Privileges and Immunities. Since a corporation is not considered a "citizen" for the purposes of the privileges and immunities clause of the Fourteenth Amendment, it need not be given any of the privileges and immunities of citizenship. Individual citizens conducting their businesses, however, would be protected by that clause. Even corporations might benefit indirectly, if a state's regulation of individual employees were held unconstitutional. When Alaska passed a statute requiring that its residents be hired in preference to new arrivals for work on oil and gas projects, employer corporations could not challenge the statute on this basis. But the act was ruled unconstitutional when it was challenged by five newly arrived workers who had been denied jobs in favor of Alaska residents (*Hicklin vs. Orbeck*, 1978). The corporations operating these projects in Alaska were thus free to hire anyone who applied for the job and was qualified, Alaska resident or not.

Equal Protection. Since the word used in this section of the Fourteenth Amendment is "person," and corporations are persons, neither they nor individuals can be denied equal protection by a state. This clause does not mean that a state cannot draw distinctions and treat different persons differently. It does mean, however, that any distinctions must be based on reasonable and rational criteria. There can be no arbitrary or invidious discrimination.

Two tests are used by the courts when violations of this clause are alleged. The strict scrutiny test is used where the regulation impacts on a fundamental right, such as freedom of speech, or where it adversely affects a "suspect class" of persons. A suspect class is one which has been subjected to past acts of discrimination, or which may have special disadvantages. Such groups might include racial, religious, or nationality minorities. Such state regulations will pass the test only if necessary to achieve a "compelling state interest," and if drawn as narrowly as possible to achieve it.

The alternative, and easier, test is the "rational basis" requirement. With no fundamental rights or suspect classes involved, a state classification would be presumed valid if there were any rational basis for it. The state's differential treatment must be related to the regulatory objective sought by the state, but if it is, it is presumed valid. The fact that other methods might be used to achieve the same result is not enough to invalidate a state's choice under this test. Many state regulations would be invalid under the first test; very few would be under this one. Most business regulations will probably be tested under this second, more generous standard.

Due Process. As was true under the Fifth Amendment, due process has both a substantive and a procedural content. Procedurally, no state can deny any person (including corporate persons) life, liberty, or property, without following a fair procedure. Since the Fourteenth Amendment does not itself spell out all the details of required criminal procedure found in the Bill of Rights, the courts have allowed some flexibility to the states in that area. For example, the Fifth Amendment requires indictment by a grand jury in serious crimes, but the states are permitted to use an alternate procedure called an **information**. The information drafted by the prosecutor/district attorney serves the same function as an indictment in informing the court and the defendant what the charges are, what facts are alleged, and what possible penalties are involved. While the details may vary from state to state and from regulation to regulation, the overall procedure must be basically fair to the affected parties.

The substantive meaning of the Fourteenth Amendment due process clause is similar to that of the Fifth Amendment. Even if a fair procedure is provided, the courts may rule that the content of the regulation makes it invalid. Such invalidity may be found because the regulation violates a specific prohibition of the Constitution or because it infringes on one of the protected rights.

Since the 1930s, most of the Justices have been more willing to defer to the state legislatures' judgments as to regulations of property and contract rights than to those which infringe on personal freedoms such as speech, press, and assembly. Some Justices and text writers continue to believe that commercial speech is less deserving of protection than noncommercial speech, and may use that distinction to validate one regulation while invalidating another. Not all Justices make these distinctions or apply them in the same way, so that the court is badly divided in many such cases. A majority may agree on the result in a case, but for quite different reasons, and there may be one or more dissenting opinions. As a result, it is often difficult to extract any rules or guidelines for future business conduct.

The *Ran-Dav's* case raises some very difficult issues regarding a state's involvement in religious practices.

RAN-DAV'S COUNTY KOSHER, INC. v. STATE
608 A.2d 1353 (NJ, 1992)

FACTS: Under regulations administered by the Division of Consumer Affairs, the State regulates the preparation, maintenance, and sale of kosher products. The regulations state that it is "an unlawful consumer practice" to sell or attempt to sell food "which is falsely represented to be Kosher." They define "Kosher" as "prepared and maintained in strict compliance with the laws and customs of the Orthodox Jewish religion." Those regulations were invoked by the Attorney General, who brought an enforcement action charging Ran-Dav's County Kosher, Inc. (County Kosher) and its principal, Arthur Weisman, with violations. The charged parties denied the allegations and claimed that the regulations violated the Religion Clauses of the federal and state constitutions. The constitutional claims were brought before the Appellate Division while the trial court retained jurisdiction of the enforcement action. A majority of the Appellate Division upheld the constitutionality of the regulations.

 JUSTICE HANDLER:

The word "kosher" (from the Hebrew "kasher") means "fit" or "ritually correct." It is used to refer to, among other things, the Jewish dietary laws. The practice of "kashrut" within Judaism serves to attain "kedusha" or holiness and is a fundamental tenet of the religion. The origin of the kosher laws can be traced back to the Torah (the first five books of the Bible), but most of the laws concerning what is kosher have developed through centuries of Talmudic debates (debates regarding the application of the principles contained in the Torah) and rulings by rabbinic scholars. The dietary laws of "kashrut" set forth rules covering: "(1) permitted and forbidden animals, (2) forbidden parts of otherwise permitted animals, (3) the methods of slaughtering and preparing permitted animals, (4) forbidden food mixtures, and (5) proportions of food mixtures prohibited ab initio but permitted *ex post facto*...." The laws of kashrut are complex and exacting. For example, animals must be slaughtered in a prescribed manner by a trained person. Meat must be "koshered" according to specifically defined soaking and salting methods to draw out the blood.... Central to the doctrine of "kashrut" is the requirement of the "mashgiah," the religious authority who must supervise kosher butchers and certify compliance with the laws of kashrut. Without proper religious supervision, certain foods are simply non-kosher, even though constituted and prepared in identical fashion to kosher foods....

Because the laws of kashrut are so complex, compliance with them is highly labor intensive. Kosher food therefore costs more than non-kosher food. Because of those higher prices, and because most consumers cannot determine whether foods labeled as "kosher" were prepared under "kosher standards," unscrupulous vendors can reap substantial profits by misleading consumers into believing their products are kosher....

The false promotion of non-kosher foods harms a variety of consumers. Observant Jews may be induced, unwittingly, to break the laws of their religion. Kosher foods are important not only to Jews but to many other persons as well. Adherents to certain other faiths, especially those forbidding the consumption of pork, purchase kosher food to comply with their own religious requirements. People with particular health problems, such as shellfish allergies, buy kosher products to avoid troublesome food. Finally, some members of the general public believe that kosher meat is superior to non-kosher meat because it is prepared under especially close scrutiny....

The constitutional strictures on government action concerning religion seek to avoid certain evils. They include discrimination among religions or between religion and nonreligion, symbolic union between government and a given religious faith or religion in general, sponsorship of the religious mission of a group, excessive entanglement between government and religion, and political divisiveness incited by the government's favoritism of a particular religious faith....

In considering whether the kosher regulations foster excessive government entanglement with religion, we initially note that they impose substantive religious standards on establishments purporting to be kosher. Specifically, the regulations contain numerous requirements relating to religious practices essential in the preparation and maintenance of kosher foods. Further, those requirements must be met "in strict compliance with the laws and customs of the Orthodox Jewish religion." Hence, the administrative scheme does more than require that businesses purporting to be under a certain type of rabbinical supervision are in fact under that type of supervision; it requires such establishments to adhere strictly to religious kosher standards in the conduct of their business and authorizes the State to monitor the adherence to those standards. As a result, Jewish law prescribing religious ritual and practice is inextricably intertwined with the secular law of the State. Further, the State itself takes on the traditional religious supervisory role, thereby partially supplanting the Jewish organizations and institutions that historically have stood as final judges of religious matters....

The sectarian nature of the regulations is further evidenced by the religious qualifications of the persons selected to enforce the regulations. The Chief of the Bureau of Enforcement is an orthodox rabbi. The Advisory Committee, which is authorized to advise the enforcement agency about compliance with the kosher regulations, consists entirely of rabbis....

The regulations at issue in this case do not constitute permissible accommodation of Orthodox Judaism. The Attorney General has not pointed to any state-imposed burdens under which Orthodox Jews currently suffer. If the regulations did not exist, observance of the laws of kashrut would go on, free of state intervention, as it has for thousands of years. The regulations merely serve to advance the form of Orthodox Judaism that the State enforces. "The principle that government may accommodate the free exercise of religion does not supersede the fundamental limitations imposed by the Establishment Clause...."

The State unquestionably has a valid interest in preventing fraud in the sale of any foods, including kosher foods. There are effective ways to achieve that end that will not offend constitutional strictures against state involvement in religion. The State can regulate the advertising and labeling of kosher products. The key to such a regulatory approach would be the religious supervision of the preparation and maintenance of products. The regulation could require those who advertise food products as "kosher" to disclose the basis on which the use of that characterization rests. Many kosher food purveyors would comply by imprinting the symbol of one of the recognized private agencies that supervise kosher compliance (e.g., "U" for the Union of Orthodox Jewish Congregations of America). Other kosher establishments could comply with a disclosure requirement by indicating other forms of rabbinical supervision. Such an approach would thus make use of the kosher foods industry's existing scheme of self-regulation....

The regulations at issue, unfortunately, are not limited to such less intrusive means to protect consumers of kosher foods. As they now stand, the regulations plainly violate constitutional standards. We therefore invalidate those portions of the regulations that impose substantive religious standards for the actual preparation and maintenance of kosher food. We do not invalidate the regulations to the extent that they may require the full and accurate disclosure by kosher establishments of the basis on which they advertise and sell their products as "kosher."

We reverse the judgment of the Appellate Division and remand the matter to the trial court for the dismissal of the State's consumer fraud complaint. We also remand to the Division of Consumer Affairs for the expeditious reformulation of the regulations in a manner consistent with this opinion.

Commerce Clause. Another very significant limitation on the regulatory power of state governments stems from the power granted to Congress under the Commerce Clause. Since one of the major purposes of the Constitution was to create a national marketplace for our people's goods and services, the states cannot unduly or unfairly interfere with interstate commerce. Similarly, the Commerce Clause limits the states' power to tax interstate business.

To be valid, state regulations cannot discriminate against interstate commerce in favor of local businesses. Interstate businesses must be given a fair chance of competition in local markets. Second, a state regulation cannot unduly burden interstate commerce. In one famous case, an Illinois statute required curved mud-flaps over the rear tires of all large trucks. The flat mud-flaps which were used to comply with the laws of all other states would not comply with the Illinois law. Nor would the curved mud-flaps comply with the other states' laws. As a result, an interstate trucker would have to drive around Illinois, or stop at the state borders to change mudflaps, or drive through and risk a ticket. The U.S. Supreme Court decided that this state law unduly burdened the interstate truckers and held it unconstitutional.

Finally, a state regulation is not valid where Congress, under the Commerce Clause, has preempted the particular subject area. The *Flood v. Kuhn* case (1972), involving baseball, is one such example; Congress has preempted the regulation of professional sports. Frequently, Congress does not specify whether it wishes to preclude state action on a particular subject, so the courts are forced to imply a congressional intent from the legislative history of the national statute and from the degree of comprehensiveness of the national regulations.

Justice Thomas's opinion in the *Oregon Waste Systems* case, which follows, discusses these "negative" implications of the commerce clause.

OREGON WASTE SYSTEMS, INC. v. DEPARTMENT OF ENVIRONMENTAL QUALITY
511 U.S. 93 (1994)

FACTS: In 1989, the state of Oregon—which already levied a wide range of fees on landfill operations to fund the state's comprehensive regulation of solid waste disposal—imposed a surcharge on the disposal within the state of solid waste generated out-of-state. The statute imposing the surcharge provided that the amount of the surcharge had to be based on the costs to the state and its political subdivisions of disposing of such out-of-state waste that was not otherwise paid for under specified statutes. A state agency set the surcharge, by rule, at $2.25 per ton. In conjunction with the surcharge, the state imposed a fee, capped at $0.85 per ton, on the in-state disposal of waste generated within the state. The operator of a solid waste landfill, and a company which transported solid waste from another state to a landfill in Oregon, alleged that the surcharge and its enabling statutes violated the Federal Constitution's commerce clause. The Court of Appeals, however, upheld the statutes and rule. The Supreme Court of Oregon affirmed.

 JUSTICE THOMAS:

The Commerce Clause provides that "the Congress shall have Power ... to regulate Commerce ... among the several States." Though phrased as a grant of regulatory power to Congress,... the Clause has long been understood to have a "negative" aspect that denies the States the power unjustifiably to discriminate against or burden the interstate flow of articles of commerce.... The Framers granted Congress plenary authority over interstate commerce in "the conviction that in order to succeed, the new Union would have to avoid the tendencies toward economic Balkanization that had plagued relations among the Colonies and later among the States under the Articles of Confederation."... "This principle that our economic unit is the Nation, which alone has the gamut of powers necessary to control of the economy,... has as its corollary that the states are not separable economic units."... Consistent with these principles, we have held that the first step in analyzing any law subject to judicial scrutiny under the negative Commerce Clause is to determine whether it "regulates evenhandedly with only 'incidental' effects on interstate commerce, or discriminates against interstate commerce."... As we use the term here, "discrimination" simply means differential treatment of in-state and out-of-state economic interests that benefits the former and burdens the latter. If a restriction on commerce is discriminatory, it is virtually per se invalid.... By contrast, nondiscriminatory regulations that have only incidental effects on interstate commerce are valid "unless the burden imposed on such commerce is clearly excessive in relation to the putative local benefits."... We deem it ... obvious here that

Oregon's $2.25 per ton surcharge is discriminatory on its face. The surcharge subjects waste from other States to a fee almost three times greater than the $0.85 per ton charge imposed on solid in-state waste. The statutory determinant for which fee applies to any particular shipment of solid waste to an Oregon landfill is whether or not the waste was "generated out-of-state."... It is well established, however, that a law is discriminatory if it "tax[es] a transaction or incident more heavily when it crosses state lines than when it occurs entirely within the State."...

Because the Oregon surcharge is discriminatory, the virtually per se rule of invalidity provides the proper legal standard here, not the *Pike* balancing test. As a result, the surcharge must be invalidated unless respondents can "show that it advances a legitimate local purpose that cannot be adequately served by reasonable nondiscriminatory alternatives."... Our cases require that justifications for discriminatory restrictions on commerce pass the "strictest scrutiny." The State's burden of justification is so heavy that "facial discrimination by itself may be a fatal defect."...

Respondents' principal defense of the higher surcharge on out-of-state waste is that it is a "compensatory tax" necessary to make shippers of such waste pay their "fair share" of the costs imposed on Oregon by the disposal of their waste in the State.... Though our cases sometimes discuss the concept of the compensatory tax as if it were a doctrine unto itself, it is merely a specific way of justifying a facially discriminatory tax as achieving a legitimate local purpose that cannot be achieved through nondiscriminatory mean.... Under that doctrine, a facially discriminatory tax that imposes on interstate commerce the rough equivalent of an identifiable and "substantially similar" tax on intrastate commerce does not offend the negative Commerce Clause.... To justify a charge on interstate commerce as a compensatory tax, a State must, as a threshold matter, "identify ... the [intrastate tax] burden for which the State is attempting to compensate."... Once that burden has been identified, the tax on interstate commerce must be shown roughly to approximate—but not exceed—the amount of the tax on intrastate commerce.... Finally, the events on which the interstate and intrastate taxes are imposed must be "substantially equivalent;" that is, they must be sufficiently similar in substance to serve as mutually exclusive "prox[ies]" for each other.... As Justice Cardozo explained for the Court in *Henneford*, under a truly compensatory tax scheme "the stranger from afar is subject to no greater burdens as a consequence of ownership than the dweller within the gates. The one pays upon one activity or incident, and the other upon another, but the sum is the same when the reckoning is closed."...

Although it is often no mean feat to determine whether a challenged tax is a compensatory tax, we have little difficulty concluding that the Oregon surcharge is not such a tax. Oregon does not impose a specific charge of at least $2.25 per ton on shippers of waste generated in Oregon, for which the out-of-state surcharge might be considered compensatory. In fact, the only analogous charge on the disposal of Oregon waste is $0.85 per ton, approximately one-third of the amount imposed on waste from other States.... Respondents' failure to identify a specific charge on intrastate commerce equal to or exceeding the surcharge is fatal to their claim....

Respondents' final argument is that Oregon has an interest in spreading the costs of the in-state disposal of Oregon waste to all Oregonians. That is, because all citizens of Oregon benefit from the proper in-state disposal of waste from Oregon, respondents claim it is only proper for Oregon to require them to bear more of the costs of disposing of such waste in the State through a higher general tax burden. At the same time, however, Oregon citizens should not be required to bear the costs of disposing of out-of-state waste, respondents claim. The necessary result of that limited cost shifting is to require shippers of out-of-state waste to bear the full costs of in-state disposal, but to permit shippers of Oregon waste to bear less than the full cost. We fail to perceive any distinction between respondents' contention and a claim that the State has an interest in reducing the costs of handling in-state waste. Our cases condemn as illegitimate, however, any governmental interest that is not "unrelated to economic protectionism,"... and regulating interstate commerce in such a way as to give those who handle domestic articles of commerce a cost advantage over their competitors handling similar items produced elsewhere constitutes such protectionism.... To give controlling effect to respondents' characterization of Oregon's tax scheme as seemingly benign cost spreading would require us to overlook the fact that the scheme necessarily incorporates a protectionist objective as well....

Respondents counter that if Oregon is engaged in any form of protectionism, it is "resource protectionism," not economic protectionism. It is true that by discouraging the flow of out-of-state waste into Oregon landfills, the higher surcharge on waste from other States conserves more space in those landfills for waste generated in Oregon. Recharacterizing the surcharge as resource protectionism hardly advances respondents' cause, however. Even assuming that landfill space is a "natural resource," "a State may not accord its own inhabitants a preferred right of access over consumers in other States to natural resources located within its borders."... As we held more than a century ago, "if the State, under the guise of exerting its police powers, should [impose a burden] ... applicable solely to articles [of commerce] ... produced or manufactured in other States, the courts would find no difficulty in holding such legislation to be in conflict with the Constitution of the United States."...

We recognize that the States have broad discretion to configure their systems of taxation as they deem appropriate.... All we intimate here is that their discretion in this regard, as in all others, is bounded by any relevant limitations of the Federal Constitution, in these cases the negative Commerce Clause. Because respondents have offered no legitimate reason to subject waste generated in other States to a discriminatory surcharge approximately three times as high as that imposed on waste generated in Oregon, the surcharge is facially invalid under the negative Commerce Clause. Accordingly, the judgment of the Oregon Supreme Court is reversed, and the cases are remanded for further proceedings not inconsistent with this opinion.

ADMINISTRATIVE AGENCIES

Origins and Functions. Often referred to as the "headless fourth branch of government," administrative agencies originated as a means to deal with the complex problems of a modern urban society. Judges and juries lack the technical expertise to solve problems in such areas as telecommunications, transportation, investment securities, and labor relations. Furthermore, court procedures tend to be technical and subject to lengthy delays.

The original idea of the independent regulatory agency was to provide a body of technical experts who could render faster decisions, based on the realities of the field, and free of the legal technicalities of the courtroom. Congress also wanted these agencies free of direct control by the President, so that they would be better able to implement the policy standards established by Congress in the statutes creating the agencies and defining their powers. The idea was for Congress to set out the basic objectives and standards, and the agencies then to implement those policies with detailed rules and individual decisions.

Originally, there was considerable concern over the extent to which Congress could lawfully delegate the legislative power given to it in Article I to these other bodies. One of the centerpieces of Franklin D. Roosevelt's New Deal, the National Industrial Recovery Act of 1933, was invalidated on these grounds in the famous "sick chicken" case, *Schechter Poultry Corp. v. United States*, 295 U.S. 495 (1935). The NIRA authorized industry groups to draw up "codes of fair competition" which could then be approved by the President. Schechter had been prosecuted for violating such a code. The Supreme Court said that Congress could not lawfully give such groups a blank check for whatever regulations they thought wise. The NIRA was declared unconstitutional. Subsequently, grants of discretion almost as broad to administrative agencies have been upheld, so that the *Schechter* rule is of little value today.

Problems. Gradually, as administrative agencies' procedures became more formalized, they were subject to many of the same criticisms that had earlier been leveled against the courts. Delays and technicalities existed in agency proceedings, too. Not all agency members were experts; some were political cronies, lacking experience in the areas they were supposed to be regulating. Many staffers drifted back and forth between agencies and private employment, creating the appearance at least of serious conflicts of interest. Questions were raised by scholars and affected parties about the fairness of a hearing where the same body was investigator, prosecutor, and judge, and was charged by Congress with implementing specific policy results.

Our national economy is strong and vibrant enough to tolerate some tinkering of this sort, but there are limits. The New Deal created agencies like a computer doing permutations of the alphabet. The 1960s and 1970s were almost as bad, and in some ways, even worse. Entire industries were subjected to bureaucratic controls—banking, transportation, communication, power. Key aspects of nearly all industries were subjected to agency control—labor relations, issuance of securities, trade practices, mergers. Nearly all businesses are subject to environmental and safety controls. Such controls are not totally evil or counterproductive; in many cases, they were adopted because of gross abuses. The total impact of such regulations, however, can be devastating. At some point, a straw breaks the camel's back; one additional regulation becomes a cost that makes the business unprofitable. The real miracle of American business is that it has persevered, and prospered, despite these massive additional costs.

Reform and Deregulation. In the late 1970s, people finally began to talk seriously about deregulating significant sectors of the economy. In part, this discussion was due to a resurgence of free market economics, but it also occurred because the regulated economy was not performing satisfactorily.

Innovation was occurring, and new jobs were being created in whitecollar, unregulated industries such as computers. Steel, autos, and transportation—burdened with stifling regulations and conflict-oriented labor relations—were in trouble. The Japanese model of labor-management cooperation was promoted as the wave of the future. Administrative rules were seen as barriers to new methods and new relationships. The nuclear power industry, for example, has been effectively killed in the United States, while it flourishes in such countries as France and Japan.

Significant deregulation has already occurred in the power, banking, and transportation industries. In other areas, agencies such as the Occupational Safety and Health Administration have a more realistic view of their function. Instead of requiring the rehanging of fire extinguishers that were an inch or two out of line with the OSHA standards, the agency has now concentrated on more serious health hazards in the workplace. At the state level, "sunset" laws are being considered, which would terminate an agency after a certain number of years unless specific legislative renewal of the agency was enacted.

No one wants to return to the days of robber barons and polluted air and water. The challenge for both business and government, as we move toward the 21st century, is to develop administrative regulations only where necessary and to make them rational and cost-effective.

ADMINISTRATIVE PROCEDURE

The following discussion focuses on the constitutional and statutory requirements for administrative action.

Requirement of a Hearing. When an agency is acting in its legislative capacity, adopting rules, it need not hold a trial-type hearing. If it does hold hearings prior to the adoption of such a rule, it is not bound by the evidence produced at the hearing, any more than Congress is in its legislative capacity. When an agency acts as a court, however, and adjudicates an individual matter, it usually can do so only after a trial-type hearing. In this capacity, it is bound by the evidence in the record, just as a court would be. Its decision must be based on that evidence and stem from that evidence. While the agency is given considerable discretion in setting the details of that hearing, it must be basically fair to those affected.

Requirement of Notice. If there is to be a trial-type hearing, the party affected must be given adequate notice to prepare for it. In practice, however, the courts have interpreted this requirement quite loosely. The evidence introduced may vary from the charges alleged, unless the variation would be unfair to the affected party.

Notice usually is sent through the mail to directly affected parties. Where a general agency decision is involved, notice is usually given through the *Federal Register*, the official bulletin for agency action.

Requirement of Confrontation. Our legal system does not favor secret accusers. Personal prejudice and envy may be motivating factors in the accusation. We want the accusers to come forward and to be available for cross-examination. We feel that truth and justice can only be served when the accusers and the accused confront each other. Otherwise, as Justice Douglas once stated, "So far as we or the Board know, the accusers may be psychopaths or venal people, ... who revel in being informers. They may bear old grudges. Under crossexamination their stories might disappear like bubbles. Their whispered confidences might turn out to be yarns conceived by twisted minds or by people who, though sincere, have poor faculties of observation and memory."

Once again, however, these general rules requiring confrontation are subject to modification under particular circumstances, through the agency's administrative discretion. The U.S. Supreme

Court ruled in 1960 that the persons who had accused state voter registrars of violations of national voting laws did not have to appear and confront the registrars. The Court felt that anonymity had to be preserved in that situation. This case (*Hannah v. Larche*, 363 U.S. 420) is clearly an exception to the general rule.

Right to Counsel. As is true in criminal proceedings, the person accused in an administrative proceeding is entitled to be represented by counsel. This requirement is also a deeply imbedded element of our common-law heritage. The right to counsel may be limited, however, where the agency is conducting an investigation, rather than adjudicating a disputed matter. In one famous case, *In re Groban*, 352 U.S. 330 (1957), the U.S. Supreme Court decided that a state fire marshal conducting an arson investigation did not have to give witnesses the right to counsel, even though they had been compelled to appear and to testify. The witnesses were not directly accused—yet. The court felt that this sort of investigation was analogous to a grand jury investigation of possible crimes, where the right to counsel has traditionally been limited.

Right to an Impartial Hearing Officer. One of the traditional concerns with administrative agencies is their alleged lack of impartiality, since they are charged with the enforcement of the statutes so as to produce the desired policy results. Part of this concern is also due to the fact that staff members may move back and forth between an agency and the industry it is trying to regulate; the fear is that such persons may become promoters rather than regulators. Legislative directions to the agency are sometimes not clear: Congress directed the original Atomic Energy Commission to promote and regulate the atomic power industry. These sorts of problems are an inevitable part of the agency regulatory process and are tolerated as part of the price of using the agency method.

Where the administrator has a direct, personal stake in the outcome of a proceeding, however, the possibility of bias is so great that the procedure, or the administrator, or both, must be changed. In one classic example, the mayors of Ohio cities were given the power to hear alleged violations of the prohibition laws. The mayor would be paid court costs only if the accused was found guilty. In *Tumey v. Ohio*, 273 U.S. 510 (1927), the U.S. Supreme Court held that this procedural arrangement violated the accused person's right to an impartial decision on the charges.

To try to separate their investigation/prosecution functions from their trial/adjudication functions, many agencies have a separate staff of hearing examiners, now called **administrative law judges** (ALJs). The prosecution staff decide whether to issue a complaint. If they do, there is a hearing before an ALJ, who must render a decision on the facts presented during the hearing.

Right to Review. Part of the agreement on using the administrative agency system, with all its ambiguities and conflicting loyalties, was an understanding that court review of these decisions would be available. Some possibility of unfairness could be tolerated, if court review were available to correct the most obvious abuses.

In many of the important agencies, such as the NLRB, the FCC, and the FTC, the agency itself—the board or commission—may review the findings and order of its ALJ prior to a court appeal. This internal agency review procedure varies somewhat from agency to agency. In some instances, the review is a limited one, "on the record:" Did the ALJ follow the statute, and is his or her order supported by evidence in the trial record? If so, the agency affirms the decision, much as an appellate court would. In other agencies, the board or commission may itself use the hearing record for making its own decision in the matter, just as if it had heard the case itself—a de novo review.

While courts are quite willing to reverse an agency's interpretation of its statute, they generally defer to the agency's findings of fact and its orders, if based on evidence in the hearing record. The agency is the expert, and its policy decisions should stand, unless they are arbitrary or biased. For the most part, courts do not have an effective check on agency decisions, since few decisions will be unsupported in the hearing record.

The *Dalton* case discusses these rules.

DALTON v. SPECTER
114 S.Ct. 1719 (1994)

FACTS: Senator Arlen Specter and others filed this action under the Administrative Procedure Act (APA) and the Defense Base Closure and Realignment Act of 1990 (1990 Act) seeking to enjoin Secretary of Defense John Dalton from carrying out the President's decision, pursuant to the 1990 Act, to close the Philadelphia Naval Shipyard. The District Court dismissed the complaint on the alternative grounds that the 1990 Act itself precluded judicial review and that the political question doctrine foreclosed judicial intervention. In affirming in part and reversing in part, the Court of Appeals held that judicial review of the closure decision was available to ensure that the Secretary and the Defense Base Closure and Realignment Commission (Commission), as participants in the selection process, had complied with the procedural mandates specified by Congress. Dalton asked for review.

 CHIEF JUSTICE REHNQUIST:

The decision to close the shipyard was the end result of an elaborate selection process prescribed by the 1990 Act. Designed "to provide a fair process that will result in the timely closure and realignment of military installations inside the United States," ... the Act provides for three successive rounds of base closings—in 1991, 1993, and 1995, respectively.... For each round, the Secretary must prepare closure and realignment recommendations, based on selection criteria he establishes after notice and an opportunity for public comment....

The Secretary submits his recommendations to Congress and to the Defense Base Closure and Realignment Commission (Commission), an independent body whose eight members are appointed by the President with the advice and consent of the Senate.... The Commission must then hold public hearings and prepare a report, containing both an assessment of the Secretary's recommendations and the Commission's own recommendations for base closures and realignments.... Within roughly three months of receiving the Secretary's recommendations, the Commission has to submit its report to the President....

In this case, respondents brought suit under the APA, alleging that the Secretary and the Commission did not follow the procedural mandates of the 1990 Act.

But here, ... the prerequisite to review under the APA—"final agency action"—is lacking. The reports submitted by the Secretary of Defense and the Commission, like the report of the Secretary of Commerce in *Franklin* "carr[y] no direct consequences" for base closings.... The action that "will directly affect" the military bases ... is taken by the President, when he submits his certification of approval to Congress. Accordingly, the Secretary's and Commission's reports serve "more like a tentative recommendation than a final and binding determination...." The reports are like the ruling of a subordinate official, not final and therefore not subject to review.... The actions of the President, in turn, are not reviewable under the APA because, as we concluded in *Franklin*, the President is not an "agency...."

First, respondents underestimate the President's authority under the Act, and the importance of his role in the base closure process. Without the President's approval no bases are closed under the Act.... The Act, in turn, does not by its terms circumscribe the President's discretion to approve or disapprove the Commission's report.... Second, and more fundamentally, respondents' argument ignores "[t]he core question" for determining finality: "whether the agency has completed its decision-making process, and whether the result of that process is one that will directly affect the parties...." That the President cannot pick and choose among bases, and must accept or reject the entire package offered by the Commission, is immaterial. What is crucial is the fact that "[t]he President, not the [Commission], takes the final action that affects" the military installations.... Accordingly, we hold that the decisions made pursuant to the 1990 Act are not reviewable under the APA....

Our decision in *Youngstown* ... does not suggest a different conclusion. In *Youngstown*, the Government disclaimed any statutory authority for the President's seizure of steel mills.... "We do not understand the Government to rely on statutory authorization for this seizure." The only basis of authority asserted was the President's inherent constitutional power as the Executive and the Commander-in-Chief of the Armed Forces.... Because no statutory authority was claimed, the case necessarily turned on whether the Constitution authorized the President's actions. *Youngstown* thus involved the conceded *absence of any* statutory authority, not a claim that the President acted in excess of such authority. The case cannot be read for the proposition that an action taken by the President in excess of his statutory authority necessarily violates the Constitution....

The 1990 Act does not at all limit the President's discretion in approving or disapproving the Commission's recommendations.... The Third Circuit seemed to believe that the President's authority to close bases depended on the Secretary's and Commission's compliance with statutory procedures. This view of the statute, however, incorrectly conflates "the duties of the Secretary and Commission" with the authority of the President. The President's authority to act is not contingent on the Secretary's and Commission's fulfillment of all the procedural requirements imposed upon them by the 1990 Act. Nothing in § 2903(e) requires the President to determine whether the Secretary or Commission committed any procedural violations in making their recommendations, nor does § 2903(e) prohibit the President from approving recommendations that are procedurally flawed. Indeed, nothing in § 2903(e) prevents the President from approving or disapproving the recommendations for whatever reason he sees fit....

How the President chooses to exercise the discretion Congress has granted him is not a matter for our review.... As we stated in *George S. Bush & Co.* ... "[n]o question of law is raised when the exercise of [the President's] discretion is challenged."

In sum, we hold that the actions of the Secretary and the Commission cannot be reviewed under the APA because they are not "final agency actions." The actions of the President cannot be reviewed under the APA because the President is not an "agency" under the Act. The claim that the President exceeded his authority under the 1990 Act is not a constitutional claim, but a statutory one. Where a statute, such as the 1990 Act, commits decision-making to the discretion of the President, judicial review of the President's decision is not available.

Respondents tell us that failure to allow judicial review here would virtually repudiate *Marbury v. Madison*, ... and nearly two centuries of constitutional adjudication. But our conclusion that judicial review is not available for respondents' claim follows from our interpretation of an Act of Congress, by which we and all federal courts are bound. The judicial power of the United States conferred by Article III of the Constitution is upheld just as surely by withholding judicial relief where Congress has permissibly foreclosed it, as it is by granting such relief where authorized by the Constitution or by statute.

The judgment of the Court of Appeals is Reversed.

QUASI-JUDICIAL PROCEDURES IN ADMINISTRATIVE AGENCIES

The National Labor Relations Board, the Federal Trade Commission, the Environmental Protection Agency, the Occupational Safety and Health Administration, and many other national and state administrative agencies daily hear disputes concerning violations of their rules and regulations. Typically, the businessperson will have more contact with administrative agencies than with the court system. The procedure for the determination of disputes in the administrative agency system is termed *quasi-judicial* because it does not have the full authority of a court and because the party being tried does not have the right to trial by jury. Nearly all decisions of administrative bodies are subject to judicial review by an appellate court.

To give the student an understanding of a typical administrative agency quasi-judicial procedure, we will follow a National Labor Relations Board case from beginning to end.

NLRB PROCEDURE IN UNFAIR LABOR PRACTICES CASES

Charge. An NLRB regional office is notified that an employer or a union is engaged in one or more unfair labor practices. This means that the employer or the union has violated the statutory rules by which both labor unions and management must conduct themselves. The complaining party is then asked to complete a **charge**, which is simply a form specifying what unfair labor practice has been committed and by whom. Once a charge is filed, a field examiner conducts an investigation. This is done to determine whether there is sufficient evidence of a violation to proceed to a formal hearing. If the field examiner does not find evidence sufficient to support further activity in the case, then the charge will be dismissed.

Formal Complaint. If the evidence found was sufficient to justify pursuing the case, then a formal complaint will be filed by the NLRB's Office of General Counsel. This complaint contains the specific allegations of wrongdoing. The employer or the labor union alleged to be in violation will be given a copy, as well as an opportunity to answer the charges.

Answer. The answer filed in this case is similar to the answer filed in a civil case. The answer may deny some allegations and admit others. Typically, allegations concerning violation of the National Labor Relations Act will be denied, and allegations concerning time and place will be admitted.

Hearing. A hearing is then scheduled at which an administrative law judge hears testimony. Witnesses are presented by both parties in a manner similar to the procedure followed in a trial of a civil lawsuit. At the end of the testimony, the parties are allowed to make summarization statements.

Findings of Fact and Conclusions of Law. The administrative law judge (ALJ) will prepare a written decision entitled "Findings of Fact and Conclusions of Law." After the ALJ has rendered a decision, either of the parties may request an appeal. This must be done within twenty days after the decision. If an appeal is not requested, the decision of the ALJ becomes final. If a request for an appeal is made, then the parties will file legal briefs to support their positions. They may request oral arguments before the five-member National Labor Relations Board in Washington, D.C.

Board Review. The Board will review the briefs of the parties, hear oral arguments, and render a decision and order. The NLRB itself has no legal power to enforce its order. If the finding is against the employer or the union and that party refuses to comply with the Board's order, then the Board must ask the U.S. Court of Appeals for a judgment to enforce its order. Or, if the employer or the union feels that the NLRB decision is incorrect or unfair, it may appeal the decision to the U.S. Court of Appeals.

Review by the U.S. Court of Appeals. The U.S. Court of Appeals will review the decision of the NLRB upon the petition of any interested party, or upon request of the NLRB if enforcement of an order of the Board is requested. The review by the court is concerned with two questions: first, was the decision of the Board supported by substantial evidence?; and second, did the Board follow the correct substantive law? If the court agrees with the Board's decision, it will order compliance. If the court disagrees with the Board, it can reverse the Board's decision and dismiss the case or send the case back for a rehearing.

Review by the Supreme Court. Either party may petition the Supreme Court of the United States for a writ of certiorari to review the decision of the U.S. Court of Appeals. If the writ of certiorari is granted, a review will be had, and the parties will have to comply with the final judgment of the U.S. Supreme Court. If the Supreme Court refuses to issue a writ of certiorari, then the judgment of the U.S. Court of Appeals is final. The failure of a party to obey a court order can be punishable as either civil or criminal contempt of court.

The procedure of the National Labor Relations Board is typical of the procedure used by most of the administrative agencies that have quasi-judicial authority. In other words, an investigation will be conducted and an initial hearing will be held before an administrative law judge, with the right of an appeal to a quasi-judicial board and with the right of a later appeal to an appellate court. The legal justification for not giving the right to trial by jury in these cases is that they are not legal trials and that the decision rendered is not a civil judgment for money. They are more like an equity injunction—an order to comply with the law, an order to pay back wages, or an order to rehire.

The flowchart on the next page shows the procedures for an unfair labor practice case before the NLRB.

SIGNIFICANCE OF THIS CHAPTER

Government regulation of business is one of the most important legal areas for the modern business manager. Many business decisions are subject to detailed, and often confusing, regulations. Likewise, entire industries may operate under an administrative agency as the watchdog of the public interest. In this context, it is important to remember that even the government must play by the rules and that court review is available where an agency oversteps its boundaries or acts in an arbitrary and unfair manner.

This chapter outlined the basic framework for government regulation of business. Other specific constitutional issues will be raised in other chapters. Questions about the constitutionality of a particular government action may be raised by the affected party, so each of us needs to know the basic rules.

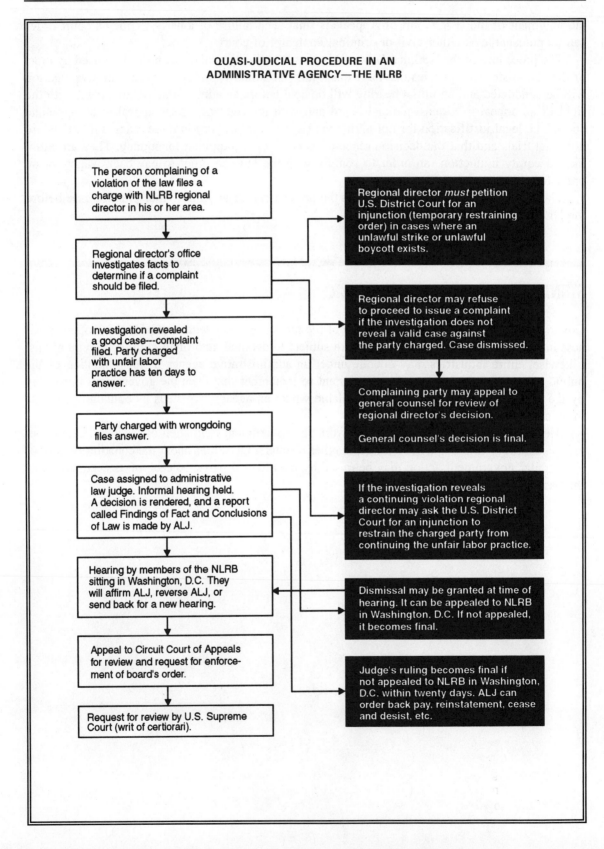

QUASI-JUDICIAL PROCEDURE IN AN
ADMINISTRATIVE AGENCY—THE NLRB

The person complaining of a violation of the law files a charge with NLRB regional director in his or her area.

Regional director's office investigates facts to determine if a complaint should be filed.

Investigation revealed a good case---complaint filed. Party charged with unfair labor practice has ten days to answer.

Party charged with wrongdoing files answer.

Case assigned to administrative law judge. Informal hearing held. A decision is rendered, and a report called Findings of Fact and Conclusions of Law is made by ALJ.

Hearing by members of the NLRB sitting in Washington, D.C. They will affirm ALJ, reverse ALJ, or send back for a new hearing.

Appeal to Circuit Court of Appeals for review and request for enforcement of board's order.

Request for review by U.S. Supreme Court (writ of certiorari).

Regional director *must* petition U.S. District Court for an injunction (temporary restraining order) in cases where an unlawful strike or unlawful boycott exists.

Regional director may refuse to proceed to issue a complaint if the investigation does not reveal a valid case against the party charged. Case dismissed.

Complaining party may appeal to general counsel for review of regional director's decision.

General counsel's decision is final.

If the investigation reveals a continuing violation regional director may ask the U.S. District Court for an injunction to restrain the charged party from continuing the unfair labor practice.

Dismissal may be granted at time of hearing. It can be appealed to NLRB in Washington, D.C. If not appealed, it becomes final.

Judge's ruling becomes final if not appealed to NLRB in Washington, D.C. within twenty days. ALJ can order back pay, reinstatement, cease and desist, etc.

PROBLEMS FOR DISCUSSION

1. Plaintiff filed a civil antitrust action, seeking an injunction and treble damages, on behalf of himself and all other purchasers of residential real estate in the prior four years in the Greater New Orleans area who had used the services of one of the defendant real estate brokers. Plaintiff alleged a conspiracy to fix commission rates and real estate prices. Defendants moved to dismiss alleging: (1) that their activities were only local in nature; (2) that there was no legal requirement that a broker be employed in the sale of real estate; and (3) that they did not usually procure financing or insurance, nor did they examine the validity of the sellers' titles. The U.S. District Court dismissed the complaint, and the Court of Appeals affirmed.

   How should the U.S. Supreme Court rule, and why?

2. The State of Arizona passed a law that prohibits railroad trains crossing through the state of Arizona to have more than seventy freight cars, or fourteen passenger cars. The Southern Pacific Railroad violated this law by having more cars than allowed and was prosecuted for violation of the law. Their defense was that the law was unconstitutional.

   How should the court rule? Is this law constitutional? Why?

3. The Gray Panthers is an organization formed to promote the rights of the elderly. The national Medicaid program provides funds to states that pay for medical treatment for the poor. An individual's benefits depend on the financial resources "available" to him or her. Some states assume ("deem") that part of a spouse's income is available to an applicant for Medicaid. As a result, some persons do not qualify for benefits at all, or qualify for reduced benefits. The Gray Panthers challenged the U.S. regulations that permit the states to deem a spouse's income to the Medicaid applicant without examining the facts of the individual case. Both the U.S. District Court and the Court of Appeals for the District of Columbia held the regulations invalid.

   Are these regulations valid? Discuss.

4. Dow Chemical Co. operates a 2,000-acre facility manufacturing chemicals at Midland, Michigan. The facility consists of numerous covered buildings, with manufacturing equipment and piping conduits located between the various buildings exposed to visual observation from the air. At all times, Dow has maintained elaborate security around the perimeter of the complex, barring ground-level public views of these areas. It also investigates any low-level flights by aircraft over the facility. Dow has not undertaken, however, to conceal all manufacturing equipment within the complex from aerial views. Dow maintains that the cost of covering its exposed equipment would be prohibitive.

   Enforcement officials of EPA, with Dow's consent, made an on-site inspection of two power plants in this complex. A subsequent EPA request for a second inspection, however, was denied, and EPA did not thereafter seek an administrative search warrant. Instead, EPA employed a commercial aerial photographer, using a standard floor-mounted, precision aerial mapping camera, to take photographs of the facility from altitudes of 12,000, 3,000, and 1,200 feet. At all times the aircraft was lawfully within navigable airspace.

   EPA did not inform Dow of this aerial photography, but when Dow became aware of it, Dow brought suit in the District Court, alleging that EPA's action violated the Fourth Amendment and was beyond EPA's statutory investigative authority. The District Court granted Dow's motion for summary judgment on the ground that EPA had no authority to take aerial photographs and that doing so was a search violating the Fourth Amendment. EPA was permanently enjoined from taking aerial photographs of Dow's premises and from disseminating, releasing, or copying the photographs already taken.

The Court of Appeals reversed, and the case was appealed to the U.S. Supreme Court. Have Dow's rights been violated? Why or why not?

5. The Minnesota Legislature enacted a statute banning the retail sale of milk in plastic non-returnable, nonrefillable containers, but permitting such sale in other nonreturnable, non-refillable containers, such as paperboard milk cartons. Clover Leaf Creamery Co. brought this action challenging the statute and contends that the statute violates the Equal Protection and Commerce Clauses of the Constitution.

The parties agree that the standard of review applicable to this case under the Equal Protection Clause is the familiar "rational basis" test. Moreover, they agree that the purposes of the Act cited by the legislature—promoting resource conservation, easily solid waste disposal problems, and conserving energy—are legitimate state purposes. Thus, the controversy in this case centers on the narrow issue of whether the legislative classification between plastic and nonplastic nonreturnable milk containers is rationally related to achievement of the statutory purposes. The Minnesota District Court, the trial court, found the statute invalid. The Minnesota Supreme Court also found the statute invalid, and the State of Minnesota appealed to the U.S. Supreme Court.
Does the statute violate the Constitution? Explain

Chapter 4
Court Systems and Civil Procedure

Legal principles are meaningless without effective mechanisms for resolving disputes and enforcing the law. In Chapter 1, we noted the two major classifications of law—procedural law and substantive law. This chapter focuses on procedural law—how courts hear cases. (Nearly all of the rest of the book discusses the various substantive law rules.) Our purpose in this chapter is not to equip you to litigate your own case. Rather, you should know what is involved in the litigation process, so that you can make a more informed decision as to when you want to litigate a dispute.

We will first examine our dual court system, then review the major steps in a civil litigation, and conclude with a brief look at two alternative methods of dispute resolution.

COURT SYSTEMS

We noted in Chapter 3 that the United States has a federal system of government, meaning that there is a national government and fifty state governments. In most nations with federal systems, there is only one national court—a supreme court, which resolves inconsistencies and disputes between the several states or regions. The U.S. is unique, in that we have a complete set of national courts, as well as the court systems in our fifty states.

Managers (and citizens) need to be aware of both systems, because cases involving business issues (and personal rights) may occur in either system. While most substantive law pertaining to business is state law, there are many national regulations which may apply, as we saw in the last chapter. In addition, there are some cases which may be filed in either system, as will be discussed in the next sections.

National Court System. The Constitution establishes only the Supreme Court, but then gives Congress the power to set up other national courts as the need arises. The national court system now also includes Courts of Appeal, District Courts, and several specialty courts, in addition to the administrative agencies which we discussed in Chapter 3. Trials are held in the District Courts or the specialty courts. Appeals go to the Courts of Appeal for the various geographic areas, or to one of the specialty appeals courts. A. final level of appeal to the Supreme Court is now nearly always at the Court's discretion.

The power of a court to hear particular kinds of case is called its **subject-matter jurisdiction**. **U.S. District Courts** have both civil and criminal subject-matter jurisdiction. They hear criminal cases where the crime charged is a violation of national law. (State crimes are tried in the appropriate state courts.) U.S. District Courts also hear civil cases which involve national substantive law, or certain classes of persons. Civil cases involving the Constitution, treaties, and national statutes, such as those dealing with patents and copyrights, are heard in the District Courts. So are cases arising under maritime or admiralty law. Cases involving the United States as a party, or the representatives to foreign governments, or one of our states against another state or its citizens or foreign persons can also be tried in District Court. However, since passage of the Eleventh Amendment, no claim against a state by persons from another state, or from another nation, can be heard in national courts.

For business persons, the most important basis for using the District Courts is **diversity of citizenship**. If all plaintiffs are citizens of states different than those of all defendants (that is, no state is represented on both sides of the case), *and* if at least $75,000 is "at issue" in the case, the District Court can hear the case, even though it involves no substantive national law at all. The District Court is an alternative place for trial, in addition to the appropriate state court or courts. If the plaintiff files such a case in the U.S. District Court, it will be tried there. If the plaintiff files in an appropriate state court, but the defendant wishes to have the case heard in District Court, the defendant can file a petition to have the case **removed** from the state court to a District Court in that state. If the defendant does not have the case removed, it will stay in the state court, be tried there, and appealed (if at all) through the state's appellate levels. If there is no national substantive law involved, and no diversity with $75,000 at stake, the civil case will be tried in a state court.

Since there is no national substantive law involved in a diversity case, the District Court will have to decide which state's law should be applied. It will do this by applying the choice of law rules of the state in which it is located. In general, questions as to the validity of a contract are decided according to the law of the place where the contract was made. Questions relating to the performance of the contract are decided according to the law of the place of performance. For torts, a court may apply the law of the place the tort was committed, or the law of the state having the greatest "grouping of contacts" with the tort. For procedural issues,, the District Court will follow the Federal Rules of Civil procedure.

The *Matimak* case involves a question of diversity of citizenship jurisdiction.

MATIMAK TRADING CO. v.
KHALILY, d/b/a UNITEX MILLS, INC. & D.A.Y. KIDS SPORTSWEAR INC.
118 F.2d 76 (Second Circuit 1997)

FACTS: Matimak is a Hong Kong corporation, and also has its principle place of business there. Unitex and D.A.Y. are both New York corporations. Matimak filed this lawsuit for breach of contract in the U.S. District Court for the Southern District of New York, on the basis of diversity of citizenship. The lawsuit was filed in 1996, before sovereignty over Hong Kong was transferred from the United Kingdom to the People's Republic of China. (Hong Kong became a "Special Administrative Region" of the PRC on July 1, 1997.) District Judge Wood herself raised the issue of the court's jurisdiction. After arguments were presented by the parties, she dismissed the case, ruling that there was no jurisdiction, since there was no "diversity," because Matimak was not a "citizen or subject" of a "foreign state," as required by the applicable statute and the U.S. Constitution. Matimak appeals.

 JUDGE McLAUGHLIN:

This is not the first time we have had to navigate what we earlier described as a "shoalstrewn area of the law."

Article III of the Constitution extends the federal judicial power to "all Cases... between a State, or citizens thereof, and foreign States, Citizens, or Subjects."... The United States Judicial Code tracks the constitutional language by providing diversity jurisdiction over any civil action arising between "citizens of a State and citizens or subjects of a foreign state." This judicial power is referred to as "alienage jurisdiction."...

Diversity of citizenship ... is determined as of the commencement of the action...

Given these building blocks, we must address three principal questions: (1) whether Hong Kong is a "foreign state"...; (2) whether Matimak is a "citizen or subject" of the United Kingdom...; and (3) whether any and all non-citizens of the United States may ipso facto invoke alienage jurisdiction against a United States citizen. Although not addressed by the parties, this last question is the focus of the dissent, and thus merits serious consideration...

Neither the Constitution nor S.1332(a)(2) defines "foreign state." However, "it has generally been held that a foreign state is one formally recognized by the executive branch of the United States government."...

For purposes of diversity jurisdiction, a corporation is a "citizen" or "subject" of the entity under whose sovereignty it was created...

When Matimak brought this suit in August 1995, Hong Kong was a "British Dependency Territory,"... and was ruled by a governor appointed by the United Kingdom. As such, it maintained some independence in its international economic and diplomatic relationship, but in matters of defense and foreign affairs remained dependent on the United Kingdom.

Hong Kong is the United States' twelfth-largest trading partner, with direct United States financial investment of almost twelve billion dollars.... Hong Kong's relationship with the United States was most recently manifested in the United States-Hong Kong Policy Act of 1992, ... which makes clear that Congress desires [U.S.-H.K.] relations to continue after July 1, 1997, when Hong Kong becomes a special administrative region in China. The Act states that "Hong Kong plays an important role in today's regional and world economy. This role is reflected in strong economic, cultural, and other ties with the United States that give the United States a strong interest in the continued vitality, prosperity, and stability of Hong Kong."...

It is clear [however] that the United States did not recognize Hong Kong as a sovereign and independent international entity....

[T]he British Nationality Act 1981 ... delineates British citizenship in detail. The Act fails to support Matimak's assertion that a Hong Kong corporation is a citizen of the United Kingdom. The Act applies only to natural persons, not corporations. The more relevant provision of British law squarely specifies that "the privileges of British nationality are not conferred on corporations formed under the laws of Hong Kong."...

At any rate, the British Nationality Act clearly distinguishes between citizens of the United Kingdom and citizens of "British Dependency Territories," who must first undergo a citizenship application procedure and fulfill certain residency requirements in the United Kingdom proper before earning British citizenship.

Matimak is not a "citizen or subject" of a foreign state. It is thus stateless. And a stateless person—the proverbial man without a country—cannot sue a United States citizen under alienage jurisdiction.

U.S. Circuit Courts of Appeal hear appeals from U.S. District Courts in their "Circuits," that is, groups of states. The U.S. Sixth Circuit, for example, consists of the states of Ohio, Michigan, Kentucky, and Tennessee. The Sixth Circuit Court of Appeals is located in Cincinnati, Ohio, and hears appeals from the U.S. District Courts in those four states. The District of Columbia Circuit Court of Appeals reviews decisions by the lower federal courts there, and also decisions by the many federal agencies located in Washington, D.C. The Court of Appeals for the Federal Circuit hears appeals from the national specialty courts, such as the Court of International Trade, the Claims Court, and also from certain agencies, such as the Patent and Trademark Office.

The Courts of Appeal have no power to try cases, only to hear appeals from lower U.S. courts and agencies.

The **U.S. Supreme Court** does have some "original jurisdiction" (to try cases that have not been heard by lower courts), but it is very limited. Article III of the Constitution states that the Supreme Court can try cases involving diplomatic personnel from another nation, and cases in which one of our states is a party. In all other cases which can be heard by the national courts, the Supreme Court has only appellate jurisdiction, as defined by Congress. In the famous *Marbury v. Madison* case (1803), the Court decided that Congress could not, by statute, increase the Court's original jurisdiction. The Supreme Court rarely uses this original jurisdiction, since the District Courts can also hear such cases.

As noted above, most cases come to the Supreme Court via a discretionary review. The party wishing review files a petition for the *writ of certiorari* with the Court. This party is called the *Petitioner*, and is listed first in the title of the Supreme Court case—no matter who was the original plaintiff. The party opposing the petition for review is called the *Respondent*, and is listed as the second party in the title of the case (the party after the "v"). If four of the nine Justices vote in favor of hearing the case, the petition for certiorari is granted, and the case will have a full review by the Court. If fewer than four vote to hear the case, the petition is not granted, and the decision of the lower court stands as the final judgment in the case. Failure to grant the petition does not mean that the Supreme Court necessarily agrees with the result reached by the lower court in the case. There may be any number of reasons why the Supreme Court Justices think that the case does not deserve their review.

State Court Systems. Each state has designed its own state court system to fit its own needs. No uniform pattern applies to all states; however, most follow a general pattern with a four-tier judicial system.

The first tier, or lowest level, of the typical state judicial system consists of *specialty courts of limited jurisdiction*. The *justice of the peace court* is perhaps the oldest of these specialty courts. Normally, this court has jurisdiction over civil cases involving small amounts of money, nonfelony criminal matters, and traffic cases in which the accused person is willing to plead guilty. Usually, there is no provision for a jury trial in this court.

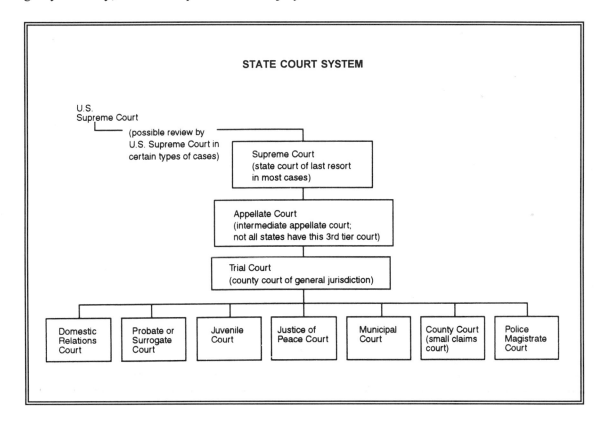

The judge in most instances serves part-time and is often not a lawyer. Court may be held in the judge's home or place of business. Many states have abolished the justice of the peace court and replaced it with a county court or a small claims court, with a full-time judge who must meet certain educational requirements. Still, these courts usually do not provide for trial by jury.

In this first tier, we also find *police magistrate courts* and *municipal courts*. Police magistrate courts are usually created to handle traffic offenses and minor criminal matters. Depending on the state, municipal courts may handle minor civil and criminal matters. Municipal courts often allow trial by jury, whereas police magistrate courts normally do not. Both courts' proceedings are usually quick and inexpensive. Most people who come before them are not represented by lawyers. They do, of course, have a right to appeal the courts' decisions.

Generally, municipal and police magistrate courts do not record all testimony and proceedings, and the appeal is made to the trial court of general jurisdiction (which is in the second tier of the state judicial system). There the case is tried **de novo**, which means that a new trial is held, rather than just a review of the record. In some states, however, a record of proceedings is kept and the appeal is directly to an appellate court for review, rather than for a retrial.

Also found in the first tier of state judicial systems are *domestic relations courts*. These courts generally handle cases involving marital relations and child custody. *Probate courts*, also known as *surrogate courts*, generally administer decedents' estates, the guardianship of minor children and persons declared incompetent to handle their own affairs, and matters involving juveniles. Some states use a separate court to hear juvenile cases. Typically there is no provision for trial by jury in domestic relations, probate, and juvenile cases. These courts usually answer to the trial court of general jurisdiction, but again some states permit appeals directly to an appellate court.

In the second of four tiers of the typical state court system, we find the *trial court with general jurisdiction*. This court may be called a district court, a superior court, a common pleas court, or (in New York) the supreme court. In most states, each county has one or more trial courts with general jurisdiction. In all states, these are courts of record, meaning proceedings are recorded. Usually there is no limit on the monetary amounts involved in cases in these courts. They handle criminal, civil, and equity matters.

The third tier in this four-tier structure is an *intermediate appellate court*. This court hears appeals from the courts below it. The appellate court is a reviewing court; no new evidence is presented to it. The court reviews the trial transcript, the testimony, and the decision of the lower court. The attorneys for each side submit written briefs of the law which they contend applies, and the court, in some cases, listens to oral arguments of the attorneys of each side. Then this court renders one of three types of decisions: to affirm the lower court's decision, to reverse the lower court's decision and give judgment to the appealing party, or to reverse the lower court's decision and remand (send) the case back to the trial court for a new trial or other proceedings in accordance with the court's opinion.

The party wishing to appeal a lower court's judgment (called the **appellant**) must allege error in the trial. For example, perhaps the trial judge allowed the jury to hear inadmissible evidence or gave the jury incorrect instructions on the law.

In some states, the title of the appellate case may be reversed from the title of the case in the lower court. For example, Smith sued Jones in the lower court. The case is titled *Smith v. Jones*. Smith won; Jones appeals. Some states now list the case as *Jones v. Smith*, with the appellant's name first.

This third tier, the intermediate appellate court, is not found in all states. It is usually needed in states with large populations and a large volume of cases.

The fourth tier of state judicial systems is the state's court of last resort. This court may be called the supreme court of errors and appeals, the supreme judicial court, the court of appeals, or simply the supreme court. Like the intermediate appellate court, this is a reviewing court; it holds no new trials. The procedure for review in this court is similar to the procedure for review at the intermediate appellate court level. This court, however, is the party's last resort for appeal in the great majority of the cases that originate in the state court system.

The decisions of a state's highest court may be reviewed by the U.S. Supreme Court if they involve questions of national law. One party's claim that the state's procedures violated due process of law, as required by the Fourteenth Amendment, would be such a case. So would a case in which the state courts had interpreted the meaning of a treaty or an act of Congress. The party making such a national law ("federal question") claim files a petition for writ of certiorari with the U.S. Supreme Court, as discussed earlier in this chapter. The Supreme Court then decides whether it should review the state case.

CIVIL PROCEDURE

Each court system has its own procedure for hearing cases. The court where the case is actually tried will use that state's rules of civil procedure. The national courts use the *Federal Rules of Civil Procedure*. Thus, holding the trial in one location or another can change any procedural rule. Questions such as whether the case can be tried to a jury, how many persons there are on the jury, how many of them the plaintiff needs to convince to get a verdict, what evidence is admissible, what privileges against testifying exist, and a whole host of similar issues may all have different answers from one court system to another. While the overall civil procedure systems may be quite similar, very often "the devil is in the details."

For these reasons, and also for the tactical advantages that may be involved in litigating in one location rather than another, the plaintiff's lawyer will try to select the most favorable place to hold the trial. Likewise, the defendant's lawyer will try to resist having the lawsuit in an unfavorable location. The key to these choices is *jurisdiction over the person.*

Jurisdiction Over the Person. No court has jurisdiction to hear cases involving anyone and everyone in the world; there are limits to a court's power to force people to appear and defend lawsuits. A person generally must have had some sort of connection with the state (or nation) where the lawsuit is filed, or with persons or things in that state, to justify holding the lawsuit there. Some of these connections are so significant that they permit any type of lawsuit to be filed in that place against the person. Other, so-called "minimum contacts" permit the filing only of lawsuits which arise out of or relate to the "contact" itself.

The significant connections in the first group are referred to as the bases for *general personal jurisdiction.* That is, the person is "generally" suable here—by anybody, from anywhere, for any sort of claim. Our system recognizes three such connections: *domicile*, *consent*, and *presence.* A person can be sued for any sort of claim where he or she has permanent residence—the person's "home state" (or country). This rule applies whether or not the person is actually physically present when the lawsuit is filed. For individuals, the location of domicile is a matter of having a residence which is considered "permanent." (See the *Keck* case problem at the end of the chapter.) For corporations, the state (or nation) of incorporation is the company's domicile. However, it is also possible for a company to acquire a second, "commercial domicile," where it has its principal place of business—its home office or major facility.

The second basis of general personal jurisdiction is consent by the litigant to have the case tried in a particular location. The plaintiff consents to have the case heard there by filing the lawsuit with the particular court. But jurisdiction over one party does not also give the court jurisdiction over the other. The problem is the defendant. The defendant may not want to consent to the plaintiff's chosen location unless there are possible benefits to *both* parties from having the case tried there. In many commercial contracts, there may be a *forum-selection clause*, which means that the parties have agreed in advance on the location for any potential lawsuit arising from the contract. (See the *Shute* case problem at the end of the chapter.)

The third basis of general personal jurisdiction is presence. An individual can be sued anywhere he or she can be personally served with process from the court. If a plaintiff discovers that you are going to Hawaii for a vacation or a conference, files a lawsuit there, and properly serves you with the court papers while you are there, you are subject to the jurisdiction of the Hawaii courts. The Hawaii courts might decide not to hear the case, on the basis of the location's being inconvenient, but if they want to hear the case, they have the jurisdiction over you to do so. Since a corporation has no physical being at all, it is deemed "present" for jurisdiction purposes anywhere it is doing a "systematic and regular part of its general business." That means that many large companies can be sued in a number of locations, even though the claim which is the basis of the lawsuit did not arise in those places.

Limited Personal Jurisdiction.

Most states in this country, and many other nations, also provide for court jurisdiction over persons who are not domiciled or present there, and have not consented to be sued there. These rules are often referred to as "*long-arm*" statutes. For our states, the U.S. Supreme Court requires that such state laws be based on certain "minimum contacts," and that allowing the lawsuit in that location will not offend traditional notions of fair play and due process.

Among the minimum contacts which have been used by various states are: making a contract there, committing a tort there, owning real property or tangible personal property there, insuring a risk there, making a contract elsewhere to deliver goods or perform services there, and serving as an officer or a director in a company formed there or having its principal place of business there. Of course, not all states have the same standards, or interpret them the same way even if they are similarly worded. These jurisdictional complexities are another reason why the parties may want to include a choice of forum clause in their commercial contract.

U.S. District Courts hearing diversity of citizenship cases have the same "long-arm" personal jurisdiction over nonresidents as the general trial courts in the state where they are located. If a state court could force the out-of-stater to appear and defend the lawsuit, so can a U.S. District Court in a diversity case. The U.S. courts' "arms" are as long as, but no longer than, those of a state trial court.

The *Hearst* case discusses these rules in the context of an Internet web site.

THE HEARST CORPORATION v. GOLDBERGER
1997 U.S. DIST. LEXIS 2065 (S.D.N.Y., 1997)

FACTS: Defendant's Internet web site is accessible to, and has been electronically "visited" by, computer users in New York. Defendant has not contracted to sell or sold any products or services to anyone in New York (or elsewhere for that matter—his "business" is not yet operational).

Hearst Corporation, owner and publisher of ESQUIRE Magazine, brought this trademark infringement action against defendant Ari Goldberger, who has established an Internet domain name and web site, "ESQWIRE.COM." Goldberger's web site exists to offer law office infrastructure network services for attorneys, but such services are not yet available, and also to provide legal information services, so far limited to information about this lawsuit. Goldberger lives in Cherry Hill, New Jersey, and works in Philadelphia.

 MAGISTRATE JUDGE PECK:

For the reasons set forth below, I recommend that the Court lacks personal jurisdiction over defendant Goldberger and therefore that the case should be transferred to the United States District Court for the District of New Jersey pursuant to 28 U.S.C. S.1406(a) and the parties' consent. Where, as here, defendant has not contracted to sell or actually sold any goods or services to New Yorkers, a finding of personal jurisdiction in New York based on an Internet web site would mean that there would be nationwide (indeed, worldwide) personal jurisdiction over anyone and everyone who establishes an Internet web site. Such nationwide jurisdiction is not consistent with traditional personal jurisdiction case law nor acceptable to the Court as a matter of policy....

The issue of personal jurisdiction and the Internet has split the federal district courts that have addressed the issue to date.... Not surprisingly, "some commentators ... believe a new body of jurisprudence is needed to address" the question of personal jurisdiction and the Internet.... Unless and until Congress or the New York legislature enacts Internet specific jurisdictional legislation, however, the Court must employ New York's existing jurisdictional statutes, CPLR Ss. 301 and 302, and analogize to presently existing, traditional, non-Internet personal jurisdiction case law....

Section 301 traditionally applies to persons actually present in New York and to corporations "doing business" in New York, "not occasionally or casually, but with a fair degree of permanence and continuity."...

It is unclear whether an individual (as opposed to a corporation or other entity) is subject to "doing business" jurisdiction under CPLR S.301 pursuant to New York law.... The Court in this case, however, need not resolve the question of whether "doing business" jurisdiction applies to an individual person. Although Hearst's complaint asserts jurisdiction under CPLR S.301 as well as S.302, ... Hearst's brief in opposition to Goldberger's motion to dismiss does not rely at all on CPLR S.301 jurisdiction.... Accordingly, the Court finds that Hearst has waived any CPLR S.301 argument....

Even if Hearst had not waived the CPLR S.301 argument and even if New York would apply CPLR S.301 "doing business" jurisdiction to an individual, S.301 jurisdiction still would be lacking. Goldberger's only contacts with New York, according to the record before the Court on this motion, are the contacts involving his ESQWIRE Internet web site and e-mail.... [T]hose contacts with New York do not even establish "transacting business" jurisdiction under CPLR S.302. Those contacts therefore do not establish "doing business" jurisdiction under CPLR S.301 either.... "The showing necessary for finding that defendant 'transacted business' and is suable on a cause of action arising from that transaction is considerably less than that needed to establish defendant's 'doing business,' which renders the defendant subject to suit on even an unrelated cause of action."...

"Section 302(a)(1) is typically invoked for a cause of action against a defendant who breaches a contract with plaintiff, ... or commits a commercial tort against plaintiff in the course of transacting business or contracting to supply goods or services in New York."...

"In order for personal jurisdiction over [Goldberger] to lie in New York ... [Goldberger] must have transacted business in this state and the cause of action must arise out of such transaction."... "The test ... is hardly a precise one; the court must look at the aggregation of defendant's activities, coupled with the selective weighing of the various actions."... Moreover, it is the "nature and quality, and not the amount of New York contacts [which] must be considered by the court."... Primary factors to consider include the physical presence of defendant in New York, the risk of loss as it effects the New York transaction, and the extent to which the contract is performed in New York.... Jurisdiction under CPLR S.302(a)(1) can exist "even though the defendant never enter[ed] New York, so long as the defendant's activities here were purposeful and there is a substantial relationship between the transaction and the claim asserted."...

The present case does not involve a contract, but rather a tort (trademark infringement) in the course of a commercial activity (i.e., Goldberger's Internet web site). It is undisputed that Goldberger created and "published" his ESQWIRE web site from the Cherry Hill, NJ—Philadelphia area, not New York.... It is also undisputed that people located in New York have accessed ("visited") Goldberger's web site.... Further, it is undisputed that Goldberger has not sold any product or services.... His Internet web site is, at most, an announcement of the future availability of his services for attorneys....

Goldberger's ESQWIRE Internet web site thus is most analogous to an advertisement in a national magazine. Like such an ad, Goldberger's Internet web site may be viewed by people in all fifty states (and all over the world too for that matter), but it is not targeted at the residents of New York or any other particular state....

New York is clear, however, that advertisements in national publications are not sufficient to provide personal jurisdiction under Section 302(a)(1)....

Even advertisements targeted at the New York market have been found to be insufficient for CPLR 302(a)(1) transaction of business jurisdiction....

It appears that Hearst has placed itself in a "Catch 22" situation. If Hearst had waited until Goldberger contracted to sell his attorney support services to New Yorkers, long arm jurisdiction likely would have been appropriate.... "New York courts may exercise personal jurisdiction over a non-domiciliary who contracts out of state to supply goods in the state, even when the goods are never shipped or supplied to the state."... But if Hearst had waited, it would have been faced with laches-type defenses and possible greater harm to its ESQUIRE trademark.... The appropriate trademark litigation strategy, however, leaves the Court without personal jurisdiction over defendant Goldberger.

This Court finds that Goldberger's ESQWIRE Internet web site is analogous to an advertisement in a national publication and thus does not constitute sufficient contacts with New York to provide the Court with personal jurisdiction over Goldberger for transacting business under CPLR S.302(a)(1).

Venue. Jurisdiction, as defined above, means the authority or power to hear a case. Technically, all courts of general jurisdiction in a state might have jurisdiction to hear a specific type of case. The question then arises, which one of those many courts which had jurisdiction *should* hear the case? **Venue** rules decide that question. Most state venue statutes provide that a lawsuit against a defendant be commenced in the defendant's county of residence or in the county in which the cause of action arose. For example, if a plaintiff in an automobile accident case filed suit in a county other than the county where the accident occurred or where the defendant resided, then the defendant could have the venue changed to one of those locations.

Venue also may be changed when the possibility of selecting a fair and impartial jury in the county where the lawsuit was filed is in question. In that case, the defendant could request a change of venue to an adjoining county. This might occur in a case involving local residents who assumed that all college students drink beer and drive at high rates of speed. In that case, it would be better to change the venue to an adjoining county where the residents are not in constant contact with college students and might not be prejudiced against students.

Pleading Stage. The first step in filing a lawsuit is the preparation of a **complaint**, sometimes called a petition or a declaration. The complaint will state the names of the parties involved. The party bringing the action is called the **plaintiff**, and the party being sued is called the **defendant**. The complaint will state the plaintiff's version of what happened, where it happened, when it happened, how it happened, and why it happened, and it will allege that it happened as the result of the defendant's wrongful acts. Then it will state what the injuries or damages were, and it will conclude with a request for an amount of money.

The attorney for the plaintiff will file this complaint with the clerk of an appropriate court. The court will issue a **summons**, which will be served on the defendant, to give notification of the lawsuit and to inform defendant when and where an appearance must be made if the defendant wishes to defend. Usually a copy of the complaint is served along with the summons so that the defendant will know the particulars of the lawsuit.

The rules for serving a summons vary for different types of lawsuits and from state to state. The most common method is service to the defendant in person by a sheriff or another authorized official. Service may also be made by registered or certified mail with a return receipt. In some jurisdictions, a summons may be legally served if it is handed to a member of the defendant's household; however, there are restrictions as to the age of the party receiving the summons. Handing the summons to the defendant's husband or wife would be proper service, but handing it to the defendant's eight-year-old child would not.

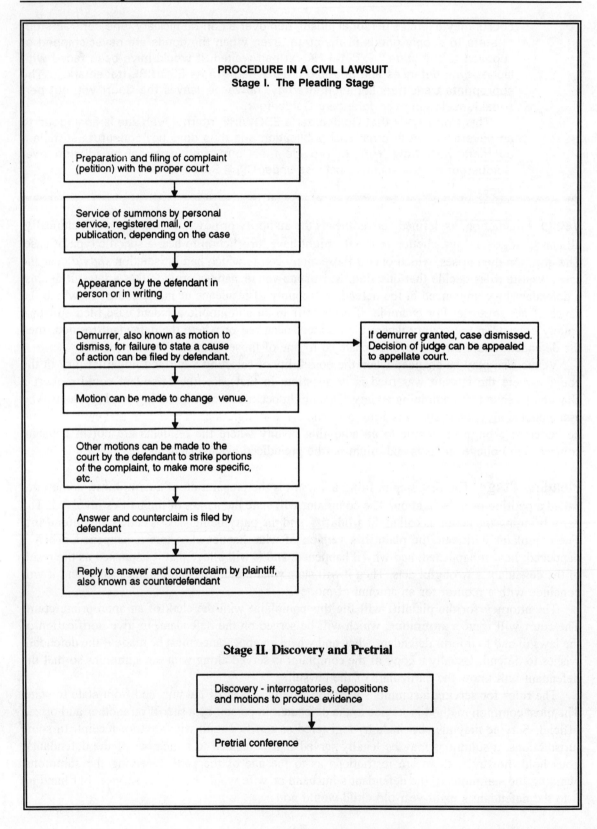

PROCEDURE IN A CIVIL LAWSUIT
Stage I. The Pleading Stage

Preparation and filing of complaint (petition) with the proper court

Service of summons by personal service, registered mail, or publication, depending on the case

Appearance by the defendant in person or in writing

Demurrer, also known as motion to dismiss, for failure to state a cause of action can be filed by defendant.

If demurrer granted, case dismissed. Decision of judge can be appealed to appellate court.

Motion can be made to change venue.

Other motions can be made to the court by the defendant to strike portions of the complaint, to make more specific, etc.

Answer and counterclaim is filed by defendant

Reply to answer and counterclaim by plaintiff, also known as counterdefendant

Stage II. Discovery and Pretrial

Discovery - interrogatories, depositions and motions to produce evidence

Pretrial conference

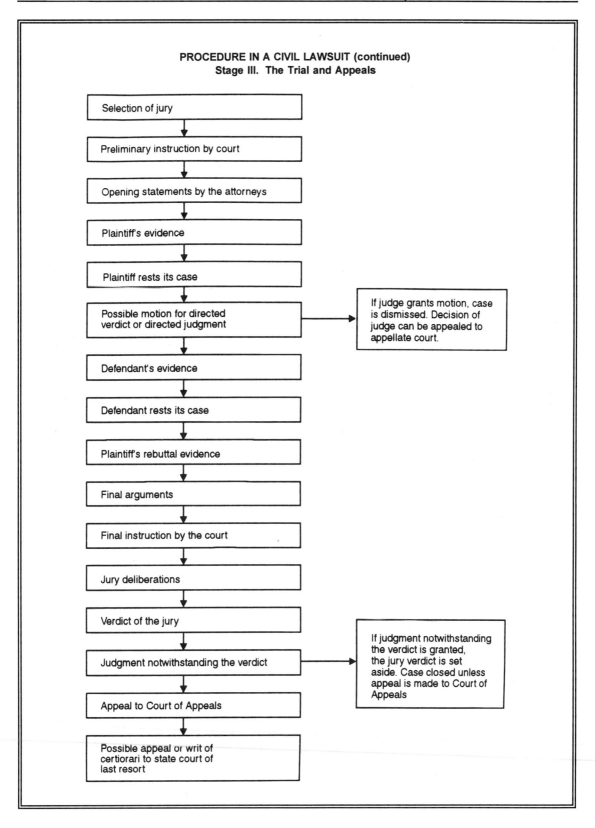

PROCEDURE IN A CIVIL LAWSUIT (continued)
Stage III. The Trial and Appeals

Selection of jury

Preliminary instruction by court

Opening statements by the attorneys

Plaintiff's evidence

Plaintiff rests its case

Possible motion for directed verdict or directed judgment → If judge grants motion, case is dismissed. Decision of judge can be appealed to appellate court.

Defendant's evidence

Defendant rests its case

Plaintiff's rebuttal evidence

Final arguments

Final instruction by the court

Jury deliberations

Verdict of the jury

Judgment notwithstanding the verdict → If judgment notwithstanding the verdict is granted, the jury verdict is set aside. Case closed unless appeal is made to Court of Appeals

Appeal to Court of Appeals

Possible appeal or writ of certiorari to state court of last resort

In many cases, the defendant will be a resident of another state. Under the long arm statutes discussed earlier, service can be made by sending a copy of the summons and the complaint by certified letter to the defendant's last known address and to the secretary of state in the state where the suit was filed.

Notice of some types of cases can he published in a local newspaper a required number of times when the whereabouts of the defendant is unknown. An example would be an adoption case in which one of the natural parents could not be located. Publication would be acceptable since the circumstances prevent service on that parent personally or by certified mail.

Once the complaint has been filed and the summons has been properly served on the defendant, the defendant must appear in court within a specified time, such as twenty days within receipt of the summons. Failure to appear either in person or by an attorney within that time will be treated as an admission of guilt, and the court will enter a default judgment against the defendant. Under certain circumstances, the defendant may have this default judgment set aside. An example occurs when the defendant can prove service of the summons was improper.

Assuming the defendant does appear as summoned, the first question he or she may raise is whether the lawsuit was filed within the proper statutory period. This period is set by the state's **statute of limitations**. For a tort action, the period will normally vary from one to five years after the date of the occurrence, depending on the law of the state where the occurrence took place. In a breach of contract case, the period may vary from five to ten years. Special provisions apply if the defendant is a governmental body. Notice of intent to sue may be required within three to six months after the occurrence, depending on applicable law.

The defendant may challenge the sufficiency of the complaint by filing a **demurrer**, or **motion to dismiss**, or attack the complaint with motions concerning jurisdiction or venue. To be legally sufficient, a complaint must state a **cause of action**. That is, the complaint filed by the plaintiff must state that the plaintiff had a specific legal right, that the defendant had a legal duty and breached it, and that the plaintiff was injured as a proximate result of the breach. This is the first of four safety valves in the trial of a civil lawsuit. If the judge finds the plaintiff did not have a specific legal right or if the defendant owed no legal duty to the plaintiff, the demurrer will be granted and the lawsuit is dismissed.

The *Stangvik* case involves a motion to dismiss.

STANGVIK v. SHILEY INC.
1 Cal.Rptr.2d 556 (CA, 1991)

FACTS: Plaintiffs, members of two families, one residing in Norway and the other in Sweden, are the wives and children of two men who received heart valve implants in the countries of their residence. The valves were designed and manufactured in California by defendant Shiley Incorporated, a California corporation. In both cases, the valves allegedly failed, and the patients died. Thereafter, plaintiffs filed suit in California against Shiley and its parent company, a Delaware corporation, alleging that the valves were defective. They sought damages based on theories of negligence, strict liability, breach of warranty, fraud, and loss of consortium. One of the complaints also sought recovery for negligent infliction of emotional distress.

Defendants moved to dismiss or stay the actions on the ground of forum non conveniens. They asserted that the cases should be tried in Sweden and Norway because it was in those countries that the plaintiffs resided, the valves were sold, decedents received medical care, the alleged fraudulent representations were made, and evidence regarding the provision of health care and other matters existed. Plaintiffs countered that California was the more convenient place of trial because the valves were designed, manufactured, tested, and packaged in California. The parties introduced conflicting evidence regarding plaintiffs' legal rights and remedies in Scandinavia, and each claimed that the most important and numerous documents and witnesses were located in the country which they asserted was the most appropriate place for trial. The trial court found in favor of defendants, concluding that California was an inconvenient forum and that Sweden and Norway provided adequate alternative forums for resolution of the actions. It stayed the actions, and retained jurisdiction to make such further orders as might become appropriate. The order was subject to seven conditions with which defendants agreed to comply. The Court of Appeal affirmed.

 JUSTICE MOSK:

Forum non conveniens is an equitable doctrine invoking the discretionary power of a court to decline to exercise the jurisdiction it has over a transitory cause of action when it believes that the action may be more appropriately and justly tried elsewhere.... We described the basis of the doctrine as follows: "There are manifest reasons for preferring residents in access to often overcrowded Courts, both in convenience and in the fact that broadly speaking it is they who pay for maintaining the Courts concerned...." [T]he injustices and the burdens on local courts and taxpayers, as well as on those leaving their work and business to serve as jurors, which can follow from an unchecked and unregulated importation of transitory causes of action for trial in this state ... require that our courts, acting upon the equitable principles, ... exercise their "discretionary power to decline to proceed in those causes of action which they conclude, on satisfactory evidence, may be more appropriately and justly tried elsewhere...."

In determining whether to grant a motion based on forum non conveniens, a court must first determine whether the alternate forum is a "suitable" place for trial. If it is, the next step is to consider the private interests of the litigants and the interests of the public in retaining the action for trial in California. The private interest factors are those that make trial and the enforceability of the ensuing judgment expeditious and relatively inexpensive, such as the ease of access to sources of proof, the cost of obtaining attendance of witnesses, and the availability of compulsory process for attendance of unwilling witnesses. The public interest factors include avoidance of overburdening local courts with congested calendars, protecting the interests of potential jurors so that they are not called upon to decide cases in which the local community has little concern, and weighing the competing interests of California and the alternate jurisdiction in the litigation....

We come, then, to an assessment of the factors discussed above. We are confronted with the somewhat anomalous situation that the parties seek to try the action in a jurisdiction which would appear to violate their interest in a convenient place for trial. Both plaintiffs and defendants are willing indeed, eager—to litigate the matter in a jurisdiction separated by an ocean and a continent from their places of residence. Although both claim that they are motivated by the convenience of the place of trial, this court, like others before it, recognizes that an additional motivating factor—and perhaps the major one—relates to the circumstance that trial in California will enhance the possibility of substantial recovery. Plaintiffs seek and defendants resist trial in the California courts substantially for this reason. In the service of this goal, they are willing to transport numerous witnesses and documents many thousand miles....

In any event, ... there was clearly substantial evidence to sustain the trial court's determination that the balance of private and public interests favors defendants under traditional rules laid down in prior cases. It is true that much, but not all, of the evidence concerning liability exists in California, but virtually all the evidence relating to damages is in Scandinavia. Since defendants have promised to supply documents in their possession if required by the Scandinavian courts, the fact that a large number of documents will be involved appears not to pose a significant inconvenience to plaintiffs. The Court of Appeal concluded that these documents could be admitted into evidence without translation, and although there was conflicting evidence on this score, its conclusion was supported by the record.

It is probable that both parties will suffer some disadvantage from trial in their home forums. For example, former employees of defendants may be beyond the jurisdiction of the Scandinavian courts and defendants may be unable to make good their promise to produce them for trial in Scandinavia. Conversely, defendants have no means by which to ensure that Scandinavian medical witnesses and others whose testimony might be important will attend the trial in California. But these problems are implicit in many cases in which forum non conveniens motions are made, and it is for the trial court to decide which party will be more inconvenienced.

The public interest factors clearly favor defendants' position. If we hold that the present cases may be tried in California, it will likely mean that the remaining 108 cases involving the Shiley valve will also be tried here. The burden on the California courts of trying these numerous complex actions is considerable. Moreover, California's interest in deterring future improper conduct by defendants would be amply vindicated if the actions filed by California resident plaintiffs resulted in judgments in their favor. Under all the circumstances, we hold that the Court of Appeal was correct in concluding that there was substantial evidence to support the trial court's determination that the private and public interest factors, on balance, justified the stays granted in these actions.

The next important pleading is the **answer**, in which the defendant must affirm or deny the allegations the plaintiff made in the complaint. The defendant may very well admit some facts, such as the time and place of the occurrence. The defendant would, however, deny allegations regarding his or her negligence. In addition to answering the plaintiff's claims, the defendant may make a claim for damages by filing a counterclaim. This is also called a cross complaint in some states. In this pleading, the defendant will allege that the plaintiff was negligent and will state a claim for damages. The plaintiff must now answer the cross complaint or counterclaim in a pleading called a reply.

A second safety valve is a motion for **summary judgment**, or judgment on the pleadings. If there are no significant fact issues in the case, as described in the pleadings, one or both parties may ask the court to enter an immediate judgment, without a trial. For instance, the defendant has a receipt or a cancelled check showing that the claim on which the plaintiff filed suit has in fact been paid. Or the defendant can demonstrate that he or she did not owe the claim in the first place; it was someone else, with a similar name. In these clear-cut cases, the court should enter a summary judgment, which is a decision on the merits of the case. Unlike the motion to dismiss (where the claim can be re-filed), the summary judgment ends the case between the parties (subject to appeal, of course).

Pretrial Stage. During the second stage of a trial, called the *pretrial stage*, the parties and their lawyers prepare the case for trial. Most major metropolitan areas have a long backlog of cases, so a case filed today may not come to trial for several years. This presents several problems. Witnesses tend to forget facts about the case as time goes by. They may die or move out of the jurisdiction, which means they cannot legally be brought back for trial.

Three general methods of discovery are used. First, each party may file interrogatories to be answered by the other. **Interrogatories** are lists of questions that probe for information about the person, the incident, and the damages. The questions must be relevant to the case, but interrogatories tend to be "fishing expeditions." They are usually not admissible as evidence in court.

Interrogatories normally are followed by depositions. A **deposition** is sworn testimony that is subject to cross-examination, and is admissible as evidence. Depositions may be taken from the parties and from witnesses, both witnesses to the incident and expert witnesses such as doctors, engineers, and economists.

Depositions basically serve two purposes. First, they discover the testimony. A party who has testified under oath will be guilty of perjury if he or she materially changes the testimony later. Second, depositions preserve the testimony in case the witness dies or moves and cannot be located. Doctors and other experts testifying in a case may not be able to appear at the trial, but their depositions can be used.

Traditionally, depositions have been taken in the presence of a court reporter, who types a record of the testimony. If the deposition has to be used at the trial, it is simply read in court. Today many courts are experimenting with videotape depositions which can be played in the courtroom. This technique can speed up trials when scheduling problems occur. Some attorneys would ask to postpone a trial rather than enter testimony read from a deposition, but they will be less hesitant to present videotaped depositions when witnesses are not available.

A third **discovery** procedure is a motion by one party to have the other party produce certain items of evidence for review. For example, the defendant may ask the plaintiff for copies of medical reports, bills, photographs, and other material that the plaintiff intends to submit at the trial.

Courts may not compel testimony or production of documents in violation of a recognized privilege of confidentiality. Such privileges may exist under a state's general common-law rules of evidence or under a specific statute. As will be more fully discussed in Chapter 5, persons cannot be required to testify as to matters which might subject them to criminal prosecution. Attorneys cannot testify about matters their clients communicated to them in confidence. Other widely recognized privileges exist for communications to the clergy, physicians, and spouses. In some states, statutes may provide privileges against disclosure for the records of teachers, newspaper reporters, accountants, and others. Generally, a privilege against disclosure can be waived by the person in whose favor it operates. A client, for instance, could waive his or her privilege and permit an attorney to testify as to matters which otherwise could not be disclosed.

After both sides have completed discovery, the court will schedule a **pretrial conference**. The purpose of the pretrial hearing is twofold. First, it enables the judge to get the attorneys representing the plaintiff and the defendant together and to determine whether or not there can be an amicable settlement. Here the judge acts more as a mediator than as a judge. When possible, the judge will encourage the parties to negotiate a settlement so the case can be dismissed before trial. If, on the other hand, a settlement appears impossible, the judge will try to determine whether any items of evidence can be admitted without objection to save time at the trial. In some jurisdictions, the judge will have the parties exchange lists of the witnesses they are going to have testify. The theory is that the trial should present no surprises and that each party should have an opportunity to know the other party's evidence. If it appears that the case will have to be tried, a trial date will be set.

Trial Stage

The actual trial of the lawsuit is a series of events which we will review in the order of their occurrence. The flowcharts on pages 84 and 85 outline the overall sequence in a civil case.

Selection of a Jury. Unless the judge is to hear a case without a jury, the first step in a trial is the selection of a jury. (Generally, there is no right to trial by jury in equity cases. Even if the parties have the right to a jury trial, they may waive it.) Traditionally, a jury was composed of twelve persons, but many jurisdictions have reduced that number to six for some cases. Selecting the jury is a very important phase of the trial. To have a fair trial, jurors must be unbiased, fair, and impartial.

A list of prospective jurors is selected at random from the eligible voters in the county where a state court lawsuit is to be tried or in the court district where a U.S. District Court suit is to be tried. Prospective jurors are called to the courtroom where attorneys for the plaintiff and the defendant question them to uncover biases or other reasons they could not serve as fair and impartial jurors. For example, the prospective jurors may be asked whether they are related to any of the parties in the lawsuit or any of the attorneys, whether they have had business dealings with the parties, or whether they know the parties socially. They may also be asked whether they have read about the cause of action in the newspapers and whether they have already formed an opinion about the guilt or innocence of the parties. This examination is called **voir dire**.

If a prospective juror admits prejudice, or if a prejudice is implied by a relationship to someone associated with the case, the prospective juror may be challenged for cause. If the court agrees that the prospective juror is prejudiced or cannot be a fair and impartial juror, the prospective juror will be dismissed. In addition to the **challenges for cause**, each side in the lawsuit will be given a certain number of **peremptory challenges**. No cause need be stated for making a peremptory challenge. The purpose of the peremptory challenge is to give each side an opportunity to dismiss certain jurors who, for one reason or another, the attorney feels may be prejudiced against his or her client. Peremptory challenges may or may not be used.

Preliminary Instructions by the Court. After the jury has been selected and seated in the jury box, the judge will give jurors preliminary instructions concerning the trial. The judge will outline the issue for trial and explain the burden of proof, the credibility of witnesses, and the manner in which the jurors should weigh the testimony they are about to hear.

Opening Statements by the Attorneys. The opening statement is not evidence; it is only a preview of coming attractions. As the complaining party, the plaintiff has the burden of proof and thus has first opening statement. In the opening statement the plaintiff's attorney tells jurors what type of case they are to hear and briefly explains what the plaintiff intends to prove. The defendant's attorney then makes an opening statement, telling the jury what the defendant expects to prove. Now the jury has an overview of the case and is ready to hear the evidence.

Plaintiff's Evidence. The plaintiff, having the burden of proof, is first to present evidence. The plaintiff's attorney calls a witness to the stand and asks this person questions; this is called **direct examination**. After this questioning, the defendant's attorney can **cross-examine** the witness to test the accuracy of the witness's statements. After the cross-examination, the plaintiff's attorney can conduct *redirect examination* to try to reestablish points challenged on cross-examination. Exhibits such as photographs, charts, documents, and articles of clothing may be submitted as evidence. This process continues until all of the plaintiff's witnesses have testified. The plaintiff will then rest his or her case.

Motion for Directed Verdict or Directed Judgment. We have now reached the third "safety valve" in the litigation. You will recall that after the complaint was filed and the summons was served, the defendant had an opportunity to file a demurrer (a motion to dismiss for failure to state a cause of action) and to have the case dismissed if in fact there was no legal right or legal duty. Now, after the plaintiff has presented evidence and rested his or her case, the defendant may make a motion for a **directed verdict** if there is a jury. If the judge feels that no issue of fact is to be decided by the jury, then the judge will direct a verdict in favor of the defendant. If there is no jury, a motion can be made for a directed judgment in favor of the defendant. If an issue of fact has been raised for the jury to decide, then the trial must go on.

Defendant's Evidence. The defendant's attorney will now call the defense witnesses, and the same process of questioning will occur. The defendant's attorney will ask questions under direct examination; the plaintiff's attorney will cross-examine; and the defendant's attorney will have an opportunity for redirect examination of the witnesses. The defendant may submit exhibits of evidentiary material for the defense. Then the defendant rests.

Plaintiff's Rebuttal Evidence. The plaintiff has the right to recall witnesses or to call additional witnesses for the sole purposes of rebutting the defendant's evidence.

Final Arguments. Since the plaintiff has the burden of proving the case against the defendant, the plaintiff is entitled to present the first closing argument. This is also called a **summation**. Here, the plaintiff's attorney reviews all the testimony and tries to convince the jurors that the plaintiff's evidence is stronger than the defendant's evidence and that the plaintiff should win. In a civil case, the jury decides not only who is right but also the amount of the verdict. Thus, the plaintiff's attorney also argues the value of the plaintiff's claim. The defendant's attorney then argues the opposite side of the case. Then the plaintiff is entitled to a final rebuttal or closing argument.

Final Instructions by the Judge. The jurors now need to know what substantive law applies to the case. The judge reads prepared instructions on the law to the jury. In most jurisdictions, the attorneys for each side prepare proposed instructions, and the judge selects those appropriate for the case. The judge may also add instructions not submitted by either attorney.

Jury Deliberations. After hearing the judge's instructions on the law, jurors are taken to the jury room. Their first order of business is to select a foreman. Then they commence deliberations.

The jury must be convinced that the plaintiff has proved his or her case by a *preponderance* of the evidence, in order to find for the plaintiff. In some civil cases, such a claim that fraud has been committed, the person alleging fraud is required to prove it by "clear and convincing" evidence. Either of these standards of proof is far short of the criminal standard: "beyond any reasonable doubt."

Verdict. When the jurors have reached agreement they return to the courtroom and the foreman reads their verdict. The verdict must be unanimous in most jurisdictions, although some states require agreement of only ten of twelve, or five of six jurors. Since civil juries decide both questions of fact and the dollar amount of the verdict, they seldom become a hung jury, which is a jury that has become deadlocked in trying to reach a unanimous verdict.

Judgment Notwithstanding the Verdict. Here we have the fourth safety valve in the system. The judge has veto power over the jury in the rare situations where the jury has obviously failed to follow the instructions on the law. At such times, the judge can disregard the verdict and enter a judgment contrary to it. In the vast majority of cases, however, the judge enters a judgment on the basis of the jury's verdict.

The trial judge also has some discretionary control over the amount of the jury's verdict. If a plaintiff's evidence clearly shows damages beyond those awarded by the jury, the trial judge may suggest an increase in the amount of the award, as an alternative to granting the plaintiff's motion for an entire new trial. If the defendant agrees with this suggestion, the award is raised. If not, a new trial is ordered. This procedure is called *additur*. Likewise, a similar suggestion can be made as to a grossly excessive award. The defendant's motion for a new trial is denied, on condition that the plaintiff agree to a reduction in the damages award. This process is called *remittitur*.

The *Honda* case challenges the constitutionality of Oregon's failure to provide for such a review of juries' punitive damages awards.

HONDA MOTOR CO., LTD. v. OBERG
114 S.Ct. 2331 (1994)

FACTS: Honda manufactured and sold the three-wheeled all-terrain vehicle that overturned while Oberg was driving it, causing him severe and permanent injuries. He brought suit alleging that Honda knew or should have known that the vehicle had an inherently and unreasonable dangerous design. The Jury found Honda liable and awarded respondent $919,390.39 in compensatory damages and punitive damages of $5,000,000. The compensatory damages, however, were reduced by 20 percent to $735,512.31, because respondent's own negligence contributed to the accident. On appeal, relying on the then recent decision in *Pacific Mut. Life Ins. Co. v. Haslip*, 499 U.S. 1, 111 S.Ct. 1032, 113 L.Ed.2d 1 (1991), Honda argued that the award of punitive damages violated the Due Process Clause of the Fourteenth Amendment, because the punitive damages were excessive and because the Oregon court lacked the power to correct excessive verdicts. The Oregon Court of Appeals affirmed, as did the Oregon Supreme Court.

 JUSTICE STEVENS:

Judicial review of the size of punitive damage awards has been a safeguard against excessive verdicts for as long as punitive damages have been awarded. One of the earliest reported cases involving exemplary damages, *Hackle v. Money*, 2 Wils. 205, 95 Eng. Rep. 768 (C.P.1763), arose out of King George III's attempt to punish the publishers of the allegedly seditious *North Briton*, No. 45. The King's agents arrested the plaintiff, a journeyman printer, in his home and detained him for six hours. Although the defendants treated the plaintiff rather well, feeding him "beefsteaks and beer, so that he suffered very little or no damages," the jury awarded him £300, an enormous sum almost 300 times the plaintiff's weekly wage. The defendant's lawyer requested a new trial, arguing that the jury's award was excessive....

Subsequent English cases, while generally deferring to the jury's determination of damages, steadfastly upheld the court's power to order new trials solely on the basis that the damages were too high....

Common law courts in the United States followed their English predecessors in providing judicial review of the size of damage awards. They too emphasized the deference ordinarily afforded jury verdicts, but they recognized that juries sometimes awarded damages so high as to require correction....

In the 19th century, both before and after the ratification of the Fourteenth Amendment, many American courts reviewed damages for "partiality" or "passion and prejudice." Nevertheless, because of the difficulty of probing juror reasoning, passion and prejudice review was, in fact, review of the amount of awards. Judges would infer passion, prejudice, or partiality from the size of the award....

Modern practice is consistent with these earlier authorities. In the federal courts and in every State, except Oregon, judges review the size of damage awards....

There is a dramatic difference between the judicial review of punitive damages awards under the common law and the scope of review available in Oregon. An Oregon trial judge, or an Oregon Appellate Court, may order a new trial if the jury was not properly instructed, if error occurred during the trial, or if there is no evidence to support any punitive damages at all. But if the defendant's only basis for relief is the *amount* of punitive damages the jury awarded, Oregon provides no procedure for reducing or setting aside that award....

In [the *Van Lom*] case, the court held that it had no power to reduce or set aside an award of both compensatory and punitive damages that was admittedly excessive. It recognized that the constitutional amendment placing a limitation on its power was a departure from the traditional common law approach. That opinion's characterization of Oregon's "lonely eminence" in this regard, ... is still an accurate portrayal of its unique position. Every other State in the Union affords postverdict judicial review of the amount of a punitive damages award, ... and subsequent decisions have reaffirmed Oregon judges' lack of authority to order new trials or other relief to remedy excessive damages....

Respondent also argues that Oregon provides adequate review, because the trial judge can overturn a punitive damage award if there is no substantial evidence to support an award of punitive damages.... This argument is unconvincing, because the review provided by Oregon courts ensures only that there is evidence to support *some* punitive damages, not that there is evidence to support the amount actually awarded. While Oregon's judicial review ensures that punitive damages are not awarded against defendants entirely innocent of conduct warranting exemplary damages, Oregon, unlike the common law, provides no assurance that those whose conduct is sanctionable by punitive damages are not subjected to punitive damages of arbitrary amounts. What we are concerned with is the possibility that a guilty defendant may be unjustly punished; evidence of guilt warranting some punishment is not a substitute for evidence providing at least a rational basis for the particular deprivation of property imposed by the State to deter future wrong doing.

Oregon's abrogation of a well-established common law protection against arbitrary deprivations of property raises a presumption that its procedures violate the Due Process Clause. As this Court has stated from its first Due Process cases, traditional practice provides a touchstone for constitutional analysis.... Because the basic procedural protections of the common law have been regarded as so fundamental, very few cases have arisen in which a party has complained of their denial. In fact, most of our Due Process decisions involve arguments that traditional procedures provide too little protection and that additional safeguards are necessary to ensure compliance with the Constitution....

Punitive damages pose an acute danger of arbitrary deprivation of property. Jury instructions typically leave the jury with wide discretion in choosing amounts, and the presentation of evidence of a defendant's net worth creates the potential that juries will use their verdicts to express biases against big businesses, particularly those without strong local presences. Judicial review of the amount awarded was one of the few procedural safeguards which the common law provided against that danger. Oregon has removed that safeguard without providing any substitute procedure and without any indication that the danger of arbitrary awards has in any way subsided over time. For these reasons, we hold that Oregon's denial of judicial review of the size of punitive damage awards violates the Due Process Clause of the Fourteenth Amendment.

Civil Appellate Procedure. After the verdict has been rendered and the judgment entered, the losing party has a right to an appeal. The procedural requirements of the court system must be followed. Notice of intent to appeal must be given within a specified time after the judgment is rendered. The procedure before the appellate court has been discussed earlier in this chapter. After all appeal procedures have been exhausted, a final judgment will be rendered, provided the court judgment has been affirmed. Of course, if there was a reversal, then we are faced with a new trial or other action in accordance with the appellate court's instructions.

In the great majority of cases, no appeal is filed, and at the end of the time allotted for filing an appeal, the judgment becomes final. Thus we come to the next step in the trial of a civil case, enforcement of the judgment.

Enforcement of Judgments. A judgment rendered against a party is worthless without a procedure to enforce and collect that judgment. In years past, persons were put in debtor's prison for failing to pay their bills, but no such procedure exists today. Now, if a person obtains a judgment for money against another person, there are basically three ways to collect that judgment. One way is for the party on whose behalf the judgment was rendered to levy **execution** on the property of the party against whom the judgment was rendered. The debtor's property that is not exempt from execution under state or national law may be seized by a law officer with a court order. It is then sold at a public sale, and the proceeds are applied against the judgment.

A second way to collect is to have the wages of the person against whom the judgment was rendered garnished, subject to the state and national laws concerning **garnishment**. There are exemptions under the national and state laws which do not allow the owner of a judgment to secure the total wages of the debtor. The judgment debtor's bank accounts may also be garnished.

The third way to collect is to secure a **lien** against property owned by the debtor. For example, a lien may be placed against real estate owned by the debtor. The debtor cannot sell and give clear title to the real estate without first paying the lien. In some cases, the property may be sold through a further court process to enforce the lien.

Full Faith and Credit. In some cases, the judgment debtor may not have enough property in the state which issued the judgment to satisfy it. If the debtor owns property in other states, it may be necessary to take the judgment from the state where the judgment was rendered to those other states and to ask for its enforcement there. When this happens, the "Full Faith and Credit Clause" in Article IV of the U.S. Constitution comes into play. This clause requires each state to give "full faith and credit" to the public acts, records, and judicial proceedings of other states. The successful judgment creditor cannot be forced to relitigate the whole case in other states to enforce the claim. Other states can, however, examine the judgment to make sure that the court that issued it had jurisdiction. If the court in the state where the judgment was rendered had jurisdiction, the other states have no choice; they must enforce the judgment just as they would one of their own. The ultimate decision as to what are adequate jurisdictional bases is made by the U.S. Supreme Court, since a matter of constitutional interpretation is at issue.

Class Actions. Traditionally, plaintiffs have pursued their claims on an individual basis. However, courts have occasionally permitted plaintiffs to represent a large class of claimants where the claims of all the parties are similar and arise out of the same occurrence. This is called a class action. The most common example of a class action is one shareholder bringing an action against a corporation for some alleged mismanagement and resulting loss. That one shareholder represents all other similar stockholders who allege similar damage. Obviously the court can hear one case more expeditiously and at less expense than hundreds or thousands of similar cases. Class actions also help overcome inequality of means. The big corporation can afford litigation more than a single plaintiff can. However, if many plaintiffs join forces, the expense is far less for each individual.

Under the current Federal Rules of Civil Procedure, four prerequisites must all be met before a class action may be maintained in the U.S. District Court:

1. The class is so numerous that joinder of all its members is impractical.

2. The class members have common questions of law or fact.

3. The claim or defense of the class representative is typical of that of the absent class members.

4. The representative will fairly and adequately protect the interests of the class.

The rules also provide that *one* of the following conditions must exist:

1. The prosecution of separate actions might result in inconsistent or varying judgments.

2. The prosecution of separate actions might in practice dispose of the interests of other members or impede their ability to protect those interests.

3. The defendant has acted or refused to act on grounds generally applicable to all members of the class, so that injunctive or declaratory relief for the whole class is appropriate.

4. The court finds that a class action is the best method to adjudicate the controversy.

If a class action based on diversity of citizenship is filed in U.S. District Court, the amount per claim must be at least $75,000. This prevents the U.S. District Courts from being flooded with class actions. The individual states also have rules for class actions, many of which are similar to the Federal Rules, with one notable exception. State courts require no minimum amount per claim. Also, many states have passed specific environmental and consumer laws authorizing class actions under certain circumstances.

ARBITRATION AND MEDIATION AS METHODS OF DISPUTE RESOLUTION

When thinking of **arbitration**, one normally thinks of labor law and the arbitration of grievances and the arbitration clauses in labor contracts. Arbitration, of course, has been used extensively as a method of settling grievance disputes in labor-management relations. However, arbitration has also been used as a method of deciding other types of disputes.

In the public bargaining sector, public employees are not allowed to strike. Thus, it is common for agreements between labor and management to be reached by submitting the offers of both parties to one or more arbitrators for a final decision as to the contract terms. This procedure is being more extensively used as unionization spreads among public employees.

Another type of arbitration has also been growing in popularity. This is the commercial arbitration of business disputes that would normally be handled in civil lawsuits, such as disputes involving a breach of contract. If such a case were filed in a civil court, there would be considerable expense for court costs and legal fees for both parties and, usually, considerable delay in getting the case to trial. Also, the typical judge does not have expertise in all fields. In commercial arbitration, the arbitrator selected often has special expertise in the area which the dispute involves. For example, the parties have a dispute concerning their obligations under a contract to build a multimillion-dollar building. Time is of the essence. The parties cannot wait six or seven years for this case to come up before a court. If the case is submitted to arbitration, they can get a decision within a very short time and then proceed in accordance with the arbitrator's decision.

In arbitration there is no set procedure, such as one would find in a court of law or even in an administrative agency. There is, however, one prerequisite to arbitration; namely, that both parties agree to submit the dispute to arbitration. This can be done by inserting an arbitration clause into the original document, such as a contract. If there is no such clause, the parties may still agree at a later date to submit a dispute to arbitration. For example, they may agree to have the case heard by a single arbitrator or by a panel of three arbitrators. If they agree to use three arbitrators, they may decide that each party will select an arbitrator of its choice and that the two arbitrators they select will choose the third arbitrator.

The American Arbitration Association was formed as a national not-for-profit association to encourage the use of arbitration in resolving disputes. It has a panel of recommended arbitrators who will hear commercial arbitration disputes. It also has panels of recommended arbitrators who will hear labor disputes.

The Federal Mediation and Conciliation Service, a governmental agency, also has a panel of recommended arbitrators for labor disputes. Both the American Arbitration Association and the Federal Mediation and Conciliation Service offer to supply the names of recommended arbitrators; the parties select the arbitrator they want and pay the arbitrator directly. Usually the two sides share the arbitrator's fee equally.

The main objections to the use of arbitration for resolving disputes are that there is no direct right of appeal and no direct power or procedure for enforcement of the arbitrator's decision.

When you agree to submit a dispute to arbitration, you also agree to abide by the arbitrator's ruling. The only exceptions would be if you could prove that the arbitrator had a financial or personal interest in the matter which prejudiced the decision, or that fraud or perjury was involved in the testimony, or that the arbitrator mistakenly failed to follow the law on a material issue. Otherwise the arbitrator's decision is final. If you can prove one of the above exceptions, a court will set aside the arbitrator's decision.

The next problem is enforcement. If the loser refuses to abide by the arbitrator's decision, the winner's only recourse is to go to court to have the arbitrator's decision enforced.

Arbitration is a fast, inexpensive method for resolving commercial disputes. However, its effectiveness depends greatly upon the attitude of the parties. Most businesses today want their legal disputes settled out of court and as cheaply and quickly as possible. Arbitration can be the answer to the need for prompt and inexpensive resolution of commercial business disputes.

Mediation, like arbitration, is also a term that traditionally has been associated with labor law and collective bargaining. However, mediation is now being used extensively to resolve court cases before they reach the trial stage. Many states have enacted legislation, or changed their court rules, to provide for mediation. Mediation in the lawsuit context is usually voluntary. However, some states give trial judges the discretion to order mediation prior to trial. The mediator may be chosen by the parties, or appointed by the court. Generally, the mediator has no power to decide the case, but merely attempts to facilitate communication between the parties about the issues in the case. The mediator may or may not make recommendations as to what would be a reasonable solution.

The more general term for arbitration, mediation, and the newer forms of non-court dispute resolution is "ADR," signifying "alternate dispute resolution." Many states have had considerable success in using ADR procedures. ADR can substantially reduce the courts' backlog of cases waiting for trial. It also reduces the expenses to the parties of following the case all the way through court trial and possible appeals. Along with ADR, many courts have also improved their procedures for scheduling trials, using more advanced computerized scheduling systems.

SIGNIFICANCE OF THIS CHAPTER

Every executive in business must realize the possibility of legal disputes and involvement in the legal process. This chapter introduced both the state and national court systems. It described the procedure of a civil lawsuit from the filing of the suit to the final appeal and enforcement of the judgment, including a discussion of the formal legal system. This chapter also reviewed dispute resolution by private arbitration, which saves time and legal expenses and is used in a large number of commercial contracts.

A basic understanding of these processes is useful in working with a lawyer to prepare a case and in deciding whether to settle or to litigate.

PROBLEMS FOR DISCUSSION

1. Cuthbert filed a $250,000 medical malpractice action against Dr. Jillian Peabody in U.S. District Court in Minisoda. Cuthbert was a resident of North Pagoda; he had gone to Minisoda, where Dr. Peabody had her offices, for treatment. Cuthbert's lawsuit was filed more than two years, but less than three years, after the negligent treatment by Dr. Peabody. Her lawyer says that the lawsuit should be dismissed because Minisoda's statute of limitations for such claims is two years. Cuthbert's lawyer says that North Pagoda's three-year statute of limitations period should be applied.

    Which lawyer is correct, and why?

2. Eulala Shute and her husband bought tickets for a cruise on the Tropicale, a ship operated by Carnival. The Shutes lived in the State of Washington and bought the tickets through a travel agent located there. The travel agent sent their payment to Carnival, at its headquarters in Miami, Florida. Carnival prepared the tickets and sent them back to the Shutes. On the face of each ticket was a statement indicating that it was subject to the conditions on the back. Statements on the back of the ticket said that the customers accepted all printed terms by accepting the ticket and that any disputes "shall be litigated, if at all, in and before a Court located in the State of Florida, USA, to the exclusion of the Courts of any other state or country."

    The Shutes boarded the ship in Los Angeles for the cruise to Puerto Vallarta, Mexico. While the ship was in international waters off the Mexican Coast, Eulala was injured when she slipped on a deck mat during a tour of the ship's galley. The Shutes filed a lawsuit in the U.S. District Court in the State of Washington. Carnival asked the court for summary judgment, on the basis of the forum-selection clause on the tickets.

    Is the "choice" clause enforceable? Why or why not?

3. Floyd Wiles, a resident of Cook County, Illinois, sued defendant Morita Iron Works Co. Ltd., a Japanese corporation which designed and manufactured the machine that allegedly caused plaintiff's injuries. Plaintiff's employer, Astro Packaging Co., is a corporation that operates plants in Hawthorne, New Jersey and Alsip, Illinois. Astro purchased four machines from defendant. Two were shipped to the New Jersey plant, and two were shipped to the Illinois plant. Plaintiff was employed at Astro's Alsip, Illinois plant. One of the machines allegedly caused personal injuries to plaintiff, for which plaintiff seeks damages from defendant.

   Morita, which has no facilities or personnel in Illinois, moves to dismiss the case.

   How should the courts rule on this motion? Discuss.

4. On June 8, Nancy Moran, then 17 years old, visited the home of Mr. and Mrs. Grigsby to meet with a number of friends, including Randy Williams, a young lady of fifteen years, who was residing with Grigsbys at the time. The group congregated in the basement, which was being used as a family room and laundry room.

   Everyone left the basement, except Nancy and Randy. Apparently these two girls were at a loss for entertainment as eventually they centered their attention on a lit Christmas-tree-shaped candle on a shelf behind the couch. The girls began to discuss whether the candle was scented. After agreeing that it was not, Randy, while remarking "Well, let's make it scented," impulsively grabbed a "drip bottle" of Faberge's Tigress cologne, which had been placed by Mrs. Grigsby in the basement for use as a laundry deodorant, and began to pour its contents onto the lower portion of the candle somewhat below the flame. Instantaneously, a burst of fire sprang out and burned Nancy's neck and breasts as she stood nearby watching but not fully aware of what her friend was doing.

   Ms. Moran brought suit against Faberge, Inc. The jury gave a verdict in favor of Ms. Moran. However, the judge granted judgment notwithstanding the verdict in favor of defendant Faberge, Inc. Plaintiff appealed.

   Did the trial judge decide correctly? Why or why not?

5. James E. Keck filed a divorce petition in Cook County, Illinois. Dolores Keck answered the complaint and asked for separate maintenance. While the Illinois case was still pending, James moved to Nevada and received a divorce through the Nevada courts. He then moved back to Illinois. The trial court upheld Dolores's claim that the Nevada decree was invalid, but the appeals court reversed, saying that the Nevada decree must be given full faith and credit.

   James lived in Nevada only two months, he returned immediately upon obtaining his decree, he retained his apartment in Chicago and returned there, he retained his job in Chicago and returned to it, he retained his Chicago bank accounts and his Illinois driver's license. Within one or two days after arriving in Nevada, he contacted a lawyer about getting a divorce.

   How should the Illinois Supreme Court decide this case? Explain.

Chapter 5

Criminal Law and Procedure

Traditionally the business manager has been less concerned about criminal law than about contract law, tort law, corporation law, and other mainstream business law subjects. However, criminal law, particularly as it applies to white-collar crimes, is becoming an area of considerable concern for business managers. Managers need to be aware of a number of business crimes. One of the newest types of business crimes is computer theft. Computer theft encompasses embezzlement of funds, theft of computer programs, and theft of confidential business information and records—all through the use and manipulation of computers and other electronic devices.

In addition to having to concern themselves with white-collar or business crimes, corporate officers and corporate directors now find that they are not only subject to civil lawsuits for their actions but that they may also be criminally liable, with resulting jail terms, or large fines.

DEFINITION OF CRIME

A **crime** can be defined as a public wrong. To maintain an orderly society, certain standards of conduct must be set which the members of society must observe. Failure to observe these standards must be enforced by some form of societal sanctions, such as fines or imprisonment. A crime may involve either the commission of a specific act or the omission or failure to act under certain circumstances. For the commission or omission of an act to be classified as a crime, the legislature, either national, state, or local, must have passed a statute or ordinance declaring the commission or omission of that act to be a crime.

Many of the acts or omissions which have been defined as crimes may also be torts. A **tort** is a private wrong for which the wronged person may recover monetary damages. A typical exam-

101

ple is the crime of assault and battery in which someone is mugged on the street. Society has decreed by statute that such acts of assault and battery against a person shall be considered crimes and shall be punished appropriately. The person who has been mugged, on the other hand, was the victim of a private wrong and has a legal right to bring a civil action at his or her own expense to recover monetary damages from the wrongdoer for the loss suffered.

CLASSIFICATIONS OF CRIME

Basically crimes may be classified as felonies or misdemeanors. There is also the crime of treason; however, it is not normally associated with business law and therefore will not be discussed here. Traditionally, **felonies** have been serious crimes, such as murder, rape, robbery, burglary, arson, theft, and larceny. A crime is not a felony, however, unless it is designated as such by the particular statute or ordinance making it a crime. Felonies are normally punishable by jail sentences of at least one year, plus possible fines.

Misdemeanors are criminal offenses other than felonies. Typically, misdemeanors are punished by small fines and/or jail sentences not exceeding one year. Normally the person who has been convicted of a misdemeanor is confined in a county jail rather than the state penitentiary. The fines imposed for misdemeanors are normally smaller than the fines imposed for felonies. There is, however, no standard that is common to all states, and different states have different crime classifications and different levels of punishment. Each state has the responsibility of creating its own criminal law. State criminal law may not, however, conflict with any applicable national law.

The *Wyant* case concerns conduct only recently defined as criminal.

STATE v. WYANT
597 N.E.2d 450 (OH, 1992)

FACTS: On May 29, 1989, appellant David Wyant and his wife rented campsite L-16 at Alum Creek State Park. On May 31, the Wyants' relatives came to join them, and rented L-17, the adjoining campsite. On June 2, Wyant rerented his site, but released the relatives' site, as they were to leave that day. Later in the day plans changed, and Wyant attempted to rerent site L-17. He was told that the site had been rented to someone else, and so he rented L-18.

Site L-17 had been rented to the complaining witnesses, Jerry White, and his girlfriend, Patricia McGowan. White and McGowan are black; everyone in the Wyant party is white. There was little contact between the groups for most of the evening of June 2nd, but sometime between 10:30 and 11:45 p.m., White went to park officials to complain of loud music coming from the Wyant campsite. A park official went to site L-16 and asked Wyant to turn off the radio. Wyant complied.

Fifteen or twenty minutes later the radio came on again, and White and McGowan heard racial epithets and threats made in a loud voice by Wyant. White and McGowan complained to park officials and left the park.

Wyant was indicted and convicted on one count of ethnic intimidation, predicated on aggravated menacing, and sentenced to one and one-half years' imprisonment. The court of appeals affirmed the conviction.

 JUSTICE BROWN:

Motive, in criminal law, is not an element of the crime.... LaFave and Scott argue that if defined narrowly enough, motive is not relevant to substantive criminal law, although procedurally it may be evidence of guilt, or, in the case of good motive, may result in leniency. Other thought-related concepts such as intent and purpose are used in the criminal law as elements of crimes or penalty-enhancing criteria, but motive itself is not punished.... "While motive may be relevant as a mitigating factor in the penalty phase, it is irrelevant to the guilt phase determination...."

There is a significant difference between why a person commits a crime and whether a person has intentionally done the acts which are made criminal. Motive is the reasons and beliefs that lead a person to act or refrain from acting. The same crime can be committed for any of a number of different motives. Enhancing a penalty because of motive therefore punishes the person's thought, rather than the person's act or criminal intent....

Some aggravating circumstances involve the identity of the victim, such as a peace officer or governmental official.... The legislature has decided, in these instances, that acts against certain individuals are more serious criminal acts. Imposing a higher penalty for killing the Governor than for killing an ordinary citizen is similar to imposing a higher penalty for stealing a painting worth $1,000 than for stealing one worth only $5.

Under the above analysis, the legislature could decide that blacks are more valuable than whites, and enhance the punishment when a black is the victim of a criminal act. Such a statute would pass First Amendment analysis because the *motive* or the thought which precipitated the attack would not be punished. However, R.C. 2927.12 could not have been written that way because such a statute would not survive analysis under the Equal Protection Clause of the Fourteenth Amendment to the United States Constitution....

Federal and state laws against discrimination in employment, housing, and education do prohibit acts committed with a discriminatory motive. However, they are analytically distinct in several ways from the statute in question here. It is the act of discrimination that is targeted, not the motive....

The freedoms of speech, press, religion, and assembly are guaranteed together in the First Amendment because they share a core value: the freedom of an individual to frame his thoughts and beliefs. The Constitution of Ohio is even more specific; it guarantees to every citizen freedom to "speak, write, and publish his sentiments on all subjects." It follows that a citizen of Ohio is free to have "sentiments on all subjects."

By enacting R.C. 2927.12, the state has infringed this basic liberty. Once the proscribed act is committed, the government criminalizes the underlying thought by enhancing the penalty based on viewpoint. This is dangerous. If the legislature can enhance a penalty for crimes committed "by reason of" racial bigotry, why not "by reason of" opposition to abortion, war, the elderly (or any other political or moral viewpoint)?....

Applying these principles, we believe that the government is not free to punish an idea, though it may punish acts motivated by the idea. It may also punish unprotected speech expressing the idea....

Conduct motivated by racial or religious bigotry can be constitutionally punished under the criminal code without resort to constructing a thought crime. In fact, the behavior which is alleged in each case before us can be punished under the criminal statutes identified in R.C. 2927.12. We agree with Justice Scalia when he observed that the government "has sufficient means at its disposal to prevent such behavior without adding the First Amendment to the fire...."

Having so held, we turn to the specific cases which are before us. Constitutional protection of thought does not shield a citizen from punishment for proscribed acts. Although the ethnic intimidation statute is invalid, the predicate offenses are punishable. As these offenses are mentioned specifically in R.C. 2927.12, they constitute lesser included offenses to ethnic intimidation.

BUSINESS CRIMES

Since this textbook focuses on business-related legal matters, our major focus here will be on crimes that are relevant to the operation of a business. The following are some typical business crimes.

Larceny. Larceny, or theft as it is commonly called, is simply the unlawful taking of another person's personal property with the intent of depriving the owner of the property. Shoplifting is an example of larceny with which the businessperson has to be concerned. Larceny is also committed by employees who carry off goods and merchandise.

Robbery. Robbery, like larceny, involves the unlawful taking of personal property. However, the unlawful taking in a robbery involves the use of force, putting other persons in fear of injury. Thus, robbery is a more serious crime than larceny since it has the potential of physical harm to individuals.

Embezzlement. With embezzlement, a person who had lawful possession of someone else's money or property used the property or money for his or her own purposes. A typical case here would be a bank employee who was in charge of certain funds and used some of the funds for personal purposes. Many embezzlers borrow money with the intent of paying it back later. In most jurisdictions, the person who takes money with the intent of returning it is still guilty of embezzlement.

The *O'Hagan* case involves an employee's wrongful use of confidential information.

UNITED STATES v. O'HAGAN
117 S.CT. 2199 (1997)

FACTS: James Herman O'Hagan was a partner in the law firm of Dorsey & Whitney in Minneapolis, Minnesota. In July 1988, Grand Metropolitan PLC (Grand Met), a company based in London, England, retained Dorsey & Whitney as local counsel to represent Grand Met regarding a potential tender offer for the common stock of the Pillsbury Company, headquartered in Minneapolis. Both Grand Met and Dorsey & Whitney took precautions to protect the confidentiality of Grand Met's tender offer plans. O'Hagan did no work on the Grand Met representation. Dorsey & Whitney withdrew from representing Grand Met on September 9, 1988. Less than a month later, on October 4, 1988, Grand Met publicly announced its tender offer for Pillsbury stock.

On August 18, 1988, while Dorsey & Whitney was still representing Grand Met, O'Hagan began purchasing call options for Pillsbury stock. Each option gave him the right to purchase 100 shares of Pillsbury stock by a specified date in September 1988. Later in August and in September, O'Hagan made additional purchases of Pillsbury call options. By the end of September, he owned 2,500 unexpired Pillsbury options, apparently more than any other individual investor. O'Hagan also purchased, in September 1988, some 5,000 shares of Pillsbury common stock, at a price just under $39 per share. When Grand Met announced its tender offer in October, the price of Pillsbury stock rose to nearly $60 per share. O'Hagan then sold his Pillsbury call options and common stock, making a profit of more than $4.3 million.

The Securities and Exchange Commission initiated an investigation into O'Hagan's transactions, culminating in a 57 count indictment. The indictment alleged that O'Hagan defrauded his law firm and its client, Grand Met, by using for his own trading purposes material, nonpublic information regarding Grand Met's planned tender offer. According to the indictment, O'Hagan used the profits he gained through this trading to conceal his previous embezzlement and conversion of unrelated client trust funds. O'Hagan was charged with 20 counts of mail fraud; 17 counts of securities fraud; 17 counts of fraudulent trading in connection with a tender offer; and 3 counts of violating federal money laundering statutes. A jury convicted O'Hagan on all 57 counts, and he was sentenced to a 41-month term of imprisonment.

A divided panel of the Court of Appeals for the Eighth Circuit reversed all of O'Hagan's convictions. [Decisions of the Courts of Appeals are in conflict on the propriety of the misappropriation theory under § 10(b) and Rule 10b-5, and on the legitimacy of Rule 14e 3(a) under § 14(e).]

JUSTICE GINSBURG:

This case concerns the interpretation and enforcement of § 10(b) and § 14(e) of the Securities Exchange Act of 1934, and rules made by the Securities and Exchange Commission pursuant to these provisions. Rule 10b-5 and Rule 14e-3(a). Two prime questions are presented. The first relates to the misappropriation of material, nonpublic information for securities trading; the second concerns fraudulent practices in the tender offer setting. In particular, we address and resolve these issues: (1) Is a person who trades in securities for personal profit, using confidential information misappropriated in breach of a fiduciary duty to the source of the information, guilty of violating § 10(b) and Rule 10b-5? (2) Did the Commission exceed its rulemaking authority by adopting Rule 14e-3(a), which proscribes trading on undisclosed information in the tender offer setting, even in the absence of a duty to disclose? Our answer to the first question is yes, and to the second question, viewed in the context of this case, no.

We address first the Court of Appeals' reversal of O'Hagan's convictions under § 10(b) and Rule 10b-5. Following the Fourth Circuit's lead ... the Eighth Circuit rejected the misappropriation theory as a basis for § 10(b) liability. We hold, in accord with several other Courts of Appeals, that criminal liability under § 10(b) may be predicated on the misappropriation theory....

The "misappropriation theory" holds that a person commits fraud "in connection with" a securities transaction, and thereby violates § 10(b) and Rule 10b-5, when he misappropriates confidential information for securities trading purposes, in breach of a duty owed to the source of the information.... Under this theory, a fiduciary's undisclosed, self-serving use of a principal's information to purchase or sell securities, in breach of a duty of loyalty and confidentiality, defrauds the principal of the exclusive use of that information. In lieu of premising liability on a fiduciary relationship between company insider and purchaser or seller of the company's stock, the misappropriation theory premises liability on a fiduciary-turned-trader's deception of those who entrusted him with access to confidential information....

We agree with the Government that misappropriation, as just defined, satisfies § 10(b)'s requirement that chargeable conduct involve a "deceptive device or contrivance" used "in connection with" the purchase or sale of securities. We observe, first, that misappropriators, as the government describes them, deal in deception. A fiduciary who "[pretends] loyalty to the principal while secretly converting the principal's information for personal gain," ... "dupes" or defrauds the principal.

Deception through nondisclosure is central to the theory of liability for which the Government seeks recognition. As counsel for the Government stated in explanation of the theory at oral argument: "To satisfy the common law rule that a trustee may not use the property that [has] been entrusted [to] him, there would have to be consent. To satisfy the requirement of the Securities Act that there be no deception, there would only have to be disclosure."

We turn next to the § 10(b) requirement that the misappropriator's deceptive use of information be "in connection with the purchase or sale of [a] security." This element is satisfied because the fiduciary's fraud is consummated, not when the fiduciary gains the confidential information, but when, without disclosure to his principal, he uses the information to purchase or sell securities. The securities transaction and the breach of duty thus coincide. This is so even though the person or entity defrauded is not the other party to the trade, but is, instead, the source of the nonpublic information.... A misappropriator who trades on the basis of material, nonpublic information, in short, gains his advantageous market position through deception; he deceives the source of the information and simultaneously harms members of the investing public....

The misappropriation theory targets information of a sort that misappropriators ordinarily capitalize upon to gain no-risk profits through the purchase or sale of securities. Should a misappropriator put such information to other use, the statute's prohibition would not be implicated. The theory does not catch all conceivable forms of fraud involving confidential information; rather, it catches fraudulent means of capitalizing on such information through securities transactions....

The misappropriation theory comports with § 10(b)'s language, which requires deception "in connection with the purchase or sale of any security," not deception of an identifiable purchaser or seller. The theory is also well-tuned to an animating purpose of the Exchange Act: to insure honest securities markets and thereby promote investor confidence.... Although informational disparity is inevitable in the securities markets, investors likely would hesitate to venture their capital in a market where trading based on misappropriated nonpublic information is unchecked by law. An investor's informational disadvantage vis-á-vis a misappropriator with material, nonpublic information stems from contrivance, not luck; it is a disadvantage that cannot be overcome with research or skill.... "If the market is thought to be systematically populated with ... transactors [trading on the basis of misappropriated information] some investors will refrain from dealing altogether, and others will incur costs to avoid dealing with such transactors or corruptly to overcome their unerodable informational advantages."...

In sum, considering the inhibiting impact on market participation of trading on misappropriated information, and the congressional purposes underlying § 10(b), it makes scant sense to hold a lawyer like O'Hagan a § 10(b) violator if he works for a law firm representing the target of a tender offer, but not if he works for a law firm representing the bidder. The text of the statute requires no such result. The misappropriation at issue here was properly made the subject of a § 10(b) charge because it meets the statutory requirement that there be "deceptive" conduct "in connection with" securities transactions....

We consider next the ground on which the Court of Appeals reversed O'Hagan's convictions for fraudulent trading in connection with a tender offer, in violation of § 14(e) of the Exchange Act and SEC Rule 14e-3(a). A sole question is before us as to these convictions: Did the Commission, as the Court of Appeals held, exceed its rule-making authority under § 14(e) when it adopted Rule 14e-3(a) without requiring a showing that the trading at issue entailed a breach of fiduciary duty? We hold that the Commission, in this regard and to the extent relevant to this case, did not exceed its authority....

Because Congress has authorized the Commission, in § 14(e), to prescribe legislative rules, we owe the Commission's judgment "more than mere deference or weight."... Therefore, in determining whether Rule 14e-3(a)'s "disclose or abstain from trading" requirement is reasonably designed to prevent fraudulent acts, we must accord the Commission's assessment "controlling weight unless [it is] arbitrary, capricious, or manifestly contrary to the statute."... In this case, we conclude, the Commission's assessment is none of these....

The judgment of the Court of Appeals for the Eighth Circuit is reversed, and the case is remanded for further proceedings consistent with this opinion.

Arson. Arson is willfully setting fire to and burning someone else's building. In old English common law, arson referred primarily to the burning of someone else's dwelling house.

Under most state statutes, arson now covers the burning of business buildings as well as dwellings. Burning one's own home or building traditionally was not arson. You had a right to tear your own building down, burn it, or destroy it in any manner as long as you didn't injure the property of others. A problem arises, however, when the building being burned is covered by fire insurance and the intent of burning it is to collect the insurance. The offense in that situation is actually criminal fraud against an insurance company.

Defrauding Consumers by Use of the Mails. It is a crime to use the mails to solicit money for fraudulent purposes. This could include schemes to sell phony corporate stocks and bonds, false statements about products which when received are not as advertised, and numerous other situations in which people use the mails to convey false information for the purpose of committing fraud. National laws also make it a crime to send pornographic materials through the mails.

Defrauding Consumers by Using False Labels, Measures, and Weights. In recent years, a number of national and state laws have been passed concerning false weights, measures, and labels. Again, intention is a key factor in this crime. A simple mistake in weight or measurement is not a crime. There must be an intent to defraud or cheat the consumer.

Forgery. Forgery is the false or fraudulent making, or the material alteration with the intent to defraud, of any writing which if it were genuine would be of legal effect and create legal liability. When we think of forgery, we typically think of a situation where one person signs another person's name to a check. Forgery also includes the changing of a legal document in such a way as to change the legal liability of the document. One of the most common acts of forgery relates to the use of credit cards. How often are you asked to furnish your driver's license or other identification when you want to use your gasoline credit card?

Credit Card Fraud. Illegal and fraudulent use of stolen credit cards has become an area of considerable concern to credit card companies. The most common problem is the theft of credit cards and then the use of the stolen credit cards by the thief for two or three days until notice goes out to retailers that the card is on a stolen list. While this does not sound like a problem that could create large losses, if one considers the number of credit cards that are stolen and then multiplies that figure by the average purchases made by the thief, it adds up to millions of dollars a year in losses to the credit card companies.

In 1971, Congress passed a law that limited an individual's liability to $50 per stolen credit card, so at least the individual cannot be liable for more than $50 per credit card stolen. However, the credit card companies do not have any limit on their loss. Another problem is just what is the crime? Is it the theft of a piece of plastic, or is it the wrongful use of the card? A number of states have passed specific statutes making it a crime to obtain property or services by using a stolen, forged, revoked, or canceled credit card.

Computer Crime. This is the newest and perhaps the most important area of criminal law of concern to business managers. Computer-related crimes range from the theft of a computer program worth thousands of dollars to the use of computers to embezzle millions of dollars. As we enter the new cashless society, electronic fund transfer systems are replacing the traditional cash and check method of payment and deposit of funds. Thus, most of our funds are stored magnetically and electronically as data in various computer memory banks, and fund transfers are made over communication circuits of various types from those computer memory banks to other computer memory banks. It is comparatively easy for a skilled and knowledgeable computer technician with access to an electronic data processing system to reprogram the computer in such a way as to shift, hide, or manipulate funds. Moreover, detection is difficult, as an erasure or an addition of data in a magnetic file leaves no traceable evidence.

Computer crimes can be classified into three general categories. The first category is the most common, and it involves the use of the computer by an insider to steal funds or property. An example of theft of property was a case in California where an employee of the Pacific Telephone and Telegraph Company who had access to the company's computer simply reprogrammed the computer to order deliveries of certain equipment to a warehouse the employee rented; then the employee would sell the equipment and pocket the money.

The second category also involves insiders using the computer. However, in this category the insiders are not using the computer to steal money or property; they are using the recordkeeping capacity of the computer to swindle and cheat outsiders out of funds. This category could be termed computer-assisted fraud. Perhaps the most appalling computer fraud case in recent years is the case of the Equity Funding Corporation of America. Certain officers of the corporation defrauded the public out of a sum estimated to exceed $2 billion. The corporation operated a life insurance company, and it claimed to have some 90,000 policyholders. In fact, its computer records would show on the printouts that it had some 90,000 policyholders; however, the problem was that nearly 60,000 of these policyholders were fictitious entries in the computer. The fraud was really very simple. The officers would enter fictitious names and addresses for policyholders in the computer and then sell the rights in these policies to reinsurance companies. These fictitious policyholders' names and records were entered in the computer under a special secret code so that a routine audit would only reveal the legitimate policyholders. In this case, the computer didn't perpetuate the fraud by electronically shifting funds or property, it was simply used in a record-keeping capacity. The real danger with this category is that managers and the public in general blindly accept computerized records and computer printouts as being accurate and truthful.

The third category of computer crime involves theft of confidential information from the computer by an outsider. There are numerous reported cases in which people with home computers were able to break security codes and gain access to major computer banks. Although many of these instances involve simple pranks, theft of confidential material from a computer by an unauthorized outsider can be a serious criminal problem. Theft of secret business data, theft of a computer program, and theft of military secrets are some examples.

Thus far, we have probably seen only the tip of the iceberg in the area of computer crime. Managers must be aware of the potential for loss and liability in this area and take appropriate precautions.

Criminal Liability of Accountants. This is also a new area of criminal law. Traditionally, professionals such as accountants, lawyers, and doctors were found liable for civil damages for malpractice but were not prosecuted criminally for acts of mere negligence. In recent years, a number of criminal cases have been brought against accountants, particularly in connection with their failure to discover and report fraud by corporate officers or employees.

In Chapter 7, we will discuss the liability of accountants and other professionals in more detail.

Commercial Bribery. In recent years, the press has exposed many cases of commercial bribery and payoffs to politicians and various cases of illegal campaign contributions. The problem in these cases is that a corporation typically makes the illegal contribution or pays the bribe. You can fine a corporation, but you can't put a corporation in jail. Shouldn't the executive who made the decision to have the corporation disobey the law also be criminally liable? Such activities by U.S corporations in other countries were the major reason behind the passage of the Foreign Corrupt Practices Act. The FCPA is discussed further in Chapter 7.

Criminal Liability of Corporate Executives. In stockholder actions against managers, corporate directors, and corporate officers, these persons have always been individually accountable in civil court for their acts of negligence in the operation of the business. With regard to criminal charges, typically the corporation is charged with the crime, and since a corporation cannot be jailed, the corporation simply paid the fine and the case was closed. There seemed to be a protective shield between the manager, corporate director, or corporate officer, and the criminal prosecutor. The first major instance in which this corporate shield was pierced was the electrical industry price-fixing conspiracy case in 1960. In that case, several corporate executives were sent to jail. This corporate shield has been disintegrating ever since.

New regulations and new laws are aiming at criminal prosecution, not of the corporate entity, an artificial person, but more realistically, of the natural persons whose decision caused the criminal act. Thus corporate executives must weigh their decisions not only on the corporate profit-loss scale but also against the possibility of personal criminal punishment. In the past, a corporate executive might have decided to violate the law because the anticipated profit of doing so exceeded the anticipated corporate fines that would have to be paid if the violation were detected.

YOUR RIGHTS UNDER CRIMINAL LAW

Your rights under criminal law are considerably different from your rights under civil law. Under civil law, if you are sued for breach of contract or for the commission of a tort, the usual remedy is monetary damages. None of us want to lose money. However, if we are unfortunate enough to have a very large judgment assessed against us and we do not have the funds to satisfy the judgment, we do have the opportunity to file for bankruptcy. A person who is adjudicated a bankrupt is free from most prior debts and in effect is born again, as far as his or her financial life is concerned. However, a person who is convicted of a crime may be jailed and/or assessed a fine, and if the crime is a felony, the person may lose certain civil rights. In some states, convicted felons lose the right to vote, the right to serve on juries, and the right to hold public office. Also, a person convicted of a crime who is also a professional practitioner, such as a lawyer, may face disbarment. Thus a criminal conviction carries with it more serious consequences than does a simple civil judgment for money. A person convicted of a crime will carry this record for life. In fact, if capital punishment is allowed, the person may lose his or her life. Thus, the guarantees that the law must give to a person charged with a crime are much greater than the guarantees which must be given in a civil trial for monetary damages.

Following are some of the guarantees that are essential in a criminal trial but need not be provided in a civil trial.

Right to a Speedy, Public Trial by Jury. The Sixth Amendment to the Constitution of the United States guarantees a speedy, public trial by jury in criminal cases. In civil cases, in large metropolitan areas, there may be a delay of several years between the time of filing a lawsuit and the time of trial. A person charged with a crime should have his or her day in court promptly. The trial must be before a jury, unless the defendant waives the right to a jury trial, and it must be public.

Presumption of Innocence. The jury in a criminal trial must be instructed by the judge that the defendant, the party charged with the crime, is innocent until proven guilty. The jury is instructed that the state or the national government, whoever the charging party may be, must prove the case against the defendant beyond a reasonable doubt. There must also, as a rule, be a unanimous verdict. In a civil case, the plaintiff must simply prove the case by a preponderance of the evidence. This means that the jury must simply believe the plaintiff's story more than it believes the defendant's story. Also, in a criminal case, the jury in most jurisdictions has only one thing to decide, and that is guilt or innocence. The punishment is normally decided by the judge or at a second deliberation of the jury. In civil cases, the jury not only decides whether the plaintiff gets a verdict or the defendant gets a verdict, but it also has the option of deciding how much money the plaintiff will be awarded.

Privilege Against Self-Incrimination. In a criminal case, the person charged with a crime cannot be forced to testify against himself or herself. This, of course, is the guarantee against self-incrimination which is provided by the Fifth Amendment of the U.S. Constitution. In an ordinary civil trial, a defendant may be required to testify or be found in civil contempt of court.

Right to Counsel. The Sixth Amendment to the U.S. Constitution provides that the accused in a criminal trial shall have the right to assistance of counsel. If the accused cannot afford an attorney, an attorney will be appointed for the accused by the court at the expense of the state. In most civil cases, no attorney is appointed for the defendant. The defendant must personally hire an attorney or act as his or her own counsel. Many metropolitan areas and many university towns now have legal aid societies which furnish free legal counsel to people who cannot afford the services of an attorney.

Right to a Miranda-Type Warning. The famous case of *Miranda v. State of Arizona*, 384 U.S. 436 (1966), initiated the so-called *Miranda*-type warning which now must be read to an accused before the accused is interrogated in any way. Briefly, the accused must be told that he or she has the right to remain silent, that he or she has the right to have an attorney present when being questioned, and that an attorney will be appointed by the court if the defendant cannot afford one. As a result of the *Miranda* decision, if the police officer failed to read the suspect his or her *Miranda* rights, any statement made by the suspect was simply not admissible in court.

The *Davis* case involves the suspect's right to counsel and the *Miranda* warning.

DAVIS v. U.S.
114 S.Ct. 2350 (1994)

FACTS:
Pool brought trouble—not to River City, but to the Charleston Naval Base. Robert Davis, a member of the United States Navy, spent the evening of October 2, 1988, shooting pool at a club on the base. Another sailor, Keith Shackleford, lost a game and a $30 wager to Davis, but Shackleford refused to pay. After the club closed, Shackleford was beaten to death with a pool cue on a loading dock behind the commissary. The body was found early the next morning.

The investigation by the Naval Investigative Service (NIS) gradually focused on Davis. Investigative agents determined that he was at the club that evening, and that he was absent without authorization from his duty station the next morning. The agents also learned that only privately owned pool cues could be removed from the club premises, and that Davis owned two cues—one of which had a bloodstain on it. The agents were told by various people that petitioner either had admitted committing the crime or had recounted details that clearly indicated his involvement in the killing.

On November 4, 1988, Davis was interviewed at the NIS office. As required by military law, the agents advised petitioner that he was a suspect in the killing, that he was not required to make a statement, that any statement could be used against him at a trial by court-martial, and that he was entitled to speak with an attorney and have an attorney present during questioning. Davis waived his rights to remain silent and to counsel, both orally and in writing.

About an hour and a half into the interview, Davis said, "Maybe I should talk to a lawyer." According to the uncontradicted testimony of one of the interviewing agents, the interview than proceeded as follows:

> "[We] made it very clear that we're not here to violate his rights, that if he wants a lawyer, then we will stop any kind of questioning with him, that we weren't going to pursue the matter unless we have it clarified is he asking for a lawyer or is he just making a comment about a lawyer, and he said, [']No, I'm not asking for a lawyer,' and then he continued on, and said, 'No, I don't want a lawyer.'"

After a short break, the agents reminded Davis of his rights to remain silent and to counsel. The interview then continued for another hour, until Davis said, "I think I want a lawyer before I say anything else." At that point, questioning ceased.

At his general court-martial, Davis moved to suppress statements made during the November 4 interview. The military judge denied the motion. Davis was convicted on one specification of unpremeditated murder. He was sentenced to confinement for life, dishonorable discharge, forfeiture of all pay and allowances, and a reduction in rank to the lowest pay grade. The convening authority approved the finding and sentence. The Navy-Marine Corps Court of Military Review affirmed.

The United States Court of Military Appeals granted discretionary review and affirmed.

 JUSTICE O'CONNOR:

The Sixth Amendment right to counsel attaches only at the initiation of adversary criminal proceedings, ... and before proceedings are initiated a suspect in a criminal investigation has no constitutional right to the assistance of counsel. Nevertheless, we held in *Miranda* ... that a suspect subject to custodial interrogation has the right to consult with an attorney and to have counsel present during questioning, and that the police must explain this right to him before questioning begins. The right to counsel established in *Miranda* was one of a "series of recommended 'procedural safeguards' ... [that] were not themselves rights protected by the Constitution but were instead measures to insure that the right against compulsory self-incrimination was protected...."

The right to counsel recognized in *Miranda* is sufficiently important to suspects in criminal investigations, we have held, that it requir[es] the special protection of the knowing and intelligent waiver standard.... If the suspect effectively waives his right to counsel after receiving the *Miranda* warnings, law enforcement officers are free to question him.... But if a suspect requests counsel at any time during the interview, he is not subject to further questioning until a lawyer has been made available or the suspect himself reinstates conversation.... This "second layer of prophylaxis for the *Miranda* right to counsel" ... is "designed to prevent police from badgering a defendant into waiving his previously asserted *Miranda* rights." To that end, we have held that a suspect who has invoked the right to counsel cannot be questioned regarding any offense unless an attorney is actually present.... "It remains clear, however, that this prohibition on further questioning—like other aspects of *Miranda*—is not itself required by the Fifth Amendment's prohibition on coerced confessions, but is instead justified only by reference to its prophylactic purpose...."

The applicability of the "rigid" prophylactic rule of *Edwards* requires courts to "determine whether the accused *actually invoked* his right to counsel...." To avoid difficulties of proof and to provide guidance to officers conducting interrogations, this is an objective inquiry.... Invocation of the *Miranda* right to counsel "requires, at a minimum, some statement that can reasonably be construed to be an expression of a desire for the assistance of an attorney...." But if a suspect makes a reference to an attorney that is ambiguous or equivocal in that a reasonable officer in light of the circumstances would have understood only that the suspect *might* be invoking the right to counsel, our precedents do not require the cessation of questioning....

Rather, the suspect must unambiguously request counsel. As we have observed, "a statement either is such an assertion of the right to counsel or it is not...." Although a suspect need not to "speak with the discrimination of an Oxford don," ... he must articulate his desire to have counsel present sufficiently clearly that a reasonable police officer in the circumstances would understand the statement to be a request for an attorney. If the statement fails to meet the requisite level of clarity, *Edwards* does not require that the officers stop questioning the suspect....

We decline petitioner's invitation to extend *Edwards* and require law enforcement officers to cease questioning immediately upon the making of an ambiguous or equivocal reference to an attorney.... The rationale underlying *Edwards* is that the police must respect a suspect's wishes regarding his right to have an attorney present during custodial interrogation. But when the officers conducting the questioning reasonably do not know whether or not the suspect wants a lawyer, a rule requiring the immediate cessation of questioning would transform the *Miranda* safeguards into wholly irrational obstacles to legitimate police investigative activity, ... because it would needlessly prevent the police from questioning a suspect in the absence of counsel, even if the suspect did not wish to have a lawyer present. Nothing in *Edwards* requires the provision of counsel to a suspect who consents to answer questions without the assistance of a lawyer. In *Miranda* itself, we expressly rejected the suggestion "that each police station must have a 'station house lawyer' present at all times to advise prisoners" ... and held instead that a suspect must be told of his right to have an attorney present and that he may not be questioned after invoking his right to counsel. We also noted that if a suspect is "indecisive in his request for counsel," the officers need not always cease questioning....

We recognize that requiring a clear assertion of the right to counsel might disadvantage some suspects who—because of fear, intimidation, lack of linguistic skills, or a variety of other reasons—will not clearly articulate their right to counsel although they actually want to have a lawyer present. But the primary protection afforded suspects subject to custodial interrogation is the *Miranda* warnings themselves. "[F]ull comprehension of the rights to remain silent and request an attorney [is] sufficient to dispel whatever coercion is inherent in the interrogation process" .... A suspect who knowingly and voluntarily waives his right to counsel after having that right explained to him has indicated his willingness to deal with the police unassisted. Although *Edwards* provides an additional protection—if a suspect subsequently requests an attorney, questioning must cease—it is one that must be affirmatively invoked by the suspect.

In considering how a suspect must invoke the right to counsel, we must consider the other side of the *Miranda* equation: the need for effective law enforcement. Although the courts ensure compliance with the *Miranda* requirements through the exclusionary rule, it is police officers who must actually decide whether or not they can question a suspect. The *Edwards* rule—questioning must cease if the suspect asks for a lawyer—provides a bright line that can be applied by officers in the real world of investigation and interrogation without unduly hampering the gathering of information. But if we were to require questioning to cease if a suspect makes a statement that might be a request for an attorney, this clarity and ease of application would be lost. Police officers would be forced to make difficult judgment calls about whether the suspect in fact wants a lawyer even though he hasn't said so, with the threat of suppression if they guess wrong. We therefore hold that, after a knowing and voluntary waiver of the *Miranda* rights, law enforcement officers may continue questioning until and unless the suspect clearly requests an attorney....

To recapitulate: We held in *Miranda* that a suspect is entitled to the assistance of counsel during custodial interrogation even though the Constitution does not provide for such assistance. We held in *Edwards* that if the suspect invokes the right to counsel at any time, the police must immediately cease questioning him until an attorney is present. But we are unwilling to create a third layer of prophylaxis to prevent police questioning when the suspect *might* want a lawyer. Unless the suspect actually requests an attorney, questioning may continue.

The courts below found that petitioner's remark to the NIS agents—"Maybe I should talk to a lawyer"—was not a request for counsel, and we see no reason to disturb that conclusion. The NIS agents therefore were not required to stop questioning petitioner, though it was entirely proper for them to clarify whether petitioner in fact wanted a lawyer. Because there is no ground for suppression of petitioner's statements, the judgment of the Court of Military Appeals is Affirmed.

No Unreasonable Searches. Persons also have the right to be secure in their private homes and places of business. The Fourth Amendment prohibits unreasonable searches and seizures of evidence.

The *Paulson* case discusses this protection.

PEOPLE v. PAULSON
265 Cal.Rptr. 579 (CA, App. 1 Dist., 1990)

FACTS: Lee Stewart Paulson appeals his conviction following his plea of nolo contendere to one count of possession of cocaine. The court suspended imposition of sentence and placed him on probation for three years on condition he serve ninety days in the county jail. He filed a timely appeal, challenging the lawfulness of the search.

On February 11, 1988, an anonymous informer tipped the Department that narcotic sales were occurring on the premises of the "My House" bar in San Francisco, and that the narcotics were kept in a safe behind the bar on the premises. A month later, on March 11, 1988, Jerry Meyer, a special investigator for the Department, went to the bar during its hours of operation, entered, identified himself, telephoned appellant (the holder of the liquor license at the premises), informed appellant he was conducting an inspection, and asked appellant to provide access to a safe and locked storage facility. When appellant arrived, Meyer, who did not have a search warrant, asked him to open the safe. Appellant did so. Meyer did not seek to obtain consent, although appellant did not object. Twenty-two bundles of cocaine, totalling 5.5 grams, were found in the safe.

 JUSTICE KLINE:

The Fourth Amendment's prohibition on unreasonable searches and seizures applies to commercial premises, as well as to private homes.... "However, unlike searches of private homes, which generally must bo conducted pursuant to a warrant in order to be reasonable under the Fourth Amendment, legislative schemes authorizing warrantless administrative searches of commercial property do not necessarily violate the Fourth Amendment.... The greater latitude to conduct warrantless inspections of commercial property reflects the fact that the expectation of privacy that the owner of commercial property enjoys in such property differs significantly from the sanctity accorded an individual's home, and that this privacy interest may, in certain circumstances, be adequately protected by regulatory schemes authorizing warrantless inspections...."

The Supreme Court has recognized an exception to the warrant requirement for administrative searches of certain "closely regulated industries which, by their very nature, require unannounced visits from government agents...." "Certain industries have such a history of government oversight that no reasonable expectation of privacy ... could exist for a proprietor over the stock of such an enterprise...." The liquor industry, the quintessential "closely regulated" business, provided the first opportunity for the Supreme Court to articulate the exception....

We need not address appellant's challenge to the use of Section 24200, because the Department does not attempt to justify the warrantless search of appellant's premises solely on the basis of the broad language of that statute; the Department relies as well on considerably more specific language in Section 24200.5. As earlier noted, Section 24200.5 provides, inter alia, that, "[n]otwithstanding the provisions of Section 24200 [relating to *discretionary* suspension or revocation]," the department *shall* revoke a license ... if a retail licensee has knowingly permitted the illegal sale, or negotiations for such sales, of controlled substances or dangerous drugs upon his licensed premises....

Permitting the sale of controlled substances or dangerous drugs on licensed premises (which, incidentally, has been adjudicated to involve moral turpitude) ... is the only public offense not itself involving alcoholic beverages requiring license revocation. Subdivision (a) of section 24200.5 therefore reflects a legislative judgment that the use of licensed premises for this purpose poses a unique threat to "the safety, welfare, health, peace, and morals of the people of the State" ... that must be dealt with more vigorously than almost all other illegal acts that may take place on licensed premises. Drugs and alcohol are both intensively regulated mind-altering substances; are both subject to abuse and addictive, are both attractive to many young persons and others who frequent licensed premises; and their adverse effects are often exacerbated when they are used at or about the same time. In other words, trafficking in dangerous drugs is a particularized criminal act warranting special attention by those charged with enforcement of laws regulating the sale of alcoholic beverages. Absent the threat of mandatory revocation, the Legislature apparently reasoned, such premises would provide a tempting venue for the sale of dangerous drugs.

For the foregoing reasons, the inspection of appellant's premises advances "a 'substantial' government interest that informs the regulatory scheme pursuant to which the inspection [was] made" and therefore satisfies the first of the three applicable criteria for a warrantless search of a closely regulated business....

The warrantless inspection also meets the second criterion because, as the United States Supreme Court has pointed out, violations of law that can be quickly concealed, such as the sale of contraband, can only be deterred by frequent and unannounced inspections. ("In this context, the prerequisite of a warrant could easily frustrate inspection; and if the necessary flexibility as to time, scope, and frequency is to be preserved, the protections afforded by a warrant would be negligible.")....

The inspection satisfies the final criterion because it was authorized by statutes—Sections 24200.5, 25753, and 25755—which collectively provide a ("constitutionally adequate substitute for a warrant").... That is, Section 24200.5 explicitly informs a licensee that "permitt[ing] the illegal sale, or negotiations for such sales, of controlled substances or dangerous drugs upon his licensed premises" is specifically prohibited.

Sections 25733 and 25755 additionally advise licensees that it is the duty of the Department and its duly authorized employees to enforce that prohibition, and that such employees are authorized to act as peace officers and may "visit and inspect the premises of any licensee at any time during which the licensee is exercising the privileges authorized by his or her license on the premises...." A licensee thus cannot help but be aware that his property will be subject to periodic inspections during business hours for the specific purpose of determining whether he is permitting the sale of controlled substances or dangerous drugs on his premises.... Therefore this is not a case in which, as a condition of doing business, the state has required a blanket submission to warrantless searches at any time or for any purpose.... The time, place,and scope of authorized inspections adequately limits the discretion of the Department's inspectors....

For the foregoing reasons, we conclude that the search in question satisfies the applicable Fourth Amendment standard of reasonableness. Accordingly, the judgment is affirmed.

Prohibition Against Double Jeopardy. In criminal trials, there is also the Fifth Amendment guarantee against double jeopardy. If a person charged with a crime has been found innocent, even though later evidence may prove that the person was in fact guilty of the crime, the person may not be tried again. The state may not appeal a verdict of not guilty. Once a person has been tried and found innocent, that is the end of the case. In a civil suit, either party may appeal a decision.

Requirement of Mens Rea. In a criminal case, a person may not be found guilty of a crime unless the person had mental intent to commit the crime. We often hear about the defense of temporary insanity in criminal cases. If a person charged with the commission of a crime did not know what he or she was doing, then the person is not guilty of the crime since there was no mental intent to commit it. Some states have a doctrine called irresistible impulse. In those states, if the person had an irresistible impulse to commit the criminal act, then the person is not guilty. The typical case here would be a husband or wife finding the spouse in bed with another person and striking or shooting them in a rage of temper.

A person who is intoxicated or under the influence of drugs may not be guilty for acts committed while in that condition. However, in such cases, the question arises as to whether the person became intoxicated or fell under the influence of drugs voluntarily or involuntarily, and whether the person was incapable of having a mental intent. If the person became intoxicated or fell under the influence of drugs voluntarily and was still capable of a mental intent, then the majority of courts would find the person guilty. For example, Sam Soak went to a party, voluntarily imbibed too much liquor, and then got into his car to drive home. While swerving down the street, Sam hit a pedestrian in the crosswalk and killed the pedestrian. Sam may very well be found guilty of manslaughter.

If the person who committed a crime was a child under the age of reason, then the child would not legally have sufficient mens rea, or mental intent, to be guilty of the crime. In most states, a child under seven years of age is presumed to be incapable of the mental intent to commit a crime. Over the age of seven years the individual child's capability of mental intent becomes an open question. Here again, the laws of the various states will differ and the particular law of the state where the crime was committed must be consulted.

CRIMINAL PROCEDURE

The procedure in a criminal trial differs considerably from the procedure in a civil trial, which we reviewed in Chapter 4. The accompanying illustration shows a typical criminal trial procedure from the investigation of a crime to the point where the person is released from prison.

In a civil case, the injured party simply secures legal counsel of his or her own choice and proceeds to file a civil lawsuit at his or her own expense. That party can control the lawsuit; that is, the injured party, the plaintiff, can settle the case out of court, pursue the case through trial, or dismiss the case entirely at any point during the proceedings. In a criminal case, the injured party simply reports the commission of a crime to the proper authority and the state or national government then takes over. The injured individual has no further control over the case.

The first step in the procedure of a criminal case is the report of the crime and the investigation. If the investigators are unable to find evidence sufficient to prosecute, then no arrest is made. Many cases will fall into the unsolved category. If the investigation does produce evidence which would support prosecution of the case, then an arrest is made. At the time of the arrest, the arresting officer must inform the person being arrested of the rights in the *Miranda* warning. After having been arrested, the person will be booked. This process involves photographing and finger-printing the subject and making up a record containing the subject's name, address, age, weight, height, and other pertinent information. The person now has a "police record."

The accused will then be entitled to an appearance before a judge. The accused is informed that he or she has the right to have counsel present. At this hearing, the judge must determine whether the person shall be released on bail or without bail, or returned to jail. If the person is to be released on bail, then the judge must set the amount of bail which must be paid or pledged to the court before the defendant is released. In many minor cases, the judge will release the person without bail.

The next step in the criminal process is to determine whether or not there is sufficient evidence to try the person for the crime charged. In serious crimes, a grand jury may be impaneled to hear evidence to determine whether or not there is sufficient cause to proceed to a regular trial. If the grand jury finds sufficient evidence, it will issue an indictment. In other cases, the prosecuting attorney will file an information, or formal statement of the charges, which will allow the case to proceed to a regular trial.

At this stage of the proceeding, the prosecutor must decide what crime the accused should be prosecuted for. Probably the prosecution and the defense will engage in the process called plea bargaining. A very typical example of plea bargaining would take place where a person was arrested for drunk driving—normally punishable by a fine, possible imprisonment, and suspension of driving privileges. If the blood alcohol test or the breath-analyzer test was borderline or just slightly over the legal limit, the prosecuting attorney will often agree to reduce the charge to speeding or reckless driving, which are lesser offenses, if the accused will plead guilty. The prosecutor realizes that the case is not too strong and thus a conviction for a lesser offense is better than a possible defense verdict on the drunken driving charge.

The next step is the arraignment hearing. Here the accused party must plead to the charges either not guilty or guilty. If the party pleads guilty, then, of course, the next step is sentencing.

If, on the other hand, the party pleads not guilty, a trial must be scheduled. The accused person has a right to a jury trial and a right to a speedy trial. After the trial, the party is either acquitted and released, or, if the jury found the party guilty, there is the possibility of appeal. The appellate court may affirm the conviction, or it may reverse and order a retrial. If the appellate procedure has been exhausted and the party has not been acquitted or released, then the party is sentenced to a jail term and/or fine. At this point, the judge may decide to put the person on probation, or to suspend the sentence, or to send the person to jail. If the person goes to jail, he or she can be paroled within a stated period of time or serve out the entire sentence, at which time he or she is released to go back into society.

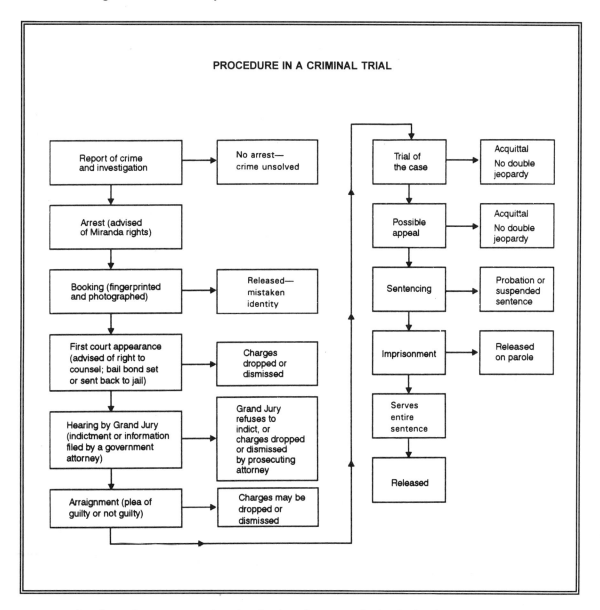

We often hear the comment that the rise in crime rates is the fault of weak judges and a weak criminal law system. It is true that a system can only be as good as the persons who operate it.

We must remember, however, that under our system of law, when a person is charged with a crime, he or she is presumed innocent until proven guilty beyond a reasonable doubt. Let us remember, too, that in most of the cases which go to trial, the crucial decision of guilty or not guilty is made, not by the judge, but by a jury of people selected at random from the community.

SIGNIFICANCE OF THIS CHAPTER

The study of criminal law was not traditionally a subject of concern for managers. However, with the increase in the volume and types of white-collar crime, criminal law becomes a real concern for business operations. This chapter reviews the various types of business-related crime and the steps and requirements of criminal procedure.

PROBLEMS FOR DISCUSSION

1. Mr.Park was the president of Acme Markets Inc., a large retail food chain, with twelve warehouses, 874 stores, and 36,000 employees. The Food and Drug Administration (FDA) advised the company and its president of unsanitary conditions in its warehouses and requested that the conditions be cleaned up. Some cleanup was done, but the warehouses still did not meet minimum standards. The U.S. government then filed a criminal action against both the company and Park for the continued violation. The company pleaded guilty, and Park pleaded not guilty. He did not feel personally responsible for the failure of other employees in the company. The trial court still found him guilty. The appeals court reversed, and the U.S. Supreme Court granted certiorari.

    Is Park guilty of a crime? Explain.

2. National Student Marketing Corporation ("Marketing") was formed in 1996. It charged fees to businesses for marketing their products and services directly to students in an "attractive package" of merchandise. Marketing stock went public in 1998 at $6 a share; five months later it was selling at $80 a share.

    Peat, Marwick, Mitchell & Co. ("Peat") became Marketing's auditors in August 1998. Anthony Natelli was the engagement partner for the account and the manager of PMM's office in Washington, D.C. Joseph Scansaroli was the audit supervisor for the account.

    Many of Marketing's fee arrangements were only oral commitments. Using their estimates of the completion of its services on the accounts, the CPA's made a 1998 year-end Adjustment for "unbilled accounts receivable" of $1.7 million and turned a loss into a profit twice that of the previous year. About $1 million of the oral commitments were written off by May 1999. Marketing's 1998 income thereby went down more than $200,000 but Scansaroli and Natelli covered this by "reversing" a deferred tax credit for about the same amount. The financial statements which were filed with a proxy statement proposing a merger with six other firms did not show any adjustment in Marketing's profit figure for 1998. A $12 million commitment from Pontiac (GM) was backdated so as to be included in the period through May 31, 1999. When Natelli questioned this practice, he was told that there was a commitment from Eastern

Airlines for a similar amount that could be included, so he let it pass. The financial statements did not show that Marketing had written off $1 million of its 1998 sales and more than $2 million of the unbilled sales for 1998 and 1999. Marketing should have showed no profit for 1999, but instead the financial statement prepared by Natelli and Scansaroli and filed with a proxy statement that was relied upon by other companies in a proposed merger showed tremendous profits and was in fact false and misleading. Anthony Natelli and Joseph Scansaroli were criminally prosecuted under Section 32(a) of the 1934 Act for willfully and knowingly making false and misleading statements in a corporation's proxy statement. Both were convicted in U.S. District Court, which imposed a one-year sentence and a $10,000 fine upon Natelli, suspending all but sixty days of imprisonment, and a one-year sentence and a $2,500 fine upon Scansaroli suspending all but ten days of the imprisonment. Both appealed.

Should their convictions be affirmed? Why or why not?

3. Nicholas Katsafanas (also known as Nick Perry) and Edward Plevel worked out a scheme to enrich themselves by the means of the computer-run state lottery. They first decided that the winning number combination (always one with three numerals) for the draw of April 24, would consist of only the numerals 4 and 6. There are eight possible three digit number combinations using only 4 or 6.

They purchased lottery tickets for all the possible number combinations from retail ticket vendors at various locations. The rigging, or "fix," took place in the studio of WTAE in Pittsburgh, Allegheny County, by means of placing counterfeit balls in the machines used in the drawing. When the winning number combination, 666, was drawn, Plevel telephoned Michael Keyser, an administrative officer in the Lottery Bureau in Harrisburg, Dauphin County. Keyser programmed 666 into the computer, and the conspirators or their agents subsequently cashed in their winning tickets.

Katsafanas and Plevel were convicted of conspiracy, theft by deception, criminal mischief, rigging a publicly exhibited contest, and perjury. They moved for a new trial. Defendants claim that they were erroneously brought to trial in Dauphin County (the locus of the computer) because none of the manipulation of the lottery equipment used to select the winning numbers took place in Dauphin County. The trial judge denied their motion and they appealed.

Have they been tried in the wrong place? Explain.

4. Charley was driving his pickup truck in Idaho when he was involved in a collision with a car. The driver of the car was killed, and Charley was seriously injured. Police officers found a pint of whiskey, almost empty, in the glove box of the pickup truck. Charley was taken to a hospital, where the smell of whiskey was detected on his breath. While he was still unconscious, a blood sample was taken. Laboratory analysis showed that Charley's blood contained about 0.17 percent alcohol. Charley was charged with involuntary manslaughter and the blood sample was used as evidence that he had been driving under the influence of liquor. On appeal, Charley contends that the seizure of the whiskey bottle and the taking of the blood sample violated his due process rights.

How should the court rule? Discuss.

5. Sheppard was arrested, tried, and convicted of murdering his wife. The trial was held in the common pleas court of Cuyahoga County, Ohio. Sheppard's conviction was affirmed by the Supreme Court of Ohio. Sheppard filed a petition for habeas corpus in U.S. District Court against the prison warden, seeking release from custody. His contention was that he was denied a fair trial because the trial judge failed to protect him from inherently prejudicial publicity which saturated the community and also because the judge allowed extensive newspaper, radio, and television coverage of his trial in the courtroom itself. The District Court ruled in favor of the petition for habeas corpus; the U.S. Court of Appeals reversed; and the Supreme Court of the United States granted certiorari.

How should the Supreme Court rule, and why?

Chapter 6
Tort Law

While business managers may face legal problems resulting from crimes, they are also fair game for a civil lawsuit. Customers may sue for injuries received if they slip or fall on the premises; they may sue for injuries resulting from defective products. Competitors may sue for alleged slander or libel, and this list could go on and on. We live in a litigious society, and if we are to survive, we must know our rights as well as our duties regarding potential lawsuits. This chapter discusses the various types of torts, and the defenses which may be raised against various claims.

DEFINITION OF A TORT

A **tort** is a civil wrong committed when one individual, having a legal duty not to invade the legal rights of another individual, breaches that legal duty, causing damage to the person, property, or reputation of that other individual. The person whose rights have been invaded and who has suffered damage may then bring action in a civil court to recover monetary damages suffered because of the invasion of rights. These rights and duties may be derived from statutory or common law. When we speak of an individual, we mean a legal individual, such as a corporation, as well as a natural individual, a human being.

A tort may also be a crime. For example, a drunken driver runs a red light and hits your car in the intersection. You have a cause of action in tort against that person for your property damage and personal injury. The drunken driver may also be prosecuted criminally for driving a motor vehicle under the influence of intoxicating beverages. Most nonintentional torts, however, are not crimes.

Also, a tortious civil wrong must be distinguished from a contractual civil wrong, where the rights and duties arise out of a specific contractual agreement. In a tort, the rights and duties are imposed by general laws which apply to others under similar circumstances, such as traffic laws and general laws of negligence.

CLASSIFICATION OF TORTS

Torts can be classified into four general categories. First, there are **intentional torts**. These are wrongs which the wrongdoers intended to commit. Second, there are **negligent torts**. These are wrongs which the wrongdoers did not mean to commit. They simply failed to act as ordinary, prudent, reasonable persons would have acted under similar circumstances. For example, in the typical automobile accident, the driver of the automobile does not mean to strike another automobile and damage it or to damage his or her own automobile. He or she was simply not careful and was not acting as a reasonable and prudent person. Third, there are **strict liability torts**. This classification comprises situations in which the law finds that the person or persons committing the torts are "strictly liable," meaning that there is no need for the plaintiff to prove negligence on the part of the defendant. The defendant is simply liable, as a matter of law, for the harmful results caused. The fourth major tort category is **vicarious liability**—one person is held liable for the torts of another, based on some relationship between them, such as employer/employee or principal/agent.

INTENTIONAL TORTS

An intentional tort is an intentional breach of one's legal duty to another person, which breach of duty invades that person's rights and causes physical or mental damage to that person or damage to that person's reputation or property.

Intentional torts can be subdivided into three categories: torts against the physical person, torts against the reputation of the person, and torts against the property of the person. Following are some of the common torts against the physical person.

Torts Against the Physical Person

Assault. An assault is an intentional act by one person which causes another person to be in immediate apprehension for his or her safety. Apprehension does not necessarily mean fear, since fear is a very subjective term. Some persons may be in apprehension for their safety without actually being frightened, whereas other persons may be frightened without justifiable cause. Courts have held that mere words are not sufficient to prove a case of assault, even if the words are provoking or insulting. Also, threats of future injury are not the basis for assault. To prove a case of assault, it must be shown that the defendant committed a specific act or acts that put the plaintiff in apprehension for his or her immediate safety, not simply future safety. Although the tort of assault is classified as an intentional tort, it is not necessary to prove that the defendant actually intended to harm the plaintiff. It is sufficient to show that a reasonable person under the circumstances would have been in apprehension for his or her safety. Assault can also be a crime as well as a tort. For example, using a gun to commit the assault would be the crime of assault with a deadly weapon.

Battery. Battery is the intentional contact or touching of another person without that person's permission and without legal justification. The contact or touching must cause injury. It is not necessary that there be a specific intent to cause harm. Nor is it necessary that the contact be directly with the person. For example, the tort of battery is committed if one person puts in motion an object that strikes another person, say, by shooting a gun or throwing a knife, or if one person strikes another person with an object in hand.

In battery cases, it is important to know that you "take the plaintiff as you find him or her." This means that you are responsible for the results of your actions even though you could not have foreseen the final result. For example, there was a case where a person struck another person on the head with an umbrella. Normally this would have resulted in a minor lump on the head, but the victim had a metal plate in his head and the blow dislodged the metal plate, forcing it into the brain, killing the victim.

Not all touching or contact is considered battery. For example, people are often bumped, pushed, and jostled when they walk through the crowded aisles of department stores or walk out of crowded sports stadiums. Here there is physical contact and touching by other persons which may cause discomfort and which may be offensive. From a legal standpoint, however, these are not considered batteries because there is an implied consent to such "touching."

Technical Battery. When we defined the tort of battery, we stated that it was the intentional contact or touching of another person without that person's permission. A technical battery occurs when the person gives consent to physical contact of one sort and then a different kind of contact occurs or the terms of the consent are exceeded. Damages may be claimed under this theory against a surgeon who performs "extra" surgical procedures while the patient is under anesthesia. In the absence of some sort of emergency, the surgeon's act is tortious and the patient could recover damages. This is a very different kind of liability than that in a malpractice action, in which the claim is that the physician did not perform the agreed treatment or procedure in accordance with reasonable professional standards.

Intentional Infliction of Mental Distress. Courts in the various states are now recognizing the intentional infliction of emotional or mental distress as a tort, without the necessity of showing either physical injury or a threat of physical contact, such as one would find in the torts of assault and battery. The tort of intentional infliction of emotional or mental distress is an entirely separate tort from the torts of assault and battery. This tort may be defined as an act or the use of words by a person with the intent of causing another person to experience anxiety, fright, terror, or some other form of emotional and mental distress.

Historically, the courts have discouraged and denied claims for emotional and mental distress unless the person had also suffered some accompanying physical injury. They thought that allowing claims for mental or emotional distress would encourage fictitious claims. Physical injury can be verified by X-ray and visual appearance. Emotional and mental distress is a very subjective claim, and until recently such injuries often could not be objectively verified. However, advances in medical science have given us more accurate methods of measuring and verifying such injuries.

The courts are still concerned about the potential for misuse of this particular tort. Generally, courts have held that in order to have recovery, it must be shown that the mental distress or disturbance is real and not simply an annoyance or hurt feelings or something of that nature. Actual mental injury must be shown. The courts also require that before one can recover for this tort, it must be shown that the conduct of the defendant has been outrageous in character and generally of a type which is intolerable in a civilized community.

False Imprisonment. False imprisonment can be defined as the intentional detention of a person without that person's permission. It is not necessary that there be actual physical detention. However, the courts have required that the detained person be detained by at least a threat of force, either expressed or implied. Also, the detention must be for more than a reasonable time.

False Arrest. False arrest is similar to false imprisonment in that it is the intentional detention of an individual without that person's permission. In the case of false arrest, the detention is imposed under an asserted legal authority. If, in fact, the person making the arrest does not have proper legal authority to do so, then we would have the tort of false arrest. In the case of false arrest, as in the case of false imprisonment, it is not necessary that the person detaining the suspect use force. For example, a person dressed in a police uniform with a badge indicating authority states to you: "You are under arrest. I am taking you to the police station." Most people would go along peacefully rather than resist arrest. If, in fact, there was no reasonable ground, no probable cause, to believe that you had committed a specific crime, then you were wrongfully deprived of your freedom, and you would have an action for false arrest and false imprisonment.

Torts Against the Reputation of the Person

Next we come to intentional torts which injure the person's reputation. These are often called defamation of character.

Libel and Slander. Libel and slander are both torts involving intentional defamation of character by the tort-feasor. **Libel** is defamation of character which can be read or seen, and **slander** is defamation of character which can be heard. In both libel and slander cases, it must be proven that a defamatory statement or defamatory material was published. In the case of libel, this means that the defamatory material was published in a book, magazine, or newspaper or in the form of a movie, pictures, a statue, or some other physical form whereby the material was seen by a person or persons other than the person about whom the material was published. If you write a personal letter to an individual and make defamatory statements about the individual in that letter, this does not constitute publication, since no one other than the individual to whom you are writing is intended to see the letter. In the case of slander, publication means that the statement was heard by someone other than the person about whom the defamatory statement was made. Thus, the simple test in slander and libel cases is: Did anyone other than the subject of the defamatory statement or material hear, read, or see the statement or material? If no third person heard, read, or saw the statement or material, then there is no slander or libel. If a third party did hear the defamatory statement or read or see the defamatory material, then we have a potential lawsuit for defamation of character.

The next issue is the truth of the defamatory statement or material. Generally speaking, truth is a defense to slander or libel. The exception is a situation where the party publishing the defamatory statement or material is doing so with a malicious intent to injure the other party. This is called a *technical tort*. An example of this would be the publication of the fact that a person now well established in society committed a crime while a teenager. Let's say that as a teenager the person stole an automobile and took it for a joyride, was arrested and convicted, and paid his or her debt to society. Then, some years later, after the person had established a good reputation in society, someone found out about this skeleton in the closet and published the information with the sole purpose of maligning the person's character. Here, even though the statement is true, it was obviously made for malicious purposes, and thus there would be a right of action for this defamation of character.

There are also cases where defamatory statements may be either absolutely **privileged** or **conditionally privileged**. Lawyers and judges may not be sued for slander for the statements made by them during the trial of a lawsuit. Also, if a member of Congress makes a defamatory statement on the floor of Congress, the legislator may not be held liable for the statement. There is also a different standard with regard to slander and libel when the statement is made about a public official or a public figure, rather than a private individual.

The amount of the verdict in slander and libel cases is often a matter of concern. For example, the famous movie and television comedian Carol Burnett was libeled by an article published in the *National Enquirer*. She brought a suit for libel against the *National Enquirer* in California Superior Court and the jury awarded a verdict of $300,000 for general damages and $1,300,000 for punitive damages. Although Burnett suffered emotional distress, she admitted she never had to have psychiatric treatment or counseling. Also, she suffered no lost income due to the libelous statements. The trial judge, responding to a motion for judgment notwithstanding the verdict, reduced the general damages to $50,000, and the California State Court of Appeals reduced the punitive damages to $150,000. There really isn't any formula for damages in slander and libel cases. The slander and libel victim typically will not have medical bills or lost wages claims, such as a person who was injured in an automobile accident might have. Also, it is usually impossible to calculate in a dollar amount the damage caused to the victim's reputation. Thus each case is going to have to be judged on its own set of facts.

The *Cubby* case discusses some of these rules.

CUBBY, INC. v. COMPUSERVE INC.
776 F. Supp. 135 (S.D.N.Y. 1991)

FACTS: CompuServe develops and provides computer-related products and services, including CompuServe Information Service ("CIS"), an online general information service or "electronic library" that subscribers may access from a personal computer or terminal. Subscribers to CIS pay a membership fee and online time usage fees, in return for which they have access to the thousands of information sources available on CIS. Subscribers may also obtain access to over 150 special interest "forums," which are comprised of electronic bulletin boards, interactive online conferences, and topical databases.

One forum available is the Journalism Forum, which focuses on the journalism industry. Cameron Communications, Inc. ("CCI"), which is independent of CompuServe, has contracted to "manage, review, create, delete, edit, and otherwise control the contents" of the Journalism Forum "in accordance with editorial and technical standards and conventions of style as established by CompuServe."

One publication available as part of the Journalism Forum is Rumorville USA, a daily newsletter that provides reports about broadcast journalism and journalists. Rumorville is published by Don Fitzpatrick Associates of San Francisco ("DFA"), which is headed by defendant Don Fitzpatrick. CompuServe has no employment, contractual, or other direct relationship with either DFA or Fitzpatrick; DFA provides Rumorville to the Journalism Forum under a contract with CCI. The contract between CCI and DFA provides that DFA "accepts total responsibility for the contents" of Rumorville. The contract also requires CCI to limit access to Rumorville to those CIS subscribers who have previously made membership arrangements directly with DFA.

CompuServe has no opportunity to review Rumorville's contents before DFA uploads it into CompuServe's computer banks, from which it is immediately available to approved CIS subscribers. CompuServe receives no part of any fees that DFA charges for access to Rumorville, nor does CompuServe compensate DFA for providing Rumorville to the Journalism Forum; the compensation CompuServe receives for making Rumorville available to its subscribers is the standard online time usage and membership fees charged to all CIS subscribers, regardless of the information services they use. CompuServe maintains that, before this action was filed, it had no notice of any complaints about the contents of the Rumorville publication or about DFA.

In 1990, plaintiffs Cubby, Inc. and Robert Blanchard developed Skuttlebut, a computer database designed to publish and distribute electronically news and gossip in the television news and radio industries. Plaintiffs intended to compete with Rumorville; subscribers gained access to Skuttlebut through their personal computers after completing subscription agreements with plaintiffs.

Plaintiffs claim that, on separate occasions in April 1990, Rumorville published false and defamatory statements relating to Skuttlebut and Blanchard, and that CompuServe carried these statements as part of the Journalism Forum. The allegedly defamatory remarks included a suggestion that individuals at Skuttlebut gained access to information first published by Rumorville "through some back door;" a statement that Blanchard was "bounced" from his previous employer, WABC; and a description of Skuttlebut as a "new start-up scam."

Plaintiffs have asserted claims against CompuServe and Fitzpatrick under New York law for libel of Blanchard, business disparagement of Skuttlebut, and unfair competition as to Skuttlebut, based largely upon the allegedly defamatory statements contained in Rumorville. CompuServe has moved for summary judgment on all claims against it. CompuServe does not dispute, solely for the purposes of this motion, that the statements relating to Skuttlebut and Blanchard were defamatory; rather, it argues that it acted as a distributor, and not a publisher, of the statements, and cannot be held liable for the statements because it did not know and had no reason to know of the statements.

 JUDGE LEISURE;

Ordinarily, "one who repeats or otherwise republishes defamatory matter is subject to liability as if he had originally published it."... With respect to entities such as news vendors, book stores, and libraries, however, "New York courts have long held that vendors and distributors of defamatory publications are not liable if they neither know nor have reason to know of the defamation."...

The requirement that a distributor must have knowledge of the contents of a publication before liability can be imposed for distributing that publication is deeply rooted in the First Amendment, made applicable to the states through the Fourteenth Amendment. "The constitutional guarantees of the freedom of speech and of the press stand in the way of imposing" strict liability on distributors for the contents of the reading materials they carry.... In *Smith*, the Court struck down an ordinance that imposed liability on a bookseller for possession of an obscene book, regardless of whether the bookseller had knowledge of the book's contents. The Court reasoned that:

> "Every bookseller would be placed under an obligation to make himself aware of the contents of every book in his shop. It would be altogether unreasonable to demand so near an approach to omniscience." And the bookseller's burden would become the public's burden, for by restricting him the public's access to reading matter would be restricted. If the contents of bookshops and periodical stands were restricted to material of which their proprietors had made an inspection, they might be depleted indeed....

Although *Smith* involved criminal liability, the First Amendment's guarantees are no less relevant to the instant action: "What a State may not constitutionally bring about by means of a criminal statute is likewise beyond the reach of its civil law of libel. The fear of damage awards ... may be markedly more inhibiting than the fear of prosecution under a criminal statute."...

CompuServe's CIS product is in essence an electronic, for-profit library that carries a vast number of publications and collects usage and membership fees from its subscribers in return for access to the publications. CompuServe and companies like it are at the forefront of the information industry revolution. High technology has markedly increased the speed with which information is gathered and processed; it is now possible for an individual and a personal computer, modem, and telephone line to have instantaneous access to thousands of news publications from across the United states and around the world. While CompuServe may decline to carry a given publication altogether, in reality, once it does decide to carry a publication, it will have little or no editorial control over that publication's contents. This is especially so when CompuServe carries the publication as part of a forum that is managed by a company unrelated to CompuServe.

With respect to the Rumorville publication, the undisputed facts are that DFA uploads the text of Rumorville into CompuServe's data banks and makes it available to approved CIS subscribers instantaneously. CompuServe has no more editorial control over such a publication than does a public library, book store, or newsstand, and it would be no more feasible for CompuServe to examine every publication it carries for potentially defamatory statements than it would be for any other distributor to do so. "First Amendment guarantees have long been recognized as protecting distributors of publications.... Obviously, the national distributor of hundreds of periodicals has no duty to monitor each issue of every periodical it distributes. Such a rule would be an impermissible burden on the First Amendment."...

Technology is rapidly transforming the information industry. A computerized database is the functional equivalent of a more traditional news vendor, and the inconsistent application of a lower standard of liability to an electronic news distributor such as CompuServe than that which is applied to a public library, book store, or newsstand would impose an undue burden on the free flow of information. Given the relevant First Amendment considerations, the appropriate standard of liability to be applied to CompuServe is whether it knew or had reason to know of the allegedly defamatory Rumorville statements....

CompuServe contends that it is undisputed that it had neither knowledge nor reason to know of the allegedly defamatory Rumorville statements, especially given the large number of publications it carries and the speed with which DFA uploads Rumorville into its computer banks and makes the publication available to CIS subscribers.... The burden is thus shifted to plaintiffs, who "must set forth specific facts showing that there is a genuine issue for trial."...

Plaintiffs have not set forth any specific facts showing that there is a genuine issue as to whether CompuServe knew or had reason to know of Rumorville's contents. Because CompuServe, as a news distributor, may not be held liable if it neither knew nor had reason to know of the allegedly defamatory Rumorville statements, summary judgment in favor of CompuServe on the libel claim is granted.

Invasion of Privacy. The area of individual privacy has been very highly publicized in recent years, and several state and national statutes have been passed concerning the individual's right to privacy. These new laws are primarily concerned with the invasion of privacy by the computer with regard to credit records and bank records which contain sensitive information about individuals. New statutes also protect employment records and school records.

In addition to the current concern about invasion of privacy by the computer and various electronic data processing procedures, there has been a concern about many more traditional invasions of the individual's privacy. One of the most common of these invasions of privacy is eavesdropping by wiretapping or other electronic devices. Such eavesdropping is a national crime as well as a tort, and it is prohibited except in the rare cases where it has been authorized by national statutory law. Another invasion of privacy is the use of a person's photograph under objectionable circumstances. Simply turning the television camera and taking pictures of the persons in the bleachers at a baseball game is not an invasion of privacy. However, if someone takes an embarrassing picture of you and uses it without your permission, you may have an action for invasion of privacy.

As with libel and slander, we again have a conflict with the constitutional protection of freedom of speech and freedom of the press. Thus, if you are involved in a matter of public interest, your rights of privacy are affected accordingly. For example, if you are involved in an automobile accident, newspaper photographers may be snapping photographs of you at the scene of the accident; or if you are arrested, the TV cameras may be directed toward you. Here you are news; thus your right of privacy must be secondary to the freedom of the press to publish the news. For similar reasons a public figure does not have the same right of privacy as an ordinary citizen.

Torts Against the Person's Property

Trespass to Real Property. The general rule of law with regard to trespass to real property is that the owner of real property has the right not only to exclusive possession of a specific piece of ground and the buildings and other things on that ground, but also to exclusive possession of the airspace above the ground and the area below the ground. The old common-law rule was that the owner of the land owned all of the airspace above the land and the area below the land all the way to the middle of the earth. This rule had to be modified when we started to use airspace for airplane travel. Now the landowner still owns the airspace above the land, subject, however, to the right of airplanes to fly through that airspace. With regard to the space below the land, the possessor of the land surface also possesses the soil and space below the surface to the extent that he or she can effectively use that soil or space, either now or in the future. When we talk about space below the land, we are talking about the ownership of the oil, gas, coal, water, and other valuable minerals and resources which may be present under the surface.

In order to have the tort of trespass to your land, it is not necessary that there be actual damage to your land. In all of the other torts previously mentioned, damage had to be proven before a recovery could be made. In the tort of trespass to land, you can sue the trespasser even though there was no actual damage and the court will award nominal damages, perhaps $1 and costs.

Trespass to Personal Property. This tort allows the owner of personal property to bring an action against a person or persons who interfere with his or her exclusive possession of an item of personal property. Unlike the plaintiff in a case involving trespass to real property, the plaintiff in a case involving trespass to personal property must show and prove monetary damage in order to get a verdict against the trespasser.

Conversion. The tort of conversion is the unlawful taking and use of personal property owned by another person. In other words, it is the conversion of another person's property to your own use. This sounds like theft. However, you will recall that in order to have theft, one has to have a mens rea, or mental intent, to steal. In the tort of conversion, the person converting the property to his or her own use does not necessarily have the intent to steal. The person may feel that he or she has the right to use the property. A good example of conversion would be a case where the branches of your neighbor's apple tree hang over the lot line so that the apples are over your property. You honestly feel that you have a right to these apples; after all, they are over your property in your airspace. After you pick the apples, your neighbor tells you that the apples belong to him and that you should give them to him. If you fail to give your neighbor the apples, you are guilty of the tort of conversion. The apples and the branches that hung over the lot line are in effect trespassing on your airspace; however, you do not have the right of ownership to them. You may, however, cut off the branches at the lot line and put them on your neighbor's land. You cannot keep them.

Deceit-Fraud. The tort of deceit, also called fraud, involves a situation where one or more parties, fraudulently and with the intent to deceive, misrepresent certain facts, either through oral or written statement or through an artifice or device of some type, and another party relies upon the misrepresentation and is damaged. Fraud in connection with the making of a contract is discussed more fully in Chapter 11.

Abuse of Civil Process. This tort involves an intentional use of the civil legal process for a purpose which is wrongful and for which the process was not designed. A person may bring a civil action against you simply to harass you and cause you the expense of defending the lawsuit, when in fact the person has no legitimate claim against you. You may sue him or her for damages as a result of this wrongful use of the civil process.

Malicious Prosecution. The tort of malicious prosecution is similar to the tort of abuse of civil process. However, it involves the criminal process. An example would be a case where the police and the court system take action against you because a person has maliciously and without probable cause sworn out a criminal complaint against you. You can sue that person for malicious prosecution and recover damages.

Interference with Economic Relations. This tort concerns your right to conduct your business free from malicious and intentional interference which might destroy the business. The free enterprise system is based on the competitive marketplace. However, competition must be kept within reasonable bounds. It is certainly permissible for one business to lower its price in an effort to competitively secure a market advantage. However, when a person or a business intentionally uses economic resources to injure another person or business for reasons other than the legal reasons for competition, the tort of interference with economic relations has been committed.

The tort of interference with economic relations also encompasses interference with contractual relations. If Johnny Rich, a nightclub owner, induces a famous entertainer to breach a contract with another nightclub to come to work for him, the employer who had a contract with the entertainer can sue Johnny Rich for interference with his contractual relations.

NEGLIGENT TORTS

Each person in society is bound to take reasonable care not to injure the person, the reputation, or the property of those persons likely to be affected by his or her behavior. Any act or omission in breach of that duty which causes damage to others may cause a person to be liable for damages to the person or persons affected by that act or omission. In the negligent tort case, the question is not, as it was with the intentional tort, whether the person intended to cause the injury or damage. The question is simply, did the person act in a negligent manner?

Definition of Negligence. The standard used to determine the absence or presence of negligence is a very simple one. The standard is, simply, did the person act in a manner similar to that in which a reasonable and prudent person would have acted under the same or similar circumstances? Would the reasonable and prudent person have foreseen the dangers of his or her action, and was the damage or injury proximately caused by the action or the failure to act of the individual being charged with the tort? The question then arises: Who is this reasonable and prudent person? The reasonable and prudent person is an imaginary person, and when deciding a case involving a negligent tort, jurors are instructed not to use themselves as examples of the reasonable and prudent person. The jurors must determine not what they individually would have done in the same or a similar situation but what that imaginary person called the reasonable and prudent person would have done. Obviously, this standard is not very precise and it is certainly subject to great variations. The standard, however, has operated very successfully over the years since it does take into consideration changes in technology and changes in societal mores which the jury will impute to the reasonable and prudent person. Also, it would be impossible to have a specific statutory code that would cover every possible act or omission which could be considered negligent. Thus, negligence continues to be decided on a case-by-case basis.

Proximate Cause. A person may commit a negligent act or may negligently fail to act under certain circumstances. However, that person will not be liable to any person who is damaged or injured as a result of such act or omission unless it can be shown that the damage or injury was proximately caused by the negligent act or omission. For a negligent act or omission to be a proximate cause of damage or injury, it must be a cause which in a natural and continuous sequence, unbroken by any intervening cause, produced the injury, and it must be a cause without which the injury would not have occurred. An example would be a motorist who was driving at a high rate of speed, hit a chuckhole, lost control of the vehicle, struck a water hydrant, breaking off the hydrant and causing the street to flood and water to flow into the basement of a house near the hydrant. The driver would be liable not only for the damage to the water hydrant, but also for the damage to the house, as that damage was proximately caused by the driver's negligence.

If, while the street was flooded, a city bus came down the street and stopped and let off an elderly lady who stepped into the water and slipped, fell, and broke her hip, would the driver of the vehicle that struck the water hydrant be responsible for her injuries? Were her injuries proximately caused by his negligence? The answer would be no. The lady was not injured as a result of a natural and continuous chain of events commencing with the motorist's negligent driving. There was an intervening cause—the negligence of the bus driver entering a dangerously flooded area and the negligence of the elderly lady stepping off the bus into the flooded street.

There are situations where the actions or omissions of more than one person are a proximate cause of damage or injury to a person or property. If two cars collide in an intersection and one of the cars strikes a legally parked car, it may be found that the negligence of both of the drivers in the collision proximately caused the damage to the parked car. Thus, it is not necessary that any one act or omission be the sole proximate cause of damage or injury.

Foreseeability. For a defendant to be liable to a plaintiff for a tortious act or omission to act, not only must the act or omission be a proximate cause of the damage or injury, but the ultimate damage or injury must also be foreseeable by the reasonable and prudent person.

The jury must be instructed by the trial judge to find each of these essential parts of the plaintiff's case, if there is to be a verdict for the plaintiff.

Jury instructions on negligence are an issue in the *Palmtag* case.

PALMTAG v. GARTNER CONST. CO.
513 N.W.2d 495 (NE, 1994)

FACTS: Plaintiff Janet Palmtag and her husband, John, hired defendant to remodel their newly purchased home under an oral arrangement, whereunder defendant was to be paid for time and materials. Defendant was given the keys to the house, and plaintiff and her husband visited the structure to monitor the progress of the work; the husband visited on a daily basis and plaintiff once or twice a week.

The house was usually left open, and the husband would be able to "just go in." According to the husband, defendant's employees never limited or restricted where he could go. Plaintiff had once met a Caroline Gartner at the house to look at tile.

The remodeling included the removal of a spiral staircase which was located in the main floor entry area and descended therefrom to the basement through a five-foot square opening.

The staircase was made up of pie-shaped treads. Attached to the narrow end of each tread was a round disk which, when stacked one on top of another, formed a center post with the treads fanned around it. The top disk fit up under the main floor landing. Working without reference to any plans, David Njus, an employee of defendant, disassembled the staircase by beginning with the top tread and working his way down. As he took out each tread and disk, the center post was whittled down.

A handrailing located around the staircase was taken out after the treads and center post were removed, leaving an empty opening in the floor. Njus also removed the plywood aprons and angle irons which were located along the underside of the landing, thus leaving the plywood floor around the opening jutting "something like a diving board out in the air."

After Njus removed the treads, aprons, and angle irons, he wondered how springy the outer edge of the flooring would be and checked it before leaving that evening by reaching up from the basement and hanging his full weight, 165 pounds on it; nothing gave way. He then hung a wire and plywood barricade across the handrailing and walked on top of the landing area; he felt no sensation of weakness in it. The landing, however, was a separate piece of wood which had been toe-nailed into the rest of the floor.

Plaintiff and her husband had arranged to meet at the house to review the remodeling work. Plaintiff, who was then eight months pregnant and weighed 200 pounds, arrived at the house at about 5 p.m. accompanied by her three-year-old son. She met and spoke briefly with Njus and an unidentified employee of defendant, who were leaving for the day.

As she walked through the entry area, she did not know the staircase had been removed, but noticed "a wire with something hanging on it" and paused approximately eight to nine inches from the wire. She then saw that the staircase was gone, at which time she was probably about a foot from the opening. Plaintiff warned her son not to get close to the stairwell. As she paused long enough for her son to pass by, the landing collapsed. As a consequence, she fell to the basement floor and landed on her seat and hands, after which her back and head hit the floor. Her face hit something on the way down.

When the husband found plaintiff, she was in extreme pain and somewhat delirious. Plaintiff could not feel the fetus move, and both she and her husband thought she had ruptured her uterus. Plaintiff was hospitalized for three days following the accident and was diagnosed as having a 20 percent compression fracture of her 12th thoracic vertebra, a torus fracture of her right wrist, a sprained left ankle, and a very painful tailbone area. As a result of the compression fracture in her back, plaintiff suffered a 20 to 25 percent permanent disability. Her pregnancy successfully came to term approximately a month after she fell.

Rejecting defendant's motions for a directed verdict and for a judgment N.O.V., the trial court entered judgment for plaintiff.

In its third and last summarized assignment of error, defendant asserts the district court incorrectly instructed the jury in that, contrary to defendant's requests, it failed to define negligence.

 JUSTICE CAPORALE:

The distinction between invitees and licensees rests on the purpose for which the invitation was extended.... If it is an invitation for the personal pleasure, convenience, or benefit of the person enjoying the privilege, the person receiving it is a licensee. But if the invitation relates to the business of the one who gives it or for the mutual advantage of a business nature for both parties, the party receiving the invitation is an invitee....

Under this "economic benefit" test of invitee status, one who enters upon land of another is not entitled to the status of invitee unless the visit is directly or indirectly connected with business dealings between them....

The only permissible inference from the undisputed facts is that plaintiff was at the jobsite for the mutual benefit of herself and defendant and that her visit served defendant's economic interest. Thus, she was, as a matter of law, an invitee....

Accordingly, the district court correctly determined plaintiff's status to be that of an invitee as a matter of law.

In its final challenge to the instructions, defendant denounces the district court's failure to define the word "negligence," arguing that such failure deprived the jury of the ability to correctly judge defendant's conduct.

But the word "negligence" appears nowhere in the instructions or verdict forms, and, therefore, its definition was not left for the jury's own interpretation; rather, the issue becomes whether the instructions given regarding defendant's standard of care correctly stated the law....

The district court advised the jury that it was plaintiff's burden to prove, among other things, that defendant had "failed to use reasonable care to protect" her from the condition described elsewhere in the instruction. That was an acceptable means of informing the jury that in order for plaintiff to recover, it was necessary that she prove that defendant had breached its described duty by having failed to exercise the requisite degree of care toward her.

The difficulty is that nowhere in its instructions did the district court define reasonable care as being that degree of caution which an ordinary, or reasonably prudent, person would exercise under like circumstances.... As a consequence, the instructions erroneously and prejudicially failed to limit the jury's consideration to the degree of caution a reasonably prudent contractor would have exercised in like circumstances.

It is true that the defendant did not ask the district court to define reasonable care, but the concept is closely related to defendant's request that the district court define negligence. In any event, while ordinarily the failure to object to instructions after they have been submitted for review will preclude raising an objection thereafter, a trial judge is nonetheless under a duty to correctly instruct on the law without any request to do so, and an appellate court may take cognizance of plain error and thus set aside a verdict because of a plainly erroneous instruction to which no previous objection was made....

Thus, the judgment of the district court must be, and hereby is, reversed and the cause remanded for further proceedings consistent with this opinion.

STRICT LIABILITY

Strict liability is liability without fault. In a strict liability case, the defendant will be liable for injuries caused by his or her actions, even though the defendant was not negligent in any way and the defendant did not intentionally injure the plaintiff. This concept of liability without fault is comparatively new in our legal system. The traditional theories of tort involve either intentional wrongful acts, or negligent acts, or omissions where the person didn't intend to injure the other party wrongfully, but through his or her carelessness or negligence the other party was injured and thus should have a right to recover. In developing the theory of no-fault or liability without fault, the courts and the legislatures are not really looking at right or wrong, but at who can best bear the cost of the loss. In other words, if you are going to engage in certain types of activities, then you must realize that persons might be injured by your activities even though you do nothing legally wrong and do not intend to hurt anyone. When you enter into certain activities you must simply be prepared to pay for the consequences of your actions, regardless of any legal fault on your part.

Whether strict liability should be applied to Pyrodyne is the issue in the next case.

KLEIN v. PYRODYNE CORP.
810 P.2d 917 (WA, 1991)

FACTS: Defendant Pyrodyne Corporation (Pyrodyne) is a general contractor for aerial fireworks at public fireworks displays. Pyrodyne contracted to procure fireworks, to provide pyrotechnic operators, and to display the fireworks at the Western Washington State Fairgrounds in Puyallup, Washington on July 4, 1987. All operators of the fireworks display were Pyrodyne employees acting within the scope of their employment duties.

During the fireworks display, one of the five-inch mortars was knocked into a horizontal position. From this position a rocket inside was ignited and discharged. The rocket flew 500 feet in a trajectory parallel to the earth and exploded near the crowd of onlookers. Plaintiffs Danny and Marion Klein were injured by the explosion. Mr. Klein's clothing was set on fire, and he suffered facial burns and serious injury to his eyes.

The Kleins brought suit against Pyrodyne under theories of products liability and strict liability. Pyrodyne filed a motion for summary judgment, which the trial court granted as to the products liability claim. The trial court denied Pyrodyne's summary judgment motion regarding the Kleins' strict liability claim, holding that Pyrodyne was strictly liable without fault and ordering summary judgment in favor of the Kleins on the issue of liability. Pyrodyne appealed.

 JUSTICE GUY:

The modern doctrine of strict liability for abnormally dangerous activities derives from ... *Rylands v. Fletcher*, 3 L.R.-H.L. 330, [1868] All E.R. 1, 12, in which the defendant's reservoir flooded mine shafts on the plaintiff's adjoining land. *Rylands v. Fletcher* has come to stand for the rule that "the defendant will be liable when he damages another by a thing or activity unduly dangerous and inappropriate to the place where it is maintained in the light of the character of that place and its surroundings...."

The basic principle of *Rylands v. Fletcher* has been accepted by the Restatement (Second) of Torts (1977).... Section 519 of the Restatement provides that any party carrying on an "abnormally dangerous activity" is strictly liable for ensuing damages. The test for what constitutes such an activity is stated in Section 520 of the Restatement. Both Restatement sections have been adopted by this court, and determination of whether an activity is an "abnormally dangerous activity" is a question of law....

Section 520 of the Restatement lists six factors that are to be considered in determining whether an activity is "abnormally dangerous." The factors are as follows:

(a) existence of a high degree of risk of some harm to the person, land, or chattels of others.

(b) likelihood that the harm that results from it will be great.

(c) inability to eliminate the risk by the exercise of reasonable care.

(d) extent to which the activity is not a matter of common usage.

(e) inappropriateness of the activity to the place where it is carried on.

(f) extent to which its value to the community is outweighed by its dangerous attributes....

The comments to Section 520 explain how these factors should be evaluated:

Any one of them is not necessarily sufficient of itself in a particular case, and ordinarily several of them will be required for strict liability. On the other hand, it is not necessary that each of them be present, especially if others weigh heavily. Because of the interplay of these various factors, it is not possible to reduce abnormally dangerous activities to any definition. The essential question is whether the risk created is so unusual, either because of its magnitude or because of the circumstances surrounding it, as to justify the imposition of strict liability for the harm that results from it, even though it is carried on with all reasonable care....

Examination of these factors persuades us that fireworks displays are abnormally dangerous activities justifying the imposition of strict liability.

We find that the factors stated in clauses (a), (b), and (c) are all present in the case of fireworks displays. Any time a person ignites rockets with the intention of sending them aloft to explode in the presence of large crowds of people, a high risk of serious personal injury or property damage is created. That risk arises because of the possibility that a rocket will malfunction or be misdirected. Furthermore, no matter how much care pyrotechnicians exercise, they cannot entirely eliminate the high risk inherent in setting off powerful explosives such as fireworks near crowds....

In sum, we find that setting off public fireworks displays satisfies four of the six conditions under the Restatement test; that is, it is an activity that is not "of common usage" and that presents an ineliminably high risk of serious bodily injury or property damage. We therefore hold that conducting public fireworks displays is an abnormally dangerous activity justifying the imposition of strict liability....

Pyrodyne argues that even if there is strict liability for fireworks, its liability under the facts of this case is cut off by the manufacturer's negligence, the existence of which we assume for purposes of evaluating the propriety of the trial court's summary judgment. According to Pyrodyne, a rocket detonated without leaving the mortar box because it was negligently manufactured. This detonation, Pyrodyne asserts, was what caused the misfire of the second rocket, which in turn resulted in the Kleins' injuries. Pyrodyne reasons that the manufacturer's negligence acted as an intervening or outside force that cuts off Pyrodyne's liability....

We note that the Restatement (Second) of Torts takes a position contrary to that advocated by Pyrodyne. Section 522 of the Restatement provides that:

> One carrying on an abnormally dangerous activity is subject to strict liability for the resulting harm although it is caused by the unexpectable (a) innocent, negligent, or reckless conduct of a third person....

The comment to Section 522 explains that "[i]f the risk [from an abnormally dangerous activity] ripens into injury, it is immaterial that the harm occurs through the unexpectable action of a human being)...."

We hold that intervening acts of third persons serve to relieve the defendant from strict liability for abnormally dangerous activities only if those acts were unforeseeable in relation to the extraordinary risk created by the activity.... The rationale for this rule is that it encourages those who conduct abnormally dangerous activities to anticipate and take precautions against the possible negligence of third persons. Where the third person's negligence is beyond the actor's control, this rule ... nonetheless imposes strict liability if the third person negligence was reasonably foreseeable. Such a result allocates the economic burden of injuries arising from the foreseeable negligence of third persons to the party best able to plan for it and to bear it—the actor carrying on the abnormally dangerous activity.

In the present case, negligence on the part of the fireworks manufacturer is readily foreseeable in relation to the extraordinary risk created by conducting a public fireworks display. Therefore, even if such negligence may properly be regarded as an intervening cause, an issue we need not decide, it cannot function to relieve Pyrodyne from liability. This is not to say, however, that in a proper case a defendant in a strict liability action could not pursue a claim against a third party and enforce a right of contribution to an extent proportionate to that party's fault.

We hold that Pyrodyne Corporation is strictly liable for all damages suffered as a result of the July 1987 fireworks display. Detonating fireworks displays constitutes an abnormally dangerous activity warranting strict liability. Public policy also supports this conclusion. Furthermore, RCW 70.77.285 mandates the payment of all damages caused by fireworks displays, regardless of whether those damages were due to the pyrotechnicians' negligence. This establishes the standard of strict liability for pyrotechnicians. Therefore, we affirm the decision of the trial court.

Strict liability has been imposed on owners or possessors of wild animals. If you keep a wild animal on your premises, you are going to be strictly liable for any damages which that animal does to other persons or to the property of other persons. The owner or possessor of hard-hooved animals, such as cattle, horses, and donkeys, may also be held strictly liable for injuries caused by those animals. The owner or possessor of a dog or a cat would not normally be liable unless he or she knows the animal to be dangerous. The common-law rule was that a dog is entitled to its first bite. This, of course, meant that until the dog has bitten someone it is not known to be dangerous. This would be true with regard to a small dog. However, if a person kept a large Doberman that was constantly growling and baring its teeth at anyone who came near to it, obviously this dog appears to have dangerous propensities, and its owner would be strictly liable for any injury or damage caused by it.

Strict liability has also been imposed on persons who are responsible for activities, the production of products, or conditions on their property which are unreasonably dangerous and which might cause injury to other persons. An example would be a construction contractor blasting out stumps or blasting hard rock in excavating for a building. If the blasting caused structural damage to nearby buildings or homes or if personal property within the buildings or homes were damaged by the concussion of the explosions, then the contractor would be strictly liable.

A third area of strict liability involves products liability. Traditionally, we had the theory of *caveat emptor*, which meant "let the buyer beware." The theory was that the buyer had a duty to inspect the goods when delivered, and unless there was intentional fraud or deceit, the buyer was simply stuck with them, if defects later appeared. This area of law has changed radically over the past forty years. Product liability is discussed in depth in Chapter 16.

VICARIOUS LIABILITY

One person may be liable for the torts of another, on the basis of some relationship between them. This doctrine provides that the boss will pay. You might also call this the "deep pocket" doctrine. Under the doctrine of *respondeat superior*, a principal may be liable for the tortious acts of an agent, provided the agent was acting in the scope of employment for the principal. Also, in the case of a simple employer-employee relationship, if the employee is acting in the scope of employment (i.e., doing the employer's job) and commits a negligent or intentional act, then the employer will be liable under the doctrine of respondeat superior. It is important to note here that the employee is still liable for his or her own actions. In other words, both employee and employer or both agent and principal could be liable in tort. This rule is discussed further in the chapter on agency.

Family members are not usually liable for each other's torts. One spouse generally can not be held liable for the other's wrongful conduct. Parents may be held liable for the torts of their children if the parent entrusts the child with a dangerous mechanism, or fails to properly supervise a child known to be violent. A parent is also liable for directing or sanctioning a child's wrong, and for torts committed while the child is acting as the parent's agent. Some states have special statutes on this point.

States disagree on the liability of social hosts for injuries caused by their guests, as seen in the *KFC* case.

JOHNSTON v. KFC NAT. MANAGEMENT CO.
788 P.2d 159 (HI, 1990)

FACTS: The employees of the Kentucky Fried Chicken (KFC), Aiea branch, had planned a Christmas party for themselves to take place on December 19, 1986. KFC management was aware of the planned party and gave approval for the party to be held on the premises of the Aiea branch after normal closing hours. Management even permitted the use of paper goods from the store and allowed the participants to eat any leftover unsold chicken. Alcoholic beverages, however, were supplied solely by the party participants.

Sandra Joan Parks was a KFC employee at another branch. Mikilani Travis, the restaurant manager of the Aiea branch and a friend of Sandra, invited Sandra to the Aiea branch Christmas party. It is alleged that Sandra was visibly intoxicated at the time she left the Aiea branch party. She managed, however, to drive to the Cuis' residence in Wahiawa.

Andrea Cui, who was 19 years old at the time, was an employee of the Aiea KFC. Though Andrea had met Sandra that evening for the first time, when Andrea invited several of her friends to continue the Christmas party at Andrea's home, Sandra joined them. Andrea brought out an ice chest containing beer which Sandra and others drank.

While the Christmas party was continuing on the Cuis' premises but outside the home, Andrea's parents, James and Marion Cui, were asleep in their bedroom.

Eventually, at an early hour in the morning of December 20th, Sandra drove home to Ward Avenue in Honolulu. She then took a shower, changed her clothes, and proceeded to drive her friend, Pinky Lan Wai, home. While driving Pinky home, Sandra drove into oncoming traffic on Kapiolani Boulevard and crashed into a moped operated by Donna Johnston. As a result of this accident, Johnston was severely and permanently injured. Johnston brought suit for damages and compensation against several defendants, including KFC, Andrea Cui, and Andrea's parents. The trial court entered summary judgments in favor of KFC, Andrea Cui, and James and Marion Cui.

 JUDGE WAKATSUKI:

Traditionally, the common law held that when a person consumes alcohol to a point of being intoxicated and injures another he is the sole proximate cause of that injury. Thus, no liability could be attributed to the supplier of the alcoholic beverages.... [H]owever, this court modified the traditional common-law rule by imposing a duty upon commercial suppliers of alcohol to injured third parties. In adopting this modification, this court relied upon "the clear trend" across the country to impose such duty, and also by reference to a statute establishing a standard of conduct for liquor licensees. However, as to the non-commercial supplier of alcoholic beverages—the social host—we find no clear judicial trend toward modifying the traditional common law, nor any statutory enactment or policy which leads this court to conclude that a change in the common law is appropriate at this time.

Many courts, faced with many different factual permutations, have dealt with the issue of social host liability. The clear trend has been a refusal to impose a duty upon a social host to protect third parties from risk of injuries that may be caused by an adult who is provided and served alcohol beverages. To date, only the courts in New Jersey and Massachusetts impose such a duty....

Among state legislatures, the "predominant trend has been to preclude social host liability...."

We fail to see any judicial trend to impose a "change in the law which has the power to so deeply affect social and business relations...."

Although we are well acquainted with the arguments for and against social host liability:

> [t]he nature of the judicial role prevents us from capably deciding the merits of social host liability. Evaluating the overall merits of social host liability, with its wide sweeping implications, requires a balancing of the costs and benefits for society as a whole, not just the parties of any one case....

Social host liability implicates changes in social relations in a society where consumption of alcohol is a pervasive and deeply rooted part of our social life....

From an economic perspective, there needs to be consideration of the effect social host liability would have on homeowners' and renters' insurance rates, and the economic impact on those not wealthy or foresighted enough to obtain such insurance.... Furthermore, cost considerations are not limited to an ultimate finding of liability against the social host. A host will, in all probability, be made a defendant in a civil suit for damages and compensation brought by a third person who is injured in a car accident involving a friend, invitee, or guest of the host who provided and served the alcoholic beverage, thereby incurring the cost of defending against such a suit even though the host may not be liable.

We hold that, as a matter of law, [defendants] owed no duty to Johnston under the facts of this case.

OTHER THEORIES OF LIABILITY FOR TORT

Res Ipsa Loquitur. The term *res ipsa loquitur* means "the thing speaks for itself." The plaintiff normally has the burden of proving that the defendant failed to act in a reasonable and prudent manner, that the accident was foreseeable, and that the damage or injury was a proximate cause of the defendant's action. Normally the plaintiff has available various types of evidence, such as skid marks and eyewitnesses.

In some cases, it is obvious that the accident would not have happened had it not been for negligence on the part of the defendant, but the plaintiff does not have access to information that would verify or prove such negligence. An example would be a situation where a person was a passenger in an airplane and the airplane struck a mountain. The plane was demolished, and all its occupants died. In this case, the next of kin of the passengers will bring suit for the wrongful deaths. However, a plaintiff here lacks access to the physical evidence needed to prove this case. We know that airplanes normally do not run into mountains and that someone's negligence probably caused the accident. The cause may have been a malfunction or a breakdown in the aircraft itself; it may have been a manufacturing defect; or it may have been a failure on the part of the airline to properly service and inspect. It may also have been pilot error or error on the part of air traffic control. In such cases, the plaintiff pleads the theory of *res ipsa loquitur*, and the burden is shifted to the defendant, to prove that they were not negligent.

Last Clear Chance Doctrine. Simply stated, this doctrine provides that the liable party is the party who had the last clear chance to avoid damage or injury to the other party. This doctrine imposes a duty upon one party to exercise care in avoiding injury to another party who has negligently placed himself or herself in a situation of danger. For example, suppose that a motorist on a very cold day started up his or her automobile, drove up to an intersection while the motor was still cold, and proceeded to pull out into the intersection. The motor died, causing the car to stall crosswise in the intersection. Cars approaching the stalled vehicle would then have a duty to exercise reasonable care to try to avoid injury to the driver who had negligently placed himself or herself in a position of peril. Thus, if an oncoming motorist could swerve to the right or the left and go around this stalled car, or could stop before hitting it, then the driver would have a duty to do so.

LIABILITY OF OWNERS AND OCCUPIERS OF LAND

Land owners and occupiers may be liable in tort under one or more of the above theories for injuries sustained by persons on the premises and by persons off the premises.

Liability to Persons Off the Premises. Torts that arise from the unreasonable or unlawful use by a person of his or her own property in such a manner as to interfere with the rights of other property owners, with resulting damage, are called *nuisance* torts.

Nuisance torts may be classified as private or public. An example of a private nuisance situation would be one in which your neighbor is an amateur inventor who produces various offensive odors and smoke that make it unpleasant for you to go outside your house. Another example would be a situation in which your neighbor has a dog that howls all night. The test with regard to a nuisance case is whether the interference with your enjoyment of your property is substantial and unreasonable and whether that interference would be offensive or inconvenient to a reasonable or prudent person. The victim may sue for money damages, an injunction, or both remedies together.

A public nuisance can be defined as the doing of something or the failure to do something as a result of which the safety, health, or morals of the public are injuriously affected. Public nuisances may be criminal as well as civil. Examples of public nuisances are the storing of explosives on a person's premises, allowing persons to smoke marijuana on the premises, and nearly any other use of the premises which could adversely affect the safety, health, or morals of the community. The shooting of fireworks in the streets is also a public nuisance. Many public nuisances may also be private nuisances. A public nuisance is an offense against the state, and as such it is subject to criminal prosecution if it is a specifically criminal act, and it may be subject to abatement by governmental order. If the public nuisance also injures private parties, those private parties may have their own actions separate from the government, since private parties are concerned with damages for their own injuries.

Liability to Persons on the Premises. As to liability for injuries to persons on the premises, most courts impose varying standards of care on the landowner, based on the legal status of the injured person.

Employees. The employer owes each employee a duty to provide a reasonably safe place in which to work. Modern statutes have substantially changed the legal rules pertaining to this duty.

Historically, if an employee was injured on the job, the employees could sue the employer for medical bills incurred and for lost wages. However, the employer had three defenses: assumption of risk, contributory negligence, and the fellow servant rule. Thus, if the employee knew the machine being operated was faulty, continued to operate it, and was injured, the employer would not be liable. Also, if the employee removed a safety guard to clean out scrap, and then forgot to replace it, and the employee was injured, the employer could defend under the doctrine of contributory negligence. If a fellow employee negligently bumped another employee, causing the first employee to fall against a machine and be injured, the employer again could successfully defend the action. The net result of the use of the traditional tort system for claims for work-related injuries to employees was that most employees simply could not collect from the employer due to these defenses, and the cost of litigation often exceeded the claimed damages. Thus, the system of no-fault compensation for employees' injuries in the course of employment was developed. Every state now has a *workers' compensation* statute. Essentially these statutes provide that if an employee is killed or injured on the job, or becomes ill or disabled due to an occupational disease, the employer or its insurance carrier will have to pay all reasonable medical bills and a percentage of the lost wages during the period of disability. A settlement, or periodic payments, will be made if the employee suffered some permanent disability, such as the loss of an eye, or the loss of a percentage of function of an arm or leg. Death benefits are payable to the deceased employee's dependents.

The key concept in workers' compensation is that it is no-fault. The employee may have negligently left the safety guard off the machine or continued to operate a machine the employee knew to be faulty, but the employee will still collect all the statutory benefits if the employee is accidentally injured.

If the employee intentionally and knowingly injures himself or herself then, normally, no benefits will be awarded.

Invitees. A similarly high duty of care is owed to business invitees—customers, clients, suppliers, and others who come onto the property with the owner's permission and for the owner's benefit. The storekeeper owes those customers a duty to provide a reasonably safe place in which to shop. The essence of this duty is based on negligence—would a reasonable store owner have been aware of the dangerous condition which caused the injury? There is thus a duty to the customer to take reasonable steps to inspect and to maintain the store or office to which customers are invited. (The *Palmtag* case earlier in the chapter illustrates this point.)

Licensees. A lesser duty of care is owed to persons who are on the premises with permission, but without providing any financial benefit to the landowner. Your social guests fall into this category. Your only duty to the guest is to warn of *known* dangers. If your guest is injured by a condition of which you were not aware, you are not liable. You do not, in other words, owe the guest a reasonably safe place in which to socialize. Of course you would be liable for any other negligence which caused injury to the guest, such as the careless handling of kerosene near an open barbecue grill.

Trespassers. The landowner's only duty towards trespassers is a negative one—not to *intentionally* cause them injury. These persons are on the property without the owner's permission, so the owner clearly owes them no affirmative duty of care. "I was hurt on your property while I was committing a tort against you, so you are liable to me!"—such a rule would seem to violate all standards of common sense and justice. One does occasionally read about decisions which seem to violate common sense, and which award damages to trespassers. Some of them may be based on the landowner's having in effect intentionally injured the trespasser, by setting traps or digging holes. Some of them may just be due to overly sympathetic judges.

In recent years, several states have passed statutes which grant landowners the right to use deadly force to repel intruders, even if there is no immediate threat to one's own life. The danger here is obvious: persons who come to the wrong door by mistake, or who are lost or otherwise seeking help, may be shot by a too-quick-on-the-trigger property owner.

There is a very different rule in most states for trespassing children—the theory of *attractive nuisance*. For example, if an old refrigerator and an old junk car are sitting on your premises, these are called attractive nuisances, because they simply invite young children to come over and climb around on them. If these children are injured, you are strictly liable for injuries to them, even though you did not intentionally do anything wrong and, in fact, the children were trespassing on your property.

OTHER TORT RULES

Defenses to Negligent Torts. There are three basic defenses to negligent torts. They are: (1) contributory negligence, or comparative negligence, depending upon the rule of law adopted by the particular state; (2) assumption of risk; and (3) act of God.

Contributory negligence on the part of the plaintiff is a complete bar to recovery by the plaintiff in a state which has adopted the contributory negligence doctrine. A simple example of contributory negligence would be a situation where Mr. Leadfoot was northbound on a through highway at a speed of 75 miles per hour in a 30-mile-per-hour zone. Ms. Badsight was driving without her glasses, which she was required to wear when driving, and, not seeing a stop sign, drove into the intersection into the side of Mr. Leadfoot's car. Obviously, Ms. Badsight was negligent for driving without prescription glasses and for failing to stop at the stop sign. Also, her negligence was a proximate cause of the accident since it directly contributed to the accident. On the other hand, Mr. Leadfoot was contributorily negligent since he was driving in excess of the speed limit and his speed was a contributing factor to the collision. Thus, in a contributory negligence state neither one will recover from the other.

Historically, the great majority of the states followed the *contributory negligence* doctrine. If the plaintiff was guilty of negligence, no matter how slight, the plaintiff could recover nothing from the defendant. This admittedly was a very harsh rule, but it was accepted by the majority of states. In recent years, there has been a trend toward the doctrine of *comparative negligence*, also referred to as comparative fault. The justification of this doctrine is that it is not as harsh as the contributory negligence doctrine, since we are not going to penalize a plaintiff and refuse to allow any recovery whatsoever simply because the plaintiff was, in the estimation of the jury, slightly negligent. Today nearly 80 percent of the states have some form of comparative fault law. Briefly, under a typical comparative fault law, a plaintiff will be entitled to recover against a defendant if the plaintiff's comparative fault is not greater than the comparative fault of the defendant or the combination of defendants. Thus, if the plaintiff's fault exceeds 50 percent, then the plaintiff will not recover at all. However, if the plaintiff's comparative fault is less than 50 percent, the plaintiff's recovery will be reduced by the percentage of the plaintiff's fault. Let's take a situation where the plaintiff's damages are $100,000, the defendant's comparative fault is 50 percent, and the plaintiff's comparative fault is 50 percent. Under the old contributory negligence doctrine, the plaintiff could recover nothing. Under the comparative fault doctrine, the plaintiff would still recover $50,000, which would be 50 percent of the plaintiff's damages. If, however, the jury found that the plaintiff's comparative fault was in excess of 50 percent (i.e., 51% or 52%), the plaintiff would recover nothing. The problem, of course, is how do you determine the percentage of fault of each party? This is a question that has to be resolved in a case-by-case basis by the jury, or by the judge if the case is being tried without a jury.

The defense of assumption of risk may be a complete defense to a plaintiff's negligent tort action. When a person is aware of the danger in a situation, yet continues to expose himself or herself to that danger and is then injured, that person cannot complain of the defendant's negligence.

The third defense is the defense of act of God. If lightning strikes a large tree in your yard, causing the tree to fall on and crush your neighbor's car, you would not be liable, as the proximate cause of the damage was a so-called act of God. Similarly, if a tornado swept your tree into your neighbor's house, you would not be liable. If, however, you had a dead tree in your backyard which you intended to cut down because the tree was rotten and dangerous and one day a strong wind toppled the tree onto your neighbor's car, then you would not be able to use the defense of act of God because you were aware of the condition of the tree and also should have been aware of the possibility that a windstorm would cause the tree to fall and do damage to others.

Immunity from Tort Action. Certain persons, organizations, and governmental bodies have traditionally been immune from tort liability under certain circumstances.

At common law, a husband could not sue his wife and a wife could not sue her husband for personal torts. The theory of courts was that such litigation would destroy family unity. Also, traditionally, a child could not sue either parent. These common-law intrafamily immunities are gradually being eroded, as the reason for immunity is no longer as strong as it used to be. Today, we generally believe that injured parties should be able to sue wrongdoers, whoever they may be. In most cases, the spouse or the child is not actually suing the other spouse or the parent, but in effect is going after insurance proceeds. The spouse or the parent is a defendant in name only.

Charitable organizations traditionally were immune to tort liability. The theory was that to impose tort liability on the funds of the charitable organization would cripple its good work and would discourage donations to the organization. This immunity is also being eroded or completely eliminated in many states. Here again, the original reasons for the immunity are no longer valid. A charitable organization today can buy liability insurance, and the cost of this insurance can be part of its regular budget. Thus, the organization needs no more protection than any other business and it should be liable for injury caused to innocent persons. An example would be the charitable hospital. A person negligently injured when a patient in a charitable hospital certainly should have the same rights of recovery in tort against the charitable hospital as he or she would have had if the injury had occurred in a profit-making hospital. In either case, the injury to the patient is the same, and the fault is the same.

The third traditional immunity is called **sovereign immunity**; simply stated, this means that the government may not be sued for its torts. The government can be defined as the U.S. government, state governments, municipal or county governments, or any governmental subdivision. The national government enacted the U.S. Tort Claims Act in 1946. This act established certain conditions for lawsuits and claims against the national government. Many states have also passed tort claims acts or other legislative acts, limiting the sovereign immunity of the state, cities, and other governmental units. Some states, however, have established dollar limits on claims that can be recovered from them. The general trend in sovereign immunity is toward its elimination. Here again, the state, city, or other governmental subdivision can purchase liability insurance and thus budget the cost on an annual basis.

No-Fault System of Automobile Tort Compensation. Traditionally, the negligent party whose negligence proximately caused injury to another person or to another person's property would be found liable in tort and would have judgment entered against him or her, provided the defendant did not have a valid defense, such as contributory negligence, assumption of risk, or act of God.

As indicated earlier in this chapter, the defense of contributory negligence as a complete defense was found to be harsh and unfair and unjust in many cases. The doctrine of comparative negligence has now replaced the traditional contributory negligence doctrine in most states.

This fault system works satisfactorily in the majority of tort cases. However, there is one specific class of tort claims—automobile accident cases—where certain states by legislative enactment have replaced the fault system with a no-fault system of compensation. The proponents of the automobile no-fault system argue that it will cut insurance rates because it will save litigation expenses, such as attorney fees and court costs. The theory of a no-fault system is simple. Each automobile owner-driver carries his or her own insurance. If that person has an accident, his or her own insurance company pays the doctor bills, lost wages, and car repair bills. The system sounds good: no attorney fees, no court costs. But what about pain and suffering, or permanent impairment? A professional basketball player earning $500,000 per year is involved in an automobile accident and has to have his right arm amputated. What kind of settlement is he entitled to? Compare the basketball player's case to a case where a school teacher is involved in a similar accident and had his right arm amputated. Should both men get the same amount since they both lost a right arm?

Critics of the no-fault system argue that no-fault statutes take away the injured person's day in court, the right to a trial by jury. To overcome this criticism, most no-fault laws allow claimants to sue in court if their injuries are serious or their damages exceed a certain dollar amount.

No-fault systems can reduce court congestion and can be an effective method for promptly resolving minor automobile property damage and nonserious injury claims.

SIGNIFICANCE OF THIS CHAPTER

We live in a legalistic society, and the law of torts is a very important area of concern for individuals and businesses. Anything we do or say in our personal or business lives could subject us to liability. This chapter reviews the various types of torts that may occur and the main defenses available against such claims.

PROBLEMS FOR DISCUSSION

1. Johnny Carson, the famous host of the "Tonight Show," had been introduced by the phrase, "Here's Johnny," since 1957. In 1967, Mr. Carson authorized the use of that phrase by a chain of restaurants and the phrase was also used for specific labels and advertising with Mr. Carson's permission. The phrase, "Here's Johnny," was not registered with the U.S. Patent Office as a trademark or as a service mark. In 1996, a corporation named "Here's Johnny Portable Toilets, Inc." was incorporated in Michigan and began doing business in Michigan. Mr. Carson filed suit for invasion of his privacy and publicity rights.

   Does Mr. Carson have a valid cause of action? How much money would you give Mr. Carson if you were the judge or jury and found in his favor?

2. Bertha L. Briney inherited her parents' farmland in Mahaska and Monroe Counties. Included was an eighty-acre tract in southwest Mahaska County where her grandparents and parents had lived. No one occupied the house thereafter. Her husband, Edward, attempted to care for the land. He kept no farm machinery thereon. The outbuildings became dilapidated.

   For about ten years, there occurred a series of trespassing and housebreaking events with loss of some household items, the breaking of windows, and "messing up of the property in general." The latest occurred June 8, prior to the event on July 16, herein involved.

   The Brineys through the years boarded up the windows and doors in an attempt to stop the intrusions. They had posted "no trespass" signs on the land several years before. The nearest one was thirty-five feet from the house. On June 11, they set "a shotgun trap" in the north bedroom. After Mr. Briney cleaned and oiled his 20-gauge shotgun, defendants took it to the old house where they secured it to an iron bed with the barrel pointed at the bedroom door. It was rigged with wire from the doorknob to the gun's trigger so it would fire when the door was opened. Briney first pointed the gun so an intruder would be hit in the stomach but at Mrs. Briney's suggestion it was lowered to the legs. He admitted he did so "because I was mad and tired of being tormented" but "he did not intend to injure anyone." He gave no explanation of why he used a loaded shell and set it to hit a person already in the house. Tin was nailed over the bedroom window. The spring gun could not be seen from the outside. No warning of its presence was posted.

   Katko lived with his wife and worked regularly as a gasoline station attendant in Eddyville, seven miles from the old house. He had observed it for several years while hunting in the area and considered it as being abandoned. Prior to July 16, Katko and McDonough had been to the premises and found several old bottles and fruit jars which they took and added to their collection of antiques. On that date about 9:30 p.m. they made a second trip to the Briney property. They entered the old house by removing a board from a porch window which was without glass. As plaintiff started to open the north bedroom door, the shotgun went off, striking him in the right leg about the ankle bone. Much of his leg, including part of the tibia, was blown away. Only by McDonough's assistance was plaintiff able to get out of the house and after crawling some distance was put in his vehicle and rushed to a doctor and then to a hospital. He remained in the hospital forty days. Katko sued.

   Have the Brineys committed a tort? Discuss.

3. Mrs. Garner entered Southwest Drugstore, found the bar of soap she wanted, took it to the cashier, paid for it, and received a sales ticket. The cashier put the soap in a small bag. Mrs. Garner walked out of the store, but before she got to her car, the manager of the store yelled out at her, telling her to stop, and accused her of stealing the bar of soap. She denied it, but he told her she would have to go back into the store with him to prove that she hadn't stolen the soap. There were a number of people in the parking lot who heard the manager's loud and rude accusations. When the manager and Mrs. Garner got back to the store, the cashier verified that Mrs. Garner had paid for the soap. Mrs. Garner was then released. She became ill and distressed as a result of the incident. She required medical treatment for her distress.

   A Mississippi statute allows a merchant to stop and question a person if the merchant has reasonable grounds to believe that the person is attempting to commit the crime of shoplifting. Mrs. Garner sued Southwest Drug Stores for false imprisonment and slander, and a verdict for $8,000 was rendered in her favor in the lower court. Southwest Drug Stores appealed.

   How should the appeals court rule, and why?

4. On August 11, four year old Joel Goode drowned in a man-made waterway or moat at Walt Disney World. He was with his mother, Marietta Goode, who noticed that he was missing shortly after 11 p.m. Approximately three hours later, Joel's body was found in five feet of water a short distance from where he had become separated from his mother. An autopsy found no evidence of foul play and established the cause of death as drowning. No one saw Joel enter the waterway.

   Joel's parents sued Walt Disney World for the wrongful death of their son. The jury returned a verdict of $1,000,000 for Joel's father, Harry Goode, and $1,000,000 for Joel's mother Marietta. The jury also determined that Disney and Joel's mother were each 50 percent negligent.

   What judgment should be given here? Explain.

5. Russo and Olive Dribble owned a large male goat, which they kept in a pen. One morning the Dribbles' two sons, aged 10 and 7, missed the school bus. Their parents had already left for work, so the boys were home alone. They let the goat out of his pen to play with him. At this point, the goat was still within the Dribbles' fenced-in front yard. When the boys went across the street to visit their friend, Mr. Pappe, the goat jumped the fence and followed them. Pappe poked the goat in the side with his cane to try to get it off his property. The goat attacked Pappe and seriously injured him. Pappe was taken to the hospital, treated for a month, and then released. He was readmitted about three months later and died about a month after that. Pappe's estate sues the Dribbles.

   Is there any basis for tort liability here? Discuss.

6. Plaintiff Page County Appliance Center, Inc. sued Honeywell, Inc. and ITT Electronic Travel Services, Inc. for nuisance and tortious interference with business relations. Defendants appeal from judgment entered on jury verdicts awarding $71,000 compensatory and $150,000 punitive damages. Honeywell appeals from a judgment rendered against it on ITT's cross-claim for indemnification.

Appliance Center has owned and operated an appliance store in Shenandoah, Iowa since 1953. In 1995, John Pearson acquired the store from his father. It sold televisions, stereos, and a variety of appliances. Before 1998, Pearson had no reception trouble with his display televisions. In early January 1998, however, ITT placed one of its computers with Central Travel Service in Shenandoah as part of a nationwide plan to lease computers to retail travel agents. Central Travel was separated by only one other business from the Appliance Center. This ITT computer was manufactured, installed, and maintained by Honeywell.

Thereafter many of Pearson's customers told him his display television pictures were bad; on two of the three channels available in Shenandoah he had a difficult time "getting a picture that was fit to watch." After unsuccessfully attempting several remedial measures, in late January 1998, he finally traced the interference to the operations of Central Travel's computer. Both defendants concede Pearson's problems were caused by radiation leaking from the Honeywell computer.

Should the trial court's decision be affirmed? Why or why not?

Chapter 7

Liability of Accountants and Other Professionals

In the previous chapter, we discussed the various types of torts that managers should be aware of, defined the types of negligence that could bring about liability claims, and discussed the defenses that could be raised against such claims. We reserved discussion of a very important area of liability for this chapter. This area of liability is often referred to as *malpractice liability* or *professional liability*.

In the previous chapter, we also noted that we live in a litigious society. That comment is certainly appropriate when we discuss malpractice or professional liability, as the number of claims made and the amounts of the various verdicts in this area of liability have increased tremendously in recent years. These claims have resulted in an enormous increase in the cost of malpractice liability insurance for professionals.

The costs associated with malpractice claims are not only payment of the claims themselves, but also the costs of legal defense. Thus, even if the professional is innocent of any wrong doing, he or she still might have to pay several thousand dollars for defense costs. Remember, even if the verdict is in your favor, the cost of your attorney for your defense is still your responsibility.

In the previous chapter, we referred to the tort known as abuse of civil process. This tort has been used successfully as a counterclaim in many malpractice cases where the plaintiff obviously did not have a valid cause of action but simply filed a lawsuit hoping for an out-of-court settlement because the professional might wish to limit adverse publicity and the costs of legal defense. In that type of case the abuse of civil process tort may well be used. However, in cases where there is reasonable evidence that malpractice did occur, the tort of abuse of civil process would not be effective, as filing of the law suit would probably not be viewed as an intentional misuse or abuse of the civil process.

In this chapter, our primary concern will be the liability of accountants. The common law applicable to accountants' liability is similar to the liability of other professionals such as physicians, attorneys, engineers, architects, and other persons classified as professionals. Accountants, however, in addition to being liable under common law principles, are also subject to liability as a result of statutory liabilities under the provisions of the national securities laws and the U.S. internal revenue laws.

COMMON LAW LIABILITY

Contract Law. The professional, whether an accountant, attorney, physician, or other professional, may be liable to the client for breach of contract if the professional fails to perform the contract with the client. An accountant or other professional sells services to clients. If the professional fails to perform the services as agreed, then the professional will be liable to the client under the theory of breach of contract. The client will be entitled to money damages sufficient to compensate the client for the out-of-pocket damages the client suffered as a result of the breach of contract by the professional. An example would be a situation where the client had contracted with an accountant to furnish a financial statement to the client's bank by a certain date, as the client had a loan commitment and guaranteed interest rate up to that date, which the accountant was aware of. If the accountant failed to deliver the financial report to the bank within the required time period, and as a result of the accountant's failure, the client's loan was turned down or the interest rate went up, then the client could sue the accountant for breach of contract and recover any out-of-pocket loss. The professional may not avoid this liability by delegating the duties to other persons. If an accountant delegates the duty of preparing your tax returns to a subordinate, the accountant will still be liable if a breach of contract occurs. Contract law will be reviewed and discussed in more detail in Part II, Contracts, which follows this chapter. The liability of accountants or other professionals to their clients under contract law is essentially the same as the liability of any party to a contract who fails to perform in accordance with the terms of the contract.

Negligence. An accountant or other professional owes a duty to the client to exercise *reasonable care* in the performance of the terms of the contract. Failure to exercise this reasonable care may be considered negligence on the part of the professional. The obvious question here is what constitutes reasonable care and what does not. Generally speaking, reasonable care has been defined as the exercise of the same degree or amount of skill and care that other similar professionals practicing in the same locality would exercise under the same or similar circumstances. The professional being judged may also be evaluated by general standards of the specific profession, as well as the standard of skill and care of similar professionals in the locality. For example, individual states have enacted codes of ethics and/or rules of professional conduct for the practice of law, the medical profession has its ethical standards, certified professional engineers have ethical codes, and Certified Public Accountants (CPAs) also have standards of care required by their profession. These standards are the generally accepted accounting principles known as GAAP, and the generally accepted auditing standards known as GAAS.

Examples of situations where a professional would be liable to his or her client for negligence would be the case of an attorney who failed to file a lawsuit for the client within the statutory period, causing the client to lose the right to receive damages from the adverse party; a physician who prescribed the wrong medication which injured the patient, or the CPA who miscalculated or made omissions or other errors in the tax report for the client, causing the client to have to pay tax penalties.

LIABILITY TO THIRD PARTIES

It is in this category of liability that the CPA is often in a more precarious liability position than other professionals. CPAs are often found liable to third parties (nonclients) who foreseeably and justifiably relied on the CPA's report to its client. In the other professions, we do not find the same degree of liability to third parties. For example, if a surgeon performs an operation and sews up the incision leaving a sponge in the wound, the only person who can claim against the surgeon is the patient, or perhaps the patient's estate or his dependents if the patient died as a result of negligence in the surgical process. Similarly in the case of an attorney, the threat of a malpractice claim is from clients, not third parties. Thus CPAs find themselves in a unique situation with regard to third party liability.

Ultramares Doctrine. Accountants do more than simply make up tax returns for clients. One of the most common tasks the accountant performs for the client is the auditing and certification of the business organization's financial reports. Obviously the accountant would be liable to the client for a mistake in the auditing and preparation and certification of a financial report if the client suffered damages as a result of the mistake, because the accountant and the client are "in privity of contract." This means they have a contractual arrangement, and therefore have responsibilities to each other.

The question arises, what happens if the client takes this audited and certified financial report to a bank to convince the bank that the client is solvent and has assets to repay the loan being requested? If the accountant negligently made a mistake in the audit and certification of the financial report and in fact the client's financial status is not as portrayed in the report, can the bank sue the accountant if they suffered damages as a result of their reliance on the report? In 1931, Chief Judge Benjamin Cardozo of the New York Court of Appeals, the highest court of the state of New York, addressed the problem of liability of accountants to third persons (nonclients) in *Ultramares Corp. v. Touche*, 174 N.E. 441 (1931). Judges in courts all over the United States followed the precedent set by that decision for many years. It was referred to as the *Ultramares* doctrine.

In the *Ultramares* case, Touche, the accounting firm, had audited the financial records of Fred Stern & Co. and prepared a financial statement as a result of the audit. Ultramares Corporation, relying on the financial statement prepared by Touche, loaned money to Fred Stern & Co. Later Fred Stern & Co. couldn't pay back the loans and declared bankruptcy. Actually Fred Stern & Co. was insolvent at the time the financial statement was made. Judge Cardozo in the *Ultramares* case stated that an accountant has a duty and responsibility not only to the client, but to all third parties who relied on their reports, if the accountant was guilty of fraud. However, if the mistake or misstatement was simply the result of negligence, then the accountant would not be liable to nonclients, that is third persons, unless the nonclient was known by the accountant to be an intended user who would be relying on the accountant's reports. This case established the *primary beneficiary* test. That is, unless the third party (nonclient) was known by the accountant to be a primary beneficiary of the accountant's work product, then the accountant would not be liable to such third party for negligence.

The *Ultramares* doctrine gave accountants a special protection that is not available to all professionals. For example, take the case of the architect who designed a building in Minneapolis, Minnesota and miscalculated the roof weight load factors. After the building was erected, the roof fell in following the first heavy snowfall, and hundreds of persons were injured. Those injured people can sue and collect damages from the architect even though the error was not the result of fraud but simply negligence. In that case, the court would find it was foreseeable that people occupying the building would be injured if the roof collapsed. The architect was aware of this potential liability when the design was made and had a duty, not only to its clients but to all foreseeable users, to design the building to withstand natural and expected roof loads such as a snowfall. Accountants under the *Ultramares* doctrine are not liable to any and all persons who might be damaged by relying on their work product.

In recent years, courts in many states have refused to follow the *Ultramares* doctrine. These courts have extended the liability of accountants beyond the client and the primary beneficiary nonclient, to nonclients who were not known to the accountant but who were in a foreseen class of users of the accountant's work product. Some courts have extended liability to foreseeable users generally. The foreseen class of users doctrine has been adopted in the *Restatement (Second) of Torts*.

Restatement (Second) of Torts. The *Restatement (Second) of Torts* was published in 1977. The relevant section reads as follows:

§552. Information Negligently Supplied for the Guidance of Others

(1) One who, in the course of his business, profession, or employment, or in any other transaction in which he has a pecuniary interest, supplies false information for the guidance of others in their business transactions, is subject to liability for pecuniary loss caused to them by their justifiable reliance upon the information, if he fails to exercise reasonable care or competence in obtaining or communicating the information.

(2) Except as stated in Subsection (3), the liability stated in Subsection (1) is limited to loss suffered

　(a) by the person or one of a limited group of persons for whose benefit and guidance he intends to supply the information or knows that the recipient intends to supply it; and

　(b) through reliance upon it in a transaction that he intends the information to influence or knows that the recipient so intends or in a substantially similar transaction.

(3) The liability of one who is under a public duty to give the information extends to loss suffered by any of the class of persons for whose benefit the duty is created, in any of the transactions in which it is intended to protect them.[1]

---

[1] Copyright ... by The American Law Institute. Reprinted with the permission of The American Law Institute.

The language of the *Restatement* expands the class of third party nonclients who can sue and recover from the accountant. The *Restatement* extends liability to certain *foreseen* beneficiaries but not to any and all *foreseeable* users of the accountant's work.

Foreseeable Users Doctrine. This doctrine is the most recent in origin and the most liberal in extending liability of the accountant. It holds that accountants may be held liable not only to nonclients who are primary beneficiaries (the *Ultramares* doctrine) or to reasonably foreseen beneficiaries (the *Restatement* concept) but also to *foreseeable third parties*. In 1983, the New Jersey Supreme Court found it was not in the public interest to give accountants the special protection against lawsuits by nonclients who were neither primary beneficiaries nor reasonably foreseen beneficiaries. Instead, the court felt accountants should be liable for their negligence to the foreseeable users of their work product, just as other professionals would be liable.

Ultramares Reaffirmed. The New York Court of Appeals in 1985 again addressed the question of liability of accountants to third persons (nonclients) in *Credit Alliance Corporation v. Arthur Andersen & Co.*, 483 N.E.2d 110. The court in that case essentially reaffirmed the original *Ultramares* doctrine and went on to list three requirements that must be met before a nonclient can hold an accountant liable for negligence. These requirements are: (1) the accountants must have been aware that their work product was to be used for a particular purpose, (2) in the furtherance of which a known party was intended to rely, and (3) some conduct on the part of the accountants linking them to that party must evidence the accountant's understanding of that party's reliance. Thus, we have a considerable difference in opinion among the various states as to the liability of accountants to third party nonclients. The accountant should be aware of which of the three legal concepts his or her state has adopted: the *Ultramares* doctrine, the *Restatement* concept, or the foreseeable users doctrine.

The *Security Pacific* case shows that the New York Court of Appeals continues to follow its earlier precedents and to refuse to extend CPAs' liability to other third parties.

SECURITY PACIFIC v. PEAT MARWICK MAIN
597 N.E.2d 1080 (NY, 1992)

FACTS: Plaintiff, an institutional lender lacking a contractual or other direct business relationship with defendant accounting firm, seeks to hold the defendant liable for alleged negligence committed by defendant's predecessor in its 1984 audit of financial statements of its client, Top Brass Enterprises, Inc. In October 1984, plaintiff, Security Pacific Business Credit, Inc. (SPBC), an asset based lender, and Bankers Trust Co. loaned Top Brass approximately $40 million on a $50 million line of credit, secured by Top Brass's accounts receivable and merchandise inventory. After Top Brass filed for bankruptcy in 1986, SPBC sued defendant Peat Marwick Main & Co., as successor to Main Hurdman. SPBC alleged that it had relied on Main Hurdman's 1984 unqualified audit opinion and financial statements, which did not accurately present the financial position of Top Brass in that they negligently overvalued Top Brass's accounts receivable and merchandise inventory. SPBC's alleged reliance is premised essentially on a telephone call from its vice president, Seiden, to Main Hurdman's audit partner, Freeman, during and with respect only to the 1984 audit process and audit work papers supplied to SPBC by Top Brass. SPBC claimed losses on the loans of at least $8 million.

 JUDGE BELLACOSA:

When accountants conduct a traditional financial audit, they undertake a duty of due care in the performance of their engagement to the party which has contracted for their services.... In "carefully circumscribed" instances, ... accountants may also incur liability to injured third parties who rely on their work, even in the absence of a direct contractual relationship between the accountants and the third party. This Court established an analytical framework for determining the applicability of this policy-based extension of common-law liability in *Credit Alliance Corp. v Andersen & Co*....: "(1) the accountants must have been aware that the financial reports were to be used for a particular purpose or purposes; (2) in the furtherance of which a known party or parties was intended to rely; and (3) there must have been some conduct on the part of the accountants linking them to that party or parties, which evinces the accountants' understanding of that party or parties' reliance...." The indicia, while distinct, are interrelated and collectively require a third party claiming harm to demonstrate a relationship or bond with the once-removed accountants "sufficiently approaching privity" based on "some conduct on the part of the accountants...."

Applying the precedents and principles to this case, we conclude that on this record plaintiff has failed to make the necessary demonstration of the existence of a relationship between the parties to this litigation "sufficiently approaching privity." In opposing Peat Marwick's motion for summary judgment, SPBC was required to produce evidentiary proof, in admissible form, of all three elements of the *Credit Alliance* analysis, warranting a trial on material questions of fact.... *It has failed to meet its burden.*

In opposing summary judgment, SPBC relies on evidence indicating that Main Hurdman was aware, before it issued its 1984 unqualified audit report, that SPBC and Top Brass were involved in negotiations for a line of credit to be secured by accounts receivable. To establish a relationship sufficiently approaching privity, particularly the indispensable linking conduct on which the parties heavily focus, SPBC primarily relies on the single phone call. It was allegedly placed by SPBC's vice president, Seiden, to Main Hurdman's audit partner, Freeman, at Top Brass's suggestion, with respect only to the 1984 audit. SPBC also relies on Main Hurdman's knowledge acquired from its own 1984 audit work papers. Notwithstanding the dissenting opinion's halving of the analysis by concentrating only on aspects of Main Hurdman's knowledge, and its dispensing with the concomitant conduct ingredient that must also be attributable to Main Hurdman in order to hold it liable, SPBC's evidence, for summary judgment purposes, fall short of the *Credit Alliance* criteria.

Fraud. An accountant may be found liable to the client or third persons for "actual" fraud. Actual fraud occurs when the accountant intentionally misstates or omits material facts intending to mislead the client or third persons who will rely on the accountant's work product. Material facts are facts that would be considered to be important to decision making based on the accountant's work product. If the client or the third party justifiably relied on the misstatement or the omission and suffered damage, then the accountant will be liable for that person's out-of-pocket damages. Also, in some cases, the courts may allow punitive damages to be awarded against the accountant. Punitive damages are a method of punishing the fraudulent wrongdoer in addition to making the wrongdoer pay for the actual damage caused by the wrong.

There are other cases where the accountant is not guilty of an intentional misstatement or omission of material facts and the accountant did not intend to mislead anyone, but the actions of the accountant were not simply negligent actions; they were grossly negligent. By this we mean the accountant was guilty of an uncaring and reckless disregard for the accuracy and possible consequences of the use of his or her work product. If there were misstatements or omission of material fact in the work product, the accountant could be found guilty of *constructive fraud*. Typically the plaintiff, who has justifiably relied on an erroneous financial report which was audited and certified by an independent accountant, where there is no evidence of actual fraud, will allege negligence, constructive fraud, and also breach of contract, thus covering all the bases.

ACCOUNTANT'S STATUTORY LIABILITIES

Securities Act of 1933. The Securities Act of 1933 requires issuers of securities to file a registration statement. This registration statement must contain financial statements and other information relating to the security. The purpose of this registration statement is to give the prospective buyers an opportunity to learn about the security before making a purchase. The 1933 Securities Act is often referred to as "The Truth in Securities Law." Chapter 37 discusses the 1933 Securities Act in more detail.

Section 11 of the 1933 Securities Act makes an accountant who provides inaccurate financial information used in a securities registration statement liable to a purchaser of the securities. Section 11(a), which specifically refers to accountants' liability, reads in part as follows:

> In case any part of the registration statement, when such part became effective, contained an untrue statement of a material fact or omitted to state a material fact required to be stated therein or necessary to make the statements therein not misleading, any person acquiring such security ... may sue ... every accountant ... who has with his consent been named as having prepared or certified any part of the registration statement.

The first question to be answered is what constitutes a material fact. Briefly, a material fact is a factual statement which would have been important to the purchaser in making the decision to purchase or not to purchase.

Once it has been determined that there has been a misstatement of a material fact or an omission of a material fact, the next question is whether the accountant exercised due diligence in the preparation of the material and whether the accountant made reasonable efforts to determine the accuracy of the factual statements prior to the time the registration statement was made available to purchasers.

Section 11 does not require the purchaser of securities issued based on a registration statement that contained misstatements of material fact or omissions of material fact to prove that the purchaser actually relied on the misstatements or omissions when purchasing the securities. Also, the purchaser doesn't have to prove the accountant/auditor was negligent. The burden is on the accountant to prove that he or she used due diligence in preparation and presentation of the material in the registration statement. Section 11 lawsuits against the accountant are also subject to a statute of limitations. The purchaser has only one year from the date the misstatement or omission is discovered, or in some cases, from the date the misstatement or omission should have been discovered. In no instance can a purchaser file suit against the accountant once a period of three years has elapsed after the securities were first offered to the public.

The *Escott v. BarChris* case explains the "due diligence" defense available to the accountant/auditor.

ESCOTT v. BARCHRIS CONSTRUCTION CORP.
283 F.Supp. 643 (NY, 1968)

FACTS: This is an action by purchasers of convertible subordinated 15-year debentures of BarChris Construction Corporation (BarChris). BarChris got into financial trouble in early 1962 and defaulted on the interest payments on the debentures. In October 1962, BarChris filed bankruptcy.

The action is brought under Section 11 of the Securities Act of 1933 (15 U.S.C. § 77k). Plaintiffs allege that the registration statement with respect to these debentures filed with the Securities and Exchange Commission, which became effective on May 16, 1961, contained material false statements and material omissions.

Defendants fall into three categories: (1) the persons who signed the registration statement; (2) the underwriters, consisting of eight investment banking firms, led by Drexel & Co. (Drexel); and (3) BarChris's auditors, Peat, Marwick, Mitchell & Co. The signers, in addition to BarChris itself, were the nine directors of BarChris, plus its controller, defendant Trilling. Defendants claim the defense of due diligence.

 DISTRICT JUDGE MCLEAN:

On the main issue of liability, the questions to be decided are: (1) did the registration statement contain false statements of fact, or did it omit to state facts which should have been stated in order to prevent it from being misleading; (2) if so, were the facts which were falsely stated or omitted "material" within the meaning of the Act; (3) if so, have defendants established their affirmative defenses?...

It is a prerequisite to liability under Section 11 of the Act that the fact which is falsely stated in a registration statement or the fact that is omitted when it should have been stated to avoid being misleading, be "material...."

The average prudent investor is not concerned with minor inaccuracies or with errors as to matters which are of no interest to him. The facts which tend to deter him from purchasing a security are facts which have an important bearing upon the nature or condition of the issuing corporation or its business.

Judged by this test, there is no doubt that many of the misstatements and omissions in this prospectus were material. This is true of all of them which relate to the state of affairs in 1961 (i.e., the overstatement of sales and gross profit for the first quarter, the understatement of contingent liabilities as of April 30, the overstatement of orders on hand and the failure to disclose the true facts with respect to officers' loans, customers' delinquencies, application of proceeds, and the prospective operation of several alleys)....

Before considering the evidence, a preliminary matter should be disposed of. The defendants do not agree among themselves as to who the "experts" were or as to the parts of the registration statement which were expertised....

To say that the entire registration statement is expertised because some lawyer prepared it would be an unreasonable construction of the statute. Neither the lawyer for the company nor the lawyer for the underwriters is an expert within the meaning of Section 11. The only expert, in the statutory sense, was Peat, Marwick, and the only parts of the registration statement which purported to be made upon the authority of an expert were the portions which purported to be made on Peat, Marwick's authority....

The underwriters other than Drexel made no investigation of the accuracy of the prospectus. One of them, Peter Morgan, had underwritten the 1959 stock issue and had been a director of BarChris. He thus had some general familiarity with its affairs, but he knew no more than the other underwriters about the debenture prospectus. They all relied upon Drexel as the "lead" underwriter.

Drexel did make an investigation. The work was in charge of Coleman, a partner of the firm, assisted by Casperson, an associate. Drexel's attorneys acted as attorneys for the entire group of underwriters. Ballard did the work, assisted by Stanton....

After Coleman was elected a director on April 17, 1961, he made no further independent investigation of the accuracy of the prospectus. He assumed that Ballard was taking care of this on his behalf as well as on behalf of the underwriters.

In April 1961, Ballard instructed Stanton to examine BarChris's minutes for the past five years and also to look at "the major contracts of the company." Stanton went to BarChris's office for that purpose on April 24. He asked Birnbaum for the minute books. He read the minutes of the board of directors and discovered interleaved in them a few minutes of executive committee meetings in 1960. He asked Kircher if there were any others. Kircher said that there had been other executive committee meetings but that the minutes had not been written up....

As to the "major contracts," all that Stanton could remember seeing was an insurance policy. Birnbaum told him that there was no file of major contracts. Stanton did not examine the agreements with Talcott. He did not examine the contracts with customers. He did not look to see what contracts comprised the backlog figure. Stanton examined no accounting records of BarChris. His visit, which lasted one day, was devoted primarily to reading the director's minutes....

The other underwriters, who did nothing and relied solely on Drexel and on the lawyers, are also bound by [their failure]. It follows that although Drexel and the other underwriters believed that those portions of the prospectus were true, they had no reasonable ground for that belief, within the meaning of the statute. Hence, they have not established their due diligence defense, except as to the 1960 audited figures.

The same conclusions must apply to Coleman. Although he participated quite actively in the earlier stages of the preparation of the prospectus and contributed questions and warnings of his own, in addition to the questions of counsel, the fact is that he stopped his participation toward the end of March 1961. He made no investigation after he became a director. When it came to verification, he relied upon his counsel to do it for him. Since counsel failed to do it, Coleman is bound by that failure. Consequently, in his case also, he has not established his due diligence defense except as to the audited 1960 figures....

Peat, Marwick's work was in general charge of a member of the firm, Cummings, and more immediately in charge of Peat, Marwick's manager, Logan. Most of the actual work was performed by a senior accountant, Berardi, who had junior assistants, one of whom was Kennedy.

Berardi was then about thirty years old. He was not yet a CPA. He had no previous experience with the bowling industry. This was his first job as a senior accountant. He could hardly have been given a more difficult assignment.

After obtaining a little background information on BarChris by talking to Logan and reviewing Peat, Marwick's work papers on its 1959 audit, Berardi examined the results of test checks of BarChris's accounting procedures which one of the junior accountants had made, and he prepared an "internal control questionnaire" and an "audit program." Thereafter, for a few days subsequent to December 30, 1960, he inspected BarChris's inventories and examined certain alley construction. Finally, on January 13, 1961, he began his auditing work, which he carried on substantially continuously until it was completed on February 24, 1961. Toward the close of the work, Logan reviewed it and made various comments and suggestions to Berardi....

The purpose of reviewing events subsequent to the date of a certified balance sheet (referred to as an S-1 review when made with reference to a registration statement) is to ascertain whether any material change has occurred in the company's financial position which should be disclosed in order to prevent the balance sheet figures from being misleading. The scope of such a review, under generally accepted auditing standards, is limited. It does not amount to a complete audit.

Peat, Marwick prepared a written program for such a review. I find that this program conformed to generally accepted auditing standards....

Berardi made the S-1 review in May 1961. He devoted a little over two days to it, a total of 20½ hours. He did not discover any of the errors or omissions pertaining to the state of affairs in 1961 which I have previously discussed at length, all of which were material. The question is whether, despite his failure to find out anything, his investigation was reasonable within the meaning of the statute.

What Berardi did was to look at a consolidated trial balance as of March 31, 1961 which had been prepared by BarChris, compare it with the audited December 31, 1960 figures, discuss with Trilling certain unfavorable developments which the comparison disclosed, and read certain minutes. He did not examine any "important financial records" other than the trial balance. As to the minutes, he read only what minutes Birnbaum gave him, which consisted only of the board of directors' minutes of BarChris. He did not read such minutes as there were of the executive committee. He did not know that there was an executive committee, hence he did not discover that Kircher had notes of executive committee minutes which had not been written up. He did not read the minutes of any subsidiary.

In substance, what Berardi did is similar to what Grant and Ballard did. He asked questions, he got answers which he considered satisfactory, and he did nothing to verify them....

There had been a material change for the worse in BarChris's financial position. That change was sufficiently serious so that the failure to disclose it made the 1960 figures misleading. Berardi did not discover it. As far as results were concerned, his S-1 review was useless.

Accountants should not be held to a standard higher than that recognized in their profession. I do not do so here. Berardi's review did not come up to that standard. He did not take some of the steps which Peat, Marwick's written program prescribed. He did not spend an adequate amount of time on a task of this magnitude. Most important of all, he was too easily satisfied with glib answers to his inquiries.

This is not to say that he should have made a complete audit. But there were enough danger signals in the materials which he did examine to require some further investigation on his part. Generally accepted accounting standards required such further investigation under these circumstances. It is not always sufficient merely to ask questions.

Here again, the burden of proof is on Peat, Marwick. I find that that burden has not been satisfied. I conclude that Peat, Marwick has not established its due diligence defense.

[Judgment for plaintiffs.]

Securities Act of 1934. The Securities Act of 1934 was passed to regulate the day to day trading of securities sold through the national stock exchanges. The 1934 Securities Act also set up the Securities and Exchange Commission. The companies regulated are typically those with more than $3,000,000 in assets and having over 500 stockholders. The 1934 Act is also covered in more detail in Chapter 37.

Under the 1934 Act, businesses whose securities are regulated are required to register their securities and to file quarterly and annual reports with the SEC. The quarterly report is called a 10-Q report and the annual report is called a 10-K report. These reports contain financial information which must be certified by an independent public accountant. These reports are available to the public.

Most suits brought against accountants under the 1934 Act are based on Section 10(b), SEC Rule 10b(5) or Section 18 of the 1934 Act. Section 10b reads as follows:

It shall be unlawful for any person, directly or indirectly, by the use of any means or instrumentality of interstate commerce or of the mails, or of any facility of any national securities exchange ... (b) To use or employ, in connection with the purchase or sale of any security registered on a national securities exchange or any security not so registered, any manipulative or deceptive device or contrivance in contravention of such rules and regulations as the commission may prescribe as necessary or appropriate in the public interest or for the protection of investors.

Section 10b allows the SEC to make further rules and regulations as necessary. Rule 10b(5) reads as follows:

It shall be unlawful for any person, directly or indirectly, by the use of any means or instrumentality of interstate commerce, or of the mails, or of any facility of any national securities exchange: (a) to employ any device, scheme, or artifice to defraud; (b) to make any untrue statement of a material fact or to omit to state a material fact necessary in order to make the statements made, in the light of the circumstances under which they were made, not misleading; or (c) to engage in any act, practice, or course of business which operates or would operate as a fraud or deceit upon any person, in connection with the purchase or sale of any security.

Section 10b and SEC Rule 10b(5) are very broad. They apply to any false statements or omissions made by the accountant, even though the statement was not made in an application document or report filed with the SEC. These provisions are primarily concerned with fraud.

Section 18 of the 1934 Act is really a disclosure provision. It only applies to statements made in applications, reports, and documents filed with the SEC. Section 18 reads as follows:

Any person who shall make or cause to be made any statement in any application, report, or document filed ... which ... was ... false or misleading with respect to any material fact, shall be liable to any person ... who, in reliance upon such statement, shall have purchased or sold a security at a price which was affected by such statement, for damages caused by such reliance, unless the person sued shall prove that he acted in good faith and had no knowledge that such statement was false or misleading.

An accountant's liability under the 1934 Act, Section 10b, or SEC Rule 10b(5) must be based on fraudulent conduct, not mere negligence. As you will recall, under the 1933 Act, the accountant was liable if there was a false statement or omission in the registration statement even though the purchaser had not relied on such statement or omission. The accountant's only defense was "due diligence." In other words, the accountant was guilty until he or she proved a defense of due diligence. The burden of proof is on the accountant under the 1933 Act.

Under Section 10b and SEC Rule 10b(5), the accountant is not liable unless fraud is proved by the purchaser. The purchaser has the burden of proving reasonable reliance on the alleged false and material statement and a financial loss as a result of such reliance. Thus the burden is entirely on the purchaser under Section 10b and SEC Rule 10b(5). Here the accountant is innocent until proven guilty.

In the following 1976 case, the Supreme Court, in a lawsuit based on Section 10b and SEC Rule 10b(5), found negligence on the part of the *Ernst & Ernst* accounting firm, but not fraud, and therefore dismissed the case against the accountants.

ERNST & ERNST v. HOCHFELDER
425 U.S. 185 (1976)

FACTS: Leston B. Nay, president and owner of 92 percent of the stock of First Securities Company of Chicago, was involved in a fraudulent securities scheme in which Hochfelder and the other plaintiffs had invested. From 1942 to 1966, Hochfelder invested in so-called escrow accounts which supposedly carried a very high interest rate. In fact, no such accounts were listed on the books of First Securities or in the disclosure filings which First Securities sent to the SEC and the Midwest Stock Exchange. Nay was using the money for his own purposes as soon as he got it. To try to hide what he was doing, Nay had a strict rule that any incoming mail addressed to him was not to be opened by anyone else, whether or not he was there at the time. The plaintiffs argued that Ernst & Ernst had failed to use proper auditing procedures on First Securities' accounts and that if they had, they would have discovered Nay's strange rule and thus the fraud. (The fraud was not discovered until 1968, when Nay committed suicide.) The U.S. District Court said that there was no case against Ernst & Ernst for *fraud* under Rule 10b(5). The Seventh Circuit Court of Appeals reversed.

 JUSTICE POWELL:

We granted certiorari to resolve the question whether a private cause of action for damages will lie under § 10(b) and Rule 10b(5) in the absence of any allegation of "scienter"—intent to deceive, manipulate, or defraud. We conclude that it will not and therefore we reverse....

Section 10(b) makes unlawful the use or employment of "any manipulative or deceptive device or contrivance" in contravention of Commission rules. The words *manipulative* or *deceptive* used in conjunction with *device* or *contrivance* suggest strongly that § 10(b) was intended to proscribe knowing or intentional misconduct....

Although the extensive legislative history of the 1934 Act is bereft of any explicit explanation of Congress' intent, we think the relevant portions of that history support our conclusion that § 10(b) was addressed to practices that involve some element of scienter and cannot be read to impose liability for negligent conduct alone.

The most relevant exposition of the provision that was to become § 10(b) was by Thomas G. Corcoran, a spokesman for the drafters. Corcoran indicated:

> Subsection (c) 9(c) of H.R. 7852—later § 10(b) says, "Thou shalt not devise any other cunning devices...." Of course, Subsection (c) is a catch-all clause to prevent manipulative devices. I do not think there is any objection to that kind of clause. The Commission should have the authority to deal with new manipulative devices.

This brief explanation of § 10(b) by a spokesman for its drafters is significant. The section was described rightly as a "catch-all" clause to enable the Commission "to deal with new manipulative (or cunning) devices." It is difficult to believe that any lawyer, legislative draftsman, or legislator would use these words if the intent was to create liability for merely negligent acts or omissions. Neither the legislative history nor the briefs supporting Hochfelder identify any usage or authority for construing "manipulative (or cunning) devices" to include negligence....

In its *amicus curiae* brief, however, the Commission contends that nothing in the language "manipulative or deceptive device or contrivance" limits its operation to knowing or intentional practices. In support of its view, the Commission cites the overall congressional purpose in the 1933 or 1934 Acts to protect investors against false and deceptive practices that might injure them.... The argument simply ignores the use of the words *manipulative*, *device*, and *contrivance*, terms that make unmistakable a congressional intent to proscribe a type of conduct quite different from negligence. Use of the word *manipulative* is especially significant.... It connotes intentional or willful conduct designed to deceive or defraud investors by controlling or artificially affecting the price of securities....

Thus, despite the broad view of Rule 10b(5) advanced by the Commission in this case, its scope cannot exceed the power granted the Commission by Congress under § 10(b).... When a statute speaks so specifically in terms of manipulation and deception, and of implementing devices and contrivances—the commonly understood terminology of intentional wrongdoing--and when its history reflects no more expansive intent, we are quite unwilling to extend the scope of the statute to negligent conduct.

The judgment of the Court of Appeals is reversed.

Section 18 does not require the proof of fraudulent conduct on the part of the accountant before the accountant may be found liable. It simply provides that if there is a false or misleading statement made by the accountant in an application, document, or report filed with the SEC, the accountant could be found liable to a purchaser of the security involved, provided the purchaser reasonably relied on the false or misleading statement and suffered a loss due to the reliance. The accountant can escape such liability by proving a lack of knowledge that the statements were either false or misleading, and that he or she acted in good faith. What constitutes good faith? This means the accountant made a reasonable effort to be truthful and did not intentionally put in false or misleading information. On the other hand, if the accountant did not actually know that the statements were false or misleading, but had been grossly negligent—he or she clearly did not follow standard procedures and was guilty of obvious misconduct in conducting the investigation-then the court would no doubt find the accountant guilty. The accountant will not be held civilly liable for simple, honest mistakes, only for mistakes that result from gross inattention and misconduct.

There is also a statute of limitations which applies to actions filed under the provisions of the 1934 Act. The same one-year and three-year limitations that apply to actions filed under the 1933 Act apply to actions filed under the 1934 Act.

RICO. In 1970, the U.S. Congress passed the Racketeer Influenced and Corrupt Organizations Act, known as RICO. The intent of this law was to control the influence of organized crime on legitimate businesses. The act has criminal penalties and civil provisions which allow the imposition of treble damages. Under this law stockholders can bring civil suits for treble damages and even get their attorney fees paid.

Originally the act was aimed at so-called organized crime, but when Congress defined the types of crimes it applied to, they included such crimes as mail fraud and fraud in the sale of securities, which were not previously considered to be the types of crimes in which so-called organized crime was involved. At any rate, this poorly and broadly worded law has been used to bring civil law suits against certified public accountants who may have been involved with a business which has been accused, but not necessarily convicted, of a pattern of racketeering activity. Almost any fraud committed by a business may be interpreted as being a violation of this act.

The *Dancor* case actually involved a negligence/malpractice claim against the accountants involved, but it was based on their failure to detect the RICO violations against *Dancor* by one of its stockholder-employees. The case is actually decided on a statute of limitations rule, but is nevertheless a good illustration of the sort of behavior that violates RICO.

DANCOR INTERNATIONAL, LTD. v. FRIEDMAN, GOLDBERG & MINTZ
681 N.E.2d 617 (Ill. App., 1997)

FACTS: Dancor International, Ltd. takes this appeal from the dismissal of its accountant malpractice action filed against Friedman, Goldberg & Mintz. The trial court granted Friedman's motion to dismiss finding that Dancor's lawsuit had not been filed within the applicable statute of limitations period. Dancor appeals from that dismissal order and from the trial court's denial of its motion to reconsider or vacate the dismissal order.

On March 24, 1993, Dancor filed a four-count complaint. Counts I and II, which were directed at defendant Friedman, respectively alleged breach of contract and professional negligence. Both counts were premised on Friedman's alleged failure, as Dancor's certified public accountants during the period of January 1987 through August 1990, to detect warehouse fraud and embezzlement committed by Arthur Corrigan, Dancor's minority shareholder, officer, director and employee, who maintained Dancor's corporate books, and Linda McGuire, Dancor's office manager and secretary. The fraud and embezzlement allegedly occurred from 1984 through the summer of 1990; and the amounts embezzled totalled approximately $1,279,000. Dancor alleged in its complaint against Friedman that Friedman was employed to audit, monitor, and issue a report regarding all the books, checks, and records maintained in the ordinary course of Dancor's business. Dancor further alleged that Friedman failed to discover and investigate forgeries on checks drawn on Dancor's accounts; altered amounts on checks drawn on Dancor's accounts; discrepancies between payees listed in the disbursement journal and the check stubs and the actual payees and indorsers of checks; check stubs marked void but which were actually cashed; and checks written on Dancor's accounts for reimbursable business expenses but which were actually for nonreimbursable personal expenses. Dancor also alleged that Friedman failed to verify warehouse statements of inventory on hand and negligently relied upon warehouse confirmations or correspondence.

Counts III and IV were directed at defendant Pam Accounting Services, Inc. who is not a party to this appeal.

On May 25, 1993, Friedman moved to dismiss Dancor's complaint because it was not filed within the time limits of the Code of Civil Procedure, which provides that actions against persons or entities registered under the Illinois Public Accounting Act must be "commenced within two years from the time the person bringing [the] action knew or should reasonably have known of such act or omission." Friedman argued that Dancor knew or should have known of Friedman's alleged acts or omissions on October 10, 1990, the date Dancor filed its federal lawsuit against Corrigan alleging RICO violations, fraudulent misrepresentation, breach of fiduciary duty, and breach of contract. Friedman argued that since Dancor's complaint was filed on May 23, 1993, rather than by October 10, 1992, it exceeded the two-year period and thus was subject to dismissal.

Attached to Friedman's motion was a copy of Dancor's 1990 federal complaint against Corrigan. That complaint, which was 35 pages long, alleged 226 specific fraudulent acts by Corrigan including use of corporate checks for personal expenses, fictitious payees, forgeries, and altered amounts on checks. Each of those alleged fraudulent acts contained specific information as to the date of the check; the recorded amount and the altered amount, where applicable; the named payee and the actual payee; and the recorded reason for the payment and the actual reason for the payment.

In response to Friedman's motion, Dancor argued that Friedman had fraudulently concealed its accounting malpractice by failing to provide Dancor with all of Dancor's records and work papers in August 1990 after Friedman resigned as Dancor's accountants. Dancor argued that due to Friedman's concealment of Dancor's accounting records, it did not discover that it had a cause of action against Friedman until August 1991 when its new accountants, Berger, Goldstein & Company received enough documentation upon which to form their professional opinion that a viable cause of action existed against Friedman.

 JUSTICE GORDON:

In the case at bar, Dancor argues that it did not know and could not have reasonably known of Friedman's negligent conduct and malpractice until it received a professional opinion to that effect from Berger, Goldstein in August 1991. Dancor contends that in a professional malpractice action, knowledge for purposes of the discovery rule does not exist until a professional opinion is rendered as to the deviation from the standard of care. We disagree. The discovery rule has never been interpreted to delay commencement of the statute of limitations until a person acquires actual knowledge of negligent conduct. Rather, it has been interpreted to delay commencement until the person has a reasonable belief that the injury was caused by wrongful conduct thereby creating an obligation to inquire further on that issue.

[W]e reject Dancor's contention that the statute of limitations did not begin to run until its new accountants rendered a professional opinion in August 1991 that Friedman's acts and omissions deviated from the standard of care. The discovery rule became operative and the statute of limitations began to run on October 10, 1990, when Dancor had enough information to put it on notice that it was injured and that injury may have been wrongfully caused by Friedman. The facts are undisputed that on October 10, 1990, Dancor had enough information to file a 35-page federal RICO complaint against Corrigan alleging warehouse fraud and embezzlement.... As discussed above, that federal complaint contained 226 separate and specific allegations of fraudulent check transactions, allegations that contained information as to names of payees and indorsers, recorded amounts and altered amounts, recorded reasons for payments and actual reasons for payments and checks recorded as void but which were actually cashed. That same information was used by Dancor to support its allegations and charge of malpractice in the instant case. Dancor charged Friedman, a certified public accounting firm hired by

Dancor to audit and monitor its books and records, with the failure to properly audit and monitor the same records and checks having the same payees and indorsers, the same dates, the same altered or divergent amounts, and the same reasons.

Based upon those records, Dancor unquestionably had sufficient knowledge to cause it to inquire further of a possible actionable wrong by Friedman in failing to detect the falsity of the accounting entries made by Corrigan. This is especially true here where the underlying federal complaint filed by Dancor demonstrated that Dancor was aware in great detail of the embezzlement scheme and the documentation supportive of that scheme. It would make no sense to presume that the paper trail that formed the basis for Dancor's federal action and its detection of Corrigan's embezzlement scheme could not also suffice to put Dancor on notice that Friedman was negligent in failing to detect Corrigan's misconduct. While Dancor may not have had full knowledge on October 10, 1990, that, in the opinion of its expert, Friedman's acts and omissions amounted to a breach of the standard of care, it is clear that the knowledge Dancor did possess at that time was sufficient to put it on notice of Friedman's possible invasion of Dancor's legally protected rights.... At that point, Dancor was required to investigate and inquire further with its new accountants and experts, Berger, Goldstein.... Under the discovery rule provision of Section 13-214.2, Dancor had two years from October 10, 1990, to make that inquiry and to file its cause of action against Friedman before that action became time barred on October 10, 1992....

Dancor's final argument on appeal is that the court erroneously dismissed its entire claim totalling $3.5 million. Dancor contends that the statute of limitations expired only as to the damages known to exist in October 1990, namely the $1.5 million embezzled by Corrigan, and not with respect to the remaining $2 million in damages discovered after October 10, 1990, the date of filing of the federal RICO action against Corrigan. Initially, we note that Dancor has not cited any authority in support of this argument, and, as such, has waived that argument on appeal....

Here, Dancor ... alleges that it did not know of the full extent of its injuries in October 1990. However, on October 10, 1990, Dancor did know that it had suffered an injury of some magnitude and was put on notice that its injury may have been wrongfully caused by Friedman. As a result, the statute of limitations began to run as to its entire claim on October 10, 1990....

For the foregoing reasons, the judgment of the circuit court of Cook County is affirmed.

Procedural Issues. In Chapter 4 we discussed procedural issues, specifically the right of the court to compel testimony or production of documents. It was pointed out that there is a recognized privilege of confidentiality for certain professions. For example, attorneys cannot be forced to reveal matters communicated to them in confidence by their clients.

The question arose as to whether a similar privilege of confidentiality exists between the client and his or her accountant. Chief Justice Burger, speaking for the Supreme Court of the United States in the case of *U.S. v. Arthur Young & Company* in 1984, found there was no privilege of confidentiality concerning an accountant's work product.

As a consequence of this case, many clients who are concerned about the confidentiality of their records will engage an attorney to handle their specific problems. The attorney then hires an accountant to assist. Thus, the accountant's work is the attorney's work product and protected by the attorney-client privilege of confidentiality.

ACCOUNTANTS' CRIMINAL LIABILITY

We briefly introduced you to the problem of criminal liability of accountants in Chapter 5, and we will now cover this area in more detail.

Securities Acts. Section 24 of the 1933 Act makes an accountant criminally liable if the accountant willfully makes a false statement regarding a material fact or willfully omits a material fact in a registration statement. The penalty can be a fine of up to $10,000, or five years in prison, or both.

Section 32(a) of the 1934 Act makes an accountant criminally liable if the accountant willfully makes a false or misleading statement regarding a material fact in a report required to be filed under the 1934 Act such as the 10K reports. The penalty can be a fine of up to $10,000, or five years in prison, or both.

Mail Fraud Statute. This statute imposes criminal liability upon persons who either send false financial statements in the U.S. mails or conspire to send false financial statements in the U.S. mail.

In the case of the *United States v. Simon*, often referred to as the *Continental Vending* case, decided by the U.S. Second Circuit in 1969, accountants were found criminally liable. That case involved violations of Section 32(a) of the 1934 Act as well as the Mail Fraud Statute.

Foreign Corrupt Practices Act. This act was passed by the U.S. Congress in 1977 to discourage payment of bribes by U.S. corporations to foreign officials for favors in business dealings.

This act prohibits both businesses registered under the provisions of the 1934 Securities Exchange Act and U.S. businesses not so registered from offering or giving anything of value to a foreign official to obtain a new business relationship or to retain a business relationship previously established. A willful violation of the provisions of this act can result in a criminal conviction with penalties of up to $100,000 and/or five years in prison for the individual or individuals involved and fines to the corporation of up to two million dollars.

Accountants are concerned with this law because it amended Section 13(b) of the Securities Exchange Act of 1934. The law now requires businesses that are registered with and report to the SEC to keep accurate and complete records of all transactions and disposition of assets. Also, the company must maintain a system of internal accounting to check on all cash payments and see that they are specifically authorized by management. The accountant is now charged with new responsibilities, which could result in severe criminal charges, if this law is violated. The SEC is the watchdog: they will investigate and then refer the case to the Justice Department for criminal prosecution if they find a violation.

Internal Revenue Code. The Internal Revenue Code provides for criminal penalties including fines and imprisonment for accountants (tax preparers) who willfully prepare false tax returns or willfully assist a client to evade taxes.

SIGNIFICANCE OF THIS CHAPTER

Accountants' legal liability as well as the legal liability of other professionals has become a real concern in recent years due to the increased amount of litigation and the increased amounts of the various awards. Future accountants must be aware of the potential liability problems they face in their profession. They must be prepared to adhere to a high standard of care in order to avoid civil and criminal liability.

PROBLEMS FOR DISCUSSION

1. Archie Starch, a famous prizefighter, was interested in investing in an oil and gas tax shelter being arranged by Minerals Corporation. Minerals went to their accounting firm and asked them to prepare an opinion letter to reassure their client, and other investors, as to the benefits of this tax shelter. The opinion letter was prepared and delivered to Minerals. When the accountants found out that the letter was being used as a sales tool, they wrote a revised, more complex letter which was sent out under the partnership name. There were both misrepresentations of material fact and omissions of material information in this letter. After a number of persons had invested in this tax shelter, the Internal Revenue Service denied deductions taken for the investment in this tax shelter. The investors now sue the accountants alleging a violation of Rule 10b(5) of the SEC.

    Who should win this case? Why?

2. An accounting firm was employed by Ace Car Rental Company to do an audit of their records and to prepare an audit statement showing the company's net worth. The client specifically requested that the accountants not audit accounts receivable. The accountant complied with that request and made an appropriate notation on the balance sheet and also qualified their audit opinion with an appropriate notation that accounts receivable had not been audited. Ajax Industries, relying on the audit report, purchased two thirds of the stock of Ace Car Rental Co. Shortly thereafter, Ace Car Rental Co. became insolvent and had to file bankruptcy. Ajax Industries then sued the accountant alleging they misrepresented the status of the accounts receivable and they should be liable for the losses Ajax suffered.

    If you were the judge, how would you rule on this case? Why?

3. The American Group engaged the accounting firm of Greene and Beane to prepare financial statements for their firm and for one of their subsidiaries, and also to express an opinion as to the most advantageous way to merge the two firms. Relying on the opinion of the accountant, the merger was consummated in accordance with the method proposed by the accountant. The merger resulted in a multimillion-dollar loss. The loss caused the filing of Chapter 11 bankruptcy, and now the trustee in the bankruptcy reorganization files suit against the accountant, alleging that the accounting method proposed by the accountant was not the usual method used by accountants in such transactions and that the accountant was guilty of malpractice. The method proposed by the accountant was not illegal and no fraud was involved. The result produced by the method was substantially the same as the result that would have been produced by the standard or normally used method.

   Should the accountant have to reimburse the firm for its loss because they proposed a merger method which was not the standard method? Discuss the responsibility of the accountant in this situation. What constitutes negligence?

4. Arnie Accountant is a CPA in the state of Illusiana. He prepared a financial statement for his client, Heavy Equipment Rentals. Arnie knew that his client was going to give the financial statement to the Bond Insurance Co. of America for their use in processing Heavy Equipment's application for a performance bond on a construction project they had been awarded. The financial statement contained material omissions and material misstatements of fact. The insurance company relied on the financial statement and issued the bond. Then Heavy Equipment Rentals took a copy of the same financial statement to First National Bank and, based on the financial statement, the bank loaned Heavy Equipment Rentals $100,000 to purchase new equipment. Later, Heavy Equipment Rentals Co. became insolvent and could not finish the construction job and could not pay the bank the balance due on the loan. Both the insurance company and the bank sued Arnie Accountant.

   Discuss the accountant's liability to the insurance company and the bank under the Ultramares Rule, the *Restatement* rule, and the foreseeability doctrine.

5. Lawrence and Theodore Colson owned shares in Hometown Telephone Answering Service, Inc. They sold their shares to Diversified Services, Inc. They accepted promissory notes from Diversified as payment. The Colsons relied on Diversified's financial statements, certified by Arthur & Company Accountants. Before the promissory notes were paid in full, Diversified became insolvent and went bankrupt. The Colsons sued Arthur & Company alleging that they did not disclose the financial picture of Diversified, in view of the fact that they did not disclose the probability that Diversified could not collect on promissory notes due to them from another corporation. The accountants showed that they had made an investigation and that the corporation that owed payments to Diversified was solvent at the time of the audit and that its business was good. The suit was brought under Section 10b of the 1934 Act and Rule 10b(5) of the SEC.

   What is the accountant's responsibility under 10b and 10b(5)? Would *Ernst & Ernst v. Hochfelder* be a precedent to be followed in this case? Explain.

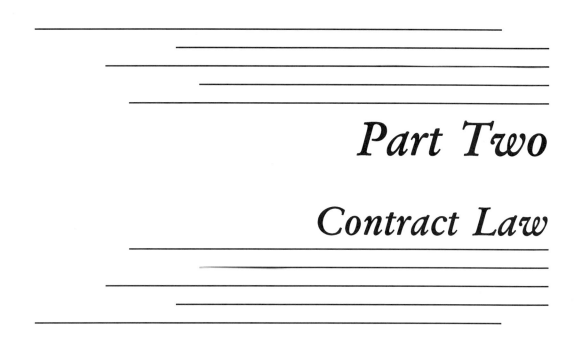

Part Two

Contract Law

Contract law affects every transaction in which an individual or a business may be involved. Every sale of goods or services to a customer is a contract. Investments made by stockholders are contracts. Purchases or rentals of land and equipment are contracts. Hiring agreements are contracts. Agreements with professional firms for advertising, accounting, and legal services are contracts. Contract law is important to you as a consumer and as a future business manager.

Contract law principles also form the basis for many other specialized bodies of law, such as sales of goods, secured transactions, and commercial paper. Although each of these other topics is covered later in this text, it is important to understand contract law principles before studying those more specific topics. Contract law is the foundation; the particular rules and exceptions for each of these specialized topics are the rooms of the house.

For these reasons, contract law is given extensive coverage in Part Two. We first give you some basic definitions and terminology and then we examine the formation of the agreement and its enforceability. We then proceed to discuss the major defenses a party may assert against liability on a contract. We also explain and discuss the situations where persons other than the two parties who made the agreement may have rights under it. We then review the various ways in which contract liability may be excused or discharged. Finally, we review the remedies available when one part breaches a contract. These seven chapters obviously cannot cover the subject in the same depth as a full year's work in law school. After studying them, however, you will have a very good overview of the major rules involved in the formation, performance, and enforcement of contracts.

Chapter 8

Contracts and Agreements

Contract law is perhaps the most basic area of civil law. Every transaction for the lease or sale of goods, land, or intangible personal property, involves principles of contract law. Contract law is the foundation upon which other areas of law are built.

For example, suppose that two persons are considering setting up a business. Whether they propose a partnership, a corporation, or any other type of organization, their venture involves principles of contract law. If employees are to be hired, any agreement between employer and employees involves contract law. The business must operate from physical premises and use machinery and equipment, and each of these necessities may be purchased or perhaps leased. Either way, principles of contract law apply.

When the organization begins transacting business, it must purchase raw materials, and those purchases involve contract law. After the raw materials are processed into products, the manufacturer's sales to wholesalers, wholesalers' subsequent sales to retailers, and retailers' sales to consumers are all controlled by principles of contract law.

Thus, we must understand the principles of contract law before we study the laws governing agency, sales, commercial paper, secured transactions, business organizations, employer-employee relations, ownership of property, and the various other areas that affect the businessperson and the daily operation of the business entity.

DEFINITION OF A CONTRACT

There are several definitions of the term **contract**. The term has been defined in various ways by legal writers in texts and treatises and by judges in court decisions. While most definitions are basically sound, the importance of the contract in our everyday existence underscores our need for a simple, uniform definition. The Uniform Commercial Code, in Section 1-201(11), defines a contract as the *"total legal obligation which results from the parties' agreement as affected by this Act and any other applicable rules of law."*

Upon reviewing this definition, we find the term *agreement* is not defined. Is an agreement always legally binding on the parties? Do all agreements create a legal obligation? Must an agreement be in writing and signed by the parties to create legal obligations? Section 1-201(3) of the UCC defines **agreement** as *"the bargain of the parties in fact as found in their language or by implication from other circumstances including course of dealing or usage of trade or course of performance as provided in this Act. Whether an agreement has legal consequences is determined by the provisions of this Act if applicable, otherwise by the law of contracts."*

The agreement is simply the bargain agreed upon by the parties. It may or may not create legal obligations against the parties, depending on the terms of the bargain and the applicable law.

For example, a promise between two friends to meet and go to the movies constitutes an agreement, since both parties agreed to meet at a certain time and place. However, the obligations created are only social and not legally enforceable.

Also, it is clear from Section 1-201(3) of the UCC that an agreement need not be in writing and signed by the parties. It can be oral, or it can even be implied from nonverbal actions of the parties. Oral contracts are fully enforceable, unless terms of the oral agreement conflict with the provisions of the Statute of Frauds. The Statute of Frauds, which requires that certain types of contracts be proved by signed writing, will be discussed in Chapter 10. As noted in Section 1-201(11) of the UCC, the contract refers to the total legal obligation that results from the agreement. The contract pertains to the legal obligations the agreement created and not the agreement itself.

BASIC REQUIREMENTS OF A VALID CONTRACT

To be fully valid and enforceable, a contract requires:

1. *That an agreement be made between the parties.* To have such an agreement, there must be an offer and an acceptance. The person making the offer is called the **offeror**, and the person to whom the offer is made is called the **offeree**. Various legal rules govern what constitutes an offer; when an offer is effective; how long an offer is effective; if an offer can be revoked and, if so, when; when an acceptance takes place; and what happens if there is a counteroffer. These rules will be discussed later in this chapter.

2. *That the agreement is supported by consideration.* For example, I promise to buy you a new car for your birthday. You gladly accept my offer. The problem is that my promise to buy you a new car on your birthday is not legally enforceable. You, the offeree, did not suffer a legal detriment; you didn't give up anything. Had I promised to give you a new car on your next birthday if you would quit smoking cigarettes, and if you accepted and did quit smoking, you

would have performed the act the offeror requested and could legally enforce my promise to buy you a new car on your birthday. Consideration will be discussed in Chapter 9.

3. *That there is legal capacity to contract.* The parties must have legal capacity to contract or the contract will be voidable by the party that lacks capacity. For example, suppose that a 16-year-old, a minor, purchases a motorcycle from a 22-year-old neighbor. The contract is legal; there was no fraud; no one took advantage of the other party. Yet under the law, the minor did not have full legal capacity to contract. The minor can change his or her mind and get his or her money back from the seller any time up until the minor reaches the age of majority and for a reasonable time thereafter. The rules concerning capacity to contract and voidability are discussed in Chapter 11.

4. *That the purpose of the contract must be legal.* A contract with a "hit man" to murder your spouse to collect the life insurance money is illegal and certainly would not be enforceable in court. However, the other three requirements were met: there was an offer and acceptance, thus an agreement; there was consideration to be paid to the hit man and benefit to be derived by the offerer; and both parties are adults. Still, all four of the requirements are necessary for a valid contract. The requirement of a legal purpose is discussed further in Chapter 12.

5. *That the agreement be in the form required by the applicable law.* A fifth requirement for a valid and enforceable contract applies only to some contracts. That is the *Statute of Frauds* requirement mentioned earlier, which states that certain agreements must be in writing to be enforceable in a court of law.

SOURCES OF CONTRACT LAW

Contract law stems from case law, the Uniform Commercial Code, and other state statutes. As noted in Chapter 1, all states have adopted the UCC except Louisiana, which has enacted only those parts of the UCC that do not conflict with its version of the Napoleonic Code.

As you study contract law, it is important to remember that the common law governs some contract transactions, and others will be governed by the Uniform Commercial Code. If the contract involves the sale of land or the sale of services, the traditional common-law rules will normally apply unless there is some specific state statutory law governing that transaction. If the transaction involves the sale of personal property, then the provisions of the Uniform Commercial Code will be applicable. Where the UCC applies, it supersedes the common-law rules. If there is no UCC rule covering a particular point, then the courts will continue to apply the general common-law rule.

The sale of land or services, in transactions not covered by any special state statutory law, normally will be covered by the general contract rules summarized by the *Restatement of Contracts*. As we noted in Chapter 1, the *Restatement* is a treatise prepared by the American Law Institute. These *Restatements* for the various areas of law are prepared in an encyclopedia-like form, giving the generally accepted rules of law on specific topics. The *Restatements* are not the actual law, only a reference to the generally applied rules.

Table 8-1

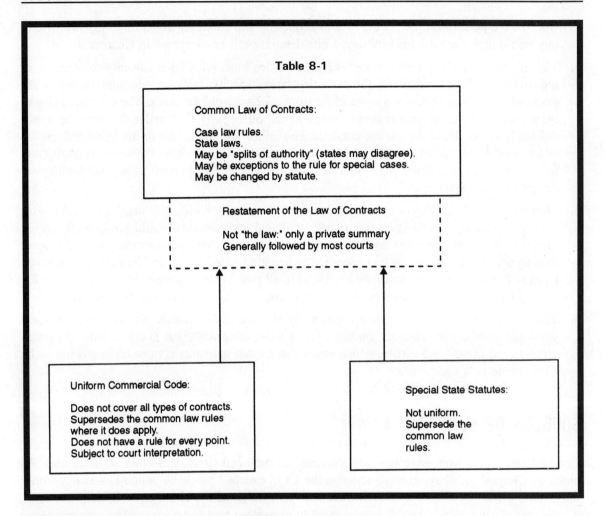

Common Law of Contracts:

Case law rules.
State laws.
May be "splits of authority" (states may disagree).
May be exceptions to the rule for special cases.
May be changed by statute.

Restatement of the Law of Contracts

Not "the law:" only a private summary
Generally followed by most courts

Uniform Commercial Code:

Does not cover all types of contracts.
Supersedes the common law rules
where it does apply.
Does not have a rule for every point.
Subject to court interpretation.

Special State Statutes:

Not uniform.
Supersede the
common law
rules.

CLASSIFICATIONS OF CONTRACTS

Contracts are classified with regard to their formation, the nature of the required acceptance, their enforceability, and the extent to which the terms of the contract have been performed. Those classifications are described by the following eleven categories.

Express Contract. An express contract is a contract, either oral or written, in which the terms of the contract are clearly and openly stated, in words.

Implied Contract. An implied contract is a contract in which the agreement between the parties was not stated orally or in writing; however, the fact that a contract was intended can be implied from the circumstances or the conduct of the parties. This type of contract is very common in everyday life. For example, suppose that you call the plumber to come fix a leaky faucet. You are at work, and you tell the plumber that the key is under the doormat. When you come home, the key is back under the doormat, the door is locked, and the faucet is repaired. You owe the plumber a reasonable fee for the repair even though you gave no oral or written promise to pay.

The fact that you called the plumber, who is in business for profit, is evidence of an implied promise to pay for services rendered.

Quasi Contract. A quasi contract is not really a contract at all, since there has been no agreement between the parties. Quasi contract is simply a remedy which the courts have developed to prevent unjust enrichment. It is an obligation implied by law rather than by the parties' conduct. In a quasi-contract situation, one party receives a benefit that had been neither ordered nor requested. Still, the law will not allow one party to be unjustly enriched at the expense of the other party. Persons cannot use a quasi contract lawsuit to recover for benefits which they voluntarily conferred on another party without that person's knowledge or consent or for benefits conferred under conditions which justify the receiving party to believe that they were a gift. Any recovery made is based solely on the extent of the unjust enrichment to the receiving party and not necessarily the loss which the plaintiff suffered.

To recover on the basis of quasi contract, the plaintiff not only must show that the defendant has been "enriched," but also that the retention of the benefit by the defendant without compensation to the plaintiff would be "unjust." This means that there must be proof that the defendant is guilty of some misconduct, or fault, or undue advantage. Money paid by mistake must nearly always be returned, since the defendant can easily do so without harm or damage. On the other hand, if someone mows your lawn by mistake while you were not at home to tell them not to do so, you have probably received a free mowing job. You don't have to pay for this "benefit," since you were in no way to blame for the other party's mistake, had no chance to prevent the mowing, and since the mowing service can't really be returned. (Try "un-mowing" a lawn sometime.)

Bilateral Contract. In a bilateral contract, one person promises to do something in exchange for a promise from another person. That person can be a human being, known in the law as a natural person, or an artificial person, such as a corporation. Generally, bilateral contracts can be oral or written. Simply stated, a bilateral contract is a promise for a promise. An example of a bilateral contract would be a situation where Phil offers to sell his car to George for $1,000. George accepts the offer. Phil has promised to sell his car to George and George has promised to buy the car for the agreed price. Thus, a promise to sell was exchanged for a promise to buy, and a bilateral contract was made.

Unilateral Contract. A unilateral contract is a contract in which a promise is made in exchange for an act or for refraining from an action. The promisor promises certain benefits if another person or persons will act in a certain way, or perhaps not to do a certain act. At any rate, there is no contract until the requested act is performed or the forbearance occurs.

A good example of a unilateral contract would be the posting of a reward for a lost dog: "I will pay $50 to anyone who will return my lost dog." No contract exists until someone shows up with the dog in response to the offer. At that point, the offeror will have to give that person the promised amount in exchange for that person's handing over the dog.

An example of a unilateral contract where the promise is made in exchange for refraining from action would be a situation where Mr. Jones had expressed an interest in bidding on a certain item at an auction. Ms. Smith was aware of this and told Mr. Jones, "I will give you $100 if you refrain from bidding on that certain item." No promise was made by Mr. Jones. When the item came up for sale, Mr. Jones refrained from bidding. He accepted the offer of Ms. Smith by *not* bidding. This example also shows the important difference between unilateral and bilateral contracts. Since Mr. Jones made no *promise* not to bid, he was thus free to do so if he wished.

Executed Contract. An executed contract is a contract wherein the obligations created by the contract have been fulfilled by the parties and nothing is left to be done. In other words, the case is closed.

Executory Contract. In an executory contract, something remains to be done. A contract can be wholly executory when there has been no performance at all yet, but each party has merely made a promise to the other. Or the contract can be partially executory when one party has performed partially or when one party has completely performed and the other has performed partially but still owes some additional performance.

Valid Contract. A contract that contains all the necessary requirements for formation and enforcement is a valid contract.

Void Contract. A void contract is not a legal contract. As the term *void* implies, the agreement which was bargained for is null and void, without legal effect. A "contract" between a person and a hit man to murder someone for insurance benefits would be an example of a void contract because the contract lacks an essential element; namely, a lawful purpose.

Voidable Contract. A contract can be classified as a voidable contract when one or both of the parties have the legal right to terminate the legal obligation. If the promisor is a minor and decides to assert that minority to avoid the contract before reaching legal age or shortly thereafter, then the contract obligation of the minor will be voided. If the party with the power to avoid liability chooses not to do so, however, the contract will be enforced.

Unenforceable Contract. An unenforceable contract is a contract which is valid in terms of its formation, but it would not be enforced in court because it does not meet some specific statutory requirement.

For example, consider an oral contract for the sale of goods over the sum of $500. Under the Statute of Frauds, such a contract must be in writing or it will not be enforced. This is not to say that oral contracts for the sale of goods over the sum of $500 are illegal or void. It simply says that in case a party to that oral contract challenges the existence of a contract, the courts will not grant a remedy unless there is a writing signed by the party against whom enforcement of the contract is sought.

Another example would be a situation where there was a valid contract which was not performed by one of the parties. However, a claim for breach of the contract might not be enforceable by the other party due to the statute of limitations. The statute of limitations requires that a lawsuit be filed within a prescribed time after the breach of contract occurs. If the party alleging a breach by the other party does not file a lawsuit in the prescribed time, the court will not enforce the contract. There are also various regulatory statutes, such as the bankruptcy act, which could affect enforceability.

FORMING A CONTRACTUAL AGREEMENT

Our basic contract formula may be stated as follows: Contract = Agreement + Consideration. That is, for promises to have legal consequences as contracts, there must be an agreement between the parties that they will have such consequences and that agreement must involve an exchange of legally sufficient considerations, or values.

This chapter examines the "Agreement" part of the formula, which may be stated as a subformula: Agreement = Offer + Acceptance. To learn whether there was a contractual agreement, we will need to know the answers to three main questions: What is an "offer?" How long is an offer open for acceptance? What is an effective acceptance?

DEFINITION OF AN OFFER

Preliminary Negotiations Distinguished from Offers. Parties may engage in extended preliminary discussions before one of them finally makes a direct business proposition to the other. Buyers typically want to compare prices and payment terms, and therefore may request such information from several prospective sellers. Sellers may have only one or a limited number of items available, but they will contact a number of prospective buyers to see whether any of them is interested. Thus, a buyer who asks, "What will you take for your car?" is only seeking price information and is not making an offer to buy. Likewise, a would-be seller who responds, "$400," is only supplying the requested information and is not making an offer to sell at that price, to this buyer, or to anyone else.

The element that distinguishes an offer from such preliminary negotiations, the thing that makes it an offer, is a promise to do business. The promise may be stated expressly, in so many words ("I'll give you $400 for your car"), or it may be implied from the language used and the surrounding facts and circumstances. This promise gives the offeree, the person to whom the offer is made, the power to change the legal relationships between the parties by accepting the offer and forming a contract. Because, typically, price quotations and advertisements do not contain such promises, they are not considered to be offers. However, stores that advertise products for sale to the public are required by state false advertising statutes and by Federal Trade Commission regulations to have "reasonable quantities" of the advertised items available for sale. They can't, in other words, rely on the general contract law rule that "advertisements are not offers" without being liable for fines under the "false advertising" laws.

Identity of Offeree. Since, as a general rule, you have no legal duty to do business with anyone unless and until a contract is made, you can as an offeror specify the person or persons to whom your offer is made. You can make the offer to as many or as few persons as you wish, on whatever basis you wish. Today, however, an offeror's power to pick and choose the persons with whom to do business is subject to some important limitations by both state and national "civil rights" acts.

Not all types of contracts, or all potential offerors, or all possible bases of "discrimination" between offerees, are covered by these acts. Each such statute must be read carefully to see exactly what forms of discrimination are prohibited. Usually it is illegal to discriminate on the basis of race, color, religion, sex, or national origin for contracts involving employment, real estate purchase or rental, or places of "public accommodation." Employment discrimination is discussed further in Chapter 41.

Communication to Offeree.
It's really no more than common sense to say that an offer has no legal effect as an offer until it has been communicated to the intended offeree or offerees. If I mail you a letter containing an offer, but then change my mind and get the letter back from the post office before it's delivered to you, no offer has been made. Even if you somehow learn what happened, there would be nothing for you to "accept." If the letter were on my desk waiting for my signature, and you or one of your agents happened to be in my office and read the letter without my having authorized you to do so, no offer would have been made to you. In other words, it's my offer, and it's not effective until I intend that it be effective.

Manner of Acceptance.
Also, since it's my offer, I determine the manner of acceptance; I tell you what you have to do to accept it. The required acceptance can be as ridiculous, as stupid, or as difficult as I choose to make it; if you want to accept, you must do so on whatever terms I specify. Of course, you are not obligated to accept my terms; you can propose your own terms or ignore the offer completely. Your counterproposal, however, does not create a contract; it is a counteroffer which has the effect of rejecting (and thus terminating) my original offer.

Where the offeror requests a return promise, that person has offered a **bilateral contract**—a promise in return for a promise. If the offeree accepts by making the requested return promise, each party is then both a **promisor** making a promise and a **promisee** receiving a promise from the other party. In order for a bilateral contract to exist, then, both parties must be bound to perform, or neither is bound. Most contracts are bilateral in form. My offer to sell you a used book is really my promise to transfer ownership of the book to you if you promise to pay me the requested contract price.

If instead the offeror requests the performance of some act, the offer is for a **unilateral contract**. A newspaper ad that states: "I offer $100 reward for the return of my lost poodle, Fifi" is offering a unilateral contract. To accept, one would have to perform the requested act—bring the lost dog back to the owner. Promising to look for the dog would not be an acceptance in this case, because that is not what the offeror requested as the price of the promise. On the other hand, since no return promise has been made, no one is obliged to look for the dog, and there is no case for breach of contract if the dog is never returned.

(Reasonably) Definite Terms Necessary.
Courts do not require that exact agreement be reached on all points for a contract to be enforceable. Obviously, the more specific and complete the terms are, the less chance there is for misunderstanding and possible lawsuit. However, the courts are aware that parties very often intend agreements but do not bother to spell out the terms completely.

At some point, however, the "terms" become so vague and indefinite that a court can only hold that there was no contract made because the parties never really agreed on anything. Confronted with an employee's claim that he had been promised "some share of the profits" of the business, a Wisconsin court had to say that there was no way for it to enforce such a "promise," since it could not know what share the parties might have had in mind.

Several of these issues are presented by the *Chang* case.

CHANG v. FIRST COLONIAL SAVINGS BANK
410 S.E. 2d 928 (VA. 1991)

FACTS: Chia T. Chang and Shin S. Chang, who resided in the Richmond area, read the following advertisement which appeared in local newspapers on November 18, 1985. The advertisement stated in part:

> You Win 2 ways
> WITH FIRST COLONIAL'S
> Savings Certificates
>
> 1 Great Gifts   2 and High Interest
>
> Savings at First Colonial is a very rewarding experience. In appreciation for your business we have Great Gifts for you to enjoy NOW—and when your investment matures you get your entire principal back PLUS GREAT INTEREST.
>
> Plan B: 3 1/2 Year Investment
> Deposit $ 14,000 and receive two
> Gifts: a Remington Shotgun and
> GE CB Radio, OR an RCA 20"
> Color-Trac TV, and $ 20,136.12
> Upon maturity in 3 1/2 years.

Relying upon this advertisement, the Changs deposited $14,000 with First Colonial Savings Bank on January 3, 1986. They received a color television that day from First Colonial and expected to receive the sum of $20,136.12 upon maturity of the deposit in three and one-half years. First Colonial also gave the Changs a certificate of deposit when they made their deposit.

When the Changs returned to liquidate the certificate of deposit upon its maturity, they were informed that the advertisement contained a typographical error and that they should have deposited $15,000 in order to receive the sum of $20,136.12 upon maturity of the certificate of deposit.

First Colonial did not inform the Changs nor were the Changs made aware that the advertisement contained an error until after the certificate of deposit had matured. First Colonial, however, did display in its lobby pamphlets which contained the correct figure when the Changs made their deposit.

The Changs instituted this proceeding in the district court seeking to recover $1,312.19, the difference between the $20,136.12 amount in the advertisement and $18,823.93, the amount that First Colonial actually paid to the Changs. The district court awarded a judgment in favor of the Changs, and First Colonial appealed that judgment to the circuit court. The circuit court held that the advertisement did not constitute an offer but was an invitation to bargain or negotiate and entered a judgment in favor of First Colonial. The Changs appeal.

⚖️ **JUSTICE HASSELL:**

The Changs argue that when members of the public reasonably rely upon a bank advertisement which offers a specific gift and dollar amount upon maturity in return for a deposit of a sum certain, and the bank fails to notify those who made deposits of an error in the advertisement until the certificate of deposit matures, then the specific term of the advertisement constitutes an offer which, when accepted, is a binding and enforceable contract. First Colonial argues, however, that the advertisement did not constitute an offer but rather was an invitation to make an offer because the advertisement was directed to the general public and required no performance on the part of the parties to whom it was directed.

The general rule followed in most states, and which we adopt, is that newspaper advertisements are not offers, but merely invitations to bargain.... However, there is a very narrow and limited exception to this rule. "[W]here the offer is clear, definite, and explicit, and leaves nothing open for negotiation, it constitutes an offer, acceptance of which will complete the contract."... [T]here can be no doubt that a positive offer may be made even by an advertisement or general notice.... The only general test which can be submitted as a guide is an inquiry whether the facts show that some performance was promised in positive terms in return for something requested.....

Applying these principles to the facts before us, we hold that the advertisement constituted an offer which was accepted when the Changs deposited their $14,000 with the Bank for a period of three and one-half years. A plain reading of the advertisement demonstrates that First Colonial's offer of the television and $20,136.12 upon maturity in three and one-half years was clear, definite, and explicit and left nothing open for negotiation.

First Colonial also argues that a contract did not exist until the Changs offered to deposit the sum of $14,000 with First Colonial and it made a counter offer which was accepted by the Changs. Pursuant to the terms of this purported counter offer, a contract was created and memorialized in the form of the certificate of deposit were not breached because such terms set forth an interest rate of 8.75 percent which the Bank used to determine that it owed the Changs $18,823.93 upon maturity of the certificate of deposit. We reject this argument because of our holding that the advertisement constituted an offer which was accepted by the Changs.

Even though the Bank's advertisement upon which the Changs relied may have contained a mistake caused by a typographical error, under the unique facts and circumstances of this case, the error does not invalidate the offer. First Colonial did not inform the Changs of this typographical error until after it had the use of the Changs' $14,000 for three and one-half years. Additionally, applying the general rule to which there are certain exceptions not applicable here, a unilateral mistake does not void an otherwise legally binding contract....

First Colonial further argues that even if the newspaper advertisement was an offer, it was a unilateral offer unsupported by consideration, and it was withdrawn before the date the Changs deposited their $14,000. We disagree.

An offer, which is usually but not always a promise, is a manifestation of a willingness to enter into a bargain.... The offer identifies the bargained for exchange ... and creates a power of acceptance in the offeree....

It is true that an offer that is not supported by consideration may be withdrawn any time before it is accepted.... However, First Colonial was required to communicate the withdrawal of the offer to the Changs before they accepted it. As we have noted, First colonial did not inform the Changs that the offer had been withdrawn or that the advertisement purportedly contained a typographical error until the Bank had used their $14,000 for three and one-half years.

We also reject First Colonial's argument that the advertisement did not create a contract because there was no meeting of the minds..... "The offeror has a right to prescribe in his offer any conditions as to time, place, quantity, mode of acceptance, or other matters, which it may please him to insert in and make a part thereof, and the acceptance to conclude the agreement must in every respect meet and correspond with the offer, neither falling within or going beyond the terms proposed, but exactly meeting them at all points and closing with these just as they stand."... When the Changs tendered their $14,000 to First Colonial for three and one-half years, they complied with all of the conditions in First Colonial's offer. Hence, there was a meeting of the minds and an enforceable contract.

Accordingly, we will reverse the judgment of the circuit court and enter final judgment here in favor of the Changs for $1,312.19 plus interest.

UCC Special Rules for Goods. The UCC (Sections 2-204, 2-305, 2-306) has liberalized this requirement to some extent for sales of goods contracts, by permitting the parties to use "requirements" or "output" as quantity terms and to leave the price term open, that is, unspecified. Even here, however, there are limits. There must be a real promise, not just an illusory one, such as, "I promise to buy as much as I want to buy." To be enforceable, the promise must be definite enough to restrict the promisor's freedom of action if the offer is accepted.

Intent to Contract. In most cases where the parties have exchanged promises, there probably has been a real "meeting of the minds;" that is, each party intended a promise in the same way that it was understood by the other. Such a mutual understanding obviously forms the contractual agreement.

There are cases, however, where one of the parties claims that no contract was ever formed because he or she did not "intend" that the promise be taken seriously—that it have contractual effect. In such cases, a court will not require the other party to prove an actual meeting of the minds; it is enough if the trier of fact is convinced that a reasonable person would have believed that the promise was seriously intended. What counts, in other words, is not what the promisor really intended but the impression that those words and actions created in the mind of the other party. If the "joke" was convincing enough to fool a reasonable person and if the other party was not aware of the joke when accepting the offer, there is a contract.

Whether there was a "meeting of the minds" is at issue in the *Higgins* case.

HIGGINS v. OIL, CHEMICAL, AND ATOMIC WORKERS
811 S.W.2d 875 (TN, 1991)

FACTS: Six former employees of Nuclear Fuel Services Company (NFS) sued their union, the Oil, Chemical and Atomic Workers International Union; Local #3-677 (the OCAW). The discharged workers alleged in their complaint that based on an agreement with the OCAW, they were entitled to receive weekly compensation from the union in an amount equal to their lost wages, plus insurance coverage for themselves and their families "until [they] were allowed or could return to work" at NFS. They further alleged that the union had breached this contract by discontinuing weekly payments while they were still unemployed.

There is no doubt that there was considerable confusion among the members who attended the March 30, 1986, meeting. At one point, someone in the back of the hall shouted that they "didn't hear the proposal back here." In response, Mr. Tolley (the Chair) attempted to restate the original motion, but he did so in an obviously oversimplified fashion saying, "The proposal was that we raise dues enough to take care of these people." There was no explanation about how long this might take, although there were additional assurances given that arbitration would be sought and that the international union would supply "the best representation ... the best lawyers that we can get" for the seven discharged members.

The OCAW denied that there was ever an enforceable contract between the union and the discharged workers, although the union concededly has made weekly payments to the plaintiffs for some twenty-two months, in an amount totalling over $300,000. The disputed question, therefore, is whether and under what circumstances the OCAW was entitled to terminate these payments.

The chancellor held that there was a valid contract between the parties. The chancellor also found that the union had breached the contract and ordered the union to resume payments to the discharged workers under terms outlined below. On appeal from the trial court, the Court of Appeals likewise concluded that there was an enforceable contract, but it expanded the terms of the judgment against the union. The OCAW appealed the decision of the Court of Appeals.

 JUSTICE DAUGHTREY:

The requirements for a valid contract are well-settled:

> While a contract may be either expressed or implied, or written or oral, it must result from a meeting of the minds of the parties in mutual assent to the terms, must be based upon a sufficient consideration, free from fraud or undue influence, not against public policy and sufficiently definite to be enforced....

The facts of this case, plainly and simply, fail to establish mutual assent. Hence, no contract between the parties ever arose.

The record establishes that the only thing on which both sides agreed was that the seven discharged workers would be "taken care of" through the payment of an amount equal to their wages and insurance premiums. The duration of payment was not specified. The plaintiffs testified that, based on the discussion at the secret meeting on March 16, they understood that the union was obligated to pay them until they were rehired, however long that took. Nevertheless, the plaintiffs admitted at trial that they knew that the assurances presented to them at the secret meeting were contingent upon a later vote by the union membership to increase dues. Hence, no contract arose as a result of the secret meeting on March 16, because under federal law the negotiating team was not authorized to bind the union membership to an increase in dues, and the plaintiffs concede that they knew this fact....

Taking all the circumstances into account, we conclude that the plaintiffs have failed to establish the degree of mutual assent necessary to give rise to a valid contract. Indeed, the facts of this case raise a legitimate question as to whether the parties intended legal consequences at all. It follows that payments made as a result of the union's commitment to support the discharged workers, based on the action of the membership on March 30, were merely a gratuity, and that no liability arose from the termination of those payments in February 1988....

Even if mutuality could be inferred from the separate events of March 16 and March 30, 1986, the resulting contract would not be enforceable.

It is undisputed that the union membership committed itself to "take care of" the discharged employees and that it did so for almost two years at considerable expense to the individual members. However, not every statement of intent of the kind made by the union in this case will rise to the level of an enforceable agreement....

It is fundamental that for a contract to be enforceable, it must be of sufficient explicitness so that a court can perceive what are the respective obligations of the parties. Applying this principle to the present case, we are convinced that ... the alleged oral contract was too indefinite to be enforced even if it fulfilled the other conditions of a valid contract.... [A]ny agreement which leaves unanswered such critical questions [as this one does] cannot by any reasonable stretch of the imagination be said to represent a real "meeting of the minds...."

In this case, the record shows that the parties intended that the plaintiffs would be "taken care of" through payments funded by a union check-off. But assuming the existence of a valid consideration for this benefit, there is no way for us to determine the essential details of that commitment. How long, for example, were the payments to continue? Were they to increase as the wages of the regular workers increased? When and under what circumstances might they be terminated?....

But even if we were to find the existence of a valid contract and impose our notion of reasonable duration on the union's obligation to perform, rather than strike down the agreement as too indefinite to be enforced, we could not uphold the decision of the Court of Appeals. Obligating the union membership to make payments until the last plaintiff reaches age 62, a period that might stretch over decades, is clearly not reasonable under the circumstances.

We hold that neither the assurances made by union officers to the plaintiffs at the secret meeting on March 16, nor the official action taken by the membership at the union meeting on March 30, gave rise to an enforceable contract between the plaintiffs and the defendant union. We therefore reverse the judgment entered by the Court of Appeals and by the trial court, enter judgment in favor of the defendant and dismiss the action with prejudice. Costs will be taxed equally.

DURATION AND TERMINATION OF OFFERS

Lapse of Time. Even though no specific termination date or length of time during which the offer will remain open is stated, the offer will not be open for acceptance forever. In such cases, the offer will terminate at the expiration of a "reasonable time." What constitutes a reasonable time depends on the facts of the particular case, and litigations will result because one party claims to have accepted in time and the other party claims that the acceptance was too late because a reasonable time had already elapsed. Where an offer is made during a person-to-person conversation, be it face-to-face or over the telephone, and nothing is stated about its being open for some period of time, the presumption is that the offer terminates when the conversation ends.

Where an offer states that it will terminate on a specific date, as in "This offer will end August 14, 1993," the day named is the last day on which an acceptance can occur. Unless facts and circumstances indicate otherwise, an acceptance which took legal effect any time on that date would form a contract. Where an offer was made by a retail store with regular business hours, it would normally have to be accepted during business hours, by the date specified in the offer. Actual communication of the acceptance to the retail store, within the specified time period, would also usually be necessary.

Where an offer sent by letter indicates that it will be open for a period of time, as in "This offer is good for thirty days," the time period normally begins to run as of the date of the writing, even though the letter is not received through the mails for several days. But if the offer says that the offeree has a certain period of time within which "to consider" or "to accept" it, the time period does not commence until the letter is delivered.

Revocability of Offers. In most cases, even though the offeror has stated that the offer will remain open for a period of time, the offeror has both the power and the right to revoke it if such a revocation takes legal effect prior to an acceptance. Since these so-called **continuing offers** are not supported by any value given by the offeree to the offeror, the offeror is not bound by his or her promise to keep the offer open. Usually, therefore, to be sure of having the promised thirty days to investigate and consider the offer, an offeree must "buy" the thirty days by forming a preliminary **option contract** with the offeror. An offeror who has received the agreed consideration in exchange for his or her "thirty-day" promise is no longer free to revoke the offer without being liable for breach of the option contract. (Note that there is still no contract on the main offer; the offeree may decide, after thinking about the main offer for the thirty days, that he or she does not wish to do business after all.)

For offers to buy or sell goods, the UCC (2-205) contains a new rule on revocability. If such an offer is made by a **merchant**, is in a signed writing, and by its terms gives assurance that it will remain open for some period of time, it is not revocable because of the lack of consideration principle explained above. The merchant is bound to keep the **firm offer** open for the time period stated, or for a reasonable time, if the offer gives such assurance but does not state a specific cutoff date; but in no case is the merchant bound for more than three months.

Implied Revocation. If an offer is revocable, it may be revoked expressly or impliedly. **Implied revocation** occurs when the court feels that underlying facts and circumstances have changed to such an extent that the agreement contemplated by the parties can no longer be made. The death or insanity of either the offeror or the offeree, for instance, impliedly revokes any outstanding offers, because one of the intended parties no longer has the capacity to contract. Likewise, the destruction of the intended subject matter of the contract operates to terminate any unaccepted offers for its purchase or sale. In a situation where a seller-offeror sells an item already offered to Buyer 1, to Buyer 2, the offeror's first offer to Buyer 1 is not terminated unless and until Buyer 1 learns of the second sale. If, in the meantime, Buyer 1 has effectively accepted the offer, the seller is bound to two contracts for the same item and will be guilty of breaching one of the contracts unless one of the buyers will accept a substitute.

Express Revocation. With an **express revocation**, the offeror's intent is usually clear enough: "I revoke;" "The deal's off;" "My offer is hereby cancelled." The main problem in these cases is not whether the offeror meant to revoke but whether the offeror's revocation took legal effect before the offeree's acceptance. If a revocation takes legal effect before the intended acceptance, there is no contract, and the would-be acceptance is only a counteroffer. If an acceptance takes legal effect first, there is a contract, and the revocation is inoperative.

Communication of Revocation. Where the parties are dealing face-to-face or over the telephone, the jury or judge must determine, as a matter of fact, which party spoke the "magic words" first. Where the parties are communicating by letter or telegram, there is an additional complexity in the case because communications may cross each other in transit—a revocation and an acceptance may be in the mail at the same time. Many such problems are solved by applying two presumptions that courts have worked out as to when communications take legal effect: generally, a revocation is not effective until it is received, while an acceptance letter takes legal effect as soon as it is mailed. In general, a letter is received when the post office finishes handling it; that is, when the letter is delivered at the place a party has designated for receipt of such communications. If you have a mailbox on your front porch and you have left a letter of acceptance of my offer in the mailbox for the mail carrier to pick up, the jury will then have to decide whether the mail carrier dropped my letter of revocation in the mailbox first and then took out your letter of acceptance, or vice versa. In the first case, there is no contract; in the second case, there is a contract.

The UCC establishes a special rule for communications to an organization for all types of contracts that it covers, such as sales of goods, secured transactions, commercial paper, and investment securities. "Organization" includes businesses, such as partnerships and corporations, and also trusts, decedents' estates, and governmental agencies. Such organizations do not receive a notice or notification until it comes to the attention of the person who is conducting the transaction, or within the time when it would have come to that person's attention if the organization had a proper procedure for handling incoming communications. If you were negotiating a UCC contract with a large automobile company, for example, your notice would not be received when the post office delivered a sack of mail to the company. Your notice would be received when it actually reached the desk of the individual you were dealing with or when it should have reached that person if the company had a proper mail handling system. This may not sound like a big difference, but it could be important. If that company executive mailed a letter accepting your offer to sell steel before your revocation letter got to the sender's desk, a contract would exist. Under prior law, and even now for non-UCC contracts, your letter of revocation would be presumed effective when received by the company, and your offer would terminate at that point.

Revocation of Offer of Unilateral Contract. There is one other conceptually difficult problem regarding revocations. This problem arises where the offeror has offered a unilateral contract. Suppose an offeree, intending to accept, has started to perform the requested act and is then notified by the offeror that the offer is revoked. There is no acceptance unless and until the offeree completes the performance requested, but shouldn't the offeree, in all fairness, be given the chance to finish? Courts disagree here; there are at least three rules. Some states, following the old common law, permit the offer to be withdrawn anytime prior to complete performance of the requested act, on the basis that every offeree should know that this can happen in a unilateral contract situation. Other courts use a rule that says an offeree's commencement of performance makes the offer irrevocable for a reasonable period of time, which gives the offeree a chance to finish the performance. If the offeree does render complete performance as requested, then the offeror must perform as promised. A few states go one step further and say that where an offeree has made substantial preparations to perform, the offeree must be given a chance to do so.

Rejection or Counteroffer. A rejection by the offeree indicates that the offeree does not wish to do business at all. A counteroffer indicates that the offeree is willing to contract, but on terms different from those stated in the original offer. Either of these responses by an offeree operates to terminate the original offer; each of them takes legal effect when it is received by the offeror. A counteroffer gives the original offeror the power to form a contract on the basis of the new terms, by accepting the counteroffer. If the offeree inquires about the possibility of alternative terms but does not indicate an unwillingness to accept the terms offered, such an inquiry is not considered a rejection.

The *Olefins* case illustrates one kind of "different terms" problem.

OLEFINS TRADING, INC. v. HAN YANG CHEMICAL CORP.
9 F.3d 282 (3rd Cir. 1993)

FACTS: Olefins is a Connecticut corporation engaged in the trading and marketing of bulk chemicals and chemical products. Han Yang Corp. is a South Korean Corporation and is engaged in the manufacture of petrochemical products. Han Yang maintains an office in New Jersey for the purpose of "sourcing" chemicals for use in its petrochemical business.

On March 13, 1991, Y.I. Han of Olefins and Shin Lee of Han Yang exchanged written confirmation letters outlining the terms of an oral contract formed by the parties on that date. Under the terms of the oral contract, Han Yang promised to purchase 4,500 metric tons ("mt") of bulk ethylene (+5% at Olefins' option) from Olefins at a price of $915/mt. Olefins promised to deliver the ethylene one month later to Han Yang's manufacturing facility in Yeosu, South Korea. Both parties agreed that payment was to be made via a letter of credit in the amount of $4,117,500. Although contested at trial, the jury found that Han Yang had promised to open this letter of credit by March 15, 1991. In addition, both parties agreed that Olefins' chemical supplier, Repsol Petroleum, would produce the ethylene and would ship it directly from Tarragona, Spain to Yeosu, South Korea.

On March 14, 1991, Olefins entered into a supply contract with Repsol for the purchase and sale of 4,500mt of ethylene in order to satisfy its obligation to Han Yang. Olefins promised to pay Repsol $890/mt for the ethylene. That same day, Olefins nominated the ship *Teviot* as the cargo vessel that would transport the ethylene from Spain to South Korea. At trial, both Olefins and Han Yang stipulated that the *Teviot* could carry exactly 4,600mt of ethylene.

Shortly after the contract was formed, however, the international market price of ethylene began to drop dramatically. By early April of 1991, the market price of ethylene was set at approximately $600/mt on a CIF basis ("cost, insurance, and freight") to South Korea, almost $300/mt less than the international market price two weeks earlier. As of April 2, 1991, Han Yang still had not opened a letter of credit as originally agreed.

On April 4, 1991, both parties orally agreed to reduce the quantity of ethylene from 4,500mt (+5%) to 4,200mt (maximum) and to discount the price from $915/mt to $900/mt. Olefins asserts that both parties also orally agreed that Han Yang would issue Olefins a "commercial credit" in the amount of $238,125 by April 5, 1991; this sum was to be paid to Olefins in the next Olefins-Han Yang transaction. Han Yang vehemently denied having assented to this latter term.

After the parties' oral negotiations concluded, Han Yang sent Olefins a revised purchase confirmation recounting the terms of the modified ethylene contract. The confirmation contained the new quantity and discounted price for the modified ethylene contract, but it did not mention the commercial credit. Olefins responded by insisting that Han Yang concede the commercial credit in the amount of $238,125 "as per agreed on the phone." Han Yang did not respond.

On April 8, 1991, Olefins sent Han Yang a letter demanding that Han Yang open a letter of credit immediately "along with a letter confirming commercial settlement of [Olefins'] estimated losses equaling U.S. $238,125." Again, Han Yang did not accede to the commercial credit term, but on April 9, 1991, Han Yang opened a letter of credit in the modified contract amount of $3,780,000 (4,200mt x $900/mt) naming Olefins as the beneficiary.

On April 19, 1991, Olefins extended an offer to Han Yang for another shipment of bulk ethylene to Yeosu, South Korea. Ostensibly, this offer was made by Olefins to enable it to recover the commercial credit from the April 4, 1991 transaction. Han Yang rejected this offer.

On April 23, 1991, the *Teviot* was loaded with 4,170mt of ethylene, bound for South Korea. Olefins asserted that Han Yang caused it to suffer actual losses under the modified contract in the amount of $195,245.55. The jury found for Olefins, but the trial judge entered a judgment for Han Yang.

 CIRCUIT JUDGE MANSMANN:

The question of whether the parties have mutually assented to a term is peculiarly a question of fact and properly placed with the fact-finder.... In returning a verdict in favor of Olefins, the jury specifically found that Han Yang had expressly agreed to issue the commercial credit to Olefins. Our task is not to disturb that finding;

rather, we must enforce the verdict unless it is not supported by the evidence in the record or is otherwise contrary to the law.

Han Yang argues that the jury verdict is contrary to the law because UCC § 2-207 prevents the commercial credit term from becoming a part of the Olefins-Han Yang contract. We disagree. We hold—consistent with the jury verdict—that because the commercial credit term was specifically agreed upon over the telephone before the parties exchanged confirmatory memoranda, UCC § 2-207 may not be utilized to exclude that term from the contract.

Section 2-207 of the UCC is designed to prescribe by law, what non-negotiated terms are to be considered a part of a contract—not to exclude those terms specifically negotiated and agreed upon. One of the main purposes of UCC § 2-207 is to facilitate oral contracts that are usually negotiated over the telephone and only later reduced to a writing. In particular, UCC § 2-207 is designed to serve as a way of dealing with conflicting or additional terms that were never a part of the bargaining process.... In other words, terms governed by UCC § 2-207 are those terms that were never expressly agreed upon; rather, they appear only later as nonnegotiated terms in confirmatory memoranda or other types of business forms purporting to "confirm" what was previously discussed orally....

This is not the situation before us. Here, Olefins and Han Yang expressly agreed to the commercial credit term. It is that agreement which must control....

Having concluded that the jury's verdict was not contrary to the law, we must now consider whether it was supported by sufficient evidence in the record. Pursuant to Rule 50(a)(1) of the Federal Rules of Civil Procedure, the court may grant a renewed motion for judgment as a matter of law if "there is no legally sufficient evidentiary basis for a reasonable jury to have found for the prevailing party...." The "legally sufficient evidentiary basis" has also been characterized as a 'minimum quantum of evidence....'' Accordingly, if there is minimally sufficient evidence to support the jury's finding that the commercial credit was an orally agreed upon term, than the court erred in granting Han Yang's Rule 50(b) motion.

At trial, Y.I. Han of Olefins testified that during the telephone conversation of April 4, 1991, Han Yang's president expressly agreed to issue a commercial credit to Olefins....

We find further support that there was an oral agreement on the commercial credit term in the testimony of Han Yang's president, Shin Lee. On cross examination, Mr. Lee was questioned abut certain notations he made on a telefax message that he had received from Olefins earlier that day....

On the basis of this testimony and the telefax messages from Olefins and Han Yang, we conclude that there is sufficient evidence in the record to provide the "legally sufficient evidentiary basis" necessary to sustain the jury's verdict.... Consequently, we find that the district court erred by granting Han Yang's renewed motion for judgment as a matter of law....

We will vacate the order of the district court granting Han Yang's renewed motion for judgment as a matter of law. We will instruct the district court to consider Han Yang's motion for a new trial to the extent that allegations of misconduct and the erroneous introduction of evidence are asserted.

REQUIREMENTS FOR AN EFFECTIVE ACCEPTANCE

When Effective. Like all other person-to-person communications, words of acceptance spoken during a conversation and heard at almost the same instant take legal effect immediately. As we have seen, most litigations arise where the parties have been negotiating by correspondence and their communications have crossed in transit.

As a convenient method of solving some of these problems, the courts have created the "mailbox rule," which states that a letter of acceptance is effective when it is *mailed*. This has the effect of placing the risk of lost, delayed, or misdelivered communications on the offeror. The rule holds that there is a contract at the instant the letter is placed in the mailbox, even though the letter is delivered late or not delivered at all.

Exceptions to the Mailbox Rule. There are several situations where a response intended as an acceptance is not effective when it is sent but only if and when it is received. Perhaps the most obvious of these is the situation where the letter does not give the offeror's correct address or does not have sufficient postage to be delivered through regular postal procedures. Here the risk of misdelivery should be borne by the offeree and the letter is an effective acceptance only when it is delivered (if it is delivered at all).

Section 40 of the *Restatement (Second) of Contracts* also indicates that there is no mailbox presumption in effect where the offeree first sends a rejection communication and then tries to accept. The second communication is only a counteroffer unless it overtakes the earlier rejection and is received by the offeror before the rejection is received.

A third exception occurs when an offer specifies that the offeror must receive the offeree's acceptance communication before the acceptance is effective. The mailbox rule is only a presumption; it applies unless the offeror says otherwise. For example, "We must have your acceptance in our main office by the close of business next Friday."

Fourth, there may be no mailbox rule where the offeree responds by using a communication means different from the means of communication that the offeror used for the offer. Generally, if the offeror did not specify the use of a particular means of communication, the offeree may use a different, but still reasonable means of communicating an acceptance, and have the acceptance effective when sent (e.g., offer by letter, acceptance-response by telegram). However, if the offeree uses another means of communication which the court feels is "unreasonable" and therefore not "intended" by the offeror, the acceptance is effective only if and when it is delivered (e.g., offer by letter, acceptance-response by carrier pigeon). Finally, if the offeror has specified *the one means* by which the acceptance must be communicated, a response by any other means is not an acceptance, but only a counteroffer.

Nature of an Effective Acceptance. Three main problems arise regarding the nature of an effective acceptance. First, what happens when an offeree responds by saying that the offeree wants to do business but adds, deletes, or modifies one or more of the terms of the offer? Second, what happens when a seller-offeree responds to an order for goods by shipping "nonconforming" (different) goods? And third, when, if ever, does silence by an offeree constitute an effective acceptance?

Offeree Changes Terms. At common law, to be an effective acceptance, a response-communication must agree exactly with the terms of the offer; courts often say it must be a "mirror image" of the offer. This mirror image rule does not mean that the acceptance must literally restate all the terms of the offer, just that it must agree with all of them. Given the right set of facts, a response as simple as "O.K." could be interpreted as an acceptance. What the rule does mean is that a response that changes one or more terms is most likely a counteroffer rather than an acceptance, so that no contract is formed when the response is sent. If, for example, an employer writes you a letter offering you a job starting June 1 and you reply, "I accept, but I can't start until June 20," at that point, you do not have a job. You have simply made a counteroffer.

As applied by the courts, this rule meant that there was no contract on the buyer's terms in the very frequently occurring situation where the buyer-offeror sends the seller an order for goods and the seller responds with an acknowledgment/invoice form which contains additional or different terms. If the seller ships the goods and the buyer receives and uses them, there is a contract on the seller's terms. The buyer's use is an acceptance of the seller's counteroffer. If the buyer refused to accept the goods on those terms (e.g., "There are no warranties, express or implied"), there is no contract and the seller will have to absorb the shipping charges. Dissatisfaction with these results led to a specific UCC provision, 2-207, to deal with this problem in the sale of goods situation.

UCC 2-207 first says that a response from the seller which indicates that the seller wants to do business is an acceptance, not a counteroffer, even though it contains terms "additional to or different from" those in the offer. The only way for the offeree (seller) to avoid this result is to make the acceptance *expressly* "conditional on assent to the additional or different terms"—in other words, to clearly make it a counteroffer.

Having thus created a contract for the sale of goods, the Code then proceeds to answer this question: on whose terms? The general rule states: "The additional terms are to be construed as proposals for addition to the contract." In other words, they are *not* part of the contract unless they are specifically agreed to by the offeror; otherwise, there is a contract on the terms of the original offer. Where *both* parties are "merchants," the additional terms become part of the contract unless: (a) the original offer said otherwise, or (b) they materially alter the original offer, or (c) the offeror objects to their inclusion within a reasonable time after the offeror has notice of them. Where the offeree-merchant has included such terms and the offeror-merchant has said nothing specific about their inclusion, the litigation will focus on whether or not the new terms "materially alter" the original offer. The *Filanto* case deals with this problem.

FILANTO S.P.A. v. CHILEWICH INTERN. CORP.
789 F.Supp. 1229 (S.D., NY, 1992)

FACTS: Chilewich International Corp. ("Chilewich") is a New York-based import-export company. In 1989, Chilewich contracted to sell footwear to Raznoexport, then a Soviet Government entity. This contract (the "Russian Contract") specified that all disputes would be resolved by arbitration before the Moscow Chamber of Commerce and Industry. To fulfill its obligations under the Russian Contract,

Chilewich contracted with Filanto, the largest Italian manufacturer of shoes and boots. There is some dispute as to the content and time of formation of that contract. Chilewich contends that a March 13, 1990, letter it sent to Filanto contains the essential terms of the contract. This letter provided that the Russian Contract was "incorporated ... as far as practicable," and specifically indicated that any arbitration should be in accordance with that contract. Filanto contends that it never accepted these terms, and that a contract was formed only by conduct at a later date. Under applicable principles of international law, Filanto contends, such a contract would not include any arbitration provisions.

In January 1991, Chilewich refused to accept 90,000 boots, causing Filanto to incur a substantial loss. Filanto filed a breach of contract suit in the District Court for the Southern District of New York. Chilewich International Corp. moved to stay the action pending arbitration in Moscow. Filanto has moved to enjoin arbitration or to order arbitration in this federal district in New York.

 CHIEF JUDGE BRIEANT:

This Court concludes that the question of whether these parties agreed to arbitrate their disputes is governed by the Arbitration Convention and its implementing legislation. That Convention, as a treaty, is the supreme law of the land, U.S. Const. Art. VI cl. 2, and controls *any* case in any American court falling within its sphere of application. Thus, any dispute involving international commercial arbitration which meets the Convention's jurisdictional requirements, whether brought in state or federal court, must be resolved with reference to that instrument....

Accordingly, the Court will apply federal law to the issue of whether an "agreement in writing" to arbitrate disputes exists between these parties....

Courts interpreting this "agreement in writing" requirement have generally started their analysis with the plain language of the Convention, which requires "an arbitral clause in a contract or an arbitration agreement, signed by the parties or contained in an exchange of letters or telegrams," Article 1(1), and have then applied that language in light of federal law, which consists of generally accepted principles of contract law, including the Uniform Commercial Code....

While Filanto apparently agrees that the March 13 Memorandum Agreement was indeed an offer, it characterizes its August 7 return of the signed Memorandum Agreement with the covering letter as a counteroffer. While defendant contends that under Uniform Commercial Code § 2-207 this action would be viewed as an acceptance with a proposal for a material modification, the Uniform Commercial Code, as previously noted, does not apply to this case because the State Department undertook to fix something that was not broken by helping to create the Sale of Goods Convention which varies from the Uniform Commercial Code in many significant ways. Instead, under this analysis, Article 19(1) of the Sale of Goods Convention would apply. That section, as the Commentary to the Sale of Goods Convention notes, reverses the rule of Uniform Commercial Code § 2-207, and reverts to the common-law rule that "A reply to an offer which purports to be an acceptance but contains additions, limitations, or other modifications is a rejection of the offer and constitutes a counter-offer...." Although the Convention, like the Uniform Commercial Code, does state that nonmaterial terms do become part of the contract unless objected to, Sale of Goods Convention Article 19(2), the Convention treats inclusion (or deletion) of an arbitration provision as "material...." The

August 7 letter, therefore, was a counteroffer which, according to Filanto, Chilewich accepted by its letter dated September 27, 1990. Though that letter refers to and acknowledges the "contractual obligations" between the parties, it is doubtful whether it can be characterized as an acceptance.

More generally, both parties seem to have lost sight of the narrow scope of the inquiry required by the Arbitration Convention.... All that this Court need do is to determine if a sufficient "agreement in writing" to arbitrate disputes exists between these parties.... Although that inquiry is informed by the provisions of the Sale of Goods Convention, the Court lacks the authority on this motion to resolve all outstanding issues between the parties. Indeed, contracts and the arbitration clauses included therein are considered to be "severable," a rule that the Sale of Goods Convention itself adopts with respect to avoidance of contracts generally.... There is therefore authority for the proposition that issues relating to existence of the contract as opposed to the existence of the arbitration clause, are issues for the arbitrators:

> "The district court reasoned that an arbitrator can derive his or her power only from a contract, so that when there is a challenge to the existence of the contract itself, the court must first decide whether there is a valid contract between the parties. Although this appears logical, it goes beyond the requirements of the statute...."

However, there are often limits to how many angels can dance on the head of a pin—even when the performance is choreographed by the distinguished courts just cited.

There seems, for example, to be some confusion in the Ninth Circuit.... There are numerous cases in the Second Circuit where the court has—out of necessity—adjudicated relevant contract issues on motions to stay or compel arbitration....

Since the issue of whether and how a contract between these parties was formed is obviously related to the issue of whether Chilewich breached any contractual obligations, the Court will direct its analysis to whether there was objective conduct evidencing an intent to be bound with respect to the arbitration provision....

The Court is satisfied on this record that there was indeed an agreement to arbitrate between these parties.

Seller Ships Nonconforming Goods. Exactly the same sort of problem, with exactly the same results under the common-law rules, is presented by the seller who responds to an order by shipping goods which do not conform to the terms of the order. Buyers were frequently placed in a situation where they either had to accept the nonconforming goods and make whatever use they could of them, paying for any modifications out of their own pocket, or send the nonconforming goods back and sustain "shut-down-the-plant" losses. (Buyer orders blue widgets; seller ships green. If buyer uses green, buyer has accepted seller's counteroffer and there is a contract for *green*.)

The UCC also has a specific provision, 2-206(1)(b), to deal with this sale of goods problem. The new Code rule states that even a shipment of nonconforming goods by the seller, in response to an order, is to be interpreted as an acceptance rather than a counteroffer. (Under the Code, in the example above, there is a contract for *blue* widgets and the seller has breached this contract and is liable for damages unless the seller sends blue widgets to the buyer within the time permitted by the contract.) The buyer is protected; whether the buyer uses nonconforming goods or rejects them and buys elsewhere, the buyer can still collect whatever damages are sustained.

Silence as Acceptance. Since, normally, an offeree has no duty to respond to an offer, the offeree's failure to respond cannot be given any particular legal significance. The offeree's silence is therefore not effective as an acceptance in most cases. The common law did, however, recognize four exceptions to this general rule.

First, where an offeree has the opportunity to reject offered services but instead takes the benefit of them, the offeree's silence does imply an acceptance. By permitting the offeror to perform services which a reasonable person should have known were not being offered for nothing, the offeree has impliedly agreed to pay a fair market price for them.

Second, where the offeror has told the offeree that he or she can accept the offer by not saying or doing anything, just by remaining silent, and the offeree *actually* does intend his or her silence to have that effect, it does.

Third, where because of previous dealings, such as a standing order with a book or record club, the offeree has indicated to the offeror that nonnotification by the offeree means that the standing order should be continued, the offeree's silence has the effect of continuing the standing order.

Finally, where nonordered merchandise is sent to the offeree and the offeree exercises "dominion" over it, this dominion has the effect of an acceptance and an implied promise to pay the offered contract price. An example would be reading an unordered book or magazine, or giving it to someone else.

The second and fourth rules have now been substantially changed because nearly all states have **unordered goods statutes**. These laws vary; the strongest ones make such unsolicited goods an absolute, out-and-out gift to the recipient, who has no obligation to return them, to pay for them, or to account for them in any way.

SIGNIFICANCE OF THIS CHAPTER

Whenever a claim for breach of contract is asserted, the other party may argue that no agreement was ever reached and thus there was no duty to perform. As we have seen, this "no agreement" argument may be made as to the entire alleged contract or only as to particular terms. When this argument is presented, the claimant must prove that an offer had been made and that it was accepted while still open for acceptance. Failure to prove any of these points means that there was no contract and, therefore, no breach and no liability.

Typically, actual cases will involve other defense arguments along with "no agreement." For discussion purposes in the remaining contracts chapters, we will assume that an agreement did exist.

The next chapter will discuss the second part of our contract formula: the requirement that the parties' agreement provides for an exchange of values or that it involves one of the recognized alternate bases for enforcement.

PROBLEMS FOR DISCUSSION

1. Compo, Inc., mailed out an advertising circular to a large number of businesses. The circular was mailed in August and was headlined "Christmas comes early at Compo." It described a list of premiums that could be selected, based on the size of an order. Deal 25E gave the customer a new LeCount convertible and fifty Dazzo cameras for only $1,000 extra with an order of $500,000 or more. The Piggie Bank ordered over $500,000 worth of computers and software and indicated that it wanted Deal 25E. Compo telephoned Piggie and told them that their order was refused. Piggie bought their computers elsewhere and now sues Compo for damages.

   What is the result, and why?

2. James Kapenis went to an open house of the plaintiffs, David and Penny Gildea. At that time Mr. Kapenis met the Gildeas' realtor, Susan Murphy. Later that evening, Mr. Kapenis met with Mrs. Murphy to discuss making a bid on the Gildea home. A purchase offer was prepared by Mrs. Murphy which contained a clause stating that the contract was "subject to buyer obtaining suitable financing interest rate no greater than 12½ percent." Mr. Kapenis signed the purchase agreement and was subsequently orally advised that the Gildeas had accepted the purchase agreement. Mr. Kapenis, Mrs. Murphy, and Mike Borschuk of Century 21 Marketplace then began a search for financing.

   Mrs. Murphy informed Mr. Kapenis about various loan programs, but because the monthly payments were too high, Mr. Kapenis stated they were unsuitable. Mike Borschuk then informed Mr. Kapenis of a loan program for a 15-year term at 12½ percent interest. Mr. Kapenis stated that the monthly payments would be too high and not assumable and that such terms were unsatisfactory. Mr. Kapenis then informed the Gildeas that he could not find suitable financing and that he was withdrawing his offer. The Gildeas subsequently filed a lawsuit, seeking specific performance of the contract.

   How should the court rule? Discuss.

3. Plaintiff was formerly a patrolman with the Nebraska State Patrol. He filed an action for overtime pay. The claim was denied. He then appealed to the district court for Lancaster County, Nebraska, and the court also denied his claim. He states he was hired on the basis of a 50-hour week and paid a stated monthly salary. Plaintiff states he worked many hours overtime and if he determined his hourly rate by dividing his monthly salary on the basis of fifty hours per week then he is entitled to $2,142.53 in overtime pay. He states that he is entitled to overtime under the theory of implied contract. He appeals.

   How should the court decide?

4. Marc Pevar asked several manufacturers for price quotes on the medium density overlay plywood which his company needed. Evans made the lowest quote, in a telephone conversation on October 12, 1995. Pevar claims that it called Evans back on October 14 and ordered the plywood. Evans admits getting the call, but denies that it accepted that order. Pevar later sent Evans a written purchase order for the plywood. This written order specified the price, quantity, and shipping instructions, but did not mention warranties or remedies for breach. On October 19, Evans sent Pevar a written acknowledgment of the order. Evans's form said that the contract was expressly conditional on Pevar's agreement to all its terms, including a disclaimer of most warranties and a limitation of remedies. Evans shipped the plywood, which was accepted and paid for by Pevar. Pevar later brought suit for breach of warranty; Evans claimed its acknowledgment form controlled the terms of the contract. Both parties moved for summary judgment.

   Who wins, and why?

5. On April 6, the defendant published the following advertisement in a Minneapolis newspaper: "SATURDAY 9 A.M. SHARP. 3 BRAND NEW FUR COATS. Worth to $100.00. First Come, First Served. $1 EACH."

   On April 13, the defendant published a similar advertisement: "SATURDAY 9 A.M. 2 BRAND NEW PASTEL MINK 3-SKIN SCARFS. Selling for $89.50. Out they go Saturday. Each ... $1.00, 1 BLACK LAPIN STOLE, Beautiful, Worth $139.50 ... $1.00. First Come, First Served."

   On each Saturday the plaintiff was the first to present himself at the appropriate counter in the defendant's store. On the first Saturday, he demanded the advertised coat, and on the second Saturday, he demanded the advertised stole. On both occasions, he indicated his readiness to pay the sales price of $1, and on both occasions, the defendant refused to sell the merchandise to the plaintiff, stating at the time of the plaintiff's first visit that by a "house rule" the offer was intended for women only and sales would not be made to men, and at the time of the second visit that the plaintiff knew the defendant's house rules. The defendant appealed the trial court's award of $138.50 damages.

   How should the appeals court rule? Explain.

6. On February 27, 1997, Rudy Turilli, owner of the Jesse James Museum at Stanton, Missouri, appeared on Joe Pyne's late-evening TV "talk show." Rudy discussed his theory that Jesse James (the famous train and bank robber) had not really been shot in the back and killed by Robert Ford in 1882 but had lived into the 1950s and had actually stayed with Rudy at his museum. During the course of the discussion, Rudy said he believed his theory so strongly that he "would pay $10,000 to anyone, yourself, Mr. Pyne, Mr. Gruber, the audience, and the network audience, to anyone who could prove me wrong."

   Stella James (Jesse's daughter-in-law) and her two daughters claimed the $10,000 on the basis of several affidavits, from persons in and acquainted with the James family, stating facts which tended to prove that Jesse was killed in 1882. Rudy refused to pay, and Stella James and her two daughters brought suit to collect the reward. Rudy appealed the judgment for the plaintiffs.

   Will Stella James collect the $10,000? Why or why not?

Chapter 9

Consideration and Unconscionability

This chapter is concerned with the second part of our contract "formula"—the requirement of "consideration." Once again, we need to know the answers to three main questions: What does the law mean by consideration? What are the basic methods of complying with this requirement? What do the courts accept as legally sufficient consideration?

We will use Uncle Ned and his nephew Johnny to provide some factually simple hypothetical examples of how the consideration rules work.

DEFINITION OF THE CONSIDERATION REQUIREMENT

Basic Definitions. In our legal system, a promise is generally not enforceable as a contract, even if it is agreed to by the promisee, unless the promise is supported by legally sufficient consideration. In other words, a completely one-sided promise of benefits (a promise of "something for nothing") does not generally bind the promisor to performance or make the promisor liable in the event of nonperformance. If Uncle Ned promises to give Johnny $5,000 as a Christmas present and then changes his mind, Johnny cannot sue and collect the $5,000, even if the promise was written and signed or was made in front of witnesses. The consideration requirement, most simply stated, means that unless *something* is given in return for the promise, the promise is not legally enforceable.

Source and Recipient of Consideration. The required consideration may be supplied by the promisee or by a third person. Uncle Ned would be contractually obligated if he had promised Johnny the $5,000 in return for a house-painting job and Johnny saw to it that the job was done, whether or not Johnny did the work. When Uncle Ned gets his house painted according to the terms of the agreement, he owes Johnny the $5,000.

Likewise, the benefits given in return for the promise may be given to the promisor or to a third person. If Uncle Ned promised the $5,000 to Johnny, if Johnny would paint H.O. Moaner's house, he is bound to pay the money if Johnny does the job. Even if no one receives anything that most people would think of as a "benefit," there is legally sufficient consideration if the promisee has assumed a *burden*, by doing something which he or she was not already legally bound to do. If Uncle Ned promises the $5,000 to Johnny, if Johnny stops smoking until age 21, and Johnny does so, Uncle Ned is legally obligated to pay the money. In each of these last two examples, Uncle Ned has received a *legal* benefit, in the sense that he got the performance he bargained for as the price for his promise, and he has therefore received consideration.

COMPLIANCE WITH THE CONSIDERATION REQUIREMENT

There are four ways in which the consideration requirement may be satisfied, so that the promisor is legally bound to perform his or her promise: (1) a bargained-for exchange of values, (2) a change of legal position by the promisee in reliance on the promise, (3) the seal, or (4) a statutory exception to the requirement. In each of the last three cases, the promise is enforced even though there was no exchange or bargain in the usual sense.

Bargained-for Exchange of Values. The basic meaning of the consideration requirement is that there must be a "bargain" for there to be a contract; promises to make gifts, with nothing given in return, are not legally enforceable. The usual method of complying with the consideration requirement, therefore, is to prove the existence of a bargain, to prove that something was given or promised in return. Since the law generally does not concern itself with whether the bargain was a good one or a bad one, but only with the question of whether there was in fact a bargain, the promisee should be able to enforce the promise by showing that there was an agreement for any sort of exchange of benefits. Note that Mr. Pitts did provide "benefits," but was unable to show any agreement for an exchange of benefits.

PITTS v. McGRAW-EDISON COMPANY
329 F.2d 412 (U.S. Sixth Circuit, 1964)

FACTS: Plaintiff was a manufacturer's representative in Memphis, Tennessee, for a period of many years prior to July 1, 1955. For approximately twenty-five years preceding that date, he sold the products of the defendant, McGraw-Edison Company, on a commission basis in an assigned territory comprising several southern states. In his capacity as a manufacturer's representative, he was an independent businessman, hiring and firing his own employees, paying his own expenses and overhead, and managing his business as he saw fit. He had no written contract with the defendant, and the defendant had no obligation to him except to compensate him on a commission basis for sales made in the assigned territory. It was terminable at will, without notice, by either party at any time. The plaintiff was free to handle any other products he desired, including those of competitors of the defendant, and he did so until early in 1954, when on his own volition and without any requirement by the defendant, he discontinued his representation of other manufacturers.

In April 1955, when the plaintiff was approximately 67 years of age, he accompanied O. Dee Harrison, the sales manager for the defendant, to Little Rock, Arkansas, for a meeting with one Paul Thurman, who had formerly worked for the plaintiff but at the time was working in the State of Arkansas as a factory representative for the defendant and others. At that meeting, Mr. Harrison told the plaintiff that the defendant was making arrangements for the plaintiff to retire at a time shortly thereafter and for Thurman to take over the plaintiff's territory, with the plaintiff receiving an overwrite commission of 1 percent from the defendant on all sales made in the territory. Thereafter the plaintiff received a letter dated July 1, 1955, from O. Dee Harrison reading in part as follows:

> Dear Lou:
>
> Whether you know it or not, you are on retirement effective July 1st. But to make the matter of retirement a little less distasteful, we are going ahead as you and I talked last time we were together by paying each month 1 percent of the ... sales from the Mississippi and Tennessee states. You will get your check each month just as you have been in the habit of getting our check on commissions. Let us hope that there is enough to help keep a few pork chops on the table and a few biscuits in the oven.
>
> We are going to keep you on the list for bulletins, Lou, so that you will know what is going on. I know that you will help Paul in every way that you can, and I know that your help will be greatly appreciated by Paul.

A letter dated July 20 also said:

> We will keep you on the mailing list and any time you can throw a little weight our way we will appreciate any effort you make, Lou. And any time you have any questions, don't be afraid to ask us about them.

The plaintiff received a check from the defendant each month regularly from July 1955 through June 1960 covering the 1 percent commission on sales in the specified territory.

On July 23, 1960, the defendant sent a letter reading in part as follows:

> Dear Mr. Pitts:
>
> I am enclosing our check #50064752 for $238.51 which, according to our records, completes the five-year series of payments to be paid after your retirement from the Company.

Pitts sued for $15,000 damages. Following a trial to the court without a jury, the District Judge held that the plaintiff was not entitled to recover any amount whatever and dismissed his complaint.

CIRCUIT JUDGE MILLER:

Plaintiff contends that the negotiations between the Company and him leading to his retirement were in substance an offer on the part of the Company that if he would retire as a manufacturer's representative on July 1, 1955, and turn over to his successor representative all of his customer account records containing valuable information on active and inactive accounts, which had been built up over a period of twenty years or more, the Company would pay him monthly thereafter a 1 percent overwrite commission on sales by the defendant in the territory which was at that time allotted to him; that after considering the offer, he accepted it and thereafter carried it out by retiring as a manufacturer's representative and turning over to his successor the stipulated records; and that the defendant breached the contract by refusing to make the payments after July 1, 1960.

In considering these contentions, it must be kept in mind that the plaintiff was an independent businessman, not an employee of the defendant. His relationship with the defendant could be terminated by either party at any time without notice and without liability therefor. The plaintiff in his testimony concedes this, and it was so found as a fact by the District Judge. Unless the plaintiff is able to establish a valid contract obligating the defendant to pay the "retirement" benefits claimed, he has no cause of action.

Assuming, without so holding, that there was a promise by the defendant to pay the plaintiff the retirement benefits claimed, we are faced with the question of what consideration passed from the plaintiff to the defendant to make this promise enforceable.

Plaintiff vigorously argues that although he did not *promise* to do anything or to refrain from doing anything, as plainly appears from the two letters, and so conceded by him, consideration nevertheless exists because of the action taken by him at the request of the defendant, namely, his retirement as a manufacturer's representative, including other manufacturers as well as the defendant, and his turning over to the defendant his personal records, pertaining to customers and sales over a period of years in the past. There would be merit in this contention if it was supported by the facts....

However, these factual contentions of the plaintiff were disputed by the evidence of the defendant. The District Judge made findings of fact that the plaintiff was not required by the terms of the letters, or by any other statements on the part of the defendant, or its agents, to do anything whatsoever; that upon his retirement of July 1, 1955, the plaintiff was free to handle the products of any other manufacturer or competitor if he so desired, to seek other employment, or to do as he pleased; that nothing in the arrangement circumscribed the plaintiff's actions or rights in any manner; and that the plaintiff was not obligated to perform any duties on behalf of the defendant. These findings are fully supported by the evidence. In fact, they were substantially conceded by the plaintiff in the cross-examination of him as a witness in which he apparently contended that he did certain things for the defendant after his retirement although he was not required to do so.

On the basis of these facts, the District Judge ruled that the payments to the plaintiff over the period of July 1, 1955, to July 1, 1960, were without consideration, were the result of voluntary action on the part of the defendant, and were mere gratuities terminable by the defendant at will.

The court also rejected Pitts's claim under promissory estoppel since "the plaintiff in no way altered his position for the worse by reason of defendant's letters of July 1 and July 20, 1955." The District Judge found as a fact that the plaintiff gave up nothing to which he was legally entitled and was restricted in no way in his activities thereafter. "Plaintiff gave up nothing in accepting retirement that he would not have lost if he had refused to accept it."

[Judgment for defendant affirmed.]

In most cases, the existence or nonexistence of a bargain can be seen pretty clearly, but the facts are somewhat ambiguous in a few situations. One of the most difficult distinctions to draw is that between a condition attached to the promise of a gift (no contract) and a burden undertaken as part of a bargain (contract).

Suppose that Uncle Ned says to Johnny, "Come over to the house Saturday night, and I'll fix you a steak dinner." Is Uncle Ned contractually obligated to provide a steak dinner when Johnny arrives as requested? No, he's not—for two reasons. First, Uncle Ned's promise is not intended by him, or reasonably understood by Johnny, as a contractual arrangement. Second, "coming over to the house" is neither intended nor understood as the price of the steak dinner.

What about the case where Uncle Ned tells Johnny, "When you get married, I'll give you $5,000," and Johnny does in fact get married? Whether Johnny's marriage supplies consideration for Uncle Ned's promise depends on the parties' intent, as derived by the court from the surrounding facts and circumstances. If Johnny already had his wedding planned and the date set and Uncle Ned was just making a promise of a cash wedding gift, there is probably no consideration for the promise and thus no contract. But if Uncle Ned is trying to induce Johnny away from life as a "swinging single," the initiative for the marriage comes from Uncle Ned rather than Johnny, and Johnny in response to the promise does as his uncle requests and gets married, Uncle Ned is contractually bound to pay the money.

Change of Position in Reliance. Most courts today accept the rule stated in Section 90 of the *Restatement (Second) of the Law of Contracts*: "A promise which the promisor should reasonably expect to induce action or forbearance of a definite and substantial character on the part of the promisee or a third person, and which does induce such action or forbearance is binding if injustice can be avoided only by enforcement of the promise." In other words, where the promisee, reasonably relying on the promise of benefits, makes a substantial change in his or her legal position, a court will estop (prevent) the promisor from using the "no consideration" argument when he or she is sued on the promise. The courts usually refer to this concept as *promissory estoppel*.

If, when Uncle Ned makes his promise of a $5,000 gift, Johnny goes out and buys a new car, which he would not have bought except for his reliance on the promise, Uncle Ned is probably estopped from asserting a no consideration defense when Johnny sues him for the money. The *Jordan* case is a real-life example of this rule in action.

JORDAN v. MOUNT SINAI HOSPITAL OF GREATER MIAMI, INC.
276 So. 2d 102 (Fla. App., 1973)

FACTS: This appeal arose from an action upon subscriptions to a charity. The trial judge found that there was adequate consideration to support the execution of the pledge agreements by Harry M. Burt, deceased. Thereupon final judgment was entered in favor of appellee and against appellants in the sum of $80,000.00,

Harry M. Burt, died November 18, 1969. The appellee filed in the probate court its claim against his estate alleging a balance of $40,000.00 due on each of two pledges. The appellants filed timely objection and the action below ensured. The trial court ruled in favor of the charity and appeal followed.

> On February 23, 1968 and May 15, 1968, the decedent, Harry M. Burt, signed and delivered to appellee two pledges of $50,000.00 each. Contemporaneous with and subsequent thereto, payments totalling $20,000.00 were made which were applied equally to each pledge. At the time of the subscriber's death, $80,000.00 remained to be paid.

> The subscription agreements were in part in the following form: "MOUNT SINAI HOSPITAL DEVELOPMENT FUND."

> "In consideration of and to induce the subscriptions of others, I (we) promise to pay to Mount Sinai Hospital of Greater Miami, Inc., or order the sum of Fifty Thousand and no/100 dollars; $5,000.00 payable herewith: Balance in nine equal annual installments commencing on _____.

> "Signature

> "Date"

 JUDGE CREWS:

The primary question is whether the consideration stated in the subscription is legally sufficient to make binding the promise of the subscriber so as to be enforceable by the promisee. The briefs of able counsel failed to cite a Florida case in point, and our independent research has not disclosed one. It is not a question, however, that has not been answered by other authorities.

A few jurisdictions have found and approved as consideration the mutual promise of subscribers. But as stated in 83 C.J.S. Subscriptions @ 5, subparagraph (3), there is definitely a conflict of authority on this point....

The connecting thread in most of these cases is that the agreement which was sought to be enforced (a voluntary promise on the part of the payor), either imposed upon the promisee some obligation which it assumed, or the requested performance of some service on the strength of the promise. When those conditions were met, there was sufficient legal consideration to uphold enforcement of the promise; for if money is promised to be paid upon the condition that the promisee will do some act or perform certain services, then the latter may, upon performance, compel payment.

While the rule is frequently stated without exception, a factual exception or additional circumstance seems to be apparent in the majority of those cases; that circumstance being one of actual reliance upon the subscription by the charitable institution....

A goodly number of jurisdictions and certain learned text writers, notably Williston and Corbin, are of the opinion that mutual promises to subscribe lack sufficient consideration to allow enforcement of charitable pledges....

"It is doubtless possible for two or more persons to make mutual promises that each will give a specified amount to a charity or other object, but in the case of ordinary charitable subscription, the promise of each subscriber is made directly to the charity, or its trustees, and it is frequently made without any reference to the subscription of others. If induced at all by previous or expected subscriptions, this inducement only affects the motive of the subscriber; it cannot be said that the previous subscriptions were given in exchange for the later one. Indeed the earlier subscriptions would be open to the objection of being past consideration so far as a later subscription was concerned."...

Additionally, it has been held that labor and expenses in obtaining other subscribers do not constitute a consideration to support a promise of charitable contribution ... and subscriptions which are conditioned upon all subscriptions for a like purpose aggregating a certain amount of money by a certain date are deemed to lack legal consideration to make them enforceable....

A majority of courts which have enforced charitable subscriptions do so on the theory of a unilateral-bilateral contract, or by applying the doctrine of promissory estoppel....

In such states neither a request in a unilateral contract nor a return promise in a bilateral contract need be expressed, because implication will suffice....

For the doctrine of promissory estoppel to be applicable, the promisor must make a promise which he should reasonably expect to induce action or forbearance of a substantial character on the part of the promisee, and where injustice could only be avoided by the enforcement of the promise.... [T]he charity must perform acts or incur expenses in reliance upon the strength of the pledge....

It is the general rule that a promise not supported by a consideration is nudum pactum and unenforceable. This rule, in its most liberal sense, is applicable to charitable subscriptions. Where there is no consideration for the promise, the strength of the promise rests solely on the will of the person making it.

It is also a respected proposition of law that an estate will be liable on the charitable subscription of a decedent. The death of a subscriber will only work a revocation of the subscription where the decedent himself might have revoked the promise at the time of death or any period prior thereto. A survey of the many jurisdictions indicates that as a matter of public policy courts will sustain subscriptions for a public object or purpose if any consideration can be found, and the courts have been willing and anxious to discover such a consideration to uphold them....

The pledges state only that they are made "in consideration of and to induce the subscriptions of others."

We view this statement as a mere gratuitous promise to a future gift lacking consideration and hence, unenforceable as a nudum pactum. We would still adhere to this proposition even if there had been evidence, which there was not, that the decedent's pledges were used to induce others to subscribe.

We are not unmindful that two or more persons may contract in an undertaking on behalf of a charitable institution so as to bind themselves to the beneficiary, but such an issue must await a determination upon facts not present in th[is] case....

The pledge cards made no specific reference as to the purpose of the gift except to indicate that it was to the "Development Fund." Appellee did not claim or assert below that the subscriber gave to some specific project or cause which was thereafter instituted in total or partial reliance on the promise of future contributions. Hence, there is no predicate upon which this court could adopt the unilateral-bilateral doctrine, to enforce a charitable pledge even if it were so inclined.

Neither can the appellee find solace in the doctrine of promissory estoppel. The record is devoid of any evidence that the promisee was induced in reliance upon decedent's promise to take any substantial action, or to forego any material right, so that an injustice could only be avoided by applying this equitable doctrine....

Courts should act with restraint in respect to the public policy arguments endeavoring to sustain a mere charitable subscription. To ascribe consideration where there is none, or to adopt any other theory which affords charities a different legal rationale than other entities, is to approve fiction.

The wisdom of such a policy, its possible detriment as well as its benefit to public bodies, may be the subject of legislative inquiry and decision.

In the interim, educational, religious, fraternal or other charitable institutions will have to depend upon the goodwill reposing in the heart of an educated, religious, fraternal or charitable disposed donor for payment of a gratuitous promise....

For the reasons stated the judgment is reversed, and the cause is remanded to the circuit court with direction to enter an order dismissing the complaint.

The Seal. As an alternative method of holding persons to promises made and accepted, the common law said that if the promise was made in writing and "sealed," there was a conclusive presumption that consideration had been given in return. Promisors, in other words, were not able to make the no consideration argument against their signed and sealed written promises. The use of the word *seal* or the initials "L.S." before or after the promisor's signature was sufficient.

Only a few states follow this rule today. In about half of the states, a seal on the signed writing supplies a rebuttal presumption of consideration, meaning that the promisor still has a chance to prove that no consideration was given for the promise. Similarly, in many states, the presence of a corporate seal on a document creates a rebuttable presumption that the document was executed by someone who had authority to act for the corporation.

In about half of the states, the presence of a seal on a signed, written document creates no presumption at all as to consideration: the promisee must prove consideration by one of the other methods. This last, "no-effect-at-all" rule is adopted by the UCC (2-203) for the sale of goods, so that many states now have two rules on the seal—one for goods and one for other contracts. The problem of the seal is further complicated by the fact that many states allow a longer "statute of limitations" period in which to bring suit where the contract is "sealed."

Statutory Exceptions to the Consideration Requirement. A respectable body of legal opinion holds that the consideration requirement has caused more problems than it has prevented, and that people should be bound to perform whatever they promised to perform, at least where the promise was made in a signed writing, whether or not the person gets anything in return. These same ideas may have been the rationale for the common-law rule on the seal; they find their modern expression in various statutes which provide that certain promises are enforceable even though no consideration was given in return. One such provision is the "firm offer" rule discussed in Chapter 8: if a merchant's signed, written offer to buy or sell goods says that the offer will remain open for acceptance, it is not revocable by the merchant even though the merchant has received no consideration for the promise to keep the offer open. Similarly, the Model Business Corporation Act, Section 17, provides that an offer to subscribe to shares of stock is not revocable for a period of six months unless otherwise agreed.

The UCC contains two other "no-consideration-required" sections that have very broad potential application (and are thus very important). UCC 1-107 permits a party to a contract to waive any claim the party may have for an alleged breach of the contract by means of a signed writing. No special form is required, and no consideration need be received by the person giving up the contract claim. Since this section is in Article 1 of the Code, it applies to all of the types of contracts covered in any other section of the Code.

UCC 2-209(1) applies only to contracts for the sale of goods, but it is also a very significant exception to the consideration requirement. It provides that any agreement modifying a preexisting contract for the sale of goods needs no consideration to be binding. Suppose that you contract to buy a new car but decide after you've driven it for two days that you'd like rear-seat stereo speakers for the radio. You call up the dealer and talk to your salesman, and the salesman promises to install the speakers for no additional charge if you bring the car in next Monday. If the jury believes your testimony that such a modification of the original car contract was agreed to, the dealer is now contractually bound to install the speakers. Without 2-209(1), the dealer would not be bound, since the dealer received no new consideration for the speakers. (Remember that this Code rule applies only to goods contracts. If you want to modify other types of contracts, such as those for land or services, there must be consideration moving both ways.)

In addition to these Code provisions, special statutory provisions applying the no-consideration-required rule to other types of contracts have been adopted by some states. The following statute, adopted by Michigan in 1941, is an example: "Agreements to Modify or Discharge Contracts, Section 1. An agreement hereafter made to change or modify, or to discharge in whole or in part, any contract, obligation, or lease, or any mortgage or other security interest in personal or real property, shall not be invalid because of the absence of consideration: Provided, that the agreement changing, modifying, or discharging such contract, obligation, lease, mortgage or security interest shall not be valid or binding unless it shall be in writing and signed by the party against whom it is sought to enforce the change, modification, or discharge."

COURTS' DEFINITIONS OF LEGALLY SUFFICIENT CONSIDERATION

Legal Sufficiency versus Adequacy. As noted previously, the courts do not generally concern themselves with whether the parties have made a "good deal" or a "bad deal;" they will enforce stupid and unreasonable contracts as well as wise and reasonable ones. To be legally sufficient, a consideration need not be "adequate," in the sense of being a reasonable estimate of a jury's idea of fair market value. Unless there are unusual circumstances, such as fraud, duress, or undue influence, it is enough that something of value was received in return as the price of the promise, even though that "something" does not seem very desirable to the judge or jury. Freedom of contract means that you have the power to make your own bargains and that you are generally bound by the bargains you make once you have agreed to them.

Courts continue to state these general rules, and yet they seem more and more willing to "remake" contracts so as to arrive at "fair" results. For one thing, the *gross* inadequacy of the consideration received by one party is *some* evidence to support that party's claim to have been defrauded or subjected to duress or undue influence. Also, where a court finds such gross inadequacy it will generally refuse to exercise its equity powers to order specific performance of the unfair contract, since "He who seeks equity must do equity." A court may even refuse to award money damages in such a case, by using the newly popular concept of "unconscionability," which means that the contract is so terribly unfair that it should not be enforced as written. For the purpose of calculating amounts due under the U.S. estate and gift taxes, the Internal Revenue Code requires examination of alleged "contracts" to make sure that each party has received "an adequate [and full] consideration in money or money's worth." For example, if Uncle Ned promises Johnny $50,000 for painting a picket fence, there may technically be a contract, but the IRS will view the transaction as a gift by Uncle Ned of the difference between $50,000 and the fair market value of the painting job.

As noted in Chapter 8, moreover, the courts do require that the promise given in return be definite enough to impose some restrictions on that party's freedom of action. An illusory promise to buy as many parts as one wants to order, imposes no real obligation to do any business at all. It seems as if a promise is being made, but there is no real commitment. An illusory promise thus does not supply consideration for a promise made in return. There is no contract in this situation, and neither party is bound to any performance. Because the buyer does not provide consideration to the seller, he would not be bound to sell them any parts at the stated price, even if they had ordered some. Their order would be an offer to buy, which the seller is absolutely free to reject if he wishes, since there was no contract originally.

The following paragraphs discuss some of the other "returns" which the courts do *not* generally accept as supplying a legally sufficient consideration.

Nominal Consideration. *Nominal* means "in name only" or "very small." "Nominal consideration" usually refers to the recital of $1 as consideration. There is nothing inherently wrong with $1 or any other very small amount as consideration for a return promise, if that amount is *in fact* intended and agreed to as the price of the bargain. Most courts, however, do not accept the mere recital of a fictitious dollar bill as legally sufficient consideration.

Good Consideration. As it appears in most legal forms ("and other good and valuable consideration"), *good* seems to be used as a synonym for *valuable* (and thus legally sufficient) consideration. However, that is not the meaning given to the term by most authoritative legal texts; they generally define *good consideration* in terms of a promise to be a "good relative," and thus *not* legally sufficient. "Nice family feelings" do not provide a legally sufficient consideration. When Johnny promises to be a "good nephew" (kind, loyal, loving, etc.) in return for Uncle Ned's promise of $5,000, there is no consideration for Uncle Ned's promise, and Uncle Ned is not contractually bound to pay the money.

Past Consideration. A promise of benefits is not changed from a gift into a contract by the fact that the promisee has given something to the promisor in a previous, separate transaction. Such so-called past consideration is no consideration for the new promise of benefits. It is this rule that requires that a modification of a preexisting contract must be supported by a new exchange of considerations in order to be enforceable, except for UCC 2-209(1). Likewise, this rule generally prevents a "good Samaritan" from enforcing a promise to repay the good Samaritan for benefits previously conferred on the promisor as a gift. Since no contract was entered into or intended at the time the benefits were originally provided, those benefits—a completed gift—constitute past consideration.

Moral Consideration. Generally, the courts treat the existence of a moral obligation in the same way that they treat past consideration. The fact that a person is morally obligated to provide certain benefits does not supply consideration for that person's promise to provide them. By most standards the person who received aid and comfort from the good Samaritan would be morally obligated to repay the good Samaritan when able to do so, but the courts do not regard this moral obligation as a legally sufficient consideration.

There are three situations where the courts *will* generally enforce a promise on the basis of some idea of moral obligation. Two of them are closely related—new promises to pay a debt barred by a discharge in bankruptcy or the running of the statute of limitations. In each of these cases the debtor has received the values the debtor contracted for but has not paid for them; in each case the debtor has a technical defense which would prevent a successful lawsuit to collect the debt. Nevertheless, when the debtor makes a new promise to pay the debt in either of these cases, most courts will hold the debtor to the new promise, even though the debtor has received no *new* consideration, on the theory that "a person ought to pay his or her debts." In most states, one or both of these new promises must be made in a signed writing to be enforceable.

The third situation relates to promises made to charitable organizations. These are almost uniformly enforceable, though the courts do not always agree on why they are. Some courts imply mutual promises between and among the donors not to revoke their pledges to the charity. Where the charity has "moved in reliance on the promises," the doctrine of promissory estoppel can be applied. An example would be hiring an architect to design a new building, or taking an option on land. Even without applying either of these ideas, some courts apparently enforce promises to charitable organizations on the basis of some underlying "moral obligation" to support good works.

Preexisting Duty. A promise to do or the actual doing of something which one is already bound to do anyway does not supply consideration for a return promise. Thus, when a landowner promises an extra bonus to a builder if the builder will get a job done on time, in accordance with the terms of the original contract, the builder cannot collect this promised bonus even if the builder does get the job done on time. The builder was already legally obligated to do so and has promised nothing new in return for the bonus. Similarly, police officers usually cannot collect rewards offered for the capture of criminals when they make the arrest in their own jurisdiction, in the line of their official duties. The following case presents the application of this rule in a slightly different factual context.

MUNDELL v. STELLMON
825 P.2d 510 (Ida.App., 1992)

FACTS: This action for declaratory judgment was brought by Eva Mundell, surviving spouse of Orie Mundell, to determine the ownership of 450 beehives which Orie had given to his son, James, prior to Orie's death. Eva claims that Orie's transfers of the beehives to James were unauthorized gifts of the Mundells' community property, and thus invalid transfers. James claims the beehives were not gifts, but were validly transferred to him as part of his compensation for working in the Mundells' beekeeping business. After a hearing, the district court determined that James had received the beehives as compensation for his labor in the Mundells' business, and thus, although the beehives had been community property, they were effectively transferred to James in consideration for his work which benefited the community business. Eva appeals this decision.

Orie and Eva Mundell owned and operated a beekeeping business consisting of approximately one thousand beehives and the equipment to service those hives. During the years 1975 though 1978 the Mundells had difficulty retaining employees in their beekeeping business. Various negative conditions of working in the beekeeping business could explain why the Mundells had difficulty maintaining an experienced staff of workers. Work in the beekeeping business is seasonal, providing income for only about six months out of the year. The majority of the work, which requires a great deal of heavy lifting, is performed outdoors, during the hot summer months. The discomfort of performing arduous physical labor in summer heat is exacerbated by the fullbody protective clothing beekeepers must wear. In spite of the protective clothing, workers are stung as many as five or six times a day while harvesting honey.

In 1978, James began working full-time in his father's and stepmother's beekeeping business. Because he had helped his father in the business throughout his youth, James had significant beekeeping experience which enabled him to provide valuable service to the Mundells' business. By the time of his father's death in July of 1988, James had worked continuously in the Mundells' beekeeping business for ten years. Initially, James was paid a salary of six hundred dollars per month. In the early 1980s, James's salary was increased to eight hundred dollars per month. In addition, James began receiving bonuses in the form of beehives. He received twenty-five to fifty beehives per year. Eventually, James was able to create new hives from his existing hives. He also purchased beehives from other beekeepers. Records submitted to the United States Agricultural Stabilization and Conservation Service (ASCS) indicated that James owned approximately 485 beehives in 1987.

The Mundells filed applications for loans from the ASCS, which is an agency of the U.S. Department of Agriculture. In order to obtain the loan, the ASCS requires that the honey producer certify the number of hives that produced the honey and the ownership of the hives. ASCS records indicate that Orie and Eva Mundell claimed ownership of 1300 hives in 1984 and 1985, 1000 in 1986, and 1010 in 1987. ASCS records indicate that James Mundell had 185 beehives in 1984, 225 beehives in 1985, 300 beehives in 1986, and 485 beehives in 1987.

Tax returns prepared by Eva Mundell indicate that, at the time of Orie's death, James owned twenty-five per cent of the total honey crop. At trial, however, Eva asserted that the hives had been gifts to James from Orie's half of the community property and were not compensatory bonuses distributed from the business.

 JUDGE SILAK:

The dispositive issue in this case is whether the beehives were given to James as a compensatory bonus for his work in the business, or as a gift from his father. Because this is a mixed question of law and fact, we will uphold the factual findings made by the district court as long as those findings are not clearly erroneous....

As a preliminary matter, we will discuss the definition of the word "bonus" as it applies to the analysis of this case. Both parties have cited the definitions listed in BLACK'S LAW DICTIONARY: "A consideration or premium paid in addition to what is strictly due. A gratuity to which the recipient has no right to make a demand.... A premium or extra or irregular remuneration in consideration of offices performed or to encourage their performance.... An extra consideration given for what is received, or something given in addition to what is ordinarily received by, or strictly due, the recipient.... An addition to salary or wages normally paid for extraordinary work. An inducement to employees to procure efficient and faithful service."... Some of the above definitions imply that a bonus may be a gift if it is a mere gratuity given without consideration. On the other hand, if there is consideration on the part of the employee such as extraordinary work, efficient and faithful service, or continuous service for a specific length of time, the bonus takes on the character of payments made in consideration of services rendered to the employer, and the employer may even become bound contractually to pay the bonus....

The district court found that James and Orie formed a contractual agreement that James would receive beehives as part of his compensation, and that the beehives which were transferred to James were given to him as bonuses to supplement his monthly wages. Though the district court did not make a specific finding, it is evident from the record that the bonuses were given, at least in part, as payment for ongoing service in an arduous, low paying, seasonal job. This evidence adequately supports the district court's finding that James's continuous service benefited the beekeeping business. In turn, this fact supports the district court's conclusion that the beehives were given to James as bonuses which were part of his total compensation.

The record also contains evidence showing that Eva was fully aware that James was receiving the beehives over the years of his employment. As noted in the presentation of facts above, Eva personally prepared James's tax returns which reflected the fact that James was the owner of the beehives given to him by his father. In addition, the ASCS documents prepared and certified by Orie and Eva, as well as James and his wife, recorded the number of beehive colonies owned by the respective parties. These records support a finding that Eva knew of and acquiesced in the transfer of the beehives to James.

The above facts in the record constitute substantial evidence supporting the conclusion of the district court....

Because we have concluded that the district court did not err in holding that the beehives were given to James Mundell, per oral contract, as compensation for his work which benefited the community, we need not consider Eva Mundell's contention that her husband had no right to divest her of her interest in their community property by making unauthorized gifts to his son.... In this case, Orie Mundell bound the community to a contract for the payment of wages and bonuses to his son. Eva Mundell's consent to the terms of the contract was not legally required; thus, her current challenge has no merit.

The final issue in this case is whether the respondents are entitled to attorney fees on appeal. The respondents assert that the appeal was brought frivolously and without foundation. We agree. This appeal has presented no meaningful issue on a question of law. Eva Mundell has merely disputed the trial court's factual findings and asked us to re-weigh conflicting evidence.... We are left with the abiding belief that this appeal was brought without foundation. Accordingly, we hold that the respondents are entitled to an award of a reasonable attorney fee on appeal, to be determined....

The judgment of the district court is affirmed. Costs and attorney fees to respondents.

Part Payment. One of the most common applications of the preexisting duty rule is in cases where a debtor offers to pay part of the debt if the creditor will accept the part payment as full satisfaction of the debt. Obviously, in most cases, the creditor is willing to agree to anything to get some cash, especially if the debt is past due and the debtor is in questionable financial condition. Does such an agreement prevent the creditor from later suing to collect the unpaid balance of the original debt? At common law, the general rule was clear: no, the creditor is not prevented from collecting the balance, because the debtor's part payment was nothing more (in fact less) than the debtor was already legally obligated to pay.

Only under special circumstances would the part payment legally discharge the debt in full. If the part payment was made and accepted by the creditor as payment in full before the debt was in fact due, the creditor would be bound by the acceptance of this "early payment." The creditor in this case did receive new consideration for the agreement to surrender the balance of the debt because the creditor had no right to receive any payment on the date that the payment was actually made. There is likewise consideration for the discharge of the entire debt if the part payment is accompanied by "some new item," received and accepted by the creditor, which the creditor was not previously legally entitled to receive. There is consideration (at least technically), and the debt is (probably) discharged, when a creditor agrees to accept a ballpoint pen and $600 in cash in full satisfaction of a $1,000 debt. Finally, where there is an honest, good faith dispute over the amount that is actually owed and the creditor agrees to take a lesser sum in full payment, the creditor is bound and the debt is discharged.

The *Myron Soik* case illustrates the "disputes" rule on past payment.

MYRON SOIK & SONS v. STOKELY USA
498 N.W.2d 897 (WI App., 1993)

FACTS: This is a class action by farmers growing corn under contract with Stokely USA, Inc., a vegetable canning company. The growers sued Stokely, claiming the company had failed to pay the amounts due them under the contracts.

The growers' claims center on a section of the 1990 corn contract providing a method of payment for "passed acreage"—corn grown by them but not taken by the company. Under the contracts, passed acreage payments were to be made from a fund set up with equal contributions from the growers and the company based on total tons harvested from all growers. Believing that the payments made by Stokely under these provisions were inadequate, the growers sued.

The plaintiff class included several growers who had retained and cashed the checks Stokely had sent to them for the 1990 crop, and the company moved for summary judgment dismissing these plaintiffs from the action. Stokely claimed that the checks had been properly calculated under the terms of the contract and that their acceptance and negotiation by the growers constituted an accord and satisfaction of the company's obligations under the contracts.

The trial court denied the motion, concluding as a matter of law that the defense of accord and satisfaction was unavailable to Stokely.

In early 1990, Stokely contracted with various Wisconsin corn growers to purchase sweet corn. The contracts were all identical and contained provisions for payment to the growers if some or all of their corn crop was "passed"—if it was fit for harvest but Stokely declined to take it. The passed acreage provisions of Stokely's 1990 Sweet Corn Contract provided as follows:

> The [Growers'] compensation for the production of sweet corn suitable for processing and fit for harvesting but not harvested at the direction of the Company shall be computed as if it were harvested....

> The [Growers] and the Company agree to share the cost of payments made for nonharvested crops ... as follows: Total payments made for non-harvested sweet corn acreage will be divided by total tons of sweet corn produced ... to establish a per ton allocation of said cost. The [Growers] will be responsible for this cost up to a maximum of $2.00 per ton. *In the event that the combined contribution of $4.00 per ton ... is not sufficient to meet total calculated non-harvested crop compensation, payment will be prorated to the extent of funds collected from the Company and [the Growers].* (Emphasis Added.)

During the 1990 harvest, Stokely "passed" some or all of the corn it had agreed to purchase from the growers. Then, after the season, Stokely notified the growers by letter that the money that had been paid into the crop compensation fund under the provisions of the contract was insufficient to pay them in full for their passed acreage crops and that, as a result, they would be receiving prorated payments:

This is to inform you that the non-harvested crop compensation fund is not sufficient this year to pay total calculated non-harvested crop compensation in full. This means your payment will be prorated to the extent the claims against the fund exceed its amount. The exact amount of the proration is now being calculated....

Details as to the proration will accompany your check.

A few days later, Stokely mailed checks in reduced amounts to the growers, along with a letter stating:

Enclosed is your Stokely USA, Inc., 1990 Sweet Corn contract payment.

Your payment has been calculated according to the formula set forth in the contract for non-harvested crops....

Unfortunately, the total fund of $1,029,375.05 is insufficient to pay claims against it in full, and as a consequence, your payment has been prorated. The proration is 53.49 percent.

Please contact me if you have any questions.

 CHIEF JUDGE EICH:

An accord and satisfaction is an agreement to discharge an existing disputed claim and constitutes a defense to an action to enforce the claim.... It is a rule "resting not only on principles of contract law but on principles of sound public policy, that is, interests of resolving disputes informally without litigation and of fairness...." In *Flambeau*, the supreme court discussed the principles underlying the rule and the protections it affords to the debtor.

The interests of fairness dictate that a creditor who cashes a check offered in full payment should be bound by the terms of the offer. The debtor's intent is known, and allowing the creditor to keep the money disregarding the debtor's conditions seems unfair.... The doctrine of accord and satisfaction includes safeguards designed to protect a creditor from an overreaching debtor: there must be a good faith dispute about the debt [and] the creditor must have reasonable notice that the check is intended to be in full satisfaction of the debt....

The *Flambeau* court also discussed the various rules that come into play when considering the defense of accord and satisfaction, two of which are relevant to our inquiry in his case:

First, the law in Wisconsin has long been that payment in full settlement of a claim which is disputed as to amount discharges the entire claim....

A second rule, also of long-standing, is that payment of part of a debt which is not disputed as to amount does not discharge the debt altogether.... The debtor's mere refusal to pay the full claim does not make it a disputed claim....

We thus consider whether there was a dispute between Stokely and the growers at the time the checks were received and cashed, and whether the growers had reasonable notice that Stokely's checks were intended by the company in full satisfaction of its obligations under the "passed acreage" provisions of the contracts....

Prior to receiving any communication from Stokely, the growers knew from the terms of their contracts that they were to be paid for "passed" acreage in an amount calculated "as if [that acreage] had been harvested," and that these payments would come from a fund comprised of equal contributions from Stokely and themselves. They also knew that in the event these contributions were insufficient to allow Stokely to pay at the "harvested crop" rate, they would receive only a pro-rata share of the amount of money actually in the fund.

Then after the harvest, the growers were informed by Stokely's first letter that their payment "this year" would have to be prorated under the contract. And in a second letter—the one enclosing the lower-than-expected checks—they were plainly advised that the amount being paid constitute "your Stokely ... 1990 Sweet Corn crop payment," and the details of the prorata calculation were explained to them.

The growers, obviously, had expected to receive a larger amount. But, armed with the above information, they nevertheless decided to cash the checks. Admittedly, the checks did not contain the words "full payment," as in Flambeau; but we do not believe such "magic language" is essential to the debtor's ability to raise the defense of accord and satisfaction. The test, after, is one of reason: "[T]he creditor must have *reasonable notice* that the check is intended to be in full satisfaction of the debt...."

We conclude on this record that: (1) at the time the checks were received and cashed a "dispute" within the meaning of the rule of accord and satisfaction existed between Stokely and the plaintiff growers, all of whom, obviously, disagreed with the company's application of the prorata clause; and (2) the correspondence preceding and accompanying the reduced payment gave the growers reasonable notice that the checks were intended as full payment under the contract. As a result, the growers' acts of accepting and cashing the checks must be considered acceptance of the tendered amount in full settlement of Stokely's obligations under the 1990 corn contracts.

UCC Rules. There have been suggestions by some legal writers that under UCC 1-107, 2-209(1), and 3-408, the cashing of a part-payment check discharges the debt in full if the check so indicates, even without the existence of a dispute. Most of the cases decided since the adoption of the Code, however, continue to apply the common law rules discussed above, without reference to any of these Code sections. It is thus not clear how a court would apply these sections if they were properly briefed and argued. It certainly appears that creditors would be much safer in sending such checks back and suing for the entire balance due. At the very least, a creditor should be aware that cashing such a check *may* cancel the right to sue for the balance of the debt.

UNCONSCIONABLE CONTRACTS

Courts have become increasingly willing to refuse enforcement of contract provisions that are not specifically illegal but which they simply don't like. Traditionally the emphasis of the common law has been on freedom of contract, or letting the parties make any sort of contractual arrangement they want so long as it is not illegal. More and more, however, recognizing that contracts in modern society do not always represent real bargaining between equals, courts have been re-writing contracts by refusing to enforce provisions which they regard as unduly harsh, oppressive, or unjust. Courts have discovered that they have always had a common-law power to refuse enforcement of such "unconscionable" provisions, even without Section 2-302 of the UCC.

SIGNIFICANCE OF THIS CHAPTER

Not all promises are contractually enforceable, even if proved to have been made and accepted. The basic idea of the consideration requirement is that a person ought not to be required to perform a promise made to another unless the promisor received something of value in return for the promise. While it is inevitable that some promisors will be disappointed in what they have received in return, that in itself is no basis for not performing their promises. But it is also true that courts are more and more willing to examine the agreement to make sure that a genuine exchange of values was promised, particularly where one of the parties lacks education and experience.

Fairness also underlies the concept of promissory estoppel as an alternate basis for enforcement. It's just not fair to let someone make the "no consideration" argument after a promise has been relied on by another party. Courts may also use the estoppel concept to prevent someone from using the Statute of Frauds to deny liability on an oral promise. The next chapter will discuss this point in more detail.

PROBLEMS FOR DISCUSSION

1. Annie Marie Porporato married John Porporato's son in 1935. The couple lived in San Francisco in a flat owned by John for a year and a half. During this period, "a close and tender relationship developed" between Annie and John. When John decided to build a new home, he also had a second home built on the property for his son and Annie. When John's wife refused to move into the main home, his son and Annie lived there. The son entered the Navy in 1942; Annie gave birth to a boy in 1943. John idolized his grandson and visited frequently. While visiting her family in Omaha, Nebraska, Annie learned that her husband had been killed in action. She decided to stay with her family and to resume her nursing career. Her father-in-law begged her to return to San Francisco and to live in the new home so that he could be near his grandson. He also told her that if she did so, he would leave her the home when he died. She returned to San Francisco, but when John died he left the home to Anita DeVincenzi, the defendant. The trial court dismissed Annie's suit for specific performance and she appeals.

    How should the appeal be decided, and why?

2. Lois McGowan claimed that her husband Wade (now deceased) had borrowed $15,000 from her and as evidence of the debt, had given her the following memorandum: "January 2, 1995. I owe my wife, Lois McGowan, $15,000. Wade H. McGowan (Seal)." In answer to specific questions in their instructions, the jury found that Wade had in fact written, signed, sealed, and delivered the memorandum. Beach, the administrator of Wade's estate, objected to the trial judge's refusal to ask the jury for a finding as to whether Wade had in fact borrowed the money. Beach appeals from a judgment in favor of Lois.

    Did the trial judge rule correctly? Explain.

3. Garth Barge had a contract with the city of Black Plains to collect and remove all materials generated within the city. Due to Black Plains's increased prestige, the number of new residences that required service rose in 1998 by 400, rather than the usual twenty to twenty-five unit increase per year. Garth went to the city council and told them about the large increase in work that he had to perform and requested a $10,000 raise to his $137,000 per year. Black Plains agreed that Garth deserved the raise, and the city modified his contract to include it. The exact same situation occurred the next year, and Black Plains again modified Garth's contract to give him a second $10,000 raise. Many of the residents of Black Plains felt that Garth should not have received the raises. Arguing that Garth was already obligated to service all of the city, a group of residents sued for the return of the additional $20,000 to the city.

   Does Garth have to return the $20,000? Why or why not?

4. During the period from 1991 to 1996 Ora Lee Williams purchased a number of household items from Walker-Thomas, for which payment was to be made in installments. The terms of each purchase were contained in a printed form contract which set forth the value of the purchased item and purported to lease the item to her for a stipulated monthly rent payment. The contract then provided, in substance, that title would remain in Walker-Thomas until the total of all the monthly payments equaled the stated value of the item, at which time Williams could take title. In the event of a default in the payment of any monthly installment, Walker-Thomas could repossess the item.

   The contract further provided that "the amount of each periodical installment payment to be made by [purchaser] to the Company under this present lease shall be inclusive of and not in addition to the amount of each installment payment to be made by [purchaser] under such prior leases, bills or accounts; *and all payments now and hereafter made by [purchaser] shall be credited pro rata on all outstanding leases, bills, and accounts* due the Company by [purchaser] at the time each such payment is made." Walker-Thomas now sues to repossess all items Williams bought.

   Should it be able to enforce this contract? Explain.

5. In this action O'Neil seeks a declaratory judgement that he is the owner of a valuable painting, allegedly the work of Peter Paul Rubens and entitled "Hunting of the Caledonian Boar...." This painting was a part of the art collection acquired by the defendants during their marriage.

   On August 18, 1998, James Paul DeLaney purportedly sold the painting to plaintiff for $10 and "other good and valuable consideration." A written contract, embodying terms of the agreement, was prepared and signed by plaintiff and James Paul DeLaney. Jeannette DeLaney was not a party to that contract. The painting was then brought to plaintiff's apartment where it was hung on the wall.

   When asked what the contract term "other good and valuable consideration" meant to him, plaintiff stated:

   > That to me and Mr. DeLaney means our friendship and favors that we have done; and as you put it earlier, the love and affection that one had for another. Mr. DeLaney didn't have any children, and I assume he looked upon me as a son.

   Under cross-examination, plaintiff was asked whether he gave James Paul DeLaney anything else other than $10 and love and affection in exchange for the painting. Plaintiff responded: "No, not really."

At the time of the sale of the painting, plaintiff believed it was worth $100,000 if not authenticated as a Rubens original,and if authenticated, several hundred thousand dollars.

Jeanette DeLaney claims an ownership interest in the painting. O'Neil says the sale to him ended her rights.

Did O'Neil buy the painting? Discuss.

6. Sam Leone worked as a foreman for Precision, which was a subcontractor on a construction project. Sam was covered under a collective bargaining contract between Precision and the construction workers' union. Sam and his wife Ella sued to enforce an alleged oral promise of a bonus of one-half of the difference between the estimated cost of the project and its actual cost. The jury found for Sam and Ella, for $17,789.28, and the trial judge refused Precision's request for a judgment notwithstanding the verdict. Precision appeals.

How should the appeals court rule? Explain.

7. Relying on the representations of Lukowitz, a representative of Red Owl Stores, that the company would set him up in business in a franchised Red Owl grocery store for a capital investment of $18,000, Hoffman and his wife did the following: sold their existing bakery business and building; bought a small grocery store, ran it for several months "to get some experience," and then resold it; took an option on the proposed site for the Red Owl store and made a down payment on the lot; moved the family's home; and rented a house in the town where the new store was to be located. Red Owl kept increasing the capital requirements, and the deal for the new store fell through without the parties ever having agreed to a contract. Hoffman and his wife sued for the damages they sustained as a result of the above transaction. The trial court ordered judgment for the plaintiffs, based on the jury's verdict, but said a new trial would be required to determine the exact amount of the loss suffered by the sale of the small grocery store. Both parties appealed.

How should this case be solved by the court?

Chapter 10

Statute of Frauds and Parol Evidence Rule

Although the parties have entered into an agreement and their agreement is supported by an exchange of legally sufficient considerations, courts, in many situations, will refuse to enforce some or all of the promises exchanged unless the alleged promises can be proved by something more than oral testimony. The Statute of Frauds requires that certain types of contractual promises be contained in a signed writing in order to be enforceable in court. The parol evidence rule prevents a party from contradicting the terms of a complete written contract, once signed, by the use of outside, or parol, evidence.

STATUTE OF FRAUDS: ORIGINS, DEVELOPMENT, AND BASIC PURPOSE

One year after the United States celebrated its bicentennial, the Statute of Frauds celebrated its tricentennial. The English Parliament passed the original statute in 1677 to deal with what was perceived to be a serious legal problem: the possibility that a court would force a party to perform a contract that had never really been made, solely on the basis of perjured oral testimony. The solution to this problem seemed simple enough: require that a contract be proved by something more than oral testimony before you enforce it. Thus, the Statute of Frauds ("An Act for Prevention of Frauds and Perjuries") was adopted. It stated that certain types of contracts would not be enforceable in court unless proved by a writing which contained the terms of the contract and which was signed by the party against whom enforcement of the contract was sought.

Parliament did not go as far as requiring that all contracts be evidenced by a signed writing to be enforceable in court. Rather, it confined this new requirement to what seemed to be "important" contracts and to other situations where intentional perjury or mistaken testimony seemed likely. As a result, the following types of contracts had to be in writing to be enforceable in court: the sale of any interest in real estate, the sale of goods worth £10 or more, any contract which by its terms could not possibly be completed within one year from the date it was made, any promise to pay the debt of another party, any promise by the executor or administrator of a decedent's estate to pay the estate's debts out of his or her own funds, any promise made "in consideration of marriage." This list formed the basis for similar statutes in nearly all of our states.

To see how the Statute of Frauds works today, we need to know the answers to three questions: What contracts are now subject to the Statute of Frauds? How does one comply with the Statute of Frauds requirement? What results follow if the Statute of Frauds applies and has not been satisfied? We will now consider each of these questions in turn.

CONTRACTS SUBJECT TO THE STATUTE OF FRAUDS

Pre-UCC Holdovers. Three provisions of the 1677 statute that have general commercial significance have, on the whole, survived in their original form: the transfer of any interest in real estate, any promise to pay the debt of another, any contract which by its terms cannot be performed within one year. Prior to the UCC, many states had also adopted a Statute of Frauds provision which required all *assignments*, or transfers, of contract rights to be made in writing. (Assignments are discussed more fully in Chapter 13.)

Real Estate Transfers. "Any interest" in land means just that: every case where one or more parties are voluntarily creating such an interest in another or divesting themselves of such an interest. Most courts agree that leases, mortgages, easements, and options on real estate are all subject to this requirement, although options might be excluded in some states. Also, most states have a statutory exception for short-term leases; if the term of an oral lease is not more than one year, the lease is enforceable. Although real estate brokers do not have an "interest" in the real estate under this section of the Statute of Frauds, in most states real estate brokers are required by a separate statutory provision to have their commission arrangements in writing to make them enforceable.

There are some definitional problems where the contract relates to things which are growing on, attached to, or contained in the land. Generally, these questions will be answered by reference to UCC 2-107. If the contract requires the seller to "sever" minerals or the like, or a structure of its materials, the contract is a sale of goods within Article 2. If the buyer is to do the severing, until the buyer does so, the contract would be assumed to deal with an "interest" in the land. Where the subject matter of the contract is timber, growing crops, "or other things attached to realty and capable of severance without material harm thereto," but not covered under the first rule, the contract is a sale of goods, regardless of who does the severing. The significance of the distinction can be seen later, in the discussion of what is a sufficient compliance with the Statute of Frauds provision which applies to the contract.

The following case involves the application of the statute of frauds to the transfer of a lease on a commercial building.

HYMAN FREIGHTWAYS v. CAROLINA FREIGHT CARRIERS CORP.
942 F.2d 500 (U.S. 8th Cir. Court of Appeals, 1991)

FACTS: Hyman and Carolina both leased space at a trucking terminal in Hillside, Illinois, from Bellemeade Development Corporation. Hyman's lease would not end until October 31, 1989, but it wanted to move to another facility. Through a real estate agent, Phyllis Sutker, Hyman and Carolina corresponded about a possible assumption of Hyman's lease by Carolina. In a letter dated July 25, 1988, Sutker told Carolina that Hyman would be vacating the property by August 31, 1988. Hyman signed a lease on its new location on or about August 1. On August 5, Carolina sent Sutker a fax which stated in part: "Please use this letter to confirm our phone conversation earlier today, wherein we agreed to assume the Lease ... between Hyman ... and Bellemeade.... The effective date of the Lease Assignment will be approximately September 15, 1988, the actual date to be determined by mutual consent once Hyman has totally vacated the leased premises. The Lessor shall prepare an assignment document immediately for the approval and signatures of all parties, including Lessee, Lessor, and Assignee."

An assignment of the lease was prepared, but the document was never signed. Hyman moved out over a three-day period, October 15-17, and gave its building keys to a Carolina employee at that time. On October 31, Carolina wrote to Hyman that it was withdrawing its offer to take over Hyman's lease. Hyman could not find anyone else to take over the lease and had to make the rest of the rental payments. Hyman sued Carolina in Minnesota state court. Carolina had the case removed to U.S. District Court, which then entered a summary judgment for Carolina. Hyman appeals.

 JUDGE GIBSON:

An assignment of the Hyman space, being for a term longer than one year, would be an interest in land that would have to be evidenced by a writing to comply with the Illinois statute of frauds.... The only writing between the parties signed by the party to be charged (Carolina) is the August 5 fax, and thus that document controls this case; either it evidences a contract or it does not. We agree with the district court that it does not because, contrary to Illinois law, the date-of-assignment term was left open for future negotiation, which makes the purported agreement unenforceable.... "When any essential term of an agreement is left to future negotiation, there is no binding contract...."

While Hyman urges that the term was identified as the date of Hyman's vacation of the premises—a date determinable by an event—we simply cannot avoid the language of the fax that the date was "to be determined by mutual consent once Hyman has totally vacated the leased premises...." That amounts to nothing more than an agreement to agree. Had the parties actually agreed to a lease assignment on the date of Hyman's vacation of the premises, they could be said to have so contracted. However, the only arguably sufficient writing (the August 5 fax) does not admit of such a simple solution.... This single correspondence in a series of negotiations is insufficient to evidence a contract for an interest in land.

We do not doubt that the parties intended to reach an agreement on a lease assignment, and perhaps at one time they even believed they had reached one. Hyman suggests that we must give effect to this intent of the parties under Illinois case law. We disagree; Hyman's authorities are distinguishable because they proceed from the existence of a contract. In this case, Hyman's argument skips a necessary step; there must first be a contract evidencing the intent of the parties before a court can effectuate that intent. We cannot take the supposed intent of the parties to create the contract and independently supply that contract's terms. The law requires a writing evidencing a contract, not a writing evidencing intent to enter into a contract. The August 5 fax is evidence only of the latter; the former simply never came about.

Promises to Pay the Debt of Another. Parliament probably included this provision because both the principal debtor and the creditor have an incentive to commit perjury in this case. Here, too, there are definitional questions to be resolved. This section does not apply to direct, "original" promises to confer benefits on a third party—only to "secondary" or supplemental promises. This section of the Statute of Frauds does not apply where the promisor's main motive in making the promise is to benefit *himself* or *herself* rather than just to "backstop" the principal debtor's credit. Finally, the section does not apply where the secondary promise is made to the principal debtor rather than to the creditor. The court must thus examine the facts to see exactly what sort of promise was allegedly made.

Contracts Impossible to Perform within One Year. The probable reason for inclusion of the "year clause" was the likelihood that the parties and witnesses would tend to forget the provisions of the contract, or would remember them differently, where the performances extended over a relatively long period of time. Thus, if on the day a contract is made, the parties can see that there is absolutely no way to perform it within one year from that date, the contract must be evidenced by a signed writing. As applied by the courts, the test is not how long the performances were likely to take or, with hindsight, how long they actually took. The test is whether there was any conceivable way that the contract *could* have been fully performed, according to its terms, within a year from the date it was made. If it *could* have been performed within a year, the oral contract is perfectly valid and perfectly enforceable in court (assuming that the jury believes the oral testimony).

Thus, an oral contract for lifetime employment, where performance is to start within one year of the date the contract is made, is enforceable, since the employee could conceivably die within the first year. But where the employee is hired for more than one year, or is not to start performing until some future date and then is to work for at least a year, the oral contract is not enforceable.

UCC Statute of Frauds Provisions. The Code contains several specific Statute of Frauds provisions. Contracts for the sale of goods worth $500 or more, investment securities, or intangible personal property worth $5,000 or more, and contracts creating a security interest or establishing a letter of credit must be evidenced by some sort of writing. In addition, "negotiable instruments" under Article 3 and "documents" under Article 7, by definition, involve signed writings with particular characteristics.

Sales of Goods for $500 or More. As defined in Section 2-105(1), goods means tangible, movable personal property, but it can also refer to things which are currently attached to land, as noted earlier in this chapter. There can be a contract for the sale of goods which do not exist yet, with the seller promising to produce them or get them from a third party prior to the delivery date specified in the contract.

In some cases, it is hard to decide whether the contract is a contract for the sale of goods or a contract for services. The distinction is very important here since there is no Statute of Frauds which is generally applicable to services contracts. If a services contract, such as a promise to construct a building on land already owned by the customer, can be performed within one year, it can be oral and still be enforceable, no matter how much money it involves. If a contract is for goods worth $500 or more, Section 2-201 applies.

A contract to buy a $600 color TV is clearly a contract for the sale of goods even if the seller also promises to deliver and "set up" the TV as part of the contract. Likewise, if you buy all the parts for a TV set in a "kit," and then hire a TV technician to put the set together for you, your contract with the technician is clearly a services contract. Many contracts are more ambiguous, however, such as your contract for the purchase of a custom-made suit from a tailor, or your contract with an artist to have your portrait painted, or your contract to have your car fixed or your house aluminum-sided, all of which involve both labor and materials. (Most probably, a court would decide that the suit and portrait contracts are primarily for goods and that the car repair and aluminum siding contracts are primarily for services.)

Sales of Investment Securities. Simply put, "investment securities" are stocks and bonds. Stock warrants and other such special devices, which are commonly traded in securities markets, would also be covered here. No dollar minimum is specified, so that every contract for the sale of securities must be in writing to be enforceable. However, nearly all the cases in point have held that this Statute of Frauds section (8-319) does not apply to your "agency" contract with your broker, so you can sue your broker for failing to follow your oral instructions. Agency law is covered in Chapter 30.

Sales of Intangible Personal Property for $5,000 or More. After eliminating goods, investment securities, and security agreements, Section 1-206 covers "personal property." Included here are the sales of such things as copyrights, patents, royalties, trademarks and trade names, and tort claims for damages. If the contract price of such items is $5,000 or more, there must be a signed writing.

Security Agreements. Where a creditor ("secured party") wishes to use a piece of personal property as collateral for the payment of some obligation, the creditor must have a written security agreement which creates or provides for such a "security interest," and the writing must be signed by the debtor. Without such a writing, the creditor has no rights against the specific collateral when the debtor defaults unless the creditor actually has possession of the collateral.

Letters of Credit. Letters of credit are widely used in international trade, where the credit standing of a buyer may not be known to the seller. Before leaving his or her country, the buyer arranges to have a bank honor drafts (orders for money) up to a certain amount. With such a written agreement from a recognized bank in the buyer's own country, the buyer can have ready access to funds from banks in a foreign country. Obviously, any such letter of credit, and any modification thereof, must be contained in a signed writing.

Modifications. Because of the common-law requirement that a document must contain all the material terms to comply with the Statute of Frauds, subsequently agreed-to modifications of such a document must also be evidenced by a signed writing to be enforceable. Such changes can be written on the original document and initialed, or a new document covering the modifications can be prepared and signed by the parties. In a real estate transaction, for example, any later agreement to modify the signed writing by changing the total contract price, the monthly payments, the acreage involved, the interest rate, or even such things as the date of possession, almost certainly has to be written to be enforced in court. The *Triple B & G, Inc.* case raises this issue.

TRIPLE B & G, INC. v. CITY OF FAIRMONT
494 N.W.2d 49 (MN App., 1992)

FACTS: Appellants Martin Luther High School and Triple B & G. Inc. are the record owners of certain real property in Martin County. Beginning in 1975, respondent City of Fairmont used property adjacent to appellants' property as a spoil site for dredge materials. Appellants allege that dredge materials escaping from the City's property have permanently damaged their property.

On February 20, 1990, appellants filed suit in Martin County District Court seeking damages and injunctive relief against the City for negligence and trespass. Trial was set for January 22, 1992. Between the filing of appellants' complaint and the time set for trial, the parties attempted to settle the dispute.

On December 3, 1991, appellants' attorney, Elton Kuderer, sent a letter to the City indicating appellants' rejection of the City's proposals. Kuderer than stated, "My clients have authorized me to propose the following settlement...." The first proposal called for appellants to sell 5.13 acres to the City for $15,390. The second called for the City to pay $7,500 in damages. The latter proposal would also require the City to allow appellants to hook up to the City's storm sewer to ensure adequate drainage. The first proposal did not include a provision for adequate drainage.

On December 11, 1991, Kuderer wrote a letter to appellants stating that the City's attorney had told him the City was not interested in acquiring the 5.13 acres at appellants' price. Instead, Kuderer said, the city made a counteroffer of $12,800. The counteroffer was confirmed in a December 16, 1991 letter from the City's attorney, Thomas Emmer, to Kuderer. In this letter, Emmer referred to the City's proposal as an "offer."

On January 17, 1992, Emmer wrote Kuderer to confirm that the City had accepted appellants' offer of December 3, 1991, to sell 5.13 acres for $15,390. Emmer's letter referenced a phone conversation between him and Kuderer on the previous day, January 16, 1992. In the phone conversation, appellants indicated their desire to get an agreement regarding drainage. In his letter to Kuderer, Emmer agreed that some arrangement regarding drainage should be made; however, Emmer stated that as far as he was concerned, the drainage concern was ancillary in nature and the lawsuit had been fully settled.

The City filed a motion to compel enforcement of the settlement on January 22, 1992. After a hearing, the trial court issued an order enforcing the settlement. Appellants filed a note of appeal.

 PRESIDING JUDGE NORTON:

Appellants contend that their settlement offer was terminated prior to the City's acceptance by way of a City counteroffer on December 16, 1991.... Respondent argues that the communication of December 16, 1991 did not constitute a counter-offer.

The characterization of this communication is not determinative of the issue. The record shows that, even after December 16, 1991, appellants continued to press the City to accept the terms of their original offer. By acting is this manner, appellants effectively renewed their original offer, reinstating the power of respondent to accept.

Appellants also assert that the alleged settlement fails to satisfy the statute of frauds. Minn. Stat. § 513.05 (1990) provides that any contract for the sale of land is void unless the contract, or some note or memorandum thereof, expressing the consideration, is in writing and subscribed by the party by whom the lease or sale is to be made.... The statute of frauds should not be applied in a rigid manner when the property description used, by itself or as amplified by other instruments or papers with which the memorandum is expressly or impliedly connected, provides an adequate guide to locate and identify the property in the light of the surrounding circumstances and in light of facts of which a court can take judicial notice....

As noted above, the parties seemed to know which property was the subject of their negotiations. Moreover, the trial court noted that establishing the boundary line would not be difficult since the location of the north, west, and south lines is known. The trial court correctly determined that the settlement satisfies the statute of frauds.

The trial court's decision that appellants and respondent settled their dispute is affirmed.

For sales of goods, however, the rules are quite different because of the wording of the applicable Code provisions. Because the signed writing here does not have to contain all the terms agreed on, or even all the material terms, oral modifications of a previous written contract for goods should be enforceable in nearly every case. The one thing Section 2-201(1) does not permit is an oral modification that increases the quantity term stated in the signed writing. (For example, the parties enter into a written contract for 1,000 bushels of wheat at $3 per bushel. They can later orally agree to raise or lower the price, to change the delivery date, or to lower the quantity to 700 bushels. What they cannot do without a new writing is to increase the quantity to 1,200 bushels. The quantity term in the original writing can't be increased orally, and 200 more bushels means $600 worth of goods, so this "modification" has to be evidenced by a new writing.) Where there was originally an enforceable oral contract for under $500 and the agreed modification brings the price to over $500, the contract as modified must be evidenced by a writing, or else the modification cannot be enforced and the original terms stand. (For example, the parties orally agree to a contract for 150 bushels of wheat at $3 per bushel. Later they agree to raise the price per bushel to $3.50, for a total price of $525. This modification must be in writing to be enforced.)

Remember from the last chapter that such modifications need no new exchange of considerations in a sale of goods case; they can be completely one-sided and still be binding under Section 2-209(1). For other types of contracts, however, remember that there has to be new consideration moving both ways for such modifications to be enforceable, even if the modifications are in writing.

Consideration Substitutes. Chapter 9 contained several examples of statutory provisions that made certain kinds of promises enforceable even without consideration. Typically, such promises will have to be contained in a signed writing to be enforceable. UCC 2-209(1) does not require modifications of a preexisting sale of goods contract to be in writing, nor, in some states, do the statutes which cover new promises to pay debts barred by the statute of limitations or by a bankruptcy discharge. (As always, of course, it's a good idea to have the promise in writing even though no statute requires it, simply because a signed written promise is easier to prove in court.)

COMPLIANCE WITH THE STATUTE OF FRAUDS

General Common-Law Rule. The method of compliance intended by the original 1677 statute was a signed writing. As interpreted by the courts, this requirement came to mean that the writing had to contain "all the material terms" and that a writing which did not clearly spell out all the important provisions of the contract was not sufficient to comply with the statute. In general, this "all-material-terms" rule continues to be used for those Statute of Frauds provisions described above as common-law "holdovers."

The all-material-terms rule can be seen operating most clearly in real estate transactions, where most courts have used the "4-P's" interpretation. To comply with the statute for real estate, the signed writing has to at least contain the Parties, the Property, the Price, and the Payment terms. If the terms are simple, a very short memorandum conceivably could contain all these elements. More typically, however, payment for real estate is to be made over an extended period of time, interest must be calculated on the unpaid balance and paid periodically, and other special provisions are agreed to. In such cases, the parties run a very real risk that a court may later find their document to be insufficient to comply with the statute.

Sale of Goods Compliance: Five Alternatives. The UCC, Section 2-201, provides five alternative methods of compliance: a signed writing, a writing in confirmation, special manufacture, admission in court, and part performance.

Unlike the common-law rule, the signed writing for the sale of goods need not contain all the material terms: "a writing is not insufficient because it omits or incorrectly states a term agreed upon." The writing must indicate that a contract for sale has been made; it must be signed by the party against whom enforcement is sought or by that party's authorized agent; and it must contain the quantity term ("the contract is not enforceable under this paragraph beyond the quantity of goods stated"). Price, packaging, and delivery terms can all be omitted and then filled in by supplementary evidence. A very simple notation on the check given for the down payment would be sufficient, for example, "Down payment on one 1989 Buick." The buyer's signature on the check binds the buyer to the contract; the seller is also bound when the seller endorses the check so that the check can be cashed or deposited to the seller's account.

Where both parties are merchants and there is no writing which evidences a contract because agreement has been reached over the telephone or in personal conversation, the Code provides a method of compliance called a "writing in confirmation." This is a brand-new Code concept, unknown in prior law. It is a "bootstrap" method: our contract becomes enforceable by me against you on the basis of a writing signed by *me*, not by you. If within a reasonable time after the oral contract has been made, one merchant sends the other a written confirmation of the contract and the confirmation is a sufficient writing against the sender-merchant, it also becomes a sufficient writing against the receiver-merchant unless the receiver-merchant sends back written notice of objection to its contents within ten days after receiving it. This Code rule is saying two things to merchants: first, to be on the safe side, always send written confirmation of the contract (preferably by registered mail) before you expend time and money in reliance on an oral agreement; and second, *read your mail!* Whether this confirmation rule applies is at issue in the *Starry* case.

STARRY CONST. CO., INC. v. MURPHY OIL USA
785 F.Supp. 1356 (D. MN, 1992)

FACTS: This case, arising in the context of the highway construction industry, involves the purported modification to a contract for the sale of asphalt cement oil. Plaintiff Starry Construction Co. (Starry) is a general contractor engaged in the business of asphalt road construction. Defendant Murphy Oil USA, Inc. (Murphy) is a supplier of asphalt cement oil, one of the materials required for installing asphalt pavement

In March 1990, Robert Billingsley, one of Murphy's sales managers, orally agreed to sell Starry 20,000 tons of asphalt cement oil for $90 per ton, excluding taxes. Murphy sent Steven Minnerath, Starry's president, a sales acknowledgment form dated April 12, 1990. That form by its terms confirms the quantity and price of Starry's order, but also contains in particular the following clauses:

> Fire, flood, strikes, differences with workmen, accidents to plants or machinery, failure of or unusual conditions surrounding the usual source of supplies of material, or other causes beyond the control of either party shall be a sufficient excuse for any delay or failure upon the part of either party to perform this order, provided, however, that such party shall notify the other with reasonable promptness as to the existence of such cause.

> If, by reason of any said causes, Murphy is unable to make deliveries to all its customers (whether under contract or not) its failure in whole or in part to make deliveries to purchaser, while delivering to others, shall not be a breach of this agreement and in such event Murphy may, but shall not be obligated to, prorate its available supply.

Starry acknowledges receiving the form, but neither signed nor returned it to Murphy. According to Minnerath, the form included additional terms that were not a part of the oral agreement. Instead, Minnerath proceeded to bid work for Starry, allegedly under the assumption that Starry and Murphy had a valid oral contract which was limited to the terms specifically agreed upon.

Toward the end of April, Minnerath determined that Starry would need more oil. He contacted Billingsley and requested an additional 5,000 tons. Billingsley said that he would "check on it" and inform Starry in a day or so. Murphy did not contact Starry. Several days later, Minnerath called Billingsley, who allegedly indicated that Murphy would sell the additional oil on the same terms and conditions as those initially agreed to. Although Starry allegedly obtained additional work based on the increased figures, Minnerath neglected to send a confirmatory memorandum of this oral modification.

During the spring and summer of 1990, Minnerath periodically communicated with Billingsley regarding the delivery of asphalt cement oil. Minnerath allegedly told Billingsley that Starry had obtained enough work to use all of the asphalt cement oil, including the additional 5,000 tons, that Murphy had agreed to provide. Minnerath claims that Billingsley never contested the quantity under the contract in their discussions.

In August 1990, Iraq invaded Kuwait. Members of the media reported that prices for all oil-based products were likely to rise substantially. During September 1990, approximately one month before the end of the 1990 paving season, Murphy began experiencing an unprecedented demand for asphalt cement oil. Essentially, Murphy's customers began requesting the full amount of oil under their contracts after the War in the Persian Gulf began, while historically they requested only 90 to 95 percent of those amounts.

Tom O'Brien, Starry's comptroller, became concerned that Murphy would not supply the additional oil. He asked Minnerath to call Billingsley and obtain a written confirmation of the modification. Minnerath did so. Billingsley allegedly responded, "Don't worry about it. I'll take care of you. I've never cheated you in the past. You are a good customer, and I treat our good customers right."

Later, Minnerath learned that Murphy was promoting Robert Billingsley and would be replacing him with Michael Palmgren. Minnerath allegedly called Billingsley once again and suggested the need to let his successor know about the agreement for 25,000 tons. Minnerath claims that Billingsley told him that he would leave a note on Palmgren's desk. Although Minnerath claims that after replacing Billingsley Palmgren acknowledged that he had seen such a note, Palmgren does not remember one.

In September 1990, Palmgren informed Starry that because of an oil crisis Murphy would be forced to allocate its supply. Consequently, Starry would not be receiving the additional 5,000 tons of oil, although Murphy did eventually supply an additional 107 tons. Believing that Murphy would inevitably provide the full 5,000 tons requested, Starry did not approach other suppliers to cover the shortfall until September 24, 1990. At that time, Starry agreed to purchase 1,000 tons of oil from Richards Asphalt Company for $117 per ton. In addition, Starry agreed to purchase another 3,000 tons from the Ashland Petroleum Company at $130 per ton on September 30, 1990.

On October 5, 1990, Minnerath, on advice of counsel, sent Palmgren a letter. That letter contains the following paragraph:

When we met on September 27, 1990, you indicated that you would get back to us with some kind of a schedule of the amount and timing for the ... [asphalt cement oil] you would give us so that we could, in turn, schedule our hot mix plants and make arrangements to purchase oil elsewhere if you would not supply us with the 25,000 ton called for by our Agreement.

The letter further provides:

We now understand that you intend to provide us with approximately fifty-four ton of oil per day, but won't guarantee its availability.

Murphy now denies that the agreement was ever modified to include an additional 5,000 tons of oil. Starry commenced this action against Murphy and asserted claims for breach of contract, equitable estoppel, promissory estoppel, and negligent misrepresentation. Murphy answered, alleging as its fourth affirmative defense that performance of the contract was commercially impracticable. Murphy now moves the Court for summary judgment and Starry moves for summary judgment as to Murphy's commercial impracticability defense.

 JUDGE MacLAUGHLIN:

Starry claims that it has in fact satisfied the merchant exception. According to Starry, Section 336.2-201(2) is satisfied if within a reasonable time after the oral contract was made Starry sent a writing confirming the contract. Starry claims that Minnerath's letter of October 5, 1990 constitutes such a writing.... That letter allegedly identifies the subject matter of the contract, and also reflects a quantity term of 25,000 tons. Further, Starry claims that the October 5, 1990 letter was sent within a reasonable time after the oral agreement was formed in the end of April 1990. Minnerath and Billingsley allegedly had built a history of trust upon verbal dealings such that written confirmation of agreements was not needed; there was therefore no reason why Minnerath would have needed to confirm the oral modification. In addition, during September 1990, Murphy still sold Starry an additional 107 tons of asphalt cement oil. Only after Murphy allegedly refused to perform the contract was there a reason for the written confirmation, which Minnerath allegedly supplied promptly thereafter....

Murphy responds in its reply that the October 5, 1990 letter is not a writing in confirmation of a contract sufficient to satisfy the statute of frauds for two reasons. First, Murphy claims that the letter was not sent within a reasonable time as a matter of law. In this case, Starry sent the letter nearly six months after formulation of the alleged oral agreement, and then only after Murphy denied the existence of any modification. During those months, the price of asphalt cement oil rose nearly 150 percent.... Murphy had also refused to provide the requested confirmation in August.... Iraq invaded Kuwait in August, causing additional instability in the market. For all of these reasons, Starry's neglect in sending the letter should be deemed unreasonable as a matter of law.

In addition, Murphy contends that the October 5, 1990 letter was not a writing "in confirmation of a contract" as required by Section 336.2-201(2). First, the letter on its face, does not confirm an agreement, but rather recognizes disagreement in that Murphy refuses to provide the additional oil. Second, it was only after Starry consulted with counsel that the letter was sent purporting to confirm the oral modification.... Because the letter was not sent in the ordinary course of business, Murphy argues that it could not confirm a contract within the meaning of Section 336.2-201(2). Consequently, Murphy was allegedly under no duty to respond to the letter.

This question thus boils down to whether the October 1990 letter satisfies the merchant exception. Although there is apparently no requirement that a letter confirming a contract be sent in the ordinary course of business, or that it take a particular form, the Court finds that under these circumstances a six-month delay in the sending of the letter was unreasonable as a matter of law. First, Starry candidly acknowledges that it has been able to find no case in which a period of more than four months was held to be reasonable under the merchant exception. The inordinate length of time alone in this case justifies holding the delay unreasonable. Moreover, the circumstances surrounding the relationship of the parties make a six-month delay unreasonable.... In this case, a writing in confirmation of the oral modification would lock the parties into a modified supply contract at a particular price. The volatility of the petroleum market, the radical fluctuations in price and supply, all counsel in favor of prompt confirmation....

In any event, Starry could have protected itself. All it needed to do was to send a letter confirming the modification; Murphy did not even need to sign it. Minnerath candidly acknowledges that he simply neglected to send one.... Moreover, Murphy's repeated refusal to provide confirmation should have indicated to Starry that Murphy did not acknowledge the existence of the modification. Thus, the Court concludes that the merchant exception is not satisfied by the October 5, 1990 letter....

Starry also argues that the statute is satisfied because there is evidence of a writing as required under Section 336.2-201(1). Starry correctly argues that as long as a quantity term is included, the form of the writing is unimportant. It "may be written in lead pencil on a scratch pad...." In this case, Starry claims that a written note which Robert Billingsley left for Michael Palmgren, stating that Murphy had agreed to provide the additional 5,000 tons of asphalt cement oil, constitutes a writing within the meaning of the statute....

Murphy responds that Starry is attempting to transform Palmgren's inability to remember a particular note into a writing sufficient to satisfy the statute. According to Murphy, the only evidence of the existence of this note is the testimony of Steven Minnerath, Starry's president. Robert Billingsley denies ever making such a note.... Palmgren does not remember seeing such a note. Murphy claims that the testimony of the plaintiff, the proponent of the alleged oral contract, should be insufficient to satisfy the statute.

To accept Starry's argument, the Court would have to rely solely upon the testimony of the proponent of the contract. This "is exactly what the statute of frauds seeks to avoid...." The oral testimony of the plaintiff does not constitute a writing sufficient to satisfy the statute of frauds. Further, even if the Court were to accept Starry's argument that there was such a note, there is no evidence that the note contained the requisite quantity term. This alleged note therefore does not satisfy the statute....

The final question in the statute of frauds analysis is whether some exception to the statute applies, making the alleged oral modification enforceable. Starry relies upon two. The first exception is contained in Section 336.2-201(3)(b).... A party against whom enforcement is sought need not actually admit that there was a contract; he only need admit the facts the legal consequence of which is a contract in order to be deprived of the statute of frauds defense....

Starry claims that three admissions by Murphy in its testimony and pleadings satisfy the statute. First, in its memorandum in support of its motion, Murphy admits having supplied Starry with an additional 107 tons of asphalt cement oil.... Second, Starry claims that Billingsley's acknowledgement that the additional oil was discussed during March 1990, combined with the evidence that Starry had received enough work to be able to use the additional amount, establishes the plausibility of Starry's claim and satisfies the purposes underlying the statute of frauds. Finally, Starry argues that an adverse credibility determination may amount to an admission.... According to Starry, Palmgren's unlikely loss of memory regarding the existence of the note satisfies the admission exception....

Starry's positions seem tenuous at best. There are at least two problems with respect to its argument that supplying 107 tons of oil constitutes an admission for statute of a contract for 5,000 tons. First, the Court cannot infer from the fact that Murphy supplied oil to Starry, a regular customer, that Murphy would not have done so without a contract because it would invalidate any allocation program. To the contrary, the statute expressly provides that the seller "may include [in its allocation program] regular customers not then under contract as well as his own requirements for further manufacture...." The only requirement is that the allocation must be fair and reasonable.... Second, the admissions exception expressly provides that "the contract is not enforceable ... beyond the quantity of goods admitted...." Assuming that there was an oral contract for an additional 5,000 tons of asphalt cement oil, that contract is enforceable only up to the 107 tons admitted.

Further, negotiations do not amount to a contract.... In order to satisfy the admissions exception, a party must admit the facts giving rise to a contract.... Notwithstanding the flexibility of the Code, it is essential that the parties intend to enter into a binding agreement.... Although the fact that the sale of additional oil may render Starry's claim more plausible, the admissions exception has clearly not been satisfied.

Starry's third argument seems the least persuasive. Credibility determinations are inappropriate when reviewing motions for summary judgment.... Regardless, Murphy's employees have denied under oath that the contract was modified. The admissions exception does not apply when the party against whom enforcement is sought denies under oath the existence of a modification....

The second exception to the statute of frauds relied upon by Starry is the equitable estoppel exception. The Uniform Commercial Code provides that unless specifically displaced by Code provisions, the principles of law and equity, including estoppel, supplement its provisions.... Minnesota courts have long held that the doctrine of equitable estoppel may limit the application of the statute of frauds....

Without addressing whether a party seeking refuge under equitable estoppel must show unconscionability, it is clear that misrepresentation of a material fact is an indispensable element.... The parties seem to acknowledge that there is no evidence of misrepresentation, either intentional or unintentional. Thus, the equitable estoppel exception does not undermine Murphy's statute of frauds defense.

After analyzing the application of the statute of frauds under the three-part inquiry, the Court finds that the statute of frauds precludes Starry's claim of an oral modification beyond the 107 tons of additional oil. The statute of frauds clearly applies, given that the contract as purportedly modified involves the sale of goods for the price of $500 or more. The statute has not been satisfied, either through the merchant exception or the allegedly lost note. Finally, the admission exception permits enforcement only for the additional 107 tons, while the estoppel exception does not apply at all. The Court will therefore grant Murphy's motion for summary judgment.

To protect the seller of goods against a potentially unfair result, UCC Section 2-201 provides a separate alternative for specially manufactured goods. Where the buyer has a change of mind and tries to cancel an oral order for custom-made goods, the seller can enforce the oral contract by convincing the jury that the goods the seller is making are "for the buyer," that the seller has substantially started to produce the goods or has made commitments to get them from someone else, and that the goods cannot be readily resold in the ordinary course of the seller's business. This situation thus raises several fact questions; basically, the jury has to be convinced that the seller will be stuck with the proverbial "white elephant" if the oral contract, actually made, is not enforced.

The oral contract is also enforceable against a party who admits its existence in pleadings, testimony, or otherwise in court. As with the "writing" alternatives, the contract is not enforceable under this provision beyond the quantity of goods admitted.

Finally, the "part performance" alternative has been substantially changed by the Code. Previously, either party could use the other's receipt and acceptance of a partial performance as evidence of a much larger contract. For example, a seller who could prove having delivered fifty bushels of wheat to a buyer who had accepted the goods might then allege that this was merely the first installment on an oral contract for 1,000 bushels of wheat; if the jury believed the seller, the seller could get the contract enforced on that basis. The drafters of the Code felt that this result circumvented the policy of the Statute of Frauds, so they provided that partial performance by one party makes the contract enforceable against the other party only to the same, *pro rata* extent. Thus, in the above example the seller can only collect the contract price for the fifty bushels of wheat delivered and accepted; the rest of the oral contract remains unenforceable. However, if the goods are an indivisible unit, such as a car or Boeing 707, the buyer's payment of part of the contract price, received and accepted by the seller, does have the effect of making the entire contract enforceable.

Compliance Alternatives Under Other Code Sections. For investment securities, the Code permits the use of these same basic alternatives, with the exception of "special manufacture." To be sufficient, a writing under this Section (8-319) must also contain the price term. The writing in confirmation procedure can be used between any buyer and seller; it is not limited to situations where both parties are, or are represented by, brokers or other securities "experts." Since these securities would normally exist in divisible units, partial performance here should nearly always result in only partial enforceability.

For security agreements, there must be a writing by which the debtor grants the secured party a security interest in the described collateral, and only if the *debtor* signs the writing will the secured party have the right to repossess and resell the collateral if the debtor goes into default. Such a writing is not required only in cases where the secured party keeps possession of the collateral ("pledge" or "pawn" transactions). Secured transactions are discussed in more detail in Chapters 18 and 19.

For sales of miscellaneous intangibles at a contract price of $5,000 or more, no alternative to the writing is provided. The signed writing must indicate that a contract has been made, must describe the subject matter of the contract, and must contain a price term.

RESULTS IF THE STATUTE OF FRAUDS APPLIES AND IT HAS NOT BEEN SATISFIED

Unenforceable in Court. In the vast majority of cases where the Statute of Frauds applies and has not been complied with, the contract is unenforceable in court. This does not mean that the contract is illegal in any way or that the parties have violated any criminal law. Nor does it mean that if the parties perform the contract in full, one of the parties can later move to rescind the performances on the basis that the contract should have been evidenced by a writing and never was. "Unenforceable" as applied here simply means that there will be no court remedy for the enforcement of such a contract, that the court will not assist either party with its sanctions for nonperformance of the contract unless the contract can be proved by the required writing.

This result is not changed by the fact that one party has relied in good faith (but stupidly) on the existence of the unenforceable oral contract. Courts do not generally feel that they are permitted to work out a result forbidden by the Statute of Frauds just because a particular plaintiff presents an appealing set of facts.

"Part Performance" Exceptions. The UCC's exceptions where part performance of an oral contract for goods or securities has taken place, have already been discussed as "alternatives." In addition, courts have worked out limited exceptions to the unenforceability result for contracts involving real estate or the one-year clause.

Where one party has in good faith conferred benefits on the other under an oral contract which is unenforceable because of the one-year clause, a court will generally permit recovery in quasi contract of the fair market value of the benefits so as to prevent "unjust enrichment." An employee who worked for three months under a two-year oral contract would thus be able to recover the fair market value of any services for which he or she had not been paid already. This exception would not, however, permit the recovery of moving expenses, bonuses, or other special compensation promised as part of the unenforceable oral agreement. The entire contract is enforceable, according to the *Restatement (Second) of Contracts*, only where one party has *fully* performed his or her obligations; that party can then enforce the other party's full return performance.

For real estate contracts, the courts have developed a doctrine called **equitable estoppel**, which prevents a party from relying on the Statute of Frauds under certain limited circumstances and thus has the effect of making an oral contract enforceable. The courts have permitted either party to enforce an oral contract where the buyer has taken possession of real estate with the seller's permission and has made substantial permanent physical improvements or (perhaps) where the buyer has taken possession and has made a part payment on the contract price. This doctrine is generally not applicable in cases where there has been only a part payment of the price or only a taking of possession by the buyer, or only "reliance" expenditures such as preparation of documents by the seller or moving expenses by the buyer.

It is never advisable to rely on the slim chance that a court will salvage your situation by applying one of the exceptions to the Statute of Frauds. The only safe course is to *get it in writing*! (And make sure the other party signs the writing!)

PAROL EVIDENCE RULE

Nature and Operation of the Rule. Just as the operation of the Statute of Frauds can be summarized in the sentence, "Get it in writing," so can the significance of the parol evidence rule be summarized by slightly modifying the sentence to read: *"Get it all in writing!"*

Although the application of the parol evidence rule may seem to produce harsh or unfair results in particular situations, the equities are not all on one side. There are sound, practical reasons for the rule's existence. It is, ultimately, another example of the courts' efforts to find and enforce the intent of the parties. The contracting parties may have engaged in extended negotiations before reaching their agreement. They may have exchanged numerous oral and written proposals and counterproposals, some accepted by the other side, some rejected. Then, at the end of this lengthy process, they signed a document which either expressly or impliedly stated that it was intended by them as the full, final, and complete written expression of their agreement.

At this point, the parol evidence rule comes into operation. Once a party has signed such a document, the rule prevents that party from unilaterally changing or modifying its terms by using parol, or outside, evidence. The document means what it says: "blue" means blue, not green; "ten tons" means ten tons, not 100 tons or ten pounds. If a term or a provision on a particular subject is not contained in the document, the presumption is that it was left out on purpose because the parties did not intend that it be included. In short, the rule operates against the "add-on-a-term" person, who is trying to say, "Yes, that's the contract I signed. Yes, that's the deal I made. But—there's something else that we agreed on that's not in the document." In general, the "add-on" person will (and should) lose this argument; parol evidence will not be admitted to change the terms of the written document.

The rule is really not saying anything more "unfair" than that a person is, generally, bound by what he or she has signed. If the document isn't "right," if it doesn't contain all the terms you have agreed on, *don't sign it*!

The *Whitney Bros.* case speaks to this point.

WHITNEY BROS. CO. v. SPRAFKIN
3 F.3d 530 (1st Cir., 1993)

FACTS: Plaintiffs/appellees are Whitney Brothers Company ("Whitney Brothers") and Griffin M. Stabler, Whitney Brothers' president, chief executive officer and director. Defendants/appellants, David C. Sprafkin and Joan Barenholtz are the trustees of the Bernard M. Barenholtz Trust, Whitney Brothers' majority shareholder. Plaintiffs sued to compel defendants to sell their stock in Whitney Brothers pursuant to a written buy/sell contract.

Whitney Brothers is a New Hampshire corporation that produces wooden learning materials. Bernard Barenholtz acquired 62.6 percent of the company's outstanding shares in 1969. Ten years later, he transferred these shares to the Bemard M. Barenholtz Trust (the "Trust") and named himself and David Sprafkin trustees. Plaintiff Griffin Stabler owns 32.7 percent of the shares, and his son, David Stabler, owns the remaining 4.7 percent.

On January 27, 1987, Whitney Brothers, the trustees, and Griffin Stabler executed a written buy/sell agreement. Under the agreement, Whitney Brothers would buy the Trust's shares within ninety days of the death of Bernard Barenholtz and buy Griffin Stabler's shares within ninety days of Stabler's death. To determine the purchase price, the parties would plug an agreed-upon appraisal into a formula to determine the purchase price. If the parties could not agree on an appraisal, they would each get their own and plug the average into the formula. The contract also provided for payment by a promissory note, with monthly installments over ten years at 10 percent interest per annum. The agreement did not mention whether prepayment of the note was permissible. Article 5, however, stated that the agreement could be altered or amended "by a writing signed by all of the shareholders."

On February 3, 1987, Bernard Barenholtz's (and defendants') attorney Samuel M. Sprafkin wrote a letter (the "February 3 letter") advising Mr. Barenholtz that the promissory note should be prepayable without penalty. After Bernard Barenholtz received the letter, the parties orally agreed to the prepayment provision. Barenholtz then placed the letter in a file with the written contract.

When Bernard Barenholtz died, on August 5, 1989, his daughter, defendant Joan Barenholtz, assumed his trustee position. A few days later, plaintiff Stabler and defendant Sprafkin discussed the contract's required stock sale. One of the parties asked E.F. Greene to update a past appraisal of Whitney Brothers. Sprafkin rejected Greene's appraisal; Whitney Brothers accepted it. Relying on Greene's appraisal, Whitney Brothers tendered to defendants a prepayable promissory note for $1,178,000 for the stock (the "September 1989 Tender").

Instead of responding immediately, defendants secured a significantly higher appraisal from Alfred Schimmel. They then rejected Whitney Brothers' tender by letter, without mentioning the note's prepayment clause. When Stabler learned of defendants' appraisal, he rejected it as too high.

After the trial the court issued an order in which it: (1) required plaintiffs to pay $1,349,343 for the stock; (2) ruled that plaintiffs could pay for the stock with a prepayable promissory note; (3) ruled that interest on the note would begin to accrue when it was executed, and not before; and (4) awarded attorneys' fees to plaintiffs based on defendants' bad faith conduct of the litigation.

 CIRCUIT JUDGE TORRUELLA:

Article 4 of the buy/sell contract provides:

> The purchase price ... *shall be paid* with a negotiable promissory note *which shall provide for* the payment of the purchase price in ten years with interest at the rate of 10 percent per annum, principal and interest payable in 120 equal, consecutive monthly payments.

(emphasis added). The agreement nowhere mentions prepayment of the proposed promissory note.

At trial, the district court conditionally allowed evidence of a subsequent oral agreement permitting prepayment of the note. Ultimately, the court admitted the evidence, finding that it was not precluded by the parol evidence rule. In the same ruling, the court found that the parties indeed entered the alleged oral agreement.

The court erred in finding the asserted oral agreement binding on the parties. Article 5 of the written buy/sell contract prohibits the parties from orally altering or amending the written contract. Under N.H. Rev. Stat. Ann. § 382-A:2-209(2), "(a) signed agreement which excludes modification or rescission except by a signed writing cannot be otherwise modified or rescinded..." While an attempted modification can constitute a waiver, that waiver can be retracted absent "a material change of position in reliance on that waiver." N.H. Rev. Stat. Ann. § 382-A:2-209(4) and (5). Here, plaintiffs allege no alteration of their position in reliance on a prepayment provision. Thus, we can find no binding waiver of Article 5 by defendants. Plaintiffs contend that since the written contract says nothing about prepayment, a subsequent agreement to allow prepayment does not constitute an alteration or amendment under Article 5. Rather, they argue that the agreement was independent of the written contract. Apparently, the district court agreed. Although the court did not explicitly address Article 5, it did conclude that a prepayment provision "does not, by its terms, vary or contradict the terms of the agreement...."

On review, we find that the district court erred in its determination. The written buy/sell contract provision regarding payment expressly contemplates payment over ten years at 10 percent interest. If plaintiffs prepay the note, they will avoid paying the 10 percent interest and thereby deviate from an express provision of the contract. Moreover, 10 percent interest over ten years amounts to a significant percentage of the contract price. Since prepayment would substantially alter the parties' financial positions under the contract, an agreement to permit prepayment constitutes an alteration under Article 5.

Furthermore, although the New Hampshire Supreme Court has never encountered this precise issue, recent holdings from that court support our conclusion....

Although these cases involve actual promissory notes, rather than agreements to make promissory notes, by finding prepayment precluded in the absence of a specific provision authorizing it, the New Hampshire Supreme Court demonstrated a belief that prepayment significantly alters the rights of the parties involved.

Finally, plaintiffs' last-ditch argument, that Sprafkin's February 3 letter constitutes a sufficient writing, needs little deliberation. Sprafkin wrote the letter to Barenholtz. Thus, it cannot be construed, as plaintiffs propose, as a written offer which plaintiffs were entitled to accept orally.

Because Article 5 of the contract precludes plaintiffs' asserted oral agreement, the district court erred in finding the note prepayable.

Situations Not Covered by the Rule. Since the purpose of the parol evidence rule is to make a final document which the parties intended to be final, the rule has no application in contract situations where no such full, final, and complete document has ever been signed. If the seller has simply given the buyer a sales receipt, or if the parties have merely exchanged letters, no such complete document exists, so all evidence is admissible to show what the parties intended to include as part of the contract. For sales of goods, a "final" writing may be "explained or supplemented," but not "contradicted," by "consistent additional terms," "unless the court finds the writing to have been intended also as a complete and exclusive statement of the terms of the agreement" (UCC, 2-202[b]). What this means in plain English is that a court *may* be a little more reluctant to apply the parol evidence rule in a sale of goods case where the contract does not contain a specific, "This is it" statement.

Again, remembering the basic purpose of the parol evidence rule, it obviously has no application in situations where the alleged modification of the terms in the document occurred *after* the document was signed. The document is presumed final as of the time it was signed. The parties may decide to modify it later, and the parol evidence rule does not prevent either of them from trying to convince a jury that such modifications were in fact agreed to. (There may, however, be both consideration and Statute of Frauds problems as to such subsequent modifications, as noted previously.)

Third, and even more obviously, the rule has no application where there are *two* contracts, one evidenced by a complete writing, the other oral. The fact that one contract is written does not prevent a party from trying to prove that there was a second, oral contract. If you buy a used car from your next-door neighbors for $900, and they also agree to let you park the car in their garage for the next six months for $10 a month, the fact that you have signed a complete written contract for the sale of the car will not prevent you from trying to prove the existence of the separate oral contract to rent the garage space. (But note that if the "garage" promise was not a *separate* rental contract, but just part of the deal for the car, and that promise was not included in the written car contract, you'd be unable to prove it was made.)

Exceptions to the Operation of the Parol Evidence Rule. Like many of the other rules of evidence, the parol evidence rule is subject to some important exceptions. That is, the trier of fact can consider parol evidence in some situations, at least for some purposes, even though a complete written document exists and even though the evidentiary facts occurred before the document was signed.

Stated most simply, parol evidence is admissible where it is being offered to help the court interpret the terms of the written contract or to show the existence of a defense against the written contract, not to *change* the terms of the written contract. The line is not always easy to draw, although in some cases the correct result seems fairly obvious.

Ambiguities. The easiest cases to decide are those where the writing makes no sense by itself, due to ambiguities, contradictory provisions, or coded "nonsense" terms. In these cases, a court must use extrinsic evidence to discover what the parties "really meant." Where both parties are engaged in a particular trade or business and certain words have acquired a customary meaning in that business, courts generally permit either party to prove that special meaning even though the words have a "plain English" meaning, too. Thus, an Oregon court permitted a seller to prove that "50 percent protein" really meant *49.50 percent* protein in the dog food business, and the seller could therefore collect the full contract price per ton for all shipments of dog food scraps with a protein content of at least 49.50 percent. For sales of goods, the UCC now permits the parties to explain or supplement a "final" writing by course of dealing, usage of trade, or course of performance.

Oral conditions. Most courts will also allow a party to show that the written contract was intended to be subject to an orally agreed-upon condition precedent, that they intended no deal at all unless and until some special condition was satisfied. Similarly, if the writing states as a fact something that is just not so, a party can usually prove the truth. For instance, if your contract to buy a new TV set not only describes the set and states the price and the payment terms, but also goes on to say that the set "has been delivered," when in fact it has not been delivered, you can prove that you didn't get the TV set as promised. (But the parol evidence rule will generally prevent you from changing "one TV" into *two* TVs, or "$600" into $450, or "TV" into stereo.)

Defenses. Courts are quite liberal in allowing proof of the existence of a defense against liability on the written contract. In most cases this is not really a "contradiction" of the writing because the writing does not usually contain such provisions as "This contract is legal" or "There was no duress." The contract may, however, contain a representation that the party signing it is of full legal age, and there are some courts which prevent a minor from asserting lack of capacity if the minor has stated otherwise in writing. (The next chapter has a more complete discussion of this point.)

SIGNIFICANCE OF THIS CHAPTER

Knowledge of the two major rules discussed in this chapter—the Statute of Frauds and the parol evidence rule—could save you and any organization you represent from many unnecessary lawsuits. This chapter contains the most significant legal "first-aid" rules in the entire book: *Get it in writing—and get it all in writing!* In some cases, you don't have any enforceable contract at all if you don't follow the rules. In other cases, you may wind up with a contract other than the one you intended if you don't follow the rules.

People tend to forget promises and guarantees once they have your contract price, or your goods, land, or services. Promises are harder to "forget" if you have them in a signed writing. Take a little extra time and write up the agreement, or rewrite it, if it doesn't state the terms correctly. If the written agreement isn't clear and understandable, you should probably have your lawyer check it over for you. Once you sign it, you'll be bound by it, so make sure you know what it says—and make sure the *other* party signs it too, and that you get a signed copy. An ounce of written "prevention" is worth several pounds of lawyers.

PROBLEMS FOR DISCUSSION

1. The plaintiff (Sinclair) alleged that on May 30, 1996, he entered into an oral contract with Sullivan Chevrolet, to serve as its sales manager for a one-year period, commencing June 6, 1996. He was to receive a salary of $1,800 per month, plus a bonus to be later agreed on but with a guaranteed minimum for the year of $30,000. In addition, Sullivan would pay his moving expenses, let him use a company car, and have a written contract for him to sign on June 6. It is further alleged that said representations were falsely made by the defendant without intention of performance, but this being unknown to the plaintiff, he quit his job in St. Louis, moved his family to Champaign, Illinois, and assumed his duties pursuant to the agreement. However, defendant did not abide by said agreement, as a result of which plaintiff terminated his employment on March 18, 1997. He claimed damages of $12,527.

   Can he collect? Explain.

2. Gisaburo Kiyose taught in the Department of East Asian Languages on the Bloomington campus of Indiana University. From 1984 to 1986, he was a teaching associate; from 1986 to April 1993, a lecturer. He received his Ph.D. in 1993 and was appointed an assistant professor. He claims that he was promised lifetime employment, beginning with a three-year appointment as assistant professor. He was notified in 1993 that he would not be reappointed for 1994-95. He further claims that he turned down five offers from other schools because of Indiana's promise. The trial court granted defendants' motion to dismiss.

   Was this ruling correct ? Why or why not?

3. Eugene Feudal brings this action against Mr. and Mrs. Trustee. The two parties had entered into an oral rental agreement which continued for several years. In September, the Trustees suddenly stopped payment. When they had not paid any rent by December, Eugene brought an action against them. The Trustees countered by claiming that they were the owners of the disputed premises, which Eugene Feudal had sold to them in an oral contract two years ago. They said that they had stopped payment when their obligation under the oral contract had been fulfilled. Mrs. Trustee testified that she had heard her husband and Feudal discussing the possibility of a sale. Mr. Trustee told his attorney that Feudal would contact him to draw up a contract.

   Was there an enforceable contract? Why or why not?

4. The plaintiffs were small independent oil dealers with their main operations in North Carolina. The defendant was a refiner, dependent almost entirely on producers for its supply of crude oil. It had for some years been selling its product to the plaintiffs. In anticipation of the oil shortage, which all parties in the industry apparently foresaw, discussions as to future supplies were held among the parties. It was contended by the plaintiffs that the defendant agreed to supply them with certain fixed quantities of gasoline. As the energy crisis deepened, the defendant's suppliers drastically reduced its supply of crude oil. The defendant accordingly proceeded to allocate on a lower percentage its deliveries to its contract customers and to notify customers such as the plaintiffs, whom it denominated noncontract customers, that it would make no further sales to them. Preliminary injunctive relief was granted in both instances. In each case the defendant appealed.

   How should the appeals court rule?

5. Kenneth Sierens and James Thompson sued Edwin Clausen for breach of two alleged oral agreements to sell them a total of 3,500 bushels of soybeans. They said they sent Clausen a written confirmation, in accordance with UCC 2201 (2). Clausen had been a farmer for thirty-four years, was then cultivating 180 acres of corn and 150 acres of soybeans, and had for the past five years sold his crops to grain elevators in both cash sales and futures contracts. The trial court held that Clausen was a farmer, and not a "merchant" for the purposes of UCC 2201(2). It dismissed the complaint, and the appellate court affirmed.

   Will the supreme court affirm? Explain.

Chapter 11
Reality of Consent

Even though a contract that appears complete has been entered into, and the agreement is enforceable under the Statute of Frauds, there may still be defenses against liability on the contract. Depending on the defense proved, the contract may be voidable at the option of one or both parties; or some parts of it, or the whole contract may be unenforceable; or the entire agreement may be void.

LACK OF CAPACITY

We consider, first, defenses based on a party's lack of capacity to contract. Capacity questions may be raised with regard to minors, insane persons, intoxicated persons, persons under the influence of drugs, aliens, American Indians, convicts, married women, and private and governmental corporations. Determinations of these questions are usually made according to the law of the place where the contract is entered into, except where real estate is involved; for realty, the law of the state where the realty is located determines capacity questions.

MINORS, OR "LEGAL INFANTS"

It is sometimes said that "minors can't make contracts." That is patently not so; minors can and do make millions of dollars' worth of contracts every day. What is distinctive about the minor's contract is that it is voidable at his or her option; the minor can later elect not to be bound by it. But make no mistake; the other party, unless that party too lacks full contractual capacity, is bound to the agreement with the minor. The common-law judges were concerned with the possibility that the "infant" might be taken advantage of, and so gave the minor the virtually absolute right of disaffirmance. Although minors today may be more sophisticated at an earlier age, this rule continues to be applied by the courts.

We need, then, to examine the scope of minors' power to disaffirm their contracts and to see when minors may be liable under five different "theories of liability."

Scope of the Minor's Power to Disaffirm. The common law set the age of legal majority at 21; until quite recently that was also the age used for full contractual capacity in nearly all states. The adoption of the Voting Rights Amendment, setting the voting age at 18, has led most states to similarly lower their age of majority to 18 (except perhaps for the age at which one can lawfully buy alcoholic beverages). Different ages, however, may still exist in some states for such matters as criminal responsibility, marriage without parental consent, and making a valid will. However, we are concerned here only with the legal capacity to make fully binding contracts.

Whatever age is established in a state, it refers strictly to chronological age. How old the minors "look," or how "experienced" they are, is completely irrelevant to minors' power to disaffirm their contracts. Equally irrelevant is the fact that the minors might be living away from their parents and are totally free of their control (i.e., emancipated).

In general, minors have the power to disaffirm any contract they make while still a minor. In some states, certain contracts are made binding against the minor by special statutes (bank accounts and life insurance contracts are typical examples), but these are special, and very limited, exceptions.

In most states, minors can disaffirm a contract any time while they are still minors and for a reasonable time after arriving at the age of majority. For contracts involving real estate, most states say that minors cannot disaffirm until reaching the age of majority, and then they have a reasonable time to elect to affirm or disaffirm. What is a reasonable time within which to disaffirm is a question to be determined by the facts of each case, with the courts paying particular attention to whether the minor was aware of the right to disaffirm.

Any words or actions which indicate the minor's intent not to be bound by the contract are sufficient notice of disaffirmance. Asking for the money back or offering to return items bought while a minor would be clear indications of an intent to disaffirm. Where the contract is completely "executory" (i.e., not performed by either side), even the minor's silence may amount to a disaffirmance. The minor's failure to confirm the unperformed contract after age 18 indicates an unwillingness to be bound by it, but the receipt and retention of benefits or the making of a payment on the contract by the former minor would probably be a ratification of the contract. Silence has the opposite implication where the minor has received the performance of the other party and has, in return, performed under the contract while still a minor, and then turns 18 but says nothing about wanting to disaffirm. In this case, silence beyond the reasonable time for disaffirmance equals ratification.

All states agree that ratification by the minor can occur only after the minor has arrived at the age of majority; otherwise, any "ratification" can be disaffirmed since it too occurred while the person was a minor. In addition to the "silence" case described above, ratification can be made by express statements, such as "I'll keep the car," or it may be implied from the retention of benefits, or from payments made after the minor has reached age 18.

Effect of Minor's Disaffirmance on the Contract. Once a minor has effectively exercised the power to disaffirm a contract, the minor can no longer be held liable for any promises made therein; the minor's contract was voidable, and the minor has elected to avoid it. Thus, where a minor purchased an automobile and promised to make installment payments for the balance of the contract price, if the minor disaffirms, then the minor is no longer liable for the balance still due. Likewise, a minor who disaffirms such a voidable contract has the legal right to receive all benefits already transferred to the other party under the contract. For example, in the car purchase case, the minor is entitled to the return of all monies already paid to the seller of the car. A minor who gave the seller a trade-in car as part of the down payment is entitled to the return of that too, or of its fair market value if the seller no longer has it.

Where the benefits given by the minor have been retransferred to third parties, the minor can generally sue such third parties and demand the return of such property. Thus, a minor who sells real estate while a minor would be able to reclaim it even as against a good faith third party who bought the real estate from the minor's buyer. As exceptions to the general third-party rule, the UCC protects good faith purchaser third parties against such claims by minors in two situations: where the minor's goods have been resold by the initial buyer to a good faith purchaser or where a promissory note or other negotiable instrument executed by a minor has gotten into the hands of a holder in due course (basically, just another name for a good faith purchaser). This HDC rule is discussed in detail in Part Five, Commercial Paper. In each of these two exception situations, the minor could not recover the instrument or the goods from the third party. The minor could, however, still use minority to avoid liability as the seller/transferor of the property.

Liability in Quasi Contract for Necessaries.

To prevent **unjust enrichment** and to provide a remedy for persons who have transferred benefits but have no enforceable contract claim for their price, the common-law courts developed the concept of **quasi contract**. While acknowledging that there is no enforceable contract claim, this theory permits a plaintiff to collect the reasonable market value of benefits that the plaintiff has conferred, "as if" a contract existed.

A minor is liable in quasi contract for the reasonable market value of "necessaries" actually furnished to the minor pursuant to the minor's now disaffirmed contract. The other party has the burden of proving that whatever was furnished was actually a necessary to the *particular* minor whom the party dealt with; proof that general categories of necessaries, such as food, clothing, shelter, or medical services, were furnished to the minor is not sufficient to establish the seller's right to recovery. It must also be shown that the minor in question had no source of supply of these items and that the items were furnished to the minor in reasonable amounts. An apartment would not be a necessary, for example, for minors who could live with their parents; and even if an apartment were a necessary for the particular minor, a ten-room penthouse would probably not be. Although the courts today are somewhat more liberal in defining necessaries, sellers of such obvious "luxury" items as stereos, TVs, and vacations probably have no case under this theory. Even where an item is found to be a necessary, the proper measure of recovery is only its fair market value (a fact question), not its contract price, and that *only* for the benefits already conferred on and used by the minor. In the case of the apartment found to be a necessary, the landlord can collect only what a jury determines to be the fair market value and only for the period of time that the minor stayed in the apartment.

Minor's Duty to Make Restitution.

Under the general rule, as applied in most states, a minor who wishes to disaffirm a contract has the duty to return to the other party whatever contract benefits are still in the minor's possession at the time of disaffirmance. In most states, the minor has no duty to reimburse the other party for that portion of the consideration which the minor has lost, wasted, or disposed of during infancy. In the classic example, a 16-year-old boy buys a new

Cadillac, drives it until he is almost 18, then "totals" it in an accident. In most states, the minor's only duty of restitution is to return the wreck; the minor is not liable for the use value of the car while the minor had it or for the extensive "depreciation" in the value of the car. Similarly, if the minor had resold the car and spent the proceeds, the minor would have nothing at all to restore but could still disaffirm the original purchase contract and get back whatever payment the minor had made to the original seller. (In short, car dealers are repeatedly warned: *"Don't sell to minors!"*) The same result—no restitution at all by the minor—occurs when the minor has received intangible benefits such as a vacation or services.

The *Mitchell* case is an example of how these rules operate to protect minors.

MITCHELL v. MITCHELL
963 S.W.2d 222 (Ky. App. 1998)

FACTS: Sherri Mitchell was injured on October 14, 1995, while traveling as a passenger in an automobile owned by her father, Donnie Fee, and operated by her husband, the appellee, Michael J. Mitchell. On October 26, 1995, Sherri, age seventeen, executed a release settling her bodily injury claim for $2,500. No conservator [guardian] was appointed at the time the release was executed.

Sherri filed a motion for declaratory judgment alleging that her incapacity at the time the release was executed rendered it null and void. The appellees argue, and the trial court agreed, that Sherri's marriage emancipated her, removing any disability she had as a minor, including the capacity to contract.

 JUDGE EMBERTON:

Ky.Rev. Stat. (KRS) 387.010 defines minor as anyone under the age of eighteen. Ordinarily, a contract executed by a minor is enforceable by the minor but may be avoided by the minor if not affirmed by him after reaching adulthood. Although the minor has the legal capacity to contract, he has the privilege of avoiding the contract.... Although there are certain exceptions to this general rule, none is applicable to this case.

A settlement agreement and release of a third-party tortfeasor has been held to be voidable by the infant.... A repudiation of the agreement requires that the minor return the consideration paid pursuant to that agreement....

The privilege bestowed upon a minor to avoid contracts made during infancy is given for policy reasons. Infants, as with other classes of disabilities, are presumed to be insufficiently mature or experienced to effectively bargain with those who have attained legal age, and any transaction which may result in a financial loss to them or in a depletion of their estates is scrutinized with care....

Marriage of the infant emancipates the minor; it does not, however, make the minor *sui juris*. In Bensinger's CoEx'rs ... the court declined to hold that an emancipated child must be bound by his contracts and followed the general rule that: "Although parental emancipation may free the infant from parental control, it does not remove all of the disabilities of infancy. It does not, for example, enlarge or affect the minor's capacity or incapacity to contract."...

The rule may seem antiquated in view of the arguable maturity of today's youth. It may seem ironic that a minor can drive a car yet not be bound by the contract to purchase that car or be responsible for his torts and crimes yet unable to settle a dispute against a tortfeasor. The distinction to be made is that too frequently a contract involves negotiation and thought beyond the maturity of most people under the age of eighteen. For the same reason we are unpersuaded by the cases cited by appellee dealing with the statute of limitations....

We cannot adopt a rule that marriage by the minor somehow classifies him as more mature and intelligent than his unmarried counterpart. We ... find that logic and common sense would not encourage such a result since marriage by a minor too frequently may itself be indicative of a lack of wisdom and maturity....

This case is reversed and remanded for an order voiding the settlement and release executed by appellant.

Estoppel to Assert Minority. As applied in most states, the above rules are hard enough on the adult seller, but even harsher results occur when minors have misrepresented their age and thus have induced the other party to contract on the assumption that they were adults.

Estoppel, remember, is the legal rule that prevents a party from denying the legal effectiveness of a previous statement, after another party has changed his or her position in reliance on the earlier statement. Shouldn't that rule be applied where the other party has made a contract in reliance on the minor's statement that the minor was of legal age to contract? Shouldn't the minor, in other words, be estopped from asserting minority in such a case? Some courts do apply estoppel against the minor here, but the majority do not. A special California statute provides a procedure for court approval of employment contracts for minor athletes and artists; the minor-employee is bound to the contract once the court approves it.

Tort Liability for Misrepresentation of Age. Minors are, as a general rule, liable for their own torts, and intentional misrepresentation is a tort—fraud. Should not the other party, having been damaged by reasonable reliance on the minor's misrepresentation of age, be able to sue the minor on a tort theory of liability even though the contract has been disaffirmed? Once again, the courts are split on this point. A slight majority still follows the older view that the minor cannot be sued in tort, where to do so would amount to holding the minor liable on his or her contract. The policy protecting the minor against unnecessary contracts is more important to most courts than the policy of holding the minor liable for torts.

It probably should also be noted at this point that a minor's parents are not generally liable for the minor's torts or the minor's contracts, although they are legally obligated to support the minor with the necessities of life. Some states do have statutes which make parents liable for their minor children's intentional torts, up to a specific dollar amount of damages.

PERSONS WHO ARE INSANE, INTOXICATED, OR DRUGGED

Contracts made by persons who lack contractual capacity because their ability to make decisions has been impaired by mental disease or defect, or by alcohol or drugs, are treated in much the same way as contracts made by minors. As a general rule, where a person's mental faculties are so impaired that the person does not understand the nature and consequences of the transaction, the resulting contract is voidable at the person's option when the person recovers, or at the option of a subsequently appointed guardian. If any such person has previously been taken before a (probate) court, adjudged incompetent to manage his or her own affairs, and had a guardian appointed, then later contracts made by that person are not just voidable but totally void. The person need take no action to disaffirm the contracts; they simply will not be recognized by the courts.

Such persons are generally liable in quasi contract for the fair market value of necessaries furnished to them during their period of disability (assuming that these needs are not already being met by a guardian), under basically the same rules as those that apply to minors. Much more strictly than with the minor, the courts require the mentally disabled person to make full restitution in money or the equivalent in order to disaffirm contracts entered into in good faith by the other party.

The *Brown* case raises these issues.

BROWN AS GUARDIAN OF MARY HALL v. FINANCIAL ENTERPRISES CORP.
188 Bankr. 476 (1995)

FACTS: On September 9, 1988, Mary Hall (the "Debtor") and her daughter, Marcia Hall, executed a promissory note in the principal amount of $24,000 payable to Financial Enterprises Corp. The note provided for a variable rate of interest, but not less than twenty-one percent (21%) annually, and was secured by a second mortgage on the Debtor's residence at 33 Fessenden Street, Mattapan, Massachusetts. The second mortgage was recorded with the Suffolk County Registry of Deeds on the same date. According to the affidavit of Stephen Hayes, Vice President of Financial, this is the only loan that Financial has ever made to the Debtor.

Ms. Hall accompanied her mother to the loan closing at Financial's office at the request of her brother, Kevin Hall, who "had arranged to borrow money from Financial to fix the porches." According to Ms. Hall, her mother neither read nor understood the contents of the loan documents that she signed. Ms. Hall co-signed the note after being asked by an agent of Financial to "sign below [her] mother's signature" so as to "make the loan go through faster."

In 1990, the Debtor fell into arrears with respect to her obligation to Financial, and Financial commenced foreclosure proceedings. However, in consideration of payments made by the Debtor, Financial agreed to forbear from foreclosing on the property.

Both Ms. Hall and her brother, Bernard Brown, stated in affidavits that their mother has been hospitalized for mental illness and depression for much of her adult life. They also stated that she is not competent to handle her own affairs. According to Ms. Hall, the Debtor has been dependent upon her children "for paper work, check writing, transportation, and dealing with the house. She has very little ability to understand these things, and this has been the situation for many years." According to Mr. Brown, the Debtor has not been competent to handle her own affairs for the last ten years.

As a result of the Debtor's alleged mental illness and incompetence, on October 5, 1994, Mr. Brown, who lives with his mother, filed a petition dated August 22, 1994, with the Probate and Family Court Department, Suffolk County, seeking appointment of himself as the Debtor's guardian and authorization to file a bankruptcy petition on her behalf. Mr. Brown was appointed temporary guardian on October 17, 1994. On February 27, 1995, the Probate Court appointed him guardian, "with authority to file Bankruptcy (sic)." His appointment was certified on May 31, 1995 after he posted the required bond.

Meanwhile, in August of 1994, because the Debtor had ceased making loan payments, Financial referred the matter to its attorney to begin foreclosure proceedings. Mr. Hayes, in his affidavit, stated, and the Debtor's counsel conceded in his memorandum opposing the motion, that Financial had no knowledge of the Debtor's alleged incompetence until foreclosure proceedings began and Financial was informed of the guardianship petition by its counsel.

After publishing a notice of the intended foreclosure sale in The Boston Globe for three successive weeks and notifying the Debtor by certified mail, Financial sold the property to itself for $50,000.00 at an auction on May 17, 1995, and executed the Memorandum of Sale as the buyer on the same day. Financial incurred legal fees and costs in the amount of approximately $6,500.00 as a result of the sale. On May 24, 1995, Financial served a notice to Quit upon the Debtor and her family.

On June 13, 1995, Mr. Brown, acting in his capacity as the Debtor's guardian, filed a Chapter 7 bankruptcy petition. On June 19, 1995, the Debtor's counsel sent a notice of rescission to Financial indicating that his client sought to rescind the loan transaction because of alleged truth in lending violations on the part of Financial. Financial, which had moved for relief from the automatic stay on June 29, 1995, denied the Debtor's request for rescission through its attorney on July 17, 1995.

On July 13, 1995, Mr. Brown brought this adversary proceeding against Financial on the Debtor's behalf.

On August 2, 1995, the Chapter 7 Trustee filed a notice of abandonment of the property pursuant to 11 U.S.C. s.554 on grounds that the property had been foreclosed prepetition and that "there would be no benefit to the estate in attempting to set aside the transfer because there is no equity for the estate in the property over the debtor's exemption and the existing liens." Accordingly, the Trustee did not object to Financial's motion for relief from stay.

At a hearing on August 2, 1995, the Court granted Financial's motion for relief from stay. On August 4, 1995, the Court allowed the Debtor's motion to convert the case from Chapter 7 to Chapter 13. The Court then stayed its order on August 2, 1995 granting Financial relief from the automatic stay and ordered the Debtor to file a Chapter 13 plan by August 9, 1995. On August 10, 1995, the Court held another hearing and continued the stay. The Court also granted the Debtor a *lis pendens* on the property and ordered the Debtor to pay Financial $500.00 per month for use and occupancy, commencing on August 18, 1995 and continuing on the 18th day of each succeeding month, pending the outcome of this adversary proceeding.

 JUDGE FEENEY:

The Debtor first argues that summary judgment should not be granted because the issue of whether the mortgage and the subsequent foreclosure sale were valid is disputed by the parties. She seeks an opportunity to present evidence of her incompetence in 1988, which, if proven, would render the mortgage invalid and Financial's foreclosure pursuant to the power of sale contained in the mortgage void. The Debtor contends that, although she would have no standing to bring this proceeding if Financial had sold the property to an "innocent third party," she retains her right to rescind based upon incompetence because Financial itself purchased to property at foreclosure. Additionally, the Debtor argues that Financial violated federal and state truth in lending laws when it extended credit to her, for which she seeks rescission of the note and mortgage as well as civil damages....

According to Financial, it had no knowledge of the Debtor's alleged incompetence until it began foreclosure proceedings. At that time, it learned only of the Debtor's present incompetence. Financial was not informed that the Debtor would raise defenses to the mortgage based upon both truth in lending violations and incompetence at the time that she granted the mortgage to Financial until after the foreclosure sale had taken place. Therefore, Financial argues, it was not required to seek the Probate Court's authorization to foreclose the mortgage....

Even though the Debtor is barred from redeeming the property and from rescinding the note on truth in lending grounds, the issue remains whether she can rescind the loan because of her alleged incompetence at the time that she signed the note and mortgage in 1988. The Debtor argues that her right to rescind based upon incompetence survives the foreclosure and may now be asserted against Financial since it is both the mortgagee and the purchaser of the property, and no bona fide purchaser has intervened in the chain of title. Financial's memorandum fails to differentiate between the right to redeem mortgaged property and the right to rescind a transaction based upon incompetence....

Where the contract has been performed in whole or in part, avoidance is permitted only on equitable terms.... Any benefits still retained the incompetent must be restored or paid for.... If the other party knew of the incompetency at the time of contracting, or if he took unfair advantage of the incompetent, consideration not received by the incompetent or dissipated without benefit to him need not be restored....

If the contract is made on fair terms and the other party has no reason to know of the incompetency, performance in whole or in part may so change the situation that the parties cannot be restored to previous positions or may otherwise render avoidance inequitable. The contract then ceases to be voidable. Where the other party, though acting in good faith, had reason to know of the incompetency at the time of contracting or performance, or where the equities can be partially adjusted by the decree, the court may grant or deny relief as the situation requires. Factors to be taken into account in such cases include not only benefits conferred and received on both sides but also the extent to which avoidance will benefit the incompetent and the extent to which others who will benefit from avoidance had opportunities to prevent the situation from arising....

Financial argues, and the Debtor concedes, that it had no knowledge of her incompetence at the time that it entered into the loan transaction with her in 1988. However, it is no defense to avoidance of the contract that one party did not know of the other's incompetence....

The Debtor has not introduced affidavits of medical experts but rather has asked the Court for additional time to produce an affidavit from her psychologist discussing her mental capacity at the time she executed the note and mortgage. However, the affidavits of both her son and daughter raise the issue of the Debtor's competence at the time of the transaction, and, therefore, a genuine issue of material fact exists. The Court denies Financial's motion for summary judgment on the issue of whether the Debtor is entitled to rescind the note and mortgage based upon incompetence....

In accordance with the foregoing, the Court concludes that Financial is entitled to judgment as a matter of law on the issues of redemption and truth in lending and therefore ALLOWS in part the defendant's motion for summary judgment. The motion is DENIED with respect to the issue of whether the Debtor can rescind the note and mortgage based upon her incompetence. At the trial scheduled for November 8, 1995, the Court shall consider testimony relating to the Debtor's competence and the total sums paid by the Debtor to financial since the inception of the loan.

ALIENS

Aliens in the United States are not generally subject to any contractual disability unless they are in the country illegally or their country is at war with ours. In either case, they will usually not be able to use our courts to enforce contracts. Aside from these two exceptional cases, some states—and even the national government—have made efforts to reserve to citizens certain rights and privileges, such as real estate ownership, practice of such professions as law and medicine, and government employment.

Aliens do not have to be given the "privileges and immunities of citizenship" under the Fourteenth Amendment, since they are obviously not citizens. But they are "persons," and thus they are protected by the due process of law clauses of the Fifth and Fourteenth Amendments and by the equal protection clause of the Fourteenth Amendment. The courts' problem, when such "citizens only" laws are challenged, is to try to decide which rights and privileges fall into which category. Voting in political elections and holding political office are obviously rights which do not have to be extended to aliens. The present tendency of the courts is to invalidate all other restrictions on aliens.

Currently, because of the large number of illegal aliens residing in this country, a significant question persists: To what extent do such persons qualify for government benefits, such as education, housing, and workers' compensation? Here again, the tendency is to require that such benefits be made available to illegal aliens, too. Even the traditional rule which denies illegal aliens access to our courts is being changed. Serious problems persist, with no easy solution in sight.

AMERICAN INDIANS

It sounds very strange to say it, some 200 years after the birth of the United States, but it is nonetheless true: The original inhabitants of this country, the American Indians, may still be subject to different legal rules because of their "national origin." This special legal status is not necessarily all bad; it may involve special privileges and immunities as well as disabilities. As an example, Albert B. LeBlanc, a full-blooded Chippewa Indian, did not have to get a commercial fishing license from the Michigan Department of Natural Resources since an 1836 treaty with the U.S. government reserved such fishing rights to the Chippewa nation. Likewise, a Navajo woman, Rosalind McClanahan, could not be required to pay Arizona state income tax on income she earned on the Navajo reservation. Inheritance of property, particularly for Indians living on reservations, may still be governed by tribal law rather than the general inheritance law of the particular state. Reservation businesses and the Bureau of Indian Affairs may engage in preferential hiring of Indians without violating the 1964 Civil Rights Act.

While the foregoing examples would probably be thought of as advantages enjoyed by Indians because of their special status, members of particular Indian tribes may still be subject to some residual contractual disabilities under old U.S. treaties and statutes.

CONVICTS

Upon conviction for certain crimes, a person may be sentenced to confinement in a U.S. or state prison. Such a sentence does not, however, mean that the person loses the general capacity to contract and to own property. Likewise, even in prison the person is still protected by the U.S. and state constitutions. Even prisoners have the capacity to appoint agents and attorneys and through them to make contracts and manage their property and affairs; such contracts made on a prisoner's behalf are, generally, fully enforceable by and against the prisoner.

Conviction of crimes involving force or fraud may, however, carry certain other disabilities. A person who has been released after having served the required sentence may be prevented from holding political (or labor union) office for some period of time. The person may also be prevented from practicing a licensed profession, such as law or medicine. Spiro Agnew, for example, was disbarred as a lawyer after pleading "no contest" to tax evasion charges.

MARRIED WOMEN

At common law, husband and wife are regarded legally as one person. As applied in contract and tort situations, this doctrine of "coverture" meant that the wife lacked the capacity to manage even her separately owned property or separate income and that no tort liability could exist between the spouses. The contracts which a married woman attempted to make were totally void. The wife could, however, obligate her *husband* in quasi contract for necessaries furnished to her for herself, their children, or their home.

In nearly all states, these rules have been changed by statute or constitution, so that a married woman enjoys the same legal rights and powers as her husband. She can own, manage, and dispose of her own property and has joint control of the jointly owned property. She, not he, is legally entitled to receive her earnings from her job. State courts have also been permitting the spouses to sue each other in tort, at least in some cases. Also, under modern interpretations, a wife would be similarly obligated in quasi contract for necessaries furnished to her husband where she had income or property and he did not.

Residues of the common-law rules remain in a few states, where a married woman may not be able to convey real estate, to mortgage jointly owned property, or act as a guarantor of someone else's debt without the husband's consent. Until 1963, Texas continued to apply the basic rules of coverture, so that a married woman lacked the capacity to contract unless she went through a special court procedure which removed her disability. Michigan continued to apply the coverture rules into the 1970s, and it did so despite Article 10, Section 1 of its 1963 constitution, which says: "The disabilities of coverture as to property are abolished." A 1982 Michigan statute appears to make the married woman liable, in most cases, where she has cosigned a contract with her husband.

The Equal Rights Amendment to the U.S. Constitution, if ever ratified, will almost certainly overturn any state laws that provide for different legal results based solely on sex.

CORPORATIONS

Private Corporations. Since corporations are "artificial" persons, existing only in the eyes of the law, they can have and exercise only those powers which the law gives them. In this sense, they have limited legal capacity; they can make contracts only in those areas of activity in which they have been authorized to be engaged. Modern corporation statutes are generally very liberal in granting corporate powers, and even if a corporation makes a contract which is outside its charter powers, most courts today do not permit either of the parties to the contract to raise that fact as a defense when sued on the contract. These matters are discussed more fully in Chapter 33.

Public (Municipal) Corporations. Like both profit and nonprofit private corporations, public corporations are creatures of limited legal authority, possessing only those powers given to them by constitutional or statutory provisions. The courts will normally not permit any enforcement of contracts made by a public corporation in excess of its powers, on the theory that to do so would injure the public through the illegal expenditures of public funds. Contracting procedures for public bodies are usually subject to very specific regulations, which must be complied with if one hopes to have an enforceable contract with them.

FRAUD AND MISTAKE

A second group of defenses centers on the idea that one of the parties did not really consent to the terms of the contract which the other wishes to enforce. While courts generally continue to require both parties to live up to the bargain they made, the problem in many cases is to discover exactly what they really did agree to. Included here are cases involving **fraud, innocent misrepresentation, undue influence, duress,** and **mistake.**

FRAUD

Many types of fraud may be crimes, so that criminal charges can be filed against the wrongdoer. False advertising and other deceptive practices may also result in administrative proceedings before the Federal Trade Commission and/or similar state bodies. We are concerned here, however, with the civil aspects of fraud, with its impact on the contract which resulted from the fraud.

Civil fraud is of two kinds: **fraud in the execution** and **fraud in the inducement**. Fraud in the execution describes a situation where one party is deceived as to the very nature of the transaction. The party is not aware that a contract is being made, or at least that he or she is making the one which the plaintiff now seeks to enforce. Elvis Presley, for example, fighting his way toward the exit from a concert hall, in the midst of a screaming mass of fans, was signing autograph books as fast as he could. One clever person shoved a folded piece of paper at him, and Elvis signed, not knowing that the unseen part of the paper contained a contract to buy a new set of *Encyclopedia Junkana*. On these facts, there is fraud in the execution, and the purported "contract" is totally void. Elvis was deceived as to the very nature of the "transaction" he was entering into, without having had a reasonable opportunity to discover the truth.

The far more common kind of civil fraud is fraud in the inducement, where the defrauded party does know that he or she is entering into a contract and does intend to enter the contract, but has been deceived as to some aspect of the contract. Usually this type of fraud involves misrepresentation of what the defrauded party is to receive. A used car falsely represented as being in A-1 mechanical condition illustrates this concept.

Although different courts may use slightly different formulations, the typical fraud case requires proof of five elements: (1) misrepresentation of a material fact, (2) knowledge of falsity, (3) intent to deceive, (4) reasonable reliance by the other party, and (5) damage to the defrauded party. Because fraud is so easily alleged by anyone having second thoughts about a contract, courts typically require proof of fraud by independent evidence which is clear and convincing.

Misrepresentation of Material Fact. A statement must contain a factual assertion to provide the basis for a fraud case. Statements of opinion are therefore not generally treated as statements of fact, so long as the statements do in fact represent the speaker's honestly held opinion. Sellers are also given some latitude in "puffing" their wares, so that such statements as, "It's the best car for the money," or, "It looks great on you," are not normally intended or understood as factual descriptions. Thus, a statement by an individual selling a used car that it is "in good shape mechanically as far as I know" would not be fraudulent unless the buyer could show that the seller knew that there were mechanical defects in the car at the time of the statement. A car dealer making the same kind of statement, however, would be making a misrepresentation of fact, since "expert opinions" are generally treated as statements of fact.

Predictions of future events over which the speaker has no control are generally not regarded as statements of fact. Where the speaker's promises concern the speaker's own future behavior, however, a misrepresentation of fact can be proved by showing that the speaker had no such intention at the time of the statements. If a buyer promises to use a piece of land for residential purposes only, there is fraud where the seller can show that the buyer had already signed construction and lease contracts for a gasoline station at the time the buyer made the "residential use" statement.

Although a party to an "arm's-length" transaction between equals generally has no affirmative duty to disclose every known fact, in several situations nondisclosure or silence can be interpreted as a fraudulent misrepresentation. The most obvious case requiring affirmative disclosure occurs when the party knowing the facts has created a mistaken belief in the mind of the other person through actions (concealment) or prior communications (which were true when spoken but have become false).

A second case requiring full disclosure occurs where the transaction is not arm's length but rather involves a **fiduciary relationship**, such as lawyer-client or guardian-ward. A lawyer who buys a piece of real estate from a client and has a resale deal with Wonder World already lined up, would have the duty to tell the client about the resale deal, whereas a buyer in an ordinary transaction would not.

A third group of cases is more difficult to define. Most courts today are increasingly willing to impose fraud remedies for nondisclosure where one party (usually the buyer) has had no reasonable opportunity to discover the truth and where the undisclosed fact is so significant that the contract might not have been made at all if the fact had been known. Examples are the house with a serious termite infestation and the used car with dangerously defective brakes.

Knowledge of Falsity. There is no fraud unless it can be shown that the speaker made a misrepresentation with knowledge that it was false. However, there are three ways to prove this "knowledge" element. One way is to show that the speaker knew the statement was a lie at the time of the statement. The speaker knew the car was not in "A-1 mechanical shape" because the day before the garage mechanic said to get rid of the car or be prepared to spend a lot of money, because it needed a lot of work.

Even if the speaker didn't actually know from personal inspection or from the mechanic that the car was in bad shape, there was "knowledge" if the speaker had "reason to know" that he or she was not telling the truth about the car's condition. Presumably, every reasonable car driver knows that a car in A-1 mechanical shape does not burn a quart of oil every 100 miles or require repeated pumping of the brake pedal to get the car to stop. A speaker who knew of these operating characteristics would certainly have reason to know that the car was not in A-1 shape.

Finally, "knowledge" can be proved by proving *lack* of knowledge. Assume that a car dealership has just taken a used car as a trade-in; no complete mechanical inspection of the car has been made. Nevertheless, when a buyer comes to the used-car lot and inquires about the car, the buyer is told that it is in "A-1 shape" and buys it on that basis. If the car has serious defects, fraud has been committed in this case. The salesperson who made the "A-1" statement knew that he or she didn't know anything at all about the car's real mechanical condition; thus the salesperson was lying and was aware of lying about the extent of information he or she had on the car.

Intent to Deceive. In most cases, knowledge of the lie and intent to deceive go so closely hand in hand that some courts do not even consider them separately. But what about the person who says, "Yes, Junior, I lied, and I knew I was lying, but I did it for your own good. But I didn't intend that you should be hurt by it. I thought things would come out all right in the end." For want of a better label, we might refer to this as the defense, Parent-Knows-Best. The few cases that have considered this argument have rejected it; the requirement is not proof of intent to injure or do harm, only of the intent to deceive. Deception for any motive, good or bad, is fraud, assuming that the other four elements are also proved.

Reasonable Reliance. Even though the liar is the nastiest person imaginable, the liar has not committed fraud unless the other party can show that he or she reasonably relied on the misrepresentation. It is not enough to show that the person was in fact deceived; the person complaining must also convince the trier of fact that it was reasonable to rely on the misstatement. There is clearly no fraud if the other party knows the truth but goes ahead and makes the contract anyway. On the other hand, reliance is reasonable where an independent verification of the representation would require considerable time, money, and effort. Where the truth is readily ascertainable, it is probably not reasonable to rely on the misstatement. If the used-car salesman tells you the car has only 25,000 miles and the odometer in the car shows the mileage is 48,000, most juries would probably decide that a reasonable person would have checked the odometer before relying on the salesperson's statement. Each case ultimately rests on its own facts.

Damage to the Defrauded Party. As a final essential part of a fraud case, the defrauded party must prove having sustained damage as a result of the misrepresentation. Suppose that a seller of land fraudulently represents that there is gold on it, and there is no gold, but there is oil. The land with oil is worth more than it would have been with gold, so the buyer probably does not have a case of fraud. (The buyer probably will not want to rescind anyway.) Even in the gold/oil case, however, the buyer has wound up with a contract different from the one the buyer intended to have, so in that sense the buyer may have suffered an "injury" which would permit the buyer to rescind if the buyer wanted to.

Generally, to justify rescission of the entire contract, the misrepresented fact must relate to an essential part of the bargain. If the defrauded party wishes to keep the contract in force and collect **"make-it-right"** or **difference-in-value-damages**, the party must prove the amount of the dollar loss which the party has sustained because of the fraud. Since fraud is an intentional tort, punitive damages (over and above the actual loss) may also be collected in many of these cases.

The *Johnson* case shows that a fraud claim may also be used as a defense, when the liar sues to enforce the contract.

JOHNSON v. HONEYWELL INFORMATION SYSTEMS, INC.
955 F.2d 409 (U.S. 6th Cir. Court of Appeals, 1992).

FACTS: Honeywell placed a help-wanted ad for a person with a college degree and "four to six years combined personnel and industrial relations experience." Mildred Johnson applied for the job. On her application, she indicated that she had a Bachelor of Arts degree from the University of Detroit and the required minimum work experience. The application form she signed stated that the submission of any false information "may be cause for immediate discharge at any time thereafter should I be employed by Honeywell." She was hired in 1976 and performed satisfactorily until mid-1983. In 1983, she was criticized by her supervisors for ineffectiveness, uncooperativeness, and unavailability by telephone. When she refused to make the suggested improvements, she was fired in November 1984. She sued for breach of contract on the basis that she could be fired only for "just cause." Her lawsuit also claimed that she had been fired in relation for being too aggressive in meeting affirmative action goals. [Affirmative action requires employees to attempt to hire and promote minorities, so that their numbers in the work force approximate their numbers in the general population.] A discharge for this reason would violate the Michigan civil rights act. While gathering evidence for the trial, Honeywell discovered that Johnson had lied on her application.

The U.S. District Court denied Honeywell's motion for a summary judgment on each claim. The trial judge felt that "after-acquired" evidence could not be used to justify the firing decision, since the evidence that Johnson had lied on her application was unknown when the decision was made. After a trial, the court did direct a verdict for Honeywell on the civil rights claim, but the jury was permitted to decide for Johnson on the breach of contract claim.

 JUDGE KEITH:

Johnson's most glaring misrepresentation involved her education. While she claimed in her employment application to have earned a Bachelor of Arts degree from the University of Detroit, Johnson actually completed only four courses at the University and audited two others.... Johnson similarly submitted false information regarding the nature and extent of her studies at Wayne State University, stating that she had studied Applied Management for one year. Wayne State had no record of her enrollment. Johnson also exaggerated some prior job descriptions and falsely claimed to have been managing some of her properties in the year between her prior job and her hiring at Honeywell....

We believe the Michigan Supreme Court would hold that just cause for termination of employment may include facts unknown to an employer at the time of dismissal, though obviously such facts would be neither the actual nor inducing cause for the discharge.

This result is principally grounded upon the holding of the Michigan Court of Appeals in *Bradley*, but it is also based on the general applicability of this rule, its common sense, and the dearth of Michigan Case Law to the contrary....

In order to provide a defense to an employer in a wrongful discharge claim, the after-acquired evidence must establish valid and legitimate reasons for the termination of employment. As a general rule, in cases of resume fraud, summary judgment will be appropriate where the misrepresentation or omission was material, directly related to measuring a candidate for employment, and was relied upon by the employer in making the hiring decision....

We do not hold that any or all misrepresentations on an employment application constitute just cause for dismissal or serve as a complete defense to a wrongful discharge action. We conclude, however, that Johnson's misrepresentations, by virtue of their nature and number, and when viewed in the context of Honeywell's express requirement of a college degree and its warning to applicants that misrepresentations may constitute cause for termination of employment, provide adequate and just cause for her dismissal as a matter of law even though they were unknown to Honeywell at the time of her discharge.

[The court also said that no remedy could be given on the civil rights claim. Someone who is hired as a doctor, but who has falsified credentials, could not later collect damages even though later fired because of race, sex, religion, or age.]

INNOCENT MISREPRESENTATION

In some cases, speakers may have honestly and reasonably believed they were telling the truth and may have had no intent to mislead anyone. Still, if the speaker in fact misrepresented the truth, damages to the other party may be as bad as if there had been fraud. The net effect is the same, whether the misrepresentation was made fraudulently or "innocently." For this reason, where the fact innocently misstated has been proved to be a very important part of the contract, most courts will permit rescission by the other party. In most states, if the misrepresented fact is not material enough to justify rescission, the contract stands as is; no damages remedy is given. In a few states, damages can be recovered even for an innocent misrepresentation, as an alternative remedy to rescission. Under the UCC rules for sales of goods, a buyer is permitted to rescind and recover the contract rice paid, *and* also collect any incidental damages incurred. Since there has been no intentional tort, punitive damages are not recoverable for innocent misrepresentation.

Both fraud and innocent misrepresentation were argued as possible theories of liability in the following case.

FIRST NAT. BANK OF LOUISVILLE v. BROOKS FARMS
821 S.W.2d 925 (TN, 1991)

FACTS: In response to a suit by the First National Bank of Louisville against Brooks Farms, the dairy farmers, for the balance due on a contract for the lease-purchase of the Harvestore silos, Brooks Farms brought a third-party action against A.O. Smith Harvestore Products, Inc. (AOSHPI), which manufactured the silos, and Hermitage Harvestore Systems, Inc. and its agent Frank Osborne (Hermitage), the dealer who sold the silos to Brooks Farms. The purchaser alleged sale of a defective product, fraudulent misrepresentation, breach of express and implied warranties, negligent design in manufacture, unfair and deceptive business acts and practices, negligent misrepresentation and innocent misrepresentation, and sued for compensatory and punitive damages. Prior to trial, all claims except those charging misrepresentation were dismissed. Brooks Farms confessed judgment in favor of the bank for the amount due. During trial, the claim of negligent misrepresentation was dismissed, and the case went to the jury on charges of fraudulent misrepresentation and innocent misrepresentation.

The substance of the purchasers' proof was that representations in advertising brochures and promotional films regarding the Harvestore system of agricultural feed storage made by the manufacturer and dealer and relied upon by the purchasers to their detriment were false. The evidence showed that the Harvestore silos did not preserve feed for Brooks Farm's dairy cattle in accordance with the representations made by Hermitage and in the advertising literature and films produced by AOSHPI. The proof showed that because feed stored in the structures lost its nutritional value the cattle produced less milk, which resulted in reduced profits to the farmers, all contrary to representations made to them.

When the Harvestore structures were purchased, Brooks Farms signed purchase orders containing language to the effect that Hermitage was an independent contractor and that none of the representations made by the dealer were binding on the manufacturer. The purchase orders also stated that the buyer had not relied upon any representations, oral or written, or any advertising in purchasing the product.

 JUDGE REID:

[D]isposition first must be made of the issues raised by AOSHPI. The manufacturer was found by the jury to be guilty of intentional or fraudulent misrepresentation, which is a cause of action based on the common law tort of deceit.... The evidence supports the jury's finding of fraud against the manufacturer and the award of punitive damages....

AOSHPI contends that since reliance is a requisite element for any cause of action based on misrepresentation, Brooks Farms cannot recover for misrepresentation because in the purchase order agreements, which contained bargained for duties and liabilities, it acknowledged and agreed not to rely upon representations made by the manufacturer or seller. The argument is that the purchasers have acknowledged that they did not rely upon representations made with regard to the quality or characteristics of the product.

Many suits have been filed against the manufacturer and their dealers by other purchasers involving essentially the same facts and circumstances as in the present case. The manufacturer in this case relies upon the same theories of liability and asserts the same defense as in the other cases....

This defense failed in *Agristor Leasing v. AOSHPI* however, when the court held correctly that Tennessee law "gives no effect to disclaimers in the presence of fraud...." With regard to the contention that there was no evidence of reliance, the courts held that the issue presented a jury question, which was resolved by the jury's general verdict against the defendant. Likewise in this case the jury verdict against AOSHPI based on fraudulent misrepresentation will be affirmed....

As previously stated, the liability of the dealer and its agent is based on innocent misrepresentation, which was made a part of the common law of Tennessee by the Court in *Lonon*, 398 S.W.2d at 240....

It appears that because of developments in the law since *Lonon*, the reasons that prompted the decision recognizing actions for pecuniary loss based on innocent misrepresentations made by a seller of chattels to the public concerning the character or quality of the chattel no longer exist. It also appears that the rights and liabilities of parties to actions based on diminished economic expectations can be better adjudicated on other legal theories. For these reasons, the approval in *Lonon* of the legal proposition set forth in formerly proposed § 552D of the *Restatement*, upon reconsideration by the Court, is found to be inappropriate and that rule as a cause of action is disapproved.

The judgment against Hermitage Harvestore System, Inc. and Frank Osborne is reversed, and the suit as to those parties is dismissed. The judgment against A.O. Smith Harvestore Products, Inc. is affirmed, and the case is remanded.

UNDUE INFLUENCE

As noted in our discussion of fraud, where any sort of fiduciary relationship exists, as in lawyer-client, guardian-ward, or doctor-patient, one of the parties to the transaction may have misused the trust and confidence which the other has given, to benefit at the other's expense. One party may rely on the advice of the trusted lawyer, doctor, or guardian as the basis for entering into a contract with that person. Where such an underlying relationship exists between the contracting parties, the courts will examine their bargain very carefully to make sure that it represents the true intent of the "subordinate" party and that all the facts had been disclosed to that party. Even without an underlying fiduciary relationship, it is possible to prove that a contract exists because of undue influence rather than by free choice, although this case is not nearly as easy to prove. Where proved, undue influence makes the contract voidable by the party of whom advantage was taken.

DURESS

Closely related to the idea of undue influence is that of **duress**. Duress means something more than just pressure or "hard selling." The most obvious cases involve violence or threats of violence against the contracting party. Threats to commence a criminal prosecution unless money is paid or promised also constitute duress, but simply threatening to bring a civil suit for money allegedly owed is not duress. While sales pressure or hard selling is not considered duress, threats of economic harm against the buyer by the seller, if the buyer does not accept seller's terms, is economic duress, and courts will recognize such threats as duress. A person can be injured by being struck by a baseball bat, but can also be injured by the misuse of economic power by an adversary. The violence-type duress makes the resulting contract totally void. Other duress makes the contract voidable by the party who was pressured into making it.

MISTAKE

The contracting parties can be "mistaken" about so many things that it is impossible to catalog all of the conceivable factual combinations. Mistakes may occur in the formation of the agreement, in writing up the deal, or in performance. Rather than a comprehensive list, what follows is a discussion of some of the most frequent kinds of mistakes: mutual mistake in basic assumptions, material unilateral mistake, mistake in integration, and mistake in performance.

Mutual Mistake in Basic Assumptions. Where both parties enter into a contract assuming the existence of some particular fact or condition which later turns out not to have been so, there is no contract at all if the fact is "basic" (material) to the contract. Efrem Zimbalist, Sr., the famous concert violinist, bought two violins which both he and the seller assumed were a genuine Stradivarius and a genuine Guarnerius. In fact, both violins were merely good copies. When he discovered the truth, Zimbalist was entitled to get his money back; neither party intended a contract for *fake* violins.

Many "mutual mistake" cases arise from a latent ambiguity in the terms of the contract; that is, a word or phrase really describes more than one thing, and each party understands it to mean something different. In the classic example, a buyer and seller contracted in England for "certain goods, to wit, 125 bales Surat cotton to arrive ex ship *Peerless* from Bombay," Unknown to either the buyer or the seller, there were *two* ships called *Peerless*, and both were in Bombay and both had some Surat cotton on board. To make the story complete, incredible though it may seem, they were both bound for London, one to arrive in October, and one in December. The buyer knew only about the "October" *Peerless*; the seller knew only about the "December" *Peerless*. When the buyer's cotton was not delivered in October and the buyer sued for breach of contract, the English court correctly held that no damages were recoverable since no contract had ever really been made. The parties were talking about two different things and had never really agreed.

There is no mistake, and thus there is a binding contract, where both parties are aware that they lack knowledge about a particular fact of condition, and take their mutual ignorance into account in setting the terms of the contract. In a Wisconsin case, the finder of a pretty stone in a field took the stone to a friend and asked the friend what he thought it was worth. The friend said he didn't know either but that he'd pay the finder $1 for it. After the sale, the stone was identified as an uncut diamond, worth $700. There was no mistake in this case, in the legal sense, since both parties were aware when they contracted that they did not know the true identity or worth of the stone.

Because much of modern commerce is based on differing estimates of the value of land, goods, and securities, most courts also adhere to a rule which says that mistake relief will not be given where the only error concerns the *value* of an item rather than its *identity*. The mistake in the *Zimbalist* case, for example, was not as to the value of fake violins but as to whether the violins were genuine or fake. This difference is probably easy enough to see in most cases, but some cases are a little harder to decide.

Material Unilateral Mistake. Generally the fact that one party to the contract has made a mistake of some sort affords no basis for relief, so long as the other party was unaware of the mistake and was acting in good faith. Most courts do, however, say that there is no contract where the mistake was so "gross" that the other party should have been aware of it. This situation arises most frequently where bids are being solicited for a certain job. Several bid offers are submitted, and one is way out of line. Courts usually will not permit the offeree to "snap up" what the offeree has good reason to know must be a mistaken bid, thus binding the honestly mistaken bidder to an unfair contract. Just how gross the mistake has to be to trigger this rule is a question of fact.

Mistake in Integration. Both the courts and the *Restatement* continue to state as the general rule that one is bound by what he or she signs. Yet, almost in the same breath, courts everywhere also continue to grant relief ("reformation") for what is commonly termed *mistake in integration*. Much of the seeming conflict between the two rules can be explained by the difference between the specifically bargained-out terms and the printed terms in a form contract. Many printed contracts use fairly standardized terms—what lawyers refer to as "boilerplate."

When you sign a form contract, you are bound by all this standardized language, as we noted in Chapter 8. On the other hand, where a specifically agreed-on term has been written up incorrectly, courts are willing to correct the error. In such a case, one party alleges that a written document is incorrect, that it does not accurately state the terms actually agreed on. If there is evidence to support this claim, a court with equity powers can "reform" the document to make it agree with the actual intent of the parties, and then enforce the document as corrected. The document is rewritten, and then enforced.

Mistake in Performance. Perhaps the most difficult case of all in which to work out a mutually fair result are those involving a "mistake in performance." Someone performs for the wrong person, or at the wrong time, or in the wrong place, or when the party was not really contractually obligated to perform at all. Where the performance involves money or a tangible object which can be easily returned, the solution is simple, the person who has received the money or other item by mistake must return it.

Where construction or demolition takes place at the wrong site, however, the problem is not so easily resolved. What does one do for the owner of the apartment house the wrecking crew tore down "by mistake"? Even if the owners are given the full fair market value of the old building, plus lost rentals, until a new one is built, they have still been the unwilling participants in a forced sale of the old building, with all sorts of possible adverse tax consequences. How about the landowners who get a new house put up on their lot "by mistake"? Should these people have to pay for removal of the house and the restoration of the pristine ecology? For these, as for many other "mistake" questions, there are no easy or universal answers.

SIGNIFICANCE OF THIS CHAPTER

The basic idea of a contract is that it is a relationship which we have entered into voluntarily, because we wished to do so. It's not something that's imposed on us by someone else; it's a relationship which we have imposed on ourselves. Where our consent to the contract has occurred because of factual misrepresentation by the other party, legal relief from the terms of the contract is available—either rescission or damages. If the misrepresentation was intentional, punitive damages should be available against the person who has committed an intentional wrong. Where no agreement ever really occurred, either because the parties were talking about two different things and didn't know that, or because they both assumed the existence of a material fact which was not so, no contract exists, and legal relief should be given. Even where only one party has made a serious mistake, there is no contract if the other is aware of the mistake. In all of these situations, what appears at first to be a contract may not be enforceable because one or both parties were unaware of the true facts.

While it is certainly true that most minors do pay their debts and meet their other contractual obligations, it is important for the other contracting party to be aware of what can happen when a contract is made with a minor. Even though the age of majority has been lowered to 18 by most states, and even though more courts are willing to permit some recourse against a minor who makes an intentional misrepresentation of age, minors still enjoy a special legal status. Courts still will give them special protection where they act innocently. If you are contracting with minors, you need to know the possible results.

Similarly, while many courts and legislatures are moving to eliminate special restrictions on legal rights and privileges, some do still remain. You also need to be aware of these possibilities, because again there can be serious legal consequences when your contract is declared void or voidable due to the other party's lack of capacity.

PROBLEMS FOR DISCUSSION

1. Dr. Oswald, a coin collector from Switzerland, was interested in Mrs. Allen's collection of Swiss coins. The parties drove to the Newburgh Savings Bank of Newburgh, New York, where two of Mrs. Allen's collections, referred to as the Swiss Coin Collection and the Rarity Coin Collection, were located in separate vault boxes. After examining and taking notes on the coins in the Swiss Coin Collection, Dr. Oswald was shown several valuable Swiss coins from the Rarity Coin Collection. He also took notes on these coins, and he later testified that he did not know that they were in a separate "collection." The evidence showed that each collection had a different key number and was housed in labeled cigar boxes.

    On the return to New York City, Dr. Oswald sat in the front seat of the car while Mrs. Allen sat in the back with Dr. Oswald's brother, Mr. Victor Oswald, and Mr. Cantarella of the Chase Manhattan Bank's Money Museum, who had helped arrange the meeting and had served as Dr. Oswald's agent. Dr. Oswald could speak practically no English and so depended on his brother to conduct the transaction. After some negotiation, a price of $50,000 was agreed upon. Apparently the parties never realized that the references to "Swiss coins" and the "Swiss Coin Collection" were ambiguous. Dr. Oswald thought the offer he had authorized his brother to make was for all of the Swiss coins, while Mrs. Allen thought she was selling only the Swiss Coin Collection and not the Swiss coins in the Rarity Coin Collection.

    Did the parties reach an agreement? Explain.

2. In December 1997, Harold M. Janinda was transferred by his employer from Denver, Colorado, to Mountain Home, Idaho. In looking for housing for his family and income-producing property, he consulted a local real estate agency. A Mr. Swearing of that agency showed him several parcels of real estate, including Mrs. Lanning's rental and residence property consisting of duplex apartments, six trailer spaces, and three-bedroom house. This property was located a short distance outside the city limit: of Mountain Home, within the county, and obtained its water supply from two shallow wells on the property.

    On January 24, 1998, Mrs. Lanning received information indicating that one of the wells was contaminated, but she did not disclose this fact to Mr. Swearingen when he asked about the water supply. About two weeks later, Janinda bought the property. Janinda now sues to rescind the contract.

    What result and why?

3. Kemper sued to rescind a bid it had submitted to do the piping work for a sewer project. The City requires that 10 percent of the bid price be posted as a bond, favor of the City, guaranteeing that the bidder would do the job for the bid price if awarded the contract. Three of Kemper's employees worked until 2 a.m. of the day the bids were due in preparing Kemper's bid. Over 1,000 different items were involved in preparing these estimates. When the work of these three men was combined and the estimates were totalled, a $301,769 item was omitted. Kemper's bid came in at $780,305. The three competing bids were $1,049,592, $1,183,000, and $1,278,895. The mistake was discovered a few hours after the bids were opened. Kemper explained what had happened and withdrew its bid, but the City accepted the bid anyway. When Kemper refused to enter into a contract at the mistaken price, the City awarded the contract to the next lowest bidder and claimed that Kemper's 10 percent bond was forfeited to the City. The trial court held that Kemper was entitled to rescind its bid and its bond.

Was this ruling correct? Explain.

4. A.N. Peddy contracted to buy certain real estate from Bessie Montgomery, a married woman. Title 34, § 73 of the Alabama Code denies a wife the power to convey or mortgage, her lands without her husband's consent. If he does not join in signing the deed or mortgage, it is void. Bessie changed her mind about selling, and, since her husband had not cosigned the land contract, she relied on the statute as a defense. When Peddy sued for specific performance of the contract, the trial court gave Bessie a summary judgment.

How should the appeals court rule?

5. Defendant Charles Edward Smith, Jr., purchased an automobile from plaintiff on 15 August 1997. On that date, defendant was 17 years old and would have his 18th birthday on 25 September 1997. Defendant executed a purchase money security agreement to finance $2,362, the balance due on the purchase price of the automobile payable in thirty installments of $99.05 each. Plaintiff subsequently assigned the purchase money security agreement to First Union National Bank. After having made eleven monthly payments pursuant to the installment loan contract, ten of which were made after his 18th birthday, defendant voluntarily returned the automobile to plaintiff and defaulted on his payment obligations. Upon default, First Union reassigned the purchase money security agreement to plaintiff, which proceeded to sell the automobile at public auction. At the time of sale, a balance was owing on the purchase money security agreement ot $1,521.52. The car was sold for $700, leaving a deficiency of $821.52. From the judgment dismissing plaintiff's complaint, plaintiff appeals.

What result on appeal, and why?

Chapter 12
Illegality and Impossibility

In the vast majority of cases, both the formation of the contract and the performances it requires are lawful. Where a bargain transaction is illegal, either in its formation or in the performances required, the court attempts to do exactly the opposite of what it normally does; instead of enforcing the intent of the parties, the court tries to frustrate it. Since the bargain is illegal in some respect, the court will try to prevent the illegality from occurring and to discourage similar illegal bargains in the future. Specific results vary from case to case, yet this policy underlies all "illegality" cases.

This chapter discusses the results which the courts work out in some of the most frequent illegality cases, as well as several examples of courts refusing to enforce contract provisions due to changed circumstances.

ILLEGAL BARGAINS

Commission of Crime or Tort. The clearest case for the application of these illegality rules occurs where the would-be contract calls for a performance specifically defined as criminal under applicable state statutory law or involves the commission of an intentional tort against some third party. In popular jargon, the arrangement between the local Big Boss and Murder, Inc., which calls for the removal of the crosstown competition, is called a contract. Clearly, the courts should not (and will not) have any part in the enforcement of such a contract, regardless of the stage of performance or nonperformance in which it is brought to the attention of the court. Whether the hit man has taken the money and has refused to perform, or has done the job in an unworkmanlike way, or the Big Boss has refused to pay for the services rendered, the court should refuse to recognize any rights or duties flowing from such a contract and simply leave these equally guilty parties where it finds them, with no relief to either. Conspiracy to commit murder is itself a crime, so very few such contracts are brought to the attention of the court.

Gambling, Lotteries, and Games of Chance.

Nearly all forms of gambling are illegal in most states, and the parties to an illegal bet are clearly in pari delicto; that is, they are equally guilty of violating the law, so that there should be no reason to prefer one over the other. Still, different legal rules are applied to the bet case. Since the illegal purpose of a bet is to pay money to the winner based on the outcome of a game, race, fight, or whatever, the courts attempt to frustrate that purpose by permitting the losers of the bets to "repent" and repudiate their bets (and get their money back) at any time before the money is actually paid to the winner. If you "see the light" only after your team has lost, you can still (legally) repudiate your bet and keep your money (or get it back from the stakeholder), as long as you indicate your intent to do so before the money is actually paid over to the winner. The same rule applies when you try unsuccessfully to fill an inside straight in poker: you can take your money back from the pot (though you may lose a lot of friends, and hands, in doing so).

Most state gambling statutes are broad enough to cover lotteries, license plate bingo, and similar games of chance; some states also have separate statutes to cover these other forms of gambling. States are also attempting to prohibit newer forms of risk taking, such as so-called chain letter and pyramid forms of selling. All of these statutes are subject to judicial interpretation as to just what they prohibit and just what the courts should refuse to enforce.

Licensing Statutes.

One study by the U.S. Labor Department estimated that over 500 different occupations required a license of some sort from at least one governmental body, including such jobs as beekeeper, rainmaker, tattoo artist, and fund-raiser. The "illegality" problem here occurs when an unlicensed person performs services for which a license is required. Should the client-customer be required to pay for the services received from the unlicensed practitioner?

Courts usually try to answer this question by first categorizing the licensing statute in question as either "regulatory" or "revenue raising." Of course, many statutes will include both legislative purposes, but what the court is trying to decide is whether the basic reason for the license is to protect persons from unqualified or unscrupulous practitioners or just to raise some money for the government. If the licensing statute contains educational and experiential requirements and specifies that a standardized test must be passed to get a license, it is pretty clearly regulatory in character. The fewer such standards it contains, the more it looks like just a revenue raiser.

Statutes licensing professionals, such as lawyers, accountants, dentists, and physicians are clearly regulatory in nature. On the other hand, a statute that required one to have a license to keep bees, but that permitted anyone to be licensed by paying $200, is only designed to raise revenue.

If a statute is regulatory in nature, the results of not being properly licensed under it are serious. In addition to being liable for whatever punishments are provided for practicing without the required license and for any malpractice against the client, unlicensed practitioners will usually be denied any recovery for the services performed even if they get licensed. On the other hand, if the statute is only designed to bring in money, the worst that will happen to unlicensed practitioners is being required to get licensed before being able to sue to recover for services already performed.

Sunday Laws. About half of the states have some sort of statute prohibiting the doing of business, or at least some types of business, on Sunday. Some of the more recently enacted statutes give the target merchants the option of closing either Sunday or Saturday. These statutes are an obvious outgrowth of the old colonial Blue Laws, which prohibited doing almost anything on Sunday except going to church. Although these laws clearly interfere with the "free exercise of religion," and clearly "establish" the Christian Sunday (in most cases) as *the* official day of rest, the U.S. Supreme Court upheld their constitutionality in 1961. However, legal challenges are still possible on other grounds, as seen in the following case.

FARAONE d/b/a/ FIVE STAR VIDEO v. CITY OF EAST PROVIDENCE
935 F.SUPP. 82 (U.S. Dist. R.I., 1996)

FACTS: This matter is before the court on plaintiff's motion for a preliminary injunction. Plaintiff, Joseph Faraone, d/b/a Five Star Video, alleges that a license "stipulation" adopted by the East Providence City Council, which prohibits the sale or rental of "any adult oriented X-rated videos on Sundays or Holidays," is preempted by state law and violates the First Amendment of the United States Constitution. The defendant, the city of East Providence, counters that the restriction placed on all Sunday/holiday sales licenses is permissible under state law and is a valid content-neutral regulation designed to serve a legitimate government interest.

The court conducted a hearing on plaintiff's motion on January 19, 1996, at which time plaintiff introduced the verified complaint and his affidavit into evidence. The defendant offered no evidence. At the conclusion of oral argument, this court granted plaintiff's motion for a preliminary injunction. This memorandum sets forth the rationale for doing so.

Plaintiff owns and operated a video rental and sale business on Willett Avenue in East Providence, Rhode Island. Plaintiff has operated his business for approximately ten years, and holds a state-issued retail license and a city-issued Sunday/holiday sales license. He rents and sells a wide range of videos, roughly ten percent of which he estimates might be considered "adult oriented" or "X-rated." Plaintiff voluntarily segregates these videos from the remaining collection and places them in a designated area of his store.

 DISTRICT JUDGE LISI:

Having considered and rejected plaintiff's State law preemption argument, this court turns its attention to his First Amendment claim.

Plaintiff contends that the stipulation attached to his Sunday/holiday sales license contravenes the First Amendment guarantee of freedom of speech because it is a content-based regulation of protected speech that does not serve any legitimate government interest. As such, plaintiff argues that the stipulation must be subjected to strict judicial scrutiny. The defendant avers that the stipulation is not aimed at the content of the banned videos; rather, that the restriction should analyzed as a "time, place, or manner regulation" aimed at the "secondary effects" of the operation of plaintiff's business "on the surrounding community." Accordingly, the defendant contends that the stipulation should be subjected to intermediate scrutiny.

In order to apply the proper level of scrutiny to the stipulation now before the court, it must first be determined whether the stipulation is "content-based" or "content-neutral." "The principal inquiry in determining content neutrality, in speech cases generally and in time, place, or manner cases in particular, is whether the government has adopted a regulation of speech because of disagreement with the message it conveys."... A municipality is not required to "steer away from content at all costs, or else risk strict scrutiny." "A regulation that serves purposes unrelated to the content of expression is deemed neutral, even if it has an incidental effect on some speakers or messages but not others."...

The defendant argues that the Sunday/holiday restriction is a permissible time, place, or manner regulation, and thus should be subject to the less exacting test of intermediate scrutiny, because it does not ban the sale or rental of these videos altogether, but rather provides that the sales or rentals may not take place on Sundays or holidays. In so doing, however, the defendant completely ignores the blatant content-based description of those items which are banned. The license stipulation here targets "adult oriented X-rated videos." The members of the East Providence City Council, the individuals responsible for monitoring compliance, and the plaintiff must refer to the message (*i.e.,* the content, of the subject videos in order to discern whether their sale or rental on Sundays or holidays is prohibited. Clearly, the stipulation is aimed at regulating the content of the speech and, therefore, must be subjected to strict judicial scrutiny.

The defendant attempts to sidestep this outcome by asserting that the stipulation is aimed at curbing the "secondary effects" of the video rental and sales business on the surrounding community. The defendant contends that it can permissibly restrict this form of speech on these grounds because of a compelling interest in "attempting to preserve the quality of urban life." In support of this contention the defendant cites to four cases...in which restrictions on adult-oriented businesses were permitted because they were designed to curb the secondary effects generated by the operations of those businesses.

In making this argument, however, the defendant offers no evidence that it researched the issue of "secondary effects" of the sale or rental of these types of videos on Sundays or holidays in East Providence, or that any such effects exist. Instead, the defendant relies on *City of Renton* for the proposition that "the First Amendment does not require a city, before enacting such an ordinance, to conduct new studies or produce evidence independent of that already generated by other cities, so long as whatever evidence the city relies upon is reasonably believed to be relevant to the problem that the city addresses."... The defendant then cites two cases, *Mitchell* and *Star Satellite*, which it contends contain evidence of secondary effects which justify deeming the stipulation content-neutral. For several reasons, however, the defendant once again misses the mark....

It is clear to this court that the secondary effects that generally underlie the regulation of adult oriented businesses—for example, "traffic congestion, parking problems, the performance of sexual acts in public, ... the littering of discarded sexually explicit materials near residential communities," ... and the increase in congestion and crime associated with the concentration of regulated uses ... are not likely to be present in this case. Here, there is no on-premises adult entertainment. Individuals who patronize plaintiff's business are on the premises for only so long as it takes to purchase or rent a videotape. Customers do not view the movies at plaintiff's store.

Accordingly, the defendant's attempt to categorize this stipulation as one which may be viewed through the lens of intermediate scrutiny must fail.

Strict scrutiny is desirable in circumstances in which restrictions on speech are content-based because "such laws 'pose the inherent risk that the Government seeks not to advance a legitimate regulatory goal, but to suppress unpopular ideas or information or manipulate the public debate through coercion rather than persuasion'."... Indeed courts generally "treat content-based regulations as 'presumptively invalid" under the First Amendment."... In order to clear this constitutional hurdle, a content-based regulation must be: (1) necessary to serve a compelling state interest, and (2) narrowly drawn to achieve that end....

In this case, the defendant has failed to rebut the presumption of invalidity. The defendant has offered no palpable justification for restricting the rental or sale of the videos on Sundays or holidays. Accordingly, I conclude that the stipulation constitutes an impermissible abrogation of the freedom of speech guaranteed by the First Amendment. Since this determination is dispositive, I need not reach plaintiff's claim that the stipulation is also impermissibly vague....

For these reasons, plaintiff's Motion for Preliminary Injunction has been granted.

Merchants who wish to remain open on Sunday have fared better by challenging these laws in state courts, under the state's own constitution, either on the "religion" ground or on the ground that the legislation arbitrarily discriminates between products and businesses.

Where there is a valid Sunday law in force, some rather surprising results may occur, as illustrated by an old New Hampshire case where two cows were sold on a Sunday with the price to be paid later. When the buyer didn't pay and the seller repossessed the cows, the seller was held liable for trespass since an absolute ownership of the cows had passed to the buyer. But when the seller sued for the contract price, the court permitted the buyer to use the illegality defense since the contract had been made on a Sunday. The court's main reason for this result was that the parties were equally guilty and should therefore have been left where they were when performance of the illegal bargain ceased—the buyer with the cows, the seller without the money. In many states today, a court would construct an "implied promise" to pay the contract price if the buyer retained the property and would say that this promise was legal because it was "made" on a weekday.

Usury. Usury is very easy to define: *it is the charging of an illegally high rate of interest.* This simple definition is not always so easy to apply to particular cases. The court must decide two subsidiary questions: What is interest, and what is an illegally high rate? State courts do not agree on the answers to these questions.

Interest is generally defined as the charge for a loan of money or for the forbearance of a debt. Since the impact on the buyer-debtor is the same in either case, and since the seller-lender ought not to be able to evade the maximum rate by merely calling interest something else, most courts today would probably hold that a "time-price differential" charged in a credit sale is in fact interest, but there are cases reaching the opposite result. Monthly service charges on revolving charge accounts have been held to be interest by nearly every court to consider the problem since

1970. Some states have specific statutes regulating these special kinds of credit arrangements and permitting the creditor to charge a higher rate of interest than that permitted by the state's general usury law. Nearly all courts agree that *bona fide* charges for separate services, such as credit reports on the debtor, appraisals of collateral, and filing fees, are valid and are not to be calculated as part of the interest charge.

How high is too high? The general usury law in most states specifies a maximum annual interest rate of from 7 to 10 percent. In most states, corporations are not protected by usury laws, and this same idea has been extended in several states to any loan to a business, incorporated or not. Small loan companies are typically governed by their own statute, which permits them to charge a much higher interest rate (usually 24 to 36%). Credit unions and other special lenders may also have their own special statutory rate. One of the main objectives of the proposed Uniform Consumer Credit Code is to simplify this hodge-podge of existing laws.

The states disagree not only on the definition of interest and the rate permitted but also on what the remedy should be when a lender tries to charge a usurious rate. At least four types of results have been worked out: (1) forfeiture of only the excessive amount of interest; (2) forfeiture of all interest; (3) forfeiture of double or triple the amount of interest charged; and (4) forfeiture of the entire debt, both principal and interest.

The *Swindell* case shows a court trying to work out a reasonable result under a usury statute.

SWINDELL v. FEDERAL NAT. MORTGAGE ASS'N.
409 S.E.2d 892 (NC, 1994)

FACTS: On 22 March 1985, plaintiffs executed an adjustable rate note secured by a deed of trust on a home for $112,500.00. The note was executed on a multistate Federal National Mortgage Association (FNMA) Uniform Instrument form, which included a provision for late payment charges. A late payment charge rate of 5 percent of the overdue payment of principal and interest was typed in a blank provided on the form.

The FNMA purchased the note from the lender, Epic Mortgage Inc. In March 1985. Skyline Mortgage Corporation succeeded Epic as servicer of the loan. On 14 October 1987, Skyline sent plaintiffs notice of uncollected late charges. When Skyline discovered that the late payment penalty rate on plaintiffs' note exceeded the legal maximum under North Carolina law, it offered to reduce the rate to four percent, pursuant to the "Loan Charges" paragraph in the note. Defendants never collected a late payment penalty from plaintiffs.

Plaintiffs filed a complaint and an amended complaint for declaratory judgment, averring the 5 percent late charge was assessed on a payment not yet due, the charge was usurious under N.C.G.S. § 24-10.1, and reduction of that rate to 4 percent was fraudulent and a material alteration discharging plaintiffs from their obligations under the note. Plaintiffs sought a judgment declaring the loan usurious, requiring defendant to forfeit all interest due under the note to FNMA or Skyline, or both, or, alternatively, discharging plaintiffs from the note pursuant to N.C.G.S. § 25-3-407. Plaintiffs further sought the court's application of N.C.G.S. § 24-2.1 and an award of all interest paid by them to any holder of the note from and after 22 March 1985 to the date of the court's order.

The trial court granted defendants' motion for summary judgment and denied that of plaintiffs. The Court of Appeals affirmed in part and reversed in part. The Court of Appeals imposed a penalty it considered consistent with the purpose of the usury statues: defendants forfeited their right to collect late charges on the loan but did not forfeit their right to receive principal and interest.

 CHIEF JUSTICE EXUM:

Chapter 24 of the General Statutes, entitled "interest," governs a number of lending transactions for which it either states maximum interest rates or excepts the transaction from such statutory constraints.... Among the "transactions" governed by this chapter is a lender's charge for a borrower's late payment, for which the statute states a maximum rate:

> **(a)** Subject to the limitations contained in subsection (b) of this section, any lender may charge a party to a loan or extension of credit governed by the provisions of G.S. 24-1.1, 24-1.2, or 24-1.1A a late payment charge as agreed upon by the parties in the loan contract.
>
> **(b)** No lender may charge a late payment charge;
>
> > **(1)** In excess of 4 percent (4%) of the amount of the payment past due....

The predecessor statute, N.C.G.S. § 24-10(e), in effect at the time plaintiffs signed their note, was essentially identical. The single statute in Chapter 24 stating penalties for charges exceeding the maximum rates stipulated in its provisions provides, in pertinent part:

> The taking, receiving, reserving or charging a greater rate of interest than permitted by this chapter or other applicable law, either before or after the interest may accrue, when knowingly done, shall be a forfeiture of the entire interest which the note or other evidence of debt carries with it, or which has been agreed to be paid thereon....

The forfeiture provisions of N.C.G.S. § 24-2 are "in the nature of a penalty intended to induce an observance of the statute, and it is the duty of the courts so to expound and apply the law as to carry out the legislative intent...." We are convinced that the General Assembly, which specified a maximum legal rate for late payment fees in N.C.G.S. § 24-10.1, considered such fees "interest" and intended to induce observance of that law through the penalty provisions of N.C.G.S. § 24-2....

The note executed by plaintiffs in actuality contemplated interest for two separable monetary transactions. The more obvious transaction was the contract for a home loan exceeding $10,000, for which the parties were free to agree on any rate of interest.... The second transaction contemplated was the cost of money retained—the delayed loan payment. A late payment fee has two purposes: to encourage the borrower to pay on time and to compensate the lender for the loss of use of the payment held for the period of the delay. In the latter case, the late payment charge is interest, for it is compensation fixed by the parties for the detention of money or for the lender's forbearance in collecting the late payment.

The elements of usury are a loan or forbearance of the collection of money, an understanding that the money owed will be paid, payment or an agreement to pay interest at a rate greater than allowed by law, and the lender's corrupt intent to receive more in interest than the legal rate permits for use of the money loaned....

> The corrupt intent required to constitute usury is simply the intentional charging of more for money lent than the law allows. Where the lender intentionally charges the borrower a greater rate of interest than the law allows and his purpose is clearly revealed on the face of the instrument, a corrupt intent to violate the usury law on the part of the lender is shown....

These four elements are all present with regard to the late payment penalty provision in plaintiffs' note. First, there was a "loan" consisting in this context of the amount of principal and interest thereon due in the allegedly overdue payment. The note's scheduled repayment of principal and interest thereon indicated the parties' expectation that each payment would eventually be made. The note provided that a payment delayed more than fifteen days would be assessed late charges at 5 percent of the payment amount, a rate that exceeded the legally permissible rate. Corrupt intent was shown simply in imposing the usurious rate. "A profit, greater than the lawful rate of interest, intentionally exacted as a bonus for the loan of money, ... is a violation of the usury laws, it matters not what form or disguise it may assume...."

The penalty for charging usurious interest, whether or not it is collected, is the "forfeiture of the entire interest which the ... evidence of debt carries with it...." In the restricted context of a late charge on a delayed payment, "forfeiture of ... interest" in no way implicates the interest on the principal. When late charges are usurious, 'the entire interest' can only signify any and all penalty fees for late payments. The penalty fee is "interest." It is compensation for the detention of money owed another, and all such compensation must be forfeited when its rate is usurious, as defined by the laws of this state....

We conclude it was the intent of the General Assembly to enforce late charges violating N.C.G.S. § 24-10.1 by the penalty provisions of N.C.G.S. § 24-2, which, under the facts of this case, require the lender's forfeit of all late charges to which it would otherwise be entitled under the terms of the loan. We accordingly hold the decision of the Court of Appeals is modified and affirmed.

Common Law Restraint of Trade. While contracts which produce unreasonable restraints of trade were illegal under common law, as they are under many modern state and national statutes, the courts have long recognized that certain types of restraints serve a legitimate business function. In two situations in particular, the courts have recognized and enforced reasonable restraints of trade. When a business is sold, the courts permit the buyer to protect the goodwill which the buyer has purchased by requiring the seller not to engage in a competing business within a reasonable geographic area for a reasonable period of time. If this restraint were not permitted, the seller could immediately regain most or all former customers by going back into business right across the street. Similarly, former employees, partners, or other business associates can be restrained from going to work for a competing firm, within reasonable area and time limits, if this is necessary to protect a former employer's goodwill, customer lists, or trade secrets.

Where the area or time limitations are unreasonable, and therefore illegal, the courts do not agree on what should happen. Some courts throw out the restraint entirely, thus giving the other party a better bargain than the party originally made. Other courts use a "blue pencil" and rewrite the limitations, so as to make them reasonable. The problem with this approach is that it encourages the buyer or employer to write in unreasonable limitations, since if these are challenged in court, they will only be made reasonable anyway.

The *Wausau* case is a recent example of these rules.

WAUSAU MEDICAL CENTER, S.C. v. ASPLUND
514 N.W.2d 34 (WI, App., 1994)

FACTS: Dr. Asplund was twice employed as a general and vascular surgeon at WMC, a multi-specialty clinic. His first employment was from August 1988 to the end of July 1989. Asplund was WMC's first vascular surgeon, and this was Asplund's first professional practice following his residency. With this employment, Asplund entered into a contract with WMC that contained a restrictive covenant. Asplund voluntarily terminated his employment and moved to Iowa to participate in a transplant program in July 1989. WMC did not have a vascular surgeon between July 1989 and August 1990.

Within a year, Asplund decided that he wanted to return to Wausau. Asplund began negotiations with WMC. The negotiations broke off at one point because Asplund wanted the restrictive covenant stricken from the new contract, and WMC refused to do so. Nevertheless, Asplund commenced a second term of employment in August 1990 after signing an employment contract that contained a restrictive covenant. The covenant, which was identical to the one contained in his first contract, stated:

> *Covenant Not to Compete.* The Employee agrees that if his employment with the Corporation is terminated for any reason, he will not engage in the practice of medicine or any phase or specialty thereof in competition with the Employer for a period of two (2) years from the date of termination of his employment within Marathon County, Wisconsin. The Employee hereby consents to an issuance of an injunction by a court of competent jurisdiction to enjoin the violation of the foregoing in addition to any other remedies available to the Corporation. In lieu of said injunction, the Corporation shall have the option to recover as liquidated damages from the Employee a sum equal to 20 percent (20%) of the total cumulative professional charges made by the Employee during the twelve-month period immediately preceding the termination date.

In September 1990, forty-five days after he started, Asplund gave WMC sixty days' notice of his employment termination. Asplund formed a service corporation, Mark Asplund, S.C., while still employed at WMC. After his employment at WMC was terminated, he began his surgery practice in Wausau as an employee of the service corporation.

Asplund originally commenced this action by seeking to have the restrictive covenant declared unenforceable. Initially, WMC obtained a five-day temporary restraining order but was later denied a temporary injunction following a hearing. WMC filed a counter-claim and a third-party complaint against Asplund and his service corporation. Asplund voluntarily dismissed his claim, making WMC the plaintiff, and he then moved for summary judgment dismissing all WMC's claims against him and the service corporation. The trial court granted summary judgment in favor of Asplund, who sought costs, which were also granted. WMC appealed.

 PRESIDING JUDGE CANE:

The following canons of construction of restrictive covenants have been adopted: (1) These restrictions are prima facie suspect, (2) they must withstand close scrutiny to pass legal muster as being reasonable, (3) they will not be construed to extend beyond their proper import or further than the language of the contract absolutely requires, and (4) they are to be construed in favor of the employee....

Under § 103.465, STATS., a covenant not to compete within a specific time and a specific territory is lawful only if the restrictions imposed are reasonably necessary for the protection of the employer. Five inquiries are made in evaluating the enforceability of a covenant not to compete. The covenant must: (1) be necessary for the protection of the employer, (2) provide a reasonable time restriction, (3) provide a reasonable territorial limit, (4) be reasonable as to the employee, and (5) be reasonable as to the general public....

Our consideration of whether the covenant not to compete was necessary to protect WMC is two-fold. First, we must look to the facts as of the time the contract was entered into. At that point, it can be argued that WMC was anticipating the unfair competition that Asplund could provide in the event that his employment was terminated. WMC's apparent concern was that Asplund's association with WMC would enhance his reputation and thereby make him a formidable competitor (i.e., that his enhanced reputation would be a special circumstance which would render the restrictive covenant reasonably necessary for the protection of WMC's business).... WMC was also concerned that it would provide Asplund with a client and referral base, which he would later take with him, again making the covenant reasonably necessary to protect WMC's business.

[W]e conclude that facts surrounding the employment itself are also to be considered. While WMC could reasonably anticipate a protectible interest, as of the signing of the contract, since Asplund was not yet provided with any clients, referrals or an enhanced reputation, WMC had not yet acquired a protectible interest. Therefore we must go on to determine whether the anticipated protectible interest was ever acquired. We conclude that it was not....

It is ... undisputed that the amount of work Asplund did in his first forty-five days of employment was sparse, to the point of concern on the part of WMC. It is further undisputed that in the remaining sixty days of his employment, after he gave his termination notice, he received very few referrals from his colleagues.

We conclude, as a matter of law, that the minimal referral contacts WMC provided Asplund with during his short tenure do not amount to a reasonable protectible interest. Further, we conclude that his short three-and-one-half-month tenure with WMC was insufficient to materially aid in his reputation. His brief employment with WMC was such that Asplund only provided "legitimate and ordinary competition of the type that a stranger could give...." Therefore, WMC did not acquire a protectible right against competition by Asplund through this brief employment on either of these bases.

WMC next argues that it acquired a protectible interest because Asplund performed unique specialized services....

[I]n order to establish a protectible interest, WMC would have to establish that Asplund's unique skills were acquired at WMC. No one disputes that Asplund acquired his vascular surgery skills prior to his employment, that there was no other vascular surgeon at WMC from whom he could enhance these unique skills, and that Asplund's short tenure at WMC prevented him from significantly improving his skills. Thus, the evidence is undisputed that Asplund did not acquire his unique skills from his employment with WMC, and, consequently, WMC did not acquire a protectible interest.

WMC's final argument regarding the restrictive covenant is that Asplund had access to competitive information at WMC and, as a result, the covenant is reasonably necessary to protect WMC. The key piece of competitive information was the patient lists....

In this case, although Asplund did not take any of this information with him, during his employment he had access to patient lists. However, Asplund, who was one of many physicians at WMC, did not have the type of control or influence over his patients so as to use this access for any competitive advantage. This was especially true in light of his surgery practice. Unlike, for example, a general practitioner, a patient's relationship with a surgeon is, hopefully, restricted to one encounter. Further, WMC did not put forth substantial efforts to acquire new patients for Asplund, and gave him very few referrals during his final sixty days there. Additionally, in his short tenure Asplund could not have established the type of "special relationship" with his patients so as to have such influence. Therefore, WMC did not acquire a protectible right to reasonably prevent competition from Asplund by virtue of his access to the patient lists....

As mentioned, restrictive covenants are suspect and must be closely scrutinized to pass legal muster as being reasonable.... Because WMC failed to prove that the covenant not to compete is reasonably necessary for the protection of WMC, we conclude that the covenant is unenforceable.... Because our conclusion is dispositive with regard to the enforceability of the covenant, we need not address WMC's remaining arguments concerning the restrictive covenant.

Improper Interference with Governmental Processes. In the wake of Watergate, with the absolutely unprecedented loss through resignation of both a President and a Vice President of the United States and with the disclosures of illegal political contributions by some of our largest national corporations, many people have been made much more aware of the possibilities for the corruption of governmental processes. Coercion or bribery of public officials is clearly illegal, and any "contract" involving such "services" would be void. *Lobbying*, on the other hand, is perfectly lawful and an essential part of the democratic process, and lobbying contracts which do not involve any improper means are valid and enforceable in court.

In most states mere failure to report a crime, called *misprison*, is no longer criminal; however, a person who actively aids in concealing a crime or agrees not to file criminal charges in return for a consideration is committing a criminal act. Perjury and jury tampering are both crimes. While at one time maintenance (stirring up litigation) was a crime, this rule has been modified as a result of the activities of such organizations as the NAACP Legal Defense Fund and Nader's Raiders. The old common-law judges were so jealous of their prerogatives that they even held arbitration agreements to be illegal "obstructions of justice," but this view has been almost completely repudiated.

The Watergate scandal has left this entire area of the law somewhat unsettled, as new legislation has been adopted to limit private political contributions and new attempts are under way to repeal the Hatch Act so as to permit political activities by employees of the U.S. government.

ILLEGALITY OR IMPOSSIBILITY AS AN EXCUSE FOR NONPERFORMANCE

Subsequent Illegality. Where the performances called for by the contract were legal when made but were subsequently made illegal by statute or administrative regulation, the now-illegal contract duties are discharged by operation of law. This is clearly the only fair result: neither party normally assumes this kind of risk, and neither ought to be forced to perform if by doing so, he or she is breaking the law. The adoption of the Eighteenth Amendment and the Volstead Act, which made it illegal to manufacture, transport, or sell alcoholic beverages, provided one illustration of this rule in effect. More current examples might involve changes in the legal rules pertaining to foreign investments, currency exchange, ownership of gold by U.S. citizens, and sales of "strategic" materials to Communist-bloc countries.

Impossibility. Where a contract specifies performance by one certain party or where the performance requires the existence of a particular thing, the death or disability of the party or the destruction of the thing will normally discharge the performance obligation through **objective impossibility**. That is, because the contract is so specific, no one at all can render the required performance. A promise to deliver "all of my tomato crop" is discharged if the tomato crop is destroyed without any fault on the part of the grower. A promise to deliver "1,000 tons of tomatoes" is probably not discharged when the grower's own crop fails, because the grower could buy other tomatoes on the market and deliver them. Where no specific thing is identified, there is only "subjective impossibility," which does not operate to discharge contract obligations.

Commercial Impracticability and Frustration. Closely related to the idea of impossibility are the ideas of **impracticability** and **frustration**. A performance may not actually be impossible to render, but it may be financially impracticable to do it, in the sense that it is stupid or nonsensical to require the performance. If a trucking company has a contract to transport a racehorse to Churchill Downs for the Kentucky Derby, and the horse dies, it would clearly be commercially impracticable to require the owner to pay the trucking company for transporting the dead horse to Churchill Downs, although that performance is not impossible. The UCC contains specific provisions, in Section 2-615, for dealing with this problem in sale of goods cases.

Frustration is closely related to impossibility. Again, the performance specified in the contract is not technically impossible, but the entire purpose or reason for making the contract no longer exists because of the happening of some unforeseeable event. The classic case of frustration involved the renting of rooms in London for exorbitant prices to enable the guests to see the coronation parade of King Edward VII. On the day designated in the "leases," there was no parade because the king had caught a cold and postponed it. Although there was nothing impossible about performance by either the landlord or the tenant, at least one English court agreed that the contract duty should be discharged.

BARGAINS AGAINST PUBLIC POLICY

Among the kinds of provisions challengeable as **against public policy** are those attempting to insulate landlords, employers, and bailees from liability for their own negligence and those which purport to waive or give up specific statutory protections. Anyone who has ever rented a house or an apartment knows that landlords' lawyers are particularly adept at coming up with objectionable lease provisions: no pets, no motorcycles, no waterbeds, no alcohol; tenant waives right to trial by jury; landlord may inspect the premises at any hour of the day or night—with or without notice to the tenant. While the landlord surely has a legitimate concern with what happens on the premises, some of the preceding seem to constitute an unwarranted intrusion into the tenant's affairs; this balance has not yet been fully and finally defined.

These are not closed categories. As society's values change, provisions which are readily accepted and enforced today may become "against public policy" and thus unenforceable. In any case where the results called for by the terms of the contract seem unduly harsh, this additional defense argument should be presented to the court. What can you lose?

The *Crawford* case involves a lease clause which says the landlord is not liable for any injury on the premises.

CRAWFORD v. BUCKNER
839 S.W.2d 754 (TN, 1992)

FACTS: On December 16, 1988, the plaintiff, Linda Crawford, rented an apartment from the defendants, Tobe McKenzie and McKenzie Development Corporation. As a condition of rental, Crawford was required to sign the defendants' standard form lease, which contained an exculpatory clause providing that:

> [t]enant agrees that the landlord, his agents and servants shall not be liable to tenant or any person claiming through tenant, for any injury to the person or loss of or damage to property for any cause. Tenant shall hold and save landlord harmless for any and all claims, suits, or judgments for any such damages or injuries however occurring.

On February 21, 1989, two months after Crawford rented her apartment, a fire started in the apartment of Debra and Larry Buckner, who lived in the apartment below the plaintiff. The fire quickly spread to the plaintiff's apartment, blocking her exit through the front, and only, door. To escape the fire, Crawford jumped from a window in her second story apartment. When she landed, the plaintiff suffered numerous injuries, partly due to the debris on the ground behind her apartment building.

Crawford later filed a tort action in Bradley County naming the Buckners, Tobe McKenzie, and McKenzie Development Corporation as defendants. The complaint alleged that the landlords were negligent in failing to maintain the fire alarm, the premises behind her apartment, and in continuing to allow the Buckners to reside at the apartment complex after numerous altercations and complaints. In addition, the plaintiff challenged the constitutionality of the Uniform Residential Landlord and Tenant Act, which prohibits lease provisions limiting a landlord's liability to a tenant. The Act was not applicable to Bradley County at that time because the legislature had limited it to counties of more than 200,000 residents. The plaintiff alleged that the limited application of the Act denied her equal protection of the law under the Fourteenth Amendment to the U.S. Constitution, and Article XI, § 8, of the Tennessee Constitution.

The landlord defendants answered that the plaintiff's action was barred by the exculpatory clause of the lease and filed a motion for summary judgment.

At the hearing on the landlords' motion for summary judgment, the trial court concluded the exculpatory clause in the lease was enforceable. The court also found that there was a rational basis for the legislature's decision to limit the Act's application to the largest counties in the state and therefore upheld the constitutionality of the Act. As a result, the landlords' motion for summary judgment was granted. The Court of Appeals affirmed.

 JUSTICE ANDERSON:

An exculpatory clause in the context of a landlord-tenant relationship refers to a clause which deprives the tenant of the right to recover damages for harm caused by the landlord's negligence by releasing the landlord from liability for future acts of negligence.

The rationale underlying the argument for enforceability of such clauses has often been based upon the doctrine of freedom of contract. Courts employing that reasoning have said:

> that the public policy in apparent conflict with the freedom of contract argument in real-estate lease exculpatory clause cases, namely, that a landlord should be liable for the negligent breach of a duty which is owed to his tenant, is subservient to the doctrine that a person has the right to freely contract about his affairs. Some cases, especially the older ones, have reasoned that the relationship of landlord and tenant is in no event a matter of public interest, but is purely a private affair, so that such clauses cannot be held void on purely public policy grounds....

However, because of the burden-shifting effect of such clauses which grant immunity from the law, it is not surprising that their validity has been challenged and that courts have reached different conclusions as to their enforceability....

The defendant contends that freedom to contract in the residential lease setting is the majority rule in the United States, and that holding exculpatory provisions in residential leases invalid on public policy grounds would require this court to adopt the minority rule. Our research of the cases in this area, however, demonstrates that there is no true majority rule. We find, as the Washington Supreme

Court found, that there is no majority rule, "only numerous conflicting decisions, decisions concerned with contracts of indemnity, cases relating to property damage under business leases, and a disposition of the courts to emasculate such exculpatory clauses by means of strict construction...."

Tennessee courts have long recognized that, subject to certain exceptions, parties may contract that one shall not be liable for his negligence to another....

Although the earlier cases recognized that there were exceptions to the rule made for the benefit of the public, no case considered the public interest issue until this Court's decision in *Olson v. Molzen*.... We held in *Olson* that if an exculpatory provision affects the public interest, it is void as against public policy, despite the general rule that parties may contract that one shall not be liable for his negligence to another....

We said that an exculpatory contract signed by a patient as a condition of receiving medical treatment is invalid as contrary to public policy and may not be pleaded as a bar to the patient's suit for negligence....

Applying the *Olson* criteria to the facts of this case, first, we conclude a residential lease concerns a business of a type that is generally thought suitable for public regulation. Our conclusion is bolstered by the fact that the legislature of this state has seen fit to regulate this area, and that other states, such as Illinois, Maryland, Massachusetts, and New York, have enacted legislation regulating the residential landlord-tenant relationship....

As a result of the essential nature of the service and the economic setting of the transaction, a residential landlord has a decisive advantage in bargaining strength against any member of the public who seeks its services. A potential tenant is usually confronted with a "take it or leave it" form contract, which the tenant is powerless to alter. The tenant's only alternative is to reject the entire transaction.

Moreover, due to its superior bargaining position, a residential landlord confronts the public with a standardized adhesion contract of exculpation, which contains no provision whereby a tenant can pay additional reasonable fees to obtain protection from the landlord's negligence. The lease in this case is a good example. In her affidavit in opposition to the defendants' motion for summary judgment, Crawford testified that she was given the defendants' standard lease form to sign, and was never offered the opportunity to pay additional reasonable fees to obtain protection from the landlords' negligence....

Finally, we conclude that by definition a residential lease places the person and the property of the tenant under the control of the landlord, subject to the risk of carelessness by the landlord and his agents. The allegations of this case ... are common examples of landlord negligence causing injury to either the person or property of the tenant. Therefore, it follows that the landlord-tenant relationship falls within the final public interest criterion set forth in *Olson*.

Accordingly, we find that the residential landlord-tenant relationship here satisfies all ... of the public interest criteria adopted in *Olson v. Molzen*....

However, the defendants insist that a residential lease between a landlord and a tenant is a purely private affair, and not a matter of public interest. We disagree. We rejected this same argument in *Olson* and find persuasive the reasoning of the Washington supreme court, which, in response to the very same argument, stated:

> [W]e are not faced merely with the theoretical duty of construing a provision in an isolated contract specifically bargained for by *one landlord and one tenant* as a purely private affair. Considered realistically, we are asked to construe an exculpa-

tory clause, the generalized use of which may have an impact upon thousands of potential tenants....

Accordingly, we hold that under the facts here, the lease clause limiting the residential landlord's liability for negligence to its tenants is void as against public policy.

SIGNIFICANCE OF THIS CHAPTER

As statutes and administrative regulations multiply, it becomes increasingly possible that contracting parties may on occasion agree to do some illegal act. Generally, for successful criminal prosecution, criminal intent must be proved. Intent is usually irrelevant, however, as far as the enforcement of an illegal bargain is concerned. Both parties are presumed to know the applicable criminal law; whether or not they do in fact is usually irrelevant—their purported contract is void or voidable. Where a statute or regulation is designed to protect one of the parties to the transaction, the courts will try to work out results that achieve that objective. Otherwise, where both parties are equally guilty, the court's general approach will be to leave all parties as is. Since either of these rules can result in the forfeiture of substantial economic values, you need to be alerted to the major types of illegality that may occur in contracting situations.

PROBLEMS FOR DISCUSSION

1. In 1998, Edwin Shaw, a tentured professor in the School of Pharmacy of Carlisle University, was fired because a cutback in funds to the pharmacy school greatly increased the pharmacy school's already existing deficit. Shaw's contract stated that he could be fired in the event of financial exigency on the part of the institution. Financial exigency was defined to include bona fide discontinuance of a program or department of instruction or reduction in size thereof. The university as a whole was not in financial trouble, and Shaw claimed that he could not be fired unless that were true.
   Can he get his job back? Explain.

2. R.E. Fuse operates a garbage collection service in the towns of Cleen and Teidy. In June 1996, he made an oral agreement with Wesley Trashy to hire him as a garbage truck driver. In November, R.E. Fuse handed Wesley a written document which stated that, upon severance of employment, Trashy would not engage in garbage collection within fifteen miles of Cleen and Teidy for a period of five years. Trashy, who knew that his signature on the document was a precondition for continued employment, signed the agreement. In September 1998, Wesley Trashy quit his job and immediately went into the garbage collection business for himself. R.E. Fuse now brings an action against Trashy for breach of contract.
   What decision? Why?

3. Sinkin Beverage Company was licensed by Blitz Beer as a wholesale distributor in 1985. The written contract which the parties signed at that time provided that either one could cancel at any time, for any reason or for no reason at all. Sinkin was the exclusive distributor for Blitz products in Suffould County 1985 to 1998, and its Blitz sales constitute a large part of its wholesale business. In 1998, Blitz notified Sinkin that the contract would be terminated in ten days. Sinkin sues for an injunction against the termination, claiming that the contract clause is unconscionable.

   Should this injunction be granted? Explain.

4. The parties executed a valid written contract by which Mr. and Mrs. Christy agreed to buy an apartment from Mrs. Pilkinton for $30,000. When the time came for performance, the purchasers, although not insolvent, were unable to raise enough money to carry out their contract. Mrs. Pilkinton, after having tendered a deed to the property, brought this suit. At the trial the defendants' evidence tended to show that, as a result of a decline in Christys' used car business, they do not possess, and cannot borrow the unpaid balance of $29,900.

   Do the Christys have a valid excuse for nonperformance? Explain.

5. Plaintiffs, desirous of purchasing a home, and defendant entered into a promissory note secured by a mortgage on the home. The promissory note was for the principal amount of $30,000 with interest at 9.5 percent per annum, for a period of five years, with monthly payments of $279.64. The mortgage agreement contained the following clause: "Balance due in five years with option to renew at current rate of interest." A statute provides that "a note, mortgage, contract, or other evidence of indebtedness shall not provide that the rate of interest initially effective may be increased for any reason whatsoever." Plaintiffs sue to have the note and mortgage declared illegal.

   How should the court rule, and why?

Chapter 13
Assignment and Third-Party Beneficiary Contracts

The problems discussed in this chapter are quite different from any we have considered so far. Here, our basic question is whether persons other than the parties who actually negotiated and agreed to the contract should be given the right to demand performance under it. The answer given by the early common law was simple: No! Today, however, courts do recognize the rights of these "strangers"—both assignees and third-party beneficiaries—at least in some situations and subject to many complicated and technical limitations.

THIRD-PARTY BENEFICIARY CONTRACTS

Basic Concepts and Definitions. A **third-party beneficiary contract** is one in which at least one of the performances called for is intended for the direct benefit of a person or persons other than the parties who actually made the contract. **Donee beneficiaries** are persons who receive this benefit as a gift, without any prior duty on anyone's part to provide them with the benefit. In most cases, persons named as the beneficiaries in life insurance policies are donees. A **creditor beneficiary** is one to whom the benefit was already owed, as a result of a prior legal relationship. If creditors have sold or financed purchases of such items as cars, appliances, or real estate to buyers who resell the as-yet-unpaid-for items to purchasers who agree to take over the payments, the creditors are third-party creditor beneficiaries of the take-over-the-payments contracts. In these cases, the creditor-beneficiary has two parties to look to for payment: the original debtor and the takeover buyer.

UCC Rule on Third-Party Beneficiaries of Warranties. The Uniform Commercial Code does not deal with third-party beneficiaries in any comprehensive way. It does, however, contain one very important third-party provision, 2-318, which provides that whatever warranties are made by a seller of goods are also by law extended to members of the buyer's family and household and to guests in the buyer's home. The section further provides that its effect cannot be limited by any contrary agreement between the seller and the buyer.

The *Harvard* case illustrates a different kind of "third party beneficiary" situation.

HARVARD LAW SCHOOL COALITION FOR CIVIL RIGHTS v. PRESIDENT AND FELLOWS OF HARVARD COLLEGE
595 N.E.2d 516 (MA, 1992)

FACTS: The plaintiffs, Harvard Law School Coalition for Civil Rights (coalition) and individual students from Harvard Law School, appeal from the dismissal of their complaint, seeking equitable relief for the allegedly discriminatory faculty hiring policies of Harvard Law School in violation of Massachusetts statutes c. 151B and c. 93, § 102.

In dismissing the complaint, the Superior Court judge ruled that the plaintiffs lacked standing under either statute and that the coalition lacked capacity to sue. The judge also denied the plaintiffs' motion to amend the complaint to add a claim under c. 151C. After judgment for the defendant, the plaintiffs appealed.

 JUSTICE LYNCH:

The plaintiffs essentially allege that, because the law school has not hired certain minorities, females, and disabled persons, they have been denied the benefit of association with an integrated faculty and therefore they have standing as "persons aggrieved" under G.L. c. 151B, § 9....

It is clear from the statute and case law that an individual has to be within the employment relationship and has to have suffered injury as a result of a prohibited practice in order to have a cause of action under § 9. On analysis, we determine that the plaintiffs are not within the employer-employee relationship and have not alleged substantial injury within the area of concern of the statute....

The judge ruled that G.L. c. 93, § 102, does not confer standing on anyone other than those whose rights have been violated. The plaintiffs argue that, as tuition-paying students, they have a contractual relationship with the law school protected by G.L. c.93, § 102.... The plaintiffs' amended complaint failed to allege that the plaintiffs had a contract with the law school in which the law school agreed not to discriminate in faculty hiring or agreed to hire valuable role models of diverse backgrounds. The only hint of any contract or agreement in the entire complaint is the allegation that the plaintiffs "as students ... are the intended beneficiaries of the agreement to employ individuals as law teachers at their school...."

The plaintiffs' contention that they are the intended beneficiaries of the employment contracts between the law school and its faculty, is also flawed. The plaintiffs are no more than incidental beneficiaries of these contracts.... Under Massachusetts law, only intended beneficiaries, not incidental beneficiaries, can enforce a contract....

The plaintiffs contend for the first time on appeal that dismissal of their complaint was erroneous because their complaint implicitly stated a claim that the law school breached a contract with them....

Nowhere in the complaint, however, is there any allegation of such a contract or facts from which the judge could have inferred the terms of such a contract. Neither is there any allegation of a breach of contract nor facts alleged that would establish one. On appeal, the plaintiffs again do not set out the provisions of the contract, nor what terms they rely on in their contractual relationship as students with the law school. Instead, they make allegations of "[c]atalogue" and "literature" without identifying those sources other than the defendant's affirmative action plan. Furthermore, at oral argument on the motion to dismiss, the plaintiffs referred to their educational contracts with the law school, not to allege a breach of contract, but to advance their argument that they had standing under that "make and enforce contracts" language under G.L. c.93, § 102. These allegations are not sufficient to support the plaintiffs' contention that there was a breach of their "contract" with the law school. Clearly, the amended complaint failed to state the essential elements of the plaintiffs' alleged contract.

Incidental Beneficiaries.

As seen in the preceding case, many courts are still quite reluctant to permit "nonparticipant" third parties to enforce contracts that they had no part in making. Such courts, therefore, demand clear proof of an intent to benefit a third party. **Incidental beneficiaries**, persons who derive some indirect benefit from a contract but cannot show such an intent on the part of the contracting parties, have no right to sue to enforce the contract.

It is not necessary that the third party be specifically named or identified at the time the contract is made. A shopkeeper-tenant was held to have enforceable rights against a contractor who had promised the owner/landlord that a remodeling job would be done "in such a way as to cause a minimum of disturbance to the daytime operations in the building." The *Harvard* case does show, however, that courts look very carefully for the contracting parties' intent.

Mutual Rescission of the Contract.

Generally, the parties to a contract can agree to call off the deal any time they want to. The problem is complicated by the presence of a third-party beneficiary: Must the original contracting parties also have consent to the rescission from the third party?

In answering this question, the *Restatement* distinguishes between the donee beneficiary and the creditor beneficiary. In the case of the donee beneficiary, the gift is considered to be complete, and therefore nonrescindable, when the contract is made. Thus, the parties to a life insurance contract, for example, cannot rescind the gift by agreeing to a change of beneficiaries unless the right to change beneficiaries has been reserved. On the other hand, where a creditor beneficiary is involved, there is a preexisting contract with the original debtor. The creditor can still demand performance from that party. The contract made for the benefit of a third-party creditor can thus be rescinded until the creditor relies on it in some way. The creditor might let the original debtor remove collateral from the state, for instance, relying on the fact that the substitute debtor was still there. Once that had happened, the original debtor and the substitute debtor would not be able to rescind their agreement.

ASSIGNMENT OF CONTRACT RIGHTS

Basic Concepts and Definitions. **Assignment** simply means transfer; the "owner" of the right to receive benefits under a contract is simply transferring this right to someone else. The transfer may itself be part of a second contract (as it usually is), or it may be made as a gift. No special language is required for an effective assignment; any manifestation of an intent to make such a transfer is sufficient. Some states require all assignments to be in writing to be enforceable; others do not. For the kinds of assignments it covers (9-102[1][b], 9-104[f], 9-106), Article 9 of the UCC requires assignments to be in writing.

Early Common Law Rule. The common law emphasized freedom of contract; no one should be required to deal with another without first agreeing to do so. Contract prohibitions against assignment were given full force and effect. An **obligor**, the person who had a duty to perform, could in effect veto an assignment by refusing to perform for the new **obligee**. Although the validity of transfers of contract rights is now generally recognized and such assignments provide the mechanisms for financing a large part of modern business, there are still many technical legal rules on this subject.

Delegation of Duties. One of the first distinctions which must be drawn is the difference between assigning a right and delegating a duty. Duties can never be assigned, only delegated, the difference being that someone who delegates his or her own duty of performance to another remains personally responsible for its proper and timely performance. In our example earlier in this chapter, if the second buyer in the take-over-the-payments deal does not make the payments as promised, the original buyer remains personally liable and can be sued by the original seller. Where a right has been validly assigned, however, the assignee completely displaces the original owner of the right, to whom performance was due. However, the original debtor is free of liability for a delegated duty only if the original obligee (creditor) agrees to the substitution of the new obligor (debtor) in place of the original one and agrees to discharge the original one. Without the obligee's consent, the performance of a duty cannot even be delegated to another person if the duty involves an individualized service or if there is a particular reason for dealing with one certain person.

The *Cosgrove* case discusses one implication of classifying a duty as "non-delegable."

COSGROVE v. MCDONNELL DOUGLAS HELICOPTER CO.
847 F.Supp. 719 (D. MN, 1994)

FACTS: The Plaintiffs' action arises from a helicopter accident which occurred on February 20, 1991, when fatigue failure caused a portion of the helicopter, which had been manufactured by a predecessor-in-interest of McDonnell Douglas Helicopter Co. ("McDonnell Douglas"), to sever the drive shaft on the aircraft, causing the craft to crash. The mechanism which resulted in the crash was not in dispute—only the fault of the parties in permitting that mechanism to exist.

At the time of the accident, the helicopter was owned by the Jacksons, had been leased by the Jacksons to Helicopter Flight, Inc. ("Helicopter Flight"), and was being piloted by Michael Cosgrove ("Cosgrove"). Each of these Plaintiffs sued McDonnell Douglas for the damages they had sustained as a result of the crash. In addition to denying its own fault, McDonnell Douglas pleaded, as an affirmative defense, that each of the Plaintiffs was comparatively at fault. McDonnell Douglas did not assert, however, a counterclaim against any of the Plaintiffs for contribution or indemnity arising from the potential joint and several liability that McDonnell Douglas might ultimately bear for the fault of a Plaintiff.

The Plaintiffs premised their action against McDonnell Douglas upon an asserted defective design of the helicopter, with attendant strict liability in tort, and upon a negligent failure on the part of McDonnell Douglas to warn. In turn, McDonnell Douglas argued that Michael Cosgrove [as the pilot], the Jacksons [as the owners and lessors] and Helicopter Flight [as the lessee] were negligent in their inspection and maintenance of the helicopter. The evidence of record was sufficient to permit the jury to conclude that proper maintenance and care by any or all of the Plaintiffs would have indicated that a fatigue failure was in progress.

Backman had been hired by the Jacksons to conduct a pre-purchase inspection of the helicopter in order to ascertain if the craft were airworthy. McDonnell Douglas contends, and the record supports a conclusion, that an approved inspection of the helicopter would have detected the site and status of the fatigue failure. Although Backman contended that such an inspection had occurred, and that the helicopter's operations manual recorded such an inspection as having been completed, the evidence was such that the Jury could have determined that no such inspection had been conducted, that the entry in the operations manual was deficient and inaccurate, and that Backman was, in part, responsible for the Plaintiffs' claimed damages. At the time of the pre-purchase inspection, Backman was an independent contractor. However, on or about January 1, 1991, Backman was hired by Helicopter Flight as a mechanic and, from that date until the date of the accident, he performed maintenance on the helicopter.

On November 4, 1993, the jury returned its special verdict which allocated the comparative fault as follows:

13. Taking all of the fault that directly caused the Plaintiffs' injuries as 100 percent, what percentage of fault do you attribute to:

a. McDonnell Douglas Helicopter Co. 65%
b. Michael Cosgrove 0
c. Steven and Beverly Jackson 10
d. Alan Backman prior to 1/1/91 15
e Alan Backman on or after 1/1/91 10
                                                        100%

At this juncture, we are only asked to consider the reallocation of Backman's 15 percent fault for the period prior to January 1, 1991, and the computation of damages for the purposes of entering judgment.

 MAGISTRATE JUDGE ERICKSON::

By its present motion, McDonnell Douglas contends that the 15 percent of fault, that the jury had attributed to Alan Backman for the period prior to January 1, 1991, should be reallocated to the Jacksons as: (1) Under 14 C.F.R § 91.405, the Jacksons had a non-delegable duty to inspect and maintain the helicopter; (2) Under the provisions of Minnesota Statutes Section 360.0216, the Jacksons should be responsible for the fault of Backman; and (3) Under the common-law of Minnesota, Backman was the agent of the Jacksons. We address each of these arguments, in turn....

In reliance upon decisional authorities under Minnesota law, McDonnell Douglas argues that 14 C.F.R. § 91.405 imposes upon the owners and operators of aircraft, including helicopters, an obligation to inspect and maintain their aircraft which cannot be delegated to others. We find the argument unconvincing.

Ordinarily, "the employer of an independent contractor is not liable for physical harm caused to another by an act or omission of the contractor or his servants...." This general principle has been substantially eroded, however, such that it "would be proper to say that the rule is now primarily important as a preamble to the catalog of its exceptions...."

Although not expressly cited by McDonnell Douglas, we understand the exception upon which it relies to be that enunciated in Restatement (Second) of Torts § 424, which provides:

> One who by statute or by administrative regulation is under a duty to provide specified safeguards or precautions for the safety of others is subject to liability to the others for whose protection the duty is imposed for harm caused by the failure of a contractor employed by him to provide such safeguards or precautions.

Specifically, McDonnell Douglas argues that, as the owners of the helicopter, the provisions of 14 C.F.R. § 91.405 imposed upon the Jacksons a non-delegable duty by requiring as follows:

> Each owner or operator of an aircraft (a) *Shall* have that aircraft inspected * * * *and shall* between required inspections * * * have discrepancies repaired as prescribed in part 43 of this chapter. [Emphasis added].

Unfortunately for the argument however, the same regulations make clear that the maintenance of an aircraft in an airworthy condition is not so exclusive to the owner or operator as to be non-delegable. In this respect, 14 C.F.R. § 91.403(A) provides:

> The owner or operator of an aircraft is primarily responsible for maintaining that aircraft in an airworthy condition, including compliance with part 39 of this chapter.

Had the regulations intended to hold owners and operators solely responsible, they would not have characterized that responsibility as being less than exclusive. Indeed, the pertinent regulations of the Federal Aviation Administration ... impose a plethora of requirements, largely expressed in obligatory "shalls" upon owners, operators, and mechanics alike, for the inspection and maintenance of aircraft, and for the documentation of such activities. In our view, the non-exclusive nature of these requirements corroborates our determination that the inspection and maintenance of aircraft is not so singularly a duty of the owner or operator that public policy dictates that it may not be delegated to others....

NOW, THEREFORE, It is ORDERED:

1. That the motion of the Defendant McDonnell Douglas to reallocate the jury's finding of 15 percent fault on Alan Backman's part, for the period before January 1, 1991, is DENIED.
2. That judgment be entered in favor of the Plaintiffs Michael Cosgrove and Luann Cosgrove in the amount of $458,869.48.
3. That judgment be entered in favor of the Plaintiffs Steven B. Jackson and Beverly S. Jackson in the amount of $13,163.70.
4. That judgment be entered in favor of the Defendant Schweitzer Aircraft Corporation.
5. That judgment be entered in favor of the Plaintiff Helicopter Flight, Inc., in the amount of $14,638.99.

Assignability of Rights. To determine whether or not rights are assignable, we must consider contracts in three categories. First, there are contracts whose rights are not assignable unless the obligor specifically agrees to the assignment. This category includes contracts involving some personal element, such as the personal service of the obligor or the personal credit or requirements of the obligee, and contracts where the performance of the duty would be materially changed if the assignment were recognized. The UCC adopts this same basic approach for sales of goods in Section 2-210(2).

Probably the vast majority of contracts fall into the second category, in which the rights are assignable unless there is a specific contract prohibition against assignment. In most cases, contract rights for such things as land, securities, or goods would be presumed to be transferable to others unless the parties had specifically agreed otherwise. Section 2-210(3) of the UCC says that in order to prohibit assignment of the right to receive goods, a contract clause must very clearly specify that result; a general prohibition of transfer of "the contract" is only effective to prohibit a delegation of duties.

The third group of contracts results from the Code's effort to make sure that businesses will be able to use their accounts as financing collateral without having to get each account debtor's consent. Section 9-318(4) says that even if the contract specifically prohibits assignment of the right to receive payment for goods sold or leased or services performed, the creditor can go ahead and assign the account anyway, without the debtor's consent; the contract provision will not be enforced. For example, when you buy your new TV on time, even getting a specific clause written into your contract will not enable you to avoid dealing with a finance company if the dealer wants to assign your contract.

As a rule, present assignments of future rights are fully effective; that is, one can effectively transfer ownership now of the right, under an existing contract, to receive a performance at some future date. However, any purported assignment of rights under a contract which does not exist yet, but is merely anticipated, is totally void. An unemployed person has not made an effective assignment by signing a contract with an employment agency which purports to assign one third of the first month's wages to the agency when it gets that person a new job. In addition, most states have specific regulatory statutes covering wage assignments and limiting the percentage share that can be assigned.

The *Smith* case presents another type of "assignability" problem.

SMITH v. BROWN
513 N.W.2d 732 (IA, 1994)

FACTS: The marriage of defendant Cathy Brown and Dennis Brown was dissolved in January 1980. The dissolution decree awarded Cathy the parties' residence until she remarried, ceased to use it as her principal residence, or the youngest child of the marriage reached eighteen. On the happening of any of these events, the decree called for the sale of the home. From the proceeds of this sale, the decree awarded Dennis $13,000 plus interest from the date of the decree. The decree then awarded Cathy the residence subject to Dennis's interest.

Cathy was awarded custody, subject to Dennis's visitation rights, of the three minor children. Dennis was ordered to pay $37.50 per child per week, the payments "becoming judgments as they accrue."

Within three months, Dennis conveyed his interest in the marital residence by special warranty deed to the plaintiffs, Gary and Sheila Smith, for $5,000. The Smiths and Cathy stipulate that the Smiths had not known Dennis prior to the execution of his special warranty deed to them in 1980. They also stipulate that the $5,000 consideration paid by the Smiths was "adequate and fair." They agree that, during the middle part of 1981, Cathy had actual and personal knowledge of the filing of the special warranty deed.

Subsequent to filing the deed, Dennis became delinquent in his child support obligations. The arrearages of $19,305, at the time of trial, exceeded the value of Dennis's interests. At the time of trial, the youngest minor child had already attained the age of 18.

The Smiths filed this declaratory judgment action seeking clarification of the parties' rights. Dennis was not made a party. Cathy answered and asserted: (1) that the lien was not assignable by Dennis, and (2) she was entitled to a setoff against the lien for Dennis's delinquent support payments.

After finding the lien was assignable and that the Smiths were assignees of all Dennis's interest in the residence, the district court declared the interest was subject to setoffs for Dennis's support payments. The Smiths asked the court to order the property sold. This was denied; the court directed the Smiths to use ordinary proceedings for enforcing the lien. Cathy appealed and the Smiths cross-appealed.

 JUSTICE HARRIS:

The trial was correct in rejecting Cathy's contention that Dennis could not assign his lien interest. In *Broyles v. Iowa Department of Social Services*, 305 N.W.2d 718, 721 (Iowa, 1981), we established that future judgments arising from dissolution-of-marriage decrees are assignable. Dennis's lien surely qualifies. When assigned, it was a present interest even though enjoyment was postponed until some future point.

A more troublesome question is whether the assigned interest was subject to setoff for the delinquent child support. According to the general rule, an assignee takes precisely what the assignor had, and assumes not only all advantages but is subject to the same defenses. Thus, the obligor can assert against the assignee all claims that would have been available against the assignor....

The Smiths recognize the rule, but point to authorities that limit it.... These same authorities point out the corollary relied upon by the Smiths. Generally, equities and defenses between the assignor and debtor arising after the assignment cannot be interposed against the assignee....

Cathy's position is greatly weakened by the fact that she is dealing with a third party. We have said that, because the rights of third parties may be implicated, "[r]eal estate titles, once fixed, should not be subjected to revision with the subsequent ebb and flow of the fortunes of former parties to the litigation...."

It is stipulated that the Smiths were unacquainted with Dennis at the time of their purchase of the lien, and that the purchase price was "adequate and fair." The Smiths had a clear right to note that the dissolution decree did not make the lien subject to further support payments and to make their purchase accordingly. The lien was not reduced by any arrearages accumulating after the assignment....

In summary, the trial court was correct in holding the plaintiffs-Smith are assignees of all interests that Dennis L. Brown had in the real estate. The trial court was correct in holding that their claim is subject to all setoffs and counterclaims to which Dennis was subject when the assignment was recorded June 24, 1980. The lien was, however, not subject to setoffs and counterclaims arising thereafter. The trial court did not err in leaving the Smiths to ordinary enforcement proceedings. Alternatively, Cathy may satisfy the lien by paying an amount equivalent to the $13,000 plus interest consistent with the 1980 divorce decree.

Due on Sale Clauses in Real Estate Mortgages. A due on sale clause does not, technically, prohibit the resale of real estate before an existing mortgage is paid off. What it does say is that when such a resale occurs, the entire remaining mortgage balance becomes immediately due and payable. As a practical result, this means that no assignment of the existing mortgage to the resale purchaser can occur; the resale purchaser will have to qualify for new financing. As interest rates soared in the late 1970s and early 1980s, mortgage lenders did not want to be bound on the twenty- and thirty-year mortgages which they had written at 6 to 9 percent interest rates. The lenders began to enforce their due on sale clauses vigorously.

Although outright prohibitions on assignment by real estate buyers would generally be enforceable, some state courts refused to enforce due on sale clauses. For a time, there was a distinction based on whether the lender was state chartered or U.S. chartered. U.S. regulations specifically recognized the validity of the due on sale, but a state lending institution, competing for the same business, might not be able to enforce the clause. As a result of the 1982 Garn-St.Germain statute passed by Congress, due on sale clauses are now generally enforceable.

Warranties of Assignor to Assignee.

Where a contract right has been transferred for value, the *Restatement* says that the assignor makes three warranties to the assignee:

1. That the assignor will do nothing to defeat or impair the value of the assignment and that he has no knowledge of any fact that would do so.
2. That the right, as assigned, actually exists and is subject to no limitations or defenses good against the assignor, except those stated or apparent.
3. That any writing given or shown to the assignee as evidence of the right is genuine and what it purports to be.

In addition, the seller/assignor of the right can be sued for breach of warranty and/or fraud for any express statements made which are not true, such as a statement that a credit check had been made on the buyer/debtor, or that the buyer/debtor had a steady job. Note, however, that there is no implied guarantee that the buyer/debtor is solvent or will in fact perform as promised. In most cases where accounts receivable are being assigned on a regular basis, as with a car dealer to a manufacturer's financing subsidiary, the assignment agreement itself will include a specific recourse provision. The assignor may have to buy back all uncollectible accounts, or none of them, or only some of them. The parties are free to work this out as they choose.

Delegation of Duty to Assignee.

Courts are not agreed as to whether, in taking the assignment, an assignee is also impliedly agreeing to perform any remaining duties owed by his assignor to the other original party. Most of the older cases say that no such promise is implied; many of the newer ones have adopted a contrary rule. In any event, all of the surrounding facts and circumstances, and especially the language of the assignment itself, will be examined to see whether such a promise should be implied. The simplest solution to this problem is to specify the result desired in the assignment itself.

For the sale of goods, the Code adopts the view of the newer cases, so that an acceptance by the assignee of a general assignment also constitutes the assignee's promise to perform all of the assignor's remaining duties, unless the language of the assignment or the circumstances indicate otherwise.

The significance of such a promise by the assignee is that nonperformance of the reciprocal duty gives (or may give) the other party an excuse for withholding the required return performance or even a basis for bringing a lawsuit against the assignee for breach of contract.

Notice to Obligor. All courts agree that, as between the assignor and the assignee, the assignment is effective when it is made, even though notice of the assignment has not been communicated to the obligor. However, notice (or its absence) does have some important legal consequences. Payment or other performance that the obligor gives to the assignor, before receiving notice that the obligation has been assigned and that the performance should now be made to the assignee, completely discharges that part of the original contract obligation. The assignee cannot sue the obligor and force a repeat performance but instead would have to sue the assignor. Similarly, the obligor can assert defenses or counterclaims against the assignee even on totally unrelated transactions between the obligor and the assignor if such claims arose before the obligor received notice of the assignment. For example, Dull buys a used car and a new car from Sharpie. Dull pays cash for the used car and finances the new car. Sharpie assigns the financing contract on the new car to the Bigger Bank. Until Dull gets notice of this assignment he can use as a defense against paying the balance due, not only any defects in the new car, but also any defects occurring in the used car. Once Dull gets notice of the assignment of his new car contract to Bigger Bank, he can use only defects in the new car as his reason for nonpayment. Any problems with the used car which arise after notice has been received will have to be taken up separately with Sharpie.

In the following case, the debtor paid the assignor *after* it received notice of the assignment.

AMERICA FIRST CREDIT UNION v. FIRST SECURITY BANK OF UTAH, N.A.
930 P.2d 1198 (UTAH, 1997)

FACTS: AFCU made a series of three loans to Renaissance, a supplier of food service to military bases under government contracts, to furnish Renaissance with working capital and to pay outstanding loans owing to AFCU and other lenders. At the time the first loan was made, Renaissance executed a security agreement with AFCU assigning as collateral a savings certificate it owned for $99,999 issued by First Security Bank. AFCU prepared a written notice of assignment, signed by Don Newsom, president and sole shareholder of Renaissance, and subsequently by an officer of First Security acknowledging receipt. The notice of assignment provided:

> We are holding as collateral on a Line of Credit Savings Certificate No. 984993 in the amount of $99,999, in the name of Renaissance Exchange. Renaissance Exchange Inc. is willing to pledge this certificate as collateral on their loan with America First Credit Union.
>
> Renaissance Exchange, Inc.
>
> [signed by Renaissance president]
>
> America First Credit Union is holding the original certificate as collateral. We would appreciate your acknowledgment of the Assignment, also confirming the balance of $99,999.00. This Assignment will be in affect [sic] until you have received written notice of our release of the Assignment. Please acknowledge the Assignment and the balance by signing below. One copy should be retained in your files.

First Security Bank of Utah

[signed by bank officer]

The savings certificate stated on its face that payment would be made to the registered owner "upon presentation and surrender of this certificate properly endorsed," and that otherwise upon maturity the account would automatically be renewed for a like period at the interest rate then offered.

At the time the second loan was made, AFCU prepared a second notice of assignment identical to the first. The certificate had previously matured and been renewed, and the new certificate number was hand-lettered by First Security on the notice of assignment to replace the original number and then signed by a First Security officer. Subsequently, First Security replaced the savings certificate with a special day-time certificate of deposit. This certificate did not state on its face that it had to be presented for payment. Consequently, in order to alert its personnel to the assignment, the bank placed a "flag" or "block" on the account in its computer system. When the certificate rolled over for the third time, First Security inadvertently removed the computer flag but did not notify AFCU of either the change in procedure or the removal of the flag.

AFCU held the certificate only as collateral on the Renaissance loan and therefore had no right to the proceeds except in the event of Renaissance's default. When the certificate matured for the third time, Newsom represented to First Security that the assignment had been released, and withdrew the proceeds of $99,999, although AFCU had not given First Security notice of release of the assignment. Newsom deposited the funds in Renaissance's AFCU checking account and subsequently paid them out. Seven months later, Renaissance defaulted with a balance of $551,529.31 owing on its third loan from AFCU, in the original amount of $675,000. AFCU demanded payment of the certificate by First Security, but the bank refused payment. AFCU then brought this suit against First Security, which in turn asserted a third-party claim against Renaissance and Don Newsom for $99,999. In a separate action, AFCU sued Newsom and Renaissance for the total balance owing on the loan. The actions were consolidated.

The trial court found that, while the notice of assignment did not contain any instructions directing First Security to take immediate action, it "recognized the assignment and the notice that payment should be made to America First Credit Union, not Renaissance Exchange, and flagged on its computer system the assignment for the certificate of deposit." The court concluded that the "totality of circumstances" gave First Security actual knowledge of the assignment which fulfilled the "reasonable notice" requirement of 9-318 (3). Therefore, the trial court ruled that AFCU had an enforceable security interest in the certificate and that First Security had breached its duty to honor that interest. The court imposed judgment against First Security accordingly and also awarded judgment in favor of AFCU against Newsom and Renaissance for the loan balance and in favor of First Security against Newsom and Renaissance for the certificate proceeds. First Security appealed to the court of appeals, which affirmed.

 JUSTICE HOWE:

First Security contends that it did not breach any duty to AFCU by paying the proceeds to Renaissance because the notice of assignment was inadequate in that it did not direct First Security to pay AFCU, and when First Security paid the proceeds to Renaissance, AFCU had no present right to them.

Section 70A-9-318 (3), Utah Code Ann. (1990) ... is identical to the Uniform Commercial Code.... This statute imposes a two-pronged notice requirement. First, notice of the assignment must be given. Second, the notice must state that payments are to be made to the assignee. First Security admits receiving notice of the assignment but contends that because it did not receive notice that payment should be made to AFCU, it was entitled to pay Renaissance. AFCU responds that the second prong of section 70A-9-318 (3) is tailored to "indirect collection" situations and therefore does not apply here....

However, the plain language of the notice of assignment, which one of First Security's officers acknowledged receiving, informed the bank of the assignment, that it would continue in force until revoked in writing, and that AFCU was holding the certificate of deposit. Furthermore, First Security knew that the certificate itself required presentation and endorsement before payment could be made. Thus payment of the certificate proceeds to Renaissance should have been impossible by First Security's own policy as long as AFCU held the certificate. When that policy changed, the computer flag on the account replaced the certificate as notice to First Security that payment was to be made to AFCU rather than to Renaissance. First Security's generation of the computer flag demonstrates that it had notice of the change in payment. Its failure to notify AFCU that the actual certificate was no longer required for payment and its erroneous removal of the computer flag were unilateral actions taken after the notice was complete and had no impact upon the duties of either party. The statute should not be read as requiring more of AFCU than what it did to apprise First Security of its continuing interest in the certificate.

We therefore hold that First Security received notice of the assignment and that payment was to be made to AFCU as required by ... 9-318 (3). Thus we affirm the finding of the trial court, upheld by the court of appeals, that First Security received "reasonable notice." By releasing the account proceeds to Renaissance while on notice of the unretracted assignment of the account as collateral for the AFCU loan, First Security breached its statutory duty to AFCU.

Notice is also significant in working out the problems encountered when the assignor has made more than one assignment of the same right. Although this should not occur and the assignor is clearly liable for breach of implied warranties to both assignees, the situation does arise and rules have been developed to deal with it. To a retailer or a construction firm caught in a temporary cash flow squeeze, a "temporary" double assignment of the accounts receivable looks like a painless solution, with no one ever being the wiser. Too often, however, the optimism is not justified and the double financing is discovered in a bankruptcy proceeding. The problem, then, is that there is only one sum of money to be paid and there are two assignee-claimants. Which one should be paid first?

The states do not agree on the answer to this question. In the states that follow the "English" rule (probably still the minority), the assignee who first gives notice to the obligor is entitled to priority of payment. In the states that follow the "American" rule, the first assignment in point of time is given priority, but subject to several exceptions where notice has not been given.

Under these exceptions, the first assignee loses if:

1. The first assignment was revocable or voidable by the assignor.
2. Payment has been made to the second assignee.
3. A judgment has been entered in favor of the second assignee.
4. A substitute contract has been negotiated by the second assignee and the debtor.
5. A specific writing representing the account, such as a savings account passbook, has been given to the second assignee.

Even in an American-rule state, therefore, it is important to give notice to the obligor immediately.

The Code will be of some help in dealing with this problem, since Article 9 covers most assignments for value as **secured transactions** and generally requires the public filing of a notice that such financing arrangements are in force in order for them to be effective against third parties. Where such a filing is required by Article 9 and has not yet occurred, a subsequent assignee of the accounts who gave value for them, had no knowledge of the first assignment, and filed its own public notice would be entitled to priority. It is, therefore, important for the first assignee to file the required public notice as well as to notify the obligor.

Availability of Defenses Against Assignee.

As it began to recognize the validity of assignments, the common law developed a rule which said that the assignee took the assigned contract right subject to all claims and defenses which the obligor could assert against the assignor. The assignee stepped into the assignor's legal shoes, and the shoes didn't get any bigger just because someone else was wearing them. While the assignee could at least cut off the obligor's claims on unrelated transactions by getting notice to that person, there was no way that the assignee could stand in any better enforcement position than assignor with respect to the assigned contract itself.

Obviously, a promise to pay money or render some other performance becomes much more uncertain and, therefore much less valuable, if it is subject to all sorts of unknown contingencies. To deal with this problem, the merchant community developed the **negotiable instrument**, which is basically just a written promise to pay money stated in a particular way. The law merchant said that if a promise to pay money was in negotiable form and was properly transferred to a good faith purchaser, then the debtor would not be able to assert most voidable-type defenses against the transferee. This was a "negotiation," not just an assignment. Where the buyer-debtor had signed a negotiable promissory note for 100 bushels of wheat which the seller had never delivered, the buyer would have to pay the amount of the note to the bank or finance company to which the note had been sold and then bring a lawsuit for breach of contract against the seller. Article 9 of the Code permitted the parties to work out this same basic result without using a negotiable instrument, by simply placing a provision to that effect, called a **waiver-of-defenses clause**, in the contract itself.

These two "exceptions"—the negotiable instrument and the waiver-of-defenses clause—came into such widespread and common use that they all but swallowed up the general rule. The result was that many, many buyers had to pay for a "dead horse"—the undelivered wheat, the fraudulently represented car, the unperformed services. As a result of the consumer movement of the 1960s and 1970s, first some of the states and then the Federal Trade Commission (FTC) adopted rules that invalidated both of these devices in consumer contracts. As the law stands today, these devices are available only where the debtor is a business or other "nonconsumer." One important loophole does remain, however: where the consumer receives a direct loan from the financing agency, and *then* gives the cash to the seller, the dead horse result still occurs. Also, if you, as a consumer, make a purchase with your Visa Card, MasterCard, or other credit card, the dead horse result could occur. In effect, the credit card company is simply loaning you the money to purchase the item, and you will have to pay the credit card company even though the purchased merchandise was defective. Some credit card companies now provide that you as a consumer can avoid the charge if you notify the credit card company within a specified time period after purchase of your desire to return the item and get credit against your account.

The *Woffard* case illustrates some of these problems.

FIRST NEW ENGLAND FINANCIAL CORP. v. WOFFARD
421 So.2d 590 (FL, 1982)

FACTS: When Woffard decided to buy a 36-foot sailing yacht from a yacht broker, the broker suggested that he contact FNEFC to finance the deal. FNEFC represented out-of-state banks which were interested in making marine loans. FNEFC approved Woffard's credit, and he signed a printed retail installment contract to buy the yacht. By its terms, the contract was simultaneously assigned to FNEFC, which reassigned it the next day to City Trust, a Connecticut bank. City Trust's name, address, and telephone number were on the contract, under that of FNEFC. Woffard got a coupon payment book from City Trust several weeks later.

On Woffard's first sea voyage, he discovered several manufacturing defects in the yacht. He notified the broker, the manufacturer, FNEFC, and City Trust. He kept making his payments for eight months, but finally stopped when no one agreed to fix the defects. City Trust and FNEFC sued for the balance due, $42,054.25. Woffard counterclaimed for the return of his $12,349.56 down payment, his monthly payments, and costs for docking and maintenance.

 JUSTICE DAUKSCH:

The Contract in the present case, entitled "Marine Security Agreement—Retail Installment Contract" contains the provision set forth in 16 CFR § 433.2:

NOTICE:

Any holder of this consumer credit contract is subject to all claims and defenses which the debtor could assert against the seller of goods or services obtained pursuant hereto or with the proceeds hereof. Recovery hereunder by the debtor shall not exceed amounts paid by the debtor hereunder.

This provision allows a consumer to set up, against one who finances a purchase, those claims and defenses which could be asserted against the seller of goods. Immediately following that provision is:

NOTICE ABOVE DOES NOT APPLY IF:

a. The amount financed ... exceeds $25,000.00. In such case, holder, nevertheless, shall be subject to all defenses which Buyer may have against Seller under this contract pursuant to the applicable State Law since the Notice above is a Federal rule rather than a State rule and does not eliminate defenses under State law.

or

b. This Consumer Contract form is used for a boat purchased primarily for commercial or business use. In such case, Buyer agrees not to assert any claim or defense arising out of this sale against Seller as a defense, counterclaim, or setoff to any action by any assignee for the unpaid balance of the total of payments or for possession of the boat.

As the amount financed in this consumer transaction exceeds $25,000.00, we look to applicable state law to determine whether appellant is subject to appellee's claims/defenses. Under Section 679.206(1), an agreement by a buyer waiving any claims/defenses against the seller is enforceable by an assignee who takes his assignment for value, in good faith and without notice of a any claim/defense. Such an agreement waiving claims/defenses often appears in the form of a waiver of defenses clause in a contract. There is no such clause in this contract. Section 679.206(1) also provides that a buyer who, as part of one transaction, signs both a negotiable instrument and a security agreement makes such an agreement waiving claims/defenses. The contract does not meet the requisites of negotiability and does not appear to be a negotiable instrument. Thus, Section 679.206(1) is inapplicable.

The contract created a purchase money security interest to be retained by the seller or seller's assignee. Section 679.206(2) provides that "when a seller retains a purchase money security interest in goods, the chapter on sales (Chapter 672) governs the sale and any disclaimer, limitation, or modification of the seller's warranties." Before reaching the merits of appellee's counterclaim for breach of warranty, governed by Chapter 672, we must first see if any other state law prevents appellee's assertion of the claim against the assignee....

An assignee has traditionally been subject to defenses or set-offs existing before an account debtor is notified of the assignments. When the account debtor's defenses on an assigned claim arise from the contract between him and the assignor, it makes no difference whether the breach giving rise to the defense occurs before or after the account debtor is notified of the assignment. The account debtor may also have claims against the assignor which arise independently of that contract: an assignee is subject to all such claims which accrue before, and free of all those which accrue after, the account debtor is notified. The account debtor may waive his right to assert claims or defenses against the assignee to the extent provided in Section 679.206.... This is in accord with the general rule in sales transactions that the assignee takes his assignment subject to the purchaser's defenses, set-offs and counterclaims against the seller....

Just as an assignee is subject to defenses and claims accruing before the obligor receives notification, so a subassignee is subject to defenses and claims accruing between the assignee and obligor before the obligor receives notice of the sub-assignment. Defenses and claims arising from the terms of the contract creating the right are available to the obligor regardless of when they accrue....

Appellee's claim of breach of warranty arose out of the terms of the contract and also accrued before receipt of notification of assignment. Testimony during trial proved that appellee told the seller that he specifically wanted to buy a sailing yacht that he could live aboard full time and also use for pleasure sailing. Appellee told the seller the yacht must be suitable for "blue water" sailing (i.e., ocean sailing). Thus, if there was a breach of warranty, it arose out of the terms of the contract (as incorporating the sale agreement) and accrued before appellee received notification of assignment, in this case by receipt of the coupon payment books....

To be effective, a seller's disclaimer of warranties in the sale of consumer goods must be part of the basis of the bargain between the parties.... The evidence indicates that appellee and seller entered into the sales agreement on the premise that the yacht was suitable for appellee's purposes. Circumstances indicate that seller's disclaimer of warranty of fitness for a particular purpose was not made a part of the bargain; to the contrary, seller's warranty of fitness for the particular purpose was an essential factor in the initial agreement between the parties.

SIGNIFICANCE OF THIS CHAPTER

Modern business operations require the free assignability of contract rights. Much business at all levels of production and distribution is done on credit, and sellers often do not have sufficient capital to do their own accounts receivable financing. The solution, of course, is to assign the accounts receivable to a bank or finance company, for cash, so that ongoing business operations can continue. Even individuals—such as inventors and authors—need to be able to assign patents and copyrights for tax, estate, and other purposes. It is also true that there are situations where performance by a substitute party is necessary or desirable. In all of these situations, the law is concerned with meeting the practical necessities of trade and commerce, while at the same time maintaining the basic terms of the original contract. For this reason, and also because many of these transactions are themselves quite involved, the legal rules for assignments are quite complex.

Modern law also needs to recognize that there are many situations where promises are made for the benefit of third parties, and rules need to be provided for these cases, too.

Both of these concepts will almost certainly apply to transactions throughout your personal and professional activities.

PROBLEMS FOR DISCUSSION

1. Vernon Siler contracted to work on a project for Mountain States. To help finance the project, he got a loan from First National and assigned to them the payment he was to receive when he finished the job for Mountain States. The written assignment was delivered to Mountain States. First National made no specific demand for payment. Mountain States paid Siler. First National then sued Mountain States for payment in accordance with the assignment by Siler. The trial court granted summary judgment in favor of First National. Defendant appealed.

   Was the trial court's ruling correct? Explain.

2. While he was walking by the Nickeldimes's house, on the public sidewalks, Frodo was attacked by the Nickeldime's dog. Frodo died as a result of the injuries he sustained. His widow, Elizabeth, sued the Nickeldimes, alleging that they had been negligent in the care and treatment of their dog. At the time of the incident, the Nickeldimes did not have a homeowner's liability insurance policy in force because their mortgage company, Esanel, had failed to purchase such insurance with the funds that the Nickeldimes had paid into their escrow account at Esanel for that purpose. Elizabeth, learning of these facts, now amends her complaint and sues Esanel, as a third-party beneficiary of the escrow agreement between Esanel and the Nickeldimes. Esanel moves to dismiss this amendment to Elizabeth's complaint.

    How should the court rule, and why?

3. Ethel Wido sued Pipeline Oil Corporation and its franchised service station operator on the New York State Thruway, Carl Pump, for failure to provide road services to her husband. Their car developed a flat tire, and a passing state trooper ordered Carl Pump to come to the aid of the stranded motorists. Carl neglected to do so, and after waiting for over two hours, Ethel's husband, a stout accountant, tried to change the tire himself. The work exhausted him, so that he collapsed. He died shortly thereafter of a heart attack.

    What is the result, and why?

4. Air Metals was a subcontractor on a construction job for Tompkins-Beckwith Co., and was required to furnish a surety bond guaranteeing its proper performance of the job. American Fire & Casualty issued the bond for Air Metals, but required that Air Metals give them a conditional assignment of all moneys due under the construction contract "in the event of default" by Air Metals. Air Metals did so, but Tompkins-Beckwith was not notified. Air Metals borrowed money from Boulevard National Bank, and gave them an absolute assignment of all moneys due or to become due, from Tompkins-Beckwith, who again were not notified. Then Air Metals defaulted on the construction contract. American Fire notified Tompkins-Beckwith of their assignment, and Tompkins-Beckwith agreed to pay them what was owed to Air Metals. Boulevard then notified Tompkins-Beckwith of their assignment, which was actually the "first" in time, since the one to American Fire was to take effect only if and when Air Metals went into default. Boulevard lost in the trial court. Boulevard appealed from the judgment for American Fire.

    How should the appeal be decided? Discuss.

5. Plaintiff-appellants Pauline and George Brown appeal from a summary judgment in favor of the three defendants, National Super Markets, Sentry Security Agency, and T. G. Watkins, a security guard employed by Sentry.

    Pauline and George Brown brought a negligence action against the defendants after Pauline was shot and seriously injured by an unknown assailant in National's parking lot. The Browns allege that the defendants have a duty to protect National's patrons both in the store and in the parking lot and that they breached that duty. Defendants denied that they have such a duty and filed a motion for summary judgment. The trial court granted the motion.

    Appellants maintain that summary judgment should not have been granted because as a matter of law their petition properly rated a claim of actionable negligence. The petition claims that in the two years prior to Mrs. Brown's assault there were sixteen incidents of reported robbery involving a firearm and seven incidents of reported strong-arm robberies as well as 136 other reported crimes on National's premises. Appellants maintain that this known criminal activity and conduct creates special facts and circumstances giving rise to a duty on behalf of the defendants to protect store patrons against assaults.

    Are the Browns correct? Explain.

6. Raymond and Connie Loftus sue for damages to their home, which they were trying to sell. Plaintiffs entered into an exclusive contract with American Realty, under which American Realty was given the exclusive right to offer plaintiff's home for sale. Plaintiffs moved out of the house, and shut off all of the appliances with the exception of the furnace.

    Under the contract, the realty company was to assume the responsibility for performing any tasks necessary for the closing of the transaction, including turning on utilities. An offer was made for plaintiffs' house, which offer was accepted by plaintiffs. Prior to the closing, American Realty hired Fitzpatrick to light the gas water heater. In opening the gas valve to the water heater, Fitzpatrick also opened an uncapped gas line. As a result, the house exploded and burned, resulting in damages totalling $22,500.

    Defendant Fitzpatrick was discharged in bankruptcy prior to trial in this matter.

    Do plaintiffs have a valid claim against American Realty? Explain.

Chapter 14
Nonperformance, Excuses, and Remedies

While the vast majority of contracts are performed according to their terms, many are not. Not all nonperformances will produce liability for breach of contract, however; in some of these cases nonperforming parties will have legal excuses for their failure. These legal excuses, or discharges of liability, can be placed in five general groupings: (1) conditions, (2) breach by other party, (3) discharge by new agreement, (4) discharge by merger, and (5) discharge by operation of law. We now proceed to consider each of these groups.

CONDITIONS

Basic Concepts and Definitions. A **condition** is an act, event, or set of facts, to which the parties have attached some special legal significance. The parties have included it in their contract, either expressly or impliedly, with the intent that its occurrence or nonoccurrence will operate to modify, suspend, or completely discharge a performance duty under the contract.

In terms of how they operate, conditions are classified as precedent, concurrent, and subsequent. A **condition precedent** prevents a contract duty from arising until it occurs. If a tailor promises that you will be personally satisfied with your new custom-made suit, and you're not satisfied, you don't have to take the suit and pay for it—no "personal satisfaction" (the condition precedent), no duty to take the suit. **Concurrent conditions**, which are usually implied by law, operate so that each party's duty to perform is conditioned on the other party's being ready, willing, and able to render the required return performance. The most typical example of concurrent conditions occurs in the cash sale transaction, but they also may arise in other contracts, as seen in the *Shaw* case.

SHAW v. MOBIL OIL CORP.
535 P.2d 756 (OR, 1975)

FACTS: In 1972 the parties entered into a service station lease and retail gasoline dealer agreement. John Shaw agreed to buy not less than 200,000 gallons of gasoline per year, and Mobil agreed to supply his requirements, up to a maximum of 500,000 gallons per year. Shaw agreed to pay rent on the station on the basis of 1.4 cents per gallon delivered, with a minimum of $470 per month. To meet the minimum rental, Mobil would have to deliver 33,572 gallons each month. In July 1973, Shaw ordered 34,000 gallons, but Mobil delivered 25,678 gallons, due to the gasoline shortage caused by the Arab oil embargo. The U.S. Energy office had required Mobil to allocate available supplies among its dealers, and Shaw's allocation was 25,678 gallons. Shaw sued for a declaratory judgment that he was not liable for the minimum rental for July. The trial court held for Mobil. Shaw appealed.

 JUSTICE DENECKE:

The law in Oregon on dependent promises, which is similar to the law in other jurisdictions, is stated in *First National Bank v. Morgan*:

> Whether covenants are dependent or independent is a question of the intention of the parties as deduced from the terms of the contract. If the parties intend that performance by each of them is in no way conditioned upon performance by the other, the covenants are independent, but if they intend performance by one to be conditioned upon performance by the other, the covenants are mutually dependent....
>
> While there is no fixed definite rule of law by which the intention in all cases can be determined, yet we must remember, as stated by Professor Williston, that, since concurrent conditions protect both parties, courts endeavor so far as is not inconsistent with the expressed intention to construe performance as concurrent conditions....

In the present case, we believe it equally apparent that the dealer undertook his obligation to pay a minimum rental in reliance on Mobil's fulfillment of its obligation to deliver the quantity of gasoline ordered by the dealer.

We conclude that the dealer's promise to pay the minimum rental was conditioned or dependent upon Mobil's delivery of the amount of gasoline ordered by the dealer.

The primary contention of Mobil and seemingly the chief reason for the trial court's decision was that under a provision of the contract Mobil was excused from delivering the quantity of gasoline ordered by the dealer because of a request to Mobil by the Federal Energy office to allocate its gasoline supply among its dealers.

Assuming that the contract does excuse Mobil from performance under these circumstances, nevertheless, the dealer is not obligated to pay the minimum rental.

The clause Mobil relies upon states:

Seller shall not be liable for loss, damage, or demurrage due to any delay or failure in performance (a) because of compliance with any order, request, or control of any governmental authority or person purporting to act therefor.

Interpreting this clause most favorably to Mobil, its meaning can be no more than that Mobil cannot be held responsible for breach of contract if it does not perform its promises because of a government request.

A party has no obligation to perform a promise that is conditioned upon the other party's performance when the other party failed to perform even though the other party's failure to perform is excused and is not a breach of contract.

[Judgment reversed.]

Conditions subsequent discharge or excuse an existing duty of performance. An automobile liability insurance policy, for example, may provide that the insurance company's duty to defend liability claims under the policy is excused where the insured admits liability for the accident. Or, a property insurance policy may specify that coverage lapses where a structure is unoccupied for more than a certain period of time. Whether a condition exists or has occurred is generally a question of fact, to be proved like any other.

Conditions of Approval or Satisfaction.

Especially in large construction contracts, the parties may specify that a third party's approval is required before the final payment has to be made. In construction, this third party is typically the architect who drew the plans and specifications for the job. Until the builder can convince the architect that the job conforms to the plans, the landowner/customer does not have to make the final payment on the contract price. Where the architect is withholding approval in bad faith, or as part of a fraudulent scheme against the builder, most courts would probably hold this condition to have been satisfied and require the landowner/customer to pay the balance due.

In some contracts, "personal satisfaction" of the buyer/customer is guaranteed: the parties' intent is that if the buyer is not satisfied, the buyer is not bound to pay the contract price. In trying to determine whether or not such a condition has been met, so that the seller can collect the contract price, the courts use two different tests: an individualized, or subjective, test and a reasonable person, or objective, test. The individualized test requires that the particular buyer be satisfied before payment is due, whereas the objective test says that if a reasonable person would be satisfied with the performance offered by the seller, the buyer must pay.

Where the contract is for an item involving personal taste, such as a custom-tailored suit, a portrait, or a statue, "personal satisfaction" probably means just that: no deal unless the individual buyer indicates that he or she is satisfied. Where the contract involves an item of everyday mechanical utility, such as a furnace, "personal satisfaction" is probably a jury question under the reasonable person test: either the furnace is working properly, or it is not; if it is, the buyer ought to be satisfied with it.

Besides the nature of the item, the other main factor considered by the courts in determining which test to use is what happens to the item if the satisfaction condition is not met. The suit, portrait, or sculpture stays with the seller; there is no unjust enrichment of the buyer, though the seller may be stuck with an unmarketable item. With something like an aluminum siding job, however, the situation is quite different, since it is somewhat uneconomical to remove aluminum siding from a house; the courts would almost certainly apply the reasonable person test to the job.

Timely Performance as a Condition Precedent. What happens when one party is late in performing or offering to perform contract obligations? Any provable damages resulting from the delay in performance should be collectible without question. But the real issue is whether or not the other party can refuse to accept the offered late performance and use the failure to perform on time as a basis for rescinding the whole contract. Courts generally consider this problem in terms of whether or not "time is of the essence," meaning that the parties have either expressly or impliedly made timely performance a condition precedent.

In a few early cases, time was presumed to be of the essence in a sale of goods, but this does not seem to be the general rule, and it is clearly not the rule for real estate or construction contracts. Where the parties have not clearly specified in the contract that time is of the essence, the court must determine, as a question of fact, whether or not such a condition precedent should be implied.

Doctrine of Substantial Performance. Courts are reluctant to excuse a party's contractual obligations completely just because the other party has committed a relatively minor breach. Just as many cases involve the simple, one-shot performances completed exactly in accordance with the contract terms, many other cases, such as construction contracts, deal with more complex performances which extend over a considerable period of time. In construction contracts, jobs are rarely completed exactly in accordance with the agreed upon plans and specifications. Should minor deviations by the builder permit the buyer to rescind the whole contract?

The courts have answered this question in the negative, by applying the doctrine of **substantial performance**. What this doctrine says is that if the builder has acted in good faith and has done the job in *substantial* compliance with the contract, the builder can enforce the contract and collect the contract price. Any damages that result from any noncompliance, no matter how trivial, can be collected by the buyer or deducted from the amount of the contractor's recovery. Perfection is not required. The buyer of a new house would not be able to rescind the contract just because the kitchen was painted green instead of blue, but the buyer could force the builder to repaint, or deduct the price of the paint job from the contract price if the builder refused.

The doctrine of substantial performance will not be applied where the builder has intentionally substituted inferior materials or used other production shortcuts in a fraudulent attempt to make extra money. Nor will it be applied where the builder has only partially, rather than substantially, performed. In such cases, buyers can rescind the whole contract. If the partially built structure has been placed on land already owned by the buyers, they are probably liable in quasi contract for the fair market value of the labor and materials, but even in this case, they can probably deduct any provable damages they have sustained.

BREACH BY OTHER PARTY

In General. When the plaintiff brings an action for breach of contract, a possible response by the defendant is the argument "You breached first." That is, the defendant argues that his or her own nonperformance was not a breach, because the plaintiff's prior nonperformance justified the defendant's refusal to perform. Although in some cases, the courts have treated the reciprocal performances as "independent," they generally accept this argument as a sufficient excuse where the prior breach by the plaintiff was a material one. It would, generally, be unfair to require the defendant to perform or hold the defendant liable for not performing if he or she has not received what the plaintiff promised to return. However, it would be equally unfair for the defendant to repudiate the whole contract and completely refuse to perform if the plaintiff has committed only a minor, relatively insignificant breach.

Under the UCC, a buyer of goods has the right to cancel the contract if the seller has committed a material breach. The buyer is then entitled to recover any payments made on the contract price, and any damages sustained because of the seller's breach.

Breach of Installment Contract. It is even more difficult to work out a fair result where the contract calls for a series of performances by one or both parties, rather than a single exchange. What should be the measure of recovery when a party partially performs and then fails to deliver one or more of the installments still due?

The courts usually try to solve this problem by first determining whether the contract is divisible or indivisible. If the contract is held to be divisible into a series of pro rata exchanges, the court will usually permit the breaching party to recover the agreed reciprocal performance, less any damages the breach has caused to the other party. An employee who quits after having worked for three months under a one-year contract would usually be able to collect the agreed contract salary for the three months worked, less any damages which the employer sustained as a result of the breach. If the contract is held to be indivisible, or "entire," a party guilty of a material breach should collect only the fair market value of any benefits retained by the other party, less damages caused by the breach.

For sales of goods, the UCC says a breach as to one installment is material, and justifies cancellation of the whole contract, if the breach "substantially impairs the value of the whole contract."

Anticipatory Repudiation. An **anticipatory repudiation** occurs when one party, by words or conduct, indicates unwillingness or inability to perform contract duties when the time for performance arrives. In other words, the party announces in advance that he or she is not going to perform as scheduled. In nearly all cases the courts treat such an unequivocal repudiation of the contract as a present breach. The injured party then has two options: to make other arrangements immediately and sue for any damages caused, or to wait and see what happens and then sue for any damages caused, if in fact performance does not occur. The courts do not apply this rule to promises to pay money at a future date; a present statement of intention not to pay a future debt normally does not accelerate the due date of the debt unless there is a special provision to that effect. The courts also normally permit a party to retract a repudiation, provided the retraction is made before the other party has substantially changed legal position because of the repudiation.

Adequate Assurance. For the sale of goods, the UCC's rules for dealing with breach and repudiation problems are substantially the same as the common-law principles discussed above. The Code does, however, give the injured party one very important new protection: the right to demand **adequate assurance**.

A breach by one of the parties to a goods contract may not be material enough in itself to justify rescission of the whole contract; for example, a two-or three-day delay in delivery of one month's shipment of goods on an installment contract. Still, such a breach may create a doubt in the mind of the other party as to whether or not the breaching party will be able and willing to continue to perform. The same is true where one party has repudiated and then retracted: Does this person mean it or not? When will this person do the same thing again?

A party who has reasonable grounds for feeling "insecure," may make a written demand that the other party furnish "adequate assurance of due performance. " So long as the insecure party is being commercially reasonable, any performance for which the agreed return has not already been received may be withheld until receipt of such adequate assurance. Where a proper demand for assurance has been made, the other party's failure to respond within a reasonable time (not over 30 days) is treated as a repudiation of the contract. At that point, the party who made the demand can go ahead and make other arrangements, without being guilty of a breach, and can sue for any damages sustained because of the other party's repudiation.

Buyer's Acceptance of Goods. Under the Code, acceptance of the goods occurs when, having had a reasonable opportunity to inspect them, the buyer indicates that they do conform to the contract, or that they are acceptable in spite of some nonconformity, or when the buyer simply fails to effectively reject them. Any act by the buyer which is inconsistent with the seller's ownership of the goods is likewise an acceptance, but if the act is wrongful as against the seller, it is an acceptance only if it is ratified by the seller. "Acceptance of a part of any commercial unit is acceptance of that entire unit."

Once the buyer has accepted the goods, they must be paid for at the contract rate. Further, the burden is now on the buyer to prove any alleged breach with respect to the accepted goods. The buyer must also prove that the seller was notified of the breach within a reasonable time after the buyer discovered it or should have discovered it. If the buyer has accepted the goods, it follows logically that they can no longer be rejected. Nor can an acceptance be revoked where the buyer knew of the nonconformity at the time of acceptance, unless the buyer accepted with the reasonable assumption that the nonconformity would be cured. Except for the foregoing provisions, acceptance does not prevent the buyer from pursuing any other remedy provided for nonconformity of the goods.

The buyer may revoke or withdraw an acceptance of any lot or commercial unit that is subsequently discovered to have a substantial nonconformity if the defect could not reasonably have been discovered before acceptance or if the buyer was induced to accept the goods by the seller's assurance that a known defect would be cured, and the seller has not seasonably cured the defect. The buyer must revoke the acceptance within a reasonable time after he or she discovers, or should have discovered, the defect "and before any substantial change in condition of the goods which is not caused by their own defects" (2-608[2]). The buyer, after having notified the seller of such a proper revocation, has the same rights against the goods as if they had been rejected initially.

The *Chancellor* case discusses some of these issues.

**CHANCELLOR DEVELOPMENT COMPANY v.
BRAND v. JACOB MOBILE HOMES, INC.**
896 S.W.2d 672 (Mo. App., 1995)

FACTS: Third-Party Plaintiffs, Louis and Debra Brand (hereinafter plaintiffs) brought this action against Third-Party Defendant, Jacob Mobile Homes, Inc. (Jacob) in two counts seeking damages for breach of contract and negligence in the sale and delivery of a mobile home. The trial court granted Jacob's motion for summary judgment on both counts. Plaintiffs appeal, asserting that genuine issues of material fact precluded summary judgment.

In count one of their third-party petition, plaintiffs alleged that they had entered into a contract with Jacob to purchase a mobile home, that the mobile home was delivered in a nonconforming and damaged condition, and that plaintiffs notified Jacob of the nonconformity, rejected delivery, and tendered the home back to Jacob. As damages for this breach of contract, they sought return of their downpayment, sales tax, and interest payments as well as reimbursement for installation and other expenses in the total amount of $13,000. In count two, plaintiffs reincorporated the allegations relating to their contract with Jacob and further alleged that Jacob or its agents negligently delivered the mobile home before the slab and driveway were prepared, resulting in damage to the mobile home.

Jacob denied the allegations and moved for summary judgment. As one of its grounds, it stated that it had repaired the damage to the home and that plaintiffs had accepted those repairs and their acceptance constituted full accord and satisfaction. In support of its motion, Jacob filed affidavits and exhibits.

Plaintiffs filed a memorandum in opposition supported by affidavits of the two plaintiffs and the subsequent purchaser of their mobile home. They asserted that summary judgment was improper because substantial fact questions remained. The trial court granted the motion.

 JUDGE CRANE:

Plaintiffs contend that in count one they stated a claim for relief for breach of contract based on a delivery of nonconforming goods. In response to Jacob's claim that plaintiffs accepted the mobile home after it was repaired, plaintiffs assert they accepted the mobile home under the reasonable assumption that the defects would be cured and that they revoked their acceptance under S.400.2-608 when the defects were not seasonably cured....

However, S.400.2-606(1)(c) RSMo 1994 provides that any act by a buyer inconsistent with seller's ownership will constitute acceptance of goods. Accordingly, if, after proper rejection, a buyer uses goods in a manner inconsistent with the seller's ownership that use nullifies the rescission and constitutes an acceptance of the goods.... Once a buyer accepts a tender, the seller acquires a right to its price on the contract terms.... A buyer's actions which are inconsistent with seller's ownership are "many and varied" and include "making payments, taking possession of the goods, use of the goods, repairing, working on them, attempts to resell them, and dealing with them in other varied ways."... Thus a buyer's acts of pricing, displaying, advertising, and selling goods after giving notice of revocation were inconsistent with seller's ownership and constituted acceptance....

A buyer's revocation of acceptance under the Uniform Commercial Code (UCC) is necessarily the buyer's recognition that the property as to which acceptance is revoked belongs to the seller.... A buyer's act of dominion over goods, including sale of the goods, is inconsistent with a buyer's claim of revocation of acceptance....

In support of its motion for summary judgment, Jacob filed the affidavit of Jacob's treasurer, Randy Clark. Clark recited that plaintiffs had purchased a mobile home from Jacob pursuant to a Delivery Agreement and Contract on November 27, 1990. He asserted that on February 27, 1991, plaintiff Louis Brand asked him if Jacob would resell his home. Clark further averred: "Defendant's Exhibit 10 is the original Contract signed by Louis Brand and me reflecting the agreement of Jacob Mobile Homes, Inc. to resell the home." He also attached the contract dated February 27, 1991, to his affidavit. This agreement was written on a preprinted purchase agreement form. However, except for the mobile home description, Brand's name and address and the signatures of Clark and Louis Brand, the preprinted form provisions were not filled in or marked. Instead, the agreement contained the following handwritten provision: "Jacob MH agrees to move home into our sales lot and attempt to sell it. Seller, Lou Brand, agrees to pay for the move and to make payments on home until sold. Jacob MH will collect sales commission from buyer of home." Jacob also filed the affidavit of a repairman it had hired who stated that on January 4, 1991, he had made the repairs the Brands had requested.

In their affidavits in opposition to the motion, plaintiffs described the damages and attested that they had notified Jacob of the damage and gave it an opportunity to repair and Jacob failed to do so. They averred that on February 27, 1991, plaintiff Louis Brand told Clark that they wanted to return the home and told Jacob the deficiencies with the home. However, neither plaintiff denied the existence or the contents of the February 27 agreement or that Louis Brand had signed it. In fact, they did not mention this agreement in their affidavits. Plaintiffs acknowledged that the trailer was subsequently moved to Jacob's premises at plaintiffs' expense.

We view the record in the light most favorable to plaintiffs and therefore assume that: (1) there was damage to the home, (2) plaintiffs notified Jacob of the damage, (3) Jacob did not repair all of the damage, and (4) plaintiffs asked to return the trailer. However, Jacob is still entitled to summary judgment on the grounds of acceptance because "any" act inconsistent with revocation of acceptance is enough to constitute acceptance under S.400.2-606(1)(c). It was undisputed that plaintiff Louis Brand signed an agreement in which Jacob agreed to move the home onto its lot and to attempt to sell it and in which plaintiff agreed to pay to move the home onto Jacob's lot and agreed to make payments on the home until it was sold. In so doing plaintiff Brand acted as an owner desiring to sell property with the help of a broker. Louis Brand's action is consistent with ownership and inconsistent with plaintiffs' claim that plaintiffs revoked acceptance. Under S.400.2-606(1)(c) this act, which is inconsistent with seller's ownership, constitutes acceptance....

The trial court's judgment is affirmed.

Buyer's Rejection of Goods. A buyer wishing to reject goods because of their nonconformity must do so within a reasonable time after delivery or tender and must "seasonably" notify the seller of the rejection. Once the buyer has rejected the goods, any exercise of ownership over them by the buyer is wrongful as against the seller. The buyer, unless entitled to retain possession under 2-711(3), is required to take reasonable care of the seller's rejected goods until the seller has had a reasonable chance to remove them. Where the buyer is a merchant and the seller does not have an agent or a place of business nearby, the buyer must follow the seller's reasonable instructions with respect to the disposition of the rejected goods. If the goods are perishable or otherwise subject to a rapid decline in value, the buyer must make reasonable efforts to resell them even if the seller has not sent instructions. Under those circumstances, it would not be fair or reasonable to permit the buyer to watch the goods spoil without making some effort to salvage them.

Seller's Right to "Cure" Defects. UCC 2-508 gives the seller a "second chance" in two situations where the buyer rejects a delivery or tender of goods because of their nonconformity to the terms of the contract. If the contract time for performance has not yet expired, the seller can seasonably notify the buyer of its intent to cure the nonconformity, and then make a conforming delivery within the contract time. For example, if the buyer rejected a tender of 500 units, because the contract called for 700 units, the seller could notify the buyer that it would deliver the full 700, and then do so within the contract period. The buyer would be required to take the second shipment of 700 units.

Where the buyer rejects goods the seller had reasonable grounds to believe would be acceptable, the seller is allowed a reasonable time *after* the contract date to substitute a conforming delivery. The purpose of this rule is to avoid unfair, "surprise" rejections, for technical reasons, where the goods are substantially conforming and would usually be accepted in the trade or business involved. As several cases have pointed out, however, the seller's right to cure is not unlimited. The seller must be acting honestly and reasonably, not trying to knowingly pass off inferior goods or to force the buyer into an acceptance.

DISCHARGE BY NEW AGREEMENT

The parties themselves created their reciprocal rights and duties by making the agreement. It's their contract, and unless the rights of third parties are involved in some way, the parties can call off their agreement anytime they both wish to do so, or they can substitute a new arrangement for the old one. There are many technical terms to describe the different types of new agreements, but they all come down to the same basic argument: "My nonperformance under the original contract was excused because we made a new deal." We now consider the main types of "new deals."

Mutual Rescission. As a rule, the parties can call off their existing contract anytime they wish, as long as they both agree to do so. This case is called a **mutual rescission**, to distinguish it from the case where the *remedy* of rescission is given to one party because of a material breach by the other. If the parties have mutually agreed to a rescission, neither can later claim that the other's nonperformance of the contract was a breach.

Where partial performance has already occurred, the mutual rescission agreement should provide for part payment or restitution. If there is no such provision in the rescission agreement, any retained benefits would almost certainly have to be paid for at fair market value.

Novation. Although the derivation and common sense meaning of the term **novation** would seem to apply to any new agreement that the parties intend to substitute for their existing contract, the courts generally apply the term only to those new arrangements that involve a substitution of parties. That is, a new debtor is substituted for the original debtor, with the consent of the creditor, or the obligation is assigned to a new creditor for whom the debtor agrees to perform.

If, in the take-over-the-payments situation discussed in the last chapter, the mortgagee/creditor agrees to accept the resale buyer as the sole obligor and to discharge the original mortgagor/debtor, there has been a novation. Whether the new agreement is called a *novation* or simply a *new contract*, it must itself be a valid contract to have the effect of discharging the original one.

Accord and Satisfaction. This term is usually applied to a situation where the obligee/creditor has agreed to accept a substituted performance, in place of the original one. For example, Dan Debtor owes Carl Creditor $1,000. Dan does not have the cash, but he does own a used car, which he offers to convey to Carl in lieu of the $1,000. Carl, of course, does not have to take the car; he can sue Dan for the $1,000 if it is not paid when due. If Carl does agree to take the car, there is an accord. At that point, the $1,000 debt is not yet discharged; if Carl does not get the car, he can sue Dan either for $1,000 or for breach of the accord. When Dan delivers the car as agreed, however, the $1,000 debt has been discharged by an "*accord and satisfaction.*"

Unfortunately, from the standpoint of clarity, courts also use the term *accord and satisfaction* to refer to situations involving part payment of a debt, especially where the debt is in dispute. (See our earlier discussion of this problem in Chapter 9.) The creditor's cashing of the "in full" check is his agreement to the "accord and satisfaction" and his acceptance of the substituted performance thereunder.

Waiver or Estoppel. A waiver is the intentional surrender of a known right or benefit; a person simply chooses not to demand that something which is due be given. Your apartment lease, for example, specifies that the rent must be paid in advance on the 1st of each month, but the landlord tells you that payment can be made by the 10th; this is a waiver of the right to insist on payment by the 1st. Ordinarily, this kind of waiver "before breach" can be retracted by proper notice to the other party, unless consideration was given for the waiver or unless the other party has made a substantial change of position in reliance on the waiver. Contrariwise, courts usually hold that a waiver of the right to sue for a breach which has already occurred does not require any new consideration to be binding. (See UCC 1-107, previously referred to in Chapter 9.) A waiver may also be inferred from a party's conduct.

Release. A release also involves the giving up of some right, but it is based on a written contract. Releases are commonly used in situations where there is a contingent or disputed liability, as in auto accident cases or in employment termination agreements. The law generally favors compromises and settlements of disputes, particularly in light of the tremendous backlog of civil litigation that is clogging the courts. Traditionally, therefore, courts have been reluctant to permit parties to avoid the effect of a release they have previously given unless there is very strong evidence of fraud, undue influence, mistake, and so on. While courts today are more and more willing to stretch a point in favor of the "little guy," they will still look for some evidence to support the claimed defense against the effect of a release.

Account Stated. The account stated is based on the same fundamental principle as accord and satisfaction: the law favors settlements. Where, after a series of transactions between them, the parties have agreed on a final statement of the net amount due. there is an account stated. No further reliance can be placed on the earlier transactions; the amount which is now due and owing is that agreed to in the account stated. An account stated can arise when the creditor sends a summary statement of the account and the debtor retains the statement without objection beyond a reasonable time. In other words, the agreement to the account stated can be implied as well as expressed.

DISCHARGE BY MERGER

In General. As used here, the doctrine of **merger** means that the prior obligation has been superseded by a "better" one, better in the sense of being easier to prove, to transfer, or to collect. Merger may be effected by a new agreement between the parties or by judgment. The three most common examples of such better legal obligations (other than a judgment) are the sealed contract, the negotiable instrument, and the secured debt. Since many states have abolished by statute the common-law effect of the seal on the presumption of consideration, there would be no merger effect in those states if a sealed contract were given in satisfaction of an unsealed one. In a state where the seal makes the contract easier to prove in court, or (perhaps) even if the seal only has the effect of keeping the debt alive for a longer time, the acceptance of a sealed contract by the creditor in place of the unsealed one should have the merger effect.

A negotiable instrument is clearly a much better form of legal obligation than an ordinary "open-book account." For example, you owe your dentist, Dr. Paul Pullit, $300 for services rendered. If he sues to collect, he will have to produce office records, witnesses, and so forth, to prove that he in fact gave you this consideration and that you agreed to pay for it at his prices. Such a collection suit would involve substantial disruption of his regular office routine and a loss of time and money, even though he would ultimately win. If he accepts your offer of a ninety-day negotiable promissory note for $250 as satisfaction of the account, he could in fact be net dollars ahead even if he is forced to sue on the note, since the note carries a presumption of consideration which you would have to overcome with evidence. Because of this fact, the note is much more readily transferable than the account. If your dentist doesn't want to wait for the ninety days and collect the interest, he will have a much easier time selling your note to a bank than he would have in assigning your account.

Finally, if the debt is made more certain of collection because the debtor gives the creditor a mortgage or other security interest against a specific piece of the debtor's property, that is clearly a better deal for the creditor. If your dentist agrees to take your new contract promise to pay $250, secured by your used car as collateral, in satisfaction of the $300 open-book amount, there has been a merger and the old account debt is discharged.

Judgment. The doctrine of **res judicata** says that once "the thing has been adjudicated," it cannot be relitigated. Whatever rights and duties may have been alleged as the result of the prior legal relationship have been superseded by the court's final judgment; the prior obligations have been merged into the judgment.

There is an important distinction between a **joint debt**, in which all debtors must be sued at the same time if they are to be held liable, and a **joint and several obligation**, in which the creditor may get a judgment against one or more of the debtors and still retain the right to sue the others. The same result would follow if the creditor released one joint debtor; such action releases the entire debt against all of the joint debtors.

DISCHARGE BY OPERATION OF LAW

Statute of Limitations. At least in most states, debts do not last forever. At some point, it becomes rather unfair for an alleged creditor to revive ancient history and begin a litigation over a matter that should have been long forgotten (and probably has been by nearly everyone else). Again, the law encourages the parties to settle their disputes and requires them to commence any necessary litigation before memories fade completely. At some point, if no action has been taken to enforce an alleged obligation, it is good public policy to declare that the debtor has a defense if that person does not wish to pay the ancient debt. This **statute of limitations** defense is a technical one, and it is not particularly favored by the courts, but where it does apply, it is a complete defense against a lawsuit based on the old debt. In most states, the limitations period for tort actions is considerably shorter than the one for contracts.

Bankruptcy; Composition with Creditors. A discharge in a bankruptcy proceeding also operates as a technical defense in favor of the debtor, as to all debts and claims provable under bankruptcy rules. This same result occurs whether the debtor has filed a "voluntary" petition with the bankruptcy court or has been forced into an "involuntary" bankruptcy by one or more creditors. (See Chapter 17.) Like the statute of limitations, a **bankruptcy discharge** is a technical defense which can be waived by the debtor when that person makes a new promise after bankruptcy to pay the old debt.

To avoid the administrative costs and (some of) the legal expenses incident to a bankruptcy proceeding, a person's creditors may, as a group, voluntarily agree to accept less than full payment in full satisfaction of their debts. A creditor cannot be forced to make such an agreement, but may wish to do so to receive payment for a higher percentage of the claim paid than if the debtor were forced through bankruptcy. Such a composition with creditors operates like an accord and satisfaction.

Illegality and Impossibility. The "subsequent illegality" and "impossibility" arguments discussed in Chapter 12 also fall into this fifth category.

GENERAL PRINCIPLES FOR CONTRACT REMEDIES

A rational decision to litigate a claim must be based on economic, psychological, and legal factors. In many cases, a party can be a legal winner (that is, get a favorable judgment) and still be an economic loser, by not being compensated for all economic losses, to say nothing of the psychological strains endured during the litigation process. The potential litigant faces the distinct possibility of not recovering all out-of-pocket expenses for court costs and attorney fees. In addition, the person's "downtime" during litigation is not compensable; that is, the plaintiff may collect "lost revenue" resulting from a breach of contract but will not collect "lost revenue" resulting from having to be in court. Also, any mental stress resulting from the pressures of the litigation process is not compensable.

Court Costs and Attorney Fees. Court costs, which include filing fees, jury fees, witness fees, and transcripts, are usually assessed against the losing party. Where a public question is involved, however, the court may decide to let the taxpayers, rather than one of the parties, bear the costs of the litigation. The trial judge generally has great discretion in determining which items of costs were really necessary to the litigation and should, therefore, be paid by the loser.

Almost alone among the legal systems of the civilized world, the common-law system did not permit victorious litigants to recover their lawyers' charges as part of court costs. In large part, this rule resulted because each lawyer-client contract was created through a private agreement, with no official fee schedule limiting the amount that could be charged. Since there was no general court control over legal fees, it was felt that the court could not properly charge them against the losing party. Lawyers' fees are still not generally included as court costs. To assess them against the losing party, there must be a specific provision to that effect in the contract of the parties or in a statute covering the kind of claim being litigated.

All of these factors should be very carefully considered by anyone contemplating litigation. Even if you win legally, you may still lose financially.

Election of Remedies. The strict application of logical principles does not always produce justice in particular cases, and the early common law always tried to be logical. Common-law rules of pleading, for example, required a plaintiff who had two alternative remedies for an alleged breach of contract to choose between them if they were "inconsistent." The two most clearly inconsistent remedies are specific performance and rescission and restitution. In the first, the plaintiff is insisting that the contract be performed as agreed; in the second, the plaintiff wants to call off the whole deal and put everything back where it was.

The plaintiff's main difficulty under these early rules was that the choice had to be made when the complaint was filed; that is, at a time when the plaintiff did not yet know whether or not a case for restitution could be proved. A court might find that the plaintiff had waited too long to rescind, for example, and deny the restitution remedy. But if the plaintiff then tried to sue for damages in a second case, the early civil procedure rules would prohibit the suit because a binding "election of remedies" had been made when the first lawsuit was filed. As a result, some plaintiffs received no remedy at all, just because they (or their lawyers) had guessed wrong initially.

Some of the injustice inherent in these rules has been removed by the adoption of civil procedure rules which permit the plaintiff to file a complaint asking for such inconsistent remedies in the alternative. ("I want *either* rescission and restitution or damages.") Such alternative pleading is possible in a majority of states and in the U.S. District Courts. Even with this liberalization, however, the plaintiff must still make an election of remedies at some point in the litigation. Such an election might mean deciding whether or not to keep the house with the leaky basement and get damages for the wet furniture and for fixing the leak, or to ask for the money back and a rescission of the house deal. If rescission is granted, no dollar damages for the wet furniture will be awarded. Because of the potential harshness of these election rules, it becomes important to know which remedies are inconsistent and thus require an election.

The best possible rule for the plaintiff is found in the UCC rules for the sale of goods, which do not require the plaintiff to make any election at all. Buyers of goods who prove their case for rescission can get their money back and also can collect all provable damages which they have sustained while the goods were in their possession.

DAMAGES

Underlying Factors. In determining the amount of compensatory damages that a plaintiff can collect for a breach of contract, the court will subject the claimed damages to four tests: **causation**, **certainty**, **foreseeability**, and **mitigation**. To be collectible, compensatory damages must meet each of these tests.

First, the plaintiff must prove that the alleged damages were caused by the breach and not by something else. Lost profits which result when a supplier fails to deliver may be recoverable, but if the plaintiff's lower sales are due to a general economic downturn, the breaching seller should not be liable because its breach did not cause the "injury."

Second, the plaintiff must be able to prove the amount of damages with *reasonable* certainty. Damages for lost profits and for mental stress are difficult to collect, in part, for this reason; courts are reluctant to permit jury speculation and sympathy to substitute for solid evidence of amount of injury. However, a plaintiff can collect "mental stress" damages even for a simple breach of contract if the right sort of case is proved.

A third significant limitation on the amount of damages awarded is that the damages sustained must have been reasonably foreseeable at the time the contract was made. That is, a party is not held legally responsible for damages that result from a breach of contract unless the party ought to have known that damages of that sort would result from the nonperformance. Damages for lost profits which result from a "shut down the plant" situation are especially difficult to collect because of the application of this foreseeability principle. Obviously, your safeguard here is to make sure that your suppliers and contractors are fully informed as to your requirements and of the consequences of their failure to perform.

Finally, it is only common sense to require the injured party to take reasonable steps to miti-gate, or hold down, losses. Even though one party has breached, it wouldn't be fair to that party to allow the other party to simply sit back and watch the damages mount up, without making any effort to get an alternative performance from someone else. The law, therefore, generally requires injured parties to make reasonable efforts to mitigate their damages.

Because a lease of real estate is a conveyance of an interest in the land as well as a contract, courts at one time did not apply the mitigation rule to landlords. Landlords could simply sue for the agreed rental price whether the tenant was using the premises or not. There is a growing trend toward removing this exception, thereby forcing the landlord to mitigate by rerenting the premises before collecting damages against a tenant who has moved out prior to the expiration of the lease.

Compensatory Damages. The basic purpose of the damages remedy is to compensate the in-jured party for the loss sustained by the other party's breach; that is, to put the injured party, so far as possible, in the place he or she would have been if the contract had been properly and fully performed. The measure of **compensatory damages** is the difference between the performance promised and the performance given; thus general compensatory damages are sometimes called **"difference-money" damages**. For example, if a used car is represented to be in "A-1 shape," and it is not, compensatory damages would give the buyer the amount of money necessary to put the car into "A-1 shape."

Special compensatory damages are awarded for losses which are further down in the chain of causation, losses over and above the difference money losses which are caused by the breach. For example, if the buyer of the above used car had to take a cab to work twice because the car wouldn't start, special compensatory damages should be given to cover the cab fare.

The general measure of the seller's damages is difference money; that is, the difference be-tween the contract price and the (lower) market price at the time and place of tender. Obviously, if another buyer pays more for the goods and the seller had only one item for sale, the seller could not collect any difference-money damages. The seller can also recover any "incidental" damages sustained because of the buyer's breach, such as additional storage charges on the goods or the cost of an advertisement needed to resell the goods. Where the buyer's breach means that the seller "loses" that sale, in the sense that the seller, a car dealer for instance, has many of the same items for sale and could have sold another one to Buyer 2, the seller should collect the profit which would have been made on that other sale as damages from Buyer 1.

If the seller has failed to deliver or the buyer has rightfully rejected or justifiably revoked an acceptance, the buyer may obtain substitute goods from another source and sue the seller for difference-money damages. The buyer may also recover any "incidental and consequential damages" which are defined as any expenses incurred in inspecting or handling the goods or obtaining substitute goods and any other reasonable expenses incident to the delay, any loss resulting from the buyer's requirements for the goods of which the seller had reason to know and which could not be avoided, and any injury to person or property resulting from breach of warranty.

As to goods which the buyer has accepted but which are nonconforming, damages may be recovered for any "loss resulting in the ordinary course of events" from the seller's breach. For a breach of warranty, the buyer may recover damages for the difference between the value of the goods accepted and what the value of the goods would have been if the warranty had been met, "unless special circumstances show proximate damages of a different amount."

Nominal Damages and Punitive Damages. Where there has been a breach of contract but the injured party is unable to show any actual losses as a result, the plaintiff will be awarded **nominal damages** (almost always $1) and court costs, provided the case is proved. Obviously, most such cases will not be litigated. But nominal damages play an important part in a case which contains the right combination of facts for **punitive damages** to be awarded. Once the injured party proves a case for breach of contract, an award of punitive damages can be added on to punish the defendant who has been guilty of repeated, willful violations of the rights of others (again, even though no actual damages can be proved). Cases involving fraudulent or other intentionally tortious conduct are particularly appropriate for punitive damage awards, as seen in the *Welch* case.

WELCH v. METRO-GOLDWYN-MAYER FILM CO.
254 Cal.Rptr. 645 (App. 2 Dist., CA, 1988)

FACTS: This lawsuit arises from the firing of the motion picture actress Raquel Welch from her starring role in the film "Cannery Row." The jury found in favor of Welch and Raquel Welch Productions, Inc. (hereinafter sometimes collectively referred to as Welch) on counts of breach of contract, conspiracy to induce breach of contract, slander, and breach of the implied covenant of good faith and fair dealing (bad faith). Welch recovered $2 million in compensatory damages and over $8 million in punitive damages from appellants Metro-Goldwyn-Mayer Film Co. (MGM), several successor corporations to MGM, David Begelman (the president of MGM) and Michael Phillips (the producer of the film).

The evidence showed that Welch appeared in about thirty films between 1965 and 1980 and had a reputation as a strong willed professional actress who sometimes clashed with directors. She was considered a sex symbol, and the only serious dramatic role was as a roller derby queen in "Kansas City Bomber." She turned down all film offers between 1977 and 1980, concentrating during that period on a television special and a television drama about an American Indian woman, for which she served as producer as well as actress.

Prior to 1980, Michael Phillips and David Ward had collaborated on two films, one of which was the Academy Award winner, "The Sting." Over several years, Phillips and Ward developed a film package based on the John Steinbeck novellas "Cannery Row" and "Sweet Thursday." Ward wrote the screenplay and was to be the director, although he had never directed a commercial film before. Phillips was to be the producer. An actor named Nick Nolte was to portray the leading male character.

Begelman insisted that an actress with a recognizable name be selected for the leading female character, a prostitute named Suzy. Numerous actresses were considered among whom were Welch and Debra Winger.

At forty years old, Welch relished the chance to direct her career towards more serious roles. She agreed to audition for the part, which was not customary for an established actress, and to perform nude scenes, which she had previously refused to do in any film.

The contract required that Welch be provided a fully equipped, "star-type" trailer for makeup purposes; her choice of hairdresser and makeup artist, on first call to her, and a wardrobe assistant. She was at first given a very small trailer, then a replacement which she also thought was inadequate. Because of this problem (and others), she did her make-up at home for three mornings before she reported for work. She was on time each day and usually had to wait for hours for her scenes.

About 5:30 p.m. on Thursday, December 18th, Begelman met in his office with Phillips and David Chasman, MGM's head of film production. Begelman was dissatisfied with the dailies he had seen of the film, but not with Welch's performance. He called the meeting because of a memorandum he had received from MGM's chairman of the board, expressing concern that the film was over budget and was in the hands of a first-time director, and suggesting that Begelman pay special attention to the problem.

Begelman began the meeting by asking Phillips, "What the hell's going on?" He also said that Phillip's and Ward's jobs were in jeopardy if the problems continued. Phillips said that shooting was beginning late because of Welch's unusual three-hour makeup period, that she had told Ward she would not come out of makeup for rehearsal, and that she had been making up at home. He further stated that he had not confronted Welch about the problem because he hoped a new makeup room which would be available the following Monday would be acceptable to her. He did not mention that Welch had made up at home for only three days.

Begelman and Chasman thought that Phillips and Ward had been intimidated by Welch. It was against studio policy for an actress to make up at home, both because it was an advantage to the production to have her available for rehearsal during the makeup period, and because of potential problems with liability and Teamsters Union drivers. Begelman ordered Phillips to tell Welch that she would be sent a letter declaring her in breach of contract, unless she made up at the studio the next morning. This was not to be deferred until Monday, and her makeup time was henceforth limited to two hours.

Welch learned of the breach letter on December 19, around noon, but continued working. Welch's agent, Michael Levy, called Begelman to complain that the letter was unnecessary. Begelman told Levy not to tell him how to run his business, and that he was not going to let Welch continue her past history of toughness with studio directors. He said the problem was curable if Welch would make up at the studio.

A letter from MGM dated December 22, indicated that the employment agreement was terminated due to Welch's failure to comply with her contractual obligations. Welch responded with a letter threatening to sue unless MGM paid the balance of $194,444 which remained due under the agreement. MGM refused.

Welch was replaced by Debra Winger in the film. Winger received $150,000 for the role. It cost almost $200,000 to replace Welch with Winger and reshoot the scenes in which Welch had appeared.

Welch received numerous inquiries from the press regarding what had happened. Many people seemed to believe that she had failed to show up for work. Industry newspapers reported that she had been fired.

An article about the incident appeared in the April 2, 1981, issue of Rolling Stone, a magazine with a weekly circulation of over 700,000 and wide readership in the motion picture industry. According to the article, Ward said that Welch was a casting mistake who was not necessarily a bad actress but was not delivering a performance he could live with. Begelman was quoted as saying: "We had a general feeling she had not lived up to her contract.... We had no alternative. It is up to the executives to tell the people in this business we will not stand for that. The producer gave her appropriate directions and she failed to obey."

Negative reviews of the film which appeared in *Variety* and *The New York Times* in February 1982 stated that Welch should feel happy she had been fired from it. The film was a major failure at the box office, and MGM lost almost $16 million on it.

The evidence established that an accusation of breaking a contract would be very damaging to an actress's reputation, as people in the industry would assume she was undependable. Welch never made another movie because of her firing from "Cannery Row." One deal fell through due to a lack of financing and the only other offers she received, to portray a Nazi and a vampire, were unacceptable. In contrast, she had made about six films between 1973 and 1980, with compensation ranging between $150,000 and $350,000. At the time of trial, in 1986, film actresses routinely received twice the 1980 level of compensation. Some stars were making from $2 to $5 million per film.

 JUSTICE WOODS:

The employment contract for Welch's services was arrived at through careful negotiations between MGM's representatives on one side and Welch's agent and attorney on the other. In addition to compensation, the contract provided for a series of conditions negotiated on behalf of Welch, such as billing; approval of nude scenes and nude stills; effect of replacement of Nolte, Ward, or Phillips; approval ... of dressing room, hairdresser and make-up artist; a wardrobe assistant and double (actress); and no make up call earlier than 6 a.m. The contract otherwise incorporated all of MGM's Standard Terms, including the "pay or play" clause, and the Basic Agreement of the Screen Actors Guild....

[W]hile the Supreme Court has not directly decided the issue, both *Tameny* and *Seaman's* provide strong support for permitting a bad faith action in the context of an employment contract. A series of decisions by the Courts of Appeal have so held, without drawing any distinction with regard to the type of employment involved....

Finally, we consider appellants' contentions that the punitive damages are excessive or duplicative as a matter of law.

As previously indicated, the jury awarded $3,750,000 against MGM and $500,000 against Phillips as punitive damages on Count II (conspiracy to induce breach of contract); $150,000 against MGM and $2,500 against Begelman as punitive damages on Count III (slander); and $3,750,000 against MGM as punitive damages against MGM on Count IV (breach of the implied covenant of good faith and fair dealing).

An award of punitive damages will be found excessive on appeal only if the record shows that it was so grossly disproportionate that it resulted from passion or prejudice.... Among the pertinent factors are the reprehensibility of the conduct, the relationship between the amounts of compensatory and punitive damages, and the wealth of the particular defendant.... Great weight is given to the determination of a trial court on motion for new trial that the damages were not excessive.... Such a ruling was made here.

The punitive damages the jury awarded were substantially less than Welch requested. As to MGM, her counsel asked the jury for $7,500,000 on the slander count and that same amount on the bad faith count. The $500,000 awarded against Phillips for bad faith was exactly what counsel requested. Counsel argued for $700,000 on the slander count, based on one dollar for each Rolling Stone subscriber.

It was stipulated below that MGM had a net worth of $215 million and Phillips of $5 million. The punitive damages thus represented 3.6 percent of MGM's net worth and 10 percent of Phillip's net worth as an individual. As to MGM, the ratio of punitive damages to compensatory damages was 2.8:1. The same ratio as to Phillips was 2.1:1....

The size of the punitive damage awards here was not inconsistent with or disproportionate to awards which have been affirmed in the past.... We realize that MGM lost money on the film and Phillip's salary for producing it was $200,000. Still, given the net worth of the defendants, their complete disregard of the likelihood that the unjustified firing would ruin Welch's film career, and the relatively high actual damages, the jury could properly conclude that appellants' conduct justified the amount of punitive damages which was awarded....

Since the various causes of action here had different elements and relied on different facts for their proof, the separate punitive damage awards were appropriate.

In any event, appellants waived this issue by permitting the case to go to the jury under a theory in which the punitive damages were to be added together.

Liquidated Damages. The general policy of the law to favor settlements of claims after they arise also operates to validate remedy provisions agreed to in advance, as part of the original contract. The parties are generally free to specify in advance what steps can be taken if their contract is breached by one of them. However, since many contracts are entered into between parties with unequal bargaining power, and since in many cases form contracts drafted by one party are used, the courts examine such **liquidated damages** provisions very carefully. These clauses must be basically fair, and a substantial forfeiture of rights must not result from a relatively minor breach.

Where a valid liquidated damages provision exists, the amount specified can be collected for a breach without any proof of actual damages.

UCC Limitation of Remedies. In accordance with its general "freedom of contract" approach, the Code permits parties to the sale of goods contract to specify what remedies will or will not be available in the event of breach. Such contract provisions are not enforceable, however, if they are unreasonable or unconscionable. One important limitation is Section 2-719(2): "Where circumstances cause an exclusive or limited remedy to fail of its essential purpose, remedy may be had as provided in this Act." If, in other words, enforcement of the contract clause would mean that the injured party wound up with no real remedy at all, the Code's remedy sections apply. Further, Subsection (3) of Section 2-719 provides that a limitation of consequential damages for personal injuries caused by defective consumer goods is prima facie unconscionable. The seller or manufacturer of the consumer goods would have a heavy presumption to overcome to make such a limitation enforceable. Where a commercial loss is caused by defective goods, there is no presumption that a contract clause limiting consequential damages is invalid. If an airline and a plane manufacturer included such a limitation in their contract, for example, the limitation would not be presumed unconscionable.

Where the contract contains a liquidated damages provision, the amount specified must be "reasonable," under essentially the same test used prior to the Code. If the amount set is unreasonably large, it is void as a penalty.

OTHER REMEDIES

In addition to the damages remedy, several other remedies may be available to the injured plaintiff, depending on the facts of the case. Most of these alternative remedies were first developed by the courts of equity to deal with situations where the "remedy at law;" that is, damages, was felt to be inadequate to solve the plaintiff's problem. The main alternative remedies for breach of contract are discussed below; certain special remedies for breach of secured financing contracts are discussed in later chapters.

Specific Performance. Where the parties have contracted for the purchase and sale of a unique item, the buyer, particularly, may want the court to specifically enforce the contract because it will usually be very hard to prove damages in the absence of an established market and because, even with damages, the buyer would still not be able to get the thing bargained for. In the eyes of the law, every piece of land is unique, so the specific performance remedy is available to either party to a real estate contract. Goods and securities are legally unique if no alternative source of supply is reasonably available. Fifty shares of stock in a small, closely held corporation might very well be unique; fifty shares of U.S. Steel would not be. A 1993 Ford is probably not unique; a 1904 Stanley Steamer almost certainly is.

As a general rule, specific performance is not available as a remedy for breach of personal services contracts for two main reasons. First, courts traditionally have been reluctant to get involved in extensive supervision of contract performances on a day-to-day basis. And second, an order forcing one person to work for another smacks of "involuntary servitude," which is prohibited by the U.S. Constitution. Because performances under construction contracts can normally be judged against an agreed set of plans and specifications, specific performance is available in such cases.

The *Bander* case illustrates some of these points.

BANDER v. GROSSMAN
611 N.Y.S.2d 985 (N.Y.Supr.Ct., 1994)

FACTS: In the summer of 1987, plaintiff looked for a sports car to purchase for interim personal use and to sell when the price rose (a practice in which he had previously engaged). The defendant had in his inventory the subject 1965 DB5 Astin-Martin convertible with left-hand drive. Plaintiff learned this particular model was one of only twenty in existence, with only forty having been made, although those twenty cars seem to turn over with more frequency than their number might suggest. Plaintiff testified he thought the car was undervalued, based upon his knowledge of sports car prices, and anticipated a price rise. A contract of sale was reached with a purchase price of $40,000, with plaintiff depositing $5,000.

The commercial agreement proceeded to unwind thereafter. The dealer could not obtain the title documents from the wholesaler from whom he had agreed to purchase the vehicle; the deposition testimony of the out-of-state wholesaler was read into evidence and confirmed that the title had been misplaced. The defendant did not transmit this explanation to plaintiff, but instead told a story about problems of getting title from a different individual. In August 1987, the defendant attempted to return the deposit, but advised that he would continue to try to resolve the title problems. Plaintiff pursued the purchase until, ultimately, in December 1987, plaintiff's lawyer wrote defendant that the contract had been breached and plaintiff would commence litigation. However, no further action was taken by plaintiff until this case was commenced in 1989, four months after defendant sold the car.

 JUDGE LEBEDEFF:

The request for specific performance raises a novel issue under the Uniform Commercial Code concerning entitlement to specific performance of a contract for the sale of unique goods with a fluctuating price. Section 2-716(1) of the Uniform Commercial Code, which is controlling, provides that "(s)pecific performance may be decreed where the goods are unique or in other proper circumstances." The jury's advisory determined that the Astin-Martin car at issue was unique.

As noted above, the car was sold prior to the commencement of this litigation for a price of $185,000 more than the $40,000 contract price, and plaintiff requests that he be granted specific performance in the form of a constructive trust impressed upon the proceeds of sale, plus interest from the date of sale. As it developed, the defendant had not sold at the "top of the market," which peaked in July of 1989, approximately two years after the original contract, when the car had a value of $335,000, which was $295,000 over the contract price. Thereafter, collectible automobile values slumped and the sale price of a comparable Astin-Martin vehicle by January of 1990 was $225,000 and, by the time of trial, was $80,000.

Clearly, plaintiff's request for an award of specific performance monetary damages is legally cognizable, for every object has a price and even rare goods are subject to economic interchangeability.... Plaintiff urges that specific performance is particularly appropriate here for UCC 2-716 has been viewed as a statute enacted to liberalize the availability of specific performance of contracts of sale as a buyers' remedy.... Nonetheless, this change does not lessen the UCC's "emphasis on the commercial feasibility of replacement" as the most desirable approach ... nor does it mean that typical equitable principles are inapplicable to consideration of the remedy....

However, both on the facts and the law, the court determines that, if equitable monetary damages are to be awarded here, that award must be based upon value at the time of trial, rather than on an earlier valuation. Traditionally, equity "give(s) relief adapted to the situation at the time of the decree."... This position is consistent with the explicit goal of the Uniform Commercial Code that its remedies are to "be liberally administered to the end that the aggrieved party may be put in as good a position as if the other party had fully performed" ... which, in the case of specific performance, has lead to confining the remedy to restoration of the equivalent of the subject goods to a plaintiff's possession.... Here, if plaintiff were to be awarded enough to be able to acquire another Astin-Martin at current prices, he would achieve the requisite equivalent.

Plaintiff has fervently, but ultimately unconvincingly, argued that the larger amount is his due. While every litigant wishes to gain a maximum economic benefit, a court of equity should not grant an award which would be "disproportionate in its harm to defendant and its assistance to plaintiff."...

[S]pecific performance rests upon the discretion of the trial court, reviewable under an abuse of discretion standard.... The use of a permissive "may" in the text of UCC 2-716 does not modify that standard in any way or change the accepted concept ... that specific performance may be declined if it is concluded such relief "would be a 'drastic' or harsh remedy." It should be noted in relation to price fluctuations that even an extreme rise in price is an insufficient reason, as a matter of law, to decline to consider this equitable remedy...but, on the other hand, neither does a mere "increase in the cost of a replacement ... merit the remedy."...

With the passage of time, specific performance becomes disfavored. For example, because goods are subject to a rapid change in condition, or the cost of maintenance of the goods is important, time may be found to have been of the essence, and even a month's delay may defeat specific performance.... Even absent such special circumstances, with a greater delay, where a defendant has changed position or taken any economic risk, the court may conclude that "the plaintiff will lose nothing but an uncontemplated opportunity to gather a windfall."... Particularly where some other transactions are available, it has been held that a "customer [for resale] may not ... refuse to cover ... and thereby speculate on the market entirely at the risk of the [defendant]."...

Turning to the facts in the instant case, the plaintiff did not sue in December of 1987, when it is likely a request for specific performance would have been granted. At that point, the defendant had disclaimed the contract and plaintiff was aware of his rights.... The court does not accept plaintiff's protest that he believed the commercial relationship was intact; the parties had already had a heated discussion and were communicating through attorneys. A more likely explanation of plaintiff's inaction is that he proceeded to complete the purchase in April of 1988 of a Ferrari Testarrosa for $128,000 and a Lamborghini for $40,000 in 1989.

In short, the plaintiff abandoned any active claim of contract enforcement by late spring of 1988. Moreover, to the extent that his two sports cars constituted "cover," he did not present any evidence as to his treatment of those cars such that the court could evaluate damages or quantify what profits he expected to make on the Astin-Martin which he regarded, in significant part, as a business transaction.... Finally, the court determines, as a matter of credibility, that plaintiff would not have pursued this matter had the price fallen below the contract price.

On this point, it is helpful to note that the initial burden of proving the proper remedy remains on the buyer.... In this instance, plaintiff's very attempt to prove qualifiable special performance damages has also proved: (a) the value of the disputed automobile was readily established by expert sources, (b) the adequacy of legal contract damages, and (c) the availability of "a substitute transaction (which) is generally a more efficient way to prevent injury than is a suit for specific performance ... [and gives] a sound economic basis for limiting the injured party to damages."...

In closing, the court does not fault plaintiff for his valiant attempt to reach for a higher level of damages. As two leading commentators have pointed out, in relation to the use of uniqueness as a basis for specific performance, the "exact dimensions [of the concepts] are not fully known."... "If only in the interest of commercial certainty, there is great wisdom in a rule of thumb that 'uniqueness' continues to cover one-of-a-kind goods and items of special sentimental value, [and] goods that have particular market significance, such as goods covered by an output contract or which are being specially manufactured."...

After full consideration of these factors, the court is satisfied that it would be inequitable and improper to grant specific performance in the form of a constructive trust upon the proceeds of sale.

Injunction. Injunction is another remedy that was developed by equity courts: a court orders someone to do something or to stop doing something. In breach of contract situations, a negative injunction may be granted to prevent a breaching party from performing for others while still under a contractual duty to perform for the plaintiff. For the reasons stated above, the plaintiff does not get a positive decree ordering the defendant to perform; the plaintiff only gets a negative order directing the defendant not to perform for others.

Rescission and Restitution. Two remedies are really involved here—calling off the deal, and returning any benefits already transferred. A court will not lightly undo the parties' whole agreement and order the restoration of benefits already given. The rescission and restitution remedy is provided only if there has been fraud, material breach, or similar failure; only if the injured party asks for this remedy with reasonable promptness; and only if the rights of third parties or other equitable factors have not intervened. The objective of "R & R" is to terminate the contract *and* to put the parties back where they were before it was made. The more difficult and complex it is to achieve this objective, the less likely it is that R & R will be used as a remedy.

Quasi Contract. Because the old common-law courts only heard cases which fell into certain categories, lawyers became somewhat creative in constructing fact combinations to fit those categories. *Quasi contract* means in essence "almost like a real contract, but not quite;" it describes a situation where a party has received and retained benefits but has made no actual promise to pay for them. It is in fact a remedy which the courts developed to prevent such a party from being "unjustly enriched." The circumstances are such that it wouldn't be fair for the person to keep the benefits without paying anything for them. The **unjust enrichment** principle is the justification for requiring a minor to pay the fair market value for necessaries received, even though the minor has exercised the option of disaffirming the contract made to pay for them. Quasi contract also applies to all sorts of other situations, such as benefits conferred on the wrong person by mistake or partial performance given to one party prior to a breach of contract.

Contract Price. The seller of goods can sue and collect the full contract price from the buyer only in certain limited situations. The seller can, of course, sue for the full price on any goods the buyer has accepted. The seller can also get the contract price for conforming goods which have been lost or damaged within a commercially reasonable time after the risk of loss passed to the buyer. Finally, the buyer owes the contract price for goods that have been identified to the contract and that cannot be resold at a reasonable price.

Possession of Goods. Where the seller discovers that the buyer is insolvent, the seller may withhold delivery of the goods, unless the buyer is prepared to pay cash, including payment for all goods already delivered under the same contract. Where the goods are already in transit, the seller can order the bailee to stop delivery if the bailee has not acknowledged the buyer's right to possession and if the buyer has not received a negotiable document of title covering the goods.

Where the goods have already been delivered on credit to an insolvent buyer, the seller has a very limited right to reclaim them. The seller must demand their return within ten days after the buyer received them, unless the buyer made a written statement of solvency within three months prior to the delivery; then the ten-day limitation does not apply. In any case, however, the seller's right of repossession is subject to the rights of buyers in the ordinary course of business or other good faith purchasers and to the rights of lien creditors. Where the seller decides on repossession, this remedy excludes all others.

If the buyer breaches before the seller has finished manufacturing the goods, the seller, if exercising "reasonable commercial judgment," has the options of completing the goods and identifying them to the contract, or of selling the unfinished goods for scrap or salvage, or of pursuing any other reasonable alternative.

A buyer in possession or control of goods that were rightfully rejected because of their nonconformity has a security interest in them for any payments already made on the price and for all reasonable expenses incurred in inspecting and handling them. The buyer can sell such goods and apply the proceeds to satisfy this claim.

SIGNIFICANCE OF THIS CHAPTER

As noted by the great Scots poet, Robert Burns, "the best laid plans of mice and men, gang aft a-glee." This chapter has indicated some of the reasons why the plans laid in a contract may "go astray." Our discussion has covered at least the main bases for excuse or discharge of a party's contractual obligations. The parties themselves may provide for such excuses, either in the original contract, or in a subsequent modifying agreement, or through their subsequent conduct. Even without express contract excuse clauses, courts will sometimes grant relief from a contract duty where the anticipated circumstances have changed very substantially. Since not every nonperformance is a breach of contract, the parties in many of these situations would be better served by a negotiated settlement than an extended litigation.

Since you are not reading this text to become lawyers, we have deemphasized most procedural aspects of the law, and concentrated instead on the nature of your rights and liabilities. The purpose of our discussion of remedies is to acquaint you with the options you may have in the event the other party is guilty of a breach of contract. Since not every remedy is available for every situation, you need an appreciation of the limits of what the courts, and your lawyer, can do for you if you are successful in proving your case. You need to know what the possible outcomes might be to make a rational decision whether or not to bring the litigation—or to continue it.

Since a court will not (and should not) give unrequested remedies, one of the lawyer's main jobs is to figure out the remedy or the combination of remedies which will best solve the client's problem. If you do go to litigation, make sure you fully understand what your options are and what your chances are of receiving each possible remedy.

PROBLEMS FOR DISCUSSION

1. For several years prior to April 30, 1992, the Storeys were partners in the petroleum products business at Cle Elum, doing business as Storey Distributing Company. On April 30, 1992, the defendants dissolved their partnership. At the time of dissolution of the partnership, defendants' account with plaintiff had a balance of $3,515.80.

    On December 27, 1993, plaintiff obtained a judgment against defendant Earl Storey for $3,735.47. Defendant William E. Storey was not a named defendant in that case. Having failed to collect that judgment, B-OK brought this suit on the same account. The trial court held for William Storey.

    Will this decision be sustained on appeal? Why or why not?

2. William E. Felch alleges, among other things, that he was employed by the defendant as a member of its faculty on a continuing basis and that contrary to and without compliance with the provisions for dismissal contained in administrative memoranda purporting to require certain hearings, the board of trustees of defendant on August 22, approved the action of its president on July 20, dismissing the plaintiff effective August 11. Plaintiff asks that "defendant be enjoined from carrying into effect the dismissal of this plaintiff as a member of the faculty ... and that the defendant may be ordered to continue plaintiff as such member of the faculty of Findlay College, Findlay, Ohio, and that defendant be ordered to pay to this plaintiff the salary therefore agreed upon."

    Should the injunction be granted? Explain.

3. Ralph Nader was scheduled to make several appearances for the Connecticut Citizens Action Group on April 28, including a noon rally in Hartford and a speech on the Storrs campus of the University of Connecticut. On April 25, he bought a ticket for Allegheny's 10:15 a.m. flight from Washington, D.C., to Hartford, which was scheduled to arrive at 11:15 a.m. His reservation was confirmed. When he arrived at the airport about five minutes before his flight, he was told there were no more seats. Only 100 seats were available for the 107 reservations which had been confirmed one hour before the flight. No one would give up a seat when Allegheny asked. Nader refused Allegheny's offer to fly him to Philadelphia, where he would have ten minutes to catch a flight due to arrive in Hartford at 12:15. He flew to Boston, where a CCAG staff member picked him up and drove him to Storrs. Nader refused the $32.41 compensation offered to him under the Civil Aeronautics Board's rules, and brought a common-law suit for damages, alleging fraudulent misrepresentation. Nader was awarded $10 compensatory damages and $25,000 punitive damages; CCAG was awarded $51 compensatory damages and $25,000 punitive damages. The Court of Appeals reversed.

   On appeal, how should the U.S. Supreme Court decide this case? Discuss.

4. By written contract, Vidal agreed to buy four used airplanes from Transcontinental Airlines. Payment was to be made by certified check on delivery of the planes, which was to occur at the Kansas City Municipal Airport on June 1. Transcontinental was ready to deliver only one plane on June 1; the other three could have been delivered sometime before July 10. No offer of performance was ever made by either party. On October 8, Vidal sued for breach of contract.

   What is the result, and why?

5. Tom sold his junk auto and salvage business, Trusty's Auto Parts, to Lem. As part of the contract, Tom agreed not to compete in the auto salvage business for a period of five years, within a radius of 100 miles. When Lem took over, he changed the business name to Loosewheel's Auto Salvage. Lem's business volume is only about half of what Tom was doing. After some investigation, Lem has learned that Tom has been buying scrap copper and aluminum wire from two of his former business contacts and has generally been buying and selling auto scrap and salvage. Lem wants to sue for breach of contract.

   What difficulties will he face in winning a lawsuit on these facts? Explain.

6. Ms. Stetzel sustained personal injuries as the result of an intersection collision in Iowa City on September 27. She was thrown sideways, and her head struck the window. She went to the University Student Health Center for treatment of her headache, was kept overnight, and was sent home the next day. Her headaches continued for several weeks, interfering with her studying; she was taking a prescribed medication for these headaches. After being pestered by an insurance adjuster, she finally signed a release on December 2, in return for $400. She admits she knew what the paper was when she signed it. Shortly thereafter, her symptoms became more serious; the headaches became more severe, she had difficulty picking things up; her eyes tired more easily; she seemed to be forgetful. Alleging that the release was invalid due to mutual mistake and/or undue influence, she sued for her injuries. The jury agreed and gave her $3,000. Defendant appeals.

   How should the appeals court rule, and why?

7. Riley purchased his new car from a Florida Ford dealer at a cost of $18,476, and Ford issued a self-styled "New Vehicle Warranty." Shortly thereafter he took the car to Robinson Brothers, an Alabama Ford dealer, for repair of a window and removal of a noise in the rear end. According to Riley, these defects were not corrected. At trial he testified that in the weeks following the requested repairs, and before the car was returned to Robinson Brothers for further repairs, these additional malfunctions developed: air conditioning did not work, speed control did not function, power seats became inoperative, the radio aerial functioned spasmodically, the rear seat did not fit, headlight panels were not synchronized, the cigarette lighter was missing, windshield wipers were defective, engine knocked upon acceleration, the transmission did not function properly, gear shift lever would not function, and the left door would not close properly.

Riley wrote to Ford setting forth in detail his complaints, and requesting Ford "to direct me to a dealer employing trained service personnel, or furnish me with someone capable of overseeing service personnel available in order to insure that the defects in my automobile are properly corrected in an expert and dependable manner." Ford dispatched a Technical Service Representative who road-tested the automobile, agreed that it was not functioning properly, and offered to take it to Robinson Brothers where he would personally supervise its repair. Riley believed he had a better idea. He sued Ford and was awarded $30,000 by a U.S. District Court jury.

What should happen when this case is appealed, and why?

Part Three

Sales of Goods

A sale of goods is one particular type of contract, so the general rules of contract law apply, unless replaced by a specific rule from the Uniform Commercial Code. We have already seen many examples of such changes in the various chapters in Part Two. There were special goods rules for offer and acceptance, consideration, Statute of Frauds, assignment, and other topics. We will not repeat all those special rules in this part.

Our focus here is the two other major areas of difference between general contract law and the UCC's rules for sales of goods. Chapter 15 discusses the rules for transferring the various ownership interests in the goods from the seller to the buyer. Chapter 15 also looks at two situations involving problems with the transfer of ownership—defects in the seller's title to the goods and claims of the bulk seller's unsecured creditors against the goods. Chapter 16 covers the very important area of products liability, one of the two or three most important legal developments in the past fifty years.

Chapter 15

Sales: Title, Risk of Loss, and Other Interests

BASIC CONCEPTS AND DEFINITIONS

UCC Coverage. Since a "sale of goods" is one specific type of contract, the general principles of contract law apply to such sales, but most of the rules relating specifically to sales of goods have been codified, supplemented, and sometimes changed by the Uniform Commercial Code. Article 2, the longest article in the Uniform Commercial Code, specifically covers sales of goods, but other portions of the UCC may also apply. If the goods are to be stored or transported as part of the transaction, Article 7 may apply. The general principles and definitions stated in Article 1 apply to all Code transactions.

Many of the special sales rules have already been discussed in the contracts chapters covering offer and acceptance, consideration, the Statute of Frauds, and assignments. This chapter and the next chapter will focus on other major areas of difference between the law of sales and general contract law.

Definitions. The basic purpose of a contract for the sale of goods is to pass the various ownership interests recognized by the Code from the seller to the buyer, for a consideration called the price. The transaction is not a gift of the goods, because the seller is receiving a price for them; it is not a bailment of the goods, because the buyer will become the owner of them. Whether a particular contract is a sale of goods or a services contract depends on which element— goods or services—predominates.

As defined in 2 105(1), **goods** means tangible, movable personal property. Investment securities, such as stocks and bonds, and other "things in action" (intangibles) are excluded from the definition of goods; specifically included are such things as growing crops, the unborn young of animals, and specially manufactured goods. Goods which are not both existing and identified when the contract is made are called **future goods**, and a contract involving such goods is a **contract to sell**. **Fungible goods** are goods whose units are indistinguishable from one another, such as grain in a grain elevator, fuel oil in a tank car, or coal in a pile.

The price is whatever value is received by the seller for the goods; it may be money, other goods, services, or land—or a promise by the buyer to deliver any of these things.

A **merchant** (2-104[1]) is defined as a person who: (a) deals in goods of the kind being sold, (b) by his or her occupation holds himself or herself out as having special knowledge about the goods or practices involved in the sale, or (c) is represented by someone who is held out as having such special knowledge. The question of whether or not a farmer is a merchant for Code purposes has not been answered uniformly by the courts.

Significance of the "Goods" Definition.

What difference does it make whether a contract is for the sale of goods, or for the sale of services, or for the sale of land? As we discussed in Chapter 10, for real estate, no oral contract except a short-term lease is enforceable, and a writing sufficient to make a real estate contract enforceable must contain all of the material terms. For services, any oral contract is fully enforceable (if proved) unless the term of the contract is definitely for over one year. For goods priced at under $500, an oral contract is enforceable; for goods priced at $500 or more, one of the five alternatives listed in UCC 2-201 must be complied with.

A second important difference was discussed in Chapter 9: For sales of goods, modifications agreed to after the contract was originally formed are binding without a new exchange of considerations, and in many cases this holds true even if the modifications are oral. For services, unless new values are exchanged, such modifications would not be binding, but the modifications can usually be oral. For land, subsequent modifications would require a new exchange of considerations and would almost certainly have to be in writing. For any type of contract, however, the parties could provide in their written contract that no oral modifications were effective.

A third important difference between sales of goods, services, and land has to do with quality guarantees: What sort of performance standards does the law require of the seller? There are some very important distinctions between goods, on the one hand, and services or land, on the other. For land, although many states now follow a different rule (at least for the seller of a new home), the original rule is that the buyer takes the land as is; unless the buyer can prove that the seller committed fraud or made a specific guarantee as part of the contract, the buyer has no case for alleged defects in the real estate. For services, unless a specific guarantee of results has been made, the buyer-customer has to prove malpractice to recover; that is, the buyer-customer has to show that the seller's performance fell below the standard of a reasonably competent practitioner. For sales of goods, however, a merchant-seller is held to an automatic quality **warranty** that the goods are merchantable, even though the merchant-seller has said nothing specific about their quality and even though the merchant-seller is not guilty of any negligence in handling or delivering the goods. A number of cases involving blood transfusions by hospitals involve the question of what is a sale of goods. As we noted in Chapter 10, in discussing the Statute of Frauds for goods, the courts try to determine which is the "dominant" part of the hybrid goods and services contract.

PASSING OF OWNERSHIP INTERESTS IN THE GOODS

One special (and somewhat complicated) problem in the law of sales is that of determining when the various ownership interests recognized by the Code pass from the seller to the buyer. The UCC recognizes six different ownership interests in the goods—**special property**, **insurable interest**, **title**, **risk of loss**, **right to possession**, and **security interest**. These six interests represent packages of rights and duties with respect to the goods. They can all exist at the same time, as to the same goods, and they may be parceled out among the seller, the buyer, and different third parties in any number of combinations. Part of the complexity in Article 2 is caused by the need to provide rules for all these situations.

The simplest case occurs when you buy a used book from a friend for cash, or items from a drugstore or grocery store. If you pay by check, things get a bit more complicated since the check will only be paid by your bank if there is enough money in the account. If you use a credit card or some other credit arrangement, the seller is taking a still greater risk of nonpayment. When you order goods by mail, as many businesses do, all sorts of things can happen while the goods are in transit. When the goods are delivered to the buyer they may not conform to the contract, and either party may decide not to go through with the deal. The Code must provide appropriate rules to deal with all of these situations.

Under the Code, most of the cases between the buyer and the seller will be "risk of loss" cases. Where third parties are involved in the litigation, the solution will nearly always depend on the location of one of the other five interests.

Presumptions. Article 2 contains a rather extensive set of statutory presumptions as to when each of the various interests in the goods passes to the buyer; the most important sections are 2-401, 2-501, and 2-509. In general, these presumptions may be overcome by the parties' specific agreement; that is, the parties are free to make any specific agreement they wish as to when a particular ownership interest will pass to the buyer, but if they say nothing, the Code presumptions apply. In most cases, the contract probably will not say anything specific about when these ownership interests pass.

One inflexible rule is stated in the Code (2-105[2]): "Goods must be both existing and identified before any interest in them can pass." In other words, even if they both agree to do so, the buyer and the seller cannot pass any interest to anyone unless the goods are both existing and identified. Once the goods come into existence and are identified as the goods for the given contract, the buyer and the seller are free to parcel out the six ownership interests in any way they choose.

Identification. Identification is the act of specifying exactly which goods are to be delivered by the seller to the buyer to satisfy the terms of a particular contract. Identification may be made by either the seller or the buyer, in any manner they agree to have it made. As an important change from prior law, the goods do not necessarily have to be in "deliverable condition" per the terms of the contract for identification to occur. If the parties so agree, individual shares of a mass of fungible goods can be "identified," and thus sold, even though these shares have not yet been parceled out. For example, the parties could agree to buy and sell one half of the fuel oil in Penn-Central Railroad car no. 35790; that would be a sufficient identification.

In the absence of any specific agreement, Section 2-501 says that identification is presumed to occur: (1) when the contract is made, if it is for goods already existing and identified in the parties' negotiations (a particular used car, for example); (2) for future goods generally, when the goods are "shipped, marked, or otherwise designated" by the seller (when the seller tags one new car in an inventory with the buyer's order number, for example); or (3) for agricultural products such as crops and the young of animals when the crops are planted and the as-yet-unborn young are conceived.

Once identification has occurred, ownership interests can then be passed to the buyer as the parties wish. "Special property" and "insurable interest" are presumed to pass to the buyer as soon as identification occurs.

Special Property. The special property interest, which the UCC gives to the buyer once particular goods have been identified to the contract, is a brand-new concept; nothing like it existed under pre-Code law. The purpose of this new Code interest is to provide some protection for the buyer, both as to the seller and as to third parties, as soon as the buyer's goods have been identified, even though the buyer is not yet technically "the owner" of the goods, that is, legal title has not yet passed to the buyer.

In addition to an "insurable interest," the buyer's special property interest gives the buyer a package of three rights against the goods:

1. The buyer has the right to inspect the goods at a reasonable time and place.

2. The buyer has the right to recover damages that the buyer sustains if a third party wrongfully interferes with the buyer's possession of the identified goods.

3. The buyer has the right to sue for possession of the identified goods where the seller refuses to deliver them and the buyer can't get substitute goods or where the seller goes insolvent within ten days after receiving the first installment on the contract price.

Insurable Interest. As soon as the goods are identified, the Code gives the buyer an "insurable interest," meaning that the buyer can then get a valid insurance policy protecting the buyer against financial losses relating to these goods. The extent to which a preexisting "blanket" insurance policy on all property "owned" by the buyer would apply to such identified goods has not yet been determined in most states. Even so, this question can be resolved by a carefully drafted policy provision.

More than one person may have an insurable interest in the same goods at the same time. This does not mean that several persons will recover for the same damages, but that several persons may suffer different financial losses when the goods are lost or damaged. Each such person has an insurable interest to the extent of his or her potential loss. The seller, for example, retains an insurable interest so long as he or she holds title to the goods or a security interest against the goods. Where the goods are shipped or stored, the carrier or the warehouse has an insurable interest in the goods while they are in its possession. Any party with an insurable interest in the goods can sue a third party who has caused a financial loss by injuring the goods.

Title. The concept of **title** generally refers to legal ownership, with all its attendant rights and liabilities. For the purpose of Article 2, however, title is given a much more restricted meaning, since most of the litigations between the buyer and the seller, and even some litigations involving third parties, are solved by using other ownership interests and the location of the legal title is irrelevant. Title is still an important concept because even under the Code many cases involving third parties will depend on whether the buyer or the seller had title to the goods at some particular point in time. Such cases might involve liability for required taxes, registration, or insurance on the goods, or liability resulting from use of the goods, or adverse claims against the goods by the creditors of the buyer or the seller.

The main presumptions as to when title passes are contained in Section 2-401; this section states a general rule and four specific applications. These presumptions are all based on common sense; if the parties want a special result, they will have to so expressly agree. On one point, however, the Code controls the parties' agreement: a seller cannot retain title to goods which have been shipped to, or delivered to, the buyer. The general rule is that title passes to the buyer "at the time and place at which the seller completes his [or her] performance with respect to the physical delivery of the goods." This rule applies even though, for financing reasons, using the goods as collateral for the unpaid balance of the purchase price, the seller has reserved a "security interest" in the goods, or even though a "document of title" (bill of lading or warehouse receipt) is to be delivered to the buyer at a different time or place. These documents are discussed more fully later in this chapter.

The four specific rules cover the two common arrangements where the goods are to be moved as part of the contract for sale and the two common situations not involving any further movement of the goods by the seller. If the contract merely authorizes the seller to make the arrangement for shipping the goods to the buyer, but it does not require the seller to deliver the goods at their destination, title is presumed to pass at the time and place of shipment. In the other "movement" case, where the seller is required to make delivery of the goods at their destination, title is not presumed to pass until there is a proper tender (offer) to deliver. A proper tender means that the seller must get the goods to the place where they are to be delivered to the buyer and give the buyer any notice reasonably necessary to enable the buyer to receive delivery.

In the two "nonmovement" cases, the goods are already at the location where the buyer is to take delivery. In one case, they are in the possession of a third party (usually a warehouse); in the other, they are in the seller's possession. If the seller is not required to move the goods but is required to deliver to the buyer a "document of title" (warehouse receipt or bill of lading) covering them, title is presumed to pass when the required document is delivered. (In this case, the seller is only required to give the buyer the document; the buyer can then go over to the warehouse whenever he or she wants to and get the goods.)

Where the seller is not required to move the goods or to deliver any documents, and the specific goods to which the contract applies have already been identified, title is presumed to pass "at the time and place of contracting;" that is, at the instant the contract is made. And the Code assumes that the place of delivery is the seller's place of business. In the typical used-car purchase, for example, "title" to the used car passes to the buyer at the instant he or she says, "I'll take it," since the seller has possession and is not required to move the car to any other location to make delivery. (In most states, this presumption would hold even though the state's motor vehicle registration requirements had not yet been complied with.)

Where title has already passed to the buyer under the above presumptions, it is passed back to the seller either by the buyer's rejection of the goods, whether the rejection is justified or not, or by the buyer's revocation of his or her previous acceptance, but only if such revocation is justified. In other words, if the buyer refuses delivery and sends the goods back, the goods again "belong to" the seller on the way back; but if the buyer has accepted the goods and then tries to revoke that acceptance by sending the goods back, title is not revested in the seller unless the buyer can show a justification for his or her action.

The *Martin* case applies these "title" rules.

MARTIN v. NAGER
469 A.2d 519 (N.J. Super., 1983)

FACTS: This controversy requires a determination of the ownership of an automobile and involves the interplay between the Motor Vehicle Certificate of Ownership Law and the Uniform Commercial Code-Sales. It arises out of a sale on consignment of a motor vehicle through an automobile dealer. Plaintiffs Rose and Gary Martin bought an automobile owned by defendant George Norton Nager through a dealer, Bellbrook Volkswagen, Inc., who converted the purchase price and is now insolvent. Plaintiffs and defendant both are victims of Bellbrook's fraud. Plaintiffs have possession of the automobile, defendant has possession of the certificate of title, Bellbrook is in bankruptcy and its two principals are in jail. The court is aware of at least twenty-one more transactions with the same or similar scenario involving Bellbrook.

In the fall of 1982, defendant placed ads in a local newspaper offering his 1975 BMW 530 automobile for sale. He received a telephone call from a salesman from Bellbrook located in Brooklawn, New Jersey, who indicated that Bellbrook had been very successful in selling fine used cars under a consignment agreement. Under this arrangement, Bellbrook would attempt to sell the automobile, absorb all the advertising costs, and arrange for financing of the sale. If it were sold, the defendant would receive an agreed price and Bellbrook would keep all proceeds of sale in excess of agreed price.

On October 18, 1982, defendant took the BMW to Bellbrook and met with one of the principals, Michael Sargent. Bellbrook was an authorized automobile dealer with a display room and a large outside area with a selection of many automobiles. Defendant agreed to accept $5,800 as his share of the sale and entered into a consignment agreement on the same date.

Defendant delivered the BMW together with the keys to Bellbrook but retained the certificate of ownership which he agreed to endorse when he was paid $5,800. He agreed to permit Bellbrook to offer for sale the BMW for a period of twenty-one days. In mid-November, defendant called Bellbrook to find out if it had any success in selling his automobile. He was informed that while the automobile had not been sold it had generated considerable interest. He agreed to leave the automobile with Bellbrook under the same conditions for another unspecified period of time.

On December 7, 1982, plaintiffs purchased defendant's vehicle from Bellbrook for $7,155. Bellbrook delivered the vehicle to the plaintiffs and assured them the certificate of title would be delivered promptly. After several unsuccessful attempts to get the certificate of title, on January 10, 1983, plaintiffs went to the Division of Motor Vehicles and, after presenting their proof of purchase, received a temporary registration which was effective only until January 31, 1983.

On January 25, 1983, defendant went to Bellbrook to retrieve his automobile since he had not been notified that it had been sold. He was shocked to learn that his automobile had been sold on December 7, 1982. He demanded his $5,800 but

Sargent indicated that he was waiting for a check to clear the bank. Sargent gave defendant a check dated January 27, 1983. The check was deposited but returned with a notation that payment had been stopped. After several unsuccessful attempts to obtain payment from Bellbrook, defendant reported the matter to the Brooklawn chief of police.

On February 24, 1983, plaintiffs filed this action to restrain defendant from repossessing the automobile and to require transfer of the certificate of title to them. An order was entered restraining the defendant from repossessing the automobile. Subsequently, on defendant's application, an order was entered restraining plaintiffs from using the automobile and requiring them to provide for its storage as well as a certificate insuring defendant as a loss payee on their insurance policy.

 JUDGE DEIGHAN:

[The Martins] contend they are buyers in the ordinary course of business. A "buyer in the ordinary course of business" is a "person who in good faith and without knowledge that the sale to him is in violation of the ownership rights or security interest of a third-party in the goods, buys in ordinary course from a person in the business of selling goods of that kind...."

Plaintiffs maintain that these sections of the UCC control the present case because defendant entrusted his BMW to Bellbrook with an express authorization to sell the automobile. Relying upon the representations of Bellbrook, plaintiffs assert they purchased the automobile in good faith without notice of the defendant's ownership interest. This, they contend, is in accord with a strong policy in New Jersey to protect buyers in the ordinary course of business and to facilitate commercial transactions.

Defendant counters by asserting that plaintiffs' purchase is in violation of the Motor Vehicle Certificate of Ownership Law...and therefore void and unenforceable. He points out that under the MVCOL, "when a used motor vehicle is sold in this state, the seller shall ... execute and deliver to the purchaser, an assignment of the certificate of ownership...." It further requires that no person shall sell or purchase any motor vehicle in this state, except in the manner and subject to the conditions provided in this chapter. Since defendant never relinquished his certificate of ownership, he asserts that the sale of the automobile to plaintiffs was in contravention of the statute, and therefore void and unenforceable....

The arduousness of this decision is due to the fact that plaintiffs and defendant are both innocent victims of the fraud perpetrated by Bellbrook. The apparent conflict between the provisions of the UCC and the MVCOL arises because the transfer of a motor vehicle, unlike the transfer of other chattels, must be made in accordance with documentary evidence executed only in the method prescribed by the MVCOL.... But these statutes should be read and construed together and given fair effect to both if possible....

The basic goals of the UCC and MVCOL are in perfect harmony; the UCC is to protect good faith purchasers and, as will be later discussed, the purpose of the MVCOL is to protect innocent purchasers of motor vehicles. Therefore, these statutes should complement and support each other rather than contradict or abrogate the other as suggested by defendant. Other jurisdictions have reconciled Sections 2-403(2), (3) of the UCC with comparable motor vehicle titling acts.

The purpose of the Motor Vehicle Certificate of Ownership Law is to regulate and control titles and possession of motor vehicles and to prevent the sale and purchase of motor vehicles with fraudulent titles.... The scheme of the motor vehicle certificates is to prevent the transfer of stolen vehicles, ... to regulate exclusively titles and evidence of ownership and to prevent fraud and theft of motor vehicles, ... and to prevent sales of automobiles to innocent purchasers by one having no legal title thereto.... The MVCOL is largely designed to protect the ordinary automobile buyer.... The act seeks to accomplish this by requiring the vendor to transmit with the delivery of the car the original bill of sale as evidence of title....

N.J.S.A. 39:10-9 requires that when a used motor vehicle is sold, the seller shall execute and deliver to the purchaser an assignment of the certificate of ownership. N.J.S.A. 39:10-11 requires that a purchaser of a motor vehicle shall, within ten days after its purchase, submit to the director evidence of the purchase. Upon presentation of the certificate, with the proper assignment and certification of the seller, a record of the transaction is made and filed by the director and a certificate of ownership issued and delivered to the buyer. N.J.S.A. 39:10-21 requires all dealers of motor vehicles to retain certificates of ownership for all motor vehicles in their possession. Failure to produce the certificate after a demand by the commissioner or his agent may result in a seizure and impounding of the motor vehicle....

On the other hand, where there is no intention to evade the statute and the parties contemplated the prompt executing and delivery of the prescribed title papers, the transaction is not to be considered void under the MVCOL merely because the papers were not delivered at the moment the bargain was struck nor when the buyer took possession of the vehicle....

Next to be considered is the UCC. Section 2-403(2) ... provides that any entrusting of possession of goods to a merchant who deals in goods of that kind gives him power to transfer all rights of the entruster to a buyer in ordinary course of business....

The UCC provisions substantially change pre-code law to enhance the protection given buyers in the ordinary course of business from dealers of such goods. Thus, under the code, delivery to a merchant for purposes of sale or resale expands the principle of prior law that delivery to a factor or dealer for such purposes confers on the latter power to make a valid sale even though made under circumstances violating the particular authority given.... Moreover, the UCC broadens pre-code law so that even a bailee, who has no authority whatever to make a sale, can confer good title to goods on a third-party, if such bailee regularly sells the same kind of goods. In addition, a sale by a merchant-intermediary in violation of the terms under which the goods were entrusted to him will, nevertheless, confer good title on a buyer in the ordinary course of business....

Under the UCC the retention of the certificate of title of the BMW by defendant and the reservation of the title as between defendant and Bellbrook is ineffective as against plaintiffs.... Defendant as an entruster gave Bellbrook "power to transfer all rights [of defendant] to a buyer in the ordinary course of business."... The sale was valid but defendant failed to execute and deliver an assignment of the certificate of ownership as required by N.J.S.A. 39:10-9....

In view of the foregoing, it is held that title to the BMW is vested in the plaintiffs. The purpose of the MVCOL is not circumvented by this holding but to the contrary is accomplished by requiring the defendant to fulfill an obligation to plaintiffs. As between the parties, a sale without an assignment of a certificate of ownership may be effective where there was no intent to evade the MVCOL....

An order may be presented by plaintiffs' attorney requiring defendant to execute and deliver the certificate of title to plaintiffs transferring title of the BMW to plaintiffs. Also, the prior order of the court requiring plaintiffs to store the motor vehicle and to carry insurance with the loss payee in favor of defendant will be vacated.

Risk of Loss. Article 2 treats "risk of loss" as a separate and distinct ownership interest. Stated most simply, risk of loss means responsibility for the goods: As between the buyer and the seller, who gets stuck for the value of the goods when they are destroyed or damaged by an "act of God" or by a third party? Who has to try to recover from the third party or from an insurance company?

Once the goods are identified, the parties can allocate the risk of loss on the goods in any way they wish. Merely giving the buyer a right to inspect the goods at a particular time and place does not postpone the passing of risk of loss, unless that result is also specified. If the parties have not made any specific agreement as to when risk of loss passes, Article 2 again provides a set of common sense presumptions.

In the two "movement" cases, the presumptions for risk of loss are basically the same as those for the passing of title. If the seller is authorized to ship but is not required to deliver, risk passes when the goods are delivered to the carrier, even though the seller has reserved the right to possession (COD shipment) or a security interest against the goods. A seller who is required to deliver keeps the risk of loss until the goods arrive at their destination and are duly tendered to the buyer.

Where the goods are in the possession of a bailee, such as a warehouse or a carrier, and are to be delivered to the buyer without further movement to another place, risk of loss passes when any one of three things happens:

1. When the buyer receives a negotiable document of title on the goods.

2. When the buyer receives a nonnegotiable document of title or other written delivery order on the goods and has had a reasonable amount of time to present the bailee with it and to pick up the goods.

3. When the bailee acknowledges the buyer's right to possession of the goods.

The reason for the difference between negotiable and nonnegotiable documents is that the negotiable document requires the carrier or the warehouse to give the goods to the bearer of the document or to the order of someone named in the document. Whether issued to the bearer or to someone's order, the document itself thus indicates that someone other than the party who originally turned over the goods may present the document and demand redelivery. Since the carrier or warehouse is alerted to this possibility from the beginning of the transaction, no extra time is allowed for the buyer to present the document. Nonnegotiable documents require that buyers be given a reasonable chance to identify themselves and explain why they, rather than the sellers, are picking up the goods.

Where the goods are in the seller's possession and the buyer is to come over and pick them up, there are two different rules as to when risk passes, depending on whether or not the seller is a merchant. Sellers who are not merchants pass risk when they tender delivery to the buyer; but sellers who are merchants do not pass risk to the buyer until actual receipt of goods by the buyer. This special "risk" rule where the seller is a merchant represents an important change from prior law.

The *Burnett* case applies these rules on risk of loss.

BURNETT v. PURTELL
1992 Ohio App. LEXIS 3467

FACTS: This appeal comes from the Painesville Municipal Court where appellant, Betty Jean Purtell, Executrix of the Estate of Lena M. Holland, was ordered to pay appellees, Richard Burnett, et. al., $6,500 plus interest at ten percent per annum from May 17, 1991.

Appellees agreed to purchase a mobile home with shed from appellant. On Saturday, March 3, 1990, appellees paid appellant $6,500 and in return were given the certificate of title to the mobile home as well as a key to the mobile home, but no keys to the shed.

At the time the certificate of title was transferred, the following items remained in the mobile home: the washer and dryer, mattress and box springs, two chairs, items in the refrigerator, and the entire contents of the shed. These items were to be retained by appellant and removed by appellant. To facilitate removal, the estate retained one key to the mobile home and the only keys to the shed.

On Sunday, March 4, 1990, the mobile home was destroyed by fire through the fault of neither party. At the time of the fire, appellant still had a key to the mobile home as well as the keys to the shed and she had not removed the contents of the mobile home nor the shed. The contents of the shed were not destroyed and have now been removed by appellant.

The referee determined that the risk of loss remained with appellant because there was no tender of delivery. Appellant objected to the conclusion of law, but the trial court overruled the objection and entered judgment in favor of appellee.

 JUDGE FORD:

First, appellant argues that because the certificate of title was transferred, appellees were given a key to the mobile home and the full purchase price was paid by appellees, that the risk of loss had shifted from appellant to appellees....

[R]isk of loss is no longer determined by who holds title....

After reviewing [the UCC], it is clear that subsection (C) applies as appellant was neither to ship the mobile home by carrier nor was the mobile home to be held by a bailee....

It is clear that neither party meets the definition of merchant and therefore the second clause of ... (C) applies.

The trial court found that there was no tender of delivery under the contract. If this determination is correct, then the risk of loss remained with appellant.... [T]ender of delivery requires that: (1) the goods be conforming, (2) the seller put and hold the goods at the buyer's disposition, and (3) the seller give the buyer any notification reasonably necessary to enable him to take delivery....

Analyzing the foregoing elements it is clear that, as the trial court stated, appellant did not tender delivery. The parties agreed that appellees would purchase the mobile home and shed from appellant. The contents of both the shed and the mobile home were to be retained by appellant and removed by appellant. At the time of the fire, appellant had not removed the items that she was required to remove from either the mobile home or the shed. Additionally, all keys to the mobile home were not surrendered and none of the keys to the shed were relinquished. Under this scenario, appellant did not tender conforming goods free of items belonging to her which remained in the trailer, nor did she put the mobile home at appellee's disposition without being fettered with the items previously enumerated. Accordingly, the trial court was correct in determining that appellant did not tender delivery within the meaning of the statute, and consequently the risk of loss remained with her....

Based on the foregoing, the judgment of the trial court is affirmed.

Where the seller's tender of delivery or the seller's delivery "fails to conform to the contract" so as to give the buyer the right to reject the goods, the risk of loss stays with the seller until the seller "cures" the problem or until the buyer agrees to accept the goods anyway. Where the buyer rightfully revokes a prior acceptance, the seller must bear any loss not covered by the buyer's insurance. Where the buyer breaches after conforming goods have been identified to the contract, but before risk has passed to the buyer, the buyer must bear any loss not covered by the seller's insurance. In these breach cases, the basic risk of loss rule is: "The bad guy loses."

If the buyer has the risk when the loss occurs, the buyer owes the seller the contract price. If the goods are identified, but then totally lost before risk has passed to the buyer, the contract is avoided. In that case, neither party has rights against the other. If there is a partial loss of identified goods before risk passes, the buyer may demand delivery of the remaining goods at a reduced price.

Right to Possession of the Goods. The Code also recognizes that a party may have title and risk of loss and yet not have an immediate "right to the goods." One obvious case where this occurs is the COD contract: When the seller ships the goods as agreed, the buyer has title, risk of loss, and a special property interest and an insurable interest in the goods, but does not yet have the right to possession because the COD term requires payment to get delivery. Another common separation of the right to possession from title and risk occurs when goods are shipped or stored by a carrier or a warehouse. Article 7 of the Code gives such persons a possessory "lien" for their services, meaning that they can hold (and if necessary sell) the goods until their charges are paid. Either the buyer or the seller may have title and risk of loss, but neither of them has the right to possession of the goods until the carrier or warehouse gets paid.

Security Interest. Finally, where the goods are being used as collateral to secure payment of the balance due on the contract price, the financing agency, which could be the seller, a bank, or other lender, has a "security interest" in them. Stated most simply, this security interest means that if the debtor defaults, the creditor (the "secured party") has the right to get possession of the goods, to resell them, and to apply the proceeds to pay off the balance due on the debt. Section 2-401(1) says that any attempt by the seller to withhold "title" on goods which are shipped or delivered to the buyer "is limited in effect to a reservation of a security interest." What the seller has to do is to make sure that there is a valid security interest. The legal requirements of such secured transactions are covered in Article 9 of the UCC; Chapters 18 and 19 will discuss secured transactions at greater length.

Special Sale Arrangements. The Code also provides specific rules to cover several frequently used special sale arrangements: sale on approval, sale or return, consignment, and sale by auction. In any situation in which one person has possession of goods which belong to someone else or which may be returned to someone else, third parties may be deceived by appearances. Creditors may rely on those goods in extending credit to the apparent owner, or a third party may wish to buy the goods from the possessor. Where the buyer has the option of returning goods even though they conform to the contract, the transaction is presumed to be a sale on approval if the buyer bought primarily for personal use and a sale or return if the goods were purchased primarily for resale to others.

In a sale on approval, the buyer has possession of someone else's goods as a bailee, to use them according to the terms of the trial contract. The seller still "owns" the goods; that is, the seller has both title and risk of loss. Title and risk do not pass to the buyer until the buyer accepts the goods, either expressly or by doing something that indicates an intent to exercise ownership, or until the agreed trial period expires with the buyer still in possession and not having notified the seller that they will be returned.

In a sale or return, title and risk pass to the buyer under the normal presumptions but with the option of returning the goods in accordance with the terms of the contract. Any such "return" is at the buyer's risk and expense, unless otherwise agreed.

In a consignment arrangement, the "buyer" (a retail store, for example) is not really a buyer at all, but rather a bailee-agent who has possession of someone else's goods and the power to sell the goods to third parties. As between this consignee (the retail store) and the consignor (a manufacturer, for example), the consignor retains title and risk on the goods until they are sold to third parties. Out of fairness to the creditors of the consignee, however, the Code says that they can treat the transaction as if it were a sale or return, unless the consignee's creditors know generally that the consignee engages in such transactions or unless the consignor publicly files a financing statement under Article 9's provisions or posts a sign on the consignee's premises in accordance with an applicable state statute.

Section 2-328 contains some special "offer and acceptance" rules for sales by **auction**. Whether the goods have to be sold to the highest bidder depends on whether the sale is **with reserve** or **without reserve**. Unless specific notice is given otherwise, it is assumed that the auction is with reserve, meaning that the auctioneer "may withdraw the goods at any time until he announces completion of the sale." When the auctioneer, Colonel Fasthammer, receives offers in the form of bids, his acceptance occurs when he raps his hammer (and hollers "Sold!") or in any other customary manner. Until the hammer falls, any bid can be withdrawn, but such a withdrawal does not revive any previous bid. In an auction without reserve, the auctioneer is making the offer and the bids are acceptances. Since the goods are already identified and (usually) no further delivery by the seller is required, title and risk would be presumed to pass to the buyer when the acceptance occurs.

SHIPMENT AND STORAGE OF GOODS

Bill of Lading—A Document of Title. Most goods shipped have no specific title registration certificates. The shipper simply delivers the goods to the common carrier with instructions to transport and deliver them, or the common carrier comes to the residence or business of the shipper and picks up the goods with instructions as to their transportation and delivery.

At the point where the shipper turns over possession to the common carrier, a document showing ownership of the particular goods is necessary. This document is called a **bill of lading** if the transportation is by land or sea, and it is called an **air bill** if the transportation is by air. The bill of lading or air bill serves as both a receipt for the goods and as a contract that states the terms of the agreement to transport and deliver the goods. Title to the goods may be transferred from the shipper to another person or organization by transferring the bill of lading or air bill.

A bill of lading or an air bill can be negotiable or nonnegotiable. If the bill is negotiable, it will state that the goods are to be delivered to the bearer of the bill or to the order of a specific person or organization. If the bill simply consigns the goods to a specific person or organization at the point of delivery, then it is nonnegotiable and it is called a **straight bill of lading** or a **straight air bill**.

The bill of lading or air bill must describe the goods. Typically, it will state the weight of the goods and describe the number of items and the content of the shipment in such a manner that the person receiving the goods will be able to identify them as those which were entrusted to the carrier for shipment.

Article 7 of the UCC contains specific provisions governing the issuance and use of bills of lading. Normally, the bill of lading is issued to the shipper. The shipper can then mail the bill of lading to the person or organization that is to receive the goods at their final destination. However, UCC Section 7-305(1) allows the shipper to request that the common carrier issue the bill of lading directly to the person or organization receiving the goods at the final destination or at any other place which the shipper may request. Obviously, situations arise where mailing the bill of lading to the receiver of the goods would be unwise. It would be better to have the bill of lading issued by the carrier directly to the person or organization receiving the goods prior to or at the time of delivery.

If the bill of lading is negotiable, then the carrier may not deliver the goods without getting the bill of lading properly indorsed by the person or organization receiving them. If the goods are shipped under a nonnegotiable bill of lading, the carrier can simply deliver them to the person or organization named as consignee in the bill, and the bill of lading need not be indorsed by the receiving party. With a nonnegotiable bill, the carrier must verify that the receiving party is in fact the party to whom the shipment was supposed to be delivered. If the carrier delivers the goods to the wrong person, the carrier will be responsible to the shipper.

Warehouse Receipts—Another Document of Title. Every warehouse that stores goods for the public must issue a **warehouse receipt** to the bailor when the bailor leaves goods for storage. There is no specific statutory form that must be used. However, the receipt must contain certain essential terms, such as the *location* of the warehouse, the *date* the receipt was issued, and the *consecutive number* of the receipt. It also must contain a statement about *delivery*. Will the goods be delivered to the *bearer* of the receipt, or to the order of a specified person? If so, the receipt is negotiable. Or, will the goods be delivered only to a specified person, thus making the receipt nonnegotiable? The rates to be charged must also be stated, and the goods must be described so that they can later be identified. The receipt must be signed by an employee or agent of the warehouse, and if any advances have been made or any liabilities incurred, an explanation must be made on the receipt. Section 7-202 of the UCC governs the contents of the warehouse receipt. The special duties of both carriers and warehouses are discussed further in Chapter 26.

Common Shipping Terms. Since in the "movement" cases the location of title and risk will probably depend on whether the seller has met contractual duties, it is important to know what certain commonly used shipping terms require the seller to do. In addition to the **COD** (collect on delivery) term discussed earlier, the abbreviations **FOB** (free on board), **FAS** (free alongside), and **CIF** (cost, insurance, and freight) are commonly used.

The FOB term is used in combination with a named city, for example, FOB Chicago. The seller's obligation is to get the goods into the possession of a carrier and to get them to the specified place. Whether this is a shipment contract or a delivery contract depends on whether "Chicago" is the seller's city or the buyer's city. If the FOB contract also specifies a vessel, car, or other vehicle, the seller must also "at his own expense and risk load the goods on board;" in other words, the seller is responsible for getting the goods into the buyer's designated carrier.

The FAS term is used in connection with a particular vessel, for example, FAS *S.S. Mariner*. The seller must deliver the goods alongside that vessel in accordance with the port's custom, or on a dock specified by the buyer; the seller must also get a receipt for the goods and tender it to the buyer so that the buyer can get a bill of lading from the vessel's operator.

The CIF contract provides the buyer with the convenience of making one lump-sum payment to the seller, after the seller has made all the arrangements for shipping the goods. The seller is obligated to pay the carrier's freight charges (or to get credit from the carrier) and to obtain the customary insurance policy on the goods while they are in transit. (A C&F contract omits the insurance requirement.) The seller then forwards to the buyer all the required paperwork: the freight receipt, the bill of lading, the insurance policy, the seller's own invoice for the package price, and a negotiable draft for the total invoice price. Normally, these papers will be sent to a bank in the buyer's city where the buyer has made credit arrangements; the bank has instructions to give the buyer the negotiable bill of lading (without which the buyer can't get the goods) only after the buyer signs the negotiable draft, thus indicating that the buyer will pay the draft when it becomes due. The bank then buys the draft from the seller and sends the seller the cash. Everyone's happy: the buyer has the goods and whatever credit period is specified in the draft in which to pay for them; the seller has the cash, with no risk of nonpayment; and the buyer's bank earns the interest rate provided for in the draft. This very common transaction shows how Articles 2, 3, 4, and 7 come together to cover the various aspects of a single commercial transaction.

"ENTRUSTING" AND BULK SALES

Two special situations involving claims by third parties against the goods have arisen frequently enough to require special legal rules. The "title" sections of Article 2 provide the rules for settling disputes which occur because of "defects" in the seller's title to the goods. "Bulk sales" problems are dealt with in Article 6.

SALE BY SELLER WITH VOID OR VOIDABLE TITLE

Defects in Seller's Title. In any number of situations, a person might possess goods which he or she doesn't own, or have a voidable title to such goods because someone else has the power to rescind a previous sale transaction. What happens when the person in possession of such goods sells them to a good faith purchaser? Which of the two innocent parties should the law protect—the original owner or the good faith purchaser? Since only one of these parties can win the litigation for ownership of the goods, the other party will sustain a loss unless he or she can find and collect against the "middleman." If you lend one of your books to a friend, and that person sells it along with some of his or her own books, either intentionally or by mistake, you can clearly sue your friend for the value of the book. The more basic question, however, is whether or not you can locate the buyer and get the book back.

The Code's basic approach to this sort of problem is to distinguish between a seller who has a "void" title (that is, no title at all) and a seller whose title to the goods is voidable because of some irregularity in that person's acquisition of the goods. Except for the very special case you are about to read, the general rule is that a person with no title passes no title to his or her buyer. Where your watch is lost, stolen, or lent and then sold by the finder, thief, or bailee, you get the watch back from the buyer if you can prove what happened, even if the buyer was acting in good faith. On the other hand, where there was in fact a sales transaction between the original owner and the seller and the original owner intended at that time to make the seller the owner of the goods, a good faith purchaser from the seller keeps the goods, even though the original sale is voidable because of minority, fraud, duress, nonpayment, or similar irregularity.

UCC 2-403(1) says that a buyer has the power to transfer a good title to a good faith purchaser even though: (a) the seller was deceived as to the buyer's identity; (b) the buyer gave the seller a bad check; (c) the parties agreed that the sale was to be for cash, and the seller didn't get the cash; or (d) the buyer committed a criminal fraud. In all these situations, the Code is saying that the seller should take the loss, unless the seller can get recourse against the original buyer; the third party/good faith purchaser from the original buyer is protected. "Good faith" is defined as "honesty in fact." "Purchase" includes any voluntary transaction creating an interest in property. "Value" includes "any consideration sufficient to support a simple contract." If a third party has taken the goods from the original buyer under these conditions, the third party owns them free and clear of the original seller's claim of fraud, nonpayment, or the like.

Appearance of Authority to Sell. Where the original owner created a situation in which it appeared to reasonable third parties that the bailee was really the owner of the goods or that the bailee had the power to sell the goods for the owner, a good faith purchaser from the bailee would keep the goods. The reason for this different result is based on the principle of estoppel. The original owner is responsible for the appearance of authority to sell. As between the original owner and an innocent third party who relied in good faith on such appearances, the innocent third party should be protected. The main problem in such a case, both before and after the adoption of the Code, has been to determine what actions by the original owner are sufficient to create this "appearance of authority" to sell.

Entrusting to a Merchant. The Code creates a conclusive presumption of such an "appearance of authority" in only one situation—an "entrusting" of possession of goods to a merchant who deals in goods of that kind. Entrusting is defined in Section 2-403(3) as including any delivery of possession or any acquiescence in retention of possession. Where such an entrusting occurs, the merchant has the *power* (not the right) to transfer all rights of the entruster to a buyer in the ordinary course of business (BIOC). If you left your watch for repair at a jewelry store that sold watches, or if you bought a new watch at the store but left it there on a layaway plan until you could pay for it, you have given the watch merchant the power to transfer all your rights in the watch to a good faith purchaser (BIOC). The buyer keeps "your" watch; you have to sue the merchant wrongfully selling your property. Notice, however, that if a thief stole your watch and left it for repair, you could still recover it from a BIOC, since the merchant had only the power to pass whatever title the thief had (none). This section thus goes further than the law ever has in protecting good faith purchasers. The *Locke* case illustrates this point.

LOCKE v. ARABI GRAIN & ELEVATOR COMPANY, INC.
399 S.E.2d 705 (Ga. App., 1990)

FACTS: Appellant Bobby Locke, CEO and principal stockholder of Leeco Farm Center, Inc., d/b/a Worthco Farm Center, hired a Mr. Hobby as Worthco's manager. It was subsequently discovered that, during some thirteen months of his tenure as manager, Hobby had sold corn stored with Worthco to appellee Arabi Grain & Elevator Company and pocketed the proceeds. There was evidence that Hobby and members of his family had previously done business with Arabi, and that Arabi did not know that Hobby was employed by Worthco.

       In January 1989, Locke, the Commodity Credit Corporation (CCC), and Leeco executed an agreement whereby the CCC and Leeco transferred to Locke all rights to the allegedly stolen corn and to all causes of action against any or all who might have acquired the corn. Locke then brought an action in trover and conversion against Arabi. Arabi answered, alleging that the purchases were made in the ordinary course of business and in good faith and without notice of any claim that plaintiff might have on the goods; and that, since the allegedly stolen goods had been entrusted to Hobby by plaintiff, Hobby had the power to transfer all rights of the entruster to the defendant. Locke moved for summary judgment, as did Arabi. The trial court entered an order denying plaintiff's motion and granting that of defendant. Locke now appeals.

 JUDGE DEEN:

Plaintiff based his case on trover and conversion. Were this a simple trover case, the outcome in favor of Plaintiff would have been abundantly clear; however, the "entrusting statutes" of the Uniform Commercial Code ... call for a different result....

       An entrusting of property, defined by S.2-403(3)...as any acquiescence by the owner of goods in the retention of those goods by another, may result in the owner's loss of title to the property if the entrustee is a merchant who deals in similar goods. Under S.2-403(2), a merchant who deals in goods of the same kind as those entrusted is empowered to convey the same title as that held by the entrustor to a buyer in the ordinary course of business. While this provision protects buyers who may be unaware of the high risk that the property is owned by another person, it limits the original owner's remedy to seeking recovery for the value of the goods from the merchant....

The general thrust of the cases involving "entrusting" of goods to a dealer is aimed at the protection of the purchaser, where the latter acts in "good faith" and the owner takes the risk by placing or leaving his chattel with a merchant of his own choosing who could convert or otherwise misdeal it.... The Georgia courts have similarly protected the good faith purchaser in the "entrusting" situations, both under the UCC ... and under the old sales law.... These latter pre-UCC cases reach the same result based in varying degrees on "estoppel" or "apparent authority" or both. The protection afforded the purchaser "is merely a special application of the broad equitable principle that where one of two innocent persons must suffer loss by reason of the fraud or deceit of another, the loss should rightly fall upon him by whose act or omission the wrongdoer has been enabled to commit the fraud."...

This court has continued to apply the statutory language in the same manner as in the cases cited in the trial court's order above. "The language of [OCGA S.11-2-403(2), (3)] is quite clear: actual entrustment to the merchant, or dealer, gives the power to transfer 'all rights of the entruster' to a buyer in the ordinary course of business."... We find no error below.

Judgment affirmed.

BULK SALES

The Problem Defined. Bulk sales also involve third parties who may have claims against the seller's goods and who wish to assert those claims even though the goods are now in the hands of a good faith purchaser. This problem, however, arises in a different context. The seller here is a merchant "whose principal business is the sale of merchandise from stock, including those who manufacture what they sell." This definition excludes farmers, contractors, and service enterprises. The seller does own the goods involved—the inventory—but instead of selling it in the normal course of business, a **bulk transfer** is made; that is, a single transfer involving a "major part" of the inventory. The problem arises because some sellers want to play "take the money and run:" they sell all their inventory to an innocent buyer, pocket the cash, and leave town without paying off their business creditors. The purpose of prior bulk sales laws and of Article 6 of the Code is to try to protect both the seller's creditors and the buyer by specifying a required procedure for bulk transfers, with the main burden of compliance placed on the bulk seller.

Basic Requirements. In most cases, the required procedure should be easy enough to follow. The buyer and seller prepare a schedule of the goods to be transferred. The seller furnishes the buyer with a list of the seller's creditors and their addresses. This list must be sworn to by the seller, and the buyer is not liable for any inaccuracies unless that person actually knows that a creditor's name has been omitted. The buyer is then responsible for notifying each listed creditor, either in person or by registered or certified mail, that the bulk transfer is to occur. This notice must be given at least ten days before the buyer takes possession of the goods or makes a payment on the price. The notice must also contain the names and business addresses of the seller and the buyer and, if provision has been made for paying off the creditors, the address to which they should send their bills for payment. If no arrangement has been made for paying off the creditors, a "long form" notice must be used, which includes the estimated total of the seller's debts, the description and location of the goods to be transferred, the address where the creditor list and property schedule may be inspected, and the consideration received by the seller for the goods. The buyer must either preserve the schedule and list for six months for inspection, or simply file this information with the specified public official.

If these steps have been followed, the buyer owns the goods free and clear of any claims of the seller's unsecured creditors, except in those few states which have adopted optional Section 6-106. This part of the Code makes the buyer personally responsible for seeing to it that the purchase price is applied to pay off the seller's creditors. If the required steps have not been followed, the seller's creditors can have the bulk goods seized and sold to satisfy their claims if they bring suit within six months after the transfer occurred or, if the transfer was "concealed," within six months after they discover what happened. In any case, a good faith purchaser from the bulk transferee owns the goods free and clear of claims of the original seller's creditors.

In those states which have adopted optional Section 6-106, the bulk buyer needs to be much more careful, since noncompliance can make the buyer personally liable to the unpaid creditors.

The *Schlussel* case discusses the relationship of these rules to a landlord's claim for rent.

SCHLUSSEL v. EMMANUEL ROTH CO.
637 A.2d 944 (N.J. Super., 1994)

FACTS: Plaintiff landlord appeals the dismissal of his claim under the Uniform Commercial Code Bulk Transfer Act, for rental payments not due and owing at the time of transfer of the assets of his tenant, defendant Emmanuel Roth Co., to defendant Novtex Corporation. The claim was rejected by the trial judge on the basis that plaintiff was not a creditor within the meaning of the act as to future rents at the time of transfer. Plaintiff also appeals a judgment entered in his favor for a rentor's lien in the amount of rent that was due as of the date of transfer reduced by the amount of Roth's security deposit. Finally, plaintiff appeals a no cause jury verdict on his claims against defendant Daniel Bird, president of Novtex, and defendants John Carpenter and Carl Funke, shareholders of Roth, for their alleged fraudulent misrepresentations that Novtex would assume the lease and alleged concealment of the removal of Roth's assets and business from the premises. Novtex cross-appeals from the rentor's lien judgment.

In October 1980, plaintiff and Roth executed a five-year lease for a portion of plaintiff's industrial building in Carlstadt. In October 1985, the lease was modified and extended to October 1995. As modified, the lease provided for an annual lease rent of $76,483.00 payable in monthly installments of $6,373.58, with a rent adjustment every two and one-half years. In addition, the lease provided for payments of a percentage of certain expenses, including taxes, insurance, and maintenance of common areas. The monthly rent was due the first of the month, but if not paid by the fifteenth of each month, a late charge would be assessed.

Pursuant to Article 15 of the lease, a default in payment of its rental obligations under the lease would occur if Roth failed to make such payments upon ten days written notice by plaintiff. Upon such default, plaintiff could terminate the lease upon five days notice, enter and repossess the premises. If so terminated, the lease established damages as either "[a] sum which represents any excess of: (i) the aggregate of the rent, impositions and additional rent for the balance of the term if the lease was not so terminated; over (ii) the net rental value of the demised premises at the effective date of such termination, both discounted at the rate of 4 percent (4%) per annum" or, at plaintiff's option, "[s]ums equal to the rent, impositions and additional rent, when the same would have been payable if not for such termination, less any net rents received by Landlord, from any reletting, after deducting all costs incurred in connection with such termination and reletting...."

Roth produced and distributed narrow fabric and trimmings at the premises. In December 1986, Carpenter and Funke purchased all of Roth's stock, and continued to operate the business. They received loans from Chemical Bank to finance this acquisition and Chemical Bank obtained a security interest in Roth's assets, which was perfected in 1987. By September 1988, the company was in financial trouble. One of the rent checks to plaintiff had bounced and, in Carpenter's words, the business was borrowing from Peter to pay Paul. Carpenter and Funke did not want to file for bankruptcy, and their alternatives were either finding a partner to allow them to continue to run the business or identifying a purchaser for the business.

In October 1988, Carpenter and Funke advised plaintiff by letter that they were seeking his help in marketing their premises. Plaintiff promoted the availability of the space to the brokerage community and Roth advertised it in the newspaper. Roth also showed the space to potential lessees.

During that time, Novtex emerged as a potential buyer for Roth. On November 9, 1988, Carpenter, Funke, and Novtex entered into an agreement for purchase of assets. Pursuant to that agreement, Novtex assumed responsibility for all of Roth's orders, including back orders and future orders, and for its inventory. It also assumed leases for five automobiles, for xerox, telex, and postage equipment, and for the telephone system. Novtex did not assume the lease with plaintiff.

Also during this November 1988 time period, Bird, Funke, and Carpenter met with plaintiff's son, Marc Schlussel. Most of the evidence presented to the jury on the fraud counts focused on whether Bird did or did not state at this meeting that, if and when the Novtex purchase was consummated, Novtex would assume Roth's lease and operate the business from Carlstadt.

The closing between Roth and Novtex occurred on January 13, 1989. As of that date, the January rent had not been paid and late fees for December's rent as well as maintenance fees had also not been paid. On January 11, 1989, plaintiff sent Roth notice of the total amount owed ($10,622). This notice was not received by Roth, however, until January 17 and pursuant to the lease, a default by Roth would not have occurred until January 22, 1989.

Pursuant to the liquidated damages provision of the lease, plaintiff calculated his damages as: (1) $85,556 unpaid base rent for 1989 plus interest of $83,422, (2) expenses as a result of the termination and reletting in the amount of $50,636 plus interest of $36,655, and (3) rental shortfall (the difference in the Roth rent and the new lease) of $137,285. No party has ever disputed these amounts and a judgment for $303,554 was entered against Roth.

Contending that he was a creditor of Roth at the time of the transfer of its assets, plaintiff claims he was entitled to notice of the transfer and to share in the proceeds that were distributed by Novtex to Roth's other creditors. He argues that Novtex, as a transferee of all of Roth's assets, is responsible for what would have been his share of the proceeds which he contends is $99,930 or 63.4 percent of that amount of the proceeds that was distributed to Roth's unsecured creditors.

 JUDGE CONLEY:

Bulk sales legislation was originally enacted around the turn of the century in response to a fraud perceived to be common: a merchant would acquire his stock in trade [on] credit, then sell his entire inventory and abscond with the proceeds leaving creditors unpaid.... Creditors had little recourse because the transfer of the goods to an innocent buyer immunized them from the reach of the seller's creditors and, even if the merchant could be found, inpersonam jurisdiction over him might not have been readily available....

It is accepted that only persons with claims at the time of the sale or transfer are included, and not persons who extend credit or whose claims come into existence after the sale or transfer. And generally, persons having liquidated claims at the time of sale or transfer are creditors entitled to protection even though their claims may not be due or payable at the time of sale.... Further, the fact that a claim may not, as of the date of transfer, have been reduced to judgment, does not preclude bulk sales laws protection. Thus, N.J.S.A. 12A:6-104(2) requires the transferor to include in the list of creditors persons known to assert a claim even though the claim may be disputed....

There is, however, little consistent treatment of what are characterized as unliquidated or contingent claims....

We focus here upon plaintiff's claim for rental obligations under the lease subsequent to termination. Both code and pre-code cases dealing with whether a landlord is a creditor within the meaning of bulk sales acts for such a claim are few and not in accord. In each case, the particular result is based upon how the claim for future rents is characterized and, in some instances, based upon an expansive view of the type of creditors covered by the act....

A contract of lease is peculiar in its nature, and differs in many respects from other contracts. Rent, as such, is an incident to, and grows out of, the use and occupancy, and is the consideration therefor. Unaccrued rent cannot be said, therefore, to be a fixed liability then absolutely owing, payable in the future, or, indeed, a "debt" of any kind, as that word seems to be used in the act. It is only an unmatured obligation to pay in the future a consideration for future enjoyment and occupancy. This cannot be said to be, properly speaking, a present debt, demand, or claim at all, as these words are apparently used in the foregoing provisions, due regard being had to the context, and cannot come within either the clause as to fixed liability then owing or a debt founded on contract....

Furthermore, in considering what type of claims were contemplated by the Legislature to entitle a "creditor" to protection, we note the act requires the seller to prepare a list of creditors "with the amounts when known" and the names of persons known to assert claims even though they may be disputed. But, contrariwise, the broad definition originally proposed, which would have included contingent or potential claims, was rejected. In this respect, the Legislature knows how to define "creditors" expansively....

We are inclined to agree with the view that a claim for future rents is beyond the scope of the bulk transfer act.... While the U.C.C. expressly includes "disputed" claims and thus clearly rejects those cases that suggest the need for a claim to be fixed and/or reduced to judgment, there is no indication the intent was to jettison the preexisting view that persons having claims that are contingent and become concrete upon the happening of subsequent events or circumstances, are not creditors within the meaning of the protections afforded the various bulk transfer acts....

Finally, we observe that New Jersey courts have consistently considered future rents as a contingent liabilities....

Even assuming plaintiff is a creditor entitled to the protection of the bulk transfer act, Novtex paid out the entire proceeds of the sale to other persons and companies who indisputably were "creditors" of Roth. It did under circumstances which indicate that the precise amounts of the claims were verified and the amounts paid were in good faith. Additionally, as evidenced by the jury verdict, Novtex had advised plaintiff several months prior to the sale that it was not assuming the lease and that it would remove Roth's assets by no later than the end of February. Other than the promise to ensure that the November and December rents would be brought current, plaintiff plainly was on notice that no further rents would be forthcoming. Not once is there any indication that prior to the sale any of the parties, including plaintiff, even contemplated the plaintiff could be a creditor within the meaning of the act for the purposes of its protections....

We, thus, affirm the dismissal of the bulk transfer act claim and the dismissal of the fraudulent misrepresentation claim. We modify the judgment pursuant to the Rentor's Lien Act to impose a lien in the amount of $10,622 upon Novtex and, as modified, affirm that judgment. We remand for the entry of an amended judgment consistent with this opinion.

Exceptions. Certain extraordinary transfers are not subject to the requirements of Article 6. Transfers pursuant to judicial processes or to satisfy certain preexisting obligations and transfers of property which is exempt from creditors' claims can be made without complying with Article 6. Article 6 also contains two exemptions that were not found in most of the old bulk sales statutes.

These two new exemptions will permit the sale of a business, including its inventories, without the necessity of compliance, where the buyer has an established, solvent business and agrees to assume the seller's debts, or where the buyer is a new enterprise organized to take over and continue the seller's business and the seller receives nothing from the bulk transfer except an interest in the new enterprise which is subordinate to the claims of the creditors. In both cases an unspecified "public notice" must be given, but otherwise these exceptions should provide considerable flexibility in reorganizing an existing business.

Tax and Other Special Statutes. In addition to the bulk sale problems discussed above, the buyer of a business will also need to be aware of possible claims against the business for unpaid taxes. Accrued social security and withholding taxes may be owed to the national government. Payments may be due to the state government for sales taxes, unemployment taxes, and workers' compensation coverage. Local real estate taxes and special assessments may not have been paid. In some cases, the tax statutes will provide that these accrued liabilities become liens against the business' assets. The buyer of the business may not be protected against such liens simply by complying with the Code's bulk sales requirements.

Also, if a transfer of real estate is involved in the sale of the business, the buyer needs to be aware of the possibility of adverse claims against the land. These matters are discussed more fully in Chapter 27. Article 6 has no application to transfers of land, only to bulk sales of inventory.

SIGNIFICANCE OF THIS CHAPTER

A modern economy cannot function effectively unless most buyers are assured that they will, in fact, own the goods they buy in good faith. The basic policy of the Code is to protect such good faith buyers against most adverse claims that might be made against the goods. Where one buys goods from a merchant-dealer in an ordinary business transaction, the Code states a conclusive presumption that the merchant was authorized to sell them if the owner voluntarily left them in the merchant's possession. Where one is buying a merchant's inventory "in bulk" and not in the ordinary course of business, Article 6 provides a relatively simple procedure to validate the transaction. In both cases, buyers are protected if they act in good faith and follow the law.

Although millions of sales contracts are made and performed each day without any problem arising, things go wrong in some cases. One of the parties fails to perform properly, or the goods are lost without the fault of either, or a third party asserts claims against the goods or otherwise tries to interfere with the transaction. The law needs to provide a set of rules to deal with these problem situations. The Code's approach is to provide a set of presumptions as to when the various ownership interests in the goods pass from the seller to the buyer or exist in favor of third parties.

As between the buyer and the seller, the most important presumptions are those dealing with risk of loss, since most such cases will involve that issue. Where one or more third parties are involved in the dispute, the case will usually require application of the presumptions for the other ownership interests: special property, insurable interest, title, right to possession, and security interest. A case pitting the seller or the buyer against a third party will usually have to be decided by applying the rules for one of these other five ownership interests. Both the parties to the sales transaction and third parties such as financing agencies thus need to know the rules governing the transfer of the various ownership interests from seller to buyer.

PROBLEMS FOR DISCUSSION

1. Freda Construction Company, working on a large electrical project, ordered three reels of burial cable from Cableus, Inc. By mistake, Cableus shipped one reel of burial cable and two reels of aerial cable, although all three cartons were labeled "burial cable." Freda's foreman rejected aerial cable but left them at the construction site because of their size and weight. Cableus was notified of the rejection but did not come out to pick up the two reels. Freda was unable to reship the two reels because of a trucker's strike. About four months later, the two reels of aerial cable were stolen from the construction site. Cableus sues for the contract price for the two cables.

   Discuss and decide.

2. Jane Zendman bought a diamond ring for $12,500 at an auction held at the gallery of Brand, Inc., on the boardwalk of Atlantic City, New Jersey.

   The ring had been entrusted to Brand by the defendant, Harry Winston, a diamond merchant located in New York City, under memorandums stating that the goods were for the jeweler's examination only and that title was not to pass until he had made his selection and had notified the defendant of his agreement to pay the stated price. Records disclosed that in the past other goods had been sent and later sold with payment accepted. A judgment in Zendman's favor in the trial court was reversed by the appellate division, and she appealed to the Court of Appeals.

   What should the decision of the appeals court be and why?

3. Stanley Jakowski bought a new automobile from Carole Chevrolet. As part of the contract, Carole promised to undercoat the car and to apply a polymer sealant to the exterior finish. When Jakowski picked up the car on May 19, these two operations had not been done. Carole realized what had happened the next day, called Jakowski and asked him to return the car for these treatments. Stanley brought the car back on May 22, and it was stolen from the lot that night, before the coatings had been applied.

   Is Carole Chevrolet liable for the theft of the car? Why?

4. Three weeks before Christmas, Fink opened a family shoe store in Buffalo, New York. In May he still had $19,000 worth of winter-style shoes. He sold 1,300 pairs for $3,549 to Rubenstein to clear his shelves of off-season shoes as well as to obtain cash to pay his debts and thus obtain credit for the purchase of new summer stock. Fink continued in business for six months after the sale, until the filing of a petition in bankruptcy in November. The plaintiff, the trustee in bankruptcy acting on behalf of the creditors, sued to hold the defendant, Jack Rubenstein, accountable under the Bulk Sales Act. The trial court held for Rubenstein, but the appellate division reversed. Rubenstein appealed.

   How should the final court of appeals decide?

5. Lamborn as the buyer and the Seggermans as the sellers entered into a written contract for the sale of "1200/50 lb. boxes Calif. Evap. apples—Extra Choice Quality—1994 crop." (The Seggermans had, in turn, made arrangements to buy 1,200 boxes of dried apples from a supplier, Rosenberg Brothers.) Lamborn was to pay 221/2 cents per pound "FOB Pacific Coast Rail Shipping Point.... Payment to be made against draft with documents attached." The Rosenbergs loaded a Southern Pacific railroad car with 1,770 boxes of dried apples and received an "order" bill of lading which provided for shipment to New York. Once they knew the apples were on the way, the Seggermans billed Lamborn for 1,200 boxes and gave Lamborn an order addressed to their delivery clerk at their place of business. Seeing these documents, Lamborn paid the contract price as agreed—$13,377. The apples never arrived in New York; they were seized en route by agents of the U.S. government, for reasons not disclosed by the court. Lamborn sued for a refund but lost in the lower court.

   If Lamborn appeals, how should the appeal court rule? Why?

Chapter 16

Warranties and Products Liability

Stop and think for a minute. How many times each day do you entrust your health and safety, and even your life, to a manufactured product? Your new electric blanket that you left on all night, the can of frozen orange juice that you opened for breakfast this morning (and the electric can opener that you used to open the orange juice), the car or bus that you used to get to school (and all the other motor vehicles that were on the highway at the same time)—a malfunction in any one of these or in thousands of other products that we encounter every day could produce sickness, injury, or even death. No product can be made absolutely safe, under any and all circumstances. Malfunctions do occur, with resulting personal injury, property damage, and financial loss. The law's function in this area is to provide the rules by which the burden of such losses will be allocated.

Earlier legal doctrine tended to "leave the loss where it was incurred;" that is, to force the injured parties to pay for their own injuries or to buy their own insurance to cover such losses. The modern legal trend, which has accelerated sharply during the last two decades, is to pass these losses back up the chain of distribution to sellers and manufacturers, as one of the costs of doing business. The net result of the modern product liability rules is that all of us as consumers will pay higher prices for products and that some of the smaller manufacturers in high-risk industries, such as chemicals and machinery, may be forced out of business because they cannot absorb these additional overhead costs. The courts' willingness to apply these modern theories of liability and to disallow traditional defenses has produced a crisis of major proportions and worldwide impact.

PLAINTIFFS, DEFENDANTS, AND THEORIES OF LIABILITY

In addition to the buyer of defective goods, other possible plaintiffs include members of the buyer's family and household, guests in the buyer's home, the buyer's employees and customers, and bystanders who have had no previous relationship with the buyer. In addition to the seller, possible defendants include the manufacturer or assembler of the product, the designer, the supplier of the defective component part, and any intermediate distributors. The availability of the manufacturer as a defendant becomes crucial in those cases where the seller is unable to pay the judgment, or where the injured buyer cannot remember where the brand name product that caused the injury was purchased, or where the injury resulted from long-continued use of the brand name product, such as lung cancer from smoking.

Modern courts have a wide selection of theories of liability which can be used to impose damages back up the chain of distribution: fraud, innocent misrepresentation, negligence, breach of express or implied warranty, and strict liability. Although these different theories of liability require different forms of proof and are subject to different defenses and different statutes of limitations, the courts are not always careful to distinguish which theory is being applied to produce liability in a particular case.

Generally, of the three major theories, negligence is the most difficult to prove from the plaintiff's standpoint, since plaintiff must prove that a specific careless act by the defendant caused plaintiff's injury. To recover based on a warranty theory, plaintiff must prove that defendant made a warranty, that it was breached, and that the breach caused plaintiff's injury. Strict liability is the easiest to prove, since plaintiff does not have to show that the defect in the goods was the result of carelessness, only that the defect existed when the goods left the defendant's control.

The Ohio court in *Grover* is trying to decide just how far "down the chain" liability extends.

GROVER v. ELI LILLY & CO.
591 N.E.2d 696 (OH, 1992)

FACTS: This case presents a certified question of state law from the United States District Court for the Northern District of Ohio, Eastern Division. For the purposes of the certified question, petitioners assert the following theory of liability based upon an agreed statement of facts. Respondents Cooper Laboratories, Inc. and Eli Lilly and Company manufactured and marketed diethylstilbestrol ("DES"), a defective prescription drug. In 1952 and 1953, June Rose ingested DES while she was pregnant. Her daughter, petitioner Candy Grover, was exposed to DES in utero and was born with injuries to her reproductive organs including the inability to carry a fetus to full term. Candy Grover subsequently delivered her son, petitioner Charles C. Grover, eleven weeks before term. Petitioners allege that as a result of his premature birth, Charles Grover suffers from cerebral palsy and other serious injuries.

Petitioners Candy Grover and Brent Grover, father of Charles and Robbie Grover, as his sons' representative, filed suit in the United States District Court for the Northern District of Ohio against Cooper Laboratories, Inc. and Eli Lilly and Company ("the pharmaceutical companies"). The pharmaceutical companies filed several motions for summary judgment, one of which states that Ohio law does not recognize a child's cause of action that is based on an actor's tortious conduct before the child was conceived. The district court certified the question to the Ohio Supreme Court.

DES was prescribed to pregnant women during the 1940s, 1950s, and 1960s to prevent miscarriage. The FDA banned its use by pregnant women in 1971 after medical studies discovered that female children exposed to the drug in utero had a high incidence of a rare type of vaginal cancer.

 JUSTICE WRIGHT:

Because the mother and the child whose injury results from her injury are uniquely interrelated, and because it is possible that the mother may not discover the extent of her own injury until she experiences difficulties during pregnancy, the facts of this case pose a novel issue. Courts and commentators refer to the child's potential cause of action in such cases as a "preconception tort...." The terminology stems from the fact that a child is pursuing liability against a party for a second injury that flows from an initial injury to the mother that occurred before the child was conceived.

Only a handful of courts have addressed whether a child has a cause of action for a preconception tort. One recurring issue is whether a child has a cause of action if a physician negligently performs a surgical procedure on the mother, such as an abortion or a Caesarean section, and the negligently performed procedure causes complications during childbirth several years later that injure the infant.... In another malpractice suit, the Illinois Supreme Court recognized that a child had a cause of action against a hospital that negligently transfused her mother with Rh positive blood eight years prior to the child's conception....

The facts of these cases are significantly different from those of the case before us. The cause of action certified to us involves the scope of liability for the manufacture of a prescription drug that allegedly has devastating side effects on the original patient's female fetus. However, this case is not about the devastating side effects of DES on the women who were exposed to it, which have indeed been well documented in medical studies and court opinions.... This case is concerned with the rippling effects of that exposure on yet another generation, when that female child reaches sexual maturity and bears a child. Because a plaintiff in Charles Grover's position cannot be injured until the original patient's child bears children, the second injury will typically have occurred more than sixteen years after the ingestion of the drug.

Several courts have addressed a fact pattern virtually identical to the facts of the case currently before this court. The New York Court of Appeals held that a child does not have a cause of action, in negligence or strict liability, against a prescription drug company based on the manufacture of DES if the child was never exposed to the drug in utero.... The court relied in part on its earlier opinion in *Albala v. New York*.... In both cases, the court was concerned with the "staggering implications of any proposition which would honor claims assuming the breach of an identifiable duty for less than a perfect birth and by what standard and the difficulty in establishing a standard or definition of perfection...." The court was troubled by the possibility that doctors would forego certain treatments of great benefit to persons already in existence out of fear of possible effects on future children....

The court noted that "the cause of action plaintiffs ask us to recognize here could not be confined without the drawing of artificial and arbitrary boundaries. For all we know, the rippling effects of DES exposure may extend for generations. It is our duty to confine liability within manageable limits. Limiting liability to those who ingested the drug or were exposed to it in utero serves this purpose."

We find the reasoning applied by the New York Court of Appeals persuasive on the issue currently before us. As an initial matter, we note that the pharmaceutical companies' conduct must be evaluated based on whether they knew or should have known of a particular risk through the exercise of ordinary care.... The marketing of prescription drugs differs significantly from other consumer goods. Each drug is tested and approved for use by the Food and Drug Administration and is selected for use by a physician who then prescribes the drug to the ultimate user. As a result, the drug manufacturer's primary responsibility is to provide adequate warnings to the physician.... The manufacturer does not breach its duty to warn—in negligence, in strict liability for breach of warranty, or in strict liability in tort—until the company knew of should have known of a particular risk through the exercise of ordinary care....

Even if knowledge of the drug's "dangerous propensities" is sufficient to create liability to the women exposed to the drug in utero, this same knowledge does not automatically justify the extension of liability to those women's children. It is one thing to say that knowledge of a propensity to harm the reproductive organs is sufficient to impose liability for a variety of different injuries to the reproductive organs. It is yet another thing to say that this generalized knowledge is sufficient to impose liability for injuries to a third party that occur twenty-eight years later.

Knowledge of a risk to one class of plaintiffs does not necessarily extend an actor's liability to every potential plaintiff. While we must assume that DES was the proximate cause of Charles Grover's injuries, an actor is not liable for every harm that may result from his actions.... An actor does not have a duty to a particular plaintiff unless the risk to that plaintiff is within the actor's "range of apprehension...." "If the actor's conduct creates such a recognizable risk of harm only to a particular class of persons, the fact that it in fact causes harm to a person of a different class, to whom the actor could not reasonably have anticipated injury, does not make the actor liable to the persons so injured...."

When a pharmaceutical company prescribes drugs to a woman, the company, under ordinary circumstances, does not have a duty to her daughter's infant who will be conceived twenty-eight years later. Charles Grover's injuries are not the result of his own exposure to the drug, but are allegedly caused by his mother's injuries from her in utero exposure to the drug. Because of the remoteness in time and causation, we hold that Charles Grover does not have an independent cause of action, and answer the district court's question in the negative. A pharmaceutical company's liability for the distribution or manufacture of a defective prescription drug does not extend to persons who were never exposed to the drug either directly or in utero.

Judgment accordingly.

FRAUD AND INNOCENT MISREPRESENTATION

The most obvious case for "product liability" is against the seller (or manufacturer) who has fraudulently misrepresented the product. The defrauder should clearly be held liable for all the losses which are caused by the misrepresentation, and probably for punitive damages as well. However, as noted in Part Two, Contract Law, fraud is easy to allege, but difficult to prove, and it probably applies to only a tiny fraction of product liability cases.

As noted in Chapter 12, most courts permit rescission (but not recovery of damages) where a buyer has been damaged because of reasonable reliance on the seller's honest, but mistaken, statement of fact. The most recent version of the *Restatement (Second) of Torts* includes a revised Section 402B, which would substantially modify this general rule for sales of goods. Under Section 402B, a seller of goods is liable for "physical harm to a consumer" which results from reliance on the seller's material misrepresentation, even though "not made fraudulently or negligently" and even though "the consumer has not bought the chattel from or entered into any contractual relation with the seller." Essentially, what this section does is to restate the law of express warranty, without the requirement of **privity** (relationship) of contract.

NEGLIGENCE

Like fraud, negligence is easy to allege but sometimes very difficult to prove. The fact that one part fails and causes injury is not much evidence of negligent manufacture, if tens of thousands of identical parts have been and are functioning properly. Indeed, in most cases such statistics would present a pretty convincing case that the manufacturer was doing an excellent job of product design, manufacture, and inspection. Where negligence can be proved against either the manufacturer or the seller or both, the injured party should be able to collect all the damages that result. Courts today generally recognize that the manufacturer's liability for negligence extends not only to the buyer of the product but also to other persons "whom he should expect to be endangered by its probable use" (if the product is not properly made). In a few situations, such as the case of the dead mouse in the bottle of cola, the courts may apply the doctrine of *res ipsa loquitur* ("the thing speaks for itself"), meaning that such things do not occur without negligent or purposeful conduct.

BREACH OF WARRANTY

Warranty is simply another word for guarantee. Depending on the facts and circumstances, the seller may make several different types of warranties on the goods being sold—warranties relating to the title to the goods or to the characteristics, qualities, or capabilities of the goods. In a simpler economy, where most sellers produced what they sold, where such manufactured goods as there were could be readily inspected and understood by the buyers, and where there was a rough equality in the bargaining power of the parties, *caveat emptor* ("let the buyer beware") may have been a workable rule for the law of sales. As products became more intricate and the distribution system became more impersonal, courts and legislatures saw the necessity of changing this early rule to provide more protection to buyers and users. It is one thing to say that Walter Woodcutter ought to be able to tell a bad ax from a good one when he deals with the village blacksmith; it is quite another to apply the same standard to a weekend hobbyist who buys a gasoline-driven chain saw from the local hardware store. The law of warranty has changed, and is still changing, to meet changes in the economy.

The UCC does not make any revolutionary changes in the law of warranties, but it does contain several provisions which extend warranty liability, or which make such liability more difficult to disclaim. The Code sections cover three types of warranties: **express**, **implied**, and **title** warranties.

Although the title warranties are not specifically labeled "implied," they are such, in the sense that they are automatically written into the transaction by the law unless the parties agree otherwise or the circumstances clearly indicate otherwise. The seller guarantees that he or she has a good title to the goods, and the right to sell them, and that there are no liens or encumbrances against them. In addition, where the seller is a merchant regularly dealing in such goods, there is also a warranty that the sale will not subject the buyer to suit by any third party claiming infringement on a patent, copyright, trademark, and the like.

EXPRESS WARRANTIES

Under the Code, express warranties are created in one of three ways:

1. An affirmation of fact or a promise, which relates to the goods and becomes part of the basis of the bargain.
2. A description of the goods.
3. A sample or model of the goods.

In each of these three cases, the assumption is that the seller and the buyer have specifically included the guarantee as an integral part of their sales contract. An express warranty is thus virtually impossible to disclaim by form language in a written sales contract. It is not necessary to prove that the seller used the word *warranty* or *guarantee*, or had the specific intent to make a warranty. If the statement is a factual one and it is made in the context of negotiations on the sales contract, it is a warranty unless the facts clearly indicate otherwise. In the case of a description, sample, or model, there is an express warranty that the goods will conform to the description, sample, or model. Even statements made in advertisements, if factual, may be held to be express warranties. An ad for "chromium steel knives," for instance, would be an express warranty that the knives are in fact made of chromium steel. On the other hand, "best deal in town" is probably not factual enough to be a warranty.

IMPLIED WARRANTY OF MERCHANTABILITY

Where the seller is a merchant with respect to the type of goods involved in the contract, there is an implied warranty that the goods are "merchantable." This is a minimum quality guarantee, defined in UCC 2-314, which is imposed on the seller unless the buyer and the seller clearly agree otherwise. Among other requirements, to be merchantable goods must at least be "fit for the ordinary purposes for which such goods are used;" be "adequately contained, packaged, and labeled as the agreement may require;" and "conform to the promises or affirmations of fact made on the container or label if any."

Prior to the adoption of the Code some courts drew a distinction between food purchased in carryout restaurants, to be consumed off the premises, and food purchased in service restaurants, where the diners ate on the premises. The latter case was held to be a services contract, not a sale of goods, and thus there was no implied warranty that food or drink purchased for consumption on the premises was "merchantable." The Code specifically repudiates this distinction, so that your hamburger must be merchantable whether you eat it on or off the restaurant premises.

Whether a particular product is merchantable is a question of fact, to be decided in each case. There is still a split of authority where an injury is caused by the presence in a food product of something which is a natural part of the food at some stage of production. For example, is a chicken sandwich which contains a chicken bone unmerchantable? Some courts would say no, since the chicken bone is a "natural" part of a chicken. The same reasoning would apply to a cherry pit in cherry pie or cherry ice cream. Other courts apply a different test: What should the consumer reasonably expect to find in the food product? Clearly, no one expects to find a sharp piece of glass in a hot dog. But neither does one expect to find a sharp piece of bone there—even though bones are a "natural" part of the beef and pork from which the hot dog is made. The "naturalness" of the object is therefore merely one fact to be considered in determining whether the food product is merchantable. Under this second test, a chicken sandwich with a bone is not merchantable, but a serving of roast chicken containing a chicken bone would be. The next case shows how these tests are applied.

Similar fact questions may arise when other products are alleged to be unmerchantable. The fact that someone was injured while a product was being used does not always mean that the product was not merchantable. The Code does not require that the goods must be perfect, or that they will do anything and everything which the buyer wishes. They need only be fit for the *ordinary* purposes for which such goods are used. Experts in design and production may be called to testify on the safety and suitability of the goods. It may be appropriate to have the use of the goods demonstrated for the judge and jury. Even if the goods are found to be defective, it is also necessary to show that the injury complained of was caused by the defect, and not by the actions of the user or someone else.

Mexicali Rose applies these rules on food warranties.

MEXICALI ROSE v. SUPERIOR COURT (CLARK)
822 P.2d 1292 (CA, 1992)

FACTS: Real party in interest (plaintiff), Jack A. Clark, was a customer at petitioners' (defendants') restaurant. He ordered a chicken enchilada and sustained throat injuries when he swallowed a one-inch chicken bone contained in the enchilada. He brought an action for damages based on theories of negligence, breach of implied warranty, and strict liability. He alleged defendant Mexicali Rose negligently left the bone in the enchilada and the food was unfit for human consumption. He also asserted he did not expect to find a bone, and it is not common knowledge there may be bones in chicken enchiladas. In addition, plaintiff sought punitive damages, alleging malice, fraud, and oppression based on the allegation defendants initially refused to obtain medical assistance for him.

The trial court overruled defendants' demurrer, but the Court of Appeal issued a writ of mandate, directing the trial court to sustain the demurrer on all causes of action. The Court of Appeal noted it was compelled, under principles of *stare decisis*, to follow the Mix rule precluding liability for injuries caused by naturally occurring substances in food.

 CHIEF JUSTICE LUCAS:

An early rule of implied warranty in cases involving foreign or adulterated food substances was adopted, as of 1960, by seventeen jurisdictions, including California.... A review of the California cases reveals that the acceptance of an implied warranty rule against manufacturers in cases involving unfit foodstuffs was based on the rationale that a manufacturer that sold food items could no longer hide behind the shield of privity to absolve itself of liability....

This same implied warranty for foreign or adulterated substances in food was extended to independent restaurant owners who purchased the food from outside manufacturers.... We imposed on the restaurateur a burden to inspect the food, reasoning that: "As between the patron, who has no means of determining whether the food served is safe for human consumption, and the seller, who has the opportunity of determining its fitness, the burden properly rests with the seller, who could have so cared for the food as to have made the injury to the customer impossible...."

A different rule developed when the injury was caused by an object deemed *natural* to the food being served. In *Mix* ... the plaintiff swallowed a fragment of chicken bone contained in a chicken pot pie he consumed in the defendant's restaurant. *Mix* affirmed the trial court order dismissing the plaintiff's complaint for negligence and breach of implied warranty. We held there could be no liability under either an implied warranty or negligence theory, explaining that the statutory implied warranty of fitness of food does not make the purveyor an insurer, but merely requires that food be reasonably fit for human consumption. Although we conceded that it is frequently a question for the jury to determine whether an injury producing substance present in food makes the food unfit for consumption, we maintained that a court in appropriate cases may find as a *matter of law* that an alleged harmful substance in food does not make the food defective or unfit for consumption. We explained our holding as follows:

> "Bones which are natural to the type of meat served cannot legitimately be called a foreign substance, and a consumer who eats meat dishes ought to anticipate and be on his guard against the presence of such bones. At least he cannot hold the restaurant keeper whose representation implied by law is that the meat dish is reasonably fit for human consumption, liable for any injury occurring as a result of the presence of a chicken bone in such chicken pie.... Certainly no liability would attach to a restaurant keeper for the serving of a T-bone steak, or a beef stew, which contained a bone natural to the type of meat served, or if a fish dish should contain a fish bone, or if a cherry pie should contain a cherry stone—although it be admitted that an ideal cherry pie would be stoneless...." We concluded as a matter of law

that a chicken pot pie containing chicken bones is reasonably fit for consumption and there could be no breach of the implied warranty....

As for the negligence claim, we concluded that because the restaurateur had no duty to offer a perfect chicken pie, he or she was not negligent in serving a pie with a bone in it.... *Mix* stated the negligence rule as follows:" [T]he restaurant keeper's obligation is limited to the exercise of the due care in the preparation and service of food furnished guests.... [A] duty of exercising due care in the furnishing and serving of food to guests exists on the part of a restaurant keeper, and ... he is liable in damages for any breach of such duty."

After recognizing the duty of care, however, the *Mix* court observed that injury due to a chicken bone in a chicken pie did not establish a lack of due care amounting to a breach of that duty. The court observed that the negligence issue involved "a question of whether or not a restaurant keeper in the exercise of due care is required to serve in every instance a perfect chicken pie, in that all bones are entirely eliminated. If the customer has no right to expect such a perfect product, and we think he is not so entitled, then it cannot be said that it was negligence on the part of the restaurant keeper to fail to furnish an entirely boneless chicken pie."

If the injury-producing substance is natural to the preparation of the food served, it can be said that it was reasonably expected by its very nature and the food cannot be determined unfit or defective. A plaintiff in such a case has no cause of action in strict liability or implied warranty. If, however, the presence of the natural substance is due to a restaurateur's failure to exercise due care in food preparation, the injured patron may sue under a negligence theory.

If the injury-causing substance is foreign to the food served, then the injured patron may also state a cause of action in implied warranty and strict liability, and the trier of fact will determine whether the substance: (i) would be reasonably expected by the average consumer, and (ii) rendered the food unfit or defective....

Thus, we conclude that to the extent *Mix* precludes a cause of action in negligence when injuries are caused by substances natural to the preparation of the food served, it is overruled.

Based on the foregoing, we affirm the Court of Appeal decision to the extent it directs the trial court to sustain defendants' demurrers to the implied warranty and strict liability causes of action, and we reverse the decision directing the demurrer to plaintiff's negligence cause of action be sustained. The cause is remanded to the Court of Appeal for further proceedings consistent with this holding.

MERCHANTABILITY OF LEASED GOODS AND OF REAL ESTATE

As noted in the last chapter, courts have been extending the merchantability concept to cover other sorts of commercial transactions. Nearly all courts which have had to decide the question have imposed an implied warranty of merchantability on a business which rents goods to others. (See the *Cucchi* case in Chapter 26.) Many states now hold sellers of new houses to a similar standard. (See the discussion in Chapter 27.) Statutes in some states now require that real estate leased for residential purposes be reasonably "habitable." (See the discussion in Chapter 28.) In each of these situations, the courts and legislatures have determined that social policy requires that at least a minimum level of quality be guaranteed to the buyer or lessee. It now seems to be only a question of time until all states adopt similar rules.

IMPLIED WARRANTY OF FITNESS

The Code has also made an important extension in the seller's liability under the implied warranty of fitness. Where this warranty applies, the seller is not only guaranteeing that the goods are of fair, average quality and that they will do what most buyers expect them to do but also that they are suitable for the *particular* needs of the given buyer. The fitness warranty does not arise unless the buyer makes known to the seller some special needs and the fact that the buyer is relying on the seller to select or furnish suitable goods to meet those special needs. Prior to the Code, this fitness warranty could not apply where the goods were sold under a brand name or a trade name; under UCC 2-315, a brand name on the goods is only one fact to be considered in determining whether the buyer relied on the seller to furnish suitable goods.

EXCLUSION OR MODIFICATION OF WARRANTIES

The Code generally makes it more difficult for the seller to disclaim warranties once they are made. For all practical purposes, it is impossible for the seller to disclaim an express warranty unless the entire transaction is renegotiated or unless the parties agree on a final written contract which does not include the express warranty and which indicates that it is intended as a complete statement of all the terms of the contract. With such a clause in the final contract, any prior express warranty would be excluded by the operation of the parol evidence section of Article 2 (2-202). Otherwise, where an express warranty has been made it overrides any attempted disclaimer of warranty to the extent that the two provisions are inconsistent.

Theoretically, at least, the implied warranties of merchantability and fitness can be disclaimed if the appropriate Code sections are complied with. As a practical matter, however, courts have been reluctant to enforce such disclaimers unless there is evidence that the buyer understood and intended that result. An example would occur where a used item is bought "as is" or where the buyer is also a business, such as TWA buying jumbo jets from Boeing. To stand *any* chance of being enforceable, the disclaimer of warranties must comply with the Code's requirements. Merchantability may be disclaimed either orally or in writing, but the word *merchantability* must be used; moreover, if the disclaimer is part of a written contract, it must be stated "conspicuously" in the writing. The fitness warranty cannot be excluded except by a writing, and the disclaimer must be a conspicuous part of the writing. UCC 1-201(10) defines *conspicuous* as being "so written that a reasonable person against whom it is to operate ought to have noticed it." A contrasting type style or color might be used to meet this requirement.

Even where all the Code's requirements for language and form of the disclaimer have been met, a court may still refuse to enforce the disclaimer on the grounds that it is an attempt to avoid the seller's basic obligations of "good faith, diligence, reasonableness, and care" (1-102[3]), or that it is "unconscionable" (2-302), or that it is against "public policy." The 1960 *Henningsen* case, from New Jersey, is perhaps the most significant single case on product liability. It started the modern trend by repudiating the "privity" requirement and by refusing to enforce the auto manufacturer's form disclaimer. Following the lead of the New Jersey court, several other states also refuse to enforce form disclaimers, at least where the buyer is a consumer, even if the disclaimer language complies with UCC requirements.

There are two other important limitations on warranty disclaimers. A seller who has made warranties to the buyer cannot "exclude or limit" the operation of Section 2-318, which extends the warranties automatically to "any natural person who is in the buyer's family or household or who is a guest in the buyer's home." Also, although Section 2-316 permits the parties to agree to limit the remedies for breach of warranty, in accordance with Sections 2-718 and 2-719, Section 2-719 states that any limitation "of consequential damages for injury to the person in the case of consumer goods is prima facie unconscionable" (and therefore not enforceable).

The Code also provides that warranties, whether expressed or implied, are to be construed as consistent with each other and cumulative, (meaning that *all* the warranties which apply on the facts are made) unless such a construction is unreasonable.

The *Morris* case shows how the Code's disclaimer provisions relate to other consumer protection statutes.

MORRIS v. MACK'S USED CARS
824 S.W.2d 538(TN, 1992)

FACTS: Darrell Morris sued the seller, Mack's Used Cars & Parts, Inc., for compensatory, treble, and punitive damages, alleging fraudulent concealment, breach of express warranty of title under T.C.A. § 47-2-312, breach of express warranty of description under T.C.A. § 47-2-313, breach of implied warranty of merchantability under T.C.A. § 47-2-314, and violation of the Tennessee Consumer Protection Act forbidding unfair or deceptive acts under T.C.A. § 47-18-104(b)(6),(7).

In September 1985, the defendant sold to Morris a vehicle described on the bill of sale as a 1979 Ford pickup truck. An older truck was traded in as a down payment, and the balance of the purchase price was financed over a term of three years with a retail installment contract and security agreement, pursuant to which the certificate of title was delivered by the defendant-seller directly to the lender. The bill of sale contained the following statement immediately above the purchaser's signature, "This unit sold as is. No warranties have been expressed or implied." At the time of sale, the truck had been wrecked or dismantled and was a "reconstructed" vehicle within the meaning of Title 55, Chapter 3, Part 2 of Tennessee Code Annotated. The seller knew but did not disclose to the purchaser that the pickup was a reconstructed vehicle. The purchaser obtained this information three years later when he received the certificate of title after paying the final installment on the sales contract. Being reconstructed reduced the vehicle's fair market value 30 to 50 percent.

The seller's defense was that the disclaimer contained in the bill of sale avoided any liability for its not disclosing to the purchaser the condition of the vehicle as revealed by the certificate of title.

The trial court agreed with the seller and dismissed the suit.

CHIEF JUSTICE REID:

The trial court and the Court of Appeals misconstrued these statutes as they relate to the Consumer Protection Act. Disclaimers permitted by § 47-2-316 of the Uniform Commercial Code (UCC) may limit or modify liability otherwise imposed by the code, but such disclaimers do not defeat separate causes of action for unfair or deceptive acts or practices under the Consumer Protection Act....

The UCC contemplates the applicability of supplemental bodies of law to commercial transactions. Section 47-1-103, T.C.A. provides the following: Unless displaced by the particular provisions of chapters 1 through 9 of this title, the principles of law and equity, including the law merchant and the law relative to capacity to contract, principal and agent, estoppel, fraud, misrepresentation, duress, coercion, mistake, bankruptcy, or other validating or invalidating cause shall supplement its provisions.

Also, the supplementary nature of the Consumer Protection Act is made clear by T.C.A. § 47-18-112, which states, "The powers and remedies provided in this part shall be cumulative and supplementary to all other powers and remedies otherwise provided by law. The invocation of one power or remedy herein shall not be construed as excluding or prohibiting the use of any other available remedy."

A seller may disclaim all implied warranties pursuant to T.C.A. § 47-2-316....

The Consumer Protection Act recognizes this right of exclusion or modification of warranties under the UCC. Section 47-18-113, T.C.A., provides:

> **Waiver of Rights.** (a) No provision of this part may be limited or waived by contract, agreement, or otherwise, notwithstanding any other provision of law to the contrary; provided, however, the provisions of this part shall not alter, amend, or repeal the provisions of the Uniform Commercial Code relative to express or implied warranties or the exclusion or modification of such warranties.

The above provision, however, also specifically precludes disclaimer of liability under the Consumer Protection Act. Furthermore, the UCC, pursuant to T.C.A. § 471-203, imposes an obligation of good faith in the performance or enforcement of every contract. Under T.C.A. § 47-1-102(3), this obligation may not be disclaimed.

Claims under the UCC and the Consumer Protection Act are distinct causes of action, with different components and defenses. The Consumer Protection Act is applicable to commercial transactions, also regulated by the UCC....

The Tennessee Consumer Protection Act is to be liberally construed to protect consumers and others from those who engage in deceptive acts or practices.... In a case similar to the one before the Court, the seller's failure to disclose to the buyer that the vehicle had been in an accident and had been repaired constituted a violation of the Consumer Protection Act. To allow the seller here to avoid liability for unfair or deceptive acts or practices by disclaiming contractual warranties under the UCC would contravene the broad remedial intent of the Consumer Protection Act.

In summary, disclaimers permitted by T.C.A. § 47-2-316 do not prevent application of the Consumer Protection Act. The Consumer Protection Act creates a separate and distinct cause of action for unfair or deceptive acts or practices.

STRICT LIABILITY IN TORT

As new case law developed during the 1960s, courts came to realize that the liability they were enforcing for product failure could no longer be properly described in terms of contract warranties. When manufacturers are held liable to retail buyers with whom they have no contract, when both manufacturers and sellers are held liable to persons other than the buyer, when both manufacturers and sellers are held liable despite clear and conspicuous written disclaimers of implied quality warranties, and when liability is imposed even before a sale is made (as in a "self-serve" store), it is no longer quite accurate to describe this liability as "breach of warranty." Most courts now recognize that this is a socially imposed, *tort* liability rather than a self-imposed, *contract* liability; in many cases, liability is being enforced despite contrary provisions in the parties' contract or even where there is no contract at all between them.

Moreover, since proof of negligence is not required and proof of the plaintiff's contributory negligence is not fatal to the case, this is a new theory of tort liability, usually described as **strict liability in tort**, or liability without fault. Historically, strict tort liability was imposed only on the keepers of dangerous wild animals and on persons who engaged in "extrahazardous activities." What the courts have done, in effect, is to extend this theory of liability to manufacturers, sellers, and renters of products, so that the supplier of a defective product will be liable for the damage it causes, irrespective of any contract. The underlying rationale for applying strict liability here is to "spread the risk." Rather than letting the loss fall totally on the unlucky user or bystander, the loss should be passed back to the manufacturer, who can then factor in such losses as another cost of production. That way, all buyers/users of the product pay a little more, but any injured persons are compensated for their injuries.

Of course, the plaintiff must still prove the case, but this is a much easier case to prove, and a much more difficult case to defend, than either negligence or breach of warranty. The fact that only this one product failed out of five million produced and used may prevent recovery for negligent manufacture, but it will not prevent recovery based on strict liability. The plaintiff need only prove that the product was made by the defendant, that it was "defective," that the defect caused the injury, and that damages have been sustained in a certain amount. The defendant can then try to show that the product was not defective, but instead failed as the result of normal wear and tear, or improper maintenance, or misuse by the plaintiff.

Although strict liability for defective products has been recognized for at least thirty years, the concept is not uniformly applied by all states. There are still differences as to what types of transactions are covered, which third parties are protected, and how possible defenses may apply. Results may vary because different triers of fact analyze similar situations in different ways. Opinions as to what constitutes a "defect," legally and factually, may differ. Is a car "defective" if its gasoline tank explodes when the car is struck from behind by another vehicle? How about a car with an unpadded dashboard? Almost by definition, if the vehicle is not made in accordance with U.S. government safety standards, it would be "defective" in the legal sense. But is the reverse also true? Does compliance with these government standards mean that the product is *not* defective? The courts have generally said "no;" compliance with government or industry standards does not necessarily prevent liability.

The *Krutsch* case discusses alleged "defects" based on design and on lack of warnings.

KRUTSCH v. WALTER H. COLLIN GmbH
495 N.W.2d 208 (MN App., 1993)

FACTS: In 1982 Federal-Hoffman, Incorporated purchased a lead extruder machine from appellant Walter H. Collin GmbH Verfahrenstechnik Und Maschinenfabric ("Collin"), a German corporation. The machine is a large hydraulic press used to make lead bullets.

Respondent John H. Krutsch, an employee of Federal-Hoffman, was operating the machine when it broke down. Federal-Hoffman had trained Krutsch in the operation of the machine, but had not trained him to repair the machine. Krutsch discussed the machine's disrepair with fellow employees, and opined that the machine was not functioning because there was air in its hydraulic cylinder and that he could fix the machine by "bleeding" the cylinder.

Krutsch consulted a partial copy of the machine's operation manual that Federal-Hoffman kept near the machine. Collin had provided Federal-Hoffman with a complete manual which included the procedure for "bleeding" the machine's hydraulic cylinder, but Federal-Hoffman kept the complete manual in its engineering office. The partial copy of the manual did not contain any information on "bleeding" the cylinder. Nevertheless, Krutsch attempted to repair the machine. He took a wrench and began to turn a pressure release bolt attached to the machine's hydraulic cylinder. The bolt contained a small hole through which fluid could flow from the cylinder. Krutsch turned the bolt too far, and highly pressurized hydraulic fluid was injected into his thumb causing severe injuries.

Krutsch sued Collin under negligence and strict liability theories. Collin asserted a contribution claim against Federal-Hoffman. Prior to the selection of a jury, Collin informed Krutsch and the trial court that it had settled its contribution claim with Federal-Hoffman, but did not provide Krutsch or the trial court with a signed copy of the settlement agreement until after the trial had begun. Federal-Hoffman did not participate in the trial.

The jury found that the machine was not defectively designed, but was defective for failure to warn and that Krutsch, Collin, and Federal-Hoffman contributed to Krutsch's injuries. The jury awarded Krutsch damages for past pain, disability, disfigurement, and emotional distress; past medical expenses; past lost earnings; future pain, disfigurement, and emotional distress; future disability, future lost earnings; and future medical expenses. The jury also awarded Krutsch's wife damages for loss of consortium. Upon Collin's motion, the trial court reduced the jury's award for future medical expenses.

 JUDGE HUSPENI:

The decision whether to grant JNOV is a pure question of law, and this court will review the trial court's decision de novo....

[JNOV] may be granted only when the evidence is so overwhelmingly on one side that reasonable minds cannot differ as to the proper outcome. In applying this standard: (1) all the evidence, including that favoring the verdict, must be taken into account; (2) the evidence is to be viewed in the light most favorable to the verdict; and (3) the court may not weigh the evidence or judge the credibility of the witnesses....

Collin claims that it is entitled to JNOV because it had no duty to warn of the dangers associated with "bleeding" the cylinder. The question of whether a product manufacturer has a duty to warn of a particular danger is a question of law....

"[A]manufacturer's duty to warn in strict liability cases extends to all reasonably foreseeable users...." However, "a manufacturer has no duty to warn when the dangers of a product are within the professional knowledge of the user...."

Collin should have foreseen that the machine would be operated by individuals who were not fully trained in the machine's maintenance and repair procedures. The dangers associated with "bleeding" the cylinder are not obvious to such a user. Thus, Collin had a duty to warn all foreseeable users of the machine of the dangers associated with "bleeding" the machine's cylinder.

Having concluded that Collin had a duty to warn, "questions of a warning's adequacy, breach, and causation are usually jury questions...." Collin claims that even if it did have a duty to warn, it satisfied that duty by providing Federal-Hoffman with a manual which included the correct procedures for "bleeding" the cylinder. Collin claims that Krutsch cannot challenge the adequacy of its warning because he never read the instructions contained in the complete manual. We disagree.

Viewing the evidence in a light most favorable to the verdict, the evidence is not so overwhelmingly on one side that reasonable minds cannot differ as to the proper outcome.... Accordingly, the trial court did not err in denying Collin's motion for JNOV.

DEFENSES AGAINST PRODUCT LIABILITY CLAIMS

As indicated previously, it may be possible to avoid liability by disproving the main element of the plaintiff's case. For negligence, a defense would be proof that reasonable care was in fact exercised throughout the production and distribution process. For warranty, liability might be avoided by proving either that no warranty was made, or that all warranties were disclaimed, or that all warranties were in fact met. For strict liability, the defense would be proving that the product was not in fact defective.

Where evidence suggests that the product failed, and personal injuries were sustained, the courts have generally been reluctant to permit the seller and the manufacturer to escape liability on a "technicality." Even misuse of the product may not be a defense, if the misuse was foreseeable by the seller and the manufacturer. They may be held liable, if they have not taken reasonable precautions, to avoid foreseeable misuses, such as providing safety devices, warnings, and detailed instructions for use of the product.

Historically, in a negligence case, contributory negligence on the part of the plaintiff was a complete defense. So was the plaintiff's voluntary assumption of a known risk. In product liability cases, these two defenses may not completely absolve the seller and the manufacturer. As noted in Chapter 6, many states have now adapted comparative negligence in place of contributory negligence. If the jury is permitted to offset the fault of the seller and the manufacturer of the defective car against the fault of the injured buyer, who happened to be speeding when the front tire fell off, clearly most of the buyer's damages will be awarded. Where the product failure occurs due to abuse or misuse, however, the defendants may be able to convince the trier of the fact that there was really no defect, no breach of warranty, and no negligence in manufacture. The machine failed not because it was defective, but because it was used constantly without proper servicing. Likewise, even where a defect exists, if the buyer continues to use the product after discovering it, without service or repair, the defendants can argue that the defect did not really *cause* the buyer's injuries.

MAGNUSON-MOSS WARRANTY ACT

One might have imagined that if any field of law under the sun required additional "protective" legislation, it was not the law of product liability. Indeed, if a problem in this field required legislative attention, it was exactly the opposite problem: how to *limit* skyrocketing product liability costs before all but the very largest manufacturers were driven out of business. Congress, however, did not see it that way. Either unaware of or unimpressed by the product liability "revolution" which had occurred during the preceding fifteen years, Congress in 1975 passed the Magnuson-Moss Warranty Act, thereby adding one more large straw to the already weakened camel's back.

The act does not provide that product warranties must be made; its basic purpose is to make warranties which are made more understandable. Warranty information must be made available prior to purchase of a product and must be displayed prominently with it. Moreover, the terms of the warranty must be stated in "plain English." The purpose of these requirements is to better enable buyers to shop for the best warranty, just as they shop for the best price and credit terms. Enforcement of the act is entrusted to the Federal Trade Commission, which has the power to adopt appropriate regulations to achieve the act's purposes.

For products costing over $15, any express warranty must be stated to be a **full warranty** or a **limited warranty**. The act provides standards for each type. A full warranty:

1. Must provide that the seller will remedy any defect, without charge, within a reasonable time.

2. Must provide that the buyer will have the choice of replacement or refund if the seller is unable to correct a defect after a reasonable number of attempts.

3. May not limit the duration of any implied warranty.

4. Must conspicuously state any clause that attempts to limit or exclude liability for consequential damages.

Such a full warranty, once made, extends for the entire time period specified, even if the product is resold. Injured third parties are protected by the warranty under its provisions and under applicable state law on warranties (UCC 2-318, for example).

Any other written warranty on a consumer product must be labeled as a limited warranty, no matter how broad its coverage or how liberal its remedies. Such a limited warranty must specify its coverage and duration, the procedures to be followed, and any mechanism provided for resolving disputes. These warranties cannot be made contingent on the consumer's return of a warranty card, or on a requirement that the goods be serviced only by authorized dealers.

Like most "remedial" legislation, the act has high-minded objectives which are impossible to oppose: to provide consumers with clearer and truer warranties and to give dissatisfied consumers a remedy for defective products. The net result in the marketplace so far has been that very few manufacturers have tried to claim that they are giving full warranties on their products, and some have stopped giving written warranties altogether. Faced with the act's uncertainties, only the very hardiest (or foolhardiest) manufacturers will run the risk of extended jousting with the FTC staff. Whether this act represents a net gain for consumers remains to be seen.

NEW STATE LEGISLATION

Confronted with manufacturers' and sellers' claims that they were being driven out of business by excessive judgments and by soaring premiums for liability insurance, state legislatures have been considering the need for statutory changes in product liability laws. Most of the product liability "crisis" is perceived to result from overexpansive judicial interpretations and overgenerous jury verdicts. Several types of changes are being considered, and, in some states, have already been adopted.

One proposal is to create a strong statutory presumption that a product is not "defective" where a claim is made a certain number of years after the initial sale of the product—ten years, for example. Under existing law, an injured party could claim that a product that had been in use for twenty or thirty years was defective and thus have the benefit of the strict liability rules. Manufacturers and sellers would also like to see a specific statutory statement of contributory negligence and assumption of risk as defenses to product liability claims, even though most courts already do apply them in appropriate cases. Manufacturers would also like to be immune from liability where they have complied with all applicable government regulations and industry standards as of the date of manufacture. This is the "state-of-the-art" argument. They do not feel that they should be held liable if they fail to recall and modify a product which has already been sold. These and similar changes are being pushed hard by producer and seller organizations. Further legislative action seems likely.

A NATIONAL PRODUCTS LIABILITY STATUTE

Since 1984, the U.S. Senate's Commerce Committee has discussed various bills which would drastically change the products liability rules in the United States. In general, these "reform" bills would require the injured party to prove that the manufacturer's or seller's negligence caused the injury, or that the injury was the result of a breach of an express warranty. These bills would thus eliminate liability based on the implied warranties of merchantability and fitness, or on strict liability in tort. They would preempt all state law on products liability under these theories. They would thus repeal nearly all of the judicial changes in this area which have occurred over the past thirty-five years. Obviously, such proposed legislative changes are of vital concern to all U.S. manufacturers and sellers of products and to any international firms interested in selling products here.

SIGNIFICANCE OF THIS CHAPTER

The product liability revolution is one of the two or three most important developments in commercial law in the last fifty years. A whole new range of potential liability exposure, of vast and unknown dimensions, has been created. Entire industries are threatened and have been forced to rethink completely their production and distribution processes. Some businesses have decided to terminate their operations. The consumer is king, with many new rights and protections. Some observers have suggested that the price (which we are all paying) may be too high. It is to deal with this question, and to strike a fair balance between rights and costs, that the state legislatures and Congress are now considering changes.

PROBLEMS FOR DISCUSSION

1. Clause bought his wife a new Plymouth as a Mother's Day present. Ten days later, while driving the car, she heard a loud noise from under the hood; she said it "felt as if something had cracked." The steering wheel spun in her hands, and the car veered sharply to the right and crashed into a brick wall. The plaintiffs sued Bloomfield (the dealer) and Chrysler (the manufacturer). The sales contract stated that the manufacturer's only warranty on the car was a promise to replace defective parts at the factory and that the warranty was given in lieu of all other warranties, express or implied. The trial court held for the plaintiffs, and the defendants appealed.

   How should the appeals court rule, and why?

2. On Saturday, April 25, at about 1 p.m., the plaintiff (Priscilla Webster), accompanied by her sister and her aunt, entered the Blue Ship Tea Room. The group was seated at a table and supplied with menus.

   This restaurant, which the plaintiff characterized as "quaint," was located in Boston "on the third floor of an old building on T Wharf, which overlooks the ocean."

   The plaintiff, who had been born and brought up in New England, ordered clam chowder and crabmeat salad. Within a few minutes, she received tidings to the effect "that there was no more clam chowder." Presently, there was set before her "a small bowl of fish chowder." "The fish chowder contained haddock, potatoes, milk, water, and seasoning. The chowder was milky in color and not clear. The haddock and potatoes were in chunks. She agitated it a little with the spoon and observed that it was a fairly full bowl. After three or four spoonfuls, she was aware that something had lodged in her throat because she couldn't swallow and couldn't clear her throat by gulping and she could feel it." This misadventure led to two esophagoscopies.

   Is Blue Ship liable for plaintiff's injury from the fish bone in her throat? Explain.

3. Baker bought a rifle from Rosemurgy. He paid for the gun even though he knew "there was something wrong with the safety" on it. He used the gun during the hunting seasons of 1989, 1990, and 1991. While he was deer hunting in 1991, he dropped the rifle, and it fired, even though the safety was in the "on" position. Baker sustained severe and permanent leg injuries. He sued Rosemurgy; Gamble-Skogmo, which had distributed the rifle to Rosemurgy; and Olin, the manufacturer. The trial court granted summary judgment for all three defendants.

   Will the trial court's ruling be upheld on appeal? Why or why not?

4. Millicent Innocent purchased a "ski weekend" vacation package at Nobby Nob Lodge. She was injured while using a rope-tow at the skiing facility operated by the Lodge. She sues the Lodge, on the theories of negligence, breach of warranty, and strict liability. The Lodge moves to dismiss all three counts of the complaint.

   How should the trial judge rule, and why?

5. Gladys Flippo went into a ladies clothing store in Batesville, operated by Rosie Goforth, and known as Mode O'Day Frock Shops of Hollywood. Mrs. Flippo tried on two pairs of pants, or slacks, which were shown to her by Mrs. Goforth. The first pair proved to be too small. When Mrs. Flippo put on the second pair, she suddenly felt a burning sensation on her thigh. She immediately removed the pants, shook them, and a spider fell to the floor. An examination of her thigh revealed a reddened area, which progressively grew worse. Mrs. Flippo was subsequently hospitalized for approximately thirty days. According to her physician, the injury was caused by the bite of a brown recluse spider. Suit for damages was instituted against Mode O'Day Frock Shops.

   Explain how the three major theories of products liability would apply to Flippo's case.

Part Four

Creditors and Debtors

Since many sales of goods are made on credit, and since goods and documents of title covering goods are frequently used as collateral in business financing arrangements, the material in Part Four logically follows Part Three. Here we review various aspects of short-term commercial financing and risks of nonpayment.

The core of the legal rules for short-term commercial financing is found in Article 9 of the UCC, "Secured Transactions." Article Nine covers all types of financing that use personal property or real estate fixtures as collateral. This very complex legal topic is covered in Chapters 18 and 19. Chapter 18 also covers the use of co-signers ("sureties") in credit transactions. To help you better appreciate the need for being a secured creditor rather than an unsecured one, the first chapter in this part summarizes the U.S. bankruptcy law. With hundreds of thousands of bankruptcies occurring each year, an unsecured creditor is taking a substantial risk of not receiving full payment. Bankruptcy is the problem; secured transactions are the solution.

Several national consumer protection statutes also limit creditors' rights. These statutes are outlined in the second half of Chapter 17.

Chapter 17

Bankruptcy and Consumer Protection

DEFINITION, GOALS, AUTHORITY, HISTORY

Bankruptcy is the process of settling the debts of persons or firms that are no longer able to meet their obligations. Under court supervision, the debtor's assets (or most of them) are collected and sold, and the proceeds are distributed to creditors. Creditors with equal priority status should receive the same proportion of their claims against the debtor. If the correct procedures have been followed, at the end of the process the debtor's obligations (or most of them) are discharged even though they have not been paid in full. The debtor gets a "fresh start."

Congress is empowered to establish uniform bankruptcy laws by the U.S. Constitution, Article I, Section 8. The first national bankruptcy law was passed in 1800. The Bankruptcy Act of 1898 was in force for eighty years, though it was substantially revised by the Chandler Act of 1938. To deal with the administrative problems that had arisen under the Bankruptcy Act and to better implement changes in consumer credit laws and in the UCC, Congress enacted the Bankruptcy Code of 1978, which became generally effective October 1, 1979.

ADMINISTRATION

The 1978 code provided for a new system of bankruptcy courts as of April 1, 1984. The plan was that each U.S. judicial district would then have a bankruptcy court as an adjunct to the U.S. District Court, with one or more bankruptcy judges, each appointed for a fourteen-year term. These courts would have jurisdiction to decide all controversies affecting the debtor or the debtor's estate. In 1982, the Supreme Court of the United States, in the *Northern Pipeline* case, found that the portion of the 1978 Bankruptcy Code that created the new system of bankruptcy courts violated Article III of the U.S. Constitution. The Court did state that its decision in this case would apply prospectively rather than retroactively, to avoid upsetting previously decided cases. In July 1984, the Bankruptcy Amendments and Federal Judgeship Act was adopted to replace those sections of the 1978 code which had been held unconstitutional. The 1984 Amendments also made many other changes in the details of bankruptcy law.

TYPES OF PROCEEDINGS

Chapter 7 of the 1978 code provides for "*straight bankruptcy*," or *liquidation*. The trustee gathers and sells the debtor's property and pays the creditors; the debtor receives a discharge from all listed debts. Generally, straight bankruptcy proceedings may be voluntary or involuntary; that is, either the debtor or the creditors may institute such proceedings. Involuntary straight bankruptcy proceedings may not be commenced against a farmer or a nonprofit corporation.

Chapter 9 provides for adjustment of the debts of municipal corporations, where this is authorized by applicable state law.

Chapter 11 gives corporations in financial difficulty a chance to "reorganize" their financial affairs by staying in business and making periodic payments to their creditors. Chapter 11 proceedings may be voluntary or involuntary. Railroads are limited to Chapter 11 procedures.

Chapter 13 permits similar debt readjustments and payoffs for individuals with regular income. Chapter 13 proceedings can only be voluntary on the part of the debtor.

Insurance companies, banks, savings and loans, and similar financial institutions are governed by their own regulatory agencies and are not subject to the Bankruptcy Code.

In 1986, Congress added Chapter 12 to the Bankruptcy Code to provide for debt adjustment plans for "family farmers." As defined, a family farmer is an individual, or individual and spouse, engaged in a farming operation, whose total debts do not exceed $1,500,000 and at least 80 percent of which arise out of farming operations. In addition, such person(s) must have received more than 50 percent of the prior year's taxable income from farming operations. A corporation or partnership is included if more than 50 percent of the equity is owned by one family, or by one family and relatives, and the family or relatives conduct the farming operation. Additionally, more than 80 percent of the firm's business assets must be related to farming operations; its debts must not exceed $1,500,000 and must be 80 percent farming related; and if a corporation, its stock must not be publicly traded. "Farming operation" is defined as including ranching, raising of crops or livestock, and production of such unprocessed farm products as milk, eggs, and wool.

Chapter 12 provides for the filing and approval of a debt readjustment plan by the family farmer. The procedure is similar in most respects to the individual plans under Chapter 13, but it is specifically tailored to the needs of farmers. The family farmer is a business operation, and thus not quite the same as the typical consumer debtor who uses Chapter 13. Likewise, family farmers probably do need a slightly different procedure than the typical business reorganization under Chapter 11. In any event, Congress decided that a special procedure was justified.

PROCEDURE

The debtor commences voluntary proceedings under Chapters 7, 9, 11, 12, or 13 by filing a petition, under the appropriate chapter, with the bankruptcy court. Spouses may file a joint petition to reduce administrative costs; the bankruptcy court has the power to allocate joint and separate property and debts.

Where the debtor has twelve or more creditors, an involuntary petition under Chapters 7 or 11 must be joined in by three of them, who must have unsecured claims totalling at least $5,000. In determining this number, employees and insiders of the debtor are not counted. Where there are fewer than twelve creditors, any one of them with an unsecured claim of $5,000 can file an involuntary petition. In addition, in an involuntary case the petitioning creditor or creditors must show either that the debtor is not paying his or her debts as they fall due or that the debtor has made a general assignment of assets for the benefit of creditors within 120 days prior to the filing of the petition.

In a voluntary case, the court's "order for relief" is automatic; this operates to stay collection proceedings against the debtor in state courts. In an involuntary petition, the court must determine whether or not relief should be ordered. Where the creditors' allegations are not proved, the debtor may be awarded court costs and damages for the lost use of property turned over to a trustee as well as actual and punitive damages if the filing was made in bad faith. Once an order for relief has been entered, the debtor is required to prepare schedules of creditors, assets, and liabilities. Where the debtor is claiming personal exemptions, a schedule of those exemptions must also be filed with the court. Based on the list of creditors, the court sends out a notification of the first creditors' meeting.

The court may appoint an interim trustee to hold and manage the debtor's property until a trustee is elected by the creditors. If the creditors fail to elect a trustee, the interim trustee continues to administer the debtor's estate. The trustee's job is to collect all the debtor's property, to separate out exempt property, to determine whether creditors' claims are secured or unsecured, and, finally, to pay off claims according to their legal priority status.

DEBTOR'S AVAILABLE PROPERTY

The 1898 act permitted each state to specify what items of property the debtor could exempt from the bankruptcy proceeding; these exemptions vary considerably from state to state. The Michigan exemptions, for example, include all family pictures, wearing apparel, "provisions and fuel" for comfortable subsistence for the family for six months, up to $1,000 of household goods and appliances, burial plots, up to $1,000 in the tools of the debtor's trade, disability insurance benefits for sickness and injury, the cash surrender value of life insurance, benefits to be paid under workers' compensation, up to $3,500 for a "homestead" exemption (the debtor's equity in the family home), and to each householder "ten sheep, two cows, five swine, one hundred hens, five roosters, and sufficient hay and grain growing or otherwise to keep such animals and poultry for six months." The foregoing list seems fairly generous if one remembers that the debtor is getting a discharge from most debts and a fresh start.

The 1978 code gives the debtor the option of choosing the state exemptions or those provided in the 1978 code, unless the particular state specified its exemptions must be used. Some thirty states have done so. For most debtors with the option, the national exemptions will be a better choice.

The exemptions of the 1978 code include a residence exemption of up to $7,500; up to $1,200 for one motor vehicle; and up to $200 per item, with a $4,000 limit on total value, for household goods, wearing apparel, appliances, books, animals, crops, or musical instruments. Additional exemptions include up to $500 in jewelry owned by the debtor or a dependent; up to $400 for any property plus up to $3,750 from any unused amount from the $7,500 residence exemptions; up to $750 for the tools or books of the debtor's or a dependent's trade; any unmatured life insurance policy owned by the debtor other than a credit life policy; up to $4,000 in cash surrender or loan value for a life insurance policy owned by the debtor and on the debtor's life; professionally prescribed health aids for the debtor and dependents; alimony and child support payments; "future earnings" such as social security and veterans' benefits, unemployment compensation, disability payments, and pension plan payments; and up to $7,500 in payments from a personal injury lawsuit. The debtor is also given the power to avoid judicial liens and nonpossessory, nonpurchase money security interests that impair his or her exemptions for most listed items of tangible personal property (but not liens against the motor vehicle).

The trustee may recover any items of property which the debtor **fraudulently transferred** to others within one year prior to the filing of the bankruptcy petition. A transfer is fraudulent if the debtor actually intended to hide the asset from his or her creditors' claims or if the debtor received less than fair consideration for the asset and was insolvent at the time (or became so as a result of the transfer). The trustee may also recover **preferential payments** made by the debtor ninety or fewer days prior to the petition. A payment is preferential if it is made for a prior unsecured debt, if it gives a creditor more than that creditor would have received in a bankruptcy proceeding, and if the debtor was insolvent at the time the payment was made. The debtor is presumed to have been insolvent during the ninety-day period, and the creditor's good faith is irrelevant. A payment is not preferential if it was made in the ordinary course of business.

The *Clark* case involves a fraudulent transfer of assets. It examines the relationship between bankruptcy and the law of fraudulent conveyances.

CLARK v. BANK OF BENTONVILLE
824 S.W.2d 358 (AK, 1992)

FACTS: This case arises out of appellants Jack and Norma Clark's conveyance of real property in Benton County, Arkansas, to appellant Gary Clark, trustee of the Jack M. Clark trust. The warranty deed conveying the property was executed on April 14, 1986, and was filed for record on May 9, 1986. On January 7, 1987, appellee Bank of Bentonville, a creditor of Jack and Norma Clark, filed this action, along with *lis pendens* notice, to set aside the transfer as a fraudulent conveyance.

On August 10, 1987, appellants Jack and Norma Clark filed a Chapter 7 bankruptcy petition in United States Bankruptcy Court for the Central District of California, San Bernardino Division. The bankruptcy court entered an order on December 30, 1987, granting Jack and Norma Clark a discharge in bankruptcy. At the close of the bankruptcy case, the bank proceeded with its previously filed fraudulent conveyance action. The chancellor denied appellants' motion to dismiss this action, and determined that the conveyance of April 14, 1986, was fraudulent. The chancellor ordered a sale of the property with the proceeds applied to appellants' debt to the bank. On June 19, 1991, the property was sold and the proceeds paid to the appellee bank.

 JUSTICE CORBIN:

On appeal, appellants raise two arguments in urging us to reverse the chancellor. First, they argue that the chancellor erred in denying their motion to dismiss because either appellants' discharge in bankruptcy or the doctrine of *res judicata* should have precluded the bank from proceeding with this action. Second, appellants argue that the chancellor erred in denying their motion for a directed verdict because the bank did not prove fraudulent intent by a preponderance of the evidence. We find no error on the part of the chancellor, and affirm his decision.

Appellants' initial argument is that the chancellor erred in allowing the bank to proceed with its fraudulent conveyance action after appellants obtained a discharge from the bankruptcy court. Appellants rely on both the discharge provisions of the bankruptcy code and the doctrine of *res judicata*. The bank does not dispute the validity of appellants' bankruptcy discharge, but argues that the bank's prepetition filing of this action created a lien on the property at issue which survived the discharge of appellants' debt to the bank.

Under Arkansas law, a general creditor who files an action to cancel a fraudulent conveyance of a debtor acquires a specific lien on the property conveyed. While the afore-cited cases involved liens on personal property, we extend the rule to include liens on real property when notice of *lis pendens* is filed. In this case, the bank created a specific lien on the property at issue when it filed its fraudulent conveyance action on January 7, 1987. 11 U.S.C. § 522(c)(2) (1979 & Supp. 1991), provides that liens which are not avoided in the bankruptcy proceeding will be preserved notwithstanding the discharge of the debtor.... Since a discharge in bankruptcy does not defeat a valid lien, the chancellor did not err in denying appellants' motion to dismiss merely because appellants' underlying debt to the bank was discharged in the bankruptcy proceeding.

Appellants also rely on the doctrine of *res judicata* in arguing that the bank should have either objected to appellants' discharge, established its status as a secured creditor, or pursued its fraudulent conveyance action during the bankruptcy proceeding. 11 U.S.C. § 727(a)(2) (1979) provides for objections to discharge based on a debtor's fraudulent transfer of property. However, this section specifically requires that the alleged fraudulent conveyance occur within one year of the debtor's bankruptcy filing.... In this case, the alleged fraudulent conveyance occurred on April 14, 1986, a date approximately fourteen months prior to appellants' bankruptcy petition filing. Therefore, under Section 727(a)(2), the bank could not have asserted a valid objection to discharge during the bankruptcy proceeding.

Appellants do not cite any authority to support their arguments that the bank had the duty to establish its secured status or pursue its fraudulent conveyance action during the bankruptcy proceeding. While the record in the case does not contain the bankruptcy proceedings, neither party disputes the fact that the bank was listed as an unsecured creditor in the bankruptcy schedule....

In this case, appellants do not allege that they had no notice of the bank's pre-petition filing of the fraudulent conveyance action. They merely assert that the bank should have taken affirmative action to preserve its lien in the proceeding. Appellants cite no authority to support their argument, and we believe the reasoning in the *Dickinson* case ... indicates that appellants, rather than the bank, had the burden of contesting the lien.

Appellants further argue that *res judicata* should bar the bank's fraudulent conveyance action because the claim was not pursued in the bankruptcy proceeding. However, the bankruptcy code does not give a creditor the power to pursue a cause of action to set aside a fraudulent conveyance.... In fact, 11 U.S.C. 362(a)(1979) imposes an automatic stay that prohibits creditors from acting against a debtor's property during the pendency of the bankruptcy proceeding.... While a trustee may elect to pursue a creditor's unsecured state law claim under 11 U.S.C. § 544(b) (1979), such an action is an exercise of the avoidance power for the benefit of all creditors. Since the bank did not have standing as a single creditor to pursue the fraudulent conveyance action during the bankruptcy proceeding, ... *res judicata* did not prohibit the bank's subsequent state court action.

CREDITORS' CLAIMS AND PRIORITIES

A claim under the 1978 code includes nearly any sort of right to payment, whether or not it is reduced to judgment, liquidated or unliquidated, fixed or contingent, matured or unmatured, disputed or undisputed, legal or equitable, secured or unsecured. It includes the right to equitable remedies where the breach also gives a right to payment. A creditor who has such a claim files a document called a **proof of claim**. A secured creditor need not do so unless the claim exceeds the value of the security and the creditor wishes to try to collect the balance in the bankruptcy proceeding. The creditor's "proof" is accepted as *prima facie* evidence of the existence and the amount of the debt, and such claims will be allowed and paid (to the extent that funds are available) unless objection is made to them by another creditor, the trustee, or the debtor. Under current practice, proofs of claim must be filed within six months after the first date set for the first meeting of creditors.

Not all claims are paid at the same time or to the same extent. Secured creditors, that is, creditors who have taken the proper steps to establish their rights against specific pieces of collateral, will be paid first from the proceeds of that collateral. If the value of their collateral is sufficient, secured creditors may be paid in full; if not, they are unsecured creditors for the remainder of their claims. In addition to the claims of secured creditors, there are other claims which are given priority under the Bankruptcy Code. Administrative expenses, including the payment of accountants, appraisers, attorneys, and trustees, are paid first; so are creditors' expenses in discovering and recovering property which the debtor has transferred or concealed.

The 1978 code changes priorities by giving second-payment status to unsecured claims for goods, services, or credit which arose in the normal course of the debtor's business between the filing of an involuntary petition and the court's order for relief or appointment of a trustee. Similarly, third priority is given to wage claims of up to $2,000 each which were earned by the debtor's employees in the ninety days preceding the filing of the petition or the cessation of business, and fourth priority is given to claims for contributions to employee benefit plans, which were earned within the prior 180 days, for up to $2,000 per employee, less any payments on wage claims. The 1984 amendments inserted a new fifth-priority claim, for up to $2,000 each, in favor of grain growers and U.S. fishermen against persons who store their products.

Consumers now have a sixth-priority claim of up to $900 per claimant for return of money deposited with the debtor for purchased or leased goods which were not delivered or for services which were not performed. Claims for unpaid taxes owed to various governmental units have been lowered to seventh-priority status. Only after all of the above priority claims have been paid in turn will the general, unsecured creditors receive any money. In most bankruptcy cases, this means that the general creditors will receive little or nothing. (And remember that the debtor is allowed to keep all "exempt" property.)

The 1978 Bankruptcy Code makes one other significant priority change. The creditors of a bankrupt partnership are now entitled to share equally with the unsecured creditors of individual partners against the partners' personal assets. Under the old rule in the Uniform Partnership Act, the firm's unpaid creditors had no claim against personal assets until all the personal creditors had been paid in full. The Bankruptcy Code also contains special rules for community property, and it gives the court general power to change priorities on equitable grounds after a hearing.

The following case discusses one of the technical priority rules from the 1978 Code.

IN RE BROUSE
110 B.R. 539 (Bkrtcy. D. CO, 1990)

FACTS: This matter comes before the Court on the Debtor's Complaint to Determine the Value of Lien and Allow the Deficiency as Unsecured. The Chapter 13 Debtor, Patricia Louise Brouse, requests an order of the Bankruptcy Court avoiding two creditors' liens pursuant to 11 U.S.C. § 506(d).

Debtor owns her residence which is valued at approximately $27,120.00. Defendant CSB Mortgage Company holds a claim against the Debtor in the sum of approximately $45,000.00, which claim is secured by a first deed of trust on the Debtor's principal residence. Defendant Colorado National Bank South holds a claim against the Debtor in the sum of approximately $9,000.00, which claim is secured by a lien on the property in a second position. Encumbrances on the Debtor's principal residence, therefore, exceed the value of the residence by approximately $26,880.00.

Pursuant to 11 U.S.C. § 506(a), CSB has a claim secured by the collateral in the sum of approximately $27,120.00 and an unsecured claim in the approximate sum of $17,880.00. Likewise, the Bank has an unsecured claim in the approximate amount of $9,000.00. Secured claims are "secured to the full extent, and only to the full extent, that there is value in the collateral actually securing the claim.... The claim against the estate is, in effect, bifurcated into secured and unsecured components."

Debtor filed a Motion to Confirm her Chapter 13 Plan and the Bank objected to the Plan because, the Bank maintains, the Plan attempts to modify its claim which is secured only by the Debtor's principal residence and such modification is in violation of 11 U.S.C. § 1322(b)(2). No other objections were filed to Debtor's Plan. Debtor filed this adversary proceeding to determine her right to avoid both liens and otherwise fix the validity, priority, and extent of the two liens on her home. Because the Debtor's Complaint in the adversary proceeding raises the identical issues to those raised in the Bank's objection to confirmation, this Court has consolidated the objection to confirmation hearing with the decision in the adversary proceeding for purposes of judicial efficiency.

 BANKRUPTCY JUDGE BROOKS:

This issue has generated many different opinions and a sharp difference in decisions, everywhere. The majority of courts addressing this issue have expressed the view which this Court adopts by this decision....

Simply stated, this Court is persuaded that the majority view allowing a debtor to employ Section 506(d) is correct in legal terms, sound in terms of statutory construction, and unavoidable under the fresh start concept of the Bankruptcy Code. *In re Folendore* best sums up the reasons for granting to debtors use of Section 506(d) to avoid certain lien claims:

> The plain language of the statute, supported by the decisions of a majority of the bankruptcy courts, inferences drawn from the 1984 amendments, and common sense, requires the ... lien be voidable whether or not [the lienor's] claim has been disallowed under section 502....

Of particular importance to this Court is the conclusion in Folendore that "the plain language of section 506(d)" ... compels allowing a debtor to avoid a lien unsecured or undersecured pursuant to Section 506(a). The language that "such lien is void" is not notably tricky or ambiguous. In determining the scope of a statute, the Court must begin with the statutory language itself. When the terms of the statute are clear, the statutory language is controlling absent exceptional circumstances....

Moreover, and perhaps equally important in this Court's opinion, the use of Section 506(d) allows a debtor to fix with certainty, clarity and finality, the relative rights and interests of the parties at the time of the bankruptcy case. This is a principal feature and purpose of the entire bankruptcy system.

> *Time to fix relative rights of debtor and secured creditor are at the time of bankruptcy.* Creditor rights, claims, and interests are, generally, to be fixed at the time of bankruptcy. That is the clear and unqualified intent of the Code and applicable case law.... There is no logical reason why that objective should be defeated by denial of access to Code tools purposely designed to fix rights as of that date....

The second issue is whether a Chapter 13 debtor is barred from using Section 506(d) by other provisions of Chapter 13, namely Section 1322(b)(2). This Court concludes that a Chapter 13 debtor is entitled to use Section 506(d) to avoid certain liens and is not barred from doing so by any provisions of Chapter 13.

Most cases dealing with a debtor's use of Section 506 are Chapter 7 cases. However, there is some treatment of this question in Chapter 13 cases and, again, the courts are split....

This Court is persuaded by and adopts the reasoning and decision of *In re Hougland* which provides, essentially, that: (1) there is no inconsistency between Sections 506 and 1322(b); (2) the prohibition of Section 1322(b)(2) against modification of "secured claims" applies only to the secured portion of claims which may be bifurcated pursuant to Section 506(a); and (3) a Chapter 13 debtor can modify through a plan the unsecured portion of a claim pursuant to Section 506(d), but cannot modify the secured portion of a claim.

Beyond the reasoning and cases which this Court adopts, one additional factor is of importance in this decision which is not otherwise discussed in the cases. That factor is an important distinction between the rights of the parties under Section 506(d) an Section 1322(b)(2).

Allowing a debtor to use Section 506(d) to avoid the lien on the unsecured portion of the debtor's principal residence does not negate the Section 1322(b)(2) prohibition of modifying the security interest in real property that is the debtor's principal residence. Section 1322(b)(2) will continue to provide protection to the holder of a security interest in a debtor's principal residence that is not provided to a holder of a security interest that is not the debtor's principal residence.

IT IS THEREFORE ORDERED that this Debtor may determine all, or portions of, claims to be secured and unsecured pursuant to 11 U.S.C. § 506(a) and may use Section 506(d) to avoid liens which represent claims in excess of the value of the collateral securing such claims.

IT IS FURTHER ORDERED that the lien securing the claim of Colorado National Bank South in the sum of $9,000.00 is hereby avoided pursuant to 11 U.S.C. § 506(d).

IT IS FURTHER ORDERED that the lien of CSB Mortgage Company is avoided in the approximate amount of $17,880.00 pursuant to Section 506(d), but that the balance of the lien securing CSB Mortgage Company's claim in the sum of $27,120.00 is not avoided pursuant to Section 506(d).

IT IS FURTHER ORDERED that Colorado National Bank South's objection to the Debtor's Plan of confirmation on the basis that the Debtor's Plan violates Section 1322(b)(2) is hereby *DISMISSED*.

IT IS FURTHER ORDERED that the Debtor's Motion to Confirm Chapter 13 Plan is hereby GRANTED.

DISCHARGE, OBJECTIONS, AND GROUNDS FOR REFUSAL

Most of the individual debtors who file under Chapter 7 will receive a discharge from most of their previous debts at the conclusion of the bankruptcy proceedings. This is the whole idea of the "fresh start." Generally, an individual can be so discharged only once within any six-year period. However, where an individual has worked out a voluntary repayment plan under Chapter 13, has paid off at least 70 percent of the claims filed under it, and has made his or her best efforts in good faith, a discharge may be granted more frequently than once in six years.

Any single creditor or the trustee acting for all of them may file an objection to a discharge. The court must then determine whether or not there is some reason for denying the discharge. The Bankruptcy Act lists several grounds for denial, including the debtor's destruction or concealment of property with the intent of delaying or defrauding creditors; destroying, concealing, falsifying, or failing to keep books and records; committing a "bankruptcy crime," such as giving a false oath or participating in bribery to obtain some special advantage; failing to explain losses or deficiencies in existing assets; and failing to obey court orders or to answer questions (but not including refusals properly based on the constitutional privilege against self-incrimination). Also, even a debtor who is entitled to a discharge may in writing waive the right to one.

Where a discharge has been properly granted, the 1978 code extends the protection given the debtor from the unpaid creditors' further collection efforts for discharged debts. The discharge, of course, voids all existing and future judgments based on such debts. The 1898 act also prohibited creditors from employing "any process" to collect discharged debts; the 1978 code forbids any act by creditors to recover such debts.

DEBTS NOT DISCHARGED

Some debts survive the bankruptcy discharge; that is, the debtor's liability still exists, and the creditor may use appropriate enforcement procedures. Such nondischargeable debts include taxes incurred for three years prior to the bankruptcy; alimony and child support payments; sums owed by a fiduciary because of fraud, misappropriation, or embezzlement; liability based on fraudulent representations or false pretenses; and liability for intentional torts ("willful and malicious injury"). As to debts in the last three groups, the creditor involved must specifically request a determination by the court that the debt is not dischargeable; if there is no such request, such debts would be discharged.

Because of the increasing frequency with which bankruptcies were being filed by recent college graduates, the 1978 code added another category of nondischargeable debts: educational loans, unless the first due date was more than five years before the filing of the bankruptcy petition or unless the continuing liability would impose an "undue hardship" on the debtor or the debtor's dependents. The 1984 amendments add liability for drunk driving to the list. Also, under the 1984 act, a debt of over $500 for luxury items bought within forty days prior to the filing, and certain cash advances of over $1,000 made within twenty days prior to filing are presumed to be nondischargeable.

REAFFIRMATION OF DEBTS

The 1978 code changes the rules on debtor's new promises to pay scheduled bankruptcy debts by adding several extra requirements for such promises to be enforceable. First, the new promises must be enforceable under the applicable state (nonbankruptcy) law; you'll recall from Chapter 10 that many states require such new promises to be made in writing. The 1978 code requires such new promises to have been made before the bankruptcy discharge becomes effective, and the code further states that such a promise may be rescinded by the debtor for sixty days after it becomes enforceable. In addition, where the debtor is an individual, the court must hold a hearing and advise the debtor of the legal effects of such a promise. The court must also tell the debtor that the promise is not required as a condition of the discharge. Where the new promise relates to a consumer debt that is not secured by real property, the court in addition must approve the promise as being in the debtor's "best interest" and not imposing an "undue hardship" or as being part of a good faith agreement for the redemption of some of the debtor's property or for the settlement of a dispute as to whether the debt was or was not dischargeable.

INDIVIDUAL REPAYMENT PLANS

An individual in financial difficulty may file a voluntary petition for "adjustment" of debts under Chapter 13 of the 1978 code and thus prevent nearly all further actions by creditors to collect their claims. This Chapter 13 procedure is available to persons who have less than $100,000 in unsecured debts, less than $350,000 in secured debts, and a "regular income." Proprietors of businesses, social security recipients, and wage earners can file under Chapter 13. Within ten days of filing the petition, the debtor must file with the court a plan which provides for payments of future income to a trustee, for full payment to creditors with priority, for equal treatment of all claims in the same class, and for retention of liens by secured creditors. Such plans usually ask for an extension of time within which to pay the debts; the plan maximum is three years unless the court grants an extension of up to five years for good cause. The debtor may also ask for a **composition** of debts in which the creditors may receive less than 100 percent of their claims.

A bankruptcy judge presides at the hearing for confirmation of the proposed plan. Unsecured creditors do not get to vote on confirming the plan, but the plan must give them at least what they would have received if the debtor had gone through a Chapter 7 bankruptcy/liquidation. Priority claimants must be paid in full, to the extent that money is available, unless these creditors agree to lesser payments. Secured creditors do get to vote on whether or not to accept the plan, but if a secured creditor disapproves, the court may confirm it anyway if the debtor gives the dissenting creditor the property that secures the claim or if the dissenting creditor retains a lien and the subject property is worth at least as much as the allowed amount of the secured claim. A secured claim against the debtor's principal residence cannot be modified by the plan; other secured claims may be. The payment arrangements of the plan itself may be modified after confirmation, subject to the above limitations, after proper notice and a hearing.

After completing the payments required by the plan, the debtor is discharged from all debts except long-term unsecured debts not covered by the plan and debts for child support, maintenance, and alimony. In cases of "hardship," where modification of the plan is not practicable and where the amounts already paid are equal to Chapter 7 liquidation values, the debtor may receive a hardship discharge if the failure to complete the plan is not his or her fault. Such a hardship discharge does not affect any nondischargeable debts under Chapter 7, or long-term debts not dealt with by the plan, whether secured or unsecured; or debts incurred without the trustee's permission after confirmation of the plan. If the plan was a composition, the debtor cannot receive a second discharge for six years unless the amounts paid were his or her best effort, made in good faith, and at least 70 percent of the required payments were made.

REORGANIZATION OF BUSINESS DEBTOR

In many cases, businesses get into financial difficulty because of dislocations in the production/distribution/collection process over which they have little, if any, control. Embargoes, wars, strikes, materials shortages, defaults by major customers, and other economic occurrences may have serious impact on a business that does not have substantial financial reserves. If a basically sound firm has a temporary cash flow problem, it probably makes sense to try to save the firm rather than push it into a Chapter 7 liquidation. Most reorganizations under Chapter 11 are designed to salvage the debtor businesses, although the creditors sometimes require management changes and the business may be run temporarily by a trustee.

The *BFP* case involves a Chapter 11 bankruptcy and an asset sale.

BFP v. RESOLUTION TRUST CORP.
114 S.Ct.1757 (1994)

FACTS: Petitioner BFP is a partnership, formed by Wayne and Marlene Pedersen and Russell Barton in 1987, for the purpose of buying a home in Newport Beach, California, from Sheldon and Ann Foreman. Petitioner took title subject to a first deed of trust in favor of Imperial Savings Association to secure payment of a loan of $356,250 made to the Pedersens in connection with petitioner's acquisition of the home. Petitioner granted a second deed of trust to the Foremans as security for a $200,000 promissory note. Subsequently, Imperial, whose loan was not being serviced, entered a notice of default under the first deed of trust and scheduled a properly noticed foreclosure sale. The foreclosure proceedings were temporarily delayed by the filing of an involuntary bankruptcy petition on behalf of petitioner. After the dismissal of that petition in June 1989, Imperial's foreclosure proceeding was completed at a foreclosure sale on July 12, 1989. The home was purchased by respondent Paul Osborne for $433,000.

In October 1989, petitioner filed for bankruptcy under Chapter 11 of the Bankruptcy Code. Acting as a debtor in possession, petitioner filed a complaint in bankruptcy court seeking to set aside the conveyance of the home to respondent Osborne on the grounds that the foreclosure sale constituted a fraudulent transfer under § 548 of the Code. Petitioner alleged that the home was actually worth over $725,000 at the time of the sale to Osborne. Acting on separate motions, the bankruptcy court dismissed the complaint as to the private respondents and granted summary judgment in favor of Imperial. The bankruptcy court found, *inter alia,* that the foreclosure sale had been conducted in compliance with California law and was neither collusive nor fraudulent. In an unpublished opinion, the District Court affirmed the bankruptcy court's granting of the private respondents' motion to dismiss. A divided bankruptcy appellate panel affirmed the bankruptcy court's entry of summary judgment for Imperial. The Court of Appeals affirmed.

 JUSTICE SCALIA:

This case presents the question whether the consideration received from a noncollusive, real estate mortgage foreclosure sale conducted in conformance with applicable state law conclusively satisfies the Bankruptcy Code's requirement that transfers of property by insolvent debtors within one year prior to the filing of a bankruptcy petition be in exchange for "a reasonably equivalent value...."

Section 548 of the Bankruptcy Code, 11 U.S.C. § 548, sets forth the powers of a trustee in bankruptcy (or, in a Chapter 11 case, a debtor in possession) to avoid fraudulent transfers. It permits to be set aside not only transfers infected by actual fraud but certain other transfers as well—so-called constructively fraudulent transfers. The constructive fraud provision at issue in this case applies to transfers by insolvent debtors. It permits avoidance if the trustee can establish: (1) that the debtor had an interest in property, (2) that a transfer of that interest occurred within one year of the filing of the bankruptcy petition, (3) that the debtor was insolvent at the time of the transfer or became insolvent as a result thereof, and (4) that the debtor received "less than a reasonably equivalent value in exchange for such transfer...." It is the last of these four elements that presents the issue in the case before us.

Section 548 applies to any "transfer," which includes "foreclosure of the debtor's equity of redemption."

Of the three critical terms "reasonably equivalent value," only the last is defined: "value" means, for purposes of § 548, "property, or satisfaction or securing of a ... debt of the debtor...." The question presented here, therefore, is whether the amount of debt (to the first and second lien holders) satisfied at the foreclosure sale (viz., a total of $433,000) is "reasonably equivalent" to the worth of the real estate conveyed. The Courts of Appeals have divided on the meaning of those undefined terms. In *Durrett v. Washington Nat. Ins. Co.*, 621 F.2d 201(1980), the Fifth Circuit, interpreting a provision of the old Bankruptcy Act analogous to § 548(a)(2), held that a foreclosure sale that yielded 57 percent of the property's fair market value could be set aside, and indicated in dicta that any such sale for less than 70 percent of fair market value should be invalidated.... This *"Durrett* rule" has continued to be applied by some courts under § 548 of the new Bankruptcy Code.... In *In re Bundles,* 856 F.2d 815, 820 (1988), the Seventh Circuit rejected the *Durrett* rule in favor of a case-by-case, "all facts and circumstances" approach to the question of reasonably equivalent value, with a *rebuttable* presumption that the foreclosure sale price is sufficient to withstand attack under § 548(a)(2).... In this case, the Ninth Circuit, agreeing with the Sixth Circuit, ... adopted the position first put forward in *In re Madrid* that the consideration received at a noncollusive, regularly conducted real estate foreclosure sale constitutes a reasonably equivalent value under § 548(a)(2)(A). The Court of Appeals acknowledged that it "necessarily part[ed] from the positions taken by the Fifth Circuit in *Durrett* ... and the Seventh Circuit in *Bundles*...."

In contrast to the approach adopted by the Ninth Circuit in the present case, both *Durrett* and *Bundles* refer to fair market value as the benchmark against which determination of reasonably equivalent value is to be measured. In the context of an otherwise lawful mortgage foreclosure sale of real estate, such reference is, in our opinion, not consistent with the text of the Bankruptcy Code. The term "fair market value," though it is a well-established concept, does not appear in § 548. In contrast, § 522, dealing with a debtor's exemptions, specifically provides that, for purposes of that section, "'value' means fair market value as of the date of the filing of the petition...." "Fair market value" also appears in the Code provision that defines the extent to which indebtedness with respect to an equity security is not forgiven for the purpose of determining whether the debtor's estate has realized taxable income.... Section 548, on the other hand, seemingly goes out of its way to avoid that standard term. It might readily have said "received less than fair market value in exchange for such transfer or obligation," or perhaps "less than a reasonable equivalent of fair market value." Instead, it used the (as far as we are aware) entirely novel phrase "reasonably equivalent value." "[I]t is generally presumed that Congress acts intentionally and purposely when it includes particular language in one section of a statute but omits it in another," and that presumption is even stronger when the omission entails the replacement of standard legal terminology with a neologism. One must suspect the language means that fair market value cannot—or at least cannot *always*—be the benchmark.

That suspicion becomes a certitude when one considers that market value, as it is commonly understood, has no applicability in the forced-sale context; indeed, it is the very *antithesis* of forced-sale value. "The market value of ... a piece of property is the price which it might be expected to bring if offered for sale in a fair market; not the price which might be obtained on a sale at public auction or a sale forced by the necessities of the owner, but such a price as would be fixed by negotiation and mutual agreement, after ample time to find a purchaser, as between a vendor who is willing (but not compelled) to sell and a purchaser who desires to buy but is not compelled to take the particular ... piece of property." Black's Law Dictionary 971 (6th ed. 1990). In short, "fair market value" presumes market conditions that, by definition, simply do not obtain in the context of a forced sale....

Neither petitioner, petitioner's *amici*, nor any federal court adopting the *Durrett* or the *Bundles* analysis has come to grips with this glaring discrepancy between the factors relevant to an appraisal of a property's market value, on the one hand, and the strictures of the foreclosure process on the other. Market value cannot be the criterion of equivalence in the foreclosure-sale context. The language of § 548(a)(2)(A) ("received less than a reasonably equivalent value in exchange") requires judicial inquiry into whether the foreclosed property was sold for a price that approximated its worth at the time of sale. An appraiser's reconstruction of "fair market value" could show what similar property would be worth if it did not have to be sold within the time and manner strictures of state-prescribed foreclosure. But property that *must* be sold within those strictures is simply *worth less*. No one would pay as much to own such property as he would pay to own real estate that could be sold at leisure and pursuant to normal marketing techniques. And it is no more realistic to ignore that characteristic of the property (the fact that state foreclosure law permits the mortgagee to sell it at forced sale) than it is to ignore other price-affecting characteristics (such as the fact that state zoning law permits the owner of the neighboring lot to open a gas station). Absent a clear statutory requirement to the contrary, we must assume the validity of this state-law regulatory background and take due account of its effect. "The existence and force and function of established institutions of local government are always in the consciousness of lawmakers and, while their weight may vary, they may never be completely overlooked in the task of interpretation...."

Fraudulent transfer law and foreclosure law enjoyed over 400 years of peaceful coexistence in Anglo-American jurisprudence until the Fifth Circuit's unprecedented 1980 decision in *Durrett.* To our knowledge, no prior decision had ever applied the "grossly inadequate price" badge of fraud under fraudulent transfer law to set aside a foreclosure sale.To say that the "reasonably equivalent value" language in the fraudulent transfer provision of the Bankruptcy Code requires a foreclosure sale to yield a certain minimum price beyond what state foreclosure law requires, is to say, in essence, that the Code has adopted *Durrett* or *Bundles*. Surely Congress has the power pursuant to its constitutional grant of authority over bankruptcy, ... to disrupt the ancient harmony that foreclosure law and fraudulent-conveyance law, those two pillars of debtor-creditor jurisprudence, have heretofore enjoyed. But absent clearer textual guidance than the phrase "reasonably equivalent value"—a phrase entirely compatible with pre-existing practice—we will not presume such a radical departure....

Federal statutes impinging upon important state interests "cannot ... be construed without regard to the implications of our dual system of government.... [W]hen the Federal Government takes over ... local radiations in the vast network of our national economic enterprise and thereby radically readjusts the balance of state and national authority, those charged with the duty of legislating [must be] reasonably explicit...." It is beyond question that an essential state interest is at issue here: we have said that "the general welfare of society is involved in the security of the titles to real estate" and the power to ensure that security "inheres in the very nature of [state] government...." Nor is there any doubt that the interpretation urged by petitioner would have a profound effect upon that interest: the title of every piece of realty purchased at foreclosure would be under a federally created cloud. (Already, title insurers have reacted to the *Durrett* rule by including specially crafted exceptions from coverage in many policies issued for properties purchased at foreclosure sales....) To displace traditional State regulation in such a manner, the federal statutory purpose must be "clear and manifest...." Otherwise, the Bankruptcy Code will be construed to adopt, rather than to displace, pre-existing state law....

For the reasons described, we decline to read the phrase "reasonably equivalent value" in § 548(a)(2) to mean, in its application to mortgage foreclosure sales, either "fair market value" or "fair foreclosure price" (whether calculated as a percentage of fair market value or otherwise). We deem, as the law has always deemed, that a fair and proper price, or a "reasonably equivalent value," for foreclosed property, is the price in fact received at the foreclosure sale, so long as all the requirements of the State's foreclosure law have been complied with.

Chapter 11 cases, like Chapter 7 liquidations, may be voluntary or involuntary; most of the same rules apply to both types of proceedings. Under Chapter 11, however, the court must appoint a creditors' committee, usually composed of the seven largest unsecured creditors. This committee examines the affairs of the business to decide whether to continue the business, or to ask the court for a liquidation, or to ask that a trustee be appointed to operate the business in place of the existing management. For the first 120 days after filing, only the debtor can propose a plan for reorganization, but the debtor would normally develop such a plan in consultation with the creditors. A debtor who files a plan within that time has a further sixty days to get the creditors to approve it. The court can reduce or extend these time periods for good cause. After the first 120 days, any party in interest (a creditor or the trustee) can propose a plan.

The proposed plan must classify claims and ownership interests and must spell out which will and which will not be impaired; it must provide equal treatment for all claims or interests in the same class unless the persons with that class of claims or interests agree otherwise; and it must provide adequate means for implementing the plan's payment arrangements. Further, where the debtor business is a corporation, the plan must require that stockholders' voting rights be protected, that no nonvoting stock be issued, and that directors and officers be selected so as to protect the interests of creditors and stockholders. Generally, the plan may modify the rights of creditors and owners, but these persons have the right to vote on whether or not to accept the plan. Normally the bankruptcy court will not confirm a reorganization plan unless it has received the required majority vote of each class of creditors or owners whose rights were modified ("impaired"). Two-thirds in dollar amount of each class of such owners must vote in favor of the plan. Each class of such creditors must approve by a majority in number and by two-thirds in the dollar amount of allowed claims. The plan may be confirmed without the consent of owners or creditors whose rights were not impaired.

It is possible for the court to confirm a plan which has not received the consent of an impaired class if the persons in that class are treated in a "fair and equitable" manner—for instance, if all members of the class will receive the full current value of their claims, or if all members of the class will receive an equal proportion of their claims, and classes whose claims and interests have lower priorities will receive nothing. In any case, dissenters are protected by the rule that they must receive from the plan at least what they would have received through a Chapter 7 liquidation.

CONSUMER PROTECTION IN CREDIT TRANSACTIONS

New Government Activism on Consumer Issues

Consumerism was surely one of the major social movements in the United States during the 1970s. The national government, and to a lesser extent the states, moved to correct what were seen as abuses by sellers and lenders. Inexperienced and unwary consumers were being pressured into paying for shoddy or undelivered merchandise, or misperformed or unperformed services. High-pressure sales tactics produced contracts with harsh and unfair provisions. Confronted with these marketplace manipulations, judges and legislators rebelled.

The *Henningsen* case (referred to in Chapter 16) is probably the single most important piece of consumer law ever written. It was the opening salvo in the product liability revolution, which has continued through the 1970s and 1980s, into the 1990s. That part of consumer protection law is discussed throughout Chapter 16.

Other aspects of the consumer protection movement have also been discussed in prior chapters. The FTC's authority over unfair trade practices and deceptive advertising is discussed in Chapter 39. The new legal rules on unordered goods and in-home sales are discussed in Chapter 8. Usury laws, limiting the rate of interest that can be charged, are covered in Chapter 12. Also discussed earlier (in Chapter 9) is the concept of "unconscionability," which courts can use to invalidate contract provisions that are grossly unfair, although not specifically illegal.

Consumer Credit Protection Act
(Truth in Lending Act)

Full Disclosure in Credit Transactions. As several philosophers have said, "knowledge is power." A consumer who was aware of the terms of a proposed credit transaction would be better able to compare them with those of other possible lenders, and to object to those which were most unfair. Congress passed the Truth in Lending Act (TILA) in 1969, as the first major part of the Consumer Credit Protection Act (CCPA), which now also includes sections on other topics, such as a consumer leasing and credit billing. A required disclosure form must be given to the consumer at or before the signing of the credit contract. It must disclose the interest rate as an annual percentage and show the total dollar figure for the "finance charge," which includes loan fees, credit report fees, and required insurance charges. TILA does not limit the amount of these charges; it only specifies that the amounts must be disclosed.

Similarly, ads for credit which mention a down payment, a monthly payment, or an interest rate must go on to specify the other terms as well.

Where the purchaser's home is used as collateral, the purchaser is given three business days after the purchase, or after the creditor gives written notice of the right to cancel, within which to rescind the whole contract. This rescission rule does not apply to the first mortgage on the home, but only to later credit contracts, such as those for home improvements.

Under its rule-making authority, the Federal Reserve Board has stated that TILA applies to any consumer transaction which calls for payment in more than four installments. This rule is found in FRB Regulation Z.

The *Franck* case discusses the TILA and FRB Regulation Z.

FRANCK v. BEDENFIELD
494 N.W.2d 840 (MI, App., 1992)

FACTS: In this case, plaintiff, Robert Franck, purchased a mortgage that had been given to Diamond by Clark and Jessie Bedenfield (hereafter defendants). Miscreants at Diamond absconded with plaintiff's investment money after assigning him the note and mortgage but without disbursing the loan funds to the Bedenfields.

Plaintiff brought suit to foreclose the Bedenfields' mortgage. Following a bench trial, the court held the debt to be valid, plaintiff being a holder in due course, but the mortgage to be invalid, plaintiff not being a bona fide purchaser for value. Both sides appeal.

 JUDGE WEAVER:

The first issue raised is whether defendants were obligated, contractually or otherwise, by execution of the note or the mortgage. Defendants contend there was no contract and also that they timely exercised their right of rescission.

The federal Truth in Lending Act (TILA) ... and Regulation Z ... both provide for rescission until three days after the latest of: (1) consummation of the transaction, (2) delivery of two copies for each borrower of the notice of right to cancel, or (3) delivery of all "material disclosures." Here, the question is whether consummation ever occurred.

This Court has previously held that when the funds of a credit transaction are never distributed to the consumer, he cannot be said to have been contractually obligated as a result of the credit transaction, and, thus, consummation cannot be said to have occurred.... Thus, even though the affirmative defense of the TILA was not pleaded, the Bedenfields' right to rescind the transaction remains effective under the TILA....

Defendants sent a letter to Diamond on January 30, 1989, expressing their intent to rescind the contract. However, in denying defendants' motion for summary disposition pursuant to MCR 2.116(C)(10), the court ruled that the letter intended to effectuate a rescission was unenforceable because Diamond was in the midst of bankruptcy proceedings, and all transactions were required to cease during the stay imposed by; such proceedings. We agree with the court's conclusion; and plaintiff's argument on appeal, that the bankruptcy stay precluded defendants' attempt to rescind the contract with regard to Diamond.

However, shortly after March 15, 1986, Diamond assigned the Bedenfields' mortgage to Franck.

Any consumer who has the right to rescind a transaction under 15 U.S.C. § 1635 may rescind the transaction with regard to any assignee of the obligation.... Thus, the Bedenfields could properly exercise their right to rescind by informing Franck of their intent to do so.... We find that defendants' motion for summary disposition alleging that they were allowed to rescind the contract under the TILA effectively rescinded the transaction....

Franck asserts that because he is a holder in due course, the TILA rescission remedy is not effective against him. However, this Court has previously ruled to the contrary regarding this issue....

After rescinding the loan transaction, the Bedenfields were not obligated to pay the note, and Franck was required to discharge the mortgage....

This resolution renders all other issues raised by the parties moot.

We amend the judgment of November 28, 1989, to strike that portion of the judgment granting Franck judgment against the Bedenfields.

Since the original TILA covered only consumer *purchases* on credit, Congress added the Consumer Leasing sections to CCPA in 1976. Leasing of cars, computers, and other equipment has become increasingly common, even for persons defined as consumers (personal users). Similar disclosures are required in these lease transactions.

Where a creditor has violated TILA or CLA, the consumer may recover twice the finance charge, but not less than $100 nor more than $1,000, plus attorneys' fees. Criminal penalties for a willful and knowing failure to comply are a fine up to $1,000, or imprisonment up to one year, or both. Because of the detail and complexities involved in complying with TILA, amendments passed in 1980 exempt a creditor from liability if the error is corrected within sixty days after it is discovered.

Credit Card Liability. Other sections of the CCPA have drastically changed the law relating to the issuance and use of credit cards. Prior to the CCPA, gasoline companies and other issuers were free to send out cards by mass mailings, using computerized lists of potential customers. Under general contract law rules, retention and use of the credit card would constitute acceptance of the issuing company's offer. The issuer's terms could include a provision making the cardholder liable for its unauthorized use. These contract provisions were sometimes enforced by the courts, at least where the merchant taking the card as payment had made a reasonable effort to verify the identity of the person using the card.

It is now unlawful to issue cards that have not been requested by the customer. Further, the customer/cardholder's liability for unauthorized use is limited to $50. Even this $50 amount is conditioned on the card issuer's compliance with CCPA's requirements. The issuer must have notified the customer of this potential $50 liability, have provided a notification form to be sent to the issuer in the event of loss or theft of the card, and have provided either a signature or photo on the card so that the merchant can identify the user. If all these requirements have been met, the customer can be held liable for up to $50 of unauthorized charges that occur before the issuer is notified that the card has been lost or stolen.

Equal Credit Opportunity Act

Originally, the problems dealt with by the Equal Credit Opportunity Act (ECOA) were denials of credit on the basis of sex or marital status. Women who had been divorced or widowed were denied credit, in many cases, because they had had no separate credit history or because they had been codebtors with their husbands, who had defaulted on the debts. Either way, they were unable to obtain credit in their own names. The ECOA now prohibits such discrimination, and also that based on race, color, religion, national origin, or age. These protections are similar to those given to employees under the national civil rights acts, as discussed in Chapter 41.

Creditors are prohibited from discouraging applications for credit, from refusing to grant a separate account to a married woman, and from asking the applicant's marital status where such a separate account is requested. Because marital property laws differ from state to state, however, a creditor may ask about marital status where collateral is required for the credit transaction. Similarly, minors cannot demand credit under ECOA, since they lack full capacity to contract and can disaffirm contracts which they make while minors.

USE OF CREDIT INFORMATION

It is true that businesses have always kept records about individuals, but recordkeeping was limited, due to the obvious problems of storage, access, and retrievability. The computer has minimized those problems, and consequently more and more information is kept about the individual. There is more possibility of error and less access by the individual to the records to determine just what they say. A major concern has been the gathering, storage, and retrieval of information about individuals by various credit bureaus and local merchants' associations, which have computerized their files and have dossiers on nearly every American adult.

Fair Credit Reporting Act. To curb the abuses of credit bureaus, Congress passed the Fair Credit Reporting Act, which became effective on April 25, 1971. The following is a summary of its major provisions.

Credit reporting agencies are authorized to furnish credit information only in connection with credit, insurance, and employment applications, a government license for which a consumer has applied, or any other business transaction in which a consumer is involved; or by written consent of the consumer concerned; or in compliance with a court order.

The reporting of adverse information more than seven years old regarding suits, arrests, and other matters is generally prohibited. However, information on bankruptcies can be made available for fourteen years, and if the inquiry concerns an application for a life insurance policy of $50,000 or more or an application for a job with an annual salary of $20,000 or more, then there is no age restriction on records and all information may be furnished. Thus, the bureaus have an excuse not to clear out the computers periodically. The reporting of adverse information from investigative reports more than three months old is generally prohibited unless the information is reverified.

All reporting agencies are required to "follow reasonable procedures to assure maximum accuracy of the information" contained in reports. The type of information which can be furnished to government agencies without a court order is limited. Upon the request of a consumer, a reporting agency must disclose to the consumer all information about him or her in the agency's files, except for medical information or the sources of the information. A person or business ordering an investigative report must notify the consumer that an investigation is being made. An agency must disclose to a consumer on request the names of persons and businesses that have been furnished credit information about the consumer in the preceding six months (two years for employment purposes).

An agency must reinvestigate information disputed by a consumer "within a reasonable period of time" unless "it has reasonable grounds to believe that the dispute by the consumer is frivolous or irrelevant." If the information is found to be inaccurate, then the agency must delete the information from the record. The consumer also has the right to have the agency put in the file a statement of not more than 100 words explaining that the information is disputed, and the agency, at the consumer's request, must send copies of the statement to the persons and businesses that had been sent the disputed information. A person or business that rejects a consumer for credit, insurance, or employment on the basis of a credit report must advise the consumer of the reason for the rejection and identify the reporting agency.

A consumer is granted the right to file a civil action in U.S. District Court to recover damages resulting from willful and negligent noncompliance with the law. Obtaining information under false pretenses for credit reporting and willfully giving out such information to unauthorized persons is punishable by a fine of up to $5,000 and imprisonment for up to one year.

As noted above, this law gives the aggrieved individual the right to file an action charging that a credit bureau, its informant, or a user of its report violated the Fair Credit Reporting Act. The violation doesn't have to be intentional, but it must have caused demonstrable financial damage. In a successful action, a consumer can collect actual damages, legal costs, and attorney's fees. For a willful violations, a credit bureau may also have to pay punitive damages and may be subject to criminal penalties.

Privacy Act. In passing the Privacy Act of 1974, Congress recognized the problems of invasion of privacy caused by governmental computer recordkeeping. The act placed many restrictions on computerized recordkeeping and the handling of computerized records by the various governmental agencies. This act applies only to the records of national governmental agencies, not to those of state agencies or private businesses. In addition to placing restrictions on governmental recordkeeping and the handling of governmental records, the act gave individuals access to such records about themselves and the right to copy, correct, and challenge personal information held by the national government. The act also prohibited the nonroutine dissemination of records without notification to the individuals involved, and it placed restrictions upon the expanded use of social security numbers.

Many states have passed privacy laws similar to the 1974 Privacy Act. These laws have placed restrictions on recordkeeping and the handling of computerized information by the various state agencies. The subject of computers and privacy is certainly a key issue in our society today. To date, the major thrust of the various privacy bills has been to regulate only national and state computerized recordkeeping, and there are still many unsolved legal problems concerning privacy and the recordkeeping practices of private business.

Electronic Funds Transfer Act. On November 10, 1978, Congress recognized the problems associated with EFT and passed the Electronic Funds Transfer Act. Congress stated that the purpose of this law was to provide a basic framework establishing the rights, liabilities, and responsibilities of participants in electronic funds transfer systems. The primary objective of the law was to ensure a basic level of protection for the individual consumer's rights.

The Electronic Funds Transfer Act allows the various states to enact more comprehensive and more protective legislation if they desire to do so. A few states have enacted regulatory legislation in the EFT area, and many others are considering such legislation.

Fair Credit Billing Act. Another area where abuses were thought to occur was disputes over charges to a credit account. Formerly, the creditor would bill charges it thought were valid, and then press the customer for payment. If the customer could not convince the creditor that disputed charges were incorrect, the creditor could report the delinquency to credit bureaus or take steps to collect the account through court process. Now, the FCBA has set up certain procedures that must be followed if there is a dispute.

The consumer-debtor has sixty days after receiving a billing to notify the creditor of any claimed errors. The creditor then has thirty days to notify the debtor of receipt of the claim. The creditor must correct the account, or investigate and explain its reasons for not correcting the account, within ninety days or two billing cycles. Claimed delinquencies cannot be reported to credit bureaus unless FCBA has been complied with. The debtor must be notified of the persons to whom the delinquency has been reported. A creditor who fails to comply with FCBA forfeits its right to collect the first $50 of the disputed amount, including finance charges.

FTC Regulation 433. Another very important consumer protection law has already been noted in Chapter 13, and will be further discussed in Chapters 19 and 22. The Federal Trade Commission adopted a rule in 1976 which abolished the "holder in due course" concept for most consumer transactions. Basically, this is the concept which says that an assignee of an account receivable which is in negotiable form, or which contains an express waiver of defenses clause, owns the account free and all clear of most common defenses that the debtor might assert to try to avoid payment. The FTC has said, in effect, that a consumer-debtor can always assert any defense which can be proved.

Fair Debt Collection Practices Act. Finally, Congress took action in 1977 to curb some of the worst abuses in the credit field—collection agencies' scare tactics and harassment. Most states had already acted to stop these abuses, and FDCPA allows these state regulations to continue if they contain adequate enforcement provisions. The national act covers only agencies that are collecting debts for others, not banks and businesses that are trying to collect their own accounts.

The FDCPA contains a number of restrictions on collection practices. The collector may not contact the consumer at work, if the employer objects, or at unusual or inconvenient times, or at all if the consumer has an attorney. The collector may not use harassing or intimidating tactics, or abusive language against any person, or false or misleading tactics. Unless so authorized by a court, the collector may not contact third parties other than a spouse, parent, or financial adviser about the account. The collector may not contact the consumer-debtor about the account after receiving a written refusal to pay, except to notify the consumer of possible actions which may be taken. A debt collector may not deposit a postdated check prior to its effective date. These are significant limitations on prior practices.

Garnishment Limitations. **Garnishment** is a court process for seizing money or property belonging to the debtor, but in the possession of third parties. Bank accounts and wages owed are typical subjects of garnishment.

Under its authority to interpret the constitutional phrase "due process of law," the U.S. Supreme Court has held that prejudgment garnishment of wages is unconstitutional *(Sniadach v. Family Finance Corp.* 395 U.S. 337). It has also said, however, that some prejudgment remedies may be permissible (*Mitchell v. W.T. Grant,* 416 U.S. 600). Prejudgment garnishment of a bank account was specifically invalidated in *North Georgia Finishing, Inc. v. Di-Chem Inc.,* 419 U.S. 601 (1975).

The CCPA also limits garnishments of wages. No more than 25 percent of an individual's wages after-tax earnings, or the amount by which the wages exceed thirty times the minimum wage, whichever is less, can be garnished. These limits do not apply if the claim is for taxes, wife or child support, or subject to an order in a bankruptcy Chapter 13 adjustment of debts.

SIGNIFICANCE OF THIS CHAPTER

Even honest and hard-working persons can suffer financial difficulties. Economic trends and technological changes can have adverse impacts on both businesses and individuals. When financial pressures become too severe, bankruptcy offers the debtor a "fresh start."

Nearly everyone is a debtor, creditor, or both, at some time during their lives. Congress and the state legislatures have moved aggressively to regulate this aspect of commercial transactions. Important new protections have been developed for the consumer-debtor. This area of the law seems sure to expand further. Every business person needs to know the current debtor-creditor rules of the game.

PROBLEMS FOR DISCUSSION

1. Michael Hemmen has no accumulated wealth. He recently obtained a divorce and his wife got everything. He has no savings account and only $40 in his checking account. He lives with his parents and pays them $60 per month for room and board. He is unemployed and has made several unsuccessful attempts to obtain a job. He does not have a car. He only has three years of college with Business Administration as his Major. He receives $90 per week unemployment. He owes $4,039 plus interest on several educational loans. The total unsecured debt less the educational loans is over $13,000.

   Is Michael entitled to a "hardship" discharge for his educational loans? Discuss.

2. James Millstone applied to Firemen's Fund Insurance for insurance on his Volkswagen bus. Firemen's issued the policy, but also ordered a credit report from O'Hanlon. About a month later, O'Hanlon furnished a report, based on information from Washington, D.C., where Millstone had previously lived. The report stated that he "was a hippie-type person with shoulder-length hair and with a beard on one occasion, who participated in many demonstrations in the Capitol, carried demonstrators back and forth to his home, where he housed them in his basement and wherever else there was room." It also said that "he was strongly suspected of being a drug user, that he was rumored by neighbors to have been evicted from three previous residences in Washington, D.C., and that he was very much disliked by his neighbors there." Based on this information, Firemen's ordered its agent to cancel the insurance policy on the VW. When the agent explained that Millstone was a highly respected assistant managing editor of the St.Louis Post-Dispatch, and that he had been a White House reporter in Washington, Firemen's withdrew its cancellation order. When O'Hanlon refused to give satisfactory answers to him about the credit report, Millstone sued. The trial court awarded $2,500 actual damages and $25,000 punitive damages, plus $12,500 attorney's fees.

   Did the trial court decide the case correctly? Explain.

3. Robert Isaac Lynn and Bonnie Marie Ryan had been married in 1991, while he was still in medical school. When they were divorced in 1999, the New Jersey court held that his medical degree and license to practice medicine were "property" and thus subject to "equitable distribution" between the spouses in the divorce proceeding. The New Jersey court then awarded Bonnie 20 percent of this "property," valued at $306,886. Robert was ordered to pay that amount ($61,377.20) in semiannual installments over the next six years. When Robert filed for bankruptcy, he indicated that he practiced medicine as a physician, but did not list his medical degree and license in his schedule of property owned. Bonnie and her attorney (Stephen Roth) objected to Robert's receiving a discharge in bankruptcy because he failed to schedule all his "property."

   Is Bonnie correct? Why or why not?

4. In November 1991, while Arland Boydston, a 40-year-old Army Lt. Colonel, married Carolyn Conner. Their financial downfall began in March 1999 when they borrowed $3,000 to start a wig business, the Chateau De Monique Wig Salon in Mineral Wells, Texas. By September, the shop's business had sharply deteriorated because of the projected closing of nearby Fort Wolters. At this time Boydston retired from the service, cutting his income by more than half, to $708 per month. Aside from his retirement income and the small amount of money the couple was taking in from the salon, the Boydstons had no other income. Mr. Boydston was also involved in a prospective low-income housing project from which he hoped to make a windfall by sharing in the net profits. In January 1991, the project fell through when FHA approval was denied, again because of the closing of Fort Wolters.

   Despite their strained financial condition, however, the Boydstons went on a spending spree which lasted from the latter part of August 1990 until they filed their petition in bankruptcy on February 15, 1991. During this six-month period, they incurred almost $32,000 in new indebtedness, the overwhelming portion of which was for luxury items and nonessential personal expenses rather than for salvaging the wig business. Merchandise purchased included a new Cadillac, a mink coat, a very expensive shotgun, a houseful of new furniture, and $1,300 in personal travel expenses. A $6,000 bank loan ostensibly intended to acquire new inventory for the wig salon was diverted to the purchase of a new home in Dallas, and on several occasions personal financial statements submitted to creditors flagrancy failed to disclose a majority of their indebtedness. Most of the debt was incurred after the Boydstons were no longer able to meet existing obligations when due, and had written at least two creditors requesting extension of payment deadlines.

During this period, $2,923.73 worth of personal merchandise was charged at Sears and $2,540.03 at Neiman Marcus. No payments were ever made on either account. Appellants claim that the factors detailed above clearly indicate a purpose to acquire merchandise on credit with no intention of paying for it. Sears also complains that, in completing a credit application with the store in November, Mrs. Boydston grossly overstated the wig salon's monthly earnings and omitted the family's major financial obligations in order to secure an extension of credit which otherwise would not have been granted. The application, however, contained only three blanks for listing present creditors.

Neiman Marcus thwarted Mrs. Boydston's discharge from any of her debts under § 14(c)(1) of the Bankruptcy Act by showing that she had altered documents pertaining to her bankruptcy for the purpose of deceiving the court and had given perjured testimony concerning the exhibits. The referee found that there was no evidence to show that Mr. Boydston participated in or knew of these changes, and granted him a discharge. The U.S. District Court affirmed.

Is this result correct? Explain.

5. Emory Catnip, driving his car on a four-lane interstate highway, hit a second car from the rear, causing the death of its driver, Hiram Dallo. Emory's car traveled 468 feet after the collision, 334 feet on the highway and another 134 feet after it left the pavement. Hiram's car traveled 382 feet after impact, 179 feet on the pavement and 203 feet off it, finally turning over. The police found a bottle of gin in Emory's car. He admitted to having taken a couple of drinks that afternoon. The accident occurred between 8:00 p.m. and 8:30 p.m. The pictures of the cars indicated a terrific impact. Emory claimed that Hiram had pulled in front of him just as he was about to pass. Hiram's widow filed a wrongful death action for $200,000 in which she alleged that Emory had been guilty of driving "carelessly, negligently, recklessly, and wantonly." After she received her judgment, Emory filed for bankruptcy.

Will this judgment be discharged by Emory's bankruptcy? Explain.

Chapter 18

Suretyship and Secured Transactions

Perhaps no single area is so crucial to the functioning of a modern economy, or so little understood by the "average" participant in the economic game, as secured financing. It is hard to imagine a modern business enterprise functioning effectively on a "cash on the barrelhead" basis; credit is the oil that keeps the economic wheels turning. Of course, some holdout consumers still insist that they always "pay cash for everything," but for most individuals this is just as much a credit economy as it is for business firms. The great majority of us will have an occasion, not just once but many times, to buy things on credit and to borrow money. Credit buying, borrowing, and financing is the name of the modern economic game, and that's what "secured transactions" are all about.

This chapter and the next are intended to convey to you the basic concepts and problems involved in secured financing and to give you some idea of what you need to do to protect your rights, either as an individual or as a businessperson. This chapter first explains the legal consequences of cosigning another person's obligations. It then focuses on the basic concepts involved in creating a "security interest" in personal property: What types of collateral may be involved? What has to be done to create a valid security interest in favor of the creditor in the debtor's property? Chapter 19 examines the requirements for "perfecting" a security interest against third-party claimants—usually the debtor's other creditors or a buyer of the collateral from the debtor. It also covers the rules for determining which creditor has the best claim to the collateral ("priority"), where there is more than one claim, and the rules for handling the collateral when the debtor defaults.

SECURITY AND PRE-CODE LAW

Creditor's Need for Security. Creditors as a group are notoriously unwanted, unloved, misunderstood, and *insecure*. A **creditor** is someone who has permitted another party to receive his or her goods, services, or other value without their having been fully paid for by return value. This other party, the **debtor,** has been permitted to enjoy the benefits of the transaction but has not yet returned the full value which was promised to the creditor. The unsecured creditor thus has only the debtor's word that he or she will fulfill that promise, subject to all the human and economic infirmities which may come "twixt the cup and the lip."

In many personal business situations, the debtor's word may be good enough. The debtor's financial standing may be such that there is little risk of nonpayment. In many other situations, the creditor has good reason to feel insecure, particularly since in the event of bankruptcy general creditors are paid only after a long line of preferred claims.

Types of Security, or Collateral. The creditor seeking the warm feeling of "security" may use any one of the three basic types of "collateral" to try to ensure the payment of the debt. A second person may be required to back up the debtor by also agreeing to pay the debt (a **surety**) or by agreeing to pay the debt if the debtor does not (a **guarantor**). The parties may agree that the creditor will have certain rights against some of the debtor's real estate if the debtor defaults. Finally, the parties may agree that the creditor will have certain rights against an item or items of personal property as collateral if the debtor defaults. It is this third situation which is defined by the UCC as a **secured transaction**.

NATURE OF SURETYSHIP

Where a lender or seller does not feel that the debtor's personal financial situation warrants the extension of credit, the lender or seller may require a **cosigner**; that is, another person who also agrees to become liable for payment of the debt. This sort of arrangement may be the only additional security the creditor requires, or it may be combined with personal property or real estate as specific collateral security for the debt. The person who actually receives the money or credit is spoken of as the **principal debtor**; the cosigner is the **surety**.

The other frequently occurring suretyship transaction involves **bonding**. Here a company issuing a surety bond promises to pay a certain sum of money if the "debtor" defaults on performance obligations. For example, with the performance bonds required of building contractors, the bonding company promises to pay the landowner/customer in the event of nonperformance or of improper performance by the builder. Because courts do not agree that such a bond also covers the claims of unpaid laborers or material suppliers, the builder may also be required to furnish a bond that specifically provides for the payment of these claims.

Many public officials, particularly those who have custody of public funds, must file bonds guaranteeing that the bonding company will replace any missing monies. Bonds are also required in many types of judicial proceedings to protect the other party and to guarantee performance of court-imposed obligations. An example is a bail bond to ensure a party's appearance for trial. Although perhaps not technically surety bonds, fidelity bonds are frequently required by employers for employees in "sensitive" jobs; specified defaults by such an employee give the employer the right to recover the amount of the bond from the bonding company.

Most courts continue to draw a distinction between *suretyship*, strictly defined, and *guaranty*. A surety makes the same promise to the creditor as does the principal debtor; the surety says, "I will pay." When the debt falls due, the creditor can sue the surety without first demanding payment from the principal debtor. A guarantor makes a different sort of promise; this person says, "If the principal debtor doesn't pay, then I'll pay." The creditor is required to demand the money from the principal debtor and to notify the guarantor of the principal debtor's default before the guarantor becomes liable to "pick up the check." The guarantor's promise is similar to the conditional contract liability of the indorser of a negotiable instrument. A **guarantor of collectibility** makes an even more limited promise; the creditor normally must get a judgment against the principal debtor and have the judgment returned unsatisfied before the guarantor of collectibility becomes liable. Many of the following legal rules, however, are applied by the courts to both suretyship and guaranty.

The nature of Ramos' promise is at issue in the *Home Federal* case.

HOME FEDERAL SAV. & LOAN ASS'N. v. RAMOS
284 Cal.Rptr. 1 (CA. App. 4 Dist., 1991)

FACTS: Defendant Ramos was president of the Ramos/Jensen Company (R/J Co.), a California corporation. R/J Co. was the general partner of a limited partnership, the Peacock Ridge Company, formed to complete the Peacock Ridge construction project. Between September 1983 and March 1985, plaintiff Home Federal loaned nearly $7.4 million to the Peacock Ridge partnership. Each of the four separate loans was personally guaranteed by Ramos.

By November 1986, financial difficulties on the project caused Peacock to default on the Home Federal loans. At that point, Peacock owed substantial sums in accrued interest and had other obligations in connection with the project. Home Federal accepted a "workout agreement" in which it forgave all but $100,000 of the interest and agreed to loan Peacock an additional $50,000. In return, Peacock promised to execute a promissory note for $150,000 secured by a personal guaranty signed by Ramos.

The workout agreement was negotiated on behalf of Peacock by Arthur Brooks, an R/J Co. employee. Thomas Lynn, a major loan officer for Home Federal, negotiated the agreement with Brooks and prepared three documents—the loan modification agreement, the promissory note and the personal guaranty—which he delivered to Brooks for the purpose of obtaining Ramos' signature. Brooks returned all three signed documents to Lynn on December 18, 1986.

The promissory note provided a signature line for "Ronald J. Ramos, President" R/J Co. as general partner of Peacock. Ramos signed the document "R.J. Ramos, Pres." The personal guaranty included the following operative language:

"In consideration of the loan from the Association to Borrower, I, Ronald J. Ramos (Guarantor), absolutely and unconditionally guarantee and promise to pay to Association, or whomever Association orders me to pay, any and all indebtedness of Borrower to Association evidenced by, or in any way connected with the loan (including but not limited to additional advances or loans) or the note, and to perform all covenants and agreements of Borrower contained in the note or any security agreement between Borrower and Association."

The signature line at the bottom of the document provided for the signature of "Ronald J. Ramos." Instead, Ramos signed it as he had signed the promissory note: "R.J. Ramos, Pres."

When Peacock defaulted on the new note and Home Federal brought suit to enforce the guaranty, Ramos defended on the ground that his signature as "Pres." indicated an intent to bind only R/J Co. and not himself personally on the guaranty. At the close of all the evidence, the trial court granted Home Federal's motion for a directed verdict. Ramos appealed.

 ASSOCIATE JUSTICE WIENER:

[O]ur function is not to determine whether factual issues remain to be resolved but rather to decide whether the trial court's interpretation of the guaranty was correct. In this regard we must interpret the document consistent with the expressed intent of the parties under an objective standard.... Would a reasonable lender in Home Federal's position have understood Ramos's conduct as indicating that only R/J Co. was to be bound? Applying this standard, we agree with the trial court that Ramos's addition of the abbreviation "Pres." after his signature did not change the legal effect of the document as Ramo's personal guaranty of Peacock's liability under the promissory note....

[A] signatory's mere addition of a title following the signature on a document otherwise purporting to be a personal guaranty does not change its personal character.... [T]itles and the like are generally terms "descriptive of the person rather than the relationship in which he signs the agreement...."

For the purposes of this case, we see no reason to articulate a blanket rule that a signatory's notation of his corporate capacity can never raise an issue as to the identity of the guarantor.... Here as in *Sebastian*, however, to interpret the document as a guaranty by the corporate principal is objectively unreasonable because the corporations were already liable without the guaranty. In *Sebastian*, West Valley was the primary lessee. Here, while R/J Co. was not the primary obligor on the note, it is well established that a general partner is personally liable for the debts of a limited partnership.... Under these circumstances, to interpret the guaranty as binding only the corporation would render it a nullity.

CONTRACT ASPECTS OF SURETYSHIP

Since suretyship is a contract, an offer and acceptance, supported by consideration, must be present. Whether or not the creditor-offeree must give notice of acceptance to the surety-offeror depends on the facts and circumstances of the particular situation. In many cases, the creditor's acceptance of the surety's offer will be obvious. Where a continuing guaranty of payment covers a number of possible transactions, many courts will require notice of a creditor's acceptance, so that the guarantor knows the extent of the obligations the creditor has undertaken.

In the simplest transaction, both the principal debtor and the surety sign the loan agreement at the same time. The bank's payment of the loan funds to the principal debtor is consideration for both promises of payment. Since a contract of guaranty is typically a "reassurance" of payment sometime after the primary debt was made, new consideration is required to bind the guarantor to the promise. This new consideration may be an extension of the time for payment, smaller monthly installments, forbearance from suit, or any other agreed modification by the creditor, but *some* new consideration has to be present to hold the guarantor liable.

The precise form in which the "backstop" promise is made may also determine whether or not the Statute of Frauds applies. Clearly the guarantor's "if-then" promise is covered, and it must be evidenced by a signed writing. Courts may not always draw the technical distinction between suretyship and guaranty, however, and they may require a writing for suretyship contracts as well. Special state statutes may also produce the same result. As always, it's a good idea to "get it in writing."

SPECIAL RIGHTS OF THE SURETY

The promise to pay someone else's debt places the surety in a rather special position. Therefore, the law gives the surety a set of special rights to produce fair ultimate results wherever possible.

Exoneration is the right of the surety to demand that the principal debtor pay the debt when it falls due and before the creditor collects it from the surety. The surety can also get a similar equity order against cosureties, forcing each to pay a proportionate share of the debt where the debtor is insolvent or otherwise in default.

The surety, after paying some or all of the debt, is entitled to **reimbursement** or **indemnification** from the debtor. This was really the debtor's obligation, and it's only fair that the debtor repay the surety. If there were two or more cosureties, any of them who paid more than a fair share is entitled to **contribution** from the cosureties, so that each surety bears the agreed proportionate part of the loss. To assist the surety in obtaining reimbursement from the principal debtor, the surety who has paid off the creditor acquires, through a process called **subrogation**, the same legal status that the creditor had. The surety automatically acquires whatever rights the creditor had in property that served as collateral for the debt, and can take whatever enforcement steps the creditor could have taken against the collateral.

DEFENSES OF THE SURETY

The law provides the surety with some special defenses because of the surety's unique situation. The surety can use some, but not all, of the defenses that can be used by the principal debtor as well as any defenses that may be personal to the surety.

Because of the surety's special legal situation, and to prevent unfair results, the courts generally hold that any of the following acts by the creditor will discharge the surety's liability.

Release of the Principal Debtor. A release of the principal debtor also releases the surety, *unless* the surety consents to such a release, or the creditor specifically reserves rights against the surety, or an arrangement is made to indemnify the surety, such as turning over to the surety sufficient collateral to cover the debt.

Where the creditor releases the principal debtor but reserves the right to sue the surety, the surety's rights against the principal debtor must be preserved too, so that the principal debtor ultimately pays.

Release of Collateral. The courts have generally said that a release of rights against property held as collateral security for the debt also will release the surety *if* it can be shown that the surety's rights are prejudiced in some material way by such release. Some courts have reached similar results where the value of the items held as collateral has been substantially diminished by negligence of the creditor.

Material Alteration of Terms. The surety agrees to assume the debt of another person under certain terms and conditions. Therefore, any material change in those terms, if not agreed to by the surety, should discharge his or her liability. Materiality here is a fact question, but changes in the amount of the debt, the maturity date, or the place of payment would almost certainly be held to be material. Most modern cases require that a surety who has been paid for acting as such must show that the change in terms prejudices the surety's rights. Friends and relatives are still automatically discharged by any material change in the terms of the surety agreement to which they do not consent.

Rejection of Tender of Payment. Where the creditor refuses a valid tender of payment by either the principal debtor or the surety, the surety is discharged. If the debtor is willing to pay the amount as agreed and the tender is refused by the creditor, it certainly wouldn't be fair for the creditor to then be able to sue the surety. If the surety's tender of payment is refused, it wouldn't be fair to extend the liability any further since the surety could have sued the principal debtor immediately if the creditor had taken the money.

Like any other party liable on a contract, the surety has available any defense which applies to the individual situation. Some examples are lack of agreement, lack of consideration, lack of contractual capacity, and fraud. However, most courts will not allow a surety sued by a creditor to use fraud by the principal debtor against the surety as a defense unless the creditor is somehow responsible for the fraud.

The special suretyship arrangement entitles the surety to assert many of the defenses of the principal debtor, especially those relating to the formation or performance of the agreement. Where a defense such as fraud or duress against the principal debtor makes the contract voidable, the surety can use the same defense if the principal debtor elects to avoid the contract. If the principal debtor elects to affirm the contract, the surety remains bound. Where the whole contract is void because of illegality, that defense would, of course, be available to the surety. Where the principal debtor's defense is a personal lack of capacity, the surety would still be bound. Such lack of capacity would in many cases be the very reason for having a cosigner. However, where a minor has disaffirmed the contract and returned the consideration received to the creditor, the surety is discharged, at least to the extent of the value of the consideration when returned. Bankruptcy of the principal debtor does not discharge the surety.

SECURED TRANSACTIONS, ARTICLE 9, UNIFORM COMMERCIAL CODE

Purpose, Policy, and General Characteristics. The basic objectives of Article 9 in the field of personal property secured financing are uniformity, unity, and simplicity. Lawyers and nonlawyers struggling with the new Code concepts and terminology may wonder whether the third objective has really been advanced very far, but it is clear that the first two have. The Code is now in force, with only relatively minor variations, in all U.S. jurisdictions except Louisiana, thus ending the pre-Code jungle of drastically conflicting state laws and the attendant conflict-of-laws problems. And even though it was necessary to make distinctions in Article 9 and to deal with different security situations and problems in different ways, such differences were placed within the context of an overall scheme of security law and their nature and effects were carefully calculated.

The following hypothetical examples show the range of Article 9's coverage:

1. Carole Consumer wants to buy a new car on credit. Whether she arranges her own financing at her bank or credit union, or signs a time payment contract which her car dealer sells to a bank or finance company, this is a "secured transaction" if the new car is used as collateral to secure payment of the balance of the purchase price.

2. Dan Debtor needs to borrow $1,500. His bank (or credit union, or finance company) will not make the loan on Dan's signature alone, but requires collateral. Dan owns an expensive stereo set and a refrigerator-freezer, which are both paid for and which his bank accepts as sufficient collateral. This is a "secured transaction."

3. Big Bennie's Appliance Store orders a shipment of new TVs on credit. This is a "secured transaction" if the credit seller (manufacturer or wholesaler) wants to use the TVs as collateral for the unpaid contract price. Alternatively, Bennie could borrow the contract price from a bank or finance company and use the TVs as collateral for the loan. Either way, since the creditor (the "secured party") wants to use the TVs as collateral, this is a "secured transaction."

4. Mr. Shatturglass (the home improvement king) needs to borrow $50,000 for added working capital. His bank (or finance company) will not lend him the money without collateral. His only available asset is his accounts receivable—the amounts due him for work performed. Whether Shatturglass merely pledges his accounts to the bank or sells the accounts outright for cash, this is a "secured transaction."

5. Freddy Farmer leases a new tractor from an equipment rental company for two years at $300 per month. At the end of the two-year lease term, Freddy has the option of buying the tractor for an additional $1. This is a "secured transaction."

In sum, all credit transactions in which personal property or a fixture is used as collateral are defined by the UCC as secured transactions.

Article 9, while "comprehensive" in intent and organization, does not embrace all the law dealing with interests in personal property. It is, after all, part of the Code; all the "General Provisions" of Article 1 apply to a particular transaction, and other parts of the Code may also be involved. For example, if the secured transaction involves a credit sale of goods, the warranty sections and other parts of Article 2 may be relevant.

The most important single piece of non-Code law applicable to financing transactions is the U.S. Bankruptcy Act; one of the main contenders that a secured creditor is trying to defeat is the trustee in bankruptcy, who is seeking the debtor's assets for *pro rata* distribution to all of the debtor's creditors. Problems as to priority of claims between the secured creditor and persons such as a garage operator who is given a statutory lien also require reference to sources outside the Code. A secured transaction involving a motor vehicle will probably require reference to the state's motor vehicle code. Moreover, in some areas the coverage of the Code will depend on prior state law, such as the definition of a "fixture," and in other areas the Code's applicability is unclear—mobile homes, for example.

General Characteristics. Like the Code generally, Article 9 is characterized by a considerable degree of "freedom of contract." Some sections contain rules that are explicitly made subject to a different agreement by the parties, usually with the words *unless otherwise agreed* (see, e.g., 9-207[2]). A few sections specifically state that they cannot be varied by the parties (see, e.g., 9-501[3]). But most of Article 9 sections contain no specific statement as to whether the parties may, by agreement, change or modify the rules the sections contain. In light of the Code's general commonsense approach and its downgrading of legal technicalities, it would seem that the parties would be given considerable latitude to "do their thing" in their own agreement, unless otherwise specified, subject only to the requirements of good faith, reasonableness, diligence, and care (the "Four Horsemen" of 1-102[3]) and to the idea of unconscionability expressed in 2-302.

The organizational pattern of Article 9 is based on a practical, step-by-step, problem-solving approach in dealing with a secured transaction. The first question we must answer is whether Article 9 applies to the transaction; the answer will be based on the 9-100 sections in Part 1 and on the general definitions contained in 1-201. Our next problem is to create a security interest in the collateral which will be effective as between the immediate parties to the transaction; here we use the 9-200 sections. Our next job is to perfect the security interest to maximize our rights against third parties; here we need to consult the 9-300s and 9-400s. Where there are conflicting claims against the collateral, we need to determine the relative priorities of these claims; for this we will use the 9-300s. And finally, in the event of a default by the debtor, we need to know what we can or must do to enforce our security interest against the collateral; these procedures are outlined in the 9-500 sections. We now proceed to consider each of these matters in greater detail.

APPLICABILITY AND DEFINITIONS

Definitions. To avoid as many ambiguities and differences in interpretation as possible, the drafters of the Code provided a set of definitions, some found in 1-201 and generally applicable throughout the Code and some contained in each article. For secured transactions the drafters felt it desirable to use new terminology which would not be encumbered and encrusted with residues from pre-Code law. The *secured party* (lender, credit seller) and the *debtor* enter into a contract (the *security agreement*) which provides that the secured party shall have a *security interest* in the described *collateral*. This is a *secured transaction* (see 9-105).

Transactions Covered. The coverage intended by the drafters of Article 9 is very broad indeed. Coverage is extended by 9-102(1):

1. To any transaction (regardless of its form) which is intended to create a security interest in personal property or fixtures including goods, documents, instruments, general intangibles, chattel paper, or accounts.

2. To any sale of accounts, or chattel paper.

In 9-102(2), the drafters reiterate their intent to cover all security interests created by contract, "including pledge, assignment, chattel mortgage, chattel trust, factor's lien, equipment trust, conditional sale, trust receipt, other lien or title retention contract and lease or consignment intended as security." The comment states that this listing of the old pre-Code security devices is illustrative only; any contractual arrangement, new or old, which is intended to create a security interest in personal property is included.

The *Brown* case resolves a conflict between these Code rules and a state agency's regulation.

BROWN v. YOUSIF
517 N.W.2d 727 (MI, 1994)

FACTS: In 1982, plaintiff James J. Brown sold his business, Lean and Tender Butcher Shop, to Prang Enterprise, Incorporated. Included in the sale was a specially designated distributor (SDD) and a specially designated merchant (SDM) liquor license. Prang paid part of the purchase price in cash and financed the remaining portion with a promissory note. However, in order to secure the payment of the note in the event of default, Prang gave plaintiff a security agreement with regard to fixtures, furniture, and equipment, as well as a reassignment of these items, including reassignment of the SDM and SDD liquor licenses, subject to approval by the LCC. Plaintiff then filed a financing statement in the appropriate offices covering "[a]ll the trade fixtures, furniture and equipment, including all the after acquired goods and chattels, which replace existing equipment only." However, it did not mention the liquor licenses or a like term (i.e., "general intangibles").

Subsequently, in 1984, Prang entered into negotiations with defendant Fakhri J. Yousif for the sale of the SDD liquor license. During this time, defendant had actual knowledge of the security interest as illustrated by defendant's attempt to obtain plaintiff's consent to the transfer before the sale. Despite plaintiff's refusal to consent to the transfer, defendant purchased the license and transferred it to his store.

In 1986, Prang transferred the remaining license, the SDM, to a David Marriot by way of a promissory note. However, when Marriot filed for bankruptcy in 1987 and defaulted in his payments to Prang, Prang/Marriot stopped making payments to plaintiff. This gave rise to plaintiff's suit against Prang and defendant. However, plaintiff eventually settled with Prang after accepting a mediated judgment of $25,000. On the other hand, plaintiff's suit against defendant sought to foreclose on the SDD liquor license pursuant to the security agreement and reassignment clause. In response, defendant moved for summary disposition relying on primarily, the LCC's rule (Rule 19) which stated:

A security agreement between a buyer and a seller of a licensed retail business, or between a debtor and a secured party, *shall not include the license* or alcoholic liquor.

The trial judge granted defendant's motion for summary disposition. The Court of Appeals reversed.

 JUSTICE RILEY:

Before turning to the enforceability of Rule 19, we find it necessary to clarify plaintiff's right and priority to the liquor license under Article 9. We begin by noting that defendant only attacks the perfection of this interest (i.e., plaintiff did not attach to the financing statement the reassignment agreement between plaintiff and Prang and the financing statement itself did not list the license or a general intangible as a collateral). Defendant does not, nor did he below, contend that plaintiff did not have a valid security interest via the security agreement signed by Prang. Nonetheless, we find that the security agreement created an effective security interest in the liquor license....

Having found a valid security interest in the liquor license, we turn to whether plaintiff was required to properly file a financing statement that either listed the license as collateral or listed the term general intangibles in order to enforce this agreement against defendant. While perfection is generally needed to enforce a security agreement covering general intangibles against other secured creditors, it is not needed against transferees who either did not give value or had knowledge of the security interest....

In the instant case, it is undisputed that a liquor license is a general intangible, it certainly is personal property and something of value as evidenced by the sale of the license for $48,342.98.... Indeed, defense counsel admitted at oral argument that a liquor license is a general intangible. Moreover, defendant is not a secured party, but is a transferee because of the transfer from Prang (transferor) to defendant (transferee). Further, despite the giving of value, defendant had actual knowledge of the security interest as evidenced by his contact with plaintiff before the transfer. Therefore, in accordance with the plain and unambiguous terms of § 9301(1)(d), plaintiff has an enforceable security interest against defendant despite his lack of proper perfection.

The question remains, however, whether a valid security interest under Article 9 can be enforced in light of the LCC rule prohibiting a lien on a liquor license....

[T]he LCC has exclusive authority to control liquor trafficking. However, the question in this case is whether the LCC has the authority to prohibit the creation of a security interest governed by Article 9 of the UCC. Despite the LCC's plenary authority to regulate liquor trafficking, we are persuaded that this authority does not allow the LCC to invalidate by *administrative rule* a portion of another duly enacted law (i.e., the UCC). Indeed, the UCC was intended as a law of general applicability that cannot be impliedly repealed by statute, let alone by administrative rule....

Moreover, the clear language of Article 9 indicates that the Legislature intended the law to be of general applicability, covering all forms of security interests in personal property, regardless of its form, except for those provided in M.C.L. §

440.9104.... Indeed, the exceptions to Article 9 as set forth in § 9104 *do not include* a liquor license and *do not exclude* rules set by the LCC. Moreover, § 9203(2) addressing the enforceability of a security interest and the applicability of other laws, does not specifically subject Article 9 to laws affecting the LCC or liquor trafficking in general. Therefore, we conclude that Article 9 grants plaintiff an enforceable security interest in this liquor license and that Rule 19 must give way to these duly enacted provisions of Article 9, a law of general applicability. Accordingly, we hold that plaintiff has an enforceable security interest in this SDD liquor license and may foreclose on this interest and seek reassignment in accordance with applicable law, subject to approval by the LCC....

We hold that § 9301(1)(d) gives plaintiff an enforceable security interest against this defendant because defendant purchased the collateral with knowledge of plaintiff's security interest. Moreover, we hold Rule 19 invalid to the extent that it conflicts with the provisions of Article 9, a law of general applicability. Accordingly, we remand to the trial court for proceedings consistent with this opinion.

Since in many cases Article 9's applicability is made dependent on the intent of the parties to the transaction, litigation frequently arises as to what the parties did intend. A third-party claimant will usually raise the question that the parties' arrangement is not effective as against third parties because it was really "intended" as a secured transaction and it was not properly filed as such. The "lease" and "consignment" cases are particularly troublesome. The problem arose so often that a special new section on consignment was added by the 1972 amendments. In general, this section requires the consignor to give the same kind of notice to other inventory financers as if it were selling on credit rather than consigning.

In 1-201(37), the Code also provides that "leases" are intended as security devices when the debtor can become the owner of the collateral by paying an additional nominal consideration.

The *Fleming* case involves this "lease" definition, as well as the rules for obtaining a deficiency judgment against the Debtor.

FLEMING v. CARROLL PUBLISHING COMPANY
581 A.2d 1219 (D.C. App., 1990)

FACTS: On December 29, 1980, Carroll Publishing Company entered into an "Equipment Lease Agreement" with three individual investors who had formed a partnership called Equity Leasing Joint Venture—80F. The lease covered certain computer hardware and software. These items were acquired through third-party vendors. Some of the software was "off-the-shelf" but at least two significant software packages were to be custom-written for Carroll by a third-party vendor. The lease term was for five years, with total payments of $87,328.25.

The lease did not provide for Carroll to purchase the equipment. In a subsequent Purchase Agreement of January 25, 1981, however, the parties agreed that "Buyer [Carroll] is hereby given the first right to purchase the Equipment at the estimated fair market value of 10 percent of the original value. Said purchase shall occur upon expiration of the lease." In addition, the Purchase Agreement provided that a "demand for purchase of the Equipment may be made by Equity or its successor or assigns at any time after the date hereof."

A series of difficulties of various kinds developed, and on August 25, 1982, Carroll wrote to Equity's agent terminating the agreement, on the ground of nondelivery of certain items called for by the lease. Up to that point, Carroll had made sixteen regular lease payments totalling $26,198.46. On February 22, 1983, Equity filed the instant suit against Carroll, seeking recovery in the amount of $61,930.11 and attorney's fees. Carroll counterclaimed, alleging nondelivery of some of the leased items and seeking damages for fraud and for breach of contract.

While the case was pending, on September 29, 1983, Equity's agent went to Carroll's office armed with a court order and repossessed a number of pieces of hardware and one item of software, located in the drive of one of the repossessed machines. Subsequently, at least some of the repossessed hardware was sold at a private sale, of which Carroll was given no form of notice.

Following a bench trial, the trial court denied Equity any relief. The court concluded first that the agreement was not a "true lease" but a security agreement governed by Article 9. It concluded further that any claims for nondelivery were the sole responsibility of third-party vendors and not Equity; hence Equity was initially within its rights in proceeding under the agreement and under Article 9. However, it held, Equity's failure to give notice to Carroll of its proposed sale of repossessed collateral barred Equity from obtaining any deficiency judgment, and any rights in the software remaining in Carroll's possession had been lost because of the subsequent modification of the software. Hence, Equity took nothing by its complaint. Nonetheless, the court interpreted the agreement to permit Equity to recover reasonable attorney's fees and costs, which it awarded in the amount of $50,636.01.

 JUDGE STEADMAN:

On appeal, Equity contends first that the trial court erred in concluding that the lease was not a "true lease" but a security agreement governed by Article 9 of the District of Columbia Uniform Commercial Code....

[I]n determining whether a lease is a "true lease" or an Article 9 security agreement, the trial court must look to the intent of the parties, which depends on "the facts of each case." The trial court's determination as to the intent of the parties is essentially one of fact,...and will not be upset unless it is "plainly wrong or without evidence to support it."... Here, the trial court recognized that the intent of the parties is essential to a determination of whether a lease is a "true lease" or security agreement and the court detailed its reasons for finding that the parties intended the lease as a security agreement. In particular, the court noted that the lease allocated to Carroll several burdens typically associated with ownership of property, such as the obligation to pay license fees and taxes on the equipment, the obligation to keep the equipment in good repair and the assumption of "the entire risk of loss of and damage to Equipment from any and every cause whatsoever." In addition, the court noted that Equity's status was as financier, rather than manufacturer or seller, and that Equity had no storage facilities for the equipment. These are among the "factors" courts use in determining whether a lease is "intended for security."... The court also noted that the total price Carroll was required to pay under the lease exceeded the purchase price of the equipment by $29,028 and that the customized system would be of little value to other potential lessees. "Under the totality of the evidence presented," the court found that the parties "intended to create a security agreement." We cannot say that this finding is "plainly wrong or without evidence to support it."

Equity contends next that, even if the lease was a security agreement, the trial court erred in barring Equity from obtaining a deficiency judgment.... To the extent that paragraph 11 of the lease can be read to permit Equity to sell repossessed equipment without giving the statutory notice to Carroll, it is unenforceable under D.C. Code Section 28:9-501(3)(b)....

Although D.C. Code Section 28:9-504(3) does not prescribe the consequences of a secured creditor's failure to notify the debtor of a proposed sale of repossessed property, we addressed this precise issue in *Randolph v. Franklin Investment Co.*... In *Randolph*, the creditor repossessed the debtor's automobile when the debtor failed to make timely payments on the automobile and the creditor sold the automobile for scrap at a private sale of which the debtor was not given notice.... The creditor then sought a deficiency judgment, which the trial court awarded. We reversed, holding broadly that "by failing to give the required notice [of] the private sale, the creditor ... is not entitled to a deficiency judgment; its recovery is limited to the proceeds of the private sale."... We noted that the notice requirement serves the two purposes of affording the debtor an opportunity to redeem the repossessed collateral before the sale and permitting the debtor to monitor the sale so as to be able to defend properly against a deficiency action.... "Because of the substantial prejudice to debtors in the absence of notice of resale," we concluded, "especially when compared to the ease with which any creditor can comply with the notice requirements, we adopt [the] strict rule" that failure to provide notice bars recovery of a deficiency judgment.... Our decision in *Randolph* was supported also by D.C. Sup. Ct. Civ. Rule 55-II(b) (1989), which states, in pertinent part, that "no deficiency judgment after repossession of personal property shall be granted unless it shall appear to the satisfaction of the Court by proper evidence that said plaintiff complied with applicable law."...

Equity contends, as a general matter, that *Randolph* ... is inapplicable to the present case because it occurred in a consumer, as opposed to a business, context. While it is true that these cases occurred in a consumer context, we find no indications in them that the "absolute preclusion" rule was not to be applicable across the board. Quite to the contrary, we specifically said in *Randolph* that "the rule of law governing the legal consequences to a secured creditor for failure to give the requisite notice of resale must be uniform for all creditors, based on the range of commercial practices realistically to be anticipated."...

The policies underlying the rule as stated in *Randolph* are not essentially different in a business context. Sitting as a panel, we see no basis for drawing the distinction urged by Equity here.

It is true that the present case is somewhat unusual in that Equity did not repossess all the collateral in Carroll's possession, nor, apparently, did it sell all the collateral it did repossess. The trial court correctly held that these facts did not thereby entitle Equity to a deficiency judgement to which it was not otherwise entitled. While a secured creditor ordinarily has the right to sue on the debt as well as proceed against the collateral, ... if he proceeds against the collateral, he is obligated to follow the applicable rule for its disposition. At least under the circumstances here, a failure to do so acts as a bar to any deficiency judgment, whatever rights the creditor may retain in the collateral itself. Case law from other jurisdictions supports this conclusion....

Although Equity lost its rights to a deficiency judgment, it does not follow that it has lost rights in the remaining collateral, and especially to the collateral not repossessed (*viz.,* the bulk of the "leased" software)....

We do not think that a bar to a deficiency judgment in itself constitutes any obstacle to the enforcement of a security interest in any collateral remaining in the debtor's possession. The policies underlying the "absolute preclusion" rule do not militate against such a result. It is one thing to deny a creditor a right to proceed against a debtor for an alleged balance owing after the debtor has been stripped of all the property securing the debt. It would be quite another to permit a debtor to continue to possess, indeed as a practical matter to own outright, a portion of the collateral although the debt remains unpaid. This would be especially unjust in the case of a debt securing, in effect, the unpaid balance of the purchase price of the collateral, as here....

The trial court's view as to Equity's limited rights in the software apparently affected its view of the available relief. It observed that "the software covered by the lease had been so substantially revised during the three years following Carroll's default that it no longer existed in an identifiable form and thus could not be returned to Plaintiffs." If Equity had no rights in post-default modifications of the software, it might well be correct that "it" (*i.e.,* the collateral as it existed at the time of default) no longer could be delivered to Equity, and, likewise, that at the time of the Order, the Court had no way of ascertaining what software "covered by the original lease" still exists. But these conclusions are brought into serious question since they seem to be an outgrowth of the unsupported assumption that Equity had no rights to any "replacements or modifications" occurring after the termination of the lease.

Accordingly, the case must be remanded for further consideration by the trial court of what rights, if any, Equity may still have with respect to the unrepossessed collateral, including replacements and modifications.

If the revisions to the form of the collateral subsequent to the termination of the lease were in breach of the security agreement or otherwise wrongful on the debtor's part, Equity would not necessarily be precluded from recovering the value of the unrepossessed collateral, any less than if the debtor following repossession of part of the collateral had deliberately or negligently destroyed the remaining unrepossessed collateral. However, we note that the trial court in its Order stated that while Equity asserted in a post-trial memorandum and that it was entitled to a money judgment for the value of the retained software, it had not "presented sufficiently exact evidence of the software's value to enable the court to make such an award." Further, the court noted, Equity had dropped its claim of wrongful conversion. These facts, depending on their precise content, may preclude a second bite at the apple.

Exclusions. Having made such brave claims for the comprehensiveness of Article 9's coverage, we must now consider the lengthy list of specific exclusions (a through k) which the Code enumerates in 9-104. Generally, these exclusions refer to liens and transactions that are outside the scope of normal financing arrangements. For example, landlords' liens, wage assignments, and transfers of insurance claims, tort claims, and bank deposits are among the exclusions. Also excluded are security interests that are subject to a supervening national statute, such as the Ship Mortgage Act of 1920. The general theme underlying these exclusions is to omit Code coverage for transactions which are not normally used in commercial situations, particularly transactions which are already adequately covered under existing law.

Conflict-of-Law Rules. Section 9-103 lays down some basic rules for dealing with multistate transactions in three situations which caused problems under prior law. The validity and perfection of security interests against accounts, general intangibles, and mobile equipment is to be determined according to the law of the state where the debtor has its chief executive office.

Where personal property of other kinds already subject to a security interest is brought into a Code state, its validity is to be determined by the law of the state where the property was located when the security interest attached. If such an interest was already perfected when the property was brought into the state, it generally remains perfected in the new state for four months, within which time it may also be perfected in that state. Where a certificate of title is issued on property under a state statute that requires notation on such a certificate in order to perfect a security interest, then perfection is governed by the law of the state that issued the certificate.

Although the adoption of the Code in all jurisdictions except Louisiana has had the effect of substantially minimizing the areas of interstate conflict, these 9-103 rules retain considerable significance. One still needs to know where to file to perfect a security interest, whether or not to have a notation made on a vehicle's certificate of title, and what to do to protect the interest where the debtor will be using the collateral in more than one state.

CLASSIFICATION OF COLLATERAL

Tangible. Collateral is classified generally into nine categories. The definitions used are essentially functional definitions, based on the nature of the item and/or the use to which it is being put by the debtor at the time the security interest attaches to it. The significance of these categories stems from the different treatment given the different types of collateral.

Such differences are observable: in the available methods of perfecting the security interest; in the place of filing and the necessity therefor; in the priority of claims against the collateral; in determining the rights of buyers from the debtor; and in the respective rights and remedies of the parties on default.

Section 9-109 recognizes four classes of "goods:"

1. "Consumer goods" if they are used or bought for use primarily for personal, family, or household purposes.

2. "Equipment" if they are used or bought for use primarily in business (including farming or a profession) or by a debtor who is a nonprofit organization or a governmental subdivision or agency or if the goods are not included in the definitions of inventory, farm products or consumer goods.

3. "Farm products" if they are crops or livestock or supplies used or produced in farming operations or if they are products of crops or livestock in their unmanufactured states, and if they are in the possession of a debtor engaged in farming operations.

4. "Inventory" if they are held by a person who holds them for sale or lease or to be furnished under contracts of service or if he has so furnished them, or if they are raw materials, work in progress, or materials used or consumed in a business.

The comment to this section makes clear that these categories are mutually exclusive. While the same goods can fall into different categories at different times, "the same property cannot at the same time and as to the same person be both equipment and inventory, for example." "Equipment" is the residuary category; if the goods do not fit one of the other definitions, they are equipment.

The *Nicolosi* case is an illustration of the differences in legal results that may flow from these differences in categorization of the collateral.

IN RE NICOLOSI
4 UCC Rptr. 111 (U.S.D.C., S.D., OH, 1966)

FACTS: Nicolosi bought a diamond engagement ring for his fiancee for $1,237.35 from Rike-Kumler Company. He executed a purchase-money security agreement for the unpaid contract price, with the ring as collateral. Rike-Kumler did not file a financing statement. Nicolosi gave the ring to his fiancee prior to his bankruptcy. After he was declared bankrupt, she called off the engagement and gave the ring to the trustee in bankruptcy. The trustee wanted to sell the ring for the benefit of all of Nicolosi's creditors; Rike-Kumler claimed priority as a secured party.

 REFEREE ANDERSON:

If the diamond ring, purchased as an engagement ring by the bankrupt, cannot be categorized as consumer goods, and therefore exempted from the notice filing requirements of the Uniform Commercial Code as adopted in Ohio, a perfected security interest does not exist....

No judicial precedents have been cited in the briefs.

Under the commercial code, collateral is divided into tangible, intangible, and documentary categories. Certainly, a diamond ring falls into the tangible category. The classes of tangible goods are distinguished by the primary use intended. Under Revised Code 1309.07 (UCC § 9-109), the four classes are "consumer goods," "equipment," "farm products," and "inventory."

The difficulty is that the code provisions use terms arising in commercial circles which have different semantical values from legal precedents. Does the fact that the purchaser bought the goods as a special gift to another person signify that it was not for his own "personal, family, or household purposes?" The trustee urges that these special facts control under the express provisions of the commercial code.

By a process of exclusion, a diamond engagement ring purchased for one's fiancee is not "equipment" bought or used in business, "farm products" used in farming operations, or "inventory" held for sale, lease, or service contracts. When the bankrupt purchased the ring, therefore, it could only have been "consumer goods" bought for use "primarily for personal use." There could be no judicial purpose to create a special class of property in derogation of the statutory principles.

Another problem is implicit, although not covered by the briefs.

By the foregoing summary analysis, it is apparent that the diamond ring, when the interest of the bankrupt attached, was consumer goods since it could have been no other class of goods. Unless the fiancee had a special status under the code provision protecting a bona fide buyer, without knowledge, for value of consumer goods, the failure to file a financing statement is not crucial. No evidence has been adduced pertinent to the scienter question.

Is a promise, as valid contractual consideration, included under the term "value?" In other words, was the ring given to his betrothed in consideration of marriage (promise for a promise)? If so, and "value" has been given, the transferee is a "buyer" under traditional concepts....

The UCC definition of "value" (because of the Code purpose of being so broad as to not derogate from the ideal ubiquitous secured creditor), very definitely covers a promise for a promise. The definition reads that "a person gives 'value' for rights if he acquires them ... (4) generally, in return for any consideration sufficient to support a simple contract."

It would seem unrealistic, nevertheless, to apply contract law concepts historically developed into the law of marriage relations in the context of new concepts developed for uniform commercial practices. They are not, in reality, the same juristic manifold. The purpose of uniformity of the code should not be defeated by the obsessions of the code drafters to be all-inclusive for secured creditors.

Even if the trustee, in behalf of the unsecured creditors, would feel inclined to insert love, romance, and morals into commercial law, he is appearing in the wrong era, and possibly the wrong court.

Ordered that the Rike-Kumler Company holds a perfected security interest in the diamond engagement ring, and the security interest attached to the proceeds realized from the sale of the goods by the trustee in bankruptcy.

Intangible. Section 9-106 defines two kinds of intangible property that may serve as collateral: **account** and **general intangible**.

"Account" means any right to payment for goods sold or leased or for services rendered which is not evidenced by an instrument or chattel paper, whether or not it has been earned by performance. "General intangibles" means any personal property (including things in action) other than goods, accounts, chattel paper, documents, instruments, and money. The distinction between an account and a contract right has been eliminated by the 1972 amendments.

Documentary. The last three general types of collateral under Article 9 are also "intangible," but they relate to rights embodied in pieces of paper which are physically transferred from party to party as the rights they represent are sold, pledged, or mortgaged. In other words, these pieces of paper are used as a convenient way of handling any transfer of these intangible rights. These three categories are "documents," "instruments," and "chattel paper." **Document** means a document of title, defined in 1201(15) as including bills of lading, warehouse receipts, and the like, covering goods in the possession of a bailee and giving the possessor of the document the right to dispose of it and of the goods it represents. **Instrument** means a negotiable instrument as defined in 3-104 (notes, drafts, checks, and certificates of deposit), or an investment security as defined in 8-102 (stocks and bonds), or any other similar writing. Under the UCC, "Chattel paper means a writing or writings which evidence both a monetary obligation and a security interest in or lease of specific goods." **Chattel paper** is thus the retail installment contract you sign when you buy your new car; you promise to pay the balance of the contract price in easy monthly installments, and the seller (or its financing agency) reserves a security interest in the goods in the event that you default. This piece of paper has value to the car dealer; it can be sold to a financing agency or used as collateral for the dealer's own loan.

Article 9 also singles out certain specific types of collateral for special treatment under some of the provisions to be discussed below. Motor vehicles, fixtures, and the proceeds derived from the sale of collateral are examples of collateral to which such special treatment is applied.

Sufficiency of Description of Collateral. Both the immediate parties to the secured transaction and third parties need to know the identity of the collateral which it covers. Thus, both the security agreement itself and any financing statement which is to be publicly filed require a description of the collateral. Once again, the drafters of Article 9 clearly express their intent that this requirement should not become encumbered with extreme technicalities and legalisms. Section 9-110 says:

> For the purpose of this Article, any description of personal property or real estate is sufficient whether or not it is specific if it reasonably identifies what is described.

The *Waychus* end-of-chapter problem, involving "farm products," provides an illustration of the "reasonableness" approach of the courts to this Article 9 requirement.

VALIDITY OF SECURITY AGREEMENT AND RIGHTS OF PARTIES THERETO

General Validity. As noted previously, both the Code generally and Article 9 specifically provide for a great deal of freedom of contract between the immediate parties to a transaction.

Section 9-201 says, in part:

> Except as otherwise provided by this Act a security agreement is effective according to its terms between the parties, against purchasers of the collateral, and against creditors.

The section then goes on to point out that Article 9 is not intended to modify in any way any existing *regulatory* legislation in the state pertaining to financial transactions.

Section 9-202 makes it clear that for the purposes of Article 9 distinctions based on whether the secured party has "title" to the collateral or "only" a lien on the collateral are no longer applicable. The parties are still free to structure their approach either way, but for the purposes of rights and remedies under Article 9 it makes no difference which form they choose to use. The location of "title" to the collateral may still be important for other reasons, however; tax, regulatory, and other non-Code liability problems may be solved by reference to the location of title.

Enforceability; Formal Requisites. Article 9 does include a "statute of frauds" requirement, 9-203(1), which states a general rule requiring a security interest to be in writing to be enforceable either against the *debtor* or against third parties. As an alternative to the writing (the "security agreement"), the secured party may keep possession of the collateral under an oral security agreement. There are also three limited exceptions to this writing requirement: the security interest of a collecting bank in items it is handling for collection (4-208); and security interests arising under Article 2 on Sales of Goods (9-113) or under Article 8 on Investment Securities (8-321).

What is a sufficient writing to make the security interest enforceable under Article 9? On its face, Section 9-203(1) is deceptively simple. It provides that the security interest is not enforceable, generally, unless "the debtor has signed a security agreement which contains a description of the collateral and in addition, when the security interest covers crops growing or to be grown or timber to be cut, a description of the land concerned." The deception arises because the term *security agreement* is itself defined in Section 9-105(1) as "an agreement which creates or provides for a security interest." In other words, to be effective as a security agreement, the writing signed by the debtor must not only *describe* the collateral; it must also *create* or *provide* for a security interest in that collateral in favor of the creditor.

FINANCING STATEMENTS

The document which is publicly filed to give notice to all the world of the existence of the security interest is called a **financing statement**. This is not the lengthy and detailed *financial* statement often required from the debtor, showing all prior credit transactions, assets, and liabilities. The Code's *financing* statement is a simple, half-page form which merely announces the existence of a security interest in certain collateral.

Contents of Financing Statement. What must a financing statement contain to be effective? Since the only purpose of the financing statement is to serve as a "red flag" to third parties who may wish to deal with the collateral, the requirements are held to a minimum. A valid financing statement must contain the signature of the debtor, the names and addresses of both the debtor and the secured party, and "a statement indicating the types, or describing the items, of collateral." In addition, where crops or fixtures are involved, there must also be a description of the real estate involved. (Remember that any description is sufficient which "reasonably identifies" the collateral.) No legal mumbo jumbo is required—no witnesses, no affidavits, no notarization. Moreover, substantial compliance is sufficient.

As previously noted, *security agreement* and *financing statement* are not used synonymously in Article 9; they are distinct terms, with distinct functions. It would be possible for a security agreement that contained the names and addresses of both parties to be filed as a valid financing statement. The disadvantage of this procedure is that it puts all the "gory details" of the transaction on the public record. But the greater potential danger to the secured party arises by attempting to have the financing statement do double duty as the security agreement. Since the typical financing statement form will not embody any agreement or provide for the creation of a security interest in the collateral, the secured party may very well wind up with an interest that is not even enforceable against the debtor. Courts are not willing to use the parties' "intent" to create a security interest, if they have not complied with Article 9.

Security Agreement for Consumer Goods
or Equipment—Motor Vehicle

(Name)   _(Street Address)_   _(City)_   _(County)_   _(State)_

("debtor"), hereby grants to ____, ("Bank"), a security interest in the following described motor vehicle:

New ☐   Use ☐

Year_____   Make_____   Mode_____   Serial No._____

together with all parts, fittings, accessories, equipment, special tools, renewals and replacements of all or any part thereof, whether now owned or here-after acquired by debtor (all hereinafter called "collateral"), to secure (i) the payment of a note dated _____, executed and delivered by debtor to Bank, in the sum of $_____, payable as to principal and interest as therein provided; (ii) further advances, to be evidenced by additional notes if such advances are made at Bank's option; (iii) all other liabilities (primary, secondary, direct, contingent, sole, joint, or general) due or to become due or which may be hereafter contracted or acquired, of debtor to Bank; and (iv) performance by debtor of the agreements hereinafter set forth.

Debtor warrants that:

1. He is or will be the owner of the collateral clear of all liens and security interests except the security interest granted herein.
2. He has the right to make this agreement.
3. He is using or will use the collateral primarily for the purpose checked below:
   ☐ Personal, family or household purposes.
   ☐ Business purposes.
4. If checked here ☐, the collateral is being acquired by debtor with the proceeds of the note and Bank is authorized to disburse said proceeds to the seller of the collateral.
5. The following statements, as checked, are true:
   (a) ☐ Debtor's place of residence is at the address hereinabove stated.
   (b) ☐ Debtor's chief place of business in Michigan is at the address hereinabove stated.
   (c) ☐ If neither (a) nor (b) is checked, debtor has no residence or place of business in Michigan but the collateral will be kept in Michigan at
   _____

   (Street Address)   (City)   (County)

Debtor agrees that he:

1. Will pay the Bank all amounts payable on the note mentioned above and all other notes held by Bank as and when the same shall be due and payable, whether at maturity, by acceleration or otherwise, and will perform all terms of said notes and this or any other security or loan agreement between debtor and Bank, and will discharge all said liabilities.
2. Will defend the collateral against the claims and demands of all persons.
3. Will insure the collateral against all hazards requested by Bank in form and amount satisfactory to Bank. If debtor fails to obtain insurance, Bank shall have the right to obtain it at debtor's expense. Debtor assigns to Bank all right to receive proceeds of insurance not exceeding the unpaid balance under the note, directs any insurer to pay all proceeds directly to Bank, and authorizes Bank to endorse any draft for the proceeds.
4. Will keep the collateral in good condition and repair, reasonable wear and tear excepted, and will permit Bank and its agents to inspect the collateral at any time.
5. Will pay as part of the debt hereby secured all amounts, including attorneys' fees, with interest thereon, paid by Bank (a) for taxes, levies, insurance, repairs to, or maintenance of the collateral, and (b) in taking possession of, disposing of or preserving the collateral after any default hereinafter described.
6. Will not permit the collateral to be removed from this state without the prior written consent of the Bank.
7. Will not (a) permit any liens or security interests (other than Bank's security interest) to attach to the collateral; (b) permit the collateral to be levied upon under any legal process; (c) dispose of the collateral without the prior written consent of Bank; (d) permit anything to be done that may impair the value of the collateral or the security intended to be afforded by this agreement.
8. Bank is hereby appointed debtor's attorney-in-fact to do all acts and things which Bank may deem necessary to perfect and continue perfected the security interest created by this security agreement and to protect the collateral.
9. Until default debtor may retain possession of the collateral and use it in any lawful manner not inconsistent with the agreements herein, or with the terms and conditions of any policy of insurance thereon.
10. Upon default by debtor in the performance of any covenant or agreement herein or in the discharge of any liability to Bank, or if any warranty should prove untrue, Bank shall have all of the rights and remedies of a secured party under the Uniform Commercial Code or other applicable law and all rights provided herein, in the notes mentioned above, or in any other applicable security or loan agreement, all of which rights and remedies shall, to the full extent permitted by law, be cumulative. Bank may require debtor to make the collateral available to Bank at a place to be designated by Bank which is reasonably convenient to Bank and debtor. Any notice of sale, disposition or other intended action by Bank, sent to debtor at the address specified above, or such other address of debtor as may from time to time be shown on Bank's records, at least five days prior to such action, shall constitute reasonable notice to debtor. The waiver of any default hereunder shall not be a waiver of any subsequent default.

All rights of Bank hereunder shall inure to the benefit of its successors and assigns; and all obligations of debtor shall bind his heirs, executors, administrators, successors and assigns. If there be more than one debtor their obligations hereunder shall be joint and several.

This agreement has been executed on _____, 19____.

_____
[Debtor]

Financing Statement
Form UCC-1

STATE OF INDIANA
FINANCING STATEMENT

UNIFORM COMMERCIAL CODE

FORM UCC-1

INSTRUCTIONS:

1. This form may be used for filings with the Secretary of State and is also suitable for the following filings with the County Recorder: consumer goods, farm equipment and farm products pursuant to IC 26-1-9-401(1)(a) & (c).
2. Please type this form. Fold only along perforation for mailing.
3. Remove Secured Party and Debtor copies and send three copies with interleaved carbon paper to the filing officer. Enclose filing fee of ___ plus an additional fee of ____ for each of the following: (i) filing of an assignment on this form; and/or (ii) each additional debtor's name over one Form UCC-3 should be used for any subsequent assignments.
4. If the space provided for any item is inadequate, the item may be continued on additional sheets, preferably 5" x 8". An additional fee of ___ is due for oversized sheets.
5. If the collateral is crops growing or to be grown, describe the collateral and also the real estate.
6. The filing officer will return the third page of this Form as an acknowledgment. Secured Party at a later time may use the third page as a Termination Statement by dating and signing the termination legend on that page.

This Financing Statement is presented to Filing Officer for filing pursuant to the Uniform Commercial Code.   Number of additional sheets presented

Debtor(s) (Last Name First) and Address(es)	Secured Party(ies) and Address(es)	For Filing Officer (Date, Time, Number, and Filing Office)
This Financing Statement covers the following types (or items) of property (include description of real estate when collateral is crops)	Name and Address of Assignee of Secured Party	
☐ Products of Collateral are also covered. (See IC 26-1-9-315)		☐ Debtor is a transmitting utility as defined in IC 26-1-9-105.

Filed with: ☐ Secretary of State   ☐ Recorder of   County

By: _____
Signature of Debtor (or Secured Party in cases covered by IC 26-1-9-402(2))
State Form 36751
FORM UCC-1 – INDIANA UNIFORM COMMERCIAL CODE
(1) FILING OFFICER COPY – ALPHABETICAL

☐ Collateral was brought into this state subject to a security interest in another jurisdiction or the Debtor's location has been changed to this state.
☐ Filed in accordance with a security agreement signed by the Debtor authorizing the Secured Party to file this statement

Approved by: Secretary of State

Continuation Statement; Termination Statement. When properly filed, the original financing statement is effective for the period it specifies, up to five years. It lapses at the end of the five-year period or sixty days after the expiration date where a shorter period is specified. "Upon such lapse, the security interest becomes unperfected" (9-403[1]).

If an extension of time is desired, a **continuation statement** may be filed by the secured party anytime within the six-month period prior to the specified expiration date or within the sixty-day grace period referred to in the preceding paragraph. The requirements for this continuation statement are absolutely minimal: "Any such continuation statement must be signed by the secured party, identify the original statement by file number, and state that the original statement is still effective." As long as it complies with the provisions each time, the secured party may renew the filing any number of times and thus preserve perfection against the collateral.

When the secured debt has been paid and the secured party has no obligation to make further advances of money or credit to the debtor, the secured party must on written demand by the debtor send the debtor a **termination statement**, saying that "he no longer claims a security interest under the financing statement, which shall be identified by file number." A termination statement signed by someone other than the secured party of record must be accompanied by a statement of assignment from the secured party of record. Where the secured party fails to send the statement within ten days after a proper demand by the debtor, the debtor can recover a penalty of $100 in addition to any loss sustained because of the secured party's refusal.

When the termination statement is presented to the filing officer, it must be noted in the index. The filing officer must then remove the financing statement, any continuation statement, and any statement of assignment or release. These are marked "terminated" and sent to the secured party. Sections 9-405 and 9-406 contain provisions for handling an "Assignment of Security Interest" and a "Release of Collateral," respectively.

RIGHTS IN THE COLLATERAL

Attachment of the Security Interest. The words **attach** and **attachment** as used in Article 9 merely refer to the coming into existence of the security interest with respect to the collateral involved. The point in time at which the security interest "attaches" to the collateral is significant for several reasons. It is at this point in time that the collateral is classified under the definitions discussed above. Some priority rules among conflicting claims to the collateral hinge on "attachment."

Section 9-203(1) also contains the rules determining when a security interest attaches. There must be an agreement, evidenced either by a writing signed by the debtor or by the creditor's possession of the collateral. Value must have been given by the secured creditor. And the debtor must have "rights" in the collateral. The security interest attaches to the collateral as soon as all three of these events have occurred unless the parties expressly agree to postpone the time of attaching. To rephrase the rules: the parties may provide that the security interest attaches to the collateral at any time *after* these three conditions exist. But even by agreement, they cannot provide for attachment *prior* to the occurrence of the three conditions.

The general rules of contract law and sales law would normally determine when the debtor had "rights" in the collateral. As pointed out in Chapter 15, for instance, UCC 2-105(2) provides: "Goods must be both existing and identified before any interest in them can pass." If you were borrowing money from your credit union to buy a new car, the credit union could not have an effective security against the new car until it had been "identified" (i.e., until you and the dealer had agreed on exactly which one you were buying). If the new car had to be ordered from the manufacturer, your credit union's security interest could not "attach" until your car was assembled and identified as yours—with your name or order number. In other words, even though a security agreement has been signed and cash or credit has been extended by the secured party, there can be no effective security interest until we know what things are being used as the collateral.

Subject to an exception for consumer goods, the Code expressly permits the parties to provide in their agreement "that collateral, whenever acquired, shall secure all obligations covered by the security agreement." For all subsequent creditors, the word is: "Look out for the person with this 'security blanket.'"

This section also permits the secured agreement to cover "future advances" of value by the secured party, whether that party is obligated to make them or has the discretion to make them.

Use of Collateral by Debtor; Statement of Account. Article 9 expressly validates financing arrangements using a debtor's inventory or accounts, and it lets the parties determine to what extent the debtor should "police" the inventory or accounts. In general, third-party creditors in such situations should be adequately protected by the requirement that a financing statement on the shifting stock of collateral be publicly filed. Where there has been no such filing and the validity of the security interest depends on possession of the collateral by the secured party, the common-law rules on "pledge" still apply.

For the protection of both the debtor and any third parties involved, Section 9-208 provides that the debtor can require the secured party to verify periodic "progress reports" on the total amount the debtor believes to be due and on the collateral which is believed to be subject to the security agreement. The secured party must comply with such a request within two weeks after it is received by sending a written correction or approval and may become liable to the debtor and to third parties if it fails to comply without "reasonable excuse." The debtor can request one such statement without charge every six months; the secured party may charge a fee of up to $10 for each additional statement.

Collateral in Possession of Secured Party. In general, Section 9-207 continues the case law rules which had been developed under the common law of pledge. Where the collateral is being held by the secured party, he or she has the obligation of using reasonable care in its custody and preservation—and of keeping collateral other than fungible goods identifiable. However, the risk of loss or damage to the collateral remains on the debtor to the extent of any deficiency in effective insurance coverage.

The secured party has the right to recover all reasonable expenses from the debtor, to hold any increase or profits (except money) received from the collateral as additional security for the debt, and to repledge the collateral so long as the debtor's right to redeem is not impaired. The secured party also has the right to use or operate the collateral to preserve it or its value, or pursuant to a court order, or in accordance with the provisions of the security agreement itself.

The secured party is liable for any loss caused by a failure to meet these obligations, but does not thereby lose the security interest in the collateral.

SIGNIFICANCE OF THIS CHAPTER

Creditors require a second party's obligation on many personal and business loans or credit sales to ensure an additional source of payment if the principal debtor defaults. Any of us may be called on to cosign for another person, or may be required to get a cosigner for our own obligation. Likewise, if we're representing the creditor company, we may want to require a cosigner. Whichever of the three parties we may be, it's nice to know the rules of the game.

Once again, the basis for suretyship law is general contract law, but some special rules apply. This chapter reviewed the special status of the surety/guarantor, the application of general contract rules, and the special rights and remedies of the surety/guarantor.

Since secured credit arrangements are so necessary and so frequently used in modern commercial society, it is important to know when and how they occur. All types of personal property may be used as collateral, and the debtor may be a single consumer or the very largest industrial corporation. The credit transaction may be structured as a sale, a loan, or a transfer of accounts receivable. For the purposes of Article 9, the form is generally irrelevant; what counts is the function—the extension of credit, with personal property used as collateral. This chapter discussed the rules for creating an effective security interest between the immediate parties. The next chapter will cover the secured party's rights against other persons who have claims against the same collateral, and the rights of both the secured party and the debtor when the debtor defaults on the credit contract.

PROBLEMS FOR DISCUSSION

1. On May 17, 1997, the bankrupt, Esther Keidel, borrowed $3,500 from the First National Bank of Wood River to finance the purchase of a mobile home. Keidel signed a security agreement with the Bank and executed a promissory note. She received from the Bank a check for $3,500 payable jointly to her, to Kenneth and Rose Mitchell (the sellers), and to Olin Employees' Credit Union (the prior lien holder). When the check was issued by the Bank, it was taken to the business office of the Credit Union, where the money changed hands and various notations were made on the old certificate of title. The bankrupt was advised immediately to apply for a new certificate of title. The bankrupt attempted to apply for a new certificate of title but failed in (and finally desisted from) her efforts.

   The petition in bankruptcy was filed on November 7, 1997. About one month later, the Bank delivered an application for a new certificate of title to the Secretary of State of Illinois. A new certificate was issued on December 15, 1997.

   The state's motor vehicle registration requires delivery of the old certificate of title and an application for a new one, with the claimed security interest noted thereon, to the Secretary of State within twenty-one days of the sale, in order to perfect the security interest.

   Who has the best claim to Esther's trailer? Explain.

2. Dallas Entertainment operated a private club known as the Music Box. Dallas sold the entire club to Follies Buffet; included was a certain cash register. The parties prepared and filed a financing statement which described the collateral as including all equipment, but which did not specifically mention the cash register. Mosley bought the cash register from Follies, and then resold it. Dallas sued Mosley for conversion and received a judgment for $950.

   During the trial, Peggy Foley, the president of Dallas, testified that Dallas had received a promissory note and a security agreement from Follies at the time of the purchase. There was an objection to the introduction of the alleged security agreement because it had not been signed, and it does not appear in the trial court record. There was no other writing.

   Does Dallas have a valid security interest? Explain.

3. Floyd McLucas and his wife wanted to buy some furniture but were told by the store that the sale could not be made to them on credit. (Floyd was 22 years old; his wife 18). Floyd was told that he needed a cosigner. He brought his friend James McWilliams to the store, and McWilliams also signed the contract. The store was still not satisfied, so Floyd brought his mother, Catherine McLucas, and she cosigned too. At that point, the sale was made. The store assigned the contract to the plaintiff, Wexler, who sued Catherine when Floyd and his wife defaulted on their payments. The trial court held for Wexler, and Catherine McLucas appealed. After the complaint was served on Catherine, Floyd had gone to Wexler's office and Wexler had agreed to let him pay off the account at $10 per week, thereby lengthening the term of the contract.

   How should this appeal be decided, and why?

4. Delilah filed for bankruptcy, listing among her secured creditors one Erlene Lertz. Erlene held a security agreement and had filed a financing statement, both of which described the collateral as "Lot 8, Lake Minotaur, and cabin at same location." Delilah leased Lot 8 and owned the cabin, so both were items of personal property rather than real estate. The trustee says that Erlene does not have a secured claim because the description of the collateral is insufficient.

   What is the result and why?

5. Denver and Gary were both officers of Sunny Mobile Homes, Inc. Both of them had indorsed several of the company's notes for loans to it. They had also signed a guaranty agreement for the loans, which stated: "Liability hereunder is not affected or impaired by any surrender, compromise, settlement, release, renewal, extension, authorization, substitution, exchange, modification, or other disposition of any said indebtedness and obligations." At one point, all of the company's outstanding loans were consolidated into one renewable note. Gary signed the renewal note, but Denver did not. Denver now claims that his liability as guarantor was discharged by a novation between the bank (lender), the company (Sunny), and Gary, since the renewal note did not include his signature.

   What result, and why?

6. From time-to-time during 1998, Waychus had borrowed money from the bank and had executed promissory notes and security agreements. A financing statement had been filed on October 17, 1998, with the recorder of Cerro Gordo County. The financing statement identified the collateral as: "All Farm Machinery, All Brood Sows & the increase, All Crops, feed, and roughage." The financing statement also contained a real estate description of land located in Floyd County, whereas Waychus, in fact, resided in Cerro Gordo County.

   Johnson, who had no actual knowledge of the bank's interest, bought hogs from Waychus. The trial court held that Johnson was subject to the bank's perfected security interest. Johnson appealed.

   How should this appeal be decided? Explain.

Chapter 19

Perfection, Priorities, and Remedies

RIGHTS OF THIRD PARTIES: PERFECTED AND UNPERFECTED SECURITY INTERESTS: PRIORITIES

Reasons for Perfection. For the purpose of Article 9, the term **perfection** is used to describe a process—the steps which a secured party must take to make the security interest effective against third parties, particularly the debtor's general creditors or their representative in an insolvency proceeding. The very idea of "security" is to have an available source of funds from which the secured debt can be paid in the event of default by the debtor; that objective is defeated if the asset in question or its proceeds are distributed *pro rata* to all creditors.

To be more specific and more technically correct, perfection of the security interest in the collateral is necessary to beat "a person who becomes a lien creditor without knowledge of the security interest and before it is perfected" (9-301[1][b]). **Lien creditor** is defined to include a creditor with a levy or attachment against the property involved, or an assignee for the benefit of creditors, or a receiver in equity, or a trustee in bankruptcy (9-301[3]). The secured party needs to perfect to prevent these people from making priority claims against that item of collateral. A secured party who has provided the purchase-money credit or loan (which enabled the debtor to purchase the collateral) does have a ten-day grace period within which to perfect a security interest and still beat out these lien creditors (9-301[2]), but as a rule, the secured party must perfect *before* the lien creditor becomes such, or lose priority. Subsections 9-301(1)(c) and (d) extend similar protection to certain unknowing transferees of goods, instruments, documents, chattel paper, accounts, and general intangibles; they too will beat the unperfected security interest of the would-be secured party to the extent that they give value without knowledge of the security interest.

Perfection will also assist the secured party in beating out some other kinds of third-party claimants, at least in some situations. But since it is possible to have more than one perfected security interest in the same collateral, and since even a perfected security interest is subordinate to certain types of third-party claims in certain situations, a secured party with a perfected security interest is not always "the first to be paid." Priorities of payment under Article 9 are discussed below.

Methods of Perfection. There are three general methods of perfection—*filing* a financing statement, *possession* of the collateral, and *automatic perfection*—plus some variations (such as different places to file for different types of collateral). Filing is effective for every type of collateral except "instruments." Filing is the only method of perfecting against accounts and general intangibles since there is nothing in these situations that can really be effectively "possessed." Possession of the item of collateral by the secured party is an effective method of perfection for all types of goods and for the "paper intangibles"—documents, instruments, and chattel paper. Since these pieces of paper are commonly dealt with in the commercial world as embodying the rights they represent, and since they are capable of being physically possessed, the drafters of Article 9 provided that a security interest in such pieces of paper could be perfected by the secured party's retention of them. Indeed, for instruments, except for a limited 21-day perfection against the debtor's other creditors, possession is the only acceptable method of perfection.

Place of Filing. The "uniformity" desired by the drafters of the Code has broken down in the requirements for a valid "filing" to give notice to third parties of the existence of a security interest against the collateral. Solid policy arguments can be made both for central filing (there's only one place to check, particularly for a mobile debtor) and for local filing (it's much more convenient). The Code originally contained a simple filing scheme: for fixtures, file with the registrar of deeds in the county where the real estate is located; for motor vehicles required to be licensed, file by making a notation on the vehicle registration certificate; for all else, file with the secretary of state. Alternatives provided in the Code, combined with the effects of having each state legislature "do its own thing," have produced some major variations in these filing requirements. Each state's filing requirements must be checked to ensure the validity of a filing there.

Where the secured party makes a good faith attempt to file but files in an improper place or in only one of two required places, the filing is nonetheless effective as to anyone who has knowledge of the contents of the financing statement and also for any types of collateral as to which the filing is correct. An effective filing is not invalidated by a change in the debtor's residence or place of business or in the location of the collateral, but some states have adopted alternative language which requires a new filing in the new county, even within the same state. **Filing** is defined as meaning *either* "[p]resentation for filing of a financing statement and tender of the filing fee" *or* "acceptance of the statement by the filing officer." (The alternative language is included just in case the local filing officer gets funny and refuses to accept your financing statement for some reason, such as "it's not in proper form.")

Automatic Perfection. For purchase-money security interests in most consumer goods, Article 9 provides a third alternative. The "purchase-money person" (the seller or the financing agency that provided the cash or credit which the debtor used to buy the collateral) is given the benefit of an "automatic" perfection as soon as that person's security interest attaches to the collateral. (This automatic perfection alternative is *not* available where the consumer good is defined as a fixture or is a motor vehicle required to be licensed.) Even without filing and with the debtor in possession of the consumer good, the purchase-money person will still be protected against nearly all other possible claimants—lien creditors, other general creditors, the trustee in bankruptcy, another dealer to whom the collateral was given, or a buyer who had knowledge of the security interest.

Aside from the common priority problems, only one sort of claimant—a **bona fide purchaser (BFP)**—takes the collateral free and clear of the unfiled purchase-money security interest. The BFP must buy without knowledge of the unfiled security interest for value, and for his or her own personal, family, or household purposes (consumer goods). Given this extensive protection of the unfiled security interest, the retailer or financier of these types of collateral can then decide whether or not protection against BFPs is worth the filing fee and the clerical expense involved in filing a financing statement. If the dealer does file, it will prevail even against a BFP, so buyers of consumer goods from other individuals do have to check these filing records to make sure that the item they are buying is indeed "free and clear." Note again that this third perfection alternative applies only to the purchase-money person; all other secured parties must file or possess to perfect.

Perfection Against Proceeds. Section 9-306 provides an extensive and careful coverage for security interests in **proceeds**, meaning "whatever is received when collateral or proceeds is sold, exchanged, collected, or otherwise disposed of. Money, checks, and the like are 'cash proceeds.' All other proceeds are 'noncash proceeds.'" The general intent of this section is to give the secured party with a security interest in collateral a similar security in anything which the debtor received from third parties in exchange for that collateral.

As a rule, unless the debtor was authorized to make the sale or exchange of the collateral, a secured party can elect to pursue the collateral in the hands of a third party as well as the proceeds in the hands of the debtor. A dealer who filed against a TV set that was bought on credit could, for example, repossess the TV from a third party to whom the set was sold if the debtor was in default under the original security agreement. The secured party will not get the debt paid twice, but will have two sources to look to for payment. This general rule is subject to several exceptions, including the **buyer in the ordinary course of business (BIOC)** who buys goods (usually from a dealer's inventory). This BIOC takes the goods free and clear of a security interest created by the seller, even though that interest is perfected and even though the BIOC knows about it. For other exceptions, see Sections 9-301, 9-308, and 9-309.

What does the secured party need to do to perfect a security interest against "proceeds?" If a financing statement which indicates that the security interest applies to proceeds as well as the original collateral has been filed, nothing more need be done; there is a continuously perfected security interest against the proceeds. Where the original financing statement does not so indicate, or where perfection against the original collateral occurred by another method, that perfection still applies to proceeds, continuously and automatically, for a ten-day grace period. Within that period, the secured party needs to file or to take possession of the proceeds to perfect.

In the event of insolvency proceedings, then, the secured party with a perfected security interest against proceeds will be able to assert rights in any of the debtor's assets that can be identified as being derived from the original collateral and in "all cash and bank accounts of the debtor," even if the cash proceeds cannot be identified because they have been commingled with other funds.

Subsection (5) of 9-306 contains a detailed set of priority rules to cover situations where "a sale of goods results in an account or chattel paper which is transferred by the seller to a secured party, and ... the goods are returned to or are repossessed by the seller or the secured party."

Perfection Against Fixtures. Many complex problems may arise where goods are attached to real estate and both the goods and the real estate are subject to the claims of financing agencies or good faith purchasers. The Code was not intended to regulate real property law, but in this area Article 9 does have an impact on real property doctrines. In general, fixtures are defined as goods which have become attached to real estate. The general law of the state where the realty is located will provide the exact definition. The Code does exclude structural materials from the "fixtures" definition.

The 1972 revision of Section 9-313 changed the rules to favor the realty claimants. First, a construction mortgagee (who makes advances of funds to finance the building of structures on the land) is given a special priority over all fixture financiers even as to such items as dishwashers and refrigerators. As to other existing interests in the real estate (such as a land contract seller or the holder of the purchase mortgage), the fixture financier must make a **fixture filing** either before or within ten days after the goods become attached to the real estate. This is a special rule for purchase-money security interests in the fixtures. Otherwise, there is a first-to-file rule for fixtures. For example, the seller of a new furnace on credit could obtain priority over the holder of an existing mortgage by making the proper fixture filing. But if the existing mortgage had already been properly recorded, a nonpurchase-money creditor who wished to use existing fixtures as collateral could not take priority over the mortgagee unless the latter agreed.

Financiers of "readily-removable factory or office machines or readily removable replacements of domestic appliances which are consumer goods" are given priority over conflicting real estate interests if their security interest is perfected before the goods become fixtures. Most stoves, refrigerators, washers, and dryers would seem to be "readily-removable;" most furnaces would not. A catchall provision indicates that a conflicting real estate interest takes priority against any security interest that is not properly perfected.

To avoid the problem that arose in states where the fixture financier did not have to file on the real estate records but merely in the *office* where real estate claims were filed, the 1972 amendments specify that a fixture filing must be made in the real estate records. It must include a legal description of the real estate to which the fixture is being attached and also the name of the real estate owner if that person is not the debtor who is using the fixture as collateral. Thus, the fixture claim should appear in any title search of the real estate records.

Priorities. For the creditor, priority of payment is what the "security" game is all about. Obviously, if the debtor had enough funds to go around, there would be no problem of who got paid first and no need for this sort of litigation. Litigation to establish priority occurs because someone who has extended credit to an insolvent debtor is going to get "stuck" for some or all of that claim against the debtor. Other types of claimants, such as good faith purchasers of collateral from the debtor, will also be interested in determining whether they hold the property in question free and clear, or subject to the claims of a creditor or creditors. Different potential claimants and different types of financing transactions combine to produce a great range of specific fact situations. Part of what appears to be a terrible complexity in Article 9's priority rules stems directly from the need to provide a number of different rules to deal with a number of quite different fact variations. We thus need to consider both the "general rules" and about fifteen special situations covered by a special priority rule.

For the first general rule on priority, we return to 9-201:

> Except as otherwise provided in this Act a security agreement is effective according to its terms between the parties, against purchasers of the collateral and against creditors.

In other words, the security agreement itself controls priority unless a Code provision covers the situation and provides otherwise. Nearly all typical priority situations are in fact covered by a Code rule, so that the security agreement itself operates only within a limited range with regard to priority rules.

The *Security Pacific* case involves the priority to be given to a landlord's lien.

SECURITY PACIFIC FINANCIAL SERVICES v. SIGNFILLED CORP.
956 P. 2d 837 (N. Mex. App. 1998)

FACTS: Security Pacific Financial Services (Security Pacific) filed a complaint against George Turner, Robert Eden, and Signfilled Corporation for collection under an installment sales contract and for replevin and declaratory relief in connection with a mobile home. The trial court ruled in favor of Security Pacific on its complaint. Signfilled Corporation appeals this ruling; George Turner and Robert Eden do not.

George Turner entered into a retail installment sales contract (the contract) and security agreement with Value Mobile Homes (Value) to purchase a mobile home. The contract granted to Value, the Seller, a security interest in the mobile home. Value assigned its rights, title, and interest in the contract to General Electric Credit Corporation (GECC). GECC was listed on the Certificate of Title for the mobile home as the first lienholder. Security Pacific then purchased the contract from GECC. The contract required Turner to pay for insurance on the mobile home, but he failed to make the required payments. When Turner was contacted by Security Pacific regarding the delinquent payments, he stated that Security Pacific should ask for payment from Robert Eden (Eden), his stepson, who was living in the mobile home. It is not clear whether Security Pacific asked Eden for the insurance payments, but no payments were made. As a result of the late insurance payments, Security Pacific issued a demand letter to Turner. In response to the demand letter, Eden told Security Pacific that he would not make the required payments unless his name was added to the contract. Security Pacific agreed to accept a credit application from Eden so that Eden's name might be added to the contract. Eden's application was approved but never consummated because Eden did not pay the required down payment. In addition, Turner was unwilling to provide his signature, which was required to allow Eden to assume the loan under the contract.

Signfilled Corporation consists of Loretta Quintana, the president of Signfilled, and Gerry Ferrara, an officer of Signfilled and Eden's sister. Quintana had been a close friend of Eden for twenty years. In July 1993, Quintana purchased all of the shares of the corporation from Eden. On July 1, 1993, Signfilled entered into a lease agreement with Eden allowing Eden to lease space on land belonging to Signfilled for placement of the mobile home. Quintana testified that Eden never paid any rent under the lease agreement and that no legal action was taken to collect the rent.

In August 1994, Signfilled gave notice to Security Pacific that it was asserting a landlord's lien against the mobile home for unpaid rent under its lease with Eden. Signfilled held an auction of the mobile home, which no one attended. Signfilled then submitted its own bid for the mobile home for the amount of the claimed landlord's lien. After Signfilled purchased the mobile home for the lien amount, Signfilled submitted documents to the Motor Vehicle Department pursuant to the claim of landlord's lien. In return, Signfilled received a Certificate of Title listing Signfilled as owner of the mobile home and removing GECC as lienholder. When Signfilled filed its landlord's lien, it knew that Turner was the owner of the mobile home, and that Security Pacific had a security interest in the mobile home.

Security Pacific received notice of Signfilled's claim of landlord's lien. Security Pacific did not receive any notice of the sale of the mobile home. In November 1994, Security Pacific received notice that title to the mobile home had been transferred from Turner to Signfilled. Security Pacific called Eden and asked him to return the mobile home, and a notice of default was sent to Turner. The contract provided that, in the event of default, the holder may pursue any rights and remedies available to the holder under the law as well as repossession and/or acceleration of Turner's indebtedness. On December 6, 1994, on the basis that Turner was in default under the terms of the contract, Security Pacific elected to accelerate the contract as allowed by its terms. Security Pacific filed its complaint against Turner, Eden, and Signfilled.

The trial court found that Security Pacific was entitled to possession of the mobile home; that Signfilled had no interest in the mobile home; that Signfilled's actions constituted wrongful conversion of the mobile home; and that Security Pacific was entitled to recovery of interest, costs, and attorney fees. Following judgment, a writ of replevin was issued for return of the mobile home to Security Pacific.

 JUDGE ALARID:

Signfilled makes various arguments pertaining to the validity of Security Pacific's interest in the mobile home. In particular, Signfilled argues that Security Pacific's interest was never perfected and the Certificate of Title was never changed to reflect Security Pacific's interest in the mobile home. As noted above, GECC held the mobile home's sales contract prior to its assignment to Security Pacific. The contract provided that the Buyer (Turner) granted to the Seller (or holder of the contract) a security interest in the mobile home and all the proceeds of the property. The security interest ensured payment and performance of Turner's obligations under the contract. Thus, the security interest was a "purchase money security interest" in that it was "taken or retained by the seller of the collateral to secure all or part of its price."...

Signfilled does not dispute GECC's status as holder of a perfected security interest. Furthermore, the fact that GECC was listed on the Certificate of Title as lienholder indicates that GECC had a perfected security interest....

The contract also provided that it could be assigned by Seller to any person or entity and that all rights granted to the Seller under the contract would apply to the assignee. GECC sold its interest in the contract to Security Pacific.... The assignment of a retail installment is valid as against those making a claim against the seller regardless of whether the assignment is filed or whether the buyer is provided notice.... As in this case, when a secured party assigns a perfected security interest there is no requirement that the assignment be filed "in order to continue the perfected status of the security interest against creditors of and transferees from the original debtor."... Therefore, Security Pacific was assigned the perfected security interest in the mobile home by GECC and the perfected status of the security interest was not altered despite the fact that Security Pacific never changed the Certificate of Title to reflect the change in lienholders.... In other words, the security interest continued to be perfected after GECC transferred the contract to Security Pacific.

Signfilled claims that its interest in the mobile home was superior to Security Pacific's interest, particularly because it perfected its lien by foreclosing on the landlord's lien and obtaining a title to the mobile home.... A landlord may assert a landlord's lien on the property of the landlord's tenants. The evidence in this case is that Eden, who was the lessee that signed the lease agreement with Signfilled, never owned the mobile home.... Accordingly, Signfilled could not assert a landlord's lien over the mobile home and Signfilled's title is invalid....

Even if Signfilled had a valid landlord's lien, the perfected purchase money security interest was superior to that landlord's lien. The security interest possessed by a Security Pacific was perfected before any interest claimed by Signfilled under a landlord's lien....

Security Pacific was entitled to relief under the replevin statute. In addition, the evidence supported the trial court's finding that Signfilled had wrongfully converted the mobile home to its own use. Security Pacific, however, would not be entitled to both the return of the mobile home under the theory of replevin and damages under the theory of conversion in the amount of the value of the mobile home at the time of conversion....

With respect to recovery in replevin, because the mobile home has been replevied by Security Pacific, the only damages left to be awarded to Security Pacific are damages for wrongful detention of the mobile home. Based on the requested findings of Security Pacific, the trial court found that the value of the mobile home on August 2, 1994, was $16,298. The only other evidence of value presented to the trial court was the value of the mobile home at the time of trial. Security Pacific's agent testified at trial that he believed the value of the mobile home at that time to be approximately $11,000.... Therefore, Security Pacific is entitled to collect $5,298 in damages from Signfilled.

One of the special priority rules (9-316) does provide that secured parties may agree among themselves as to their relative priority positions. Such an arrangement, of course, would be effective only as between the parties who agreed to it.

A second look at 9-301 indicates that even a secured party with an unfiled, unperfected security interest receives some protection in terms of priority. If the interest has attached to the collateral, the secured party does have rights in the collateral as against the debtor, and generally that interest will take priority as against buyers of the collateral or lien creditors who have *knowledge* of the security interest when they become such.

Section 9-312 is the basic priorities section. It provides the general rules for determining priorities between conflicting security interests in the same collateral; it spells out special purchase-money rules for inventory and noninventory collateral; it provides a special priority rule where "crops" are used as collateral; and it cross-references other sections containing special priority rules.

The general priority rules from 9-312(5) are simple and logical. As between competing perfected interests, priority is determined according to the time of filing or perfection. For example, Mabel is shopping for a new car. She agrees to buy a particular car from Big Bennie's dealership. Mabel goes to her credit union and borrows $8,000 to buy the car, giving her credit union a security interest against the car. The credit union files a financing statement which identifies the new car as collateral. Mabel then goes back to Bennie's and signs a purchase-money security agreement for the car—buying it on credit. Bennie's gives her the car, and then files a financing statement (without checking the records under Mabel's name). Mabel then drives back to her credit union and picks up her $8,000 check. Even though Bennie's security interest was *perfected* first, Mabel's credit union takes priority if she defaults on these two obligations. The credit union *filed* first, even though their interest was perfected after Bennie's. Bennie should have checked the records before giving Mabel the car.

So long as neither security interest has been perfected, priority is given in the order in which they attached to the collateral.

For the purpose of applying these priority rules, the date of filing or perfection as to the collateral is also the effective date as to any proceeds of that collateral.

Special purchase-money rules for inventory and noninventory collateral are set out in 9-312(3) and (4). A purchase-money security interest in inventory collateral has priority over a conflicting security interest in the same collateral if the purchase-money security interest is perfected when the debtor gets possession of the collateral; *and* written notification of the purchase-money security interest is received by any other "known" or "filed" secured party before the debtor gets possession of the collateral; *and* the notification states that the purchase-money person has or intends to acquire a purchase-money security interest in the debtor's inventory, "describing such inventory by item of type." Because there is much less of a commingling problem with noninventory collateral, the purchase-money person's requirements for priority in such collateral are much simpler. The interest just has to have been perfected when the debtor takes possession of the noninventory collateral, or within ten days thereafter. Under this rule, Bennie could take priority over Mabel's credit union (in our last example) if he filed within the ten-day period.

As the *James Talcott* case shows, a creditor can lose collateral to a security interest already on file, if these rules are not followed.

JAMES TALCOTT, INC. v. FRANKLIN NATIONAL BANK OF MINNEAPOLIS
194 N.W.2d 775 (MN, 1972)

FACTS: This is an appeal taken from a summary judgment in favor of defendant, Franklin National Bank of Minneapolis. The action was commenced for the recovery of possession of several motor vehicles, or their value, in which plaintiff, James Talcott, Inc., claimed a superior security interest.

On February 20, 1968, Noyes Paving Company, hereinafter refereed to as "debtor" entered into a conditional sales contract with Northern Contracting Company as seller, covering the purchase on an installment basis, of two dump trucks and other construction equipment. On that same day, the seller assigned without recourse, the conditional sales contract to plaintiff, together with all sums payable thereunder and all right, title, and interest in and to the equipment covered by the contract. On February 21, 1968, a financing statement was filed with the secretary of state naming Noyes Paving as debtor, Northern Contracting Company as secured party, and James Talcott, as assignee of the secured party. The financing statement covered the following items of property: "Construction Equipment, Motor Vehicles."

On May 1, debtor entered into an equipment lease with defendant bank covering one dump truck; and on May 31, a similar lease agreement was entered into between the same parties covering two additional dump trucks and other equipment. Each lease provided that debtor, if not in default, could purchase the leased goods at the end of the lease term for the sum of $1. Defendant did not at that time file a financing statement regarding the equipment described in the two lease agreements.

During the latter part of the year 1968, debtor experienced difficulty in making payments on the conditional sales contract. On January 20, 1969, debtor and plaintiff entered into an agreement extending the time for payment. In consideration of the extension granted, debtor gave plaintiff a security interest *"in all goods (as defined in Article 9 of the Uniform Commercial Code) whether now owned or hereafter acquired."* No additional financing statement was filed in connection with the extension agreement of January 30. At that time, plaintiff did not know of the existence of the motor vehicles and other equipment listed in defendant's two equipment leases and did not rely upon their existence in entering into the extension agreement.

Following the date of the extension agreement, debtor ran into more financial difficulty and defaulted in payments with respect to both the conditional sales contract and the equipment leases. On May 21, 1970, copies of the leases were filed by defendant bank as financing statements with the secretary of state. Sometime during May 1970, defendant repossessed the equipment in question and this action ensued. The precise date on which defendant made the repossession is not clear from the record. The parties agreed that it took place during the month of May 1970. All of the equipment was located with the exception of one item. By agreement between plaintiff and defendant, the equipment was sold, and the proceeds were placed in a special account pending the outcome of this case.

 JUSTICE HACKEY:

1. Were the leases security agreements?

This question is extremely significant because plaintiff's right to recovery is dependent upon a finding that the lease agreements between defendant and debtor were, in effect, security agreements....

The language of the code specifically determines whether or not a lease creates a security interest in the collateral.... The words of that section are unequivocal. An option given to the lessee to purchase the leased property for a nominal consideration does make the lease one intended for security. Hence, the options to buy the equipment in the instant case for the combined sum of $2, a nominal amount when compared to the total rental of $73,303.32, created security interests. The leases in question were precisely the type that Article 9 was intended to cover (i.e., transactions in goods which were in substance, although not in form security agreements)....

2. Did the debtor "own" the leased property so that it was included as secured property under plaintiff's security agreement?

This question is a part of the critical issue in the case in as much as the second security agreement between plaintiff and debtor (the extension agreement of January 30, 1969) gave plaintiff a security interest in "all goods ... whether now owned or hereafter acquired" by debtor. The issue turns on whether or not debtor can be deemed to have owned the leased property at the time it entered into the extension agreement....

[T]he draftsmen of the code intended that its provisions should not be circumvented by manipulation of the locus of title. For this reason, consignment sales, conditional sales, and other arrangements or devices whereby title is retained in the seller for a period following possession by the debtor are all treated under Article 9 as though the title had been transferred to the debtor and the creditor-seller had retained only a security interest in the goods. For the purpose of analyzing rights of ownership under Article 9, we hold, based up on the stipulated facts of this case, that defendant had only a security interest in the equipment despite a purported reservation of title and that debtor "owned" the equipment at the time that the extension agreement was executed.

3. Was the description of the secured property, as it appeared in the extension agreement, sufficient to meet the requirements of Article 9; that is, did the description reasonably identify what was being described?

The description of the collateral in the extension agreement did what it was meant to do—namely, it included all of the goods then owned, or to be owned in the future by the debtor. The term "goods" was defined to be those goods as comprehended within the meaning of Article 9 of the code. The definition selected is embodied in the statue, a definition that is used and applied frequently. The parties sought to create a security interest in substantially all of the debtor's property. That is what was stated, and that is what was meant. The parties did not particularize any further, and the statute does not require it....

A security agreement should not be held unenforceable unless it is so ambiguous that its meaning cannot reasonably be construed from the language of the agreement itself. Such a test appears to have been intended by the draftsmen of the code and should be applied in this case. We fail to find an impelling reason why we should not approve the description used in this case, and we hold that it suffices within the terms of the statute. We further hold specifically that the description used in the extension agreement between debtor and plaintiff includes the equipment financed by defendant bank.

4. Was the financing statement, filed at the time the first security agreement was assigned to plaintiff, sufficient to reflect a security interest in the property covered by the extension agreement?

Section 336.402(1) provides that "[a] financing statement may be filed before a security agreement is made or a security interest otherwise attaches." This is what happened in the instant case. The financing statement filed February 21, 1968, met all requirements of the code since it described by type ("Construction Equipment, Motor Vehicles") not only the property covered by the original sales agreement which was assigned to plaintiff but also the property, which likewise consisted of motor vehicles and construction equipment, financed by defendant. The code does not require a reference in the financing statement to after-acquired property....

The whole purpose of notice filing would be nullified if a financing statement had to be filed whenever a new transaction took place between a secured party and a debtor. Once a financing statement is on file describing property by type, the entire world is warned, not only that the secured party may already have a security interest in the property of that type (as did plaintiff in the property originally financed), but that it may later acquire a perfected security interest in property of the same type acquired by the debtor in the future. When the debtor does acquire more property of the type referred to in the financing statement already on file, and when a security interest attaches to that property, the perfection is instantaneous and automatic....

5. Priority....

Defendant's security interest did attach first, but (assuming it was filed after repossession) it was not perfected.

Plaintiff's security interest attached later—actually after its filing had occurred. But neither of these factors is material in the application of the first-to-perfect rule. Accordingly, when the conflict arose (still assuming it was before defendant had filed), plaintiff was entitled to priority. Once plaintiff's priority had been acquired, no subsequent filing by defendant (more than 10 days after debtor received possession) could alter the situation. Moreover, even if ... 312(5)(a) should apply, plaintiff would still have priority under the first-to-file rule as its filing preceded defendant's by many months....

The summary judgment for defendant is reversed, and the matter is remanded with directions to enter judgment for plaintiff....

Some other sections containing special priority rules have already been referred to above: 9-301, dealing with unperfected security interests and lien creditors; 9-306, covering proceeds and repossessions; 9-307, on good faith purchasers of goods (more on this in the next section of this chapter); 9-313, on fixtures; 9-316, on contractual subordination. For the sake of brevity, the remaining special priority rules are summarized:

Section 4-208 gives a bank which has given credit against an item being handled for collection a high-priority security interest against the item itself and any accompanying documents, even without a separate security agreement and without filing.

Section 9-304 provides a set of special rules for dealing with instruments, documents, and goods covered by documents, including a provision for limited and temporary (21 days) perfection without filing and without possession.

Section 9-308 provides a special rule protecting BFPs of chattel paper or nonnegotiable instruments where the conflicting security interest is perfected under 9-304's rules on permissive filing or temporary perfection.

Section 9-309 preserves the superior rights of good faith buyers of negotiable pieces of paper—instruments, documents, and investment securities; filing under Article 9 is not notice of the security interest to these parties.

Section 9-310 grants priority to any lien created by statute or case law in favor of a person who furnishes services or materials with respect to goods subject to a security interest.

Section 9-314 adopts a set of detailed rules for dealing with the common problem of *accessions* where goods become installed in or affixed to other goods, for example, the new motor in the old car; these rules are similar to the 1962 fixture rules.

Section 9-315 attempts to cover the situation where goods are commingled or processed so that they lose their distinct identity; the general idea is that the security interest continues against the mass or product; where there is more than one such security interest, they have equal priority and share pro rata in the product.

Protection for Certain Good Faith Purchasers.

Section 9-307 contains two special rules designed for the protection of good faith purchasers of goods. These rules were referred to in the preceding section of this chapter; and the *Nicolosi* case in Chapter 18 illustrates their application in one fact situation.

Subsection (1) of 9-307 protects the "buyer in the ordinary course of business," who is defined by 1-201(9) as follows:

"Buyer in ordinary course of business" means a person who in good faith and without knowledge that the sale to him is in violation of the ownership rights or security interest of a third party in the goods buys in ordinary course from a person in the business of selling goods of that kind.

Stated more simply, the BIOC is a buyer from a dealer's inventory. The BIOC "takes free of a security interest created by his seller even though the security interest is perfected and even though the buyer knows of its existence."

The limitations inherent in 9-307(1) have been brought out by several car dealer cases. In one such case, the Supreme Court of New Hampshire held that BIOC Jones was not protected under either 9-307(1) or (2) because a security interest had not been created by his seller and because the bank's security interest had been filed. Jones had bought the car in good faith from the dealer to whom it had been resold by the original buyer. When the original buyer went into default on his installment payments, the bank sued to foreclose on its security interest and won.

Moreover, where the BIOC not only knows of the existence of a security interest but also knows that the sale to him is in *violation* of it, he takes subject to the security interest.

Section 9-307(1) also specifically excludes from its protection "a person buying farm products from a person engaged in farming operations." Thus, buyer Johnson did not get BIOC protection in the *Waychus* problem in Chapter 18.

Equally significant is the limitation which 9-307(2) places on the operation of the automatic perfection alternative for consumer goods. Where the secured party is relying on automatic perfection, a BFP takes free of the security interest if buying without knowledge and for personal, family, or household purposes.

As seen in the *M & I* case, movable collateral presents some tricky questions for both creditors and buyers.

M & I WESTERN STATE BANK v. WILSON
493 N.W.2d 387(WI App., 1992)

FACTS: Darin Treleven appeals from a judgment of the trial court which awarded possession of a truck owned by Marilyn A. Wilson to the M & I Western State Bank (bank).

The bank holds a security interest in a 1978 Peterbilt truck owned by Wilson. Treleven repaired the truck seven times, each time releasing the vehicle to Wilson so she could earn the money to pay Treleven for the repairs. The repairs were invoiced between November 20, 1990 and April 23, 1991.

After Wilson defaulted on her payments to the bank, the bank commenced a replevin action. The parties made a repayment agreement; however, Wilson again defaulted and the bank obtained a judgment of replevin on April 9, 1990. The sheriff attempted to enforce the judgment but was unable to locate the truck. On May 12, 1991, employees of the bank saw the vehicle and followed it to Treleven's place of business, D.T. Truck Repair, Inc. The sheriff again tried to serve the writ of execution, but Treleven refused to release the vehicle, asserting that he held a mechanic's lien for services rendered.

After the attempted levy, the bank filed a second replevin action to determine who was entitled to possession of the truck and named Treleven as a third-party defendant. At the date of the hearing, Treleven still was owed $3497.26 for the repairs plus $1273.10 for interest and storage as of the date of the hearing, January 30, 1992. The bank's balance as of January 2, 1992 was $3032.16. The bank's estimate of the value of the truck is approximately $3000. If this estimate is correct, only the lien with first priority would be paid from the proceeds of the sale of the truck.

 JUDGE ANDERSON:

No Wisconsin court has decided whether the lien is lost once the mechanic conditionally releases the vehicle to the owner. The general and modern rule can be found in RESTATEMENT OF SECURITY §80 (1941). This rule states that when the bailor (owner) is under an obligation to return the vehicle to the lienor (mechanic), the lien is revived upon the recovery of the vehicle, subject only to the interests of bona fide purchasers for value and attaching or levying creditors who do not have notice of the lienor's interest....

Once the mechanic's lien arises, in most circumstances, the later conditional release does no further damage to the prior creditor and actually can be advantageous to the creditor. For example, in a case such as this where the vehicle is necessary to the owner's business, the conditional release allows the owner to generate cash to pay off the mechanic's lien and make payments on the creditor's prior loan. If the mechanic were forced to keep possession of the vehicle, the owner would be unable to raise the cash to pay off either the mechanic or the creditor.

The circumstance where a prior creditor could be damaged by the conditional release also is covered by the Restatement. If a prior creditor does not have notice of the mechanic's lien and goes through the expense of levying upon the vehicle while it is in the owner's possession, then the levying creditor is accorded the same protection as the bona fide purchaser for value or the new attaching creditor. This rule gives the prior creditor a "window of opportunity" to levy, but the mechanic can protect the lien by notifying prior creditors of the conditional release arrangement.

For the reasons stated above, we reject the bank's argument that a conditional release of the vehicle destroys the lien as to all third parties. Instead, we adopt the Restatement's rule that upon a conditional release, the lien is enforceable against all parties except a bona fide purchaser for value or a subsequent attaching or levying creditor who has no notice of the mechanic's interest. Upon the resumption of possession, the lien is revived and retains its priority as before the release, except it is subordinate to the bona fide purchaser or attaching or levying creditor. Applying this rule to the facts of the case, it is apparent that the mechanic's lien is superior to the bank's security interest. The fact that the truck was found at the mechanic's place of business well after the repairs were made supports Treleven's claim that the release of the vehicle was conditional. Furthermore, the bank is not afforded the protection given to the levying creditor because the sheriff levied upon the vehicle while it was in Treleven's possession, and thus had notice of Treleven's interest.

Because Treleven's lien was not waived by the conditional release under Section 77941(1), Stats., we next must examine whether the conditional release destroyed the lien's priority under Section 409.310, Stats. Neither party addressed this issue, but commentary and cases interpreting UCC § 9-310, the model upon which Section 409.310 is based, make clear that the possession requirement of this statute is separate from any possession requirement of the underlying mechanic's lien.

The question then becomes whether the resumption of possession will allow Section 409.310, Stats., to be applied to give the mechanic's lien priority. The statute's language does not tell us whether continuous possession is required. When a statute is ambiguous, we must look to other sources to determine legislative intent.... Among the few courts that have decided this issue, the jurisdictions do not agree as to the effect of resuming possession under § 9-310....

Wisconsin case law decided prior to the enactment of Section 409.310, Stats., gave priority to a mechanic's lien over a prior security interest.... Wisconsin's enactment of Section 409.310 did not expressly state that its effect was to displace prior law in this area. Commentary to the UCC reveals the drafter's view that § 9-310 was to reverse prior case law which subordinated the mechanic's lien to prior security interests, but it does not state how the rule was to affect prior decisions holding the mechanic's lien superior.... Because Wisconsin's prior case law and Section 409.310 can be read in a consistent manner, we decline to interpret the statute otherwise.

Finally, but not least importantly, the plain language of Section 409.310, Stats., gives priority to the mechanic "in possession." It does not require "continuous possession" or "retained possession." We must construe laws relating to mechanics liens in a way to accomplish their equitable purpose of aiding mechanics in obtaining compensation....

[W]e are not concerned with formulating a national standard and do not need to look at other federal laws interpreting "possession" under Wisconsin law, we must interpret Section 409.310, Stats., in a way that aids the mechanic in obtaining compensation. It is not in a mechanic's best interest to interpret "possession" in Section 409.310 as "continuous possession," and we decline to do so. Therefore, because Treleven was in possession of the vehicle at the time the bank's lien was enforced, Treleven's mechanic's lien had priority over the bank's interest under Section 409.310.

Debtor's Defenses Against Assignee. The great bulk of time-sale contracts are not held by the seller until maturity, but are transferred or "assigned" to a bank or other financing agency. The early common law absolutely prohibited such assignments since it was felt that they forced the debtor to do business with a stranger. Only within the last hundred years has their validity been accepted, and traces of the absolute common law prohibition have survived almost to our own day.

One of the most significant common law rules developed to protect account debtors in the assignment situation is the one that makes the assignee subject to all defenses the debtor has against the assignor (seller). The assignee steps into the assignor's shoes—they don't get any larger just because someone else is wearing them; if they pinch a little bit, too bad. For its own protection, the financial community has been able to get statutes passed in some states which modify this general rule. The seller could also insulate the financing agency from most of the debtor's usual defenses (nondelivery, defective merchandise, fraud in the inducement) by having the debtor sign a negotiable instrument and then negotiating it to the financing agency as a "holder in due course."

The drafters of Article 9 continued the general rule on debtors' defenses against the assignee in substantially unchanged form, in 9-318(1). As under the common law, therefore, the account debtor can assert any defense under the assigned contract against the assignee, and can use any defense or claim against the assignor on totally unrelated matters, until receiving notice that the account has been assigned. For example, Biff Baker buys two cars, one new and one used, from Able's Auto Sales. Biff pays cash for the used car and finances the new car over thirty-six months. Able's Auto assigns the financing contract to the E-Z Money Company. If anything goes wrong with *either* car, Biff can use that defect (breach of warranty) as a defense when he is sued by E-Z Money, up to the point when Biff is notified of the assignment. After that, Biff can only assert claims he has under the new-car contract against E-Z, and he has to go back to Able's Auto for any claims on the used car that arise after Biff gets notice.

The references in 9-318(1) to Section 9-206 are important because 9-206 specifically validates a contractual agreement by the debtor-buyer "that he will not assert against an assignee any claim or defense which he may have against the seller." For an assignee to claim the protection afforded by this section, it must take the assignment "for value, in good faith, and without notice of claim or defense." Moreover, this section does not prevent the debtor from asserting defenses that could be asserted against the holder in due course of a negotiable instrument, such as minority, illegality, and fraud in the execution. And finally, and perhaps most significantly, 9-206 states that it is subject to "any statute or decision which establishes a different rule for buyers of consumer goods."

If a state wishes to modify the seeming harshness of this third section to protect consumers, this is easily done, either legislatively or judicially. Massachusetts took the lead by passing the bill that abolished the "holder in due course" concept for consumer sales; most states have now adopted such legislation. Under its rule-making powers, the FTC held extensive hearings and then adopted an "unfair method of competition" rule at the national level. As a result, the "holder in due course" doctrine has been largely removed from the consumer-sales field. Such waiver clauses are valid for nonconsumer buyers (who, presumably, are better able to take care of themselves from a legal and contractual standpoint).

Section 9-206 makes it clear that any "disclaimer, limitation or modification of the seller's warranties" must be made in accordance with Article 2 and not under this section.

The *Woffard* case in Chapter 13 was an illustration of these UCC rules on debtor's defenses.

DEFAULT AND REMEDIES

Most of our discussion of secured transactions in this chapter has concerned the problems confronted by the secured party when third-party claimants contest the right to "priority" against the collateral. Most of Article 9 is directed toward those problems, but Part 5, Default, does step into the transaction between the immediate parties, to regulate the rights and remedies as between them in the event that the debtor defaults.

Cumulative Remedies; Minimum Requirements After Default. Section 9-501(1) makes clear the intent of the UCC drafters that the secured party should be entitled to pursue all available remedies until the debt is satisfied. The secured party has the rights and remedies provided by Part 5 and 9-207, those provided in the security agreement itself (subject to the limitations in 9-501[3]), and "any available judicial procedure" for debt enforcement under applicable state law. "The rights and remedies referred to in this subsection are cumulative" (9-501[1]).

Similarly, the debtor has the rights and remedies provided in Part 5, in Section 9-207, and in the security agreement. The policy of the Code and of Article 9 is to provide substantial freedom of contract between the immediate parties to the particular transaction. That policy is continued, to a degree, as regards default procedures, but 9-501(3) imposes a set of "minimum procedural requirements" on default, for the protection of the debtor. In addition to these prescribed minima, the parties' freedom to agree to "whatever they want" may also be limited by 1-102[3] and 2-302, as noted above.

The objective in these default sections, then, is to balance the rights and remedies of both parties and to ensure that the debtor is protected by requiring that certain steps be taken when default occurs. *Default*, however, is not specifically defined; its definition is left to the agreement itself and to generally applicable legal principles.

Collection. On default, or whenever so agreed, the secured party has the right to notify an account debtor or the obligor on an instrument to start making payments directly and the right to take control of any proceeds under Section 9-306. This rule applies even though the assignor, called the "debtor" in the security agreement, was previously making the collections and then remitting them to the secured party.

Where the agreement provides that the secured party is entitled to charge back against the debtor any "uncollected" collateral and the secured party elects to collect personally, that must be done "in a commercially reasonable manner." The reasonable expenses incurred in the collection process can be recovered from the assignor-debtor. Provision is also made for both "deficiency" and "surplus" situations (9-502[2]):

> If the security agreement secures an indebtedness, the secured party must account to the debtor for any surplus, and unless otherwise agreed, the debtor is liable for any deficiency. But, if the underlying transaction was a sale of accounts or chattel paper, the debtor is entitled to any surplus or is liable for any deficiency only if the security agreement so provides.

Repossession. The creditor's classic remedy on default has been to "repo" the collateral. This remedy is continued for the secured party, pretty much as it existed under prior law, by 9-503:

> Unless otherwise agreed, a secured party has on default the right to take possession of the collateral. In taking possession a secured party may proceed without judicial process if this can be done without breach of the peace or may proceed by action.

Traditionally, the main question in these cases has been the definition of what constitutes a "breach of the peace" by the creditor repossessing without court order. Parked on the street or in a public parking lot, the debtor's car seems to be fair game for the repo person. Even if it's in the debtor's driveway or parked on private property, the repo person can probably still seize it and drive or tow it away. The line of demarcation seems to be the point at which the repo person opens a door or gate, either by force or fraud, or threatens the debtor in any way. These lines of decision under prior law will presumably continue under 9-503.

Section 9-503 also provides two new repo alternatives:

> If the security agreement so provides the secured party may require the debtor to assemble the collateral and make it available to the secured party at a place to be designated by the secured party which is reasonably convenient to both parties.

And:

> Without removal a secured party may render equipment unusable, and may dispose of collateral on the debtor's premises under Section 9-504.

These two provisions give the secured party additional options under the general right to repossession.

Repossession without notice to the debtor is at issue in the next case.

SALISBURY LIVESTOCK v.
COLORADO CENTRAL CREDIT UNION
793 P.2d 470 (WY, 1990)

FACTS: Salisbury Livestock Company (Salisbury Livestock) initiated a trespass action in response to Colorado Central's repossession of vehicles owned by George Salisbury, III (young Salisbury) from Wyoming property of Salisbury Livestock. Salisbury Livestock is a family corporation run by young Salisbury's father, George Salisbury, Jr.; it is registered in Wyoming and possesses land in Wyoming and Colorado. The disputed repossession of the vehicles took place on Salisbury Livestock's Ladder Ranch, which is on the Wyoming side of the Wyoming-Colorado state border.

Young Salisbury had pledged the repossessed vehicles, along with three others, as collateral for a $13,000 loan from Colorado Central in October 1984. This loan was made while he was living in the Denver area. He defaulted on the loan in March 1986. He had defaulted on the loan once before, in October 1985, and Colorado Central had repossessed one of his vehicles, which he subsequently redeemed. Colorado Central had then given young Salisbury an extension until February 15, 1986 meaning that he paid only interest from October 1985 until February 1986. He made the February,1986 payment, but did not make any further payments.

At some time in early 1986, young Salisbury left Denver and returned to Slater, Colorado, where he resided near the Salisbury Livestock Wyoming property on which his mother and father lived. Colorado Central sent notice of default to his Slater, Colorado mailing address in May 1986, but did not receive a response. In July 1986, Colorado Central decided to repossess the vehicles pledged as security on the loan. Welzheimer, Colorado Central's credit manager, hired C.A.R.S.-U.S.A., a car repossession company, to retrieve the vehicles.

On the evening of July 27, 1986, C.A.R.S.-U.S A. owner Clark and employees Srock and Boling (and one other C.A.R.S.-U.S.A. employee not made a party to the action) left Denver with two tow trucks to repossess young Salisbury's vehicles. Before leaving Denver, Clark had called young Salisbury's Slater, Colorado home and received directions for finding it from an unidentified woman. The repossession crew arrived at young Salisbury's home about 5:00 the next morning. They found one of the vehicles, a van, parked just off the highway in front of the house and with the key in the ignition. Clark looked inside a small shed or garage on the property and scouted the area around the house for the other vehicles, but did not find them.

Taking the van, they drove a short distance back up the road they had just traveled, Colorado Highway 129, to a large "Salisbury" sign that had been mentioned as a landmark by the unidentified woman Clark talked to on the telephone, and which they had noticed on their way to young Salisbury's home. The sign was adjacent to a private drive or roadway. Although they could not see any vehicles from the highway, the repossession crew turned down the drive. After traveling about fifty yards, they spotted several vehicles in the ranch yard. When they reached the vehicles, they identified two from their assignment form, a Corvette and a conversion van. They pushed the Corvette onto the drive so that they could reach it with one tow truck, backed up to the conversion van with the other tow truck, hooked both vehicles up, and towed them away.

At the time, it was light, and appellees reported that they heard people stirring in a nearby building. They did not attempt to obtain permission to enter the property or to take the vehicles. Clark testified that he did not plan on contacting anyone as it was his intention to avoid a confrontation. George Salisbury, Jr. testified that after the repossession, he discovered that the repossessors had apparently broken a two-by-four that was lying on the ground near the repossessed vehicles.

After the repossession, young Salisbury explained his financial problems to his father. The two agreed on a loan that permitted young Salisbury to redeem the vehicles on August 4, 1986, with a check drafted by his father. Salisbury Livestock, owner of the Wyoming property from which the Corvette and conversion van were towed, then initiated this trespass action. The trial court granted Colorado Central's motion for a directed verdict. Salisbury appealed.

 JUSTICE GOLDEN:

[W]e agree with the statement that "courts disfavor self-help repossession because, if abused, it invades the legitimate conflict resolution function of the courts".... While recognizing that W.S. 34-21-962 extends a conditional self-help privilege to secured parties, we will read the statute narrowly to reduce the risk to the public of extra judicial conflict resolution. Although it is apparent that the self-help remedy is efficient for creditors and results in reduced costs of credit for debtors, ... we must seek a reasonable balancing of that interest against private property interests and society's interest in tranquillity.

We then look to the language of W.S. 34-21-962 to establish the parameters of the protection it offers to secured parties who seek to repossess collateral without judicial process. The statute provides in pertinent part that "[i]n taking possession a secured party may proceed without judicial process if this can be done without breach of the peace...." Obviously, the key to whether a self-help repossession is privileged by the statute is whether the peace has been breached. Colorado Central agrees, but argues that the facts demonstrate that there was no breach of the peace. Salisbury Livestock would have us define breach of the peace as including simple trespass.

W.S. 34-21-962 does not define breach of the peace, and there is no definition offered elsewhere in the Wyoming statutes that address rights of secured parties. In our review of decisions from other jurisdictions, we find no consistently applied definition but agree with the analysis of the Utah Supreme Court ... that, "[c]ourts have struggled in determining when a creditor's trespass onto a debtor's property rises to the level of a breach of the peace. The two primary factors considered in making this determination are the potential for immediate violence and the nature of the premises intruded upon." These factors are interrelated in that the potential for violence increases as the creditor's trespass comes closer to a dwelling, and we will focus our analysis on them. It is necessary to evaluate the facts of each case to determine whether a breach of the peace has occurred....

We agree with the trial court that the Restatement (Second) of Torts § 198 reasonableness requirement provides appropriate criteria for evaluating whether a creditor's entry has breached the peace. If, as here, there was no confrontation and the timing and manner, including notice or lack of notice, are found reasonable, the entry is privileged. If the jury should find that the manner or timing of this entry was unreasonable because it may have triggered a breach of the peace, it in effect finds the entry a breach of the peace and unprivileged. We foresee the possibility that a rational jury could reach the conclusion that this entry was unreasonable....

[W]e cannot agree with Colorado Central's assertion that there can be no finding of a breach of the peace because there was no confrontation. Confrontation or violence is not necessary to finding a breach of the peace. The possibility of immediate violence is sufficient.... Two elements of this case create questions which we believe might lead reasonable jurors to a conclusion at odds with the trial court's directed verdict. First, this was an entry onto the premises of a third party not privy to the loan agreement. Particularly if there was no knowledge of young Salisbury's consent to repossession, this could trigger a breach of the peace. The few reported cases involving repossession from third party properties suggest that such entry is acceptable.... However, these cases do not address third party residential property. When entry onto third party property is coupled with the second unusual element, the location and the setting of this repossession, the possibility of a different verdict becomes more apparent.

We have not located any cases addressing a creditor's entry into the secluded ranchyard of an isolated ranch where the vehicles sought are not even visible from a public place. The few cases involve urban or suburban driveways, urban parking lots, or business premises.... We believe that the location and setting of this entry to repossess is sufficiently distinct, and the privacy expectations of rural resident sufficiently different, that a jury should weigh the reasonableness of this entry, or whether the peace may have been breached by a real possibility of imminent violence, or even by mere entry into these premises: the area next to the residence in a secluded ranchyard.

Because there are factual questions on which reasonable minds may differ, it was error to grant the motion for a directed verdict. The jury must determine whether the peace was breached by this creditor's entry because of the premises entered or the real possibility of immediate violence given the setting and location of the repossession. The reasonableness of the time and manner of the entry must be considered in the context of the third party property status and the rural setting. Whether notice is necessary is also an appropriate consideration when evaluating the manner of repossession. If either time or manner, or both, are found unreasonable then the entry is not privileged....

We need not, and so do not, reach the question of exemplary damages. Any question of damages awaits a prerequisite finding that the repossessors committed an unprivileged trespass.

Reversed and remanded for a new trial.

Disposition. After default by the debtor, the secured party has the right to dispose of the collateral and to apply the proceeds—first, to pay all reasonable selling expenses; second, to satisfy the security interest; and third, to pay any subordinate security interest as to which a written demand for payment is received prior to distribution of the proceeds. Where there is an underlying debt, "the secured party must account to the debtor for any surplus, and, unless otherwise agreed, the debtor is liable for any deficiency." But if the transaction was a sale of accounts or chattel paper, "the debtor is entitled to any surplus or is liable for any deficiency only if the security agreement so provides."

As regards the disposition itself, Section 9-504 allows maximum flexibility as to details. The disposition may be made by public or private sale, in one or more contracts, as a unit or in parcels, at any time and place, and on any terms. The secured party may sell the collateral at any public sale, or at a private sale if the collateral is of a type sold in a recognized market or subject to widely distributed standard price quotations. This considerable flexibility is, however, subject to a basic good faith limitation: "every aspect of the disposition including the method, manner, time, place and terms must be commercially reasonable." Except where the collateral is perishable, or threatens to decline speedily in value, or is customarily sold on a recognized market, the secured party must give the debtor reasonable notification of the intended sale. Except for consumer goods, notification must also be sent to any other secured party who has filed against the collateral or whose interest is known to the secured party. The debtor can thus challenge the legal effects of the sale either under the **commercially reasonable** requirement or on the basis that he or she did not get **reasonable notification**. The issue is most often raised when the debtor is sued for a deficiency judgment, where the secured party says that the sale did not bring enough to pay off the debt.

Section 9-504(4) deals with the rights acquired by the purchaser of the collateral at the disposition sale. The disposition gives the purchaser all rights of the debtor, and it discharges the security interest under which the sale was made and any subordinate interest or lien. Even though the secured party does not follow proper sale procedures, the purchaser is protected at a public sale if there is no knowledge of the defects in the sale or collusion, and in any other case if acting in good faith.

Compulsory Disposition. A secured party who has repossessed the collateral *must* dispose of it in accordance with Section 9-504 where the consumer-debtor has paid 60 percent of the cash price or of the loan and has not signed *after default* a statement renouncing or modifying his or her rights under Part 5. If the secured party fails to comply with this section within ninety days after taking possession, the debtor may either sue for conversion of the collateral or recover damages and a penalty as specified under 9-507(1).

Except for the above consumer goods situation, a secured party who is in possession of the collateral may propose *after default* that he or she will retain it in satisfaction of the debt. The secured party must send written notice of this "proposal" to the debtor and, except for consumer goods, to any other secured party who has filed or who is known to the secured party with possession. The debtor or any secured party entitled to notification has twenty-one days from receipt of the notification to object in writing to the proposal; any other secured party claiming an interest in the collateral has twenty-one days from the time that secured party one obtained possession of the collateral. If anyone does object, secured party one cannot retain the collateral as proposed but must dispose of it under 9-504; if there is no objection, the secured party can keep the collateral in satisfaction of the obligation.

Redemption by Debtor. At any time before the secured party has disposed or contracted to dispose of the collateral under 9-504 or has discharged the obligation by retention of the collateral under 9-505(2), the debtor or any other secured party has the right to redeem the collateral. To redeem, there must be a tender to the secured party of: (a) all obligations secured by the collateral; (b) "the expenses reasonably incurred by the secured party in retaking, holding, and preparing the collateral for disposition, in arranging for the sale;" and (c) "to the extent provided in the agreement and not prohibited by law, his reasonable attorneys' fees and legal expenses."

The debtor or any other secured party may agree *in writing, after default*, to waive this right to redeem.

Secured Party Liability for Failure to Comply. Section 9-507 does two things. It defines more precisely the requirement that the secured party proceed after default in a "commercially reasonable" manner and it provides remedies for the debtor where the secured party does not proceed in accordance with the provisions of Part 5.

Section 9-507(2) establishes several principles regarding "commercial reasonableness," and the debtor's right to recover for a secured party's violation of the default provisions of Part 5. Where such violation has occurred:

1. [D]isposition may be ordered or restrained on appropriate terms and conditions.

2. If the disposition has occurred, the debtor or any person entitled to notification or whose security interest has been made known to the secured party prior to disposition has a right to recover from the secured party any loss caused by a failure to comply with the provisions of this Part.

3. If the collateral is consumer goods, the debtor has a right to recover in any event an amount not less than the credit service charge plus 10 percent of the principal amount of the debt or the time price differential plus 10 percent of the cash price.

These Code sections thus provide significant protections for both consumer and nonconsumer debtors even after they have gone into default on their obligations under a security agreement.

SIGNIFICANCE OF THIS CHAPTER

Since debtors do default with some frequency, creditors need to be assured that they will have priority claims against "their" pieces of collateral. This priority is really the whole purpose of structuring the credit arrangement as a secured transaction. The entire motive for being a *secured* creditor is to have a specific source of funds in the event the debtor defaults, rather than having to rely on the debtor's general financial condition. Creditors thus need to know what to do to establish priority and what payment sequences the Code provides.

Similarly, both debtors and creditors need to be aware of their rights when a default does occur. In general, a secured creditor who is proceeding in a reasonable manner is well protected by Article 9. On the other hand, the Code also tries to assure that the debtor is treated fairly, even though guilty of a default. Because abuses occurred in the past, Article 9 gives consumer debtors the right to recover a penalty in the event their secured parties do not follow proper procedures. The Code has attempted to strike a fair balance between the parties in this very common and very important commercial transaction.

PROBLEMS FOR DISCUSSION

1. Ned Ninepins, owner of Lucky Lane bowling alley, bought six automatic pinsetters from Leisure Equipment, Inc. He entered into a retail installment contract with the seller which specified that upon default the total contract price would become due. After several payments Ned defaulted, and six months later Leisure Equipment, Inc. brought a foreclosure action against him. Under a warrant of seizure, the local sheriff entered the building and rendered the pinsetters inoperative but left them in their place. Ned counterclaimed for damages, arguing that personal property had been converted and that the sheriff's failure to remove the seized equipment made it impossible for Ned to use the building in any other way.

    Was the seizure legal? Explain.

2. While Nancy Raffa and her husband were entertaining friends in their home at Lighthouse Point, her Cadillac Eldorado was taken by a "collection agent" (the repo man). She was over a month behind in making the 16th of thirty-six monthly payments on the car. The car was gone when Mrs. Raffa and her guests came out of the house, and she said she was embarrassed by the incident. She has paid off the loan and retrieved the car and now sues for compensatory and punitive damages for wrongful repossession. She claims that the repo man committed an unlawful trespass and that the Dania Bank failed to give her specific notice of their intent to repo the car. The trial court granted summary judgment for the defendants. Nancy appealed.

    How should the appeals court decide, and why?

3. On June 15, NCR sold a new cash register to Edmond Carroll who was doing business as the "Kozy Kitchen" in Canton, Massachusetts. This sale was designated as conditional sale. The cash register was delivered sometime between November 19 and November 25. NCR filed financing statements on December 20 and 21. Meanwhile, Caroll had borrowed $1,911 from Firestone on November 18 and had executed a security agreement covering the following goods, chattels, and automobiles namely: The business located at and numbered 574 Washington Street, Canton, MA together with all its goodwill, fixtures, equipment, and merchandise. The fixtures specifically consist of the following: *All contents of luncheonette including equipment such as: booths and tables, stand and counter, tables, chairs, booths, steam tables, salad unit, potato peeler, U.S. slicer, range, case fryer, compressor, bobtail, milk dispenser, Silex, 100 class air conditioner, signs, pastry case, mixer, dishes, silverware, tables, hot fudge, Haven Ex., 2-door station wagon 1957 Ford a57R107215* together with property and articles now and which may hereafter be used or mixed with added or attached to and/or substituted for any of the foregoing described property." Firestone filed financing statements on November 18 and 25 which identified the collateral with the italicized words. When Carroll went into default on both contracts, Firestone repossessed and sold the contents of the luncheonette including the cash register. NCR sued for the tort of conversion of "its" cash register. The lower court held for NCR.

    Does NCR have priority as to the cash register? Explain.

4. Becky Miller, MBA, decided to open a Texaco station. She purchased equipment from Leek Oil Equipment Company, for which she delivered to the seller a promissory note for $3,000. Under the conditional sales agreement, she was to pay monthly installments and title to the equipment would remain with the seller until the entire purchase price was paid. After making three payments she defaulted. Leek repossessed the equipment estimated to be worth $2,000, credited the promissory note for this amount, and sued Becky for another $1,000. Becky protests, claiming that the repossession wipes out the entire debt.

   What is the decision? Discuss.

5. Pedro Agricola, a farmer, bought a pickup for which he executed a promissory note to Flatland Bank. The note was secured by a properly executed and perfected security agreement. Pedro also had other loans outstanding with Flatland Bank which were secured by mortgages on other equipment and on his sixteen pigs. Two years later Pedro borrowed money from his neighbor Lilly White and gave her a promissory note but soon afterward he defaulted on both notes. Lilly took possession of the truck, claiming that the bank should satisfy its claim by taking possession of Pedro's other assets, namely the ten-year-old equipment and the sixteen two-year-old pigs.

   Who has prior claim on the truck? Why?

Part Five

Commercial Paper

Part Five deals with credit, but with a different aspect of the credit transaction than Part Four. Whereas the main focus of Part Four was on setting up the credit arrangement in a way that assures payment, this part deals with the problems involved in using non-money pieces of paper as a method of payment. Article Three of the UCC calls these pieces of paper *commercial paper*; the earlier term was *negotiable instruments*.

Nearly everyone is familiar with the use of personal checks as a payment instrument. The check is one form of commercial paper. This part covers the various types of liability on such instruments, the rules for enforcement of those liabilities, and the circumstances that will discharge such liabilities. Chapter 23 also covers the relationship between the customer and a bank where such instruments are deposited, or against which they have been issued.

Many students have signed promissory notes in loan transactions—for school expenses, car purchases, and the like. The promissory note is another form of commercial paper. Because it is a promise to pay, rather than an order to a bank to pay, some of the rules for a note are different than those for a check. These differences are also covered in this part.

The rules for dealing with these pieces of paper used as substitutes for money are complex, but very important to business operations. Millions of checks circulate through the banking system every day. Promissory notes are a key part of short-term financing arrangements, both for individuals and for businesses. A basic understanding of commercial paper rules is important to help you avoid or minimize liability, and to protect your rights in transactions where these pieces of paper are used.

Chapter 20

Types of Instruments, Requirements of Negotiability

Negotiable instruments were developed by Western European merchants several centuries ago to meet the needs of trade and commerce. Highwaymen and bandits made carrying large sums of money a risky operation. Goods and services conceivably could have been purchased on the buyer's credit, but that arrangement also entailed substantial risks of nonpayment in the days before Dun & Bradstreet and credit bureaus. What the merchant wanted was something as acceptable as money in most commercial transactions, that could be carried from place to place more safely than currency.

Through custom and usage, merchants and their special commercial courts came to agree that instruments written in the proper form would have the characteristics they desired. These traits were:

1. Such instruments would be freely transferable from person to person (under the old English common law, at least, a transferee of contract rights could not sue the debtor directly).

2. They would be presumed to have been issued for value, and the debtor would have the burden of proving otherwise.

3. The debtor would not be able to assert certain defenses (generally, "voidable" defenses) when a good faith purchaser ("holder in due course") sued to enforce an instrument and to collect the money.

Negotiable instruments law, as part of the law merchant, was assimilated into English common law during the 17th and 18th centuries. An English statute codifying these practices was passed in 1882, and in 1896, the Uniform Negotiable Instruments Law (NIL) was proposed and later adopted by nearly all states in the United States. The UCC's Article 3, Commercial Paper, now supersedes the NIL. Article 4, Bank Deposits and Collections, brings together the rules regarding bank processing of such instruments. More recently, several states and the FTC have adopted new rules eliminating the "no defenses" result where the instrument was executed by a consumer-debtor. Articles 3 and 4 were substantially amended in 1990. Article 4A on funds transfers was submitted to the states in 1989.

MAJOR LEGAL ISSUES

Negotiable instruments law is technical and complex and tends to confuse many beginners. Since it's so easy to get lost in the details of the cases and the UCC provisions, the student needs an overall picture of what's happening in these situations. One or more persons allegedly have signed a piece of paper that contains some sort of promise to pay money, and the plaintiff is trying to collect the money. The primary significance of that piece of paper's being *negotiable* is that a person to whom it was transferred as a good faith purchaser can force a party who is liable on it to pay the money even though that party has a defense against liability. If the instrument is negotiable, and it gets into the hands of the special sort of *bona fide* purchaser called a **holder in due course (HDC)**, a business debtor who had signed it would have to pay it as promised. This is true even when the merchandise or services exchanged for the instrument were never delivered or were misrepresented. In other words, a negotiable instrument in the hands of an HDC can be enforced as written, despite the existence of certain defenses. The instrument's negotiability prevents the defendant from using some defenses, such as fraud or nonperformance, to avoid paying the HDC.

In analyzing a negotiable instruments problem, then, we need to determine whether or not this special "negotiability" result should occur. Should the person who signed the instrument have to pay it, even if the goods or services for which it was issued were not delivered or were misrepresented? First, to get these special negotiability results, the instrument must be in negotiable form. It must comply with the requirements for negotiability, as discussed later in this chapter. If the instrument is not negotiable, any defense against liability on it can be asserted as a reason for not paying it.

Second, to collect against a particular person, plaintiff must prove that that person is liable on the instrument in some way. In most cases, liability is based either on a defendant's having signed the instrument, thereby making a contractual promise to pay it, or having transferred it for value, thereby assuming certain implied warranties as to is validity. In some cases, a tort theory based on negligence or conversion may also be used to collect the amount of the instrument from a particular defendant. It's not enough, in other words, for plaintiff to prove that he or she is the proper party to be paid. To collect against a particular person, the plaintiff must prove that that person is liable, under some theory, for payment of the instrument. These theories of liability are discussed in Chapter 21.

Third, in order for the plaintiff to enforce the instrument and collect the money, the terms of the instrument must make the plaintiff the holder of the instrument. It must have been issued to the plaintiff or properly transferred ("negotiated") to the plaintiff. The requirements for becoming "holder" of these instruments are discussed in Chapter 22. If the plaintiff is not a holder, the plaintiff should not collect on the instrument.

Fourth, if some of the persons who may be liable on the instrument have defenses against liability (reasons for not paying it), the plaintiff must also qualify as a "holder in due course" in order to overcome certain defenses and collect the money anyway. What it takes to become a holder in due course (HDC) is also discussed in Chapter 22. If the plaintiff is not an HDC of the negotiable instrument, any defense that can be proved can be used to defeat or reduce the plaintiff's recovery on the instrument. If there are no reasons for not paying the instrument, plaintiff collects merely by being a holder. The significance of HDC status relates to cases where there are reasons for not paying the instrument or disputes over its ownership.

Finally, since some defenses against liability can be asserted against HDCs and some cannot, we need to know which are which. These two types of defenses are discussed in Chapter 22, along with the events that discharge a party's liability on a negotiable instrument.

Text discussion in these chapters will follow the applicable sections of Article 3 of the UCC, which covers all these points in some detail. The cases in this area will focus on interpretation of the Code sections in particular fact situations.

TYPES OF COMMERCIAL PAPER

When someone issues a negotiable instrument in exchange for cash, goods, or services, the instrument is written in either of two basic ways. It may be a *promise* by the issuer to pay the indicated amount, or it may be an *order* to someone else (a bank, or some other party who owes the issuer money) to pay the stated amount. The UCC says that a promise is an "undertaking to pay." An "I.O.U." is therefore not a negotiable instrument, even though it is in writing and signed, because it is merely an "acknowledgement" of the debt. An order is defined as "an instruction to pay." If you have a checking account, look at your checks—they don't say "Please pay," just "Pay." Some smart lawyer might otherwise try to argue that the use of courteous language made the "order" only a "request," and that the check was thus not negotiable.

The Code identifies several specific types of commercial paper. A **note** is a promise by a **maker** to pay money to a payee. A **certificate of deposit** is "an acknowledgment by a bank" of receipt of money and a promise to repay it. A **draft** (or bill of exchange) is an order from a **drawer** directed to a drawee and ordering the drawee to pay the stated amount of money to a named payee. A **check** is an order directed to a bank as drawee and indicating that the money is to be paid "on demand," that is, anytime the payee requests it.

In addition to these four basic types, several special kinds of negotiable instruments are widely used. **Installment notes** are frequently used for credit purchases of appliances, cars, and other large consumer items. Rather than being payable all at once, an installment note specifies monthly required payments. **Mortgage notes** are typically used in connection with the purchase of real estate. Again, monthly payments on the real estate mortgage are usually required. Businesses buying goods on credit also use the **trade acceptance**, which is a form of draft. Rather than ordering a bank to pay, the trade acceptance orders the buyer of the goods to pay the contract price of the goods, plus interest for the agreed credit period. The seller issues the trade acceptance as the drawer; the buyer is the drawee, who is ordered to pay the amount stated to the seller, as payee. When the buyer signs this order as well, meaning that the buyer promises to pay it according to its terms, the seller can then sell the trade acceptance to a bank (usually a bank where the buyer of the goods has established credit). The buyer of the goods gets the time to pay for the goods, the seller of the goods gets cash, and the buyer of the trade acceptance gets the interest on it, plus any discount. Trade acceptances are very useful where the seller of the goods cannot afford to carry the buyer as an account receivable for the length of time the buyer requires. A **cer-**

tified check operates in much the same way as a trade acceptance. The order to pay the money is directed to the drawee bank. When the drawee bank agrees that it will pay the check, it "certifies" the check by writing its name on the face of the check. At that point, the bank has directly promised to pay the check. A **cashier's check** is a check written by a bank ordering itself to pay the stated amount. Again, the bank is directly liable for payment of the cashier's check.

Types of Commercial Paper
Note (Promissory Note)

$ _____   _____, 19 ___
                        City   Date

On demand, for value received, I/We promise to pay to the order

of _____

the sum of _____ Dollars,

at _____,
     Address

together with interest at the rate of _____ per year. If lawsuit be commenced to enforce payment of this note, I promise to pay such added sum as the court may determine as reasonable attorney's fees in connection with said lawsuit.

_____

_____

Draft (Bill of Exchange)

TRADE ACCEPTANCE

NO. _____

BIGGER BANK

_____   _____
City of drawer   Date

On _____, pay to the order of OURSELVES

_____DOLLARS ($ _____)

The transaction which gives rise to this instrument is the purchase of goods by the Acceptor from the Drawer.

TO: _____
Name of Drawee

Street Address

City of Drawee

Date Payable on ____ Bank

Location ____ Acceptor

Signature of Drawer

BY _____
by

Article 3 of the Code specifically excludes "investment securities" (stocks and bonds) from its coverage, along with money and "documents of title." Article 8 covers investment securities, and documents of title are covered in Article 7. Both securities and documents may be issued in "negotiable" form, but they are not used as money substitutes in the same way as "negotiable instruments."

STATE v. FAMILY BANK OF HALLANDALE
623 So. 2d 474 (FL, 1993)

FACTS: The Department of Transportation awarded a contract to Ted's Sheds, Inc., for several metal buildings to be used at various service plazas on the Florida Turnpike. Ted's Sheds provided a Ft. Lauderdale address during the bidding process. When the buildings were delivered, the State received an invoice from Ted's Sheds, Inc., listing its address as Bonita Springs, Florida. The state approved the invoices for payment and, on February 5, 1987, the Comptroller issued a warrant, for $16,932 payable to the order of Ted's Sheds and sent it to the Ft. Lauderdale, Florida, address listed on the original bid.

On February 12, 1987, Ted's Sheds of Broward, Inc., presented the original warrant to Seminole National Bank. The warrant was endorsed "Ted's Sheds of Broward, Inc.," and was credited by the bank. Sometime thereafter, the agents of Ted's Sheds Inc, in Bonita Springs stated that they had not received the warrant and requested a duplicate warrant. It was then discovered that there were two Ted's Sheds, one in Ft. Lauderdale known as Ted's Sheds of Broward, Inc." and one in Bonita Springs, known as "Ted's Sheds, Inc." These separate legal entitles shared common corporate officers. On February 19, 1987, the Comptroller placed a stop payment on the original warrant, issued a duplicate warrant to Ted's Sheds and mailed it to Ted's Sheds Inc., in Bonita Springs. Subsequently, the Federal Reserve Bank of Miami returned the original warrant to the bank indicating that payment had been stopped by the state treasurer.

The bank initiated this action some fourteen months after the original warrant was returned. In the intervening time, Ted's Sheds of Broward, Inc., was involuntarily dissolved. The bank argued that it had no knowledge of the stop payment order and asserted that it was a "holder in due course" entitled to reimbursement by the State of Florida on the theory that state warrants are negotiable instruments. The State maintained that state warrants are not negotiable instruments under the Uniform Commercial Code and, thus, the bank was not entitled to repayment of these funds by the people of the State of Florida. The trial court entered summary judgment in favor of the bank as holder for value of a state warrant. On appeal, the district court affirmed.

  JUSTICE McDONALD:

A brief examination of the meaning and use of warrants is desirable before addressing the issues in this case. In connection with state funds, the term "warrant" has a well-defined meaning. Warrants are devices, prescribed by law, for drawing money from the state treasury. They are orders issued by the official whose duty it is to pass on claims to the treasurer to pay a specified sum from the treasury for the persons and purposes specified.... A warrant is not an order to pay absolutely, rather it is generally prime facie evidence of indebtedness payable out of a particular fund or appropriation.... Warrants have been regarded as negotiable in the restricted sense of the term in that they have the quality of easy or simple transferability.... But, in fact, there is much pre-code authority that a warrant possesses all of the qualities of negotiable paper but one (i.e., unlike negotiable paper, it is open to any defense which might have been made to the claim in the hands of the original holder).... Warrants drawn for ordinary governmental expenses are licenses authorizing payment and are not intended to have all the qualities of commercial paper. Warrants do not represent a pledge of the general credit of the issuing body, but are instruments authorized for convenience in conducting ordinary business and as a means of anticipating revenue.

A warrant is best characterized as a chose in action, payable when funds are available for its purpose. This court has held that there is a "vast distinction" between warrants and bonds.... A bond is basically an acknowledgement of indebtedness and a promise to pay, while a warrant is an order or direction to pay. The most noteworthy distinction between the two instruments is that a bond generally constitutes an absolute order to pay, while warrants generally are an order to pay out of a particular fund. Also, before the adoption of the Uniform Commercial Code, the point of distinction most often emphasized by the courts was the negotiability of bonds and the nonnegotiability of warrants.... "A bond is a negotiable instrument, while a warrant is nonnegotiable. A warrant is subject at all times to the defenses it would be subject to were it in the hands of the original payee—not so with a negotiable bond."

Prior to the adoption of the Uniform Commercial Code in Florida, warrants issued by sovereign governmental entities were expressly declared nonnegotiable for public policy reasons.... Under the pre-code law, the Uniform Negotiable Instruments Law (NIL) governed the negotiability of commercial paper.... During this stage, the law was clear, and there was no question as to the nonnegotiability of state treasury warrants.... The general rule regarding warrants under pre-code law expressly provided that a warrant drawn by a proper officer on the state treasury was not a negotiable instrument in the sense of the law merchant.... There are several reasons for this rule under the Uniform Negotiable Instruments Law; primarily, warrants are paid out of a particular fund and, therefore, are not unconditional. However, even though some warrants may have been in negotiable form under the NIL, Florida was among several jurisdictions that, because of public policy reasons, followed the rule that government warrants are not to be regarded as negotiable commercial paper so as to be free of all legal and equitable defenses of the particular governmental entity when in the hands of a holder in due course.... In its simplest terms, the public policy holding state warrants to be nonnegotiable instruments is the state's way of protecting the public treasury from crookedness and shady deals by dishonest officials. Warrants serve the dual purpose of safeguarding the public treasury and protecting the treasurer as to payments made in compliance there with.... "[W]arrants, because of the nature of their creation, the purposes for which issued, the informal manner of their issue, the danger of mistakes, fraud, want of consideration, etc., are not given the protection of negotiable instruments." [T]he policy of allowing the government to assert defenses against a holder of a warrant must outweigh any innocent purchaser notions; otherwise a few dishonest officials could bankrupt an entire town. "It would overwhelm municipalities with ruin to hold that such warrants or orders have the qualities of negotiable paper, especially that quality which protects an innocent holder for value from defenses of which he has no notice, actual or constructive...."

We hold that the district court erred in its finding that the Florida Legislature, in adopting the Uniform Commercial Code, intended to declare warrants to be commercial paper and abandon the public policy of nonnegotiability of governmental warrants....

The Family Bank of Hallandale is not a holder in due course because the state treasury warrant involved is not a negotiable instrument to which the Uniform Commercial Code applies. As a result, the Family Bank took the warrant subject to the State's defense that it had issued a valid stop payment order.

REQUIREMENTS OF NEGOTIABILITY

Negotiability is strictly a matter of form. If an instrument is written to comply with the requirements of UCC 3-104(a), it is negotiable; if not, it is not negotiable, though it may be enforceable as an ordinary written contract. *Negotiability*, in other words, does not depend on the parties' intent, or their agreement, or their understanding, but on their compliance with the Code's requirements. The drafters of the Code have expressed this policy very clearly in several of their earlier official comments.

The courts were thus directed not to produce the very special negotiability results unless the debtor has signed a writing which clearly conforms to Article 3's requirements.

What are these requirements? They are listed in Section 3-104(a); the writing must:

1. Be signed by the maker or drawer.

2. Contain an unconditional promise or order to pay a fixed amount of money, with or without interest or other charges.

3. Be payable on demand or at a definite time.

4. Be payable to order or to bearer at the time it is issued or first comes into possession of a holder.

5. Not state any other undertaking or instruction by the person promising or ordering payment to do any act in addition to the payment of money.

Each of these requirements is further defined and explained in other Code sections. Often, the defendant-debtor will argue against liability, claiming that the signed instrument is not negotiable. If true, the plaintiff creditor would be subject to any provable defense.

SIGNED BY MAKER OR DRAWER

Signed, in the general definitions section of Article 1, includes "any symbol executed or adopted by a party with present intention to authenticate a writing." Thus, a signature need not be written out fully in script; it can be printed, typed, stamped, initialed, or reproduced mechanically by a checkwriter. Because of the special characteristics of negotiable instruments, Sections 3-401(a) states a very important rule for them: "A person is not liable on an instrument unless the person signed the instrument," or (ii) "the person is represented by an agent ... who signed...." A person may be liable on some other basis to the plaintiff, but cannot be liable *on an instrument* unless that person's signature is on the instrument, though it does not necessarily have to appear at the bottom. It may be made by trade name, assumed name, mark (X), or even thumbprint. It may be made by a properly authorized agent, though the agent may be held personally liable to subsequent holders of the instrument if the agent does not clearly indicate that the signing is being done only on behalf of the principal. Where someone who is not authorized to sign another's name does so, the signature operates as that of "the unauthorized signer in favor of any person who in good faith pays the instrument or takes it for value" (3-403).

The application of these rules to Ms. Shulof, a corporate officer, is discussed in the following case.

FINNISH FUR SALES v. JULIETTE SHULOF FURS
770 F.Supp. 139 (S.D., NY, 1991)

FACTS: This is an action to collect sums allegedly owed in connection with furs purchased at two auctions in Vantaa, Finland. Plaintiff Finnish Fur Sales Co., Ltd.("FFS"), asserts its claim of failure to pay for and clear 2,469 fox pelts against defendants Juliette Shulof Furs, Inc. ("JSF"), and George Shulof. Plaintiff Okobank Osuuspankkien Keskuspankki Oy ("Okobank") asserts its claim of failure to honor a bill of exchange against defendants JSF and Juliette Shulof.

Defendants George and Juliette Shulof asked the Court for summary judgment dismissing the individual claims against each of them. Plaintiffs opposed defendants' motion and asked for summary judgment against all defendants.

FFS is a limited company organized under Finnish law, which sells fur pelts raised by Finnish breeders at public auctions held several times each year. The auctions are conducted under certain Conditions of Sale ("Conditions"), which are listed in the auction catalogue, a copy of which is given to each prospective bidder in advance of the auction. A one-page English translation of the Conditions appears on the inside front cover of the catalogue.

JSF is a New York corporation that has conducted a fur dealing business for approximately fifteen years. George Shulof, an officer of JSF, has been in the fur business since 1935. Mr. Shulof attended the FFS auctions held in Vantaa, Finland, in January and May 1987. He purchased over $500,000 worth of skins at the January auction, and some $700,000 worth of skins at the May auction. It is undisputed that at each auction he was the actual bidder. JSF had not sent a bidder to the FFS auctions during the twenty-five-year period from 1959 to 1984, but Mr. Shulof had personally attended the FFS auction in December 1986.

The parties apparently do not dispute the fact that JSF paid for and cleared the majority of the skins purchased at the two 1987 auctions, with the exception of 2,469 fox pelts worth $290,048.17. The parties also do not dispute that JSF made certain payments against the uncleared skins, leaving an unpaid balance of $202,416.85, plus interest.

Between December 1987 and December 1988, JSF gave FFS resale instructions regarding a number of the uncleared skins. FFS asserts that it was unable to sell the skins at the minimum resale prices set by JSF. Thereafter, FFS decided to liquidate JSF's account, to which JSF agreed in March 1989. FFS sold the remaining uncleared skins at its May and September 1989 auctions. FFS alleges damages of $153,502.39.

FFS claims that, in addition to the liability of JSF, Mr. Shulof is personally liable for this debt, based on Finnish law, the custom and practice of the fur trade, and the provisions of Section 4 of the Conditions. Section 4 provides:

> Any person bidding at the auction shall stand surety as for his own debt until full payment is made for purchased merchandise. If he has made the bid on behalf of another person, he is jointly and severally liable with the person for the purchase.

George Shulof denies any personal liability on the grounds, *inter alia,* that the provision is unenforceable under both New York and Finnish law.

Okobank's claim arises from a line of credit arranged by FFS in November 1988 to allow JSF to clear some of the remaining skins. JSF made a cash down payment and accepted a bill of exchange (the "Bill of Exchange") for $30,328.39, due February 7, 1989.

According to plaintiffs, in January 1989, Okobank became holder in due course of the Bill of Exchange, which was presented for collection on or about February 7, 1989, at Bank Leumi in New York, but was dishonored. As of July 31, 1990, Okobank claimed principal and interest due amounting to $37,480.90.

The Bill of Exchange was signed "Juliette A. Shulof" above the printed name "Juliette Shulof Furs Inc." Okobank contends, and Mrs. Shulof denies, that this signature renders Mrs. Shulof liable in her individual capacity.

 DISTRICT JUDGE LEISURE:

Section 15 of the Conditions provides that "[t]hese conditions are governed by Finnish law." Choice of law clauses are routinely enforced by the courts of this Circuit, "if there is a reasonable basis for the choice...."

Finland's contacts with the transactions at issue are substantial, rendering the choice of law clause enforceable unless a strong public policy of New York is impaired by the application of Finnish law....

FFS's expert, Vesa Majamaa ... a Doctor of Law and Professor of the Faculty of Law at the University of Helsinki, gives as his opinion that the provision of Section 4 of the Conditions imposing personal liability upon the bidder, regardless of whether he bids on behalf of another, is valid both as a term of the particular auctions at issue and as a general principle of Finnish and Scandinavian auction law....

According to Majamaa, it is commonly accepted in Scandinavia that a bidder, by making a bid, accepts those conditions which have been announced at the auction....

Majamaa also notes that under Danish law, which he maintains would be applied by a Finnish court in the absence of Finnish decisional or legislative law on point, "it is taken for granted that someone who has bid on merchandise on someone else's account is responsible for the transaction, as he would be for his own obligation, together with his superior.... Hence the auction buyer's responsibility is not secondary, as is, for example, the responsibility of a guarantor...."

[A] perusal of the Conditions reveals that their entire text is only a single page long, and that all of the Conditions, including Section 4, are printed in the same size print, which, although small, is legible. The catalogue was made available to Mr. Shulof at the beginning of the four-day period prior to the auction during which potential bidders were allowed to inspect the furs. Although Mr. Shulof contends that the urgent need to inspect large numbers of furs prevented him from reading the one-page list of Conditions, he admits that he knew where they were located in the catalogue and that he did read some of the Conditions before bidding. Further, Mr. Shulof does not dispute the fact that he was given a copy of the same Conditions at the time of the 1986 auction he attended.

Under these circumstances, it seems unlikely that a New York court would refuse to enforce Section 4 in an arm's length commercial transaction involving a sophisticated defendant accustomed to bidding at fur auctions. Moreover, even if a New York court would not enforce such a provision in a transaction to which New York law clearly applied, this Court does not find New York's interest in protecting one of its residents against personal liability as a corporate officer to constitute so fundamental a policy that New York courts would refuse to enforce a contrary rule of foreign law....

Thus, Mr. Shulof must be held jointly and severally liable with JSF for any damages owed to FFS for the furs purchased at its 1987 auctions, and his motion for summary judgment is denied....

The parties agree that New York law governs the issue of the liability of Juliette Shulof on the Bill of Exchange, which was executed and payable in New York. The parties do not dispute that the Bill of Exchange is a negotiable instrument, and therefore subject to the provisions of Article 3 of the Uniform Commercial Code, as adopted by the state of New York.

The relevant section of the Code is § 3-403, which governs signatures by authorized representatives....

In the case at bar, Mrs. Shulof signed as "Juliette A. Shulof" above a typed name of "Juliette Shulof Furs Inc.," which had been typed in by the preparer of the instrument, FFS. The cases interpreting signatures of this type demonstrate the special treatment of negotiable instruments under New York law. As reflected in the discussion in an earlier section of this opinion, New York has, as a general rule, a policy against imposing personal liability on corporate officers if the circumstances are ambiguous. However, this policy gives way before the policy considerations underlying N.Y.U.C.C. § 3-403, which "aims to foster certainty and definiteness in the law of commercial paper, requirements deriving from the 'necessity for takers of negotiable instruments to tell at a glance whose obligation they hold....'"

Construing Section 3-403(2), the New York Court of Appeals held that "the basic law is that resort to extrinsic proof is impermissible when the face of the instrument itself does not serve to put its holder on notice of the limited liability of a signer...."

The Court finds the case at bar to be analogous to the holdings in *Javeri* and *Rotuba*. It is undisputed that Okobank never dealt with either of the Shulofs or JSF. Mrs. Shulof offers no evidence sufficient to raise a triable issue of fact as to either Okobank's status as a holder in due course or her allegations of fraud in the inducement on the part of FFS. Accordingly, the Court finds that Mrs. Shulof's signature on the Bill of Exchange did not give notice that she signed in a representative capacity only, and therefore she is personally liable for the amount of the bill. Her motion for summary judgment is denied, and the motion of Okobank for summary judgment against Juliette Shulof is granted.

UNCONDITIONAL PROMISE OR ORDER

Section 3-206 lists a number of rules for determining when a promise or an order is or is not "unconditional;" most of these rules are designed to meet particular problems which have come up in prior cases. Instruments frequently refer to the transaction out of which they arose, or to the consideration received or to be received for them, or to the fact that payment is secured by mortgage or otherwise. Within limits, the Code permits such references; the promise or order is still "unconditional," and the instrument is still negotiable. But when a promise or order states that it is "subject to or governed by" any other agreement, it is conditional and thus not negotiable. (The instrument may still be enforced like any ordinary written contract, however; "not negotiable" just means that the plaintiff's claim is subject to any defense that the defendant can prove.)

Similar rules are stated about the source of funds to pay the instrument. Generally, an instrument that is to be paid only out of a particular fund is conditional (and therefore not negotiable).

FIXED AMOUNT

The Code also provides some detailed rules for determining when the amount to be paid is a fixed amount. Most typical provisions regarding interest, installment payments, and discounts or penalties for early payment require only a little mathematics to determine the amount due and are thus permissible. The interest rates and other percentages must be specified, however, so that the calculations can be made from the information appearing on the face of the instrument. Many instruments, particularly promissory notes, will include a provision requiring the payment of collection costs and attorney fees if the debtor defaults and litigation is necessary; the Code validates such provisions. Aside from the fact that "attorneys" drafted the Code, the rationale for this provision is that the basic sum due at maturity is "certain" and that these additional costs arise only because of the debtor's default.

OF MONEY

Money is defined in the general definitions section of the Code as "a medium of exchange authorized or adopted by a domestic or foreign government as a part of its currency." The "official governmental currency" test is broader than just saying "legal tender;" thus an instrument is payable in "money" even though it is payable in the United States in foreign currency. Unless it specifies otherwise, such an instrument may be paid in dollars equivalent to the stated amount of foreign currency on the due date.

NO OTHER PROMISE OR ORDER
EXCEPT AS ARTICLE 3 AUTHORIZES

Negotiable instruments used to be described as "couriers without luggage." The obligations they imposed were to be stated clearly and simply; thus any language providing for performances in addition to the payment of money was to be regarded with suspicion. The UCC continues that same basic policy, but does state some rules more specifically. Section 3-104 lists provisions permitted to be included in (or omitted from) an instrument without destroying its negotiability. Provisions relating to collateral given to secure payment of the instrument may be included.

Section 3-104 also permits the inclusion of terms that waive the benefit of any law intended to protect debtors and by which the debtor authorizes the creditor to go into court on the debtor's behalf and "confess judgment" (admit that the debtor owes the money). Many states would probably not permit their consumer protection laws to be overridden in this way, and only a few states recognize the confession of judgment procedure. Section 3-104 merely permits such provisions where they are otherwise lawful. An instrument need not state the consideration received for it, nor need it include any indication of where it was drawn or where it is to be paid.

PAYABLE ON DEMAND OR AT A DEFINITE TIME

For an instrument to be negotiable, its amount must be certain and the holder must be able to determine when the money may be demanded. Where the instrument is payable "on demand," the money is due whenever the holder asks for it. **Demand instruments** include those payable "at sight" or "at the will of the holder" (essentially the same thing as saying "on demand") and those in which no time for payment is stated. Checks, for example, usually do not include any statement as to when they are to be paid, so they are assumed to be demand instruments.

The rules for determining whether an instrument is payable at a definite time are a little more complicated. The clearest cases are those where the instrument is payable on or before a stated date or at a fixed period after a stated date. Also fairly easy to decide are those where the instruments are payable at a fixed period after sight. The **acceleration clause** and the **extension clause**, two provisions frequently inserted in instruments, may cause some difficulties with respect to the "definite time" requirement. An acceleration clause advances the due date; an extension clause delays it.

The UCC permits the use of acceleration clauses, within reason. If the acceleration of the date for payment can be made by the maker, a note is essentially payable "on or before" the due date, and thus still negotiable. Payment must be made at least by the due date, but can be made earlier if the maker so wishes. If acceleration of the due date can be made by the holder of the instrument, such acceleration must be made in good faith. The holder must honestly believe that "the prospect of payment or performance is impaired." A default in paying several monthly installments, or perhaps only one installment, could produce such a good faith belief. The holder's good faith is presumed here; the party against whom the acceleration is occurring must prove that the holder acted in bad faith in advancing the due date. An instrument could also specify that acceleration would occur automatically when a specified event happens, such as filing of bankruptcy by the debtor, or sale of its business assets, or similar occurrences.

Since the holder of an instrument could always extend the time for payment anyway, giving the holder express permission to do so in the instrument does not affect its negotiability. If the maker is given an express option to extend the time for payment, it must be for a specified additional time. Similarly, if there is a provision for an automatic extension of the time for payment, it must be for a specified additional time. In these latter two cases, there is thus still a known date on which payment can definitely be demanded. If the holder is doing the extending, he or she can demand payment by simply refusing to give any further extensions. With both extensions and accelerations, the drafters of the Code wanted to give the parties some flexibility in making their payment arrangements, but subject always to reasonableness and good faith.

The *Waller* case involves these rules.

WALLER v. MARYLAND NAT'L. BANK
620 A.2d 381 (MD App., 1993)

FACTS: Earthtech is a Maryland corporation with technical expertise in earth measurement systems. In the early 1980s, Earthtech sought to develop two pieces of sophisticated equipment. In order to achieve this goal, Earthtech required additional working capital. On 16 February 1983, Earthtech obtained a loan from MNB for $50,000 evidenced by a Revolving Note which provided for a continuing line of credit. This Revolving Note also stated that it was payable "on demand." This note was executed by Earthtech's officers: Waller, President; John Millhiser, Vice President; and Jeffrey Bloom, Vice President. Each officer also personally and unconditionally guaranteed payment of Earthtech's obligations to MNB.

On 20 May 1983, Earthtech obtained a second loan for $5,000 from MNB. This loan was evidenced by an Installment Note and was payable in thirty-five equal monthly installments.

The parties' relationship appeared to run smoothly until late April 1984 when Earthtech requested an additional loan from MNB to cover its May payroll. MNB denied Earthtech's request. Subsequently, during the afternoon of 30 April 1984, Gary Tyrrell, an MNB officer, arrived at Earthtech's offices and requested that Earthtech's officers execute indemnity deeds of trust (IDOTs) on their residences in favor of MNB. Earthtech's officers were surprised and reminded Tyrrell that MNB already possessed adequate security for its loans. The officers refused to sign the IDOTS and, after much discussion, Tyrrell agreed to return the next morning in order to give the officers additional time to consider MNB's request.

The following day, 1 May 1984, Tyrrell arrived at Earthtech's offices by mid-morning and immediately presented Earthtech's officers with a letter demanding repayment of the outstanding balance on the Revolving Note. Earthtech was unable to meet this demand. As a consequence, on 9 May 1984, MNB advised Earthtech that it was also in default of the Installment Note because it included a cross default provision which provided that a default by Earthtech under any agreement with MNB could result in default under *all* agreements between Earthtech and MNB. MNB, therefore, was invoking its right under the agreement to accelerate and demand payment of the outstanding principal and accrued interest of the Installment Note.

In early May 1984, Waller learned that she required an emergency hysterectomy. She entered the hospital on 8 May and underwent surgery the following day. Waller resumed active involvement in Earthtech, on a part-time basis, on 5 June 1984 and began working full-time on 11 June 1984. Appellants claim that MNB agreed to forbear from taking any action against Earthtech for the period of Waller's recovery. MNB, in contrast, claims that the forbearance agreement was contingent upon Earthtech's officers executing IDOTs on their residences in favor of MNB.

On 7 June 1984, MNB filed confessed judgment actions against Earthtech and its officers. Subsequently, Earthtech and MNB entered into a Workout Agreement. Under the Workout Agreement, Earthtech agreed to repay the full balance of the outstanding loans by mid-October 1984. In return, MNB agreed to dismiss the confessed judgment actions. For some reason, not clear from the record extract, the Workout Agreement was never signed by both parties, but they operated as if the agreement had full effect.

Earthtech voluntarily accelerated the repayment period and MNB was repaid in full by 21 August 1984. Approximately three weeks later, on 13 September 1984, MNB dismissed the confessed judgment actions.

On 30 April 1987, appellants, Earthtech, Inc. and its president and chief executive officer, Muriel Jennings Waller, filed a six count complaint against Maryland National Bank (MNB), appellee, in the Circuit Court for Baltimore City.

> **Count I:** Earthtech and Waller alleged breach of contract for violation by MNB of its duty of good faith and fair dealing;
>
> **Count II:** Earthtech and Waller alleged "negligent breach of contract;"
>
> **Count III:** Earthtech and Waller alleged conversion;
>
> **Count IV:** Earthtech alleged breach of contract, claiming a breach of alleged forbearance and workout agreements;
>
> **Count V:** Earthtech alleged intentional interference with contractual and business relations; and
>
> **Count VI:** Waller alleged intentional infliction of emotional distress.

MNB filed a motion to dismiss for failure to state a claim upon which relief can be granted, and a motion for summary judgment. The circuit court granted MNB's motion to dismiss the claim for punitive damages under Count I and dismissed Count VI in its entirety. Later, the circuit court granted summary judgments on all the other claims.

Earthtech and Waller appealed.

 JUDGE HARRELL:

Appellants first argue that the circuit court erred because it failed to consider that MNB, as a party to a contract, was subject to a good faith duty not only in the *enforcement* of the Revolving Note, but also in its *performance*. Appellants claim that MNB breached its duty of good faith in the performance of the contract by engaging in "collection activities" prior to MNB explicitly demanding payment of the Revolving Note....

Maryland law implies a duty of good faith and fair dealing in certain contracts....

This duty simply prohibits one party to a contract from acting in such a manner as to prevent the other party from performing his obligations under the contract.... Thus, the duty of good faith merely obligates a lender to exercise good faith in performing its contractual obligations; it does not obligate a lender to take affirmative actions that the lender is clearly not required to take under its loan documents....

The implied duty of good faith does not change the terms of the contract. In addition, when the language of a contract is plain and unambiguous, there is no room for construction by the court. "The clear and unambiguous language of an agreement will not give way to what the parties thought that the agreement meant or intended it to mean." The actual contract, therefore, is the starting point for our analysis.

Appellants and MNB entered into a loan agreement on 2 February 1983 that was evidenced by the Revolving Note. The clear and unambiguous language of the Revolving Note provides, in pertinent part:

> ON demand, the Undersigned (whether one or more than one) promises jointly and severally, if more than one) to pay to the order of MARYLAND NATIONAL BANK (the "Bank") the principal sum of fifty thousand and 00/100 Dollars (the "Principal Sum") or so much thereof as shall have been actually advanced by the Bank to the Undersigned....

As discussed [above], the Revolving Note was clearly a demand note. As a demand note, it was payable immediately, without demand.... A demand loan may be called at any time by the lender because there is no fixed dated of maturity.... Although § 1-208 of the Commercial Law Article imposes a general requirement of good faith in an option to accelerate at will, the Official Comment states, "Obviously this section has no application to demand instruments or obligations whose very nature permits call at any time with or without reason."

In addition, the weight of authority in other jurisdictions holds that the good faith requirement does not apply to a lender's decision to call a demand note....

In summary, the Revolving Note was clearly a demand note, as evidenced by its clear and unambiguous language. A demand note by its very nature may be called at any time by the holder, with or without reason. Therefore, the circuit court did not err in holding that MNB was not required to act in good faith and thereby impose a reasonableness standard upon MNB's conduct. Instead, MNB could enforce the plain terms of the contract and call the demand note at anytime, with or without reason. The circuit court's grant of summary judgment as to Count I was proper.

PAYABLE TO ORDER OR TO BEARER

These are "the magic words of negotiability;" they indicate clearly that an instrument is intended to pass freely from hand-to-hand, to circulate in commerce as a money substitute. Section 3-109 specifies the words and phrases used to achieve these results. **Bearer instruments** include those made payable to bearer, to the order of bearer, to a specified person or bearer, to cash, to the order or cash, or "otherwise indicates that it is not payable to an identified person." An instrument which indicates that the person in possession of it is entitled to payment is a bearer instrument. The revised Article 3 also says that an instrument which does not state a payee is bearer paper.

Order instruments are those payable to the order of any identified person, or to an identified person or order.

Section 3-110 states that a person may be "identified" in any way on the instrument, including name, number, office, or account number.

The revised Article 3 does allow a check to be negotiable even if it is not payable to order or bearer, as long as it meets all the other requirements.

The *Larsen* case shows that even a non-negotiable instrument is still subject to many other Code provisions, including Article 9.

LARSEN v. FIRST BANK
515 N.W. 2d 804 (NE, 1994)

FACTS: The plaintiffs-appellees, Edward W. Larsen, Carmelita A. Larsen, Candice Marie Larsen Ishii, Dennis E. Larsen, and Linda Marie Larsen, allege that the defendant-appellant, First Bank converted a certain note in which the aforementioned Larsens had a security interest by breaching an agreement to protect said interest. The district court granted the Larsens a partial summary judgment, holding First Bank liable, and subsequently sustained the Larsens' motion for a directed verdict made at the close of all the evidence at the trial on the issue of damages. First Bank appealed.

The Larsens held 50 percent of the common stock in Roger L. Hass, Inc., a dissolved Nebraska corporation, in which the other 50 percent of the stock was held by Roger Hass. In 1982, the Hass corporation sold substantially all of its assets to Financial Service Company, which, in addition to paying $50,000 in cash, executed a promissory note payable to the order of the Hass corporation in the sum of $159,052.50. The note incorporated the provisions of an agreement between Financial Service and Roger Hass and recited that said agreement provided for the cancellation and satisfaction of the note without payment, should certain events come to pass.

Although the Larsens, as owners of half of the Hass corporation's stock, were entitled to half of the $50,000, Roger Hass kept it all. He later, on August 16, 1982, assigned "all [his] right, title, and interest" in the Financial Service note to First Bank as security for an unrelated personal loan.

On January 10, 1983, Roger Hass executed three promissory notes payable to the Larsens in the amounts of $25,000, $13,564, and $5,481.51. The $25,000 note represented the Larsens' share of the cash Financial Service had paid toward the purchase of the assets of the Hass corporation. The other two notes were related to amounts Roger Hass owed the Larsens on other dealings.

In order to secure his notes to the Larsens, Roger Hass, in April 1983, executed in their favor a junior assignment of his 50-percent "beneficial interest" in the proceeds from the Financial Service promissory note "subject to a previous pledge dated August 16, 1982, by [the Hass corporation] to [First Bank]." Also executed was an agreement entitled "Junior Pledge Agreement for Security," which recites that it was entered into by "the Common SHAREHOLDERS OF [the Hass corporation] and [First Bank]."

After reciting Roger Hass' obligations to the Larsens, the existence of his notes to the Larsens, and the respective interests of the Larsens and Roger Hass in the Hass corporation prior to the sale of its assets, the junior pledge agreement recognizes the Larsens' second lien on Roger Haas' 50-percent interest in the proceeds of the Financial Service note which was specifically made junior to Roger Hass' pledge to First Bank. It further declares it to be the intention and understanding of the parties that all the proceeds received from Financial Service be distributed pro rata to the shareholders pursuant to their respective percentages of stock ownership. First Bank agreed that as a condition precedent to the effectiveness of the pledge given by the Hass corporation on August 16, 1982, the Larsens' 50-percent interest would not be encumbered or set off against any prior debts it was owed by the Hass corporation or Roger Hass personally and that it would not jeopardize the second lien the Larsens held on Roger Hass' beneficial interest in the note.

Undaunted by his existing debt Roger Hass, in February 1985, executed two promissory notes to Ralston Bank for a total of $12,500, which were secured by a deed of trust on his home. Sometime prior to April 23, 1986, Roger Hass sold his home and asked Ralston Bank to release the deed of trust, offering to assign his interest in the Financial Service promissory note as collateral. An officer of Ralston Bank contacted First Bank and was assured, notwithstanding the existence of the above-described junior pledge agreement, that if the First Bank debt were paid, there would be no prior liens or claims on Roger Hass' 50-percent interest in the proceeds of the Financial Service note.

On April 23, 1986, Roger Hass executed a $46,865.70 promissory note payable to Ralston Bank and an assignment of his interest in the Financial Service note. Of the proceeds, $13,583.22 was used to refinance Robert Hass' prior notes to Ralston Bank; the remaining $33,273.48 was paid to First Bank in discharge of its lien on Roger Hass' interest in the Financial Service note. The next day, at which time Roger Hass was $46,035.17 in debt to the Larsens, First Bank released its assignment of the possession of the note, Ralston Bank, using the note as security, lent Roger Hass an additional $12,969.35. At some point, Roger Hass' 50-percent beneficial interest in the payments from the Financial Service promissory note produced a payment of $54,164.22 to Ralston Bank.

The Larsens learned of Roger Hass' assignment of the Financial Service note to Ralston Bank sometime after the event, at which time the Larsens demanded that First Bank either deliver possession of the Financial Service promissory note to them or pay them its fair market value. Receiving neither, nor any funds from Roger Hass' 50-percent beneficial interest in the proceeds of the note, the Larsens instituted this suit.

 JUSTICE CAPORALE:

The question as to whether the Larsens perfected a security interest in the Financial Service note is controlled by Article 9 of the Nebraska version of the Uniform Commercial Code. With an exception not relevant to our analysis, the article at the time of the execution of the junior pledge agreement applied, as it does now, "to any transaction (regardless of its form) which is intended to create a security interest in ... documents, instruments, general intangibles, chattel paper [and] to security interests created by contract including pledge, assignment ... intended as security...."

First Bank is correct in its assertion that incorporation into the note of the agreement between Financial Service and Roger Hass described in Part II above makes the note something other than an unconditional promise to pay and thus makes it something other than a "negotiable instrument," as defined in Neb. UCC 3-104....

However, that does not mean that the Financial Service note was or is a "general intangible," as First bank claims. A general intangible was at the relevant time and continues to be defined as "any personal property (including things in action) other than goods, accounts, chattel paper, documents, instruments, and money...."

A document which is not a "negotiable instrument" might then and may now nonetheless qualify as an "instrument" which, unless the context of Article 9 otherwise requires, then included and continues to include "a negotiable instrument or any other writing which evidences a right to the payment of money and is not itself a security agreement or lease and is of a type which is in ordinary course of business transferred by delivery with any necessary endorsement or assignment...."

There are a number of cases not involving installment or executory contracts for the sale of real estate which hold that a promissory note not qualifying as a negotiable instrument was nonetheless an instrument within the purview of Article 9....

We conclude that a separate promissory note which is not a negotiable instrument may nonetheless be an instrument and hold, as the district court implicitly did, that the Financial Service note is an instrument and not a general intangible.

The distinction is an important one, for to perfect a security interest in a general intangible, one was at the relevant time, and still is, required to file a financing statement.... However, with certain exceptions not involved here, the only way one could then, or can now, perfect a security interest in an instrument is by taking possession of the document.... Additionally, so far as is relevant, Neb. UCC § 9-305 ... provided and provides: "A security interest in ... instruments ... may be perfected by the secured party's taking possession of the collateral. If such collateral ... is held by a bailee, the secured party is deemed to have possession from the time the bailee receives notification of the secured party's interest."

The net effect of §§ 9-304 and 9-305, then, is to permit a bailee to take possession of an instrument for the benefit of a secured party. Here, First Bank perfected its superior security interest in the Financial Service note by taking possession of it on its own behalf and then agreed that as a condition precedent to the effectiveness of the prior pledge given it by the Hass corporation, it would not jeopardize the junior lien held by the Larsens. It thereby committed itself to possess the note not only on its own behalf, but as a bailee for the benefit of the Larsens. That agreement necessarily required that once First Bank had recovered its debt, it would deliver the Financial Service note to the Larsens or come to some other arrangement with them. First Bank simply ignored the existence of its agreement with the Larsens and breached it by giving possession of the note to Ralston Bank without any regard for the Larsens' security interest in it.

SIGNIFICANCE OF THIS CHAPTER

The special negotiability results can occur only where the written promise to pay money is in negotiable form: a written, unconditional promise or order to pay a sum certain in money, signed by the maker or drawer, payable on demand or at a definite time, payable to order or to bearer, and containing no other promise or order not authorized by the provisions of Article 3. The special holder in due course status, which is explained in Chapter 22, can only exist with respect to negotiable instruments. As a general rule, even an assignee who takes an account receivable in good faith and for value holds it subject to any defense which the debtor had against liability on the underlying contract. To prevent the debtor from asserting most voidable-type defenses, the instrument must be in negotiable form. Unless it is, the holder's good faith and lack of notice of the defenses are irrelevant.

On the other hand, just because an instrument is nonnegotiable does not mean that it is totally invalid. If the debtor has no defenses to assert anyway, or is estopped to assert them, the holder of the nonnegotiable instrument will get the money represented by the instrument.

The requirements for negotiability are simply the first hurdle that the plaintiff must clear in establishing the special elimination-of-defenses result.

PROBLEMS FOR DISCUSSION

1. Charter sued to foreclose on a note and mortgage given by Holly Hill. The note contained the following provision: "The terms of said mortgage are by this reference made a part thereof." Rogers and Blythe had sold to Holly Hill, received the note and mortgage, and then assigned both to Charter. Holly Hill alleged that Rogers and Blythe had committed fraud in the sale. The trial court entered summary judgment against Holly Hill, since it ruled that Charter was a holder in due course of a negotiable instrument.

   How should the Appeals Court rule? Why?

2. Barton signed a promissory note for $3,000 which would become due and payable "upon evidence of an acceptable permanent loan of $290,000 for Barton-Ludwig Cains Hill Place Office Building, Atlanta, Georgia, from one of SHRAM's investors and upon acceptance of the commitment by the undersigned." Barton admitted that SHRAM did get such a loan commitment and that Barton did execute the commitment. Barton claimed, however, that since the loan had not in fact been made, he didn't owe the $3,000 loan fee. The trial court entered judgment for SHRAM on the pleadings. Barton appealed.

   Is the note negotiable? Can Barton avoid paying it? Explain.

3. Albert and Dora Ingel had an aluminum siding job done on their home by Allied Aluminum Associates, Inc. In payment, they executed a promissory note for $1,890. The note, together with a certificate indicating that the job had been completed, was transferred for value to the plaintiff. After making several monthly payments, the Ingels alleged that the job had not been done properly and that Allied was guilty of breach of warranties, breach of contract, and/or fraud. C.I.T. sued for the balance due, claiming that it was a holder in due course, and recovered $1,630.12 in the trial court. The Ingels appealed, alleging that the note was nonnegotiable and that the holder (C.I.T.) was subject to any defense that the Ingels could prove.

    Are they correct? Why or why not?

4. Aztec Properties, Inc. executed a promissory note payable to Union Planters National Bank of Memphis in exchange for a $50,000 loan. The promisor agreed to pay the promisee $50,000, "in constant United States Dollars adjusted for inflation (deflation)" with interest at 10 percent per annum. The adjusted principal was to be calculated according to a formula contained in the note, to wit:

    > Amount of principal due shall equal the amount of original principal multiplied by the consumer price index adjustment factor. This adjustment factor shall be computed by dividing the consumer price index at maturity by the consumer price index on date of borrowing. Said consumer price index numbers shall be for the most recent month available preceding borrowing and maturity dates. This consumer price index shall be the index not seasonally adjusted for all items as reported by the United States Department of Labor.

    On maturity of the note, Aztec Properties repaid to the bank $50,000, with discounted interest at the rate 9.875 percent, in the amount of $419.35 (which is an effective yield of 9.96% per annum), but the borrower refused to pay the additional "indexed principal" of $500 based on the inflation adjustment formula.

    The bank sued Aztec Properties for the "indexed principal" together with interest from maturity at the rate of 10 percent per annum. Both parties filed motions for summary judgment.

    Who should win, and why?

5. Defendants entered into a franchise agreement with Great Lakes Nursery Corporation. Defendants, as the franchisees, were to grow and sell nursery stock and Christmas trees. The Nursery was to provide and to deliver 65,000 trees as planting stock for the purchase price of $9,500. The franchisor, the Nursery, under the agreement was to provide the number, size, and variety therein specified, as well as to furnish replanting stock, chemicals, fertilizers, and other articles to be used in the production and sale of the trees; to root prune the trees; and to provide technical training and supervision necessary for the planting, shearing, pruning, marketing, and sale, and other technical information affecting the growth, production, harvest, and sale of the trees.

Contemporaneously with the franchise agreement, the defendants, as makers, executed two promissory notes, each in the amount of $6,412. The notes were payable "to Great Lakes Nursery Corp." Nursery indorsed the notes to "First Investment Company or order."

Defendants made no further payments on their notes for the reason that the Nursery had failed to perform in accordance with the franchise agreement. First Investment sued to collect on the two notes. In their answer, defendants pleaded a failure of consideration as an affirmative defense.

What result and why?

Chapter 21
Liabilities of Parties

H aving determined that an instrument is negotiable, and that the plaintiff is the holder of it, we next need to ascertain whether or not the defendant is liable on it and, if so, the nature of that liability. Negotiable instruments combine property and contract concepts, so liability may stem from the contract a person has made concerning the instrument or from that person's transferral of a piece of property. In addition, persons who intentionally or negligently cause loss to others when dealing with such instruments may be held liable on a tort theory. We now proceed to examine each of these types of liability.

DISTINCTIONS BETWEEN PRIMARY AND SECONDARY LIABILITY

Primary Contract Liability. Someone who has made a direct, unqualified promise to pay an instrument when it is due has assumed **primary contract liability** on the instrument. Only two parties make such a primary promise—the *maker* of a promissory note and the *acceptor* of a draft or check. Where the draft has not been presented to the drawee (or drawee bank) and accepted (certified) by the drawee, *no one* has primary contract liability on the draft or check. The draft or check is an *order* to the drawee to pay, and the drawer's normal assumption is that the order will be honored by the drawee.

If the payee or some later holder of the draft has some doubts about whether or not it will be honored, or if the payee refuses to send merchandise or to perform services without receiving a certified check, then the instrument can be presented to the drawee to find out whether or not the drawee will agree to pay it when it is presented for payment. A drawee who agrees to the order and directly promises to pay the money when due, writes "accepted" or "certified" on the instrument, signs his or her name, and gives the instrument back to the holder. By doing this, the drawee becomes an acceptor with primary contract liability; until the drawee does this, no one has primary contract liability on the draft or check, and the drawee or drawee bank is not liable on the instrument at all—to anyone.

How these rules apply to money orders is at issue in the following case.

TRUMP PLAZA ASSOCIATES v. HAAS
692 A.2d 86 (N.J. Super., 1997)

FACTS: Plaintiff Trump Plaza Associates, d/b/a/ Trump Plaza Hotel and Casino appeals from a summary judgment dismissing its complaint against defendant Meridian Bank, New Jersey (Meridian). In its complaint, Trump alleges that Meridian unlawfully stopped payment on a personal money order the bank had issued to a James Haas, Jr., in the amount of $35,000. Haas cashed the personal money order at Trump's casino for gaming proceeds. Trump returned the money order to Meridian, the drawee bank. Meridian refused to honor the money order, marking it "payment stopped," since Haas had insufficient funds in his account with Meridian to cover the $35,000 instrument.

In dismissing the complaint, the motion judge concluded that the money order was a personal check and that Meridian had not "accepted" it under the provisions of the Uniform Commercial Code.

On appeal, Trump argues that: (1) Meridian could not stop payment on the money order, "prejudicing the rights of a holder in due course;" (2) Meridian "accepted" the money order by marking it "payment stopped" and by use of its printed name and logo on the face of the instrument; (3) as a holder in due course, Trump "should not suffer due to Meridian's negligence" in issuing the instrument; and (4) *Newman v. First Nat'l Bank of Toms River*, relied on by the motion judge, is distinguishable or should be overturned. We reject the arguments and affirm.

On December 13, 1994, Haas deposited two checks in the amount of $20,000 and $22,000, respectively, into the Meridian account of J.E. Haas—Mid-Way Equipment Co. The checks were drawn on a Mid-Way Equipment Co. account at Commerce Bank. Meridian credited the J.E. Haas—Mid-Way Equipment Co. account for the full amount of the two checks and forwarded them to Commerce Bank for payment.

On December 15, 1994, Haas purchased a $35,000 personal money order from Meridian. Meridian's name and logo are printed on the upper left-hand side of the money order. The money order is also stamped: "NOT VALID FOR MORE THAN $35,000." It is made payable to the order of "Jim Haas;" it is not clear from the record when the name of the payee "Jim Haas" was inserted.

Haas signed the money order in the bottom right-hand corner of the document. On December 15, 1994, he presented the signed instrument to Trump and was given $35,000 in cash for use at Trump's gaming tables.

On December 16, 1994, the Mid-Way Equipment Co. checks drawn on the Commerce Bank account were returned to Meridian unpaid with a notation that the Mid-Way Equipment Co. account had been closed. Meridian debited its J.E. Haas-Mid-Way Equipment Co. account for the amount of the returned checks which resulted in a $38,584 overdraft. On December 20, 1994, Trump presented Haas' personal money order to Meridian for payment. Meridian dishonored the order, placing a "payment stopped" notation on it, since the J.E. Haas-Mid-Way Equipment Co. account contained insufficient funds to cover the amount of the money order. It was thereupon returned to Trump's bank.

 JUDGE HAVEY:

Th[e] statutory scheme makes clear that, despite a payee's expectation that the drawee bank will pay a check, the bank has no obligation to the check holder to pay it unless and until the bank has accepted it.... Even if the drawee "arbitrarily dishonors a check, the payee or holder ordinarily has no cause of action against the drawee bank on the instrument."...

Although acceptance of an instrument is generally manifested by such words as "accepted" in the case of a draft, or "certified" in the case of a check, the Code expressly provides that an acceptance may consist of the drawee's signature alone.... However, it is essential that the instrument at least contain the signature of the drawee.... The money order purchased by [Haas] was not signed by any authorized representative of the bank, nor did it bear the signature of the bank. The mere fact that the printed name of the bank appeared on the face of the money order was not sufficient to constitute its signature and therefore was not an acceptance of the instrument for payment within the purview of N.J.S.A. 12A:3-401(1)....

We agree with the motion judge that *Newman* is dispositive. Although *Newman* involved a customer's stop-payment, and not a stop-payment or dishonor by the drawee bank, its holding turns on the concept of "acceptance" of the personal money order by the drawee bank as a predicate to its obligation to honor the instrument. That analysis applies here. Meridian did not "accept" or "certify" the personal money order prior to its dishonor. There is no "signature" of Meridian on the face of the instrument, nor is there any other indication that Meridian "assented in writing to the order of the drawer."... The mere fact that Meridian's name and logo were printed on the instrument "was not sufficient to constitute its signature and therefore was not an acceptance of the instrument for payment within the purview of N.J.S.A. 12A:3-401(1)."... In our view, the name and logo were nothing more than a commercially acceptable means of identifying the institution issuing the instrument.

Further, we reject plaintiff's argument that Meridian accepted the money order by stamping "payment stopped" on its face. Meridian's action in stamping the money order "payment stopped" is in fact a clear and obvious indication of an intent to dishonor the instrument, and nothing more. It logically cannot be deemed to constitute acceptance. Moreover, the fact the money order was stamped "NOT VALID FOR MORE THAN $35,000" does not change the result. This notation can be fairly deemed merely as an expression of limitation on the authority of the party signing and delivering the money order. It certainly cannot be deemed a "signed engagement to honor the draft as presented."...

Finally, we reject Trump's argument that acceptance is shown by the fact that the purchase of the money order was a "sale" and that the money order was drawn not on Mid-Way Equipment Co.'s but Meridian's account. In *Newman* ... we did not focus upon the fund created to pay the money order. Instead, we adopted the rationale ... that in purchasing a money order an individual deposits a sum with a bank and essentially receives one blank check....

The 1995 revisions to Articles 3 and 4, although not directly applicable here, lend support to our holding and the continued viability of Newman's analysis and result. Revised N.J.S.A. 12A:3-104f defines a check to include a money order: "An instrument may be a check even though it is described on its face by another term, such as 'money order'."... The inclusion of personal money orders within the definition of an ordinary check (at Revised Section 3-104f) rather than inclusion as a form of cashier's check (at Section 3-411) means that such money orders are subject to customer stop payment orders and can be dishonored like an ordinary check. This applies only to money orders signed by the purchaser as drawer; of course a bank money order or similar bank draft (drawn by the issuing bank) would be treated as a cashier's or teller's check....

It is true that a number of courts have held a personal money order should be treated like a cashier's check; therefore, a bank, on its own initiative, may not stop payment on a personal money order it has issued....

In our view, these cases should be given little weight. As stated, the revisions to Article 3 of the UCC that define a personal money order as a check mean that the purchaser or drawer of a personal money order may stop payment on it and "the drawee may dishonor it without liability to the holder."... Thus, these revisions would change the reasoning and the result of such cases as *Sequoyah State Bank*....

Trump next argues that, as a holder in due course of the money order "it should not suffer due to Meridian's negligence in issuing the instrument as [Meridian] did not follow its own procedure nor use ordinary care." This claim is predicated on the fact that Meridian purportedly failed to follow its own internal procedures requiring that, before a money order is sold, there are sufficient funds in the customer's account to cover it.

Trump's status as a holder in due course meant that it took the instrument free from essentially all claims by others and all defenses of any party to the instrument with whom the holder has not dealt.... But these rights and protections do not come into play unless and until the drawee bank accepts the instrument.... Absent acceptance of the instrument by Meridian, Trump's sole remedy is against Haas, the drawer of the purchase money order.

Moreover, we are satisfied that any claim of negligence based on Meridian's failure to adhere to its internal procedures was subsumed by former N.J.S.A. 12A:4-402, which makes a payor bank liable to its "customer" for damages proximately caused by the "wrongful dishonor of an item." Only the purchaser of a personal money order, the "customer," has a claim when the dishonor occurs through the "mistake" of the payor bank....

It is true that N.J.S.A. 12A:1-103 provides that "principles of law and equity" supplement the UCC, unless displaced by particular provisions.... This provision may be interpreted as permitting a claim of negligence under the UCC absent a specific provision preempting such a claim. But a party asserting that a bank has acted negligently must demonstrate that the bank owed a duty to that party which has been breached ... and that there is a causal connection between the bank's action and the party's loss....

[H]ere Meridian breached no statutory standard of care owed to its customer expressly established by the UCC.

Affirmed.

Secondary Contract Liability. A party with *secondary contract liability* does not expect to pay the instrument; if everything goes right, someone else will pay. The drawer's signature on the instrument implies a kind of backstop promise: I'll pay if necessary—*if* you make a proper, timely presentment of the instrument to the person who is supposed to pay, *and if* that person dishonors the instrument, *and if* you give me proper notice of the dishonor, *then* bring it to me and I'll give you your money. This kind of "if-then" promise is quite different from that of the party who simply says, "I'll pay." Drawers of drafts and checks and indorsers of all types of negotiable instruments make this secondary contract promise. (Even though the new Article 3 no longer calls the drawer a "secondary party," the nature of the drawer's promise is the same.) Furthermore, the drawer of a noncheck draft or any indorser may *disclaim* even this secondary promise by drawing or indorsing "without recourse." If the instrument is an international draft governed by foreign law, there may be a further requirement. The holder may also have to send the drawer and indorser a **protest**, which is an official notarized statement of the fact of dishonor.

Failure to Meet Conditions. Implicit in the conditional promise of the drawer or indorser is the idea that if the above conditions are not met, the secondary liability is excused. For a drawer, this is true only to a limited extent. An unexcused failure to make a proper presentment or to send a notice of dishonor excuses the drawer only where the drawer "is deprived of funds maintained with the drawee or payor bank to cover the instrument" because the drawee or payor bank becomes insolvent during the delay. The drawer is now entitled to receive notice of dishonor only where a draft was accepted by a non-bank drawee, and then dishonored.

When a bank insolvency occurs, the drawer can avoid any further liability for instruments by making a written assignment to the holder of any rights against the insolvent drawee bank. As a practical matter, this means that few drawers will be excused by a holder's failure to present or to give notice of dishonor. As to indorsers, any unexcused delay in complying with the requirements for presentment or notice is a complete discharge. Adhering to these requirements thus becomes very important to the holder. The holder must make sure that the secondary contract liability of drawers and indorsers is preserved, to keep them available if the instrument is dishonored. (On many notes, there will be a waiver of these requirements.) The details of these requirements are spelled out in various other provisions of Article 3.

PRESENTMENT, NOTICE OF DISHONOR, PROTEST

Presentment is the holder's demand for acceptance or payment of the instrument. It may be made by mail, through a clearinghouse, or in person at the place specified. The party to whom presentment is made may require the presenter to show the instrument, to provide personal identification, to note a receipt for partial or full payment on the instrument, and to surrender the instrument if it is paid in full.

When should presentment be made? If the instrument is payable on a specific date, presentment is also due then. If it is payable "after sight," it must "either be presented for acceptance or negotiated within a reasonable time after date or issue whichever is later." To enforce the instrument against a secondary party, presentment of any other instrument "is due within a reasonable time after such party becomes liable thereon." For an uncertified, domestic check, a "reasonable time" was *presumed* to be thirty days after date or issue, whichever is later, for the drawer to be held liable; for an indorser, seven days after the indorsement. (These presumptions do not appear in the revised Article 3.) If presentment is due on a day which is not a full business day for either party, it is postponed to the next day that is a full business day for both. Presentment must be made at a reasonable hour; if it is made at a bank, it must be during its banking day.

In some cases, the holder is required to present the instrument in order to hold secondary parties liable on it. In other situations, presentment is optional. Presentment for acceptance is necessary to charge the drawers and indorsers of a draft: (1) where it so provides, (2) where it is payable elsewhere than at the residence or place of business of the drawee, or (3) where its date of payment depends upon such presentment. Any other draft payable on a stated date may be presented for acceptance at the option of the holder.

Presentment for payment is necessary to charge any indorser, of any sort of instrument. To charge any drawer, or the acceptor of a draft payable at a bank, or the maker of a note payable at a bank, presentment for payment is required. As noted above, however, such drawers, acceptors, and makers are discharged only to a limited extent if the required presentment for payment is not made or is delayed. Only in the situation where they are deprived of funds due to the insolvency of the drawee or payor bank, during the delay period, will they be excused from further liability on the instrument.

Dishonor of the instrument occurs when it is properly presented and acceptance or payment is refused. The party to whom presentment is made has only a limited period to decide whether to pay or to accept. The time to decide whether or not to accept is limited to the close of the next business day, but the holder has the option of extending that deadline by one extra business day.

Payment, if requested, can be deferred "pending reasonable examination to determine whether it is properly payable," but only until the close of business on the day of presentment. There are only two exceptions to this "pay-same-day" rule: first, where the party to pay agrees to an earlier time for payment; second, where "documentary drafts" are being presented under a "letter of credit." In letter of credit cases, the bank to which such drafts are presented may defer honor until "the third banking day following receipt of the documents."

Where an instrument has not been properly indorsed, returning it to the holder to obtain the required indorsement is not a dishonor, but a bank may or may not certify the instrument before returning it for the proper indorsement.

Since a check is a demand instrument which is normally intended to have only limited circulation and then to be paid, the drawee bank "has no obligation to certify a check." The bank's refusal to pay the check would, of course, be a dishonor. The holder is entitled to have the instrument accepted as presented and can treat any variation or qualification in the acceptance as a dishonor. If the holder does agree to take the acceptance with the changed terms, that act discharges the drawer and indorser. The holder then has only the obligation of the drawee/acceptor according to the changed terms. In this situation, the holder must decide which course is more likely to produce the money.

Notice Requirements. Something has obviously gone wrong when a proper presentment has been made and the instrument has been dishonored; the original expectations of the parties have somehow been frustrated. Where such dishonor occurs, the drawer of a draft or check and indorsers of any sort of instrument are entitled to receive prompt notice so that they can take steps to protect their rights. Notice is usually given by the holder, but 3-503(b) says that it may be given by "any other party who can be compelled to pay the instrument," such as a prior indorser.

"Any reasonable manner" of notification is sufficient; even oral notice is permitted, if it can be proved. The Code also specifically recognizes the validity of the common banking procedure of simply returning the item with a stamp or attached ticket indicating the dishonor, or just sending back a debit notice to the party who gave the instrument to the bank. Banks must give such required notice before their "midnight deadline," which means that a bank must send the word back up the line to others by midnight of the next banking day after the day of dishonor or the day of its own receipt from some other party of notice of dishonor. Nonbank parties are given until midnight of the *third* business day following dishonor or their receipt of notice.

Since a "written notice is given when sent although it is not received," it is important to be able to prove exactly when letters were posted or telegrams given to the telegraph company. Once properly given, "notice operates for the benefit of all parties who have rights on the instrument against the party notified." If a holder sent notice to prior indorsers Archie and Bernice, for example, Bernice's rights against Archie would be preserved even though *she* didn't send Archie any notice.

The effect of delaying notice of dishonor is seen in the *First Union* case.

FIRST UNION NAT. v. FIRST FLORIDA BANK
616 So.2d 1168 (FL, App.2 Dist., 1993)

FACTS: First Union National Bank appeals a monetary judgment in favor of First Florida Bank, N.A. The lawsuit was filed to determine whether the payor bank, First Florida, or the presenting bank, Union Bank, should be responsible for a dishonored check.

Victor Elias had a bank account with First Florida. On August 13, 1986, he wrote a $10,000 check payable to National Computer Consultants, Inc. National Computer endorsed the check and deposited the check in its account with Union Bank. Union Bank posted the check to National Computers account on Thursday, August 14.

Union Bank presented this check to First Florida on the following day at the local clearinghouse. At the clearinghouse, Union Bank was credited $10,000 and First Florida was debited $10,000. The clearinghouse forwarded the check to First Florida.

On August 14, Mr. Ellias gave a verbal stop-payment order to First Florida. Under statutory provisions discussed later in this opinion, First Florida had until midnight Monday, August 18, to notify Union Bank of its intention to dishonor this check. As a result, First Florida took steps on Monday, August 18, to return the check to Union Bank via the clearinghouse. The check was returned to the clearinghouse on either August 18 or August 19. Unfortunately, First Florida misrouted the check when it returned the item to the clearinghouse by addressing it to the wrong bank. That bank received the misrouted check and returned it to First Florida through the clearinghouse on August 20. First Florida did not return the check to the clearinghouse for Union Bank until August 21.

In addition to returning the check, First Florida attempted to give Union bank notice of dishonor. In August 1986, First Florida was a member of a service offered by Security Pacific to give notice of dishonor on checks over $2,500. Security Pacific provided notice through a computer system to banks participating in its service. It telephonically informed nonmember banks of dishonored checks. Union Bank was not a member of the Security Pacific system. First Florida did not request Security Pacific to give notice of dishonor to Union Bank until 5:54 p.m. on August 18, 1986. Security Pacific gave that notice by telephone at 11:40 a.m. on August 19, 1986. The midnight deadline was midnight deadline was midnight on August 18.

In the trial court, First Florida sued Union Bank for reimbursement of this check. Reimbursement was requested because the debits and credits at the clearinghouse had left responsibility for this check with First Florida. Union Bank argued that First Florida was responsible for this check because First Florida had not given timely notice of dishonor by telephone and the check was not timely returned by first Florida to Union Bank. The trial court determined that Sections 673.508 and 674.302, Florida Statutes (1985), should be controlled by a "rule of reasonableness." It decided that First Florida's efforts to provide telephonic notice had been reasonable and ordered Union Bank to reimburse First Florida $10,000, plus interest and costs.

 JUDGE ALTENBERND:

By the midnight deadline, First Florida had delivered the check to the clearinghouse, but had routed this item to the wrong bank. It had notified Security Pacific of its intention to dishonor the check, but Security Pacific had not notified Union Bank. These efforts were insufficient to negate the payor bank's responsibility for the check.

The payor bank must bear the responsibility of its error in misrouting this item. Section 674.301(4)(a) provides that an item received, through a clearinghouse is returned "when it is delivered to the presenting or last collecting bank or to the clearinghouse or is sent or delivered in accordance with its rules." First Florida argues that it returned the check to the clearinghouse, and that its erroneous instructions to deliver the check to the wrong bank are irrelevant. The trial court rejected this argument and we agree with the trial court. The applicable rules and regulations of the Clearinghouse Association of Florida required a return item to be enclosed in an envelope indicating the identity of the "first endorsing member." Union Bank was the first endorsing member. By placing the check in an envelope to another bank, First Florida did not satisfy the rules of the local clearinghouse. The purposes of these statutes can be fulfilled only if they are interpreted to require delivery to the clearinghouse in a manner reasonably designed to result in an item's return to the presenting or last collecting bank.... In light of the substantial violation of the procedures established by the local clearinghouse, First Florida did not effectively return the item by the midnight deadline.

First Florida's telephonic notification was also deficient because Union Bank did not receive it prior to the midnight deadline. First Florida argues that it provided notice of dishonor when it notified Security Pacific. We recognize that notice of dishonor may be given in any reasonable manner.... Nevertheless, Security Pacific was clearly the agent of First Florida, not Union Bank. Union Bank was not a member of the Security Pacific system of notification. Thus, Union Bank did not receive oral notice of dishonor until it received the telephone call on Tuesday, after the midnight deadline.

The trial court acknowledged that First Florida had not fully satisfied these notice requirements prior to the midnight deadline, but was convinced that such noncompliance should not automatically place responsibility on First Florida. First Florida persuasively argued that the telephone call on Tuesday morning had a practical effect similar to an actual return of the check to the clearinghouse on the preceding day. Moreover, there was evidence that funds were disbursed from the National Computer account at Union Bank prior to the expiration of the normal hold period. First Florida maintains that the monetary problem for the two banks could have been avoided if Union Bank had utilized different procedures. The trial court concluded that the midnight deadline, under these circumstances, did not create a rule of strict liability but rather a rule requiring reasonable compliance. It concluded that First Florida had attempted reasonable compliance with the requirements for telephonic notification and that the loss should be borne by Union Bank.

No Florida court has ever expressly held that the midnight deadline is a bright line rule that places responsibility for such a loss on the payor bank. In *First National Bank of Fla.v. Brandon State Bank, 377 So.2d 990*..., this court held that the payor bank could revoke a provisional settlement of a check by either a timely notice of dishonor or a timely return of the item. In that case, the item was timely returned to the federal reserve but the notice of dishonor was not timely given. We held that the timely return of the check allowed the payor bank to avoid responsibility for the check. We at least implied that the payor bank would have had responsibility if neither option had been timely satisfied....

In other states, it is well-established that Sections 4-301 and 4-302 of the Uniform Commercial Code create a statutory doctrine of strict accountability by the payor bank to the presenting bank if notice is not accomplished within the midnight deadline.... Under this doctrine, the payor bank is liable to the presenting bank for the full face amount of the check, absent a successful defense. This bright line test has been adopted under the rationale that the banking industry will better function with a rule establishing across-the-board certainty rather than case-by-case equity. We see no reason to depart from this application of the Uniform Commercial Code.

Because First Florida presented no evidence in the trial court which might justify another basis for recovery from Union Bank, we reverse the judgment with instructions to enter judgment in favor of Union Bank.

Excuse for Failure to Meet Conditions. Parties with secondary contract liability may still be held liable on an instrument where there is an excuse for a delay in meeting these requirements or for a failure to meet them at all. If a holder does not know that an instrument has been accelerated by a prior holder, for example, a delay in making presentment would be excused. Similarly, where a delay is due to "circumstances beyond [his] control," a party has an excuse for late notice, so long as that person "exercised reasonable diligence after the cause of the delay ceased to operate."

Presentment is entirely excused where: (1) the party to be charged has waived it; (2) there is no reason to expect the instrument to be paid or accepted, such as when the drawer of a check issues a stop pay order to his or her drawee bank; or (3) the requirement cannot be met by "reasonable diligence." Presentment is also excused by the death or subsequent insolvency of the maker or acceptor, or where payment is refused but not for want of proper presentment. In line with general commercial understanding, a waiver of presentment is also a waiver of notice. If the waiver language is part of the body of the instrument, it is binding on all secondary parties; if it is written above the signature of an indorser, it binds only that person. Notice may also be excused by a separate waiver. Either requirement may also be excused by the terms of the instrument itself.

OTHER TYPES OF LIABILITY

Liability of Accommodation Parties and Guarantors. In many cases, the person desiring a loan or credit may not have sufficient income or assets to make the creditor feel reasonably secure about receiving repayment when it is due. One form of additional security that can be used is to have another person, someone who does have a good credit rating, also promise to pay the debt. These "backstop" promises on negotiable instruments can take several forms.

An **accommodation party** is someone who has signed an instrument in some capacity (maker, indorser, acceptor) to lend his or her credit standing to another party to the instrument. Common sense and the Code dictate that the accommodation party be liable in whatever capacity he or she signs to third parties who take the instrument for value. If Jones can't get a bank loan in his own name and his friend Smith agrees to cosign the note with him as a joint maker, Smith (the accommodation party) is liable to third parties as a maker. Had Smith indorsed the note after Jones signed as a sole maker, Smith would be liable to third parties as an indorser (and entitled to presentment and notice). Generally, these results occur even if the third party knows that Smith signed only to accommodate Jones. As between Smith and Jones, however, Smith has the right to demand reimbursement from Jones if Smith has to pay a third party, regardless of the order or the capacity in which they signed the instrument. The debt is really owed by Jones, and Jones should repay Smith.

Words of guarantee may also be added to a signature. **Payment guaranteed** means that the holder of the instrument can present it directly to the person so signing if it is not paid when due. In other words, the person making the guarantee is directly and immediately liable when the primary debtor defaults. **Collection guaranteed** means that before the signer/guarantor is obligated to pay, the holder must first get a judgment against the maker or acceptor and show that the judgment is uncollectible. Where an indorser so guarantees payment or collection, presentment, notice, and protest are waived as to that indorser.

Warranty Liability. In addition to assuming contract liability by signing an instrument, a person may assume warranty liability by dealing with it as a piece of property. Warranty liability is imposed by the Code in two types of transactions—transfers of ownership of instruments and presentments of instruments for payment or acceptance. Where a person transfers an instrument and receives consideration in return, that person makes five warranties about the instrument. This person is not collecting final payment, but is simply transferring ownership of the instrument to someone else. If the transferee is a donee, receiving the instrument as a gift, the transferor makes no warranties. However, if the transferee is buying the instrument from the transferor, the five transfer warranties are made by the transferor. The details of these five transfer warranties are explained in the next section.

A person who presents the instrument for payment or acceptance (discussed earlier in this chapter) also makes warranties to the party who in good faith pays or accepts. Someone who takes the instrument to the party who is supposed to pay it and gets the money from that party should at least make a guarantee that he or she is the proper party to be paid. The Code implies such a guarantee, as well as certain guarantees about the genuineness of the instrument. If the instrument is being presented for acceptance, the presenter is asking for a direct promise to pay it when it is finally presented for payment. In this case too, the presenter should be required to guarantee ownership and validity, and the Code so requires. The details of the three presentment warranties are also spelled out below.

Transfer Warranties. Because the parties are dealing with the instrument as a piece of property, the Code provides that certain implied warranties are made when the instrument is transferred for value. Just as implied warranties are imposed against the seller of goods under Article 2, so, too, five implied warranties are imposed on the person who transfers an instrument and receives consideration. If the transfer is by indorsement, these five warranties run to all subsequent good faith holders of the instrument; if the transfer is by delivery alone, they run only to the immediate transferee. If the instrument is payable to someone's order, that person must indorse it to negotiate it to someone else. No indorsement is required to transfer a bearer instrument, but the transferor will often indorse anyway.

The transferor for value warrants:

1. That the warrantor is a person entitled to enforce the instrument.

2. That all signatures are authentic and authorized.

3. That the instrument has not been altered.

4. That no prior party who is liable on the instrument has a defense or claim which is good as against the warrantor.

5. That the warrantor has no knowledge of any insolvency proceeding instituted with respect to the maker, acceptor, or drawer of an unaccepted draft.

These warranties may be disclaimed by agreement between the immediate parties, but an indorser cannot escape such warranty liability to subsequent holders unless the disclaimer is part of the indorsement. Such a disclaimer might be stated as, "without warranty of any kind." These warranties may not be disclaimed by the transferor of a check.

The *Oak Park* case shows the liability which can rise from indorsing a check for a friend.

OAK PARK CURRENCY EXCHANGE, INC. v. MAROPOULOS
363 N.E.2d 54 (IL, 1977)

FACTS: Oak Park Currency Exchange, Inc. (plaintiff) brought action against James Maropoulos (defendant). Plaintiff's theory was that a check for $3,564 had been indorsed by defendant and cashed by plaintiff and that the prior indorsement of the payee was a forgery. After all of the evidence was presented, the trial court directed a jury verdict for defendant. Plaintiff appeals.

Defendant testified that on several occasions, his friend, John Bugay, had asked for assistance in cashing checks. On these occasions, defendant had accompanied Bugay to a bank where defendant transacted his business and had indorsed the check as a favor. On July 24, 1971, Bugay again requested assistance in cashing a check. Defendant suggested that they go to plaintiff currency exchange where defendant often transacted business and was known to plaintiff's employees. The check in question was a certified check drawn on American National Bank payable to the order of "Henry Sherman, Inc." and endorsed "Henry Sherman" on the reverse side.

Defendant testified that at the currency exchange he identified himself and asked the clerk if she would cash his friend's check. Though she was not the woman with whom he usually dealt, she recognized him. She answered that she would cash the check if defendant would indorse it. He indorsed the check and handed it to the clerk. He observed that she examined both sides of the check. She then handed him the money. He did not count this but gave it immediately to Bugay. Defendant testified unequivocally that he received no money from Bugay in return for his help.

Some time later a claim was made against plaintiff by Belmont National Bank where plaintiff had deposited the check because the indorsement "Henry Sherman" had been forged. Plaintiff determined that it was liable to the bank and paid the claim. Subsequently plaintiff filed this action.

 JUSTICE GOLDBERG:

In its judgment order directing the verdict, the trial court found that defendant was an accommodation indorser and as such made no warranty to plaintiff under the Uniform Commercial Code ... and that payment of the check discharged all indorsers so that defendant was not liable to plaintiff on his indorsement.

In this court, plaintiff urges that defendant breached his warranty of good title when he obtained payment of a check on which the payee's indorsement was forged and that there was sufficient evidence to support a directed verdict in favor of plaintiff. Plaintiff's contentions are based exclusively on Section 3-417(1) [now 3-417(a)] of the Code. Defendant contends that an accommodation indorser does not make warranties under ... 3-417(1) and that the trial court properly directed a verdict for defendant.

A party who signs an instrument "for the purpose of lending his name to another party to" ... that instrument is an accommodation party.... Such a party "is liable in the capacity in which he has signed...." Therefore defendant is an accommodation indorser and would be liable to plaintiff under his indorser's contract, provided that he had received timely notice that the check had been presented to the drawee bank and dishonored.... Because these conditions precedent to the contractual liability of an indorser have not been met, defendant is not liable on his contract as an accommodation indorser.

Furthermore, the drawee bank, American National, did not dishonor the check but paid it. This operated to discharge the liability of defendant as an accommodation indorser....

The portion of the Code upon which plaintiff seeks to hold defendant liable is Section 3-417 entitled "Warranties on Presentment and Transfer...." As shown above, the parties both confine their arguments to Subsection 3-417(1) of the Code and the judgment order refers specifically thereto. Section 3-417(1) sets out warranties which run only to a party who "pays or accepts" an instrument upon presentment.... We note that presentment is defined as "a demand for acceptance or payment made upon the maker, acceptor, drawee, or other payor...." As applied to the instant case, the warranties contained in Section 3-417(1) are limited to run only to the payor bank and not to any other transferee who acquired the check. In the case before us, plaintiff is not a payor or acceptor of the draft. This interpretation is strongly supported by the official comment which details the reasons for distinguishing warranties made to a payor or acceptor of an instrument from those made to a transferee.... The case before us involves a transferee, not a party who paid or accepted the instrument. Thus it appears that reliance by plaintiff upon Subsection 3-417(1) was misplaced. The authorities cited by plaintiff do not support its contention as all of these cases were decided before the effective date of the Code.

Defendant has cited no case bearing directly upon the situation before us. Our research has not disclosed any case construing this aspect of the pertinent subsection of the Code. Aside from the enactment itself and the comments above cited, we found only dicta to the effect that by this subsection the warranties pertaining to authenticity of indorsements run only "to a person who in good faith pays or accepts" ... the instrument....

An additional theory requires affirmance of the judgment appealed from. Subsection 3-417(2) [now 3-416(a)] of the Code provides that one "who transfers an instrument and receives consideration warrants to his transferee ..." that he has good title.... The Illinois comments to this portion of the Code confirm that this warranty is made only by any party who transfers an instrument for consideration....

The evidence presented in the case at bar establishes that defendant received no consideration for his indorsement. Though Mrs. Panveno testified that she saw Bugay hand defendant some money as the two left the currency exchange, she also testified that defendant stated that he was doing a favor for his friend; that she was not paying close attention to the two men and that she did not watch them as they walked away from her. Thus, her testimony was considerably weakened by her own qualifying statements and it was strongly and directly contradicted by the positive and unshaken testimony of defendant that he received nothing in return for his assistance. The simple fact standing alone that this witness saw Bugay hand some money to defendant, even if proved, would have no legal significance without additional proof of some type showing that the payment was consideration for defendant's indorsement....

In our opinion, the trial court correctly determined that no contrary verdict based on the testimony offered by plaintiff could ever stand and properly directed a verdict for defendant.

[Judgment affirmed.]

Presentment Warranties. Primarily to assure that the proper party gets the money, Article 3 also imposes three warranties when the instrument is presented for payment or acceptance. These three warranties are imposed on both the person who obtains the payment or acceptance and on any prior transferor.

The warranties on presentment of an unaccepted draft to the drawee are:

1. That the warrantor is, or was at the time of transfer, a person entitled to enforce the draft or authorized to act for someone who is or was.

2. That the warrantor has no knowledge of any unauthorized signature of the drawer.

3. That the draft has not been altered.

The result under (b) is to ensure fairness and is based on the old English case of *Price v. Neal*, 3 Burr. 1354 (1762). The idea is that at some point payment should be "final;" the Code draws this line at the point where payment is made to a holder in due course, acting in good faith. If the drawee isn't sharp enough to catch the fact that the drawer's signature has been forged, it's simply not fair to permit recovery of the money paid to a holder in due course who was acting in good faith. Probably the most typical situation where the money has to be paid back and the instrument has to be kicked back up the chain of title is the case where a required indorsement is missing, so that the person making the presentment did not really have a "good title." The *Steinroe* case discusses these presentment warranties.

STEINROE INCOME TRUST v. CONTINENTAL BANK N.A.
606 N.E.2d 503 (Ill. App., 1992)

FACTS: After the death of her husband, Mary B. Dybas filed a claim on her husband's life insurance policy. In early 1987, the insurance company sent Dybas a check for approximately $100,000. This check was stolen by an unidentified culprit before it reached Dybas.

In February 1987, the culprit used the insurance check to open an account with the plaintiff investment company, Steinroe Income Trust. The culprit assumed the identity of Howard Brest, who had died in Quincy, Illinois. Although the only payee on the insurance check was Dybas, the Steinroe account was opened as a joint account in the names of Dybas and Brest. Of course, the indorsements on the back of the check in the names of Dybas and Brest were phony as were the signatures that appeared on the application forms for the Steinroe account.

Three days later, the culprit called Steinroe and received confirmation that the insurance check had cleared. The next day, the culprit went to Steinroe's office and presented a letter, purportedly signed in the names of Dybas and Brest, requesting that nearly all of the proceeds in the account be redeemed. The culprit asked that Steinroe have a redemption check ready for him to pick up in another three days. Steinroe prepared the redemption check in the amount of $87,500 and made it payable to Dybas and Brest. The redemption check was drawn on the State Street Bank where Steinroe maintained its bank accounts.

The culprit picked up the redemption check and, having previously opened an account with Continental Bank in the name of Howard Brest, promptly deposited the redemption check into this account. Again, the indorsements of Brest and Dybas on the back of the redemption check were phony. Continental Bank stamped the check "P.E.G." (prior [e]ndorsements guaranteed) and presented the check to State Street Bank. State Street Bank paid the check and charged Steinroe's account.

The culprit then absconded with the proceeds in the account with Continental Bank.

Meanwhile, Dybas contacted the insurance company explaining that she never received the insurance check. The insurance company issued her another check and then filed suit against Steinroe to recover for the loss on the insurance check. Steinroe agreed to settle the claim and paid the insurance company approximately $100,000. Steinroe, in turn, asked the State Street Bank to recredit its account for the amount that was paid on the redemption check. State Street Bank refused to do so. Steinroe then filed suit against Continental Bank to recover for the loss on the redemption check.

In the trial court, the parties stipulated to the facts and each side moved for summary judgment. Continental Bank argued in its motion that Steinroe did not have standing to enforce the presentment warranties under Sections 3-417(1)(a) and 4-207(1)(a). The trial court disagreed and entered the summary judgment in favor of plaintiff on other grounds. Defendant filed this appeal.

 JUDGE LORENZ:

According to the express language of the sections, a party had standing to enforce the presentment warranties only if it could be deemed the "payor bank" or "other payor" who pays or accepts. We now consider whether Steinroe, as the drawer of the redemption check, had standing to enforce the presentment warranties.

It is clear that Steinroe did not have standing as a "payor bank." The State Street Bank, not Steinroe, was the "payor bank" on the redemption check.

However, at the time of the proceedings below, it was somewhat unclear whether Steinroe, as the drawer of the redemption check, could be deemed an "other payor" and thereby satisfy the standing requirements. In fact, the parties set forth case law from across the country which presented a majority and minority view on this question. The majority view provided that the language "other payor" required a narrow construction which excluded the drawer of a check. Continental Bank argued that the court should apply this majority view and cited in support thereof *Oak Park Currency Exchange*.... The minority view provided that the language "other payor" required a broad construction which included the drawer of a check. Steinroe argued that the court should apply this minority view and cited the leading case in support thereof, *Sun 'N Sand, Inc*....

We note that, after the parties filed their briefs, Sections 3-417 and 4-207 were amended.... The comments to the amended Section 3-417 addressed the question concerning application of the majority and minority view:

> "In *Sun 'N Sand*, ... the court held that under former Section 3-417(1) a warranty was made to the drawer of a check when the check was presented to the drawee for payment. The result in that case is rejected."...

Therefore, we also reject Steinroe's argument for application of the minority view as represented by *Sun 'N Sand*. We hold that Steinroe, as the drawer of the redemption check, did not have standing to enforce the presentment warranties under either the former or amended Sections 3-417 and 4-207. The judgment in favor of Steinroe is reversed and judgment is entered in favor of Continental Bank.

Tort Liability. Article 3 also has special sections imposing liability for the torts of negligence and conversion. Section 3-406 says:

> A person whose failure to exercise ordinary care substantially contributes to an alteration of the instrument or to the making of a forged signature ... is precluded from asserting the alteration or the forgery against a person who in good faith pays the instrument or takes it for value or for collection.

If you fill out a check with a blank space after "Six" and before "dollars," and you also leave a blank where you write "$ 6.00" and if someone alters that check to read "Six Hundred" and the check is paid by your bank, you could not claim the alteration as a basis for having the bank put $594 back in your account. However, if the words *six* and *hundred* were written in ink of a different color, or if the handwritings were obviously dissimilar, your counterargument would be that the bank had not paid the check in good faith or had not exercised reasonable care in doing so.

Another fairly typical case of this sort would involve the negligence of a business that printed its checks on a checkwriter. If the business had not taken reasonable precautions to prevent unauthorized persons from using the checkwriter, it could not assert their lack of authority where the drawee bank had paid the checks in good faith. The net result of this section is that the negligent party is stuck with the loss, unless that party can find and recover from the person who inserted the alteration or the unauthorized signature.

As with other types of personal property, a person who deals with an instrument in a manner inconsistent with the rights of the true owner commits the tort of conversion. Section 3-420 says that an instrument is also converted if it is taken by transfer, other than a negotiation, from a person not entitled to enforce it, or if a bank makes or obtains payment of it for a person not entitled to payment. If any of these things occurs, the amount of tort damages the owner can collect against the wrongdoer will usually be the face amount of the instrument.

SIGNIFICANCE OF THIS CHAPTER

Both plaintiffs and defendants, creditors and debtors, need to know the circumstances under which they could become liable on a negotiable instrument. These rules are complicated, since they encompass different types of liability. Perhaps no other single topic so clearly combines all the basic legal concepts: contracts, property, tort, and crime.

Although negotiable instruments are involved in many fraudulent schemes where criminal prosecution could occur, this chapter examined civil, rather than criminal, liability. We covered the contract liabilities of makers of notes, drawers and acceptors of drafts and checks, and indorsers of all types of instruments. Our discussion included warranties made by persons who transfer instruments for value or who present them for payment or acceptance, and tort liability for negligence or conversion. While these liabilities are primarily based on the provisions of Article 3 of the UCC, liabilities may also arise under general legal principles.

Because liability is easy to incur and hard to disclaim, extreme care should be exercised in signing, handling, transferring, and verifying all negotiable instruments.

PROBLEMS FOR DISCUSSION

1. The Reverend Stuart F. Gast and his wife, Elizabeth, contracted to sell a house to Mark and Gertrude Hanna. Pursuant to the contract, the Hannas bought a fire insurance policy on the property, with the proceeds payable to the Gasts in the event of loss or damage. After a fire damaged the building, an amount of $3,435.92 was agreed on as the settlement. American Insurance Company issued a draft in that amount, drawn on itself, payable through Berks County Trust Company, and naming the insurance adjuster, the Gasts, and the Hannas as payees. The adjuster indorsed the draft, but when the Gasts' attorney sent the note to the Hannas for their signature, they forged the Gasts' indorsements, cashed the draft, and absconded with the money. The Gasts sued the drawee for conversion.

   Should they recover? Why or why not?

2. Kerr, Mott, and Thurston signed a promissory note, all three signing in the lower right-hand corner. The note was dated December 29, 1993, and stated that it was for 180 days, due on June 18, 1994. The bank admitted that Thurston's credit was insufficient to support a loan in any amount. Kerr and Mott argued that they were only accommodation parties, but the bank president testified that they said "they had a percentage interest in this production." After default, demand for payment was sent to each of these three persons by letters dated January 15, 1995.

   Are Kerr and Mott primarily liable, as makers of the note? Explain.

3. Sylvio, an independent insurance agent, received a check for $28,000, payable to one of his customers, Cobber Taxi Company. The check was issued by Rely Insurance Company to settle a claim filed by Cobber. Sylvio fraudulently indorsed the check with Cobber's name and then added his own indorsement. Sylvio then gave the check to his brother Lem, and told Lem to use it as the initial deposit to the account of a car-rental business the brothers were starting up. Lem did so. Sylvio later withdrew these funds from the partnership account for his own use. Rely sued the bank where the check had been deposited. That bank sued Lem and the car-rental partnership.

   How should the court decide these lawsuits? Explain.

4. Billie Biggert had been buying sheep for her sheep ranch for several years from the Tremont Livestock Company, represented by Kevin Mummar. In 1999, Kevin told Billie that Tremont needed to buy back 100 sheep, so she sold them to him. Kevin gave her a check on Tremont's bank account for $42,000, which he had signed on behalf of Tremont. Billie thought Kevin was a partner, and therefore authorized to sign checks for Tremont, but in fact, he was only an employee in a sole proprietorship.

   Billie deposited the check in her account, but when it was presented to Tremont's bank for payment, payment was refused because Kevin had no authority to sign checks on the account. When she got the check back, Billie immediately called up Tremont's bank to find out what the problem was. The bank's cashier told Billie to send the check through again and "we'll get the problem straightened out." Billie did so, but the bank bounced the check again. Tremont itself is now in bankruptcy, and Kevin is nowhere to be found.

   Can Billie collect on this check against Tremont's bank? Discuss.

5. John B. Hane was the assignee-holder of a note issued by Theta Electronics Laboratories, Inc., in the amount of $15,377.07, plus 6 percent interest. The note, dated August 10, 1994, provided that the first monthly payment of $320.47 would be due on January 10, 1995. The note contained an acceleration clause. Gerald M. Exten, Emil L. O'Neil, James W. Hane, and their wives all indorsed the note. The original payees, George B. and Marguerite F. Thompson, assigned the note without recourse to Hane on November 26, 1995. Some $2,222.13 had been paid on the note up to that point. Exten had originally been the corporate president of Theta but had been removed in April or May 1995. Although no more than six payments were made (through June 1995), Hane took no action until June 7, 1997, when he filed a confession of judgment against all of the indorsers except the Thompsons. The Extens demanded and received a trial on the merits, after which the judge found them not liable. Hane appeals.

   What result, and why?

Chapter 22

Negotiation, Holders in Due Course, and Defenses

We now have an instrument which is negotiable and on which one or more parties are liable as signers. To get the special "negotiability" results, however, a plaintiff seeking to enforce the instrument must meet an additional set of requirements. Unless the plaintiff has taken the instrument through a special form of transfer called *negotiation* and under circumstances that qualify the plaintiff as a "holder in due course," our plaintiff holds the instrument subject to all the defenses and claims that would be available against the assignee of a simple written contract. Only a person with the rights of an HDC holds the negotiable instrument free of adverse claims and defenses.

NEGOTIATION

Today, as indicated in Chapter 13, most contracts can be assigned. Only a negotiable instrument, however, can be "negotiated." **Negotiation** is a transfer in such form that the transferee becomes a holder. There must be physical delivery of the instrument and, if the instrument is payable to order, it must be indorsed. A **holder** is a person who is in possession of an instrument "drawn, issued, or indorsed to him or to his order or to bearer or in blank." Where you make your check payable to "cash," or where you indorse your paycheck on the back by simply signing your name, any person who subsequently gains possession of the instrument is a holder, even without any further indorsements. Not every holder is a holder in due course, however. That status depends on the circumstances under which the holder acquired the instrument.

Where an instrument is drawn to someone's order (your rent check to your landlord, for example) or is indorsed to someone's order (you indorsed a dividend check to your bank as payment on a loan), negotiation cannot occur unless the person to whose order the instrument is now payable has properly indorsed the instrument. In other words, the finder of an unindorsed order instrument would not be a holder nor would any subsequent transferee from the finder. The missing required indorsement breaks the "chain of title" to the instrument, so that no later person, even though in possession of the instrument itself, is a "holder."

To qualify as a holder in due course so as to own an instrument free of most claims and defenses, a person must first be a holder. The proper indorsement of an order instrument is therefore crucial to the HDC status of later possessors. If you simply sign your name on the back of your paycheck and then lose it on the way to the bank, the finder would not be an HDC (since that person gave no value for it), but the finder would be a *holder* and the store where he or she used it to buy merchandise could qualify as an HDC. The net result is that you lose the value represented by your paycheck just as if you had cashed it and then lost the cash.

To change this example: If you lost your paycheck before you indorsed it, the finder would not be a holder and neither would the store, even if the finder forged your indorsement on the back of the check. The net result is that you get your money back and the store gets stuck. For this reason, many stores and banks are reluctant to cash checks where the person asking for the money is not the original payee.

INDORSEMENT

General Rules. An indorsement is made by signing your name on the instrument, normally on the back. An indorser could sign on the front of the instrument, but this would entail the risk of being held liable as a co-maker of the note or as a co-drawer of the draft if that's what the signature seemed to be. As a rule, unless the instrument clearly indicates that a signature is made in some other capacity, it is an indorsement. It is usually assumed that indorsers are liable "in the order in which they indorse, which is presumed to be the order in which their signatures appear on the instrument." Where an instrument has been transferred so many times that there is no room on it for further indorsements, these may be made on a "permanently" attached piece of paper called an **allonge**.

An indorsement is effective for negotiation only when it conveys the entire amount due on the instrument. Any attempt to indorse over only part of what's due is not a negotiation; it is, rather, a partial assignment. (Therefore, no transferee under such a partial indorsement could be an HDC.) Where the name of the person to whose order the instrument is payable is misspelled or otherwise incorrect, he or she may indorse with the incorrect name or the correct name or both. Anyone giving value for the instrument can require the double indorsement of both the incorrect and the correct names. Unless the instrument is already payable to the bearer, any transferee for value can demand that the transferor indorse.

Where an instrument is payable to two or more persons jointly ("pay to the order of Jones and Green"), all of them must indorse to be able to negotiate the instrument. Where an instrument is payable to two or more persons in the alternative ("pay to the order of Jones or Green"), the single indorsement of either of them is sufficient to negotiate it.

Impostors and Defrauders. Article 3 contains some very special rules to cover situations where instruments are issued to impostors, crooked employees and agents, and other defrauders. In the impostor case, someone who is not Henry Forge comes into your office, says "I am Henry

Forge," convinces you that he is, and persuades you to enter into a transaction that results in your making out a check payable to the order of "Henry Forge." He tricked you. The Code says that *anyone* can effectively indorse this instrument by signing "Henry Forge." The fake Henry Forge can do so. If he loses it or it's stolen from him, the thief or finder can indorse "Henry Forge" and effectively negotiate the instrument. This doesn't mean that some or all of these persons can't be prosecuted criminally; it just means that subsequent transferees can be holders and can therefore qualify as HDCs if they meet all of the other requirements.

The same rule applies where a corporation's bookkeeper or payroll clerk "pads the payroll" with extra fake names and then indorses and cashes these extra checks. The crook's indorsements in the names of the named payees are effective; the drawee bank honoring these checks when presented has paid the right party; and the corporation is stuck unless it can get the money back from the crook. Most simply, the Code's rule for these cases is: "The sucker always pays!"

The Code also provides for similar results where the negotiation of an instrument is subject to rescission because of minority or other incapacity, illegality, breach of duty, or fraud, duress, or mistake. Such a negotiation is at least temporarily effective, and these "defects" in the transaction cannot be used to recover the instrument from a later HDC. A minor's negotiation of an instrument, for example, would make all later transferees "holders," so that one of them could qualify as an HDC. If there were a subsequent HDC in the chain of title, the minor could not get the instrument back; if there were no subsequent HDC, the minor could recover the instrument from the current holder. In either case, the minor could use minority as a defense against having to actually pay the instrument.

The "impostor" rules are applied in the *Hinkle* case.

HINKLE v. CORNWELL QUALITY TOOL CO.
532 N.E.2d 772 (OH App., 1987)

FACTS: This case involves the appeal and cross-appeal of G.F. Hinkle, dba Akron Novelty Co., and Cornwell Quality Tool Co., respectively. Cornwell's subrogee, Royal Insurance Company, intervened in the trial action and joins Cornwell in its appeal. Defendants-cross-appellees, Centran Bank and County of Summit have filed cross-appellee briefs.

Linda Zelnar embezzled $57,000 from Akron Novelty while she was employed there as a bookkeeper. She was discovered and discharged.

Rather than prosecuting her for the crime of embezzlement, the Summit County Prosecutor's office referred Zelnar to its pretrial diversion program. After giving Zelnar a psychological examination, the director of the program, Mark Tully, enrolled her in the diversion program. One of the requirements of her participation in the program was her restitution of the stolen funds.

Zelnar told Tully she would be able to return Akron Novelty's funds by refinancing her home and borrowing from her parents. Zelnar presented Tully with two checks on two different occasions—one for $20,000 and a second for $37,000. The testimony contained in the trial transcript and depositions indicates that Hinkle had some concerns as to whether the first check was good. He had Tully and

Zelnar got Centran to assure that there were sufficient funds in her account to cover the check. This Centran did. Zelnar got the second check for $37,000 certified. Hinkle deposited both checks in the accounts from which the funds had originally been taken.

Linda Zelnar was discharged from Akron Novelty on April 6, 1984. On April 30, 1984, she was employed, through Kelly Services, as an accounts payable clerk for Cornwell Quality Tools. She was eventually hired directly by Cornwell, and filled out an application listing previous employment, including Akron Novelty. However, Cornwell never made its own inquiries into her previous employment relying on the assumption that Kelly Services had already done so.

Zelnar's duties included the personal preparation of checks to Cornwell's creditors. While employed at Cornwell, Zelnar conceived a plan to embezzle money to pay back Hinkle, as well as for her own use. She established an account at Centran Bank in the name of "Linda R. Zelnar dba 'Model.'" She also purchased a kit and made a rubber stamp that read "For Deposit Only, Model."

Cornwell had regularly done business with Model Industries, Inc. of Chicago. When mailing more than one check, it was Cornwell's policy to make the first check in a group payable with the full name and address of the payee. The remaining checks were made payable only to "Model." Over a three-month period, Zelnar prepared six checks payable to "Model," which were drawn on Cornwell's account at First National Bank. She presented the checks for the proper drawers' signatures and then took the checks, endorsed them with the stamp, and deposited them in the account at Centran. All six of the checks were accepted for payment by First National which charged them to Cornwell's account.

Zelnar drew two checks on the Centran account that were payable to Hinkle. When Centran notified Zelnar that one of the checks was going to be returned for uncollected funds, Zelnar obtained a letter from Centran explaining the delay, and gave the letter to Mr. Tully of the diversion program. Zelnar was concerned because a check returned for insufficient funds would result in her ouster from the program. When the embezzlement scheme was discovered, the funds remaining in the Centran account were frozen and then returned to Cornwell.

Cornwell filed a complaint, seeking to enjoin the funds in the Centran account, and an amended complaint, alleging that Centran failed to exercise ordinary care in the establishment of the account and collection of the checks. Royal Insurance Company, which paid Cornwell $50,000, intervened in the suit as subrogee. Royal charged Centran and First National with conversion, pursuant to R.C. 1303.55 (UCC 3-419), and alleged that Centran failed to exercise ordinary care in the establishment of the account and collection of the checks. Centran filed motions for summary judgment against both plaintiffs. First National was voluntarily dismissed from the suit.

The trial court granted summary judgment to Centran.

 JUDGE CACIOPPO:

Application of the impostor rule ... deems a forgery effective to pass good title to a negotiable instrument. The rule is an exception to the strict liability imposed on a bank that pays on a forged indorsement. The loss is shifted to the drawer because the responsibility for the payment can be attributed more to the drawer's actions than to the bank's failure to obtain a proper indorsement....

"The principle followed is that the loss should fall upon the employer as a risk of his business enterprise rather than upon the subsequent holder or drawee. The reasons are that the employer is normally in a better position to prevent such forgeries by reasonable care in the selection or supervision of his employees, or, if he is not, is at least in a better position to cover the loss by fidelity insurance; and that the cost of such insurance is properly an expense of his business rather than of the business of the holder or drawee."

To receive the protection of this rule, Centran has to meet both prongs of the statute, i.e.:

1. That Linda Zelnar supplied the name of the payee, "Model," to her employer, Cornwell.

2. That Linda Zelnar intended the payee, "Model," to have no interest in the checks.

In its attempt to meet the first prong, Centran uses a strained and contorted line of reasoning. Centran claims that the entity "Model" was fictitious because Cornwell did not do business with any entity designated as such. For the purposes of the rule, a forger using the name of a fictitious payee obviously shows the name was "supplied" to employer.

Cornwell did, however, do business with "Model Industries, Inc." of Chicago. The record shows that "Model" cannot be considered a fictitious entity, and even if it were, it would have been "created" by Cornwell itself. Zelnar stated in her deposition that it was company policy to abbreviate the names of payees such as Model Industries, Inc.

It was Cornwell's practice in a situation where several invoices were to be paid to one supplier on a single day—as was the case with Model Industries which was a constant supplier to Cornwell—that only the first check in the group would bear the full name and address of the payee. This check would be inserted in the window of the envelope, while the other checks would bear only the abbreviated name of the payee. There was nothing extraordinary about her use of the word "Model" on the following checks, particularly since the invoices to which they applied were perfectly genuine. Thus, it is inaccurate to say that "Cornwell never had done business with the fictitious entity called 'Model'...." As used on these checks, "Model" clearly pertained to Model Industries, Inc. of Chicago, from which the invoices attached to them had been received....

To escape the application of the first prong of the rule, Cornwell uses a more plausible argument as to when an employee can be considered to have "supplied" the name of the payee. Specifically, the issue is whether an employee can "supply" a payee's name when the check is issued to a real person in payment of a genuine obligation of the employer. Several courts have held that where a check is issued to a bona fide creditor who had furnished legitimate invoices, the employee's action amounts to no more than theft of the check. An employee cannot be said to have "supplied" the name of a payee in the course of a normal business transaction that would have occurred in any event....

The second prong of the rule requires that, in supplying the name, the employee must intend that the named payee have no interest in the check. Linda Zelnar freely admitted that, at the time she presented the checks to her superiors for their signatures, she never intended the true payee, Model Industries, Inc. of Chicago, to have any interest in the check.

Having met the requirements of ... UCC 3-405[1][C], the forgery must be considered effective to pass good title on the instrument, and Cornwell must bear the loss. Therefore, summary judgment was appropriate in this case.

Cornwell raises a second issue, asserting that the negligence of Centran precludes the benefits of R.C. 1303.41, making summary judgment improper. Cornwell claims that, in spite of Centran's relief from statutory liability by operation of R.C. 1303.41, a triable issue of fact remained as to Centran's actual negligence in failing to exercise ordinary care in the transaction.

There are three Code provisions which allow a bank to escape strict liability for paying on a forged indorsement. R.C. 1303.42 (UCC 3-406) and R.C. 1304.29 (UCC 4-406) both specifically provide that where the drawer asserts and can prove that the bank failed to exercise reasonable commercial standards in handling the check, the bank loses its protection. R.C. 1303.41 (UCC 3-405) is silent on the issue of the bank's lack of care. We do not believe this silence to be inadvertent. The policy statements provided in the Official Comment denote an intent to place the loss on the party best able to prevent it.

The interpretation of Section 3-405 as an *absolute* loss allocation device is also more consistent with the recognition that this section was conceived as a "banker's provision *intended to narrow the liability of banks* and broaden the responsibility of their customers."

Such a "banker's provision" was not likely to have been intended to leave the banks open to common-law liability. Therefore, since the Supreme Court has clearly expressed faith in and support of the policies advanced by the drafters, it can safely be said that R.C. 1303.41 (UCC 3-405) displaces any negligence claims against the depositary bank, common-law or otherwise.

Since it was clear that Centran Bank met the requirements of R.C. 1303.41(A)(3), and that R.C. 1303.41(A)(3) is an absolute defense, regardless of negligence on the part of a bank, the trial court acted properly in granting Centran Bank's motion for summary judgment.

TYPES OF INDORSEMENT

Every indorsement has at least three features: the method it requires for making further negotiations, or at least the next one; the nature of the liability it imposes on the indorser; and the kind of restrictions, if any, which it attempts to place on further transfers. These three features may be combined in various ways.

Blank Indorsements and Special Indorsements. The last indorsement controls the status of the instrument as order paper or bearer paper, regardless of the form in which it was originally issued. A **blank indorsement** consists merely of the indorser's signature: "John Smith." If the last or the only indorsement is a blank indorsement, the instrument is now **bearer paper** and may be negotiated henceforth by delivery, without further indorsement. A **special indorsement** names the next transferee: "Pay to Judy Jones. John Smith." Regardless of how it was originally made payable, this instrument is now **order paper,** and Judy must indorse to negotiate the instrument further. (Note that the words of negotiability—*order* or *bearer*—do not have to be used in an indorsement; the preceding example is payable to the order of Judy Jones.)

Qualified and Unqualified Indorsements. An indorser may disclaim secondary contract liability by using the words "without recourse" or similar language. This is called a **qualified indorsement**. If such language is not used, the indorsement is unqualified, meaning that the indorser is assuming the normal secondary contract liability—to pay the instrument on dishonor.

Restrictive Indorsements. Indorsers sometimes attempt, in various ways, to restrict or limit the further negotiation of an instrument. Under the Code's rules, some such restrictions are fully effective, some are partially effective, and some are without legal effect. Section 3-206(a) states that no indorser can effectively prohibit the further negotiation of a negotiable instrument. If John Smith indorsed "Pay only Judy Jones" or "Pay Judy Jones and no one else," the "only" language is completely ineffective. Judy can indorse and renegotiate the instrument just as if John had indorsed "Pay to the order of Judy Jones."

The promise or order contained in the body of the instrument itself cannot be conditional without destroying its negotiability. This is not true, however, of indorsements. Conditions can be included in indorsements without affecting an instrument's negotiability. However, the Code makes such conditions effective only as between the immediate parties.

For example, Biff Bosox buys a new TV from Big Bennie's Appliance Store. As payment, Biff indorses his payroll check: "Pay to Big Bennie if he delivers one new Zenith TV to my home. Biff Bosox." Bennie is not supposed to get the money unless he delivers the TV as promised. The Code says that no later holder of the instrument is responsible for verifying that he has done so before taking the instrument. If Bennie has not delivered the TV but gets the money from someone anyway, that later holder of the instrument may still be an HDC. In contrast, all subsequent holders other than intermediary banks are fully bound by such language in the indorsement as "For deposit only" or "For collection." It is very hard to imagine a situation where a nonbank person taking an instrument after such an indorsement could ever qualify as an HDC. Such language clearly indicates that the instrument is intended to circulate only through the bank collection process.

Where the restrictive indorsement indicates that the proceeds are to be paid to one person for the benefit of another ("Pay to Ollie Orkin for the benefit of Shirley Trample"), only the first taker after the indorsement is bound by it. To be a holder for value so as to (perhaps) qualify as an HDC, the immediate transferee must pay any value given "consistently with the indorsement." Unless later holders of the instrument actually know that the trustee or other fiduciary has misapplied these funds, they are not affected in any way by the "benefit" type of restrictive indorsement.

HOLDER IN DUE COURSE

Generally. The essence of the whole concept of negotiability is the elimination or nonassertability of most common defenses when the instrument gets into the hands of a good faith purchaser. The technical term for such a bona fide purchaser (BFP) in the negotiable instruments context is **holder in due course**. The requirements for becoming an HDC are set out in Section 3-302, and then they are more specifically defined in other sections. Whether or not a particular person has met this set of requirements presents a complex combination of legal and factual issues which have been subject to considerable litigation. Since, as previously noted, consumer debtors are now permitted to assert any defense they may have against anyone, HDC status has become virtually meaningless in consumer transactions. For businesses, however, these issues are still vital where merchandise has been fraudulently misrepresented or has not been delivered at all. Whether a business debtor will be able to assert such defenses or will be forced to pay for the proverbial "dead horse," will depend on a later holder's status as an HDC.

A holder in due course first has to be a holder (as discussed above) and also must have taken the instrument for value, and in good faith, and without notice that it is overdue or has been dishonored or of any defense against or claim to it on the part of any person. Section 3-302 also contains several specific rules: a purchaser of a limited interest in an instrument can be an HDC only to that extent; and a person cannot become an HDC by buying an instrument at a judicial sale or as part of a bulk transaction not in the ordinary course of business or by acquiring it through legal process or in taking over an estate.

Value. Value, as used here, is a much more limited concept than "consideration." A holder for value must have performed the agreed consideration for the note. If Axle Greez promises to buy a certain promissory note from Henna Rinz for $600, there is a contract, but Axle is not a holder for value until he actually pays Henna the $600. If he is notified of an existing defense before he pays, he can't become an HDC. A person who acquires security interests or other liens against instruments, other than by judicial process, is a holder for value. So is a person who takes the instrument "as payment of or as security for an antecedent claim against any person whether or not the claim is due." Similarly, someone who makes an "irrevocable obligation to a third party" (a binding agreement for an extension of credit, for example) is thereby a holder for value. Finally, value is given by giving another negotiable instrument. In the above example, if Axle had given Henna his check for $600 in payment for the promissory note he bought from her, Axle would be a holder for value of the note.

Good Faith. Article 3 contains no special definition of good faith other than in the general definitions Section 1-201[19]. It is a subjective test to be applied by the trier of fact: "honesty in fact in the conduct or transaction concerned." Such facts as the relationship between the parties, the size of any discount from the face amount of the instrument, the proximity of the transfer to the instrument's due date, the appearance of the instrument, and the time and place of the transfer would be relevant in deciding whether a particular holder had bought in "good faith."

No Notice of Claim or Defense. Article 3 does contain several specific rules for determining when a purchaser has **notice** that an instrument is overdue, has been dishonored, or is subject to a claim or defense. The basic rule is nothing more than common sense: A purchaser has notice of a claim or defense where the instrument bears "such apparent evidence of forgery or alteration," or is otherwise so "irregular or incomplete as to call into question its authenticity." Where a fiduciary has negotiated an instrument for his or her own benefit, the purchaser must have had knowledge of that fact when taking the instrument. Remember the difference between "knowledge" and "notice;" **knowledge** means actual, "inside-the-head" information, whereas **notice** includes both acts from which a reasonable person should infer other information and the receipt of notices containing information, whether those notices are actually read or not. Knowledge is therefore only one form of "notice." This section does say that the filing or recording of a document does not of itself constitute notice so as to prevent a person from being an HDC. It also says that for notice to be effective, it must be received "at a time and in a manner that gives a reasonable opportunity to act on it."

The application of these HDC rules can be seen in the *Northwestern* case.

NORTHWESTERN NAT. INS. CO. v. MAGGIO
976 F.2d 320 (7th Cir. 1992)

FACTS: This diversity suit on a promissory note was brought by Northwestern National Insurance Company against the note's maker, Anthony Maggio. The district court, holding that Northwestern was a holder in due course and had therefore taken the note free of any defenses Maggio might have had to a suit by the promisee, gave judgment for Northwestern on the latter's motion for summary judgment.

In 1981, Maggio had purchased a limited partnership in a new venture created by a former astronaut to develop an optoelectronic scanner designed to provide perimeter security for sprawling properties such as airfields, oil fields, and pipelines. As consideration for his partnership interest, Maggio gave the partnership a non-interest-bearing note for $55,000 maturing October 31, 1990. The partnership negotiated the note to a venture-capital company that in turn negotiated it to Goldman Sachs which in 1988 negotiated it to Northwestern, along with other notes of the limited partners, at a 50 percent discount. When the note matured on October 31, 1990, Northwestern demanded payment from Maggio of the full face amount. He refused.

 CIRCUIT JUDGE POSNER:

Maggio claims that he was induced to purchase the limited partnership by fraud. If so, he has, of course, a claim against the partnership itself and perhaps the general partner and others, but he has no claim against Northwestern if the latter is a holder in due course. It is not if (so far as relevant here) it either did not take the note "in good faith" or "purchas[ed] it as part of a bulk transaction not in the regular course of business of the transferor." We take up these questions in reverse order, and ignore Maggio's frivolous argument of judicial estoppel. The note recites, and the parties agree, that disputes concerning it are to be resolved under the law of Arizona, where the partnership was formed.

The rarely litigated bulk-transfer exception identifies a narrow class of transactions where the purchaser of the (otherwise) negotiable instrument ought to be suspicious that the seller may be trying to thwart promisors' defenses and prefer one creditor over others, or committing outright fraud (the transferee might be a successor of the transferor), perhaps en route to bankruptcy. The existence of those defenses makes the promisors creditors; the wholesale transfer of their notes to a "holder in due course" would extinguish the promisors' claims; and the fact that the transfer is not in the ordinary course of business reinforces the inference that the transfer is an attempt to extinguish creditors' claims.... There is no indication that the sale by Goldman Sachs of the limited partners' notes to Northwestern was of this character. Bulk transfer it was, but there is no evidence that Goldman Sachs, a large investment bank, was acting outside the ordinary course of its business in making such a transfer....

The more substantial issue is whether the 50 percent discount at which Northwestern bought the note should have made Northwestern inquire into the possible existence of defenses. Maggio does not argue that the discount itself established bad faith-only that it was a sufficiently suspicious circumstance to make Northwestern guilty of ostrich conduct, or more precisely to raise a jury issue and thus forestall summary judgment. Bad faith is a conscious state but it includes the deliberate avoidance of inquiry by one who fears what inquiry would bring to light....

Northwestern reminds us that a noninterest-bearing note at fixed maturity *must* sell at a discount.... No one will pay $1,000 today for the right to receive $1,000 in two years, and Northwestern bought Maggio's note from Goldman Sachs two years before it was to mature. But a 50 percent discount on a note bought two years before maturity implies an interest rate of about 40 percent a year, and Maggio asks us to infer that no one would compensate the buyer of a note at such a rate unless the promisor had defenses (we do not know whether Goldman Sachs was a holder in due course). But this overlooks an obvious reason for the discount besides compensation for the time value of Northwestern's money-the risk that Maggio, even if he had no defenses to a suit for collection brought by the original promisee, would raise some anyway, as he has done, or wouldn't have the assets to pay the note when it matured. A bird in the hand is said to be worth two in the bush. Goldman Sachs got the bird in the hand; Northwestern got the two birds in the bush.

The fact that a note is sold at a discount is thus not in itself a suspicious circumstance that triggers a duty of inquiry by the buyer.... This would hardly be worth saying but for a sentence in an opinion by the Supreme Court of Arizona that, because this case is governed by Arizona law, we must take with more than ordinary seriousness: "That fact alone [that the note was purchased at a 33% discount] is sufficient to alert a prospective purchaser to a possible defense" *Stewart v. Thorton* 116 Ariz. 107.... Well, but as in other cases in which such dicta appear ... that fact didn't stand alone. The note had been sold (at the discount) within the 48-hour period in which the buyer of the property in exchange for which the note was issued was entitled under Arizona law to rescind the purchase. The court held that the buyer of the note was charged with knowing the law and therefore would be assumed to have known when it bought the note that the maker had a defense against the note's seller (the promisee). The discount merely reinforced the inference of knowledge. In our case, the discount stands alone.

"[A]lone ...." It is *conceivable* that by use of this word the Supreme Court of Arizona intended to revolutionize the law of negotiable instruments, bore a large hole in negotiability, and thereby raise transaction costs in financial markets. But nothing in the opinion besides that one word suggests any such perverse ambition. Judicial opinions are frequently drafted in haste, with imperfect foresight, and without due regard for the possibility that words or phrases or sentences may be taken out of context and treated as doctrines. We shouldn't like this done to our opinions and are therefore reluctant to do it to the opinions of other courts. No court, even a federal court in a diversity suit, is obliged to treat a dictum of another court (or, for that matter, its own dicta) as binding precedent.... The dictum in *Stewart* does not persuade us that the courts of Arizona would hold that the purchase of a promissory note at a discount is alone enough to defeat negotiability by requiring the buyer to determine whether, were he the original promisee, the promisor would have a defense to a suit for collection. We add that no court in Arizona (or for that matter anywhere else) has ever cited *Stewart* for that proposition, though the case is now fifteen years old.

No Notice that Instrument is Overdue. Section 3-304 provides a few rules for determining when an instrument is "overdue." With a demand instrument, rather than one with a specific due date, it's overdue after a demand for payment has already been made by a prior holder or after more than a reasonable time from the date issued. The section contains a presumption that ninety days is such a reasonable time for an uncertified check payable in the United States, but it does not contain similar guidelines for drafts or notes. (Presumably, the reasonable time for these other instruments would be longer than that for an uncertified check.)

The purchaser who is aware that a prior acceleration of the due date has been made also has such notice. Finally, there is notice that an instrument is overdue when the purchaser has reason to know that part of the principal is overdue (a missed installment payment, for example) or that "there is an uncured default in payment of another instrument of the same series." There is no stated rule for the most obvious case: the stated due date is July 1, and you buy the instrument on July 2. You can clearly see that the instrument is overdue when you buy it, and you are not an HDC.

SHELTER RULE

Under the Code, a transferee of a negotiable instrument (including one who is not even a holder), in most instances, receives whatever rights its transferor had. A holder who is not an HDC (a donee, for example) would nevertheless have whatever enforcement rights the transferor had. Because of this general rule, any holder of an instrument after an HDC succeeds to all the rights of the HDC, even though the later holder or holders don't personally meet all the requirements for being an HDC. The donee of the instrument can't personally qualify as an HDC, because he or she gave no value for it. But if the donor or some prior party was an HDC, the donee would have all the rights to the instrument that the HDC did. In simplest terms, once there is an HDC in an instrument's chain of title, all later holders of the instrument receive the "shelter" of that person's HDC status even though they can't meet the HDC tests personally.

There are two exceptions to this shelter rule. A person who is a party to some fraud or illegality affecting an instrument cannot improve his or her legal position by transferring the instrument to an HDC and then reacquiring it. Nor can a person who has notice of a claim or defense to an instrument, then transfers the instrument to an HDC, and then later reacquires the instrument.

The shelter rule is applied in the *Manufacturers* case.

MANUFACTURERS HANOVER TRUST v. ROBINSON
597 N.Y.S.2d 986 (Sup.Ct. 1993)

FACTS: Defendants are limited partners in 600 Grant Street Associates Limited Partnership which was organized to acquire, own and operate a commercial office building in Pittsburgh, Pennsylvania. In connection with the purchase of their interests, defendants made cash down payments and executed promissory notes payable to the order of the Partnership for the balance.

Defendants allege that they were induced to invest in the Partnership as a result of certain misrepresentations made by the sponsor of the transaction, Integrated Resources, Inc., which allegedly failed to advise defendants of the presence of asbestos throughout the building and misrepresented that at the time of the sale there were 2.23 million square feet of vacant office space in downtown Pittsburgh, when in fact the vacant space was in excess of twelve million square feet.

In June and September 1986, plaintiff Manufacturers Hanover Trust Company acquired thirty-nine of the promissory notes as collateral for an $80,000,000 loan made to the Partnership by it and five other banks for which it acted as agent.

Manufacturers alleges that in 1986 it accepted only the notes of limited partners who had met certain financial criteria, and then only if the notes were not in default. It also asserts that the Partnership represented and warranted that none of the notes were overdue or had been dishonored and that no defense against or claim to the notes existed. Manufacturers also allegedly conducted a credit check of each limited partner who had executed a note.

Plaintiff asserts that at the time of the delivery of the notes to it in 1986, thirty-seven were indorsed in blank by an officer of Marine Midland Bank, N. A. in the following form:

> *"PAY TO THE ORDER OF*
>
> *WITHOUT RECOURSE*
>
> *MARINE MIDLAND BANK, N.A.*
>
> *BY (signature of officer)*

Two of the notes were similarly indorsed in blank by an officer of Security Pacific National Bank. Previously the notes had been indorsed by the Partnership to these two banks.

An exception to this scenario was the note made by defendant Russell D. Robinson, which was pledged in 1987 and indorsed the Partnership directly to Manufacturers.

Defendants were promised by the Partnership and integrated in documents dated December 5, 1984 and March 15, 1985, that in the event of a reduction in the highest marginal federal income tax bracket, the purchase price of the property would be reduced, and the limited partners would be entitled to a reduction of their required capital contribution to the Partnership. The October 1986 tax code amendments effected a reduction in such tax bracket, thereby triggering the capital reduction. The limited partners were notified that as a result they would receive a rebate of $21,552 per unit, which would be paid in annual installments in March 1988, 1989, 1990, and 1991. Integrated filed for bankruptcy thereafter in February 1990 and the promised capital reduction payments for the years 1990 and 1991 were never made.

In August 1990, Manufacturers removed the notes from its vault to inventory them, allegedly in anticipation of litigation. For reasons that are unclear, the removing bank officers then allegedly stamped on the thirty-nine notes held in blank "600 GRANT STREET ASSOCIATES LIMITED PARTNERSHIP" in the blank space of each of the above mentioned indorsements, and then placed the following indorsement on these notes:

"600 Grant Street Associates Limited Partnership without recourse

By: Manufacturers Hanover Trust Company as Agent, Attorney-in-fact for

600 Grant Street Associates Limited Partnership

By: (signature of officer) Vice President"

Claiming that the notes were negotiated to it in 1986 and that it then took possession of them for value, in good faith and without knowledge of any claim or defense, Manufacturers moved for summary judgment asserting that it was a holder in due course thereof.

 JUSTICE LEHNER:

Manufacturers contends that its 1986 holder in due course status was unaffected by the 1990 indorsements because there was no delivery of the instruments to the Partnership. However, Manufacturers functioned in a dual role, acting for itself and as the Partnership's agent. Once the notes were indorsed in favor of the Partnership, only the Partnership had the right to negotiate them. Manufacturers accomplished this by receiving the notes as the Partnership's agent and indorsing them in blank in that same capacity. The indorsement stamp used states that Manufacturers was signing as "Agent, Attorney-in-fact for 600 Grant Street Associates Limited Partnership" Therefore, albeit only for a brief period, the notes were upon such negotiation owned by the Partnership, although if the allegations against it are proven, not as a holder in due course.

What then was Manufacturers' status when the notes were then renegotiated to it? It contends that even if it did not reacquire the notes as a holder in due course in 1990, summary judgment is still appropriate under the "Shelter Rule" embodied in UCC § 3-201(1), which provides: "Transfer of an instrument vests in the transferee such rights as the transferor has therein, except that a transferee who has himself been a party to any fraud or illegality affecting the instrument or who as a prior holder had notice of a defense or claim against it cannot improve his position by taking from a later holder in due course."

Under the Shelter Rule, a transferee obtains the rights, not the status, of the prior holder in due course.

The Shelter Rule is designed to guarantee a holder in due course a ready market for its negotiable instrument....

"Thus, when a transferee takes an instrument from a holder in due course the transferee takes free from all claims and defenses to the same extent as did the holder in due course even if the transferee is aware of those claims and defenses. If this was not the rule, a holder in due course could be deprived of a market for the instrument if the obligor widely disseminated notice of a claim or defense ... [which would] harm the holder in due course by destroying the market for the instrument...."

The purpose behind this shelter principle is to protect the holder in due course so that he can sell what he has purchased. The statute therefore permits a holder with notice of defenses to acquire the rights of a holder in due course.

The Shelter Rule, however, does not necessarily protect Manufacturers under the facts at bar. When the Partnership acquired title to the notes in 1990, it was allegedly a party to the asserted fraud and a prior holder who had notice of defenses against the notes. Therefore, if the allegations against it are proven, the Partnership is not eligible for the Shelter Rule protection or holder in due course status. Hence, the question arises whether Manufacturers can be sheltered under UCC § 3-201(1) if its transferor is specifically denied that protection.

In Hawkland and Lawrence ... the authors state: "A question existed under the NIL and exists under the Code as well as to whether a purchaser from a party who was denied protection of the shelter provision because he was a party to a fraud or illegality (or, under the Code, had notice of a defense or claim) obtains merely the rights of his transferor or whether he can succeed to the rights of a previous holder in due course. Assume A made a note payable to B, who with notice of a defense transferred the note to C, a holder in due course. If C transferred the note to B who resold it to D, would D be entitled to C's rights or is he limited to B's rights? Under the NIL, it was unclear whether the exclusion from the shelter provision was personal to B or extended to anyone deriving title from B. Section 58 of the NIL provided that any holder except a party to fraud or illegality who derived title through a holder in due course obtained the rights of the holder in due course. From this it could be implied that only B himself was denied the protection. Apparently B could thus transfer the instrument to a relative who would then take free of the claim or defense. Any such result would be unfortunate. Fortunately, the language of Section 3-201 militates in favor of the contrary result. Under Subsection 3-201(1) the transfer vests in the transferee, D, all of the rights of his transferor, B. Since B was not entitled to C's rights as a holder in due course, D would not be entitled to these rights either."

Since the same policy consideration in favor of a holder in due course does not apply to a party to a fraud or a prior holder who had knowledge of defenses, if the Partnership is found to have fallen within the exceptions of the Shelter Rule, it is consistent with the statutory policy to prohibit it from improving its position and the market for its instrument by also denying any transferee acquiring the notes from it (in this case Manufacturers) shelter under the statute. The fact that Manufacturers was a prior holder in due course does not aid it under the language of the section.

Why Manufacturers indorsed the notes as it did in 1990 remains a mystery. Absent such indorsements, it could, based on the facts set forth in the submitted papers, enforce the notes as a holder in due course. But, as a consequence of its inexplicable unilateral actions it faces losing that substantive right, without having procured any seeming benefit from the indorsements, as the court finds no statutory provision governing commercial paper that entitles plaintiff, as a matter of law, to the rights of a holder in due course under the unusual circumstances presented herein.

Accordingly, as there are numerous questions of fact concerning the Partnership's alleged fraudulent acts and Manufacturer's knowledge in 1990 of asserted defenses and claims, the motion for summary judgment, except as to the Robinson note, is denied.

With respect to the Robinson note, which was endorsed directly to plaintiff in 1987, there is no evidence that plaintiff then had knowledge of any defense or infirmity with respect thereto, and thus it became a holder in due course upon acquiring the note. Consequently, plaintiff is entitled to summary judgment against Robinson for the outstanding principal on the note, plus interest, with the claim for attorneys' fees to be severed for an assessment of damages after the filing of a note of issue and statement of readiness.

DEFENSES

The merchant community's main purpose in developing negotiable instruments and the main significance of negotiability today is the nonassertability of most common defenses against liability when an instrument gets into the hands of an HDC. HDC status does not, however, eliminate all defenses. Some defenses can still be asserted against an HDC and, if proved, will defeat or reduce recovery on an instrument. Those defenses that cannot be asserted against an HDC or an HHDC (a holder through a holder in due course) are called personal or limited defenses. Personal defenses can still be asserted against anyone who is not an HDC or a holder through an HDC.

Those defenses that can be used against anyone, including an HDC or an HHDC, are called real or universal defenses. The most obvious example of these defenses is forgery; certainly a person whose name has been forged on an instrument should not be required to pay it, even to an HDC. The basic distinction is between void-type defenses (= real) and voidable type defenses (= personal), except for minority, which is recognized as a real defense. If a defense is one which "makes the obligation a nullity," it is a real defense. If there is no contract, there is no contract— even if the instrument is in the hands of an HDC. On the other hand, if a defense merely relates to some problem between two of the parties on an instrument, it is a personal defense, and it cannot be asserted against an HDC.

REAL DEFENSES

Article 3's main list of real defenses is found in Section 3-305. In addition, 3-403 (unauthorized signatures) and 3-407 (alteration) describe real defenses.

Unauthorized Signature or Forgery. When someone signs your name to an instrument without your permission, you're not liable, even to an HDC. The result is the same whether your name is simply forged or whether it is signed with an indication of agency authority that doesn't exist.

The section says that this unauthorized signature is "wholly inoperative" against you unless you ratify it or are estopped by your conduct from denying its validity. It is, however, effective to impose full liability on the instrument against the forger, in favor of someone who pays or takes the instrument in good faith.

Material Alteration. Where the contract of any party to an instrument has been changed "in any respect" by an alteration, Section 3-407 says that the alteration is material. If this material alteration is also fraudulent, the party whose contract is changed is discharged from further liability on the instrument unless that person assents to the change or is estopped from asserting it. As the one exception to this rule, an HDC can still enforce the instrument "according to its original terms," that is, the terms prior to the alteration. A nonmaterial or nonfraudulent alteration does not discharge any party.

As an example of these rules, if you signed a blank check and lost it, and the finder filled in $600 as the amount, an HDC could force you to pay the $600. If you signed a check and filled it in for $6.00, and someone found or stole the check and altered it to read $600, an HDC could force you to pay only the original $6.00. However, if you filled in the amount spaces with blanks after the number 6 and the word Six, so that the thief or finder could very easily add "00" and "Hundred," you would be estopped from asserting the alteration and would have to pay the full $600.

Minority. Although minority or infancy generally results in a voidable obligation rather than a void one, Section 3-305 makes it a real defense to liability on a negotiable instrument. Infancy is a defense to the same extent that it would be against liability on a simple contract. In other words, infancy can be asserted against an HDC. On the other hand, since this section distinguishes between "defenses" and "claims" and states that an HDC owns the instrument free of all adverse ownership claims, the minor cannot get back the instrument that he or she signed. Remember that the indorsement sections make the minor's indorsement fully effective to transfer ownership of the instrument, so that there can be later HDCs in the chain of title.

Other Incapacity. As to other types of contractual incapacity, 3-305 makes these a real defense only if they void the contract ("nullify the obligation of the obligor"). This rule thus refers us to the applicable state law on insanity, aliens, married women, and so on, as discussed in Chapter 11. Unauthorized acts by corporations or governmental agencies which resulted in the issuance of negotiable instruments would probably also fall into this category.

Void-Type Duress. Duress may be either a real or a personal defense, depending on whether it results in a void or a voidable obligation. "Gun-to-the-head" duress "renders the obligation of the party a nullity" and can thus be asserted against an HDC. The "threat-of-criminal-prosecution" type of duress would make a contract only voidable, not void, and thus it cannot be asserted against an HDC.

Void-Type Illegality. Where some part of a transaction violates a criminal statute, the state's statutory and case law may make the contract involved either void or voidable. Section 3-305 again refers us to these state law distinctions to see whether the particular illegality is a real or only a personal defense.

The *Kedzie* case illustrates this point.

KEDZIE AND 103rd CURRENCY EXCHANGE v. HODGE
619 N.E.2d 732 (IL, 1993)

FACTS: Pursuant to a written "work order, " Fred Fentress agreed to install a "flood control system" at the home of Eric and Beulah Hodge of Chicago for $900. In partial payment for the work, Beulah Hodge drafted a personal check payable to "Fred Fentress-A-OK Plumbing" for $500 from the Hodges' joint account at Citicorp Savings.

The system's components were not delivered to the Hodge's home as scheduled. And, when Fentress failed to appear on the date set for installation, Eric Hodge telephoned him to announce the contract "cancelled." Hodge also told Fentress that he would order Citicorp Savings not to pay the check Fentress had been given.

Records of Citicorp Savings confirm acknowledgment of a stop-payment order entered the same day.

Nevertheless, Fentress presented the check at the Kedzie & 103rd Street Currency Exchange, endorsing it as "sole owner" of A-OK Plumbing, and obtained payment. However, when the Currency Exchange later presented the check for payment at Citicorp Savings, payment was refused in accordance with the stop-payment order.

The Currency Exchange, alleging it was a holder in due course, then sued Beulah Hodge, as drawer of the check, and Fentress for the amount stated. Hodge, in turn, filed a counterclaim against Fentress. Hodge also moved to dismiss the Currency Exchange's action against her. The disposition of Hodge's motion gives rise to this appeal.

Hodge asserted a defense provided by Section 3-305 of the Uniform Commercial Code. Under that section, the claim of a holder in due course of a negotiable instrument may be barred based on "illegality of the transaction." Hodge contended Fentress was not a licensed plumber as was required under the Illinois Plumbing License Law. The director of licensing and registration of the Chicago department of buildings and the keeper of plumbing licensing records of the Illinois Department of Public Health provided affidavits supporting that contention.

The circuit court granted the motion and dismissed the Currency Exchange's action against Hodge. The appellate court, with one justice dissenting, affirmed.

 JUDGE FREEMAN:

The issue of "illegality" arises "under a variety of statutes...." In view of the diverse constructions to which statutory enactments are given, "illegality" is, accordingly, a matter "left to the local law...." Even so, it is only when an obligation is made "entirely null and void" under "local law" that "illegality" exists as one of the "real defenses" under Section 3-305 to defeat a claim of a holder in due course.... In effect, the obligation must be no obligation at all. If it is "merely voidable" at the election of the obligor, the defense is unavailable....

Historically, this court has recognized "illegality" to arise only in view of legislative declaration affecting both the underlying contract or transaction and instrument exchanged upon it.... A contract or transaction which is void must certainly negate the obligation to pay arising from it as between the contracting parties.... But, unless an instrument memorializing the obligation is also made void, an innocent third party who has no knowledge of the circumstances of the initial contract or transaction may yet claim payment of it against the drawer or maker.

The holder in due course concept is intended to facilitate commercial transactions by eliminating the need for "elaborate investigation" of the nature of the circumstances for which an instrument is initially exchanged or of its drafting.... If "illegality" means simply negation of the initial obligation to pay, a holder in due course enjoys no more protection than a party to the original contract or transaction. The "real" defense of "illegality" is reduced to a "personal" one....

It is, therefore, not enough simply to conclude that the initial obligation to pay arising from a void contract or transaction is void. Negation of that obligation as between the contracting parties has little bearing on whether a holder in due course of an instrument arising from the contract or transaction should nevertheless be permitted to make a claim for payment.

The "local law" of this State has been formulated upon this court's recognition, in cases predating the UCC, of legislative prerogative regarding negotiable instruments. In adopting the UCC and, in particular, Section 3-305, our legislature chose to confer upon a holder in due course of a negotiable instrument considerable protection against claims by persons to it. Our legislature also continues to declare certain obligations void because of the circumstances of the agreements from which they arise and without regard to the status of who may claim ownership.... The selective negation of obligations reflects a legislative aim to declare what will and will not give rise to "illegality" in cases now governed by UCC. As legislative direction indicates which obligations are always void, legislative silence indicates when the protection afforded a holder in due course must be honored.

We therefore reaffirm, today, the view this court has consistently recognized in cases predating the UCC. Unless the instrument arising from a contract or transaction is, itself, made void by statute, the "illegality" defense under Section 3-305 is not available to bar the claim of a holder in due course.

To determine whether Hodge is entitled to a judgment of dismissal, we need not engage in an analysis aimed at characterizing the contract between Fentress and the Hodges. Whether the underlying contract should be considered void because Fentress was not licensed as required by the Illinois Plumbing License Law is not dispositive of the Currency Exchange's right, as a holder in due course, to claim payment of the check. It is relevant only to determine whether the Illinois Plumbing License Law provides that any obligation arising from a contract for plumbing services made in violation of its requirements is void. It does not.

For the reasons stated, the judgments of the appellate and circuit courts are reversed, and the cause is remanded to the circuit court for further proceeding.

Fraud in the Execution. The most obvious example of fraud in the execution occurs when the nature of the instrument itself is misrepresented. You are told you're merely signing a receipt for delivery of merchandise, or an authorization form for repairs on your car, but the document is folded, or covered, or switched, so that you can't see it's really a negotiable instrument. The section also extends this defense to the case where you do know you're signing a negotiable instrument but you don't have a reasonable opportunity to obtain knowledge of its "essential terms." In either of these cases, you must show that your ignorance of the character and terms of the instrument was "excusable ignorance"—in other words, that you acted reasonably under the circumstances. This is a fact question, depending on such things as the signer's age, education, business experience, and literacy; the nature of the representations made to the signer and the signer's reasons for relying on them; the availability of independent information; and the need to act quickly. If your ignorance was "excusable," you have a real defense, good even as against an HDC; otherwise, you don't.

Discharge in Bankruptcy. Section 3-305 also spells out a result that should be obvious anyway: the debtor's discharge in bankruptcy or other insolvency proceedings can be asserted against anyone, even the HDC of a negotiable instrument signed by the debtor.

Notice of Other Discharge. A holder can't qualify as an HDC after taking the instrument with notice that *all* parties have been discharged. But it's possible to become an HDC with notice that one or more parties have been discharged, as long as there's no notice that *all* have been. The holder then qualifies as an HDC as to the remaining parties, but can't collect against the ones known to have been discharged when the instrument was transferred. Discharge of an indorser by cancelling his or her signature would be a typical example of this rule. The HDC couldn't collect against that indorser, but would still be an HDC as to all the remaining parties.

Personal Defenses

Since Section 3-305 says that an HDC can enforce an instrument free of "all defenses except" those listed, any other defense against liability on the instrument is only a personal defense. Some of these personal defenses are listed below.

Ordinary Contract Defenses. Any defense a party could assert in a simple contract suit can be asserted against anyone who does not have the rights of an HDC. This general rule would include such things as undue influence, breach of contract by the plaintiff (including any counterclaim by the defendant), and set-offs which the defendant might have from unrelated transactions.

Consideration Defenses. Section 3-303 mentions "issued without consideration" specifically because there is an initial presumption that the negotiable instrument was issued for legally sufficient consideration. If it was not, or if the promised consideration was not properly delivered, the burden of proving the defense is on the defendant. These consideration defenses are only personal ones, and thus they can't be used against an HDC.

Voidable Defenses. Tying back into Section 3-305, any defense based on lack of capacity, duress, or illegality which does not "render the obligation of the party a nullity" (void) is only a personal defense. Remember that minority is a real defense even though the minor's contracts are voidable rather than void.

Fraud in the Inducement. In contrast to fraud in the execution, fraud in the inducement, which is the typical fraud case, provides only a personal defense. Here the party does know that he or she is entering into a contract but is deceived as to the consideration to be received or the other terms and conditions of the contract. Fraud in the inducement also exists where a party could reasonably have discovered the nature of the contract that was signed, but simply didn't bother to read it. The contract was misrepresented, but on the fact there's only a personal defense, and so the HDC collects. Where the parties are consumers, the result in the case would be reversed under the new FTC regulations.

Delivery Defenses. Numerous cases involve irregularities in the delivery or completion of an instrument. Where an instrument has been signed or indorsed in bearer form, the fact that it has been negotiated by a thief or finder will not prevent a later party from being an HDC and collecting on the instrument. The fact that you just signed your check as drawer, intending to fill in the payee's name and the amount later, and that the check was completed by a thief or finder, won't change this result; the HDC still collects. An HDC would also collect where you signed a check and delivered it to your intended payee with instructions to fill in the amount you owed, but your payee filled it in for a larger, unauthorized amount. Finally, an HDC is also protected where a check had been properly filled in and delivered, but delivered subject to some oral condition which is not expressed in the instrument. If the condition is not fulfilled, a defense exists which could be asserted only against someone not having the rights of an HDC.

Agency Defenses. Where someone signing on behalf of a corporation, a partnership, or an individual has general authority to sign negotiable instruments, the fact that a particular instrument was improperly signed is only a personal defense.

FTC REGULATION

Since the courts decided in the early 1970s that the Federal Trade Commission (FTC) could issue rules with industry-wide application, the FTC has been much more vigorous in the consumer protection field. One of the most important and widely discussed FTC rules relates to the HDC status of holders of consumer installment sales contracts. While the rule does not say so in so many words, the net effect is that in most cases all of a consumer's defenses are real defenses. Likewise, no waiver-of-defenses clause in an installment contract for the purchase of goods or services is effective against the consumer-buyer. Holders and assignees are thus remitted to their position under the old common law: The assignee "steps into the shoes of the assignor" and is subject to all available defenses that can be proved by the debtor. While the exact dimensions of this FTC rule are still subject to litigation, revolving charge accounts (such as a Sears charge account) signed before August 1, 1977, and credit card accounts have been exempted from its operation.

ESTOPPEL

It has been, and still is, true that a person with a claim or defense may be estopped by his or her conduct from asserting it. This is as true of real defenses as of personal defenses. If you typically signed your checks with a rubber stamp, and you lost the stamp and didn't bother to alert your bank, you probably ought to get stuck when your bank continues to honor the checks that someone else has prepared in your name with your lost signature stamp. Estoppel clearly applies where you have made out your check or note in such a way as to permit alteration very easily (large, inviting gaps after words and numbers, for example). A more interesting question for litigation is whether gullible persons ought to be permitted to assert the new FTC rule to avoid liability on the notes they signed, or should at some point also be estopped to assert the FTC rule, as well.

DISCHARGE

In addition to the defenses discussed above and the conditions precedent to indorsers' liability discussed in Chapter 21, parties may be discharged from liability on an instrument in several other ways.

Payment. The most obvious and most frequent method of discharge is payment of the instrument to the holder. Perhaps the most important rule for most of us found in Section 3-310(b)(1): "Payment ... of the check results in discharge of the obligation to the extent of the amount of the check." In other words, when your check is paid by your bank, you are discharged of both liability on the check and liability on the underlying debt for which it was given as payment. The one danger point here is that this discharge is not effective against a later HDC of the instrument if the HDC does not have notice of it. If you pay your promissory note, but you don't get it back from the holder, and there's no indication on it that it has been paid or that it's overdue, a later HDC could make you pay it again.

Tender of Payment. Where payment is offered to a holder on or after the due date of the instrument and the holder refuses payment for some reason, the party offering full payment is discharged only to the extent of any additional interest, court costs, or attorney fees later incurred. This rule also applies where the maker or acceptor of a non-demand instrument is ready and able to make payment on the due date at the place or places specified in the instrument, and payment is not demanded by the holder. The holder's refusal of tender discharges any party who has a right of recourse against the party making the tender.

Simple Contract Discharge. As between themselves, any two parties can agree that the liability of one to the other is discharged by any mechanism that is sufficient to discharge liability on a simple contract. All the forms of new agreements discussed in Chapter 14 also apply here: novation, rescission, release, waiver, and accord and satisfaction. Once again, no HDC unaware of these arrangements is bound by them.

Cancellation or Renunciation. As a special negotiable instruments rule, Section 3-604 provides that any holder may discharge any party from further liability on an instrument by destruction or mutilation of the instrument, by cancelling the party's signature, by surrendering the instrument to the party, or by a separate writing signed and delivered to the party. All of these but the last would seem to be sufficient to put third parties on notice of the discharge.

Reacquisition Rules. Because of the very special nature of indorsers' liability, Section 3-207 provides specific rules for the discharge of intermediate parties where someone reacquires an instrument. As against the reacquirer, such parties are discharged. If Arnie, Bernice, and Carole have signed an instrument as indorsers and Arnie reacquires it, he can't sue Bernice or Carole. Arnie could, however, renegotiate the instrument to Donald, who could sue Bernice or Carole if he qualified as an HDC. On the other hand, if Arnie crossed out the signatures of Bernice and Carole, Donald would be on notice that they had been discharged and so he could not sue them either.

Suretyship Rules. As is true under the law of suretyship generally (see Chapter 18), a holder of an obligation who impairs someone's rights of recourse or repayment from another person discharges the party whose rights are impaired. In the above example, if Donald had crossed out Bernice's signature, he would have discharged her from liability on the instrument, thus impairing Carole's rights against Bernice, and so Carole would have also been discharged. A holder can avoid such an "automatic discharge" by expressly reserving rights against the other party (Carole), but when he (Donald) does so, that has the effect of preserving the right of secondary recourse (by Carole against Bernice). Donald can say: "I won't sue Bernice, but I reserve my right to sue Carole." This also preserves Carole's rights to sue Bernice if Carole has to pay Donald.

Likewise, where some piece of property is being used as collateral for an obligation, and through the negligence or intentional conduct of the holder its value is lessened or lost, secondary parties are discharged to that extent.

SIGNIFICANCE OF THIS CHAPTER

Since the major purpose of the merchant community in developing negotiable instruments was to protect holders in due course to whom they had been transferred, and to permit HDCs to enforce them free of most common defenses, an understanding of how one becomes an HDC is crucial to understanding the uses and the significance of commercial paper.

The requirements for HDC status are relatively easy to list but sometimes more difficult in specific fact situations. Always, to be an HDC, one must first be a holder, which means that there can be no required indorsements missing. The holder's good faith is usually assumed, but circumstances may indicate otherwise. It is usually easy enough to determine whether the holder has given value for the instrument. Most litigations seem to center on whether or not the holder had notice of a claim or defense when the instrument was acquired. Generally, one who acquires an instrument from an HDC acquires all the HDC's rights to enforce it, even if the acquirer cannot personally qualify as an HDC. This Shelter Rule thus further protects the HDC, by providing greater marketability for the instrument. Although FTC Regulation 433 has made HDC status less significant in most consumer transactions, it is still very important in all other commercial transactions involving negotiable instruments.

Even HDCs will not necessarily collect every instrument from any party whose name appears on it. Some defenses, such as forgery and material alteration, involve such fundamental irregularities that they can be used against any plaintiff, including an HDC. Others, such as fraud in the inducement, are primarily just difficulties between two of the parties to the instrument and should not be available when an HDC sues to enforce the instrument. Under FTC Regulation 433, consumers are generally able to assert any defense that they can prove to defeat or reduce the claim of any plaintiff. For nonconsumers who have signed negotiable instruments, the distinction between real and personal defenses continues to be important.

In addition to defenses against liability that may be available, both claimants and obligors need to know the circumstances under which an existing liability may be discharged. Here, too, an HDC may be prevented from collecting the instrument from a particular party because that party's liability has been discharged.

PROBLEMS FOR DISCUSSION

1. Middle Georgia bought some stolen cattle at an auction sale and paid for them with a check. When it learned that the cattle were stolen, it ordered its bank to stop payment on the check. Meanwhile, the plaintiff bank had cashed the check for the seller. When payment was refused by the drawee bank, the plaintiff bank sued the drawer, Middle Georgia. Middle Georgia appealed from the trial court's decision against it.

   How should the Appeals Court rule? Explain.

2. Money Mart cashes payroll and government checks for a fee. Epicycle Corporation is a Colorado employer that pays its employees by check. On February 16, Epicycle issued a payroll check, payable to John Cronin, in the amount of $278.59. During the term of his employment, Cronin had borrowed money from Epicycle to be offset by subsequent wages.

   The sequence of events is not clear, but Cronin's employment was terminated, and an Epicycle employee who was unaware of Cronin's indebtedness gave Cronin his final payroll check. Epicycle ordered payment on the check stopped. Cronin cashed the check at one of Money Mart's locations on February 22. Money Mart deposited the check, sending it through normal banking channels. The check was returned to Money Mart marked "Payment Stopped."

   Money Mart brought suit for the amount of the check, claiming that as a holder in due course of the dishonored check, it was entitled to collect from Epicycle.

   Is Money Mart correct? Explain.

3. Graff & Sons, a real estate brokerage partnership represented Fred Klomann in his trading of certain real estate for the Countryside Shopping Plaza. The firm owed Klomann $13,000 as a result and Robert Graff (a partner) gave him three notes, one for $5,000 and two for $4,000 each. Klomann hired Graff & Sons to manage the shopping center and orally promised that the commissions which the firm earned for that work could be offset against the amount that Graff owed him. Robert Graff estimated that his salary of $300 a month (total $14,700) more than offset the firm's debt to Klomann. Klomann specially indorsed the notes to his daughter, Candace Klomann. She examined them and then handed them back to her father so that he could collect them for her. Klomann later scratched out Candace's name, inserted his wife Georgia's name, and delivered the notes to Georgia. Georgia sued to collect. The trial court ruled that the money earned by Robert as manager of the shopping center could not be offset against the money that Graff & Sons owed Klomann and it entered a summary judgment for Georgia.

    Is the trial court correct? Why or Why not?

4. On October 31, Armand Korzenik's law firm had received $15,000 in trade acceptances from its client, Southern New England Distributing Corporation, "as a retainer for services to be performed." Korzenik had been retained by Southern on October 25 in connection with certain antitrust litigation. He did some work for Southern from October 25 to October 31, but there was no evidence as to its value. He also paid co-counsel in the antitrust case some money, but there was no indication of the specific amount. Korzenik sued to collect on two of the trade acceptances due November 1 and December 1, in a total amount of $1,900. Southern had defrauded Supreme, although Korzenik didn't know that when he took the trade acceptances. The lower courts found for Southern New England Distributing Corporation.

    What decision on appeal, and why?

5. Apparently as a result of irregularities in its earlier dealings with customers, Kroyden Industries was under an injunctive order from a New Jersey court not to engage in certain sales practices in connection with the sale of carpeting. In violation of this injunction an employee of Kroyden told Andrew and Anna Berenyi that they could have $1,100 worth of new carpeting in their home if they referred other customers to Kroyden. The Berenyi's bought the carpeting and signed a negotiable promissory note for $1,521, with the understanding that they would receive credit for each referral they made. The note was negotiated to plaintiff, a holder in due course. When the note was signed neither the state nor the FTC had a consumer protection regulation in force. Anna Berenyi appeals from a trial court judgment for the plaintiff; Andrew is now deceased.

    How should the appeal be decided? Explain.

Chapter 23

Bank Deposits and Collections

Commercial banking in the United States is a huge industry. The nation's 10,000-plus commercial banks hold over $1 *trillion* in assets. Banks are responsible for funding many business purchases of land, buildings, and equipment and also provide many other services to business. The banking industry has been subjected to a considerable amount of governmental regulation, but the early 1980s saw a movement toward de-regulation of many banking operations. This chapter will not attempt to cover all of the various banking regulations but will focus instead on Article 4 of the UCC, Bank Deposits and Collections. Article 4 sets out the basic legal rules for the relationship between a bank and its customers and for the processing of negotiable (and non-negotiable) instruments.

CHECKS: THE COLLECTION PROCESS

Clearinghouses and Federal Reserve Banks. The next time you get back a cancelled check that you've sent to an out-of-state creditor (a book club or a record club, for example), take a look at its reverse side. All of those funny multicolored stamps indicate that your humble little check has passed through several banks, and goodness knows how many computers, on its way back to you.

If both the payee and the drawer do business at the same bank, the collection process is quite simple: out of one account and into the other. If both are in the same city, but are customers of different banks, a local clearinghouse association of banks probably handles the collection of the check. At the end of each business day, if a bank has presented more (total dollar) items for payment than have been presented against it, it gets a check for the difference from the clearinghouse. If the reverse is true, it writes a check for the total dollar difference to the clearinghouse.

Many "correspondent" bank arrangements also exist for collecting checks and other items, particularly between large metropolitan banks and smaller banks in the same region. The small local bank receiving a check for collection would forward it to its large correspondent bank, which would in turn present it directly to the payor bank or would forward it through one of the thirteen federal reserve banks if the payor bank were located in a different federal reserve district.

Your check to your out-of-state creditor might pass through a local bank, a large nearby metropolitan bank, a federal reserve bank in that district, a federal reserve bank in your district, a large metropolitan bank close to your bank, and finally get presented at your bank for payment (by which time you had better have the money in your account). Over $50 million worth of checks is probably "floating" through this national collection process on any given day. In 1990, when Article 4 was revised, the American Bankers Association estimated that fifty billion checks were being written each year. It's therefore obvious that banks (and their customers) need a set of legal rules to ensure that this process goes smoothly.

The *Campbell Leasing* case illustrates some of the legal problems which may occur when the collection process doesn't "go smoothly."

CAMPBELL LEASING, INC. v. FDIC
901 F.2d 1244 (5th Cir. 1990)

FACTS: Appellants Campbell Leasing, Inc., Eagle Airlines, Inc., and George A. Day challenge the district court's entry of summary judgment on a promissory note in favor of the Federal Deposit Insurance Corporation (FDIC) and NCNB Texas National Bank (NCNB).

On February 16, 1984, Campbell Leasing, Inc. executed a promissory note in the amount of $136,804.24, plus interest, payable to RepublicBank Brownwood. To secure payment of the note, Campbell Leasing granted RepublicBank a security interest in a 1979 Piper airplane. RepublicBank also obtained the personal guarantee of George A. Day.

In May of 1986, Campbell Leasing defaulted on the note. RepublicBank accelerated the maturity of the note after Campbell Leasing failed to cure its default. On June 12, 1986, RepublicBank seized the airplane but did not gain possession of its maintenance records or flight logs. The seizure prompted appellants to file this lawsuit. RepublicBank counterclaimed for payment of the note, plus interest, costs, and attorneys' fees.

On July 29 1988, the successor to RepublicBank, First RepublicBank Brownwood, N.A. was declared insolvent and closed. The Comptroller of Currency appointed the FDIC as receiver. The FDIC entered into a purchase and assumption agreement with a federally established bridge bank, which purchased the promissory note, security agreement, and guarantee at issue in this case. The bridge bank became NCNB Texas National Bank.

In August of 1988, the FDIC and NCNB removed the case to federal court and filed a motion for summary judgment.

The district court granted summary judgment for NCNB and the FDIC, concluding that all of the appellants' claims and affirmative defenses were barred by the holder in due course doctrine.

 CHIEF JUDGE CLARK:

The federal holder in due course doctrine bars the makers of promissory notes from asserting various "personal" defenses against the FDIC in connection with purchase and assumption transactions involving insolvent banks.... The protection extends to subsequent holders of the notes....

In this case, the appellants assert various defenses and counterclaims to liability on the note. They contend that RepublicBank tortiously interfered with their efforts to lease the Piper airplane to a third party and delayed too long after the plane's seizure before attempting to sell it. They maintain that the note could have been completely discharged absent RepublicBank's wrongful actions. They also claim that RepublicBank elected to keep the airplane in full satisfaction of the note and caused Day to suffer mental and emotional distress. Because these are "personal" rather than "real" defenses to liability on the note ... the FDIC and NCNB as holders in due course acquired the note free of these claims....

The appellants ... argue that the FDIC and NCNB do not qualify as holders in due course under Texas law because they acquired the note in a bulk transaction by legal process and had notice that the note was overdue.... We reject these contentions.

We find no logical reason to limit federal holder in due course protection to the FDIC in its corporate capacity, to the exclusion of its receivership function. In its corporate capacity, the FDIC is obligated to protect the depositors of a failed bank, while the FDIC as receiver must also protect the bank's creditors and shareholders.... In both cases, the holder in due course doctrine enables the FDIC to efficiently and effectively fulfill its role, thus minimizing the harm to depositors, creditors, and shareholders.... We conclude that the FDIC enjoys holder in due course status as a matter of federal common law whether it is acting in its corporate or its receivership capacity.

In addition, the FDIC and subsequent note holders enjoy holder in due course status whether or not they satisfy the technical requirements of state law. The court in *Wood* assumed that the FDIC did not qualify as a holder in due course under state law, yet it still held that the FDIC was entitled to the protections of a holder in due course as a matter of federal common law.... We reached the same conclusion with respect to the FDIC....: This rule "promotes the necessary uniformity of law in this area while it counters individual state laws that would frustrate [basic FDIC objectives]...."

However, the district court erred in granting summary judgment against the appellants on all their claims. The appellants have a statutory right to continue their action against the FDIC as receiver for First RepublicBank on their claims of tortious interference with contract, breach of the Campbell Leasing security agreement, and intentional infliction of mental and emotional distress.... While the holder in due course doctrine prevents the appellants from asserting these claims as a set-off to liability on the note, it does not prevent the appellants from trying these claims to the district court, liquidating the amount of damages, and subsequently receiving a prorata share of First RepublicBank's remaining assets along with the bank's other creditors.... We therefore must vacate that part of the district court's judgment dismissing the appellants' breach of contract and tort claims and remand for additional proceedings....

The summary judgment proof amply demonstrates that the FDIC and NCNB have acted in a commercially reasonable manner with respect to the aircraft. Nothing in the Texas Uniform Commercial Code establishes a set time limit for disposing of repossessed collateral, except for consumer goods.... The FDIC and NCNB have reasonably waited to sell the airplane until the appellants come forward with the maintenance records and flight logs. These records are essential in order to obtain the highest and best price for the aircraft. The appellants have also contributed to prolonging the process by keeping the FDIC and NCNB in continuous litigation on this matter. We reject as disingenuous appellants' suggestion at oral argument that they at all times desired that the FDIC and NCNB sell the airplane. Finally, the appellants produced no evidence to support their allegation that the FDIC and NCNB have allowed the airplane to deteriorate or to be damaged. The district court properly granted summary judgment in favor of the FDIC and NCNB on this issue.

We vacate that part of the district court's judgment dismissing the appellants' claims against the FDIC as receiver for First RepublicBank for tortious interference with contract, breach of the security agreement, and infliction of emotional distress, and we remand for further proceedings consistent with this opinion. We affirm the judgment in all other respects.

Banks Under Article 4. To better spell out the rights and duties of banks in the collection process, Article 4 defines different categories of banks according to their function in the various stages of that process. A **depositary bank** is "the first bank to take an item even though it is also the payor bank," unless the item is presented for immediate payment over the counter. (The depositor, usually the payee/creditor of the drawer, or possibly a later holder of the instrument, takes the item to his or her bank and either cashes it or deposits it.)

The **payor bank** is the bank which is the drawee of a draft. (In the simplest case, where both the drawer and the "depositor" have accounts at the same bank, no other banks will be involved.) An **intermediary bank** is any bank "to which an item is transferred in course of collection except the depositary or payor bank." (In our earlier example, the correspondent banks and the federal reserve banks would be intermediary banks.)

Where the depository bank is not also the payor bank, it and all intermediary banks are also called **collecting banks**. (They're collecting, or trying to collect, your paycheck for you.) The last bank in the collection process, the one that actually presents the item to the payor/drawee for payment, is called the **presenting bank**. (A payor bank presenting the item to itself is excluded from this definition.)

DEPOSITOR AND DEPOSITARY BANK

Agency Relationship. In the normal transaction, the depositor remains the owner of the check or other item which is being processed for collection by his or her bank. This rule protects the depositary and intermediary banks by leaving all the risks of ownership of the item with the depositor.

All the banks in the collection process are protected so long as they exercise reasonable care in processing the item. This basic rule applies unless there is a clear agreement otherwise, regardless of the form of the indorsement or of the fact that the depositor is permitted to make withdrawals against these funds.

Withdrawals of Deposited Funds. A cash deposit can be withdrawn "as a matter of right" at the opening of the next banking day following its receipt by the bank unless the bank has the right to offset the deposited funds against amounts owed it by the depositor/customer. Where the deposit is in the form of a check or other instrument, however, the credit to the customer's account is only **provisional**; that is, the credit is subject to revocation if the instrument is not honored when it is presented to the drawee bank. The depositor/customer thus does not have the right to withdraw these funds until the depositary bank has received a "final statement" for the item (4-214 and 4-215). Where the depositary bank is also the payor bank and the item is paid from the drawer's account, the depositor/customer has the right to withdraw the funds at the opening of the second banking day following receipt of the item.

CUSTOMER/DEPOSITOR/HOLDER (AND COLLECTING BANKS AS AGENTS) AND PAYOR BANKS

As between the holder of an instrument who is trying to collect on it and the payor/drawee bank that is supposedly going to pay it when it's presented, the most important rule is found in Article 3: "A check or other draft does not of itself operate as an assignment of any funds in the hands of the drawee available for its payment, and the drawee is not liable on the instrument until the drawee accepts it" (3-408). Even if the money is in the drawer's checking account, in other words, the drawee bank owes no direct duty to the *holder* to pay the instrument. The drawee bank may be liable to its customer, the drawer, for a wrongful dishonor of the instrument, but that does not mean that the holder/depositor has any direct claim against the payor bank.

Obviously, a drawee bank which has certified a check or accepted a draft is primarily liable on it to the holder thereof and can be sued if it doesn't pay the check or draft when it is properly presented.

CUSTOMER/DEPOSITOR/HOLDER AND DRAWER

If a deposited item is not paid, for whatever reason, the holder who deposited the item for collection may proceed against the drawer on the basis of secondary contract liability, subject to the rules discussed in Chapter 21. In addition, the depositor/holder may have a case against one or more of the collecting banks, where their negligent mishandling of the instrument was the reason for its dishonor. However, a collecting bank is not liable solely on the basis of some prior bank's mishandling of the instrument; its own negligence must be established.

DRAWER/CUSTOMER AND DRAWEE/PAYOR BANK

Article 4 also provides some detailed rules for handling the problems that may occur between a drawer and the drawee bank.

Charging Items Against Customer's Account. The drawee bank has a general contractual duty to its drawer/customer to pay items when presented, assuming that there are sufficient funds in the account. As a general rule, when the drawee bank does pay such items in good faith, it can charge the items against the customer's account. Even if an item causes an overdraft to a customer's account, the drawee/payor bank may honor the item anyway, and it has a claim against its customer for the amount of the overdraft.

The general rule for paying overdrafts is, however, subject to some important exceptions. The key phrase in Section 4-401 is "properly payable from that account." If the drawer's signature has been forged, the instrument is *not* "properly payable" from the drawer's account, and the bank will have to put the money back even if it paid in good faith. The same result occurs where the required signature of an indorser is forged; the money must be returned to the drawer's account because the bank has not paid the right party. If the instrument has been materially altered, the bank that has paid it can charge the drawer's account only "according to the original tenor of the altered item." The drawer's own negligence may prevent the assertion of any of these irregularities against the drawee bank unless the bank was also negligent in paying the item; that is, the bank did not pay in good faith and according to reasonable commercial standards. These rules are at issue in the next case.

TRUST CO. BANK v. STATE OF ALABAMA (TRS)
420 So.2d 10 (AL, 1982)

FACTS: State of Alabama, Teachers' Retirement System of Alabama (TRS), and others filed suit against defendant, Trust Company Bank, a Georgia chartered state bank, for breach of statutory warranty under §7-4-207. Between February 1972 and August 1980, plaintiff, State of Alabama, issued warrants on the Alabama state treasury for retirement benefits to Jacob T. Williams, a retired teacher who died 7 January 1971. The warrants were sent through the United States mail to the payee in Gadsden, Alabama, at the address printed on the warrants. Defendant, as a collecting bank, from time to time presented to the treasurer of the State of Alabama for payment certain of those warrants drawn on the Teachers' Retirement System Funds on deposit with the state treasurer and received payment for them in spite of the fact they bore forged indorsements of the payee, in breach of the warranty provided by §7-4-207.

In its answer, the Bank admitted the breach, but denied liability on the basis of one of several affirmative defenses: (1) those warrants presented and paid more than six years next before the filing of this action were barred by the statute of limitations, (2) plaintiffs failed to make a claim for breach of warranty within a reasonable time after they learned or should have learned of the breach, and (3) plaintiffs are barred from asserting the forgery because they were guilty of negligence substantially contributing to the making of the forged indorsements.

The trial court granted plaintiffs' motion for summary judgment and entered judgment in their behalf for the sum of $28,115.24 plus interest and denied the Bank's motion for summary judgment. This appeal by the Bank is from the 8 October 1981 order.

Jacob T. Williams, a teacher and principal in the Gadsden city school system, became a member of TRS on 25 January 1941 and continued a member thereof until his death. He retired on disability in December 1968, at which time TRS began sending monthly retirement warrants payable to him to 804 North Eighth Street, Gadsden. Although he died on 7 January 1971, the retirement system was not notified of his death and continued to send his retirement benefits to his home address noted above.

Beginning in November 1973, Lewis Williams, a resident of Atlanta and the son of Jacob T. Williams, deposited these warrants into his, Lewis', account with defendant Bank in Atlanta, after first forging the indorsement of his deceased father. Lewis continued this practice monthly until 31 December 1979, by which time TRS warrants totalling $28,115.24 had been deposited into his account.

On or about 1 October 1980, the U.S. Postal Service Inspector at Gadsden contacted the superintendent of schools there and informed him the retirement benefit checks were being mailed and delivered to a person whom the post office suspected was deceased: Jacob T. Williams. The superintendent confirmed Mr. William's death and immediately notified the Teachers' Retirement System in Montgomery. TRS turned the matter over to the Alabama Bureau of Investigation and notified the state treasurer of the forgeries. Following an indictment of Lewis Williams, the state treasurer made a demand upon the Bank for repayment of the warrants. The Bank refused to do so. As a result, plaintiffs filed this suit.

 JUSTICE EMBRY:

Appellant Bank's first assignment of error is that the trial court erred in failing to grant its motion for summary judgment based on the assertion of the statute of limitations as a bar to recovery for warrants paid prior to 6 March 1975, more than six years before this action was filed. The Bank's contention is that TRS cannot recover for the warrants paid prior to 6 March 1975 because, as a matter of law, any recovery is barred by § 6-2-34, 7-2-34, Code 1975, which provides: "The following must be commenced within six years: (9) Actions upon any simple contract or specialty not specifically enumerated in this section." We agree and reverse as to that question.

The Alabama Uniform Commercial Code ... does not have an express statute of limitations governing actions for breach of warranty; the general statute of limitations governing action on contracts controls....

The period of limitation governing this cause of action begins to run from the time of the wrongful payment, not from the time of the discovery of the breach....

The plaintiffs contend that: (1) the sole limitation upon actions for breach of warranty is §7-4-207(4) [now 4-207(d)], providing that an action for breach of warranty must be brought within a reasonable time after learning of the breach; and (2) if the six-year statute is applicable, it is tolled by the fraud of the forger until discovery of that fraud. We find both of these contentions erroneous. First, § 7-4-207 is a separate limitation in the nature of laches or estoppel, quite different from the ordinary statute of limitations. Second, plaintiffs' cause of action is against *the Bank* for breach of warranty, not fraud. In this case, we do not find any evidence that the Bank committed fraud in connection with its breach of warranty....

We need not address the issue of negligence or whether the claim for breach of warranty was made within a reasonable time, because a thorough review of the record indicates there are triable issues of fact with respect to appellant's contentions. In light of this, we conclude that summary judgment was inappropriate. The law in Alabama is clear, and there is little need for citation of authority for the rule, that summary judgment is only proper where it is clear what the truth is; there must not be a genuine issue as to any material fact....

For the reasons stated, this case is remanded to the trial court for trial on its merits except as to those claims involving the warrants presented, and paid, more than six years next before the filing of this action. Further, judgment as to those warrants should be entered in favor of the Trust Company Bank by the trial court upon the receipt of certificate of judgment.

Wrongful Dishonor. Whether mistakenly ("computer error") or intentionally, the drawee bank may dishonor an instrument which it should have paid. When this happens, the drawer is at least temporarily embarrassed since his or her good credit is impugned when the check bounces. If this happens by an honest mistake, Article 4 protects the drawee bank by providing that the drawer can recover only damages which were "proximately caused" and "actually proved;" there will be no punitive damages, in other words, for a simple mistake by the drawee bank. Further, the dishonor of a check is not per se defamation of a drawer's reputation, so that actual damages must be proved there too. Finally, damages resulting from the arrest and prosecution of the drawer under an "insufficient funds" criminal statute may be recovered from the drawee bank *if* they are proved to have been proximately caused by the dishonor.

The issue in the *Osten Meat* case is whether the bank had legal grounds for dishonoring the letter of credit it had issued.

OSTEN MEAT v. FIRST OF AMERICA
517 N.W.2d 742 (MI App., 1994)

FACTS: Plaintiff appeals from a judgment of the circuit court entered in favor of defendant on plaintiff's claim against defendant for wrongful dishonor of a letter of credit.

On May 17, 1989, at the request of its customer, Swenehart's Zero Foods, Inc., defendant issued an irrevocable stand-by letter of credit for the benefit of plaintiff. The letter of credit provided that defendant would honor one or more sight drafts, not exceeding $150,000 in total, accompanied by:

1. Copy of unpaid invoice(s) from May 16, 1989 or subsequently.

2. An affidavit purportedly executed by an officer of Osten Meat Co. reading exactly as follows:

Reference is made to Letter of Credit No. 65469 issued by First of America Bank-Southeast Michigan, N.A. in favor of Osten Meat Co.

The undersigned deposes and says:

1. Swenehart's Zero Foods has failed to pay in full for the shipment of merchandise described in the attached invoice(s).

2. The amount of the attached sight draft is not in excess of the amount owed to Osten Meat Co. by Swenehart's Zero Foods.

The letter of credit also provided that the original of the letter of credit must be submitted whenever a partial draw on the letter of credit was requested.

On or about January 25, 1990, plaintiff requested a full draw of $150,000 pursuant to the letter of credit. With the request, plaintiff submitted: (1) a sight draft in the amount of $150,000, and (2) copies of invoices from plaintiff to Swenehart's after May 16, 1989. An affidavit of Werner Osten, the president of plaintiff.

In a letter dated February 5, 1990, defendant advised plaintiff that it would not honor the letter of credit because of the following discrepancies:

1. Original Letter of Credit No. 65469 not presented as required.

2. Documents inconsistent with one another:

   Invoices reference Letter of Credit Number different than sworn affidavit.

3. Invoices 57040-00—$6,076.69 marked PAID, 48439-00—$24,384.26 marked PAID, Check #2248 55922-00—$7,000.00 marked PAID, Personal Money Order #501548.

Plaintiff did not resubmit documents before the letter of credit expired.

 PRESIDING JUDGE SAWYER:

To resolve the dispute, we must first determine the Michigan standard for determining whether documents submitted in conjunction with a draw on a letter of credit are sufficient. Two standards have emerged in other jurisdictions, namely, (1) strict compliance with the terms of the letter of credit, and (2) mere substantial compliance. This appears to present a question of first impression in Michigan. However, we are persuaded that the defendant is correct that we should follow the rule of strict compliance.

A letter of credit is "an engagement by a bank ... made at the request of a customer ... that the [bank] will honor drafts or other demands for payment upon compliance with the conditions specified in the credit...."

A letter of credit is a contract between the bank and the beneficiary of the credit that is separate and distinct from the commercial contract between the beneficiary, usually the seller, and the bank's customer, usually the buyer.... The letter of credit is not tied to or dependent upon the underlying commercial transaction, and in determining whether to pay, the bank looks only at the letter and the documentation the beneficiary presents to determine whether the documentation meets the requirements in the letter....

There is no Michigan statute or case law that illuminates what standard is to be used in determining whether documents submitted by a beneficiary are in compliance with the terms of the letter of credit. Nor is there a standard set forth in the

Uniform Customs and Practice for Documentary Credits (1983 rev.), International Chamber of Commerce, Brochure No. 400 (UCP), which frequently governs letters of credit and which does so in this case....

Case law outside Michigan is split on the issue. The majority position is that the standard is one of strict compliance: the papers, documents, and shipping descriptions must be as stated in the letter of credit.... This standard leaves "no room for documents which are almost the same or which will do just as well...."

A minority of cases do hold that a beneficiary's reasonable or substantial performance of the letter's requirements will do.... We are persuaded that the majority position that a letter of credit must be strictly construed and performed precisely in accordance with its terms is the appropriate rule and should be followed in Michigan.

In a letter of credit transaction, the issuing bank's duty with respect to a letter of credit is purely ministerial. The bank's representative, who knows nothing of the parties, the underlying transaction, or the practices of the industry concerned, checks presented documents carefully against the requirements of the credit. Under a strict compliance standard, if the documents comply, the draft is paid. If there is a discrepancy between the requirements of the letter of credit and the submitted documents, the draft is not paid and the beneficiary is notified of the reason for the dishonor. The beneficiary then has the right to resubmit the correct documents before the credit expires.

A substantial-compliance standard would impose a duty on the bank to investigate the underlying transaction whenever a discrepancy is found between the documents submitted and the credit to determine whether a discrepancy is significant. Such a duty would negate the credit's advantages, that is, its independence from the underlying transaction and the predictability and swiftness of the determination to honor or dishonor a draw request....

Indeed, ultimately, a strict-compliance standard should prove to make the processing of letter of credit transactions more efficient rather than less because a beneficiary will know precisely what documentation must be submitted in support of the draw on the letter of credit and may promptly correct any defects found in those documents. On the other hand, accepting a mere "substantial compliance" standard would cause the waters to be muddied. Each transaction would open itself to questions by the issuer of the letter of credit whether the documentation submitted was sufficient. This would result in delays because it would not be sufficient to answer the question whether there is strict compliance with the terms and conditions of the letter of credit. Rather a determination would have to be made whether the less-than-full compliance would nevertheless be sufficient, a question that might often require the solicitation of legal advice. Similarly, such disputes might often end in litigation, further impairing the efficacy of letter of credit transactions. In the long run, we are persuaded that the majority rule of strict compliance makes sense and will make the handling of letter of credit transactions more efficient, both from a commercial and a legal viewpoint....

[D]efendant's dishonor of the sight draft was proper if any of the defects cited as reasons for the dishonor are appropriate....

The third reason cited by defendant for dishonoring the draft was that certain invoices submitted with the draft had been marked paid, while the terms of the letter of credit allowed for a draft to be made only for payment of unpaid invoices. Thus, defendant argues, the representation in the affidavit that the invoices were unpaid and the notation on the invoices that they were, in fact, paid created an inconsistency that warranted dishonoring the draft....

Thus, the letter of credit, through its adoption of the UCP, requires that all documents submitted with the draft in support of the letter of credit be consistent on their face and that the submission of inconsistent documents is not in accordance with the terms and conditions of the letter of credit. Thus, the letter of credit did require that all documentation being submitted be consistent with each other on their face. Because the notations on the invoices indicating that they had been paid were inconsistent with the statement in the affidavit that all the attached invoices were unpaid, as well as being inconsistent with the requirements of the letter of credit that the invoices be unpaid, those invoices do not conform with the consistency requirement found in Article 15. Accordingly, they did not strictly comply with the terms and conditions of the letter of credit, and defendant acted properly in refusing to consider those invoices in determining whether there was compliance with the letter of credit.

Stop Payment Orders. A check is an order by the customer/drawer to the drawee/payor bank to pay money to the order of the named payee. At least until the check is certified by the drawee bank, the drawer has the right to stop payment, in other words, to countermand the original order. An oral stop-pay order is valid for only fourteen calendar days unless it is reconfirmed in writing within that period. A written stop-pay order is valid for six months unless it is similarly reconfirmed. In either case, the stop-pay order must be received by the drawee/ payor bank "at a time and in a manner that affords the bank a reasonable opportunity to act on it before any action by the bank with respect to the item" (4-403).

If the drawee/payor bank pays the item anyway, it can still charge its customer's account unless the customer can prove having suffered a loss as a result. (That would be the case, for example, where the customer had a defense which was valid against the holder, so that the holder really shouldn't have gotten the money. The bank would have to put that money back in its customer's account.) Obviously, once a check has been certified, the customer loses the right to stop payment.

The next case discusses these issues.

NEW COVENANT COMM. CH. v. FED. NAT. BANK
734 P.2d 1318 (OK App., 1987)

FACTS: On June 30, 1982, the defendant, Federal National Bank and Trust Company of Shawnee, Oklahoma ("Bank"), issued a cashier's check in the amount of $325,000 to the New Covenant Community Church ("Church") and Living Way Ministries Church ("Living Way") as payees. Living Way was the purchaser of the cashier's check and a named payee. Living Way promptly negotiated and endorsed the cashier's check to Church in satisfaction of a previously incurred obligation. On July 1, 1982, with proper endorsement, Church deposited the check in its account with the Penn Square Bank in Oklahoma City. The following day, July 2, 1982, Penn Square Bank was closed by the Federal Deposit Insurance Corporation.

Immediately upon learning of the demise of Penn Square Bank, both Church and Living Way made demand on Bank to stop payment on the cashier's check. Bank informed them it could not stop payment. The check was presented to Bank for payment sometime after July 2, 1982. Due to the failure of Penn Square Bank, Church lost $215,262.20 of the $325,000.

Church then brought this action against Bank for recovery of the $215,262.20 and punitive damages in the amount of $1,000,000. Bank filed an answer and its dismissal motion based on grounds set out above. The trial court sustained the motion. From that order, Church appeals. Living Way was not a party below or to this appeal.

 JUDGE GARRETT:

The Oklahoma Code Comment following 12A O.S.A. § 4-403, in pertinent part, is as follows:

> Any ... notice or stop-order received by, ... a payor bank, whether or not effective under other rules of law to terminate, suspend or modify the bank's right or duty to pay an item ... comes too late to so terminate, suspend or modify such right or duty if the ... notice or stop-order ... is received ... and a reasonable time for the bank to act thereon expires or the setoff is exercised after the bank has....
>
> (a) accepted or certified the item....

Section 3410(1) defines acceptance as the "drawee's signed engagement to honor the draft as presented.... It becomes operative when completed by delivery or notification."

Here, the drawee Bank's signed engagement to honor the draft was contemporaneous with its act of issuing the cashier's check. That is, it both issued and accepted the check at the same time. The acceptance became operative upon delivery of the check to Living Way and Church. Living Way, as stated, endorsed its rights in the check to Church. Thus, any stop payment order from Church which came after the date of issuance of the check on June 30, 1982, came after the check was accepted, and violated the provisions of § 4-303(1)(a). We hold that under the UCC as applied to the facts at bar, Church could not have requested a stop order to Bank after June 30, 1982, because it came after the acceptance of the check by the defendant Bank....

As a general rule, neither a bank nor a bank customer may order a stop payment on a cashier's check.

We are not persuaded by Church's argument to apply the common law where the Uniform Commercial Code is silent. The Official Comment to 12A O.S.A. 1981 3-101 states:

> The Article [3 of the UCC governing the case at bar] represents a complete revision and modernization of the Uniform Negotiable Instruments Law.... Needless to say, in the fifty odd years of the history of that statute [codifying common-law principles], there have been vast changes in the commercial practices relating to the handling of negotiable instruments. The need for revision was felt for some years before the present project was undertaken.

We find no UCC, contractual or common-law duty to Church was breached by Bank. Therefore, that portion of the trial court order sustaining the defendant Bank's motion to dismiss for failure to state a claim upon which relief could be granted is affirmed.

Having thus ruled on the Appellant church's first proposition, we need not address its proposition regarding the statute of limitations.

Stale Checks. Where an uncertified check has been circulating for more than six months, the drawee/payor bank is under no obligation to its checking account customer to pay the check. The bank may dishonor the check without any liability for damage even if there is enough money in the account to cover it. If the bank does pay the stale check, in good faith, it may charge the item against its customer account. It's completely up to the bank, as long as the bank acts in good faith.

Customer's Death or Incompetence. The Code's rules generally protect a bank from liability in the case where the customer dies or becomes legally incompetent. "Neither death nor incompetence of a customer revokes [a bank's] authority to accept, pay, collect or account until the bank knows of the fact of death or of an adjudication of incompetence and has reasonable opportunity to act on it" (4-405). Moreover, a bank, even after learning of its customer's death, may pay or certify previously issued checks for a period of ten days, unless ordered not to by someone claiming an interest in the account. A customer's bankruptcy probably does not terminate the bank's authority to process items until the bank has knowledge or notice of it.

Customer's Duty to Inspect Statements. When a bank makes available an itemized statement and the cancelled items, its customer has a duty to exercise reasonable care and promptness in inspecting the charges and reporting any improper ones to the bank. Failure to do so may prevent a customer from forcing the bank to put money back in the account where an item has been altered or paid over a forged signature or indorsement. However, if the bank failed to exercise ordinary care in paying an item (for example, if it paid an item that was obviously altered), the customer could still force the bank to put the money back into the account. Finally, whether the customer, the bank, or both were guilty of negligence, this section protects the bank by imposing a one-year statute of limitations period for claims of alteration or forgery of the drawer's signature. In other words, if you don't notify the bank of irregularities within that time period, you can't make it put the money back in your account even if your signature on the check was forged. The lesson is clear: *Read your bank statement and verify your checks right away.*

Bank's Right to Subrogation. The drawee/payor bank is further protected by being subrogated to the rights of other parties where it has made a payment despite a stop order or under other circumstances where the drawer or maker has "a basis for objection." Where such an "improper" payment has occurred, the bank steps into the shoes of: (1) an HDC, as against the drawer or maker; (2) the payee or any other holder, as against the drawer or maker, either on the paid item itself or on the underlying transaction; and (3) the drawer or maker, as against the payee or any other holder on the underlying transaction. In other words, if the bank has paid someone when it should not have done so, it shouldn't get stuck for the money but should have recourse against another party. The only problem may be finding that other party.

ELECTRONIC FUNDS TRANSFER

Just as the use of checks and credit cards has made us, to a very large extent, a "cashless" society, use of computer-controlled electronic funds transfer (EFT) systems could make us a "checkless" society. With billions of checks being processed each year, the practical need for such a system is very clear. Properly implemented, it could speed payments, reduce errors, and lower costs. However, EFT presents its own set of problems, which the law is just beginning to confront.

Some phases of EFT are already in widespread use; probably the most common is the "24-hour money machine," located at bank branches and even many supermarkets, where a customer can use a magnetic card to receive cash, make deposits, pay bills, and transfer funds between accounts. Another frequently used EFT system makes direct deposits of paychecks to employees' bank accounts. More recently, banks have begun to offer their customers the option of paying bills with a telephone call to the bank's computer system; this method saves the customer's time and money. Not yet widely adopted is the most revolutionary EFT system: immediate payment from the customer's checking account through point-of-sale computer terminals located in stores.

It's not hard to imagine some of the problems involved in implementing each of these EFT systems. Inevitably, some customers who fear that they will lose control of their money will resist the change. Some workers like to see their actual paycheck, if only for a few minutes on the way to the bank. (Anyone who has ever been paid by an employer in cash can probably appreciate the different feeling you get from being able to actually see what you've earned in your own hands.)

The money machines are a great convenience, but they also involve security risks late at night and the possibility of lost cards and unauthorized withdrawals. The major difficulty involved with the point-of-sale payment, aside from the loss of the float period which would exist if the bills were totalled once a month and mailed out, is preserving consumer defenses where defective merchandise or services are delivered.

New legal rules to deal with these and other problems have been proposed, both as amendments to the UCC and as separate legislation. New laws have such provisions as: (1) the bank must send each customer a written agreement which includes rights of EFT card users, (2) the bank must provide a monthly statement of all EFT transactions to the customer, (3) the customer must be given a receipt for each EFT transaction, (4) the bank is liable for unauthorized use of the EFT card in the machine unless the customer has been negligent, (5) the bank may not send out unsolicited EFT cards unless the recipients are already its customers, and (6) the bank may not release a customer's financial records without the customer's permission or a court order. These statutes may provide civil and criminal penalties for violation by the bank.

The entire area of electronic funds transfer will continue to challenge the ingenuity of judges, lawyers, and legislators.

SIGNIFICANCE OF THIS CHAPTER

Since most individuals and nearly all businesses issue and receive checks in significant numbers, we must have a clear set of rules for processing these instruments. Article 4 of the UCC supplements the general rules for commercial paper found in Article 3 by outlining the relationships between check issuers, check depositors, and the banks involved in the check collection process. Article 4 spells out the rules for charging a customer's checking account and the circumstances under which the drawee bank has to put the money back in the account. In general, in dealing with their customers, banks will not incur liability if they act in good faith and with reasonable care. Even if they do, however, they may still be liable in cases involving forgery or alteration of instruments. For customer-depositors, it is important to have adequate internal financial controls and to verify bank statements and canceled items promptly.

PROBLEMS FOR DISCUSSION

1. On October 10, Granite drew a check against its account at Hempstead, made payable to Overseas Equipment Company. Five days later, when Overseas notified Granite that it had not received the check, Granite issued a written stop-pay order on the check and directed Hempstead to simply wire the funds directly to Overseas. Hempstead did so. Granite never renewed its stop-pay order. On November 10, the original check was presented for payment. Without any notice or inquiry to Granite, Hempstead simply paid the stale check and charged Granite's account.

   Was Hempstead correct in doing so? Explain.

2. K.C. Jones, the manager of Cairo's branch in Cunningham, was authorized to draw checks against Cairo's account. From September 30, 1998, to March 6, 1999, Jones drew 101 checks for various amounts to various customers of Cairo. Jones forged the customers' signatures on ten of these checks and cashed them. As to these checks, Cairo made no claim for reimbursement from its bank. As to the other ninety-one checks, after forging the customers' indorsements, Jones used the co-op's own restrictive endorsement stamp, which read: "Pay to the order of First Bank, Cunningham, Kansas. For Deposit only, Cairo Co-Op Equity Exchange, Farmer's Co-Op." Jones got a total of $46,564.46 in cash at the bank for these checks. The trial court granted summary judgment for the bank, and Cairo appealed.

   Should Cairo win its appeal? Why or why not?

3. John Mahoney had prepared Antone Silvia's tax returns for over twenty-five years. Mahoney would make out the return and a check for any tax due to the IRS and would then take the documents to Silvia for his signature. In 1987, "apparently in need of some extra cash," Mahoney added $7,000 of nonexistent business profits to Silvia's return, thereby increasing Silvia's tax liability from about $2,000 to $4,625. Mahoney made out one of Silvia's checks to "Internal Revenue Services" and had Silvia sign the check and the return. Mahoney then added "by John J. Mahoney" in the space for the payee's name, indorsed the check "Internal Revenue Services by John J. Mahoney," and exchanged Silvia's check for several cashier's checks at Industrial National Bank. Mahoney used these cashier's checks to pay his personal creditors. Silvia did not notice the alterations made by his accountant when he received the canceled check with his bank statement in February 1988. Silvia first became aware of the problem in April 1989, when the IRS notified him that he had not paid his taxes for 1987. By that time, Mahoney had died. Silvia sued Industrial to force it to recredit his account. The trial court held for the bank; Silvia appealed.

   How should the Appeals Court rule? Explain.

4. Edward and Christine McSweeney, husband and wife, opened a joint checking account with the plaintiff bank in September 1996. Overdrafts commenced almost immediately, but the plaintiff regularly honored the checks. Edward gave the plaintiff two notes, totalling $181,000, to cover the overdrafts and some loans which the bank had made to him. The notes were given in April 1998. Between then and July 1998, when the account was closed, 195 checks were written, totalling $99,063.74. Christine wrote 95, totalling $16,811.43; Edward wrote 100, totalling $82,252.31. After deducting deposits to the account, the cumulative overdraft for this period was $75,983.06. The bank sued Edward on the two notes and sued both McSweeneys for the later overdrafts. The trial court gave summary judgment against Edward on both theories, but refused to enter summary judgment against Christine. Plaintiff bank appeals from this refusal.

   Is Christine liable? Why or why not?

5. On February 27, 1996, FJS Electronics, Inc., trading as Multi-Teck, drew a check in the amount of $1,844.98 on Fidelity Bank. The number of the check was 896 and the payee was Multilayer Computer Circuits. On March 9, 1996, Mr. Frank Suttill, president of Multi-Teck, called Fidelity on the telephone and requested payment on check number 896 be stopped. Mrs. Roanna M. Sanders took the stop payment order. The amount given by Suttill was $1,844.48; otherwise the information he provided was essentially correct. A confirmation notice was subsequently sent to Multi-Teck, reciting the inaccurate amount. and Multi-Teck confirmed all the information it contained. The confirmation notice also contained the request, "PLEASE ENSURE AMOUNT IS CORRECT." The Bank used a computer to pull checks on which stop payment requests had been made. The computer keyed on the amount of the check which was typed in computer digits by the depository Bank on the bottom of each check. The Bank's computer program was designed so that all digits of the amount of the stop payment request had to agree with the computer digits of the amount on the bottom of the check before the check was pulled. The Bank's computer was not programmed to pull checks where there was a discrepancy in a digit of the amount of the stop payment request and the computer digits of the amount on the bottom of the check nor was it designed for stop payment purposes to read the number of the check. The Bank received approximately 100 to 150 stop payment requests a day during 1996.

   On March 15, 1996, check No. 896 was paid by Fidelity, and Multi-Teck's account was charged. This charge resulted in a loss of $1,844.98 to Multi-Teck. The trial court held for Multi-Teck.

   Was the trial court correct? Discuss.

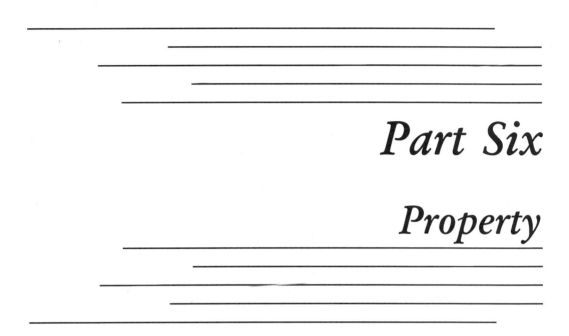

Part Six

Property

The law governing the acquisition, ownership, and disposition of property, both real and personal, is basic to the management of business and of nearly all our personal affairs. Real property cannot be picked up and carried with us from place-to-place, and mere possession is not a presumption of ownership. Also, more than one person may have an ownership interest in real or personal property. Thus, ownership rights have to be defined and different forms of ownership are needed to fit the various situations that may arise in co-ownership.

In our society, we often rent or borrow personal property and lease real property. We need to know the rights and duties each party has in those transactions. Also, since many areas in which we live and work have become densely populated, we can no longer do with our property as we wish if it offends or injures our neighbors. We must, therefore, have land use and environmental regulations. For all these reasons, it is important to understand property rights.

In Part Six, we review the methods of acquisition and disposition of real and personal property and define the various forms of ownership. We examine the law regarding rental or use of personal property belonging to someone else (bailments), scrutinize the rights and duties of landlords and tenants, discuss zoning laws and environmental regulations and how they affect the use of land. We also discuss the increasingly important laws relating to the ownership of intellectual property.

Chapter 24

Forms of Co-Ownership; Personal Property

HUMAN RIGHTS, PROPERTY RIGHTS, AND PERSONAL RIGHTS

You'll often hear people, particularly proponents of regulatory and wealth redistribution schemes, say that "human rights are more important than property rights." That statement is illogical and ridiculous. The *things* that are the subject matter of property rights—cars, books, TVs, parcels of real estate—have no "rights" at all, in and of themselves. Property rights belong to persons, including human beings, corporate persons, and various other kinds of legal entities. Among the most important rights of human beings are property rights—the right to acquire, possess, use, enjoy, and dispose of the things which are the subject of those rights. Your TV set has no "rights;" you do: the rights to acquire it, to watch it when you want to, to turn it off when you want to study, and to sell it or give it away (when it's paid for).

At least equally important is your property right in the results of your labor—the money and other rewards you earn through your physical and mental efforts. Those things are yours because you worked for them, and your "property rights" protect your freedom to save or spend, as you see fit, when you wish, where you wish. Property rights are very important to all of us. They enable us to enjoy music, art, poetry, literature, and all sorts of leisure and productive activity. In short, they are a large part of what separates us from the beasts of the jungle and makes life worth living.

DEFINITION AND CLASSIFICATIONS

Property may be defined as the bundle of rights concerning a specific parcel of land or any other thing of value, tangible or intangible, visible or invisible. Some of the rights included in this bundle are the right to possess, to use, to sell, to lease, to dispose of, or to destroy the land or thing in a legal way, and the right to exclude others from trespassing or interfering with the land or thing.

Since property may be described as the bundle of rights concerning land or a thing, we often find that we do not have absolute or unconditional property, since someone else may have certain rights in the land or thing. For example, the owner of a parcel of land may say, "That is my property," but the parcel of land may be leased to a tenant. Thus, the tenant has property rights in the land—the right to use it and the right to use the proceeds from it according to the terms of the lease contract. Also, a public utility company may have an easement across the parcel of land, allowing it to come in and repair or replace underground or overhead power lines. An **easement** is simply a right to enter someone else's land for a specific purpose. If there are mineral, oil, or gas deposits on the land, those deposits may be owned by a person or persons other than the landowner. Moreover, if the purchaser of the land took out a purchase-money mortgage (i.e., a loan to buy the land), the mortgagee has certain rights in the land as security for payment of the mortgage. Thus, it is not uncommon for several persons to have property rights in the same land.

The *Lewis* case examines the public's rights on private property.

LEWIS v. COLORADO ROCKIES BASEBALL CLUB, LTD.
941 P.2d 266 (Colo., 1997)

FACTS: The Colorado Rockies Baseball Club, Ltd. (Rockies) appeal a judgment by the Denver District Court finding that certain areas around Coors Field baseball stadium are public forum property for free speech purposes and that the Rockies' policies preventing the sale and distribution of any materials in those areas were not reasonable time, place, and manner restrictions. The district court granted an injunction against the Rockies precluding it from restricting vendors in those areas.

Robert Lewis and Bert Matthews (Publishers) publish and distribute "alternative" baseball programs and scorecards outside Coors Field during Colorado Rockies' baseball games. The Rockies lease Coors Field and its surrounding walkways and sidewalks from the Denver Metropolitan Major League Baseball Stadium District, a public entity. Coors Field is a newly constructed baseball stadium that opened for the 1995 baseball season. The Rockies have a long term concession agreement with ARA Leisure Services, Inc. (ARAMARK) which grants ARAMARK exclusive concession rights on the leased premises both inside and outside the stadium. Thus, the Rockies prohibit the sale or distribution of any materials by other vendors in these areas.

During the 1995 baseball season, the Publishers and their vendors were harassed and ticketed for trespass while attempting to distribute programs in certain areas around Coors Field. The specific areas in dispute are the North Walkway, the

Wynkoop Walkway, and the walkway between gates D and E. The North Walkway runs perpendicular from the northeast side of the stadium into and through a paid parking lot, is physically separated from the closest city street by a concrete retaining wall, and is connected by a stairway to the public sidewalk on 22nd Street. The Wynkoop Walkway runs perpendicular from the southeast side of the stadium from gate E to 19th Street. The disputed portion of the Wynkoop Walkway includes the pedestrian footbridge that runs over 20th Street to gate E. The third disputed area is the walkway between gate D and gate E from the corner of Blake and 20th Streets along the third base side of Coors Field.

JUSTICE MULLARKEY:

The federal protection of free speech is guaranteed only against abridgment by the government.... Here, however, the Rockies concede that the restrictions in this case constitute state action such that the constitutional protection of free speech is implicated. While the Rockies are a private entity, Coors Field and the surrounding sidewalks and walkways at issue are owned by a public entity, the Stadium District. Thus the Rockies' policies are subject to applicable constitutional constraints....

Apparently relying on the rational articulated in *Grace*, the district court determined that the sidewalks and walkways surrounding Coors Field are public forum property because "sidewalks and walkways have traditionally been public" and because "Coors Field and its environs are fully integrated into the downtown area." With respect to the North Walkway, however, the district court specifically found that only the first three hundred feet of the North Walkway heading east from the stadium are public.

The Rockies argue that the district court erred as a matter of law when it ruled that the areas in dispute were traditional public forum property. Relying in large part on the Supreme Court's holding in *Kokinda*, the Rockies contend that the disputed areas serve only as a means of ingress and egress for Coors Field patrons. According to the Rockies, the caselaw upon which the district court based its decision pertains only to ordinary public parks, streets, and perimeter sidewalks adjacent to public streets, and does not pertain to what it characterizes as interior, on-premises walkways at issue in this case. We disagree.

Contrary to the Rockies' argument, the record supports the conclusion that, unlike the postal sidewalk in *Kokinda*, the areas in dispute here are not properly categorized as interior, on-premises walkways. In fact, the sidewalks and walkways surrounding Coors Field were specifically designed to be integrated into downtown Denver's street grid. As such, the sidewalks are not used solely for ingress and egress to the stadium but connect with, and essentially function in the same manner as, the municipal sidewalks throughout the downtown area. Further, as in *Grace*, the architectural design and layout of the sidewalks and walkways fail to indicate to the public that they have entered a private area. In this sense, the location of the area in question is important because "separation from acknowledged public areas may serve to indicate that the separated area is ... subject to greater restriction."...

We agree with the Publishers that to a pedestrian standing at the corner of 20th and Blake Streets there is no significant difference between the Blake Street sidewalk, which the Rockies concede is a public forum, and the walkway between gates D & E, which the Rockies claim is not a public forum. Therefore, the disputed area between gates D and E is functionally indistinguishable from the ordinary public sidewalk adjacent to the Blake Street gates. We reach the same conclusion as to the Wynkoop Walkway. The exhibits reveal that the physical characteristics of the Whykoop Walkway fail to indicate to the public that it is a private area.

As noted by the district court, the Rockies' strongest argument under the federal public forum analysis is with the North Walkway. The North Walkway is fifty to sixty feet below the grade level of the surrounding streets with a retaining wall running almost its entire length along Wazee Street. The North Walkway leads from gate A to a paid parking lot that is completely encircled by a security fence. Because gate A and the adjacent outfield portion of the stadium are at the same grade below Wazee Street, the North Walkway is level with gate A. Thus, much of the North Walkway is not easily accessible to the general public. Although the North Walkway is physically separated from the closest city street, it is not completely isolated from the public. A concrete stairway leads from the street level to the North Walkway in front of gate A. The district court concluded that at least part of the North Walkway was a public forum. More specifically, the district court ruled that the area directly in front of gate A and that portion of the North Walkway extending to the east away from gate A, "perhaps as far as three hundred feet" was a public forum. We agree....

The Rockies have identified a number of government interests justifying the restrictive policies at issue. These include concerns about premises liability, crowd control, safety, pedestrian movement, and maximizing revenue. The district court acknowledged that the first four interests articulated by the Rockies were valid and significant, but specifically rejected the notion that economic concerns were appropriate considerations in a free speech analysis....

In this case, we have already concluded that the sidewalks and walkways at issue are public forum property. The Rockies appear to argue that they have some greater interest in generating revenue in the disputed areas because the areas happen to be adjacent to Coors Field, a concededly non-public commercial venture. We find, however, that the ability of the Rockies to generate revenue in these disputed areas is no more significant than that of the Publishers. Further, even if we were to consider the Rockies' economic interest in maximizing revenue, the Rockies have failed to present any concrete evidence that the restrictions in place are necessary to protect them from any significant harm. Therefore, we agree with the district court that the economic interests of the Rockies are not an appropriate consideration at the "significant government interest" stage of a free speech analysis....

The district court found that the Rockies' total ban on vending or distributing was not logically related to the interests of safety and crowd control. The district court pointed out that gate D, which the Rockies concede is the busiest and most congested gate area, had the fewest restrictions in place. Thus, the district court concluded that the total ban on vending in the disputed areas was not narrowly tailored to serve the interests of crowd control, safety, and pedestrian movement....

In conclusion, we find that the district court correctly enjoined the Rockies from enforcing its total ban on vending in various areas around Coors Field. The disputed areas in question are traditional public forum property under a First Amendment free speech analysis. Therefore, the Rockies had the burden of showing that the restrictions on free speech were narrowly tailored to advance significant government interests and that the restrictions left open ample alternative channels of communication. We agree with the district court that the Rockies failed to meet that burden and that the Rockies' policies violated the First Amendment of the United States

Constitution. The policies at issue were not reasonable time, place, and manner restrictions because they were not narrowly tailored and they did not allow for ample alternative channels of communication. Accordingly, we affirm the ruling of the district court to enjoin the Rockies from banning the Publishers from distributing their alternative baseball programs in the disputed areas around Coors Field.

We tend to think of property in terms of tangible and visible objects or things, such as cars, furniture, houses, and land. However, property can be intangible things, such as patents granted by the U.S. patent office or copyrights granted by the U.S. copyright office. Here the property is simply the right to prevent others from using an invention or copying a book, song, or other copyrighted material, and to secure damages from those persons who do so without permission. Patents, copyrights, and other forms of "intellectual property" will be discussed in the next chapter.

Real Property. When we speak of **real property**, we are referring to land, buildings, or permanent fixtures which have been erected on or affixed to the land. Crops, trees, or any other objects that are growing on land are generally considered real property until they are severed from the land.

Personal Property. This term designates anything of value that is subject to ownership and is not classified as real property. **Personal property** can be divided into two classifications, tangible and intangible. **Tangible personal property** includes such items as animals, furniture, books, clothes, jewelry, and business inventories. **Intangible personal property** includes a person's rights in patents, copyrights, shares of corporate stock, insurance policies, and many similar contract rights.

Public Property. **Public property** designates the land and things that are owned by the national government, a state government, a city, or some other political subdivision. Those things are, therefore, considered to be owned by the public. This classification includes parks, public buildings, and the national archives.

Private Property. In contrast to public property, this **private property** belongs to an individual, a corporation, or other private legal entity. The property of Notre Dame University is private property, whereas the property of Iowa State University is public property.

TYPES OF OWNERSHIP

Ownership in Severalty. This is ownership in the name of one person, with no one else having any legal interest in the real or personal property involved.

Tenancy in Common. Here, there are two or more co-owners of real or personal property. Under this type of co-ownership, the co-owners or co-tenants have equal rights to possess and use the property. A co-owner's interest in a tenancy in common may be transferred by a last will and testament. It may be sold without the consent of the other co-owners, and is subject to judicial sale by a creditor who has secured a judgment against the owner.

Tenants in common need not be equal owners. For example, Grandfather had a will which said that all of his property would be divided equally among his children and that any deceased child's share should go to that child's children. When Grandfather died, only one of his children survived him. However, one of the deceased children had five children and the other had four. Thus, one-third of Grandfather's real and personal property went to his surviving child, and the third which was willed to each of his other children was co-owned by their children. All of the heirs are tenants in common, yet the tenants in common do not have equal shares.

In this example, the heirs could continue as tenants in common and any rents or profits from the property would have to be divided in proportion to the share of each person. Alternatively, the entire property or parts of the property could be sold and the money received from the sale would be divided according to each person's proportionate share. In some cases, the property itself might be divided.

In addition to arising from inherited property, tenancy in common may arise when title to real or personal property is transferred to two or more persons and it is not declared to be joint tenancy or tenancy by the entirety.

Don Kohler is claiming "his half" of property allegedly held in tenancy in common.

KOHLER v. FLYNN
493 N.W.2d 647 (ND, 1992)

FACTS: Don Kohler appeals a judgment dismissing his claim against Tangula Flynn for division of assets and debts after their cohabitation ended.

Don and Tangula began living together in May 1990. They kept separate checking accounts, although Don deposited a disputed amount of his sporadic earnings in Tangula's account, resulting in what the trial court termed a "common pot arrangement." The couple bought a mobile home in Tangula's name, with Don making the down payment and Tangula making subsequent payments. They occasionally paid one another's debts, including some incurred before they lived together. Intending to marry, Don and Tangula became engaged and bought an engagement ring for her.

In November 1990, the couple separated, not having married. Soon after, the mobile home and the engagement ring were destroyed by a fire. Tangula collected the fire insurance proceeds.

Don sued Tangula for an accounting of indebtedness and "an equitable share of their joint properties in the form of money," claiming that "the expenditures and pooling of monies and assets were done in anticipation of marriage which did not take place." Tangula counterclaimed, also seeking damages for her expenditures for Don's benefit, for some damage that Don did to the mobile home when he left and for personal property allegedly taken by Don.

After a trial without a jury, the trial court recognized that Don's claim was in the nature of "an audit or an accounting," but found the couple's funds to be "hopelessly intermingled."

The trial court concluded that Don and Tangula "parted with essentially the same assets, or their replacements, they had when they entered into the arrangement." The court dismissed both claims.

 JUSTICE MESCHKE:

This is not a "palimony" case like the notorious decision in *Marvin v. Marvin*.... The *Marvin* plaintiff gave up an entertainment career to live with a well-known actor for seven years, and she sought a share of the actor's property for her services as a "companion, homemaker, housekeeper, and cook...." One scholar summarizes the *Marvin* holding: "The meaning of the Marvin case thus seems to be that living together out of wedlock, *at least for a substantial period*, gives rise to claims on the part of both parties to share in each other's property on some unspecified equitable basis...." Here, Don and Tangula lived together for only six months, anything but "a substantial period," and neither gave up any personal or professional opportunity. Even if we were to consider the *Marvin* precedent, it has no bearing on this case.

Our law on equitable distribution of martial property in a divorce does not fit the breakup of an engagement or living arrangement.... Rather, this case is controlled by the law on partition of property. ND 32-16-01 says:

> When several cotenants hold and are in possession of real or personal property as partners, joint tenants, or tenants in common, in which one or more of them have an estate or inheritance, or for life or lives, or for years, an action may be brought by one or more of such persons for a partition thereof according to the respective rights of the persons interested therein....

Thus, outside of marriage, judicial division of property ordinarily depends on common ownership. In this case, Don and Tangula did not hold any property "as partners, joint tenants, or tenants in common." Thus, Don and Tangula do not qualify for judicial division of their accumulated assets, debts, and mutual gifts.

The general rule is that "[c]ohabitants may bring an action for partition of their property where the[ir] intention was clearly to own their property jointly. Conversely, mere cohabitation is not enough to support a right to partition in the absence of actual joint ownership...." If live-in companions intend to share property, they should express that intention in writing. In this case, their is neither evidence nor a finding that Don auld Tangula intended to own any property together.

The parties argue whether the engagement ring was an unconditional gift. Don cites the view, existing in many states, that an engagement ring is a conditional gift, returnable if the engagement is broken without justification by the donee or terminated by consent and sometimes irrespective of fault.... In some states, a specific statute governs the return of gifts made in contemplation of a marriage that does not take place.... Don alleges that "the ring was thought of as Don's by Tangula," despite the fact that "she did not return it to him" when they separated. Don also claims that Tangula had the risk of the ring's loss by fire while it was in her possession, so that he is entitled to recover its value instead of its return. Tangula counters that Don deserves nothing more, because "[s]he paid on the ring while they were together, and ... would have returned it if she still had it, but the [trial] Court found it to be an unconditional gift." Besides, she says, she lost much more in value than the insurance reimbursed her.

Because the engagement ring was destroyed in the fire and is unavailable, we cannot consider its return. Furthermore, the trial court ruled that, factually neither party was indebted to the other. Since the court found that Don and Tangula each left "with essentially the same assets" they had when they began living together, the possibility of fault by one of the parties in ending the engagement is not relevant to this case.

North Dakota law defines a "gift" as "a transfer of personal property made voluntarily and without consideration...." For a valid gift *inter vivos*, we have said:

> There must be an intention on the part of the donor to relinquish the right of dominion on one hand and to create it on the other, and the delivery must be not only of possession but also of the dominion and control of the property. To have the effect of a valid gift, therefore, the transfer of possession and title must be absolute and go into immediate effect, so far as the donor can make it so by intent and delivery, and must be so complete that if he again resumes control over it without consent of the donee he becomes liable as a trespasser....

Here, both parties acknowledge that Don bought the ring for Tangula, despite her installment payments on it while they were together. Regardless of other arguments about the ring, the findings of the trial court control this case. Applying the law of gifts, the trial court found that "whenever one party used identifiable funds belonging to that party for some purchase that was considered as belonging to the other party, that no loan was being made nor was there any expectation of receiving an ownership interest in the item purchased. If anything, they were unconditional mutual gifts."

Joint Tenancy.

Joint tenancy is a second form of co-ownership in which land or personal property is owned by two or more persons. These persons enjoy equal rights to share in the use and profits of the property involved, but if any one of the joint tenants dies, the entire property passes to the surviving joint tenants. The interest of a joint tenant cannot be willed to the joint tenant's heirs because the deceased's interest terminates at death.

Joint tenants may sell and convey their separate shares in the joint tenancy. If this is done, the joint tenancy is severed, and the tenants or co-owners become tenants in common. Also, a joint tenant's interest is subject to the rights of creditors. The creditors of one joint tenant may secure judgment and have that co-owner's interest sold and the joint tenancy severed.

Historically, joint tenancy was only applicable to real estate. Today, however, one can have joint tenancy in almost any type of personal property—including bank accounts, stock shares, and automobiles.

Many states have passed specific joint tenancy statutes which modify the common-law concept, and thus the applicable state law must be referred to in any case involving a joint tenancy relationship.

These rules are discussed in the next case.

MATTER OF ESTATE OF WILLIAMS
515 N.W.2d 552 (IA App., 1994)

FACTS: The executor appeals the district court's order sustaining the objection to the exclusion of a certificate of deposit from the decedent's estate. The executor argues the district court erred in finding the certificate of deposit had been held by the decedent as a sole depositorship and not as a joint tenancy with full right of survivorship in the executor. In the alternative, the executor contends the certificate of deposit was held as a tenancy in common.

Elva H. Williams died testate on January 28, 1992. Her last will and testament left her entire estate in equal shares to her nine nieces and nephews. Pursuant to her will, one of her nephews, Arlo J. Jones, was nominated and appointed as executor.

The probate inventory listed three certificates of deposit in the amounts of $2,000, $2,000, and $36,130, held in joint tenancy between Williams and Jones. Four other devisees, Derrel Tow, Ronald Tow, Steven Tow, and Lucinda Kane, filed objections to the final report relating to these three certificates.

After a hearing, the district court found the two smaller certificates of deposit had been held in joint tenancy, but the larger certificate of deposit had been held as a sole depositorship. The court sustained the objections related to the $36,130 certificate of deposit but overruled the remaining objections. Jones appeals.

 JUDGE SCHLEGEL:

The contested certificate of deposit in the amount of $36,130, was originally opened by Elva Williams in January 1980. This certificate of deposit was initially issued by the now defunct First Federal Savings and Loan Association of Estherville and Emmetsburg (First Federal). In July 1980, Arlo Jones's name was added to the certificate of deposit at Elva William's' request. Jones signed the signature for the certificate of deposit.

When First Federal failed, its certificates of deposit were purchased by Swea City State Bank. The exact date of purchase was not part of the evidence, however, the trial court found the purchase took place in June 1990. The record indicates the certificate of deposit was changed at First Federal to a joint tenancy certificate at the request of Elva Williams and was transferred over to the Swea City State Bank as a joint certificate when the bank took over First Federal's assets.

The certificate of deposit in question was issued by Swea City State Bank on December 30, 1991, and was held in the names of "Elva Williams or Arlo Jones." The law concerning ownership of accounts in a state bank which are payable to one or more persons is contained in Iowa Code Section 524.806 (1991) which states:

Deposit in the names of two or more individuals.

When a deposit is made in any state bank in the names of two or more individuals, payable to any one or more of them, or payable to the survivor or survivors, the deposit, including interest, or any part thereof, *may be paid to any one or more of the individuals whether the others be living or not,* and the receipt or acquittance of the individuals so paid is a valid and sufficient release and discharge to the state bank for any payment so made. (Emphasis added.)

The Iowa Supreme Court has determined that Section 524.806 "was enacted to protect the depository bank rather than to establish ownership of the deposit...." However, the court specifically stated that this section "has the effect of converting the presumption in favor of tenancy in common, which would otherwise exist, to a presumption in favor of joint tenancy...."

The statute creates a rebuttable presumption that the depositor intends to create a joint tenancy when he makes a deposit in the names of two individuals, payable to either, or payable to either or the survivor....

The resulting rule is that a bank deposit in the name of alternate payees becomes the property of the surviving payee upon the depositor's death in the absence of extrinsic evidence showing that the depositor had a contrary intention. When substantial evidence is offered in an effort to establish a contrary intention, an issue of fact is generated. However, when the evidence offered to show a contrary intention is not substantial, a joint tenancy exists as a matter of law....

Having reviewed the evidence in the record, we conclude the objecters-appellees have failed to offer substantial evidence lo rebut the presumption of joint tenancy ownership. The evidence to the contrary is slight, not substantial. Accordingly, the joint tenancy exists as a matter of law....

The objectors ... argue the joint tenancy signature card signed at First Federal was not signed by both Elva Williams and Arlo Jones at the same time. This argument is without merit. It is not necessary that both parties sign at the same time. The "four unities" common-law rule with regard to the creation of a joint tenancy does not apply in Iowa....

In accordance with the above discussion, we reverse the district court's order sustaining the objection to the exclusion of the certificate of deposit from the decedent's estate. The district court erred in finding the certificate of deposit had been held by the decedent as a sole depositorship and not as a joint tenancy with full right of survivorship in the executor. The certificate of deposit of $36,130 was owned in joint tenancy as a matter of law, in light of the objectors-appellees' failure to establish by substantial evidence the decedent-depositor's contrary intention.

Tenancy by the Entirety. **Tenancy by the entirety** is essentially a joint tenancy with the right of survivorship; however, the co-owners must be husband and wife to each other. The characteristic which distinguishes the two forms of property ownership is that tenancy by the entirety cannot be changed except by joint action of the husband and wife during their lifetimes, whereas a joint tenancy is terminated when any one of the tenants conveys his or her interest, or when a levy of execution is made by a creditor against a joint tenant's interest. If a husband and wife take title to a home as tenants by the entireties and the husband has a judgment rendered against him for damages that result from an automobile accident, the person who was awarded the damages cannot have the judgment executed against the home. If, however, both the husband and wife are jointly liable on a debt, then the creditor may secure a judgment and execute it against the home.

Like joint tenancy, tenancy by the entirety was historically confined to real estate ownership and did not extend to ownership of personal property. However, some states have extended the concept to personal property. About twenty states recognize tenancy by the entirety, but here again the state laws are not uniform and the individual state law must be referred to in each case.

The *Parcel* case discusses these rules.

U.S. v. PARCEL OF REAL PROPERTY
949 F.2d 73 (3rd Cir., 1991)

FACTS: The United States appeals from an order dismissing its complaint seeking civil forfeiture of property containing a pharmacy that was used for the illegal distribution of prescription drugs. The pharmacy was owned as a tenancy by the entireties by a husband, who was convicted for the illegal activities, and his wife, who did not know about or consent to this use of the property. The district court held that the United States was not entitled at this time to forfeiture of any interest in the property.

In 1989, the United States filed a complaint seeking civil forfeiture of property in Pittsburgh, Pennsylvania, on which the Pentown Pharmacy, Inc. was located. The complaint alleged that the property in question was transferred to A. Leonard Bernstein and his wife, Linda M. Bernstein, in October 1979. The complaint asserted that A. Leonard Bernstein, the president of the pharmacy, has used the property for the illegal diversion of various pharmaceutical drugs from 1984 to 1987. The affidavit submitted in support of the complaint asserted the following facts. Dr. Albert T. Smith, who was convicted of drug-related offenses, initially informed the Drug Enforcement Administration that Mr. Bernstein was involved in the illegal diversion of pharmaceutical drugs at the pharmacy. Dr. Smith subsequently engaged in a consensually recorded conversation with Mr. Bernstein at the pharmacy. During that conversation, Mr. Bernstein discussed the illegal diversion of Percocet and Dilaudid, two Schedule II drugs. Mr. Bernstein also gave Dr. Smith a prescription vial containing Percocet tablets.

In May 1987, a confidential source informed law enforcement authorities that he or she had purchased various controlled substances from Mr. Bernstein without a prescription for the past three to four years. Between May 1987 and October 1987, the confidential informant made five controlled purchases of Schedule III and Schedule IV drugs from Mr. Bernstein at the Pentown Pharmacy without presenting a prescription. After obtaining a warrant, DEA agents searched the pharmacy and recovered $47,000 in cash including bills bearing serial numbers matching those used by the confidential informant in making the controlled purchases. Mr. Bernstein was subsequently indicted by a federal grand jury for fifty-one drug-related offenses. He eventually pled guilty to nine counts and was sentenced to ten years imprisonment.

CIRCUIT JUDGE ALITO:

[I]f property is used to commit or facilitate a drug offense, the statute calls for forfeiture of any interest in that property except for the interest of an innocent owner.

Unfortunately the statutory language does not clearly reveal what interest, if any, is subject to forfeiture in a case such as this. Indeed, the statutory language is susceptible to diametrically opposed interpretations. Because each spouse in a tenancy by the entireties is regarded as owning the whole estate, it may be argued as the government initially suggested in the district court, that forfeiture of the guilty spouse's interest means forfeiture of the whole estate and consequently leaves nothing for the innocent spouse. On the other hand, it may be argued, as the district court reasoned, that the innocent spouse's retention of his or her interest in the tenancy means retention of the whole estate and therefore leaves nothing for the government to obtain by forfeiture. Intermediate interpretations—such as the government's contention earlier in this case that one-half of the property should be forfeited—are also possible.

Looking beyond the statutory language, we find nothing in the legislative history that provides an answer to the specific question presented here. The legislative history does show clearly that 21 U.S.C. § 881(A)(7) and other new forfeiture provisions were added in 1984 because Congress felt that strong forfeiture laws were badly needed to combat rampant drug offenses.... At the same time, however, the insertion of the innocent owner defense in 21 U.S.C. § 881(a)(7) shows that Congress did not want to extinguish the interests of innocent owners, and nothing in the legislative history discloses precisely how Congress wanted to balance the interest in forfeiture and the interest of an innocent owner in the circumstances presented by the case now before us.

Without any definitive guidance in the statutory language or the legislative history, we believe that we should adopt the interpretation that best serves the two goals that 21 U.S.C. § 881(a)(7) was intended to promote: forfeiture of the property used in committing drug offenses and preservation of the property rights of innocent owners. In the present case, the innocent owner held title as a tenant by the entireties. As a tenant by the entireties, Mrs. Bernstein had the right to possess and use the whole property during her life and right to obtain title in fee simple absolute if her cotenant predeceased her. Similarly, she had protection against a unilateral conveyance by her cotenant of his interest in the estate, as well as protection against a levy upon the property by any creditor of her cotenant....

The range of possible interpretations that we must consider has been substantially narrowed as a result of the position taken by the government in its motion to alter or amend the judgment and on appeal. The government maintains that it is now entitled to forfeiture of Mr. Bernstein's interest in the tenancy by the entireties but that Mrs. Bernstein may retain full and exclusive use of the property during her life, protection against any alienation without her consent or any attempt to levy upon her husband's former interest, and the right to obtain title in fee simple absolute if her husband predeceases her. In light of the government's position, we need not consider possible interpretations of the statute that would result in a greater degree of forfeiture. Instead, we may limit our consideration to the interpretation now advanced by the government and those interpretations that would result in a lessor degree of forfeiture.

Two such interpretations have been suggested. As noted earlier, the Bernsteins argue that the complaint should simply be dismissed, and thus they appear to contend that the government may not obtain forfeiture of any interest in the property either now or at any future time. The district court, and the Eleventh Circuit decision on which the district court relied, concluded that in a situation such as this the government is not entitled to the forfeiture of any interest from the tenants by the entireties but that the government may file a *lis pendens* and thereby preserve its right to seek forfeiture of any separate interest in the property that might later be acquired by the guilty spouse due to either the death of the innocent spouse or the severance of the estate....

We believe that the interpretation advanced by the government best serves the dual purposes of 21 U.S.C. § 881(a)(7). This interpretation permits the immediate forfeiture of the interest of the guilty spouse and thus serves the goal of forfeiting property used in illegal drug activities. At the same time, this interpretation fully protects all of the property rights that the innocent owner enjoyed under the tenancy by the entireties. The innocent owner retains full use and possession (indeed, exclusive use and possession) of the property during his or her lifetime. The innocent owner is also protected against any conveyance without his or her consent or any attempt to levy upon the interest formerly held by the guilty spouse. In addition, the innocent owner retains the right to obtain title in fee simple absolute if he or she is predeceased by the guilty spouse....

Accordingly, we hold that the district court erred in dismissing the complaint in this case. On remand, the district court should determine whether Mr. Bernstein's interest is subject to forfeiture irrespective of Mrs. Bernstein's innocent owner defense. If the court decides that it is, the court should enter an order forfeiting that interest but preserving Mrs. Bernstein's right to full and exclusive use and possession of the property during her life, her protection against conveyance of or execution by third parties upon her husband's former interest, and her survivorship right.

Community Property. The main feature of the community property system is that most property acquired after marriage by either the husband or the wife automatically becomes the common property of the husband and wife. Under the common law, if a husband earned $50,000 per year, he was legally obligated to provide the necessities for his wife's support with that amount; however, his wife had no rights in any money over and above the amount required to provide these necessities. Also, under the common law, if a wife were employed outside the home, her income was also her husband's. Under the community property theory, most income and property acquired by either spouse is owned by both, share and share alike. Probable exceptions to the co-ownership rule would be property acquired by gift or inheritance, or property received in exchange for property owned by one of the parties prior to the marriage. Income earned during the marriage by separately owned property may or may not be community property, depending on the state.

The community property system is a statutory type of ownership which, if adopted by a specific state, will cover all persons in the relationship of husband and wife who are subject to the laws of that state. Unlike the previous types of ownership discussed in this chapter, it is not voluntary. Also, the states that have adopted this form of ownership have not followed any uniform pattern. Answers to such questions as whether a spouse's share in community property will descend to his or her heirs or will automatically go to the surviving spouse, or whether or not the spouse's share is subject to levy of execution of creditors, or how the property is to be divided in case of divorce, must be determined by looking at the specific statute of the state involved. The nine states that have community property laws are Arizona, California, Idaho, Louisiana, New Mexico, Nevada, Texas, Washington, and Wisconsin.

Condominium Ownership. Today we are seeing a rapid growth in condominium ownership, which is a combination of ownership in severalty and tenancy in common. Condominiums are multiple-unit buildings or developments of several buildings where an owner owns an individual unit, and all of these owners share the land and common areas used by all tenants as tenants in common. The owners of the various individual apartments or buildings pay a management fee to a condominium corporation to manage the complex and to keep the common areas repaired and cleaned.

Nearly all of the states have enacted some type of condominium law to regulate condominium ownership and construction. These laws vary from state to state, and a person should be familiar with the particular state condominium law before making any decisions regarding condominium ownership or construction.

Condominium owners are joint owners of the common areas, and as such are liable on a pro rata basis for costs, expenses, and even liability for claims for damages arising out of the use of the common areas.

Time-Sharing Ownership. This property concept has been developed in recent years, particularly for resort properties.

The theory of **time-sharing ownership** is very simple. In the past, you purchased a condominium in Florida, hoping to rent it out for most of the year and to reserve it for yourself for two months in the winter. The problem was that the capital investment was quite sizable. Now, you can simply buy the right to use a condominium unit in a resort area for a specific period of time, perhaps two weeks a year; the other fifty weeks are sold to other individuals. You have purchased two weeks' use per year for your life or forever, as the case may be. You can trade your two weeks to one of the other time-share owners if you want to use the property at a different time, or you can sell or lease your right to use it. The obvious benefit of time-sharing ownership is that you have to pay only a fraction of the total value of the unit, yet you own an exclusive right to use it for a specific time every year.

As with condominium ownership, state laws regulating this type of ownership vary, so before any decision is made regarding such purchases, the laws of the state where the real estate is located should be reviewed.

CHANGES IN FORM

Personal Property to Real Property

When purchasing a home the buyer may ask, "Do these drapes go with the house?" "Does this chandelier stay with the house?" "Does the carpet in the family room go with the house?" The crucial legal question here is whether or not these items, which were once personal property, now have become fixtures to the real property, and thus an inseparable part of the real property.

Here again, the specific law of the state in which the property is located will determine whether a particular item is still movable personal property, or whether it has become a fixture and part of the real property.

Affixation. Has the item become permanently affixed to the land or the building? If an item has been attached to the land or the building in such a manner that it cannot be removed without damaging the building or the land or the item itself, then the item is considered part of the real property. If carpet is glued to the concrete slab in the family room of a house, it is typically considered part of the real estate and no longer personal property, since removing the carpet would leave a bare, unusable floor and would no doubt destroy the carpet. Drapes or curtains can normally be removed from curtain rods or other types of hangers without damaging either the curtains or the fixtures upon which they are hanging. However, the curtain rods themselves are considered permanent fixtures because they are permanently attached to the wall and cannot be removed without leaving holes in it.

Intent. What was the intent of the owner of the personal property when the personal property was affixed to the real property? Here, we may go beyond the actual physical method of affixing the property and look to the owner's intention when the property was affixed. Did the owner intend to add the fixture to the real property or to maintain it as personal property? If a person rents a store building and installs a freezer, counters, showcases, and other equipment necessary to run the store, will these items be considered personal property, or will they be part of the real estate? The freezer may be anchored to the floor with bolts to prevent vibration, and the counters may be anchored to the floor so that they will not move when people lean against them. Usually, if a person affixes personal property to the land or building of another, the owner of the land or building becomes the owner of the affixed items. But in a situation such as the above, most courts would probably say that the tenant remains the owner of the items even though it becomes necessary to unbolt them from the floor or to disconnect electric wires or water pipes before the items can be removed from the building. It is normally not the intent of the business tenant to make a gift of such items to the landlord, and the landlord has either expressly or impliedly agreed to such removals.

Business Records. How is the property being carried on the books of the business? Is it still considered as personal property, or is it considered as an improvement of the real estate? Business records can be used as evidence of the parties' intent.

Intent is really the most important test. However, in many cases there is no evidence of intent other than the actual method of affixing the items to the real estate.

Courts are generally more liberal in permitting removal of items attached for the tenant's specific business or agricultural use, or to add to the comfort and convenience of a residence. In all of these situations, however, it is advisable to have a clause in the lease specifying which items are removable by the tenant and are not to be considered part of the realty, even though there is evidence of permanent attachment.

Real Property to Personal Property

When a fixture is severed from the real estate, it becomes personal property. A built-in stove in your kitchen is considered part of the real estate and goes with the house. However, if you decide to replace it with a new one, once the old stove has been physically severed from the real estate it returns to the status of personal property. Growing timber or crops are part of the real estate; however, once they are severed from the ground they become personal property. They can be sold, as "goods" under the UCC, without already having been physically detached from the land. Coal in the ground is part of the real estate; however, when it is mined and severed from the ground it becomes personal property.

ACQUISITION OF TITLE TO PERSONAL PROPERTY

Title to personal property may be acquired in several different ways. Acquisition may be the result of voluntary action on the part of the former owner and the new owner, or it may occur simply by the operation of the law. Following are some of the common methods of acquisition of title to personal property.

Purchase. When you go to the grocery store and buy groceries for the week, you have acquired personal property by purchase. No certificate of title is attached to each item in your grocery sack; mere possession is evidence of title to such items. If you purchase an automobile, a motorcycle, or a motor home, the seller will give you a bill of sale, which must be presented to a specific state authority, so that title to the vehicle is registered in your name on state records. If you purchase the equipment and trade fixtures of a business, you will normally require that a bill of sale specifically describes each item or object which is part of the purchase. This bill of sale does not need to be recorded with the state or county; however, it will be your evidence of title.

Gift. Title to personal property may be transferred from one person to other persons by gift. A gift is a voluntary action on the part of the giver, with no expectation of consideration from the person receiving the gift. The transfer of personal property by gift can be divided into three basic classifications. An **inter vivos** gift is a gift made by a living person to another living person. A gift **causa mortis** is a gift which is given in contemplation of the giver's death. A **testamentary gift** is a gift which is given in a person's will.

The three types of gifts differ mainly with regard to revocability. Once an *inter vivos* gift has been delivered, it is generally irrevocable. Since a gift *causa mortis* is made in contemplation of death, if the giver recovers, then the giver can have the property back. The *causa mortis* gift may be revoked by the giver during the giver's lifetime and it may be revoked if the recipient dies before the giver dies. A *testamentary gift* may be revoked by revoking or amending the will.

The question often arises as to when an *inter vivos* gift becomes effective. Two tests must be met. First, it must be shown that the giver intended to divest certain rights in the property. It is not necessary that all rights be given for a gift to be valid. For example, an owner of corporate stock may give the dividends of the stock to another person, but retain ownership of the actual shares of stock. Intent may be evidenced by a written statement, by actions of the giver, or by other documents such as the signature card for a joint bank account.

The second test of a gift is delivery. **Delivery** is simply the transfer of possession or control from one person to another. Delivery does not have to be made to the recipient of the gift; it can be made to a third person as agent or trustee for the recipient. A bank will often be the trustee for the recipient if the recipient is a minor or if the recipient is an elderly person who is incapable of handling the property. The key with regard to delivery is that the giver surrenders all rights to possession and control of the property that is the subject of the gift. In some instances, you cannot pick the gift up and hand it to the recipient. With an automobile, for example, delivery would consist of handing over the keys. This would be called symbolic delivery. If the gift involves intangible property, then delivery would consist of turning over some document which transfers title to the intangible property to the donee, such as an assignment of a patent or a copyright or a properly indorsed stock certificate.

Uniform Gifts to Minors Act. In the past, many parents who wanted to give money to their children would set up a savings account in a bank in the name of the minor child. The account would show one of the parents as parent and guardian, and normally the money could be taken out of the account only by the parent. The question arose as to whether or not there was an actual gift, since the parent still retained control over the property. Was there really delivery? The Uniform Gifts to Minors Act (UGMA) was drafted to set up a procedure for making legal gifts to minors. This act has been adopted in nearly all of the states. It provides a method for making gifts of money and of registered and unregistered securities to minors.

If the gift is money, the money may simply be deposited in a bank in the name of the giver or some other adult, or of some corporate trustee, such as a bank, with the statement that the party in whose name the account is registered is a custodian for the minor under the UGMA. If the gift is a registered security, then the giver registers the security as custodian for the minor under the UGMA. If the security is unregistered, it has to be delivered to another adult or to a bank or some other financial institution as trustee, together with a statement of the gift and an acknowledgment accepting the role of custodian of the security for and on behalf of the minor. The custodian has very broad powers as to the use and disposition of the property. The property can be exchanged or sold without the permission of the minor who is the beneficiary of the gift. Of course, the custodian is not permitted to use any of the property or any of the proceeds for personal benefit.

Uniform Anatomical Gift Act. Traditionally, we do not think of the human body or parts of the human body as things of monetary value, so we were not concerned about property rights to our body or various parts of our body. Now that medical technology has developed processes for transplanting parts of one body to another body, the law must treat the human body and the parts thereof as property, and establish some procedure for making gifts of the human body or its parts. Under the Uniform Anatomical Gift Act (UAGA), people eighteen years of age or older may make a gift of their entire body or any specified part of their body. However, the gift does not take effect until the death of the giver. Such gifts are revocable at any time. They are usually included in the giver's last will and testament. Also, many states have included an anatomical gift statement on the back of the driver's license. Persons wishing to donate their bodies or specific organs can so specify and sign and date the statement in the presence of two witnesses, who must also sign.

People also may sell or donate blood, a kidney, an eye, or some other organ, the loss of which does not automatically cause death. Such gifts are not covered by the UAGA since they are not given at death.

Inheritance. As indicated previously, you may become the owner of personal property as a result of a specific bequest in a deceased person's will. You may also become the owner of personal property through the process of **intestate succession**. This means that you are an heir under state statute and that you will receive a designated share of the decedent's personal property if there is no valid will which disposes of it.

Accession. **Accession** simply means an addition to what you already have. An example of accession would be a situation where the lawn mower which your neighbor borrowed for the weekend broke down and he had to have it repaired. When your neighbor returned the lawn mower to you, you became the owner of the repairs by accession.

Problems of this type of acquisition of personal property arise when accession of considerable value is made without the property owner's consent and when the original item has been changed or altered so that identification is difficult. A trespasser cuts down small trees on my land, makes rustic lawn chairs from the trees, and sets up a stand along the highway to sell the lawn chairs. Who owns the lawn chairs which were previously my timber? There is no simple answer to this question because the courts have not agreed on one solution, especially if the original material was taken as the result of an innocent mistake. If, on the other hand, the taking was intentional and wrongful, the original owner will no doubt be awarded the chairs.

Possession. Title to personal property may be acquired in some instances by simply taking possession of an item and exercising rights of ownership and control over that item. Following are some common situations where title by possession could be legally exercised.

Wildlife. Title to fish, birds, or wild animals may, in some instances, be acquired simply by taking possession and control of the fish, birds, or animals. Title by possession can only occur, however, where the fish, birds, or animals are not owned by another party or where such action would not violate national, state, or local laws for the conservation and protection of wildlife. If you trespass upon a farmer's land and catch fish in the farmer's private pond, the fish belong to the farmer, not you. If you go hunting when it is not legal to hunt a certain species of animal, then you will not be allowed to keep the slain animal, and you may have to pay a fine for your wrongful action.

Abandoned Personal Property. An item of personal property has been abandoned if the owner has intentionally and voluntarily relinquished control and possession of the item and has not transferred the title to the item in any manner to another person. The intent of the owner is simply to have nothing more to do with the item. The issue of whether or not the article has been abandoned will be a fact question in each case.

Lost or Mislaid Property. **Lost property** is property the owner accidentally dropped or property that was accidentally separated from the owner. The owner has no knowledge of the location of the lost property. **Mislaid property** is property which was voluntarily and intentionally placed somewhere by the owner and then forgotten. Lost or mislaid personal property, unlike abandoned personal property, is still the property of the owner who lost or mislaid it. However, it is generally held that the finder of lost property has a right to possession and control until the item is claimed by the true owner, if the item is found in a publicly accessible place, such as a street, a parking lot, or a store. On the other hand, if you find a billfold in an office or an apartment, the courts will generally say that the landowner or occupier has the right to possession of the billfold. Mislaid property generally stays with the owner or occupier of the place where it was discovered.

The identity of the lost or mislaid item is also a factor in determining who has the better right to possession. A lost billfold will normally have the owner's identification in it, whereas a wristwatch that fell off the owner's wrist when the band broke would not be so identifiable. Courts may also consider the status of the finder. Trespassers usually have to turn over any property they find; so do employees whose jobs include such a duty.

Many states have finders' statutes which enable the finder to become the new owner of lost or mislaid property by advertising or posting notices. If the owner does not return and claim the property within the statutory period, usually one year, the finder can become the new owner. Some of these statutes require the finder to pay the state part of the value of the item.

Confusion. Title to personal property may be acquired when the property of different owners is so intermingled that the property of the individual owners cannot be identified or separated and returned to the specific owners. **Confusion** is most common when dealing with such fungible goods as corn, wheat, milk, and oil.

If three persons owning 1,000 bushels of wheat of the same grade and quality agree to intermingle their property for purposes of storage, there would be no problem since the intermingling was voluntary. Each party will simply have a one-third ownership in the total volume of wheat. The problem involving title to personal property arises where one owner intentionally and wrongfully intermingles goods with those of another person so that the goods of each owner can no longer be separated or distinguished. The majority of the courts, in a case where the commingling was deliberate and wrongful and without the permission of the other party, will simply grant the innocent party title to the entire volume of goods. The wrongdoer is punished by being deprived of any further right or title to the property. If the intermingling of the goods is not an intentional and wrongful act, and if the goods are of the same kind and quality, courts will usually hold that each owner now owns a proportionate share of the total mixed goods.

Creation. Property is created when a new invention is made, when a new song or book is written, or when a new painting is created. These creations are the result of intellectual production. In title by creation, you are intellectually creating a new idea in which the law grants property rights. The patent law gives inventors certain property rights in the inventions they create, and the copyright law gives writers, composers, and producers of other copyrightable material certain property rights in their creations. These points are developed in more detail in the next chapter.

SIGNIFICANCE OF THIS CHAPTER

Ownership of property is one of the most basic concepts of the law. At one time, it was said that "possession is nine-tenths of the law," but in a civilized society we must have rules regarding the ownership of property, how it can be transferred, and who inherits what rights. Possession in itself may not mean very much. Suppose, for example, that you found a wristwatch with a broken band. Obviously it accidentally fell off the person's arm when the band broke. Is the watch yours because you physically possess it? Clearly not. It is also important to understand the concept of the bundle of rights, as many things we say we own are not wholly owned by us; that is, we do not own all the rights in that thing. Another very important question concerns things that may be attached to, or detached from, real estate. Landlords and tenants, and buyers and sellers of land, need to know which things are part of the land. As a tenant, before you attach any item of personal property, get permission from the landlord to do so, reserve the right to remove the item, and "get it in writing."

PROBLEMS FOR DISCUSSION

1. Sergeant Morrison was the sergeant in command of an infantry squad on a search and destroy mission in Vietnam. They were searching a cave in the hills and found $150,000 in U.S. currency and a large sum of South Vietnamese money. The Sergeant turned all the money over to his superiors as representatives of the government of the United States. Now Sergeant Morrison files claim in the U.S. Claims Court alleging that he was the finder and he should be entitled to the money.

   Who is entitled to this money? Why?

2. Arthur Evans had rented a safe-deposit box in which he had stored valuables. His niece, Mrs. Kellows, had worked for the family since she was 16, and she continued to care for Evans until he died. Before Evans went into the hospital, just prior to his death, he gave the keys to the box to Kellows. Reverend Cummings visited Evans shortly before he died, and Evans told Cummings that he was giving $10,000 to the church and that he had given the rest of his possessions and the keys to the safe-deposit box to Kellows. The executor considered the contents of the safe-deposit box, valued at approximately $80,000, to be assets of the estate and not the specific property of Kellows. Kellows filed objections, stating that there had been a gift and that she owned the contents of the box. She had the keys; however, her name was not on the rental agreement and the bank had no notice that she had any interest in the box.

   Who owns the box contents, and why?

3. Plaintiff and defendant bought a house in 1982 and separated in 1996. The husband was seeking a divorce. The wife was seeking a separation and opposed a divorce on religious grounds. The husband had refused to share their marital home with the plaintiff, either by selling the house and dividing the proceeds, by paying the plaintiff her share of the equity of the house, or by renting the premises and dividing the proceeds. In support of his position, the husband pointed out that the property in question was held under a tenancy by the entirety which gave both him and his wife an indefeasible right of survivorship, but gave him the exclusive right to possession and control during his lifetime. He stated that he would grant the plaintiff one half of the equity in the house if she would grant him an uncontested divorce. She sued for her half.

   What result, and why?

4. Kalyvakis was employed as an assistant steward aboard the T.S.S. Olympia, a passenger ocean liner. While the ship was moored at a pier in New York City taking on passengers for a cruise, Kalyvakis found $3,010 in U.S. currency lying scattered on the floor of the men's restroom on the upper deck. He turned the money over to the chief steward to hold for the owner of the money, should he come and claim it. Now three years have elapsed, no one has even made a claim for the money, and Kalyvakis asks that the money be returned to him. The T.S.S. Olympia owner, a Greek corporation, refused to turn over the money, so Mr. Kalyvakis sued.

   What should the court decide? Explain.

5. Eyesore Products sells a "kit" for assembly of a large steel farm silo for storage of grain. The kit includes 100 steel sheets, some 7,000 bolts and nuts, and a sealant. Eyesore's dealers assemble the kit for the customers, on a concrete slab that weighs about 65 tons. The silo is 22 feet in diameter, 72 feet high, weighs 32 tons, and costs about $40,000.

Kansas levies a sales tax on building materials used for the alteration or improvement of real estate. Eyesore claims that it does not have to collect this tax on its silo sales, because it is selling personal property, and that the silos remain personal property after they are assembled.

Are Eyesore silo kits subject to the sales tax? Explain.

Chapter 25
Intellectual Property

It can be argued—with some justification—that "intellectual property" is the most important part of our modern internationalized economy. The term includes all those products of the human intellect that have potential commercial value. Many of our nation's major exports are based on "intellectual property." Films, TV programs, music, and books are protected (usually) by copyright law. Franchisors of hamburgers and fried chicken rely on trademark protection to distinguish their heavily-advertised products from domestic and foreign competitors, and the chicken colonel likewise uses trade secret law to protect his "eleven secret herbs and spices." Certain formulas for cola drinks and drug products are also trade secrets. Alternatively, such formulas may be patented. Sellers of computers, jet planes, office furniture, automotive equipment, and similar goods have patents on various product designs and manufacturing processes. Intellectual property law thus provides protection for significant business assets that are the basis of many companies' competitive advantages. Understanding intellectual property law is therefore a key part of effective management in today's global business environment.

This chapter covers the four major subjects of intellectual property law—trade secrets, patents, copyrights, and trademarks. "Trade dress" law is included as a sub-part of trademark law. The chapter concludes with a brief overview of some of the international dimensions of intellectual property law.

TRADE SECRET LAW

Unlike the other three major areas of intellectual property law, which are now governed primarily by national statutes and regulations, trade secret law is still basically state law. Originally part of the common law of "unfair competition" (which is discussed in Chapter 39), trade secret law is now subject to statutory definition in most states. About three-fourths of the states have adopted the Uniform Trade Secrets Act, a brief (but somewhat complex) statute defining the owner's rights and providing for monetary and injunctive relief.

Definition of Trade Secret. A "trade secret" is created when a business expends time or money to develop a concept or information which has commercial value, is kept confidential, and is not generally known in the trade. It is, in other words, a *secret* "competitive advantage." According to the U.T.S.Act, such information may include "a formula, pattern, compilation, program, device, method, technique, or process."

When deciding whether a particular set of data qualifies as a trade secret, courts usually consider several questions. To what extent are other businesses also aware of this information? Is this information widely shared within the company claiming the trade secret? What measures have been taken by the claimant company to preserve the secrecy of the information? How valuable is the information to the claimant company? How difficult would it be for competitors to (lawfully) acquire or duplicate the information? In light of these tests, one can understand the extreme security precautions taken by the cola drink company and the fried chicken franchisor to protect their product formulas. Each one of these examples is a multi-billion-dollar global enterprise, with thousands of employees, but with only two or three persons knowing the treasured product formula.

Misappropriation. The UTSA says that a trade secret is misappropriated (and legal remedies can therefore be sought) in two circumstances. First, when it is acquired "by a person who knows or has reason to know that the trade secret was acquired by improper means." If the acquirer was buying the trade secret from a known industrial spy, there would be "reason to know" that it had been improperly acquired.

Second, misappropriation includes disclosure or use, without the owner's consent, by three groups of persons: (a) any person who used improper means to acquire knowledge of the secret; or (b) any person who knew or had reason to know that his [her] knowledge of the secret was derived from a person who had learned it by improper means or who owed the secret's owner a duty to keep the secret, or was acquired "under circumstances giving rise to a duty to maintain its secrecy or limit its use;" or (c) any person who, before any material change in his [her] position, knew or had reason to know that knowledge of the secret had been acquired by "accident or mistake."

With these comprehensive definitions, the UTSA is thus trying to cover all the possible circumstances where wrongful use of the trade secret has occurred. The key to *wrongful* use is the unauthorized taking of someone else's trade secret. There is no violation if a second person independently develops a second version of the formula or process. Even if the second person discovers the trade secret by "reverse engineering" the first's product, there is no violation.

Trade secret law does not guarantee that no one else can manufacture and sell your product, only that they cannot use *your* secret process to do so. If you want exclusive rights to make and sell something, you need a patent or a copyright. This lack of protection against independent duplication is the major danger in relying on trade secret law.

Enforcement. Where misappropriation has occurred, an injunction may be issued to prevent further wrongful use or disclosure. Money damages may be awarded to the secret owner for any loss sustained as a result of the misappropriation. For intentional conduct, punitive damages may also be awarded. Criminal laws against theft and embezzlement may also be applicable to some wrongful takings.

Prevention. New employees ought to be required to sign confidentiality agreements as part of the hiring process. Clear disclosure policies, as to which persons within the company have a need to know which trade secrets, need to be developed and monitored. Policies also need to be developed and enforced as to the presence of non-employees on the business premises. Company records which might contain trade secret information need to be carefully maintained. Exit interviews, reminding employees who are leaving of their post-employment obligations, are probably also a good idea.

PATENT LAW

The Constitution (Article I, Section 8) gives Congress the power "To promote the progress of science and useful arts, by securing for limited times to authors and inventors the exclusive right to their respective writings and discoveries." Using this grant of authority, Congress has passed statutes providing for patents and copyrights, and establishing the process for awarding them. The first patent law was enacted in 1790, and has been subject to only three major revisions—1793, 1836, and 1952.

Definition of Patent. A patent gives the owner the exclusive right to make and sell the invention for the "limited times" specified by Congress. There are three basic categories of patents: **product or process patents**, **design patents**, and **plant patents**.

It is the product or process patent that most people are thinking of when they use the term "patent." This first category applies to any "process, machine, manufacture, or composition of matter," and to improvements on any of these things. These are patents for the proverbial "better mousetrap." The inventor's rights extend for twenty years. Because of the extensive government testing requirements for new drugs and medical devices, before they can be sold, 1984 amendments to the patent law permit a five-year extension of protection for these products, under certain conditions.

Design patents are granted to protect developers of original, ornamental product designs. The designer has exclusive rights of use for fourteen years. Plant patents are granted to promote agricultural progress by protecting the rights of persons who develop distinctive new plants by methods other than improved seeds. The Supreme Court decided in 1980 that developers of other new life forms (bacertia) could apply for product or process patents, even though they might not be eligible for a plant patent.

Patentability. What does the inventor have to show to qualify for a patent? No one can own an idea, so Einstein could not have patented $E=mc^2$. Likewise, patents cannot be granted for naturally-occurring plants or animals, or for the "laws of nature." Printed matter and business methods are not patentable, although the former may be protectable by copyright. Ultimately, the Supreme Court will decide where to draw these lines.

For a product or process patent, the invention must be **new**, **useful**, and **non-obvious**. "New" in this context means, generally, that the invention was previously unknown—that no one has previously patented it or disclosed it through publication. Here again, there are some difficult, technical questions as to exactly what was known and when, where, and by whom it was known. "Useful" means that the inventor must show that the invention produces a specific, substantial beneficial result. "Non-obvious" means that the invention would not have been apparent to someone skilled in the particular field or industry. This third requirement causes particular difficulty when a patent claim is made for a new combination of elements which were already well-known. On this point as well, the courts will have to make case-by-case decisions.

Diamond v. Diehr involves some of these issues.

DIAMOND v. DIEHR
101 S.Ct. 1048 (1981)

FACTS: Diehr and Lutton filed a patent application for a process for making rubber products. Raw, uncured synthetic rubber is subjected to heat and pressure in a mold. The problem is to make sure that the finished product is not over-cured or under-cured. The industry has used a time and temperature formula, the well-known Arrhenius equation, to calculate the time for the product to remain in the mold. Because the precise temperature in the mold could not be measured, finished products often come out over-cured or under-cured.

Diehr and Lutton's improved process measures the temperature in the mold constantly and feeds this information into a computer, which then repeatedly calculates the curing time, using the Arrhenius equation. The patent application was denied by an examiner, whose decision was upheld by the Patent Office Board of Appeals. The Court of Customs and Patent Appeals said the patent could be granted. Sydney Diamond, the then Commissioner of Patents, asked for certiorari.

 JUSTICE REHNQUIST:

The Patent Act of 1793 defined statutory subject matter as "any new and useful art, machine, manufacture, or composition of matter, or any new or useful improvement thereof."... Not until the patent laws were recodified in 1952 did Congress replace the word "art" with the word "process." It is that latter word which we confront today, and in order to determine its meaning, we may not be unmindful of the Committee Reports accompanying the 1952 Act which inform us that Congress intended statutory subject matter to "include anything under the sun that is made by man."...

Analyzing [applicants'] claims according to the ... statements from our cases, we think that a physical and chemical process for molding precision synthetic rubber products falls within the S.101 categories of possibly patentable subject matter. That [applicants'] claims involve the transformation of an article, in this case, raw uncured synthetic rubber, into a different state or thing cannot be disputed. The [applicants'] claims describe in detail a step-by-step method for accomplishing such, beginning with the loading of a mold with raw uncured rubber and ending with the eventual opening of the press at the conclusion of the cure. Industrial processes such as this are the type which have historically been eligible to receive the protection of our patent laws.

Our conclusion regarding [applicants'] claims is not altered by the fact that in several steps of the process a mathematical equation and a programmed digital computer are used. This Court has undoubtedly recognized limits to S.101 and every discovery is not embraced within the statutory terms. Excluded from such patent protection are laws of nature, physical phenomena, and abstract ideas.... "A principle, in the abstract, is a fundamental truth; an original cause; a motive; these cannot be patented, as no one can claim in either of them an exclusive right."...

The [applicants] here do not seek to patent a mathematical formula. Instead, they seek patent protection for a process of curing synthetic rubber. Their process admittedly employs a well known mathematical equation, but they do not seek to pre-empt the use of that equation. Rather, they seek only to foreclose from others the use of that equation in conjunction with all of the other steps in their claimed process. These include installing rubber in a press, closing the mold, constantly determining the temperature of the mold, constantly recalculating the appropriate cure time through the use of the formula and digital computer, and automatically opening the press at the proper time. Obviously, one does not need a "computer" to cure natural or synthetic rubber, but if the computer use incorporated in the process patent significantly lessens the possibility of "overcuring" or "undercuring," the process as a whole does not thereby become unpatentable subject matter....

Because we do not view [applicants'] claims as an attempt to patent a mathematical formula, but rather to be drawn to an industrial process for the molding of rubber products, we affirm the judgment of the Court of Customs and Patents Appeals.

For a design patent, the claimant must show the design's "ornamentality," rather than the "utility" required for a product or process patent. The "novelty" and "nonobviousness" requirements are the same. For a plant patent, the claimant must show the "distinctiveness" of the new plant, that is, that its characteristics are clearly different from those of existing types. Here again, the other two requirements are the same, but "nonobvious" in this context may mean little more than "distinctive."

Application Process. As indicated in the *Diehr* case, a person claiming a patent files an application with the Patent and Trademark Office. The application must disclose, with words and diagrams, how to make and use the invention. Further, it must also explain how the invention differs from already known devices and processes (the "prior art" in the field). Finally, it must state precisely exactly what aspects of the invention are to be protected by the patent—the "claim." (As explained by Justice Rehnquist, Diehr and Lutton were not trying to patent the Arrhenius equation, just its *application* as part of their unique process for curing rubber.)

Typically, there will be a considerable exchange of documents between the PTO and the inventor, as objections are raised and modifications to the application are made. As also noted in the *Diehr* case, there is an appeals process if the patent is denied.

Scope of Protection. Once granted, the patent gives the owner the right to prevent others from making or selling the invention within the United States. Since patents are still granted nation by nation, further applications will have to be filed in each country where protection is sought.

Getting overseas protection may thus be a lengthy and expensive process, especially since procedures and protections may be quite different from nation to nation. These points will be discussed further in the last section of this chapter.

Since the patent process involves public disclosure of the invention, including how to make it and what it does, all the world now has access to this information. Anyone and everyone can now try to engineer their way around the patent, by trying to produce the same benefits with a different device or process.

Companies thus need to weigh very carefully the respective costs and benefits of patent protection versus trade secret protection.

Infringement. When a lawsuit claiming infringement is filed, the court will focus very closely on the claims made in the patent. Do they describe the allegedly offending device or product, as well as the patented one? As one court stated the test, the question is whether the defendant's product or process "performs substantially the same overall function or work, in substantially the same way, to obtain substantially the same overall result."

Infringement may occur by making, selling, or using a sufficiently similar product or process. Making, selling, or using a smaller, unpatented part of the patented product or process would not be a violation of the patent-holder's rights. Other persons are still free to use the Arrhenius equation in other contexts, despite the process patent held by Diehr and Lutton. Good faith and ignorance are generally not excuses, although they may result in lower damages against the infringer.

Once a patented item has been sold to a buyer, that person may of course use it, *and* re-sell it. It is likewise clear that the buyer may repair the purchased patented item, without violating the patent-holder's rights. The difficulty is drawing the line between *repairing* an existing item, and building a *new* one. Since only the patent-holder has the right to "make" the patented item, making a new one would violate the holder's patent rights. Here too, some difficult legal and factual lines must be drawn by the courts.

Enforcement and Remedies. The Patent Act provides for a combination of remedies where infringement has occurred. The patent owner is entitled to an injunction against further wrongful manufacture, sale or use. Damages are awarded to compensate the plaintiff's loss, in an amount at least equal to what would have been a reasonable royalty for use of the patent, plus interest. In an appropriate case (as for example, where the defendant has willfully infringed), damages may be trebled. Court costs will be awarded, but attorney fees are given only in "exceptional" cases. In design patent cases, the infringer's profits derived from the wrongful copying may be recovered by the patent owner.

COPYRIGHT LAW

The very first Congress also passed a copyright act in 1790. Major revisions occurred in 1831, 1870, 1909, and 1976. Important changes in the law were also made when the U.S. acceded to the international copyright treaty (the Berne Convention) in 1989.

Definition of Copyright. "Copyright" is exactly what the word says: the *right* to *copy* a tangible creative work, or "work of authorship." The underlying idea is not protected, only the specific manner or form in which it is expressed. No one can copyright the idea of having a chapter on

"Intellectual Property" in a Business Law book, but we *do* have a copyright on the words you are reading at this very moment. Copyright gives the author the exclusive right to copy or reproduce the work for the statutory period, which is now generally the life of the author plus fifty years.

Copyrightability. While the constitutional provision speaks of "writings," that word has been given a very broad interpretation. The Copyright Act of 1976 says that "works of authorship" include "literary works; musical works, including any accompanying words; dramatic works, including any accompanying music; pantomimes and choreographic works; pictorial, graphic, sculptural works; motion pictures and other audiovisual works; sound recordings; and architectural works." (Computer programs on microchips can also be protected, under the Semiconductor Chip Protection Act of 1984. The "chip" rules are quite different from normal copyright, although the same office administers both statutes.)

That's an impressive listing, but it is not intended to be exclusive. Protection is given to any original work of authorship which is expressed in tangible form and is capable of being communicated. The three requirements for copyright protection are that the work be *original,* that it be expressed in a *tangible medium,* and that it contain some element of *creativity.* It is the third requirement that distinguishes the copyrightability of the telephone book yellow pages from the non-copyrightability of the white pages. There is no "creativity" in an alphabetical listing of the names of people who have telephone numbers. There is at least some "creativity" in deciding how to categorize the multitude of businesses and services that are listed in the yellow pages.

What, then, is not copyrightable? The 1976 Act says that protection cannot be given to "any idea, procedure, process, system, method of operation, concept, principle, or discovery." Such information will therefore have to be protected, if at all, as a trade secret, or perhaps with a process patent.

Registration Process. Unlike patent rights, which require registration for protection, copyright protection exists from the moment when the author puts the "work" into a tangible form. These very lines are protected by copyright as they are being typed on the IBM laptop and are appearing on the computer screen. From that instant, only we—as the authors (and our publisher, to whom we have contractually transferred the right to publish)—have the right to reproduce these words, in this sequence.

Why then bother with registration at all? Registering the work with the U.S. Copyright Office is a necessary prerequisite to filing a lawsuit against an alleged infringer. In other words, although the author's exclusive right to copy the work is protected, he or she cannot sue to enforce that right without first having registered the copyright.

In addition, registration does give the author important advantages when it is necessary to sue an infringer. The copyright for a registered work is presumed valid. Registration prior to infringement permits the copyright owner to recover statutory damages (up to $100,000) without any proof of actual damages, and in appropriate cases, attorney fees.

On the "cost" side of the cost-benefit analysis, copyright registration (unlike patent registration) is simple, fast, and inexpensive. The author fills out the proper form and sends it, together with two copies of the work (or appropriate "identifying material" for non-printed works) and a $20 fee, to the Copyright Office. Since independent duplication does not violate copyright law, there is no need to search all the "prior art" (as is necessary for the issuance of a patent) to make sure there is no duplication. Consequently, registration is all but automatic. Unless there is an obvious omission or error on the form, it and the work will be filed, and a certificate of copyright will be issued to the author.

Scope of Protection. The author (or an assignee) is protected against unauthorized copying of the work. The author of a play has the exclusive right to have the play publicly performed. Authors of pictures and sculptures have exclusive rights to display their works to the public.

As previously noted, the normal protection period is the life of the author (or authors), plus fifty years. However, in the case of a "work for hire" the employer of the author owns the copyright for seventy-five years after the first publication of the work, or 100 years after the creation of the work, whichever comes first. A person who fits the common-law definition of employee (discussed in Chapter 30) is presumed to create any "works" which fall within the scope of employment, for the benefit of the employer. Likewise, an independent contractor (also discussed in Chapter 30) specifically hired, by written contract, to create certain types of works, also turns over copyright to the employer. Among the types of works specified in the 1976 Act are textbooks, tests, and test answers. If we had specifically hired someone to prepare the test questions for this book, we would own the copyright on the tests.

Infringement. Since there is no protection against independent production of a very similar work, there would be no infringement in such a case. Conceivably, a person who had never read this chapter could develop an analysis of "intellectual property" very similar to ours, and write a very similar chapter. If that were the case, we would have no claim for copyright infringement. Nor would we have a case if someone did read this chapter, but then wrote a different analysis of intellectual property. The *Amistad* problem at the end of the chapter raises this "similarity" issue.

Fair Use. One of the most important concepts in copyright law is the doctrine of *fair use.* The basic idea here is that the copying is not done to exploit the work commercially, and is incidental to some other legitimate purpose. According to the 1976 Act, these purposes include "criticism, comment, news reporting, teaching (including multiple copies for classroom use), scholarship, or research." **But**—whether any particular use is "fair" ultimately depends on the court's analysis of the facts of the particular case.

The statute specifies that the factors to be considered will include (at least): "(1) the purpose and character of the use, including whether such use is of a commercial nature or is for nonprofit educational purposes; (2) the nature of the copyrighted work; (3) the amount and substantiality of the portion used in relation to the copyrighted work as a whole; and (4) the effect of the use upon the potential market for or value of the copyrighted work."

Using these tests, a U.S. Court of Appeals decided that a private, for-profit copy shop which was preparing "course packs" based on professors' reading lists was violating the copyright law. Presumably, the students could have each made personal photocopies without violating the law, or the professor could have made the copies and distributed them. But using the third party processor, who was making a profit on selling the course packs, pushed the case over the line.

Parodies. Another difficult copyright problem arises when a copyrighted work is parodied by someone else. By definition ("a song sung alongside another"—from the Greek), a parody involves the use of the parodied work. How much such "use" is *fair* use? Clearly, there must be enough "use" to identify the work being parodied. On the other hand, the claimed parody should not just use the copyrighted work "to get attention" or "to avoid the drudgery in working up something fresh." This difficult line-drawing is illustrated by the *Dr. Seuss* problem at the end of the chapter.

The *Hormel Foods* case discusses several of these copyright issues, including the parody problem.

HORMEL FOODS CORP. v. JIM HENSON PRODUCTIONS, INC.
73 F.3d 497 (2 Cir. 1996)

FACTS: Hormel Foods Corporation appeals from a judgment of the United States District Court for the Southern District of New York denying Hormel's request for a permanent injunction against Jim Henson Productions, Inc., after a full bench trial on the merits. Hormel originally contended that Henson's use of the character "Spa'am" in its upcoming movie and related merchandise would infringe and/or dilute Hormel's trademark in the luncheon meat SPAM, but now limits its argument to the merchandising use. With respect to that use, Hormel argues that the district court erred in finding no infringement and that it misinterpreted New York's anti-dilution statute.

Since 1937, Hormel has used the trademark name "SPAM" to market its luncheon meat. It is beyond dispute that SPAM is a distinctive, widely recognized mark. Under that name, Hormel has sold over five billion cans of meat in the United States alone and spent millions of dollars to advertise its product.

In February 1996, Henson planned to release the film "Muppet Treasure Island," which features Henson's widely popular cast of puppets, known collectively as the "Muppets." The film uses some of Henson's most familiar characters, including Kermit the Frog, Miss Piggy, and Fozzie Bear. A number of additional characters have been created for this production, among whom is Spa'am, the subject of this litigation. The similarity between the name "Spa'am" and Hormel's mark is not accidental. In Henson's film, Spa'am is the high priest of a tribe of wild boars that worships Miss Piggy as its Queen Sha Ka La Ka La. Although the name "Spa'am" is mentioned only once in the entire movie, Henson hopes to poke a little fun at Hormel's famous luncheon meat by associating its processed, gelatinous block with a humorously wild beast.

However, the executives at Hormel are not amused. They worry that sales of SPAM will drop off if it is linked with "evil in porcine form." Spa'am, however, is not the boarish Beelzebub that Hormel seems to fear. The district court credited and relied upon the testimony of Anne Devereaux Jordan, an expert in children's literature, to find that Spa'am is a positive figure in the context of the movie as a whole—even if he is not "classically handsome." Indeed, Spa'am is a comic character who "seems childish rather than evil." Although he is humorously threatening in his first appearance, he comes to befriend the Muppets and helps them escape from the film's villain, Long John Silver. By film's end, "Spa'am is shown sailing away with the other Muppets as good humor and camaraderie reign."

Hormel also expresses concern that even comic association with an unclean "grotesque" boar will call into question the purity and high quality of its meat product. But the district court found no evidence that Spa'am was unhygienic. At worst, he might be described as "untidy." Moreover, by now Hormel should be inured to any such ridicule. Although SPAM is in fact made from pork shoulder and ham meat, and the name itself supposedly is a portmanteau word for spiced ham, countless jokes have played off the public's unfounded suspicion that SPAM is a product of less than savory ingredients. In a recent newspaper column it was noted that "In one little can, SPAM contains the five major food groups: Snouts, Ears, Feet, Tails, Brains." In view of the more or less humorous takeoffs such as these, one might think Hormel would welcome the association with a genuine source of pork. Nevertheless, on July 25, 1995, Hormel filed this suit alleging both trademark infringement and dilution.

 CIRCUIT JUDGE VAN GRAAFEILAND:

There is little doubt that SPAM is a distinctive, widely recognized trademark. Hormel has sold over five billion cans of its luncheon meat under the SPAM mark and invested millions of dollars in advertising. As a result, Hormel has a 75 percent share of the canned meat market and SPAM is eaten in 30 percent of all American homes. Thus, SPAM truly is a household name. In the usual trademark case, such an undeniably strong mark would be a factor favoring the trademark plaintiff. The more deeply a plaintiff's mark is embedded in the consumer's mind, the more likely it is that the defendant's mark will conjur up the image of the plaintiff's product instead of that of the junior user....

However, this does not always lead to confusion.... "[W]here the plaintiff's mark is being used as part of a jest or commentary, ... [and] both plaintiff['s] and defendant's marks are strong, well recognized, and clearly associated in the consumers' mind with a particular distinct ethic,... confusion is avoided...." Indeed, a parody depends on a lack of confusion to make its point. "A parody must convey two simultaneous—and contradictory—messages: that it is the original, but also that it is not the original and is instead a parody."...

We find, therefore, that the clarity of Henson's parodic intent, the widespread familiarity with Henson's Muppet parodies, and the strength of Hormel's mark, all weigh strongly against the likelihood of confusion as to source or sponsorship between Hormel's mark and the name "Spa'am." Moreover, this reasoning applies to both use of the Spa'am character likeness alone and use of the likeness and name together on Henson's movie merchandise....

Although Henson's wild boar puppet in no way resembles Hormel's luncheon meat or SPAM-man, Hormel contends that depiction of the puppet alone will conjure up the name "Spa'am," because consumers will associate the name that appears in the movie and media with the figure on Henson's merchandise. Thus, Hormel argues, use of the puppet likeness alone is in essence no different than its use in conjunction with its name. However, even combined use of the name and likeness does not present a strong case of similarity. Viewed alone, of course, the names "Spa'am" and "SPAM" bear more than a passing resemblance. Indeed, Henson's parody depends on the correspondence between the two. However, there are also some significant differences. "Spa'am" is divided in two by an apostrophe and it contains two a's instead of one. In addition, Spa'am is pronounced as two distinct syllables, SPAM only one....

Our finding that the marks are dissimilar in practice is buttressed by the fact that Henson and Hormel occupy distinct merchandising markets. The district court found that SPAM merchandise and Muppet merchandise featuring Spa'am "clearly

... derive their associations from a primary product—luncheon meat, in the case of SPAM, and a Muppet motion picture, in the case of Spa'am."... It noted that "purchasers of SPAM merchandise would generally be consumers of the luncheon meat," ... and that "consumers of merchandise bearing the likeness and/or name of Spa'am will buy it because they like Spa'am, the Muppets, and/or Muppet Treasure Island." Thus, the separation between the markets for luncheon meat and puppet entertainment carries over into the secondary merchandising market....

There is very little likelihood that Henson's parody will weaken the association between the mark SPAM and Hormel's luncheon meat. Instead, like other spoofs, Henson's parody will "tend[] to increase public identification" of Hormel's mark with Hormel....

This conclusion is strengthened when we consider that Henson's parody undermines any superficial similarities the marks might share. As we noted above, the name "Spa'am" will always appear next to the character likeness and the words "Muppet Treasure Island." This dissimilarity alone could defeat Hormel's blurring claim, for in order to establish dilution by blurring, the two marks must not only be similar, they "must be 'very' or 'substantially' similar."... Moreover, Henson is not using the name "Spa'am" as a product brand name. Rather, Spa'am is a character in products branded with Henson's own trademark "Muppet Treasure Island." This tends to dissipate the fear that SPAM will no longer be considered a unique product identifier. Viewed against the backdrop of Henson's transparent parodic intent and the contextual dissimilarity between the two marks, it is clear that use of the name "Spa'am" does not blur Hormel's mark....

Dilution may also occur by tarnishment. A trademark may be tarnished when it is "linked to products of shoddy quality, or is portrayed in an unwholesome or unsavory context," with the result that "the public will associate the lack of quality or lack of prestige in the defendant's goods with the plaintiff's unrelated goods." The mark may also be tarnished if it loses its ability to serve as a "wholesome identifier" of plaintiff's product....

Hormel argues that the image of Spa'am, as a "grotesque," "untidy" wild boar will "inspire negative and unsavory associations with SPAM luncheon meat." Both Hormel and *Amicus Curiae* rely heavily on our recent decision in *Deere, supra,* for the proposition that products that "poke fun at widely recognized marks of noncompeting products, risk diluting the selling power of the mark that is made fun of."... Their reliance is misplaced....

Therefore, in the instant case, where: (1) there is no evidence that Henson's use will cause negative associations, (2) Henson is not a direct competitor, and (3) the parody inheres in the product, we find that there is no likelihood of dilution under a tarnishment theory....

We affirm the district court's denial of injunctive relief.

Enforcement and Remedies. Just as for patent infringement, injunctive relief is available to the copyright owner. In addition, the allegedly infringing copies and the equipment used to produce them may be seized under court order ("impounded") for the duration of the trial, and then destroyed if the plaintiff wins the case. As a further special action, importation of infringing copies may be prohibited by the court, or by the U.S. Customs Service.

The 1976 Act provides for the recovery of both the plaintiff's actual damages and the defendant's illegally-earned profits, to the extent these two do not overlap. (The plaintiff only has to prove defendant's gross profits; the defendant has the burden of proving any related expenses, to try to reduce the amount of the award.) If the copyright was registered prior to the infringement, the plaintiff may elect to receive statutory damages instead, without having to prove any actual loss at all. The court is empowered to award whatever amount is "just," with a minimum of $500 and a maximum of $20,000. For unknowing or mistaken infringement ("innocent" infringement), a defendant who acted in good faith can get the statutory damages reduced to $200. Contrariwise, if the defendant's infringement was willful, the court may award statutory damages up to $100,000.

Court costs will also be awarded. Reasonable attorneys' fees may be awarded to the winning party, at the court's discretion. Unlike the rules for patent and trademark cases, where attorneys' fees are awarded only in "exceptional" cases, the court has the power to do so in any copyright case.

Criminal prosecution is also possible against willful infringers. Conviction may result in a fine up to $10,000, or imprisonment for up to one year. Conviction will also mean impoundment and destruction of the infringing copies. Because record and tape copying has become big business, 1982 amendments add harsher penalties for these "pirates"—fines up to $250,000, and up to five years in prison.

TRADEMARK LAW

Artisans and craftsmen who take pride in their work have long used the practice of identifying their goods with some distinctive mark or symbol. One source indicates statutes regulating this "trademark" practice as early as the thirteenth century. The early common law rules were directed primarily against a second producer's copying the mark of the original producer, in order to take advantage of the first's good reputation. Such "passing off" would be unfair both to the first producer and to the buyers.

Unlike patent and copyright, there is no express constitutional grant of "trademark" authority to Congress. The commerce clause is therefore the basis for national regulation in this area. The current statute is the Trademark Act of 1946, commonly know as the Lanham Act.

Definition. As was true historically, a trademark is a word, symbol, or other device used to identify the source of goods. Since the sale of services is such a large part of our modern economy, service marks have been developed to identify the source of services. They too are protected under the Lanham Act.

"**Trade dress**" refers to the total appearance of a product, including its size, shape, texture, color, and graphics. Such trade dress, when it is *nonfunctional* and *distinctive* (or has acquired a *secondary meaning*) is protected by law against copying. These rules are discussed further in Chapter 39, as part of the law of unfair competition.

Registration. Unlike the rules for patents, the basis for trademark protection is actual use of the mark in connection with the sale of a product, rather than the registration of the mark. Common law rules protect the first user of a distinctive mark in connection with the sale of a product or service within a given geographic area.

Registration with the U.S. Patent and Trademark Office does, however, provide important benefits. It gives "constructive" notice to all persons marketing in the U.S. that the mark has been claimed. Thus, no later user of the registered mark can claim to be doing so in "good faith." Further, the validity of the registered mark becomes *incontestable* after five years. In addition, when it becomes necessary to enforce the registered mark, the national courts can be used, even without diversity of citizenship.

Even though a mark does not qualify for listing in the "primary register," because not distinctive, it may still be listed in the "supplemental register," if the mark is capable of becoming distinctive. Such supplementary registration may be advisable, in order to protect use of the mark in other nations. Another nation might permit registration of the mark there, but require that it first be registered in its "home" country. U.S. "supplemental registration" meets this requirement.

For smaller companies operating within a single state, registration with the appropriate state official there may be sufficient.

Scope of Protection. What, then, can be registered as a trademark? As seen in the *Qualitex* case, which follows this section, the Lanham Act permits registration of any "word, name, symbol, or device, or any combination thereof." The mark must be inherently distinctive, or have acquired a secondary meaning (i.e., buyers associate the non-distinctive mark with the product or service of a particular seller).

In the classic categorization of marks stated by one court, there are four types: *arbitrary* or *fanciful* marks, *suggestive* marks, *descriptive* marks, and *generic* marks. "Kodak" is the classic arbitrary mark—a word which has no meaning at all, apart from its use as a trademark. One source suggests that "Roach Motel" would be a suggestive mark for an insect trap. Both of these kinds of marks are distinctive, and thus registrable.

On the other hand, descriptive marks cannot be protected unless a secondary meaning is proved. A generic term cannot be protected, even if a secondary meaning has been developed. If a term within one of the other categories comes to be used generically, trademark protection may be lost. This has happened to "aspirin" and "cellophane," for example. Xerox Corporation publishes advertisements every year to remind users that "Xerox" is a specific, copyrighted term, not a generic term for "copier."

The *Qualitex* case involves the issue of whether a color can be registered as a trademark.

QUALITEX CO. v. JACOBSON PRODUCTS
514 U.S. 159 (1995)

FACTS: Qualitex manufactures pads for the clothes presses used by dry cleaners. Since the 1950s, it has used a special shade of greenish-gold color ("brass #6587") to identify its product. (The National Bureau of Standards indicated that, with good lighting, the average person can distinguish some *five million* shades of the 300 colors for which there are verbal designations.) Many dry cleaners were small, family-owned businesses, staffed primarily by recent immigrants, many of whom had limited English-language skills. They thus relied on the green-gold color to identify (and purchase) Qualitex's product.

In 1989, Jacobson Products began selling a competing press pad, which was colored a similar green-gold. Qualitex filed a lawsuit, then subsequently registered its green-gold color as a trademark and added a count to the complaint alleging trademark infringement. The U.S. District Court awarded damages, and ordered Jacobson to stop passing off its product as Qualitex's. On appeal, the Ninth Circuit Court of Appeals upheld the award of damages and the injunction, but cancelled Qualitex's trademark, on the basis that a "mere color" could not be trademarked. Other Circuits had decided this issue both ways, so the Supreme Court granted Qualitex's petition for certiorari.

 JUSTICE BREYER:

The question in this case is whether the Trademark Act of 1946 (Lanham Act) ... permits the registration of a trademark that consists, purely and simply, of a color. We conclude that, sometimes, a color will meet ordinary legal trademark requirements. And, when it does so, no special legal rule prevents color alone from serving as a trademark.:..

Both the language of the Act and the basic underlying principles of trademark law would seem to include color within the universe of things that can qualify as a trademark. The language of the Lanham Act describes that universe in the broadest of terms. It says that trademarks "include any word, name, symbol, or device, or any combination thereof."... Since humans beings might use as a "symbol" or "device" almost anything at all that is capable of carrying meaning, this language, read literally, is not restrictive. The courts and the Patent and Trademark Office have authorized for use as a mark a particular shape..., a particular sound..., and even a particular scent.... If a shape, a sound, and a fragrance can act as symbols why, one might ask, can a color not do the same?

A color is also capable of satisfying the more important part of the statutory definition of a trademark, which requires that a person "use" or "intend to use" the mark "to identify and distinguish his or her goods, including a unique product, from those manufactured or sold by others and to indicate the source of the goods, even if that source is unknown." True, a product's color is unlike "fanciful," "arbitrary," or "suggestive" words or designs, which almost automatically tell a customer that they refer to a brand.... But, over time, customers may come to treat a particular color on a product or its packaging ... as signifying a brand. And, if so, that color would have come to identify and distinguish the goods (i.e., "to indicate" their "source") much in the way that descriptive words on a product ... can come to indicate a product's origin.... In this circumstance, trademark law says that the word ... although not inherently distinctive, has developed "secondary meaning."... Again, one might ask, if trademark law permits a descriptive word with secondary meaning to act as a mark, why would it not permit a color, under similar circumstances, to do the same? We cannot find in the basic objectives of trademark law any obvious theoretical objection to the use of color as a trademark,-where that color has attained "secondary meaning" and therefore identifies and distinguishes a particular brand (and thus indicates its "source")....

Having determined that a color may sometimes meet the basic legal requirements for use as a trademark and that respondent Jacobson's arguments do not justify a special legal rule preventing color alone from serving as a trademark (and, in light of the District Court's here undisputed findings that Qualitex's use of the green-gold color on its press pads meets the basic trademark requirements), we conclude that the Ninth Circuit erred in barring Qualitex's use of color as a trademark. For these reasons, the judgment of the Ninth Circuit is Reversed.

Infringement. Infringement occurs when a second seller (such as Jacobson) uses a mark which is so similar to the first user's trademark that buyers are likely to be confused as to the source of the second product or service. The owner of the original trademark does not have to prove that any consumer has actually been confused, only that there is a reasonable likelihood of such confusion. Thus, all the facts need to be considered, such as the similarity of the marks, the similarity of the goods or services being sold, and the similarity of marketing channels used. If there *is* evidence of buyers' actually having been confused, that would normally be sufficient evidence of a "likelihood" of confusion.

Enforcement and Remedies. The remedy package for trademark violations is much the same as those for other intellectual property rights violations: injunction, destruction of violating materials, damages, and attorneys' fees. Damages here include *both* the plaintiff's losses *and* the defendant's profits. The court has the discretion to adjust the award of (gross) profits up or down, to make sure that it is neither inadequate nor a "penalty." Likewise, the court may award up to three times the plaintiff's proved losses, if there is an indication that the actual losses were greater.

Here too, a trademark owner may be able to prevent the importation of infringing goods. However, if the goods have been lawfully manufactured and sold overseas, it may not be possible to do so. This problem is discussed more fully in the next section.

INTERNATIONAL ASPECTS

Two international problems with respect to the use of intellectual property arise with enough frequency to justify further discussion here. The first problem is the unauthorized importation into the U.S. of properly produced goods. The second is the unauthorized use of intellectual property to make and sell goods in other countries.

Gray Market Goods. The first problem is usually described as the sale of "gray market goods." The goods themselves have been properly produced, either by the owner of the intellectual property, or by a licensee. The irregularity (the "gray-ness") arises from someone's violation of the original understanding on how the goods were to be distributed.

This situation arises because manufacturing costs, especially wages and environmental compliance, are substantially lower in many nations than they are here. A foreign licensee might be able to produce the same item for 60 percent of the U.S. cost, add on a 10 percent profit, and sell to a local distributor in that nation. The distributor adds on a 10 percent profit, and 10 percent for shipping costs to the U.S., and can still significantly undercut the U.S. producers. Alternatively, the U.S. producer sells goods to a foreign distributor, with a large discount because the buyer will assume all advertising and other distribution costs. Rather than reselling the product there, however, the foreign distributor brings it back to the U.S., for sale here at a discounted price. U.S. consumers (and large discount stores) are happy with these arrangements, but the U.S. producers are not.

Can the U.S. producer, as owner or licensee of the intellectual property connected to the product, prevent these "re-importations," these "Lassies" who always come home? The only answer to this complex question is "Sometimes." The *Quality King* case addresses the problem in the context of copyrighted product labels.

QUALITY KING DISTRIB. v. L'ANZA RESEARCH INTERN.
118 S.Ct. 1125 (1998)

FACTS: L'Anza manufactures hair care products, which it advertises heavily and for which it charges premium prices. In the U.S., L'Anza sells exclusively to distributors who have agreed to resell only within their geographic areas and only to authorized retailers, such as barber shops, beauty salons, and hair-care schools. L'Anza provides special training to these retailers. For its foreign sales, however, L'Anza has no similar promotion or advertising activities. Prices to its foreign distributors are thus 35 percent to 40 percent lower than those charged here.

In 1992 and 1993, L'Anza's U.K. distributor sold three shipments of goods to a buyer in Malta. Each shipment contained several tons of L'Anza's products, with copyrighted labels attached. It is not clear from the record whether this was a resale, or a direct sale through the U.K. distributor as agent. Some of these goods were purchased by Quality King, reshipped to the U.S., and sold to unauthorized distributors in California. The U.S. District Court for the Central District of California granted summary judgment for L'Anza, and the Ninth Circuit affirmed. Quality King asked for certiorari.

 JUSTICE STEVENS:

Section 106 (3) of the Copyright Act of 1976 ... gives the owner of a copyright the exclusive right to distribute copies of a copyrighted work. That exclusive right is expressly limited, however, by the provisions of SS. 107 through 120. Section 602(a) gives the copyright owner the right to prohibit the unauthorized importation of copies. The question presented by this case is whether the right granted by S.602(a) is also limited by SS. 107 through 120. More narrowly, the question is whether the "first sale" doctrine endorsed by S.109(a) is applicable to imported copies....

This is an unusual copyright case because L'Anza does not claim that anyone has made unauthorized copies of its copyrighted labels. Instead, L'Anza is primarily interested in protecting the integrity of its method of marketing the products to which the labels are affixed. Although the labels themselves have only a limited creative component, our interpretation of the relevant statutory provisions would apply equally to a case involving more familiar copyrighted materials such as sound recordings or books....

The most relevant portion of S.602(a) provides:

> "Importation into the United States, without the authority of the owner of the copyright under this title, of copies or phonorecords of a work that have been acquired outside the United States is an infringement of the exclusive right to distribute copies or phonorecords under Section 106, actionable under Section 501...."

It is significant that this provision does not categorically prohibit the unauthorized importation of copyrighted materials. Instead, it provides that such importation is an infringement of the exclusive right to distribute copies "under Section 106."... [T]he exclusive right to distribute is a limited right. The introductory language in S.106 expressly states that all of the exclusive rights granted by that section— including, of course, the distribution right granted by subsection (3)—are limited by the provisions of SS. 107 through 120. One of those limitations ... is provided by the terms of S.109(a), which expressly permit the owner of a lawfully made copy to sell that copy "(n)otwithstanding the provisions of Section 106(3)."

After the first sale of a copyrighted item "lawfully made under this title," any subsequent purchaser, whether from a domestic or from a foreign reseller, is obviously an "owner" of that item. Read literally, S.109(a) unambiguously states that such an owner "is entitled, without the authority of the copyright owner, to sell" that item. Moreover, since S.602(a) merely provides that unauthorized importation is an infringement of an exclusive right "under Section 106," and since that limited right does not encompass resales by lawful owners, the literal text of S.602(a) is simply inapplicable to both domestic and foreign owners of L'Anza's products who decide to import them and resell them in the United States....

The judgment of the Court of Appeals is reversed.

 JUSTICE GINSBURG (concurring):

This case involves a "round trip" journey, travel of the copies in question from the United States to places abroad, then back again. I join the Court's opinion recognizing that we do not today resolve cases in which the allegedly infringing imports were manufactured abroad....

In 1988, in the *K-Mart* case, a five-Justice majority of the Supreme Court said that the U.S. owner of a trademark could prevent the unauthorized importation of goods that had been lawfully produced by an overseas licensee.

Pirated Intellectual Property. The second problem involves the out-and-out pirating of intellectual property by foreign producers. This is a huge problem; there are varying estimates of how many tens of billions or hundreds of billions of pirated products are sold each year. Governments of other nations vary in the vigor with which they enforce the intellectual property rights of foreign owners (or even those of their own citizens). In 1996, for example, the U.S. government threatened to impose trade sanctions against China for failing to protect intellectual property rights, especially rights on computer software.

Treaties/Conventions. To try to deal with the problem of international enforcement of intellectual property rights, several multi-nation treaties (usually referred to as *conventions*) have been negotiated. Included here are the Berne Convention (for copyrights), the EC Patent Convention, the European Patent Convention, the Paris Convention (all IP forms), the Patent Cooperation Treaty, the Universal Copyright Convention, the Vienna Trademark Registration Treaty, and others. Many nations have signed on to one or more of these agreements. Even within a nation which has agreed to the relevant treaty or convention, the IP owner still needs to be aware of significant differences in local laws, and in the effectiveness of local enforcement.

SIGNIFICANCE OF THIS CHAPTER

It is difficult to imagine any single legal topic of more importance to today's global economy than intellectual property rights. Intellectual property is the source of significant competitive advantages for most companies. Protection of these major corporate assets has to be of primary concern to managers. This chapter provides an overview of the rules for doing so.

PROBLEMS FOR DISCUSSION

1. For over thirty years, Pepperidge Farm has sold its popular "Goldfish" snack crackers. They are fish-shaped, golden in color, and available in several flavors. They have a small, but distinct, share of the snack cracker market.

   Nabisco, a huge producer of crackers and other snack foods, plans to introduce a small cheese-flavored cracker shaped like various animals, including a golden-colored fish. Pepperidge Farm sued to enjoin the sale of the new Nabisco crackers.

   Should the injunction be granted? Why or why not?

2. Apple Computer manufactures and markets personal computers, related peripheral equipment, and computer programs. Franklin Computers makes and sells the ACE 100 personal computer, designed to be "Apple compatible," so that Apple software could be used on the ACE 100.

   Franklin admitted copying the Apple computer programs. Its vice president of engineering stated that it was not "feasible" for Franklin to create its own programs, and that there can be no infringement because Apple's programs are not copyrightable.

   If Apple sues, what result, and why?

3. Between 1931 and his death in 1991, Theodore Geisel wrote and published forty-seven children's books, with total world-wide sales of some thirty-five million copies. Geisel used "Dr. Seuss" as his pen name. One of his most popular characters was the "Cat in the Hat," who wore a large, floppy, red-and-white stovepipe hat.

   In 1995, Alan Katz and Chris Wrinn produced a satire on the O.J. Simpson murder trial, titled "The Cat NOT in the Hat." They used a rhyming style similar to Geisel's to tell the O.J. story, and O.J. is pictured thirteen times wearing the Cat's distinctive stovepipe hat.

   Dr. Seuss Enterprises sued, to enjoin distribution of "The Cat NOT in the Hat." Should an injunction be issued by the court? Explain.

4. After three years of research, Chase Riboud wrote a historical novel ("Echo of Lions") loosely based on the story of the revolt on the slave ship *Amistad*. Published in 1989, her book sold about 500,000 copies. She then tried to interest movie studios, including Steven Spielberg's company, in doing a film version. In 1993, Punch Productions took a two-year option on the film rights, but then abandoned the project when no major studio showed any interest. In 1996, Spielberg announced that he would make the movie "Amistad." His named screenplay-writer was David Franzoni, who had been involved in trying to sell the "Echo of Lions" project. In October 1997, shortly before the release of the Spielberg film, Riboud filed suit for an injunction.

   What sort of analysis should the court do in deciding whether or not to enjoin the showing of the film? Discuss.

5. Vicki Company, a Michigan corporation, owns the nationally registered trademark "LeGance" for its high-priced line of jewelry. Vicki has learned that a large shipment of jewelry bearing its trademark, produced by one of its European licensees who is authorized to make sales only within the European Community, is headed for the U.S.

   What steps should Vicki take to protect its rights? Explain.

Chapter 26

Bailments and Carriers

In addition to professional bailees such as the carriers and warehouses mentioned in Chapter 15, many other businesses and individuals are frequently involved in **bailments**.

Have you ever loaned your car to a friend? Have you ever taken your stereo back to the dealer for repairs? Have you ever checked your coat and hat at a restaurant? These are all bailments. A bailment exists when the possessor of personal property gives possession and control to another person with the agreement that there is no transfer of title to the object and that the transfer of possession is temporary. The person who is giving up possession is a **bailor**, and the person who is receiving the personal property is a **bailee**.

ESSENTIAL ELEMENTS OF BAILMENT

Four essential elements must be present to create a bailment: (1) an agreement between the parties, (2) possession by the bailor of the object to be bailed, (3) delivery to the bailee of the object to be bailed, and (4) a duty on the part of the bailee to return the object to either the bailor or to someone else as instructed by the bailor.

Agreement. The first essential of a bailment, an agreement between parties, can be expressed either orally or in writing, or it may be implied from the facts and circumstances of the situation. An express agreement of bailment would normally cover the consideration, if any, to the bailor for the use of the bailed property or to the bailee for caring for it; what the property is going to be used for or how it is going to be used; when, where, and how the bailed item is to be returned to the bailor, delivered to someone else, or disposed of in some other manner; and the rights and duties of the parties.

In a simple situation, such as leaving your coat with the attendant in a cloakroom, you normally receive a token with a number on it. This is your receipt for the coat you entrusted to the cloakroom attendant, and normally when you hand this token back to the attendant you would get your coat. There is an implied agreement of bailment when you hand the attendant the coat: the attendant knows you are not transferring title and that your intent is to have the coat returned to you. The attendant is also aware of his or her duty to take care not to damage the coat.

If you rent a car from a car rental agency, you will sign a rental agreement. The contract you sign is an agreement of bailment because it will specify the consideration that you will pay for the use of the car, the restrictions on its use, when and where the car is to be returned, and specific details as to the rights and duties of the parties in case of damage to the car or damage to a third party.

Possession by the Bailor. To have a bailment, the bailor must have possession of the object to be bailed. The bailor need not be the owner of the property. In fact, the bailor may be a bailee. For example, as the bailee of the car you rented from Hertz, you may entrust it to a parking attendant and thus become its bailor, as to the parking lot.

Delivery of the Object to be Bailed. There must be delivery of the object to be bailed from the bailor to the bailee, and the bailee must accept delivery of the object. As noted earlier, size, weight, and location prevent some items of personal property from being physically handed over to another person. Instead, we may have **constructive delivery**, such as handing a person the keys to a rental car in the parking lot and telling the person to go ahead and take the car. Where the bailed property contains other items, there is no bailment as to those items unless the bailee knows, or has reason to know, of their existence.

For example, suppose that a friend loans you a car to drive downtown. The friend asks you to bring it back to the parking garage, park it in an assigned space, and return the keys before 5 p.m. After making some purchases downtown, you open the trunk and find a pocket-size radio with earphones, the type used by joggers. You take it out and use it. Obviously the radio was not part of the car and it is not bailed property. You are using it without permission.

Bailee's Duty to Return Object to Bailor. The bailee must have a duty to return the personal property to the bailor, to deliver the property to a third person, or to dispose of the property in accordance with the bailor's wishes. Assume that you rent a U-Haul truck to move your household goods from Los Angeles to New York. As the bailee, you will have a duty to return the specific property, the truck, to the bailor or to any person the bailor may designate. In this case, let's say that the bailor does not have an office in New York City, and therefore the bailor directs you to deliver the truck to a specific location in New York City where an employee of the bailor will pick it up and drive it back. The important factor here is that the object is still the bailor's property and that the bailee has the duty to give up possession of the object at the time and place that the bailor designates.

GENERAL LEGAL RULES

Types of Bailments. Basically, there are three types of bailments. First, there is a type where both parties benefit from the bailment. Before leaving school, you rent a rug shampooer from a rental agency to clean your apartment to get your security deposit back. You are paying to use the rug shampooer so the bailor benefits and, in exchange for your payment, you receive the right to possess, use, and control the rug shampooer for a specified time.

In the second type of bailment the bailor is the only person who benefits from the arrangement. For example, your neighbor is going to the store where you bought your stereo and you ask that person to take your stereo back for adjustment. Your neighbor agrees, and you deliver the set to him for the purpose of taking it to the store for repairs. Obviously, your neighbor is doing you a favor for no personal gain.

A third type of bailment is one where only the bailee benefits. Your roommate borrows your car for the evening. No payment is to be made; the bailment is simply for the benefit of the bailee. In each of these last two situations, there is a bailment even though there is no contract.

Bailments also can be classified into two major categories: **gratuitous bailments**, where no fee is charged for the use or care of the bailed object, and bailments where a fee is charged. Bailments made in exchange for payment can be further broken down into two areas: **commercial bailors** such as automobile or equipment rental companies, and **professional bailees**, such as common carriers, innkeepers (hotels and motels), and warehouses. Professional bailees will be discussed in detail later in this chapter.

Custody. Businesspeople need to understand the difference between bailments and custody situations where a bailment will not exist. By knowing what creates a bailment, business owners can reduce liability for damage or theft of customers' property by avoiding situations in which they would become bailees. For example, in the typical university parking lot you either pay by the month or get a claim check upon entering and pay when leaving. Since you park your own car and keep the keys, no bailment exists. You have not entrusted your car to the parking lot owner; you simply rent space. If, however, a parking lot attendant gives you a claim check, takes your car, parks it, and retains the keys, then there is a delivery to and acceptance by the bailee. In the case involving the university parking lot, there was no delivery to the bailee or acceptance by the bailee. You simply drove your car in and parked it.

Rights of the Bailee. Since a bailment is based on an express or implied agreement between two parties, each party has rights and duties with regard to the use, care, and eventual return of the object of the bailment. The bailee has the right to possess, use, and control the object during the period of the bailment, subject to any legal restrictions and to the restrictions in any express or implied agreement. For example, a garage to which you had given your car for repairs would not have the right to make any other use of it.

Duty of Care for the Bailed Property. The general rule is that the bailee must take reasonable care of the bailed object while it is in the bailee's possession and control. If something happens to the bailed object, does the bailee have to reimburse the bailor for the cost of repairs if damaged, or the value of the object if it was lost or stolen? If, in fact, the bailee exercised reasonable care and still the damage or loss occurred, the bailee owes nothing to the bailor. If, however, the bailee failed to use reasonable care, then the bailee would be liable to the bailor for the damages or the value of the object if lost or stolen.

Now the question is: How much care is reasonable? The courts look at various factors when determining what level of care is reasonable. First, what type of bailment is involved? Is it a mutual benefit bailment, a bailment solely for the benefit of bailee, or a bailment solely for the benefit of the bailor? Next, courts consider the type of object and, when appropriate, the skill level of the bailee.

In the case where the bailment is for the sole benefit of the bailor, the bailee must still use reasonable care, but again, what is reasonable depends on the circumstances and the facts.

The *Commercial Union* case discusses these rules.

COMMERCIAL UNION INSURANCE CO. v. BOHEMIA RIVER ASSOCIATES, LTD.
855 F.Supp. 802 (D.MD., 1991)

FACTS: Presently before the Court are several motions for summary judgment. The twenty plaintiffs in this consolidated admiralty case are the owners of yachts that were either destroyed or damaged by fire at the Bohemia Bay Yacht Harbour ("marina") in Chesapeake City, Maryland, on January 6, 1989. Plaintiffs seek recovery from six defendants, five of whom were allegedly involved in the construction, development, or operation of the marina.

The difficulty with this admiralty case is that "the marina" was not a traditional marina. That is, instead of having one entity or individual own and run the facility, Bohemia Bay Yacht Harbour was developed as a "condominium marina." Individuals owned their slips, while the condo association maintained the common areas, including all of the piers. The plaintiffs in this case either owned or rented their slips.

 JUDGE SMALKIN:

Defendants NPI, Condo Association, BRA, and BYS assert that there are no facts allowing the plaintiffs and their insurers to allege claims under a bailment contract. All of the plaintiffs who leased their slips pursuant to a Slip Rental Agreement argue the existence of a bailment relationship, which they claim arose through the lease agreement. Additionally, plaintiff Brian Hard, owner of slip F-8, asserts a claim under a bailment theory.

Generally, a contract for the storage or repair of a boat constitutes a bailment agreement.... In admiralty law, a bailor makes out a rebuttable presumption of negligence if the bailor proves that the bailed article was delivered in good condition and was returned damaged or not at all.... The burden of proof then shifts to the defendant/bailee who may rebut the presumption of negligence by showing that either the disaster was in no way attributable to the defendant's negligence, or that the defendant did indeed exercise the requisite care....

The parties disagree as to whether a bailment requires exclusive control by the bailee. As plaintiffs note, the exclusive control requirement has been relaxed somewhat when the owner of the boat has access to it in dry storage.... But, as is true with the general law of bailment, the majority of the admiralty cases consider the bailee's exclusive right to possess the boat a major factor which points in the direction of an admiralty bailment.... The rebuttable presumption of negligence given a bailor makes sense if the bailee has exclusive control, because it is then the bailee who is in the best position to explain the loss.

Plaintiffs' failure to assert that either the marina or any of the defendants had the exclusive right to control the vessels, is, in itself, enough to deny them the benefit of the bailment presumption.... All of the plaintiffs who claim that there was a bailment in this case rented or owned water slips, and all but one plaintiff rented pursuant to a Slip Rental Agreement.

There is a distinction in the admiralty cases between what is essentially a mere lease and a bailment. A lease is an agreement to pay a fee for the opportunity to tie a boat at an assigned slip ... while a bailment is a contract for storage or repair.... A plain reading of the lease agreements in this case indicates that the parties were contemplating a contract for the leasing of space at the marina.

According to some of the plaintiffs, defendant NPI served as the marina's management company and "undertook to perform certain services for yachts which entered into storage agreements with the marina ... including keeping a general eye on the yachts, boarding them to correct obviously unsafe conditions such as failure of bilge pumps, etc."... The Slip Rental Agreement in this case explicitly provides for the lease of space, and it does not list any other services. Additionally, because these alleged services were purportedly for the benefit of all of the areas leased, it is highly unlikely that the services arose out of the Slip Rental Agreement.... In any event, these alleged duties undertaken by the marina do not transform the lease agreement into a bailment contract, given the lack of exclusivity of possession. The plaintiffs who rented their slips were admittedly involved with a condominium regime, not the typical boat storage and repair bailment contract which is common in maritime affairs.

The above analysis applies with equal force to those plaintiffs who owned their slips, including plaintiff Hard. In addition, the Court has found no authority, and plaintiffs point to none, applying the bailment presumption where the article in question is located on the plaintiff's own property. Accordingly, the motions for partial and complete summary judgment will be granted as to all claims based on a bailment contract.

Bailee's Contract Liability. In view of the uncertainty about what the common-law liability of the bailee may be, in certain circumstances, it is advisable to specify the bailee's liability in the bailment contract. This is especially true for a commercial bailee, such as a garage or a repair shop. A parking garage will normally have a disclaimer clause in the bailment contract stating that the garage will not be responsible for theft of or damage to the automobile while the automobile is in its custody. Typically, this clause is printed on a parking ticket which you receive as you enter the parking lot. Also, the terms are in very small print. This disclaimer clause may be effective in relieving the bailee of liability for damage to your car if the clause is called to your attention when you leave the car, except in cases where the bailee or its agents or employees negligently or willfully damage the bailed property. If the parking attendant backed your car into a post, for example, the bailee would be liable for the damages, even though a clause in the bailment contract disclaimed all liability. If, on the other hand, the brakes of another parked car failed and that car ran into your parked car, no negligence would be attributed to the bailee or its employees or agents; the disclaimer clause would relieve the bailee of liability.

Some courts have held such disclaimer clauses to be against public policy, and thus not effective in limiting the professional bailee's liability.

The other extreme in contract clauses concerns the bailee's assumption of full liability for the bailed object. If you take your diamond ring to the jeweler for cleaning, the jeweler may issue a bailment contract which is, in effect, an insurance policy for the safety of your ring. If the jewelry store is broken into and your ring is stolen, the jeweler or its insurance company will reimburse you for the value of the ring. Rental contracts for cars, trailers, and equipment typically contain similar clauses, which purport to make the bailee liable for any loss to the property. They may or may not be fully effective.

Bailor's Liability for Defects. The traditional bailment litigation is that of a bailor suing a bailee for loss of or damage to the bailed property. Even though the amounts involved in many of these cases are relatively small, the results are important to the parties.

More and more, people are renting all kinds of items from professional rental companies. Hundreds of thousands of cars are rented each year. Many businesses have discovered that it is more economical to rent trucks when they need them than to own and maintain their own fleets. College students rent furniture, TVs, and refrigerators. Do-it-yourselfers rent all types of tools and equipment. Businesses rent computers, software, and other office equipment. As a result, legal rules have been formulated to deal with cases in which the rented property is defective in some way and causes injury to the bailee or to third persons. Most recently, an entire Article (2A) has been added to the Uniform Commercial Code to provide a more complete set of rules for such leases of personal property.

Where the bailor simply loans an item to a friend, the bailor's only duty is to inform the friend-bailee of any known hazards or defects in the item. The bailor has no obligation to inspect the item or to discover existing defects. If the bailee has been informed of all known defects, the bailor has no further liability.

In the mutual benefit bailment, the bailor's obligation is much more extensive. Most courts that have looked at this problem in recent years have applied to the professional bailor the same three theories of product liability that are applied to the seller of goods. In such cases, a bailor may be held liable for negligence because of a failure to exercise reasonable care in maintaining, servicing, and inspecting equipment which is being rented for immediate use. The bailor may also be held liable for breach of warranty—either express warranty or the implied warranties of merchantability and fitness. The most recent development has been the extension to professional bailors of warranty liability under Article 2A of the UCC. Many courts also apply strict liability to professional bailors of products.

Some of these rules are discussed in the *Cucchi* case.

CUCCHI v. ROLLINS PROTECTIVE SERVICES CO.
574 A.2d 565 (PA, 1990)

FACTS: In July 1973, Anthony and Grace Cucchi leased a burglar alarm system for their home. The Rollins salesman told Anthony that the system was "state of the art" and "almost unbeatable." The written contract signed by the Cucchis contained a clause which limited Rollins' liability to $250 for any loss caused by the system's failure to operate. However, this contract also stated that it would not become effective until signed by Rollins' home office, and it was never so signed.

The Cucchis' house was burglarized in 1984. The alarm system did not work, and some $36,000 worth of property was taken. The Cucchis sued, alleging negligence, breach of warranty, and strict liability. The trial court held that strict liability did not apply to this case. After trial, the trial judge directed a verdict for Rollins on the negligence count, but permitted the jury to consider the Cucchis' claims for express and implied warranty. The jury awarded Grace Cucchi $20,000 and Anthony $10,000. On appeal, the Superior Court reversed on the basis that the UCC's four-year statute of limitations applied and that the lawsuit had been filed more than four years after the lease commenced. The Cucchis appealed to the State Supreme Court.

 JUSTICE LARSEN:

[M]ost (but not all) courts that have considered the issue have concluded that Article 2 of the UCC, ... should be judicially extended to other sorts of transactions in goods, including various forms of leases, ... because ... there are sufficient economic and practical similarities between sales and leases of goods to apply at least some of the provisions of Article 2 ... to lease transactions....

Many consumers and businesses are leasing goods rather than buying them.... By leasing goods, parties achieve substantially the same result as by buying and selling. The essence of both transactions is that the lessee/buyer seeks to acquire the right to use goods and the lessor/seller seeks to sell the right to use the goods.... Considering that a large volume of commercial transactions is being cast in the form of a lease instead of a sale, and that leases reach the same economic result as sales, it would be illogical to apply a different set of rules to leases than to sales where there is no justification for doing so....

[L]essees rely upon implied and express representations of lessors as to the quality, merchantability, and fitness of goods to the same extent and in the same manner as buyers rely upon similar representations by sellers.... Accordingly, we hold ... that the express and implied warranty provisions of Article 2 ... apply to transactions involving the lease of goods....

Considering the nature of the transaction involved in this case, and the respective interests of the lessor and lessee, we have no difficulty finding that the express and implied warranties made by Rollins explicitly extended to future performance of the burglar alarm system and that discovery of the breach had to await the time of performance....

[T]he very nature of a conventional lease of goods with monthly payments by the lessee and the continuous obligation of the lessor to service and repair, especially where (as here) the goods are to be returned in working order to the lessor at the end of the lease, supports a finding that the future performance of the goods has been warranted, and that the goods will continue to operate and remain fit for their ordinary and intended use.

Bailee's Statutory Liability. In certain types of bailments, the bailee has a statutory duty rather than a common-law duty of care. Common carriers and innkeepers are by law held to a higher degree of care with regard to bailed property. Some states also have special statutes for parking lots, repair shops, dry cleaners, and other specific categories of bailees. Such statutes typically give the bailee a lien for services performed and the power to sell the property, if necessary, to enforce the lien.

PROFESSIONAL BAILEES: SPECIAL RULES AND REGULATIONS

Common carriers, warehouses, and innkeepers are referred to as professional bailees, and as such, they are subject to certain special rules and regulations.

Common Carriers

A **common carrier** is an organization, such as a railroad, a truckline, an airline, a bus company, a moving company, a pipeline, or any other type of business, that presents itself to the public as a transporter of goods or people. A common carrier must be licensed by the Interstate Commerce Commission (ICC) if it transports goods or persons over state lines, and it also has to be licensed by the commerce commissions of the various states where it operates. The license designates the routes and territory over which the common carrier is allowed to travel and do business. The common carrier may also be restricted to the transportation of a certain type of cargo. For example, the large household-moving companies move only household goods and do not have to accept commercial goods for transportation. The rates of the common carrier may be subject to ICC regulation and the various state commerce commissions. Airlines, railroads, and bus lines are common carriers that carry passengers as well as goods. In the past, their rates were strictly regulated; however, the trend now is toward deregulation, which allows competition among the carriers.

Common Carrier of Goods—Special Duty of Care. The basic difference between the duty of care required of the bailee in the ordinary bailment and that required in the common carrier bailment is that the bailee in an ordinary bailment must use reasonable care for the care and protection of the bailed goods, whereas the common carrier is by law virtually an **absolute insurer** of the goods being transported from the time that it receives the goods until it delivers them to their final destination. This is a very high duty of care, and there have been many instances where liability has been imposed for goods lost or damaged in transportation or delivery despite the fact that the common carrier used reasonable care.

The common carrier is strictly liable for damage to the bailor's goods while they are in its possession. At first glance, this rule may seem very harsh since loss or damage to goods could be caused by elements beyond the control or foreseeability of the common carrier. For this reason, five exceptions to the strict liability, or absolute insurer, rule have been adopted to reduce the common carrier's liability in certain circumstances. These exceptions are for damage to goods or the loss of goods which is caused:

1. *By an act of God.* For example, a tornado destroys the shipment.

2. *By action of a public enemy.* This would include damage in a war by enemy forces.

3. *By an order of public authority.* For example, if goods in shipment were in close proximity to a radiation leak from a nuclear power plant, the public authorities might condemn the shipment and have it disposed of.

4. *By the inherent nature of the goods.* For example, if goods are perishable, the bailor who is contracting to have them transported must notify the bailee of the problem, and the bailee may not want to accept the goods unless it has proper facilities for refrigeration and some guarantee of speedy transportation and delivery.

5. *By the bailor's negligence in packaging or crating.* This one is the most frequently used exception.

The courts tend to be very strict in their interpretation of the five exceptions. As a rule, for the carrier to avoid liability, the loss or damage must be due solely to one of the five excepted causes.

The following case is an example of the courts' interpretation of these rules.

MULAY PLASTICS, INC. v.
GRAND TRUNK WESTERN RAILROAD COMPANY
822 F.2d 676 (Seventh Circuit, 1987)

FACTS: Mulay's injection molding machine suffered damage from undetermined causes while being shipped. Mulay sued the shipper, the rigger, and the carrier under the common law, the Uniform Commercial Code, and the Carmack Amendment. The jury found for defendants. Mulay contended that the jury's verdict was not supported by the evidence and was inherently contradictory. The trial judge declined to grant a new trial or judgment notwithstanding the verdict and Mulay appeals.

Mulay purchased a massive piece of machinery, a used injection-molding machine, from Prestolite in February of 1981. Prestolite had used the machine for eleven years and sold it to Mulay "as-is." The injection-molding machine consisted of an injection end, a clamp end, and a base. The clamp end and base were shipped as a single unit (the "machine") from Prestolite's plant in Bay City, Michigan, to Mulay's in Addison, Illinois. Together, the clamp end and base are twenty-seven feet long and fifteen feet high and weigh about seventy-five tons. The clamp end itself, which rests on the base, weighs fifty tons. Mulay hired Dobson to move the machine from the Prestolite plant to a Grand Trunk railway siding and to load it on a Grand Trunk flatcar.

Mulay took no part in transporting the machine, leaving the disassembly, loading, rigging, and carriage to the defendants. Dobson brought the machine by truck from Prestolite's plant to Grand Trunk's siding and loaded it by crane onto the flatcar. Dobson blocked and bolted the base of the machine to the flatcar but did not block the clamp end, leaving it simply in its position atop the base. Thus, the six one-inch steel bolts and two one and one-quarter inch steel sleeve dowels which held the clamp end in place during operation were the only things holding the clamp end in place during shipment besides gravity and friction. The bolts guarded against vertical movement and the dowels against horizontal. The bolts and dowels can only be seen if a sheet metal cover is removed from the sides of the machine.

Grand Trunk's car man saw the machine four times. He took rough measurements of it in Prestolite's plant. He made a general inspection after it was loaded on the flatcar. Dobson's rigging foreman told him then how the machine would be secured and told him that there were parts above the base. He inspected it after rigging was finished and again before it left the siding. He approved the machine for transport as rigged.

Grand Trunk then transported it as far as Markham, Illinois. The machine was twice weighed underway at weigh stations of the Illinois Central Gulf Railroad Company. Illinois Central both times issued a weigh bill with instructions not to exceed thirty miles per hour, because the machine exceeded Illinois Central weight requirements for that type of load, flatcar and track. Signs were put on the flatcar with the legend, "Do Not Hump." "Humping" means coupling railway cars at speeds greater than four miles per hour.

In Markham, the unit was found to be severely damaged. The clamp end had come loose and moved almost six feet, damaging the machine in various ways. No one ever determined when the clamp end had moved. The bolts had been cut in half by the clamp end's movement. One witness testified that the dowels were found intact at the bottom of the flatcar. Another testified that the dowels were sheared.

 CIRCUIT JUDGE ESCHBACH:

The jury found for Grand Trunk on the Carmack Amendment count and for Prestolite on the UCC count. Mulay argues as follows: The parties agree that the machine was delivered to Grand Trunk undamaged and became damaged en route. Therefore, the jury must have found that Grand Trunk proved its affirmative defense, which required finding that the damage was caused by a "latent or hidden defect in the machine." Thus, the machine was delivered to Grand Trunk with a latent defect. But on the UCC count, the jury must have found that Prestolite delivered the machine free from defects. The two findings are contradictory.

Setting aside for a moment the wording of the instructions, we note first that a verdict for Grand Trunk on the Carmack Amendment count and a verdict for Prestolite on the UCC count are not inconsistent under the law. Grand Trunk establishes its defense if it proves that the damage was caused by an "inherent vice" of the machine. Prestolite wins unless Mulay shows that Prestolite did not "duly deliver" the machine. To say that verdicts for each defendant are inconsistent would be to say that the shipper's duty to "duly deliver" the goods includes the duty to ensure that the goods will not suffer damage as a result of an "inherent vice." Particularly here, where the machine was sold as-is, that would require more of the shipper than the UCC intends. Whenever goods suffer damage because of an inherent vice, the shipper would be liable, even where he sold the goods "as-is."...

Prestolite had performed the little that was required of it to ship the goods, which was to open a wall at its plant so Dobson could remove the machine. As discussed above, the jury was entitled to find that the damage was not a result of negligence on the part of Prestolite, that the dowels had been in securely in place when the machine left Prestolite.

At least where, as here, a nonmerchant shipper sells the goods "as-is," thus disavowing liability for hidden faults in the goods, the risk that they will suffer damage as a result of a latent, inherent vice is one that belongs with the risk of loss of the shipment. Mulay bought the machine "as-is," arranged for the rigging and shipping of the machine, knew how the machine would be shipped, and accepted the risk of loss during shipment. Prestolite would not have been liable if the machine had broken down the first time that Mulay used it. We will not hold that Prestolite did not "duly deliver" the machine and thus that the risk of loss did not pass to Mulay because Prestolite did not inspect the dowels where, as discussed below, the jury could find that inspecting the dowels or even blocking the clamp end would not have prevented the damage.

We turn to Grand Trunk. The Carmack Amendment absolves the carrier from liability when it can show both that it was not negligent and that the damage resulted from an inherent vice of the goods. The jury was entitled to find that Grand Trunk was not negligent, as discussed above.

As to the second prong of Grand Trunk's defense, in some cases it is clear what damage from an inherent vice of goods means. Foods rot; iron rusts; some wines simply do not travel well. Where the carrier is not negligent in handling such goods, he is not held liable for the rot, rust or deterioration. An inherent vice, then, could be understood to mean a quality of the goods that causes damage to the goods during transport even in the absence of negligence. There was evidence that such a quality was present in this case, as discussed above. Although the machine appeared solid and was normally securely held together by dowels, the dowels had a tendency to slip out during rail transport and permit the clamp end to shift on the base.

Returning to the discussion of the question whether the jury's verdicts were inconsistent under the particular instructions in this case, the reason for the tension is that the instructions use the word "defect" to refer both to an inherent vice of the goods for Carmack Amendment purposes and to a failure of the shipper to duly deliver the goods for UCC purposes and thus hazard conflating two distinct concepts. Under the instructions, an inherent vice is a "latent or hidden defect;" goods that are not [duly] delivered have a "defect." The jury found the machine to have the former but not the latter.

We reconcile the two findings by holding that the jury was entitled to find that where the goods had a "latent or hidden defect" for the purposes of the Carmack Amendment count, they did not necessarily have a "defect" for the purposes of the UCC count. In other words, the jurors could have decided that the tendency of the dowels to slip loose and permit the clamp end to shift was a "latent defect" for which the carrier was not responsible, but at the same time that condition was not a "defect" the presence of which meant that the shipper did not duly deliver the goods. The word defect would not be given the same meaning in the two instructions. That is not illogical; indeed, the word must be given different meanings in order to interpret the instructions accurately to reflect the law. This is a strained reading of the instructions, but a correct one. Such an understanding of the instructions is consistent with the law underlying the instructions and with the evidence in the case. As the trial judge put it, "You cannot, in Gertrude Stein terms, say, 'a defect is a defect is a defect.'..."

Liability Among Connecting Carriers. One problem that seems to come up constantly is that of the liability of the initial bailee versus the liability of the various connecting carriers or subbailees. If you were shipping goods from New York City to Los Angeles, you would make a bailment contract with a shipper-bailee in New York City, and that shipper would accept the goods for transportation and final delivery. However, as we learned, common carriers are limited in the routes and territory over which they can operate. Therefore, the New York common carrier might transfer the goods to several connecting common carriers before the goods are finally delivered in Los Angeles. Assume that the goods were in good condition when the bailor delivered them to the bailee carrier but were severely damaged when they finally were delivered in Los Angeles. Who damaged them—the original bailee, one of the connecting carriers, or the delivering carrier?

Obviously, in many cases, it is impossible to know which of the carriers caused the damage. Since there is strict liability for damage to the goods, the bailor may collect the full amount for the loss, and may make the claim against either the initial bailee or the delivering bailee. The bailee to whom the claim is made may, in turn, seek restitution from the other carriers involved. Thus, without proof as to which carrier actually caused the loss, the loss may be shared by all of the parties that handled the goods.

Common Carrier of Passengers—Special Duty of Care. What is the duty of the common carrier when the objects of transportation are persons rather than goods? Common carriers, such as railroads, airlines, and buses, that transport human beings, are not held to be absolute insurers of the safety of their passengers; however, their duty of care for their passengers' safety is still very high. The injured passenger must prove that the common carrier was guilty of at least some negligence.

Common Carrier—Right to Limit Liability to Bailor. In the absence of any specific state or national law or regulation, a common carrier has the right to limit its liability to its own negligence. Rather than accepting the strict liability or absolute safety standard, the carrier may include a limited liability provision in its contract with the shipper-bailor, provided, however, that the shipper-bailor is given a reduced rate in exchange for accepting the carrier's limited liability. In other words, if the shipper-bailor and the carrier-bailee agree to a limited liability contract, the courts generally will enforce the contract unless fraud, duress, or unconscionability was involved in the transaction. If the shipper-bailor so requests, however, the carrier-bailee must accept the shipment from the shipper-bailor with full liability, charging the full rate.

The common carrier may also make an agreement with the shipper regarding the value of the goods being shipped. Generally, the courts will accept this figure for loss purposes unless the amount appears unreasonable. Specific regulations of the Interstate Commerce Commission have further limited the liability of certain common carriers which transport goods in interstate commerce. These regulations do not affect the legal liability of the carrier for loss or damage. The liability is still strict liability with the exceptions previously noted. These regulations simply place a limit on the amount that the carrier must pay for loss of or damage to the goods.

If the shipper-bailor desires protection up to the full value of the goods, then the shipper-bailor may buy value insurance from the carrier or the carrier's insurance company. Specific regulations also limit the liability of common carriers that handle commercial freight rather than household goods. The value per pound is usually less for commercial freight. It should also be noted that the Interstate Commerce Commission regulations will change from time to time.

Shipper-bailors should make themselves aware of the pertinent regulations. Although Interstate Commerce Commission regulations govern the transportation of goods and persons in interstate commerce within the United States, many common carriers carry passengers and goods by air and sea outside the territorial limits of the United States. Thus, there is a need for treaties and regulations that limit the liability of common carriers involved in international commerce and travel. The Warsaw Convention is a treaty that limits the liability of airlines carrying passengers in international travel. The Carriage of Goods by Sea Act similarly limits the liability of carriers operating in international waters.

Common carriers of passengers, such as airlines, railroads, and bus lines, are required to have certain facilities for carrying the passengers' baggage. Regulations stipulate the number of bags that each passenger can transport and the maximum weight of each bag or the maximum weight of each passengers' total baggage. If baggage exceeds the weight limit or if the number of bags checked exceeds the allowable number, an added fare is charged. Limits have also been set on the common carrier's liability for loss of or damage to the baggage. The common carrier is not an absolute insurer of the passenger's baggage, but is responsible only for its negligence in its handling. Such negligence is defined as a lack of reasonable care in handling the baggage.

Bill of Lading. Except for automobiles, boats, airplanes, and other personal property which must be specifically licensed to be used, the owner of personal property normally does not have a specific ownership document for such property. This explains the expression, "Possession is nine tenths of the law." In other words, it is assumed that people own the objects in their possession unless such ownership is challenged by another person. Thus, for most of the goods that are shipped, such as household or commercial, there are no specific title registration certificates. The shipper-bailor simply delivers the goods to the common carrier with instructions to transport and deliver them, or the common carrier comes to the residence or business of the shipper and picks up the goods with instructions as to their transportation and delivery.

At the point where the shipper-bailor turns over possession to the common carrier-bailee, a document showing ownership of the particular goods is necessary. This document is called a **bill of lading** if the transportation is by land or sea, and it is called an **air bill** if the transportation is by air. The bill of lading or air bill serves as both a receipt for the goods and as a contract which states the terms of the agreement to transport and deliver the goods. Title to the goods may be transferred from the shipper to another person or organization by transferring the bill of lading or air bill.

A bill of lading or an air bill can be negotiable or nonnegotiable. If the bill is to be negotiable, it will state that the goods are to be delivered to the bearer of the bill or to the order of a specific person or organization. If the bill simply consigns the goods to a specific person or organization at the point of delivery, then it is nonnegotiable and it is called a **straight bill of lading** or a **straight air bill**.

The bill of lading or air bill must describe the goods. Typically, it will state the weight of the goods and describe the number of items and the content of the shipment in such a manner that the person receiving the goods will be able to identify them as those which were entrusted to the carrier for shipment.

Article 7 of the Uniform Commercial Code, Warehouse Receipts, Bills of Lading, and other Documents of Title, contains specific provisions governing the issuance and use of bills of lading and warehouse receipts. Normally, the bill of lading is issued to the shipper-bailor. The shipper-bailor can then mail the bill of lading to the person or organization that is to receive the goods at their final destination. However, Uniform Commercial Code Section 7-305(1) allows the shipper to request that the common carrier issue the bill of lading directly to the person or organization receiving the goods at the final destination or at any other place the shipper-bailor may request. Obviously, situations arise where mailing the bill of lading to the receiver of the goods would be unwise. It would be better to have the bill of lading issued by the carrier directly to the person or organization receiving the goods prior to or at the time of delivery.

If the bill of lading is negotiable, then the carrier may not deliver the goods without getting the bill of lading properly indorsed by the person or organization receiving them. If the goods are shipped under a nonnegotiable bill of lading, the carrier can simply deliver them to the person or organization named as consignee in the bill, and the bill of lading need not be indorsed by the receiving party. With a nonnegotiable bill, the carrier must verify that the receiving party is in fact the party to whom the shipment was supposed to be delivered. If the carrier delivers the goods to the wrong person, the carrier will be responsible to the shipper-bailor.

Warehouses

A public warehouse presents itself to the public as a business engaged in storing goods for members of the public for a fee. A private warehouse is a storage business that is not open to the public, but only leases storage space to one person or company or to a select number of persons or companies.

Warehouse Duties. A warehouse is liable for damage to or loss of the goods being stored by the bailor only if the warehouse fails to exercise reasonable care in their storage or handling. The warehouse is generally not held to the same standard of care as that required of the common carrier. What constitutes reasonable care has to be resolved in each case. The care required to store goods subject to damage or to deterioration by freezing would certainly be different from the care required to store lawn furniture for the winter. Fragile goods require more care than nonfragile goods. Stacking heavy cartons on top of fragile antique tables would not be reasonable care. Thus, the standard of care depends on the type and condition of the goods being stored, and the warehouse must provide facilities suitable for the goods being stored.

Warehouse Rights. The public warehouse is entitled to a lien for the amount of the storage charges on the goods stored by the bailor. If the stored goods are not picked up by the bailor at the designated time, the warehouse, after giving proper legal notice to the owner or to any other person having an interest in the goods, may sell the goods to pay off the lien. Most states have specific laws relating to the operation of warehouses and setting out the rights and duties of warehouses with regard to the claiming of liens for storage fees and with regard to the sale of stored goods to satisfy their bills.

Limitations of Liability. Like common carriers, warehouses may arrive at an agreement with the bailor on the values of the items being stored, and the courts will generally accept these figures assessing losses unless the amounts appear unreasonable. Warehouses may also limit their liability as to the amount which they will pay if stored goods are lost or damaged. Such a limit on liability is a contractual agreement between the bailor and the warehouse. The warehouse gives the bailor a reduced rate, and the bailor agrees to a maximum amount for which the warehouse will be liable if the stored item is lost or damaged. The warehouse's liability limit must be stated for each item or each unit of weight and not simply as a standard dollar amount per customer.

Warehouse Receipts. Every warehouse which stores goods for the public must issue a **warehouse receipt** to the bailor when the bailor leaves goods for storage. There is no specific statutory form that must be used. However, the receipt must contain certain essential terms, such as the *location* of the warehouse, the *date* the receipt was issued, and the *consecutive number* of the receipt. It also must contain a statement about *delivery*. Will the goods be delivered to the bearer of the receipt, or to the order of a specified person? If so, the receipt is negotiable, or, will the goods be delivered only to a specified person, thus making the receipt nonnegotiable? The rates to be charged must also be stated, and the goods must be described so that they can later be identified. The receipt must be signed by an employee or agent of the warehouse, and if any advances have been made or any liabilities incurred, an explanation must be made on the receipt. Section 7-202 of the Uniform Commercial Code governs the contents of the warehouse receipt.

Innkeepers

An **innkeeper**, more commonly known today as a hotelkeeper, is any person or organization that operates a hotel, motel, or other business that offers sleeping and living accommodations to transient persons. Owners of an apartment complex are not innkeepers, since they are not in the business of offering sleeping and living accommodations to transient persons.

Liability for Goods. Traditionally, the innkeeper was an insurer of the safety of the goods of its guests. The innkeeper's liability was subject to exceptions similar to those applicable to the liability of the common carrier for the bailor's goods. Thus, the innkeeper was not liable for damage to the guest's goods caused by an act of God, a public enemy, the nature of the goods, some act of a public authority, or negligence or fault of the guest, who in this instance is the bailor. Today, most states have passed laws to limit the common law liabilities of the innkeeper. Many statutes allow the innkeeper to limit its liability by posting a notice of the limitations. Frequently, a notice will be placed on the door of a hotel room or a card will be left in the room which states that the hotel will not be responsible for the theft of money, jewelry, or similar valuables. It advises guests to deposit these valuables with the innkeeper to be put in its safe until they are ready to leave.

Other states besides New York have enacted laws that limit the maximum amount for which an innkeeper can be held liable. Such a law might say that the innkeeper cannot be held liable for any amount in excess of $500 for loss or damage to the goods of a single guest. Some states have simply reduced the high standard of care that the common law required of innkeepers to a standard of ordinary care, basically the same care that any bailee must use with regard to bailed property. In no case, however, can an innkeeper be held liable for more than the actual value of the guest's goods. Moreover, the innkeeper is not liable for any consequential damages that may result from damage to or loss of the guest's property. For example, a manufacturer's representative rents a hotel room and has two suitcases of samples used to demonstrate products to prospective customers. The innkeeper could be responsible for the value of the samples and the suitcases, but would not be liable for any lost sales caused by the representative's inability to show samples to prospective customers. The *Bhattal* case examines some of these rules.

BHATTAL v. GRAND HYATT—NEW YORK
563 F. Supp. 277 (S.D.N.Y., 1983)

FACTS: Defendant, an innkeeper, seeks summary judgment in its favor in this alienage case, regulated by New York law. Plaintiffs, residents and citizens of India, registered as guests in defendant's Grand Hyatt Hotel in Midtown Manhattan on July 19, 1981, and were assigned Room 2946.

Following the customary practice in first class hotels in this City of the sort operated by defendant, plaintiffs turned over to the bell captain various pieces of personal luggage, which are now said to have contained valuables of great significance, and this luggage was duly transferred by defendant's employees to plaintiffs' assigned hotel room.

Plaintiffs did not request that any of their valuables be placed in the safe depository provided by the hotel, nor did they enter into any "special agreement" with the hotel concerning their valuables, as is contemplated by S.200 of the New York General Business Law.

Shortly after arriving at their room with the luggage, plaintiffs left the hotel for luncheon with friends, locking their door with a key provided by defendant. On returning early the same evening, plaintiffs discovered that their luggage and the contents thereof were missing.

 DISTRICT JUDGE BRIEANT:

All things in the modern world which go wrong for reasons other than the application of Murphy's Law, seem to go wrong because of a particular sort of mechanical malevolence known as "computer error." Apparently defendant's front desk relies heavily on computer support, and as a result of computer error, employees of defendant transported plaintiffs' luggage from plaintiffs' room to JFK International Airport, along with the luggage of aircraft crew members of Saudi Arabian nationality, who had previously occupied Room 2946. In other words, the computer omitted to notice that the room had been vacated and relet to plaintiffs, and hotel employees responding to computer direction, included plaintiffs' luggage along with the other luggage of the departing prior guests. This is not to suggest that the Grand Hyatt-New York is a hotbed house, but apparently it was operating at 100 percent occupancy with no lost time between the departure of the Saudi Arabian aircraft crew members who had previously occupied the room, and the arrival of plaintiffs.

Needless to say, plaintiffs' luggage departed for Saudi Arabia and has not since been seen. A missing pearl is always a pearl of the finest water, and accordingly plaintiffs demand damages in the amount of $250,000, together with costs and attorneys fees....

The motion thereby presents the question of whether [the] statutes limit the liability of an innkeeper, in a case where the innkeeper, by his own agents, intentionally and without justification, took custody and control of plaintiffs' luggage and contents, without plaintiffs' authorization, and intentionally, although inadvertently, caused the luggage to be transported to Saudi Arabia. The Court concludes that the statutes do not extend so far as to protect the innkeeper under these facts.

Essentially what has taken place here is a common law conversion of property by defendant's agents. A fair reading of the amended complaint as amplified by the papers submitted on this motion indicates that plaintiffs state a claim for unintentional conversion under New York law, although not specifically so labelled.... Intentional use of property beyond the authority which an owner confers upon a user or in violation of instructions given is a conversion....

Here, defendant's employees entered plaintiffs' locked room, without plaintiffs' permission or knowledge, and removed their luggage, commingled it with the luggage of the Saudi Arabian aircraft crew members and placed it on a bus headed for Kennedy Airport. The court infers that if the luggage was not stolen at Kennedy Airport, it arrived in Saudi Arabia and was eventually stolen by a Saudi thief who still had the use of at least one good hand. In this instance, the intentional acts of the defendant clearly constituted conversion under New York law.

Sections 200 and 201 of the New York General Business Law were adopted in the middle of the nineteenth century to relieve an innkeeper from his liability at common law as an insurer of property of a guest lost by theft, caused without negligence or fault of the guest.... These statutes and the cases cited thereunder by the defendant extend to the situation where there is a mysterious disappearance of valuable property, either as a result of a theft by an employee of the hotel—or a trespass or theft by an unrelated party, for whose acts the innkeeper is not responsible. The statutes are also intended to protect the innkeeper from the danger of fraud on the part of a guest in a situation where the property said to have disappeared never existed at all, or was taken or stolen by or with the privity of the guest....

The reason for providing a hotel safe in compliance with S.200 and the reason for limiting a hotel's liability under S.201 is to protect against just such situations. When a hotel room is let to a guest, the innkeeper has lost a large measure of control and supervision over the hotel room and its contents. While housekeeping and security staff can enter the room at reasonable hours and on notice to any persons present therein, essentially, for most of the time at least, property of guest which is present in a hotel room can be said to be under the exclusive dominion and control of the hotel guest, rather than the innkeeper.

We have been cited to no case extending the limited immunity provided by statute against the common law liability of innkeepers, where the liability sought to be founded on the innkeeper was based on the exercise of unlawful dominion and control by the innkeeper himself, or his agents and employees acting in the course of their employment; as contrasted with mysterious disappearances due to causes unknown, or criminal acts of third parties or employees acting for themselves rather than for the employer. As noted above, it was only for the latter class of cases that the statutes granted immunity.

Since Ss 200 and 201 of the New York General Business Law operate in derogation of the common law liability of an innkeeper as insurer, courts have traditionally construed their application strictly....

Applying this rationale to the case at bar, the Court is compelled to conclude that Ss 200 and 201 do not limit the liability of an innkeeper for its conversion of guests' property. In this case, the plaintiff's luggage was not converted or stolen from the hotel by means of an employee theft or a fraud perpetrated by a third party.... Rather, employees of the defendant, acting within the scope of their employment and relying on the accuracy of their employer's computer, intentionally converted the luggage of the plaintiffs by removing it from plaintiff's room and delivering it to an aircraft bound for Saudi Arabia. The theft (by unknown parties) occurred after the conversion....

[U]nder New York law, applicable here, absent proof of malicious intent on the part of the defendant, a party cannot recover damages for mental anguish, humiliation or emotional distress caused by conversion of a chattel.... There is no evidence to suggest that the defendant acted maliciously or willfully in converting the luggage of the plaintiffs. The employees of the defendant acted in good faith, in reliance upon the instructions of a computer. Although the propriety of placing such blind faith in a mere piece of unthinking machinery is questionable, it is clear that the conversion of the plaintiffs' luggage was not the result of malice. Therefore, damages for mental anguish or consequential damages arising from re-vaccination, etc., allegedly suffered as a result of the conversion are not recoverable. Absent malicious conduct, the proper measure of damages for conversion is the fair market value of the converted property at the time and place of the conversion, plus interest....

The remaining issue, which is the amount of plaintiffs' damages, requires a plenary hearing at which the parties will be free to introduce evidence as to the nature of the converted property and its fair market value at the time and place of conversion.

Innkeeper—Special Rights. The innkeeper is given a lien on all goods brought onto the premises by the guest for the charges for the accommodations. In most states, the innkeeper can hold those goods until the guest's debt is paid, and the innkeeper can ultimately sell those goods to enforce the lien.

SIGNIFICANCE OF THIS CHAPTER

Every person either has been or will be a bailor and a bailee. Most bailments in which we are involved from day to day are gratuitous, such as loaning a book to a friend or letting neighbors use a lawn mower while theirs is getting repaired. Remember, even though no money changes hands, a bailment still exists in those situations, and there is a possibility of legal action if the bailed object is lost, stolen, damaged, or totally destroyed. If the bailment is a business agreement with a professional bailee, such as a common carrier, a warehouse, or an innkeeper, then there are special rules and regulations which will govern the parties' rights and duties.

Prospective bailors and bailees should understand these rules and regulations and also realize that the various states may have other special regulations affecting their rights and duties.

PROBLEMS FOR DISCUSSION

1. Francisco Cintrone was injured when the brakes failed on a 1999 Ford truck which his employer had leased from Hertz. Cintrone had driven the truck for three days during the previous week. Cintrone said he had complained to Hertz each day about the brakes. When the accident occurred, Cintrone was a passenger in the truck; the driver was Robert Sottilare. Sottilare said that prior to the accident he had had no difficulty with the brakes; "they wasn't perfect;" "they were a little low, but they held." Both men were injured when the top of the truck hit a low bridge; the brakes had failed completely. The trial judge refused to charge the jury on Cintrone's breach of warranty claim, and the jury found for Hertz on the negligence claim, apparently feeling that neither party had been guilty of any negligence. Cintrone appealed.

   Who wins on appeal, and why?

2. On December 24, Mae Theobald came to the Crystal Palace Barber and Beauty Shop, owned by Guy and Helen Satterthwaite, for a permanent wave. There were three rooms at Crystal: the front room was the waiting room; the middle room was the beauty shop; and the back room was the barbershop. Persons on the street could see into the waiting room through the front window, but persons in the waiting room could not see into the beauty shop, or vice versa. Mae was wearing her new fur coat. When Helen called her to come into the beauty shop, Mae hung her coat on a hook in the waiting room. On a prior visit, Mae had asked Helen whether it was safe to leave her coat there and Helen had told her that it was safe, that nothing had been stolen in twenty years. This time Mae's coat was stolen. The trial court gave Mae $300, the value of the coat, on the basis that there had been a bailment and that the waiting room was not a safe place since there was no bell or other warning device on the front door and since the waiting room was visible from the street. Guy and Helen appealed.

   How should the appeal be decided? Explain.

3. Harvey Smith parked his car on a parking lot owned by Sarbov Parking, Inc. He drove up, took his claim check from the automatic machine, parked his car, and took the keys. His car was about 100 feet from the attendant's office, which had windows on all sides. The lot was well lighted. Later that evening an unidentified customer told the attendant that something was happening to one of the cars on the lot. The attendant went over to Harvey's car and saw a man looking under the hood. The man told the attendant that something was wrong with the car, which was his brother's, and that he was trying to fix it. The attendant made no further inquiry or observation, nor did he call the police, as he had been told to do if he saw a car being tampered with by unknown persons. When Harvey got back, the transmission was missing from his car. When Harvey sued, Sarbov Parking denied liability on the basis that no bailment had been established.

   What is the result here, and why?

4. Mindy, age 12, and her mother were visiting Mindy's grandparents, who were staying at the Beefeaters Tables Motel. At around 2:30 p.m., Mindy left the swimming pool area at the back of the motel and went to look at the rock garden and statue on the premises of the adjoining restaurant, the Beefeaters Tables Inn. Although both businesses had the same name, the inn was operated by a separate company and was not open for business at the time. Mindy spent several minutes looking at the inn's rock garden and statue. As she was skipping back to the motel, she was struck by a car in the driveway that separated the inn from the motel. Because of the shrubbery and other decorations, neither Mindy nor the driver could see each other. There was no warning sign to either pedestrians or drivers. Mindy sues the motel and the inn. Both deny liability on the grounds that she was not a guest, that she was trespassing on the inn's property, and that she was guilty of contributory negligence.

   Can Mindy recover for her injuries? Discuss.

5. Soby Construction Company is engaged in road building and other heavy construction projects. It hired Skjonsby Truck Line, Inc. to transport a large Caterpillar tractor from one of its job sites to another. The tractor was damaged when the truck carrying it slipped off the dirt road at the job site, causing the tractor to break the tie-down chains holding it and to roll upside down. In its complaint Soby Construction Company alleged: (1) that Syonsby's driver had negligently loaded the tractor, and/or (2) that he had negligently operated the truck. In its answer, Skjonsby denied that it had been negligent in any way and said that the accident was due to Soby Construction Company's negligence in constructing and/or maintaining the road on its job site. At the trial, Soby Construction Company offered no proof of specific negligence. Defendant moved to dismiss.

   How should the court rule, and why?

Chapter 27
Real Property—
Acquisition of Ownership

The law concerning the rights and duties of the owners of real property differs considerably from the law concerning the rights and duties of the owners of personal property. Some objects of personal property can be transported from state to state, or even from country to country.

When dealing with real property, we are concerned with land and with the permanent fixtures and buildings attached to it. The land cannot be picked up and taken across state lines; it is part of the earth's surface. The fixtures and buildings on the land may depreciate, burn down, or otherwise be destroyed; however, the land itself remains basically the same, century after century. Also, the land cannot be possessed physically in the same way that an item of personal property is possessed.

NATURE OF REAL PROPERTY

Real property is a term that describes the *bundle of rights* to a specific parcel of land. It includes not only buildings and permanent fixtures attached to the surface of the land, but also rights to the ground below the surface of the land and rights to the air and sky above the land. Thus, the owner of a parcel of land has rights to the airspace above that parcel, to water on it, to things growing on or attached to its surface, and to the minerals, underground waters, and whatever else may be found below its surface.

Airspace. Technically, the owners of a tract of land, and therefore of the airspace above it, could prevent anyone from trespassing into their airspace. This presented a problem since landowners could have restricted the large volume of interstate or even international air travel, so the

American Law Institute formulated a rule to govern trespasses into the airspace above a land-owner's parcel of land. That rule states that such an overflight is privileged if it is made at a reasonable height and if it is in accordance with all applicable government regulations. For example, the Federal Aviation Administration (FAA) regulations state that no aircraft may fly over a congested (populated) area at an altitude of less than 1,000 feet, and no aircraft may fly over a non-congested (farmland) area at an altitude of less than 500 feet. These rules do allow an exception for helicopters if they are operated without hazard and in accordance with specific regulations. An example would be the use of a helicopter for medical rescue operations in a congested populated area and the use of helicopters for crop spraying in a noncongested farm area.

The most obvious area of real property is the surface of the land. In Chapter 24, we discussed the question of when fixtures become real property and how certain things that are part of real property, such as growing crops, may be severed from the real property to become personal property. The rules are fairly clear concerning most of the land surface and the buildings, fixtures, trees, and other growing objects, which are generally affixed and stay affixed to it until they are severed by people or by an act of God. The water that is present on the land surface is in constant motion, and it changes course and swells and shrinks in height and width with the seasons and the years.

Water. Water rights, called **riparian rights**, are a concern of those who own land which abuts a lake, river, or other body of water. Generally, the owner of the land next to a stream, river or lake may take or use the water as needed for natural and domestic purposes on the land adjoining the water. For example, the water could be taken for use in irrigation, for washing, or drinking purposes. A riparian owner would not, however, have the right to divert the entire stream and thus deprive landowners downstream of its use. Riparian rights also concern the property boundary lines of land next to a river, stream, or lake. Does your ownership extend to the edge of the river, ten feet out into the river, or just where? The river or stream will run at different levels depending on the time of year. The general rule is that the property line will be at the point of normal flow of the river or stream. The law concerning riparian rights varies from state to state, because different areas of the country have different problems regarding water. In areas where water is scarce and irrigation is a necessity, rules governing the use of water from running streams will be strict. Also, different problems are involved if the property abuts a creek rather than a navigable river. In addition, many national and state statutes govern what a riparian landowner can or cannot do which might affect water quality.

The next case deals with a conflict between Wyoming law and Indian water rights.

IN RE BIG HORN RIVER SYSTEM
835 P.2d 273 (WY, 1992)

FACTS: The State of Wyoming and non-Indian water users appeal from a judgment entered by the district court which: (1) decreed that the Shoshone and Northern Arapaho Tribes on the Wind River Indian Reservation may change the use of their reserved water right as they deem advisable without regard to Wyoming water law, and (2) substituted the tribal water agency for the state engineer as the administrator of both reserved and state-permitted water rights within the Wind River Indian Reservation.

This is another appeal of an ongoing general adjudication of all water rights in the Big Horn River System, involving over 20,000 claimants. Because of its size and complexity, the adjudication is being conducted in phases. The dispute presently before this court relates to the interpretation of the amended judgment and decree entered on May 24, 1985, by Judge Alan B. Johnson (the 1985 decree) involving Phase 1, wherein the Tribes were granted the right to divert water for agricultural purposes on reservation land historically irrigated, as well as on reservation land included within certain future projects. In *Big Horn I*, this court affirmed the 1985 decree, granting the Tribes the right to divert water from the Big Horn River System for agricultural purposes and subsuming livestock, municipal, domestic, and commercial uses within those purposes. This court also affirmed the district court's finding that an instream flow right for fisheries was not a subsuming use. The United States Supreme Court affirmed the *Big Horn I* decision in 1989. After the United States Supreme Court affirmed the Wyoming Supreme Court's decision, the Tribes announced their intent to dedicate a portion of their reserved water right, which had been awarded for future projects, to instream flow for fisheries and other nonsubsumed uses in the Wind River. To that end, the Tribes adopted a Wind River Interim Water Code, created the Wind River Water Resources Control Board, and, on April 12, 1990, granted themselves Instream Flow Permit No. 90-001, which authorized the dedication for the 1990 irrigation season of up to 252 cfs of water in the Wind River for "fisheries restoration and enhancement, recreational uses, ground water recharge downstream benefits to irrigators and other water users."

Shortly after the issuance of Permit No. 90-001, the Tribes complained to the state engineer that the diversion of water by holders of state-awarded water rights caused the Wind River flows to be less than that amount authorized by the permit. The state engineer informed the Tribes that their permit was unenforceable because the Tribes had been awarded only the right to divert water and that any change in the use of future project water covered by their reserved water right must be made following a diversion. The Tribes nevertheless thereafter requested that the state-awarded water rights of Midvale Irrigation District be curtailed so that the instream flows could be maintained. The state engineer refused to honor this request, which he viewed as being an unlawful selective call.

On July 30, 1990, the Tribes filed a motion in the district court for an order to show cause why the state engineer should not be held in contempt, why he should not be relieved of his duties, and why a special master should not be appointed to enforce the Tribes' reserved water right. The State filed its own motion for a determination of certain administrative matters. The district court referred the motions to a special master for a report. The special master agreed to hear all the issues raised except for the contempt issue involving the state engineer.

After hearing oral arguments on exceptions to the special master's report, the district court entered its judgment and decree on March 11, 1991, declaring that the Tribes were entitled to use their reserved water right on the reservation as they deemed advisable, including instream flow use, without regard to Wyoming water law.

JUSTICE MACY:

Our opinion clearly and unequivocally stated that the Tribes had the right to use a quantified amount of water on their reservation solely for agricultural and subsumed purposes and not for instream purposes. If we had intended to specify what the water could be used for merely as a methodology to determine the amount of water the Tribes could use for any purpose, we would have said so. The contrary is unmistakable. See the dissenting opinions of Justice Thomas and Judge Hanscum in *Big Horn I*, wherein they stated that they would have allowed the Tribes to use the water for any purpose appropriate to the progress and development of the reservation rather than limiting the uses to those mentioned in the majority opinion. It is not necessary for us to discuss the Tribes' alternative contention that principles of federal law do not limit the uses to which they may put their water or the State's contention that the 1983 decision and the 1985 decree are not final orders. *Big Horn I*, having been affirmed by the United States Supreme Court, is final and controlling. The Tribes do not have the unfettered right to use their quantified amount of future project water for any purpose they desire.

We must now consider whether the district court erred when it decreed that the Tribes may change the use of their reserved future project water right from agriculture to any other purpose, including instream flows, without regard to Wyoming water law. The Tribes' first contention is that judgment and decree no. 8 in the 1983 decision gave them the right to change the "use of the water covered by their reserved water rights" in any manner in which they deemed advisable. This position is simply not tenable. Our decision in *Big Horn I* is controlling. As we previously stated, the Tribes reliance upon the 1983 decision for this proposition is not justified. It makes no sense whatsoever for this court to limit the use of the water for agricultural purposes and then to permit the Tribes to unilaterally change that use.

The Tribes also contend that this court held that federal and not state law applied when we stated in *Big Horn I*, "the decree entered in the instant case does not require application of state water law to the Indian reservation...." We do not disagree with this statement; however, the statement cannot be taken out of context. We made this statement in acknowledgment that the Tribes had a reserved right by treaty to the use of Wyoming water for agricultural purposes which was not dependent upon state law or procedures and which did not need to be adjudicated pursuant to our statutory scheme. We clearly stated, "Federal law has not preempted state oversight of reserved water rights...."

The Wyoming legislature has for good reason precluded water right holders from unilaterally dedicating water to maintain instream flows. Water is the lifeblood of Wyoming. It is a scarce resource which must be effectively managed and efficiently used to meet the various demands of society. Wyoming's founding fathers also recognized the necessity of having state control over this vital resource.... Our decision today recognizes only that which has been the traditional wisdom relating to Wyoming water: Water is simply too precious to the well being of society to permit water right holders unfettered control over its use....

Article 1, § 31 of the Wyoming Constitution recognizes that state control of water is essential to the development and prosperity of Wyoming. To this end, the constitution declares that "[t]he water of all natural streams, springs, lakes, or other collections of still water" within the boundaries of Wyoming is the property of the state.... The constitution provides for the administration of state water....

As is apparent from the text of the constitution, the state engineer is a constitutionally designated officer of the executive branch of government. He is appointed by the governor and must be approved by the senate as an individual who is qualified to fulfill the position's requirements. The state engineer is responsible for general supervising both the use of state water and such subordinate officers as are associated with its distribution....

Neither the constitution nor the statutes contemplate that a district court should have the authority to remove or replace the state engineer as the administrator of Wyoming water.... The state engineer is an executive officer appointed by and subject to removal by only the governor of Wyoming.... The district court's primary role in the instant case was to adjudicate the nature, extent, and relative priority of competing water interests in the Big Horn River System.... We hold that the district court had no inherent equitable enforcement authority, as argued by the Tribes, to effectuate a *de facto* removal and replacement of the state engineer as the administrator of state water within the reservation. A contrary position would result in a most unbalanced and unworkable form of government. The district court's action violated not only the separation of powers doctrine embodied in the Wyoming Constitution, but also the constitutional charge that the state engineer shall have "general supervision of the waters of the state...."

This court addressed the role of the state engineer as the administrator of the Tribes' reserved water right in *Big Horn I*. We limited the state engineer's authority as the administrator in two respects. We initially acknowledged that the Indian reserved water right existed independent of state law and procedure regarding the perfection of usufructuary rights to Wyoming water. We then determined that the state engineer, as the monitor of the Indian reserved water right, could not shut down tribal headgates once he believed that the Tribes had exceeded either the nature or the extent of their decreed right. We explained that, assuming cooperative efforts were of no avail, the state engineer would have to seek judicial enforcement of the decree against the United States and the Tribes....

Our present decision is consistent with the duties and limitations imposed upon the state engineer in *Big Horn I*. The state engineer remains responsible to distribute the water within the Big Horn River System according to the nature, extent, and priority of right. When the nature, extent, and priority of the Indian reserved water right are clear and not respected by state appropriators, the state engineer must exercise his authority over the state appropriators to see that the tribal right is observed. When, on the other hand, it is impossible to determine if the tribal right is being violated because the right itself is in some respect ill-defined, the state engineer should promptly seek clarification from the district court so that appropriate remedial action, if needed, may be undertaken.... Should the state engineer determine that the Tribes violated the decree, he should execute an enforcement action as outlined in *Big Horn I* and summarized in the preceding paragraph.

Minerals. With regard to what lies under the land's surface, the law covering minerals, such as coal or metals, is quite clear. If you own the land, you own everything below the surface unless the mineral rights were previously sold to someone else. Such sales of mineral rights are very common in Texas, Oklahoma, and other oil-producing states. If there is oil under your land and your neighbor's land, how much do you own? How much does your neighbor own? If you pump out the pool under your land, will you be taking your neighbor's oil? Since liquids seek their own level, you cannot just separate and take your part of the oil beneath your area of land if the pool extends beyond the boundaries of your property. Thus, the courts have often been called upon to resolve disputes as the ownership of oil and gas taken from below the surface of the ground. Now, an entire area of the law, known as "oil and gas law," specifically addresses the problems of oil and gas ownership. While this is an area of interest, time and space do not permit a further discussion of this area of the law in this text.

Land Description and Title Registration. Personal property can be described fairly easily—for example, "a red 1990 Dodge two-door sedan." People can readily recognize the personal property in question by that description. On the other hand, if a man says that he owns 300 acres of land, we must have some method of description to designate the boundaries of the land. Moreover, the method of description must be similar to the method used to describe the adjoining parcels of land. For these reasons, some type of uniform system for describing and identifying land became necessary.

Basically there are two methods of land description—the **metes and bounds description** and the **rectangular survey description**. The metes and bounds description is the traditional method. It involves picking a starting point and marking it with a permanent stake or post so that it can always be referred to and then simply measuring distances and angles until you return to the starting point. This system was used for land description in the original thirteen states of the United States.

In 1875, the U.S. government adopted a rectangular survey system which is now used in most of the states. This system divides the land into rectangular squares called sections. These sections are divided into quarter sections and can be further subdivided as needed. A section is a square mile. Where the rectangular survey system has been adopted, there will be maps or plats of the entire surface area of the land in a county, divided into one-mile squares. Records of such plats are filed in the county courthouse. If the land involved lies within the limits of a city or town, it will be divided further into various subdivisions, which in turn are subdivided into lots.

Unlike personal property, for which physical possession is a strong indicator of ownership, ownership of land is proved by registration of title. If you purchase land, you will be given a deed transferring ownership from the previous owner to you. This deed has to be filed or registered with the proper authority in the county where the land is located. The title will then be a public record, and anyone may check the county records to find out who owns that particular tract of land. Land registration is also needed for taxation purposes. Real estate is a prime source of tax revenue for municipal, county, and state governments, and an *ad valorem* tax is imposed upon the registered title holder of a tract of land.

TYPES OF RIGHTS TO OWNERSHIP IN REAL PROPERTY

All of the rights of ownership to most objects of personal property are typically owned by one person. Seldom would a person have only a life interest in a book, a chair, or an automobile. This, of course, is because personal property typically does not have perpetual life; most items of personal property will fall apart, rot, or be destroyed in some other manner over time. Land, however, will always be there. This explains the need for a different set of ownership rights for real property than for personal property.

Fee Simple Estate. **Fee simple title** is the best title that an owner can have. This means that the owner has all of the rights associated with a parcel of real property, and that the owner has these rights forever. The owner of the fee simple estate can sell all of these rights in the real property, or any part thereof. When the owner dies, the heirs will inherit the fee simple estate, and the title can be passed on through generations.

Life Estate. A **life estate** is an interest in real property that is limited to the life of the person or persons to whom the life estate was granted. The owner of the life estate may not sell the real property or cause permanent injury to it. The owner of the life estate simply has the right to use the real property and the right to profit from it during his lifetime. An owner of a life estate may be viewed as a tenant who has free rent until he or she dies. When the life estate owner dies, ownership of the real property will either revert to the owner who gave the life estate or, if that owner is now dead, it will go to that owner's heirs or to whomever that owner has designated in his or her will.

Leasehold Estate. The owner of a **leasehold estate** has the right to occupy and use the described real property. A leasehold estate may be for a specified period, such as a year or ten years, or it may be a **tenancy at will**, which means that either the tenant or the owner-landlord may terminate the leasehold at any time without reason, simply by giving a required notice. If you rent an apartment during the school year and you sign a lease, you will have acquired a leasehold interest in real property. Leasehold estates are discussed more fully in the next chapter.

Easements. **Easements** may also be described as rights-of-way over real property. If you buy a lot in a subdivision on which you intend to build a home, no doubt there will be an easement across the back of the lot for the use of public utilities. The easement will allow the water company, the electric company, and the gas company to come upon that specific area of land and erect poles, dig trenches for water lines, bury cable lines, and do other tasks associated with their business. You still own the land covered by an easement, but the easement allows another person or persons to come upon that portion of the land for certain purposes. An easement is an interest in real property which is usually evidenced by a written document called a **deed of easement**, and this deed must be registered with the appropriate county official in the county where the real property is located. An exception to this general rule is called an **easement by prescription**. Here there is no written easement and, in fact, there is no agreement that there should be an easement. This is simply a situation where the owner of the land has allowed another person or persons to use a certain portion of the land continuously for a number of years, and the owner is now legally unable to deny the rights of that person or persons to continue to use the land. Most states have a specific statutory time before an easement by prescription will be effective.

The *Stoesser* case illustrates these rules.

STOESSER v. SHORE DRIVE PARTNERSHIP
494 N.W.2d 204 (WI, 1993)

FACTS: The plaintiffs-appellants (hereinafter "subdivision owners") are non-riparian land-owners in the O-Tan-Kah Subdivision. The defendants-respondents (hereinafter "partnership") are riparian landowners along Lake Beulah having purchased its riparian land on September 15, 1989. The partnership operates a bar and restaurant known as the "Dockside." The subdivision owners claim the right to use the partnership's lakeshore to exercise riparian rights that were reserved in a 1939 warranty deed from their predecessors in title to the partnership's predecessor in title. The relevant portion of the deed states:

> The parties of the first part reserve for themselves, their heirs and assigns and the owners in O-Tan-Kah Subdivision and any owners along the channel, the use of the channel as a means of ingress and egress, and also reserving to themselves and such owners, the right in common with the parties of the second part for themselves and guests to use the lake shore for bathing, boating or kindred purposes....

Each year after the 1939 deed was executed, the partnership and its predecessors in interest installed a pier on the lakeshore frontage. In the spring of 1989, the subdivision owners, for the first time since the execution of the 1939 deed, exercised the riparian rights they claimed by erecting a pier abutting the shore of the partnership's property. On April 7, 1990, the subdivision owners again erected their pier on the partnership's lakeshore. That same day the partnership removed the subdivision owners' pier claiming the sudivision owners had no right to erect a pier on its property.

The subdivision owners commenced this action on May 25, 1990, alleging that they had "lake rights ... to swim, dock boats, and erect a pier along the shores of Lake Beulah." They no longer claim the right to maintain a pier. The subdivision owners sought declaratory relief setting forth their rights in the lake frontage of Lake Beulah and an injunction to prevent the partnership from placing a pier or other structure which would interfere with the subdivision owners' rights to use the lakeshore. The subdivision owners also requested compensatory and punitive damages.

 JUSTICE WILCOX:

A riparian owner is one who holds title to land abutting a body of water.... Riparian owners have certain rights, known as riparian rights, based upon title to the ownership of the bank or upland.... Riparian rights are not common to the citizens at large, but exist as natural and inherent incidents of the ownership of riparian land....

The riparian rights relevant to this case are the right of access to a lake and the privilege that goes along with that right to use the lake and lakeshore for bathing, boating, and kindred purposes.

None of the subdivision owners who are plaintiffs in this case own riparian land. The subdivision owners claim riparian rights through the easement reserved in the 1939 deed.

It is clear that the mere fact that one owns property abutting a natural body of water presumptively confers certain rights.... However, one who acquires land abutting a body of water may acquire no more than is conveyed by his deed....

In the instant case, the partnership claims exclusive rights to use its lakeshore. However, the partnership's predecessor in interest, granted an easement to the subdivision owners allowing them to use the lakeshore for bathing, boating, or kindred purposes. This easement was a part of the partnership's predecessors' deed which was recorded in the Walworth County Register of Deeds office on March 23, 1939. The easement was recorded and gave notice to subsequent purchasers of the subdivision owners' rights. The easement bound future owners.

An easement has been defined ... as a liberty, privilege, or advantage in land without profit and existing distinct from the ownership of the land.... In the case of an easement, title does not pass but only the right to a limited use of the land of another.... The subdivision owners did not become riparian owners based upon the easement; but they did obtain the right to use the partnership's lakeshore to access Lake Beulah for bathing, boating, and kindred purposes.

All members of the public have the right to use Lake Beulah for swimming, bathing and boating purposes subject to regulation by the legislature and state agencies. The state holds the lake bed and water in trust for the public. However, members of the public do not have the right to access Lake Beulah by way of the partnership's private property....

Public policy supports the rule that riparian rights can be conveyed by easement. A deed, like any instrument, should not be rewritten by the court. If the court could rewrite or invalidate private contractual agreements, it would destroy the certainty upon which contracting parties are entitled to reply....

We conclude that riparian rights can be conveyed by easement to non-riparian owners. In the instant case, the intent of the parties was that the subdivision owners have access to Lake Beulah by way of partnership property. The easement is valid and reserved for the subdivision owners the right of access to Lake Beulah.

Profits. In the law of real property, a **profit** is the right to remove part of someone else's land; for example, timber, crops, or minerals. Most modern cases treat profits under the same general rules as are applied to easements. Like easements, a profit may be **appurtenant**, attached to the ownership of other land, or **in gross**, owned by someone other than the adjoining landowner, without regard to whether or not that someone owns other real estate. An example of an appurtenant profit would be a neighbor who has the right to cut as much wood as he needs for his fireplace. A profit in gross would exist where the landowner has simply sold or given someone the right to remove firewood from the land. Complex legal problems can arise when the owner of a profit tries to convey it to someone else.

Licenses. A **license** is permission to enter upon the real property of another person. It is not an easement since it is not truly an interest in real property, but simply temporary permission to go upon another person's real property for a specific purpose. A friend has an apple orchard, for example, and agrees to sell you all of the apples in the orchard for a specific price. Part of the agreement is that you will have to go into the orchard, pick the apples, and take them to market. You do not have a permanent easement to traverse that area at a later time or for any other reason.

Dower Rights. Under the common law, a widow had **dower rights** in her husband's real property. This meant that she had a life estate in one-third of all the real property the husband had owned during his lifetime, provided she had not signed away her dower rights in a transfer of any of that real property to another person. The purpose of the dower interest was to ensure that the widow would have some means to support herself if her husband died. In those days, a woman typically was not a wage earner outside the home.

The widow's dower interest is still recognized in some states. However, some states have limited it to only that real property the husband owned at the time of his decease, thus preventing the widow from claiming an interest in real property which the husband had transferred to others during his lifetime. Other states simply give the wife a statutory share of all the property in the deceased husband's estate.

Curtesy Rights. Under the common law, the husband, upon the death of his wife, was entitled to a life estate in all of the real property his wife owned which was subject to inheritance. One requirement had to be met before the husband was granted curtesy rights: a child who could have inherited the real property had to have been born alive. Most states have replaced the common-law right of curtesy with specific statutory provisions concerning a husband's right in his wife's estate.

Liens Against Real Property. A **lien** is a claim which some person or persons may have had against an owner of real property for the payment of some debt, obligation, or duty. A lien may be either voluntary or involuntary. An example of a **voluntary lien** would be the lien of a mortgage which is created when the owner of real estate borrows money and pledges the real estate as security for repayment of the loan. The lending institution, the mortgagee, then files the mortgage agreement with the county recorder in the county where the land is located, and thus it has a lien against the property. The owner of the real property cannot sell the real property and give clear title until the mortgage lien is satisfied by full payment or unless the mortgagee agrees to let a new buyer assume the present mortgage lien, which means that the new buyer will have to pay off the mortgage.

Examples of **involuntary liens** include a tax lien, a judgment lien, and a mechanic's lien. If the owner of real property fails to pay the property taxes, then the property taxes become a lien against the real property. As with a mortgage, the real property may not be sold with a clear title unless the lien is paid off. A **judgment lien** would involve a situation where the owner of real property has been sued, the court has rendered a judgment against the owner, and the owner has not paid off the judgment. A **mechanic's lien** is a lien of a person or persons who furnish building materials and/or labor for the improvement of the owner's real property. Here again, the real property cannot be sold with a clear title unless the mechanic's lien is paid off. Mechanic's lien provisions differ from state to state. In some states, if a mechanic's lien is not satisfied within a specified period of time, the person holding the mechanic's lien may sue the owner, get a judgment, and have the real property sold at a sheriff's auction to satisfy the lien. Since mechanic's lien statutes differ from state to state, it is advisable to find out what the law is in your state. Otherwise, you might find your home sold for a very minor debt.

ACQUISITION OF OWNERSHIP TO REAL PROPERTY

Legislative Grant. Real property may be acquired by legislative grant from the national government or by a patent. A patent is a document similar to a deed which the government issues to convey a portion of the public lands to one or more persons. In the early days of this nation, the national Homestead Act allowed settlers to establish their homestead on public land, and after the passage of a specified period of time and compliance with the requirements of the act, the homesteader would be granted a patent to this land.

Purchase. Real property may be acquired by purchase. This, of course, is the most common method of acquisition.

Inheritance. Real property may be acquired by inheritance. You may inherit land from your parents, grandparents, or other persons who die and name you in their will, or if you are the legal heir, you would inherit by intestate succession.

Gift. Owners of land may decide to give a certain parcel of land to their children, to some other person or persons, or to some charity during their lifetime. A gift is not valid unless there is a proper deed which evidences a transfer of title from the donor, or giver, to the donee, that is, the person receiving the gift.

Accretion. Accretion simply means that the owner of land has acquired more land because of a change in the course of a river or stream that runs alongside the property. For example, over a period of years sand and soil have been deposited on your side of a stream, thus increasing the actual land that you can use. A stream may also recede, giving more land between the previous bank and the present level of the stream.

Adverse Possession. After you use or occupy real property continuously for a statutory period of time, the original owner loses the right to object to your possession of the land. By your possession, which was adverse to the owner's interests, and the failure of the owner to enforce his or her rights to evict you, you have acquired ownership by **adverse possession**.

Eminent Domain. This method of acquiring land applies to governmental entities, such as school districts, cities, states, and the national government. This method of acquisition, **eminent domain**, also is often referred to as **condemnation**. It is the right of government to take private property for the use of the public. The owner of the private property must be paid a fair amount for the land taken.

Dedication. Acquisition through dedication is also a method of acquiring land, but applies only to governmental entities. A real estate developer of a new subdivision dedicates the streets to the city. The streets then become public property. **Dedication** is a gift by the landowner to a governmental entity, and it is an effective acquisition only if the governmental entity accepts the gift. For example, a person may want to dedicate certain land to a city for use as a park that will be named after the donor. The city may or may not accept the gift with that condition. If the gift is accepted, then appropriate documents are executed and the land becomes public property that is owned and maintained by the city.

PROCESS OF TRANSFER OF OWNERSHIP

The transfer of land from the present owner or owners to the acquiring owner or owners must be evidenced by a written document which can be recorded in the records of the county where the land is located.

Deeds. The transfer document used in an acquisition by purchase or by gift is a **deed**. This is a written document which is signed by the owner of the real property and which conveys or transfers the owner's rights, title, and interest in specifically described real estate to the person or persons who are acquiring the ownership. The present owner or owners are called the **grantors** and the person or persons acquiring ownership are called the **grantees**. The grantors must sign the deed in the presence of a notary public who will verify that they signed it. The deed may be in the form of a **warranty deed** or a **quit-claim deed**.

In a warranty deed, the grantor expressly guarantees that the ownership being transferred is free from the claims of others. That is, the grantor guarantees to the grantee that the grantor is transferring a clear and merchantable title. A quit-claim deed states that the grantor is transferring all of his or her rights, title, and interest in the real property to the grantee, but the grantor makes no guarantee that the grantee will have a clear title free from the claims of others.

The grantor or grantors in a warranty deed may reserve some rights or may make the warranty subject to certain rights of others. For example, the grantors in a warranty deed may reserve subsurface mineral rights. Then, if oil is ever found under the land, it belongs to the grantor. If there is a mortgage on the land, the grantor-seller may deed the title subject to the rights of the mortgagee, normally a bank or other lending institution. Thus, the new purchaser gets title subject to the lien of the mortgage. If there are private restrictions on the real estate, the deed will transfer title subject to those restrictions. Since taxes are a lien, the deed will also specify that the transfer of title is subject to unpaid taxes if any remain unpaid at the time of the transfer of title.

Warranties of Title. The person transferring title, the grantor, is presumed to have made certain warranties of title even though those warranties were not expressly stated in the deed. The grantor warrants that he or she owns the real property which is being conveyed free from restrictions, such as unpaid taxes, an unpaid mortgage, easements, or any other liens against the real property. The grantor also warrants that he or she has the right to convey the property and is not restricted with regard to the right to make the conveyance. In the case of the transfer of title by a corporation, the officers signing the deed warrant that they have authority to act for the corporation. It is good practice for the purchaser to have the corporate officers furnish a resolution whereby the corporation's board of directors had authorized those officers to sign a transfer of title for the corporation. The grantor also guarantees that the land is not encumbered by any right or interest other than the liens or easements stated in the deed. Thus, the grantor is guaranteeing that the purchaser will have the right to enjoy the use of the property without interference by the grantors or others at a later date.

Even though the grantor guarantees that the buyer is being given a clear title and will have the right to undisturbed enjoyment of the premises, free from liens and encumbrances other than those shown in the deed, the buyer should request further assurances. After all, should there be problems later, the grantor who made those guarantees may have spent the money that the buyer paid for the real property, may have moved out of the area, may have died, may have filed bankruptcy, or may simply be judgment proof. Before consummating the purchase of real property, the buyer should require from the seller either an **abstract of title** showing good and merchantable title certified to the date of the closing of the transaction, or a **policy of title insurance** for the real estate.

An abstract of title is a history of the title to a piece of real estate. Usually beginning with the original transfer from the U.S. government to the homesteader, it then contains brief copies of every deed, mortgage, or other document that affects the transfer of the title from that date to the present. It also contains copies of any liens or encumbrances that have been filed against the real property. The abstract of title, however, only covers those documents that have been recorded in the county recorder's office in the county where the real property is situated. It does not cover any unrecorded documents which may have been agreed upon by parties involved in the chain of title.

The **abstractor,** the person preparing the abstract, does not certify that the title is clear from liens and encumbrances and is merchantable. The abstract must be taken to an attorney who will examine the chain of title and then give an opinion stating whether or not the title is merchantable and what liens and encumbrances may be effective against it.

A policy of title insurance is an insurance policy which states that if any person or persons later challenges the title, the insurance company will pay the cost of any judgment against you and will pay the legal fees and court costs required to defend any action brought by the person or persons claiming title against you. Before the title insurance company issues a title insurance policy, it first searches the title and verifies that the title is clear of liens and encumbrances and is merchantable. If it feels that the title is clear and merchantable, it will issue a policy of title insurance.

The warranties made by the seller-grantor, the issuance of a title insurance policy, and the preparation and examination of an abstract of title do not protect the buyer against any defects in the improvements on the real property, such as the house, the garage, or the other buildings on it. The courts originally used the doctrine of **caveat emptor** with regard to the condition of the improvements on the real property. *Caveat emptor* means "Let the buyer beware." Buyers have an opportunity to examine the real property, and if they do not request any express warranties or agreement as to the buildings, then they get what they see. Of course, an exception exists where there was fraud or misinterpretation by the seller in the sale of the real property. If the seller lied to the buyer about some material fact and this concerned a condition that the buyer could not have checked with the use of ordinary inspection methods, then the courts will simply void the transaction. The buyer also may be able to secure additional monetary damages.

Another exception to the general rule of *caveat emptor* with regard to the buildings on the real property being transferred may occur when a new home has been constructed on the real property. Many states have specific laws that make the builder responsible for defects in the new home for a specific period of time, usually one year. Since this is a matter of state law, the buyer of real property should either secure an express warranty from the seller or check the statutory law in the given state.

National Regulation. The U.S. Real Estate Settlement Procedures Act (RESPA), which was passed in 1974, requires the disclosure of the costs of a real estate transaction to the buyer prior to the consummation of such a transaction. The costs that must be disclosed are the loan origination fees, loan discount points, appraisal fees, attorney's fees, inspection fees, charges for title search or title insurance, and land survey fee. The purpose of this law is primarily to let buyers know just what they are paying for.

RESPA also prohibits certain practices which are not in the best interests of the buyer. The lending institution is not allowed to give a kickback to any person for referring the borrower to them, to charge or accept fees except for services actually performed, or to require that the borrower purchase title insurance from any specific title insurance company that the lender prefers. The parties also cannot be forced to use an attorney that the lending institution selects. They are free to hire one of their own choosing.

FINANCING OF REAL ESTATE TRANSACTIONS

The great majority of real estate transactions involve some type of financing arrangement, since few people have the cash required in exchange for the title to real property. Financing can be handled through either a land contract or a real estate mortgage.

Land Contracts

A **land contract** is an agreement between a buyer and a seller regarding the purchase of a parcel of land. The contract is a conditional sale of the land subject to payment of the purchase price by the buyer. Typically, the buyer will make a down payment and will agree to make periodic payments of interest and principal for a specified period of time, either until the entire balance of the principal is paid or until the principal balance is paid down to a level where the buyer can secure a real estate mortgage from a lending institution. The down payment required for a land contract transaction is often less than that required in a transaction involving a real estate mortgage.

The buyer in a land contract transaction does not acquire a fee simple title to the land until the entire contract purchase price has been paid. The seller retains the fee simple title, and if the buyer breaches the terms of the contract, either by not making the scheduled payments or by breaching other terms of the contract, the seller may give the buyer notice of the breach, reenter the premises, and evict the buyer from possession. In some instances, the buyer's down payment and other payments may be forfeited. Some states, however, follow the same procedure in the foreclosure of a land contract as in the foreclosure of a mortgage after default.

Upon execution of a land contract, the buyer is entitled to possession and control of the land and the improvements thereon. The buyer is the equitable owner of the rights to possess and control the land, subject to the legal rights of the fee simple titleholder who is selling the real property. In other words, the buyer may not use the real property in any way he or she wants to; however, the buyer does have the duty to keep the premises insured against fire and other risks of loss. The buyer may not add to or tear down the improvements without the specific permission of the seller. The buyer has the right to use, control, and enjoy the land and improvements, but may not materially change the land or improvements.

The primary difference between land contracts and real property mortgages is this: in a real estate purchase involving a mortgage, the buyer receives fee simple title to the real estate and executes a mortgage to secure the payment of the loan which a bank or other lending institution has made for the purchase of the real estate. The seller is then paid off and deeds over all of his or her property rights in the real property. In the land contract transaction, the seller still holds property rights, and thus a certain amount of control, until the last payment has been made on the contract.

Real Estate Mortgages

A real estate mortgage is a document wherein the owner of real property pledges that real property as security for the payment of a debt or some other obligation. The owner of the property, who is called the **mortgagor**, does not transfer title to the land in this document; the **mortgagee**, normally a bank or other lending institution, obtains a nonpossessory interest in the real estate. If the debt or obligation is not satisfied within the required time period or in accordance with the conditions for repayment set out in the mortgage document, the mortgagee may commence legal proceedings to foreclose on the mortgage and to have the real property sold at a sheriff's sale. The proceeds will then be applied to the balance owed on the mortgage. The owner-mortgagor will receive any proceeds from the sale of the real property that are left after the payment of the mortgage balance, plus reasonable attorney's fees and court costs.

Purchase-Money Mortgage. A **purchase-money mortgage** is a mortgage that is executed to obtain money to purchase the land that is to be pledged in the mortgage. Typically, an individual or individuals contemplating the purchase of a home will go to a bank or other lending institution and get a commitment to lend them money for the purchase of a certain piece of property. Then, relying on that commitment the individual or individuals will negotiate the purchase of the real estate. After all preliminary legal matters have been taken care of, the seller will convey the title to the buyer, and the buyer will sign a purchase-money mortgage with the bank or other lending institution. The financial institution will, in turn, pay the amount of the loan to the seller or to the seller's mortgagee if there is a mortgage on the property at the time it is sold.

Nonpurchase-Money Mortgage. This mortgage is executed on real property, not for the purpose of purchasing the real property. For example, your parents own their home, debt-free, and need money to send you to college. Thus, they borrow money from a financial institution and pledge their home in the form of a mortgage to secure the repayment of this money.

Construction Mortgage. This mortgage is used when the mortgagor-owner owns a parcel of land and wants to construct a building or buildings on the land. The bank or other lending institution will review the owner's building plans and building estimates, and if it approves them it will make a commitment to lend a certain sum to the mortgagor. Typically, the agreement is not to pay the entire amount out in a lump sum, as would be done with a purchase-money mortgage, but to pay out portions of the loan as necessary to pay the costs of construction. When construction has been completed, the loan funds will be paid in full to the mortgagor or his or her assigns. The procedure for payment and/or foreclosure is the same as that of any other mortgage.

Filing and Recording Requirements. A mortgage need not be filed or recorded in any public office for its lien to be valid between the mortgagor and the mortgagee. However, if a mortgage is not filed and recorded in the office of the recorder of the county where the real property is located, the mortgagee's lien will not be superior to any subsequent liens which may be placed against the real property. For example, an individual borrows money, executes a promissory note, and signs a mortgage on the real property, but the mortgagee doesn't file and record the mortgage. The property owner, the mortgagor, makes improvements to the real property but does not pay for them, so a mechanic's lien is filed against the real property, or perhaps a judgment was rendered against the owner as the result of an automobile accident. If the mortgage was not filed and recorded properly, it would not have priority over the mechanic's lien or the judgment. Thus, immediately after a mortgage is executed, it is very important to file and record the mortgage with the recorder of the county where the real property is located.

The *Claflin* case discusses a series of "irregularities" in a mortgage transaction.

CLAFLIN v. COMMERCIAL STATE BANK
487 N.W.2d 242 (MI App., 1992)

FACTS: Appellant Margaret Claflin seeks review of a judgment dismissing her claims against respondent Commercial State Bank of Two Harbors. Margaret sought to have set aside two mortgages the Bank had taken in exchange for loans granted to her son, Gregory, while he held record title to her home. Margaret also sought punitive damages. After presentation of Margaret's evidence in the jury trial, the Bank's motion for a directed verdict was granted, dismissing all counts. The trial court held that the Bank had no duty to investigate beyond the record title and that there was no evidence of any willful action by the Bank against Margaret.

Greg's parents, Margaret and Amos Claflin, bought the real estate in question (the "Property") in 1973. The Property consists of a two story home on about forty acres in rural Two Harbors, Minnesota. In 1988, Amos died. Greg and his wife Mary returned to Two Harbors for Amos' funeral and decided to relocate there.

By January 1990, Greg convinced his mother to sign two documents. One was a note (the "Note") which Greg drafted by copying portions of the mortgage he and Mary gave her parents. Greg had his mother come to his office to sign the Note and have it notarized. Margaret's testimony indicates that she did not consider whether the Note should be recorded against the Property; she believed it was "official" because it was notarized.

Mother and son also went to the county recorder's office. There, Greg obtained a blank Minnesota Uniform Conveyancing Quit Claim Deed which he prepared, and had his mother execute before a notary. By this deed, which was duly recorded, Margaret quit claimed the Property to Greg. Both documents were executed and notarized on January 25, 1990; only the deed was recorded.

On February 2, 1990, Greg applied to the Bank for a loan to be secured by a mortgage on the Property (the "mortgage loan"). He told Bank Vice President Lance Schwanke that the purpose of the loan was to consolidate unsecured debt. Greg obtained a loan application and had his wife sign it before it was completed.

Schwanke went to Greg and Mary's home with the mortgage loan documents on the evening of February 9, 1990. The evidence demonstrates that portions of these documents were not completed when Mary signed them. While it is not clear what information was contained at that time, none of the completed documents in evidence contain the street address of the Property; they contain a lengthy legal description. Mary testified that she did not read the documents, but simply executed them that evening. Mary and her infant son left Minnesota on February 13, 1990, to reside with Mary's parents in Philadelphia.

The mortgage loan documents were then dated March 21, 1990, and notarized by Schwanke, who had in fact witnessed the signatures on a much earlier date. The proceeds were disbursed to Greg, mainly through fourteen cashier's checks issued to various unsecured creditors. Additional cashier's checks were disbursed for expenses related to the mortgage. After April 13, 1990, only $1,300 of the original $45,000 remained undisbursed.

One evening in June of 1990, Mary, still in Philadelphia, learned that Greg had acquired a new truck. Mary immediately called Schwanke at home regarding the source of these funds. Mary then learned for the first time that the documents she signed for Greg in February placed a mortgage on Margaret's home. Mary immediately insisted that all disbursements be stopped. Mary then arranged a trip to Minnesota.

When Mary arrived the Claflin family held a meeting. Margaret learned for the first time that Greg had mortgaged the Property, contrary to their understanding. Mary learned that Margaret had conveyed the Property to Greg in a secret deal. Margaret retained an attorney who insisted that Greg and Mary immediately convey the Property back to Margaret. Greg and Mary gave Margaret a warranty deed, duly recorded on June 27, 1990.

Margaret then sought to assume the mortgage loan, submitting a financial statement to the Bank. The Bank instead elected to accelerate the mortgage loan, which contained a due-on-sale clause, because the property had been conveyed to Margaret. On September 10, 1990, Schwanke wrote to Greg and Mary indicating that the mortgage loan was more than sixty days past due. Seven days later, the Bank's attorneys prepared a Notice of Mortgage Foreclosure Sale scheduled for November 14, 1990. On October 26, 1990, Margaret brought this suit against the Bank.

 JUDGE NORTON:

Minnesota law requires every conveyance of real estate to be recorded; unrecorded conveyances shall be void against any subsequent purchaser in good faith for valuable consideration.... Under the recording act, a purchaser in good faith is one who gives consideration without actual, implied or constructive notice of the inconsistent outstanding rights of others.... The purpose of the recording act is to protect those who purchase real estate in reliance upon the record.... Implied notice has been found where one has "actual knowledge of facts which would put one on further inquiry...."

If one is aware that someone other than the vendor is living on the land, one has a duty to inquire concerning the rights of the inhabitant of the property and is chargeable with notice of all facts which such inquiry would disclose.... One is not a bona fide purchaser if one had knowledge of facts which ought to have put one on an inquiry that would have led to knowledge of a conveyance....

A purchaser who has actual, implied or constructive notice of the outstanding rights of another is not a bona fide purchaser entitled to the protection of the recording act.... Actual, open possession and use of property puts a subsequent purchaser on inquiry notice of the possessor's rights in the property.... Actual possession of real property is notice to all the world of the title and rights of the person so in possession and also of all facts connected therewith which reasonable inquiry would have developed.... Implied notice differs from constructive notice arising from the record of instruments because the record is notice only of what appears upon its face....

In Minnesota, clear, actual, exclusive possession of the granted premises by the grantor, even after delivery and recording of the deed, is notice against purchasers and mortgagees of the grantor's possible interest in the property....

In order to have status as a bona fide purchaser the mortgagee's inquiry must be directed to the person in possession; inquiry of the mortgagor, who may have reason to conceal the truth, is not sufficient. The supreme court has stated, "Having made no inquiry, [the bank] is chargeable with notice of the actual condition of the title to the land."

Schwanke testified that he never contacted Margaret, although he knew she was living on the Property. Schwanke also acted to ensure that only Greg would be contacted by the others involved. Schwanke knew the title opinion contained an exception for the rights of occupants but he ignored it as "boilerplate." The Bank argues that it satisfied its duty of inquiry by asking Greg what interest his mother has in the Property. We disagree. Greg told the bank that his mother was simply living there with his permission. The Bank knowingly prevented and avoided inquiry directed to Margaret. The evidence demonstrates that, had the Bank inquired of Margaret, it could have learned that she asserted a superior interest. The Bank is therefore chargeable with notice of Margaret's unrecorded interests....

In summary, most of the evidence presented clearly supports Margaret's claims; contrary evidence was generally impeached. Schwanke admitted that he had Mary pre-sign documents which were not complete, which were completed and notarized much later, and that he had previously made false statements about that. Schwanke admitted that he ignored the title opinion exception regarding the rights of occupants. He admitted that he inquired only of Greg regarding Margaret's possible rights in the Property. Greg admitted that he and his mother had intended to create a life estate. We must accept that evidence as true, including the reasonable inferences which may be drawn therefrom....

In addition to her claim that the mortgage is invalid against her interests, Margaret sought punitive damages based on the Bank's conduct in taking the mortgage....

The evidence establishes that the Bank was more than disinterested in Margaret's rights. The Bank, through Schwanke, not only avoided but actually prevented inquiry directed to Margaret. These acts effectively prevented her from learning that the Bank planned to grant Greg a mortgage loan against the Property. This cause of action arose when the mortgage became an encumbrance against the Property in March 1990. Therefore, while the Bank's conduct may demonstrate deliberate disregard for Margaret's rights, the standard applicable here is that of willful indifference. We hold that Margaret presented sufficient evidence to support a verdict that the Bank acted with willful indifference to her rights.

Defaults by the Mortgagor. The mortgagor may be in default on the mortgage by failing to pay the mortgage payments, the real property taxes, or the payments for insurance against fire and extended coverage as they become due, or by doing an act which would endanger the security interest of the mortgagee.

If the mortgagor fails to make the mortgage payments when they become due or defaults in any of the other ways just stated, then the mortgagee may file a suit of foreclosure against the mortgagor. At that time, the entire balance of the mortgage is due and payable, and if the court awards the mortgagee a judgment of foreclosure, the property will be sold at a sheriff's sale. The proceeds of the sale of the real estate will be applied first to the unpaid balance of the mortgage plus interest and to the legal fees and court costs of the foreclosure suit, and the balance will then be paid to the mortgagor. If the sale does not bring enough money to pay off the mortgage debt, the mortgagor will remain liable for the unpaid balance of the mortgage.

This procedure appears to be very one-sided in favor of the mortgagee, the lending institution. However, most lending institutions proceed with a foreclosure suit only in situations where the mortgagor has demonstrated a continued pattern of default. Moreover, many states have enacted statutes that allow the mortgagor to get a delay of foreclosure in certain hardship cases. Another statutory procedure that favors the mortgagor is called the **right of redemption**. This is the mortgagor's statutory right to repurchase the real estate within a specified time after the foreclosure. In other words, a mortgagor who can get the money together can have the property back for the amount for which it was sold plus the expenses incurred in the foreclosure and sale.

In the case where the real property was sold by the sheriff, the sheriff is authorized by law to execute to the purchaser a sheriff's deed which is free and clear of the mortgage lien.

TRUSTS

Nature. A **trust** is any arrangement whereby the owner of property transfers its ownership to a natural or corporate person, called the **trustee**, who is instructed to hold the property for the benefit of a person or persons who are designated as **beneficiaries**. A trust can be created for any purpose that is legal and not against public policy. The owner of the property interest that is being transferred must instruct the trustee as to how that interest is to be administered for the beneficiaries. For example, an owner of an interest in property may transfer that interest to the trustee for a person's benefit and may instruct the trustee to distribute only the earnings on the property and not to distribute the principal, or corpus, of the trust until a later date. It is important that the trustee have specific instructions as to how the property is to be administered for the beneficiaries.

Types. Trusts are divided into two basic categories. A **living trust**, also called an *inter vivos trust*, is a trust that takes effect, and is administered during the lifetime of the transferor of the property. A **testamentary trust** is created prior to the death of the person who sets it up but does not take effect until that person's death. These voluntary arrangements should be distinguished from a "constructive trust" which is a remedy for the fraudulent acquisition of property, imposed by a court of equity in favor of the real or intended owner. Equity says that the defrauder holds the property "in trust" for the rightful owner.

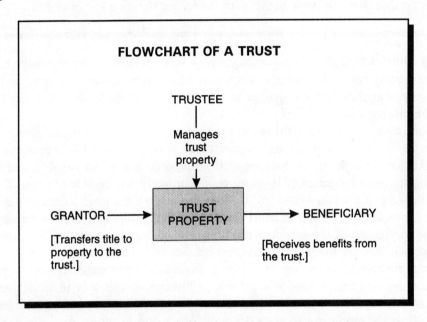

FLOWCHART OF A TRUST

TRUSTEE

Manages
trust
property

GRANTOR   →   **TRUST PROPERTY**   →   BENEFICIARY

[Transfers title to property to the trust.]

[Receives benefits from the trust.]

Creation. A trust is not necessarily a contract, since no consideration is required from the beneficiaries. It is in effect a gift from the giver, also called the **settlor**, to the beneficiary through a middle person; namely, the trustee. To create an express trust, there must be a written document, which is normally called a **trust agreement** or a **deed of trust**. While it is not necessary for any specific language to be used, certain requirements must be met. If the trust involves an interest in land, then the Statute of Frauds requires that the details of the transfer of that interest be set out in writing.

There is also a limit to how long a trust may exist before the interest vests in beneficiaries. The rule to be complied with here is called **the rule against perpetuities**. This rule prohibits a person from creating a trust that remains in existence forever. A general statement of the rule is that an interest in property, if conveyed for the benefit of a beneficiary, must be turned over or vested in the beneficiary no more than twenty-one years plus the period of gestation of a new life after the expiration of the life or lives of some person or persons who were in being when the trust was created. There are exceptions to this rule if the purpose of the trust is charitable. Most states have a statutory maximum time during which a trust may remain operative. Here the specific state laws would govern.

Revocability. An *inter vivos trust* may be declared either revocable or irrevocable. If a person sets up an **irrevocable trust** for the benefit of beneficiaries, then that person, the settlor, may not revoke or change the trust at a later date. Such a trust may be modified, with the consent of all the beneficiaries, provided such modification would not frustrate its original intent. However, this would only be possible in exceptional circumstances, as the courts will not allow a change in a trust if this would change the trust's original intended purpose. If the settlor sets up a **revocable trust**, this means that this person transfers title to certain property to a trustee for the benefit of specific beneficiaries, but may at any time change his or her mind and take back the corpus of the trust from the trustee.

Many wealthy persons deed property over to a trustee so that the trustee can manage it for them. Thus, these persons are both settlor and beneficiary. Having a professional manage their property relieves them of the responsibilities of management, and gives them the income, less a managerial service charge. If such a trust is revocable, the settlor can terminate the trust at any time.

Testamentary trusts do not become effective until the death of the settlor, and they are not revocable after the settlor's death. But anytime before the settlor's death, such a trust may be revoked simply by changing the last will and testament that contains or refers to it.

Trustee—Rights and Obligations.

A trustee can be an individual or an institution, such as a bank, a trust company, or a similar financial institution. The trustee is governed by a given state's laws concerning the handling of trust funds. A trustee generally has the right to make decisions concerning the investment of the trust corpus in accordance with the settlor's directions, provided those directions are not contrary to the law of the particular jurisdiction. For example, a trustee must generally invest trust funds more conservatively than he or she would invest personal funds.

A trustee may not commingle the property of a trust with property that the trustee owns individually or with property that the trustee is administering as the trustee of another trust. Generally speaking, the trustee owes a duty of loyalty to the beneficiaries; that is, the trustee's job is to conserve the corpus for the beneficiaries' benefit and yet to secure the best income and growth possible. The trustee will be required to use the skill, judgment, and care reasonably expected of a person in that capacity. Banks, trust companies, and other corporate trustees will of course be required to use a high degree of skill, care, and judgment in the management of trusts since that is their profession. An individual who is acting as a trustee would not be required to use the same high degree of skill, care, and judgment but would be required to use reasonable care and judgment in the handling of the trust funds. Most trusts involving large sums of money or property will be administered by corporate trustees who have professional investment knowledge and expertise.

The next case examines an Indian claim under an alleged trust created by their ancestors.

CHILDREN OF THE CHIPPEWA, OTTAWA, AND POTAWATOMY TRIBES v. THE UNIVERSITY OF MICHIGAN
305 N.W.2d 522 (MI, 1981)

FACTS: On September 29, 1817, the Treaty of Fort Meigs was executed. The Chippewa, Ottawa, and Potawatomy Tribes were signatories of the first part, and the government of the United States of America was the signatory of the second part. The treaty was drafted entirely by the representative of the United States. The defendant, the University of Michigan, was not a party to the treaty.

Notwithstanding this latter fact, the plaintiffs, who are descendants of the members of the signatory Indian Tribes, brought an action in equity before the

Circuit Court of Washtenaw County seeking to have a trust declared in their favor against defendant based on the provisions of this treaty. The trial court denied plaintiffs' request for a declaration of a trust in their favor. Plaintiffs appealed.

 PER CURIAM:

The original complaint was filed August 5, 1971. It was claimed that Article 16 of the treaty created a trust whereby certain land, belonging to the Indians, was conveyed to defendant for purposes of ensuring that the Indians and their descendants would receive an education in the European fashion. In support of this contention, the complaint cited certain alleged historical events, including the vesting of title of the conveyed parcels of land in the defendant; the then-University president Lewis Cass's appointment of two trustees to locate and survey these lands; the patenting of these lands to defendant by the government of the United States in 1824; and the release by one Church of St. Anne of its interest of the lands in favor of defendant.

The inclusion of St. Anne's Church in the complaint was occasioned by the plaintiffs' assertion that the treaty compelled the church to provide for the primary and secondary education of the Indians. The complaint then contends that the treaty imposed a concomitant duty upon defendant to ensure the Indians' college education. It is then claimed that the aforementioned conveyance by the church to the defendant merged the foregoing duties wholly into defendant's realm of responsibility....

The treaty provision that is the primary focus of the present dispute, Article 16, reads:

> Some of the Ottawa, Chippewa, and Potawatomy Tribes, being attached to the Catholic religion, and believing they may wish some of their children hereafter educated, do grant to the rector of the Catholic church of St. Anne of Detroit, for the use of the said church, and to the corporation of the college at Detroit, for the use of the said college, to be retained or sold, as the said rector and corporation may judge expedient, each, one-half of three sections of land, to contain 640 acres, on the river Raisin, at a place called Macon; and three sections of land not yet located, which tracts were reserved, for the use of the said Indians, by the treaty of Detroit, on 1,807; and the superintendent of Indian affairs, in the territory of Michigan, is authorized, on the part of the said Indians, to select the said tracts of land.

Trial commenced on August 21, 1978. During the trial, numerous exhibits were received along with much expert testimony from all sides. On February 28, 1979, the trial judge issued a meticulously researched and well drafted written opinion, thoroughly discussing the historical and procedural facets of this novel action and carefully setting forth the law which he believed controlling of this case. The opinion denied relief on all counts.

We have painstakingly reviewed the findings of fact in that opinion and agree with the trial judge in respect to those findings. The task of leaping back over 160 years in time is most difficult, and the trial judge is to be commended for his efforts in that regard....

It is first asserted that the trial judge erred in finding that the Indians could not have owned fee simple title to any lands conveyed from the year 1790 forward. In so ruling, the trial court found *Oneida Indian Nation v. County of Oneida*, 414 U.S.

661 ... (1974), to be dispositive. We agree. The thrust of *Oneida* is that the 1790 Nonintercourse Act created a right of occupancy rather than a title in fee simple in the Indians as to lands held by them. The trial court held that the federal government possesses power to convey the fee as to lands occupied by Indian Tribes and all questions with respect to rights of occupancy and conditions of extinguishment of Indian title are solely for the federal government. The trial court went on to say:

> This court will concede that in 1817 the Indians could have imposed an express trust on the lands possessed by them and granted to the Church and College by the 1817 Treaty, but this simply was not done at that time.

Given this recognition by the trial court, it is difficult to understand the plaintiffs' argument on the issue. The trial court's ultimate decision obviates further discussion in any event....

A third issue raised by plaintiffs is whether the trial court was justified in holding that Article 16 of the Treaty of Fort Meigs constituted a gift of lands to Father Richard and to defendant. We believe that it did....

The operative language in Article 16 provides that some of the plaintiffs' forefathers: "do grant to the ... church ... for the use of the said church, and to the ... college ... for the use of the said college, *to be retained or sold, as the said rector and corporation may judge expedient*...." (Emphasis added.)

Clearly, the grant itself is a completed one and not conditional in nature. Nor do its terms encompass more than one transaction. The land is donated jointly to the church, and to the corporation. The later division of the parcels was a consequence of Father Richard's discretion, a discretion Article 16 allowed him to exercise.

The evidence points to an almost reverential attitude toward Father Richard on the Indians' part. This attitude was commingled with an attitude of filial affection. The evidence also points to a clear donative intent on the Indians' part as regards Father Richard and encompasses a similar attitude toward the educational institution which the Indians very properly regarded as an extension of Father Richard's personality and influence.

We disagree with plaintiffs' continued assertions that the treaty, and particularly Article 16, were the sole product of Lewis Cass's efforts. The evidence does not support such a contention in any way. Rather, the treaty was the cumulative result of extended negotiations involving many leaders on both sides.

Both the expert testimony and the language of the treaty itself reflect the likelihood of a present donative intent on the part of the Indians at the time of the treaty's execution....

The next claim of error challenges the trial court's decision that Article 16 created no express trust in the Indians' favor.

It is a general principle of trust law that a trust is created only if the settlor manifests an intention to create a trust, and it is essential that there be an explicit declaration of trust accompanied by a transfer of property to one for the benefit of another.... Further, an express trust in real property must be in writing, under the hand of the party to be charged....

We find that the plaintiffs' substantive arguments in support of the theory of an express trust are based on speculation and irrelevancy....

The last claim on appeal concerns the issue of a constructive trust. The trial court rejected this theory for several reasons: (1) the university was not a party to the negotiations and committed no misconduct in the treaty negotiations; (2) the

Indians were represented by competent interpreters and a trusted Indian agent; (3) the United States evidenced no unjust conduct at the negotiations, its main intent being to secure a cession of a significant area in Ohio; (4) the Article 16 land was of minimal value when conveyed and when the university tried to sell it; and (5) the two cases cited by plaintiffs are distinguishable. We agree.

In a pristinely humane world, it might be honorable and fair to compel defendant to offer comprehensive scholarships in gratitude for the 1817 conveyance. Certainly, the cost of higher education is subject to the rigors of inflation as are all other things, and the plaintiffs, like everyone else, could benefit by the financial assistance they seek. However, constructive trusts are not used to requite obligations imposed by conscience alone. Rather, they are imposed solely where a balancing of equities discloses that it would be unfair to act otherwise. Where, as here, the language of the treaty and the historical evidence reflect a gift *inter vivos* and nothing more, the imposition of a constructive trust is neither equitably nor legally desirable.

Based on the foregoing, it is readily apparent that the judgment of the trial court should be and the same is hereby affirmed. No costs, questions of novel impression, and public significance being involved.

SIGNIFICANCE OF THIS CHAPTER

Everyone needs to understand the various rights involved in ownership of real property, since both individuals and businesses may become parties to many legal relationships involving land. This chapter attempts to answer many of the questions that relate to the ownership and transfer of real property.

PROBLEMS FOR DISCUSSION

1. The Fontainebleau Hotel is a large, luxury, beachfront hotel in Miami Beach, Florida. The Fontainebleau Hotel Corporation decided to build a fourteen-story tower addition to the hotel. The Eden Roc Hotel is also a large, luxury, beachfront hotel which adjoins the Fontainebleau on the north. If this addition is built, it will block the sun to the Eden Roc. During the winter months, from around 2 P.M. for the remainder of the day, the shadow of the addition will extend over the cabana, swimming pool, and sunbathing areas of the Eden Roc, which are located in the southern portion of its property. The Eden Roc files suit to secure an injunction to enjoin the Fontainebleau from building this addition. The city had issued a building permit and the Fontainebleau had complied with all existing zoning and building requirements.

    How should the court rule, and why?

2. J.P. Acker, Jr., brought this declaratory judgment action against M.M. Guinn to determine whether certain mineral rights passed under a deed executed in 1981. The deed conveyed "an undivided one-half interest in and to all of the oil, gas, and other minerals in and under, and that may be produced from" a tract of 86½ acres in Cherokee County. Acker, who held through the grantee, claimed that the deed included an interest in the iron ore on the land; Guinn, who held under the grantor, said that the deed did not include the iron ore. Over the years, the main use made of iron ore from Cherokee County had been as a foundation base for road construction; iron ore was also used in the manufacture of cement. Because of its high silica content, this iron ore had to be mixed with other ores to make pig iron. The ore deposits were solid beds, varying in thickness from a few inches to three or four feet. There were outcrops of the ore deposits at some places, and the deposits ranged in depth to as much as 50 feet below the surface. The ore had to be strip-mined, which would destroy or substantially impair the use of the surface for farming, ranching, or timber production. The trial court granted Acker's motion for summary judgment; the court of civil appeals reversed.

How should the Supreme Court rule, and why?

3. In 1957, James and Dolly Brown, husband and wife, purchased eighty acres of land from William and Faith Bost, joint tenants. The Bosts gave the Browns a statutory warranty deed. The deed was absolute on its face, and it purported to convey an estate in fee simple. In fact, a prior owner in the chain of title had conveyed a two-thirds interest in the mineral rights in 1947. This prior conveyance was not discovered in title searches which the Bosts had done in 1968 and 1988, when they used the land as collateral for loans. Faith Bost died in 1984; William had died earlier. Maureen Lober was appointed as executor of Faith's estate. On May 8, 1994, the Browns granted a coal option to the Consolidated Coal Company for $6,000. On May 4, 1995, the Browns learned that they owned only one-third of the coal rights. They accepted $2,000 from the coal company and then sued Faith's estate for damages of $4,000. The trial court dismissed the lawsuit, holding that only the first two warranties in the Bosts' deed had been breached, that this had occurred in 1957, when the deed was delivered, and that the claim was thus barred by the ten-year statute of limitations. The Browns appealed.

Do the Browns still have a claim? Explain.

4. The city of Renton built a concrete reservoir. About once a year, from 1968 to 1999, the city had to drain and clean the reservoir to prevent the buildup of contamination. The wastewater pipe ran from the base of the reservoir and was discharged into a small gully. The wastewater then ran down into a small stream, which crossed Downie's land. Downie bought his two acres in 1991; it was then "unused, unimproved, unoccupied, unfenced, and covered with underbrush and second growth trees." In 1998, Downie dammed up the stream and created a one-third acre pond, which he stocked with 25,000 fish. The city's cleaning of the reservoir in September 1999 resulted in the discharge of wastewater, debris, and mud into Downie's pond. The trial court dismissed Downie's suit for an injunction, holding that the city had acquired an easement by prescription. Downie appealed.

What result, and why?

5. Medlin died in 1999, survived by his wife Minnie and nine children. Five of the children sued Minnie and the other four children for a declaratory judgment interpreting T.W.'s will. The will gave Minnie all of T.W.'s property "to have the use and benefit of the same during her natural life, and at her death, all of such property in her hands shall completely vest in my children, share and share alike." In another paragraph, the will gave Minnie "the full and complete management, use, and enjoyment of all of my property during her said lifetime, including all rents and revenues to be derived therefrom." The plaintiffs argued that Minnie received only a limited life estate, for her use and benefit, rather than a general life estate and that, similarly, the rents and revenues earned during her lifetime were not hers absolutely but were only to be used for her reasonable support. The trial court rejected both of these arguments. The plaintiffs appealed.

What was Minnie's ownership interest in the land? Explain.

Chapter 28

Real Property— Landlord and Tenant

The problems, rights, and duties involved in the landlord-tenant relationship are very relevant to the students reading this textbook, as nearly all of you are involved in such a relationship. A student who lives in a dormitory is part of a landlord-tenant relationship in which the university is the landlord and the student is the tenant. For a student who lives in an apartment, the landlord is the owner of the apartment complex. In this chapter, we will try to answer some of the questions that are often asked about the landlord-tenant relationship. We will start by looking at tenancy—the right of the tenant, or lessee—to occupy the premises.

TYPES OF TENANCIES

Tenancies at Will. The simplest form of tenancy, **tenancy at will**, occurs when the landlord allows the tenant to occupy the premises and there is no agreement as to a specific time period. Either the landlord or the tenant may terminate the tenancy at any time. Also, a tenancy at will is automatically terminated by the death of either party.

Most states require that the terminating party give the other party advance notice. The length of this notice varies from state to state, but thirty days is typical. This, of course, assumes that the rent has been paid. If the tenant fails to pay the rent, then the landlord can simply give the tenant notice that the lease has been terminated for that reason. In this situation, a different notice requirement would be imposed.

No reason need be given to terminate the tenancy at will. Landlords may terminate the tenancy at will simply because they do not want a tenant living there any longer. Tenants, on the other hand, may terminate it simply because they want to move out.

Tenancies for a Specified Period. The great majority of residential tenancies are for a period of one year. In a college community, however, the period of tenancy may be governed by the school year. For example, the landlord may lease an apartment from August to May to one student and then lease the apartment for two months during the summer to a student going to summer school. A commercial lease, for reasons of expediency, usually will be for a period longer than one year. A tenancy for a specified time is automatically terminated by the expiration of its term, and there is no requirement that either party give any notice. Both parties are aware of the term, and when the term ends, the tenancy ends.

Normally, tenancies for a specified period will be in writing because it is in the best interest of both parties to have written evidence of their agreement and the term of the tenancy. In this type of tenancy, neither the landlord nor the tenant may terminate the tenancy until the term expires, unless the tenant fails to pay the rent when due, in which case the landlord may terminate the tenancy, or unless one of the parties fails to live up to the requirements of the agreement, in which case the other party may terminate the tenancy based on that breach of the agreement. For example, if the landlord turns off the heat in subzero weather, the tenant certainly would have a right to terminate the lease and to move out of the premises since it would be unsafe to continue to live there.

Tenancies by Sufferance. This type of tenancy occurs after the tenancy for a specified period expires. For example, a student had a ten-month lease which expired on May 31. The student had a duty to move out on May 31, but for one reason or another needed to continue to occupy the premises. The student then became a tenant by sufferance. The landlord may treat the tenant by sufferance as a trespasser and have that person evicted, or the landlord may work out some type of rental agreement with such a tenant for the period of time that the tenant needs to stay. Until a landlord issues an eviction notice, or until the landlord and tenant agree to a new term of tenancy, the status of the tenant is that of a tenant by sufferance.

NATURE OF A LEASE

The **lease** is a contract, and thus must comply with the requirements for the formation and enforcement of a contract. There must be an *offer*, *acceptance*, *consideration*, *capacity to contract*, and *lawful purpose*. The lease contract may be oral or written. If it is oral and for a term exceeding one year, it will not be legally enforceable in most states. A few states, however, allow the enforcement of oral lease contracts for a period up to three years.

Many tenants have the misconception that an oral lease is better for them than a written one. Actually, a written lease provides better protection for both parties. In a written lease, the rights and duties of both parties are stated, and the landlord cannot raise the rent, evict the tenant, or impose any new rules during the term of the lease. In a college town where living space is limited, these protections can be very important. A written lease also prevents the tenant from moving out during the term of the lease except where the landlord has breached duties under terms of the lease. If the landlord fails to comply with the terms of the lease, then the tenant can move out legally, or force the landlord to comply with the terms, or sue for damages.

The lease agreement gives the tenant-lessee the right to occupy, use, and enjoy the apartment or the parcel of land and the improvements thereon, as defined in the agreement. Since the intent is not to permanently convey any rights to the lessee, the agreement must state when the landlord is allowed to retake possession. It must also state the consideration—how much rent the tenant is required to pay. The lease should specify what security deposit must be paid and when rental payments are due and to whom they are to be paid. There will also be lease terms which govern the tenant's use, enjoyment, and possession of the premises, and which preserve the landlord's right of inspection. Other terms may be inserted in a lease agreement. Many landlords do not want animals on the premises and, therefore, have a clause in the lease that prohibits the tenant from having a pet. Another common clause restricts the subletting of the premises. Normally, the tenant may sublet the premises to another person, provided the landlord agrees to the sublease. Landlords also frequently include clauses that purport to limit their liability for accidents on the premises.

LANDLORD'S RIGHTS AND OBLIGATIONS

Once a lease agreement has been made, either orally or in writing, the landlord has a duty to give the tenant possession of the premises specified in the lease agreement. The landlord also has the duty not to interfere with the right of the tenant to use, possess, and enjoy the premises for the term of the agreement, provided that the tenant does not breach any of the conditions or covenants of the lease, and provided that the tenant pays the rent as scheduled in the lease agreement. The landlord also has the right to inspect the premises at reasonable times, with the tenant's permission, to see that the premises are not being mistreated or damaged.

Condition of Premises. Under the common law, the landlord did not have to worry about the condition of the premises at the time they were rented to a tenant. The tenant was subject to the rule of *caveat emptor* and simply took the premises as they were or refused to rent them. If the premises were filthy or infested with rats and other vermin and the tenant knowingly agreed to take them, then the tenant assumed the risk and the landlord would not be responsible for injuries and damages that the tenant might suffer as a result of living in the premises. The rule of *caveat emptor* has generally been replaced by the rule of *caveat vendor*—that is, "Let the seller (in this case, the landlord) beware." The landlord-tenant relationship has become the target of many consumer groups. As a result, many states, cities, and counties have enacted housing codes which set minimum standards with regard to the rental of premises for residential occupancy. Most cities and counties now have housing inspectors who will respond to the complaints of tenants. These inspectors check to see that rental units are in fact safe, habitable, and free from dangers such as bare electrical wires, or other unhealthy and unsanitary conditions.

Injuries. In many recent cases, landlords have been found civilly liable for injury to tenants because the landlords failed to provide sufficient security, or because the landlords' employees were responsible for theft from or injury to tenants. Whether or not the landlord is liable, in such cases, depends heavily on the circumstances. If the apartment complex advertises that it provides security for its tenants, then it has assumed that duty; if, however, no security has been promised or provided, then the tenant will be faced with *caveat emptor*. As to theft, the landlord will normally have a clause in the lease stating that the landlord is not responsible for theft. If an employee of the landlord commits a crime against a tenant, then the landlord will allege that the person who perpetrated the crime was not acting as an agent or employee, and that the employer is not responsible for criminal acts of employees. We must, however, keep in mind that the pendulum of the law is swinging in favor of the consumer-tenant and against the seller-landlord.

The wise landlord will insure adequately against such situations, as this is still a questionable area of landlord's rights and obligations.

The *Spitzak* case is a recent example of how these rules work.

SPITZAK v. HYLANDS, LTD.
500 N.W.2d 154 (MN App., 1993)

FACTS: Appellant Patricia Spitzak and her children, Anthony, age 10, and Amy, age 13, reside at The Hylands in Rochester, Minnesota. The Hylands is a complex of townhouses owned by respondent The Hylands, Ltd., and managed by respondent Pembco. The relationship between respondents and appellant is that of landlord/tenant.

On July 27, 1988, Anthony was upstairs in his room playing Nintendo with two other boys. His mother had gone out for the evening and his sister was downstairs with a friend. Chad Quandt, a friend of Anthony's, was riding his bicycle across the grounds of The Hylands on his way to the Spitzaks' residence when he met four teenagers. The teenagers, who had been drinking, threatened Chad and tried to beat him up. Chad fled to the Spitzaks' apartment and told Amy Spitzak that the teenagers attacked him. Amy went outside to investigate.

While still upstairs, Anthony overheard the teenagers yelling for Chad to come out of the apartment. Fearing for Chad's safety, Anthony went downstairs, locked the door, and began shutting all the windows. While Anthony was shutting one of the windows, Terry Vale struck the window with his fist from the outside and broke it. A shard of glass from the broken window flew into Anthony's eye. As a result, Anthony's eye had to be surgically removed.

Appellant brought this action to recover damages for injuries sustained by Anthony. On these facts, the trial court found there was no special relationship between Anthony and respondents that would give rise to a duty to protect Anthony from harm caused by third parties. Furthermore, the trial court also found the third party act resulting in harm to Anthony was not foreseeable. The trial court granted summary judgment in favor of respondents.

 JUDGE RANDALL:

To maintain a claim for negligence, a plaintiff must show: (1) a duty, (2) a breach of that duty, (3) a causal connection between breach of duty and injury, and (4) injury in fact.... Generally, the existence of a legal duty is for the court to determine as a matter of law....

In the absence of a special relationship, there is no duty to control the conduct of a third person to prevent him from causing physical harm to another.... "Whether a duty is imposed depends, therefore, on the relationship of the parties and the foreseeable risk involved...."

If the law is to impose a duty on A to protect B from C's criminal acts, the law usually looks for a special relationship between A and B, a situation where B has in some way entrusted his or her safety to A and A has accepted that entrustment. This special relationship also assumes that the harm presented by C is something A is in a position to protect against and should be expected to protect against....

Although the standard for delineating acceptable and unacceptable risks has not been clearly defined, ... at the very least, the risk must be greater than "that presented out on the street and in the neighborhood generally" before a duty will be imposed. In this case, appellant does not claim that the apartment complex owned and managed by respondents presents a "particular focus or unique opportunity for criminals and their criminal activities...." Nor does appellant argue that tenants at The Hylands are exposed to a greater risk than that in the neighborhood generally. The trial court properly found that appellant failed to meet its threshold burden of establishing the existence of a special relationship duty....

Notwithstanding the lack of a special relationship in this case, the landlord-tenant relationship between appellant and respondents may serve to impose some duty of care on respondents.... However, given the facts in the record, the criminal act which resulted in injury to Anthony is not the type of act which respondents could reasonably be expected to prevent.... Nothing in the record suggests that The Hylands is particularly susceptible to roving bands of teenagers looking for a fight with tenants.

Even where a duty to protect exists, the duty only extends to foreseeable acts. Generally, the issue of foreseeability is for the trial court to decide.... The test of foreseeability is whether respondents were aware of facts indicating the tenants were being exposed to unreasonable risk of harm. Or, as stated another way,

> The common-law test of duty is the probability or foreseeability of injury to the plaintiff. As stated by Chief Justice Cardozo, "The risk reasonably to be perceived defines the duty to be obeyed, and risk imports relation; it is risk to another or to others within the range of apprehension...."

The trial court found that respondents could not have foreseen the teenagers' actions which resulted in injury. We agree. Although appellant submitted some general evidence of reports of crime in the area, there is no evidence indicating The Hylands is a known high crime complex. Nor is there evidence that a series of similar incidents occurred at or around The Hylands which respondents knew of or at least should have been aware.... The harm suffered by appellant was simply not foreseeable. Therefore, respondents owed no duty to prevent that harm.

The trial court properly concluded that, on these facts, respondents owed no special duty to protect appellant's son Anthony from third parties. Appellant failed to establish that tenants at The Hylands were subjected to unacceptable risks as the result of third party criminal activity. No special relationship existed between the parties which would have given rise to a duty to protect Anthony. Further, the third party criminal act which caused the injury was not foreseeable to respondents. We affirm the trial court's grant of summary judgment in favor of respondent.

TENANT'S RIGHTS AND OBLIGATIONS

The most important right that a tenant has is what the law terms **quiet enjoyment** of the premises. This means that, with a few exceptions, tenants have the right to use the house or apartment they are renting in generally the same manner as if they owned the premises. To be more specific, if you are a tenant, you may invite anyone you wish to visit you, and you may carry on any activities which are not forbidden by the lease or by law. The key here is reasonable use of the premises. For example, you rent a house with a large yard and the house is a considerable distance from other houses. In that case, you can play your stereo as loud as you want to and have loud parties, as long as you do not destroy or damage the rented property. On the other hand, if you live in an apartment building, your right to play the stereo loud and to have loud parties would be limited. As the tenant in an apartment, you not only have the right to quiet enjoyment of the premises, but you also have an obligation not to unreasonably disturb the other tenants, who also have the right to quiet enjoyment of the premises. The tenant should always read the fine print in the lease agreement, as the agreement may prohibit many activities which are not expressly forbidden by law, and such provisions are contractual and will generally be enforced by courts.

Landlord Inspections. As stated earlier, the landlord has a right to inspect the rented premises. However, during the period of the lease the landlord does not have the right to enter the house or apartment at will and without the tenant's permission. The landlord who is going to inspect the premises must do so at reasonable times that will not interfere with the quiet enjoyment of the premises by the tenant. A landlord could be civilly liable in a trespass action for forcing entry into the rented premises or for entering the rented premises periodically when the tenant is not at home simply to snoop.

Repairs. Another common problem experienced by tenants is that of liability for repairs. What repairs are the landlord's duty, and what repairs are the duty of the tenant? The landlord's obligation to make repairs inside the rented house or apartment will vary from state to state and from locality to locality, and may also be dictated by the terms of the lease. As a general rule, however, the landlord is required to make major repairs except where the damage is caused by the tenant's negligence. If the tenant is having a wild party and something is thrown through the window, the tenant will be obligated to replace the window. If a windstorm blows off part of the roofing and water drips through the ceiling causing the plaster to fall, the landlord will be responsible for repairs.

A rule of thumb in these cases would be that the tenant has a duty to make minor repairs to keep the premises in as good a condition as when they were rented, excluding, of course, normal wear and tear. Most landlords require a security deposit for use in making such minor repairs when the tenant vacates the premises. If the tenant's furniture marked up the walls, then the tenant would be obligated to have the walls repainted in order to cover the damage. If the furnace broke down, that is a major repair which would be the landlord's obligation.

The next case discusses the consequences of the landlord's failure to make repairs.

P.H. INVESTMENT v. OLIVER
818 P.2d 1018 (UT, 1991)

FACTS: This is an unlawful detainer action by P.H. Investment (the landlord) against Cathy Oliver (the tenant) based upon nonpayment of rent. Because of the deteriorated condition of the premises, the tenant argued that she owed no rent and counter-claimed for a rebate of rent paid. At trial, an officer with the Salt Lake City Building and Housing Services testified that there were forty-two housing code violations on the rental premises. The violations included numerous electrical violations; a hazardous stairway without handrails; holes in the walls in every room; dilapidated and rotted floors and carpets; a collapsed bathroom ceilng; a collapsed bedroom ceiling; leaking faucets, shower, and toilets; broken and missing windows; no bathroom door; and inadequate protection from weather. The inspector declared the building a public nuisance and ordered it repaired or demolished.

The trial court granted judgment to the landlord against the tenant for rent, treble damages, and costs of court, together with an order of restitution of the premises. The tenant received an offset against the judgment for the value of her deposit, but her rent rebate counterclaim was dismissed. The court of appeals affirmed by a divided court.

 JUSTICE DURHAM:

Under contract principles, relief for a breach in the warranty of habitability is based on a failure of consideration rather than on some theory of eviction. As a result, the tenant should not have to vacate the premises to raise the claim. Especially where there is a shortage of rental housing, and given the cost and inconvenience of relocation, little would be accomplished if the tenant's only remedy for a breach of the warranty of habitability required vacation of the premises before taking action to recover for the breach. Thus, many courts allow the tenant to remain in possession, withhold rent installments accruing after the landlord's breach, and then raise the landlord's breach of the warranty of habitability as a counterclaim or defense when the landlord brings an eviction action for failure to pay rent.... We hold that no legal doctrine, substantive or procedural, bars a tenant from raising this critical issue in an unlawful detainer action in this jurisdiction.

Utah's unlawful detainer statute ... takes away the landlord's common-law right to use self-help to remove a tenant. The statute grants the landlord a summary court proceeding to evict a tenant who has violated some express or implied provision of the lease. The statute provides five instances in which the tenant is in unlawful detainer, including the situation where the tenant defaults in the payment of rent and remains In possession.... The remedy for a successful landlord is restitution of the premises, treble damages, and recovery for waste or rent due.... If the unlawful detainer action is based on default in payment of rent, the judgment will also mandate forfeiture of the lease....

[T]his court has recognized a defendant-tenant's right to raise proper counter-claims in unlawful detainer cases. The legislature, too, apparently has recognized this right.... Under the concept of dependence of covenants, a breach of the warranty of habitability is directly relevant to the issue of possession.... Having recognized a warranty of habitability, we conclude that a breach of that warranty must necessarily give rise to a counterclaim in an unlawful detainer action; otherwise, the tenant would be required to vacate before being able to raise the breach, a result entirely inconsistent with the policy behind our adoption of the implied warranty. While the state does have a significant interest in preserving a speedy repossession remedy, that interest is not strong enough to warrant a deprivation of a meaningful opportunity to raise a breach of the warranty of habitability. We reject, therefore, any limitation on the tenant's ability to raise a breach of the warranty of habitability as a defense or counterclaim to a landlord's unlawful detainer action for possession.

The trial court held, as a matter of law, that the tenant had waived any defense or cause of action under a theory of warranty of habitability by agreeing to rent the premises in their deteriorated condition. Courts disagree on the propriety of waivers with regard to the warrant of habitability. A majority of courts prohibit them, reasoning that such a shift of responsibility is contrary to public policy....

In the present case, the tenant is typical of the individuals we sought to protect by adopting the warranty of habitability. Ms. Oliver is a woman with little or no resources or income, with seven children, and pregnant with an eighth at the time of this action.... Because of a lack of bargaining power, low-income tenants often have no meaningful choice but to accept and continue to live in substandard housing. To protect persons similarly situated, our approach will invalidate boiler-plate language, eliminate any duty of inspection, and protect against uninformed waivers of any latent defects. Moreover, because we will permit only express waivers of specifically listed defects, our approach should have the advantage of preventing much of the case-by-case litigation on the subject of implied waivers which may be generated by adherence to the Restatement approach. Our approach is, in this way, a workable compromise between those courts disallowing all waivers and those following the Restatement's broader language permitting implied waivers. Although we seek to protect parties' freedom to contract as they see fit, we must also recognize the undesirability of permitting landlords to lease uninhabitable dwellings.

On remand, the trial court will need to determine if any specific defects were expressly waived by the tenant when she moved in. The burden of proving the waiver should be on the landlord. If such a waiver was made, the trial court will then need to determine if the waiver was contrary to public policy or unconscionable under comment of the Restatement. The burden of proving this issue is on the tenant. We note that a finding upholding such a waiver must be supported by evidence that: (1) the waiver was express, and (2) the express waiver listed the specific defects waived.

The tenant's rights as to heat, water, and electricity will depend primarily upon the lease. If a landlord who is to provide heat turns the thermostats down to an unsafe or intolerable temperature, then the tenant may terminate the lease and leave, or pay to heat the premises and deduct the cost from the rent, or report the landlord to the local housing authority.

Tenant's Property. Another question that often arises is: Who bears the responsibility for the loss of the tenant's furniture, clothing, and personal effects if the rented apartment or house burns down? The lease will often expressly state that the tenants assume responsibility for carrying fire insurance on their personal belongings. If there is no such agreement in the lease, then the courts will usually hold the landlord responsible for damages to the tenants' contents if the fire or other damage was caused as a result of the landlord's negligence. The wise thing for the tenants to do is to carry renter's insurance on their contents, as the law and the obligation of the landlord will vary from jurisdiction to jurisdiction and with the situation. Also, it is often difficult to determine who, if anyone, was negligent in a major fire or catastrophe.

Physical Alterations. Another common question concerns the extent to which tenants can make changes or additions, such as putting pictures on the walls, installing shelves, or changing curtain rods. Again, the lease often specifies that tenants may not paint the premises, hang pictures, or make any alterations to the premises without the landlord's permission. If there is no such provision in the lease, then a reasonableness rule applies. If tenants make any major additions, such as bookshelves, a room divider, or other fixtures, the landlord automatically becomes the owner of those fixtures when the tenants leave, unless the fixtures can be removed without causing any damage to the rented property.

TERMINATION OF THE LEASE

If the lease is for a fixed period of time, it is rather difficult for the tenant to break it. However, a landlord and a tenant can always end the lease by mutual agreement, regardless of its terms. Thus, if the tenant and the landlord agree that the tenant may move out before the lease expires, then the lease may be terminated by mutual consent. It is a good idea to put this in writing to prevent the landlord from coming back later and trying to enforce the lease.

Breach of Lease. The tenant may also terminate the lease without the landlord's agreement if the landlord has interfered with the tenant's quiet enjoyment or if the landlord has in some way failed to meet obligations specified in the lease and such failure has caused the premises to be uninhabitable or below minimum health standards.

The landlord can evict a tenant for nonpayment of rent. The landlord can evict a tenant if the tenant stays in possession of the premises after the term of the lease has expired, or if the tenant violates the rules and regulations of the lease. For example, if your lease states that no pets are allowed and you keep a cat, the landlord can evict you unless you get rid of it.

The *McCray* case discusses the landlord's retaking of the premises when the tenant still has personal property on the premises.

McCRAY v. CARSTENSEN
492 N.W.2d 444 (IA App., 1992)

FACTS: Plaintiffs executed a lease to rent commercial real estate from defendants. The lease stated the premises were to be used "only for a bar serving a limited number of food items." The term of the lease was for a one-year period beginning on May 1, 1989, and terminating on April 30, 1990. In a default situation, the lease provided plaintiffs were to receive a ten-day notice prior to cancellation or forfeiture of the lease.

Plaintiffs began doing business on May 29, 1989, and continued to do business until March of 1990. They operated the business as a bar which featured seminude female dancers. During its operation, however, plaintiffs had problems concerning a dance permit. In March 1990, plaintiffs lost their dance permit. Determining it to be economically infeasible to continue operation without the female dancers, plaintiffs closed their bar. Plaintiffs testified at trial they continued to apply for permits necessary to reopen the bar.

On several occasions in late March and the first week of April 1990, defendants observed plaintiffs' business was not open during normal operating hours. In addition, the rent payment was over one month late, and defendants had received several requests from utility companies for access to the premises to shut off services. Defendants were also aware of plaintiffs' inability to obtain a dance permit. During this same period of time, defendants informed plaintiffs of a rent increase at the expiration of the lease. Plaintiffs expressly rejected renewal of the lease. Plaintiffs' final application for a dance permit was also denied in early April. Consequently, plaintiffs ceased efforts to obtain the permits necessary to reopen the bar.

Defendants took possession of the premises on April 7, 1990. The record shows defendants failed to provide notice of default and changed the locks on the premises. On April 18, 1990, defendants leased the premises to a third party.

Plaintiffs did not return to the premises until mid-April at which time they found the locks had been changed. Plaintiffs then contacted defendants and requested the return of their personal property. This was the only time plaintiffs contacted defendants with regard to the release of their property. Defendants asked them to contact the new tenant and stated there should be no problems with the return of their property. Upon contacting the new tenant, plaintiffs were requested to submit a list of their possessions. The new tenant explained he needed the list to verify ownership because several individuals were claiming rights to property on the premises. At no time did the new tenant refuse to return items to plaintiffs. Plaintiffs never submitted a list, and they never contacted defendants with regard to any problems with the return of their property. On November 19, 1990, however, plaintiffs filed a petition at law alleging conversion of their personal property.

On October 30, 1991, the trial court filed its order in favor of defendants. The trial court rejected plaintiffs' argument they were denied return of their property.

The trial court concluded the actions of defendants did not constitute conversion. It determined defendants took possession of the premises after plaintiffs has abandoned the premises. Plaintiffs appealed.

 JUDGE HAYDEN:

The Iowa Supreme Court has defined conversion as "the act of wrongful control or dominion over another's personal property in denial of or inconsistent with that person's possessory right to the property...." The fact defendants locked plaintiffs out of the premises does not necessarily involve sufficient interference with plaintiffs' personal property to constitute conversion because defendants were willing to allow plaintiffs to access the premises for the purpose of removing their property.... The following factors should be considered in determining the seriousness of the interference:

(a) The extent and duration of the actor's exercise of dominion or control.
(b) The actor's intent to assert a right in fact inconsistent with the other's right of control.
(c) The actor's good faith.
(d) The extent and duration of the resulting interference with the other's right of control.
(e) The harm done to the chattel.
(f) The inconvenience and expense caused to the other....

The fact defendants failed to provide notice of default does not alone determine whether they converted the property. The issue is whether defendants' actions so seriously interfered with plaintiffs' rights as to require them to pay full value of the property. The following facts support the conclusion defendants are not liable.

Evidence shows plaintiffs contacted defendants only one time to discuss the return of their personal property. Defendants asked plaintiffs to contact the new tenant and foresaw no problems with the return of the property. The new tenant merely asked plaintiffs to provide a list of their property as proof of ownership prior to turning over the equipment. The period during which the property was in defendants' possession is due to plaintiffs' failure to retrieve it. The record shows plaintiffs failed to provide such a list to the new tenant and never contacted defendants with any complaints about the return of their property. At all times, defendants were willing to release the property and had no intent on denying access to plaintiffs.

The good faith of defendants is another consideration in assessing the seriousness of the interference.... We agree with the trial court conclusion defendants acted in good faith when they took possession of the premises. Defendants did not assert any rights inconsistent with plaintiffs' rights over the personal property. Defendants also acted in good faith through their efforts to relet the premises....

Finally, we determine the personal property of plaintiffs was not harmed. Evidence shows the items still remain in the building. There is no evidence to show plaintiffs were refused the right to remove their personal property. The new tenant merely requested a list of property in order to establish ownership....

Defendants retook possession of the real estate for several reasons. Although the lockout occurred approximately three weeks before the expiration of the lease, it was evident plaintiffs would not reopen their business. The bar had been closed during regular business hours of a tavern for some time, rent was more than a month overdue, and plaintiffs had failed to pay other bills, such as utilities, for which they were responsible under the terms of the lease. In addition, evidence shows plaintiffs ceased their efforts to obtain a dance permit as soon as they learned rent would be increasing at the end of April.

We determine plaintiffs failed to meet their burden showing there was any distinct act of wrongful control exercised over their personal property.... Defendants' actions did not rise to the level of conversion. The record shows defendants would have willingly released plaintiffs' property. We conclude defendants never interfered so seriously as to constitute a denial of plaintiffs' right to their personal property. We affirm the trial court.

Security Deposits. Most leases provide that a lessee must pay a security deposit when the lease is signed. This security deposit is to be held by the landlord and to be applied to any repairs required as a result of damage caused by the tenant other than normal wear and tear and for clean up after the tenant leaves, if the premises are not in a reasonably clean condition. Two problems exist. First, the landlord takes two or three hundred dollars of each tenant's money and holds it for the lease period, which may be a year or longer. During that time, the landlord can invest this money and secure interest on it. Some states require landlords to pay interest to tenants on the security deposit when it is returned. Most states, however, still do not have such a requirement. Thus, a landlord with 100 apartments has a large amount of cash to invest, and the landlord can earn a good income from the tenants' money.

The second problem is what type of repairs and what type of cleanup should come out of the security deposit. Some landlords use the money for improvements such as repainting the entire apartment or purchasing new curtains on the contention that the walls were chipped or the drapes were stained. Obviously the walls could be patched and painted as necessary, but the landlord is not entitled to a complete paint job at the expense of the tenant. The same principle applies to the curtains and drapes. Cleaning may be allowable, but not the purchase of new drapes. The landlord is not supposed to gain by getting an improvement. The problem is that the landlord has the security deposit, and he or she often refuses to return it, alleging it was used for repairs and cleanup. For years tenants simply grumbled but did not go to court since the cost of paying a lawyer, court costs, and other expenses made collecting too expensive for the amount of money involved. Most jurisdictions now have small claims courts where the tenant can, for a minimal filing fee, file a lawsuit and have the case heard promptly. Landlord-tenant cases comprise a major portion of the court calendar in most small claims courts.

Landlord's Damages. Where a tenant simply defaults in the payment of rent, the landlord may file suit to evict and to collect the back rent. Depending on the particular state, the landlord may be entitled to hold the tenant's possessions under a "landlord lien statute."

The *Bender* case reviews the landlord's right to attach a tenant's possessions for nonpayment of back rent, as opposed to the right to evict the tenant.

BENDER v. NORTH MERIDIAN MOBILE HOME PARK
63 So.2d 385 (Mississippi, 1994)

FACTS: Richard Bender entered into a six month lease on July 13, 1987, to rent trailer No. 4 from North Meridian Mobile Home Park, Inc., (landlord). The lease specified that the rent was $195.00 per month, but did not state when such rent was due.

Bender paid rent at various intervals and in varying amounts. Bender was behind on his rent from the beginning of the lease. Bender testified that no one complained about the way that he paid his rent. However, Lannie Ritter testified that he had talked with Bender many times about getting his rent paid. Through the end of November 1987, Bender was in arrears in the amount of $165.00

The facts are disputed as to when Bender was locked out of the trailer. Bender testified that he had gone by to see Mr. Ritter on December 5, 1987, so that he would know that he was planning on bringing partial payment of the rent. He stated that he went to see Mr. Ritter because Mrs. Ritter had come by his trailer earlier to see if he had anything toward the rent. Bender stated that later that day when he returned to make a payment towards rent that he was locked out of his trailer. Bender testified that he received the eviction notice after he had been locked out of the trailer. Bender stated that all these events occurred on the same day.

After finding that the locks had been changed on the trailer, Bender stated that he went to see Mr. Ritter and attempted to give him some money towards rent, but Mr. Ritter would not accept it. Bender testified that Ritter told him not to come back to the trailer park, and if he did he would be shot as a trespasser. Bender testified that he made several pleas with Mr. Ritter to allow him in the trailer to get some medication for his back injury but Ritter refused. Bender stated that he returned to the trailer three or four days after he had been locked out (December 8 or 9, 1987) to get some papers for the Social Security Administration. He testified that he was not allowed to take any other items from the trailer.

Lannie Ritter did not testify at trial, but his deposition was admitted into evidence. Ritter testified that he and Clyde Rose decided that Bender must be evicted. Ritter testified that he served Bender with the eviction notice on December 5, 1987. He stated that he did not take further action until December 8 or 9, 1987. On either December 8 or 9 Ritter stated that he changed the locks on the trailer Bender was renting while Bender was away. Ritter stated that when Bender came back to the trailer park, he wanted to be let back in his trailer. Ritter stated that his wife went to the trailer with Bender and allowed him to get his medication out of the trailer. Ritter stated that the day after he locked Bender out of the trailer he (Bender) returned to the trailer park and threatened him with a gun. Ritter stated that when he threatened to call the sheriff, Bender left the trailer park. Ritter said that was the last time that he saw Bender.

Landlord kept Bender's property locked in the rental trailer No. 4 for about two months, until some date in February. At that time, landlord moved Bender's property to a storage trailer and prepared an inventory. Bender's property remained in the storage trailer until May or June 1988. The landlord sold the inventoried items at a general rummage sale in June 1988. An advertisement announcing the rummage sale was published in the local newspaper, but no reference was made to Bender's possessions being put up for sale. Bender was not notified of the sale. According to the landlord, the rummage sale of all items, including the inventoried property of the tenant, brought in thirty-five ($35.00) dollars.

The trial court in its final judgment specifically denied all relief prayed for by Bender against both Lannie Ritter and Clyde Rose, individually.

 JUSTICE PITTMAN:

Bender asserted that he was wrongfully evicted. The landlord stated that it had a landlord's lien pursuant to Miss. Code Ann. S.89-7-51(2) for non-payment of rent....

Bender argued that the Landlord Lien Statute S.89-7-51 does not provide for the ejectment of a tenant from the leased premises for failure to pay rent. This Court agrees. Section 89-7-51(2) is not an alternative remedy for removal of a tenant from the leased premises as the lower court stated. Section 89-7-51(2) gives a landlord a subordinate lien on all articles of personal property.

The landlord's reliance on the Landlord Lien Statute as some form of legal process or sanction to eject the tenant from his home was misplaced. There is nothing in the statute that indicates that a landlord is allowed to resort to lockout. The statute specifically states the means by which the lien should be enforced. The last sentence of S. 89-7-51(2) states "All of the provisions of law as to attachment for rent and proceedings thereunder shall be applicable with reference to the lessor's lien under this subsection." This means that in order for the landlord to enforce his statutorily created lien on the tenant's personal property they must follow the attachment for rent statutes. Sections 89-7-55 through 89-7-125 set forth how a landlord attaches for rent. The landlord clearly did not follow this procedure. Since S.89-7-51(2) did not provide for the actions taken by the landlord, the Court finds that the trial court erred in finding that Bender was properly evicted.

Not only were landlord's actions of lockout not allowed by statute, but case law also prohibited the action. This Court has held that a landlord could not regain possession of leased premises by breaking in or by threats of personal violence or the exercise of such violence, but where the lease provided for reentry by the landlord for tenant's failure to pay rent, the landlord may exercise such reentry if done so without breaking in, violence or threats of violence....

The lease between the landlord and tenant in [this] case ... had no provision which would have allowed the landlord to regain possession without notice and hearing. Since there was no such provision, the landlord should have used the statutory process and not resorted to a self-help procedure....

Bender argued that the trial court erred in assessing the amount of damages for conversion. At the trial of the case ... landlord introduced an inventory done by the landlord's manager about two months after Bender's property was locked up in his trailer. Bender's testimony as to what specific items were in the trailer and their value differed vastly from the inventory made by landlord.

Bender argued that a review of the record would clearly show that the trial court erred in its findings. Bender introduced an exhibit that listed the items he claimed were in the trailer at the time of landlord's seizure of property. This exhibit stated a total value of the listed items at $4,793.00. Bender testified that the seized property was worth at least $3,500. Bender introduced ten photographs which portrayed items of personal property that Bender alleged were in the trailer at the time of the seizure by landlord.

The trial court found that "there was no credible evidence produced at trial convincing the court as to the value of said possessions, whatever they were, at the time of conversion." However, the trial court assessed Bender's conversion damages at $296.45. This was the same amount that the court found Bender owed to landlord for past due rent and deposit....

After reviewing the record, there is nothing to indicate that the trial judge was manifestly wrong in his damage assessment for conversion. As the trier of fact, the trial judge determined the value of items that he believed to be in the trailer. The Court finds this assignment of error to be without merit....

This Court reverses the lower court's finding that Bender was not wrongfully evicted. We leave to the lower court to determine whether or not Bender suffered any damages from this wrongful eviction. We affirm the lower court's conversion damage assessment. Accordingly, the Court affirms in part and reverses in part.

What happens if the tenant moves out of the leased premises before the end of the lease? The landlord may sue the tenant for any unpaid rent due at the time the tenant moved out, and for the balance of the rent due under the lease. What is the landlord's duty to mitigate, that is, to lessen, the amount due from the lessee by re-renting the premises to someone else? Traditionally, the landlord did not have a duty to re-rent the premises and thus mitigate the loss. The trend in the recent landlord-tenant cases involving residential leases reflects a change in judicial thinking. Recent cases require the landlord in residential leases to make at least a reasonable effort to re-rent the premises and thereby mitigate the damages.

With regard to commercial leases, the courts will not feel so sorry for the lessee. In a commercial lease situation, the lease agreement is usually negotiated, with each party having legal counsel. Also, in a commercial lease situation, the parties will be on a more equal footing financially. Thus, the landlord may be able to collect the rent for the balance of the lease without trying to re-rent the commercial building.

SIGNIFICANCE OF THIS CHAPTER

Most people will be involved in a lease at some time, either as a tenant or as a landlord. This chapter reviews the contents of a lease and discusses the rights and duties of the tenant and the landlord.

PROBLEMS FOR DISCUSSION

1. Two tenants living in an apartment complex commenced legal actions against the landlord to recover damages for personal injuries they suffered in accidents which occurred in common passageways of the apartment complex. Tenant McCutcheon fell down an unlighted stairway, and tenant Fuller fell down an exterior wooden stairway. Both alleged negligence in maintenance by the landlord. In both cases the landlord defended on the basis of an exculpatory clause in the lease which said that the landlord would not be liable for any injury to the lessee or his family. The plaintiffs are asking the court to declare this exculpatory clause to be against public policy and thus invalid.

   How should the court rule? Why?

2. Rienecker leased a single-family house from Agnes Roseberry in 1990. Agnes had just had some remodeling done on the house, including the installation of a new roof. The roofers had removed the gutters from the front of the house but had not reinstalled them. Without gutters, water ran off the front side of the roof onto the front steps. On January 9, 1991, ice had accumulated on the steps and Rienecker worked that afternoon to clean them off. Gary Borders arrived at about 4 p.m. in response to a dinner invitation. When Gary left that evening, about 9 p.m., he slipped and fell on the icy steps, and sustained personal injuries. Gary sued Agnes. He appealed from a trial court ruling that Agnes owed no duty to a social guest of the tenant in a single-family house where the injury was the result of a known hazard.

   What result, and why?

3. The Village Green is a housing complex of 629 units in the Baldwin Hills area of Los Angeles. It was built in 1942 and was operated as an apartment complex until 1973, when it was converted to a condominium development. As part of the condominium conversion, the developer drafted and recorded a declaration of CC and Rs [Covenants, Conditions, and Restrictions] which run with the property and which contain a prohibition against residency by anyone under the age of 18. The CC and Rs also establish the Village Green Owners Association (Association) and authorize it to enforce the regulations set forth therein. The Association is a nonprofit organization whose membership consists of all owners of units at Village Green.

   John and Denise O'Connor bought a two-bedroom unit in Village Green in 1995. On July 4, 1998, their son Gavin was born. Shortly thereafter, the Association gave them written notice that the presence of their son Gavin in the unit constituted a violation of the CC and Rs and directed them to discontinue having Gavin live there.

   After making unsuccessful attempts to find other suitable housing, the O'Connors filed a complaint against the Association seeking to have the age restriction declared invalid and to enjoin its enforcement. They alleged that the age restriction violated the state's Civil Rights Act. The action was dismissed and the O'Connors appealed.

   Are these age restrictions valid? Discuss.

4. Kirsch and her son moved into a ground floor apartment in a building owned by Mendez. Mendez employed Middleton as caretaker for the building. Kirsch lived there for one month before she was required to sign a one-year lease. The lease contained a clause disclaiming the landlord's liability for any damage done by plumbing, gas, steam, water, or other pipes. Kirsch did not read this clause at the time, nor was it explained to her. Her apartment had

a "sleeve" for an air conditioning unit, but there was no air conditioning unit. Instead, a piece of cardboard covered the opening where the unit would have been. Hickman and Cramer moved into the apartment above Kirsch's in November. Their air conditioner was also missing, and during the winter they filed about fifty complaints with Middleton about the cardboard blowing off the hole and letting in cold air. Middleton did nothing about the problem. Kirsch received a call at work telling her to come back to her apartment. A copper tube in the baseboard radiation system had broken, and her apartment was flooded with water. The cold air coming in upstairs had apparently frozen the pipe, and it broke. Kirsch was paid by her insurance company, State Farm, and it sued Mendez's insurance company, Home. State Farm won a jury verdict, but the trial court entered a judgment notwithstanding the verdict for Home. State Farm appealed.

Is the disclaimer in the lease effective here? Explain.

5. Helen Fisher owns a three-story building located at 117 North Washington Avenue in Minneapolis. The first floor is leased to a commercial sauna and massage parlor, and the second and third floors are each studio/loft apartments. Stacey Greene and two roommates leased the second floor.

The building entrance, facing Washington Avenue, is not locked and opens into a small vestibule. Inside the vestibule one door opens into the sauna and another onto a stairway leading up to the lofts. A door on the second floor opens off the stairway into Greene's loft, and the stairway continues up to the third floor.

On January 1, 1999, appellant Renae Rullman attended an impromptu New Year's party in Greene's loft apartment. Because the building had no intercom or buzzer system, guests entered by knocking on the door at the bottom of the stairway and waiting for someone to walk down the stairs to open the door. The deposition testimony varied on the type of door and lock but was consistent that the door did not lock automatically upon closing. The depositions were also conflicting as to whether the door at the top of the stairs could be effectively locked. In the early evening, Greene followed departing guests down the stairs to make sure the door was locked because she worried about security, particularly the "sauna situation." She states that she became "frustrated," however, because guests "were always going in and out," and stopped checking the door. Rullman arrived with a group of friends shortly after midnight.

Greene stated in a deposition that she recognized everyone at the party except for one man. Rullman said she did not know the man either, but "he was there mingling, like everybody else," and she assumed he was a guest. Greene said that even though he was a stranger she thought at the time, "it's New Year's Eve, if he's okay, then we'll welcome him." She stated that the unknown man was not doing anything improper. None of the other guests knew the man or how he had come to the party.

Rullman danced with the man and introduced him to Greene as "Leon." When she went to use the bathroom, located at the back of the loft away from the area of the party, the man followed her, pushed her into the bathroom, beat her, broke her jaw, and sexually assaulted her. Another guest interrupted the attack, but the man fled and was never apprehended or identified.

Rullman brought this personal injury action, contending that Fisher was negligent in failing to maintain reasonable security and security devices in the building. The trial court granted a summary judgment in favor of the landlord. Plaintiff appealed.

Is the landlord liable for this assault? Why or why not?

Chapter 29

Real Property—
Environmental Regulation

This chapter deals with the many problems involved in the use of real estate by its owner. The initial reaction from most people is: "It's my land, and I ought to be able to use it as I see fit." If we look back to the era of our grandfathers, or perhaps our great-grandfathers, we would find that owners of real estate could use their land in any way that they saw fit, provided their use did not cause a **nuisance**, as defined by law. Such a nuisance would do harm to the neighboring property owners or would interfere with their peaceable use and enjoyment of their real estate. There were no restrictions on house sizes, on the erection of fences or any outbuildings, on the number of families housed on a property, or on the use of a home to operate a beauty shop, a barbershop, a small appliance repair shop, or some similar type of business. In those days, we did not have the density problem or the traffic problem that we have today in most cities. Plenty of land was available, and far fewer people were making a demand for its use. Yet, cities grew and grew—in most cases, without a master plan. Thus, we ended up with industrial plants, apartment complexes, and scattered commercial buildings in single-family residential areas.

LAND USE REGULATION

The increased population density in our cities has brought environmental problems—contaminated air and water, solid waste pollution, traffic congestion, and noise pollution. To solve such problems, we have had to resort to governmental regulation of the use of various land areas. Today most cities develop industrial parks and encourage industry to build and operate within these areas. Most cities have developed zoning ordinances which restrict the use of the land in various areas. For example, single-family dwellings will be allowed in some areas, two-family dwellings will be allowed in other areas, multifamily dwellings, such as large apartment houses will be allowed in still other areas, and commercial businesses will be excluded from certain areas.

At first glance, this may seem unfair to the owner of real estate, since under these ordinances the owner is limited to the uses prescribed by the law. It is true that zoning ordinances do take away certain rights of the individual owner. However, when one looks at the overall picture, it is clear that some type of land use regulation is in the best interest of all the residents of the city. Such regulation guarantees a more peaceful enjoyment of the owners' premises for the purposes that are allowed in an area, and it also preserves the property values for the owners in that area. For example, if you live in an area of single-family dwellings, you certainly would object to having a developer put an apartment complex next to your home since this would increase the traffic in front of your residence, create a parking problem, and generally reduce the value of your real estate.

The first zoning law in the United States was an ordinance adopted in 1916 by New York City. It regulated both the location and the use of buildings in the city. The basic constitutionality of zoning laws was upheld as a valid exercise of the local government's police power in the landmark case of *Euclid v. Ambler Realty Co.*, which was decided by the U.S. Supreme Court in 1926. Zoning and land use restrictions of other kinds may still be held unconstitutional, if they unreasonably interfere with a property owner's rights or if they violate some other constitutional restriction.

Zoning Defined. Zoning can be defined as the division of a city, a township, or a county, or other governmental unit into specific districts for the purpose of regulating the type of building structure that may be built in each district, the placement of the buildings upon the land, and the permitted use or uses of the buildings and the land. For example, certain districts will be zoned R-1, which means that only single-family residential buildings would be allowed in them. Two-family buildings would be allowed in an R-2 district. Multifamily buildings, such as apartment houses, would be allowed in an R-3 district. A G-B district would allow general businesses, such as office buildings, stores, shopping centers, motels, and hotels. An L-I would allow light industry, such as assembly-type factories and warehouses. H-I zoning would allow heavy industry, such as manufacturing plants, with the potential for noise and air pollution. Typically, these industrial districts are located as far away from residential areas as possible. The use of the identifying terms R-1, R-2, R-3, G-B, L-I, and H-I is not universal. Some areas classify their zoning districts alphabetically, referring, for example, to A or B districts, or use other methods to identify their various zoning districts.

Within each zoning district there may be further regulations regarding the architecture, the location, and the occupancy of buildings. Examples of such regulations are restrictions on the height of buildings and regulations specifying a minimum distance from the front, side, and rear property lines within which no building may be constructed. This type of regulation helps control the density of buildings and protects property owners from encroachment upon their airspace and access to sunlight. For example, a neighbor would not be allowed to construct a sixteen-foot fence that blocks your view or blocks sunlight from your windows, or to build an addition that brings the neighbor's house right up to your property line and thus reduces the space between the houses.

Most cities or counties now have specific building construction codes, primarily for safety and health purposes. These codes regulate construction methods and the use of construction materials, and typically set a minimum standard for the area. Building codes will differ throughout the country because different standards are dictated by regional characteristics, such as temperature, the density of buildings, the possibility of earthquakes, and freezing and thawing problems.

In addition to physical regulations regarding the structure and placement of buildings, many zoning districts may have regulations concerning businesses that may be undesirable to property owners. For example, certain districts may not allow bars or the selling of intoxicating beverages, or may exclude funeral homes or cemeteries.

One of the problems that has plagued city planners is that zoning must be prospective rather than retroactive in effect. If a zoning ordinance zones a certain area exclusively for single-family residential dwellings, the little corner grocery store or the lady who has her beauty shop in her home cannot be forced to cease doing business. Thus, most zoning laws have a grandfather clause which allows a business that was in the area before the passage of the zoning ordinance to operate until it is sold or disposed of in some other manner.

Another exception to zoning regulations is the **variance**. Often there are situations where the strict adherence to a zoning regulation would cause undue hardship to a property owner. In such situations, the regulatory agency can grant a variance to allow the land to be used in a manner not in strict conformance with the zoning regulation. Variances are, however, not automatic but are granted only in exceptional situations.

The *Lucas* case discusses the "outer limits" of the government's power to regulate land use.

LUCAS v. SOUTH CAROLINA COASTAL COUNCIL
112 S.Ct. 2886 (1992)

FACTS: In 1986, David Lucas bought two lots on the Isle of Palms (an island east of Charleston, South Carolina) for $975,000. He hired an architect to draw up plans for a single-family home on each lot. Two years later, the state passed the Beachfront Management Act. The BMA prohibited owners from building "occupiable improvements" within twenty feet of the coast at any point where erosion had occurred within the last forty years. It was thus illegal for Lucas to build any sort of dwelling on either of his island lots.

Lucas sued, claiming that his lots had been "taken," and that the Constitution required compensation be paid by the state. The state trial court agreed, deciding that the lots were worth $1,232,387.50. The state supreme court reversed. Lucas asked the U.S. Supreme Court for further review.

 JUSTICE SCALIA:

Justice Holmes recognized ... that if the protection against physical appropriations of private property was to be meaningfully enforced, the government's power to redefine the range of interests included in the ownership of property was necessarily constrained by constitutional limits.... If, instead, the uses of private property were subject to unbridled, uncompensated qualification under the police power, "the natural tendency of human nature [would be] to extend the qualification more and more until at last private property disappear[ed]."... "[W]hile property may be regulated to a certain extent, if regulation goes too far it will be recognized as a taking."

In 70-odd years of ... "regulatory takings" jurisprudence, we have generally eschewed any "set formula" for determining how far is too far, preferring to "engag[e] in ... essentially ad hoc, factual inquiries."... We have, however, described at least two discrete categories of regulatory action as compensable without case-specific inquiry into the public interest advanced in support of the restraint. The first encompasses regulations that compel the property owner to suffer a physical "invasion" of his property....

The second situation in which we have found categorical treatment appropriate is where regulation denies all economically beneficial or productive use of land....

We have never set forth the justification for this rule. Perhaps it is simply ... that total deprivation of beneficial use is, from the landowner's point of view, the equivalent of a physical appropriation....

It seems unlikely that common-law principles would have prevented the erection of any habitable or productive improvements on land; they rarely support prohibition of the "essential use" of land.... [T]o win this case ... South Carolina must identify background principles of nuisance and property law that prohibit the uses [Lucas] now intends in the circumstances in which the property is presently found. Only on this showing can the State fairly claim that, in proscribing all such beneficial uses, the Beachfront Management Act is taking nothing.

[Judgment is reversed, and case is remanded to the South Carolina trial court for further proceedings.]

Private Restrictive Covenants. Zoning laws are usually general in character and often do not cover certain specific areas of land use. For example, zoning laws do not forbid the parking of large boats or campers in a driveway, yet such action may be unsightly and disturbing to the adjoining residents. Thus, a land developer may place certain restrictions in the land deeds to protect the value of the real estate in a new residential subdivision. When the land is being developed and sold, the contract of sale and deed will contain certain restrictions, such as the requirement to submit house plans not only to the public agency for a building permit but also to a committee in the subdivision for its approval. Other restrictions might ban outside clotheslines, the construction of outbuildings, the construction of fences without prior approval, and the parking of boats and campers on driveways. Homeowners who violate these restrictions may be taken to court. The court may enjoin further violations and cause the party to tear down the building or fence, move the camper or trailer, or perhaps pay damages to neighbors if damages to them were incurred. Failure to comply with the court order could result in fines and/or imprisonment for civil contempt of court.

Thus, we have public zoning and private restrictive zoning. Before purchasing any parcel of real estate, purchasers should be aware not only of public zoning restrictions but of any private restrictions which may affect their future use of this land.

Other Land Use Regulations. As we learned earlier in this chapter, each state has inherent rights to exercise police power to regulate private property for the public interest, convenience, and necessity. The states have delegated this regulatory power to the local governments: namely, counties and cities.

In addition to zoning regulations, housing codes, and building codes, most cities and counties now have subdivision controls and regulations, since housing density is becoming more and more of a problem. When a group of new homes is to be built in an area, there must be a preliminary investigation to determine whether any health or other environmental hazard will be caused by this new group of dwellings. Today, many subdivisions are being created in areas where there are no public sewage systems or public water systems. In such areas, it is important to make sure that the soil will allow proper drainage and filtering of wastes from the septic tanks of the new dwellings. It must also be determined that the water supply will not be contaminated by the septic systems.

In the following case, Ms. Nahrstedt is complaining about another sort of restriction.

NAHRSTEDT v. LAKESIDE VILLAGE CONDO.
11 Cal. Rptr.2d 299 (CA App. 2 Dist., 1992)

FACTS: This action concerns: (1) a plaintiff who wishes to continue living with her three pet cats in the condominium she owns; (2) a provision in the recorded covenants, conditions, and restrictions ("CC & R's") governing that condominium, which prohibits owners of the units in her condominium project from keeping most types of pets; and (3) the authority of the board of directors of her homeowners association to levy monetary fines on homeowners who violate that pet restriction. Natore Nahrstedt filed this action to obtain, among other things, a declaration that she: (1) is entitled to keep her pets in her condominium, notwithstanding the CC & R's; and (2) has no legal obligation to pay the fines which have been assessed against her for her refusal to move her cats out of her condominium. Plaintiff appeals from a judgment of dismissal which was entered after the trial court sustained, without leave to amend, demurrers to all six causes of action in plaintiff's original complaint.

 ASSOCIATE JUSTICE CROSSKEY:

Plaintiff's first cause of action is for invasion of privacy. In it she alleges that Article VII, Section 11 of the CC & R's for the condominium project provides in part: "No animals (which shall mean dogs and cats), livestock, reptiles, or poultry shall be kept in any unit except that usual and ordinary domestic fish and birds (and [sic] inside bird cages) may be kept as household pets within any unit; provided: (a) they are not kept, bred, or raised for commercial purposes or in unreasonable numbers; and (b) prior written approval of the Board [of Directors of the Condominium Association] is first obtained. As used herein, 'unreasonable numbers' shall be determined by the Board, but in no event shall such term be construed so as to permit the maintenance by any owner of more than two (2) pets per unit. The Association shall have the right to prohibit maintenance of any pet which constitutes, in the opinion of the Board, a nuisance to any other owner."

Plaintiff alleges that her three cats at all times remain inside her unit and are noiseless and not a nuisance; that beginning in July 1988, defendants peered into and entered her condominium without a compelling reason to do so and in violation of the California Constitution's provision for privacy, found in Article 1, Section 1 thereof; that defendants have harassed plaintiff by assessing penalties against her in increasingly large amounts, (beginning with $25/month and increasing in steps to $500/month), to penalize her for keeping her pet cats; and that the assessments are in violation of the CC & R's and in violation of her right to privacy.....

The question of whether the pet restriction at issue in the case before us is an enforceable equitable servitude under Civil Code Section 1354 is a mixed issue of law and fact which can only be resolved in the context of the particular circumstances of this case....

[T]he enforceability of the pet restriction will be decided in the trial court after the taking of evidence as to the relevant circumstances of this case. Restrictions in CC & R's regarding the ownership and possession of pets are reasonable and therefore are enforceable under Civil Code Section 1354 when they prohibit conduct which, while otherwise lawful, in fact interferes with, or has a reasonable likelihood of interfering with, the rights of other condominium owners to the peaceful and quiet enjoyment of their property.

Defendants argue that the blanket pet restriction they seek to enforce against plaintiff is reasonable and enforceable because it avoids a situation where they must always take a "wait and see" position on pets and then litigate over pets that are causing problems in the condominium project. We reject this contention.... Plaintiff's condominium home is her castle and her enjoyment of it should be by the least restrictive means possible, conducive with a harmonious communal living arrangement. Second, if carried to its logical conclusion, defendants' argument could be used to support all-inclusive bans on such diverse things as stereo equipment, social gatherings and visitors between the ages of two and eighteen. We cannot envision the courts finding that blanket restrictions against such things are reasonable; yet it is certainly conceivable that allowing Fluffin, Muffin, and Ruffin to live inside plaintiff's condominium will pose less of a threat to the peace and quiet of the parties' communal living arrangement than would stereo equipment, parties, or young visitors.

As a final observation on the issue of Civil Code Section 1354, "reasonableness," we note its effect on defendants' contention that by purchasing a unit in the condominium project, plaintiff agreed to and became bound by the pet restriction and should not now be heard to complain of it. The contention is without merit because under Section 1354, defendants can only enforce restrictions in CC & R's that are reasonable. Thus, if the pet restriction at issue here is found to be unreasonable as applied to plaintiff because plaintiff's conduct in keeping her cats has not interfered with and does not have a reasonable likelihood of interfering with, the rights of other owners to the peaceful and quiet enjoyment of their property, then by the very terms of Section 1354, it is not enforceable against plaintiff, even though she bought her unit with at least constructive knowledge that keeping cats in the project was forbidden....

Plaintiff should have been given an opportunity to revise the invasion of privacy cause of action by limiting it to the allegations regarding defendants' peering into and entering her home. She should also have been given the opportunity to advance these allegations as a basis for a cause of action for trespass. The other allegations pertaining to the pet restriction should be included in plaintiff's cause of action for declaratory relief, as a basis for her assertion that such a restriction is unreasonable and therefore unenforceable under Civil Code Section 1354....

[I]t appears to this court that the fines levied against plaintiff are not proper under the authority given to the Board in the portion of the CC & R's relied upon by defendants to support their demurrer to this fifth cause of action. We must therefore conclude that, absent such support in other positions of the CC & R's, not only did the trial court err in sustaining a demurrer to this cause of action (with or without leave to amend, but a request by plaintiff for a summary adjudication of issues on the question of the fines would, on the basis of the record before us, have to be resolved in her favor...

The judgment of dismissal is reversed and, as to Homeowner's Association, a writ of mandate shall issue directing the trial court to vacate its order sustaining demurrers without leave to amend and to enter a new and different order. The cause is remanded to the trial court for further proceedings consistent with the views expressed herein. Costs on appeal to plaintiff.

ENVIRONMENTAL CONCERNS

The freedom of landowners to use their property as they wish was a cherished right in our country for many years. One day, only a few decades ago, people saw that our streams, rivers, and lakes had become polluted to such an extent that we could not enjoy the waters and that the air had become hazy, smelly, and acrid, often burning our eyes. The landscape was cluttered with old car bodies, beer cans, and solid waste of every description. Citizen groups began calling for governmental regulation of the environment.

On the national level, Congress passed the National Environmental Policy Act and created the Environmental Protection Agency to act as the watchdog against continued pollution of our air, water, and land. Congress also passed legislation to control specific areas of pollution, such as the Clean Air Act, the Water Pollution Control Act, the Noise Control Act, and the Solid Waste Disposal Act.

Many states, counties, and cities have enacted environmental laws, and in some instances these laws have set even more stringent pollution standards than the national pollution laws. Many states have also created their own environmental protection agencies to control and regulate pollution within their boundaries. A recent development in the control of solid waste pollution has been the passage of so-called bottle bills by several states. These laws require stores to take deposits from the customer on beverage containers and to return the deposit when the cans or bottles are returned empty. These same laws have also banned the use of pull-top cans for beverages.

Further environmental problems have been caused by the expansion of our cities into what was previously the domain of the farmer. No cattle or hog feedlot is pleasing to the nostrils, and we must accept the fact that such farming operations are not desirable next door to a residential area. What happens when the city expands to the point where the rights of the parties conflict? There are no easy answers.

One of the strongest environmental statutes is CERCLA—the Comprehensive Environmental Response, Compensation, and Liability Act. CERCLA imposes cleanup costs on those causing pollution.

The *Fleet Factors* case discusses the nature of liability under CERCLA.

U.S. v. FLEET FACTORS CORP.
901 F.2d 1550 (11th Cir., 1990)

FACTS: In 1976, Swainsboro Print Works ("SPW"), a cloth print facility, entered into a factoring agreement with Fleet in which Fleet agreed to advance funds against the assignment of SPW's accounts receivable. As collateral for these advances, Fleet also obtained a security interest in SPW's textile facility and all of its equipment, inventory, and fixtures. In August 1979, SPW filed for bankruptcy under Chapter 11. The factoring agreement between SPW and Fleet continued with court approval. In early 1981, Fleet ceased advancing funds to SPW because SPW's debt to Fleet exceeded Fleet's estimate of the value of SPW's accounts receivable. On February 27, 1981, SPW ceased operations and began to liquidate its inventory. Fleet continued to collect on the accounts receivable assigned to it under the Chapter 11 factoring agreement. In December 1981, SPW was adjudicated a bankrupt under Chapter 7, and a trustee assumed title and control of the facility.

In May 1982, Fleet foreclosed on its security interest in some of SPW's inventory and equipment, and contracted with Baldwin Industrial Liquidators ("Baldwin") to conduct an auction of the collateral. Baldwin sold the material "as is" and "in place" on June 22, 1982; the removal of the items was the responsibility of the purchasers. On August 31, 1982, Fleet allegedly contracted with Nix Riggers ("Nix") to remove the unsold equipment in consideration for leaving the premises "broom clean." Nix testified in deposition that he understood that he had been given a "free hand" by Fleet or Baldwin to do whatever was necessary at the facility by the end of December 1983.

On January 20, 1984, the Environmental Protection Agency inspected the facility and found 700 fifty-five gallon drums containing toxic chemicals and forty-four truckloads of material containing asbestos. The EPA incurred costs of nearly $400,000 in responding to the environmental threat at SPW. On July 7, 1987, the facility was conveyed to Emanuel County, Georgia, at a foreclosure sale resulting from SPW's failure to pay state and county taxes.

The government sued Horowitz and Newton, the two principal officers and stockholders of SPW, and Fleet to recover the cost of cleaning up the hazardous waste. The district court granted the government's summary judgment motion with respect to the liability of Horowitz and Newton for the cost of removing the hazardous waste in the drums. The government's motion with respect to Fleet's liability, and the liability of Horowitz and Newton for the asbestos removal costs was denied. Fleet's motion for summary judgment was also denied. Fleet subsequently brought this appeal challenging the court's denial of its motion for summary judgment.

CIRCUIT JUDGE KRAVITCH:

The Comprehensive Environmental Response Compensation and Liability Act was enacted by Congress in response to the environmental and public health hazards caused by the improper disposal of hazardous wastes.... The essential policy underlying CERCLA is to place the ultimate responsibility for cleaning up hazardous waste on "those responsible for problems caused by the disposal of chemical poison...." Accordingly, CERCLA authorizes the federal government to clean up hazardous waste dump sites and recover the cost of the effort from certain categories of responsible parties....

The parties liable for costs incurred by the government in responding to an environmental hazard are: (1) the present owners and operators of a facility where hazardous wastes were released or are in danger of being released, (2) the owners or operators of a facility at the time the hazardous wastes were disposed, (3) the person or entity that arranged for the treatment or disposal of substances at the facility, and (4) the person or entity that transported the substances to the facility....

CERCLA holds the owner or operator of a facility containing hazardous waste strictly liable to the United States for expenses incurred in responding to the environmental and health hazards posed by the waste in that facility.... This provision of the statute targets those individuals presently "owning or operating such facilit[ies]...." In order to effectuate the goals of the statute, we will construe the present owner and operator of a facility as that individual or entity owning or operating the facility at the time the plaintiff initiated the lawsuit by filing a complaint....

CERCLA also imposes liability on "any person who at the time of disposal of any hazardous substance owned or operated any ... facility at which such hazardous substances were disposed of...." CERCLA excludes from the definition of "owner or operator" any "person, who, without participating in the management of a ... facility, holds indicia of ownership primarily to protect his security interest in the ... facility...." Fleet has the burden of establishing its entitlement to this exemption.... There is no dispute that Fleet had an "indicia of ownership" in the facility through its deed of trust to SPW, and that this interest was held primarily to protect its security interest in the facility. The critical issue is whether Fleet participated in management sufficiently to incur liability under the statute....

Although similar, the phrase "participating in the management" and the term "operator" are not congruent. Under the standard we adopt today, a secured creditor may incur Section 9607(a)(2) liability, without being an operator, by participating in the financial management of a facility to a degree indicating a capacity to influence the corporation's treatment of hazardous wastes. It is not necessary for the secured creditor actually to involve itself in the day-to-day operations of the facility in order to be liable—although such conduct will certainly lead to the loss of the protection of the statutory exemption. Nor is it necessary for the secured creditor to participate in management decisions relating to hazardous waste. Rather, a secured creditor will be liable if its involvement with the management of the facility is sufficiently broad to support the inference that it could affect hazardous waste disposal decisions if it so chose....

This construction of the secured creditor exemption, while less permissive than that of the trial court, is broader than that urged by the government and, therefore, should give lenders some latitude in their dealings with debtors without exposing themselves to potential liability. Nothing in our discussion should preclude a secured creditor from monitoring any aspect of a debtor's business. Likewise, a secured creditor can become involved in occasional and discrete financial decisions relating to the protection of its security interest without incurring liability....

Our ruling today should encourage potential creditors to investigate thoroughly the waste treatment systems and policies of potential debtors. If the treatment systems seem inadequate, the risk of CERCLA liability will be weighed into the terms of the loan agreement. Creditors, therefore, will incur no greater risk than they bargained for and debtors, aware that inadequate hazardous waste treatment will have a significant adverse impact on their loan terms, will have powerful incentives to improve their handling of hazardous wastes....

We agree with the court below that the government has alleged sufficient facts to hold Fleet liable under Section 9607(a)(2). From 1976 until SPW ceased printing operations on February 27, 1981, Fleet's involvement with the facility was within the parameters of the secured creditor exemption to liability. During this period, Fleet regularly advanced funds to SPW against the assignment of SPW's accounts receivable, paid and arranged for security deposits for SPW's Georgia utility services, and informed SPW that it would not advance any more money when it determined that its advanced sums exceeded the value of SPW's accounts receivable.

Fleet's involvement with SPW, according to the government, increased substantially after SPW ceased printing operations at the Georgia plant on February 27, 1981, and began to wind down its affairs. Fleet required SPW to seek its approval before shipping its goods to customers, established the price for excess inventory, dictated when and to whom the finished goods should be shipped, determined when employees should be laid off supervised the activity of the office administrator at the site, received, and processed SPW's employment and tax forms, controlled access to the facility, and contracted with Baldwin to dispose of the fixtures and equipment at SPW. These facts, if proved, are sufficient to remove Fleet from the protection of the secured creditor exemption. Fleet's involvement in the financial management of the facility was pervasive, if not complete. Furthermore, the government's allegations indicate that Fleet was also involved in the operational management of the facility. Either of these allegations is sufficient as a matter of law to impose CERCLA liability on a secured creditor.

EMINENT DOMAIN

The Fifth Amendment in the Bill of Rights of the U.S. Constitution provides that the national government shall not take private property without the payment of just compensation. The Fourteenth Amendment extended this provision to the various states. The states also have similar provisions in their constitutions, allowing them to exercise the power of eminent domain if just compensation is paid to the property owner.

Most simply stated, the power of eminent domain is the power of government to take real estate from a private owner for the use of the public. This very basic governmental power is necessary for the government to function properly and efficiently. For example, if the government is building a highway across the state, the highway must be laid out in as straight a line as possible, considering the topography of the land. It would not be in the best interest of the public if the highway had to jog around various pieces of property whose owners had decided not to sell to the government. The power of eminent domain is also used to acquire land for new school buildings, public parks, public housing projects, and other public buildings and projects.

The government simply must have the right to take over private property when doing so serves the best interest of the public. The owner of such property does, however, have a right to just compensation. The two key problems are: (1) that the land may be taken only for a public purpose, and (2) that the owner must receive just compensation. What constitutes a public purpose is often a question that must be resolved in the courts. What constitutes just compensation is also not an easy question to resolve in many cases, and thus a lawsuit may be filed and a jury called upon to decide the issue.

The next case is an important recent example of the relationship between "taking" and "regulating."

RYBACHEK v. U.S. E.P.A.
904 F.2d 1276 (9th Cir. 1990)

FACTS: Placer mining is one of the four basic methods of mining metal ores; it involves the mining of alluvial or glacial deposits of loose gravel, sand, soil, clay, or mud called "placers." These placers often contain particles of gold and other heavy minerals. Placer miners excavate the gold-bearing material (paydirt) from the placer deposit after removing the surface vegetation and non-gold-bearing gravel (overburden). The gold is then separated from the other materials in the paydirt by a gravity separation process known as "sluicing."

In the sluicing process, a miner places the ore in an on-site washing plant (usually a sluice box) which has small submerged dams (riffles) attached to its bottom. he causes water to be run over the paydirt in the sluice box; when the heavier materials (including gold) fall, they are caught by the riffles. The lighter sand, dirt, and clay particles are left suspended in the wastewater released from the sluice box.

Placer mining typically is conducted directly in streambeds or an adjacent property. The water usually enters the sluice box through gravity, but may sometimes also enter through the use of pumping equipment. At some point after the process described above, the water in the sluice box is discharged. The discharges from placer mining can have aesthetic and water-quality impacts on waters both in the immediate vicinity and downstream. Toxic metals, including arsenic, cadmium, lead, zinc, and copper, have been found at a higher concentration in streams where mining occurs than in non-mining streams.

It is the treatment of the sluice-box discharge water before it reenters a natural water course that is at the heart of this case.

Congress enacted the Clean Water Act to "restore and maintain the chemical, physical, and biological integrity of the Nation's waters." Under the Act, the EPA must impose and enforce technology-based effluent limitations and standards through individual National Pollutant Discharge Elimination System ("NPDES") permits. These permits contain specific terms and conditions, as well as numerical discharge limits, which govern the activities of pollutant dischargers. Through the Clean Water Act, Congress has directed the EPA to incorporate into the permits increasingly stringent technology-based effluent limitations.

Congress specified a number of means for the EPA to impose and to enforce these limitations in NPDES permits. For instance, it requires the Agency to establish effluent limitations requiring dischargers to use the "best practicable control technology currently available" ("BPT"') within an industry. These limits are to represent "the average of the best" treatment technology performance in an industrial category. The EPA is further required to promulgate limitations both for discharge of toxic pollutants by mandating that an industry use the "best available technology economically achievable" ("BCT"); the congressionally imposed deadline for promulgation of these limitations was March 31, 1989.

In addition, new pollution sources in an industry must meet a separate set of standards called new-source performance standards ("NSPS"). These standards limit the discharge of pollutants by new sources based on the "best available demonstrated control technology" ("BDT"). Finally, the EPA is authorized to establish best management practices ("BMPs") "to control plant site runoff, spillage or leaks, sludge or waste disposal, and drainage from raw material storage" in order to diminish the amount of toxic pollutants flowing into receiving waters....

On November 20, 1985, proceeding under the Clean Water Act, the EPA proposed regulations for placer mining. For most mines processing fewer than 500 cubic yards of ore per day ("yd^3/day"), the EPA proposed BPT effluent limitations of 0.2 milliliters per litre ("ml/l") of discharge for settleable solids and 2,000 milligrams per litre ("mg/l") for total suspended solids. For mines processing more than 500 yd^3/day of ore, the EPA proposed more-stringent BCT and BAT limitations, as well as new-source performance standards (NSPS) prohibiting the discharge of processed wastewater. Twice during the rulemaking process, the Agency published notices of new information and requested public comment on additional financial and technical data.

As a result of its studies, the comments received during the review-and-comment periods, and new studies undertaken in response to the submitted comment, the EPA promulgated final effluent-limitation guidelines and standards on May 24, 1988. The EPA established a BPT limitation, based upon simple-settling technology, for settleable solids of 0.2 ml/l for virtually all mines. The final rule also established BAT limitations and NSPS, based on recirculation technology, restricting the flow of processed wastewater that could be discharged. In addition, the EPA promulgated five BMP's to control discharge due to mine drainage and infiltration.

The Alaska Miners Association ("AMA") and Stanley and Rosalie Rybachek petitioned for review of the EPA's regulations.

 CIRCUIT JUDGE O'SCANNLAIN:

In a dubious reincarnation of the 1890's world of Yukon poet Robert Service, we deal here a century later with "strange things done in the midnight sun by the men who moil for gold." We are asked to determine the validity of Environmental Protection Agency regulations under the Clean Water Act which govern placer mining and have particular impact on the gold-rich streambeds of Alaska. Because the regulations are complex and the issues raised are multitudinous, our opinion (written, alas, in arid prose) is outlined in some detail....

The parties dispute whether placer mining is even subject to regulation under the Clean Water Act.

The Act charges the EPA with developing comprehensive programs aimed at "preventing, reducing, or eliminating the pollution of the navigable waters and ground waters and improving the sanitary condition of surface and underground waters...." To assist the EPA in this program development, Congress made unlawful "the discharge of any pollutant by any person" except as in compliance with the Clean Water Act.... It defined "discharge of a pollutant," in part, as "any addition of any pollutant to navigable waters from any point source...."

The AMA seizes upon this statutory scheme to argue that placer miming is not subject to regulation under the Clean Water Act for at least two reasons: (1) placer mines do not discharge into "navigable waters;" and (2) placer mining does not "add" pollutants to water within the meaning of the Act. We reject both of these arguments and find that the EPA did not exceed the scope of its authority under the Clean Water Act in promulgating the challenged regulations.

First, the Clean Water Act covers the waters at issue here. Congress views broadly the words "navigable waters" in the Clean Water Act: it has defined them simply as "the waters of the United States, including the territorial seas...." Here, the parties agree that placer mines discharge into nearby streams and rivers. These are clearly among "the waters of the United States."

Second, we will not strike down the EPA's finding that placer mining discharges pollutants within the meaning of the Act. Placer miners excavate the dirt and gravel in and around waterways, extract any gold, and discharge the dirt and other non-gold material into the water....

Petitioners challenge the merits of the EPA's regulations on a number of grounds; indeed, virtually every aspect of the regulations is attacked. To the extent the regulations may be divided into component parts (e.g., the BPT limitations, the BAT limitations, and new source criteria), we address petitioners' arguments along those lines.

We turn first to petitioners' argument that the EPA erred in its determination that settling ponds are the best practicable control technology currently available (BPT) within the placer mining industry. There is no dispute that settling ponds are currently available pollution control technology; in fact, the AMA concedes that they are now used by almost all miners. Rather, petitioners contend that the EPA failed to use a "cost-benefit analysis" in determining that settling ponds were BPT for placer mining. They also argue that the EPA failed to consider costs when it set forth BPT limitations governing settleable solids for small mines.

The Clean Water Act controls when and how the EPA should require BPT. Under 33 U.S.C. § 1311(b)(1)(A), the Act requires "effluent limitations for point sources ... which shall require the application of the best practicable control technology currently available [BPT]." Under this section, the EPA is to determine whether a technology is BPT; the factors it considers "shall include ... total cost of the technology in relation to effluent reduction to be achieved from it, the age of equipment, engineering aspects, non-water quality environmental impact ... and such other factors as the Administrator deems appropriate...."

From this statutory language, it is "plain that, as a general rule, the EPA is required to consider the costs and benefits of a proposed technology in its inquiry to determine the BPT...." The EPA has broad discretion in weighing these competing factors.... It may determine that a technology is not BPT on the basis of this cost-benefit analysis only when the costs are "wholly disportionate" to the potential effluent-reduction benefits....

The EPA has not acted arbitrarily or capriciously in setting forth [the] criteria for new-source placer mines. According to the AMA, these criteria make it likely that certain placer mines, which in the past have been mined periodically, will be considered new sources and therefore will require full review of their permits. That may be so, but the EPA might have chosen more restrictive criteria that would have insured that all placer mines would be considered new sources *every time* the miners moved during the normal course of operations or reinstalled the mines each spring. The EPA instead chose a middle path and developed factors which the reviewing authority will "take into account" in determining whether a particular mine is a new source. This approach, which allows for an ad hoc, case-by-case application of the criteria, cannot fairly be said to be overbroad....

Finally, we turn to the Rybacheks' argument that the regulations promulgated by the EPA constitute a taking under the Fifth Amendment. They seek just compensation for this alleged taking. There are at least two flaws in the Rybacheks' argument.

First, no takings claim here is ripe for judicial resolution. A taking occurs in this context only when the EPA's regulations are applied to particular property.... Because the Rybacheks do not claim that a particular item of their property has been taken by the EPA's final rule, a takings claim is unripe....

Second, ours is an inappropriate forum for such a takings claim. Our jurisdiction over the challenge to EPA regulations comes from a particular statutory grant.... Congress has specified other fora for resolution of claims against the United States that seek just compensation for a taking.... Thus, our authority for hearing the petitioners' challenges to the EPA's regulations does not suffice to hear a taking claim.

The EPA regulations contested here are not the most rousing words ever written about gold mining. Consider, for instance, the excitement missing from the technical discussion above:

> Gold! We leapt from our benches! Gold! We sprang from our stools.
> Gold! We wheeled in the furrow, fired with the faith of fools.
> Fearless, unfound, unfitted, far from the night and the cold,
> Heard we the clarion summons, followed the master-lure—Gold!
> Men from the sands of the Sunland; men from the woods of the West;
> Men from the farms and the cities, into the Northland we pressed.
> Graybeards and striplings and women, good men and bad men and bold,
> Leaving our homes and our loved ones, crying exultantly—"Gold!"

R. Service, *The Trail of Ninety-Eight, in Collected Poems of Robert Service 144* (1940).

Gold! The trail of the 1990's may be burdened by twentieth century laws and regulations, but the promise Service sings still awaits those who persevere.

Petitions for review denied.

SIGNIFICANCE OF THIS CHAPTER

From the early 1960s, we have seen a movement in the United States to save the environment, to clean the air and water, to control solid waste dumping, and to stop other forms of pollution. We finally realized the results of uncontrolled and unregulated land use, which had occurred over a period of many years, and which left many cities with unnecessary traffic congestion problems, fire and safety hazards, and lowered property values. Most cities, both large and small, now have a system of land use regulation as well as local regulation of environmental problems. National and state governments have moved aggressively against the many different forms of environmental pollution.

This chapter gives an overview of the law concerning these areas of concern. All citizens must realize the importance of this type of regulation and the continued need for regulation in the areas of land use and environment.

PROBLEMS FOR DISCUSSION

1. Sandy Snidely, doing business as the Misfit Cleaners, had his business property condemned by the State Highway Commission to make way for a new road. Sandy says he was told that he would be given a relocation payment but would not be compensated for any equipment left in the building. Relying on this advice, he removed his dry cleaning equipment. Because of the age and nature of the equipment and because of changes in the city's laws and building codes, Sandy says that he was prohibited from relocating his business in the city and that the equipment now has only scrap value. Sandy did accept a relocation payment, but now he says that he is also entitled to the difference in value of the equipment resulting from the condemnation of his business location. The state says that he can't have both.

   Who's right, and why?

2. The City Council of Burbank passed an ordinance making it illegal for jet aircraft to take off from the Hollywood-Burbank Airport between the hours of 11 p.m. and 7 a.m. The only regularly scheduled flight affected by the ordinance was an intrastate flight of Pacific Southwest Airlines which originated in Oakland and departed from the Hollywood-Burbank Airport for San Diego every Sunday night at 11:30 p.m. The plaintiff, Lockheed, brought suit for an injunction against enforcement of the ordinance, alleging that it was invalid under the Commerce Clause and the Supremacy Clause of the U.S. Constitution. The U.S. District Court granted the injunction, and the U.S. Court of Appeals affirmed. The City of Burbank appealed.

   Is the city regulation valid? Why or why not?

3. The small retirement community of Youngtown was founded in 1954, just off the Phoenix-Wickenburg Highway (Grand Avenue), about fourteen or fifteen miles west of the urban area of Phoenix. Farming operations had been conducted in the area since 1911, and Spur's predecessors had started a feedlot about two and one-half miles south of Youngtown in 1956. By 1989, there were twenty-five cattle feeding or dairy operations in the area. In 1989, Del Webb began planning the development of a large retirement community, Sun City, and purchased some 20,000 acres of land south of Grand Avenue and directly east of Youngtown. One year later, 450 to 500 homes were completed or under construction. The units just south of Grand Avenue sold well, but sales resistance increased as the location of the homes got closer and closer to the feedlots. By 1992, Spur had expanded its operation from thirty-five to 114 acres. By 1993, Del Webb's housing manager said that it was impossible to sell any home in the southwestern portion of Del Webb's land. By 1997, the properties were within 500 feet of each other at one point, and Spur was feeding between 20,000 and 30,000 head of cattle on its lots, producing over a million pounds of wet manure per day. Del Webb sued to enjoin Spur as a public nuisance, due to the flies and odor. The trial court entered an injunction, and Spur appealed.

   Should the injunction be upheld? Explain.

4. Residents of Hillcrest Heights sued to enjoin defendants from erecting two apartment buildings on a platted lot owned by defendants and located in Hillcrest Heights Subdivision. Plaintiffs contended that defendants' proposed apartment buildings would violate the subdivision's protective covenants, based upon the following clause of the covenants: "A. All lots in this subdivision shall be Residential One (R-1) only...."

   Defendants admitted that this clause standing alone would prohibit the construction of the proposed apartment buildings. They contend, however, that since another clause in the restrictive covenants incorporates an existing zoning classification that allows apartment buildings, the apartment buildings would not violate the protective covenants. The clause relied on by defendants provides as follows:

   "L. None of the foregoing shall be construed as conflicting with any terms or regulations of the present or future Jefferson County zoning ordinance which shall form a part of this instrument and shall govern their use of all land herein described."

   The trial court entered judgment for plaintiffs.

   Does a zoning ordinance supersede any and all private restrictions on land used?

5. Mr. Reer requested a building permit to establish a "Good Times Pizza" parlor in the City of Midland. After the city's building inspector told Reer that a carryout restaurant was not a permissible use in the Business A zoning district where Reer proposed to build, Reer's request for an interpretation of the zoning ordinance was heard by the zoning board of appeals on March 29. By a three-to-one vote, the board determined that a carryout pizzeria was a permissible use. On April 19, the city attorney requested the board to reconsider. The board took no action. On April 28, Reer obtained a building permit and began extensive renovation of the building he proposed to convert into a pizzeria. He also entered into a ten-year lease of the building.

On May 17, the zoning board of appeals again took no action to reconsider. On June 6, a group of citizens filed suit against the city asking for a review of the zoning board's interpretation, contending that the notice requirement of the zoning ordinance had not been followed before the board's prior determination. After stipulation for another hearing following proper notice was entered into by the parties, the zoning board reconsidered its prior interpretation on June 28. By a four-to-zero vote, the board found a carryout pizzeria was not a permissible use.

Subsequently, the trial court affirmed the zoning board's interpretation. On grounds of estoppel the trial judge enjoined the city from enforcing the ordinance. However, the trial court granted a group of private citizens, plaintiffs Talcott, Burks, and Boots, an injunction enjoining Reer from operating the pizzeria. Mr. Reer appealed.

Does the zoning ordinance prevent Rear's pizzeria?

Part Seven

Business Associations

Persons who intend to start a business may choose which of the various types of business associations to use in conducting their business. These choices range from the sole proprietorship, which is the least expensive to create, and is not subject to extensive regulation, but has the disadvantage of unlimited liability against the owner; to the corporation, which is more expensive to create, and may be subject to more extensive regulation, but which offers limited liability. Part Seven reviews the various types of business associations and discusses the pros and cons of each. In Part Seven, we also discuss the law of agency which allows us to have others, our agents, conduct business on our behalf. Finally, we examine the issues of corporate social responsibility and business ethics.

Chapter 30
Agency Law

Agency is a very ancient and very important legal concept. Agency law and contract law describe the two most basic legal relationships. On this foundation many of the other, more specialized legal relationships are erected. The modern law of agency can be traced to the Roman law concerning the owner and slave; the law merchant, a private system of rules and courts which traders and merchants established to govern themselves during the Middle Ages; and the English common law. Because individuals and businesses everywhere must on many occasions conduct their affairs through others, every legal system must somehow deal with the concept of agency. Every contract entered into by corporations and partnerships and many of the contracts made by individuals and unincorporated associations involve the principles of agency law.

Although the law of agency obviously has very great "commercial" significance, it is not covered in the Uniform Commercial Code. One reason for this omission may be that when the Uniform Commercial Code was formulated, the basic rules of agency law were already pretty well agreed on by the states and were already summarized in the *Restatement of the Law of Agency, Second*. The *Restatement* does not have the force of law, but it is considered to be an authoritative source and it is followed most of the time by most courts.

BASIC DEFINITIONS

An agent is one who has been authorized to act for another person, to conduct that other person's business dealings with one or more third parties. The person who authorizes another as agent is called the **principal**. The "third party" is the other person with whom the negotiations are to be conducted. The third party may also be represented in the transaction by an agent. Since all corporations must rely on human beings to conduct their actual business affairs, any contract between two corporations will be negotiated and finalized (and performed) by their agents.

An **employee** is a person who has been hired by someone to do a particular job for that person. Employees, as such, do not have the power to act as agents and make contracts with third persons on behalf of their employer. The same person, however, may be both an agent and an employee. The sales clerk in a retail store is clearly an employee of the store, but is also an agent, with the authority to make sales to customers and to receive payment for the goods sold. A friend taking your coat to the dry cleaners for you would be your agent, but not your employee. A factory worker with no authority to deal with third parties is an employee, but not also an agent.

Before we look at the various ways in which the agency relationship can be created (and terminated), it is necessary to distinguish another arrangement that involves the use of others to conduct one's affairs—the independent contractor.

INDEPENDENT CONTRACTORS

Independent Contractors Distinguished from Agents/Employees. As a rule, a person who employs an independent contractor to perform services is liable neither for torts committed by the independent contractor in performing the job nor for subcontracts made by the independent contractor to get the job done. Independent contractors are, of course, liable for their own torts (and for the torts of their agents and employees) and for their own contracts. Litigation frequently arises, however, when the independent contractor has gone out of business, or lacks the financial resources to cover a substantial claim, or is simply out of the jurisdiction and not available, or at least not conveniently available, for suit. The key issue in these cases is whether the relationship in question was really an independent contractor-employer relationship, which results in nonliability, or was a principal-agent or employer-employee relationship, which results in the principal/employer's being held liable in tort and/or contract.

The primary test used by the courts to distinguish these legal relationships is the degree of control the employer/principal exercises over the person in the middle; that is, the independent contractor or the agent/ employee. The general idea is that with independent contractors the employer contracts only for results and leaves the details of the job to the independent contractors, although given the right set of facts, these too could be agents/employees.

Put in the simplest terms, a person using an independent contractor controls *what* gets done, but the independent contractor decides *how* it gets done. With an agent/employee, the principal/employer not only determines *what* gets done but also has the power to determine *how* it gets done. If you hire an employee to help you put aluminum siding on your house, you can tell that person what size hammer to use, what size nails to use, where to place the nails, and so on. If you hire Mr. Shatturglas, "the aluminum siding king," to do the job for you, you contract only for a good, skillful job, and Shatturglas determines the nail placement and all the other details of how the job gets done.

The nature of the relationship the parties have created is essentially a fact question, for determination by the court. The label that the parties have attached to that relationship is not conclusive, nor is the "intent" of the parties, nor is what the parties "thought" they were creating. The facts speak for themselves in each case, since the parties may easily be mistaken as to what the law is or they may be attempting to avoid legal responsibilities by using the independent contractor label as a smokescreen. Among the factors which a court may consider significant are "whether the one employed is engaged in a distinct business, whether in the locality the work is usually done under supervision or by a specialist without supervision, skill required, furnishing of tools and equipment, time limit of employment, method of payment, whether [the] work is a part of [the] regular business of [the] employer, whether [the] parties believe they are creating one or the other relationship, and whether the principal is or is not in business."

The *Zimmerman* case illustrates the application of these tests.

ZIMMERMAN v. ELM HILL MARINA
839 S.W.2d 760 (TN App., 1992)

FACTS: Plaintiff, Emily Zimmerman, appeals from the trial court's order granting the defendant Elm Hill Marina's motion for summary judgment. Also named as defendants are Ed Rafalowski, individually and dba Elm Hill Marina, L & R Incorporated dba Elm Hill Marina, Brentwood Bodyguard and Security, Inc., and Roy Tanner.

Elm Hill Marina entered into a lease agreement with the Secretary of the Army for the Marina to operate a business within the J. Percy Priest Dam and Reservoir Project Area. The lease, which authorized the Marina to furnish docking facilities for privately owned boats, prohibited the Marina from using the premises or permitting them to be used for "any illegal or immoral business or purpose" and from permitting upon the premises "any activity which would constitute a nuisance."

Under a separate agreement, the defendant, Brentwood Bodyguard and Security, Inc. provided security services for the Marina. The defendant, Roy Tanner, was employed by the security company as a guard.

At about 10:30 a.m. on Sunday, March 26, 1989, Roy Tanner, while on duty at the Marina, observed Plaintiff's decedent, Dr. Daniel P. McCoy, go from the parking lot to his boat. According to Mr. Tanner, Dr. McCoy was staggering and did not have good control of his faculties. Dr. McCoy fell while getting out of his car, while crossing the parking lot, and again while approaching the Marina ramp. Dr. McCoy then crawled out on the pier to his boat and passed out on its bow. Mr. Tanner followed Dr. McCoy to make sure he did not fall in the water and drown. Mr. Tanner then returned to his normal duties.

Another witness observed Dr. McCoy lying on the deck of his boat at about 11:30 a.m. the same day. The witness stated that Dr. McCoy appeared to be intoxicated in that when he tried to sit up, he would fall over and hit his head on the deck. The witness also reported that at about 3:45 p.m. he saw Dr. McCoy's keys, t-shirt, and newspaper, but he did not see Dr. McCoy.

On Monday, March 27, 1989, Dr. McCoy's body was found in Percy Priest Lake. An autopsy revealed that his death was caused by drowning and that his blood alcohol level was 0.26 percent.

Plaintiff, the personal representative of Dr. McCoy's estate and the guardian of his sole surviving heir at law, filed this lawsuit against the defendants for Dr. McCoy's death. Plaintiff's theory of liability as to the Marina was predicated on the argument that the lease agreement between the Marina and the Secretary of the Army created a duty to Dr. McCoy in tort. Specifically, Plaintiff argued that the duty was not to permit the premises to be used for any illegal purpose and not to permit upon the premises any nuisance. Because Dr. McCoy's level of intoxication was illegal and constituted a nuisance, Plaintiff reasoned, the Marina breached its duty to Dr. McCoy by failing to deny him access to the Marina and, thus, proximately caused his death. Further, Plaintiff argued that the Marina was liable under the theory of respondeat superior in that the Marina's agents, the security company and Roy Tanner, breached the aforementioned duty.

 JUDGE FARMER:

This court has held that "the doctrine of respondeat superior applies only when the relation of master and servant is shown to exist between the wrongdoer and the person sought to be charged with the injury resulting from the wrong...."

In determining liability under the theory of respondeat superior, the courts have recognized the decisive question to be whether the defendant had the power or right to control the wrongdoer's specific conduct or manner of doing work.... The question of control is one of fact, and each case must depend on its own facts.... Factors considered by this Court have included, but are not limited to, whether the defendant paid the worker's salary and Social Security taxes; whether the defendant provided the worker with employee benefits, such as an optional retirement fund; and whether the defendant had the power to terminate the worker's employment at that time....

In support of its motion for summary judgment, the Marina submitted the affidavit of its president, Edward C. Rafalowski. In his affidavit, Mr. Rafalowski stated that the Marina entered into a contract with the security company to provide security services for the Marina on an independent contractor basis. Additionally, he stated that the Marina did not control the manner in which the security guard performed his duties nor did it pay the security guard. Instead, pursuant to the contract, the Marina paid the security company, which in turn paid the security guard.

Plaintiff filed a memorandum in opposition to the Marina's motion for summary judgment. In her memorandum, Plaintiff neither contradicted the affidavit of Mr. Rafalowski nor filed opposing affidavits or depositions thereto. On appeal, Plaintiff chooses to rely on her pleadings and on the written contract between the Marina and the security company. Although this contract clearly specifies that the security company is an independent contractor, Plaintiff points to provisions which state that the Marina will set the schedule of the hours and numbers of guards needed, that the Marina will make payments to the security company, and that the security guards will perform their services pursuant to guidelines furnished by the Marina. We note, however, that this last provision reiterates that the security company and its guards are independent contractors....

Plaintiff has failed to respond by affidavit or otherwise setting forth facts which would show that either the security company or security guard was an employee of the Marina. Once the Marina filed its affidavit demonstrating an independent contractor relationship, Plaintiff's reliance on her pleadings and the security agreement was insufficient to create a genuine issue of fact regarding an essential element of her claim, the theory of respondeat superior. Further, in her amended complaint Plaintiff alleged that Roy Tanner was an employee of the security company, and the Marina admitted this fact in its answer. Since this fact was admitted, Plaintiff cannot now take a position to the contrary. Under these circumstances, we hold that the trial court did not err in granting the Marina's motion for summary judgment.

Independent Contractors Under Statutes Regulating Employer-Employee Relationships.

The nonliability aspects of the independent contractor relationship as compared to the agent/employee relationship tend to make businesses and individuals prefer to conduct their affairs through independent contractors whenever possible. However, the tort and contract areas are not the only places where the law deals differently with independent contractors and their employers. In general, employers of independent contractors escape regulation under statutes designed to "protect" employees. Employers of independent contractors do not have to withhold state or national income tax, do not have to withhold or pay social security taxes, do not have to pay unemployment compensation taxes, do not have to provide workers' compensation coverage for the independent contractors, and are not subject to minimum wage or employment discrimination statutes. Moreover, independent contractors have no rights to organization and collective bargaining under the National Labor Relations Act.

Statutes often contain their own definition, for their purposes, of who is an "employee" and who is an "independent contractor." Typically the board or agency charged with the enforcement of such a statute may make its own administrative determination as to who is subject to the statute's provisions, and often employers have to challenge the board or agency in court if they wish to claim an exemption for independent contractors employed by them.

Franchisees as Independent Contractors.

A business that sells a widely advertised product or service through local franchised "dealers" (e.g., McDonald's, Kentucky Fried Chicken, and General Motors) must avoid overstepping the boundaries that separate the independent contractor relationship from the principal-agent relationship. The business wants to minimize its legal liability and regulatory exposures by using independent contractors to sell its products or services. At the same time, however, it wants to ensure that certain quality standards are met by each franchisee-dealer. The dilemma is that the greater the degree of "quality control" it exercises, the more likely it is that the franchisee will be held to be an agent-employee rather than an independent contractor for both liability and regulatory purposes. Ultimately, each case presents a fact question for the court.

Exceptions to the Nonliability Rule for Contracts and Torts of Independent Contractors.

There are at least three well-recognized exceptions to the nonliability aspects of employing independent contractors.

(1) Contracts by the Independent Contractor.

Nearly all states have mechanic's lien statutes, which provide that persons who supply labor or materials for improvements on real estate can file claims against the real estate if they are not paid. These laws generally do not make the owners of the real estate personally liable for the debts their independent contractors owe to laborers or materialmen, but the results have almost the same effect: owners must pay off the claims to clear the title to the real estate. Of course, the landowner who is forced to pay off such third-party claims can recover from the independent contractor, if the contractor is still solvent and available for suit.

(2) Extra-Hazardous Activities.

Where the work for which the contractor is hired involves a clear risk of injury to others, the employer will be liable when such injuries occur. Examples of such activities include construction of dams and reservoirs, blasting, excavations near a highway, spraying of poisons, clearing land by fire, and razing buildings. These kinds of operations call for special precautions, and the employer should remain liable for any contractor negligence where such jobs are being done.

Both the "extra-hazardous" and the "retained control" exceptions are discussed in the *Szymanski* case.

SZYMANSKI v. K-MART CORP.
493 N.W.2d 460 (MI App.,1992)

FACTS: Plaintiff John M. Szymanski, an employee of Cadillac Window Cleaning Company, was injured when he fell from a scaffold suspended approximately forty feet above the ground while washing windows at defendant K-Mart Corporation's world head-quarters. Plaintiff and the two other men who were on the scaffold with him were not wearing safety belts or safety lines. Plaintiff subsequently brought suit against defendant and, after a jury trial, was awarded $1,306,250 in damages. Defendant appeals the judgment.

 PER CURIAM:

Generally, an employer of an independent contractor is not liable for the contrac-tor's negligence or the negligence of its employees.... However, an exception to the general rule exists when the work performed by the contractor is inherently dan-gerous. Another exception exists where the employer or landowner retains control of the work being performed by the independent contractor.... Although the inher-ently dangerous activity doctrine usually applies when third parties claim injury, the doctrine has been applied where, as in this case, the claimant is an employee of the independent contractor....

In this case, the trial court relied on both exceptions in denying defendant's motion for a directed verdict. First, the trial court found that the activity of working on a scaffold high above the ground was inherently dangerous. Secondly, with regard to the issue of control, the trial court noted:

> K-Mart gave Cadillac a store room, some equipment, the name tags, keys to the stairwell and towers, and Cadillac employees could eat in the cafeteria, there was no written contract and the work—that the employees were occasionally told what windows to clean. In this instance, the signs of control are not strong, ... but the Court will conclude once again that it's a jury question....

We disagree with the trial court with regard to the issue of control....

The evidence in this case does not support such a finding of control. There was no indication from the testimony that K-Mart directed Cadillac regarding the manner in which the job was to be performed or that K-Mart had any control with regard to the manner in which the scaffold was assembled and used....

We also conclude that the trial court erred in denying defendant's motion for a directed verdict based on the doctrine of inherently dangerous activity.

The inherently dangerous activity doctrine provides an exception to the general rule of nonliability by the employer of an independent contractor. Under the doctrine, liability may be imposed when "the work contracted for is likely to create a peculiar risk of physical harm or if the work involves a special danger inherent in or normal to the work that the employer reasonably should have known about at the inception of the contract...." The risk or danger must be recognizable in advance (i.e., at the time the contract is made).... [L]iability should not be imposed where a new risk is created in the performance of the work and the risk was not reasonably contemplated at the time of the contract....

Similarly, liability should not be imposed where the activity involved was not unusual, the risk was not unique, "reasonable safeguards against injury could readily have been provided by well-recognized safety measures" and the employer selected a responsible experienced contractor....

The activity performed by plaintiff in this case, washing windows forty feet above the ground while on a scaffold suspended from the side of a building, is an activity that presents a possibility of serious injury unless special precautions are taken. However, as noted by plaintiffs expert at trial, any danger of serious physical injury from this activity could have been prevented by the use of well-recognized safety measures (i.e., safety belts and safety lines). The risk of injury was not inherent to the work being done, but was created by the failure to use well-recognized safety measures.... [T]he evidence presented at trial, even when viewed in the light most favorable to plaintiff, could not have permitted reasonable minds to conclude that the activity at issue was inherently dangerous.

Plaintiff argues that the verdict in his favor should nevertheless be upheld because the jury found defendant to be independently negligent. Although plaintiff's complaint alleges negligence on the part of defendant in failing to hire a competent contractor, failing to supervise its employees and contractors, and so on, the jury was only instructed with regard to the issues of control and inherently dangerous activity. These are the theories that plaintiff argued during his opening statement and closing argument. Accordingly, we reject plaintiff's argument on appeal.

Our resolution of the previous issues makes it unnecessary for us to address the other issues raised by defendant.

---

(3) Nondelegable Duties. Nondelegable duties may be created by statute, by contract, or by case law. In Chapter 13, we discussed contractual duties that could not be delegated due to their personal nature. Statutory and case-law rules create nondelegable duties on the part of a railroad to keep its crossings in good repair, a city to keep its streets in good repair, a business to provide a safe place for employees and customers, and others. In each of these cases, the employer can be held liable for the negligence of a contractor hired to perform the duty, at least where the negligence relates directly to the job itself. Of course, the employer could also be held liable for any personal negligence, such as providing the contractor with improper plans for the job or hiring a contractor who was not qualified to do the job. Most courts would also disallow the exemption where the employer reserved the right to supervise, or did in fact supervise, the performance of the job.

Personal Negligence by Employer of Independent Contractor. Quite apart from the issue of employer's liability for torts by the independent contractor, the employer can clearly be held liable for his or her own torts. The employer is liable for any personal negligence in connection with the work being done. The employer can be held liable for negligence in failing to select a qualified contractor, or for failing to require the contractor to take needed safety precautions, or for inadequate instructions or equipment furnished to the contractor. If the employer directs or controls part of the job, negligence in doing so would also make the employer liable. The employer would also be held negligent for failing to make a proper inspection after the job was done to make sure it had been done properly. In any of these cases, the negligence is the employer's own, not that of the independent contractor.

CREATION OF THE AGENCY RELATIONSHIP

In General. The agency relationship is created by the mutual consent of the parties thereto, the principal and the agent, but whether it exists or not depends on the legal significance of what the parties actually said and did rather than what they "really intended." In other words, a court may find that agency exists even though the parties did not really intend that result. As a general rule, agency may be created by oral or written words or by conduct. There is no generally applicable Statute of Frauds section for agency agreements, although many states require written authority if the agent is to execute real estate documents for his or her principal. Depending on the state, other particular types of agency agreements may also have to be in writing. A signed, written statement of agency authority is usually called a **power of attorney**, making the agent an "attorney in fact" for his or her principal as to the matters contained in the document.

Although agency is usually based on a contract, with the agent being compensated for his or her services, the relationship can also exist without any contract at all. For example, your roommate agrees to take your coat to the cleaner for you, as he or she is going to the cleaner anyway. Your roommate is acting as your agent when he or she makes the contract with the cleaner to have the coat cleaned, even though he or she is just doing it as a favor, with no compensation at all. If the cleaner ruins your coat, you could sue it for breach of contract. An agency was created. Your agent made an offer on your behalf, and the cleaner accepted the coat for cleaning. You would not, however, be able to sue your roommate for breach of contract if he or she decided not to take your coat to the cleaner after all, since there was no agency contract.

Since the agent is to contract on behalf of the principal, the principal is the party who must have contractual capacity. Principals who are minors have the same rights of disaffirmance as they would have if they had made a contract in person, including the right to disaffirm whatever contract they may have made with their agents. The fact that agents are minors or lack capacity for some other reason would not generally have any impact on the contracts they made on behalf of their principals. However, agents who are minors can disaffirm any employment contract they made with their principals.

The burden of proving that an agency relationship exists is on the person alleging it, typically the third party who dealt with the alleged agent. The third party has no case against the alleged principal unless it can be shown that the principal gave the agent the authority to do the acts in question. To hold the principal liable for the agent's actions, the third party must show that the agent had **express authority**, **implied authority**, **apparent authority**, or **authority by ratification**.

Express Authority. Express authority is authority which has been given specifically, in so many words. Orally or in writing, the principal has told the agent to perform some specific act: "Sell my GM stock"; or "Go over to the lumberyard and buy us ten more two-by-fours." In these simple examples it's pretty clear what is intended, but there are many situations where the principal's meaning is not so easy to determine. Where the words used are more general, or where the agent is to conduct a series of complicated transactions, or where the agent is left "in charge" for a period of time, a court may be called on to see whether the principal's instructions did or did not include the acts in question.

The *Restatement of the Law of Agency, Second*, is of some help here, at least as to what is involved in "managing" a business. Section 73 lists these things: buying supplies and equipment, making repairs, hiring and firing employees, selling goods held for sale, paying and receiving payment of debts, and doing those things that are incidental, usual, necessary, or ordinary in such a business.

The courts are generally very reluctant to imply the power to issue negotiable instruments, since such a power, quite literally, gives the agent a blank check with the principal's name on it. As a general rule, third parties should not take such instruments signed by an alleged agent unless these parties have so dealt with the agent in the past or unless they have a clear, express statement of authority from the principal.

Implied Authority. Not every detail needs to be stated expressly for actual authority to exist. Once an agent has been given the express authority to do a particular job, the implication is that the principal also intended the agent to have the authority to do whatever was necessary and appropriate to get the main job done. By implication, the agent has the authority to take care of all incidental details. Also, when an emergency threatens the success of the enterprise, the agent on the spot, in charge of the principal's affairs, is assumed to have the authority to meet and deal with the emergency. And finally, implied authority may exist on the basis of a course of prior transactions between the principal and the agent or on the basis of custom in their trade or business.

Any implied authority which might otherwise exist would be negated by express instructions to the contrary, but third parties might still be able to rely on the "appearance" of authority unless they were aware of the specific instructions.

In addition to these fundamental ideas on implied authority, many rules as to whether particular powers have been given to the agent are generally agreed on, through long-established usage and custom and by expression in the *Restatement of Agency*. For instance, once an agency relationship has been established, notice to the agent is effectively notice to the principal, as to those facts related to the conduct of the agency. Likewise, admissions by the agent, as to matters within the scope of that person's authority, bind the principal. And, although there are some earlier cases to the contrary, most courts today would probably hold the principal liable for representations made by the agent about the subject matter of the agency.

Third parties dealing with agents should be particularly careful about making payments to them, since the courts are reluctant to imply the power to receive payment unless there is a clear industry custom or a history of prior dealing between the parties. Store clerks who sell merchandise usually have the power to receive payments; traveling salespersons who merely solicit orders for goods or services usually do not. An agent who does have authority to receive payments can only accept money, checks (usually), or credit cards (in accordance with the principal's policies).

The agent cannot take other forms of property or services in payment unless expressly authorized to do so.

Apparent Authority. Even though the principal did not actually give the alleged agent the express or implied authority to do the acts in question, the principal may be held liable nonetheless if he or she has created the "appearance" of authority. That is, if the principal has created a situation where it appears to a reasonable third party that the agent was authorized to do what he or she did, the principal is estopped to deny that an agency relationship existed once the third party has changed legal position in reliance on the appearances. This may also be called agency by estoppel.

Apparent authority may arise where secret instructions or limitations of authority are communicated to the agent but not to third parties. Or it may arise where actual authority was terminated (as where the agent was fired) but third parties were not notified of the termination. Apparent authority may also arise from some other business relationship between the "principal" and the "agent" and even in a situation where there is no business relationship between them at all.

Ratification. Finally, the principal may be held liable for an agent's actions on the basis of ratification. Where the agent acted without authority but the principal wishes to accept the results of the agent's action anyway, the principal has the power to do so. In most states the principal must act to ratify before the third party discovers the agent's lack of authority and decides to repudiate the contract. If the principal does so, the third party ends up with exactly the contract he thought he was making and should have no basis for complaint.

Ratification may be express ("I agree to be bound on this contract"), or it may be implied from the principal's retention of the benefits of the unauthorized transaction or from other conduct of the principal which indicates an intent to be bound to the contract. Obviously, the principal must have knowledge of the transaction when it speaks or acts to ratify; the principal generally will not be held to have ratified something it did not know about. Equally obvious, the principal has to ratify the entire transaction; the principal can't just accept the benefits and refuse to assume the reciprocal obligations. Generally, when the principal does ratify an unauthorized contract, the courts say that the principal has also agreed to accept responsibility for whatever conduct of the agent produced the contract, including false warranties and fraud.

Ratification, like any of the other cases against the alleged principal, must be proved by evidence; agency is not necessarily assumed just because some other relationship exists. Generally, to be ratifiable, the act must be one which the principal could have authorized when it was done and when it is ratified.

UNDISCLOSED PRINCIPAL

A principal is "undisclosed" when the third party is unaware of the principal's existence or identity; that is, the third party either doesn't know that an agent is being dealt with or knows that an agent is being dealt with but doesn't know whom the agent represents. In most cases it probably makes no difference to the third party who is being dealt with, as long as the third party gets the contracted return performance. An undisclosed principal is given substantially the same rights to enforce the contract as are given to a disclosed principal.

Because in certain circumstances it would be unfair to force the third party to do business with an undisclosed principal, the courts have worked out some limitations. These limitations are much the same as the limitations covering the assignment of contract rights. For instance, a third party cannot be forced to perform personal services for an undisclosed principal, or to loan an undisclosed principal money, or to sell to an undisclosed principal on credit. In such cases the third party's rights might be prejudiced by being forced to do business with someone other than the party believed to have been contracted with—the agent. A court may also refuse to force the third party to perform for an undisclosed principal where both the principal and the agent are aware that the third party would have refused to make the contract if the principal's identity had been disclosed.

To make sure that the third party's rights are fully protected, the third party is given the choice of holding *either* the agent or the undisclosed principal liable for the promised return performance, once the third party discovers the principal's identity. This election may be made either expressly or impliedly, after the principal become known. The undisclosed principal is not liable to the third party under such an election where the third party had already received full performance under the contract, where the principal has already settled accounts with the agent on the basis of conduct by the third party, or where the principal's name does not appear on a negotiable instrument (because of the special liability rules for negotiable instruments).

PRINCIPAL'S LIABILITY FOR AGENT'S TORTS

When a person conducts affairs through agents or employees, the doctrine of *respondeat superior* holds the person liable for any wrongs they commit in trying to accomplish that person's business. Agents or employees are, of course, always liable for their own torts; the only question is whether the torts were committed within the "scope of employment" or the "scope of authority," so that the principal/employer is also liable. This is a form of vicarious liability—that is, liability for the wrongful acts of another, not for one's own conduct.

The main question to be decided in such cases is one of fact: Was the tort committed by the agent or employee within the scope of employment? If the answer is yes, both the principal/ employer and the agent/employee are liable for the tort; if the answer is no, the agent/employee is liable but the principal/employer is not. An agent/employee may have been within the "scope of employment" even where that person violated direct instructions, so long as the trier of fact feels that the agent or employee was attempting to accomplish the assigned job. On the other hand, if agents are "off on a frolic of their own," or "doing their own thing," the principal is not liable for their actions. The "frolic" rule, however, may be subject to special motor vehicle statutory liabilities.

Two other important variables in deciding the scope of authority question are the character and the location of the tort. If the tort was intentionally committed, rather than just negligence, the agent/employee may have been motivated by personal reasons rather than the employer's needs; if the intentional tort was so motivated, the employer ought not be held liable. The place where the tort occurred may be important in proving its connection with the principal/employer's business. However, acts on the "premises" may not be within the scope of employment. These fact issues are discussed in the following case, which involves charges of sexual harassment by supervisors.

BURLINGTON INDUSTRIES v. ELLERTH
118 S.Ct. 2257 (1998)

FACTS: From March 1993 until May 1994, Kimberly Ellerth worked in a two-person office in Chicago, as a salesperson in one of Burlington's five divisions. She alleges constant sexual harassment by Ted Slowik, her second-level supervisor. Slowik was a unit vice-president within the division; he had authority to hire and promote, subject to his supervisor's approval.

Ellerth emphasized three specific instances: an invitation to a hotel lounge while they were both on a business trip, at which time Slowik told her to "loosen up," and warned her "you know, Kim, I could make your life very hard or very easy at Burlington"; a promotion interview during which Slowik told her she was not "loose enough," and then rubbed her knee—and told her after she got the promotion "you're gonna be out there with men who work in factories, and they certainly like women with pretty legs"; and two business telephone calls, during which he said "I don't have time for you right now, Kim—unless you want to tell me what you're wearing" and "are you wearing shorter skirts yet, Kim, because it would make your job a whole heck of a lot easier." Even though she knew that Burlington had an anti-harassment policy, she told no one in authority about these incidents.

The U.S. District Court for the Northern District of Illinois granted summary judgment for Burlington. The Seventh Circuit, sitting en banc, reversed.

 JUSTICE KENNEDY:

We decide whether, under Title VII of the Civil Rights Act of 1964 ... an employee who refuses the unwelcome and threatening sexual advances of a supervisor, yet suffers no adverse, tangible job consequences, can recover against the employer without showing the employer is negligent or otherwise at fault for the supervisor's actions....

We must decide ... whether an employer has vicarious liability when a supervisor creates a hostile work environment by making explicit threats to alter a subordinate's terms or conditions of employment, based on sex, but does not fulfill the threat. We turn to the principles of agency law, for the term "employer" is defined under Title VII to include "agents."...

[T]he Restatement (Second) of Agency (1957) ... is a useful beginning point for a discussion of general agency principles.... Since our decision in *Meritor*, federal courts have explored agency principles, and we find useful instruction in their decisions, noting that "common-law principles may not be transferable in all their particulars to Title VII."... The EEOC has issued Guidelines governing sexual harassment claims under Title VII, but they provide little guidance on the issue of employer liability for supervisor harassment....

An employer may be liable for both negligent and intentional torts committed by an employee within the scope of his or her employment. Sexual harassment under Title VII presupposes intentional conduct. While early decisions absolved employers of liability for the intentional torts of their employees, the law now imposes liability where the employee's "purpose, however misguided, is wholly or in part to further the master's business."... In applying the scope of employment principles to intentional torts, however, it is accepted that "it is less likely that a willful tort will properly be held to be in the course of employment and that the liability of the master for such torts will naturally be more limited."... The Restatement defines conduct, including an intentional tort, to be within the scope of employment when "actuated, at least in part, by a purpose to serve the [employer]," even if it is forbidden by the employer.... For example, when a salesperson lies to a customer to make a sale, the tortious conduct is within the scope of employment because it benefits the employer by increasing sales, even though it may violate the employer's policies....

[A] supervisor acting out of gender-based animus or a desire to fulfill sexual urges may not be actuated by a purpose to serve the employer.... The harassing supervisor often acts for personal motives, motives unrelated and even antithetical to the objectives of the employer.... There are instances, of course, where a supervisor engages in unlawful discrimination with the purpose, mistaken or otherwise, to serve the employer....

The concept of scope of employment has not always been construed to require a motive to serve the employer....

The general rule is that sexual harassment by a supervisor is not conduct within the scope of employment.

Scope of employment does not define the only basis for employer liability under agency principles. In limited circumstances, agency principles impose liability on employers even where employees commit torts outside the scope of employment. The principles are set forth in the much-cited S.219(2) of the Restatement: "(2) A master is not subject to liability for the torts of his servants acting outside the scope of their employment unless ... (d) the servant ... was aided in accomplishing the tort by the existence of the agency relation."...

We turn to the "aided in the agency relation" standard. In a sense, most workplace tortfeasors are aided in accomplishing their tortious objective by the existence of the agency relation: Proximity and regular contact may afford a captive pool of potential victims.... Were this to satisfy the aided in the agency relation standard, an employer would be subject to vicarious liability not only for all supervisor harassment, but also for all co-worker harassment, a result enforced by neither the EEOC nor any court of appeals to have considered the issue.... The aided in the agency relation standard, therefore, requires the existence of something more than the employment relation itself....

Whether the agency relation aids in commission of supervisor harassment which does not culminate in a tangible employment action is less obvious. Application of the standard is made difficult by its malleable terminology, which can be read to either expand or limit liability in the context of supervisor harassment. On the one hand, a supervisor's power and authority invests his or her harassing conduct with a particular threatening character, and in this sense, a supervisor is always aided by the agency relation.... On the other hand, there are acts of harassment a supervisor might commit which might be the same acts a co employee would commit, and there may be some circumstances where the supervisor's status makes little difference....

In order to accommodate the agency principles of vicarious liability for harm caused by misuse of supervisory authority, as well as Title VII's equally basic policies of encouraging forethought by employers and saving action by objecting employees, we adopt the following holding.... An employer is subject to vicarious liability to a victimized employee for an actionable hostile environment created by a supervisor with immediate (or successively higher) authority over the employee. When no tangible employment action is taken, a defending employer may raise an affirmative defense to liability or damages, subject to proof by a preponderance of the evidence.... The defense comprises two necessary elements: (a) that the employer exercised reasonable care to prevent and correct promptly any sexually harassing behavior, and (b) that the plaintiff employee unreasonably failed to take advantage of any preventative or corrective opportunities provided by the employer or to avoid harm otherwise. While proof that an employer had promulgated an anti-harassment policy with complaint procedure is not necessary in every instance as a matter of law, the need for a stated policy suitable to the employment circumstances may appropriately be addressed in any case when litigating the first element of the defense. And while proof that an employee failed to fulfill the corresponding obligation of reasonable care to avoid harm is not limited to showing any unreasonable failure to use any complaint procedure provided by the employer, a demonstration of such failure will normally suffice to satisfy the employer's burden under the second element of the defense. No affirmative defense is available, however, when the supervisor's harassment culminates in a tangible employment action, such as discharge, demotion, or undesirable reassignment....

For these reasons, we will affirm the judgment of the Court of Appeals, reversing the grant of summary judgment against Ellerth. On remand, the District Court will have the opportunity to decide whether it would be appropriate to allow Ellerth to amend her pleading or supplement her discovery.

DUTIES AND LIABILITIES OF PRINCIPAL TO AGENT

Principal's Duty to Compensate Agent. Many of the cases in which an agent is suing a principal involve the principal's duty to compensate the agent. It is assumed that the principal owes the agent whatever salary or commission was agreed on for doing the acts required, and it is also assumed that the principal should reimburse the agent for any expenses which the agent reasonably and necessarily incurred in carrying out the principal's instructions. If the agent is to pay expenses, this should be stated in the contract. In the absence of any specific agreement, it is also assumed that the agent should be reimbursed for any personal loss or damage sustained as a result of following the principal's instructions.

Special compensation rules apply to real estate brokers. Usually the broker does not actually have the power to sell the listed property but only to conduct negotiations with prospective buyers. The broker, therefore, has normally earned the commission by "bringing in a deal," that is, when the broker produces a buyer who is ready, willing, and able to meet the purchase terms specified by the seller in the listing agreement.

Principal's Liability for Breach of Agency Contract. If the principal wrongfully prevents the agent from carrying out their contract and thus earning the agreed compensation, the principal, like any other employer, is liable to the agent for breach. Some of these cases involve an unjustified discharge of the agent; others result from the principal's improper interference with the agent's conduct of the agency, such as failing to provide the agent with new price and product information or attempting to impose arbitrary and discriminatory paperwork requirements.

If the agent fails to meet duties under the contract, the principal may be justified in firing the agent. Generally, if the agency has not been set up for a specific period of time, and therefore is "at will," the agent may be fired at any time, with or without reason, and the agent will have no case for breach of contract. The courts in many states have recognized limitations on the "at-will" employment doctrine. Some of the state legislatures are considering legislation to prohibit arbitrary dismissals of "at-will" employees. The law on this point is changing very rapidly. Lawsuits may be filed claiming breach of express or implied contract, or under various tort theories.

The *Johnson* case discusses these issues.

JOHNSON v. MORTON THIOKOL, INC.
818 P.2d 997 (UT, 1991)

FACTS: Plaintiff Billy Johnson sought to recover damages resulting from the involuntary termination of his employment. From an entry of summary judgment in favor of defendant Morton Thiokol, Inc. ("Thiokol"), Johnson appeals.

Johnson was hired by Thiokol on February 12, 1979, as a process inspector and was continuously employed at Thiokol until the date of his termination, July 20, 1988. At no time during his employment did he enter into an express contract with Thiokol which restricted Thiokol's ability to terminate his employment. Throughout Johnson's tenure, Thiokol published and distributed an employee handbook. The text of the handbook contains several pages prescribing Thiokol's policy concerning employee disciplinary, appraisal, and grievance procedures. In administering Johnson's nine employee appraisals, Thiokol complied with the procedures set out in the handbook. However, the introduction of the handbook contains clear and conspicuous language stating that the provisions of the manual are not intended to operate as terms of an employment contract.

In the beginning of July 1988, Thiokol implemented a leak check test procedure for verifying the proper placement and seal of Thiokol's redesigned O-rings, which are used in space shuttle rocket motors. Johnson, although he had not received adequate training regarding the new process, was assigned to inspect the leak check test procedure. For the three weeks prior to the date of the incident which resulted in his termination, Johnson and all members of the inspection crews worked mandatory overtime in order to meet Air Force-imposed deadlines. In connection with these deadlines, the inspectors were urged by upper management to avoid shut-down orders because such orders would result in unacceptable scheduling pressure.

When Johnson arrived at work on July 8, 1988, the technicians were involved in setting up five simultaneous operations. It had become common practice to perform numerous operations simultaneously even though there was only one inspector assigned to the building. An inspector was required to witness each operation, but due to the simultaneous "setups," it was impossible for one inspector to observe each procedure. Johnson therefore prioritized those areas where actual observations were made. At one point, he was notified that a setup had been completed. He glanced at the setup but did not complete the 39-step procedure. However, he verified that he had completed the appropriate inspection. Due to the inadequate inspection, Johnson failed to notice that certain hoses had been improperly installed.

The next day, during a routine test operation, excess pressure caused by the improperly installed hoses forced the O-rings out of their groove and damaged some insulation lining on the motor. The damage required that the test motor be disassembled to make repairs, causing a twenty-day delay in the test firing of the rocket motor. The incident resulted in an investigation by NASA officials and was highly publicized in both the local and national news media. Johnson and the employee who installed the hoses were terminated.

Johnson was terminated pursuant to the procedures set out in the employee handbook. After his termination, he initiated grievance procedures which were also conducted in accordance with the handbook. The grievance was denied on the ground that Johnson was terminated for "careless or inefficient performance of duty," a ground which, according to the handbook, can result in termination.

 CHIEF JUSTICE HALL:

There are issues concerning ... implied-in-fact employee contracts ... that have yet to be addressed.... It is clear that the employee has the burden of establishing the existence of an implied-in-fact contract provision; that is, the employee must show that although there was no express contract provision to this effect, the parties nevertheless agree that the employment would not be at will. If the parties actually intended such an agreement and the agreement is of such a nature that it is possible to operate as a contract term, a court will give effect to the parties' intentions by enforcing the agreement as an implied-in-fact contract provision. The existence of such an agreement is a question of fact which turns on the objective manifestations of the parties' intent. As a question of fact, the intent of the parties is primarily a jury question. However, if the evidence presented is such that no reasonable jury could conclude that the parties agreed to limit the employer's right to terminate the employee, it is appropriate for a court to decide the issue as a matter of law.

We have also addressed the nature of indefinite-term employment relationships with implied-in-fact contract provisions which limit an employer's right to terminate an employee.... [I]f an employee manual is to be considered part of an employment contract, the terms should be considered terms of a unilateral contract. Several jurisdictions have taken such an approach. Under a unilateral contract analysis, an employer's promise of employment under certain terms and for an indefinite period constitutes both the terms of the employment contract and the employer's consideration for the employment contract. The employee's performance of service pursuant to the employer's offer constitutes both the employee's acceptance of the offer and the employee's consideration for the contract. Therefore, for an implied-in-fact contract term to exist, it must meet the requirements for an offer of a unilateral contract. There must be a manifestation of the employer's intent that is communicated to the employee and sufficiently definite to operate as a contract provision. Furthermore, the manifestation of the employer's intent must be of such a nature that the employee can reasonably believe that the employer is making an offer of employment other than employment at will. The unilateral nature of such an employment contract is important because it affects the flexibility of the employment relationship....

Indeed, such an approach is consistent with our case law ... where we have held that the terms of an employee manual may constitute terms of an employment contract even when the employees do not receive the manual until after they are hired.

However, it is not clear what type of evidence is sufficient to raise a triable issue concerning the mentions of the parties and therefore the existence of an implied-in-fact contract term. In cases where we have held that there is a triable issue regarding the existence of such a term, we have based our decision upon express statements of the employer....

Applying these principles to the instant case, it is clear that the trial judge was correct in ruling as a matter of law that no implied contract provision existed limiting Thiokol's right to terminate Johnson. Johnson's allegations are insufficient to create a triable issue concerning whether Johnson could reasonably believe that Thiokol intended to modify the employment relationship to provide that an employee could be terminated only for good cause. This can be seen by examining the specific allegations upon which Johnson bases his claim. Johnson argues that an implied-in-fact contract term providing that he should be terminated only for good cause is evidenced by the procedures set out in the handbook for appraisals, discipline, and grievances; the administration of its annual employee performance evaluation program; Johnson's and Thiokol's joint use of the grievance procedures; and Thiokol's use of the grievance procedures; and Thiokol's stated good cause reason for terminating Johnson.

It is to be observed that Johnson's reliance on the terms of the employee handbook is misplaced. We have held that the terms of employee manuals may raise triable issues concerning the existence of an implied-in-fact contract. However, the manual presently at issue contains clear and conspicuous language disclaiming any contractual liability and stating Thiokol's intent to maintain an at-will relationship with its employees.... Given this language, the only reasonable conclusion an employee or a juror could reach concerning Thiokol's intention is that Thiokol intended to retain the right to discharge for any reason. Treating the handbook as part of the employment contract, traditional rules of contract interpretation would require us to read the handbook as a whole, harmonizing all of the provisions. Therefore, the procedures in the handbook for terminating an employee must be read in light of the language in the disclaimer which clearly reserved the right to discharge for any reason. Under such an approach, the most Johnson is entitled to is the right to challenge his termination under the handbook's procedures, not the right to be fired only for good cause. We also note that a number of jurisdictions have held that a clear and conspicuous disclaimer, as a matter of law, prevents employee manuals or other like material from being considered as implied-in-fact contract terms.

Therefore, at the time the handbook was first distributed to Johnson, his employment was at will. While it is true that subsequent expressed or implied agreements could have modified the at-will employment relationship, in the instant case the remaining allegations are insufficient to raise a triable issue concerning a subsequent modification. Aside from the handbook itself, Johnson relies only on the fact that Thiokol complied with the procedures in the handbook during his annual employee appraisals and his termination. However, by complying with the handbook Thiokol did nothing that was inconsistent with the at-will employment relationship established when the handbook was first distributed to Johnson. It cannot be reasonably concluded, therefore, that Thiokol's actions communicated an intention to alter an employment relationship that existed at the time the handbook was distributed. The trial court was correct in granting summary judgment on the ground that no implied-in-fact contract provision existed between Thiokol and Johnson.

Principal's Liability for Defamation. One way to avoid liability for wrongful or discriminatory discharge of an agent or employee is to show that that there was cause for the discharge. To prove that the discharged person's job performance had been unsatisfactory, the principal/employer usually has to produce a written record of warnings and reprimands. Employers are thus motivated to document all wrongful or improper employee actions in each individual's personnel file, just in case. In doing so, however, the employer faces something of a dilemma, since liability can also arise when defamatory statements about the employee are communicated to a third person.

The problem arises in many cases when a former employer is asked for a reference on one of its former employees. In answering such requests, the former employer must make sure that any statements made are absolutely true, and can be verified if necessary.

Employers' Liability Under Workers' Compensation. As noted in Chapter 6, an employer may also be held liable for an employee's on-the-job injuries. The employer owes a duty to provide a reasonably safe workplace. This duty is now expressed in state workers' compensation statutes, under which the employer is presumed to be liable for any job-related injuries. These statutes, and the state courts' decisions interpreting them, are not completely uniform. Chronic, long-term conditions such as black lung disease, and asbestosis, and mental illness resulting from job pressures, may or may not be covered. In general, state courts have been quite liberal in applying statutory coverage.

FIDUCIARY DUTIES OF AGENT TO PRINCIPAL

In General. The agency relationship is based upon the trust and confidence that the principal has placed in the agent by giving the agent the power to manage the principal's affairs. The agent is thus a fiduciary, owing to the principal a duty of honesty and fair dealing in their relationship. The following specific aspects of this fiduciary duty may be easier to remember if you recall the boy scout's pledge: "Trustworthy, Loyal, Helpful, Friendly, Courteous, Kind, Obedient, Cheerful, Thrifty, Brave, Clean, and Reverent." Nearly all of these desirable characteristics of a successful scout also apply to the agent.

Loyalty and Good Faith. Loyalty to the principal's interests and good faith in dealing with that person are the most basic parts of the agent's fiduciary duty. Under the rule that a person "cannot faithfully serve two masters," an agent is prohibited from representing two persons with opposing interests, such as the two parties of a business transaction, unless both of them know of the dual agency and agree to it. A principal who does not know of the dual agency can rescind the resulting transaction upon learning the truth. Likewise, the agent can neither buy from or sell to himself or herself nor derive any other secret benefit from conducting the principal's affairs. The receipt of secret bribes, payoffs, or presents by the agent from third parties will justify dismissal of the agent and may also involve civil or criminal penalties against the agent.

A related problem, and one which arises with some frequency in a technological society, is the conflict between employer and employee over who owns patents developed by the employee and other "secret" information used by the employee on the job (for example, customer lists). Courts generally hold that the fiduciary duty does not end simply because employment is terminated, and thus the employee (or agent) does not have the right to use formulas, processes, customer lists, or other trade secrets in competition with a former employer. As to patented devices and processes which the employee developed on the job, the employee may become the owner by having them patented in his or her own name, but the employer has a "shop right" to make use of them in the employer's business without paying royalties. Specific language in the employment contract will probably head off most of these problems.

Employment contracts may also contain an agreement by the agent/ employee not to compete with the principal/employer after the relationship is terminated. As noted in Chapter 12, such agreements are lawful and enforceable so long as the area and the duration of the restraint are both reasonable. If an unreasonable restraint is included, courts are split as to what should happen. Some courts refuse to enforce the unreasonable restraint at all; others are willing to rewrite it so as to make it reasonable. If the employer materially breaches the employment contract, as by wrongfully discharging the employee, a court could decide that such a restraint clause in the contract was no longer enforceable by the employer. In the absence of such an agreement, an employee (after termination) could go to work for a competitor, but would still not be able to use the former employer's trade secrets.

Care and Skill in a Calling. A person, after accepting appointment as an agent, has the duty to use that degree of care and skill possessed by a reasonably competent practitioner in that line of business. A salesperson, for example, would be required to have and to exercise the knowledge, training, and diligence of "average" salespersons in the field involved. The existence of this duty means that an agent can be held liable for **misfeasance** (not doing lawful acts in a proper manner), **malfeasance** (doing a wrongful act), or **nonfeasance** (not being diligent in performing the job).

Personal Performance. A person is chosen as an agent of a principal, and placed in a position of trust and confidence, on the basis of his or her unique personal characteristics. It therefore follows logically that the agent owes a duty to use those personal qualities in performing the assigned job and that the agent should not be able to delegate to others the exercise of his or her discretionary powers as an agent. Absent any specific agreement, delegation by the agent is permitted only where the nature of the business requires it, or where a known and established custom permits it, or where the delegation involves purely ministerial or mechanical acts (such as answering the telephone or typing correspondence). Except in these situations, the principal will not be liable to third parties for the acts of such "subagents," and their appointment by the original agent would be a breach of his or her duty to the principal.

Obedience to Instructions and Good Conduct. Like the boy scout, a good agent is obedient. The agent must obey the principal's instructions, even if they seem stupid or unreasonable; this control over methods, remember, is the main distinction between the agent/employee and the independent contractor. In general, the agent's only excuses for not obeying instructions are that they require doing something illegal or that it has become impossible to comply with them. The law is not too clear on the degree to which agents must subject themselves to personal danger to comply with the principal's instructions, although the *Restatement of Agency* does indicate that agents can disregard such instructions to "protect the agent's own superior interests." It is clear that the agent will have to follow instructions that are merely "unreasonable," unless the relationship involves an agency coupled with an interest and the unreasonable instructions would interfere with the agent's rights in the subject matter of the agency.

As far as third parties are concerned, the agent is the principal. This holds true particularly for agents who represent business concerns. The image and reputation of a business are in large part determined by the way its agents and employees conduct themselves toward third parties. The agent, and to some extent even the employee, therefore owes a duty of "good conduct." This requirement clearly covers on-the-job conduct, so things like dress codes can be enforced if they are reasonably and uniformly applied (see the cases in Chapter 41). The *Restatement of Agency* also indicates that this duty extends to off-the-job conduct that might affect the principal's business, such as the conduct of the bank teller who becomes known in the community as the "patron of the races." The exact degree to which agents can be legally required to surrender their personality to keep their jobs remains an open question.

Use of Principal's Property. The agent is liable for any misuse of property which the principal has entrusted to the agent or which comes into the agent's possession in the course of acting as agent. As part of this duty, the agent is not to commingle money or other property of the principal with personal money or other property, and the agent is required to provide the principal with correct and reasonably detailed statements of account.

The agent also has a duty to communicate to the principal any information that the agent possesses which might materially affect the agency.

Principal's Ratification of Agent's Unauthorized Act. Typically where the principal has a clear choice and ratifies with full knowledge that the agent's actions were unauthorized, the agent is excused of any further liability to the principal. The *Restatement* says that the agent will remain liable for breach of duty either where the principal "is obliged to affirm the act in order to protect his own interest" or where the principal is induced to ratify by the agent's fraud or duress.

LIABILITY OF AGENT TO THIRD PARTY

Agent Acts Beyond Authority. In most cases, when the agent in a disclosed agency transaction acts beyond the scope of his or her authority, so that the third party has no contract with the principal, the third party has no contract with the agent either. In these states the third party's remedy against the agent is a tort claim for fraud, provided the agent knowingly misrepresented his or her authority, or a case for breach by the agent of an "implied warranty of authority." As a rule, it is assumed that the agent makes such a warranty to the third party. There is no such warranty, however, if the third party knew that the agent was unauthorized, or if the agent in good faith disclosed to the third party all the facts regarding the extent of the authority, or if the contract contains a disclaimer of the agent's liability. In a minority of states the agent could also be sued directly on the contract the agent was not authorized to make for the principal.

Principal Nonexistent or Incompetent. The two most common examples of the "nonexistent" principal are the corporation which has not yet been formed and the unincorporated association, which is usually not recognized as a separate legal person. In these cases, the agent is personally liable on the contracts made with the third party, even if the third party knows of the "nonexistence," unless the contracts specifically exempt the agent from personal liability.

Where the principal totally lacks contractual capacity at the time the contract is made, for instance a person who has been judicially declared insane, most courts will probably arrive at the same result as would be reached if the principal were "nonexistent." Also, the agent would clearly be liable if the agent fraudulently misrepresented or concealed the principal's lack of capacity. Where the principal has merely exercised an option to disaffirm the contract, however, the results are not so clear-cut, but even in such cases many courts would hold the agent liable. The majority rule seems to be that the agent impliedly warrants the principal's existence and the agent's authority, but does not impliedly warrant the principal's capacity or solvency.

Agent Pledges Personal Credit. An agent who has pledged his or her personal credit on the contract, as surety for the principal, is also clearly liable to the third party. This occurs very frequently where the agent is acting on behalf of a small, brand-new corporation that has not yet established its own credit standing; in such cases the third party will often demand that the agent-promoter-shareholder cosign the contract. If the agent does so, the agent is liable according to the terms of the contract.

Because this situation is so common, the agent may also be held personally liable where the contract language or the signatures on the contract indicate his or her liability. If it appears that the agent was a party (or the other party) to the contract, the agent may be prevented by the parol evidence rule from proving otherwise. If the principal's name does not appear on a negotiable instrument and the agent's does, the agent is liable on it and the principal is not. To avoid these unintended results, the agent should always sign "Peter Principal, by Jane Able, agent"—thus clearly indicating that he or she is signing in a representative capacity.

Agent Commits Tort Against Third Party. As stated earlier in the chapter, an agent is personally liable for the torts the agent commits against third parties. Where the agent's tort was within the scope of authority, the third party can sue *both* the agent and the principal and they are both liable, although the third party cannot collect damages twice.

As a rule, the agent is not liable to third parties for breach of a duty which is owed only to the principal, at least if the breach involves only nonfeasance or misfeasance.

Undisclosed Principal. As also indicated earlier, where the existence of identity of the principal is not disclosed at the time the contract is made, the third party has the option of holding the agent personally liable on the contract. The courts do not agree on when the third party must make an election to hold one to the exclusion of the other, although of course all do agree that no double recovery is permitted. The only way for an agent to avoid being held liable on this basis is to disclose the principal when the contract is made.

LIABILITY OF THIRD PARTY TO AGENT

Agent Suing on His or Her Own Behalf. There are only a few situations where the agent will sue the third party on his or her own behalf. If the agent was also made a party to the original contract, or if the agent owns the contract rights by assignment from the principal, the agent can sue the third party. The agent can also sue a third party for wrongful interference in the contractual relationship between the agent and the principal or for any other tort the third party commits against the agent. Finally, where the agent has delivered money or goods to the third party under circumstances in which the third party would be unjustly enriched at the agent's expense (e.g., the agent by mistake pays the third party more than the principal owes the third party), the agent can sue in his or her own name to prevent such unjust enrichment.

Agent Suing for the Principal. Generally, an agent cannot sue in his or her own name to enforce a contract that the agent made on behalf of the principal; the principal has to sue the third party. If specifically authorized to do so, an agent may be able to bring suit as an agent for collection, and an assignment may be made to such an agent for the purpose of collection only. An agent can also sue on the principal's behalf to recover goods the agent delivered to the third party by mistake or for interference by the third party with the agent's possession of the principal's goods.

Thus, while the main agency is the third party's suit against the principal, based on an alleged contract or on the agent's tort, any of the three parties to this relationship may have a case against either of the other two.

TERMINATION OF THE AGENCY RELATIONSHIP

In discussing the termination of the agency relationship, we must first distinguish between the principal's *power* to terminate and the principal's *right* to do so. As a rule, the principal has the power to terminate the agency at any time by *revocation*, provided the principal gives proper notice of termination to the agent and to third parties. Whether the principal also has the right to do so depends on the principal's arrangement with the agent. If there is a contract between them, the principal's wrongful termination may make the principal liable to the agent for breach, even though the agent's power to make contracts with third parties has been effectively terminated. The same distinction applies to the agent; the agent can effectively terminate the relationship at any time by simply *refusing* to continue as agent but may be liable to the principal for breach of contract.

The agency relationship may also be terminated, without liability for breach, by mutual *agreement* between the principal and the agent, by *fulfillment* of the purpose of the agency, or by *expiration* of an agreed duration. An agency may also be terminated without liability by the same sort of "impossibility" excuses as apply to contracts generally: the *death, insanity,* or *bankruptcy* of either party; the subsequent *illegality* of the agency's purpose; the *destruction* of the subject matter of the agency; a substantial *change* in business conditions; or war.

Notice of Termination. Generally, where termination has occurred by the act of either the principal or the agent, or by their mutual agreement, notice of the termination must be given to third parties. Otherwise, the agent may still have apparent authority to continue business as usual. Any third party who has actually dealt with the agent as an agent in the past must be given actual notice, either orally or in writing. A newspaper ad or similar "constructive notice" is sufficient for all other third parties, whether or not they ever read the ad or have it called to their attention. Where the termination of an agency occurs by "operation of law," no notice at all need be given to third parties, except that an insane principal is bound on contracts made by third parties in good faith before that person is judicially declared incompetent or before the third parties receive other notice of the principal's incapacity.

Agency Coupled with an Interest. As an exception to the general rule that gives the principal the power to revoke an agency at any time, the principal cannot revoke an agency in which the agent has a personal interest in the subject matter—an **agency coupled with an interest**. This phrase describes the cases where the agent is more than just a hired hand, where there is some other underlying relationship between the parties—most typically, a debtor-creditor relationship. The agency power has been given to the agent as the creditor of the principal, to try to make sure that the agent gets paid. In such cases, the principal cannot revoke the agent's power and the agent's power is not terminated by the subsequent incapacity of either party.

Following the precedent established by Chief Justice Marshall in the *Hunt* case, most courts have said that the agent's power is terminated by the principal's death unless the principal has also transferred some sort of ownership interest in the subject matter to the agent. In other words, if the principal had merely authorized the agent to sell a specific piece of property to pay the principal's debt to the agent, the principal's death would terminate the power to sell; if the principal had given the agent a mortgage on the property (an "interest") plus the power to sell, the principal's death would not terminate that power.

Since the intent of the parties is basically the same in both cases, some modern decisions do not follow this distinction and hold that either a power given as security or a power "coupled with an interest" would survive the principal's death.

Such powers to sell collateral in the event of default would be terminated by the principal's bankruptcy, unless a proper filing of the security agreement or a financing statement has been made, or other steps have been taken in accordance with bankruptcy law to establish priority over other creditors.

SIGNIFICANCE OF THIS CHAPTER

Many business activities are carried on through other persons. Each of us, living in a complex society, needs to be aware of the basic rules for determining when one person is responsible for the actions of another. An important distinction exists between principals who employ agents and persons who employ independent contractors. Likewise, there are different rules for determining contract and tort liability for the actions of agents. Since we will all be dealing with and through agents on many occasions, we need to know how these basic rules work.

Since many of us will be employed as agents and will also be employing agents of our own, we also need to know the rights and duties that exist between principal and agent. Whether we are acting as agents or are the third parties with whom the agents are dealing, we should be aware of the rights and duties involved in that relationship as well. Although the major litigation pattern is a suit by the third party against the principal, based on actions of the agent, any of the three parties involved may have grounds for a suit against either of the others.

PROBLEMS FOR DISCUSSION

1. Alfred Dale, owner of an apartment house in Bismark, bought three folding beds from Sears for installation in his apartments. The beds were designed to fold up into the wall when not in use; six heavy coil springs on each bed made it easier to raise or lower. Dale had his "handyman," Chris Nelson, install one of the beds in Mrs. Holum's apartment in the fall of 1994. After she moved out, Dale and his wife occupied that apartment and used the bed. In December, the apartment was rented to Claude Newman. On February 28, 1995, after Newman had gone to bed, the bed folded up with Newman inside.

    In installing the bed, Nelson had used ordinary wood screws rather than the seven lag screws which were designed to hold the bed in place as it was raised up and lowered down. The lag screws which came with the bed had a holding power four times that of the wood screws used by Nelson.

    The trial court dismissed the action against Sears since there was no indication that the bed had been negligently designed or manufactured. It also held that Dale was not liable for Nelson's improper installation. Newman appealed.

    How should the appeal be decided, and why?

2. Defendant J.C. Penney Co. hired plaintiff David Patton in 1979. Plaintiff worked in Eugene until 1990 when he was transferred to Portland where he worked as a merchandising manager. In 1998 the store manager, defendant McKay, told plaintiff to break off a social relationship with a female coemployee. Plaintiff responded by telling McKay that he did not socialize with the coemployee at work and that he intended to continue seeing her on his own time. Apparently, the social relationship did not interfere with the plaintiff's performance at work, for during this time he earned several awards for "Merchant of the Month" and one for "Merchant of the Year."

    McKay later, while interrogating other employees about whether plaintiff had broken off the relationship, made statements to the effect that if plaintiff wanted to keep working he had to discontinue the relationship. Although no written or unwritten policy, rule, or regulation proscribed socializing between employees, other employees told plaintiff that McKay disfavored plaintiff's fraternization with the female coemployee. Nevertheless, plaintiff continued seeing the coemployee. When McKay warned plaintiff in late 1998 that his job performance was unsatisfactory and that he would be fired if there was no improvement, plaintiff asked for a transfer to another department. McKay denied the request. In February, McKay terminated plaintiff's employment for unsatisfactory job performance. The district manager, defendant Chapin, approved the termination.

    Does Patton have a case for wrongful discharge? Explain.

3. On December 23, Mr. Kanelles entered the Hotel Ohio, operated by Mrs. Ida Locke, in downtown Cleveland. The one man who was in the lobby (it was 1:00 a.m.) got up out of his chair, came over to the registration desk, had Kanelles register, got a room key, and gave it to him. Kanelles then said he wanted to leave his valuables in the hotel safe, so he gave the man a diamond pin, two $5.00 checks, and $484 in cash. The man gave him a receipt signed: "Mrs. Locke—Hotel Ohio, J.C. Clemens." The man (Clemens) was merely a roomer in the hotel, and he left during the night with Kanelles' valuables. When Mrs. Locke failed to make good the loss, Kanelles sued her.

   How should this case be decided? Explain.

4. Parke Davis, a pharmaceutical manufacturer, employed Neil Stuempges as one of its Minneapolis sales representatives from 1978 until February 25, 1994, when it asked him to resign or be fired. During the first fifteen years of his employment, Stuempges had never been disparaged for his lack of ability as a salesperson and had even received commendations over the years for his outstanding sales record.

   In July 1993, Robert Jones became the new district manager of the Minneapolis area in which Stuempges' sales territory was located. From the beginning, they clashed in their approaches to a number of issues.

   On February 25, 1994, at Jones's request, Stuempges met with him and Donald Burgett, Jones's immediate supervisor. At this meeting, Stuempges was asked to resign and was promised a good recommendation if he did so. If he refused to resign, however, Jones told him that he would be "blackballed" in the industry. Shortly thereafter, Stuempges submitted his resignation.

   On March 5, 1994, Stuempges sought assistance in finding another job through Sales Consultants, Inc., an employment agency specializing in sales personnel. He was interviewed by Robert Hammer, at which time he listed Parke Davis as his most recent employer and Jones as his most recent supervisor and gave him permission for Sales Consultants to check his references at Parke Davis. Hammer called Jones for a reference. Jones told Hammer that Stuempges was a poor salesman, not industrious, hard to motivate, could not sell, and that he had been fired and had not just resigned. Hammer refused to try to place Stuempges in a job as a result of this poor recommendation. Stuempges sued Parke Davis & Company alleging he had been defamed by Parke Davis employees.

   Has Parke Davis defamed Stuempges? Discuss.

5. Plaintiffs, Wagner Brothers, operate four retail clothing stores in the greater New York City area. Defendant Appendagez, Inc. is a Massachusetts corporation which manufactured and sold wholesale a line of jeans, tops, and sweaters under the brand name "Faded Glory."

   The Wagners wished to feature the "Faded Glory" line at their new Cedarhurst location, which was in a high-income, sophisticated area. Aaron Wagner telephoned the corporate offices of Appendagez and asked to be placed in communication with the Appendagez salesman covering that area. This inquiry produced a visit, at the Cedarhurst location, from one Alan Friedman, who identified himself to Aaron Wagner as the Long Island salesman for Appendagez. Upon hearing of the other three stores, Friedman advised that he would write orders for all four stores, billing them through the Wagner Brothers Haberdashery account in Cedarhurst, so that the Wagners could examine the entire line at one time and there would be only one billing address. The Wagners agreed to this procedure. A number of orders were placed with Appendagez, through Friedman, for the four stores. To the extent that those orders were unfilled, they form the subject matter of this action.

   Orders were written up by Friedman on a printed order form prepared by Appendagez. There is no statement to the effect that orders are subject to acceptance by Appendagez at Norwood before they become binding upon the seller. Some sellers in the industry had such a statement on their order forms; others did not.

   The Wagners sued for breach of contract.

   How should this case be analyzed? Explain.

Chapter 31
Partnership Law

NATURE OF PARTNERSHIP

Origin. The partnership is perhaps the oldest and most common form of business organization involving more than one person. The partnership form of organization dates as far back as the Middle Ages and perhaps even before that. Traditionally, the partnership was a nonstatutory form of business organization, whose creation was comparatively simple, inexpensive and informal.

The body of law governing the partnership business organization was developed on a case-by-case basis throughout the court system over the years. Whenever law is developed by the case method, there are bound to be variations in decisions by different judges, a lack of uniformity from state to state, and a lack of real clarity as to what the law is on a particular point. Thus, the National Conference of Commissioners on Uniform State Laws, which was referred to in an earlier chapter, drafted the Uniform Partnership Act (UPA) in 1914. The purpose of this act was to clarify and codify the maze of court decisions on partnership law into a workable statutory form. The great majority of the states have adopted the UPA. Thus, references will be made to the UPA throughout this chapter.

A revised version of the UPA has recently been presented to the states by the Commissioners. Although it has been criticized by some commentators, most states will probably adopt the revised UPA.

Legal Entity. Under the common law, a partnership was not considered a separate legal entity, or person, but merely a collection of persons who were doing business together. There was no separate "it," but merely "them." In contrast, a corporation is clearly a separate legal person, even though "it" has no actual physical existence. All a corporation's business affairs are conducted in its name, even though it must use agents.

Failure to recognize a partnership as a separate entity makes the conduct of its business unnecessarily cumbersome. At common law, for example, a partnership could not hold title to real estate in its firm name; it had to be held in the name of one or more partners. Suits by or against large partnerships can be terribly complex if the rules require each partner to be specifically named. And so on.

Recognizing these problems, the UPA's drafters reached a compromise. For certain purposes, but not completely, the partnership is now recognized as a separate entity. Its property is treated as separate from that of the individual partners (as discussed later in the chapter), and it can own real estate in the firm name if it wishes. It keeps separate books and records and prepares separate (informational) tax returns. It does not, however, pay a separate income tax, as it would if it were a separate entity. Many states, with newer civil procedure rules, now also permit suits by or against a partnership in the firm name. Separate bankruptcy proceedings can also be instituted by or against a partnership.

Definition. Section 6 of the UPA defines a **partnership** as follows: "a partnership is an association of two or more persons to carry on as co-owners of a business for profit." This definition contains several requirements which must be met before there can be a partnership. First, the partnership must be an association of two or more persons. The word *association* implies that an agreement has been made. Thus, we are talking about contract law with regard to whether or not a legal agreement exists. Second, the association must consist of two or more persons. A person can be a natural person or a legal entity such as a corporation. Third, persons must carry on a business as co-owners. A partnership is not simply two or more people working together; it must be two or more people, each of whom has some rights of ownership in the business. It is not required that all of these people have equal rights of ownership; however, each must be a co-owner. Finally, the business must be for profit. This rules out the many organizations which have been established for religious, charitable, educational, and other not-for-profit purposes.

It is interesting to note that for tax purposes the Internal Revenue Code, Section 761(a) defines a partnership as a "syndicate, group, pool, joint venture, or other unincorporated organization through ... which any business ... is carried on, and which is not ... a corporation or a trust or estate." The IRS is not concerned about the rights and duties between partners or between partners and third persons; it is only trying to classify business organizations for taxing purposes.

Joint Ventures. A **joint venture** is similar to a partnership in that it also involves two or more persons who are engaged in some business activity. Joint ventures differ from partnerships mainly in purpose and duration. A partnership is created to carry on a business for profit for an indefinite period of time and is dissolved by the death or resignation of one of the partners. A joint venture, on the other hand, is created to conduct a specific business activity over a specific period of time. An example of a joint venture would be a situation where two persons purchased an apartment house as an investment for resale and hired a manager to run it until it was sold. The purpose of this venture is specific, and the duration is limited. No general agency is created between the parties; they are simply joint investors. Deciding whether a joint venture has been created usually presents the court with some difficult fact questions.

A **syndicate**, like a partnership, involves two or more persons who are involved in some business activity. However, a syndicate differs from a partnership in that, like a joint venture, it is formed for a specific business activity and a specific duration. The parties involved in a syndicate can be classified as investors rather than as persons carrying on a business as co-owners. A syndicate was defined in the case of *Hambleton v. Rhind*, 84 Md. 456, as "[A]n association of individuals, formed for the purpose of conducting and carrying out some particular business transaction, ordinarily of a financial character in which the members are mutually interested."

The terms *group* and *pool* as used in Section 761(a) are really just Internal Revenue Code language used to describe a group of people who are participating in a business activity or a situation where people pool their money to conduct a business for profit.

Qualifications of Partners.

Part I, Section 2 of the Uniform Partnership Act states that the word *persons* includes individuals, partners, corporations, and other associations. This means that not only individuals but also corporations, partnerships, and other associations may be partners in a partnership. Since the individual states may have specific rules and regulations regarding participation in partnerships by corporations, other partnerships, and other associations, whether these can be partners depends on state law.

Any natural person having the capacity to contract can become a partner. In Part II, Contracts, we dealt with the question of what persons are competent to contract. Insane persons may not become partners. Minors do not have full contractual capacity; however, they may become partners in a partnership. But, as with simple contracts, minors have the right to disaffirm their partnership contracts at any time before they reach majority and for a reasonable time thereafter. By such disaffirmance, a minor may avoid certain liability to partnership creditors. Also, a minor who disaffirms the partnership agreement is generally entitled to get back his or her capital investment and share of the profits up to that time, provided that such a distribution will not adversely affect the interest of existing partnership creditors. In some states, the disaffirming minor may be able to withdraw capital *before* creditors are paid.

Since a partnership is a voluntary association, the general rule is that no one can be forced to become a partner with another; there must be an agreement to be partners. This rule is summed up in the Latin phrase: *delectus personae* (choice of persons). Each of us has the right to choose the persons with whom we will be partners, and we're not partners unless we agree to be partners. In contrast, the shares of stock in a corporation are presumed to be fully and freely transferable, so that a person could become involved in a corporate business with someone who was a total stranger, of unknown abilities and personality.

Classification.

Partnerships may be classified as **general partnerships** or **limited partnerships**. The general partnership is the more common form. It is a partnership in which all of the partners have unlimited liability for partnership debts. A limited partnership is a partnership in which one or more of the partners are general partners with unlimited liability. However, one or more of the other partners are limited partners, and their liabilities for partnership debts are limited to the extent of their investment in the partnership. Like persons who buy stock in a corporation, they cannot be liable for more than their investment in the business.

Partnerships may be further classified as **trading** or **nontrading partnerships**. A trading partnership is engaged in the business of buying or selling goods or real estate for a profit. A nontrading partnership is a business which provides services, such as a law partnership or an accounting partnership.

The law of limited partnerships will be dealt with in detail in Chapter 32.

CREATING A GENERAL PARTNERSHIP

The "association" requirement in Section 6 of the UPA means that for a partnership to exist there must be some sort of agreement among the persons involved in it. As is true under general contract law, however, this agreement may be express—either oral or written—or implied. Most courts would refuse to enforce, at least as between the partners themselves, an oral partnership agreement that was to last longer than one year. The Statute of Frauds might also be applicable where the partnership agreement called for the transfer of land, goods over $500, or miscellaneous intangibles over $5,000.

Intent. Although the parties' intent is certainly important in creating a partnership, it is not conclusive. If the parties wanted to create a partnership but left out one of the required elements, they did not form a partnership. Likewise, if the parties did not intend to create a partnership but in fact voluntarily entered into a relationship which contained all of the elements of a partnership, they become partners. No state action is required to form a partnership, though most states do require some sort of registration of the firm, at least where it is using a fictitious name. Failure to register under such a statute does not preclude a firm's existence, though it may prevent the firm from suing.

Estoppel. Section 16 of the UPA provides that persons who are not actual partners as to each other may be held liable to third parties as if they were partners where they have held themselves out as partners or where they have consented to having another hold them out as partners and where the third party has relied on such representations in making a decision to extend credit to the firm. Where the representation of partnership has been made publicly, no specific proof of reliance is required; reliance is assumed. Section 16 calls this sort of situation a "*partnership by estoppel.*"

The *Tralmer* case raises some of these issues.

TRALMER SALES AND SERVICE, INC. v. ERICKSON
521 N.W.2d 182 (WI App., 1994)

FACTS: Section 815.18, STATS., allows debtors to claim certain property as exempt from execution. This case involves a judgment creditor's challenge to the debtors' claim that property comes within the business property exemption.

The Ericksons own their home in Tomah, Wisconsin. In 1990, Sandra obtained a state permit to operate a bed and breakfast, the "Victoriana," in their home. Tralmer, a building contractor, provided home-improvement labor and materials to the Ericksons in 1990 and 1991. The Ericksons failed to pay the balance due Tralmer. In December 1991, Tralmer took judgment against them for $11,637.23. On March 1992, the county sheriff levied execution on goods in the Ericksons' home.

In April 1992, the Ericksons affirmatively claimed that all the items seized were exempt from execution, some as business property under § 815.18(3)(b), STATS, and the rest as consumer goods under § 815.18 (3)(d). They requested an appraisal of the property under § 815.19(1), STATS., and received it in June. In early July, they moved for an order, determining their right to the claimed exemptions.

While the judgment was still unsatisfied, Sandra sold and gave away some unseized property still in their possession. In late July, Tralmer moved the court to appoint a supplementary receiver to exercise control over the goods still in the Ericksons' possession and to prohibit them from amending the claim they had filed in April. In August, the Ericksons amended their claim of exemptions, asserting that some items they originally claimed as exempt consumer goods were actually exempt business property and some items they originally claimed as exempt business property were actually exempt consumer goods. The sheriff has not sold or disposed of the seized property.

Following hearings in September, the trial court: (1) concluded that the Ericksons were entitled to claim business property exemptions because the Victoriana was a business, (2) determined that some seized items were business property and the rest were consumer goods, (3) denied Tralmer's motion to prohibit the Ericksons from amending their claimed exemptions, (4) denied Tralmer's motion to appoint a receiver, and (5) required the Ericksons to designate and select their claimed exemptions within ten days of the last hearing. They did so, claiming as exempt $9,862.50 worth of consumer goods and $14,707.50 worth of business property. Tralmer appeals.

 JUSTICE GARTZKE:

We begin our discussion by acknowledging the legislature's charge to the courts in § 815.18(1), STATS.: "This section shall be construed to secure its full benefit to debtors and to advance the humane purpose of preserving to debtors and their dependents the means of obtaining a livelihood, the enjoyment of property necessary to sustain life and the opportunity to avoid becoming public charges."

The direction in § 815.18(1), STATS., is consistent with judicial decisions over the years requiring a liberal construction of the exemption laws in favor of the debtor....

Tralmer argues that if the Victoriana was a business, it was a partnership consisting of Sandra and Daniel, and therefore the Ericksons cannot claim business exemptions under § 815.18(3)(b).... Section 815.18(3)(b) allows a debtor to exempt up to $7,500 worth of business property used in the business of the "debtor." Section 815.18(2)(c) defines a debtor as "an individual;" the definition excludes a "partnership."

Because the exemption statute does not define a partnership, we look to ch. 178, STATS., the Uniform Partnership Act, for guidance. That act defines a partnership as "an association of two or more persons to carry on as co-owners a business for profit...." Case law establishes the elements the contracting parties must satisfy to create a partnership. The parties must: (1) intend to form a bona fide partnership and accept the accompanying legal requirements and duties, (2) have a community of interest in the capital employed, (3) have an equal voice in the partnership's management, and (4) share and distribute profits and losses.... If any of the four elements is not satisfied, the parties have not created a partnership.

Because it claims that a partnership exists, Tralmer bears the burden of proof.... Tralmer fails to meet its burden. It has not established the existence of the first element, that the Ericksons intended to create a partnership.

To establish the first element, Tralmer relies on Daniel's testimony that "[t]his is a partnership as it relates to a marriage; she and I lived in that house and we operated it on that basis." Tralmer also relies on Sandra's testimony:

Q. [You] ran this business as a partnership with your husband, did you not?

A. [We] were into it together just as we are in marri[age] that-in the partnership in that sense.

Q. All right. So it was a partnership between you and your husband, something the two of you engaged in together.

A. Yes, we did it together.

The trial court made no explicit finding that Daniel and Sandra used "partnership" simply to mean their marriage rather than a business organization. However, we may assume that the trial court decided the missing finding consistently with its order.... The court concluded that the Ericksons are entitled to claim property under the business exemption. Only a debtor can claim exemptions under § 815. 18, STATS., and, under § 815.18(2)(c), a partnership is not a debtor. We infer that the trial court concluded that Daniel and Sandra used "partnership" to mean their marriage.

Other evidence supports the trial court's implied finding that the Ericksons used "partnership" in its marriage sense. Their 1990 and 1991 tax returns describe the bed and breakfast as a sole proprietorship and name Sandra the sole proprietor....

Tralmer argues that even if the Ericksons did not create a partnership, they publicly held themselves out as a partnership and are therefore estopped under 178.13(1), STATS., from claiming otherwise. Tralmer claims that the Ericksons represented the Victoriana as a partnership by naming Sandra and Daniel as its hosts in advertising brochures....

Tralmer's estoppel claim fails. A party claiming partnership by statutory estoppel must prove the elements of estoppel.... Reliance is an element of estoppel under § 178.13(1), STATS. Tralmer did not establish that it relied on the Ericksons' advertising brochures when it extended credit to them.

Contents of Partnership Agreement. A **partnership agreement**, also called articles of partnership or articles of copartnership, should contain the basic provisions required to form a contract as a partnership agreement is in fact a contract. In addition to these basic provisions, there will usually be certain provisions which relate to the type of business and to special problems connected with the management of that particular business. For example, a considerable number of the provisions in the articles of partnership of a large law firm would not be found in the articles of partnership of a family manufacturing firm.

PARTNERS' MUTUAL RIGHTS AND DUTIES

Right to Participate in Management Decisions. In a general partnership, unless there is a specific agreement to the contrary, each partner has the right to participate in the partnership's management activities and management decisions. Each partner also has an equal vote with the other partners in the management and decision-making of the partnership. Here a partnership differs from a corporation, since in a corporation a stockholder will have votes for directors in proportion to ownership of stock, whereas in a partnership every partner has an equal voice and vote regardless of the amount of money or services the partner has contributed to the business.

With regard to day-to-day business decisions, it is not uncommon for partners to delegate certain decision-making authority to a managing partner. This partner will act as a general manager of the business. In a large law or accounting firm, for example, it is not possible for the partners to get together daily to make decisions on business matters. Typically the partners will meet on a regular basis to make policy and general management decisions other than the day-to-day decisions which are delegated to the managing partner. Usually a simple majority vote is needed on such matters. Certain types of decisions, however, require unanimous action of the partners. These include decisions involving an amendment of the original articles of partnership, the addition of a new partner, major changes in the business activities of the partnership, and any changes in the division of profits. Again, we must emphasize that a partnership is a contractual arrangement and that the partners may, if they so desire, provide in the partnership agreement that certain changes shall require only a majority vote, a two-thirds vote, a unanimous vote, and so on. Again, we emphasize the desirability of having specific provisions in the partnership agreement to cover these kinds of matters. Especially where there are only two partners, provisions should be included for deciding issues on which the partners are evenly divided.

Right to Share Profits and Duty to Share Losses. Generally speaking, each partner has a right to share in the profits of the partnership and is liable for its losses. The problem to be resolved is how much each partner's share is. If there is no agreement with regard to the sharing of profits, then the partners would share equally. However, it is best to have an agreement specifying a formula for sharing profits. This formula can be based on the various partners' contributions of capital and/or services.

If there is no specific agreement on the sharing of losses, then the partners will share losses in the same ratio as they share profits. However, if there is a formula for sharing losses, then that formula will be followed as between the partners. A partner with a large income from other sources might be willing to accept a larger allocation of losses, since such losses would be set off against the other income for tax purposes. Once determined, the profit-sharing ratio must be applied to all aspects of the firm's business. These rules are used in the *Frank* case.

FRANK v. BIRKY
817 P.2d 696 (Mont., 1991)

FACTS: On July 1, 1978, Lawrence Birky (appellant/defendant) and Alan Frank (respondent/plaintiff) entered into a written partnership agreement to engage in the general business of logging and related industries. The agreement provided in part that the initial capital of the partnership would be contributed equally, that individual capital accounts would be kept for each partner, and that in the event of termination the assets would be divided equally. In October 1983, Frank filed a complaint in the District Court alleging that Birky had breached the partnership agreement, requesting that the court dissolve the partnership and that the court award Frank his partnership share plus damages.

On October 21, 1985, the parties stipulated to bifurcate the trial; first to determine the scope of the partnership and then to resolve the issue of accounting and distribution. Judgment on the scope of the partnership was entered September 26, 1986. The partnership was determined to be composed of the following assets: 1976 Barko Loader mounted on a Kenworth truck complete with winch; 1978 Kenworth Truck and Trailer; 1978 450 Timberjack rubber-tire Skidder with chains, air compressor and fuel tank. The District Court found that the partnership was dissolved by mutual agreement in May 1983 and ordered that the above property be divided equally between the parties. For the second phase, a Special Master was appointed by the court to provide an accounting of the partnership property. During presentation of evidence to the Special Master a dispute arose concerning the court's order that the property be divided equally and whether Birky would be precluded from offering evidence of capital contributions. Birky was unable to provide books containing a record of individual capital accounts and admitted that such a record did not exist.

Thereafter the Special Master completed his findings and the District Court adopted the findings of the Special Master, which included the following distribution of the partnership property:

1. The Barko loader (sold by Birky for $42,000).
    $9,000 allowed to Birky for repairs necessary to promulgate the sale.
    $15,500 to Frank.
    $15,500 retained by Birky.

2. The Kenworth truck and trailer (sold for $42,000).
    $21,000 to Frank.
    $21,000 retained by Birky (including responsibility for collecting $6,000 owed by purchaser).

3. The Timberjack Skidder (Value of $40,000 at dissolution).
    $20,000 owed Frank by Birky who retained control and later sold.

4. Profits, wages and other compensation generated during the partnership. $22,325.00 owed Frank by Birky.

Birky believes the equal distribution of the assets as delineated above is inequitable in light of the evidence presented.

 JUSTICE MCDONOUGH::

First, appellant Birky contends that the court committed prejudicial error by ordering (in the absence of individual capital accounts on the partnership books) the capital contributions of the partners to be deemed equal.... Birky argues that by failing to remunerate him for his alleged capital contributions the District Court has circumvented the mandate of [the U.P.A.] Birky further argues that to ignore the capital contributions creates an inequitable distribution of the property which results in the unjust enrichment of Frank. A substantial portion of his alleged capital contributions would have to be proved by parol or extrinsic evidence....

Birky contends that the court abused its discretion by not allowing him to present evidence pertaining to his capital contributions other than the business records.

In the dissolution of a partnership and the sale and distribution of the partnership's assets, a partner against whom an action was brought and who failed to keep records [is] estopped from objecting to the court's finding of value of each party's contribution to the venture.... Here Birky kept the records of the partnership. We conclude that the court did not abuse its discretion in refusing to allow parol or extrinsic evidence to be presented by Birky in determining capital contributions.

The ultimate determination of capital contribution to the partnership is a question of fact to be determined by the District Court. Rule 52(a), M.R.Civ.P., requires that findings of facts be upheld unless they are found to be clearly erroneous....

The District Court stated that in deciding to deem the contributions equal in the absence of partnership records, consideration was given [to] "...the fact that the Defendant was primarily responsible for maintaining the books of the partnership, the passage of time, the confusing and incomplete evidence relating to this issue at the initial hearing and other factors."

There are ample facts in the record to support the District Court's finding that the capital contributions should be deemed equal. First, the partnership agreement itself clearly indicates that the contributions would be equal. Second, in the event that contributions were made they were to be documented in the capital accounts as part of the partnership records. As previously indicated, there were no such records. Third, the record of the proceeding before the District Court reflects evidence to support such a finding. The findings as supported above are not clearly erroneous and therefore cannot be set aside.

The appellant raises the additional claim that the manner in which the court provided the accounting and distribution of the partnership was inconsistent with the evidence on record. We disagree. Specifically, the appellant finds error with the District Court's reliance on expert testimony, the court's lack of consideration of draws taken by Frank, the court's lack of consideration of partnership obligations, and the court's valuation of the skidder. Each of these four related issues is a question of fact to be determined by the trial court....

Both parties had opportunity to present expert testimony and thereby opportunity to provide a manner for the court to calculate the value of wages and profits generated by the partnership. The appellant takes exception with the court's acceptance of Frank's experts' method. Both experts testified that it was difficult to impossible to accurately verify the partnership's expenses. The finder of fact weighs the evidence and we conclude the findings are not clearly erroneous and are therefore affirmed.

Lastly, appellant asks for review of the determination of the value of the skidder because he believes it was valued at an improper date. It is uncontested that the net value of assets is generally made at or near the time of dissolution.... The appellant argues that to follow the general rule achieves an inequitable result and that an exception should be made. Once again, decisions regarding valuation of partnership property will be overturned only if they are clearly erroneous. The decision of the court to adhere to the general rule is not clearly erroneous.

Affirmed.

Rights to Salary or Other Compensation. A partner is not, as a matter of right, entitled to a salary or to other compensation for the services he or she renders to the partnership. Absent an agreement that provides for salaries to the various partners, it is assumed that the partners have agreed to share the profits. Obviously, salaries would reduce the total profits. Thus, if salaries or other forms of compensation are contemplated, then a special agreement should be made with regard to these items. It is not uncommon for partners to be paid regular salaries, with profits then being distributed at the end of the calendar or fiscal year. No partner is entitled to receive secret profits, but only the agreed share.

Right to Inspect Partnership Books of Account. Each partner has the right to inspect the partnership books and to make copies of those books for his or her own records. The partnership books must be kept at the principal office of the partnership unless the partnership agreement specifies otherwise.

Rights in Partnership Property. Section 8 of the Uniform Partnership Act indicates that all property which is contributed when the partnership is formed and all property which the partnership later acquires by purchase or otherwise is considered partnership property and not the property of any individual partner. Whether a particular asset has been contributed to the firm is a question of fact. Partners may permit the firm to use their personal assets, as for example, space in a building or a vehicle or other piece of equipment. The name listed on the deed or other registration document is some evidence on this question, but certainly not conclusive, since firm assets are sometimes held in the name of one or more individual partners. The fact that the firm is paying taxes, insurance, and license fees on the asset is likewise not conclusive, since these are sometimes paid by the firm in place of a monthly rental to the partner-owner. If there is a specific agreement, either in the articles of partnership or elsewhere, that should nearly always control. In the absence of a specific agreement, the way the asset is treated in the firm's books is probably the best indicator of ownership.

Section 24 of the UPA says that a partner has three property rights in the firm: (1) rights as to specific pieces of the firm's property, (2) an "interest" in the firm, and (3) the right to participate in management. We have already discussed a partner's management rights. What about the other two of these "property rights"?

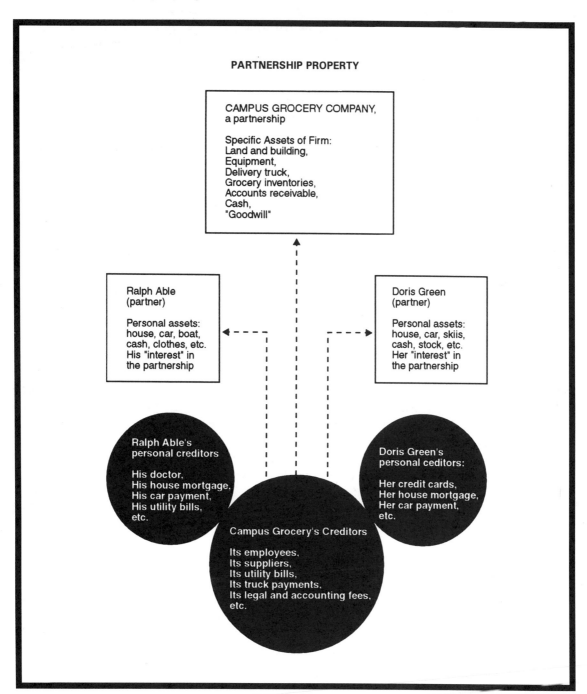

As to specific pieces of property owned by the firm, the partners are co-owners in a special form of joint ownership known as "tenancy in partnership." As defined in Section 25, this co-ownership gives each partner an equal right to possess and use the firm's assets for the firm's business. A partner has no right to make any personal use of the firm's assets for personal purposes. A partner would have to get the other partners' permission to take the firm's delivery truck on a camping trip, for instance. Further, this right to make business use of the firm's property is personal in each partner, and cannot be transferred to anyone else by an individual partner. Of course, the firm's rights of ownership of its assets can be sold to someone else by the firm. It's just that a single partner cannot *separately* transfer that person's individual right to use the asset as a partner. As a corollary to that rule, the personal creditor of an individual partner has no claim against any specific firm asset. Partnership assets, in other words, cannot be seized and sold to satisfy personal claims against individual partners. Partnership creditors can seize the firm's assets; creditors of the partners as individuals cannot do so.

When a partner dies, that partner's right in specific firm assets passes to the surviving partner or partners, for partnership purposes. When such a dissolution occurs, the firm will either be terminated or continued. In either case, the firm's assets will stay in the firm. There may be a pay-out to the estate of the deceased partner by the firm, as part of the process of settling up accounts, but the firm's assets as such do not pass directly into the deceased partner's estate.

What is being paid over to the deceased partner's estate is actually the third thing mentioned in UPA Section 24: the partner's "interest in the partnership." This phrase has a very precise, technical meaning in the UPA. It means a partner's "share of the profits and surplus." This right to receive money from the firm (profits and surplus) is an item of property owned by each partner as an individual. This claim against the firm for money can thus be voluntarily transferred, or assigned, by each partner, without the consent of the other partners. Likewise, this claim for money can be garnisheed by the creditor of an individual partner. *Neither a voluntary assignment nor a garnishment order ("charging order") automatically dissolves the firm.* In either case, the firm is free to continue its business; one partner's share of the profits is simply being paid to someone else. *That other person is not a partner, has no liability as a partner, and has no right to participate in management.* An assignee is not even entitled to receive periodic information on the firm's business or to inspect the books. Further, the assignee can ask for an accounting, if the firm is dissolved, only back to the time of the assignment. Where a court has entered a charging order against a partner's interest, the court can require any information from the firm that is necessary to make sure its order is being obeyed. Where the partner's interest is transferred either voluntarily or involuntarily, the transferee may petition a court for a dissolution. Such a petition could be filed at any time if the partnership is one at will. If the partnership agreement specified a duration, the transferee could petition for dissolution at the end of that period.

Right to Return of Capital Contributions. Section 18 of the Uniform Partnership Act provides that absent any agreement to the contrary among the partners, each partner shall be legally entitled to repayment of any capital contribution to the partnership. The repayment of capital contributions is considered a liability of the partnership. Unless otherwise agreed, a partner is not entitled to interest on a capital contribution. If, however, a partner contributes more than the required share, then the amount in excess of the required contribution will be treated as a loan, and interest will be paid on it.

Right to Repayment of Expenses. Each partner has a right to be indemnified for payments which he or she makes and personal liabilities which he or she reasonably incurs in the ordinary and proper conduct of the partnership business or in order to preserve the partnership business or its property.

Right to Decide Who Will be a Partner. No new partners may be admitted to a partnership without the consent of all present partners unless there is an agreed procedure to the contrary in the partnership agreement.

Duties of One Partner to the Other Partner. Each partner is an agent of the partnership and thus, in effect, an agent of every other partner in the partnership. As an agent, the partner has a fiduciary relationship with the partnership and with the other partners. This relationship carries with it a number of duties. Among these duties are the following:

1. A partner must be loyal to the partnership and to his or her partners. A partner may not conduct business that will conflict with the partnership unless he or she has the other partner's permission to do so.
2. A partner has a duty to account to the other partners.
3. A partner must use reasonable care in conducting partnership business.
4. If the activities in which a partner engages or the information which a partner has acquired may affect the partnership, the partner has a duty to keep the other partners advised of them.
5. A partner has a legal duty to abide by the terms of the partnership agreement.

LIABILITIES OF THE PARTNERSHIP

Contracts. Unless there is a contrary agreement, every partner in a general partnership is an agent of the partnership for the purpose of conducting the partnership's business. It is not uncommon for articles of partnership to limit or to restrict the agency power of the various partners. This is an agreement between the partners, and such internal limitations or restrictions among the partners themselves would not relieve the partnership of liability to a third person who dealt with a partner who exceeded them unless that third person knew that the partner was limited in his or her authority. Since, generally speaking, each partner is an agent of the partnership, the basic law of agency is applicable to the relationship between partners and third persons.

It is a general rule of agency that third persons who deal with an agent have the duty to ascertain the nature and the extent of the alleged agent's authority. Third persons cannot simply rely on a person's statement that he or she is an agent and has certain authority. In the case of a partnership, if a third person verifies that a person is a partner, then the third person has a right to believe that the partner-agent has the normal authority of a partner unless he or she is told otherwise. In other words, if a partnership is going to restrict or limit a partner's authority, then the partnership is responsible for notifying all persons who might be dealing with the partner-agent that the partner-agent does not have the full authority that would ordinarily be expected of a person in that capacity.

The partnership is also a principal and the individual partner an agent with regard to any information that the individual partnership may secure which relates to the partnership's business affairs. If a partner acquires certain information, then the partnership as the principal is automatically charged with the same information. It is also a general rule of agency that statements and representations made by an agent will bind the principal even though the statements may be untrue, provided the statements were made in the course of the agent's business for the principal and provided the statements were within the normally expected authority of such an agent.

Limitations on a Partner's Authority by Law. Since each partner is an agent of the partnership, it would seem that as long as a partner's acts or transactions are within the scope of the partnership business, then the partnership would be liable for the contracts made by a partner on behalf of the partnership. However, there are a number of legal limitations on the authority of individual partners to act for the partnership.

The first such limitation concerns a partner's right to act as an agent with regard to the purchase and conveyance of real estate. Section 10 of the Uniform Partnership Act deals with the right to convey real property owned by the partnership. Where the partnership holds title to real property in the partnership name, any partner may convey the title to that property by a deed executed in the partnership name by that partner as agent. However, if the other partners have not authorized the partner to make such a conveyance, then the partnership can recover the property from the persons to whom it was conveyed. An exception would be made to this right of the partnership to recover the property where the person to whom the conveyance was made transferred the title to an innocent third person who had no knowledge of the situation. Then the innocent third person would prevail over the partnership, provided there was not fraud in the transaction. Another exception would be made where certain acts or past practices of the partnership had created the apparent authority of the particular agent to convey the real estate.

The only safe way to purchase real estate from a partnership is to secure both a deed signed by one of the partners and a resolution signed by all of the partners which authorizes the sale of the real estate and also authorizes a specific partner to sign on behalf of the partnership.

Section 9(3) of the Uniform Partnership Act sets out these further restrictions:

Unless authorized by the other partners or unless they have abandoned the business, one or more but less than all the partners have no authority to: **(a)** assign the partnership property in trust for creditors or on the assignee's promise to pay the debts of the partnership, **(b)** dispose of the good-will of the business, **(c)** do any other act which would make it impossible to carry on the ordinary business of a partnership, **(d)** confess a judgment, and **(e)** submit a partnership claim or liability to arbitration or reference.

Section 9(4) of the UPA further confirms that no act of a partner in contravention of a restriction on the partner's authority shall bind the partnership to persons having knowledge of the restriction. Thus, as indicated previously, if there are so-called internal restrictions on the power and authority of a partnership's various agents and if those restrictions have been revealed to third persons, such third persons have no recourse against the partnership for the partner's unauthorized acts.

Authority to Hire and Fire Employees. Going back to the basic authority of the partner, as set out in Section 9 of the Uniform Partnership Act, every partner is an agent of the partnership for the purpose of its business. Every act of a partner, including the execution in the partnership name of any instrument apparently necessary for carrying on the business of the partnership in the usual way, binds the partnership, unless the partner has no authority to act for the partnership in that particular matter and the person with whom he is dealing knows of the lack of authority.

The articles of partnership could very well state that certain partners are charged with the duty of hiring and firing personnel and that the other partners have no direct authority to do so but have the right to be consulted on matters concerning the employment and tenure of personnel. For example, in a fifty-partner law or accounting firm, you could not have each and every partner hiring and firing as he or she saw fit. In a two- or three-member partnership, on the other hand, each of the partners may be involved in the hiring and firing of personnel.

Absent an agreement to the contrary between partners, each partner would have the authority to hire persons whose services were reasonably necessary to carry on the partnership business and the further authority to bind the partnership for a reasonable salary for such persons. Each partner would also have the right to dismiss any employee whose services he or she felt were not reasonably necessary to carry on the partnership business. One can immediately see the problems that could arise if such authority were exercised in a firm with a large number of partners. This is why some internal agreement between the partners should specify which partner or partners have the authority to hire and fire personnel and should restrict the other partners accordingly.

Borrowing Money and Mortgaging the Partnership Property. Going back to the general authority clause to which we referred briefly, any partner has the authority to borrow money and execute a mortgage on behalf of the partnership, provided this is done for the purpose of carrying on the partnership business in the usual way. The Uniform Partnership Act does not differentiate between the authority of an agent in a trading partnership and that of an agent in a nontrading partnership. However, in interpreting a partner's authority, courts in many jurisdictions have generally found that partners in a trading partnership which is engaged in buying and selling goods and property have greater implied and apparent authority to buy and sell property, to borrow in the partnership name, and to indorse or execute negotiable instruments in the partnership name if this is reasonably necessary to carry on the partnership business.

In partnerships that are considered to be engaged in a nontrading business, such as law firms or accounting firms, courts generally do not feel that individual partners should have the implied and apparent authority to borrow money or to execute or indorse negotiable instruments in the partnership name. Generally speaking, courts have held that the partners in nontrading partnerships do not have the authority to bind the partnership in such situations unless it was customary to do so in a given partnership or unless there was an actual necessity to do so. Thus trading partnerships are governed by standards different from the standards that govern partners in nontrading partnerships, insofar as their authority with relation to third parties is concerned.

Lawsuits Involving Partnerships. Under the common law, a partnership was not a legal entity, and therefore a partnership could not sue or be sued in the partnership name. If a third person wanted to sue a partnership, the complaint had to name all of the partners as individual defendants, and each partner had to be individually served with a summons. This could be accomplished without too much effort when dealing with simple father-son partnerships or three- or four-member partnerships. However, if it had to be done with a modern accounting firm having more than a hundred partners, not all of whom lived in the same jurisdiction, the chore could prove very frustrating. Many states have enacted statutes that allow a partnership to be sued as an entity by simply naming the partnership by its firm name. These statutes also allow a partnership to bring action as a legal entity against third persons. Most statutes, however, require that the partners be named as defendants and be served personally with process if this is at all possible. Most statutes also permit the petitioner to secure a judgment against the partnership if the petitioner served at least one of the partners even though several other partners were not served. In a case where the partnership entity was sued and at least one of the partners was named and served process, the judgment can be collected from the partnership assets. However, any judgment amount not collectible from the partnership assets cannot be collected from the individual partners unless the individual partners were sued, made a party to the law suit, and properly served with a summons.

Getting a judgment against a partnership is the first step. The next step is to collect it. Section 40(h) of the Uniform Partnership Act states: "When partnership property and the individual properties of the partners are in possession of a court for distribution, partnership creditors shall have priority on partnership property and separate creditors on individual property, saving the rights of lien or secured creditors as heretofore." In other words, lienholders and secured creditors come first; the partner's individual creditors for his or her individual bills come next; and then the balance can be taken for partnership debts. The new Bankruptcy Code which became law in October 1979 changes the law of distribution with regard to the assets of partners. It provides that in a case concerning a partnership, if the assets of the partnership are insufficient to satisfy the claims allowed, then each general partner in the partnership will be liable to the trustee in bankruptcy for the full amount of the deficiency. Thus, in the case of a bankrupt partnership the trustee in bankruptcy may now seek to recover the entire deficiency from any one of the general partners on a pro rata basis with the partner's personal creditors.

Torts. Section 13 of the Uniform Partnership Act provides that when a partner is acting in the ordinary course of the business of the partnership or is acting with the authority of the co-partners of the partnership, then if that partner commits a tort, the partnership will be liable for damages to the same extent that the partner committing the tort was liable. If, however, the injured person was another partner in the partnership, then the partnership would not be liable for the claims of the injured partner.

What if the person who committed the tort was not a partner, but was an employee of the partnership? The UPA does not specifically state that the partnership is liable for the torts of its employees. However, Section 4(3) of the UPA states that the law of agency shall apply under this act. Thus, the partnership is the employer and is liable for the tortious acts of its employees, provided the employee was acting within the scope of employment.

Section 15 of the Uniform Partnership Act provides that all partners are liable not only jointly but severally for any liability chargeable to the partnership under Section 13 of the UPA. Thus, if there are insufficient funds in the partnership to pay the damages resulting from the tort, then the partners may jointly pay for the loss. Or, if the partnership has no assets and one partner has personal assets and the others do not, that partner may be held severally liable for the entire loss. This should be a serious concern whenever you enter into a general partnership, as you could end up losing your personal assets, such as your home and your life savings, simply because of the negligence of some other person. This is one of the primary reasons that persons with individual assets over and above their investment in the business should consider being a limited partner in a limited partnership or forming a corporation. If there are unexpected tort losses, the most you as an investor will lose is your original investment, not your home and your life savings. It is, of course, recommended that the partnership carry liability insurance to cover tort losses. However, people sometimes forget to pay insurance policy premiums when due, and often the loss exceeds the policy limits.

Crimes. As previously stated, under the common law a partnership was not viewed as a legal entity, and it could not sue or be sued. Any legal action had to be taken by or against the individual partners. Thus, if the partnership was not a legal entity, it could neither commit nor be charged with a crime. Again, most states have now enacted statutes which allow a partnership to be sued as a legal entity by simply naming the partnership by its firm name. Many states have gone further and found that a partnership can be a legal entity for criminal purposes and can be guilty of a crime. The criminal penalty is simply a fine to be paid by the partnership from partnership funds. The nonacting partners normally could not be jailed for a crime committed by the partnership, particularly if the crime requires proof of a specific wrongful intent. If the partners are to be punished, they must be separately charged and have separate trials.

An individual partner who commits a crime while in the course of activities on behalf of and in the scope of the partnership will be criminally liable. But neither the partnership as an entity nor any other partner will be criminally liable unless the other partner or partners and/or the partnership participated in the criminal actions. For example, Jerry Jones is a partner in Jones and Son Construction. Jerry is discussing a construction bid with a client, and they get into a heated argument. Jerry, an ex-professional boxer now weighing 275 pounds, strikes the client in the face, breaking his glasses and injuring him. Jerry is arrested for criminal assault and battery. Neither the two other partners nor the partnership is guilty of any crime, although they could very likely be held liable in tort.

Let's change the facts. Say Jerry was hired as an "enforcer" to "convince" clients to accept the bids from Jones and Son Construction, and it was understood by the partners that Jerry would use force to get a desired result, a signed contract. In that case, the other partners would be found to be accessories to the criminal act and would be criminally liable.

Some of these issues are raised in the *Kansallis* case.

KANSALLIS FINANCE LTD. v. FERN
659 N.E.2d 731 (Mass., 1996)

FACTS: The United States Court of Appeals for the First Circuit has certified to this court, the following two questions of State law:

"**1.**   Under Massachusetts law, to find that a certain act is within the scope of a partnership for the purpose of applying the doctrine of vicarious liability, must a plaintiff show, inter alia, that the act was taken at least in part with the intent to serve or benefit the partnership?

"**2.**   May defendants be found vicariously liable for authorized conduct by their partner that violated Mass.Gen.L. ch. 93A, even if they were entirely unaware of and uninvolved with that conduct?"

The questions arise out of an appeal by Kansallis Finance Ltd. (plaintiff) from a trial in the United States District Court for the District of Massachusetts. The Court of Appeals stated that the first question concerns an issue on which an apparent conflict exists in Massachusetts precedent, and that the second question concerns a separate issue on which there is no controlling Massachusetts precedent.

Stephen Jones and the four defendants were law partners in Massachusetts when, in connection with a loan and lease financing transaction, the plaintiff sought and obtained an opinion letter from Jones. In the order of certification, the Court of Appeals states that the letter, executed in Massachusetts and issued on "Fern, Anderson, Donahue, Jones & Sabatt, P.A." letterhead, "contained several intentional misrepresentations concerning the transaction and was part of a conspiracy by Jones and others (though not any of the defendants here) to defraud Kansallis." Although Jones did not personally sign the letter, he arranged for a third party to do so, and both the District Court judge and the jury found that Jones adopted or ratified the issuance of the letter. Jones was later convicted on criminal charges for his part in the fraud, but the plaintiff was unable to collect its $880,000 loss from Jones or his coconspirators.

In an effort to recover its loss, the plaintiff brought suit in the United States District Court for the District of Massachusetts seeking compensation from Jones's law partners on the theory that the partners were liable for the damage caused by the fraudulent letter. Advancing the claim on essentially three grounds, the plaintiff asserted that defendants are liable for the letter because: (1) the defendants gave Jones apparent authority to issue the letter; (2) Jones acted within the scope of the partnership in issuing the letter; and (3) the issuance of the letter violated G.L.c. 93A, under which the partners are vicariously liable. The District Court submitted the first two common law claims to the jury and reserved the c. 93A count to itself. Both the judge and jury, for different reasons, decided that defendants were not liable for Jones's conduct. The Court of Appeals affirmed both the judge's and the jury's factual findings and certified two questions to this court in order to resolve the legal issues.

 JUDGE FRIED:

The parties have cited to us cases from this and other jurisdictions, as well as general principles set out in the Restatement (Second) of Agency and in the Uniform Partnership Act.... Whatever difficulties this array of authorities presents may in part be attributed to the fact that the issue of vicarious liability has engendered somewhat divergent formulations in the several different contexts in which it has arisen. The genus here is agency, and two of its species, for which there are special rules for determining vicarious liability, are partnership and master-servant.

In the context of a partnership, the person acting and the persons who might be held liable for his actions usually stand on an equal footing and may be thought of as equally implicated in a joint enterprise.... By contrast, the law of the vicarious liability of a master for the acts of his servant grew up in circumstances where the actor was often in a subordinate position and had a limited interest in the enterprise which he assists.... In the partnership context, while each partner is the agent of the partnership, he also stands in the role of a principal—a reciprocity that is lacking in the master-servant relation. Finally, there is an important practical distinction between determining vicarious liability for harms that come about through the victim's voluntary interactions with the purported agent—as in the case of contracts, of fraud and of misrepresentation—and those that are inflicted on a victim who has made no choice to deal with the agent, as in the case of an accident, an assault or a trespass. Only in the former instance is the inquiry into apparent authority particularly apt, since where the victim transacts business with the agent, the victim's ability to assess the agent's authority will bear on whether and in what ways he chooses to deal with him.... By contrast, where the victim has not chosen to deal with the agent by whose act he suffers harm—as in an automobile accident—the scope of employment seems the natural determinant of vicarious liability, and that is where the concept has had its most usual application....

Standing behind these diverse concepts of vicarious liability is a principle that helps to rationalize them. This is the principle that as between two innocent parties—the principal-master and the third party—the principal-master who for his own purposes places another in a position to do harm to a third party should bear the loss.... A principal who requires an agent to transact his business, and can only get that business done if third parties deal with the agent as if with the principal, cannot complain if the innocent third party suffers loss by reason of the agent's act. Similarly, the master who must put an instrument into his servant's hands in order to get his business done, must also bear the loss if the servant causes harm to a stranger in the use of that instrument as the business is transacted....

Accordingly, if we take the first certified question to ask whether a partner must necessarily at least in part act for the benefit of the partnership if the partnership is to be liable for his actions, the answer is "no." But the answer is "no" only because under our law—and the law of partnership and agency generally—there are two routes by which vicarious liability may be found. If the partner has apparent authority to do the act, that will be sufficient to ground vicarious liability, whether or not he acted to benefit the partnership. It is only where there is no apparent authority, which is what the jury found on the common law counts here, that there may yet be vicarious liability on the alternative ground requiring such an intent to benefit the partnership. Since there is no evidence that Jones was acting to benefit the partnership, the District Court's judgment for the defendants on the common law counts accords with our statutes and precedents. The jury instructions on the common law claims were correct.

The second question asks whether there must be a finding that the partners were at all aware of or involved in Jones's misconduct before they may be held liable to Jones's victim under G.L.c. 93A. This question raises a difficulty of a different order, because it arises under a statute...which was designed to offer broader and more comprehensive relief to victims of dishonesty than may be available at common law.... Accordingly, it is not surprising that neither the statutory language nor our cases suggest that vicarious liability under the statute is measured by any less comprehensive standards than those we have set out above in considering the common law cause of action. Plaintiffs point out for example that c. 93A recoveries are routinely had against corporate defendants, all of whom, of course, have been landed in liability by the acts—often not actually authorized—of their agents....

As G.L.c. 93A, S.1, defines "persons" subject to liability under S.11 to include both partnerships and corporations, the standard for determining liability under c. 93A is the same for both. Vicarious liability may be imposed by either of the two routes that we have set out above with respect to the common law cause of action. Neither route contains a requirement of awareness or personal involvement by the person held vicariously liable beyond that implicit in the two sets of rules themselves: (a) did the actor have apparent or actual authority for the acts on which liability is predicated, or (b) did the actor act within the scope of the partnership business with some intent to benefit the partnership. To the extent that either of these tests is met, there is liability under the statute.

Accordingly, the simple answer to the second question—whether a defendant may be vicariously liable under c.93A for conduct of which it was entirely unaware and with which it was entirely uninvolved—is "yes."

The statute does, however, by its terms make a distinction between cases where simple compensatory damages are paid to the plaintiff and where there are double or treble—that is, punitive—damages. In those latter cases, the statute requires that the court find that "the act or practice was a willful or knowing violation." Thus the Legislature envisaged multiple damage awards against those defendants with a higher degree of culpability than that sufficient to ground simple liability....

We must, however, approach this question with some caution, lest we unsettle a large body of accepted practice under c. 93A. As we have noted, the definition section of c. 93A equates partnerships to corporations and natural persons; and S.13 of the Uniform Partnership Act makes partnerships liable for penalties incurred by an errant partner. Moreover, our cases have routinely held corporations liable for multiple damages because of the knowing and wilful acts of their agents. Nevertheless, we are not persuaded that partners should automatically be equated to corporations for the purpose of assessing multiple damages for the knowing and wilful act of their agents. A corporation is an impersonal entity that can act only through agents, and so requiring some measure of personal culpability would exempt businesses operating in corporate form from multiple damages. Partnerships differ from corporations in that those held vicariously liable for multiple damages are often themselves natural persons, capable of personal culpability. It makes sense then to consider the partners' knowledge or wilfulness. Moreover, corporations exist in part just to insulate from and limit the liability of natural persons associated with them as investors, while partners are generally subject to unlimited personal liability....

There are few State courts which have addressed specifically the liability of innocent partners for penalties arising out of the fraudulent act of their copartner. Of the six States that have addressed this issue, Texas, Maryland, and Missouri hold innocent partners liable for punitive damages, and New Mexico, Indiana and Hawaii do not.

We acknowledge that to make such a distinction between corporations on the one hand and partnerships and perhaps other natural persons in the position of master or principal on the other engrafts on the statute a middle degree of responsibility, and we shall not lay out here a comprehensive set of rules to govern this heretofore unexplored territory. It is only in the course of further adjudication that the courts can develop a sensible approach to this freshly raised problem. Suffice it to say that the jury's finding that there was no apparent authority in this case, although the trial judge did not feel bound by it in reaching his own conclusions under c. 93A, might have some bearing on whether double or triple damages are appropriate....

To summarize, we hold that under the law of the Commonwealth a partnership may be liable by one of two routes for the unauthorized acts of a partner: if there is apparent authority, or if the partner acts within the scope of the partnership at least in part to benefit the partnership. Where there is neither apparent authority nor action intended at least in part to benefit the partnership, there cannot be vicarious liability. Accordingly, we answer the first question "no," but only because even if a partner acts with no purpose to benefit the partnership, vicarious liability may yet be appropriate, if he is clothed with apparent authority. In this case, however, the jury found that there was no apparent authority. We answer the second question "yes," but add that, while c. 93A permits a finding that an innocent and uninvolved partner may be vicariously liable for the acts of his partner, some further showing of culpability or involvement must be made to justify multiple damages.

Breach of Trust. As previously stated, each partner is an agent of the other partners. As such, each is responsible for the acts or omissions of the other partners, provided such acts or omissions are in the ordinary course of business of the partnership. If any partner acting in the course of the partnership business, or acting within the scope of apparent authority, receives money or property of a third person and misapplies it, or if the partnership has money or property in its custody and such money or property is misapplied by one of the partners, then in both situations the partnership is liable and must make good the loss.

DISSOLUTION, WINDING UP, AND TERMINATION

A partnership is based on a contract, which may be superseded by the parties' later actions. The firm may be dissolved by agreement of the partners, by acts of the partners, by a decree of court, or by operation of law. In the case of a partnership with a specific time span, it is dissolved at the end of the stipulated period of time. The partnership contract does, however, differ from many other contracts in that it concerns not only the contractual relationship between the parties to the contract but also the contractual relationship between the partnership and its various creditors. Thus, even though the partners may decide to dissolve their contractual relationship between themselves, the partnership is not really terminated until all of its debts are paid and all of its assets are distributed. This procedure is commonly called "winding up." Once the winding-up process has been completed, the partnership is considered terminated. Thus we have a three-step process: dissolution, winding up, and termination.

Dissolution is defined by Section 29 of the Uniform Partnership Act as "the change in the relation of the partners caused by any partner ceasing to be associated in the carrying on as distinguished from the winding up of the business." This change in relation can be voluntary or involuntary. An example of voluntary dissolution would be one in which the partners simply decide to end their relationship and go their separate ways. An example of involuntary dissolution would be one which occurred because a partner died or became mentally or physically incapacitated.

The key legal point to remember is that dissolution in itself does not terminate the partnership entity. Dissolution may trigger the next step; namely the winding-up process. During the winding-up process, the partnership agreement is still legally in force. However, the authority of each partner to act as an agent of the partnership has been legally terminated except as necessary to wind up partnership affairs.

By Agreement. The partners may decide to dissolve their partnership for various reasons. This decision must be unanimous unless the partnership agreement specifies otherwise. For example, the agreement could specify that only a majority vote of the partners is needed to dissolve the partnership. Remember, a partnership is a voluntary association, so it can be dissolved by voluntary agreement.

Acts of the Partners. Various actions by one or more partners may also cause dissolution.

1. **Withdrawal by a Partner.** If a partner withdraws from the business, that action causes a dissolution of the partnership. This does not necessarily mean that the business will have to be terminated. If the partnership agreement has been drawn with this problem in mind, it will contain provisions that give the remaining partners the right to buy the withdrawing partner's interest so that they can continue the business.

   Although a partner has the power to withdraw from the partnership for any reason that he or she may choose, the withdrawing partner may still be liable to the remaining partners for breach of contract. After all, the partnership agreement is a contract, and if its breach causes damage to the other contracting parties, then the violating party should be liable for such damages. Here again, a well-drawn partnership agreement should anticipate and provide a solution for such problems.

2. **Expulsion of a Partner.** Section 31(1)(d) of the Uniform Partnership Act states that a partnership is dissolved "by the expulsion of any partner from the business bona fide in accordance with such a power conferred by the agreement between the partners." Thus, if the agreement provides for the expulsion of a member under certain circumstances and the remaining partners exercise that power for good and valid cause, then the partnership is dissolved.

3. **Death of a Partner.** The Uniform Partnership Act, Section 31(4), states that the death of any partner will cause dissolution.

4. **Bankruptcy of a Partner.** The Uniform Partnership Act, Section 31(5), states that the bankruptcy of any partner will cause dissolution.

5. **Addition of a Partner.** The addition of a partner dissolves the partnership, technically, but in few situations would there be a winding up and termination.

6. **Assignment of a Partner's Interest for the Benefit of Creditors.** Under the old common law rule, the voluntary or involuntary sale or assignment of a partner's interest would have dissolved the partnership. Section 27 of the Uniform Partnership Act specifically provides that neither a voluntary nor an involuntary sale for the benefit of creditors automatically dissolves the partnership. The creditors will simply receive the profits which the partner would have received. If, however, a dissolution did occur, then the assignees would get the capital interest of the partner. A few states still follow the old common-law rule of automatic dissolution.

   As a general rule of law, a partnership is dissolved whenever its membership changes. When informed of this rule of law, the lay-person asks, "If this is true, then how do large law firm and accounting firm partnerships handle the problem, as they are constantly bringing in partners, retiring partners, and so forth?" The answer is that the partnership agreement of such firms specifies the procedure to be followed in case of expulsion, voluntary withdrawal, the addition, death, or retirement of a partner, or any other change in membership. In effect, the old partnership is technically dissolved and reorganized in accordance with the provisions of the agreement each time such a situation occurs.

Operation of Law. The Uniform Partnership Act, Section 31(3) states, "Dissolution is caused: By any event which makes it unlawful for the business of the partnership to be carried on or for the members to carry it on in the partnership." This simply means that if by either legislative enactment or a court decision the business that the partnership was carrying on is no longer legal, then the partnership is dissolved by operation of the law. To refer to Part II, Contracts, the partnership agreement is then an illegal bargain and therefore void. As an illustration, let's say that a partnership is operating a casino in Atlantic City and the gaming commission takes away its license or the gambling law is repealed, making gambling illegal. The partnership will then be dissolved by operation of law.

Court Decree. Often circumstances arise that require a court to determine whether or not a partnership should be dissolved. For example, if an affliction has caused a partner to be of unsound mind and incapable of handling the partnership's affairs, then a remaining partner may petition the court to order the dissolution of the partnership. A court determination might also be desirable if one of partners has become a drunkard or a drug addict and no longer assumes his or her share of the work and responsibility but refuses to dissolve the partnership voluntarily. Or, if fewer than the number of partners required for voluntary dissolution under the agreement will agree to dissolution, then the partners requesting dissolution may request that the court review the situation.

Expiration. A partnership may be created for a specified period of time, such as one, five, or ten years. When that period expires, the contract of partnership is dissolved.

After Dissolution. Dissolution does not change either the existing liability of the partnership or the existing liabilities of the individual partners. Dissolution may be likened to the death of an individual. The person dies, and then an administrator is appointed to settle the affairs of the deceased's estate. The administration of the deceased's estate is a process similar to the winding up process previously referred to.

The rights of the partners may be likened to the rights of the heirs of a deceased person's estate. The partners have a right to an accounting to see that their interests are being handled properly, and after all the debts have been paid, whatever is left is distributed to them.

All partnership creditors and all other persons who have any current relationship with the partnership should be notified of the dissolution immediately. If these persons are not notified and if they continue to deal with the business after dissolution, the partnership and the individual partners may be liable as if the transactions had occurred prior to dissolution. Thus, once the decision has been made to dissolve the partnership, or once an act of dissolution has occurred, or once a court decree of dissolution has been entered, the first step is to notify in writing everyone who could possibly be concerned with the dissolution and termination of the business.

There are different liability rules for withdrawing and incoming partners. The withdrawing partner remains fully personally liable for all debts of the firm which were incurred prior to withdrawal. Even if there is an agreement that the continuing partners will pay off all existing liabilities without any further contribution from the withdrawing partner, the third-party creditors are not bound by such agreement. Third-party creditors of the firm can, if necessary, impose full personal liability on any person who was a member of the firm when the debt was incurred. To avoid such continuing liability, the withdrawing partner would have to get the agreement of the third-party creditors of the firm. Notice of dissolution, in other words, does not terminate *existing* liabilities; it merely avoids additional *future* liabilities.

The incoming partner will, of course, assume full personal liability for all debts of the firm incurred after becoming a member. As to preexisting debts of the firm, the incoming partner is liable only to the extent of any capital contribution. Here again, if the firm's creditors wanted to have the new partner assume full liability for preexisting debts, a specific agreement to that effect would be necessary.

Winding Up. Winding up, the second step in ending a partnership, is the process of liquidating the partnership assets, that is, selling the real and personal property the partnership owned, collecting any outstanding accounts, paying any outstanding debts, and closing out any loose ends of the business— cancelling orders not yet delivered, canceling any lease or rental agreements, terminating any relationships that the partnership may have had with persons who were not partners, and so on.

After all the outstanding accounts have been collected, all the assets have been turned into cash, and all the outstanding bills and claims against the partnership have been paid and settled, then any cash remaining has to be divided among the partners. First, if any of the partners have loaned money to the partnership, those loans are repaid with whatever interest was agreed on. Next, the partners will be given back their initial investment. Finally, if there is still some cash left, it will be divided among the partners as profits, and the distribution will be in the same proportions as the distribution of profits in the past and in accordance with the proportions set out in the partnership agreement.

The preceding discussion of the dissolution assumes that the assets of the partnership exceed its outstanding debts. This, of course, is not always the situation of a dissolved partnership which is in the process of winding up. If the assets are insufficient to pay its debts, then the personal assets of the various partners may be called upon to pay them. It must be noted, however, that the personal creditors of an individual partner with personal debts may have priority over creditors who are attempting to collect partnership debts from that partner. If a bankruptcy proceeding is instituted, both groups of creditors will have equal priority against a partner's personal assets, as previously noted.

The Uniform Partnership Act, Section 35(1)(a), allows a partner to do "any act appropriate for winding up partnership affairs or completing transactions unfinished at dissolution." Thus, the winding up can be done by any of the partners, or by a partner whom the other partners designate as the winding up partner, or by an outsider who is appointed as a receiver for the purpose of winding up the partnership and making the final distribution of its assets. Where one partner has wrongfully caused the dissolution, the other partners have the right to do the winding up.

Continuing the Business. As indicated previously, the dissolution of a partnership does not automatically mean the termination of its business. Among the common situations that cause dissolution are the death or withdrawal of a partner. In such cases the remaining partners do not necessarily want to terminate the business. Winding-up in such situations will simply be an internal process of buying out the interest of the deceased or withdrawing partner and of making appropriate bookkeeping changes for the reorganization and continued operation of the business. Creditors and persons dealing with the firm may not even know that any changes were made when a partnership has been legally dissolved by death of one of the partners. However, if a partner withdraws from the firm, it is wise to so notify all creditors and all persons and firms that deal with the partnership.

Remember, in a general partnership each partner is an agent of the partnership. While dissolution terminates that relationship as between the partners, people who have been doing business with the partnership will not know that the person who has withdrawn is no longer a partner. Until such third parties are notified otherwise, the partnership may be liable for certain acts and dealings of the former partner. Thus, even though the business is to continue after dissolution, it is still necessary to give proper notification of the dissolution to all creditors and all persons who might be dealing with the continuing business.

The *Gull* case focuses on the rights of the withdrawing partner.

GULL v. VAN EPPS
517 N.W.2d 531 (WI App., 1994)

FACTS: Jerome E. Gull, Ruth E. Van Epps, and David L. Berth practiced law in an at-will partnership from January 1, 1984, until Gull withdrew effective December 31, 1987. Gull continued to serve his clients in the partnership offices until February 19, 1988, when he opened his own office in the same city. He took with him his clients and his files.

Despite serious attempts, the parties were unable to wind up the affairs of the partnership. Gull began this action for an accounting December 11, 1990. On December 10, 1991, during trial, the parties stipulated to Gull's share of the accounts receivable and the furniture, furnishings and library. However, the parties were unable to settle Gull's claim that he is entitled to his customary percentage of the "profits" of the partnership earned during the wind-up period, January 1, 1988 to December 10, 1991.

On December 23, 1992, the trial court entered judgment in favor of Gull according to the stipulation. However, the court denied Gull's claim for any share of the fees earned by Van Epps and Werth during the wind-up period. The court concluded that it would be unethical fee-splitting for Van Epps and Werth to share such fees with Gull.

 JUDGE SUNDBY:

We first address the fee-splitting issue. Van Epps and Berth cite Wisconsin Supreme Court Rule 20:1.5(e) (Callaghan 1994) which provides in part: "A division of fees between lawyers *who are not in the same firm* may be made only if: ..." (Emphasis added.) None of the enumerated exceptions apply here.

Section 178.25(2), STATS., of the Uniform Partnership Act, provides: "On dissolution the partnership is not terminated, but continues until the winding up of partnership affairs is completed." After Gull's withdrawal, the partnership was dissolved, but until its affairs were wound up, the partnership remained intact for that purpose. Supreme Court Rule 20:1.5(e) does not apply to the division of fees concluding the affairs of the partnership because, until that process is completed, the lawyers are in the same firm. We recognize that winding up the affairs of a law partnership involves non-economic responsibilities which the partners have to their clients. The discharge of those responsibilities does not present issues in this appeal.

We next consider Gull's claim that he consented to the continuation of the partnership and therefore ... he may elect to share in the "profits" of the partnership earned after dissolution. We construe his claim to extend to fees earned by Van Epps and Werth on new work contracted for and performed during wind-up....

While fees from new work normally do not belong to a dissolved partnership, ... all partners of the dissolved firm are generally entitled to share in fees for predissolution work in progress earned after dissolution, even if the client has exercised a right to discharge the attorney or attorneys who are sharing in the fees.... The dissolution of a partnership operates only with respect to future transactions; the partnership continues as to all existing matters until they are terminated.... On dissolution, the partnership remains in existence for the purpose of performing existing executory contracts.... The partnership entity continues in existence after dissolution until termination.... Until termination of the partnership, the interests of the partners in partnership assets, profits, liabilities and losses do not change....

Perhaps the most difficult problem with regard to completion of work in progress concerns compensation for the partner who must complete the work.... Section 178.15(6), STATS., and U.P.A. § 18(F) (1914) provide: "No partner is entitled to remuneration for acting in the partnership business, except that a surviving partner is entitled to reasonable compensation for his services in winding up the partnership affairs." Section 178.15(6) allows extra compensation only when the partnership is dissolved due to the death of a partner and there is a surviving partner. It appears to be the rule in inter vivos cases—those in which a partner retires or withdraws—that the partner who completes work in progress is not entitled to any compensation beyond the fee he or she would have received for that work had the partnership not dissolved.... However, the former partners of a dissolved law firm are entitled to reasonable overhead expenses, excluding partners' salaries, attributable to the production of postdissolution partnership income....

We therefore conclude that during wind-up, net fees from work in progress by Van Epps, Werth and Gull constitute an asset of the partnership and shall be allocated to each partner according to the partnership formula without any additional compensation to any partner.

When law partners cannot agree as to how the affairs of the law partnership are to be wound up, judicial resources in accomplishing wind-up may be considerably strained, depending on the size of the partnership and the nature of the partnership's practice. Fortunately, the trial court has broad discretion to accomplish a fair accounting between the parties because an action for the dissolution of a partnership and the liquidation of its affairs is a proceeding in equity.... We affirm the portion of the judgment based upon the parties' stipulation and reverse the judgment as to Gull's claim to fees earned during the wind-up, and remand for the trial court to apply ch. 178, STATS, and its equitable powers to complete the wind-up of the affairs of this law partnership.

SIGNIFICANCE OF THIS CHAPTER

The partnership is still the most simple and most commonly used form of business organization for small businesses. It is, therefore, important for the future business person to know what a partnership is, how a partnership is created, and how it can be terminated, either by some intentional act of the partners or some unexpected event such as death of a partner.

Once a partnership is created and begins transacting business, many problems regarding day-to-day operation may arise. It becomes important to know what each partner's rights and duties are. This chapter sets out the partners' rights and duties in managing the business, to each other, and also to third persons.

PROBLEMS FOR DISCUSSION

1. C.N. Stroud and Earl Freeman were equal partners in a grocery business known as Stroud's Food Center. During 1992, 1993, and 1994, the plaintiff regularly sold bread to the store. Several months prior to February 1995, Stroud told one of the plaintiff's agents that he did not want any more of its bread in the store and that he would not be personally responsible for any more bread purchases from it. From February 6 through February 25, 1995, the plaintiff sold $171.04 worth of bread to the store through this agent. The partnership was dissolved and Stroud took over the business and paid off all of its existing debts ($12,014.45) except for "his" half of the bread bill, $85.52. The plaintiff recovered a judgment for $171.04, and Stroud appealed.

   Was the trial court correct? Discuss.

2. Ellingson was the receiver of the landlord; the suit was to enforce a lease executed by a partnership. Barneson, one of the partners, disputed his personal liability on the lease because it was executed by the firm before he became a member. After Barneson became a general partner in the firm, it subleased the premises in question for a time, collected rent from the sublessee, and paid its own rent to the landlord. The firm owed $2,374.13 for the period from March 1, 1992 to January 25, 1993. The trial court judgment imposed full liability on Barneson along with the other general partners.

   Does Barneson have a basis for an appeal? Why or why not?

3. Daniel Phillips and Isadore Harris were equal partners in a business known as Dan's Used Cars. Neither of them owned a personal car. They had agreed that Harris would use the firm's cars for transportation to and from home. He could demonstrate and sell such cars, and they had "for sale" signs placed in them at various times. He could also use such cars to visit other dealerships and buy cars for the firm's inventory and to stop at the Department of Motor Vehicles so that necessary paperwork could be done for the firm's business. On January 7, while driving one of the firm's cars, Harris hit a car driven by Smith, which in turn hit a car driven by Dolores Cook. Harris was on his way home at the time. About a week later, the partnership was terminated. Dolores and her husband, Marshall, sued the partnership and received a judgment. Phillips appealed.

   Is Phillips liable? Explain.

4. Amerco got a judgment against Jerry Bohonus, who was acting as his own attorney. The trial court ruled that his attempt to appeal from the summary judgment was not timely, and granted Amerco's request for a charging order against Bohonus's interest in a partnership. As part of that process, the trial court ordered a sale of Bohonus's interest in the assets of the partnership, which included a liquor license. The sheriff proceeded with the sale. Bohonus appeals,

    What result, and why?

5. Anna Reid began this action against Haley and her two other partners, alleging that she had dissolved the firm and asking for a distribution of assets. Reid died after the lawsuit was commenced, and her executors were substituted as plaintiffs. Reid had written a letter to her partners, which stated in part: "I hereby notify you that I am terminating the partnership...." Meetings were held, but the partners were unable to agree on a plan for liquidation or on the respective rights of the partners. At that point, Reid started this lawsuit. The partnership agreement gave the surviving partners the right to purchase the interest of a deceased partner, but it contained no such provision in the event that a partner dropped out voluntarily. The chancellor held that Reid's letter did not dissolve the firm but that her death did. He also held that the other partners could exercise their buy-out option by paying her estate $29,165.48 plus Reid's 70 percent of the income up to dissolution. Reid's executors appealed.

    How should the appeals court rule? Discuss.

Chapter 32
Limited Partnerships and Other Organizational Forms

LIMITED PARTNERSHIPS

A limited partnership differs from a general partnership in two major respects. First, a limited partnership allows certain partners to have limited liability for the debts and other liabilities of the partnership. Second, a general partnership may be formed by an express oral or written agreement or by an implied agreement, whereas a limited partnership agreement must be in writing, must conform to the statutory requirements for the formation of such a partnership, and must receive state approval.

Statutes. The National Conference of Commissioners on Uniform State Laws, after finding that limited partnership laws varied from state to state, recognized the need for uniformity. In 1916, the commissioners drafted the Uniform Limited Partnership Act. This act was adopted by every state except Louisiana, which has its own limited partnership law.

In 1976, the commissioners revised the Uniform Limited Partnership Act. Nearly all states have adopted the revised act, but it is still important to note what state is involved and whether the new act or the old act is the effective statutory law in that state. Our primary focus in this chapter will be the Revised Uniform Limited Partnership Act (RULPA), and the available alternatives to the limited partnership.

Use. Limited partnerships have become a very popular form of business organization for persons who wish to invest but want limited liability, and who also wish to have their profits treated as partnership profits and not as corporate profits subject to the corporate income tax. There is no income tax on the profits of a limited partnership. The partners divide the profits in accordance with the partnership agreement. The partnership files with the Internal Revenue Service a partnership return which is merely an informational return. The individual partner's profit is then shown on his or her income tax return, and the individual pays tax on that profit along with the tax on his or her other income. The limited partnership form of business organization is found mostly in so-called tax shelter ventures, such as land development organizations, oil exploration ventures, and cattle feeding ventures.

Definition. Section 101(7) of the Revised Uniform Limited Partnership Act (RULPA) defines a limited partnership as a "partnership formed by two or more persons ... having as members one or more general partners and one or more limited partners." Thus, each limited partnership must have at least one general partner with unlimited liability for the business of the partnership and at least one partner with limited liability. The limited partner, like a stockholder in a corporation, cannot be liable for more than his or her investment. However, unlike the corporation stockholder, who has a voice in the control of the business through votes for directors based on the number of shares owned, the limited partner has no voice in the control of the business. In fact, a limited partner who does take a part in the management or control of the business may be held personally liable for the firm's debts. Thus, if a limited partner wants to retain complete limited liability, he or she should not become involved in any way in the operation of the business.

Under RULPA, a limited partner who acts substantially like a general partner is liable as a general partner to all the firm's creditors. But if the limited partner merely participates in control, he or she has full liability only to those third parties with actual knowledge of that participation.

Creation. A limited partnership certificate must be prepared. This certificate must state the name of the limited partnership—for example, Wildcat Oil Exploration Associates, Ltd. If the Revised Uniform Limited Partnership Act of 1976 has been adopted by the state where the limited partnership is being formed, then the name of the limited partnership would have to be Wildcat Oil Exploration Associates, Limited Partnership. In other words, the letters *Ltd.* are no longer allowed since many consumers do not know what *Ltd.* means. If the words *Limited Partnership* are written out in full, the public should be aware of the limited liability of some partners.

Next, the certificate must state the purpose of the limited partnership. In this case the purpose would be to conduct oil explorations in the state of Texas. The principal place of business of the limited partnership, the names and addresses of each general and limited partner, the duration of the partnership, and the amount of the contribution that is to be received from each partner must also be stated. Other requirements include a statement as to whether additional partners can be admitted to the partnership and whether the limited partners may sell and assign their interests to other persons. The limited partnership certificate must be filed and recorded in a designated office such as the office of the county recorder or the county clerk in the county where the principal office is located. This filing gives persons who deal with the limited partnership public notice as to the items of information that are provided on the certificate of limited partnership. In most states it is also necessary to file the limited partnership certificate with a state authority such as the secretary of state's office.

Once the limited partnership certificate has been filed and recorded, the limited partnership may proceed to do business. If the statutory requirements were properly adhered to, the limited partners should be free from liability beyond their investment. However, the partners may desire to draft more detailed articles of partnership in order to provide for matters not considered in the limited partnership certificate.

Defective Formation. What happens if the business associates fail to comply with the required procedures for becoming a limited partnership? Of course, any of them who are doing anything knowingly, with fraudulent intent, would be fully liable personally for all claims against the firm. But suppose one or more of the associates is acting in good faith, assuming that he or she is a limited partner, when in fact the statutory requirements have not been met. What happens to those good faith investors?

Potentially, each investor in the business would have full, unlimited personal liability for all the debts of the business. If they have failed to achieve the status of a limited partnership, they must then be general partners in a general partnership. They meet all the definitional elements as a partnership, so they will be held liable as general partners. Recognizing that this result is potentially unfair to an investor who acts in good faith, the old Uniform Limited Partnership Act (ULPA) included an "escape hatch" in Section 11. Such an investor is not held personally liable if he or she promptly renounces any interest in the profits of the business as soon as the mistake is discovered.

The Revised ULPA gives an investor a choice. When he or she discovers the mistake, he or she can either withdraw from future equity participation in the firm, or file a proper limited partnership certificate or an amendment, to correct the error. This rule is probably more fair to the investor, since it would permit the firm to proceed as planned once the correction was made. RULPA does provide, however, that such an investor continues to be fully personally liable to persons who thought the investor was a general partner before the correction was made.

General Partners' Rights and Duties. The general partner or partners have essentially the same rights and duties as any partner in a general partnership insofar as the partnership's day-to-day business operations are concerned. There is, however, one difference. Such partners cannot, on their own, take in other general partners or other limited partners unless this right has been granted to them in the limited partnership certificate.

The *Bennett* case examines the nature of a "managing" partner's fiduciary duties.

MATTER OF BENNETT
989 F.2d 779 (5th Cir., 1993)

FACTS: This appeal arises out of an adversary proceeding in a bankruptcy case, in which the bankruptcy court entered an order granting a discharge to the Appellee, Archie Bennett, Jr., over the objection of the Appellants that certain of Mr. Bennett's debts were not dischargeable. In support of their argument, the Appellants rely solely on 11 U.S.C. § 523(a)(4), which provides that debts resulting from a defalcation by the debtor while acting in a fiduciary capacity are not dischargeable in bankruptcy. This Court must decide whether Bennett, as the managing partner of the managing partner of the limited partnership, owed a sufficient fiduciary duty to the limited partners to satisfy the strict requirements of 11 U.S.C. § 523(a)(4). This is a case of first impression in this Circuit.

In approximately March of 1980, Bennett and the Appellants formed a Texas limited partnership known as Mariner/Greenspoint, Ltd. ("MG"). The Appellants in this case are and were at all relevant times, limited partners of MG. The sole general partner of MG was another limited partnership, known as Mariner Interest No. 20, Ltd. ("No. 20"). The sole general partner of No. 20 was the Appellee, Archie Bennett, Jr.

Under the terms of the MG partnership agreement, the general partner, No. 20, was charged with management of the partnership and had full, exclusive, and complete authority and discretion to manage, control, and make all decisions affecting the purposes of the partnership and to take any action required to effectuate the purpose of the partnership. Bennett, as the sole general partner of No. 20, was the only individual with the power or authority to direct the affairs of No. 20 and MG, and was prohibited by the MG partnership agreement from voluntarily withdrawing as the general partner of No. 20.

The purpose of the MG partnership was to construct and operate a Marriott hotel near the Greenspoint Mall in Houston, Texas. The partnership obtained $22 million in capital contributions and loans, to cover the cost of constructing the hotel. The MG partnership agreement required the general partner to contribute cash, as necessary, for the costs of constructing, equipping, and furnishing the hotel, to the extent such costs exceeded the $22 million previously raised. As an incentive, the agreement also provided that the general partner was eligible to receive a cash distribution of up to $4 million if the project was completed for less than the projected $22 million. However, prior to taking any distribution for savings in the construction of the hotel, the general partner was required both to construct the hotel and to provide all equipment necessary so that it could operate as a "first-class hotel."

At some point early on in the business venture, Bennett retained a corporation, known as Mariner Corporation, to perform his duties as the general partner of No. 20 and, in turn, its duties as general partner of MG. Mariner Corporation was 100 percent owned by Bennett. The officers and employees of Mariner Corporation acted on Bennett's behalf in performing their duties and were aware that, if the project was completed under budget, the savings would be paid directly to Bennett.

Mariner Corporation obtained bids for the construction of the hotel from a number of general contractors. All of the bids initially submitted were at least $1 million over the budgeted amount of $22 million. After these bids were received, Mariner Corporation entered into negotiations with one of the contractors, Eaves Construction. Subsequently, Eaves dropped its bid price by $1 million and was awarded the contract. Eaves was not able to obtain a bond on the project, however, due to its lack of financial strength and lack of a sufficient track record on large projects. Bennett told Eaves that it could have the job without a bond, if it reduced its general contractor's fee by one-half. Eaves agreed and reduced its fee by an additional $250,000.

The hotel was completed on time, and opened in January of 1981. At that time Bennett made a $1 million distribution to himself, for completing the project for less than the budgeted $22 million.

Subsequently, several problems with the hotel came to light. First, in approximately April of 1981, mildew began to occur in the guest rooms of the hotel. This mildew was evidently caused by a "negative pressure" problem, which in turn was caused by the design of the heating, ventilation, and air conditioning (HVAC) system in the hotel. As a result of the mildew problem, virtually all of the guest rooms in the hotel had to be revinyled and resheetrocked twice, during 1981 and 1982.

The bankruptcy court found that the mildew problem at the hotel was a continuous construction problem that the general partner had an obligation to fix and pay for under the terms of the MG partnership agreement. The court found that the first round of repairs was performed at the expense of the general contractor. The second round, however, was charged, by the general partner, to the partnership earnings. The limited partners' share of this cost was $72,000.

The bankruptcy court also reviewed numerous equipment leases that were entered into by the general partner for the purpose of providing various types of equipment to the hotel. The court found that, under the partnership agreement, the general partner had an obligation to equip and furnish the hotel with the $22 million budgeted amount. The court found, with respect to some but not all of these leases, that the general partner had charged them to the partnership, instead of paying for them out of the construction budget. The court also found that Bennett had failed to properly disclose these leases to the limited partners, or to obtain their approval for them. The court determined that the amount wrongfully charged to the limited partners for these equipment leases was $832,204.40.

The bankruptcy court concluded that the misapplication of partnership funds to pay for the mildew repairs and the equipment leases described above were the result of defalcations by the general partner of MG in the total amount of $904,204.40. The court also found that No. 20, as the sole general partner of MG, was a fiduciary to the limited partners of MG, for purposes of Section 523(a)(4). The bankruptcy court noted that while Texas courts have not extended the partnership relationship generally to encompass the type of fiduciary duty envisioned by Section 523(a)(4), an exception exists for the managing partner of a partnership, who owes to his co-partners, "one of the highest fiduciary duties recognized in law."

The bankruptcy court also found, however, that Bennett, as the general partner of the general partner, did not owe a fiduciary duty to the limited partners of MG.

The district court, in a brief opinion, affirmed the order of the bankruptcy court granting a discharge to Bennett.

 JUDGE PRADO:

The first issue that we address is whether the scope of the fiduciary duty owed by the managing general partner of a limited partnership to the limited partners is sufficient to meet the narrow requirements of Section 523(a)(4). Next, we must decide if such a duty also applies to the managing partner of the managing partner.

A number of courts have addressed the issue of whether a partner generally owes the type of fiduciary duty contemplated by Section 523(a)(4) to his co-partners. The courts are split on this issue with approximately half finding that such a fiduciary duty is owed, and the other half finding that it is not....

In determining whether a particular debtor was acting in a fiduciary capacity for purposes of Section 523(a)(4), the Court must look to both state and federal law.

The scope of the concept of fiduciary under 11 U.S.C. § 523(a)(4) is a question of federal law; however, state law is important in determining whether or not a trust obligation exists....

The controlling law in this case is Texas law. Therefore, this Court must look to Texas law in order to determine what obligations are imposed on the managing general partner of a limited partnership with respect to the limited partners. The Court must then decide whether the obligations imposed under state law are sufficient to meet the federal law requirements of "fiduciary capacity" under Section 523(a)(4)....

Significantly, the specific duties imposed by the Texas courts on managing partners pursuant to this line of cases are the same as those imposed on trustees. They include the duty of loyalty ... and the duty to "deal with one another with the utmost good faith and most scrupulous honesty...." As the court in *Crenshaw* stated, when a general partner is in complete control of the assets and affairs of a limited partnership:

> [His] conduct must be measured by standards exacting the utmost fidelity.... Not only is it [the general partner's] duty to administer the partnership affairs solely for the benefit of the partnership, he is not permitted to place himself in a position where it would be for his own benefit to violate this duty....

We find, as the Ninth Circuit did in *Ragsdale*, that these obligations are more than a fiduciary relationship created in response to some wrongdoing. Texas law clearly and expressly imposes trust obligations on managing partners of limited partnerships and these obligations are sufficient to meet the narrow requirements of Section 523(a)(4).

However, this is only the first step in the analysis, because it is undisputed that Bennett was not the managing partner of MG. He was instead, the managing partner *of the managing partner* of MG. Therefore, this Court must now address the more difficult question of whether Texas law imposes these same trust-type obligations on the managing partner in a two-tiered partnership arrangement (i.e., the managing partner of the managing partner)....

In reviewing the line of cases that gave rise to the rule in Texas that the managing partner of a partnership owes to his copartners the highest fiduciary obligations known at law, it is clear that the issue of control has always been the critical fact looked to by the courts in imposing this high level of responsibility....

[I]n *Meinhard v. Salmon*, a case cited extensively in Texas and elsewhere for establishing the fundamental fiduciary duty rules governing managing partners, Justice Cardozo focused on the control that one "coadventurer" exercised over the business enterprise at issue:

> The very fact that Salmon was in control with exclusive powers of direction charged him the more obviously with the duty of disclosure....

The court observed: [T]here may be no abuse of special opportunities growing out of a special trust as manager or agent.... Salmon had put himself in a position in which thought of self was to be renounced, however hard the abnegation. He was much more than a coadventurer. He was a managing coadventurer. For him and for those like him the rule of undivided loyalty is relentless and supreme....

Therefore, again in the *Meinhard* case the fact of control or management is vital to the court's analysis....

The *Crenshaw* court, analyzing the issue in a manner consistent with the way in which Texas jurisprudence has developed in this area, concluded that ... the managing partner of the managing partner of the limited partnership, owed to the limited partners the highest fiduciary duty known at law, a duty analogous to that owed by a trustee to the beneficiaries of the trust.... Therefore, based on the holding in *Crenshaw* and the cases cited therein, we find that Bennett, as the managing partner of the managing partner, owed to the MG limited partners "the highest fiduciary duty recognized in the law." We find further that this fiduciary obligation is sufficient to meet the requirement of Section 523(a)(4)....

In conclusion, we find that the question of the nondischargeability of Bennett's debts to the limited partners under 11 U.S.C. § 523(a)(4) was wrongly decided. We therefore reverse the decisions of the bankruptcy and district courts on that issue and render judgment in favor of the limited partners in the amount of $1,904,204.40.

Limited Partners' Rights and Duties. Basically the limited partner has no specific duties. He or she is simply an investor. However, Section 305 of the Revised Uniform Limited Partnership Act gives the limited partner the right to inspect and copy the partnership certificate, list of partners, tax returns, and partnership agreement. The limited partner also has the right to demand full information on all matters affecting the partnership. Thus, the limited partner may not have a voice as such in the management of the limited partnership, but he or she need not stand by and watch as fraudulent or wasteful acts are being committed by the general partner. In addition, a limited partner may petition a court of proper jurisdiction to have a dissolution and winding up of the limited partnership. If that occurs, the limited partner is entitled to receive a share of the profits as income and may also be entitled to have his or her contribution returned in accordance with the limited partnership certificate, subject of course to any exceptions under local law. As an alternative to a lawsuit for dissolution, RULPA permits a limited partner to bring a derivative suit for damages on behalf of the firm. Such a suit might be brought against a general partner for injuries caused to the firm by a breach of fiduciary duty.

The *Norwest* case involves the use of loan guarantees by general partners in a limited partnership.

NORWEST BANK v. CHRISTIANSON
494 N.W.2d 165 (N.D. 1992)

FACTS: James D. Christianson, Christopher A. Carlson, and James P. Beck appealed from a judgment finding them liable on guaranties to Norwest Bank North Dakota, N.A., in the amount of $132,654.90.

In 1985, Soo Hotel Associates [Soo], a limited partnership in which Christianson, Carlson, and Beck [Partners] are general partners, executed a promissory note in favor of Norwest Bank North Dakota, N.A.,[Norwest] in the amount of $132,500.00. The note was secured by a mortgage in the amount of $132,500.00

on real property owned by Soo in downtown Bismarck. Both the note and the mortgage were signed by Partners. Additionally, at the time the loan was negotiated, Partners were asked to sign personal and unconditional guaranties in the event Soo, as the mortgagor, defaulted. Partners claimed that at the time of the loan negotiation, Thomas Gietzen, a loan officer with Norwest, advised them that there was sufficient equity in the real estate for which the bank was taking the mortgage to cover the indebtedness, and regardless, Norwest would only pursue the personal guaranties if the real estate value turned out to be less than the balance due on the note. Partners claimed they were assured that Norwest would only pursue the personal guaranties if a deficiency existed after sale of the real estate. Gietzen, by way of affidavit, denies any such conversation took place, and the guaranty agreements signed individually by Partners make no provisions which would support Partners' contention.

After several renewals, the note became due in late 1991. In early 1992, Norwest commenced an action against Partners on their personal guaranties without foreclosing on the real estate on which Soo's note was secured.

Partners admitted Soo's default in repayment, admitted signing the personal guaranties, and attested to the genuineness of the guaranties as proffered by Norwest. The trial court resolved the legal issues against Partners and granted Norwest's motion for summary judgment.

 JUSTICE VANDE WALLE:

Partners contend that after a mortgagor's default, a mortgagee may sue the guarantors of the mortgagor's debt, but the recovery is limited to the difference between the amount owed and the fair market value of the mortgaged real estate if the mortgagee does not first foreclose on the real estate.

In *First Interstate Bank of Fargo v. Larson* ... we held that the anti-deficiency statute, NDCC § 32-19-07, applies to general partners who guaranty their partnership's notes which are secured by a mortgage. Because a general partner's guaranty is not a separate obligation from the underlying note, the general partner's liability is not founded on the guaranty, but on the note itself. Therefore, a mortgagee suing on a general partner's guaranty after the partnership's (mortgagor's) default, is subject to the rights and limitations enumerated in the anti-deficiency statute. *Larson* would have been dispositive of this appeal, but we specifically held that its application would be applied prospectively only. As the mortgage, note, and guaranties were signed by Partners in 1985, *Larson*, decided in 1991, has no bearing on their case....

In 1985, the law with respect to the liability of general partners as a result of their guaranties of the partnership's mortgage, was controlled by the Court's decision in *Mandan Sec. Bank v. Heinsohn*.... In *Heinsohn*, the majority of this Court held that a general partner who personally guaranteed payment of a partnership note secured by a mortgage, changed the nature of the partner's obligation on the debts and as a result the partner was not only jointly liable on the note, but was jointly and severally liable on the guaranty. Because the liability of the general partner on the guaranty was not founded on the underlying note secured by the mortgage, the anti-deficiency statute did not preclude recovery on the individual guaranty and the creditor could collect on the guaranty without first foreclosing on the real property....

Applying the law at the time the contract was entered into, Partners' obligation of repayment is not founded on the note, but on their personal guaranties.... Therefore, the anti-deficiency statutes do not apply to this action, and Norwest is not bound by their limited options upon the default of the mortgagor.... Norwest is free to collect the entire amount guaranteed jointly and severally by Partners without first resorting to foreclosing on the real estate, and without limiting its recovery to the difference between the fair market value of the real estate and the amount due on the note.

Dissolution, Winding Up, and Termination.

In Chapter 31, it was noted that the death, bankruptcy, or withdrawal of a partner were causes for dissolution of the partnership. These rules do not apply to a limited partnership. Since limited partners are simply limited liability investors, they have no voice in management, and are not liable for more than their investment. Thus, there is no specific loss to the limited partnership if a limited partner dies or becomes bankrupt. For these reasons, the substitution of a new limited partner for an old limited partner or the addition of a limited partner will not cause dissolution of a limited partnership. Only if all the limited partners have either died or withdrawn and no substitutions have been made would the death or withdrawal of limited partners necessitate the dissolution of a limited partnership. A limited partnership must have a minimum of one limited partner. Without the limited partner there is no limited partnership.

The death or withdrawal of a general partner from a limited partnership will cause the limited partnership to be dissolved unless there is a provision in the certificate to substitute another person for the deceased or withdrawing general partner.

Thus, a limited partnership will normally not be dissolved until the general partners or their replacements decide to dissolve the partnership or until a specific term expires, if the limited partnership was created for a specified term.

Although the limited partnership need not be dissolved upon the death or withdrawal of a general partner if provisions were made for that partner's replacement, the limited partnership still has to file and record an amended limited partnership certificate to inform the public of the change. If a limited partner dies or withdraws and is not replaced, no amendments need be filed and recorded. However, if another person is substituted or added as a limited partner, then the certificate must be amended. Also, if a limited partnership decides to go into a different business or to make any other major changes in the business which concern matters covered in its certificate, it must file and record an amended certificate that gives the public full notice of these changes. Section 24 of the Uniform Limited Partnership Act specifies the various changes in the business that require an amended certificate be filed.

Under RULPA, amendments to the certificate must be filed within thirty days after: (1) the admission of a new partner, (2) the withdrawal of a partner, (3) the continuation of the firm's operations after a judicial dissolution due to withdrawal of the last general partner, or (4) any change in a partner's contribution to the firm. Changes in the addresses of limited partners need only be filed once a year.

R.U.L.P.A. Changes.

The Revised ULPA has now been adopted by nearly all states. A major reason for the revision of the Uniform Limited Partnership Act was to clarify the question of control. The 1916 ULPA states that a limited partner may not participate in the control of the limited partnership. A limited partner who does participate in the control of the business will be treated in the same way as a general partner and thus will lose limited liability. The problem is simply what is control. Can a limited partner make suggestions to the general partner? Can a limited partner have a vote? Conflicting court decisions have been reached in the various states as to what a limited partner may or may not do insofar as participation in the control of the business is concerned. Some states even amended their limited partnership statute to grant limited partners a right to vote on certain types of major business decisions.

Because of the concern over the growing nonuniformity of the Uniform Limited Partnership laws, the Revised ULPA was drafted. This act specifically allows the limited partner to do certain acts with the understanding that these acts do not constitute participation in the control of the business. The following acts are permitted by the Revised ULPA:

1. Being a contractor for, or an agent of, the partnership.

2. Consulting with and advising a partner with respect to the business.

3. Acting as a surety for the partnership.

4. Approving or disapproving of an amendment to the partnership agreement.

5. Voting on such matters as dissolution, winding up, the transfer of all or substantially all of the assets, the incurrence of debt other than in the ordinary course of business, a change in the nature of the business, and the removal of a general partner.

In addition to allowing the limited partner to do the above acts, the Revised ULPA also provides that if a limited partner does actively participate in the control of the partnership by doing acts other than those mentioned above, the limited partner will only be liable to those persons who did business with the partnership and who had knowledge of the limited partner's participation in its control. The Revised ULPA also makes some general changes in the filing requirements for limited partnerships. It requires that the certificate of limited partnership be filed in the office of the secretary of state in the state where the limited partnership is doing business, and it also requires that the limited partnership designate a resident in the state where it is doing business as the registered agent for the service of process for lawsuits which may be filed against it. These requirements are similar to the filing requirements for corporations.

The original ULPA restricted the limited partner's capital contribution to cash or other property. Under the Revised ULPA the limited partner may contribute services as a capital contribution as well as or in place of cash or other property. This is a very important change, since it means that the consulting expertise or other specialized talents of limited partners can now be contributed as a capital contribution to a limited partnership.

Another change in the Revised ULPA was previously referred to. That change requires that the full words limited partnership be used in the firm name rather than the abbreviation "Ltd.," which is allowed under the original ULPA.

OTHER ORGANIZATIONAL FORMS

Subchapter S Corporation

Subchapter S corporations are mentioned briefly in Chapter 33. Subchapter S is simply a subdivision of the Internal Revenue Code which permits small close corporations to be exempt from payment of corporate income tax. The shareholders are allocated shares of the profits and then declare those profits as income. Also, if the corporation has losses, the shareholder can deduct his or her share of those losses from other personal income. The corporation files a corporate tax return, but it is simply an informational return similar to the return required to be filed by a general partnership. Thus, the shareholders gain the benefits of incorporation, such as limited liability, ease of transferability of their interest, and perpetual duration, but are not subjected to double taxation. There is no separate taxation of corporate income and a second tax when dividends are distributed as individual income.

Subchapter S status is a tax status granted by the Internal Revenue Service, upon application and IRS approval. There are several requirements which a corporation must meet before it will be granted subchapter S status by the Internal Revenue Service. The first requirement refers to the number of shareholders. A subchapter S corporation can have no more than thirty-five shareholders. Second, the corporation can have only one class of stock. Third, the corporation must be a U.S. corporation. And fourth, shareholders may not be nonresident aliens or nonhuman entities, such as other corporations. However, there is an exception for estates and trusts, as they may be shareholders in a subchapter S corporation.

There are also limitations as to the percentage of non-U.S. income and investment income the corporation may receive and still retain subchapter S status. Another requirement is that all shareholders must join in the application for subchapter S status. However, if the shareholders decide to terminate the subchapter S status, they may do so. Only the consent of a majority of the stockholders is needed for revocation of subchapter S status.

Subchapter S status is advantageous only as long as it is in the best interests of the shareholders from a tax standpoint. For example, if the shareholders in a small corporation were three shareholders who all had other incomes that put them in the top tax bracket for their individual income taxes, then they would not want subchapter S status. Their preference would be to have the corporation profits taxed at corporation tax levels and then have the after-tax profits reinvested, rather than distributed as dividends. Then later, when they wanted to take their money out of the corporation, they could sell their stock and only have to pay capital gains taxes. However, if the corporation was sustaining losses, the three shareholders might want to use S status, so that they could offset the losses against their other income.

Joint Stock Company

The *joint stock company* is a form of business organization in which the management of the business is placed in the hands of trustees or directors. Shares represented by certificates are then issued to the members of the company, who are in effect, joint owners of the enterprise. These certificate holders then elect the board of directors or the board of trustees. Like the shares of a corporation, the shares or certificates are transferable, and their transfer does not cause dissolution, as it would in a partnership. Also, the death of a shareholder does not dissolve the organization, as would be the case for a partnership. The joint stock company exists for the period of time stated in its bylaws. In reality, the joint stock company is a partnership; however, it has many of the advantages of the corporation. Its principle disadvantage is that there is still unlimited personal liability, as in a partnership. Depending on the state statute, the joint stock company may or may not be considered a legal entity for purposes of litigation.

One may wonder why the law recognizes a business organization such as the joint stock company. The joint stock company is a compromise between the partnership and the corporation. It has the partnership's tax advantages since it pays no separate corporation tax, and it has the corporation's advantages of transferability and duration, but it also has the partnership's disadvantage of unlimited liability. At one time, the joint stock company was a popular form of business. However, with the advent of the subchapter S corporation, it no longer has great appeal.

Business Trust

The **business trust**, or the **Massachusetts trust**, as it is often called, is a business organization where title to certain property is deeded over to a trustee or a board of trustees who manage and operate the business for the benefit of those parties who contributed property in the form of money or other assets to the trust. The people who contributed money or other assets to the trust are called **beneficiaries**. They no longer have any legal title to the trust corpus; however, they do have an equitable or beneficial interest in the trust. They are given trust certificates as evidence of their interest in it. As beneficiaries of the trust, the certificate holders will receive the profits from the operations and investments of the trust properties. However, the key factor is that the certificate holders do not have any right to control the enterprise. If, in fact, they do have a right to control the actions of the trustees, the courts will normally hold that the business is a partnership and not a trust.

The main purpose of the business trust is to ensure limited liability to the beneficiaries and yet avoid some of the statutory regulations and reporting procedures of a corporation.

This form of business organization, like the joint stock company, is not used extensively today.

Cooperative Association

One often hears of farm co-ops or student co-ops. A **cooperative association** is a union of individuals formed for the purpose of operating an enterprise to make profits or to provide benefits for its members. If it is a profit-making business, the legal rules governing it will be very similar to those that govern a partnership or a joint venture.

If a cooperative is nonprofit and unincorporated, the legal rules governing it are quite different, particularly those relating to the personal liability of the associates. Personal liability for the contract and tort debts of the organization is not automatically assumed on the basis of membership in a nonprofit cooperative. The liability of individual members must be based on proof of an agency relationship; that is, the members whom it is sought to hold personally liable must be shown to have authorized the liability-producing act. Such personal authorization may be proved by showing that the act in question is part of the organization's purposes, or that the act was specifically authorized by the persons sought to be held liable, or that those persons were active participants in the act.

The status of an individual member is at issue in the *Cox* case.

COX v. THEE EVERGREEN CHURCH
836 S.W.2d 167 (TX, 1992)

FACTS: Karen Cox (Cox) was a member of Thee Evergreen Church (Evergreen), an unincorporated charitable association. Cox had been a member for four years and held a position on Evergreen's administrative board. On November 4, 1986, Cox dropped her son off at a "mothers day out" program, for which she paid a nominal fee, operated on Evergreen premises by volunteer members of the church. Upon entering the church, Cox slipped and fell, injuring her back and head. Cox brought an action against Evergreen alleging negligence and gross negligence. The trial court granted a motion for summary judgment filed on behalf of Evergreen on the ground that a member of an unincorporated charitable association lacks standing to maintain an action against the association. The court of appeals affirmed.

 JUSTICE HIGHTOWER:

An unincorporated association is a voluntary group of persons, without a charter, formed by mutual consent for the purpose of promoting a common enterprise or prosecuting a common objective.... Historically, unincorporated associations were not considered separate legal entities and had no existence apart from their individual members.... Because of the lack of a separate legal status, it was generally considered that unincorporated associations could only hold property through the intervention of trustees.... For the same reason, a judgment could not be rendered against such an association....

Consequent to the lack of legal identity, special rules arose concerning liability in actions involving unincorporated associations. In regard to contracts, members incurring the debt on behalf of the association or assenting to its creation were personally liable.... In regard to tort actions, member liability depended upon such factors as the nature of the association and the individual member's involvement in the conduct giving rise to the cause of action....

The rule of law also developed that an unincorporated association was not liable to one of its members for damages occasioned by the wrongful act of another member or agent of the association.... Such immunity was grounded on the concept that the injured member and the association were regarded as coprincipals, with the tort feasor as their common agent. The wrongful conduct was thus "imputed" to the plaintiff for purposes of his action against the association.... In effect, it was considered that the plaintiff was suing himself.... It is this rule of law that Evergreen contends precludes Cox's claim.

Cox advances three arguments for allowing her to maintain a cause of action. First, Cox argues that the common-law principles have been modified by a series of statutes concerning suits by and against unincorporated joint stock companies and associations....

Cox next looks to Rule 28 of the Texas Rules of Civil Procedure. Rule 28 has been interpreted as treating unincorporated associations as legal entities, at least to the extent of obtaining and enforcing judgments against them....

Lastly, Cox argues that the common-law principle precluding her from bringing a negligence action solely because of her membership in the association should be abolished. We agree.

As discussed above, an unincorporated association was historically not liable to one of its members for damages occasioned by the wrongful act of another member or agent of the association.... This court, however, has recognized various situations in which membership alone is an insufficient reason to preclude a member of an unincorporated association from asserting a cause of action against the association....

So what remains of the early common-law rules regarding unincorporated associations and the imputed negligence doctrine? Apparently, very little. We allow suits by and against unincorporated associations in their own name.... We allow non-members to bring suits, including those for negligence, against unincorporated associations.... We allow members to sue unincorporated associations for acts committed that are strictly adverse to the member's interests.... We allow members to sue unincorporated associations when the association conspires to bring about or ratifies the wrongful conduct....We refuse to apply the imputed negligence doctrine in the analogous joint enterprise context when there is no business or pecuniary purpose.... And lastly, a number of states allow suits against unincorporated associations by their members for injuries resulting from the association's negligence.... Nevertheless, one vestige of the common law survives—our obedience to an ancient precept automatically imputing the negligence of an unincorporated association to an injured member. Considering the development of the law in regard to our treatment of unincorporated associations, ... combined with our refusal to apply the imputed negligence doctrine in other contexts, ... we perceive no compelling reason for retaining this remnant of the original common-law rules.... Consequently, we hold that a member of an unincorporated charitable association is not precluded from bringing a negligence action against the association solely because of the individual's membership in the association. Any assets of the unincorporated charitable association, held either by the association or in trust by a member of the association, may be reached in satisfaction of a judgment against the association.

For these reasons, we reverse the judgment of the court of appeals and remand this cause to the trial court for further proceedings.

LIMITED LIABILITY COMPANIES (LLCs)

History and mythology abound with stories of searches for the ultimate prize. Jason and the Argonauts searched for the Golden Fleece. King Arthur's Knights of the Round Table searched for the Holy Grail. Columbus searched for the Indies. Henry Cabot searched for the Northwest Passage.

Like these historical and mythical searchers, investors seek the ultimate organizational form for their business ventures. Generally, they want single taxation of profits, limited liability, transferability of ownership interests, perpetual existence, and professional management. Finding an organizational form which embodies all of these desired features has been difficult, to say the least.

The corporation provides four of the five characteristics, but is subject to potentially devastating double taxation. It pays its own income taxes on its profits, and its stockholders are then taxed again when those profits are distributed as dividends. Subchapter S offers relief from this double tax, as noted above, but is subject to many limitations. Limited partnership offers single taxation, but the investors cannot actively participate in management, dissolution may occur, and someone has to assume unlimited personal liability. The joint stock company and the business trust have limited utility, as noted above. So what is the answer?

Under German law, the answer is the GmbH (*Geschellschaft mit beschrenkter Haftung*)—an enterprise with limited liability. By analogy, the GmbH is an "incorporated partnership." Members can exercise full management authority and still enjoy limited liability. Similar business organizations exist in other countries—the *Limitada* in most Latin American countries, for example. No comparable organizational form was available in this country until 1977, when Wyoming passed an act authorizing the formation of limited liability companies. The act was apparently passed in response to the request of an oil company.

Although adopted by one state (with a very small population), LLCs remained virtually unknown until 1988. In that year, the IRS issued Revenue Ruling 88-76, which said that LLCs would be treated as partnerships for IRS purposes. A Wyoming LLC, in other words, would not be subject to double taxation on profits. With that Ruling, the floodgates opened, and 40+ states passed statutes authorizing the formation of LLCs.

Just what is an LLC? It is a business organization in which the members have limited liability, but are not subject to double taxation on profits. To gain this favorable tax treatment, the IRS says that an organization may not possess more than two of the following four characteristics: limited liability, continuity of life, free transferability of interest, and central management. Since limited liability is the much-sought-after "Holy Grail," along with single taxation, an LLC can possess only one of the other three characteristics. In practice, that means that limitations must be placed on two of the three remaining features. If the organization has unlimited life, then there must be restrictions on the transfer of ownership interests and on centralized management. If there is to be free transferability of ownership interests, then there must be restrictions on unlimited life and on centralized management. If there is to be centralized management (as in a corporation), then there must be restrictions on free transferability of ownership interests and unlimited life. Just how restrictive these various "restrictions" have to be for tax purposes, remains an open question. There will necessarily be much litigation until all these complications are sorted out. Until there are definitive rulings, LLCs will remain a somewhat risky organizational form.

The next case shows the kind of technical questions that are likely to arise.

WATER, WASTE & LAND, INC. v. LANHAM; CLARK; and PREFERRED INCOME INVESTORS, L.L.C.
955 P.2d (Colo., 1998)

FACTS: Water, Waste, & Land, Inc., the petitioner, is a land development and engineering company doing business under the name "Westec." At the time of the events in this case, Donald Lanham and Larry Clark were managers and also members of Preferred Income Investors, L.L.C. The Company is a limited liability company organized under the Colorado Limited Liability Company Act.

In March 1995, Clark contacted Westec about the possibility of hiring Westec to perform engineering work in connection with a development project which involved the construction of a fast-food restaurant known as Taco Cabana. In the course of preliminary discussions, Clark gave his business card to representatives of Westec. The business card included Lanham's address, which was also the address listed as the Company's principal office and place of business in its articles or organization filed with the secretary of state. While the Company's name was not on the business card, the letters "P.I.I." appeared above the address on the card. However, there was no indication as to what the acronym meant or that P.I.I. was a limited liability company.

After further negotiations, an oral agreement was reached concerning Westec's involvement with the Company's restaurant project. Clark instructed Westec to send a written proposal of its work to Lanham and the proposal was sent in April 1995. On August 2, 1995, Westec sent Lanham a form of contract, which Lanham was to execute and return to Westec. Although Westec never received a signed contract, in mid-August it did receive verbal authorization from Clark to begin work. Westec completed the engineering work and sent a bill for $9,183.40 to Lanham. No payments were made on the bill.

Westec filed a claim in county court against Clark and Lanham individually as well as against the Company. At trial, the company admitted liability for the amount claimed by Westec. The county court entered judgment in favor of Westec. Based on its findings, the county court ruled that: (1) Clark was an agent of both Lanham and the Company with "authority to obligate ... Lanham and the Company," (2) a valid and binding contract existed for the work, (3) Westec "did not have knowledge of any business entity" and only dealt with Clark and Lanham "on a personal basis," and (4) Westec understood Clark to be Lanham's agent and therefore "Clark is not personally liable." Accordingly, the county court dismissed Clark from the suit, concluding he could not be held personally liable, and entered judgment in the amount of $9,183 against Lanham and the Company. Lanham appealed.

JUSTICE SCOTT:

The district court interpreted the LLC Act's notice provision ... as putting Westec on constructive notice of Lanham's agency relationship with the Company. In essence, this course of analysis assumed that the LLC Act displaced certain common law agency doctrines, at least insofar as these doctrines otherwise would be applicable to suits by third parties seeking to hold the agents of a limited liability company liable for their personal actions as agents.

We hold, however, that the statutory notice provision applies only where a third party seeks to impose liability on an LLC's members or managers simply due to their status as members or managers of the LLC. When a third party sues a manager or member of an LLC under an agency theory, the principles of agency law apply notwithstanding the LLC Act's statutory notice rules.

Under the common law of agency, an agent is liable on a contract entered on behalf of a principal if the principal is not fully disclosed. In other words, an agent who negotiates a contract with a third party can be sued for any breach of the contract unless the agent discloses both the fact that he or she is acting on behalf of a principal and the identity of the principal. As a leading treatise explains:

"If both the existence and identity of the agent's principal are fully disclosed to the other party, the agent does not become a party to any contract which he negotiates.... But where the principal is partially disclosed (*i.e.*, the existence of a principal is known but his identity is not), it is usually inferred that the agent is a party to the contract...."

These principles lead us to conclude that the district court erred in substituting its own factual determinations for the findings of the county court. If the district court had held a trial de novo, its conclusion that the initials "P.I.I." on Clark's business card sufficiently alerted Westec's representatives to the fact of Clark's agency relationship with the Company and to the Company's identity would be entitled to deference if supported by evidence in the record. However, we see the evidence as sufficient to support the county court's finding to the contrary. Indeed, neither the business card nor the unsigned contract documents, both of which are of obvious significance in evaluating whether Westec knew the identity of the entity represented by Clark and Lanham, are in the record before us. We are, therefore, bound to accept the county court's finding that Westec did not know Clark was acting as an agent for the Company or that the initials "P.I.I." stood for "Preferred Income Investors," a limited liability company registered under Colorado law. For the same reason, the district court erred in concluding that Clark was not acting as Lanham's agent. The trial record was sufficient to support the county court's finding that Clark was an agent for Lanham and this conclusion should not have been disturbed by the district court.

In light of the partially disclosed principal doctrine, the county court's determination that Clark and Lanham failed to disclose the existence as well as the identity of the limited liability company they represented is dispositive under the common law of agency. Still, if the General Assembly has altered the common law rules applicable to this case by adopting the LLC Act, then these rules must yield in favor of the statute. We conclude, however, that the LLC Act's notice provision was not intended to alter the partially disclosed principal doctrine.

Section 7-80-208, C.R.S. (1997) states: "The fact that the articles of organization are on file in the office of the secretary of state is notice that the limited liability company is a limited liability company and is notice of all other facts set forth therein which are required to be set forth in the articles of organization."

In order to relieve Lanham of liability, this provision would have to be read to establish a conclusive presumption that a third party who deals with the agent of a limited liability company always has constructive notice of the existence of the agent's principal. We are not persuaded that the statute can bear such an interpretation.

Such a construction exaggerates the plain meaning of the language in the statute. Section 7-80-208 could be read to state that third parties who deal with a limited liability company are always on constructive notice of the company's limited liability status, without regard to whether any part of the company's name or even the fact of its existence has been disclosed. However, an equally plausible interpretation of the words used in the statute is that once the limited liability company's name is known to the third party, constructive notice of the company's limited liability status has been given, as well as the fact that managers and members will not be liable simply due to their status as members.

Moreover, the broad interpretation urged by Lanham would be an invitation to fraud, because it would leave the agent of a limited liability company free to mislead third parties into the belief that the agent would bear personal financial responsibility under any contract, when in fact, recovery would be limited to the assets of a limited liability company not known to the third party at the time the contract was made. While Westec has not alleged that Clark or Lanham deliberately tried to conceal the Company's identity or status as a limited liability company, Lanham's construction would open the door to sharp practices and outright fraud. We may presume that in adopting Section 7-80-208, the General Assembly did not intend to create a safe harbor for deceit.... For this reason alone, a broad reading of the notice provision would be suspect.

In addition, statutes in derogation of the common law are to be strictly construed.... For the reasons outlined above, the interpretation urged by Lanham would be a radical departure from the settled rules of agency under the common law. If the legislature had intended a departure of such magnitude, its desires would have to be expressed more clearly....

Under our interpretation, Section 7-80-208 still offers significant protection to the members of a limited liability company. The notice provision protects the members from suit based on their status as members, as opposed to their acts as agents of the corporate entity. If a third party such as Westec had tried to pierce the corporate veil to hold Clark and Lanham personally responsible for the Company's contractual debt based on the fact that they were members of the LLC, section 7-80-208 would protect them from liability. The distinction between the use of an agency theory and the doctrine of piercing the corporate or limited liability company veil is significant....

For these reasons, we conclude that where an agent fails to disclose either the fact that he is acting on behalf of a principal or the identity of the principal, the notice provision of our LLC Act ... cannot relieve the agent of liability to a third party. When a third party deals with an agent acting on behalf of a limited liability company, the existence and identity of which has been disclosed, the third party is conclusively presumed to know that the entity is a limited liability company and not a partnership or some other type of business organization. Where the third party does not know the identity of the principal entity, however, the situation is fundamentally different because the third party is without notice and the law does not contemplate that he has any way of finding the relevant records.

If Clark or Lanham had told Westec's representatives that they were acting on behalf of an entity known as "Preferred Income Investors, LLC," the failure to disclose the fact that the entity was a limited liability company would be irrelevant by virtue of the statute, which provides that the articles of organization operate as constructive notice of the company's limited liability form. The county court, however, found that Lanham and Clark did not identify Preferred Income Investors, LLC, as the principal in the transaction. The "missing link" between the limited disclosure made by Clark and the protection of the notice statute was the failure to state that "P.I.I." the Company, stood for "Preferred Income Investors, LLC....

Accordingly, the judgment of the district court is reversed and this case is remanded to that court with instructions that it reinstate the judgment of the county court.

SIGNIFICANCE OF THIS CHAPTER

In the last few decades, limited partnerships have become a very important form of business organization, particularly for use in tax shelter business operations. It is therefore important for the businessperson to know what a limited partnership is, how it is formed, what the limited partners can and cannot do and still retain limited liability status, and also how a limited partnership can be terminated. While the limited partnership is certainly the most significant of these alternative forms of organization, there are several other possibilities. Since the rights and liabilities of the associates vary from one form to another, this chapter has also included a summary of the differences between the joint stock company, the business trust, the for-profit unincorporated association, the LLC, and the nonprofit unincorporated association. Not only the associates, but also the third parties dealing with various organizations, need to know the basic rules for who can do what and who's liable for what.

PROBLEMS FOR DISCUSSION

1. Ricardo de Escamilla was raising beans on a farm near Escondido when he organized Hacienda Farms, a limited partnership, with James Russell and H.W. Andrews. Russell and Andrews were the limited partners; Ricardo was the general partner. Hacienda Farms operated only from February to December 1993, when it went bankrupt. Holzman, Hacienda's trustee in bankruptcy, sought to hold Russell and Andrews personally liable for its debts.

    Russell and Andrews had participated substantially in the operation of Hacienda Farms. When asked whether he had had conversations with them prior to deciding to plant tomatoes, Ricardo said: "We also conferred and agreed as to what crops we would put in." He also said: "There ... was never any crop that was planted or contemplated in planting that wasn't thoroughly discussed and agreed upon by the three of us; particularly Andrews and myself." In fact, Andrews and Russell overruled de Escamilla on the planting of peppers, watermelons, and eggplant. They also asked him to resign as manager of Hacienda and replaced him with Harry Miller. Russell and Andrews also seemed to have control of Hacienda's finances.

The two men had absolute power to withdraw all the partnership funds in the banks without the knowledge or consent of the general partner. Either Russell or Andrews could take control of the business from de Escamilla by refusing to sign checks for bills contracted by him and thus limit his activities in the management of the business. They were active in dictating the crops to be planted, some of them against the wish of de Escamilla.

Are Russell and Andrews personally liable for the debts of the business? Why or why not?

2. Plaintiff was injured by carbon monoxide fumes while attending a fish fry at Post 650. The petition alleges that the defendants, American Legion Post No. 650 Realty Co., Inc., and the individual members of the American Legion Post No. 650 "jointly and severally, conducted or caused to be conducted within said building a social affair known as a fish fry for which they charged each person attending the sum of one dollar ($1)," and that "defendants, each of them, were negligent in failing to provide a safe heating system in the building; in equipping and maintaining the building with a defective heating system; in failing to adequately inspect said heating system; in failing to provide proper ventilation in the building; and in failing to warn invitees in the building, including decedent, of the presence of carbon monoxide fumes therein."

Are the individual members of Post 650 personally liable, as well as the organization? Explain.

3. Steinberg and his two general partners owned eighty-four acres of land in Baltimore County, which land they had encumbered with $365,000 worth of mortgages. To get operating capital, they solicited investments from persons who would become limited partners.

Allen, the plaintiff's husband, was one of those solicited. He said that he and his wife would not be interested in any construction project but that they would be interested in a land deal. Mrs. Allen sent a check for $10,000, after being assured that they were investing in land and that the building operation on that land would be separate. The partnership agreement which Mrs. Allen signed had been redrafted by her husband so that the definition of the firm's business was "the ownership and promotion for development of a tract of land" rather than "the ownership and development of a tract of land." Through various manipulations, the general partners had the firm assume $275,000 worth of utility installation costs and also mortgaged part of the tract for $140,000, all without the knowledge or consent of the limited partners. The firm's assets were lost, and Mrs. Allen sued the general partners for an accounting and for damages resulting from their mismanagement. She appealed from the trial court's dismissal of her suit.

How should the appeals court rule? Discuss.

4. Michael Halb was killed by Bernie Wells when Michael surprised Bernie in the process of robbing Michael's home. Michael's estate sued Bernie and his live-in lady friend, Lili Hamel, in a wrongful death action. Bernie and Lili had lived together for five years, during which time he frequently went out late at night, had no regular job, filed tax returns showing several hundred thousand dollars of income each year, and bought a million-dollar house and several expensive cars. Bernie told Lili he was in the "gold and silver business." He installed a metal smelting furnace in their garage. Lili handled the inventories, filed the tax returns which listed "cost of goods sold" although no invoices were ever received, and generally kept the books. When Bernie was caught, he had over 3,000 stolen items in their basement. Lili says she's not a crook and didn't know what Bernie was doing.

Is there any basis on which Lili can be held liable for Bernie's actions? Discuss.

5. Dr. Vidricksen intended, when he turned over to Thom $25,000 in July 1992, to become a limited partner with Thom, the general manager, in a Chevrolet car agency business at Dunsmuir, California. Articles of partnership were drawn up, but no effort was made to comply with the California statutory requirement of recording a certificate of limited partnership. Bankruptcy overtook Thom in September 1994. Apparently the agency developed financial difficulties in March 1994, and the doctor consulted successively two different lawyers. From them, although they could not represent him because of conflict of interest, he did learn he had a problem; to wit, whether in his venture he had attained a real limited partnership and therefore limited liability under California law.

On September 19, 1994 (eight days after the bankruptcy proceedings started), Dr. Vidricksen filed in the bankruptcy proceedings a renunciation under Section 15511 of the Corporations Code of California, that state's version of the ULPA.

Is the doctor now free of liability? Explain.

Chapter 33

Corporations—Nature, Formation, and Powers

A corporation is called a legal person or a legal entity. It may also be called a child of the state, since its birth, existence, and termination are regulated by statutory law. Upon the completion of certain requirements a state will grant a charter of incorporation which is in effect a birth certificate for the corporation. The corporation must abide by the specific statutory law during its existence, and if the corporation is to be terminated, then the termination must comply with the statutory law. Each state has specific statutes governing the creation, regulation, and termination of corporations and also regulating corporations created in other states but doing local business in that state.

The Model Business Corporation Act (MBCA) was drafted by the Committee of Corporation Laws of the Section of Corporation Banking and Business Law of the American Bar Association in 1950 with the hope that the various states would pattern their state corporate statutes after the Model Act. The Model Act is similar to the Uniform Acts we have discussed earlier in the text in that they are not law until adopted by a specific state legislature. The Model Act has been reviewed and revised periodically, and in 1984 the committee completed a comprehensive revision of the Model Act.

CLASSIFICATIONS OF CORPORATIONS

Private Corporation for Profit. This is the most common type of corporation. Such a corporation is created for the purpose of conducting private, nongovernmental business.

Private corporations for profit may be further classified as **close corporations** or **publicly held corporations**. A close corporation is a corporation where the stock is owned by a small

743

number of shareholders and the stock is not offered for sale to the general public. It is called a close corporation because it is closed to the general public. Its shares are not for sale on any stock exchange. A publicly held corporation is a corporation whose shares are offered for sale to the general public. These shares of stock are traded regularly on the various stock exchanges.

Publicly held corporations must comply with very strict rules and regulations as to their procedure in offering their shares of stock for sale to the public. These rules and regulations are made and enforced by the various State Securities Commissions as well as the national Securities Exchange Commission. These procedures and requirements will be discussed further in Chapter 37.

A subclassification of the close corporation is the **subchapter S corporation**, discussed in the last chapter.

Government Corporation. This is a corporation created for governmental purposes. An example would be a municipal corporation, a school corporation, and other corporations created by the state government or the national government for governmental purposes.

Not-for-Profit Corporation. This is a corporation created for a civic, charitable, or educational purpose. For example, a fraternity or sorority, if incorporated, would be incorporated as a not-for-profit corporation, since its purposes would be social and civic rather than the conduct of a profit-making business. Special tax considerations are given to not-for-profit corporations.

Domestic Corporation. In the state where it was originally incorporated, a corporation is a domestic corporation. Acting in any other state, it is doing so as a "foreign" corporation.

Foreign Corporation. This is a corporation which is incorporated in one state and is doing business in another state. Foreign corporations must file certain documents and pay certain fees before doing local business in states other than the state in which they are incorporated. This topic is discussed in more detail later in the chapter.

Professional Corporation. Many states now have specific incorporation laws which allow the incorporation of certain professionals; for example, a medical corporation. Such a corporation can be one doctor or many doctors. Dentists, veterinarians, architects, accountants, and lawyers may also incorporate their businesses under professional corporation statutes. Typically there are different requirements for incorporation and different provisions for regulation under the professional corporation statutes.

FORMATION OF THE CORPORATION

Incorporators. Incorporators are the persons who actually apply to the state for the incorporation of a business. The incorporators sign a document, usually called **articles of incorporation,** and file it with the secretary of state of the state where they are requesting incorporation. Some states require the incorporators to be citizens of the incorporation state; others do not. The Model Business Corporation Act, which has been followed by many states, now allows a single incorporator to apply. Thus an individual may incorporate a business and may be the sole shareholder.

Procedure for Incorporation. While each state has its own individual incorporation statute, the requirements for incorporation are similar in all states. Generally speaking, the incorporator or incorporators execute and sign articles of incorporation and file this document with the appropriate state official, usually the secretary of state. A filing fee is required, which, of course, varies from state to state. The corporation division of the secretary of state's office will review the articles, and if they comply with the applicable statute, the secretary of state's office will issue a certificate of incorporation which officially gives birth to the corporation. Many states require that a minimum amount of capital be paid into the corporation before it can legally commence business. Some states require that the articles of incorporation be filed in the recorder's office of any county where the corporation holds real estate, or where it has its home office.

1. **Name.** The corporation, like a new baby, must be given a legal name. The incorporators are free to choose nearly any name, so long as it is not the same as or similar to the name of another corporation doing business in the state. Thus, before approving a name for the corporation, the state must run a check of all the corporations on file to find out whether this name is the same as or similar to the names of other corporations. Also, the name of the corporation must include the word *Incorporated* or the abbreviation Inc., so that people will know that when they deal with this organization they are dealing with a limited liability organization.

2. **The purpose for which the corporation is formed.** The purpose for which the corporation is formed can be stated in general terms. In most states it is not necessary to state the specific business the corporation intends to participate in. For example, the purpose may be stated as follows: "to transact any and all lawful business for which a corporation may be incorporated" (under the specific state corporation act).

3. **The address of the corporation's principal office and the name of its registered agent.** The principal office, of course, will be the mailing address for all corporate correspondence, and the resident agent is the person who can officially accept service of process for lawsuits against the corporation.

4. **The duration of the corporation.** A corporation has perpetual existence unless its articles of incorporation provide otherwise.

5. **Issuance of shares of stock.** The incorporator or incorporators must here state the total number of shares of stock the corporation requests authority to issue, the number of shares of stock that are to have a par value, and the number of shares that are to have no par value. If there are to be different classes of stock, different series of stock, and different rights and preferences with regard to different classes of stock, then this information must also be provided. Some states require the names and addresses of the original subscribers to the capital stock and the amount of their subscriptions.

6. **Directors and officers and qualifications of directors.** Many states require the articles of incorporation to include the names of the members of the first board of directors, and often the names of the officers of the corporation are also required. Most states do not require their corporations' directors to be residents of that state.

7. **Provisions for regulation of business and conduct of affairs of the corporation.** Many states require specific statements as to the conduct and scheduling of annual and special meetings of shareholders and directors and as to other provisions concerning the conduct of the business.

8. Requirements prior to doing business. Many states have specific requirements that must be complied with prior to the commencement of business by the corporation. The most common requirement is the payment of a minimum amount of money, typically $1,000, by subscribers to the corporation before the corporation commences doing business.

Charter as Contract.
When the articles are approved or the corporate charter is issued by the state of incorporation, a "contract" is formed between the state and the corporation. As a contract, the corporate charter is protected by Article I, Section 10 of the U.S. Constitution, which prohibits a state from passing any law "impairing the obligation of contracts." In the days when each corporate charter was the result of a special statute, this decision barred much state regulation of corporations. Today, however, general corporation laws contain provisions that reserve to the state the power to amend or repeal the statute. The state's power to change the corporate rules thus becomes part of every contract formed with every corporation pursuant to the statute.

The corporate charter also acts as a contract between the corporation and its stockholders, in the sense that it states the nature of the corporation's business. The bylaws adopted by the corporation also become part of this contract. To avoid unnecessary litigation, clear procedures for amending the corporate charter/articles and the corporate bylaws should be spelled out, and the power to amend should be specifically stated.

Other Obligations.
The obligations of the corporation to its home state do not end with the issuance of the charter. Typically annual reports to the state are required, and the corporation must pay an annual fee for the privilege of exercising its corporate powers. Corporation statutes usually provide for suspension or termination of the corporation's privileges for noncompliance with these annual requirements, at least where the default continues for an extended period of time.

The *Lyman Lumber* case shows the kind of complications that arise when this happens.

LYMAN LUMBER CO. v. FAVORITE CONST. CO.
524 N.W.2d 484 (MN App., 1994)

FACTS: Appellant Lyman Lumber Company commenced this action seeking a declaration that a judgment entered against Favorite Construction Company in 1983 and subsequently renewed in 1993 was a lien against real estate owned by respondent property owners. Lyman Lumber challenges summary judgment for respondents, arguing that the district court erred when it determined that the renewed judgment was void. The district court determined that the court had lacked personal jurisdiction over Favorite Construction in the action to renew the 1983 judgment because the Secretary of State had administratively dissolved that corporation prior to commencement of the judgment renewal action. Lyman Lumber has appealed.

In 1982 and 1983, Lyman Lumber furnished materials to Favorite Construction, a Minnesota corporation, for the improvement of four lots in Dakota County. Favorite Construction delivered checks to Lyman Lumber for the materials and, in exchange, Lyman Lumber delivered mechanic's lien waivers to Favorite Construction. After Favorite Construction's checks were dishonored, Lyman Lumber commenced an action to recover the amount due for the materials. On May 18, 1983, judgment in the amount of $44,097.19 was entered and docketed in favor of Lyman Lumber and against Favorite Construction.

In 1992, Lyman Lumber discovered that Favorite Construction had been the record owner of four additional parcels of real estate in Dakota County when the judgment was docketed in 1983. Lyman Lumber then gave written notice of the 1983 judgment to the subsequent owners of those properties and demanded payment. Respondents, the property owners and Universal Title Insurance Company (Universal Title), refused to pay Lyman Lumber.

Lyman Lumber commenced an action in district court to renew the 1983 judgment and lien against Favorite Construction (the renewal action). On February 9, 1993, judgment was entered, extending for ten years the 1983 judgment and lien. Lyman Lumber then commenced this action in district court to declare that the 1983 judgment and the renewed judgment constituted a valid lien against the above property, and to foreclose the lien against the property (the lien action). In each action, Lyman Lumber served Favorite Construction by serving process upon the Secretary of State according to Minn. Stat. § 302A.901 (1992).

 JUDGE NORTON:

The district court determined that because the Secretary of State dissolved Favorite Construction as a corporation in 1991, service of process upon the Secretary of State in 1992 did not constitute personal service on Favorite Construction. The district court's decision involves application of the following statutory provision for administrative dissolution of corporations that fail, as did Favorite Construction, to file annual registration statements:

A corporation that has failed for three consecutive years to file a registration pursuant to the requirements of subdivision 1, has been notified of the failure pursuant to subdivision 4, and has failed to file the delinquent registration during the 60-day period described in subdivision 4, shall be dissolved by the secretary of state.... A corporation dissolved in this manner is not entitled to the benefits of Section 302A.781....

The district court construed the term "dissolved" in Section 302A.821 to be an unambiguous direction that a corporation so dissolved was dead, had "ceased to exist as a corporation," and was not subject to suit. We disagree. This section contains provisions, as do other sections of the Act, that compel a conclusion that a corporation remains subject to suit after an administrative dissolution. The district court erred when it failed to construe the term "dissolved" in Section 302A.821 in relation to other sections of the Act that govern dissolution of a corporation.... Further, 1993 amendments to Sections 302A.821 and 302A.901 demonstrate that the Act has always recognized a cause of action against an administratively-dissolved corporation. We begin our analysis with the Act prior to the 1993 amendments.

Minn. Stat. § 302A.821 is not, nor has it ever been, contained in or referred to by the collection of statutes that the Act separates into a section titled "Dissolution...." Significantly, the legislature has not listed Minn. Stat. §302A.821 in the section of the Act titled "Methods of dissolution," which provides:

A corporation may be dissolved:

(a) By the incorporators pursuant to Section 302A.711;

(b) By the shareholders pursuant to Sections 302A.721 to 302A.7291; or

(c) By order of a court pursuant to Sections 302A.741 to 302A.765....

Minn. Stat. § 302A.821, subd. 6, refers to administrative dissolution by the Secretary of State as a "penalty." The Reporter's comments explain that this section facilitates the state's recordkeeping and provides an "incentive for ... dormant corporations to use the simplified dissolution proceedings of this act in order to end the corporate existence...."

Thus, this section provides an incentive to corporations to update the records kept by the Secretary of State and a penalty for those corporations that fail to do so. The district court's interpretation that administrative dissolution under Section 302A.821 provides for an immediate cessation of the corporate existence and an immediate bar to creditor actions against the corporation undermines this purpose and provides, instead, the easiest means of corporate dissolution and a quicker bar to creditor remedies than provided by other methods of dissolution.

The Act sets forth detailed procedures for a corporation to follow before it may file articles of dissolution to terminate the corporation's existence, or for a court to follow before it may order a decree of dissolution to terminate the corporation's existence.... Each procedure provides for payment or expiration of creditor claims and an affirmative statement by the corporation, or finding by the court, that the corporation has followed all notice requirements in the statute....

Significantly, the Act explicitly bars claims when a corporation or court dissolves a corporation through filing articles of dissolution or a decree of dissolution. Further, the Act provides a means whereby a creditor or claimant whose claims have been barred under those sections may apply to a court to allow a claim "against the corporation" within one year after articles of dissolution have been filed or a decree of dissolution has been entered.

Unlike the above circumstances, the Act does not contain a provision barring creditors' claims when a corporation is administratively dissolved by the Secretary of State under Minn. Stat. § 302A.821, such as Favorite Construction was here. In fact, Section 302A.821 explicitly clarifies that a corporation dissolved pursuant to that statute "is not entitled to the benefits of Section 302A.781...." One benefit under Minn. Stat. § 302A.781 is that a creditor is limited to one year within which to bring an action against a dissolved "corporation...." The creditor must show "good cause" why it did not previously file the claim.... As Lyman Lumber points out, if the administratively-dissolved corporation immediately ceases to exist and cannot be sued thereafter, then the provision in Section 302A.821, Subdivision 6(b), that the "corporation dissolved in this manner is not entitled to the benefits of Section 302A.781" is meaningless. Thus, the district court erroneously construed Minn. Stat. § 302A.821 to create an immediate bar to creditor claims against Favorite Construction, an administratively- dissolved corporation....

The fact that an administratively-dissolved corporation can be retroactively reinstated further supports a conclusion that the corporation has not completely ceased to exist and is still subject to suit. In 1992, the legislature amended Section 302A.821 to add a provision for retroactive reinstatement of corporations that had been administratively dissolved by the Secretary of State after September 1, 1991.... This provision is applicable here because the Secretary of State dissolved

Favorite Construction on October 16, 1991. Significantly, retroactive reinstatement of a corporation "returns the corporation *to active status* as of the date of the statutory dissolution...." The term "active status" implies that the corporation had some status, an "inactive status," during the period of administrative dissolution.

Courts in other states have held that the effect of a reinstatement statute is to make the dissolution of a corporation a suspension of corporate privileges rather than a termination of the corporate existence.

CORPORATION AS PERSON AND CITIZEN

The corporation is, by definition, a legal person. As such, it enjoys the same constitutional protections as human persons. Under the Fifth Amendment, its life, liberty, and property cannot be taken, without due process of law, by the national government or any of its agencies. Under the Fourteenth Amendment, the same due process protection exists against the state governments. Likewise, states cannot deny corporate persons the equal protection of the law. (*Equal* here does not mean identical. It only means that distinctions must have a rational basis; arbitrary, invidious discrimination against corporations is prohibited.)

Corporations are not considered citizens for the purpose of Fourteenth Amendment "privileges and immunities of citizenship." Most obviously, this means that corporations cannot vote in political elections, hold political office, or serve on juries. More important, corporations do not have a citizen's right to conduct business in states other than the domicile state. Corporations wishing to do local business in a second state must secure that state's permission to do so; human persons, as citizens, are exempt from this requirement. These points are discussed more fully later in this chapter.

To determine whether or not diversity of citizenship exists (so that an ordinary civil case may be brought into U.S. District Court), a corporation is considered to be a "citizen" of its state of incorporation. Courts have also recognized that a corporation may acquire a kind of "double citizenship" in the state where it has its principal place of business. If any of the opposing parties in a litigation were a citizen of either of those two states, there would not be complete diversity of citizenship, and the case could not be brought into the U.S. courts on that basis, no matter how large an amount was involved.

DEFECTIVE FORMATION

Mistakes are sometimes made during the incorporation process. Forms are filled out incorrectly, or some procedural step is omitted. The effect of such errors on the corporation's existence varies, depending on the seriousness of the mistake and on the intent of the human beings who were representing the corporation.

De Jure Corporation. Perfection is not required in order to attain full de jure corporate status. As long as any errors are minor, immaterial ones, the corporation's existence cannot be challenged by anyone, including the state of incorporation. Substantial compliance with all mandatory state requirements, in good faith, is all that is required. A mistake as to the last digit in the zip code on the corporation's mailing address would almost certainly be of this nature. If the corporation's name, street number, city, county, and state were correct, its mail would be delivered despite the (slightly) incorrect zip code.

De Facto Corporation. Even though the mandatory requirements of the corporation law have not been substantially complied with, so that the corporation has not attained de jure status, the corporation's de facto ("in fact") existence may nevertheless be recognized. Only very limited challenges against a de facto corporation are permitted. Subscribers cannot be forced to take and pay for stock in a de facto corporation; they are entitled to full de jure status. The state of incorporation, in a direct proceeding (usually called a *quo warranto*—"by whose authority") can force the suspension of a de facto corporation's business until the error is corrected. In order to attain de facto status, the promoters/incorporators must have made a good faith attempt to comply with a statute under which the corporation could be organized; they must be in at least "colorable" compliance with the statutory requirements (no mandatory step has been omitted); and the corporation must actually have used its powers. The stockholders of a de facto corporation have limited liability, and the de facto corporation can conduct its business free of third-party challenges.

Corporation by Estoppel. Courts sometimes apply the principle of estoppel against persons who have received benefits from a purported, but really nonexistent, corporation. The recipient of goods and services should have to pay for them, whether or not the provider was validly organized as a corporation. Similarly, insiders who were responsible for the defective organization but then dealt with it to their advantage should be prevented from asserting its defects.

The principle of estoppel can also be used to prevent persons who have held themselves out as a corporation from later trying to deny they were in fact a corporation.

No Corporation; Partnership Liability. Where the promoters acted in bad faith, or omitted a mandatory procedural step, or for any other reason failed to achieve at least de facto status for the corporation, the result is partnership liability for all the business associates. In such situations stockholders could be held fully liable personally for all the debts of the business. Persons trying to assert claims against the corporation would normally not be estopped from proving that it was not really a corporation and that all associates in the enterprise were personally liable for its torts and contracts.

SEPARATE CORPORATE ENTITY/ PIERCING THE CORPORATE VEIL

Once a corporation has been successfully organized, it is recognized as a separate and distinct legal person or entity. It owns its own property, makes its own contracts, and pays its own taxes. So long as a corporation's separate identity is preserved by the persons who operate the corporation, that identity should be respected and upheld by the courts and other agencies of government. The fact that all of a corporation's stock is held by only a few persons is not, in itself, a basis for disregarding the separate corporate entity. A court should take this drastic step only where the corporation is being used to produce illegal or fraudulent results or where its human operators are themselves disregarding its existence. Severe under-capitalization of the new corporation may lead a court to infer fraud on the part of its organizers.

Some regulatory and taxation statutes permit enforcement agencies to impose liability on other persons for acts by a corporation. Although this is not quite the same as piercing the corporate veil, in effect the separate corporate entity is disregarded.

In the next case, the "piercing" argument is raised against the director of a successor non-profit corporation.

IGL-WIS. AWNING TENT v. GREATER MILWAUKEE
520 N.W.2d 279 (WI App., 1994)

FACTS: In 1990, Wisconsin Awning rented tents and other equipment to Milwaukee Unlimited, Ltd., a nonprofit corporation organized under Chapter 181, STATS., in connection with Milwaukee Unlimited's production of a hydroplane boat race at the Milwaukee lakefront that summer. Wisconsin Awning's bill was never paid, and, on March 11, 1991, Wisconsin Awning obtained a default judgment against Milwaukee Unlimited for $35,486.63, plus costs. Subsequently, Milwaukee Unlimited was dissolved, and Greater Milwaukee, also a nonprofit corporation organized under Chapter 181, STATS., was formed by, among others, Beemster, who had been a director and vice-president of Milwaukee Unlimited. Beemster was also a director of Greater Milwaukee. Greater Milwaukee produced a hydroplane boat race at the Milwaukee lakefront in the summer of 1991.

Alleging that Greater Milwaukee was but a continuation of Milwaukee Unlimited, Wisconsin Awning sued Greater Milwaukee and Beemster to recover on the judgment against Milwaukee Unlimited. After a bench trial, the trial court held that Greater Milwaukee and Beemster were liable for Milwaukee Unlimited's debt to Wisconsin Awning.

Defendants appealed.

 JUDGE FINE:

It is black-letter law that a new corporation is liable for the debts of an old corporation if the succession is just one of form so that the new corporation "is in reality, however it may be in law, a mere continuation of the old corporation...." Thus, "although technically, as a matter of law, a new corporation may be created, yet, if the old corporation ceases to exist, and all its assets and franchises are acquired by the new, which is in reality a mere continuation of the old ... the new corporation is deemed to have impliedly assumed, and is liable upon, all the obligations of the old...." Wisconsin law is similar....

These principles, designed to prevent avoidance of legitimate obligations, ... also apply to nonprofit corporations....

Following a bench trial, the trial court here found that: "there was an identity of management and control" of the two corporations; Greater Milwaukee used

Milwaukee Unlimited's "equipment and information" in producing the 1991 race; Greater Milwaukee used Milwaukee Unlimited's telephone number; and Greater Milwaukee "was located in the suite next to" Milwaukee Unlimited's former offices. Additionally, referring to what it characterized as the "transformation" from Milwaukee Unlimited to Greater Milwaukee, the trial court also found: "For all intents and purposes, only the name of the business changed. The identical organization in substance continued to operate with the same persons, equipment, files, and purpose of putting on the 1991 boat races." These findings are not "clearly erroneous," ... and support the trial court's conclusion that Greater Milwaukee was but a continuation of Milwaukee Unlimited, and therefore liable for Milwaukee Unlimited's debt to Wisconsin Awning. We affirm the trial court on this issue....

The trial court pierced the corporate veil of both Milwaukee Unlimited and Greater Milwaukee, and found Beemster liable for the corporations' debt to Wisconsin Awning..... Beemster argues that he was immune from suit under both §§ 181.287 and 181.297, STATS. We agree.

Both Greater Milwaukee and Milwaukee Unlimited were non-stock corporations organized under Chapter 181, STATS. Section 181.287 grants immunity from suit by creditors to officers and directors of Chapter 181 corporations. Beemster is a director of Greater Milwaukee, and was an officer and director of Milwaukee Unlimited. Further, Wisconsin Awning does not contend that Beemster was not a "volunteer" *vis a vis* both corporations.... (A "volunteer means a natural person, other than an employee [*sic*] of the corporation, who provides services to or on behalf of the corporation without compensation.") Nevertheless, Wisconsin Awning contends that Beemster is liable for the judgment against Milwaukee Unlimited ... because the trial court found that Beemster's role in forming Greater Milwaukee was "'a dishonest and unjust act' in contravention of [Wisconsin Awning]'s legal rights, (i.e., execution of the judgement [*sic*]" against Milwaukee Unlimited), ... and was "dishonest manipulation in contravention" of Wisconsin Awning's "legal rights."

The phrase "wilful misconduct" is not defined in either § 181.287(1)(d), STATS., or § 181.297(2)(b), STATS. Whether actions constitute "wilful misconduct" so as to render inapplicable the immunity granted by §§ 181.287 and 181.297, STATS., is a question of law that we determine *de novo*....

The trial court based its conclusions that Beemster's conduct was "dishonest," "unjust," and "manipulat[ive]" in the context of its decision whether to pierce the corporate veil. A creditor's attempt to impose personal liability on a corporate director or officer for the corporation's debt "resulting solely from his or her status as a director or officer," § 181.287, STATS., however, does not encounter the immunity interposed by this provision unless the corporate veil is first pierced. This requires proof of, among other things, a "dishonest and unjust act in contravention of [the] plaintiff's legal rights...."

If the immunity granted by § 181.287, STATS., could be circumvented by a showing sufficient to pierce the corporate veil, the "wilful misconduct" exception in Subsection (l)(d) would be rendered superfluous, and the immunity would be illusory, thus violating one of the fundamental tenets of statutory interpretation.... Accordingly, to bypass § 181.287 immunity, a creditor must show something other than the "dishonest and unjust act in contravention of [the] plaintiff's legal rights" necessary to pierce the corporate veil. Given the injunction that cases should be decided on the narrowest possible grounds, we need not define the precise contours of the "wilful misconduct" exception. In light of the broad policy of protecting those who labor in the vineyards of nonprofit corporations that underlies §§ 181.287 and

181.297, STATS., however, we conclude that, in the context of this case at least, in order to establish "wilful misconduct," as that term is used in § 181.287(1)(d), Wisconsin Awning had to show that Beemster's predominant motive was to prevent it from realizing on a collectable debt.

Wisconsin Awning's proof failed in two respects. First, there is absolutely no evidence to support the trial court's finding that Beemster's role either in the dissolution of Milwaukee Unlimited or the formation of Greater Milwaukee was dishonest. Thus, the trial court's finding in this regard is "clearly erroneous." Second, the trial court did not find, nor could it from the evidence in the record, that Beemster's predominant motive in organizing Greater Milwaukee was to avoid payment of the debt to Wisconsin Awning. Rather, the overwhelming evidence is to the contrary—Beemster's primary purpose was to be able to stage boat races in the summer of 1991. Thus, there is no evidence in the record that any of the few assets Milwaukee Unlimited had at the time Greater Milwaukee was formed were transferred to Greater Milwaukee in order to cheat Wisconsin Awning. That portion of the judgment imposing liability on Beemster for the judgment against Milwaukee Unlimited is reversed....

Judgment and order affirmed in part, reversed in part, and cause remanded.

CORPORATE POWERS

Since a corporation is a creature of the law, it possesses only those powers given to it by the law. It can only do those things it has been authorized to do. Authorization for particular acts of a corporation must be found either in its state's corporation statute or in its own charter. Powers that result from the corporation's existence as a legal person, such as the power to sue and be sued in its corporate name and the power to hold and convey property, are called inherent powers. These powers and others specifically stated in the corporation statute are also referred to as statutory powers. All corporations formed in the state have them.

Express powers are the powers specifically granted to a particular corporation by its charter. Many states permit such powers to be stated very broadly for example, "to conduct any lawful business which may be conducted by corporations in this state." Corporations also have implied powers; that is, the powers that are necessary and appropriate to help carry out their express powers. Where a corporation has not used a very broad statement of its express powers, litigation may occur over whether a particular corporate activity is or is not within its implied powers.

Problems have arisen, for example, over whether a corporation has the inherent or implied power to reacquire its own shares of stock, to be a partner in a partnership, to acquire shares of stock in other corporations not in the same line of business, and to make charitable contributions. Some state corporation statutes contain a long list of things that corporations formed thereunder are permitted to do. Section 302 of the MBCA contains such a list. If the corporation's powers/purpose clause has been stated as "any lawful business," there should be little chance of a successful court challenge to any of the above activities. While some state statutes are still rather restrictive, the modern tendency seems to be to take a liberal view of the corporation's powers. If specific investors/promoters wish to limit *their* corporation's operations, they would be free to do so by adopting a restrictive purpose clause and statement of powers.

Acts that do not fall within one of the above categories are said to be **ultra vires**, "outside" the corporation's powers. Courts have not agreed as to what should happen when a corporation engages in such unauthorized activity. The modern tendency is to severely limit such challenges to corporate acts. If a contract has been fully performed by both parties, neither party can raise the *ultra vires* claim so as to force rescission. If a contract is completely executory, neither party can sue for enforcement. Where only one party has performed, the courts disagree on what should happen; most courts permit the party that has performed to enforce the contract. In any case, the state should be able to enjoin the performance of unauthorized acts; a shareholder should be able to sue for an injunction and damages, and the corporation itself should be able to collect damages against the directors and officers who were responsible for the violation of the charter. Both the MCBA and the Revised MCBA follow this modern approach.

PROMOTERS

Definition. The classic definition of a **promoter** is found in the *Old Dominion* case: "those who undertake to form a corporation and to procure for it the rights, instrumentalities, and capital by which it is to carry out the purposes set forth in its charter and to establish it as fully able to do business." The promoters are the "idea people"; they conceive the idea of incorporation, and then they attempt to implement it. The incorporators, the persons who sign the documents specifically requesting the state of incorporation to recognize the corporation's existence, may or may not be promoters. Persons whose only function in the incorporation process is a professional one, such as lawyers, accountants, or engineers, are not necessarily promoters. The promoters are the driving force behind the corporation.

Liability Inter Se. As between themselves, promoters are in a sense partners, or at least joint venturers. Once agreement has been reached as to what will be done and how it will be done, they owe each other a fiduciary duty. This fiduciary duty does not arise, however, unless and until some agreement has been reached. A person who discloses a "good idea" to another person before any agreement has been reached therefore runs the risk that the other person will appropriate the idea without compensation.

Liability to the Corporation and/or Shareholders. Promoters also occupy a fiduciary relationship to their corporation and its subscribers/shareholders. Promoters should, of course, recover all reasonable expenses they have incurred during the incorporation process. They are not, however, entitled to retain secret profits which they have made during the incorporation process, for example, by reselling assets to the corporation for more than they paid for them. Full disclosure of such proposed profits must be made. The question is: To whom? By the majority rule, disclosure to only the original promoters/subscribers is not sufficient, at least where there is a plan to sell more shares to the public. Full disclosure must be made to an independent (nonpromoters) board of directors, or to all subscribers, or to all shareholders, unless the promoters making the profits have themselves subscribed to all the shares to be issued.

Corporation's Liability on Promoter's Contracts. Since the corporation does not yet legally exist, the promoters cannot be its agents when they make preincorporation contracts. The promo-

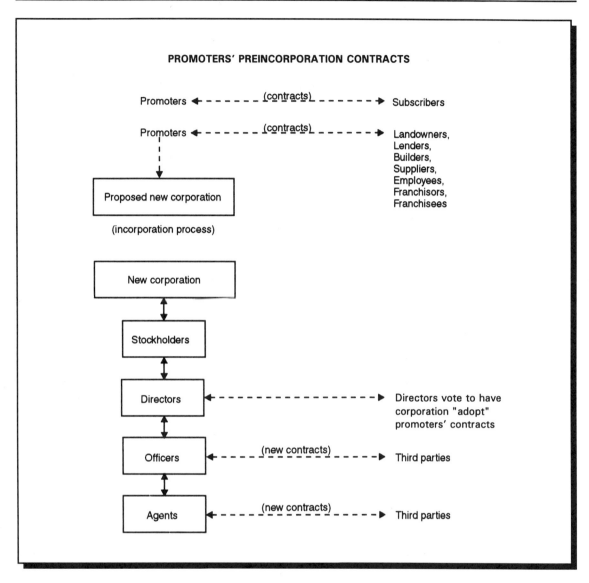

PROMOTERS' PREINCORPORATION CONTRACTS

ters are thus personally liable on all preincorporation contracts (with suppliers, landlords, employees, and so on) unless and until the new corporation comes into existence and "adopts" these contracts as its own. If and when that happens, the states disagree on whether the promoter's liability on the contract is impliedly discharged. If the third party knew that the corporation had not yet been formed and did intend to deal with it through the promoter, and the corporation then comes into existence and adopts the contract, there would seem to be no reason to hold the promoter liable any further. Both parties got exactly the contract they intended and wanted. Some states so hold, but others do not. In this other group of states, the promoter is not discharged unless the third party agrees to a novation, either expressly or impliedly agreeing to accept the corporation in place of the promoter and to discharge the promoter. This second rule seems to give the third party more than he bargained for and more than the promoter originally agreed to. Because of these uncertainties, the preincorporation contract should be very carefully drafted, with a specific statement on when the promoter's liability ends.

FOREIGN CORPORATIONS

Definition. When we see the term **foreign corporation** we normally think of a corporation from some country other than the United States. Actually any corporation for profit, organized and created in one state and doing business in another state, is a foreign corporation. For example, a corporation organized and created in Illinois is a foreign corporation when it is transacting intrastate business in Wisconsin or Iowa. Corporations organized in foreign countries and doing business in a state of the United States would technically be classified as **alien corporations** but are also usually regulated as foreign corporations. Simply stated, any corporation not organized in the specific state in which it is doing local business or requesting to do local business is a foreign corporation insofar as that state's law is concerned. A corporation organized and doing business in the state in which it is organized is termed a **domestic corporation**. Thus, a corporation can be both a domestic corporation and a foreign corporation, depending upon where it is doing business.

Degrees of "Doing Business." A foreign corporation may be subject to the jurisdiction of a state other than the state of incorporation for litigation, for taxation, or for regulation, on the basis of having done business in the second state. The degree of "doing business" necessary to sustain jurisdiction is not the same, however, in the three cases. One transaction may be sufficient to provide jurisdiction for litigation relating to that transaction. For taxation, the event or relationship being taxed must have occurred within the taxing state. For a corporation to be subject to a second state's regulatory system for foreign corporations, it must conduct some more substantial amount of local business in that state.

Jurisdiction for Litigation. If a foreign corporation has been granted a certificate of authority and it does business within a state, then the foreign corporation must designate a person or another corporation as a resident agent for the service of process. Thus, there is no problem in securing service of process against a foreign corporation that is admitted and qualified to do business in the state.

A problem arises when a foreign corporation is doing business within a state but has not secured a certificate of authority and does not have an office or any employees or agents within the state boundaries. In Chapter 4, we indicated that most states now have long arm civil procedure statutes. These statutes allow service of process upon foreign corporations even though they have not registered and have not appointed an agent to receive service of process within the state. Some statutes provide for service of process to the litigation state's secretary of state (who will then forward the notice to the defendant foreign corporation). Other statutes require the plaintiff to send copies of the summons and complaint directly to the out-of-state corporate defendant, by registered or certified mail. In any event, for the long arm process to be constitutionally valid, the defendant foreign corporation must have had some "minimum contact" with persons or property in the plaintiff's state. Exactly how minimal these contacts can be is not yet completely clear, as seen in the next case.

UNITED ROPE DISTRIBUTORS. INC. v. KIMBERLY LINE
770 F.Supp. 128 (S.D. NY, 1991)

FACTS: Plaintiff United Rope Distributors is a Delaware Corporation with its principal place of business in Minnesota. Defendant and third-party plaintiff Kim-Sail, Ltd. is a Cayman Islands corporation with its principal place of business in New York City. Third-party defendant Seatriumph is a Liberian corporation with its principal place of business in Greece.

At the time of the events giving rise to this action, Seatriumph was the owner of the M.V. Katia. Seatriumph had chartered the Katia to a Danish company, Copenship A/S, under a head charter in January 1988. Copenship A/S had in turn subchartered the vessel to Kim-Sail in October 1988.

In November of 1988, Kim-Sail, through its general agent in New York, Kersten Shipping Agency, Inc., accepted 300,000 bales of twine from Sisalana, S.A. of Salvador, Brazil, for shipment to United Rope Distributors in Superior, Wisconsin. The twine was loaded onto the Katia beginning on November 5, 1988 in Salvador, Brazil. The cargo was never delivered because the Katia sank on or about November 25, 1988.

United Rope Distributors brought this admiralty action against Kim-Sail for damages arising from the loss of the cargo. Kim-Sail impleaded Seatriumph, seeking indemnity or contribution for any liability Kim-Sail is found to have to United Rope Distributors. Seatriumph moved to dismiss the third-party complaint on the ground that the court lacked personal jurisdiction over it.

The Katia called at New York in December of 1986 and April of 1987.

In August, 1982, Seatriumph and four other borrowers borrowed $2.5 million from Bank of America International Trust and Savings Association, a California bank. The loan agreement provided for payment to be made in United States dollars at that bank's New York branch. On September 22, 1982, Seatriumph granted a $3.1 million mortgage on the Katia to the bank in order to secure the loans. The mortgage was recorded on that date in a Certificate of Ownership and Encumbrance registered in Seatriumph's name at Liberia's Bureau of Maritime Affairs in New York City. The loan was completely paid off on September 30, 1988.

Seatriumph's head charter with Copenship required all hire thereunder to be paid in United States dollars. More importantly, the head charter also provided that hire was to be paid to the owner's bankers in New York, specifically:

> continental bank international, new york branch ... 520 madison avenue, new york, n.y. 10022 ... attention miss eileen pierson ... in favour of m.v. "katia."

Michael Petropoulos, the president of Seatriumph, affirmed in affidavits that Seatriumph has never had a bank account in New York. Rather, the bank account designated in the head charter for receipt of hire was held by Richmond Investments Ltd., which had agreed with Seatriumph's managing agent, Global Ship Management Ltd. to receive the Katia's charter hire. Richmond, according to Petropoulos, was not a collection agent for Seatriumph but "simply had an account in New York which Richmond agreed (with Global) could be used from time to time for the receipt of funds." In addition, Petropoulos stated that not all of Seatriumph's hire and freight was paid in New York by wire transfer into Richmond's New York account; Seatriumph also used an account which it held at Continental Bank in Pireaus, Greece as well as Global's account in Pireaus. A substantial amount of the Katia's charter hire and freights was paid into the Richmond account in New York.

Petropoulos admitted at his deposition that he had signed the signature card to open Richmond's account into which Seatriumph's hire was paid. Ownership and control of Richmond, Seatriumph, and Global Ship Management overlap. Although Michael Petropoulos in an earlier affidavit sought to distance himself from Richmond, saying that he "believe[d]" that "Richmond Investments Ltd. was in the business of receiving charter hire for various ships," the directors of Richmond are Michael Petropoulos, C. Petropoulos (his mother), and D. Petropoulos. The directors of Seatriumph are Michael Petropoulos, C. Petropoulos, and A. Dousladzi. C. Petropoulos is also Seatriumph 's vice-president. C. Petropoulos and A. Dousladzi are also directors of Global Ship Management. Michael Petropoulos is not an officer or director of Global Ship Management.

Seatriumph paid expenses out of the Richmond account as well as receiving hire into it. Checks were signed by Michael Petropoulos on the New York account of Richmond, as payments made on behalf of Seatriumph, from December 17, 1987 through December 19, 1988. These checks were payments for various expenses of the Katia. Petropoulos also sent telexes to Continental Bank in New York which were instructions from Richmond to make payments on behalf of Seatriumph. The last one was sent on February 22, 1989. From December 1987 through February 1989, Richmond wrote 107 checks and made forty-seven wire transfers on its New York bank account on behalf of Seatriumph.

Richmond received no consideration for allowing the Katia's managers to use its New York bank account. Seatriumph last used the Richmond account on February 22, 1989. The account was closed on instruction from Petropoulos sent on March 20, 1989 (five days after the third-party complaint was served), and the balance in the account was transferred to another account at the same bank in New York, in the name of Med Investments, of which Petropoulos was also a principal.

In addition to these critical financial activities, Kim-Sail points to certain activities by a New York broker, Kersten, involving the Katia or Seatriumph. Kersten, as intermediate broker, negotiated two charters of the Katia in 1987.

From April 16, 1987 to July 2, 1987, Kersten collected six installments of a charterer's hire under a time charter of the Katia it had brokered and sent them to the Richmond account at Continental Bank in New York, which it was told was Seatriumph's account. Seatriumph responds that Kersten was never its broker or agent but was always an intermediate broker that simply received hire and remitted it per instructions of Seatriumph's Copenhagen broker.

 JUDGE CEDARBAUM:

In *Omni Capital Int'l v. Rudolf Wolff & Co.*, the Supreme Court held, in a case arising under a federal statute which did not provide for service of process on party not an inhabitant of or found within the forum state, that under Fed.R.Civ.P. (4)(e), the forum state's long-arm statutes control amenability to suit in the federal courts.... Although this is a suit in admiralty, and not a federal question action, the same principle applies. Therefore, in the absence of a federal statute authorizing service of process beyond the state, I must look to the New York longarm statutes to determine whether I can exercise personal jurisdiction over Seatriumph....

Kim-Sail argues that this court has personal jurisdiction over Seatriumph under Sections 301 and 302(a)(3) of the New York Civil Practice Law and Rules ("CPLR") and because Seatriumph has consented to be sued in this forum....

In order to be subject to personal jurisdiction under CPLR § 301, a non-resident defendant must be "engaged in such a continuous and systematic course of "doing business" [in New York] as to warrant a finding of its "presence" in this jurisdiction.... A foreign corporation may be subject to jurisdiction in New York under § 301 when a separate corporation, acting with its authority and for its substantial benefit, carries out activities in New York that are "sufficiently important to the foreign corporation that if it did not have a representative to perform them, the corporation's own officials would undertake to perform substantially similar services...." A New York representative of a non-resident defendant need not be an official agent for its activities to subject the defendant to personal jurisdiction in New York.... Kim-Sail has made a *prima facie* showing that the systematic financial activities of Richmond in New York in behalf of Seatriumph were carried out with Seatriumph's authority and for its substantial benefit. These activities were sufficiently important to Seatriumph that if it had not had Richmond to perform them, its own officials would have had to perform substantially similar services. Indeed, its own official directed the activities as an official of Richmond....

The only business of Seatriumph was owning and operating the Katia. When it sank, the Katia had been under a time charter to Copenship since January of 1988. Thus, most of Seatriumph's activity ... consisted of paying the expenses of the Katia and receiving its hire. These activities were carried out in New York by Richmond on behalf of Seatriumph.

The Katia's hire constituted substantially all of Seatriumph's profits. Seatriumph required in its head charter with Copenship that all hire be paid in New York City. Indeed, Seatriumph normally required all charterers to pay hire and freight to it via Richmond's account in New York City.... Thus, Seatriumph, in operating the Katia, arranged through its charters to receive virtually all of its income in New York City. This arrangement, combined with Seatriumph's use of Richmond's bank account to make payments for most of the expenses of the Katia, constitutes activity within New York sufficient to make Seatriumph subject to personal jurisdiction as a corporation doing business in New York....

Seatriumph argues that having a New York bank account does not by itself constitute doing business in New York, an unexceptionable proposition. The cases on which Seatriumph relies, however, did not involve bank accounts for the receipt of substantially all of the income of a foreign corporation....

Here, Seatriumph had control over its money held in Richmond's account in New York. In addition, Seatriumph purposefully chose New York as the location to receive its hire.

Seatriumph also argues that even if these facts establish that it was doing business in New York, all activity in New York had ceased by March 15, 1989, when the third-party complaint was filed. Hire was last paid to Seatriumph in the New York account on November 10, 1988, and money was last paid out of that account on behalf of Seatriumph on February 22, 1989, three weeks before the third-party complaint was filed. However, Richmond maintained the account until March 20, 1989, five days after the third-party complaint was filed. On March 30, 1989, under the signature of Petropoulos, Richmond's account was transferred to an account in the same New York bank, in the name of Med Investments, of which Petropoulos was also a principal. Under these circumstances, I find that Seatriumph's ties to New York still existed as of the date of the filing of the third-party complaint.

Finally, requiring Seatriumph to defend this suit in New York does not "offend 'traditional notions of fair play and substantial justice'...."

Because I find that Seatriumph is doing business in New York, it is unnecessary to consider the other grounds advanced by Kim-Sail as a basis for personal jurisdiction over Seatriumph....

For the reasons discussed above, Seatriumph's motion to dismiss the third-party complaint for lack of personal jurisdiction is denied.

Jurisdiction for Taxation. To tax a foreign corporation, the taxing state must show that the corporation has entered into the relationship, within the state, which the tax is designed to reach. Further, if challenged on constitutional grounds, the taxing state must show that the tax does not unfairly discriminate against interstate commerce. Where multistate relationships are involved, some rational apportionment formula must be used to allocate appropriate taxable shares to each state.

With real estate that a foreign corporation owns in the taxing state, the relationship, or "nexus," is clear. The foreign corporation, like any other landowner, will have to pay the assessed real estate taxes. Where personal property of a foreign corporation is being taxed, conflicts may arise if the property is being used in more than one state. For example, trucking companies, airlines, and railroads all have equipment that simply cannot stay in one place all year long. How much of their equipment can be taxed by each of the states where the equipment lands or travels? No uniform or standardized formula for taxing personal property is used in all states. The threat of multiple taxation continues to be a problem for corporations using property in more than one state.

Many difficulties also exist in the area of income taxation. Each state of course wants to tax as much of the foreign corporation's income as possible. In a landmark case the U.S. Supreme Court upheld the state of Minnesota in its taxation of income that the Northwestern States Portland Cement Company derived from sales in interstate commerce rather than intrastate business. After the decision in that case Congress enacted the interstate income law, which provides that a tax cannot be imposed on net income of a person or a corporation engaged in interstate business where the only activity of the person or the corporation is to solicit orders for the sale of tangible personal property, the orders are sent outside the state for approval or rejection, and approved orders are shipped or delivered from a point outside the state. The law also exempts income that a foreign corporation derives from selling or soliciting sales through independent contractors, even though the independent contractor may have an office within the state. There will continue to be many litigations in this area, since the revenue needs of the taxing state must be balanced against the discriminatory effect of the tax on interstate commerce and since the tax statute must provide a rational apportionment formula for multistate income.

The *Mobil Oil* case is one of the key precedents on taxation of multinational corporations.

MOBIL OIL CORPORATION v.
COMMISSIONER OF TAXES OF VERMONT
445 U.S. 425 (1980)

FACTS: Appellant Mobil Oil Corporation is a corporation organized under the laws of the state of New York. It has its principal place of business and its "commercial domicile" in New York City. It is authorized to do business in Vermont.

Mobil engages in an integrated petroleum business, ranging from exploration for petroleum reserves to production, refining, transportation, and distribution and sale of petroleum and petroleum products. It also engages in related chemical and mining enterprises. It does business in over forty of our states and in the District of Columbia as well as in a number of foreign countries.

Much of appellant's business abroad is conducted through wholly and partly owned subsidiaries and affiliates. Many of these are corporations organized under the laws of foreign nations; a number, however, are domestically incorporated in states other than Vermont. None of appellant's subsidiaries or affiliates conducts business in Vermont, and appellant's shareholdings in those corporations are controlled and managed elsewhere, presumably from the headquarters in New York City.

In Vermont, appellant's business activities are confined to wholesale and retail marketing of petroleum and related products. Mobil has no oil or gas production or refineries within the state. Although appellant's business activity in Vermont is by no means insignificant, it forms but a small part of the corporation's worldwide enterprise.

Vermont imposes an annual net income tax on every corporation doing business within the state. Under its scheme, net income is defined as the taxable income of the taxpayer "under the laws of the United States." If a taxpayer corporation does business both within and without Vermont, the state taxes only that portion of the net income attributable to it under a three-factor apportionment formula. In order to determine that portion, net income is multiplied by a fraction representing the arithmetic average of the ratios of sales, payroll, and property values within Vermont to those of the corporation as a whole.

 JUSTICE BLACKMUN:

In this case, we are called upon to consider constitutional limits on a nondomiciliary state's taxation of income received by a domestic corporation in the form of dividends from subsidiaries and affiliates doing business abroad. The state of Vermont imposed a tax, calculated by means of an apportionment formula, upon appellant's so-called foreign source dividend income for the taxable years 1970, 1971, and 1972. The Supreme Court of Vermont sustained that tax....

It long has been established that the income of a business operating in interstate commerce is not immune from fairly apportioned state taxation.... For a state to tax income generated in interstate commerce, the due process clause of the Fourteenth Amendment imposes two requirements: a "minimal connection" between the interstate activities and the taxing state, and a rational relationship between the income attributed to the state and the intrastate values of the enterprise.... The requisite "nexus" is supplied if the corporation avails itself of the "substantial privilege of carrying on business" within the state; and "[t]he fact that a tax is contingent upon events brought to pass without a state does not destroy the nexus between such a tax and transactions within a state for which the tax is an exaction."

We do not understand appellant to contest these general principles.... What appellant does seek to establish, in the due process phase of its argument, is that its dividend income must be excepted from the general principle of apportionability because it lacks a satisfactory nexus with appellant's business activities in Vermont. To carve that out as an exception, appellant must demonstrate something about the nature of this income that distinguishes it from operating income, a proper portion of which the state concededly may tax. From appellant's argument we discern two potential differentiating factors: the "foreign source" of the income, and the fact that it is received in the form of dividends from subsidiaries and affiliates.

The argument that the source of the income precludes its taxability runs contrary to precedent. In the past, apportionability often has been challenged by the contention that income earned in one state may not be taxed in another if the source of the income may be ascertained by separate geographical accounting. The court has rejected that contention so long as the intrastate and extrastate activities formed part of a single unitary business....

The court has applied the same rationale to businesses operating both here and abroad....

[T]he linchpin of apportionability in the field of state income taxation is the unitary business principle. In accord with this principle, what appellant must show in order to establish that its dividend income is not subject to an apportioned tax in Vermont is that the income was earned in the course of activities unrelated to the sale of petroleum products in that state.... [A]ppellant has made no effort to demonstrate that the foreign operations of its subsidiaries and affiliates are distinct in any business or economic sense from its petroleum sales activities in Vermont. Indeed, all indications in the record are to the contrary, since it appears that these foreign activities are part of appellant's integrated petroleum enterprise. In the absence of any proof of discrete business enterprise, Vermont was entitled to conclude that the dividend income's foreign source did not destroy the requisite nexus with in-state activities....

Nor do we find particularly persuasive Mobil's attempt to identify a separate business in its holding company function. So long as dividends from subsidiaries and affiliates reflect profits derived from a functionally integrated enterprise, those dividends are income to the parent earned in a unitary business. One must look principally at the underlying activity, not at the form of investment, to determine the propriety of apportionability....

In addition to its due process challenge, appellant contends that Vermont's tax imposes a burden on interstate and foreign commerce by subjecting appellant's dividend income to a substantial risk of multiple taxation....

Mobil no doubt enjoys privileges and protections conferred by New York law with respect to ownership of its stock holdings, and its activities in that state no doubt supply some nexus for jurisdiction to tax.... But there is no reason in theory why that power should be exclusive when the dividends reflect income from a unitary business, part of which is conducted in other states.... Since Vermont seeks to tax income, not ownership, we hold that its interest in taxing a proportionate share of appellant's dividend income is not overridden by any interest of the state of commercial domicile....

In sum, appellant has failed to demonstrate any sound basis, under either the due process clause or the Commerce Clause, for establishing a constitutional preference for allocation of its foreign source dividend income to the state of commercial domicile. Because the issue has not been presented, we need not, and do not, decide what the constituent elements of a fair apportionment formula applicable to such income would be. We do hold, however, that Vermont is not precluded from taxing its proportionate share.

The judgment of the Supreme Court of Vermont is affirmed.

Jurisdiction for Regulation.

Since a foreign corporation is not a "citizen" under the Fourteenth Amendment, it has no right to transact intrastate business in states other than the state of its creation. However, all of the states have provisions in their corporation laws which allow foreign corporations to do intrastate business upon compliance with certain filing and licensing requirements. Moreover, a foreign corporation may transact interstate business across a state's borders without being required to file and comply with the state's requirements for foreign corporations.

Interstate commerce, that is, commerce among the states, is regulated by the national government under the authority of the Interstate Commerce Clause of the U.S. Constitution (Article I, Section 8). The individual states may not interfere with, burden, or discriminate against interstate commerce by their laws or regulations. The question which then arises is: What is interstate commerce, and what is intrastate commerce? The Model Business Corporation Act sets out some general guidelines as to the activities of foreign corporations which will not be regarded as doing business in a state and will not require filing as a foreign corporation. These activities include selling goods through an independent contractor in another state; soliciting or procuring by mail orders which will be accepted in a home state rather than in the state where they are solicited; conducting isolated transactions; maintaining a bank account; maintaining an office or agency for the transfer, exchange, and registration of the corporation's securities; holding meetings of directors or shareholders; maintaining or defending a lawsuit; or taking out loans or mortgages.

The common element in all of these examples is that the foreign corporation is not intending to conduct a long-term business in the state; does not have employees, agents, or property within the state; and thus is dealing in interstate commerce only. Section 15.01 of the revised MBCA specifically states that the list it sets out is not exclusive. There is no clear rule of thumb as to what is and what is not interstate commerce. Thus, each case is going to have to review separately the amount of business conducted, the type of business conducted, the time span, and so on.

Procedure for Admission.

Chapter 15 of the revised MBCA sets out procedures for the admission of foreign corporations and regulations concerning the doing of local business in a particular state. Similar provisions have been adopted generally by most of the states. However, it must be remembered that this was a "model" act and that not all states adopted it verbatim. Many states have made specific changes to take care of specific problems.

Generally speaking, a foreign corporation doing local business within a state must apply for a certificate of authority. Such an application will normally require the name of the corporation, when and where it was incorporated, the names and addresses of the directors and corporate officers, a breakdown of the number and types of shares issued, and authorization the corporation has regarding the further issuance of stock. The corporation will also be required to estimate the value of the property, both real and personal, that it intends to own within the state and the gross amount of the business that it will transact within the state in the coming year. In addition, it will have to designate some person within the state to be the registered agent upon whom service of process for lawsuits can be made, and it will have to maintain a registered office within the state. A license fee must accompany the application. This license fee will differ from state to state. A franchise tax may be assessed annually, based on the corporation's property within the state and the business it conducts there. The foreign corporation must file an annual report similar to the annual reports filed by domestic corporations. A state may not, however, impose restrictions which violate basic constitutional protections.

Penalties. The Model Business Corporation Act states that a foreign corporation that transacts business within a state without first obtaining a certificate of authority will not be permitted to bring any lawsuit in a court of that state until it has obtained a certificate of authority. The compliance with the requirements for the certificate of authority can be retroactive, thus allowing the corporation to sue on transactions that were consummated prior to the granting of the certificate of authority.

The Model Act goes on to state that the failure of a foreign corporation to obtain a certificate of authority to transact business in a state will not impair the validity of any contracts or acts of the corporation and will not prevent the corporation from defending any action brought against it in a court in the state. Thus, a corporation does not have the right to bring action as a plaintiff in the courts in a state where it is not authorized to do business; however, it does have the right to defend itself.

The foreign corporation will, of course, be liable for all fees and franchise taxes which it would have paid had it duly applied for a certificate of authority and received it. Also, many states have statutory penalties for doing business without first obtaining permission. These penalties may be fines imposed upon the corporation or its individual officers, directors, or resident agents. Another penalty imposed by some states is to make the officers, the directors, and any agents involved in contracts personally liable on the contracts, in effect taking away the corporate shield against liability. Again, it must be noted that not all states adopted the earlier MBCA in its entirety, and thus there are still differences in the treatment of foreign corporations that fail to comply with the requirements of a particular state. Before doing business in a state, a foreign corporation should check out the state's law carefully.

SIGNIFICANCE OF THIS CHAPTER

The corporation is not only for big business. It is an organizational form that can be used by small family businesses, farmers, and professionals, such as doctors, accountants, lawyers, and architects. Nonprofit organizations also may have corporate status.

This chapter first discusses classifications of corporations, and then goes through a typical procedure to be followed in establishing a corporation. The chapter discusses what happens when a mistake is made, and who may be liable. Corporate powers also are discussed.

Nearly all large corporations do business in more than one state, and thus are foreign corporations when they do business in states other than the state that granted their charter. This chapter defines what a foreign corporation is, reviews the filing procedures for registration as a foreign corporation, discusses the rights and duties a foreign corporation has, and reviews the penalty for failure of a foreign corporation to comply with the registration and filing procedures.

Any corporation operating across state lines needs to be aware of these rules, since the consequences of noncompliance can be very serious. Not being licensed as required can result in the invalidation of contracts made in the other state. Failure to pay properly assessed taxes can result in large fines. Failure to defend a properly filed lawsuit can result in a default judgment, which can then be brought to the corporation's home state and enforced. For some of these violations, the human beings representing the foreign corporation may be subject to fines and/or imprisonment. Foreign corporation rules should definitely be factored into the decision to do business in another state.

PROBLEMS FOR DISCUSSION

1. Plaintiff-appellant, John Hyland, M.D., claiming a violation of the Age Discrimination in Employment Act (ADEA) alleges that he was forced to resign as an employee, officer, and director of defendant-appellee, New Haven Radiology Associates, P.C. ("NHRA") because he was 51 years of age. Following extensive discovery, NHRA, a professional corporation, moved for summary judgment, asserting that Hyland lacked the necessary standing to invoke the protections afforded by the ADEA. Applying an "economic realities" test, the District Court granted the motion, finding that NHRA "amounts to a partnership in all but name," and that Hyland was, in effect, a partner in the enterprise. According to the District Court, Hyland therefore was not an employee entitled to claim the benefits provided by the ADEA.

   Appellant and four other radiologists organized NHRA in 1992 as a professional services corporation under the laws of the state of Connecticut to conduct the practice of radiology. Pursuant to the terms of a stockholder's agreement, each of the five founding members contributed the same amount of capital for equal shares in the corporation and an equal voice in management. Profits and losses were divided evenly among the members, all of whom served as corporate officers and directors. The stockholders agreed that stock could be held only by shareholder-members, who were required to be licensed physicians. Upon the death, withdrawal or termination of any member, the member or his estate was required to sell, and NHRA to purchase, that shareholder's stock at a price fixed in accordance with the valuation provisions of the agreement. No stock could be held in the corporation by a nonmember or nonemployee. The stockholders' agreement provided for the admission to membership of additional "Stockholder-Employees," who would enjoy the benefits of the corporation and participate in the management of its affairs equally with the other shareholders.

Is Hyland "really" still a "partner," so that he has no claim as an "employee" under ADEA? Explain.

2. Rochester Leasing, a New York corporation with its principal place of business in Rochester, New York, was in the business of leasing machines and equipment. Schilling, located in Tennessee, had leased twenty-five postage stamp vending machines at $55.35 a month for five years. The machines were delivered, but Schilling claimed that he had been defrauded by the salesman of a Florida company which had initially arranged the lease contract. Schilling refused to pay, and Rochester sued. Rochester was not registered to do business as a foreign corporation in Tennessee. It had no agents or employees there, and all dealings with it in this case had been by mail. The lease contract had been approved by Rochester at its New York office and had provided that all payments should be made there. The trial court dismissed the suit because Rochester was not registered to do business; the court of appeals affirmed; and Rochester then appealed to the Supreme Court.

How should the Tennessee Supreme Court rule, and why?

3. Prior to March 17, Dr. Valencia and eight other medical doctors agreed to staff the emergency room at St. Mary's. On that date, the doctors executed articles of incorporation for Mercy Medical Associates, Inc. On April 6, the articles were approved by the secretary of state. Eugene Birt was treated by Dr. Valencia on May 13, at which time Birt claims malpractice occurred. On May 13, Associates had not received the required certificate of registration from the Board of Medical Registration and Examination, because they had not sent the board a copy of their corporate bylaws. When Birt sued for malpractice, he named the eight nontreating doctors along with Dr. Valencia, St. Mary's, and Associates. Birt appeals from a summary judgment for the eight doctors.

4. Peter Maxwell and his wife Helen were the founders, controlling stockholders, and principal officers of Hi Life Products, Inc. They each owned 47.5 percent of the stock. Helen's sister, Marlene Sadler, and her husband Alan also worked for Hi Life. Marlene and Alan each owned 2.5 percent of Hi Life's stock. Hi Life's board of directors consisted of Peter, Helen, and Alan.

On March 9, 1997, Peter was injured while operating a mixing machine at the Hi Life factory. He suffered a broken arm, cuts, and burns. Surgery was required, and a metal plate was installed in his forearm. State law required employers to have workers' compensation insurance to cover such injuries, but Hi Life had not purchased the required coverage. Peter first consulted with the company's attorney (Brown), who recommended that he retain his own personal lawyer. Peter then hired an outside attorney (Pico), who wrote attorney Brown a letter stating that Peter had a claim for $125,000. Hi Life's directors had a special meeting, from which Peter excused himself. Attorney Brown recommended a settlement of Peter's claim for $122,500. Helen and Alan approved the settlement, and Hi Life paid Peter the $122,500. Hi Life deducted this amount as a business expense in calculating its taxable income for 1997. Peter did not report the $122,500 as income, since Section 104(a)(2) of the Internal Revenue Code said that money received as damages for personal injury is not taxable. The Commissioner argued that the payment was really just a disguised dividend, which would not be deductible by the corporation but which would be taxable income to Peter. The Commissioner determined that Peter and Helen owed $64,185 and that Hi Life owed $58,800. Both the Maxwells and Hi Life petitioned the Tax Court for review of the Commissioner's decision.

Who is right on this tax issue, and why?

5. Ill health forced James Bukacek to sell his dairy business. His personal problems resulted in a divorce from his wife, Virginia. His financial affairs were also in bad shape. The sheriff was advertising his 300-acre farm for sale, to pay three judgments; he owed the state $15,000 for back taxes; and his mortgage payment was overdue. Bukacek was also unable to exercise the option which Virginia had given him on the 180 acres she owned. At this point, Bukacek went to see Buttram "about saving 'my farm.'" Together with Kelly and Wyatt, they agreed to organize Pell City Farms, Inc. Bukacek conveyed his 300 acres to Pell City, which also exercised the option on Virginia's 180 acres. Pell City (or its promoters) paid off all the back claims and personally assumed the old mortgage and executed a new one. When the deeds from James and Virginia were executed, Pell City's articles had not been filed with the local judge of probate, as required by Alabama law. James filed an action to quiet title to the land in himself, since Pell City was not incorporated and therefore could not take title. The trial court held for Pell City, and James appealed.

How should his appeal be decided? Explain.

Chapter 34

Corporations—Stocks and Stockholders

The legal structure of a corporation differs substantially from that of a partnership. As discussed in Chapter 31, each partner is assumed to have an equal voice in managing the business, the right to an equal share of the profits, and the liability for an equal share of the losses. If necessary, any partner can be forced to pay the firm's debts in full. Each partner is assumed to be a general agent of the firm, with full authority to conduct all of its normal business operations. The partners' investments in the firm are governed by their own partnership agreement. These management and ownership rights and liabilities inhere in each partner individually, as the result of their partnership agreement. Partnership status cannot be transferred to someone else by the act of a single partner.

Corporate Ownership. Nearly all these ownership and management rules are different for a corporation. The primary mechanism for corporation investment and control purposes is the share of stock. A corporation, as a separate legal person, can of course borrow money in much the same way as an individual or a partnership can. The equity investment in the corporation, however, is done by buying shares of stock. The investor agrees to buy a certain number of shares and receives a certificate indicating how many shares have been purchased. The investor, now a "stockholder" or "shareholder," has the right to vote the number of shares owned at stockholders' meetings. The investor also has the right to receive dividends, as earned and declared, based on the number of shares owned. While the stockholder is not considered an agent of the corporation, and generally has no authority to conduct its business operations, shares of stock are assumed to be freely transferable. The shares can be sold to someone else without the consent of the other shareholders or of the corporation, and the transferee becomes a shareholder with the same rights as all other shareholders.

As a separate legal person, the corporation owns its own assets. Individual stockholders have no right to possess or use these assets just because they are stockholders. Their shares of stock simply make them the "owners" of proportionate parts of the corporation's net worth.

As the *Engstrand* case shows, a corporation's stockholders do not normally have any personal rights against third parties who have dealt with their corporation.

ENGSTRAND v. WEST DES MOINES STATE BANK
516 N.W.2d 797 (IA, 1994)

FACTS: The Engstrand family owned a wholesale boat company in Ankeny called Ralph's Distributing Company (Ralph's). Ralph, Mark, and Michael Engstrand were the sole shareholders in Ralph's. Ralph's expanded into the retail business by opening a Des Moines store called Des Moines Boating Center (DMBC), a wholly owned subsidiary of Ralph's. A second retail operation, called Boatland, was opened in Lincoln, Nebraska. Boatland was also owned solely by Ralph's.

Because of a combination of adverse factors, the businesses fell on hard times, and in 1988 the companies showed a loss of $600,000. In December 1988, the two retail establishments, DMBC and Boatland, filed bankruptcy under Chapter 11. The cases were subsequently ordered into Chapter 7 liquidations by the bankruptcy court, and various creditors began to scramble to claim their collateral.

The retail buildings and grounds were packed with inventory, including boats and boating accessories. Many secured creditors attempted to pick up their collateral from the premises. In the meantime, the defendant bank began to dictate the disposition of the collateral in which it had a security interest.

In July 1989, this suit was filed against West Bank and Boats Unlimited. The plaintiffs alleged that West Bank was negligent in its lending relationship with the plaintiffs, negligent in failing to allow the plaintiffs an active role in the liquidation, and negligent in failing to dispose of the collateral in a commercially reasonable manner. The plaintiffs also alleged that the bank breached a fiduciary duty to the plaintiffs.

The court granted a directed verdict in favor of Boats Unlimited, but a jury returned substantial verdicts against the bank. The court entered a judgment notwithstanding that verdict, and the plaintiffs appealed.

 JUSTICE LARSON:

The issues on appeal in this case are whether the court erred in ruling as a matter of law that the bank did not owe a fiduciary duty to the plaintiffs and ruling that neither the bank nor Boats Unlimited owed a "special duty" to the plaintiff shareholders to allow them to sue for alleged wrongs committed against the corporations.... The issue in a companion appeal Is whether the bank properly foreclosed a real estate mortgage given as additional security....

The nature of a two-party relationship may be enough in itself to create a fiduciary duty. For example, a fiduciary duty arises between attorneys and clients, guardians and wards, and principals and agents.... This, however, is not true as to a bank's relationship with its customers, whether they are borrowers or depositors. The banking-customer relationship does not automatically create a fiduciary duty.

Here, the bank agreed to make a loan on certain conditions, and the plaintiffs agreed to accept the loan with those conditions. The bank was acting on its own behalf and not on behalf of the plaintiffs in a confidential or trust relationship.

There was no evidence that the bank was acting as an advisor to the plaintiffs or that it exercised any influence over the plaintiffs' business except to enforce its loan agreement.

Viewing the evidence in the light most favorable to the verdict, we agree that it is not sufficient to create a fiduciary relationship, and the court correctly directed a verdict on this issue.

II. The Special Duty Issue.

The district court ruled as a matter of law that the defendants owed to the plaintiffs no "special duty" that would permit a direct suit as shareholders. On that basis, the court granted a judgment notwithstanding the verdict in favor of the defendants....

The Engstrands were shareholders in Ralph's, which was, in turn, the sole shareholder of the retail businesses known as Des Moines Boating and Boatland. Thus, all claims by these plaintiffs are as shareholders, either in Ralph's or through Ralph's' ownership of the shares in the retail outlets. All of the plaintiffs' claims arise out of wrongs allegedly committed against the corporations. They claim that they may pursue these claims in their own right because the defendants owed them a "special duty" because the bank had agreed that the plaintiffs would be actively involved in the liquidation of their assets and because they had personally guaranteed the corporations' indebtedness.

We have recognized that,

> [a]s a matter of general corporate law, shareholders have no claim for injuries to their corporations by third parties unless within the context of a derivative action.

There is, however, a well-recognized exception to the general rule: a shareholder has an individual cause of action if the harm to the corporation also damaged the shareholder in his capacity as an individual rather than as a shareholder....

... [T]he test is best stated in the disjunctive: in order to bring an individual cause of action for direct injuries a shareholder must show that the third-party owed him a special duty *or* that he suffered an injury separate and distinct from that suffered by the other shareholders....

As one court has noted,

> [t]here are several well-founded reasons why a stockholder is precluded from asserting a personal right of action against a third party whose actions have caused damage to the corporation. In such a case, it is the corporation that has suffered direct injury, and any damage resulting to the stockholder is merely indirect; such damage is normally reflected only in the decreased value of his stock. In addition, however, the rule requiring that such a claim be pursued on behalf of the corporation and for its benefit prevents a multiplicity of suits by the various stockholders and assures that the corporation will be bound by the result of the litigation. Finally, by requiring the suit to be maintained for the corporation's benefit, any proceeds re-

sulting from the litigation will be treated as corporate assets and available to satisfy both creditors' and other stockholders' claims....

The court in *Nicholson* [a precedent case] also rejected an argument for a special duty based upon the shareholder's guaranty of a corporate obligation....
As one authority has noted,

[a]ny other rule might result in as many suits against the wrongdoer as there were shareholders in the corporation. If damages to a shareholder result indirectly, as the result of an injury to the corporation, and not directly, the shareholder cannot sue as an individual....

The Engstrands raised a similar "special duty" argument in a federal suit against one of their boat suppliers. A summary judgment in favor of the defendant was affirmed by the eighth circuit on the ground that a special duty was not established....
In this case, the suit was not on the guaranty agreement itself. While the wrong complained of, the alleged unreasonable disposition of the collateral, indirectly affected these plaintiffs, it was a wrong against the corporation.
Because the evidence, even when viewed in the light most favorable to the plaintiffs, fails to establish a special duty so as to permit this action on behalf of the shareholders, the court properly entered the judgment notwithstanding the verdict. This disposition makes it unnecessary to address any of the additional issues raised by the parties.
Affirmed.

CLASSES OF STOCK

In small corporations there is normally only one type of stock. Typically all of the shares in a small corporation have the same value and all of the shareholders have the same rights. This is not true in large corporations where it is not uncommon to have several classes and series of stock. Some stock may have a par value, and other stock may have no-par value. Some stock may have voting rights, and other stock may not have voting rights. Some stock may be preferred, and other stock may be common.

Common Stock. This is the basic class of stock issued by corporations. Typically a shareholder has one vote for each share of stock and the shareholder is entitled to receive a *pro rata* share of the corporation's profits in the form of dividends. The common stockholder is given no guarantees, no special preference. If the business succeeds, the common stockholders receive dividends and their share value will increase. If the business fails, the common stockholders get no return on their investment and they may lose the investment itself, as they share in the balance of the assets after creditors and preferred stockholders have been paid off.

Preferred Stock. As the term indicates, this class of stockholders gets special preference. Typically the preferred stockholder receives a specific, guaranteed dividend before any dividends are paid to the persons owning the corporation's common stock. In case of dissolution of the corporation the preferred stockholders get their money back before any money is returned to the common stockholders.

The preferred stockholder is not a creditor of the corporation, and normally the dividend on preferred stock does not have to be paid if the board of directors decides not to declare a dividend.

Cumulative Preferred Stock. In some lean years the corporation may not have enough profits to declare a dividend for either the preferred stockholders or the common stockholder. This question then arises: Does the preferred stockholder lose out on the unpaid dividend for such years? Unless the articles of incorporation state otherwise, the unpaid dividends on preferred stock would accumulate. Thus, it is important that preferred stock be declared either noncumulative or cumulative. If the preferred stock is noncumulative, then, of course, if no dividends are declared by the board of directors during a given year, the preferred stockholders simply lose out for that year. If the stock is cumulative, then the next year they will get the past year's dividends plus the new year's dividends before any money is distributed to the common stockholders.

Participating Preferred Stock. The preferred stockholder has the advantage of receiving dividends prior to the distribution of dividends to the common stockholder. Typically, however, the preferred stockholder is entitled to receive only a specific, guaranteed dividend, for example, 6 percent. If the corporation had a good year, the amount left to divide among the common stockholders might well exceed the percentage awarded to the preferred stockholders. However, if the preferred stockholder has participating preferred stock, then the preferred stockholder would share in the amount divided after the common stockholders received a dividend equal to the dividend paid to the preferred stockholders. Thus, if the preferred stockholders get 6 percent on their stock, then the common stockholders would get 6 percent on their stock and if there was extra money left over, it would be shared equally on a *pro rata* basis between the two classes of shared stock. This special feature would have to be expressly stated.

In addition to the cumulative or noncumulative and participating or nonparticipating provisions of preferred stock, it is not uncommon to find **redeemable** or **convertible** provisions. Such provisions say, in effect, that at the election of the corporation or of the stockholder, preferred shares may be converted into another class of shares or may be redeemable by the corporation.

Par Value and No-Par-Value Stock. A corporation may issue stock with or without a par value. The certificates for par value stock state an amount which must be paid per share for the stock by the subscriber. The amount paid per share of no-par-value stock is simply determined by the board of directors.

The issuance of par value stock often creates misunderstanding. For example, if a new corporation issues 1,000 shares at a par value of $100 each and you buy ten shares at $100 each, you will be given stock certificates that show a face value of $1,000. The corporation, however, proceeds to buy equipment and inventory and to pay the expenses of incorporation and other expenses of doing business, and thus the corporation no longer has a net worth of $100,000 or 1,000 times $100 per share of par value stock. As a result, even though your certificate of stock shows a par value of $100 per share, you could not necessarily sell the stock for $100 per share as the stock is now only worth 1/1000 of the net worth or book value of the corporation. The revised Model Business Corporation Act eliminates the concept of par value.

ISSUANCE OF SHARES

Authorized Stock. This term describes the number of shares and the kind of stock that the corporation is authorized to issue. The original charter issued to the corporation by the state of its creation states the number of shares authorized and also the kind of shares authorized. If the corporation desires to increase its authority to issue more shares or different kinds of stock it must apply to the state of its creation. Such approval will be granted if the request complies with the requirements of the state's corporation laws. A minimal filing fee will be charged.

Unissued Stock. This term refers to the authorized stock that is not yet issued.

Issued Stock. This term refers to the shares of stock that have been sold and delivered to shareholders. It includes shares that have been reacquired by the corporation as treasury shares.

Outstanding Stock. This term describes that stock that has been issued and is currently owned by stockholders.

Treasury Stock. This term refers to stock that was issued to shareholders and was later repurchased by the corporation. Treasury stock must be paid for with the corporation's surplus funds; the corporation cannot use original capital funds to repurchase stock. Also, the shares of treasury stock, while they are held in the corporation's name, are not votable, and such shares cannot earn dividends. Treasury stock may be resold, held, or canceled. Canceling these shares reduces the number of shares issued, and the corporation can then issue new stock as long as it does not exceed the total number of shares authorized. The revised MBCA provides that such shares become authorized, unissued stock, unless their reissue is prohibited by the articles of incorporation.

SUBSCRIPTIONS FOR SHARES

One of the promoters' most important preincorporation functions is to make arrangements for acquiring the capital necessary to commence the firm's business. Persons making preincorporation offers to buy shares of the firm's stock are called **subscribers**. Since these offers are made to the corporation, they cannot be accepted until after incorporation. Unfortunately, in many cases proposed corporations fail before they ever commence business or after a very short period of operation. If there are unpaid creditors of the now insolvent corporation, it thus becomes very important to know exactly when subscribers become liable for their shares, and the extent of that liability.

Revocable Offer. The general rule is that a stock subscription, like any offer, is revocable prior to acceptance. This rule creates problems for the promoters, since they can't count on having any set amount of capital until the corporation is formed and accepts the subscription offers. Some courts have found particular subscriptions to be irrevocable because the promoters' efforts provided consideration for an implied promise by the subscriber not to revoke. Some cases find mutual promise between the several subscribers not to revoke. Section 17 of the MBCA, which has been adopted in many states, makes the subscription offer irrevocable for six months without consideration. Of course, where fraud was committed against the subscriber, the offer can be revoked despite Section 17 or the presence of consideration. The revised MBCA contains a similar provision.

Implied Conditions Precedent.
For a subscriber to be held liable on a subscription contract, the courts have generally agreed that three conditions must be met. First, the corporation must be fully organized de jure. Second, it must be substantially like the one proposed to the subscriber. And finally, the shares subscribed for must be legally issuable by the corporation (in other words, must not be shares representing an oversubscription).

Express Conditions Precedent/Subscriptions on Special Terms.
Some potential subscribers may not be interested in investing in the proposed corporation unless certain return promises are made. These special promises could relate to the corporation's method of operation, the location of its place of business, or other matters. What happens when the corporation is organized, accepts the subscriptions, but goes into bankruptcy before it builds its main plant in Keokuk, as it promised one subscriber? Is that subscriber liable anyway, or was the "plant in Keokuk" an express condition precedent which has not been fulfilled? As between risk-taking investors and unpaid corporate creditors, the equities are all with the creditors. Courts will try as hard as possible to label these special deals as *subscriptions on special terms*, so as to hold the subscriber liable for the full price of the contracted shares. After paying in full, the subscriber then has a claim for damages, if any can be proved, for the corporation's breach of its promise to build the plant. If the parties' intent and the "no contract if no plant" results are spelled out clearly enough in the subscription, the subscriber may avoid liability.

Subscription versus Contract to Purchase Shares.
Particularly in cases where the stock is being paid for in installments, it may also be important to distinguish between a subscription and a contract to purchase shares. A subscriber becomes liable for the full price of the shares when the subscription offer is effectively accepted by the corporation. A purchaser does not become a shareholder (and thus become liable for the price of the shares) until a certificate is delivered or tendered. Where corporations have gone into bankruptcy before issuance of the certificates, many courts have held that the purchasers were excused from further liability because they would never receive their certificates. Subscribers in such a case would be bound to pay any balance due on their shares.

Once again, in figuring out which is which, it's a question of the parties' intent and of some legal presumptions and rules. Prior to incorporation, the transaction can only be a subscription, not a purchase. After incorporation, the agreement to buy original, unissued shares may be either. Generally, a purchase is an individual agreement, whereas a subscription may involve several purchasers. If there is any ambiguity at all, most courts will try to impose full liability by classifying the transaction as a subscription. The revised MBCA makes all postincorporation agreements "contracts."

Minimum Liability Equals Full Par Value.
In some instances subscribers may not be willing to pay the full par value per share, and the promoters may agree to sell shares at a discount. This is a dangerous practice at best, since all states agree, on one theory or another, that every subscriber must pay at least the full par value for each share taken. One early case held that the corporation's capital was a sort of "trust fund" for the benefit of its creditors. A few states analyze the discount to subscribers as a fraud on the firm's creditors. The most sensible analysis simply

says that payment of at least full par is the price the state demands for the privilege of doing business in the corporate form with limited personal liability.

Under any of these theories, creditors can force payment of the difference between the discounted contract price and the full par value. Creditors who knew about the discount when they extended credit, however, might have some difficulty in recovering in a fraud theory state. Stockholders who have paid full par for their shares might also sue to force the discounter to pay up. In some cases the corporation itself or the state of incorporation may bring the suit.

In addition to the original subscriber who bought at a discount (whether or not still a stockholder), possible defendants include knowing transferees of the discounted shares, the directors who approved the sale, and the promoters. As states adopt the revised MBCA, these lawsuits will be almost completely eliminated, since there will be no "par value" for shares.

Creditors in a fraud theory state must also prove that they "relied" on some misrepresentation of the amount of the debtor corporation's capital.

Payment in Property or Services. Another potential area of liability arises when shares are paid for with noncash items. Property or services, to be valid payment for shares, must be usable by the corporation in operating its business. Generally, promises to perform services or to deliver property in the future do not constitute proper payment for shares, and subscribers who receive shares in exchange for such promises could be sued for the full par value of the shares they receive. The revised MBCA permits payment with promissory notes and with promises to perform services.

Complications arise not only from questions as to whether or not the corporation was authorized to receive the noncash items but also as to the valuation of those items. States use two very different rules in determining whether at least full par has been paid. The Model Act and most of the newer corporation statutes have adopted the *good faith rule*: the valuation of the board of directors is conclusive. Whatever the board says the property or services were worth binds the corporation and all its creditors, unless the board was acting fraudulently or was grossly negligent. Some of the states still follow the older *true value rule*, which holds that any such noncash item had a true market value when it was transferred to the firm in payment for shares, that such value presents a question of fact, and that a jury can thus determine the true value of the noncash item. The result of this rule is that jurors are second-guessing the parties, sometimes after a lapse of several years, on the basis of less than perfect information.

No-Par Shares. As noted above, no-par stock does not have any specific dollar figure indicated on the share certificate. Thus, most "valuation" problems are avoided when no-par stock is exchanged for a noncash item. Most statutes permit no-par shares to be issued for such consideration as is agreed to by the directors (or the existing stockholders). The no-par's price is thus permitted to fluctuate with market conditions, and the no-par stockholders would not be held liable for any "discount." No-par shares cannot, however, be issued as a gift. Moreover, there is case law that indicates that after the initial issue, if the price paid for no-par is not "fair" to the existing stockholders, they can bring suit to enjoin the dilution of their interest in the firm's net assets. Again, this difference in treatment will be eliminated under the revised MBCA, which eliminates the idea of par value.

Treasury Shares. Treasury shares (which were issued but then reacquired by the corporation) generally may be resold for any consideration fixed by the board of directors. Once again, there should be no "valuation" problem or "discount" liability as long as the directors were acting in good faith. The revised MBCA simply makes such stock additional authorized but unissued shares.

Shares Issued by Going Concern. What if the corporation needs additional capital after it has been in operation for some period of time? If it still has original, unissued par stock, can it sell that stock to investors at the market price, or is it still bound to receive at least par value per share? Only in a few states do the corporation statutes recognize this problem and specifically permit the directors, in this case, to sell par stock at the going market price. This problem, too, should be solved by the adoption of the revised MBCA.

Repurchase of Shares. Having required the payment of at least par value per share by subscribers/investors, courts do not want these risktakers to be able to escape easily if the firm gets into financial difficulties. Creditors should be paid in full before stockholders recover any part of their investment. Thus, a contract for the repurchase of shares is valid only if the corporation has earned surplus when the contract is made, and for such a contract to be enforceable in court by the shareholder, the corporation must also have earned surplus when payment is to be made to the shareholder. At both points in time, the earned surplus shown on the books must be sufficient to cover the repurchase.

REGISTRATION AND TRANSFER OF SHARES

Registration. Many securities issues must be registered with either the Securities and Exchange Commission, a similar state agency, or both. This is a very complex area of the law. Chapter 37 discusses the nature of these registration requirements and the potential liabilities involved.

Mechanics of Transfer. Article 8 of the UCC contains many of the rules covering the transfer of corporate securities (both stocks and bonds). Many customary practices are also involved—stockbrokers' rules for dealing with each other and their customers, regulations adopted by the stock exchanges, and administrative rulings from the SEC. Large corporations usually appoint a bank or trust company to act as their **transfer agent**; that is, to record transfer of their securities and to issue new certificates in the new owners' names. Securities, particularly bonds, may also be issued in bearer form, in which case ownership transfers are not registered with the corporation. **Bearer bonds** are often called **coupon bonds**, since interest coupons attached to such bonds must be clipped and sent in by the bondholder in order to receive the interest due on the bonds.

The revised MBCA does not require that a corporation issue paper certificates as evidence of ownership of its shares. Most corporations have done so, and continue to do so, but computerized share transfers may become more popular in the near future. If used, share certificates provide proof of ownership of the shares they represent and furnish a handy means of dealing with the shares. When shares are sold, the certificate is indorsed over to the buyer or simply indorsed in blank. When shares are used as collateral in a credit transaction, the certificate is usually left with the creditor.

As discussed in Chapter 10, every contract for the sale of investment securities is subject to the Statute of Frauds rules in UCC 8-319. The contract is not enforceable unless the party against whom enforcement is sought (or an authorized agent) has signed a writing containing the quantity of the particular security being bought and sold and a statement of the price or a means of ascertaining the price. As an alternative, either party may send the other a writing in confirmation of their oral contract. If the confirmation is sufficient against the sender and if the receiver does not send back written notice of objection to its contents within ten days after receipt, the confirmation does satisfy the writing requirement against the receiver as well as against the sender. Where a payment for the securities has been accepted or securities have been delivered to the buyer, the oral contract is enforceable by the person who has given the partial performance to the same extent that performance has been accepted. Finally, an oral contract for the sale of securities is enforceable to the extent that it is admitted in court.

Someone who transfers a certificate for value warrants to the purchaser that: (1) the transfer is effective and rightful; (2) the certificate is genuine and has not been materially altered; and (3) the transferor knows of no fact that would impair the validity of the certificate. However, if the transfer is made by an intermediary, that person warrants only that the transfer is authorized and is made in good faith.

Registration of Transfer. Where securities have been issued in registered form, the corporation may continue to treat as owner the person whom they have registered as owner. That registered owner would, for instance, continue to receive dividends on the shares. A buyer of registered shares, therefore, may wish to have the transfer of ownership registered on the corporation's books. The corporation has a duty to do so if: (1) the certificate has been properly indorsed; (2) reasonable assurance is given that the indorsement is valid; (3) no adverse ownership claims to the shares have been presented to the corporation and are still pending; (4) all applicable tax laws have been satisfied; and (5) the transfer was in fact rightful or was made to a bona fide purchaser who received the certificate free of adverse claims. A bona fide purchaser (BFP) of the certificate is a person who took it for value, in good faith, and without notice of any adverse claims. In order for the transferee to receive this BFP protection, the certificate must have been issued in bearer form or have been properly indorsed.

Lost or Stolen Securities. Where the missing securities were in bearer form or had been properly indorsed by the former registered owner, a good faith purchaser from the thief or finder owns the securities. If registered securities are involved, the *bona fide* purchaser (BFP) is entitled to be registered on the corporation's books as the new owner.

Where the securities were in registered form but the thief or finder forged the indorsement/ assignment of the owner, the BFP does not own the certificates and must return them. If the BFP sends in an old certificate to the transfer agent, however, and the old certificate is canceled and a new one issued to the BFP, the BFP does own the new certificate. In this last situation the former owner has a claim against the corporation and its transfer agent for not catching the forgery. Because of the potential liabilities resulting from such a "double issuance" of a new certificate, corporations will uniformly require that persons who claim that their certificates have been lost or stolen post bonds protecting the corporation against the "reappearance" of the missing securities.

Restrictions. Corporate securities are generally freely transferable by the owner. In special situations, however, the persons operating the firm may wish to place limitations on the retransfer of its stock. In a small closely held corporation, for example, the stockholders might want to give the corporation itself or the other stockholders a right of first refusal before any stock is resold to outsiders. Similarly, there might be a requirement that shares issued to key employees be resold to the firm rather than to outsiders when the employment ends. For such restrictions to be effective against buyers who don't know about them, they must be noted conspicuously on the certificate.

SHAREHOLDER RIGHTS

Vested Rights. As noted in Chapter 33, the charter of the corporation is a contract. This means that the shareholders' rights the charter establishes cannot be changed without their consent. Where the power to amend the articles and the bylaws has been reserved, however, and the amendment procedure is followed, changes can be made in the respective rights and liabilities of the stockholders.

Preemptive Rights. One right recognized in many older cases is the right to maintain one's proportionate investment in the corporation. The original stock issue gave each stockholder a certain percentage of the votes and of any dividends declared. To protect this relationship among the stockholders, courts required that existing stockholders be given a right of first refusal for a proportionate part of any new issue. That is, the new stock had to be offered to existing stockholders first, before it could be sold to others. Courts did not agree as to whether this "preemptive right" also applied to originally authorized but unissued stock.

Insistence on such preemptive rights makes it very difficult for a firm to authorize a new stock issue for executive bonuses, acquisition of assets, mergers with other firms, or other possible business needs. The modern tendency is to limit or eliminate such preemptive rights unless they are specifically provided for in the articles or by agreement among the stockholders.

Voting Rights. In most states, corporations are permitted to issue both voting and nonvoting stock. As previously noted, typically common stock has the right to vote, while preferred stock does not. Unlike partnerships, where each *partner* is presumed to have one vote regardless of the amount invested, in corporations each *share* is entitled to one vote.

To facilitate minority representation on the board of directors, some corporations provide for cumulative voting. (In some states, in fact, cumulative voting for directors is required by law.) Under this voting system, all directors' vacancies that are to be filled in a given year are voted for at the same time, with each share having as many votes as there are directors to be elected. The idea is that by massing their votes for only one (or a few) candidates, minority stockholders may be able to get at least some representation on the board. A seat on the board enables the minority to obtain information and to present alternative proposals and views. To find out how many shares they need to assemble to be assured of electing their candidates, minority stockholders can use the following formula:

$$X = \frac{a \times c + 1}{b + 1}$$

where X equals the number of shares needed, a equals the number of shares voting in the election, b equals the number of directors to be elected, and c equals the number of directors the minority want to elect.

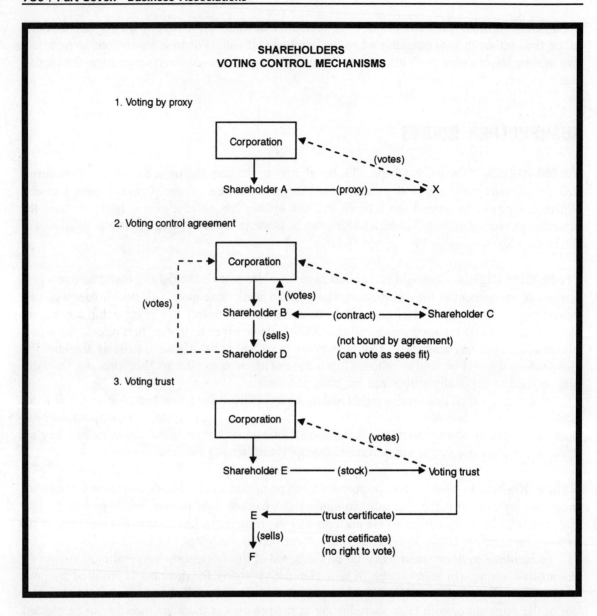

SHAREHOLDERS
VOTING CONTROL MECHANISMS

1. Voting by proxy

Corporation
(votes)
Shareholder A ————(proxy)————► X

2. Voting control agreement

Corporation
(votes)
(votes)
Shareholder B ◄————(contract)————► Shareholder C
(sells)
Shareholder D

(not bound by agreement)
(can vote as sees fit)

3. Voting trust

Corporation
(votes)
Shareholder E ————(stock)————► Voting trust

E ◄————(trust certificate)————
(sells)
F

(trust cetificate)
(no right to vote)

Voting Control Mechanisms. To assemble the number of shares needed to obtain board representation or to gain or maintain control, shareholder groups can use one of three devices: the proxy, the voting control agreement, or the voting trust. A **proxy** is merely a revocable agency authority to vote shares. Changing conditions or new information could lead stockholders to withdraw their proxies or to give later proxies to the opposing side. Proxies thus do not provide a very stable coalition.

Some or all of the stockholders, particularly in closely held corporations, may enter into **voting control agreements**. Such agreements usually provide for reciprocal voting for the board of directors; A, B, and C agree to vote for each other, so that each retains a seat on the board. Such agreements are permitted in most states, at least for a limited period of time. They are not, however, binding on the corporation or on unknowing transferees of stock. A stockholder wishing to break up such an agreement could simply transfer shares to a BFP, who would then be free to vote them as he or she pleased.

The **voting trust** is the most durable arrangement for accumulating the votes necessary to maintain control of a corporation. Stockholders, the corporation itself, and transferees are all bound by the voting trust, since shares of stock are actually turned over to the voting trustees, who are registered as the owners of the shares on the corporation's books. In return for their shares, the (former) stockholders receive voting trust certificates, which give them all the rights of stockholders *except* the right to vote. Many voting trusts are set up by demand of the firm's creditors, as a condition to the extension of further credit. The creditors want to assure continuity of management, and a voting trust is a good way to do so.

The *Sanders* case explains the "writing" requirements for voting agreements.

SANDERS v. McMULLEN
868 F.2d 1465 (5th Cir., 1989)

FACTS: The Houston Sports Association (HSA) is a Texas corporation that owns and operates the Astrodome and the Houston Astros Baseball Club. In 1979, the defendant-appellee, John J. McMullen, formed the Houston Astros Limited Partnership (HALP) to purchase the capital stock of HSA from its creditors. McMullen was a general partner of HALP and personally owned 25 percent of the partnership. His family owned an additional 8 percent. The plaintiff, Don A. Sanders, as one of twenty-five other investors, owned a 2 percent interest in HALP.

After the 1980 baseball season, investors sought to oust McMullen as a general partner of HALP, and the organization was dissolved. HSA, however, was recapitalized and the partners of HALP received HSA stock. The result was that McMullen controlled 34 percent of the stock and became Chairman of the Board. Sanders still owned 2 percent.

In 1984, minority shareholders tried to enter a voting agreement with 51 percent of the stockholders to remove McMullen from management of HSA. Sanders' 2 percent interest was included in the 51 percent, but he decided to withdraw from the agreement, leaving the shareholders with only 49 percent. Sanders claims he agreed to withdraw because of promises made by McMullen. McMullen was able to retain control of HSA, and even purchased more shares when the organization was restructured. McMullen then controlled 63 percent of the shares and Sanders increased his share to 13 percent with a $4 million stock purchase.

Sanders contends that McMullen promised him the following items in exchange for withdrawing from the voting trust:

(1)   Participation in all management decisions involving the baseball team.

(2)   Access to all operational information.

(3)   The baseball manager and staff would be advised of Sanders' status.

(4)   Participation in league meetings, World Series, and All Star Game activities.

(5)   Access to all baseball facilities.

(6) Inclusion of his shares in the control block for any sale.

(7) McMullen would vote his shares to keep Sanders on the Board of Directors.

Sanders contends that he purchased the additional stock and withdrew from the voting trust that would have ousted McMullen in reliance on these promises. A continuing shareholder's agreement and a collateral agreement were both signed by the parties. The agreements represented Sanders' additional investment of $4 million. The promises are not contained in the documents or mentioned on the stock certificates.

In November 1986, Sanders was not reelected to the Board of Directors of HSA and McMullen sent him a letter stating that he was not entitled to any special privileges as a shareholder. Sanders sued McMullen for breaching the agreement and for fraudulent misrepresentation. He sought specific performance or an injunction requiring McMullen to honor his agreement. The trial court stated that Sanders wanted McMullen to purchase his shares for a 100 percent profit, but this remark is disputed by Sanders' attorneys, who say he seeks only fair market value. An expert witness testified that the value of Sanders' stock is considerably lower if it is not part of the control block.

The trial court granted McMullen's motion for summary judgment, finding that there was no genuine issue of material fact.

 CIRCUIT JUDGE GEE:

Summary judgment is appropriate when there is no genuine issue of material fact for the jury to decide. In this case, the trial court examined the evidence and determined that any agreement between McMullen and Sanders was a "voting agreement" that fell under the Texas Business Corporation Act, Article 2.30(B).

This statute ... requires, in rather verbose fashion, three things:

(1) A writing.

(2) A deposit of a counterpart at the corporation's main office.

(3) Reference to the agreement on the certificates.

The trial court determined that the oral agreement between McMullen and Sanders was a "voting agreement" subject to the requirements of Article 2.30(13). Since the promises were not in writing, the court granted summary judgment on the issue. The trial court treated all of the issues as constituting a voting agreement, although not all of them related to voting. In fact, of the seven alleged promises, only the one that required McMullen to vote his shares so as to keep Sanders on the Board is without question controlled by Article 2.30(B). The trial court's summary judgment on alleged promises not relating to the voting of shares is therefore reversed and remanded.

With regard to the alleged agreement that McMullen vote so as to keep Sanders on the Board, the appellant argues that the doctrine of part performance removes it from the statute of frauds. The part performance by Sanders would be his purchase of the shares. The appellant contends McMullen's alleged agreement would then be enforceable without meeting the writing requirement of Article 2.30(B).

The appellant's argument is not persuasive. Part performance must be specifically referable to an agreement. As Cardozo wrote,

> There must be performance "unequivocally referable" to the agreement, performance which alone and without the aid of words of promise is unintelligible or at least extraordinary unless as an incident of ownership, assured, if not existing....

The other cause of action, fraudulent misrepresentation, sounds in tort. The order of the trial court fails completely to address the fraud complaint....

Perhaps the trial court considered the tort claim moot since the contract claim failed. This, however, would not eliminate the tort claim....

Alternatively, both in its original complaint and on appeal, the appellant sought specific enforcement of the agreement or an injunction. The trial court will be able to consider these remedies on remand. The plaintiff has stated a cause of action on the tort claim, and granting the motion for summary judgment was error....

Summary judgment for the appellee on the alleged promise of McMullen to vote so as to keep Sanders on the Board is AFFIRMED. The agreement was properly characterized as a voting agreement subject to the strictures of the Texas Business Corporation Act, Article 2.30(B). The appellee, however, has presented a prima facie case for fraudulent misrepresentation. All alleged promises not relating to the voting of shares must therefore be heard at trial. The trial court's grant of summary judgment on these issues is therefore

REVERSED and the cause is REMANDED.

Dividend Rights. Many persons who invest in corporate stock are mainly motivated by the expectation of dividends. The firm's directors generally determine the timing and amount of dividends, subject to the requirements of the particular state. Most states require that there be earned surplus before dividends may be lawfully declared and paid, but a few states permit the payment of dividends from current earnings even though prior years' losses have not been made up. Once declared, cash dividends become debts of the corporation. If a dividend has been illegally declared, the directors who voted in favor are jointly and severally liable for the entire amount of the dividend. All of the states agree that shareholders who know that a dividend was illegal can be forced to return it, but there is disagreement as to whether innocent stockholders can also be forced to return an illegal dividend.

Stock dividends are not debts of the corporation, and they may be rescinded by the board before the new shares are issued.

Access to Information. Stockholders have the right to receive information regarding the operation of "their" corporation. This right, however, is not unlimited. All of the states agree that financial information, such as the firm's annual balance sheet and its profit and loss statement should be available to the stockholders. There is some disagreement as to when an individual stockholder should have access to other information, particularly the firm's general books and business records. With unlimited rights of access, minority stockholders might be able to disrupt normal business operations. Competitors could simply buy one share of a firm's stock and then demand access to all of its trade secrets, formulas, and customer lists. "Junk mailers" of various sorts could buy one share and ask for lists of stockholders. For these reasons, courts have generally required that a stockholder must have a "proper purpose" in asking for access to corporate books and records. Some states require ownership of a certain percentage of a class of stock, and some also require that the stock have been owned for some minimum period of time (such as six months) prior to the demand for information. Where the demand is proper and the officers refuse to provide the information, some statutes make them liable for 10 percent of the value of the stock owned, in addition to any other appropriate remedy to which the stockholder may be entitled. The revised MBCA makes the corporation liable for the stockholder's legal fees in getting a court order for inspection, unless the corporation had a good faith doubt about the stockholder's right to inspect.

Management Rights. In small, closely held corporations, where the stockholders are also the directors, officers, and managers, the stockholders may participate in the daily operations of the business. With large corporations like IBM or GM, however, stockholders will usually have only one annual meeting to attend. Special meetings other than the regular annual meeting may be called, but only after proper notice has been sent to all of the stockholders so that they all have a chance to attend. The Model Act specifies that a quorum at a stockholders' meeting is a majority of the voting shares (represented in person or by proxy), unless the articles of the particular firm specify a lower percentage. Some of the newer statutes permit the stockholders to transact business if any shares are represented, as long as proper notice has been sent. Once a quorum has been established, stockholders cannot prevent the transaction of business by leaving the meeting and then having someone make another quorum call.

The main item of business to be transacted at the stockholders' meeting is the election of directors. As noted above, the cumulative voting system may be used. In most cases the slate of candidates proposed by management is elected without much, if any, opposition. Where a firm has had bad financial results, dissident stockholders may propose their own slate of directors and try to take control of the firm. Each side will solicit support from the rest of the stockholders through personal letters, ads in the *Wall Street Journal*, and other methods. The SEC has extensive regulations on the solicitation and use of proxies in such control battles.

The stockholders generally have no say in making ordinary business decisions for "their" company. By custom and statute, the responsibility for day-to-day management is vested in the board of directors, which in turn delegates much of this authority to the officers. The directors and officers are usually called on to report to the stockholders at the annual meeting, and the stockholders can question them at that time about the decisions made during the year. The stockholders will also usually vote on the selection of the corporation's outside auditors. The independent CPA firm auditing the corporation's books provides another source of information to the stockholders and another method of checking on the directors' and officers' conduct of the firm's business. If changes in a corporation's bylaws are proposed, those will also have to be voted on by the stockholders. Extraordinary business decisions, such as amending the articles to change the nature of the firm's business or voluntary dissolution of the corporation, or merger or consolidation with another company, must also be presented for stockholder vote. While the Model Act now requires only a majority vote on such extraordinary decisions, many states still require a two-thirds or even a three-fourths favorable vote.

Generally, the majority stockholders have the right to determine corporate policy as they see fit, through the directors they elect and through the officers those directors appoint. The majority control group, however, must act within the limits set by the charter and must act in good faith as far as the rights of the minority stockholders are concerned. Several cases have held that the majority control group occupies a fiduciary position with respect to the minority and that its acts can be challenged where it is abusing its control powers.

The *Chambers* case applies some of the SEC's proxy regulations to a directors' election.

CHAMBERS v. BRIGGS & STRATTON CORP.
863 F.Supp. 900 (E.D. WI 1994)

FACTS: The plaintiff, Joseph G. Chambers, a shareholder of seventeen shares of stock in the defendant corporation, Briggs & Stratton Corporation, commenced this action for declaratory and injunctive relief on September 14, 1994. Along with his complaint, Mr. Chambers filed a "Motion for Temporary Restraining Order/Preliminary Injunction."

The defendant's annual meeting was scheduled to be held on October 19, 1994. On September 8, 1994, the defendant sent to shareholders a "Notice of Annual Meeting of Shareholders," a "Proxy Statement" and a form of proxy. One of the items of business identified in the notice and proxy statement is the election of directors. Three of the nine seats on the defendant's board of directors are now up for election.

The proxy statement identifies the three candidates put forth as nominees by the current directors, but it omits the name of William P. Dixon, who the plaintiff claims he nominated pursuant to Article II, Section 2.01 of the defendant's by-laws. Mr. Dixon is described by the plaintiff as a lawyer who has formerly served as commissioner of banking of Wisconsin, chief of staff to United States Senator Gary Hart, and the United States alternative executive director to the World Bank.

Notwithstanding the fact that Mr. Dixon had been properly nominated in accordance with Article II, Section 2.01, his name was not included in the proxy statement or the form of proxy that was mailed to the shareholders by the defendant on September 8, 1994. Mr. Chambers alleges that this omission renders the proxy materials materially false and misleading under the regulations of the Securities and Exchange Commission ["SEC"], namely, 17 C.F.R. § 240.14a-9. As a result of such material omission, the plaintiff contends that the defendant may acquire a sufficient number of proxies such that Mr. Dixon will not gain election to the board of directors.

 DISTRICT JUDGE GORDON:

In order to obtain a preliminary injunction, the plaintiff has the burden to show "some likelihood of success" on its claim.... The plaintiff claims that the defendant's proxy materials violate Section 14(a) of the Securities Exchange Act, 15 U.S.C. § 78n(a), and the regulations promulgated thereunder in that they contain a material omission—namely, the materials do not disclose that Mr. Dixon is a candidate for director....

The United States Supreme Court has held that "an omitted fact is material if there is a substantial likelihood that a reasonable shareholder would consider it important in deciding how to vote." This standard does not require proof of a substantial likelihood that disclosure of the omitted fact would have caused the reasonable investor to change his vote. What the standard does contemplate is a showing of a substantial likelihood that, under all of the circumstances, the omitted fact would have assumed actual significance in the deliberations of the reasonable shareholder. Put another way, there must be a substantial likelihood that disclosure of the omitted fact would have been viewed by the reasonable investor as having significantly altered the "total mix" of information made available....

The plaintiff argues that the above standard is met by the omission of Mr. Dixon's name in the defendant's proxy statement and form of proxy as a candidate for director because the omission makes the shareholders think that they have only three choices (the three candidates nominated by the board) for the three open seats on the board of directors.

In response, the defendant argues that Mr. Chambers has no likelihood of succeeding on the merits because the relief he seeks is contrary to the regulatory scheme embodied in the SEC's rules which place upon Mr. Chambers—not the company—the responsibility of disseminating information concerning opposition candidates....

Contrary to the defendant's reading, I believe that these regulations place upon the **defendant** the obligation of disclosing in its proxy statement the existence of candidates who are not nominated by management. In instances involving the election of directors, persons other than management are obligated to disclose information only concerning their own nominees under Instruction 5 to § 229.401(a) and Item 7 of § 240.14a-101. However, this same limitation does not apply to solicitations by management. Rather, the express language of Instruction 5 to § 229.401(a) and Item 7 of § 240.14a-101 requires management to provide information as to: (1) directors, (2) persons nominated for election, and (3) persons chosen by management. Had the SEC intended the same limitation to apply to solicitations by both management and persons other than management, it would not have distinguished between the two types of solicitations as it did in these regulations....

For these reasons, I conclude that Mr. Chambers has a likelihood of succeeding on the merits of his claim that the defendant's failure to disclose Mr. Dixon's candidacy was a material omission under 17 C.F.R. § 240.14a-9....

Since the defendant's proxy statement contained a material omission, the shareholder vote will go forward on the basis of potentially misleading information unless the court grants the plaintiff's request for injunctive relief. The Supreme Court has recognized the "use of solicitation which is materially misleading poses the kind of irreparable injury to stockholders which can justify injunctive relief prior to a shareholder's meeting...."

Given the overriding public interest in the full and accurate disclosure of information to shareholders of public corporations to ensure that a shareholder's vote is based upon accurate and complete information, I believe that this factor weighs in favor of granting a preliminary injunction. Allowing a shareholder vote based on incomplete and inaccurate information undermines the purpose underlying SEC Rule 14a-9.

II. RELIEF

The plaintiff has demonstrated all of the prerequisites for preliminary injunctive relief in connection with the defendant's failure to identify Mr. Dixon as a candidate in its proxy statement. I have determined that this constituted a material omission under 17 C.F.R. § 240.14a-9. I conclude that the plaintiff's request for a preliminary injunction must be granted in part. I have considered the several forms of relief sought by the plaintiff in this action and have determined that the equitable course is to require the defendant to cure the material omission in its **proxy statement**. In addition, the defendant will be directed not to vote any **proxy** it solicited prior to October 1, 1994, at the annual meeting of its shareholders.

Consistent with the identification of its own nominees in the initial proxy statement, Briggs & Stratton Corporation's revised proxy statement should name Mr. Dixon and include the following information: (1) Mr. Dixon's age (50); (2) that he is presently a partner in the law firm of Davis, Miner, Barnhill & Galland, P.D. in Madison, Wisconsin; (3) that he served as the commissioner of banking of Wisconsin from 1983 to 1985; (4) that he served as chief of staff to United States Senator Gary Hart in 1987; and (5) that he served as the alternative executive director to the World Bank from 1977 to 1979.

I decline Mr. Chambers' invitation to require Briggs & Stratton Corporation to disseminate a new proxy **form** that identifies Mr. Dixon as a candidate. Mr. Chambers is entitled to have Briggs & Stratton Corporation correct its proxy **statement**, but the corporation does not have to provide its shareholders with the form which solicits an actual proxy for Mr. Chambers' nominee. In other words, after (or simultaneously with) the transmission of a corrected proxy statement, the defendant is free to submit to its shareholders a proxy form which invites shareholders to select the nominees favored by Briggs & Stratton Corporation. If Mr. Chambers chooses to seek proxies from shareholders, he has to do so at his own expense.

EXTRAORDINARY BUSINESS DECISIONS

Substantial changes in economic circumstances or regulatory policies may indicate the need for a firm to expand or to terminate its business. The Model Act and most state statutes contain fairly detailed procedures to cover each of these special situations and the stockholders' role in deciding how to deal with them.

Methods of Expansion. In addition to growing gradually by selling more of its product or service year by year, a corporation may wish to expand rapidly by entering into various sorts of combinations with other firms. It may wish to buy or lease all the assets of a second firm. It may wish to merge or consolidate with one or more other firms. Or it may wish to simply buy a controlling stock interest in other firms.

In general, the legality of any of the above sorts of combinations would be tested under the national antitrust laws if the firm is engaged in interstate commerce or if its activities have a substantial impact on interstate commerce. Even if a combination met all of the state procedural requirements, the Federal Trade Commission or the U.S. attorney general could still prevent the combination if it would have substantial anticompetitive effects. Antitrust law is discussed more thoroughly in Chapters 38 and 39.

Purchase or Lease of Assets. Where one corporation buys or leases all the existing assets of another, there is no change in the corporate identity of either; they both continue to exist as before. The seller or lessor firm has simply decided to liquidate its operations in one line of business and to reinvest in funds and efforts elsewhere. A TV manufacturer, for example, feels that the present and future competition is too tough, so it sells its TV manufacturing assets and starts making business machines. The stockholders of the seller or lessor firm must approve this extraordinary transaction by majority vote, after recommendation and proper notice of the special meeting from the board of directors. Once shareholder authorization has been given, however, the board may cancel the sale or lease, if conditions change, without further shareholder action. Assuming that all actions have been taken in good faith, the creditors of the seller or lessor firm would have no basis for objecting to the transaction. Since the buyer or lessee is paying fair value for the assets, it should own them free and clear of the seller/lessor's creditors.

Merger and Consolidation. Two or more firms may decide to combine by means of a merger or a consolidation. In a **merger**, one of the original firms survives and the others end. In a consolidation all of the original firms end; a new corporation is formed, and the original ones all become parts of it. In either case, all assets and all liabilities are turned over to the surviving firm. In each case, the Model Act requires approval by the board and by a majority of each class of stock entitled to vote as a class. Since all liabilities are being assumed by the survivor firm, consent of the creditors of the original firms would generally not be required.

Purchase of Controlling Stock Interest. Where the directors of X Corporation decide to have X buy a controlling stock interest in Y Corporation, both firms continue to exist as before. X Corporation offers to buy shares from Y's stockholders. This is a **tender offer** and is subject to extensive regulations by the SEC and the states. See Chapter 37 for further discussion of this concept.

Rights of Dissenting Shareholders. The Model Act requires approval by majority stockholder vote in the case of sale or lease of all the firm's assets, merger, or consolidation. In the tender offer, each stockholder makes an individual decision as to whether to sell at the price offered. Generally, consent of the firm's creditors is not required. But what about the minority shareholders who object to this drastic change in their firm's operations?

The revised Model Act tries to protect the minority by providing a mandatory buy-out procedure. Prior to attendance at the special stockholders' meeting, the dissenter must file written notice of objection to the proposed action. At the meeting, of course, the dissenter must not vote for the proposal. If the proposal is passed by the necessary majority vote, the dissenter may then file a written demand with the firm for payment of the fair value of his or her shares as of the day prior to the vote, "excluding any appreciation or depreciation in anticipation of such corporation action." This demand for payment must be made within the time period specified in the notice sent by the corporation to the dissenters. The theory of this procedure is that the individual should not be forced to maintain an investment in a substantially different firm.

This procedure is discussed in the *First American* case.

FIRST AMERICAN BANK v. SHIVERS
629 A.2d 1334 (MD App. 1993)

FACTS: On or about 29 March 1988, First American Bank of Maryland (First American or the Bank), appellant, entered into a merger agreement with FABM Acquisition Bank. The proposal was constructed with First American as the surviving, or successor, bank. On 25 May 1988, Rufus W. Shivers (the Shareholder), appellee, voted by proxy his 1,178 shares of First American common stock against the proposed merger. His objection was to no avail, however, as he and his fellow dissentients comprised less than the number of the Bank's shareholders needed to defeat the proposal. The merger was approved on 14 June 1988.

Some time in August 1988 the Bank sent, by regular mail, a "Notice of Effective Date of Merger" to its shareholders. The notice was dated 8 August 1988 but there is no evidence as to when the notice was actually mailed. The notice informed the shareholders that the merger was approved on 14 June and became effective on 8 August. The notice also stated that objecting shareholders who did not perfect their "dissenter's rights" would be entitled to receive only the amount offered by the Bank for each share of First American stock.

Finally, the notice directed shareholders who had voted against the merger and desired to perfect their dissenter's rights to follow the procedures set forth in FI §3-719. By perfecting dissenter's rights within the thirty-day time frame indicated in that section, an objecting shareholder can elect to receive the appraised fair value of the shares rather than accept the dollar amount per share offered by the successor bank. The offered price per share was $42.00. The fair market value of the Bank's shares was eventually determined to be $55.00 per share.

The thirty-day period in the instant case began on 8 August 1988 and ended on 7 September 1988. The Shareholder, however, was away from his Alexandria, Virginia home on out-of-town trips for over half of those thirty days. On 11 August, he embarked on a thirteen-day business trip to several locations around the country; he returned home on 23 August. He left again on 2 September to oversee rental property that he owned in Delaware. He returned home from that trip on 6 September. He opened and read the 8 August 1988 Notice of Effective Date of Merger on 8 September, one day after the statutory time period ended. In his answers to the Bank's interrogatories in this litigation, the Shareholder explained that his two out-of-town trips and the large quantity of mail that accumulated during those trips contributed to the delay in discovering the 8 August 1988 notice.

The Shareholder read the notice on the evening of 8 September. The next morning, he called the office of the Bank's corporate secretary, Nancy R. Lewis, whose name and number appeared on the notice. Because Ms. Lewis was not in her office, the Shareholder spoke to an unidentified woman. He explained to this person the circumstances surrounding his discovery of the merger notice, his status as a dissenting shareholder, and his desire to inform Ms. Lewis of these facts. Later that day, the Shareholder sent a letter addressed to Ms. Lewis, explaining the events leading to his discovery of the notice and expressing his desire to maintain his dissenter's rights. He added that his stock certificates were then being used as security for a loan, but that he would immediately take action to obtain them.

One week later, the Shareholder spoke to Ms. Lewis by telephone to restate his position as a dissenting shareholder and explain again the reason for his delay in perfecting his dissenter's rights. On 21 and 26 September 1988, however, the Shareholder received letters from the Bank's president, Paul G. Adams, III, denying his requests for fair value for his shares.

The Shareholder filed a complaint against the Bank in the Circuit Court for Montgomery County on 8 August 1991. He sought to be included among the Bank's list of objecting stockholders who had perfected their dissenter's rights and to receive the fair value for his shares. The Shareholder based his claim on the Bank's failure to send the merger notice via certified mail pursuant to CA § 3-207(b), which, he asserted, applied to bank mergers by way of FI § 1-201.

The Bank argued that the Financial Institutions Article contained specific provisions that prevailed over the Corporations and Associations Article, rendering CA § 3-207 inapplicable.

By order dated 27 October 1992, the court granted the Shareholder's motion for summary judgment, denied the Bank's motion for summary judgment, and awarded the Shareholder $64,790.00 plus prejudgment interest from 14 June 1988 and postjudgment interest. The Bank appealed on 16 November 1992.

 JUDGE HARRELL:

This appeal presents a statutory interpretation question of first impression in Maryland: In what manner must a bank provide notice of the effective date of its merger with another bank to a shareholder who has objected to that merger, so that the shareholder may timely exercise his statutory right to receive the fair market value of his shares?

The Financial Institutions Article of the Annotated Code of Maryland contains specific provisions governing mergers of banks. Section 3-719 of the article sets forth the procedures that a stockholder who objects to an approved merger must follow to perfect his right to fair value of his shares....

The Financial Institutions Article is silent on the questions of who is to give bank shareholders notice of a merger's effective date and in what manner such notice is to be given.

The Maryland General Corporation Law, on the other hand, not only imposes specific duties on objecting stockholders with regard to exercising their statutory rights generally, but also provides clear directions to a successor corporation with regard to providing notice of the event that triggers the time period within which the stockholders may exercise those rights.

The Bank's first argument is simple: There is no certified mail requirement in the merger provisions of the Financial Institutions Article, §§ 3-701 to 3-721. In the Bank's view, these provisions set forth a statutory scheme that is self-contained and completely separate from that found in the Corporations and Associations Article (sometimes hereinafter referred to as the Corporations Article). As support for that assertion, the Bank refers not to the Financial Institutions Article itself, but rather to a provision of the Corporations Article. As indicated earlier, CA § 1-102(d)(1) directs that when a provision relating to a specific class of corporations conflicts with a general provision of the Corporations Article, the specific provision will govern. According to the Bank, FI § 3-719, which relates specifically to bank mergers, conflicts with CA § 3-207, which is part of the general corporation law. Thus, the Bank asserts, § 3-719 governs and, because it is silent on what manner of notice a bank must use to notify shareholders, it does not require a bank to use certified mail.

The Bank also refers us to several other sections that it contends demonstrate that the merger provisions of the Corporations Article are not intended to apply automatically to bank mergers and that the bank merger laws are self-contained. For example, FI § 3-713 governs the effect of a transfer of assets, and states, "Consummation of a transfer of assets has the effects provided in § 3-115 of the Corporations and Associations Article." The Bank posits that if the provisions of the Corporations Article automatically applied to bank mergers then § 3-713's specific incorporation of CA § 3-115 would be unnecessary. As an additional example, the Bank points to FI § 3-708(c), which states that a merger must be approved by the affirmative vote of two-thirds of the stockholders. CA § 3-105 contains the exact same requirement. If, the Bank inquires, the provisions of the Corporations Article "are to be construed as instant gap-fillers" in the Financial Institutions Article, why did the identical requirement need to be stated in both articles?

Although we agree with the Bank's assertion that the bank merger provisions of the Financial Institutions Article represent the General Assembly's separate treatment of this particular class of corporations, we disagree that these provisions are self-contained and not governed in any respect by the general corporation law. We believe, as did the circuit court, that the plain language of FI § 1-201 compels the conclusion that CA § 3-207(b) requires a bank to use personal delivery or certified mail as the manner of sending notice of the effective date of a merger to the bank's shareholders....

In sum, we hold that, pursuant to FI § 1-201 and CA § 3-207(b), a bank must notify its objecting shareholders of the effective date of an approved merger by delivering the notice personally or mailing it by certified mail, return receipt requested. This conclusion follows seamlessly and naturally from the plain and unambiguous language of FI § 1-201. It also affords the same protection to dissenting shareholders of a bank that is given to dissenting shareholders of an ordinary corporation. Absent an express directive to the contrary from the legislature, we see no basis for differentiating between such similar classes of dissenting stockholders with regard to the protection of their dissenter's rights. Objecting shareholders of a merging corporation clearly are entitled to be notified, in a specified manner, of the date of the event—the acceptance by the State Department of Assessments and Taxation of the articles of merger—that triggers the running of the period within which such shareholders must perfect their statutory rights. We believe that, in the absence of any statute or other law providing otherwise, dissenting shareholders of a merging bank are entitled to the same notice, in the same specified manner, of the analogous triggering event—the date the merger becomes effective....

Technical or not, the requirement of certified mail is mandated by CA § 3-207(b). The breach of this requirement renders the given notice ineffective....

> For that reason, the Shareholder's alleged lack of diligence is of no moment. He did not receive notice consistent with the requirements of the Maryland Code. Accordingly, we affirm the circuit court's grant of summary judgment in the Shareholder's favor.

Dissolution. Assuming that it retained the power to amend, the legislature of the state of incorporation would presumably have the power to terminate the existence of that state's corporations. The state's attorney general or corporation commissioner could ask a court to decree dissolution where a corporation was in continuing default on its duties to file reports and to pay taxes and fees. In those rare cases where the articles did not provide for perpetual existence, the end of the specified time period or the occurrence of the specified event would cause a dissolution of the firm. The shareholders may act voluntarily to terminate their corporation, either by unanimous action or by majority vote, after a recommendation from the board of directors. Normally courts will not interfere with the shareholders' decision.

Modern corporation law treats a dissolved corporation in much the same way as a dissolved partnership. That is, the corporation continues to operate for the limited purpose of winding up its affairs—collecting money owed to it, selling off its assets, and paying off its creditors. After the creditors have been paid in full, the preferred stockholders have the first claim on any assets remaining and then, finally, the common stockholders are paid.

Reorganization. Financial reorganizations under the Bankruptcy Act were covered in Chapter 17. An attempt may be made to save the firm by adjusting its debts, or the firm may be dissolved and its assets used to pay off as many claims as possible according to bankruptcy priorities.

SHAREHOLDER LAWSUITS

Individual shareholders can of course bring lawsuits, as individuals, to enforce their rights as shareholders. They may sue to enforce their right to dividends, to vote, to subscribe to additional shares, to receive corporate information, and other similar stockholder rights. A group of shareholders together may file a class action lawsuit if they meet the test outlined in Chapter 2. Such lawsuits by one or more shareholders are directed against the corporation, and any remedies given are directed against the corporation and for the benefit of the stockholders

Derivative Suits. In certain extraordinary situations, individual stockholders may be able to bring lawsuits on behalf of their corporation. In these cases, they are suing for their own benefit only indirectly; the real plaintiff is the corporation. Any remedies given are for the corporation and against the third parties who are defendants—directors, officers, majority shareholders, or outsiders. Any benefits received by the corporation as plaintiff will indirectly benefit the shareholders who brought the case, but the primary purpose of the lawsuit is to protect the corporation.

Normally, of course, the shareholders have no right as such to manage the corporation directly. That rule would include the lack of stockholder authority to decide to bring a lawsuit on behalf of the corporation. What then are the "extraordinary circumstances" that justify a derivative suit? Typically, the wrongdoers are officers, directors, or majority stockholders. Because they control the corporation's decision-making process, the corporation is unlikely to sue. If there is an independent board of directors which could take action to correct the problem (as by firing an officer), the stockholder must make a demand to the board that it act. If such a demand would be "futile," because the wrongdoers also control the board, the stockholder can proceed to file the derivative lawsuit without making any demand. If a demand is made and the board decides that the corporation should sue, the complaining stockholders could not bring a second lawsuit in the name of the corporation. If a demand is made and the board decides that the corporation should not sue, that decision would also prevent the complaining stockholders from bringing a derivative suit. If the board is acting in good faith, its business judgment in deciding that the corporation should not sue would be upheld by the courts. Of course, if the board is the alleged wrongdoer, its decision that the corporation should not sue would not prevent the complaining shareholders from bringing the derivative suit against the board itself.

Some corporations have attempted to use a special board committee—the "stockholder litigation committee"—to convince the courts that it acted in good faith. Use of such a separate committee will not necessarily prevent a court from second-guessing the board's decision not to sue. Where a derivative lawsuit is successful, the corporation will probably be ordered to reimburse the complaining stockholders for any reasonable litigation expenses, including attorneys' fees. On the other hand, where the lawsuit is unsuccessful and has been brought without "reasonable cause," many corporation statutes require the complaining stockholders to pay the *defendants'* litigation expenses, including attorneys' fees.

SIGNIFICANCE OF THIS CHAPTER

This chapter defines and discusses the various kinds of stock that corporations may issue, the process of subscribing to purchase shares, the issuance and transfer of such shares, and shareholders' rights. Thus, this chapter provides an overview of the methods by which stockholders own and control a corporation.

Corporations also have financial difficulties and often must be dissolved or perhaps reorganized under bankruptcy law, and procedures are needed for these changes. Also, corporations often desire to expand by purchasing other corporations and merging them within the parent corporation. This chapter also reviews these procedures and the rights of the stockholders in these matters.

PROBLEMS FOR DISCUSSION

1. Uriah Grant sues the Peppy Pickle Company, challenging the validity of an amendment to Peppy's articles of incorporation. Grant owned 3,000 shares of $1 par preferred 8 percent cumulative stock in Peppy. Dividends had not been declared (or paid) on Peppy's preferred stock for ten years. Peppy's articles had expressly reserved the power to amend. Pursuant to the amendment procedure, a majority of Peppy's stockholders voted to cancel the old preferred shares and to issue one new preferred share of 10 percent cumulative preferred for each two old shares. The amendment also canceled the accumulated but undeclared dividends for the ten years. Grant says that it would be unconstitutional to interpret this amendment so as to deprive him of accrued property rights.

   What is the result, and why?

2. On August 5, 1997, the plaintiff (Wilkes) filed a bill in equity for declaratory judgment in the Probate Court for Berkshire County, naming as defendants T. Edward Quinn (Quinn), Leon L. Riche (Riche), the First Agricultural Bank of Berkshire County, and Frank Sutherland MacShane as executors under the will of Lawrence R. Connor (Connor), and the Springside Nursing Home, Inc. (Springside or the corporation). Wilkes alleged that he, Quinn, Riche, and Dr. Hubert A. Pipkin (Pipkin) entered into a partnership agreement in 1991, prior to the incorporation of Springside, which agreement was breached in 1997 when Wilkes's salary was terminated and he was voted out as an officer and director of the corporation. Wilkes sought, among other forms of relief, damages in the amount of the salary he would have received had he continued as a director and officer of Springside subsequent to March 1997.

   A judge of the probate court referred the suit to a master, who, after a lengthy hearing, issued his final report in late 1997. Wilkes's objections to the master's report were overruled after a hearing, and the master's report was confirmed in late 1998. A judgment was entered dismissing Wilkes's action on the merits. The state supreme court granted direct appellate renew.

   How should Wilkes' appeal be decided? Discuss.

3. Danny Donaho owned 25 percent of the stock in Loyalty Electric Corporation and was its vice president, but he was not on the board of directors. The other 75 percent of the stock was owned by Larry Hoddy, who was president and chairman of the board. In 1998 Larry put his sons, Kenny and Lennie, who worked for Loyalty, on the board and gave them each 25 shares. The board then voted to buy Larry's remaining twenty-five shares for $1,000 a share. At a special stockholders' meeting, Danny learned of the repurchase for the first time and voted against a resolution approving it. Danny then offered his twenty-five shares to Loyalty for $1,000 a share. Loyalty refused to buy Danny's shares. Danny died, and his widow, Ufemia, brings a lawsuit challenging the validity of this repurchase of Larry's shares.

   What is the result, and why?

4. Wallazz Eaton owned and operated a frozen foods business. He organized a corporation and transferred the business to it in return for 4,500 shares of $10 par stock. The corporations commissioner required that 1,022 shares of the stock be placed in escrow and not transferred without his written consent; 1,022 shares were put in escrow in Eaton's name, and the other 3,478 shares were issued directly to him. The plaintiff had a judgment against the corporation for $21,246.42, of which some $15,000 was still unpaid. The corporation was insolvent. The trial court found that the value of the transferred business was $34,780.83 and gave the plaintiff a judgment against Eaton for $10,219.17. Because it had failed to make a finding that the plaintiff relied on some misrepresentation in connection with the watered stock, the trial court granted Eaton a new trial. The Plaintiff appealed the order granting a new trial.

What ruling on appeal, and why?

5. On July 3, Pillsbury attended a meeting of a group involved in a so-called Honeywell Project. He had long opposed the Vietnam War, but it was at this meeting that he first learned of Honeywell's involvement as a manufacturer of antipersonnel fragmentation bombs. "Upset" and "shocked" by this information, he determined to stop Honeywell's munitions production. On July 14, he told his fiscal agent to buy 100 shares of Honeywell. The agent, not knowing that Pillsbury wanted the shares in his own name, put them in the name of Quad & Co., a family holding company, as he always did. Upon learning that the 100 shares had not been registered in his name, Pillsbury bought one share in his own name. Meanwhile, he learned that his grandmother's trust, of which he was a beneficiary, owned 242 Honeywell shares. He then made a written demand that Honeywell give him its original shareholder ledger, its current shareholder ledger, and "all corporate records dealing with weapons and munitions manufacture." Honeywell refused, and Pillsbury filed a petition to order disclosure. He appealed from the trial court's denial of his petition.

Is he entitled to the information? Explain.

Chapter 35

Corporations— Management Duties

DIRECTORS

Authority and Qualifications. The directors are given management control of the normal business operations of the corporation. They are more than just agents for the shareholders, since a large part of their authority and duties flows from the state's corporation statute. Shareholders may try to influence or replace the directors, but shareholders as such have no right to participate in corporate management. So long as the directors are acting in good faith and within the statute, articles, and bylaws, they have exclusive control of the corporation's ordinary business decisions.

Older statutes required three or more directors. Recognizing the reality of the "one-person" corporation, modern corporation codes require only one director. Some states still require directors to be shareholders and/or residents of the state of incorporation. Again, the modern tendency, as seen in Section 8.02 of the revised MBCA, is to require neither unless the articles or bylaws of the particular corporation so specify. In other words, let each corporation decide for itself what qualifications its directors must have.

Selection and Removal. As noted in the last chapter, selection of the board of directors is the shareholders' most important management function. While some states require cumulative voting, most statutes permit it but do not require it. Most states also permit corporations to provide for staggered terms for directors, similar to those of U.S. Senators. Electing only part of the board each year provides continuity of management and also prevents an outside group from taking over the board all at once, in one election.

The rule in most states is that directors may be removed by the shareholders at any time, with or without cause. Directors, in other words, serve at the pleasure of the shareholders. In this sense, they are like agents. In a few states, such as New York, directors can be removed only if good cause is shown. In any corporation where cumulative voting is in force, a director could not be removed unless he or she failed to get enough votes to win a seat under the cumulative voting system.

Nearly all statutes provide for the replacement of directors by the remaining board members, where vacancies occur, at least until the next shareholders' meeting at which directors are elected. These procedural steps must be followed exactly.

Meetings of the Board. The general rule is that the directors must meet as a board to take official action for the corporation. Proxy voting is not permitted. Most states today permit the directors to meet outside the state of incorporation; this allows the board to select the most convenient location. Some modern statutes are even more flexible; they permit the directors to have a "meeting" by means of a conference telephone call. Some statutes also permit the directors to take official action by means of a signed document: if they all read and sign the same document, why require them to waste transportation facilities to come together in a meeting room?

Section 8.25 of the revised MBCA and the laws in some states permit the directors to designate some board members as an executive committee and to delegate some decision-making authority to the smaller committee. Other similar committees may also be created. The modern tendency is toward flexible management.

If a director wishes to dissent from a decision of the board, the normal rule is that the dissent must be officially entered in the minutes of the board. Otherwise, concurrence with the majority decision is presumed. This rule is significant where a later lawsuit challenges board actions.

Power and Duties. As noted previously, some extraordinary business decisions are left to the shareholders, but the directors have exclusive control of the ordinary business of the firm. In making these ordinary business decisions, the directors are given the widest possible discretion as long as they are acting in good faith. The individual directors are selected for their business skill and judgment, and courts do not feel that they should second-guess the directors when the directors exercise that judgment. There is, therefore, a very strong presumption in favor of the directors' decisions unless some abuse is shown.

This principle of nonintervention in corporate affairs is summarized as the "**business judgment rule**." The business decisions of the directors cannot be challenged in court so long as the directors are acting in good faith and with reasonable care. They cannot guarantee satisfactory results for the corporation in every case; there are too many uncertainties and factors beyond their control. All that can be required of directors is that they are honest and diligent. If they are, but nevertheless make a bad decision, they should not be held liable for the unfavorable results. The business judgment rule underlies the *Shlensky* case in Chapter 36.

On the other hand, where there is evidence that the directors are acting in a totally arbitrary and capricious way, to the corporation's detriment, their actions may be overturned. Henry Ford's arbitrary policy on dividends was successfully challenged by the stockholders in the *Dodge* case in the next chapter.

The following case looks at the business judgment rule in the context of a hostile takeover attempt. The directors' defensive tactics are being questioned.

PARAMOUNT COMMUNICATIONS v. QVC NETWORK
637 A.2d 34 (DE Supr. 1993)

FACTS: This appeal is a review of an order of the Court of Chancery dated November 24, 1993 (the "November 24 Order"), preliminarily enjoining certain defensive measures designed to facilitate a so-called strategic alliance between Viacom Inc. and Paramount Communications Inc. approved by the board of directors of Paramount and to thwart an unsolicited, more valuable, tender offer by QVC Network Inc.

Paramount is a Delaware corporation with its principal offices in New York City. Approximately 118 million shares of Paramount's common stock are outstanding and traded on the New York Stock Exchange. The majority of Paramount's stock is publicly held by numerous unaffiliated investors. Paramount owns and operates a diverse group of entertainment businesses, including motion picture and television studios, book publishers, professional sports teams, and amusement parks.

There are fifteen persons serving on the Paramount Board. Four directors are officer-employees of Paramount: Martin S. Davis ("Davis"), Paramount's Chairman and Chief Executive Officer since 1983; Donald Oresman ("Oresman"), Executive Vice President, Chief Administrative Officer, and General Counsel; Stanley R. Jaffe, President and Chief Operating Officer; and Ronald L. Nelson, Executive Vice President and Chief Financial Officer. Paramount's 11 outside directors are distinguished and experienced business persons who are present or former senior executives of public corporations or financial institutions.

Viacom is a Delaware corporation with its headquarters in Massachusetts. Viacom is controlled by Sumner M. Redstone ("Redstone"), its Chairman and Chief Executive Officer, who owns indirectly approximately 85.2 percent of Viacom's voting Class A stock and approximately 69.2 percent of Viacom's nonvoting Class B stock through National Amusements, Inc. ("NAI"), an entity 91.7 percent owned by Redstone. Viacom has a wide range of entertainment operations, including a number of well-known cable television channels such as MTV, Nickelodeon, Showtime, and The Movie Channel. Viacom's equity co-investors in the Paramount-Viacom transaction include NYNEX Corporation and Blockbuster Entertainment Corporation.

QVC is a Delaware corporation with its headquarters in West Chester, PA. QVC has several large stockholders, including Liberty Media Corporation, Comcast Corporation, Advance Publications, Inc., and Cox Enterprises Inc. Barry Diller ("Diller"), the Chairman and Chief Executive Officer of QVC, is also a substantial stockholder. QVC sells a variety of merchandise through a televised shopping channel. QVC has several equity co-investors in its proposed combination with Paramount including BellSouth Corporation and Comcast Corporation.

QVC and certain stockholders of Paramount commenced separate actions (later consolidated) in the Court of Chancery seeking preliminary and permanent injunctive relief against Paramount, certain members of the Paramount Board, and Viacom. This action arises out of a proposed acquisition of Paramount by Viacom through a tender offer followed by a second-step merger (the "Paramount-Viacom transaction"), and a competing unsolicited tender offer by QVC. The Court of Chancery granted a preliminary injunction.

The Court of Chancery found that the Paramount directors violated their fiduciary duties by favoring the Paramount-Viacom transaction over the more valuable unsolicited offer of QVC. The Court of Chancery preliminarily enjoined Paramount and the individual defendants (the "Paramount defendants") from amending or modifying Paramount's stockholder rights agreement (the "Rights Agreement"), including the redemption of the Rights, or taking other action to facilitate the consummation of the pending tender offer by Viacom or any proposed second-step merger; including the Merger Agreement between Paramount and Viacom dated September 12, 1993 (the "Original Merger Agreement"), as amended on October 24, 1993 (the "Amended Merger Agreement"). Viacom and the Paramount defendants were enjoined from taking any action to exercise any provision of the Stock Option Agreement between Paramount and Viacom dated September 12, 1993 (the "Stock Option Agreement"), as amended on October 24, 1993. The Court of Chancery did not grant preliminary injunctive relief as to the termination fee provided for the benefit of Viacom in Section 8.05 of the Original Merger Agreement and the Amended Merger Agreement (the "Termination Fee").

 CHIEF JUSTICE VEASEY:

The General Corporation Law of the State of Delaware and the decisions of this Court have repeatedly recognized the fundamental principle that the management of the business and affairs of a Delaware corporation is entrusted to its directors, who are the duly elected and authorized representatives of the stockholders.... Under normal circumstances, neither the courts nor the stockholders should interfere with the managerial decisions of the directors. The business judgment rule embodies the deference to which such decisions are entitled....

Nevertheless, there are rare situations which mandate that a court take a more direct and active role in overseeing the decisions made and actions taken by directors. In these situations, a court subjects the directors' conduct to enhanced scrutiny to ensure that it is reasonable. The decisions of this Court have clearly established the circumstances where such enhanced scrutiny will be applied.... The case at bar implicates two such circumstances: (1) the approval of a transaction resulting in a sale of control, and (2) the adoption of defensive measures in response to a threat to corporate control....

In the case before us, the public stockholders (in the aggregate) currently own a majority of Paramount's voting stock. Control of the corporation is not vested in a single person, entity, or group, but vested in the fluid aggregation of unaffiliated stockholders. In the event the Paramount-Viacom transaction is consummated, the public stockholders will receive cash and a minority equity voting position in the surviving corporation. Following such consummation, there will be a controlling stockholder who will have the voting power to: (a) elect directors, (b) cause a break-up of the corporation, (c) merge it with another company, (d) cash-out the public stockholders, (e) amend the certificate of incorporation, (f) sell all or substantially all of the corporate assets, or (g) otherwise alter materially the nature of the corporation and the public stockholders' interests. Irrespective of the present Paramount Board's vision of a long-term strategic alliance with Viacom, the proposed sale of control would provide the new controlling stockholder with the power to alter that vision.

Because of the intended sale of control, the Paramount-Viacom transaction has economic consequences of considerable significance to the Paramount stockholders. Once control has shifted, the current Paramount stockholders will have no leverage in the future to demand another control premium. As a result, the Paramount stockholders are entitled to receive, and should receive, a control premium and/or protective devices of significant value. There being no such protective provisions in the Viacom-Paramount transaction, the Paramount directors had an obligation to take the maximum advantage of the current opportunity to realize for the stockholders the best value reasonably available.

The consequences of a sale of control impose special obligations on the directors of a corporation. In particular, they have the obligation of acting reasonably to seek the transaction offering the best value reasonably available to the stockholders. The courts will apply enhanced scrutiny to ensure that the directors have acted reasonably. The obligations of the directors and the enhanced scrutiny of the courts are well-established by the decisions of this Court. The directors' fiduciary duties in a sale of control context are those which generally attach. In short, "the directors must act in accordance with their fundamental duties of care and loyalty...."

The key features of an enhanced scrutiny test are: (a) a judicial determination regarding the adequacy of the decision making process employed by the directors, including the information on which the directors based their decision; and (b) a judicial examination of the reasonableness of the directors' action in light of the circumstances then existing. The directors have the burden of proving that they were adequately informed and acted reasonably.

Although an enhanced scrutiny test involves a review of the reasonableness of the substantive merits of a board's actions, a court should not ignore the complexity of the directors' task in a sale of control. There are many business and financial considerations implicated in investigating and selecting the best value reasonably available. The board of directors is the corporate decision making body best equipped to make these judgments. Accordingly, a court applying enhanced judicial scrutiny should be deciding whether the directors made a **reasonable** decision, not a **perfect** decision. If a board selected one of several reasonable alternatives, a court should not second-guess that choice even though it might have decided otherwise or subsequent events may have cast doubt on the board's determination. Thus, courts will not substitute their business judgment for that of the directors, but will determine if the directors' decision was, on balance, within a range of reasonableness....

Accordingly, when a corporation undertakes a transaction which will cause: (a) a change in corporate control; or (b) a breakup of the corporate entity, the directors' obligation is to seek the best value reasonably available to the stockholders. This obligation arises because the effect of the Viacom-Paramount transaction, if consummated, is to shift control of Paramount from the public stockholders to a controlling stockholder, Viacom. Neither *Time-Warner* nor any other decision of this Court holds that a "break-up" of the company is essential to give rise to this obligation where there is a sale of control.

Under the facts of this case, the Paramount directors had the obligation: (a) to be diligent and vigilant in examining critically the Paramount-Viacom transaction and the QVC tender offers; (b) to act in good faith; (c) to obtain, and act with due care on, all material information reasonably available, including information necessary to compare the two offers to determine which of these transactions, or an alternative course of action, would provide the best value reasonable available to the stockholders; and (d) to negotiate actively and in good faith with both Viacom and QVC to that end.

Having decided to sell control of the corporation, the Paramount directors were required to evaluate critically whether or not all material aspects of the Paramount-Viacom transaction (separately and in the aggregate) were reasonable and in the best interests of the Paramount stockholders in light of current circumstances, including: the change of control premium, the Stock Option Agreement, the Termination Fee, the coercive nature of both the Viacom and QVC tender offers, the No-Shop Provision, and the proposed disparate use of the Rights Agreement as to the Viacom and QVC tender offers, respectively.

These obligations necessarily implicated various issues, including the questions of whether or not those provisions and other aspects of the Paramount-Viacom transaction (separately and in the aggregate): (a) adversely affected the value provided to the Paramount stockholders; (b) inhibited or encouraged alternative bids; (c) were enforceable contractual obligations in light of the directors' fiduciary duties; and (d) in the end would advance or retard the Paramount directors' obligation to secure for the Paramount stockholders the best value reasonably available under the circumstances.

The Paramount defendants contend that they were precluded by certain contractual provisions, including the No-Shop Provision, from negotiating with QVC or seeking alternatives. Such provisions, whether or not they are presumptively valid in the abstract, may not validly define or limit the directors' fiduciary duties under Delaware law or prevent the Paramount directors from carrying out their fiduciary duties under Delaware law. To the extent such provisions are inconsistent with those duties, they are invalid and unenforceable....

The Paramount directors made the decision on September 12,1993, that, in their judgment, a strategic merger with Viacom on the economic terms of the Original Merger Agreement was in the best interests of Paramount and its stockholders. Those terms provided a modest change of control premium to the stockholders. The directors also decided at that time that it was appropriate to agree to certain defensive measures (the Stock Option Agreement, the Termination Fee, and the No-Shop Provision) insisted upon by Viacom as part of that economic transaction. Those defensive measures, coupled with the sale of control and subsequent disparate treatment of competing bidders, implicated the judicial scrutiny of *Unocal, Revlon, Macmillan*, and their progeny. We conclude that the Paramount directors' process was not reasonable, and the result achieved for the stockholders was not reasonable under the circumstances.

When entering into the Original Merger Agreement, and thereafter, the Paramount Board clearly gave insufficient attention to the potential consequences of the defensive measures demanded by Viacom. The Stock Option Agreement had a number of unusual and potentially "draconian": provisions, including the Note Feature and the Put Feature. Furthermore, the Termination Fee, whether or not unreasonable by itself, clearly made Paramount less attractive to other bidders, when coupled with the Stock Option Agreement. Finally, the No-Shop Provision inhibited the Paramount Board's ability to negotiate with other potential bidders, particularly QVC which had already expressed an interest in Paramount.

Throughout the applicable time period, and especially from the first QVC merger proposal on September 20 through the Paramount Board meeting on November 15,

QVC's interest in Paramount provided the **opportunity** for the Paramount Board to seek significantly higher value for the Paramount stockholders than that being offered by Viacom. QVC persistently demonstrated its intention to meet and exceed the Viacom offers, and frequently expressed its willingness to negotiate possible further increases.

The Paramount directors had the opportunity in the October 23-24 time frame, when the Original Merger Agreement was renegotiated, to take appropriate action to modify the improper defensive measures as well as to improve the economic terms of the Paramount-Viacom transaction. Under the circumstances existing at that time, it should have been clear to the Paramount Board that the Stock Option Agreement, coupled with the Termination Fee and the No-Shop Clause, were impeding the realization of the best value reasonably available to the Paramount stockholders. Nevertheless, the Paramount Board made no effort to eliminate or modify these counterproductive devices, and instead continued to cling to its vision of a strategic alliance with Viacom. Moreover, based on advice from the Paramount management, the Paramount directors considered the QVC offer to be "conditional" and asserted that they were precluded by the No-Shop Provision from seeking more information from, or negotiating with, QVC.

By November 12, 1993, the value of the revised QVC offer on its face exceeded that of the Viacom offer by over $1 billion at then current values. This significant disparity of value cannot be justified on the basis of the directors' vision of future strategy, primarily because the change of control would supplant the authority of the current Paramount Board to continue to hold and implement their strategic vision in any meaningful way. Moreover, their uninformed process had deprived their strategic vision of much of its credibility....

When the Paramount directors met on November 15 to consider QVC's increased tender offer, they remained prisoners of their own misconceptions and missed opportunities to eliminate the restrictions they had imposed on themselves. Yet, it was not "too late" to reconsider negotiating with QVC. The circumstances existing on November 16 made it clear that the defensive measures, taken as a whole, were problematic: (a) the No-Shop Provision could not define or limit their fiduciary duties; (b) the Stock Option Agreement had become "draconian;" and (c) the Termination Fee, in context with all the circumstances, was similarly deterring the realization of possibly higher bids. Nevertheless, the Paramount directors remained paralyzed by their uninformed belief that the QVC offer was "illusory." This final opportunity to negotiate on the stockholders' behalf and to fulfill their obligation to seek the best value reasonably available was thereby squandered....

The realization of the best value reasonably available to the stockholders became the Paramount directors' primary obligation under these facts in light of the change of control. That obligation was not satisfied, and the Paramount Board's process was deficient. The directors' initial hope and expectation for a strategic alliance with Viacom was allowed to dominate their decision making process to the point where the arsenal of defensive measures established at the outset was perpetuated (not modified or eliminated) when the situation was dramatically altered. QVC's unsolicited bid presented the opportunity for significantly greater value for the stockholders and enhanced negotiating leverage for the directors. Rather than seizing those opportunities, the Paramount directors chose to wall themselves off from material information which was reasonably available and to hide behind the defensive measures as a rationalization for refusing to negotiate with QVC or seeking other alternatives. Their view of the strategic alliance likewise became an empty rationalization as the opportunities for higher value for the stockholders continued to develop. For the reasons set forth herein, the November 24, 1993, Order of the Court of Chancery has been AFFIRMED, and this matter has been REMANDED for proceedings consistent herewith, as set forth in the December 9, 1993, Order of this Court.

The directors are fiduciaries, and as such, they owe their corporation and its stockholders responsibility and loyalty. Responsibility means that the directors must be more than just personally honest; they must "direct." They must be diligent and careful in managing the firm's business. They are responsible for knowing what's going on, and they may be held personally liable if they don't know but should. These requirements are explained in detail by Delaware's Chancellor Allen in the *Caremark* case.

IN RE CAREMARK INTERNATIONAL, INC. DERIVATIVE LITIGATION
698 A.2d 959 (Del. Ch., 1996)

FACTS: Pending is a motion to approve as fair and reasonable a proposed settlement of a consolidated derivative action on behalf of Caremark International, Inc. The suit involves claims that the members of Caremark's board of directors breached their fiduciary duty of care to Caremark in connection with alleged violations by Caremark employees of federal and state laws and regulations applicable to health care providers. As a result of the alleged violations, Caremark was subject to an extensive four year investigation by the United States Department of Health and Human Services and the Department of Justice. In 1994 Caremark was charged in an indictment with multiple felonies. It thereafter entered into a number of agreements with the Department of Justice and others. Those agreements included a plea agreement in which Caremark pleaded guilty to a single felony of mail fraud and agreed to pay civil and criminal fines. Subsequently, Caremark agreed to make reimbursements to various private and public parties. In all, the payments that Caremark has been required to make total approximately $250 million.

This suit was filed in 1994, purporting to seek on behalf of the company recovery of these losses from the individual defendants who constitute the board of directors of Caremark. The parties now propose that it be settled and, after notice to Caremark shareholders, a hearing on the fairness of the proposal was held on August 16, 1996.

Caremark, a Delaware corporation with its headquarters in Northbrook, Illinois, was created in November 1992 when it was spun-off from Baxter International, Inc. and became a publicly held company listed on the New York Stock Exchange. The business practices that created the problem pre-dated the spin-off. During the relevant period Caremark was involved in two main health care business segments, providing patient care and managed care services. As part of its patient care business, which accounted for the majority of Caremark's revenues, Caremark provided alternative site health care services, including infusion therapy, growth hormone therapy, HIV/AIDS-related treatments and hemophilia therapy. Caremark's managed care services included prescription drug programs and the operation of multi-specialty group practices.

A substantial part of the revenues generated by Caremark's businesses is derived from third party payments, insurers, and Medicare and Medicaid reimbursement programs. The latter source of payments are subject to the terms of the Anti-Referral Payments Law ("ARPL") which prohibits health care providers from paying any form of remuneration to induce the referral of Medicare or Medicaid patients. From its inception, Caremark entered into a variety of agreements with hospitals, physicians, and health care providers for advice and services, as well as distribution agreements with drug manufacturers, as had its predecessor prior to 1992. Specifically, Caremark did have a practice of entering into contracts for services (e.g., consultation agreements and research grants) with physicians at least some of whom prescribed or recommended services or products that Caremark provided to Medicare recipients and other patients. Such contracts were not prohibited by the ARPL but they obviously raised a possibility of unlawful "kickbacks."

As early as 1989, Caremark's predecessor issued an internal "Guide to Contractual Relationships" to govern its employees in entering into contracts with physicians and hospitals. The guide tended to be reviewed annually by lawyers and updated. Each version of the Guide stated as Caremark's and its predecessor's policy that no payments would be made in exchange for or to induce patient referrals. But what one might deem a prohibited quid pro quo was not always clear. Due to a scarcity of court decisions interpreting the ARPL, however, Caremark repeatedly publicly stated that there was uncertainty concerning Caremark's interpretation of the law.

To clarify the scope of the ARPL, the United States Department of Health and Human Services ("HHS") issued "safe harbor" regulations in July 1991 stating conditions under which financial relationships between health care service providers and patient referral sources, such as physicians, would not violate the ARPL. Caremark contends that the narrowly drawn regulations gave limited guidance as to the legality of many of the agreements used by Caremark that did not fall within the safe-harbor. Caremark's predecessor, however, amended many of its standard forms of agreement with health care providers and revised the Guide in an apparent attempt to comply with the new regulations.

In August 1991, the HHS Office of the Inspector General ("OIG") initiated an investigation of Caremark's predecessor. Caremark's predecessor was served with a subpoena requiring the production of documents, including contracts between Caremark's predecessor and physicians [Quality Service Agreements ("QSAs")]. Under the QSAs, Caremark's predecessor appears to have paid physicians fees for monitoring patients under Caremark's predecessor's care, including Medicare and Medicaid recipients. Sometimes apparently those monitoring patients were referring physicians, which raised ARPL concerns.

In March 1992, the Department of Justice ("DOJ") joined the OIG investigation and separate investigations were commenced by several additional federal and state agencies.

During the relevant period, Caremark had approximately 7,000 employees and ninety branch operations. It had a decentralized management structure. By May 1991, however, Caremark asserts that it had begun making attempts to centralize its management structure in order to increase supervision over its branch operations.

The first action taken by management, as a result of the initiation of the OIG investigation, was an announcement that as of October 1, 1991, Caremark's predecessor would no longer pay management fees to physicians for services to Medicare and Medicaid patients. Despite this decision, Caremark asserts that its management, pursuant to advice, did not believe that such payments were illegal under the existing laws and regulations.

During this period, Caremark's Board took several additional steps consistent with an effort to assure compliance with company policies concerning the ARPL and the contractual forms in the Guide. In April 1992, Caremark published a fourth revised version of its Guide apparently designed to assure that its agreements either complied with the ARPL and regulations or excluded Medicare and Medicaid patients altogether. In addition, in September 1992, Caremark instituted a policy requiring its regional officers, Zone Presidents, to approve each contractual relationship entered into by Caremark with a physician.

Although there is evidence that inside and outside counsel had advised Caremark's directors that their contracts were in accord with the law, Caremark recognized that some uncertainty respecting the correct interpretation of the law existed. In its 1992 annual report, Caremark disclosed the ongoing government investigations, acknowledged that if penalties were imposed on the company they could have a material adverse effect of Caremark's business, and stated that no assurance could be given that its interpretation of the ARPL would prevail if challenged.

Throughout the period of the government investigations, Caremark had an internal audit plan designed to assure compliance with business and ethics policies. In addition, Caremark employed Price Waterhouse as its outside auditor. On February 8, 1993, the Ethics Committee of Caremark's Board received and reviewed an outside auditors report by Price Waterhouse which concluded that there were no material weaknesses in Caremark's control structure. Despite the positive findings of Price Waterhouse, however, on April 20, 1993, the Audit & Ethics Committee adopted a new internal audit charter requiring a comprehensive review of compliance policies and the compilation of an employee ethics handbook concerning such policies.

The Board appears to have been informed about this project and other efforts to assure compliance with the law. For example, Caremark's management reported to the Board that Caremark's sales force was receiving an ongoing education regarding the ARPL and the proper use of Caremark's form contracts which had been approved by in-house counsel. On July 27, 1993, the new ethics manual, expressly prohibiting payments in exchange for referrals and requiring employees to report all illegal conduct to a toll free confidential ethics hotline, was approved and allegedly disseminated. The record suggests that Caremark continued these policies in subsequent years, causing employees to be given revised versions of the ethics manual and requiring them to participate in training sessions concerning compliance with the law.

During 1993, Caremark took several additional steps which appear to have been aimed at increasing management supervision. These steps included new policies requiring local branch managers to secure home office approval for all disbursements under agreements with health care providers and to certify compliance with the ethics program. In addition, the chief financial officer was appointed to serve as Caremark's compliance officer. In 1994, a fifth revised Guide was published.

CHANCELLOR ALLEN:

A motion of this type requires the court to assess the strengths and weaknesses of the claims asserted in light of the discovery record and to evaluate the fairness and adequacy of the consideration offered to the corporation in exchange for the release of all claims made or arising from the facts alleged. The ultimate issue then is whether the proposed settlement appears to be fair to the corporation and its absent shareholders. In this effort the court does not determine contested facts, but evaluates the claims and defenses on the discovery record to achieve a sense of the relative strengths of the parties' positions.... In doing this, in most instances, the court is constrained by the absence of a truly adversarial process, since inevitably both sides support the settlement and legally assisted objectors are rare. Thus, the facts stated hereafter represent the court's effort to understand the context of the motion from the discovery record, but do not deserve the respect that judicial findings after trial are customarily accorded.

Legally, evaluation of the central claim made entails consideration of the legal standard governing a board of directors' obligation to supervise or monitor corporate performance. For the reasons set forth below I conclude, in light of the discovery record, that there is a very low probability that it would be determined that the directors of Caremark breached any duty to appropriately monitor and supervise the enterprise. Indeed the record tends to show an active consideration by Caremark management and its Board of the Caremark structures and programs that ultimately led to the company's indictment and to the large financial losses incurred in the settlement of those claims. It does not tend to show knowing or intentional violation of law. Neither the fact that the Board, although advised by lawyers and accountants, did not accurately predict the severe consequences to the company that would ultimately follow from the deployment by the company of the strategies and practices that ultimately led to this liability, nor the scale of the liability, gives rise to an inference of breach of any duty imposed by corporation law upon the directors of Caremark....

The complaint charges the director defendants with breach of their duty of attention or care in connection with the on-going operation of the corporation's business. The claim is that the directors allowed a situation to develop and continue which exposed the corporation to enormous legal liability and that in so doing they violated a duty to be active monitors of corporate performance. The complaint thus does not charge either director self-dealing or the more difficult loyalty-type problems arising from cases of suspect director motivation, such as entrenchment or sale of control contexts. The theory here advanced is possibly the most difficult theory in corporation law upon which a plaintiff might hope to win a judgment....

Director liability for a breach of the duty to exercise appropriate attention may, in theory, arise in two distinct contexts. First, such liability may be said to follow from a board decision that results in a loss because that decision was ill advised or "negligent." Second, liability to the corporation for a loss may be said to arise from an unconsidered failure of the board to act in circumstances in which due attention would, arguably, have prevented the loss.... The first class of cases will typically be subject to review under the director-protective business judgment rule, assuming the decision made was the product of a process that was either deliberately considered in good faith or was otherwise rational.... What should be understood, but may not widely be understood by courts or commentators who are not often required to face such questions, is that compliance with a director's duty of care can never appropriately be judicially determined by reference to the content of the board decision that leads to a corporate loss, apart from consideration of the good faith or rationality of the process employed. That is, whether a judge or jury considering the matter after the fact, believes a decision substantively wrong, or degrees of wrong extending through "stupid" to "egregious" or "irrational" provides no ground for director liability, so long as the court determines that the process employed was either rational or employed in a good faith effort to advance corporate interests. To employ a different rule—one that permitted an "objective" evaluation of the decision—would expose directors to substantive second guessing by ill-equipped judges or juries, which would, in the long-run, be injurious to investor interests. Thus, the business judgment rule is process oriented and informed by a deep respect for all good faith board decisions.

Indeed, one wonders on what moral basis might shareholders attack a good faith business decision of a director as "unreasonable" or "irrational." Where a director in fact exercises a good faith effort to be informed and to exercise appropriate judgment, he or she should be deemed to satisfy fully the duty of attention. If the shareholders thought themselves entitled to some other quality of judgment than such a director produces in the good faith exercise of the powers of office, then the shareholders should have elected other directors....

The second class of cases in which director liability for inattention is theoretically possible entail circumstances in which a loss eventuates not from a decision but, from unconsidered inaction. Most of the decisions that a corporation, acting through its human agents, makes are, of course, not the subject of director attention. Legally, the board itself will be required only to authorize the most significant corporate acts or transactions: mergers, changes in capital structure, fundamental changes in business, appointment and compensation of the CEO, etc. As the facts of this case graphically demonstrate, ordinary business decisions that are made by officers and employees deeper in the interior of the organization can, however, vitally affect the welfare of the corporation and its ability to achieve its various strategic and financial goals. If this case did not prove the point itself, recent business history would. Recall for example the displacement of senior management and much of the board of Salomon, Inc.; the replacement of senior management of Kidder, Peabody following the discovery of large trading losses resulting from phantom trades by a highly compensated trader; or the extensive financial loss and reputational injury suffered by Prudential Insurance as a result its junior officers' misrepresentations in connection with the distribution of limited partnership interests. Financial and organizational disasters such as these raise the question, what is the board's responsibility with respect to the organization and monitoring of the enterprise to assure that the corporation functions within the law to achieve its purposes?

Modernly this question has been given special importance by an increasing tendency, especially under federal law, to employ the criminal law to assure corporate compliance with external legal requirements, including environmental, financial, employee and product safety as well as assorted other health and safety regulations. In 1991, pursuant to the Sentencing Reform Act of 1984, the United States Sentencing Commission adopted Organizational Sentencing Guidelines which impact importantly on the prospective effect these criminal sanctions might have on business corporations. The Guidelines set forth a uniform sentencing structure for organizations to be sentenced for violation of federal criminal statutes and provide for penalties that equal or often massively exceed those previously imposed on corporations. The Guidelines offer powerful incentives for corporations today to have in place compliance programs to detect violations of law, promptly to report violations to appropriate public officials when discovered, and to take prompt, voluntary remedial efforts...

Can it be said today that, absent some ground giving rise to suspicion of violation of law, that corporate directors have no duty to assure that a corporate information gathering and reporting systems exists which represents a good faith attempt to provide senior management and the Board with information respecting material acts, events or conditions within the corporation, including compliance with applicable statutes and regulations? I certainly do not believe so.... [A]bsent grounds to suspect deception, neither corporate boards nor senior officers can be charged with wrongdoing simply for assuming the integrity of employees and the honesty of their dealings on the company's behalf....

Obviously the level of detail that is appropriate for such an information system is a question of business judgment. And obviously too, no rationally designed information and reporting system will remove the possibility that the corporation will violate laws or regulations, or that senior officers or directors may nevertheless sometimes be misled or otherwise fail reasonably to detect acts material to the corporation's compliance with the law. But it is important that the board exercise a good faith judgment that the corporation's information and reporting system is in concept and design adequate to assure the board that appropriate information will come to its attention in a timely manner as a matter of ordinary operations, so that it may satisfy its responsibility.

Thus, I am of the view that a director's obligation includes a duty to attempt in good faith to assure that a corporate information and reporting system, which the board concludes is adequate, exists, and that failure to do so under some circumstances may, in theory at least, render a director liable for losses caused by noncompliance with applicable legal standards. I now turn to an analysis of the claims asserted with this concept of the directors' duty of care, as a duty satisfied in part by assurance of adequate information flows to the board, in mind.

On balance, after reviewing an extensive record in this case, including numerous documents and three depositions, I conclude that this settlement is fair and reasonable. In light of the fact that the Caremark Board already has a functioning committee charged with overseeing corporate compliance, the changes in corporate practice that are presented as consideration for the settlement do not impress one as very significant. Nonetheless, that consideration appears fully adequate to support dismissal of the derivative claims of director fault asserted, because those claims find no substantial evidentiary support in the record and quite likely were susceptible to a motion to dismiss in all events.

In order to show that the Caremark directors breached their duty of care by failing adequately to control Caremark's employees, plaintiffs would have to show either: (1) that the directors knew, or (2) should have known that violations of law were occurring and, in either event (3) that the directors took no steps in a good faith effort to prevent or remedy that situation, and (4) that such failure proximately resulted in the losses complained of....

Here the record supplies essentially no evidence that the director defendants were guilty of a sustained failure to exercise their oversight function. To the contrary, insofar as I am able to tell on this record, the corporation's information systems appear to have represented a good faith attempt to be informed of relevant facts. If the directors did not know the specifics of the activities that lead to the indictments, they cannot be faulted.

The liability that eventuated in this instance was huge. But the fact that it resulted from a violation of criminal law alone does not create a breach of fiduciary duty by directors. The record at this stage does not support the conclusion that the defendants either lacked good faith in the exercise of their monitoring responsibilities or conscientiously permitted a known violation of law by the corporation to occur. The claims asserted against them must be viewed at this stage as extremely weak....

The proposed settlement provides very modest benefits. Under the settlement agreement, plaintiffs have been given express assurances that Caremark will have a more centralized, active supervisory system in the future. Specifically, the settlement mandates duties to be performed by the newly named Compliance and Ethics Committee on an ongoing basis and increases the responsibility for monitoring compliance with the law at the lower levels of management. In adopting the resolutions required under the settlement, Caremark has further clarified its policies concerning the prohibition of providing remuneration for referrals. These appear to be positive consequences of the settlement of the claims brought by the plaintiffs, even if they are not highly significant. Nonetheless, given the weakness of the plaintiffs' claims the proposed settlement appears to be an adequate, reasonable, and beneficial outcome for all of the parties. Thus, the proposed settlement will be approved.

A fiduciary must also be loyal. This means at least that the director cannot use his or her position for personal gain at the expense of the corporation. Most states today permit the directors to set their own compensation, but courts would be willing to review such arrangements to make sure there was no abuse of discretion. In any case where the director is dealing with the corporation and receiving a personal benefit, the transaction would be subject to very close judicial review.

One specific aspect of the duty of loyalty owed by directors and officers is described as the **corporate opportunity** rule. A director or officer may not take, for personal benefit, a business opportunity which should rightfully belong to the corporation. If the director or officer does so, a court will order any profits from the "opportunity" turned over to the corporation. In deciding whether the opportunity rightfully belongs to the corporation, the courts will examine whether: (1) it is within the scope of the corporation's business; (2) the director or officer learned of the opportunity while acting as such; and (3) corporate funds, equipment, or personnel were used to develop the opportunity. Under the strictest application of the rule, if any of these three conditions exist, the opportunity belongs to the corporation.

The following case is an example of the doctrine.

LANGE v. LANGE
520 N.W.2d 113 (IA, 1994)

FACTS: Madison Holding Company, was owned and controlled by two brothers, Elmer Lange and Jean Lange. Upon Elmer's death, Jean—the sole surviving director—took action to wrest control of the corporation from Elmer's widow (and executor) and daughters, plaintiffs Beth Lange, Mary Beth Williams, and Martha Jean Lange. This litigation ensued.

In the early 1970s, Jean and Elmer Lange, in equal partnership, acquired a majority interest in the Union State Bank of Winterset, Iowa. They decided some years later that formation of a bank holding company would reap desired tax benefits. Such a move required the holding company to own 80 percent of the bank's outstanding stock. Thus Jean and Elmer purchased an equal number of additional shares until collectively they owned more than 80 percent of the bank. They then activated the Madison Holding Company.

At the time the holding company was formed, Jean and Elmer's equal number of bank shares were exchanged for shares of common stock in the company on a one-for-one basis. The company assumed the brothers' debts associated with acquisition of the bank stock. Because Jean transferred $120,000 more debt into the company than Elmer, the company issued Elmer 1,200 more shares of preferred stock, at a par value of $100, to Elmer's side of the family. Thus Elmer's family owned 61.84 percent of the company and Jean's family owned 48.16 percent.

Despite the imbalance in stock ownership, the brothers treated one another as equal partners. The record clearly reveals that they intended to equalize their stock holdings at some future time. The family members, other than the brothers, were apparently unaware of the disparity.

One way to equalize formal ownership was for the company to redeem $120,000 of Elmer's preferred stock. In 1982, the company issued two $15,000 checks to Elmer to advance the equalization process. At the time, the bank—like many other Iowa financial institutions—found its very existence threatened by the farm crisis. Its precarious financial position rendered the proposed stock redemption unwise. Thus Elmer returned the $30,000 to the company.

A year later the brothers executed a buy/sell agreement to provide for disposition of company stock upon the death of either of them. The agreement gave the surviving brother an option to purchase common and preferred stock from the deceased brother's wife. The agreement was signed by Elmer, Jean, and their wives Beth and Jeanne.

In 1985 Elmer again set out to formally restore the fifty-fifty partnership. His accountant advised that the company could issue $120,000 in additional preferred shares to Jean, or Jean could purchase 600 preferred shares from Elmer. Jean testified that he and Elmer discussed the accountant's recommendations sometime in 1986 or 1987 and that Elmer agreed to sell Jean 600 shares of preferred stock for $60,000. The transfer was never completed, however, because of continuing concern over the bank's financial stability. On eleven separate occasions during this time period, the brothers invested equal sums—totalling nearly $750,000 each—to keep the bank afloat. Despite the continued discrepancy in share ownership, the brothers always operated with the understanding that they were equal partners in the enterprise.

Elmer died on May 6, 1990. He left one-half of his estate to his widow, Beth, and the other half equally to his two daughters, Mary Beth and Martha. These heirs soon learned of the disparity in stock ownership and Elmer's unsuccessful attempt to equalize it. Elmer and Jean's longtime attorney, John Schulte, drafted an agreement acknowledging Jean and Elmer's intentions and proposing Jean's purchase of 600 shares of preferred stock at $100 per share. Jean's family signed the agreement, but Elmer's did not. Upon advice of separate counsel, Elmer's heirs expressed their desire to retain majority ownership of the company.

Throughout the brothers' partnership, Jean had assumed responsibility for day-to-day bank management. Elmer supervised other joint ventures. Jean thus became concerned that the bank would be mismanaged or sold if Elmer's heirs continued to insist on majority control. In February 1991, he passed a corporate resolution calling for the redemption of 1,600 shares of preferred stock and 1054 shares of common stock from Elmer's estate. Later that month he appointed his son, Gene, director of the company to assume the position vacated by Elmer. The two then amended the earlier resolution by enlarging the proposed redemption of preferred shares by 250. The next day, the directors authorized the issuance of 2,000 shares of common stock to Jean in exchange for existing debt.

In August and September of 1991, Jean made an individual purchase of 400 shares of the bank's common stock from outside shareholders. This purchase represented 10 percent of the bank's 4,000 outstanding common shares.

In April 1991, plaintiffs filed suit alleging Jean had breached his fiduciary duty to the corporation shareholders by causing the issuance of 2000 shares of common stock to himself and by attempting to redeem portions of Elmer's common and preferred stock. Defendants counterclaimed, seeking specific performance of the agreement for the sale of 600 preferred shares from Elmer's estate.

Following bench trial, the court ruled that the 1990 agreement drawn by Schulte represented a valid exercise of Jean's option to purchase under the 1983 buy/sell agreement. It therefore ordered Elmer's estate to transfer 600 shares of preferred stock to Jean in exchange for $60,000. The court voided the issuance of the 2,000 additional common stock shares, concluding the action was taken by Jean for the wrongful purpose of acquiring control of the company. It went on to find the attempted redemption of 1,760 shares of Elmer's preferred stock "technically and legally valid" but voided the transaction as an inequitable attempt by Jean to upset the balance in ownership between the two families. Finally, the court rejected plaintiffs' amended posttrial claim that Jean usurped a "corporate opportunity" by individually buying 400 additional shares of bank stock. This appeal and cross appeal followed.

⚖️ **JUSTICE NEUMAN:**

Plaintiffs argue that the district court erred in finding that Jean breached no fiduciary duty by buying additional bank stock for his own account and the account of his personal holding company. Plaintiffs assert that such purchases, without notice to them or to the company, amounted to a usurpation of a "corporate opportunity." We disagree.

As a fiduciary, a corporate director may not secure a business opportunity that in all fairness should belong to the corporation.... Plaintiffs assert that because the holding company's only purpose was bank ownership, the opportunity to purchase additional bank shares was "essential" to the company's business and of practical importance to it. They therefore claim that Jean breached his fiduciary duty by taking advantage of the stock purchase without prior notice to the company. Defendants respond that no corporate opportunity existed and, even if it had, the company could not have availed itself of the opportunity....

As the court noted, the shares Jean purchased in no way jeopardized the company's significant majority ownership of the bank. The company did not need the stock for the conduct of its business because it had already surpassed the 80 percent ownership threshold necessary to obtain the tax benefits for which it was formed. Moreover, defendants tendered substantial proof that the company had no expectancy regarding the 400 additional shares....

The record further reveals, and plaintiffs fully admit, that the company was not financially positioned to purchase the 400 shares. Given this circumstance, and so long as the acquisition was not made with corporate funds, Jean was entitled to treat the opportunity as his own.... The records reveals that Jean used his own funds to make the stock purchases. Thus we affirm the district court's finding that the record does not contain the proof necessary to sustain a corporate opportunity claim....

The district court struck down Jean's issuance of 2,000 additional shares of common stock on the ground the action was taken for the sole purpose of obtaining control of the company. Defendants urge on cross-appeal that the court's ruling is in error because a legitimate business purpose existed for the transaction.

We are guided in our analysis by the general rule set out by the Maryland Court of Special Appeals in *Mountain Manor Realty, Inc. v. Buccheri*:

> Directors may not exploit their official position to manipulate the issue of shares *solely* to perpetuate their own control of the corporation.... But an issue of stock that has the collateral effect of enhancing the power of incumbent management is not invalid if the transaction has as its principal purpose some proper corporate goal.... And management has not only the right but the duty to resist by all lawful means persons whose attempt to win control of the corporation, if successful, would harm the corporate enterprise....

The district court found that issuance of the 2,000 additional shares was undertaken solely for the personal advantage of Jean's family to obtain control of the corporation. Jean asserted at trial, and argues on appeal, that his primary interest In issuing the stock was keeping the bank out of the control of those who "have no expertise in the banking business whatsoever." He also expressed concern that Elmer's family would sell the bank to outsiders, thereby threatening the positions of its managers. The record, however, does not bear out Jean's concerns.

Although plaintiffs admit their prior lack of involvement in the bank's operations, nothing other than Jean's bare assertions suggest that they could not competently oversee its management. Indeed, Beth and her sisters own a bank in Jefferson. Mary Beth is director of her husband's company and of a community college in Kansas. In addition, defendants tendered no competent evidence that plaintiffs intended to sell the bank. On the contrary, Beth testified that she had complete confidence in the bank's president, James Herrick, and the way the bank was being managed by him and other bank officers. Jean's fear, therefore, appears to be based on nothing more than speculation. Like the district court, we are not convinced that actions based on speculation can be equated with actions motivated by a "legitimate corporate purpose."

The district court's position is strengthened by this court's observations in *Carlson v. Ringgold County Mut. Tel. Co.*, 252 Iowa 748, 108 N.W.2d 478 (1961). There we said:

> It is a fraud for directors of a corporation, without the knowledge and consent of other stockholders, to subscribe for and to take the unissued stock to the enrichment of themselves and the detriment of the other stockholders....

In short, the court did not err in voiding the common stock issue.

To summarize, we affirm the district court's order enforcing Jean's right under the 1983 buy/sell agreement to purchase 600 shares of preferred stock held by Elmer. We likewise affirm the court's decision to void the company's issuance of 2,000 shares of common stock to Jean, at his direction, as action undertaken to advance his personal interest rather than a legitimate corporate purpose. While we disagree with that portion of the court's decision that would interpret the corporate by-laws to permit partial redemption by the company of Elmer's preferred shares, and reverse the court's ruling to that extent, we affirm the court's ultimate refusal to enforce the redemption on equitable grounds. Finally, we affirm the court's finding of insufficient proof on plaintiffs' posttrial claim regarding Jean's alleged usurpation of a corporate opportunity.

Affirmed in part and reversed in part on the appeal; affirmed on the cross appeal.

OFFICERS

Authority. To a more limited extent, the firm's officers may also get some of their authority from the state's corporation statute. For the most part, the officers derive their authority from the corporation's articles and bylaws and from specific board resolutions. The states do not agree on the amount of power which is given to the corporation's president merely by appointment as such. In some states, the president is presumed to be a kind of "general manager," with automatic authority to make all contracts that are within the scope of the firm's normal business. In other states, the corporation president is only a figurehead, unless specific powers have been given to the officeholder by articles, bylaws, or resolution. Third parties need to check carefully on whether the individual with whom they are negotiating has authority to bind the corporation. In no state would the president have the authority to execute unusual or extraordinary contracts without specific resolutions.

As the next case shows, the powers of corporate officers may also be subject to limitations in other state regulations.

UNITED ACCOUNTS, INC. v. TELADVANTAGE, INC.
524 N.W.2d 605 (ND, 1994)

FACTS: Teladvantage, Inc., acting through an officer and stockholder, appealed an order denying its motion for relief from a final summary judgment.

This is a sequel to *United Accounts, Inc. v. Teladvantage, Inc.*, 499 N.W.2d 115 (ND, 1993) (*Teladvantage I*), where the North Dakota Supreme Court affirmed a summary judgment for United Accounts. After remand, again acting through Martin E. O'Connor, not an attorney, Teladvantage moved for relief from the judgment, claiming that it mistakenly failed to respond to the original motion for summary judgment. The trial court denied relief, noting that Teladvantage deliberately chose not to respond although it was properly notified and had an officer present at the hearing. Teladvantage appeals with a notice of appeal and an appellant's brief, both signed by O'Connor, who is not licensed to practice law.

 PER CURIAM:

United Accounts' responsive brief points out that no cost bond has been filed and that O'Connor continues to act for the corporation despite our warning in *Teladvantage I* at 117, n. 1, that a corporation "cannot appear pro se, and must be represented by counsel in court proceedings...." "Except as otherwise provided by state law or supreme court rule, a person may not practice law, act as an attorney or counselor at law in this state, or commence, conduct, or defend in any court of record of this state, any action or proceeding in which he is not a party concerned ...." No statute or rule permits an unlicensed agent to litigate for a corporation. Therefore, on our own initiative, we summarily dismiss this appeal.

The appellant's brief filed by O'Connor asserts that our prior opinion was wrong and that O'Connor may nevertheless represent the corporation. O'Connor cites a South Dakota trial court opinion that likened a corporation to a person for equal protection, and there allowed a corporation to appear through a stockholder not licensed to practice law.

A trial court decision, particularly one in a different case and from another jurisdiction, is not authoritative.... ("The decisions of lower courts are not binding upon appellate courts.") We reject O'Connor's inartful argument.

It is well established that a corporation does not have a constitutional right to litigate through agents who are not licensed to practice law. In Hawaii, the "prevailing rule" has also been that "a corporation cannot appear and represent itself either in proper person or by its officers...." Moreover, in that case, the Hawaiian Supreme Court rejected a constitutional claim, as well, and held that a natural person and a corporation are not similarly situated for litigation.... ("It has been the law for the better part of two centuries, for example, that a corporation may appear in the federal courts only through licensed counsel.")

O'Connor is not entitled to file a brief for his corporation in this or any other legal action. We reject the brief and summarily dismiss this appeal as frivolous.

A failure to comply with proper appellate procedure is also grounds for dismissal.... ("Failure of an appellant to take any step ... is ground only for such action as the court deems appropriate, which may include dismissal of the appeal.") NDRAppP 7 requires a cost bond unless "exempted by law," by "fil[ing] a supersedeas bond or other undertaking which includes security for the payment of costs on appeal," or by obtaining a written waiver from the appellee. United Accounts has been prejudiced because Teladvantage has not given security for payment of any costs awarded to United Accounts. Teladvantage has made no effort to cure this defect or to justify its failure.

Since O'Connor has persisted, after warning, in a frivolous effort to represent his corporation in court though not licensed to do so, and has not filed the required cost bond, we summarily dismiss this appeal.

Selection, Compensation, and Removal. Corporate officers are selected by the board of directors unless the articles provide otherwise. Officers are usually appointed for one-year renewable terms, but they continue to serve at the will of the board. In other words, the general rule is that the board can remove an officer at any time, with or without cause. If an officer is removed without good cause, his or her employment contract with the firm would probably require compensation for the remainder of the appointment period, but he or she would no longer be permitted to function as a corporate officer. Most modern corporation statutes do not require more than one officer, though there may be requirements that more than one person sign certain documents for the corporation (deeds to land, for example). Specific board of directors' action on all major personnel decisions might help avoid some employee lawsuits.

Officers' compensation is determined by the board of directors, and their decision will generally not be second-guessed by a court. A director who is also an officer should not be present when the directors set the salary for his or her office. As with any other decision where the board's business judgment is involved, there are limits to the discretion that is given to the board with regard to officers' compensation.

Liabilities of Directors and Officers. Most of the specific sources of directors' and officers' liability have already been discussed, in this and previous chapters. Directors are liable for the issuance of watered stock and for the declaration of illegal dividends. They may be held liable for refusing a stockholder's justified demand for corporate information or for breaching their fiduciary duty by self-dealing or by stealing a corporate opportunity. Directors and officers may also incur liability under state regulatory statutes for failure to file required reports and income statements. Under the national securities laws (see Chapter 37), such corporate insiders as directors and officers may be held liable for making personal profits at the expense of the corporation or its shareholders. And directors and officers may be held liable to their firm and its shareholders for failing to take reasonable care in the operation of its business.

In recent years, directors and officers have also been subjected to an increasing criminal liability exposure. Criminal prosecutions against the directors and officers responsible for antitrust and other regulatory violations have been becoming more common, as have prison terms for persons convicted of willful violations.

Foreign Corrupt Practices Act. After SEC investigations disclosed that over 300 U.S. firms had made various kinds of payments and gifts to foreign officials to get contracts or favorable regulations, Congress passed the Foreign Corrupt Practices Act (FCPA) in 1977. The FCPA amends the 1934 Securities Exchange Act in three main areas: a U.S. firm, whether or not subject to the 1934 Act's registration and disclosure requirements, is prohibited from bribing foreign officials to misuse their official position to benefit the firm; a firm subject to the 1934 Act must maintain books and records which, in reasonable detail, accurately and fairly reflect the firm's transactions and must also maintain a system of internal accounting controls which reasonably ensures that transactions are properly executed and recorded and that corporate assets are protected. New criminal penalties of up to $2 million for the firm and of up to $100,000 each for the individuals involved may be imposed for willful violations. This is a very important new area of potential liability for both corporate and noncorporate managers, but its exact dimensions will not be known until there have been more court interpretations of the FCPA.

SIGNIFICANCE OF THIS CHAPTER

The corporation is simply a legal entity, a piece of paper, a charter from the state. Thus, it must be managed by people. This chapter identifies those people as directors and officers and reviews the process of their selection and removal, and their powers, duties, authority, compensation, and possible personal liability.

Persons in these positions must be aware of the limits on their authority and the potential sources of personal and corporate liability. Persons dealing with the corporation, either as stockholders or creditors, also need to know these "rules of the game."

PROBLEMS FOR DISCUSSION

1. Audit Services, a collection agency, sued on behalf of three union trust funds for monies owing pursuant to certain collective bargaining agreements and declarations of trust. Roy Winslow, Elmo Road's general manager, signed the collective agreements for the corporation, which was then obligated to make certain payments to the pension and welfare trusts for its employees' benefit. Elmo Road made these payments from April to October 1992, and then stopped. When further payments were refused, the trust funds assigned their claims to the plaintiff, which sued for $31,842.53 due, plus $1,802.02 attorney fees. The trial court gave judgment for Elmo Road, holding that Winslow had no express, implied, or apparent authority to sign for the corporation. Plaintiff appealed.
    How should the appeals court decide? Explain.

2. Harry Smith, a minority stockholder in Alabama Dry Docks and Shipbuilding Company, Inc., brought a stockholder's derivative suit to recover for the corporation allegedly excessive salaries and bonuses paid to four of its director-officers. Smith tried to get the other directors and stockholders to take action on this matter, but they refused to do so. He then brought this derivative suit on behalf of the corporation. He appealed from the trial court's dismissal of the suit on demurrer.

    Did the complaint state a valid cause of action against the directors and officers? Discuss.

3. Alex Hozer and his wife Glitta owned a sailboat. Glitta called Tinker Yachts, Inc. to inquire about selling the boat. Tinker agreed to do so for a 10 percent commission. Harold Hite saw the boat at Tinker's, displayed on a boat trailer, and agreed to buy the boat and trailer for $45,000. Harold dealt with a salesman, John Russ. Russ telephoned Glitta, and she agreed to the $45,000 price. Harold gave Russ a check for $5,000, which was deposited in Tinker's bank. Later, he came back with a check for the $40,000 balance, and took delivery of the boat and trailer. The Hozers did not own the boat trailer which had been given to Harold. When the mistake was discovered, Tinker's president, Eddy Otfar, asked the Hozers to buy the trailer, so that their buyer Harold could keep it. The Hozers refused and demanded their money. They now sue Tinker and Otfar for fraud and conversion.

    Otfar moves for summary judgment, claiming there is no basis for a claim against him.
    How should the court rule? Explain.

4. The bylaws of Ozone Onion Farms, Inc. specify a maximum of eleven directors; there is no indication of any minimum number. Handel, Bach, Mozart, and eight other persons were serving on the board of directors when a special stockholders' meeting was called. Mozart owned 1,400 of the 2,700 shares of stock outstanding. The vote was 1,400 to 1,300 to remove all eleven directors. Mozart, his wife, and Lemming were then elected as directors. The state's statute provided that a corporation must have at least three directors and that the term of a director could not be shortened by amending the bylaws to decrease the number of directors. Handel and Bach file suit, challenging the removal and election.

    What is the result, and why?

5. The court of chancery granted a preliminary injunction to the plaintiffs (collectively "Mesa"), enjoining an exchange offer of the defendant, Unocal Corporation, for its own stock. The trial court concluded that a selective exchange offer, excluding Mesa, was legally impermissible. The factual findings of the vice chancellor establish that Unocal's board, consisting of a majority of independent directors, acted in good faith, and after reasonable investigation found that Mesa's tender offer was both inadequate and coercive.

    On April 8, 1995, Mesa, the owner of approximately 13 percent of Unocal's stock, commenced a two-tier "front loaded" cash tender offer for 64 million shares, or approximately 37 percent, of Unocal's outstanding stock at a price of $54 per share. The "back-end" was designed to eliminate the remaining publicly held shares by an exchange of securities purportedly worth $54 per share. However, pursuant to an order entered by the United States District Court for the Central District of California on April 26, 1995, Mesa issued a supplemental proxy statement to Unocal's stockholders disclosing that the securities offered in the second-step merger would be highly subordinated and that Unocal's capitalization would differ significantly from its present structure. Unocal has rather aptly termed such securities "junk bonds."

    Should this injunction be upheld when Unocal appeals? Why or why not?

Chapter 36

Ethics in Business and Corporate Social Responsibility

In Chapter 1, we discussed the relationship between two great ethical principles—Truthfulness and Fairness—and the Law. In the intervening chapters, you have seen many examples of these two ethical principles in action. Chapter 4 showed that the limitations on "long-arm" jurisdiction are based on fairness. So are many of the constitutional limitations discussed in Chapter 3. Many of the procedural protections discussed in Chapter 5 are also based on fairness to the criminal accused. Chapter 6's test for negligence liability—"reasonable" conduct—is also a kind of fairness standard. The doctrines of promissory estoppel and unconscionability in Chapter 9, and equitable estoppel in Chapter 10, are based on fairness. Sanctions for untruthfulness are discussed in Chapter 11. The concept of "unconscionability"—gross unfairness—underlies all of the law of sales of goods, and arguably, all of the Uniform Commercial Code. The imposition of standards of fiduciary duty, involving Truth and Fairness, on partners and members of closely held corporations, provides other examples of the Law's recognition of ethical duties.

There is thus a considerable overlap between Law and Ethics. To the extent that a corporation merely complies with these legal requirements, it is doing only the required (social) minimum. Some would argue that that is enough; that the corporation's sole reason for existence is to make a profit for its shareholders. There is, however, also a strong argument that business institutions must play a more activist role in the salvation of the planet.

If a business firm is to move beyond compliance with its legal obligations, and assume ethical-moral obligations as well, several tough questions have to be answered. First, who is going to decide what ethical obligations will be met? Second, by what standards will these decisions be made? And third, how and by whom will such decisions be implemented?

CORPORATE DECISIONS ON SOCIAL RESPONSIBILITY

The first question requires a balancing of the powers of the directors with those of the stockholders. One of the earliest "social responsibility" cases arose as a dispute over the Ford Motor Company's dividend policy under Henry Ford I. Henry apparently distrusted "Eastern bankers" and feared that borrowing money might mean losing control of his company. He also had certain altruistic ideas about "sharing the wealth" generated by Ford's assembly line with its employees and customers. As a result, he told his hand-picked Ford directors not to declare further special dividends. In fact, regular and special dividends totalling more than twenty times the original investment in the company had already been declared and paid. A 2,000+ percent return on investment would be considered quite good by most stockholders, but not so by the "Dodge boys." The Dodge brothers, minority stockholders, challenged Ford's dividend policy in the Michigan courts. Henry's testimony to his vision of "corporate social responsibility" astounded the Dodges' lawyer—and lost the case.

DODGE v. FORD MOTOR CO.
170 N.W. 668 (MI, 1919)

FACTS: Minority stockholders sued to force the directors to declare an additional special dividend. Horace and John Dodge, the plaintiffs, were two of the original stockholders in Ford Motor Company, along with Horace Rackham, James Couzens, and Henry Ford himself. On the capitalization of $2 million, Ford Motor had been paying a quarterly dividend equal to 60 percent per year; it had also paid out a total of $41 million in special dividends. Ford Motor still had a capital surplus of nearly $112 million, however, and sales and profits were up. Henry now proposed a massive capital expansion to produce iron and steel (the Rouge plant) as well as a lowering of the price of the Model T from $440 to $360. At one point, Henry was quoted as saying: "My ambition is to employ still more men, to spread the benefits of this industrial system to the greatest possible number, to help them build up their lives and their homes. To do this, we are putting the greatest share of our profits back in the business." Ford Motor appealed from the trial court's decision ordering payment of a special dividend and enjoining the building of the Rouge plant.

 JUSTICE OSTRANDER:

The rule which will govern courts in deciding these questions is not in dispute....

> It is a well-recognized principle of law that the directors of a corporation, and they alone, have the power to declare a dividend of the earnings of the corporation, and to determine its amount.... Courts of equity will not interfere in the management of the directors unless it is clearly made to appear that they are guilty of fraud or misappropriation of the corporate funds, or refuse to declare a dividend when the corporation has a surplus of net profits which it can, without detriment to its business,

divide among its stockholders, and when a refusal to do so would amount to such an abuse of discretion as would constitute a fraud, or breach of that good faith which they are bound to exercise towards the stockholders....

It is the contention of plaintiffs that the apparent effect of the plan is intended to be the continued and continuing effect of it and that it is deliberately proposed, not of record and not by official corporate declaration, but nevertheless proposed, to continue the corporation henceforth as a semieleemosynary institution and not as a business institution. In support of this contention they point to the attitude and to the expressions of Mr. Henry Ford.

Mr. Henry Ford is the dominant force in the business of the Ford Motor Company. No plan of operations could be adopted unless he consented, and no board of directors can be elected whom he does not favor. One of the directors of the company has no stock. One share was assigned to him to qualify him for the position, but it is not claimed that he owns it. A business, one of the largest in the world, and one of the most profitable, has been built up. It employs many men, at good pay....

With regard to dividends, the company paid 60 percent on its capitalization of two million dollars, or $1,200,000, leaving $58,000,000 to reinvest for the growth of the company. This is Mr. Ford's policy at present, and it is understood that the other stockholders cheerfully accede to this plan.

He had made up his mind in the summer of 1916 that no dividends other than the regular dividends should be paid, "for the present."

> "**Q.** For how long? Had you fixed in your mind any time in the future, when you were going to pay—
>
> "**A.** No.
>
> "**Q.** That was indefinite in the future?
>
> "**A.** That was indefinite, yes, sir."

The record, and especially the testimony of Mr. Ford, convinces that he has to some extent the attitude towards shareholders of one who has dispensed and distributed to them large gains, and that they should be content to take what he chooses to give. His testimony creates the impression, also, that he thinks the Ford Motor Company has made too much money, has had too large profits, and that although large profits might be still earned, a sharing of them with the public, by reducing the price of the output of the company, ought to be undertaken. We have no doubt that certain sentiments, philanthropic and altruistic, creditable to Mr. Ford, had large influence in determining the policy to be pursued by the Ford Motor Company—the policy which has been herein referred to. It is said by his counsel that—

> Although a manufacturing corporation cannot engage in humanitarian works as its principal business, the fact that it is organized for profit does not prevent the existence of implied powers to carry on with humanitarian motives such charitable works as are incidental to the main business of the corporation.

And again:

> As the expenditures complained of are being made in an expansion of the business which the company is organized to carry on, and for purposes within the powers of the corporation as hereinbefore shown, the question is as to whether such expenditures are rendered illegal because influenced to some extent by humanitarian motives and purposes on the part of the members of the board of directors....

We do not draw in question, nor do counsel for the plaintiffs do so, the validity of the general propositions stated by counsel nor the soundness of the opinions delivered in the cases cited. The case presented here is not like any of them. The difference between an incidental humanitarian expenditure of corporate funds for the benefit of the employees, like the building of a hospital for their use and the employment of agencies for the betterment of their condition, and a general purpose and plan to benefit mankind at the expense of others, is obvious. There should be no confusion (of which there is evidence) of the duties which Mr. Ford conceives that he and the stockholders owe to the general public and the duties which in law he and his codirectors owe to protesting, minority stockholders. A business corporation is organized and carried on primarily for the profit of the stockholders. The powers of the directors are to be employed for that end. The discretion of directors is to be exercised in the choice of means to attain that end and does not extend to a change in the end itself, to the reduction of profits, or to the nondistribution of profits among stockholders in order to devote them to other purposes.

There is committed to the discretion of directors a discretion to be exercised in good faith, the infinite details of business, including the wages which shall be paid to employees, the number of hours they shall work, the conditions under which labor shall be carried on, and the prices for which products shall be offered to the public. It is said by appellants that the motives of the board members are not material and will not be inquired into by the court so long as their acts are within their lawful powers. As we have pointed out, and the proposition does not require argument to sustain it, it is not within the lawful powers of a board of directors to shape and conduct the affairs of a corporation for the merely incidental benefit of shareholders and for the primary purpose of benefiting others, and no one will contend that if the avowed purpose of defendant directors was to sacrifice the interests of shareholders it would not be the duty of the courts to interfere.

We are not, however, persuaded that we should interfere with the proposed expansion of the business of the Ford Motor Company. In view of the fact that the selling price of products may be increased at any time, the ultimate results of the larger business cannot be certainly estimated. The judges are not business experts. It is recognized that plans must often be made for a long future, for expected competition, for a continuing as well as an immediately profitable venture. The experience of the Ford Motor Company is evidence of capable management of its affairs. It may be noticed, incidentally, that it took from the public the money required for the execution of its plan and that the very considerable salaries paid to Mr. Ford and to certain executive officers and employees were not diminished. We are not satisfied that the alleged motives of the directors, in so far as they are reflected in the conduct of the business, menace the interests of shareholders. It is enough to say, perhaps, that the court of equity is at all times open to complaining shareholders having a just grievance....

The decree of the court below fixing and determining the specific amount ($19,275,385.96) to be distributed to the stockholders is affirmed. In other respects, except as to the allowance of costs, the said decree is reversed. Plaintiffs will recover interest at 5 percent per annum upon their proportional share of said dividend from the date of the decree of the lower court. Appellants will tax the costs of their appeal, and two thirds of the amount thereof will be paid by plaintiffs. No other costs are allowed.

While Henry I and the company lost on the dividend issue, they at least prevailed on building the River Rouge plant complex. Building a new plant, the Michigan court felt, was clearly the sort of business decision left to the discretion of the corporation's board of directors. The presumption in favor of the directors' dividend policy, on the other hand, was overcome by Henry's testimony of altruistic intent. "Doing good" with the stockholders' money was not within the directors' discretion. If they wanted to give away their own money, after they received their own dividends, fine and dandy. But Henry and his directors could not use the company as a vehicle for their personal share-the-wealth schemes.

Today, either by court decision or by statute, most states permit charitable donations (in appropriate amounts) by business firms. This sort of building of "good will" has become customary, and is clearly recognized by the tax laws, which permit deductions for charitable gifts. It would still be an open question, however, as to whether this gift-giving custom would be broad enough to cover a new Henry Ford case. It may now be permissible to make small corporate gifts of cash to appropriate charities. That principle would not necessarily cover a situation where the company's directors were making basic policy decisions such as product pricing, wage levels, and dividend declaration on the basis of personal altruism.

Consideration of "social responsibility" factors, however, within the context of the *corporation's* best interests—both long-term and short-term—is almost certainly appropriate. Taking social concerns into account was held to be within the directors' "business judgment" in the next case.

SHLENSKY v. WRIGLEY
237 N.E.2d 776 (IL, 1968)

FACTS: Plaintiff is a minority stockholder of defendant corporation, Chicago National League Ball Club (Inc.), a Delaware corporation with its principal place of business in Chicago, Illinois. Defendant corporation owns and operates the major league professional baseball team known as the Chicago Cubs. The corporation also engages in the operation of Wrigley Field, the Cubs' home park, the concessionaire sales during Cubs' home games, television and radio broadcasts of Cubs' home games, the leasing of the field for football games and other events and receives its share, as visiting team, of admission moneys from games played in other National League stadia. The individual defendants are directors of the Cubs and have served for varying periods of years. Defendant Phillp K. Wrigley is also president of the corporation and owner of approximately 80 percent of the stock therein.

Plaintiff alleges that since night baseball was first played in 1935, nineteen of the twenty major league teams have scheduled night games. In 1966, out of a total of 1,620 games in the major leagues, 932 were played at night. Plaintiff alleges that every member of the major leagues, other than the Cubs, scheduled substantially all of its home games in 1966 at night, exclusive of opening days, Saturdays, Sundays, holidays, and days prohibited by league rules. Allegedly this has been done for the specific purpose of maximizing attendance and thereby maximizing revenue and income.

The Cubs, in the years 1961-65, sustained operating losses from its direct baseball operations. Plaintiff attributes those losses to inadequate attendance at Cubs' home games. He concludes that if the directors continue to refuse to install lights at Wrigley Field and schedule night baseball games, the Cubs will continue to sustain comparable losses and its financial condition will continue to deteriorate.

Plaintiff further alleges that defendant Wrigley has refused to install lights, not because of interest in the welfare of the corporation but because of his personal opinions "that baseball is a 'daytime sport' and that the installation of lights and night baseball games will have a deteriorating effect upon the surrounding neighborhood."

 JUSTICE SULLIVAN:

The question on appeal is whether plaintiff's amended complaint states a cause of action. It is plaintiff's position that fraud, illegality, and conflict of interest are not the only bases for a stockholder's derivative action against the directors. Contrariwise, defendants argue that the courts will not step in and interfere with honest business judgment of the directors unless there is a showing of fraud, illegality, or conflict of interest.

The cases in this area are numerous, and each differs from the others on a factual basis. However, the courts have pronounced certain ground rules which appear in all cases and which are then applied to the given factual situation. The court in *Wheeler v. Pullman Iron and Steel Company* ... said:

> It is, however, fundamental in the law of corporations, that the majority of its stockholders shall control the policy of the corporation, and regulate and govern the lawful exercise of its franchise and business.... Every one purchasing or subscribing for stock in a corporation impliedly agrees that he will be bound by the acts and proceedings done or sanctioned by a majority of the shareholders, or by the agents of the corporation duly chosen by such majority, within the scope of the powers conferred by the charter, and courts of equity will not undertake to control the policy or business methods of a corporation, although it may be seen that a wiser policy might be adopted and the business more successful if other methods were pursued. The majority of shares of its stock, or the agents by the holders thereof lawfully chosen, must be permitted to control the business of the corporation in their discretion, when not in violation of its charter or some public law, or corruptly and fraudulently subversive of the rights and interests of the corporation or of a shareholder....

Plaintiff in the instant case argues that the directors are acting for reasons unrelated to the financial interest and welfare of the Cubs. However, we are not satisfied that the motives assigned to Philip K. Wrigley, and through him to the other directors, are contrary to the best interests of the corporation and the stockholders. By these thoughts we do not mean to say that we have decided that the decision of the directors was a correct one. That is beyond our jurisdiction and ability. We are merely saying that the decision is one properly before directors, and motives alleged in the amended complaint showed no fraud, illegality, or conflict of interest in their making of that decision.

While all the courts do not insist that one or more of the three elements must be present for a stockholder's derivative action to lie, nevertheless we feel that unless the conduct of the defendants at least borders on one of the elements, the courts should not interfere....

We feel that plaintiff's amended complaint was also defective in failing to allege damage to the corporation....

There is no allegation that the night games played by the other nineteen teams enhanced their financial position or that the profits, if any, of those teams were directly related to the number of night games scheduled....

Finally, we do not agree with plaintiff's contention that failure to follow the example of the other major clubs in scheduling night games constituted negligence. Plaintiff made no allegation that these teams' night schedules were profitable or that the purpose for which night baseball had been undertaken was fulfilled. Furthermore, it cannot be said that directors, even those of corporations that are losing money, must follow the lead of the other corporations in the field. Directors are elected for their business capabilities and judgment, and the courts cannot require them to forego their judgment because of the decisions of directors of other companies. Courts may not decide these questions in the absence of a clear showing of dereliction of duty on the part of the specific directors, and mere failure to "follow the crowd" is not such a dereliction.

For the foregoing reasons the order of dismissal entered by the trial court is affirmed.

Stockholder Votes. A corporate social responsibility issue confronted Dow Chemical, the primary manufacturer of napalm—jellied gasoline—which is dropped from the air on enemy troops. In 1968, an article appeared in *Business Week*, titled "Why Dow Continues to Make Napalm." It was quite profitable, apparently, but the Dow management said they would make it even if it were not, as the company's patriotic duty to support our troops who were fighting and dying in Viet Nam. Shortly after the article appeared, a group calling itself the "Medical Committee for Human Rights" somehow acquired a few shares of Dow stock and demanded a stockholder vote on an amendment to the company's Articles. The following lawsuit ensued.

MEDICAL COMMITTEE FOR HUMAN RIGHTS v. SEC
432 F.2d 659 (U.S. District of Columbia Circuit, 1970)

FACTS: On March 11, 1968, Dr. Quentin Young, the national chairman of the Medical Committee, wrote to the secretary of the Dow Chemical Company, stating that the committee had received a few shares of Dow's stock as a gift and asking permission to introduce an amendment to the company's charter at the annual meeting. The amendment would have prohibited Dow from making napalm. The committee was late in making its request, and Dow refused to waive the time limit set by the corporate bylaws. On January 6, 1969, the committee made a timely demand for inclusion of the proposed amendment in Dow's proxy statement for that year's shareholders' meeting. Dow refused to do so, relying on the SEC's proxy rules which said that proposals could be omitted if they were "primarily for the purpose of promoting general economic, political, racial, religious, social or similar causes" or if they requested that "the management take action with respect to a matter relating to the conduct of the ordinary business operations" of the corporation. On February 18, the chief counsel of the SEC's Division of Corporate Finance sent a letter to both parties which said that the division would "not recommend any action ... if this proposal is omitted from the management's proxy material." On April 2, the SEC approved this "no action" recommendation. The Medical Committee appealed.

 JUDGE TAMM:

[Much of Judge Tamm's opinion dealt with the question of whether such a "no action" decision by the SEC was reviewable by a Court of Appeals. He decided that the very strong presumption in favor of judicial review of administrative action had not been overcome in this case and that this was in effect a "final order" and thus ready for review. The SEC's proxy procedures were also sufficiently adversarial and formal in nature to permit court review of the results. Tamm also felt that the SEC had not done an adequate job of explaining its decision.]

[T]he Commission has not deigned to address itself to any possible grounds for allowing management to exclude this proposal from its proxy statement. We confess to a similar puzzlement as to how the Commission reached the result which it did, and thus we are forced to remand the controversy for a more illuminating consideration and decision.... In aid of this consideration on remand, we feel constrained to explain our difficulties with the position taken by the company and endorsed by the Commission.

It is obvious to the point of banality to restate the proposition that Congress intended by its enactment of Section 14 of the Securities Exchange Act of 1934 to give true vitality to the concept of corporate democracy. The depth of this commitment is reflected in the strong language employed in the legislative history: ... "Fair corporate suffrage is an important right that should attach to every equity security bought on a public exchange. Managements of properties owned by the investing public should not be permitted to perpetuate themselves by the misuse of corporate proxies...."

These two exceptions are, on their face, consistent with the legislative purpose underlying Section 14; for it seems fair to infer that Congress desired to make proxy solicitations a vehicle for corporate democracy rather than an all purpose forum for malcontented shareholders to vent their spleen about irrelevant matters, and also realized that management cannot exercise its specialized talents effectively if corporate investors assert the power to dictate the minutiae of daily business decision. However, it is also apparent that the two exceptions ... can be construed so as to permit the exclusion of practically any shareholder proposal....

Close examination of the company's arguments only increases doubt as to the reasoning processes which led the Commission to this result.
[Reversed and remanded to SEC.]

Ethical Principles. The second difficulty in deciding to implement a policy of corporate social responsibility is to establish the standards by which corporate actions will be judged. The legal profession has its Code of Professional Responsibility, which is enforced and explained by state bar organizations and their committees on professional responsibility. There is a similar code for judicial conduct. Accountants have adopted standards and principles for judging their work. The medical profession at least has the broad conduct outlines of the Hippocratic Oath ("First, Do No Harm.")

Other than the vague requirement of reasonable business judgment, there are really no similar standards or agencies for judging business conduct. To be sure, the Federal Trade Commission may sanction "unfair trade practices" and "unfair methods of competition," as we will see in Chapter 39. Those are legal standards, however, rather than primarily ethical ones. Other than making charitable contributions, what kinds of socially responsible conduct should a corporation undertake? How are its standards for ethical corporate decision-making to be established?

One starting point might be the set of "consensus ethical values" which came out of a conference on ethics in business, held at the University of Nebraska in 1989. In addition to the two great principles of Truthfulness and Fairness which we discussed in Chapter 1, eight others were listed. Included are Integrity, Promise-keeping, Loyalty, Compassion, Respect, Responsible Citizenship, Excellence, and Accountability. Discussing major corporate policy decisions in terms of these ten ethical standards would certainly help in producing socially responsible behavior.

Even using such standards as a benchmark, there will still be differences of opinion in how they apply to a particular case, especially since some of them may sometimes conflict. Dow Chemical, for example, felt that its decision to keep producing napalm was an exercise of Responsible Citizenship and Promise-keeping (it had a contract with the government). Dow's critics were arguing that the production of this horrible weapon showed a lack of Compassion and Respect for human beings, who would be the targets of the napalm bombs. Even allowing for such disagreements, and possible conflicts among the standards, couching the corporation's policy debates in these terms has to improve its level of ethical behavior.

Ethical Tests. Over the centuries, philosophers have developed a variety of tests for judging one's behavior. While these were generally phrased in terms of the behavior of individual human beings, some tests may be useful for corporate management.

The great German philosopher, Immanuel Kant, developed what came to be called the "Universal Imperative." A person was to act in such a way that the conduct could be universalized. That is, when deciding to do a certain act, ask yourself the questions "would I want everyone to behave this way?" If the answer is yes, proceed as planned; if the answer is no, rethink your plan.

Kant's Universal Imperative is not all that different from a principle found in all of the world's major religions, and based on reciprocity. We are advised to treat other people as we would want them to treat us—that is, with respect and compassion. Business application of this "Golden Rule" has begun in the area of employee relations, as a part of the realization that a firm's work force can be a prime source of competitive advantage. In a sense, this rule also underlies the "Quality" movement, or "customer focus," about which so much has been written. Customers may not in fact "always" be right, but listening respectfully to their comments and complaints may help to ensure repeat purchases. Splashy ads and hard sells may work for a while, but are usually not going to build brand loyalty. Focusing on both employees and customers as human beings can help build the long-term relationships needed for survival in today's global marketplace.

Jeremy Bentham, John Stuart Mill, and others developed a philosophical system called Utilitarianism. A decision on a course of action should be made so as to produce "the greatest good for the greatest number." This decision process involves a weighing of the burdens and the benefits which the proposed course of action will entail. Stating corporate policy decisions in these terms may be quite useful. The formula recognizes that a proposed course of action may impact some people and organizations negatively. Looking at corporate policies in this way would require a consideration of the interests of the various "stakeholders"—employees, customers, suppliers, communities, perhaps even competitors. Thinking about a corporate decision in terms of its probable impact on each group would at least ensure that potential negative impacts had been considered in arriving at the final decision.

Another attempt at finding a "bottom-line" standard for corporate decisions is usually described as the "Publicity Test." Would you be proud to have your decision widely known, to have it published on the front pages of local and national newspapers where it could be seen by your family, friends. and colleagues? If not, perhaps you should rethink your decision. Using this test would certainly improve the ethical quality of many (or at least some) corporate decisions.

One final ethical test deserves mention. It is directly responsive to the frequent criticism that U.S. corporate managements are far too concerned with short-term financial results, to the detriment of long-range company and societal interests. The test was eloquently stated by Leon Shenandoah, Chief of the Onondaga Nation and Moderator of the Iroquois Confederacy:

> Look behind you. See your sons and daughters. They are your future. Look farther, and you will see your sons' and your daughters' children even into the Seventh Generation. That's the way we were taught. Think about it. You yourself are a Seventh Generation.

If each of us were to adopt this standard of "Connectedness," behaviors both corporate and personal would surely change for the better.

Implementation of Social Responsibility Policies. Obviously, an overall strategy for corporate social responsibility will need to be decided at the highest level—the board of directors. It will normally be advisable to involve the stockholders early in the decision process—at least for advice and counsel, if not for actual ratification of the directors' decision. The policy will also benefit from employee comments and suggestions, so they too should be involved at an early stage. In unionized companies, care needs to be taken so that management's actions are not seen as a unilateral attempt to change the "wages, hours, and terms and conditions of employment" which are subject to a collective bargaining agreement. This issue will be discussed in more detail in Chapter 40, but there is at least one disturbing ruling which held that an employer violated the National Labor Relations Act by involving employees in "quality circles." Many employees view any workplace change as a threat. If they're at least getting along under the present system, they worry that they won't even be able to do that under a new system. The need for change and the scope and nature of the change need to be carefully explained. It should be made clear that the objective is to improve the workplace atmosphere, to create a more worker-friendly environment, rather than to impose added new obligations. Rules and general policies will still be required, but they can certainly be administered and applied with a bit of humanity. To the greatest extent possible, allowance should be made for individual situations.

The *Thomas* case illustrates one sort of "individual situation."

THOMAS v. REVIEW BOARD OF
INDIANA EMPLOYMENT SECURITY DIVISION
101 S. Ct.1425 (1981)

FACTS: Thomas terminated his employment in the Blaw-Knox Foundry and Machinery Company when he was transferred from the roll foundry to a department that produced turrets for military tanks. He claimed his religious beliefs prevented him from participating in the production of war materials, so he quit his job. He then applied for unemployment compensation benefits from the state fund, since he was "unemployed." The Review Board denied him compensation benefits, because he had quit his job voluntarily, for personal reasons. The Indiana Court of Appeals ordered payment of benefits, but the Indiana Supreme Court reversed. Thomas petitioned the U.S. Supreme Court for further review.

 CHIEF JUSTICE BURGER:

Where the state conditions receipt of an important benefit upon conduct proscribed by a religious faith, or where it denies such a benefit because of conduct mandated by religious belief, thereby putting substantial pressure on an adherent to modify his behavior and to violate his beliefs, a burden upon religion exists. While the compulsion may be indirect, the infringement upon free exercise is nonetheless substantial....

The mere fact that the petitioner's religious practice is burdened by a governmental program does not mean that an exemption accommodating his practice must be granted. The state may justify an inroad on religious liberty by showing that it is the least restrictive means of achieving some compelling state interest. However, it is still true that "[t]he essence of all that has been said and written on the subject is that only those interests of the highest order can overbalance legitimate claims to the free exercise of religion...."

The purposes urged to sustain the disqualifying provision of the Indiana unemployment compensation scheme are twofold: (1) to avoid the widespread unemployment and the consequent burden on the fund resulting if people were permitted to leave jobs for "personal" reasons, and (2) to avoid detailed probing by employers into job applicants' religious beliefs. These are by no means unimportant considerations.... [However, we must conclude that the interests advanced by the state do not justify the burden placed on free exercise of religion.

There is no evidence in the record to indicate that the number of people who find themselves in the predicament of choosing between benefits and religious beliefs is large enough to create widespread unemployment, or even to seriously affect unemployment—and no such claim was advanced by the Review Board. Similarly, although detailed inquiry by employers into applicants' religious beliefs is undesirable, there is no evidence in the record to indicate that such inquiries will occur in Indiana, or that they have occurred in any of the states that extend benefits to people in the petitioner's position. Nor is there any reason to believe that the number of people terminating employment for religious reasons will be so great as to motivate employers to make such inquiries.

Neither of the interests advanced is sufficiently compelling to justify the burden upon Thomas' religious liberty. Accordingly, Thomas is entitled to receive benefits unless, as the state contends and the Indiana court held, such payment would violate the Establishment Clause.

The [Review Board] contends that to compel benefit payments to Thomas involves the state in fostering a religious faith. There is, in a sense, a "benefit" to Thomas deriving from his religious beliefs, but this manifests no more than the tension between the two Religious Clauses which the Court resolved in *Sherbert* [the prior case dealing with this issue]....

Unless we are prepared to overrule *Sherbert*..., Thomas cannot be denied the benefits due him on the basis of the findings of the referee, the Review Board and the Indiana Court of Appeals that he terminated his employment because of his religious convictions.

There are many other very complicated ethical/moral issues involved in managing today's diverse workforce. Companies may need to rethink their policies on such matters as monitoring electronic mail, drug testing, off-work conduct, and other such "privacy" issues. The legal rules on these questions are still under development, but there does seem to be a clear trend in favor of worker privacy rights. Restrictive policies should be adopted only after careful consideration, and only if the company is convinced it can demonstrate a legitimate business need for the restriction.

CORPORATE SOCIAL AUDIT

In the past decade we have seen a process called **social auditing** emerge. Business managers who are concerned about corporate social responsibility seem convinced of the need for an accounting or audit procedure to determine just what is being done within their firm, whether the efforts are cost effective and aimed toward the proper goals for that particular firm, and whether the efforts are sufficient considering the resources involved.

The late 60s and 70s brought a great concern on the part of investors, consumers, and employees regarding the social activities of corporations. Management is beginning to realize that social responsibility can be profitable. Companies are becoming more concerned about their social image, and many have found that internal social audits give them information to use in their annual reports. Thus, favorable social audit results as well as favorable financial results are often shown in these annual reports.

How does a social audit differ from a financial audit? The answer is simple. In a financial audit there are standards of the profession and standards of law that must be adhered to; in a social audit, there are no standards of social responsibility, but there are basic legal standards regarding pollution, safety, and employment discrimination. However, as we have said before, social responsibility means performance beyond that which is legally required. The real purpose of the social audit is not to compare what you are doing to some standard of the profession. Rather, its purpose is to see what is presently being done in your firm in the area of social responsibility, then to serve as an aid in reviewing those findings, setting goals, and preparing long-range policies which can be implemented and reviewed in the future. Remember, corporate social responsibility is more than giving gifts to the United Way or to the local symphony group. It is real concern for employees, their needs, and their desires; it is better customer relations, a better product, and a better and safer working environment, as well as many other areas of internal and external corporate activities previously commented on in this chapter.

A social audit is not required by law. It is simply a voluntary act of management. Management may take whatever action it pleases as a result of the audit. Of course, any violations of the law revealed by the audit must be corrected.

ETHICS: THE BOTTOM LINE FOR THE 21st CENTURY

On March 15, 1995, a feature story titled "The Bottom Line on Ethics" appeared in *U.S. News & World Report*. It began by stating that the public perception of American Business was very low: only Government scored lower in public opinion polls. The bulk of the story then went on to present the reality of current business practice, which largely contradicts the very negative public image.

More than half of the largest corporations are teaching ethics to their employees. Another study of sixty "corporate giants" finds improvement in all categories of corporate social responsibility, including charitable giving. The reasons given for these changes include some of those discussed above—pressure from consumers, response to public-relations disasters, personal religious and moral beliefs of business executives. One other important source of change is also noted. The national guidelines for criminal sentencing provide lighter penalties for corporate violators that have ethics programs in place, or that agree to implement them. In effect, the ethics program's existence is taken as evidence that any violation by the company was a mistake, rather than intentional conduct—thus the lighter sentence. Whatever the motivation, the resulting demand for ethics education for managers has made it a "boom industry," says Charles Hickman of the American Assembly of Collegiate Schools of Business. It seems that many managers see no inherent conflict between "doing good" and "doing well." Indeed, it may even be that there is a considerable synergy between "doing the right thing" and "the bottom line."

SIGNIFICANCE OF THIS CHAPTER

In this chapter we have defined business ethics and corporate social responsibility, discussed the pros and cons of corporate social responsibility, and introduced a relatively new concept, the corporate social audit.

Since there is no enforceable code of business ethics or social responsibility, each manager has to develop a personal sense of moral consciousness to identify ethical issues that may be involved in the decision-making process. Managers need values that will help them consider the ethical issues as well as the traditional profit motives when making business decisions.

Businesspersons live in a very competitive environment, and it is often easy to justify wrongful actions, especially if the wrongful action produced a profit. Hopefully this chapter will show future business managers the need for the inclusion of ethical considerations as well as profit considerations in our business decision-making. It is not true that ethical decisions are less profitable. In fact, corporations that have practiced corporate social responsibility in their daily decision-making usually find their public image is much better than their less socially responsible competitors. In the long run, the socially conscious corporations may very well come out ahead.

PROBLEMS FOR DISCUSSION

1. Smith Company made a contribution of $1,500 to Princeton University. Over the years, Smith had contributed to the local community chest, to Upsala College in East Orange, and to Newark University. Smith manufactured valves, fire hydrants, and special equipment for the water and gas industries. Barlow and other stockholders challenged the legality of the Princeton gift, since such gifts were neither expressly authorized nor (the stockholders claimed) impliedly authorized. Smith Co. filed a declaratory judgment action in the chancery division, which upheld the gift. The stockholders appealed.

    How should the appeals court decide? Explain.

2. Big Bucks Bakery Company makes cookies for various organizations to sell for fund-raising drives. After mixing a 1,000-pound batch of dough it was noted that a large box of rodent poison had been knocked over and got into the batter. One of the company chemists said the concentration would not be enough to cause a fatality, and it could not be detected by taste. People might get nauseated and possibly vomit, but the chemist didn't feel they would ever know where it came from. The problem is that the chemist tested the current batch, and that batch had no sign of the poison. The poisoned batch could have been made into cookies yesterday, last week, or any time in the last month. That was the last time anyone noticed the box of rodent poison being on the shelf and full. What do they do— close their eyes, or recall all the cookies baked in the last month?

    Discuss the company's legal and ethical duties.

3. Mary Beth Whitehead agreed to bear a child for the Sterns in return for $10,000. She was artificially inseminated with Mr. Stern's sperm, and the child was born nine months later. Mrs. Whitehead during this period had changed her mind. She renounced the contract, and began a custody fight for the child. After a long and bitter struggle, the trial court awarded custody to the Stems, and terminated Mrs. Whitehead's visitation and parental rights. Meanwhile, still married to Mr. Whitehead, she had become pregnant by Mr. Gould, whom she married after she divorced Mr. Whitehead. She appealed to the State Supreme Court.

    How will the court rule? Should this sort of contract be enforced by the courts?

4. Zord's market position was being heavily eroded by competition from domestic and foreign manufacturers of subcompact cars. The President of Zord was determined to regain Zord's share of the market by having a new subcompact, the Dento, in production by 1990.

When Zord engineers crash-tested an early model of the Dento, they found that when the automobile was struck from the rear at twenty miles per hour, the gas tank regularly ruptured. Stray sparks could then ignite the spraying gasoline, engulf the car in flames and possibly burn the trapped occupants.

Nonetheless, Zord management decided for several reasons to go ahead with production of the Dento as designed. First, the design met all applicable federal laws and standards then in effect. Secondly, the Dento was comparable in safety to other cars being produced by the auto industry. Third, an internal Zord's study indicated that the social costs of improving the design outweighed the social benefits. According to the study it was estimated that a maximum of 180 deaths might result if the Dento design were not changed. For purposes of cost/benefit analysis the federal government at that time put a value of $200,000 on a human life. Consequently, the study reasoned, saving 180 lives was worth about a total of $36 million to society. On the other hand, improving the 11 million Dentos then being planned would cost about $11 per car for a total investment of $121 million. Since the social cost of $121 million outweighed the social benefit of $36 million, the study concluded that improving the Dento design would not be cost-effective from a societal point of view.

Hilda Hapless was horribly burned when the Dento in which she was riding was rear-ended by a truck. She sues Zord and its managers for damages.

How will the courts decide, and why?

5. Ms. Trotti placed her purse in her locker when she arrived for work. She testified that she snapped the lock closed and then pulled on it to make sure it was locked. When she returned to her locker during her afternoon break, she discovered the lock hanging open. Searching through her locker, she further discovered her personal items in her purse in considerable disorder. Nothing was missing from either the locker or the purse. The store manager testified that, in the company of three junior administrators at the store, he had that afternoon searched the lockers because of a suspicion raised by the appellants' security personnel that an unidentified employee, not the appellee, had stolen a watch. The manager and his assistants were also searching for missing price-marking guns. Ms. Trotti further testified that, as she left the employee's locker area after discovering her locker open, she heard the manager suggest to his assistants, "Let's get busy again." The manager testified that none of the parties searched through employees' personal effects.

Ms. Trotti approached the manager later that day and asked if he had searched employees' lockers and/or her purse. The manager initially denied either kind of search and maintained this denial for approximately one month. At that time, the manager then admitted having searched the employees' lockers and further mentioned that they had, in fact, searched the appellee's purse, later saying that he meant that they had searched only her locker and not her purse.

Ms. Trotti then sued her employer for an invasion of her privacy. The jury awarded $8,000 for actual damages and $100,000 for punitive damages. K-Mart appealed.

Should the award be upheld? Why or why not?

Part Eight

Government Regulation

Today, nearly every business transaction is subject to some form of government regulation—at least in this country. We have examined many of these already, as they applied to the specific legal topics being discussed in the various chapters. Chapter 3 provided a general overview of the constitutional limitations on government regulation, and of the development and procedure of the agencies that administer these regulations. Chapter 29 covered the very important area of environmental regulation. So, in a sense, we have been looking at "Government Regulation" throughout the book.

Part Eight focuses on three major areas of business activity which are subject to comprehensive national regulation: securities transactions, marketing tactics, and employment practices. Chapter 37 outlines the rules for the issuance of and trading in securities. Chapters 38 and 39 deal with the legal rules which place limits on competitive strategies and tactics. Chapter 40 covers the still-important area of union-management relations. Chapter 41 discusses the principal points of concern in the government's efforts to eliminate discrimination in the workplace. Violations in these areas have the potential to cause serious adverse impacts on the offending business, so managers need to be particularly sensitive to the legal rules applicable here.

Chapter 37
Securities Law

The securities industry is one of the most heavily regulated areas of business. With certain exceptions, both the original issue of securities and subsequent trading are subject to detailed and complicated regulations at both the national and state levels. These regulations impose duties and liabilities not only on buyers and sellers of securities but also on the corporate issuer, its officers and directors, and its attorneys, accountants, and other experts. Noncompliance may result in serious civil and criminal penalties as well as the loss of millions of dollars of value.

STATE REGULATION OF SECURITIES

The great surge of economic development during the late 1800s and early 1900s and the greatly increased use of the corporate form of business organization brought with them many abuses. Promoters of dubious background and resources sold investments to a gullible public in all sort of "speculative schemes which have no more basis than as many feet of blue sky," as one judge put it. To deal with these abuses, the states passed blue-sky laws, regulating transactions in securities. Standing alone, the state laws were not very effective. Some states had no such law; others did not enforce their statute very effectively. The simplest method for the fraudulent promoter was to operate across state lines from a "friendly" state, beyond the reach of state officials who were trying to enforce their statute. Moreover, the early state laws had many exemptions and were thus relatively easy to evade. Finally, since enforcement depended primarily on the victims' willingness to pursue a lawsuit, the promoters who did get "caught" could escape simply by reaching a financial settlement with the plaintiffs in the lawsuit.

Since the national securities laws specifically permit concurrent regulation by the several states, blue-sky statutes are on the books in nearly all states. The effectiveness with which these statutes are enforced still varies. About half the states have adopted the Uniform Securities Act. It attempts to combine three types of state regulation:

1. *Antifraud provisions*, which prohibit fraud in the sale of securities and provide for injunctions and criminal penalties.

2. *Full-disclosure provisions*, similar to those in the national act, which require the disclosure of all material information to prospective purchasers of the security.

3. *Broker-licensing provisions*, which require registration and licensing for persons marketing securities.

The *Hartman* case discusses a claim under the Uniform Securities Act. Notice that Ms. Hartman also alleged violations of national stock exchange and securities dealers rules, RICO, and added a claim for common-law negligence.

HARTMAN v. SHEARSON LEHMAN HUTTON, INC.
486 N.W.2d 53 (MI App. 1992)

FACTS: This dispute is premised on plaintiff's dissatisfaction with financial services rendered her now deceased father, Joseph Walker, by defendant Shearson Lehman Hutton, Inc., and its agent, defendant William J. Konchal. Plaintiff alleged various counts, including claims of negligent estate planning, that the decedent was sold securities unsuitable for his investment purposes, that defendant engaged in excessive trading in the decedent's account, and violation of the Racketeer Influenced and Corrupt Organizations Act.

Plaintiff appeals from an order of the circuit court granting summary disposition in favor of defendants.

 PER CURIAM:

Plaintiff ... argues on appeal that the trial court erred in granting defendants' motion for summary disposition. We disagree. First, we conclude that the trial court correctly determined that there was no genuine issue of material fact concerning Count I of the complaint, plaintiff's claim of negligent estate planning. The trial court determined, after reviewing the deposition testimony and affidavit of Konchal, that there was no evidence to support the claim that Konchal ever gave estate planning advice to Walker and that plaintiff failed to produce any affidavits or other documentary evidence in support of her claim. A genuine issue of material fact does not exist in the absence of contradictory evidence brought forth by the nonmoving party. The nonmoving party may not merely rely on the allegations or denials contained in the pleadings....

Turning to count II of the complaint, that defendant Konchal had recommended an unsuitable investment for Walker in light of his investment objectives, we again conclude that summary disposition was appropriate. First, plaintiff argues that the cause of action for selling unsuitable securities may be found in the provisions of ... M.S.A. § 19.776(204)(a)(1)(M), which authorizes the revocation of the registration of a broker for recommending to a customer the purchase, sale, or exchange of a security without reasonable grounds to believe that the recommendation is suitable for the customer on the basis of the customer's circumstances as known by the broker. However, § 204(h) specifically states that a violation of § 204 does not subject a registrant to civil liability to a customer, except to the extent that the violation is contrary to some other provision of the Uniform Securities Act.... Thus by the explicit terms of the statute, plaintiffs reliance on § 204 to establish a cause of action for selling unsuitable securities is frivolous.

Plaintiff also argues that the claim of selling unsuitable securities also can be based on violations of the rules promulgated by the New York Stock Exchange (NYSE) and the National Association of Securities Dealers (NASD). We disagree. With regard to this issue, we are persuaded by the reasoning of Judge (now Justice) Boyle in *Kirkland v. E.F. Hutton & Co., Inc.*, ... who held that there is no private cause of action by a customer against a broker for violations of the NASD and NYSE rules.

Further, it appears that plaintiff also relies upon the Securities and Exchange Act of 1934 in support of her claim that the defendant had recommended unsuitable investments. However, we need not determine whether a cause of action for selling unsuitable securities is created under the Securities and Exchange Act of 1934, or the rules promulgated thereunder, because Congress has vested the federal courts with exclusive jurisdiction to resolve claims arising under the 1934 act....

Finally, with respect to plaintiffs unsuitability claim, to the extent that plaintiff argues that she is stating a negligence claim and is merely relying on the above statutes and rules to establish the standard of conduct required of a stockbroker, we could agree that those restrictions on stockbrokers would be probative of the issue but nevertheless agree with defendants that there exists no genuine issue of material fact concerning any such claim of negligence with respect to defendant Konchal selling unsuitable securities to the decedent. Specifically, plaintiff has produced no evidence to support a claim that Konchal recommended a sale or purchase that was unsuitable for the investment aims of the decedent. In fact, plaintiff, in her deposition, testified that she had no knowledge whether defendant Konchal had recommended to Walker that he engage in the securities transactions that did occur. Furthermore, Konchal's affidavit does not disclose that he recommended any particular course of action to Walker, but that he merely had executed the "unequivocal directive" of Walker to engage in the transactions. Accordingly, even assuming that a stockbroker's recommendation that a client engage in a securities transaction that is unsuitable for the investment goals of the client gives rise to a common-law negligence action, plaintiff has produced no facts supporting the conclusion that Konchal had affirmatively recommended that Walker engage in the complained-of transactions. Further, at least with respect to the subsequent reinvestment, there has been no claim that the transaction was unsuitable. Therefore, the trial court correctly granted summary disposition of this count.

Turning to the claim of excessive trading, or "churning," we again agree with defendants that summary disposition was appropriate. To establish churning, it is necessary to show that the stockbroker has control of the account and that there has been excessive trading in it.... In the case at bar, plaintiff has produced no facts to support a conclusion that Konchal controlled Walker's account. In fact, as discussed above, the only facts of record indicate that Walker approached Konchal with a specific investment plan in mind, to sell the stockholdings Walker had accumulated over the years and to reinvest the proceeds in other investment vehicles.

Furthermore, while it is true that Walker, over the period of several months, did change his investment portfolio, the total number of trades involved were relatively few. Accordingly, we conclude that there is no genuine issue of material fact.

Finally, plaintiff argues that the trial court erred in granting summary disposition in favor of defendants of plaintiff's claim under the Racketeer Influenced and Corrupt Organizations Act.... The record is utterly devoid of any evidence that would support a conclusion that defendants engaged in securities fraud or otherwise committed acts that could give rise to a RICO claim. Plaintiff's RICO claim is so lacking in merit that it requires neither reversal nor discussion.

Affirmed.

Most of the states that have not adopted the Uniform Securities Act have at least adopted a full-disclosure statute. Even with the Uniform Act in force, an individual state would have difficulty in preventing securities frauds without the cooperation of other states.

As businesses merged, reorganized, and relocated, many states became concerned with the possibility of the loss of jobs. The older industrial states of the Northeast and Midwest were particularly unhappy about the movement of factories to the South and Southwest. Several states tried to protect their businesses from being taken over by outside companies by passing statutes which imposed certain requirements which the offeror company had to meet before the buy-out could occur. The validity of the Indiana anti-takeover statute was upheld by the U.S. Supreme Court in 1987, even though an earlier decision had held the Illinois act unconstitutional.

NATIONAL REGULATION OF SECURITIES

The fantastic boom times of the 1920s turned into the depression of the 1930s. Many an investment bubble was punctured by the great stock market crash of 1929. The 1929 crash exposed to the public for the first time the widespread price manipulations and credit abuses that had characterized the stock market of the 1920s. The first New Deal Congress passed the two main pieces of national securities legislation—the Securities Act of 1933 and the Securities Exchange Act of 1934. Other legislation followed, such as the Public Utility Holding Company Act of 1935, the Trust Indenture Act of 1939, the Investment Company Act of 1940, and the Investment Advisors Act of 1940. More recently, Congress passed the Securities Investor Protection Act of 1970 (designed to protect investors against the insolvency of their stockbroker) and the 1975 Amendments to the 1933 Act, which extend the antifraud provisions of the act to dealers in municipal securities.

The SEC. The Securities Act of 1933 entrusted enforcement to the Federal Trade Commission, but Congress decided by the next year that this specialized area needed its own specialized regulatory body. The Securities Exchange Act of 1934 thus created the Securities and Exchange Commission and gave it the responsibility for enforcing both acts. Over the years the SEC has accumulated jurisdiction under the various other new securities laws, and it also exercises important functions in corporate reorganizations in bankruptcy proceedings.

The SEC is headed by five commissioners, appointed for staggered five year terms by the President with the advice and consent of the Senate. No more than three commissioners may be members of the same political party, but the President does have the power to name the Commission's chairperson. The SEC's headquarters is in Washington, but it has regional offices throughout the country, particularly in the large cities where corporate financing operations are concentrated. The commissioners are assisted by a large organizational staff of lawyers, accountants, economists, securities analysts, and other experts.

GOING PUBLIC: THE 1933 SECURITIES ACT

Basic Purposes. The 1933 Act was aimed solely at the first offering of a securities issue, not at later trading on the stock exchanges or over-the-counter. Its primary objective was *truth in securities*: to provide the potential investor with all the information needed to make a rational decision when purchasing a security. Patterned in large part after the English Companies Act of 1900, the 1933 Act did not provide for governmental "approval" of securities, in the sense of deciding whether they were good or bad investments. Its main objective was to require full disclosure by the offering company, so that the potential investor could make an informed decision. Only secondarily did the 1933 Act prohibit fraud and deceit in securities transactions generally.

Even this somewhat limited approach was a big change from the common-law rules. You will recall from Chapter 11 that mere nondisclosure was not usually regarded as a fraudulent misrepresentation unless some special facts were present in the case. The 1933 Act imposed on the offering corporation a positive legal duty to speak out and tell the truth, and the whole truth, about the offered security.

Definition of "Security." The costs of complying with the full-disclosure requirement can be very high. When paying lawyers, accountants, experts, printers, and others, a quarter of a million dollars doesn't go very far. Since these costs have to be deducted from profits, promoters are always looking for "moneymaking" schemes that don't have to comply with the requirements of the 1933 Act.

Only **"securities"** are covered by the 1933 Act, but the courts have given that term a very broad definition. So does the Act:

> The term "security" means any note, stock, treasury stock, bond, debenture, evidence of indebtedness, certificate of interest or participation in any profit-sharing agreement, collateral-trust certificate, preorganization certificate or subscription, transferable share, investment contract, voting-trust certificate, certificate of deposit for a security, fractional undivided interest in oil, gas, or other mineral rights, or, in general, any interest or instrument commonly known as a "security," or any certificate of interest or participation in, temporary or interim certificate for, receipt for, guarantee of, or warrant or right to subscribe to or purchase, any of the foregoing....

With that definition, it's hard to imagine any investment that's not a "security," but as the following case shows, some business investments are not covered.

GOTHAM PRINT v. AMERICAN SPEEDY PRINTING CENTERS
863 F.Supp. 447 (E.D. MI, 1994)

FACTS: This action arises out of transactions and events surrounding a "Master Franchise Agreement" between Plaintiff GOTHAM PRINT, INC. and Defendant AMERICAN SPEEDY PRINTING CENTERS, INC. ("ASPCI"). The individual Defendants, Vernon Buchanan, William McIntyre, Jr., and Gerald Bergler are all present and/or former directors/officers of ASPCI.

ASPCI was in the business of franchising printing stores throughout the United States and other countries. In 1986, pursuant to a plan to expand the growth of the company, ASPCI began contracting with third parties to act as "middlemen" or "distributors" to develop new franchises and to support existing franchises through a series of "Master Franchise Distributorships." It appears that Master Franchise Distributors were given a geographic area in which to develop new ASPCI franchises. They also directed the functions of existing franchises in the territory. In turn, the Master Franchisees were entitled to a percentage of the franchise royalties paid by the franchisees to ASPCI.

With respect to the Master Franchise Agreement at issue in this lawsuit, in June of 1990, Thomas Tybinka, the president of Gotham Print, Inc., and another Gotham-affiliated individual, Tony Romano, met with Defendant Vernon Buchanan, the chairman of the board of directors and CEO of ASPCI, in ASPCI's offices in Bloomfield Hills, Michigan, to discuss the prospects of purchasing an ASPCI Master Franchise Distributorship in the New York City region. These discussions continued in July 1990.

According to Plaintiff's First Amended Complaint, a principal point of negotiation regarding Gotham Print's purchase of a Master Franchise Distributorship was the particular geographic region to be covered. Gotham wanted the territory to include all New York City zip codes, plus a part of New Jersey and two counties in Connecticut. Gotham was to have the exclusive right to control ASPCI franchise development in the geographical area. Gotham also was promised a working capital loan from ASPCI in the amount of $150,000.

On July 12, 1990, Defendants Buchanan, Bergler and Shovlin again met with Messrs. Tybinka and Romano. A proposed Master Franchise Agreement, which called for Gotham's payment of $1,800,000 to ASPCI, was presented to Tybinka and Romano to review. This draft Agreement provided for Gotham's exclusive rights to the New Jersey and Connecticut areas, as well as all New York City zip codes. Tybinka and Romano were also promised, both orally and in writing, the $150,000 working capital loan they wanted. More details were worked on at a meeting held on August 23, 1990.

The parties met again a few days later to sign the final Master Franchise Agreement. However, the promised Connecticut territory was not included in the Agreement, nor was the promise of $150,000 working capital loan. The Defendants represented that amendments would be made to the Agreement. Mr. Tybinka executed the Agreement on behalf of Gotham. However, as a result of the omissions of the Connecticut territory and working capital loan provisions, only half of the required

$250,000 down payment was given by Gotham; the balance of the downpayment was being withheld until such time as Connecticut was added and the working capital loan was arranged. As for the remaining $1,550,000 of the $1,800,000 purchase price, this amount was covered by two promissory notes for $775,000 each executed by Mr. Tybinka.

Plaintiff claims that during the pre-contract negotiations pertaining to the Master Franchise Agreement, Defendants made false representations on past successes of other then-existing Master Franchise Distributorships and provided Plaintiff with false and misleading financial projections for a New York City Distributorship. Gotham further contends that from the very beginning of the negotiations, Defendant Buchanan knew that the Connecticut area and two zip code areas of New York City, which Gotham desired and which was promised to Gotham in the proposed Master Franchise Agreement, were already under contract to other Master Franchise Distributorships, but Buchanan failed to reveal this information to Gotham's representatives. Gotham also contends that the Defendants fraudulently misrepresented the financial strength of ASPCI and failed to reveal to Plaintiff that ASPCI was considering filing for bankruptcy at the time of the negotiations and also failed to reveal that ASPCI was being sued by several other Master Franchise Distributors.

Based upon the above allegations of fraud, Gotham filed a four-count Amended Complaint alleging two federal claims: securities fraud in violation of Section 10(b) of the Securities Exchange Act of 1934, and Rule 10b(5) and violation of Section 1962(a) and (c) of the Racketeer Influenced and Corrupt Organizations Act. Plaintiff also has alleged two state common law fraud claims: conspiracy to commit fraudulent misrepresentation (Count III) and fraudulent misrepresentation (Count IV).

Defendant ASPCI has filed a counterclaim/third-party claim against Plaintiff Gotham Print, Inc. and its president Thomas Tybinka based upon nonpayment of two promissory notes dated August 25, 1990, each in the face amount of $775,000.

 DISTRICT JUDGE ROSEN:

Plaintiff claims violation of Section 10(b) of the Securities Exchange Act of 1934 ... and Rule 10b(5)....

The elements necessary to state a claim of securities fraud under Section 10(b)/ Rule 10b(5) claim are: (1) use of jurisdictional means, (2) to implement a deceptive or manipulative practice (with scienter), (3) in connection with, (4) the purchase or sale, (5) *of a security*, (6) causing, (7) damages....

Neither the 1934 Act nor the Securities Act of 1933 ... provides a definition of "investment contract." However, the Supreme Court has filled in this gap in the statutes.

In *SEC v. Howey Co.*, ... the Court held that whether an "investment contract" interest exists required a demonstration that the business venture called for: (1) an investment of money, (2) in a common enterprise, (3) with profits to come solely from the efforts of others.... The "profits coming *solely* from the efforts of others" element has been slightly modified in the ensuing years since *Howey*. In *SEC v. Glenn W. Turner Enterprises* ... the Ninth Circuit replaced the "*solely* from the efforts of others" portion of the *Howey* test with one requiring a showing that:

the efforts made by those other than the investor are the undeniably significant ones, those essential managerial efforts which affect the failure or success of the enterprise....

By application of the principles extracted from the foregoing decisions, courts have virtually unanimously concluded that franchise and distributorship arrangements are not "investment contracts," and, hence, not securities within the meaning of the federal securities laws....

In all of these franchise/distributorship cases, the courts found that in such business arrangements, the managerial efforts are those of the franchisee, not solely, primarily, or in any large part the efforts of "others."

Plaintiff does not dispute this result in a "traditional" franchise arrangement. However, Gotham contends that the Master Franchise Agreement at issue in this case is different from a "traditional" franchise in that as the "Master Franchisee," its profits *did* derive from the efforts of others—the franchisees of the Speedy Printing businesses developed, or to be developed, in Gotham's territory. An analysis of Gotham's Master Franchise Agreement, however, demonstrates that, contrary to Plaintiff's assertions, from the inception of the Agreement, Gotham as Master Franchisee was intended as much more than a mere "passive" investor.

The Master Franchise Agreement contemplates that profits, if any, will be derived, if not primarily, then at least in large part, from the managerial/entrepreneurial efforts of Gotham. While Plaintiff correctly asserts that the work of franchisees will contribute to Gotham's profits, it overlooks the important first step to Gotham's earning a share of the money generated by the franchisees (i.e., that it is *Gotham's* entrepreneurial efforts in recruiting Speedy Printing franchisees in the territory that enables Gotham to have any claim to its percentage of franchisee monies). In other words, without Gotham recruiting franchisees, Gotham would have no right to profits, whatsoever.

Further, as provided in the Agreement, Gotham was to itself operate ten franchises in the territory. As expressly provided in the Master Franchise Agreement ... Gotham's and ASPCI's rights and obligations with respect to these ten franchises were to be governed by ASPCI's standard (traditional) Franchise and License Agreements, and thus, clearly within the scope of the law developed for "traditional" franchises.

With respect to Gotham's development of new franchises in the territory, the Agreement sets forth particular managerial duties which Gotham, as Master Franchisee was obligated to perform....

Where, as here, a franchisee/plaintiff retains duties with respect to hiring and firing of personnel, maintenance of good customer relations, and day-to-day business promotion and salesmanship, even though the franchisor retains certain rights, such as the right to specify the decor of the store, operating hours, store location, quality of merchandise and physical arrangement of equipment within the store, no "investment contract" exists....

For all of the foregoing reasons, the Court finds that the Master Franchise/ Distributorship relationship between Gotham and ASPCI was not an investment in a venture premised on a reasonable expectation of profits to be derived from the entrepreneurial or managerial efforts of others. The Master Franchise Agreement

> clearly contemplated Gotham's substantial active participation. Therefore, no "security" within the meaning of the federal securities laws exists and, accordingly, Plaintiff's Count I must be dismissed.

New "multilevel" schemes have continued to arise. Many states now have statutes regulating franchise investments which prohibit or strictly limit the use of such multilevel plans. Given the ingenuity of promoters, the definition of a security has to be flexible.

Exemptions. Not every offering of securities is subject to the 1933 Act. Some *types* of securities and some *transactions* in securities are exempted. These exemptions only eliminate the need to register the security through SEC procedures; the antifraud (and other) provisions still apply.

Short-term commercial paper, ordinarily bought by banks rather than being issued to the general public, is exempt from SEC registration. Securities issued by governmental agencies and nonprofit organizations, such as churches and schools, are exempt. Transactions that involve only a private offering or that are exclusively intrastate in nature are exempt; in both of these cases the process of qualifying the securities for the exemption requires expert advice. Most individual sales of securities are exempt; the 1933 Act is aimed at the issuer, underwriter, and broker making the initial offering. The SEC is authorized by statute to provide a simplified registration procedure for issues that do not involve more than a minimal amount, currently set at $1,500,000.

Registration Statement and Prospectus. The corporation issuing nonexempt securities must file multiple copies of a **registration statement** with the SEC, before offering the securities for sale to investors. The registration statement is the basic document for making "**full disclosure**." It must include such information as the company's business, organizational structure, and financial structure and condition; how the proceeds of the new issue are to be used; agreements for the distribution of the new issue; and extraordinary business contracts. The registration statement must be signed by the issuing company, its principal officers, at least a majority of the board of directors, and any expert named as having prepared or certified part of the statement. Certified financial statements for the current year and the last two years must also be filed.

The registration statement becomes effective twenty days after filing unless the SEC advances the effective date or requires further data, in which case the twenty days starts again when the supplement is filed. Technically, the SEC doesn't have the power to "disapprove" a security because it's a bad investment, but by delaying and by requiring many negative disclosure statements, the SEC can certainly try to discourage the issuer. Where there are any delays in the final effective date, all materials in the registration statement must be reviewed to make sure they are still completely accurate.

The **prospectus** contains most of the information noted above, but not necessarily all of the exhibits or all of the details on how the securities are to be distributed. The prospectus is the document given directly to offeree-buyers. Like the registration statement, it must be accurate and complete; literally true information which is misleading in the context in which it is stated is a violation.

Rescission by Investors. Section 12(2) of the 1933 Act permits investors to rescind their transactions if they can prove that false statements or significant omissions were made "by means of a prospectus or oral communication." This section is especially favorable to investors, since they do not have to prove fraud; mere negligence, if proved, permits rescission. Likewise, the investor-plaintiff need not prove personal reliance on the false statement.

Section 12(2) became very popular with plaintiffs after the 1976 ruling by the U.S. Supreme Court in the *Hochfelder* case. Investors, alleging a negligent audit, sued Ernst & Ernst. The claim was based on Section 10(b) of the 1934 Act and S.E.C. Rule 10(b)5. The Supreme Court decided that 10(b) required proof of fraud, not just professional negligence.

Since Section 12(2) of the 1933 Act only requires proof of negligence, dissatisfied investors began to allege that it had been violated, in their claims, rather than Section 10(b) of the 1934 Act. Courts disagreed as to whether Section 12(2) applied to *all* securities transactions, or only to initial public offerings (IPOs). The disagreement was resolved in a 5-to-4 Supreme Court decisions—*Alloyd*—in 1995.

GUSTAFSON et al. v. ALLOYD CO., INC.
63 U.S.L.W 4165 (U.S. S.Ct., 1995)

FACTS: Petitioners (collectively Gustafson), the sole shareholders of Alloyd, Inc., sold substantially all of its stock to respondents and other buyers in a private sale agreement. The purchase price included a payment reflecting an estimated increase in the company's net worth from the end of the previous year through the closing, since hard financial data was unavailable. The contract provided that if a year-end audit and financial statements revealed variances between estimated and actual increased value, the disappointed party would receive an adjustment. As a result of the audit, respondents were entitled to recover an adjustment, but instead sought relief under § 12(2) of the Securities Act of 1933, which gives buyers an express right of rescission against sellers who make material misstatements or omissions "by means of a prospectus." In granting Gustafson's motion for summary judgment, the District Court held that § 12(2) claims can only arise out of initial stock offerings and not a private sale agreement. The Court of Appeals vacated the judgment and remanded the case. The sellers petitioned for Supreme Court review.

 JUSTICE KENNEDY:

Under § 12(2) of the Securities Act of 1933 buyers have an express cause of action for rescission against sellers who make material misstatements or omissions "by means of a prospectus." The question presented is whether this right of rescission extends to a private, secondary transaction, on the theory that recitations in the purchase agreement are part of a "prospectus...."

Three sections of the 1933 Act are critical in resolving the definitional question on which the case turns: § 2(10), which defines a prospectus; § 10, which sets forth the information that must be contained in a prospectus; and § 12, which imposes liability based on misstatements in a prospectus. In seeking to interpret the term "prospectus," we adopt the premise that the term should be construed, if possible, to give it a consistent meaning throughout the Act. That principle follows from our duty to construe statutes, not isolated provisions....

Although § 10 does not define what a prospectus is, it does instruct us what a prospectus cannot be if the Act is to be interpreted as a symmetrical and coherent regulatory scheme, one in which the operative words have a consistent meaning throughout. There is no dispute that the contract in this case was not required to contain the information contained in a registration statement and that no statutory exemption was required to take the document out of § 10's coverage.... It follows that the contract is not a prospectus under § 10. That does not mean that a document ceases to be a prospectus whenever it omits a required piece of information. It does mean that a document is not a prospectus within the meaning of that section if, absent an exemption, it need not comply with § 10's requirements in the first place.

An examination of § 10 reveals that, whatever else "prospectus" may mean, the term is confined to a document that, absent an overriding exemption, must include the "information contained in the registration statement." By and large, only public offerings by an issuer of a security, or by controlling shareholders of an issuer, require the preparation and filing of registration statements..... It follows, we conclude, that a prospectus under § 10 is confined to documents related to public offerings by an issuer or its controlling shareholders.

This much (the meaning of prospectus in § 10) seems not to be in dispute. Where the courts are in disagreement is with the implications of this proposition for the entirety of the Act, and for § 12 in particular.... We conclude that the term "prospectus" must have the same meaning under §§ 10 and 12. In so holding, we do not, as the dissent by JUSTICE GINSBURG suggests, make the mistake of treating § 10 as a definitional section.... Instead, we find in § 10 guidance and instruction for giving the term a consistent meaning throughout the Act.

The Securities Act of 1933, like every Act of Congress, should not be read as a series of unrelated and isolated provisions. Only last term we adhered to the "normal rule of statutory construction" that "identical words used in different parts of the same act are intended to have the same meaning...." That principle applies here. If the contract before us is not a prospectus for purposes of § 10—as all must and do concede—it is not a prospectus for purposes of § 12 either.

The conclusion that prospectus has the same meaning, and refers to the same types of communications (public offers by an issuer or its controlling shareholders), in both § 10 and § 12 is reinforced by an examination of the structure of the 1933 Act. Sections 4 and 5 of the Act together require a seller to file a registration statement and to issue a prospectus for certain defined types of sales.... Sections 7 and 10 of the Act set forth the information required in the registration statement and the prospectus.... Section 11 provides for liability on account of false registration statements; § 12(2) for liability based on misstatements in prospectuses....

Following the most natural and symmetrical reading, just as the liability imposed by § 11 flows from the requirements imposed by § 5 and § 7 providing for the filing and content of registration statements, the liability imposed by § 12(2), cannot attach unless there is an obligation to distribute the prospectus in the first place (or unless there is an exemption).

Our interpretation is further confirmed by a reexamination of § 12 itself. The section contains an important guide to the correct resolution of the case. By its terms, § 12(2) exempts from its coverage prospectuses relating to the sales of government-issued securities.... If Congress intended § 12(2) to create liability for misstatements contained in any written communication relating to the sale of a security—including secondary market transactions—there is no ready explanation for exempting government-issued securities from the reach of the right to rescind granted by § 12(2). Why would Congress grant immunity to a private seller from liability in a rescission suit for no reason other than that the seller's misstatements happen to relate to securities issued by a governmental entity? No reason is apparent. The anomaly disappears, however, when the term "prospectus" relates only to documents that offer securities sold to the public by an issuer. The exemption for government-issued securities makes perfect sense on that view, for it then becomes a precise and appropriate means of giving immunity to governmental authorities.

The primary innovation of the 1933 Act was the creation of federal duties—for the most part, registration and disclosure obligations—in connection with public offerings.... We are reluctant to conclude that § 12(2) creates vast additional liabilities that are quite independent of the new substantive obligations the Act imposes. It is more reasonable to interpret the liability provisions of the 1933 Act as designed for the primary purpose of providing remedies for violations of the obligations it had created. Indeed, §§ 11 and 12(1)—the statutory neighbors of § 12(2)—afford remedies for violations of those obligations.... Under our interpretation of "prospectus," § 12(2) in similar manner is linked to the new duties created by the Act....

It is understandable that Congress would provide buyers with a right to rescind, without proof of fraud or reliance, as to misstatements contained in a document prepared with care, following well established procedures relating to investigations with due diligence and in the context of a public offering by an issuer or its controlling shareholders. It is not plausible to infer that Congress created this extensive liability for every casual communication between buyer and seller in the secondary market. It is often difficult, if not altogether impractical, for those engaged in casual communications not to omit some fact that would, if included, qualify the accuracy of a statement. Under Alloyd's view, any casual communication between buyer and seller in the aftermarket could give rise to an action for rescission, with no evidence of fraud on the part of the seller or reliance on the part of the buyer. In many instances, buyers in practical effect would have an option to rescind, impairing the stability of past transactions where neither fraud nor detrimental reliance on misstatements or omissions occurred. We find no basis for interpreting the statute to reach so far....

In light of the care that Congress took to justify the imposition of liability without proof of either fraud or reliance on "those whose moral responsibility to the public is particularly heavy"—the "originators of securities"—we cannot conclude that Congress would have extended that liability to every private or secondary sale without a whisper of explanation....

In sum, the word "prospectus" is a term of art referring to a document that describes a public offering of securities by an issuer or controlling shareholder. The contract of sale, and its recitations, were not held out to the public and were not a prospectus as the term is used in the 1933 Act.

The judgment of the Court of Appeals is reversed, and the case is remanded for further proceedings consistent with this opinion.

Antifraud Provisions. In addition to its disclosure requirements, the 1933 Act also contains a very broad prohibition in Section 17 against securities fraud. This section covers "any device, scheme, or artifice to defraud" and "any transaction, practice, or course of business which operates or would operate as a fraud or deceit upon the purchaser." It includes both false statements and material omissions which make otherwise true statements misleading. Securities that are exempt from registration are not exempt from these antifraud provisions.

BEING PUBLIC: THE 1934
SECURITIES EXCHANGE ACT

Basic Purposes. While the 1933 Act dealt primarily with the initial offering of a securities issue, the 1934 Act attempted to deal with the abuses and manipulations that occurred once the stock got into the market. The original basis for regulation was that the security was traded on one of the national stock exchanges and was clearly "interstate commerce." More recent amendments require registration where the corporation has total assets of $1 million or more and a class of equity securities held by 500 or more persons. (Bonds are not equity securities; bondholders are creditors, so a company could have a class of bonds held by more than 500 persons and not have to register under the 1934 Act.) Once these minimum standards apply, the corporation and its stockholders become subject to all sorts of burdensome and costly regulations. For this reason, there has been a considerable movement in recent years to "go private"; that is, to buy back enough shares to reduce the number of stockholders below 500 and "deregister" the stock.

If the 1934 Act applies, the stock must be registered with the SEC, and if the stock is traded on an exchange, it must be registered with the exchange as well. These registration requirements are similar to those under the 1933 Act. In addition, certified annual reports must be filed each year, disclosing such matters as management changes, important legal proceedings, significant asset changes, and other material business events.

Ownership and Proxy Regulations. The SEC has adopted extensive regulations to prevent injury to the corporation or its shareholders by a few dominant "insiders" or by an outside group trying to take control. Within ten days after becoming the **beneficial owner** of more than 5 percent of a registered equity security, the owner must file a disclosure statement with the SEC and send copies to the issuing corporation and to any stock exchange on which the shares are traded. The owner must disclose who he or she is, why he or she bought the shares, how many shares are owned, and where the funds came from to buy them. Updated reports must be filed ten days after the end of any month in which the owner has changed the amount of holdings.

Such beneficial owners must turn over to the corporation any **short-swing profits** if the owner holds more than 10 percent of the stock. Short-swing profits result from the purchase and sale of their company's shares within a six-month period. A stockholder with only 9 percent ownership could keep the profits. The corporation's directors and officers are also covered by this rule (Section 16 of the 1934 Act). If the buying and selling transactions extend beyond six months, all of these persons (directors, officers, 10 percent owners) could keep their profits. The reason for this short-swing rule is that insiders should not be allowed to take financial advantage of inside corporate information until there is a fair chance for it to be circulated to all investors.

In recent years there have been many criminal prosecutions of persons who used insider information to make a profit in the stock market. The question arises as to just who is an "insider." The Supreme Court has generally said that, to be an "insider," the person must owe a duty to shareholders.

Whether they are the existing management insiders or a group of outsiders seeking to gain control, persons soliciting proxies from stockholders must file an extensive disclosure statement with the SEC. This information must also be available to the stockholders being solicited. Since the 1968 Amendments to the 1934 Act, similar disclosures must be made in connection with a cash offer to the stockholders to buy all or part of a class of shares. The SEC's proxy rules also attempt to promote "shareholder democracy" by requiring management to include most shareholder proposals in the company's proxy statement and to provide shareholder lists or send out supporting material for the sponsors of such proposals. The *Chambers* case in Chapter 34 illustrated a stockholder's use of these rules.

Antifraud Provisions. While all of the foregoing rules are important and have probably contributed to better corporate management, the most sweeping and revolutionary section of the 1934 Act is 10(b), the antifraud section. Together with the SEC's Rule 10b(5), as interpreted by the courts, this section potentially covers nearly any aspect of the securities markets one can imagine. It applies not only to the actual buyers and sellers of securities but to all other involved parties as well. It applies not only to the actual purchase and sale of securities but to *any* transaction *in connection with* their purchase and sale. It includes transactions in any securities, whether or not they are required to be listed and whether or not they are traded on an exchange. It covers much more than just common law fraud, including such things as failure to comply with other securities law requirements, arbitrary withholding of dividends, breaches of fiduciary duty, and disclosure of too much or too little information.

Rule 10b(5) reads as follows:

It shall be unlawful for any person, directly or indirectly, by the use of any means or instrumentality of interstate commerce, or of the mails, or of any facility of any national securities exchange,

(a) to employ any device, scheme, or artifice to defraud.

(b) to make any untrue statement of a material fact or to omit to state a material fact necessary in order to make the statements made, in the light of the circumstances under which they were made, not misleading.

(c) to engage in any act, practice, or course of business which operates or would operate as a fraud or deceit upon any person, in connection with the purchase or sale of any security.

As noted earlier, this rule's application was narrowed considerably in 1976, when the Supreme Court held that it applied only to cases of fraud.

Remedies, Liabilities, and Penalties. The SEC uses a variety of court and administrative remedies to enforce the securities laws. It may seek an injunction to halt the sale of unregistered securities. It may ask a court to order the return of illegally received profits. Administratively, it may try to prevent employment of known violators by securities firms. The SEC enters into many voluntary settlements ("consent decrees") with firms and individuals accused of violations. The accused does not admit guilt but agrees to refrain from certain specified practices, or to do certain things, in the future. Sometimes a penalty is accepted as part of the consent decree; sometimes not. Since the courts are usually quite lenient with securities law violators, the SEC feels these consent decrees are justified in many cases.

Under Rule 2(e) of its rules of practice, the SEC may also bring disciplinary proceedings against professionals, such as accountants and attorneys, who are involved in securities transactions under the Commission's jurisdiction. The SEC, after giving the accused offender the opportunity for a hearing on the charges, may revoke the privilege of practicing before the Commission. Persons who lack the qualifications to represent others, or who have engaged in unethical professional conduct or otherwise lack character or integrity, or who have willfully violated or aided and abetted violations of the securities laws, may be prohibited from appearing before the Commission. Rule 2(e) also provides for automatic suspension of any attorney who has been suspended or disbarred, and any person whose state license has been suspended or revoked, and any person who has been convicted of a felony or of a misdemeanor involving moral turpitude. Temporary suspension may also occur where a professional has been subjected to an injunction against further violations of the securities laws. Commencing in 1975, the SEC has used this rule against corporate officers who also happened to be accountants or attorneys. In such a case, the corporate officer who could not practice before the SEC would be unable to sign the required filing documents for his company, and would thus be prevented from continuing to serve as the officer required to sign those documents. Since the Rule states that it applies to "any person," the SEC could conceivably try to apply it to officers who were neither accountants nor attorneys. Further litigation on the validity and scope of this Rule seems inevitable.

Individual investors who have been damaged financially as a result of violations of the securities laws may bring their own lawsuits against those responsible. The problem of suing for individual relief is the same here as in any other case—legal fees. It will undoubtedly cost several thousand dollars to get a securities case instituted, and perhaps as much as $50,000 to see it through all the possible appeals and rehearings. Class action lawsuits are still possible, although the U.S. Supreme Court ruled in 1974 that each member of a "class" of potential plaintiffs has to be notified personally of the lawsuit, so that he or she can decide whether to join in as a plaintiff. Where such a class action is brought, with thousands of plaintiffs, including large institutional investors, damages can add up to millions of dollars very quickly.

Both the 1933 Act and the 1934 Act provide for criminal penalties—up to five years in prison and fines of up to $10,000 for most violations. Failure to file any report under the 1984 Act makes the issuing corporation liable for a fine of $100 per day until the required filing occurs. (A corporation can't be imprisoned, of course, but it can certainly be fined and enjoined.) Criminal cases are brought for the SEC by the U.S. Justice Department, so these two agencies must work together to prepare and present an effective criminal case. The *United States v. Natelli* case is one of the rare criminal cases that have been brought against accountants for securities law violations.

Defenses to Civil Liability. There are several possible defenses which may be used to avoid liability under the securities laws. First, the 1933 Act has a relatively short statute of limitations: Suit must be brought within one year from the discovery of the violation or from the date when it would have been discovered using reasonable diligence; in no case, however, can suit be brought more than three years after the sale. With many analysts constantly studying the markets, most large frauds would probably be discovered within that time, but in the *Hochfelder* case Nay defrauded people for twenty-five years and was "discovered" only when he committed suicide.

It's at least theoretically possible for the courts to hold that a particular misstatement or omission was not material, but that is unlikely if investors have in fact sustained damage. The definition of *materiality* used in *Escott, Texas Gulf Sulphur*, and similar cases is quite liberal: "any fact which *might* reasonably affect the value of the security."

The *Davidson* case explains the "reliance" element in the plaintiff's case.

DAVIDSON v. WILSON
973 F.2d (8th Cir., 1992)

FACTS: Appellants, Robert L. Davidson and Guenther R. Roth, commenced this action in May 1989, against appellees Thomas C. Wilson ("Wilson"), Winthrop Securities Company, Inc. ("Winthrop Securities"), and Winthrop Financial Associates ("Winthrop Financial"), a limited partnership. Wilson acted as agent on behalf of Winthrop Securities. The latter, in turn, was owned by Winthrop Financial. Davidson and Roth claim they were wrongfully induced by appellees to invest in Wilcap Holding Limited Partnership ("Wilcap") by appellees' misrepresentations concerning allocations of tax losses, rates of return, and cash distributions available to the investor. The seven-count complaint included the following claims: violations of the Securities Exchange Act of 1934 and Rule 10b(5); violations of Sections 17 and 12 of the Securities Act of 1933; violations of the securities laws of Minnesota and Massachusetts; RICO violations; common-law misrepresentation; and breaches of fiduciary duty.

Wilcap was formed for the sole purpose of purchasing 1,000 units in another limited partnership known as Winthrop California Investors Limited Partnership (WCI), a limited partnership which owns real estate in California. Winthrop Financial, which, as indicated *supra*, owns Winthrop Securities, is the general partner of Wilcap. Limited partnership units in Wilcap were a separate syndication pursuant to which benefits arising from special allocations of cash distributions and tax losses by appellees were promised. Davidson and Roth each contend that Wilson fraudulently promised the special allocations of tax losses and the cash distributions in order to induce each of appellants to invest in the Wilcap partnership.

Davidson is a wealthy real estate development lawyer who is a partner in a Minneapolis law firm. He has been practicing law for approximately thirty-five years and is experienced in both investments and commercial law practice. Davidson initially became aware of the Wilcap investment opportunity when he was contacted by one of his former accountants—James Weichert—who had discussed the investment with Wilson. During a three-way telephone conversation on September 19, 1986, involving Weichert, Wilson, and Davidson, the latter states that Wilson informed him that a $105,000 investment in Wilcap made in September, 1986 would provide Davidson a 1986 tax loss of approximately $132,000 and annual cash flow distributions of $6,000 in 1986, and $7,000 in 1987, and, thereafter, cash flow distributions which would annually increase at the rate of 6 percent per year until the project's end in 1996. In addition, Davidson claims that Wilson told Weichert and himself during that discussion on the telephone that Davidson would receive a total of $200,000 in cash distributions over the ten-year life of the project and would realize $195,000 to $200,000 from the sale of the residual interest in the project.

In a subsequent three-way telephone conference among the same three persons on September 24, 1986, Davidson says that Wilson said that written confirmation of the special allocations under Wilcap could not yet be provided by him, Winthrop Financial or Winthrop Securities, and that Wilson also stated that if he (Wilson) did get new numbers, "he would have to rescind all sales and start over" and Wilson did not want to incur that expense. After Davidson requested written verification of new cash flow numbers, Wilson, according to Davidson, stated that the numbers were not yet available in writing but stated that Davidson would soon receive written confirmation of the "new numbers."

Davidson asserts that on September 24, 1986, Wilson also provided information about the underlying transaction—the WCI investment. According to Davidson, it was the latter information which led Davidson—who acknowledges he is experienced in real estate transactions—to conclude that Wilcap could deliver the promised benefits. Wilson, according to Davidson, informed the latter during the September 24, 1986 discussion that Wilson and his partners had purchased 1,000 units in WCI without even considering the tax ramifications. Wilson allegedly represented that an attractive feature of the Wilcap investment was that appellees could offer a combination of tax benefits and cash flows because they were specially allocated by the general partner of Wilcap—Winthrop Financial.

In this appeal, appellants challenge the granting by the district court of summary judgment as to all of their claims other than those for breach of fiduciary duty and violations of RICO.

 SENIOR DISTRICT JUDGE KAUFMAN:

As a threshold matter, Davidson and Roth assert that genuine issues of material fact precluded the lower court from granting summary judgment. However, the district court's Opinions and Orders of March 6, 1990 and of April 10, 1991 reveal full acceptance by that court of Davidson's and Roth's versions of the facts, and that court's determination, as a matter of law, that notwithstanding the alleged oral misrepresentations made by Wilson, Davidson's and Roth's reliance upon those representations was unjustified because Davidson and Roth, as sophisticated investors, should have been on notice not to rely upon those representations. That is so, reasoned the court below, because Davidson and Roth acknowledged in their affidavits that they each had copies of the Subscription Agreement prior to making their investments. The district court, referring to the numerous caveats and disclaimers contained in the Subscription Agreement as well as the references in it to other documents, determined that such references made a sophisticated investor's reliance upon contrary oral representations unreasonable as a matter of law.

Thus, the key issue in this appeal is whether the lower court's determination that such reliance was unjustifiable as a matter of law is correct....

In a misrepresentation claim made under Rule 10b(5), a plaintiff must establish that the defendant, with scienter, made a false representation of material fact, upon which plaintiff justifiably relied to his detriment, in connection with the purchase or sale of a security.... Justifiable reliance is not a theory of contributory negligence;

rather, it is a limitation on a Rule 10b(5) action which insures that there is a causal connection between the misrepresentation and the plaintiff's harm....

Based upon a review of the cases from other circuits, the Tenth Circuit in *Zobrist* observed that whether reliance is justifiable depends upon the specific factual situation. That review yielded the following relevant factors in determining whether reliance was justifiable:

> (1) the sophistication and expertise of the plaintiff in financial and securities matters, (2) the existence of long standing business or personal relationships, (3) access to the relevant information, (4) the existence of a fiduciary relationship; (5) concealment of the fraud; (6) the opportunity to detect the fraud, (7) whether the plaintiff initiated the stock transaction or sought to expedite the transaction, and (8) the generality or specificity of the misrepresentations....

"No single factor is determinative; all relevant factors must be considered and balanced to determine whether reliance was justified...."

In this case, Davidson and Roth acknowledge that they are each sophisticated investors. Davidson had never dealt with Wilson before although Wilson apparently was known to Davidson's former accountant—Weichert—who also acted as an advisor to Davidson in the transaction at issue. As to Roth, he had been a client of Wilson and Winthrop Securities. Shaw, acting as Roth's agent, had purchased "several" real estate investments from Wilson; however, there is no indication that there necessarily was a longstanding, close relationship of trust between Roth (or, more particularly, his agent) and Wilson.

As to the factor of access to relevant information, Davidson and Roth have admitted that they each did have access to information which repeatedly indicated the existence of two other memoranda and which described, in general terms, the contents of those memoranda and made reference to specific attachments thereto. However, Davidson and Roth assert that although they repeatedly questioned Wilson about such documents, they were told that there were no such documents.

The district court determined, and we agree, that no fiduciary relationship existed between Davidson and Roth and the appellees at the time the alleged misrepresentations were made. Indeed, Davidson and Roth do not press before this Court the contention made below that appellees breached their fiduciary duty.

There is no indication in the record in this case that appellees concealed the alleged fraud. As emphasized *supra*, the Subscription Agreement contained disclaimers and other warnings stated in the strongest of terms. In addition, that Agreement explicitly referred to memoranda which Wilson stated did not exist.

As to whether Davidson and Roth had the opportunity to detect the fraud, the record reveals that they each were on notice that Wilson's oral assertions contradicting the Subscription Agreement were cause for concern. Davidson and Roth both assert that they raised such worries with Wilson and were told that no such written documents existed.

In this case, Wilson apparently initiated the transaction rather than Davidson or Roth. Finally, the misrepresentations were quite specific—tax losses and cash distributions of specific amounts were promised. Also the Subscription Agreement contained explicit disclaimers regarding the specific dollar values associated with the investment.

Application of the eight factors enumerated in *Zobrist* dictates the conclusion that a sophisticated investor, confronted with a written document which contained repeated references to two other documents—which the investor had been orally informed did not exist—and that also contained explicit disclaimers concerning representations as to dollar values associated with the investment, did not justifiably rely upon any contradictory oral representations. There was seemingly ample reason for David and Roth to take the position, that they would not move ahead and make investment payments until such references and representations were clarified to their satisfaction. Thus, we agree with the district court that, based upon the facts of this case, appellants' claimed reliance upon Wilson's oral representations was unjustifiable as a matter of law.

Justifiable reliance is also a necessary element to state a claim under the two state securities laws relied upon by appellants; therefore, the lack of justifiable reliance which negates appellants' Rule 10b(5) claims also dooms their state securities laws claims. Appellants concede that a required element of their fraud claims under Minnesota common law is justifiable reliance. Nevertheless, they assert that under Minnesota law, "reliance on an oral representation is unjustified as a matter of law only if the written contract directly contradicts the oral representation ... [W]here there [is] not a direct contradiction between the prior oral representation and the terms of the written contract, the question of justifiable reliance [is] for the trier of fact...." But [that rule] is of little or no assistance to appellants in this case because the oral representations did directly contradict the terms of the written contract (e.g., on the one hand, specific dollars amounts were orally promised; on the other hand, the written contract disavowed the ability to predict specific dollar amounts)....

In sum, for the reasons stated in this opinion, the two Opinions and Orders of the District Court are affirmed.

Due Diligence. Probably the most important defense, and the one most open to interpretation, is the "due diligence" defense. This defense may be proved by any person other than the issuing corporation. As to parts of a registration statement not based on an expert's authority, the defendant is not liable if he or she can show that he or she "had, after reasonable investigation, reasonable ground to believe and did believe, at the time such part of the registration statement became effective, that the statements therein were true" (and not misleading). The standard of reasonableness specified is "that required of a prudent person in the management of his or her own property."

As to the "expertised" sections of the registration statement (those certified by CPAs, engineers, or appraisers, for example), the defendant is not liable if he or she "had no reasonable ground to believe, and did not believe," that the statements were untrue or misleading. In other words, the statements made by experts can be relied on unless the defendant knew or reasonably should have known that the statements were false or misleading. However, lawyers are not necessarily "experts" on everything, under this definition. The court in the *Escott* case (excerpted in Chapter 7) rejected the defendants' claim that they could rely on everything in the registration statement because it had been prepared by lawyers. Under this definition, lawyers would only be experts as to specifically legal questions; for example, the nature of the company's contingent liabilities.

SIGNIFICANCE OF THIS CHAPTER

Regulation of the issuance and sale of securities is a very important phase of government regulation on both the state and national level. It is not only the very rich, who obviously have access to excellent legal advice and valuable market information, who invest in securities. Investors include people from all walks of life and from all income levels. They must be protected from persons who would defraud them or take their money by deceptive practices. Also, the public buyer should be protected against the "insider" who because of special knowledge would get an unfair advantage as to new stock issues, stock splits, and similar material developments.

From the issuing company's standpoint, compliance with the securities law is burdensome in time, effort, and money. There are no easy shortcuts. But full and accurate compliance is clearly in the company's best interests. For all responsible individuals, the company's compliance should be checked and rechecked to avoid the possibility of ruinous damage suits by angry investors.

PROBLEMS FOR DISCUSSION

1. The SEC asked for an injunction to stop the sale of unregistered "securities" and to prohibit fraudulent practices in connection with their sale. The U.S. District Court denied the injunction, and the SEC appealed.

   Koscot was one of the subsidiaries of Glen W. Turner Enterprises; it was organized as a multilevel network of distributors for a line of cosmetics. Distributors received cash bonuses ranging up to $3,000 for each new person who was brought into the plan and advanced up the distribution chain. Prospective distributors were introduced to the plan at "Opportunity Meetings," which were to be run exactly according to a company-prepared script. Distributors were told to dress and live as if they had a very large income, so as to impress the prospects. At the Opportunity Meetings, films were shown, speeches were made, and high-pressure sales tactics were used to try to get the prospects to "make a decision."

   How should the SEC's appeal be decided, and why?

2. Piano Company was a closely held South Carolina corporation. It had only four shareholders—Huey, Louis, Dewey, and Donald. From the time it was incorporated in 1986, it had been unprofitable. In 1994 Donald, who was the only shareholder actively involved in Piano's management, learned that certain market changes would make Piano very profitable. Donald persuaded the other three shareholders to sell their shares to him, without disclosing his new information. All of these representations and statements were made in person by Donald; he sent no letters, and he did not use the telephone.

   Do the other three shareholders have a case against Donald under Section 10(b) of the 1934 Act? Discuss.

3. Chiarella was a printer by trade. he worked as a "markup man" in the New York composing room of Pandick Press, a financial printer. Among documents that Chiarella handled were five announcements of corporate takeover bids. When these documents were delivered to the printer, the identities of the acquiring and target corporations were concealed by blank spaces or false names. The true names were sent to the printer on the night of the final printing.

   Chiarella, however, was able to deduce the names of the target companies before the final printing from other information contained in the documents. Without disclosing his knowledge, he purchased stock in the target companies and sold shares immediately after the takeover attempts were made public. By this method, he realized a gain of slightly more than $30,000 in the course of fourteen months.

   Has Chiarella violated the Securities Acts? Why or why not?

4. Merry Lyncher, a stockbroker, developed what she thought was a surefire scheme for making money in the market. After study, she picked stocks she thought were sure to go down in price and placed "sell" orders with other brokers. She told them that she owned these shares; otherwise, they would have required a margin deposit or refused the orders altogether. Her plan was to buy the stocks when the price went down so that she'd have them by the time she was required to deliver them. Unfortunately, the stocks she selected rose sharply in price and she defaulted on her sales contracts. The other brokers were forced to buy in at the higher market prices to cover sales to their customers, and they now sue Merry for securities fraud. Merry contends that she is not liable, since Section 17(a)(1) of the 1933 Act only protects *investors*, not brokers. Has Merry violated the securities acts? Discuss.

5. Plaintiffs have sued defendant, Transamerica Corporation, for having purchased from them Class A and Class B stock of the Axton-Fisher Tobacco Company at $40 and $12 per share, respectively, pursuant to a written offer dated November 12, 1998, which Transamerica made to all minority stockholders. The complaint alleges that at the time of the sale the true value of the Class A stock was more than $200 per share and such value of the Class B stock was in excess of $100 per share. Plaintiffs allege Transamerica deceived them into selling their shares.

   The complaint further alleges that prior to the time when Transamerica made its offer, it had determined to purchase as many Class A and Class B shares as possible and thereafter to convert its Class A stock into Class B stock, to redeem the remaining Class A stock, and as a final step, to merge or dissolve Axton-Fisher, to the end it might capture for itself the increased but undisclosed value of the Axton-Fisher inventory, all of which Transamerica did. Under these circumstances, the complaint alleges, Transamerica was under a fiduciary duty as a majority stockholder to inform the minority stockholders that the real value of the Axton-Fisher inventory was in excess of $17,000,000; that its earnings were improving; and that Transamerica had determined upon a plan which had as its ultimate objective the merger or dissolution of Axton-Fisher; and that if Transamerica had made known these facts to plaintiffs, they would not have sold their stock.

   Have plaintiffs stated a valid claim? Explain.

Chapter 38
Antitrust Law

BASIC POLICY AND INTERPRETATION OF THE SHERMAN ACT

It's hard to say whether Senator John Sherman of Ohio would be pleased with the growth of his century-old offspring. The Sherman Antitrust Act was passed in 1890 as the first attempt by the national government to deal with the perceived abuses of market power by the giant industrial corporations which had grown up after the Civil War.

In the broadest possible language, the Sherman Act stated: "Every contract, combination in the form of trust or otherwise, or conspiracy, in restraint of trade or commerce among the several states, or with foreign nations, is hereby declared to be illegal." Section 2 of the act defined another broad category of offenses: "Every person who shall monopolize, or attempt to monopolize, or combine or conspire with any other person or persons, to monopolize any part of the trade or commerce among the several States, or with foreign nations, shall be deemed guilty of a misdemeanor." The act was clearly aimed at the giant concentrations of economic power which existed in many industries—the "trusts." Firms which should have been competing against each other were working together and were in many cases tied together organizationally through voting trusts (see Chapter 34). Quite clearly, the act was intended to reach such anticompetitive schemes as price-fixing, bid-rigging, and market-splitting.

The continuing dilemma of antitrust interpretation is whether or not the act was intended to go beyond those obvious, specific practices to prohibit "bigness" as such. If one company competes aggressively, builds a better product at lower cost, and succeeds in getting nearly all the potential customers to deal with it, has it violated the antitrust laws? Stated most simply, is market success illegal? This is where opinions diverge.

There are two opposing schools of thought on the basic meaning and purpose of the Sherman Act and the other antitrust laws: for want of better terminology, the **legal school** and the **eco-**

nomic school. The dispute is not quite as simple as the terms suggest, since some economists support the "legal" view and many lawyers and judges take the "economic" view. The legal approach starts with the premise that size alone is not made illegal by the Sherman Act; there is specific support for this approach in the 1890 debates in Congress. To be guilty of an antitrust violation, a company must be shown to have actually abused its position of market power. What counts are the methods used and the intent of those using them. Free and fair competition means that there will be winners *and losers* in the marketplace; the winners should not be penalized if they've won "fair and square." This view of antitrust emphasizes protecting the *process* of competition rather than trying to ensure the survival of specific *competitors*. If customers want to deal with GM and IBM, should the government step in to "preserve" other car makers and computer manufacturers? Supporters of the legal approach would answer no.

The economic approach starts from the premise that large concentrations of economic power are bad *per se*, that our democratic society is endangered by such power blocks, and that Congress intended the antitrust laws as a vehicle for preserving an economic structure which embraces a number of smaller independent economic units. In this view, economic efficiencies may at times have to be sacrificed to preserve this sort of market structure. The Robinson-Patman Act of 1936 (sometimes referred to as the "anti-chainstore act") clearly points in this direction. What counts in this approach is the market structure; large size and market dominance are inherently bad. There is an antitrust violation if a company has the *potential* power to abuse, whether or not it has actually been guilty of any specific abuse. This view of antitrust is clearly most concerned with protecting *competitors*, even to the point of insulating them from the rigors of effective competition.

Unfortunately for students, teachers, lawyers, and most of all for business firms, the antitrust laws have been interpreted *both* ways by various courts with various combinations of judges. Depending in large part on the basic policy view taken by a majority of the justices on the U.S. Supreme Court, a given course of business conduct may or may not be deemed to violate the antitrust laws. If the results in some of the cases and problems in this chapter and the next seem to conflict, that's because they probably do conflict.

Penalties for Violation. These basic questions of interpretation are of more than academic interest to the business community because of the broad reach of the antitrust statutes and the serious penalties that may be imposed for violations. The three basic enforcement mechanisms are *criminal prosecution, civil suit by the U.S. government* (the Justice Department or the Federal Trade Commission), and *civil suit by private parties*.

Criminal cases are usually instituted by the Justice Department only for conduct which is deemed to be illegal per se (without any test of "reasonableness"), such as price-fixing. If convicted, a corporation now faces a fine of up to $10 million. For individuals, criminal penalties include a fine of up to $350,000 and/or a maximum of three years in jail. Historically, jail sentences were rarely imposed, but there is some evidence that the courts' attitude has been changing. Executives served more time in jail for price-fixing in 1978 than in the entire preceding eighty-seven years of the Sherman Act's existence. The Justice Department was also able to establish in the electrical industry price-fixing cases in the 1960s that it does not have to accept a *nolo contendere* ("no contest") plea to the criminal charges. This last point is important because a plea of guilty can be used by a civil plaintiff to help prove a case for damages; a *nolo* plea does not admit guilt.

Because of the much higher standard of proof required in a criminal case (beyond any reasonable doubt) and the general reluctance of juries to subject someone to the chance of prison for nonviolent, business-related conduct, the Justice Department and the FTC prefer to file civil actions in many cases. Anticompetitive conduct may be enjoined; divestiture may be ordered where an illegal merger has taken place; and other civil remedies may be involved. In 1974, for instance, the FTC agreed to a settlement of its complaint against Xerox, by the terms of which Xerox was required to make its entire portfolio of about 2,000 patents available to any other firm that wanted to enter the copier market. Much of the fear of antitrust lawsuits stems from the fact that private parties can recover treble damages plus reasonable attorney fees. This measure of damages is a very real incentive to litigate, and thus a significant deterrent to antitrust violations.

Monopoly Power in One Company. In the first big case under the Sherman Act, the Sugar Trust, which controlled about 98 percent of the U.S. production, escaped liability when the Supreme Court held that manufacturing was not "commerce" and was therefore not covered by the act. This interpretation was soon overruled, and in the famous *Standard Oil* case of 1911 a majority of five justices voted to apply a "rule of reason" in antitrust cases. The Standard Oil majority correctly concluded that a literal reading of the act ("every contract") would produce absurd results since every business contract "restrains" trade in the sense of denying a particular business opportunity to others. (If you contract to buy Smith's used car, Smith has "foreclosed" others from selling you a used car, unless you need more than one. Likewise, you have "foreclosed" Smith's opportunity to sell his used car to other buyers.) Clearly, the act must have been aimed at something other than these normal business contracts with their normal business consequences While the majority adopted a reasonableness test, they did not really apply it to the facts of the *Standard Oil* case, and ordered the combination split up without much investigation of actual economic performance.

In the landmark *Alcoa* case in 1945, Circuit Judge Hand stated that monopoly power was illegal *per se*, regardless of how it had been attained and regardless of whether or not it had been abused. The case had been started in 1937 in U.S. District Court, where Judge Caffey heard 155 witnesses, viewed 1,803 exhibits, and produced a trial record of 58,000 pages. After four years the court decided that Alcoa was not guilty on any of the 140 criminal counts. Hand and the Second Circuit Court of Appeals reversed Judge Caffey on *one* count and took that as the opportunity to radically reinterpret the Sherman Act. The appeals court found a monopoly by a very restrictive definition of the relevant market, which excluded aluminum made from reprocessed scrap and aluminum produced abroad. While the *Alcoa* decision was not reviewed by the Supreme Court, the principle stated there was generally accepted in the Supreme Court's 1946 decision in the *American Tobacco* case. Obviously a court's determination of the dimensions of the "relevant market" may be decisive in deciding whether or not there is a "monopoly."

In the 1960s and 1970s, the government filed monopolization charges against such industrial giants as IBM and AT&T, and threatened several times to try to break up GM. In the early 1970s, the late Senator Philip Hart of Michigan sponsored an "Industrial Reorganization Act" which would have created a new government agency with the power to restructure industries where an *oligopoly* existed. An oligopoly was defined as four or fewer firms controlling over 50 percent of a market. In the late 1970s, as the energy crisis worsened, several states passed laws prohibiting oil companies (the large refiners) from also owning retail gas stations. Also, the FTC's long-pending case against the four large cereal makers, charging a "shared monopoly" in violation of the Sherman Act, was finally dismissed. Such a theory would have opened many firms to prosecution.

The case filed by the Justice Department in 1998 against Microsoft charged that the defendant was abusing its monopoly position in personal computer operating systems. As of early 1999, the trial was still proceeding.

Attempts to Monopolize. Section 2 of the Sherman Act also prohibits attempts to monopolize. Courts have disagreed as to what must be proved to show a violation of this section. Generally, it is necessary to show a specific intent to monopolize, but it is not necessary to show that the defendant already has monopoly power. The charge is that the defendant is *attempting* to achieve monopoly power. Disagreement exists over whether a "dangerous probability" of success in acquiring monopoly power must also be shown. Some courts have required this element; others have not. This other group of courts have found violations where the intent was coupled with an attempt to acquire a monopoly. Sometimes, in the second group of cases, the courts did not even seem too worried about establishing the relevant market. The *Queen City* case is a recent example of the court's application of Section 2, as well as Section 1.

QUEEN CITY PIZZA, INC. v. DOMINO'S PIZZA, INC.
124 F.3d 430 (Third Circuit, 1997).

FACTS: Domino's Pizza, Inc. is a fast-food service company that sells pizza through a national network of over 4200 stores. Domino's Pizza owns and operates approximately 700 of these stores. Independent franchisees own and operate the remaining 3,500. Domino's Pizza, Inc. is the second largest pizza company in the United States, with revenues in excess of $1.8 billion per year.

A franchisee joins the Domino's system by executing a standard franchise agreement with Domino's Pizza, Inc. Under the franchise agreement, the franchisee receives the right to sell pizza under the "Domino's" name and format. In return, Domino's Pizza receives franchise fees and royalties.

The essence of a successful nationwide fast-food chain is product uniformity and consistency. Uniformity benefits franchisees because customers can purchase pizza from any Domino's store and be certain the pizza will taste exactly like the Domino's pizza with which they are familiar. This means that individual franchisees need not build up their own good will. Uniformity also benefits the franchisor. It ensures the brand name will continue to attract and hold customers, increasing franchise fees and royalties.

For these reasons, Section 12.2 of the Domino's Pizza standard franchise agreement requires that all pizza ingredients, beverages, and packaging materials used by a Domino's franchisee conform to the standards set by Domino's Pizza, Inc. Section 12.2 also provides that Domino's Pizza, Inc. "may in our sole discretion require that ingredients, supplies and materials used in the preparation, packaging, and delivery of pizza be purchased exclusively from us or from approved suppliers or distributors." Domino's Pizza reserves the right "to impose reasonable limitations on the number of approved suppliers or distributors of any product." To enforce these rights, Domino's Pizza, Inc. retains the power to inspect franchisee stores and to test materials and ingredients. Section 12.2 is subject to a reasonableness clause providing that Domino's Pizza, Inc. must "exercise reasonable judgment with respect to all determinations to be made by us under the terms of this Agreement."

Under the standard franchise agreement, Domino's Pizza, Inc. sells approximately 90 percent of the $500 million in ingredients and supplies used by Domino's franchisees. These sales, worth some $450 million per year, form a significant part of Domino's Pizza, Inc.'s profits. Franchisees purchase only 10 percent of their ingredients and supplies from outside sources. With the exception of fresh dough, Domino's Pizza, Inc. does not manufacture the products it sells to franchisees. Instead, it purchases these products from approved suppliers and then resells them to the franchisees at a markup.

The plaintiffs in this case are eleven Domino's franchisees and the International Franchise Advisory Council, Inc. ("IFAC"), a Michigan corporation consisting of approximately 40 percent of the Domino's franchisees in the United States, formed to promote their common interests. The plaintiffs contend that Domino's Pizza, Inc. has a monopoly in "the $500 million aftermarket for sales of supplies to Domino's franchisees" and has used its monopoly power to unreasonably restrain trade, limit competition, and extract supra-competitive profits. Plaintiffs point to several actions by Domino's Pizza, Inc. to support their claims.

 CIRCUIT JUDGE SCIRICA:

Plaintiffs assert six distinct antitrust claims on appeal. First, plaintiffs allege Domino's Pizza, Inc. has monopolized the market in pizza supplies and ingredients for use in Domino's stores, in violation of S.2 of the Sherman Act.... In support of this contention, plaintiffs allege Domino's Pizza, Inc. has sufficient market power to control prices and exclude competition in this market. Second, plaintiffs contend Domino's Pizza, Inc. has attempted to monopolize the market for Domino's pizza supplies and ingredients, in violation of S.2 of the Sherman Act. Third, plaintiffs allege Domino's Pizza, Inc.'s exclusive dealing arrangements have unreasonably restrained trade in violation of S.1 of the Sherman Act.... Fourth, plaintiffs allege Domino's Pizza, Inc. imposed an unlawful tying arrangement by requiring franchisees to buy ingredients and supplies from them as a condition of obtaining fresh dough, in violation of the Sherman Act S.1.... Fifth, plaintiffs allege Domino's Pizza, Inc. imposed an unlawful tying arrangement by requiring franchisees to buy ingredients and supplies "as a condition of their continued enjoyment of rights and services under their Standard Franchise Agreement," in violation of S.1 of the Sherman Act.... Sixth, plaintiffs allege Domino's Pizza, Inc. has monopoly power in a relevant "market for reasonably interchangeable franchise opportunities facing prospective franchisees," in violation of S.2 of the Sherman Act....

The district court dismissed plaintiffs' S.2 monopoly claims for failure to plead a valid relevant market. Plaintiffs suggest the "ingredients, supplies, materials, and distribution services used by and in the operation of Domino's pizza stores" constitutes a relevant market for antitrust purposes. We disagree....

Were we to accept plaintiffs' relevant market, virtually all franchise tying agreements requiring the franchisee to purchase inputs such as ingredients and supplies from the franchisor would violate antitrust law. Courts and legal commentators have long recognized that franchise tying contracts are an essential and important aspect of the franchise form of business organization because they reduce agency costs and prevent franchisees from free riding—offering products of sub-standard quality insufficient to maintain the reputation value of the franchise product while benefiting from the quality control efforts of other actors in the franchise system. Franchising is a bedrock of the American economy. More than one third of all dollars spent in retailing transactions in the United States are paid to franchise outlets. We do not believe the antitrust laws were designed to erect a serious barrier to this form of business organization....

The purpose of the Sherman Act "is not to protect businesses from the working of the market; it is to protect the public from the failure of the market."... Here, plaintiffs' acceptance of a franchise package that included purchase requirements and contractual restrictions is consistent with the existence of a competitive market in which franchises are valued, in part, according to the terms of the proposed franchise agreement and the availability of alternative franchise opportunities. Plaintiffs need not have become Domino's franchisees. If the contractual restrictions in Section 12.2 of the general franchise agreement were viewed as overly burdensome or risky at the time they were proposed, plaintiffs could have purchased a different form of restaurant, or made some alternative investment. They chose not to do so. Unlike the plaintiffs in *Kodak*, plaintiffs here must purchase products from Domino's Pizza not because of Domino's market power over a unique product, but because they are bound by contract to do so. If Domino's Pizza, Inc. acted unreasonably when, under the franchise agreement, it restricted plaintiffs' ability to purchase supplies from other sources, plaintiffs' remedy, if any, is in contract, not under the antitrust laws....

Plaintiffs' claim for attempt to monopolize fails for the same reasons. To prevail on an attempted monopolization claim under S.2 of the Sherman Act, "a plaintiff must prove that the defendant: (1) engaged in predatory or anticompetitive conduct, with (2) specific intent to monopolize, and with (3) a dangerous probability of achieving monopoly power."... In order to determine whether there is a dangerous probability of monopolization, a court must inquire "into the relevant product and geographic market and the defendant's economic power in that market."...

Plaintiffs' attempted monopoly claim is predicated on the identical proposed relevant market underlying its monopoly claim: a market in the ingredients, supplies, and materials used by Domino's pizza stores. Because the products within this proposed market are interchangeable with other products outside of the proposed market, the claim was properly dismissed....

Plaintiffs allege Domino's Pizza, Inc. imposed an unlawful tie-in arrangement by requiring franchisees to buy ingredients and supplies "as a condition of their continue enjoyment of rights and services under their Standard Franchise Agreement," in violation of S.1 of the Sherman Act.... This claim is meritless. Though plaintiffs complain of an illegal tie-in arrangement, they have failed to point to any particular tying product or service over which Domino's Pizza, Inc. has market power. Domino's Pizza's control over plaintiffs' "continued enjoyment of rights and services under their Standard Franchise Agreement" is not a "market." Rather, it is a function of Domino's contractual powers under the franchise agreement to terminate the participation of franchisees in the franchise system if they violate the agreement. Because plaintiffs failed to plead any relevant tying market, the claim was properly dismissed....

Plaintiffs also contend the district court held that the availability of contract remedies prohibited recovery under antitrust laws. But this misstates the district court's holding. The district court held that Domino's Pizza's ability to block franchisees from purchasing ingredients from other sources stemmed from its exercise of contractual powers, not market power, and the remedy for this problem lies, if at all, under contract law. The court did not say that as a matter of law the availability of common law remedies prohibits recovery under an antitrust theory. We see no error.

Concerted Activities Among Competitors. When competing companies get together to fix prices, limit output, or divide markets, the antitrust violation is clear. These practices are so inherently anticompetitive that they are classified as **per se violations**; that is, there is generally no "rule of reason" defense available. In the 1927 *Trenton Potteries* case, the U.S. Supreme Court held that the defendants' good motives and the reasonableness of the prices they set were both irrelevant; the power to fix reasonable prices was also the power to fix unreasonable prices at some future time. In 1940, in the *Socony-Vacuum Oil* case, the Court said that the government did not have to prove that the defendants had been successful in raising prices, only that they had conspired with the intent to do so. In a 1933 decision that stands virtually alone, the Supreme Court did rule in favor of coal producers who had entered into a "reasonable" price and output agreement; in the midst of a terrible depression, reasonable cooperation in the industry was permitted.

One of the most troublesome "conspiracy" areas involves the cooperative activities of trade associations, especially the collection and reporting of price information. The government's problem in these cases is to prevent the trade association from being used as a price-fixing mechanism while permitting legitimate cooperative activities. In cases dealing with manufacturers of sugar, lumber, and linseed oil, the Supreme Court has indicated that "reporting" of specific prices charged to specific customers is probably evidence of an agreement to charge everyone the same prices. In a case involving cement manufacturers, the Court permitted such reporting, where there was a history of some firms delivering extra, "free" cement, billing the customer, and splitting the extra profits with the contractor.

Another difficult problem relates to the proof necessary to substantiate the conspiracy charge. Price uniformity, in and of itself, does not necessarily indicate the existence of a conspiracy, especially where similar increases can be shown to have stemmed from uniformly increased costs of production and delivery. On the other hand, specific instances of joint price increases and reductions, when new firms entered the market, were held to show a conspiracy based on **conscious parallelism** in the 1946 *American Tobacco* case. This doctrine was limited by the 1954 *Theatre Enterprises* decision, which stated that parallel business behavior was not itself illegal nor was it conclusive proof of an illegal conspiracy. In most such cases the existence of a conspiracy is for the jury to decide.

The court makes that finding in the *Palmer* case.

PALMER v. BRG OF GEORGIA, INC.
111 S.CT. 401 (1990)

FACTS: In preparation for the 1985 Georgia Bar Examination, Jay Palmer and other law students contracted to take a bar review course offered by respondent BRG of Georgia, Inc. (BRG). In this litigation, they contend that the price of BRG's course was enhanced by reason of an unlawful agreement between BRG and respondent Harcourt Brace Jovanovich Legal and Professional Publications (HBJ), the Nation's largest provider of bar review materials and lecture services.

HBJ began offering a Georgia bar review course on a limited basis in 1976, and was in direct, and often intense, competition with BRG during the period from 1977-1979. BRG and HBJ were the two main providers of bar review courses in Georgia during this time period. In early 1980, they entered into an agreement that gave BRG an exclusive license to market HBJ's material in Georgia and to use its trade name "Bar/Bri." The parties agreed that HBJ would not compete with BRG in Georgia and that BRG would not compete with HBJ outside of Georgia. Under the agreement HBJ received $100 per student enrolled by BRG and 40 percent of all revenues over $350. Immediately after the 1980 agreement, the price of BRG's course was increased from $150 to over $400.

On petitioners' motion for partial summary judgment as to the § 1 counts in the complaint and respondents' motion for summary judgment, the District Court held that the agreement was lawful. The United States Court of Appeals for the Eleventh Circuit, with one judge dissenting, agreed with the District Court that per se unlawful horizontal price fixing required an explicit agreement on prices to be charged or that one party have the right to be consulted about the other's prices. The Court of Appeals also agreed with the District Court that to prove a per se violation under a geographic market allocation theory, petitioners had to show that respondents had subdivided some relevant market in which they had previously competed. The Court of Appeals denied a petition for rehearing en banc that had been supported by the United States.

 PER CURIAM:

In *United States v. Socony-Vacuum Oil Co.* ..., we held that an agreement among competitors to engage in a program of buying surplus gasoline on the spot market in order to prevent prices from falling sharply was unlawful, even though there was no direct agreement on the actual prices to be maintained. We explained that "[u]nder the Sherman Act a combination formed for the purpose and with the effect of raising, depressing, fixing, pegging, or stabilizing the price of a commodity in interstate or foreign commerce is illegal *per se*...."

The revenue-sharing formula in the 1980 agreement between BRG and HBJ, coupled with the price increase that took place immediately after the parties agreed to cease competing with each other in 1980, indicates that this agreement was "formed for the purpose and with the effect of raising" the price of the bar review course. It was, therefore, plainly incorrect for the District Court to enter summary judgment in respondents' favor. Moreover, it is equally clear that the District Court and the Court of Appeals erred when they assumed that an allocation of markets or submarkets by competitors is not unlawful unless the market in which the two previously competed is divided between them.

In *United States v. Topco Associates, Inc.* ... (1972), we held that agreements between competitors to allocate territories to minimize competition are illegal:

> "One of the classic examples of a per se violation of § 1 is an agreement between competitors at the same level of the market structure to allocate territories in order to minimize competition.... This Court has reiterated time and time again that '[h]orizontal territorial limitations ... are naked restraints of trade with no purpose except stifling of competition.' Such limitations are *per se* violations of the Sherman Act})...."

The defendants in *Topco* had never competed in the same market, but had simply agreed to allocate markets. Here, HBJ and BRG had previously competed in the Georgia market; under their allocation agreement, BRG received that market, while HBJ received the remainder of the United States. Each agreed not to compete in the other's territories. Such agreements are anticompetitive regardless of whether the parties split a market within which both do business or whether they merely reserve one market for one and another for the other. Thus, the 1980 agreement between HBJ and BRG was unlawful on its face.

The petition for a writ of certiorari is granted, the judgment of the Court of Appeals is reversed, and the case is remanded for further proceedings consistent with this opinion.

Resale Price Maintenance and Refusals to Deal. For many years the manufacturers of some products have attempted in various ways to maintain control over the prices at which retailers sell the products, usually by establishing a minimum retail price The U.S Supreme Court decided in 1911 in the *Dr. Miles* case that such contracts between a drug manufacturer and distributors were illegal under the Sherman Act. In 1919, however. the Court held in the *Colgate* case that a manufacturer could establish unilaterally the retail prices for its products and could announce in advance that it would refuse to deal with anyone who sold the product for less than the announced price. And in the 1926 *General Electric* case, the Court said that a consignor-manufacturer (which still had title to the products) was free to set any retail price it wanted to, since the retailer was simply acting as the manufacturer's agent and was bound to follow its instructions in selling the product.

Believing that a manufacturer had a legitimate interest in maintaining the "quality image" of its product and in protecting its established dealer network from discounters' price wars, most states passed so-called fair trade laws by 1940. Congress passed the Miller-Tydings Amendment to the Sherman Act in 1937 to exempt such state laws from antitrust, but the U.S. Supreme Court ruled in 1951 that the amendment applied only where the retailer had *voluntarily* agreed to the resale prices. Congress then passed the McGuire Amendment to the FTC Act in 1952, so that *non-signer plans* (if one retailer in a state agreed to the minimum prices, all retailers in that state were bound to adhere to them) were also exempt from antitrust. Even with this legislative support, manufacturers found it very difficult to "police" their minimum prices, and they could not prevent an interstate shipment of goods at a lower price from a non-fair trade state. Moreover, at least ten state courts had declared the nonsigner plans to be a violation of their state constitutions by 1957. In 1975 Congress brought the fair trade movement to an end by repealing the 1937 and 1952 amendments; nearly any fair trade arrangement would now be an antitrust violation.

What about refusals to deal, as possible antitrust violations? Except for certain businesses which are bound to deal with all members of the public on an equal basis, such as innkeepers and common carriers, it is generally assumed that a business is free to decide with whom it will deal and on what terms. This principle was applied to antitrust in the *Colgate* case. In the 1960, *Parke, Davis* case, however, the Court said that where the manufacturer **entwined** its wholesalers and retailers in a policing arrangement it had created an illegal conspiracy under the Sherman Act.

Courts continue to examine both of these restrictions very closely. The *State Oil* case in Chapter 1 showed the Supreme Court deciding that agreements setting maximum resale prices would no longer be *per se* violations.

Territorial and Other Distribution Restrictions. Manufacturers may wish to restrict resales by their wholesalers or retailers. The manufacturer may get its distributor to agree not to resell the product outside a particular geographical area or not to resell to a particular class of customers. For example, the manufacturer may want to handle all sales of the product to the government or to institutional buyers, such as schools and hospitals. Where the manufacturer has granted exclusive sales territories to its several distributors, it doesn't want them stepping on each other's toes. Rather than having its distributors compete with each other for the same set of customers, it wants each of them to compete with other suppliers' products—within their assigned area. These restrictions are designed to increase *inter*brand competition, at the expense of intrabrand competition. The legal validity of such restrictions under the antitrust laws was upheld by the Supreme Court in 1977.

But as the next case shows, cooperative arrangements with independent dealers continue to face antitrust challenges.

ATLANTIC RICHFIELD CO. v. USA PETROLEUM CO.
110 S. Ct. 1184 (1990)

FACTS: Atlantic Richfield Co. (ARCO), a large integrated oil company, operates company-owned retail stations and franchises stations to dealers. ARCO urged its dealers to match the retail prices of independents like USA. ARCO gave its dealers temporary allowances and also reduced their costs by eliminating credit card sales. As a result, ARCO and its dealers increased market share to the detriment of USA and similar independents. USA sued, alleging a conspiracy to set maximum retail prices, a *per se* violation of Section 1 of the Sherman Act. The District Court granted summary judgment for ARCO, but the Ninth Circuit reversed.

⚖️ **JUSTICE BRENNAN:**

A private plaintiff may not recover damages under § 4 of the Clayton Act merely by showing "injury causally linked to an illegal presence in the market." Instead, a plaintiff must prove the existence of "antitrust injury, which is to say injury of the type the antitrust laws were intended to prevent and that flows from that which makes defendants' acts unlawful...." [I]njury, although causally related to an antitrust violation, nevertheless will not qualify as "antitrust injury" unless it is attributable to an anti-competitive aspect of the practice under scrutiny, "since [i]t is inimical to [the antitrust] laws to award damages for losses stemming from continued competition...."

When a firm, or even a group of firms adhering to a vertical agreement, lowers prices but maintains them above predatory levels, the business lost by rivals cannot be viewed as an "anti-competitive" consequence of the claimed violation. A firm complaining about the harm it suffers from nonpredatory price competition "is really claiming that it [is] unable to raise prices...." This is not antitrust injury; indeed, "cutting prices in order to increase business often is the very essence of competition...." "The antitrust laws were enacted for the protection of competition, not competitors...." "To hold that the antitrust laws protect competitors from the loss of profits would, in effect, render illegal any decision by a firm to cut prices in order to increase market share...."

We also reject [USA's] suggestion that no antitrust injury need be shown where a per se violation is involved. The per se rule is a method of determining whether § 1 of the Sherman Act has been violated, but it does not indicate whether a private plaintiff has suffered antitrust injury and thus whether he may recover damages under § 4 of the Clayton Act....

The purpose of the antitrust injury requirement is different. It ensures that the harm claimed by the plaintiff corresponds to the rationale for finding a violation of the antitrust laws in the first place, and it prevents losses that stem from competition from supporting suits by private plaintiffs for either damages or equitable relief. Actions per se unlawful under the antitrust laws may nonetheless have some procompetitive effects, and private parties might suffer losses therefrom....

We decline to dilute the antitrust injury requirement here because we find that there is no need to encourage private enforcement by competitors of the rule against vertical, maximum price-fixing. If such a scheme causes ... anticompetitive consequences ..., consumers and the manufacturer's own dealers may bring suit....

[USA] has failed to demonstrate that it has suffered any antitrust injury.

CLAYTON ACT

Section 1 of the Sherman Act of 1890 had stated: "Every contract, combination in the form of a trust or otherwise, or conspiracy, in restraint of trade or commerce among the several states, or with foreign nations, is hereby declared to be illegal." The *Standard Oil* case added the rule of reason when judging these contracts and combinations. Still, courts lacked a real definition or classification of what was illegal and what was legal. This need for specific classifications of contracts or combinations which may be illegal brought about the passage of the Clayton Act in 1914. The important sections of the Clayton Act which affect antitrust are Sections 2, 3, 7, and 8.

Section 2 prohibits price discrimination, subject to certain exclusions and exceptions. Price discrimination is simply selling products of the same kind and quality to different customers for different prices. This topic will be discussed in the next chapter.

Tying Contracts and Exclusive Dealing Agreements. Section 3 prohibits tying contracts and exclusive dealing agreements. A **tying contract** is an arrangement whereby the customer is required to buy a product or service it may not want in order to buy the product it does want; in the retail trade, this is sometimes referred to as **full-line forcing**. Tying contracts, said the Supreme Court in the 1958 *Northern Pacific Railway* case, are presumed to be illegal "because of their pernicious effect on competition and lack of any redeeming virtue." Unless some very special facts are present, tying contracts are hard to justify. The following case illustrates some of these rules.

VIRTUAL MAINTENANCE, INC. v. PRIME COMPUTER, INC.
957 F.2d 1318 (Sixth Circuit, 1992).

FACTS: Defendant Prime Computer, Inc. appeals the district court's denial of its motion for judgment notwithstanding the verdict or a new trial following a jury's general verdict in favor of plaintiff Virtual Maintenance, Inc. in this antitrust action. The jury found that Prime's sale of certain computer software support services in conjunction with computer hardware maintenance for Prime's 50 Series minicomputers amounted to an illegal tying arrangement in violation of Section 1 of the Sherman Act. The jury awarded Virtual $8,453,000 in compensatory damages, which the district court trebled under the antitrust statute for a total award of $25,359,000. The district court then issued an injunction prohibiting Prime from enforcing a contract provision requiring the purchase of Prime's hardware maintenance with its software support services and declaring void any Prime hardware maintenance contracts with customers using "Ford-required CAD/CAM applications."

Prime manufactures and markets computer systems, distributes software, and provides hardware maintenance services for those systems. One of Prime's hardware systems is the Prime 50 Series minicomputer. In the general market for computers and software, Prime competes with companies such as IBM, UNISYS, NCR, DEC, Hewlett-Packard, and Data General. All large companies that sell computers and software provide hardware maintenance for their own computers.

Part of Prime's business is to supply companies with Computer Aided Design/ Computer Aided Manufacturing Systems ("CAD/CAM") used in product design. Prime also distributes software for the CAD/CAM systems and accounts for approximately 11 percent of the general CAD/CAM software sold throughout the world, making it the second largest vendor of CAD/CAM in the world.

One software design program distributed by Prime, called PDGS, was created by Ford Motor Company. A general version of PDGS is widely available from other distributors. Ford licenses Prime as the exclusive distributor of a modified version of PDGS used in automotive design under a year-to-year contract. Ford frequently updates PDGS and requires all companies that provide it with design services to use the most current version of PDGS in order to facilitate translation of the designs into Ford's identical PDGS software.

Although Ford's version of PDGS runs only on Prime's 50 Series minicomputers, it can be translated to other systems at a higher cost. The Prime 50 Series computer is in use in approximately 23,000 systems worldwide. Software compatible with the 50 Series accounts for approximately 3 percent of the worldwide CAD/CAM market, and Ford's PDGS software accounts for an even smaller percentage of the total CAD/CAM market. Approximately 350-400 of the 23,000 Prime 50 Series computers, or about 2 percent, are capable of using PDGS.

In addition to distributing Ford's PDGS software, Prime distributes revisions, modifications, updates, and support services (collectively "software support") for general CAD/CAM software. Prime also distributes software support for PDGS software, offering it to Ford's design suppliers as part of a package that includes hardware maintenance on the 50 Series minicomputers. The cost of the package is $16,000 per year for each installation. Customers are free to buy the software support separately from the hardware maintenance, but the cost to purchase software support without the maintenance package varies from $80,000 to $160,000 per year for each installation.

Virtual sued Prime, claiming that Prime's marketing strategy of linking its software support with hardware maintenance on 50 Series computers amounted to an illegal tying arrangement in violation of the antitrust laws. Virtual alleged that purchase of software support for general CAD/CAM and/or Ford-required CAD/CAM software (the tying product) was conditioned on the purchase of hardware maintenance for Prime 50 Series computers (the tied product). Virtual claimed that this tie-in unlawfully restricted its ability to compete with Prime in the 50 Series hardware maintenance market.

Prior to trial, Prime moved for summary judgment claiming that there was no genuine issue of material fact regarding whether it had sufficient economic power in the market for the tying product to restrain competition appreciably in the tied product market. The district court determined that genuine issues of material fact were present as to the definition of the relevant product market and denied Prime's motion for summary judgment. At trial, the jury found in favor of Virtual.

The district court denied Prime's motion for j.n.o.v. or a new trial and issued an injunction prohibiting Prime from continuing its practice of selling software support with hardware maintenance.

 CIRCUIT JUDGE SUHRHEINRICH:

A tying arrangement clearly exists here because the large price differential between software support alone and the software support/hardware maintenance package induces all rational buyers of Prime's software support to accept its hardware maintenance. It is also clear that two separate products or services, software support and hardware maintenance, are involved in this case due to the evidence of separate consumer demand for each product.... We therefore turn to the issue of Prime's economic power in the tying product market.

The second element of a per se tying case is proof of sufficient economic power in the tying market to affect appreciably the competition in the tied market. Such economic power exists when the tying party enjoys some significant advantage in the tying product market, not enjoyed by its competitors, that enables it to condition the availability of the tying item on acceptance of the tied item.... If this market power over consumers is not present, then purchasers of the tying product can simply turn to other sources of supply, and the attempted tie will ultimately collapse for want of takers.

The market power inquiry has both a product and a geographic dimension. Because the relevant market provides the framework against which economic power can be measured, defining the product and geographic markets is a threshold requirement.... The parties agree that the relevant geographic market is the entire world. Virtual submits, however, that we need not determine the relevant product market because Prime's market power is established by evidence that Prime was able to force an appreciable number of customers to submit to the tie. Virtual claims that when "forcing" is present...the Sherman Act is violated....

Virtual is mistaken. Proof that a defendant forced a consumer to accept a tying arrangement is not alone adequate to establish an illegal tie. Rather, "forcing" is simply a proxy for determining whether the seller has conditioned the tying product on acceptance of the tied product. Evident of "forcing" is necessary to show that a tie exists between two products, but is not sufficient to establish that the tie is illegal. Proof of such conduct does not establish per se illegality since not all ties are illegal.

Indeed, if proof of forcing alone were sufficient to establish an illegal tie, the Supreme Court's market analysis in Jefferson Parish would have been superfluous.... Similarly, Virtual must show that Prime is able to force customers to buy its software support plus hardware maintenance because of its market power over the tying product. Thus evidence of "forcing" without market power over the tying product does not establish an antitrust violation....

We find no error in the legal adequacy of the district court's first market definition. However, this market definition required the jury to find that Prime possessed power over price or "market power" in the sale of all software suitable for CAD/CAM purposes. Viewing the evidence in the light most favorable to Virtual, Prime possessed at most an 11 percent share of this market. This market share is insufficient to confer market power....

Prime contends that the second market instruction defined the tying product market too narrowly as a matter of law. Prime claims that the market definition of "Ford-required CAD/CAM" must fail because this market is limited to PDGS, a single manufacturer's brand of software. We agree....

Even if we accepted Virtual's lock-in argument, it seems unlikely that a large consumer like Ford would be "locked-in" by Prime when Ford controls the license to PDGS. The lock-in theory is viable only when the producer can charge its customer monopoly prices without fear of being replaced by competitors due to the customer's substantial investments. Ford's control of the product it is allegedly being forced to buy precludes Prime from maintaining the market share necessary to charge monopoly prices. Market power cannot be sustained absent the ability to maintain market share....

Even assuming that Prime had market power over consumers of its own brand of software, Prime's tie foreclosed competition for hardware maintenance of at most the 400 50 Series systems capable of using PDGS.... ("A defendant must have market power [over the tying product] before its conduct can be shown to have an adverse effect on competition [in the tied product market].") The foreclosure of 400 computer systems out of the thousands of systems in the worldwide market for computer hardware maintenance is insignificant as a matter of law. Consequently, Prime's tie-in did not have anticompetitive effects in the general hardware maintenance market. "Without a showing of actual adverse effect on competition, [Virtual] cannot make out a case under the antitrust laws, and no such showing has been made."... There is insufficient evidence to support the jury verdict under the rule of reason.

The judgment of the trial court is reversed because it is based upon an erroneous determination of the fundamental issue of relevant product market. A j.n.o.v. is entered for Prime because the facts presented show that Prime lacks market power in the interbrand market for general CAD/CAM software. Moreover, there is no proof that Prime's conduct had a substantial anticompetitive effect in the general market for computer hardware maintenance. Therefore, the award of damages and the injunction are vacated.

Exclusive dealing arrangements should be analyzed quite differently from tying contracts, since in many situations both the seller and the buyer benefit from such commitments. The buyer has an assured supply and protection against price fluctuations; the seller has an assured market and can plan production more realistically. Such agreements therefore must be tested on a case-by-case basis, under the rule of reason. The motives of the parties are important and so is the impact of the particular agreement on the relevant market.

Mergers

Section 7 of the Clayton Act prohibits certain mergers where the effect of the merger may be to substantially lessen competition.

Mergers may be divided into three basic classifications: (1) horizontal mergers, (2) vertical mergers, and (3) conglomerate mergers. A **horizontal merger** occurs when two competing firms merge. For example, one retail grocery chain merges with another retail grocery chain, both of whom compete in the same geographic area. A **vertical merger** is one in which a manufacturer merges with a wholesale distributor or a retail chain, which does business in the same product market as the manufacturer. For example, a manufacturer of shoes owns no retail outlets so it merges with a company that runs a chain of retail stores selling shoes. A **conglomerate merger** is a merger where the acquiring firm is not in the same line of commerce as the firm being acquired, and thus the acquired firm was neither a competitor nor a supplier nor a former customer. An example of a conglomerate merger would be in the situation where a firm that manufactures bicycles buys a company that makes water beds. The key question in all three of these types of mergers is whether or not the merger may substantially lessen competition.

Section 7 of the Clayton Act of 1914 was largely ineffective during its first forty years on the statute books due to restrictive Supreme Court interpretations and a lack of enforcement vigor. Section 7, in its original version, established a kind of per se rule which prohibited any acquisition by a company of a controlling stock interest in a competitor. In several cases in the 1920s and 1930s, the Supreme Court held that an acquisition of a competitor's assets was not prohibited. The *GM/DuPont* case, filed in 1949, resulted in a drastic reinterpretation of the original Section 7, but it really set no precedent because Congress had in the meantime passed the 1950 Celler-Kefauver Amendment, which substantially reworked Section 7.

The amended Section 7 covered one corporation's acquisition of the stock or the assets of another "where in any line of commerce in any section of the country, the effect of such acquisition may be substantially to lessen competition, or to tend to create a monopoly." This new version clearly established an **incipiency test**; the acquisition was illegal if there was a reasonable probability that it would have future anticompetitive effects.

Using the revised Section 7, the government was able to stop the proposed merger of Bethlehem Steel and Youngstown Sheet & Tube in 1958 (but Youngstown was subsequently merged into Lykes and Lykes into LTV). The first case to come to the Supreme Court under the new Section 7 was the Brown Shoe acquisition of Kinney Shoes, a merger which had both vertical and horizontal aspects, since both companies were manufacturers and retailers. Using a very restrictive definition of the market which excluded shoe retailers such as Sears, Montgomery Ward, and J.C. Penney and ignoring the fact that Kinney stores bought *more* shoes from independent manufacturers after the merger than it had before, the Supreme Court found the merger illegal.

To resolve some of the uncertainty as to which mergers would be challenged, the Justice Department in 1968 issued its merger "guidelines." These guidelines did little more than summarize the existing case law.

In 1982 the Federal Trade Commission issued their revised horizontal merger guidelines and in 1984 the Justice Department issued their revised horizontal merger guidelines. On April 2, 1992, the U.S. Department of Justice and the Federal Trade Commission jointly issued new and revised horizontal merger guidelines. These new guidelines jointly issued by the Justice Department and the Federal Trade Commission outline the present enforcement policy of both the Justice Department and the Federal Trade Commission concerning horizontal acquisitions and mergers subject to Section 7 of the Clayton Act, as amended. These new guidelines described the specific standards and the analytical process which will be used to determine whether to challenge a horizontal merger. One of the key factors in the decision making process is to determine what the post-merger market concentration will be and the anticipated increase in market concentration which might result from such a merger. These guidelines use a mathematical formula—the Herfindahl-Hirschman Index (HHI) to describe the approximate level of concentration already existing in an industry. If the level is too high, the proposed merger will probably be challenged. The market share of each existing competitor is squared and these figures are totalled. If the total is 1,000 or less, indicating a relatively unconcentrated market, the proposed merger will probably not be challenged. If the total is over 1,800, the Justice Department or the Federal Trade Commission would probably object. Between these figures, the agency involved will evaluate the amount of concentration the proposed merger would add to the industry. The market shares of the proposed merger partners will be added together and squared, and totalled with the other firms' squared market shares. The original total will be subtracted from this new total to see how many points have been added. If more than 100 points would be added to the HHI, the merger will probably be challenged; under 50, probably not. Between these extremes, the agency will weigh other industry factors and then decide whether to permit the merger or to challenge it. Vertical and conglomerate mergers are generally not viewed as posing serious marketplace threats by the Justice Department and the Federal Trade Commission.

Interlocking Directorates

Section 8 of the Clayton Act prohibits certain interlocking directorates. An **interlocking directorate** exists when a person is a director in any two or more competing corporations. Section 8 would prohibit an interlocking directorate if any one of the corporations has capital, surplus, and undivided profits aggregating more than $1 million, and if companies are engaged in commerce, and if they are not banks, banking associations, trust companies, or common carriers.

Similar to the history of proceedings on Section 7 violations, there were very few proceedings against "interlocking" directors for the first forty years after the Clayton Act was passed. Cases against W.T. Grant and Sears, Roebuck & Co. were decided in 1953, and Section 8 of the Clayton Act was revived. A District Court forced the common director of Sears and B. F Goodrich to resign from the Sears board, and five years later the same District Court held that its decree would be violated if the same person served on the Goodrich board and as a director of Sears' Savings and Profit Sharing Pension Fund. There was renewed emphasis on enforcement of this section in the 1970s, and a common director of Chrysler and General Electric was forced to resign from the GE board because both companies made air conditioners. Potentially, there is a considerable area of antitrust violation under this section.

FEDERAL TRADE COMMISSION ACT

In 1914 the U.S. Congress not only passed the Clayton Act but in the same session passed the Federal Trade Commission Act. This act created a new administrative agency with very broad powers in the area of trade regulation. The FTC has the responsibility of investigating alleged violations of Sections 2, 3, 7, and 8 of the Clayton Act and has the authority to issue cease and desist orders to stop certain illegal practices and activities. Failure to comply with a cease and desist order from the Federal Trade Commission can result in fines of up to $10,000 for each day the violation continues.

In the next chapter, we will discuss the Robinson-Patman Act, which amended Section 2 of the Clayton Act, and also Section 5 of the Federal Trade Commission Act, which prohibits unfair and deceptive trade practices.

SIGNIFICANCE OF THIS CHAPTER

The antitrust laws are significant because to maintain a competitive marketplace we must prevent anticompetitive schemes, such as price-fixing, market splitting, resale price maintenance, and tying contracts. The antitrust, or perhaps better phrased, the antimonopoly, laws try to prevent anticompetitive actions which may restrain competition. All business managers need at least a general knowledge of the purpose and coverage of the antitrust laws. This chapter provides the future business manager with that knowledge.

PROBLEMS FOR DISCUSSION

1. Morton Salt Company was the largest producer of salt for industrial and commercial uses. It also manufactured and sold various machines for the utilization of salt in production processes. One such machine, the Mixator, dissolved rock salt into a brine for industrial use. Another, the Saltomatic, injected salt tablets into canned food products during the canning process. Morton held patents on both machines. It leased about 800 Mixators and about 100 Saltomatics. In each lease there was a clause which required the lessee to purchase all salt used in the machine from Morton. The United States brings a civil suit for an injunction to prevent the use of such restrictive clauses in the leases, alleging violation of Section 1 of the Sherman Act and Section 3 of the Clayton Act.

    What is the result, and why?

2. The United States brought cases against ten corporations and five individuals. The corporations were three banks and their three respective holding companies, and four mutual life insurance companies. The five individuals each served on the board of directors of one of the banks or bank holding companies and one of the insurance companies. It was stipulated that the interlocked banks and insurance companies compete in the interstate market for mortgage and real estate loans.

    The government asserts that interlocking directorates between banks and insurance companies violate Section 8 of the Clayton Act.

    Is this a correct interpretation? Why or why not?

3. California Standard and its wholly owned subsidiary, Standard Stations, Inc., entered into exclusive supplier contracts with some 16 percent of the retail gasoline stations in seven western states. Cal/Standard was the largest gasoline retailer in the area, with over 20 percent of the sales. The next six largest competitors had over 40 percent of the sales; over seventy small companies shared the remaining sales. The nearly 6,000 independent dealers (16 percent of the area's retailers) who had signed such exclusive contracts bought over $57 million worth of gasoline and over $8 million worth of other products from Cal/Standard. The government sought a declaratory judgment that these contracts were illegal under Section 3 of the Clayton Act.

    How should the court rule, and why?

4. Sylvania Inc. manufactures and sells television sets through its Home Entertainment Products Division. Prior to 1992, like most other television manufacturers, Sylvania sold its televisions to independent or company-owned distributors who in turn resold to a large and diverse group of retailers. Prompted by a decline in its market share to a relatively insignificant 1 percent to 2 percent of national television sales, Sylvania conducted an intensive reassessment of its marketing strategy, and in 1992 it adopted the franchise plan challenged here. Sylvania phased out its wholesale distributors and began to sell its televisions directly to a smaller and more select group of franchised retailers. An acknowledged purpose of the change was to decrease the number of competing Sylvania retailers in the hope of attracting the more aggressive and competent retailers thought necessary to the improvement of the company's market position. To this end, Sylvania limited the number of franchises granted for any given area and required each franchisee to sell his Sylvania products only from the location or locations at which he was franchised. A franchise did not constitute an exclusive territory, and Sylvania retained sole discretion to increase the number of retailers in an area in light of the success or failure of existing retailers in developing their market.

When Sylvania franchised a new dealer in San Francisco, one of its existing dealers there sued, claiming that the Sylvania franchise restrictions violated Section 1 of the Sherman Act.

Will this claim be upheld in court? Why or why not?

5. Copperweld Corp. purchased the Regal division from Lear Siegler; the sale agreement bound Lear Siegler and its subsidiaries not to compete with Regal in the United States for five years. Copperweld then transferred Regal's assets to a newly formed, wholly owned Pennsylvania corporation, petitioner Regal Tube Co. The new subsidiary continued to conduct its manufacturing operations in Chicago but shared Copperweld's corporate headquarters in Pittsburgh.

One of Copperweld's competitors sued, claiming that the joint marketing plan of Copperweld and Regal was a conspiracy under Section 1 of the Sherman Act.

How should the court decide, and why?

Chapter 39
Trade Practices Law

UNFAIR TRADE PRACTICES
UNDER THE COMMON LAW

Even the common law placed some limits on the methods that one firm could use to attract customers from its competitors. Where a contract already existed, a third party that induced either of the contracting parties to breach was guilty of a tort. Tort law also recognized a wrong called **product disparagement**, a sort of commercial libel; it is only in recent years, with FTC approval, that comparative ads have begun to name the "other product." Both competitor and customer may suffer injury if one firm "passes off" its product for that of a competitor.

TRADEMARK PROTECTIONS

Trademarks serve to identify the source of products. **Service marks** do the same job for sellers of services. **"Trade dress"**—distinctive packaging and labelling—may also be used by a product seller to differentiate its products. These forms of intangible property are often referred to as "intellectual property," along with such other forms as patents, copyrights, and trade secrets. The legal rules for intellectual property protection were covered in some detail in Chapter 25.

Within the United States, trademarks are protected under the Lanham Act of 1946. Owners of trademarks can register them with the U.S. Patent and Trademark Office. After five years, the validity of the listed trademark can no longer be challenged by other persons. Registration does need to be renewed after ten years.

Third parties who infringe on a trademark may be liable for lost profits suffered by the trademark owner because of the infringement. Alternatively, damages may be measured by the third party's wrongful profits. The trademark owner can normally get an injunction to stop the infringement. The Lanham Act also prohibits false advertising, as seen in the next case.

SANDOZ PHARMACEUTICALS CORP. v. RICHARDSON-VICKS, INC.
902 F.2d 222 (Third Circuit, 1990)

FACTS: This appeal, from an order of the district court denying plaintiff/appellant Sandoz Pharmaceuticals Corp.'s request for a preliminary injunction against defendant/appellee Richardson-Vicks, Inc., is another installment in the cough syrup marketing wars. Sandoz alleges that Vicks's representations about its product, Vicks Pediatric Formula 44, constituted false and deceptive advertising in violation of section 43(a) of the Lanham Act.

At the nub of the controversy is Vick's assertion that Pediatric 44 starts to work the instant it is swallowed. Sandoz alleges that the representations about the instant action of the product are false. It also alleges that such representations constitute per se violations of the Lanham Act, given Vicks's failure to disclose, on Pediatric 44's label, that the demulcents which theoretically effectuate the immediate relief are intended to be active yet are not approved by the Food and Drug Administration. Additionally, Sandoz challenges Vicks's advertising claims that Pediatric 44 is superior to its competitors.

After an extensive hearing, the district court found that Sandoz: (1) had failed to meet its burden of proving that any of Vicks's advertising claims was false or misleading, and (2) had not proved irreparable injury.

 CIRCUIT JUDGE BECKER

Our conclusions depend on the resolution of an interesting legal issue arising out of the interface between the Lanham Act and the Food, Drug and Cosmetic Act.... The controversy centers on whether a Lanham Act plaintiff needs to show only that the defendant's advertising claims of its own drug's effectiveness are inadequately substantiated under FDA guidelines, or whether the plaintiff must also show that the claims are literally false or are misleading to the public. For the reasons that follow, we conclude that the additional proof that a defendant's claims are literally false or actually misleading is necessary to sustain a Lanham Act claim....

Three different federal statutory schemes regulate OTC [over-the-counter] drug marketing, but the interplay among the statutes is somewhat ambiguous. The primary regulatory system covering prescription and non-prescription drugs was created by the Food, Drug and Cosmetic Act.... Under the FD & C Act, a "new" drug may not be marketed and sold in the United States without prior approval by the FDA. To obtain this approval, an applicant must demonstrate, by the presentation of substantial evidence, that the drug is safe and effective for the uses recommended in its labeling....

The approval process usually consists of three stages of review. First, the FDA appoints an advisory review panel of independent qualified experts. This panel submits a recommendation to the FDA stating whether a drug is or is not safe and effective for its designated purposes or whether there is insufficient evidence upon which to base a recommendation. Second, the FDA publishes a tentative "final monograph" presenting its initial position on the drug's safety and effectiveness. Third, after an extensive comment and review period, the FDA publishes a final monograph that establishes the conditions under which a drug is considered safe and effective.... Once a final monograph goes into effect, it is illegal to sell a drug described therein unless it conforms therewith....

Public regulation of trade competition beyond antitrust violations is vested by the Federal Trade Commission Act ... in the Federal Trade Commission.... The FTC Act prohibits "unfair methods of competition," including advertisements containing false or misleading representations or material omissions.... The Supreme Court and other federal courts have given an expansive reading to both the scope of the FTC Act and the powers granted to the FTC thereunder.... This expansive view of the FTC's capacity to define and regulate unfair trade practices is premised upon the FTC's "familiarity with the expectations and beliefs of the public, acquired by long experience."...

To a certain degree, the jurisdictions of the FDA and the FTC overlap in the regulation of OTC drug marketing. The FDA's authority in this field derives from the requirement that no drug may be sold in the United States unless it has FDA approval, and then only within the standards set by the FDA. The FTC's authority derives from its power to regulate any false or deceptive advertising or unfair trade practices, even in the OTC drug industry. To resolve issues of enforcement resulting from this concurrent jurisdiction, in 1971 the FDA and the FTC agreed to a division of regulatory authority: the FDA regulates the labeling of OTC drugs while the FTC monitors the advertising for these drugs....

The third relevant statute in the field of OTC drug marketing is the statute at issue in this case, the Lanham Act. The Lanham Act creates a civil remedy for the use of a "false or misleading description of fact, or false or misleading representation of fact" in connection with the sale of goods in interstate commerce....

After initial uncertainty as to the statute's reach, with some believing it to be little more than a codification of the common law action for deceitful advertising, it is now settled that it creates a new statutory tort of broader scope, which requires neither proof of literal or obvious falsehood, nor of intent to deceive.... "S.43(a) of the Lanham Act encompasses more than blatant falsehoods. It embraces 'innuendo, indirect intimations, and ambiguous suggestions' evidenced by the consuming public's misapprehension of the hard facts underlying an advertisement."...

The first question of law we must address is whether a plaintiff can prevail under the Lanham Act by showing simply that the defendant's advertising claims about the effectiveness of its OTC drug are inadequately substantiated under federal guidelines, without also showing that the claims are literally false or are misleading to the consuming public. Sandoz's prime contention on appeal is that it can.

The FTC has the authority under Sections 5 and 12 of the FTC Act ... to find that an inadequately substantiated advertising claim regarding a non-prescription drug is deceptive or misleading, and thus illegal.... Sandoz argues that the language in the FTC Act prohibiting "any false advertising" is functionally indistinguishable from the language in the Lanham Act prohibiting "any false description or representation."... Therefore, according to Sandoz, "it would be absurd" to conclude that an inadequately substantiated claim can violate Sections 5 and 12 of the FTC Act but not Section 43(a) of the Lanham Act....

The key distinctions between the FTC and a Lanham Act plaintiff turns on the burdens of proof and the deference accorded these respective litigants. The FTC, as a plaintiff, can rely on its own determination of deceptiveness. In contrast, a Lanham Act plaintiff must prove deceptiveness in court. As the Supreme Court has stated:

> As an administrative agency which deals continually with cases in the area, the [FTC] is often in a better position than are courts to determine when a practice is "deceptive" within the meaning of the Act. This Court has frequently stated that the [FTC's] judgment is to be given great weight by reviewing courts. This admonition is especially true with respect to allegedly deceptive advertising since the finding of a S.5 violation in this field rests so heavily on inference and pragmatic judgment....

Sandoz's invitation to blur the distinctions between the FTC and a Lanham Act plaintiff would require us to ignore the separate jurisprudence that has evolved under each Act, and the sound reasoning that underlies it. We decline the invitation. We hold that it is not sufficient for a Lanham Act plaintiff to show only that the defendant's advertising claims of its own drug's effectiveness are inadequately substantiated under FDA guidelines; the plaintiff must also show that the claims are literally false or misleading to the public....

Sandoz takes issue with the district court's conclusion that it had failed to meet its burden of proof. The district court relied on the lack of a consumer survey, which is a common mode of proof in these cases. Sandoz submits that consumer surveys or some other surrogate for the FTC's expertise are needed only when an advertising claim is ambiguous, not when it is clear but inadequately substantiated. However, there is not legal support for Sandoz's theory....

As noted above, Sandoz failed to advance actual evidence of consumer misinterpretation. Furthermore, Sandoz's counsel in oral argument before this court admitted that Sandoz had not proven either that the ingredient in Pediatric 44 designed to shield cough receptors was ineffective or that Vicks's advertising claim was literally false. The district court carefully analyzed the evidence of Vicks's theoretical and empirical justifications for its advertising claims, and we cannot say that its finding that Sandoz did not establish that consumers were misled was clearly erroneous. The court had ample evidence before it, including the contents of Vicks's advertisements, the statements of multiple experts, and the results of various tests performed using Pediatric 44....

For the foregoing reasons, the district court's findings of fact are not clearly erroneous, and it was correct in rejecting Sandoz's legal claims. It is clear, therefore, that the district court did not abuse its discretion in finding that Sandoz could not prove a likelihood of success on the merits. The judgment of the district court will be affirmed.

The U.S. Courts of Appeal were badly divided on the question of protection of the use of a color to identify a product. The traditional rule was that a color cannot be trademarked, and that therefore anyone can use any color for its own product, even if another manufacturer was using that same color first. In one famous case, however, the Federal Circuit Court of Appeals held that a maker of home insulation could not use pink for its fiberglass product, since there would be a likelihood of confusion with a competing Owens-Corning product. Owens-Corning had done extensive TV advertising to get buyers to identify pink insulation as its product, and the second manufacturer was simply trying to get a free ride on Owens-Corning's good will. This disagreement was resolved by the *Qualitex* decision, which appears in Chapter 25.

The *Two Pesos* case presents another kind of claim for trade dress infringement.

TWO PESOS, INC. v. TACO CABANA, INC.
112 S.Ct. 2753 (1992)

FACTS: Respondent Taco Cabana, Inc., operates a chain of fast-food restaurants in Texas. The restaurants serve Mexican food. The first Taco Cabana restaurant was opened in San Antonio in September 1978, and five more restaurants had been opened in San Antonio by 1985. Taco Cabana describes its Mexican trade dress as:

> "a festive eating atmosphere having interior dining and patio areas decorated with artifacts, bright colors, paintings, and murals. The patio includes interior and exterior areas with the interior patio capable of being sealed off from the outside patio by overhead garage doors. The stepped exterior of the building is a festive and vivid color scheme using top border paint and neon stripes. Bright awnings and umbrellas continue the theme."

In December 1985, a Two Pesos, Inc., restaurant was opened in Houston. Two Pesos adopted a motif very similar to the foregoing description of Taco Cabana's trade dress. Two Pesos restaurants expanded rapidly in Houston and other markets, but did not enter San Antonio. In 1986, Taco Cabana entered the Houston and Austin markets and expanded into other Texas cities, including Dallas and El Paso where Two Pesos was also doing business.

In 1987, Taco Cabana sued Two Pesos in the United States District Court for the Southern District of Texas for trade dress infringement under § 43(a) of the Lanham Act. Because, as the jury was told, Taco Cabana's trade dress was protected if it either was inherently distinctive or had acquired a secondary meaning, judgment was entered awarding damages to Taco Cabana. The Court of Appeals affirmed.

 JUSTICE WHITE:

Engrafting onto § 43(a) a requirement of secondary meaning for inherently distinctive trade dress ... would undermine the purposes of the Lanham Act. Protection of trade dress, no less than of trademarks, serves the Act's purpose to "secure to the owner of the mark the goodwill of his business and to protect the ability of consumers to distinguish among competing producers. National protection of trademarks is desirable, Congress concluded, because trademarks foster competition and the maintenance of quality by securing to the producer the benefits of good reputation...." By making more difficult the identification of a producer with its product, a secondary meaning requirement for a non-descriptive trade dress would hinder improving or maintaining the producer's competitive position.

Suggestions that under the [Court of Appeals' rule] the initial user of any shape or design would cut off competition from products of like design and shape are not persuasive. Only nonfunctional, distinctive trade dress is protected under § 43(a). The Fifth Circuit holds that a design is legally functional, and thus unprotectable, if it is one of a limited number of equally efficient options available to competitors and free competition would be unduly hindered by according the design trademark protection.... This serves to assure that competition will not be stifled by the exhaustion of a limited number of trade dresses.

On the other hand, adding a secondary meaning requirement could have anticompetitive effects, creating particular burdens on the start-up of small companies. It would present special difficulties for a business, such as respondent, that seeks to start a new product in a limited area and then expand into new markets. Denying protection for inherently distinctive non-functional trade dress until after secondary meaning has been established would allow a competitor, which has not adopted a distinctive trade dress of its own, to appropriate the originator's dress in other markets and to deter the originator from expanding into and competing in these areas.

As noted above, petitioner concedes that protecting an inherently distinctive trade dress from its inception may be critical to new entrants to the market and that withholding protection until secondary meaning has been established would be contrary to the goals of the Lanham Act. Petitioner specifically suggests, however, that the solution is to dispense with the requirement of secondary meaning for a reasonable, but brief period at the outset of the use of a trade dress.... If § 43(a) does not require secondary meaning at the outset of a business' adoption of trade dress, there is no basis in the statute to support the suggestion that such a requirement comes into being after some unspecified time.

We agree with the Court of Appeals that proof of secondary meaning is not required to prevail on a claim under § 43(a) of the Lanham Act where the trade dress at issue is inherently distinctive, and accordingly the judgment of that court is affirmed.

THE FTC AND UNFAIR TRADE PRACTICES

Section 5 of the Federal Trade Commission Act of 1914 prohibited unfair methods of competition and unfair or deceptive acts or practices. The FTC's original enforcement emphasis was against deceptive advertising. Many of the states had statutes that outlawed deceptive advertising, but enforcement varied from state to state. This sort of violation obviously injured both competitors and consumers, so it was probably a good place to start. While the FTC's approach to unfair methods of competition has become much broader over the years, especially since the 1970s, it continues to be alert for false and deceptive advertising.

A "comparative" commercial is being tested in the following case.

KRAFT, INC. v. FEDERAL TRADE COMMISSION
970 F.2d 311 (Seventh Circuit, 1992).

FACTS: The FTC determined that Kraft, in an advertising campaign, had misrepresented information regarding the amount of calcium contained in Kraft Singles American Pasteurized Process Cheese Food ("Singles") relative to the calcium content in five ounces of milk and in imitation cheese slices. The FTC ordered Kraft to cease and desist from making these misrepresentations and Kraft filed this petition for review.

Three categories of cheese compete in the individually wrapped process slice market: process cheese food slices, imitation slices, and substitute slices. Process cheese food slices, also known as "dairy slices," must contain at least 51 percent natural cheese by federal regulation. Imitation cheese slices, by contrast, contain little or no natural cheese and consist primarily of water, vegetable oil, flavoring agents, and fortifying agents. While imitation slices are as healthy as process cheese food slices in some nutrient categories, they are as a whole considered "nutritionally inferior" and must carry the label "imitation." Substitute slices fit somewhere in between; they fall short of the natural cheese content of process cheese food slices yet are nutritionally superior to imitation slices. Consistent with FTC usage, we refer to both imitation and substitute slices as "imitation" slices.

Kraft Singles are process cheese food slices. In the early 1980s, Kraft began losing market share to an increasing number of imitation slices that were advertised as both less expense and equally nutritious as dairy slices like Singles. Kraft responded with a series of advertisements, collectively known as the "Five Ounces of Milk" campaign, designed to inform consumers that Kraft Singles cost more than imitation slices because they are made from five ounces of milk rather than less expense ingredients. The ads also focused on the calcium content of Kraft Singles in an effort to capitalize on growing consumer interest in adequate calcium consumption.

The FTC filed a complaint against Kraft charging that this advertising campaign materially misrepresented the calcium content and relative calcium benefit of Kraft Singles. The FTC Act makes it unlawful to engage in unfair or deceptive commercial practices, or to induce consumers to purchase certain products through advertising that is misleading in a material respect. Thus, an advertisement is deceptive under the Act if it is likely to mislead consumers, acting reasonably under the circumstances, in a material respect. In implementing this standard, the Commission examines the overall net impression of an ad and engages in a three-part inquiry: (1) what claims are conveyed in the ad, (2) are those claims false or misleading, and (3) are those claims material to prospective consumers.

Two facts are critical to understanding the allegations against Kraft. First, although Kraft does use five ounces of milk in making each Kraft Single, roughly 30 percent of the calcium contained in the milk is lost during processing. Second, the vast majority of imitation slices sold in the United States contain 15 percent of the U.S. Recommended Daily Allowance (RDA) of calcium per ounce, roughly the same amount contained in Kraft Singles. Specifically then, the FTC complaint alleged that the challenged advertisements made two implied claims, neither of which was true: (1) that a slice of Kraft Singles contains the same amount of calcium as five ounces of milk (the "milk equivalency" claim), and (2) that Kraft Singles contain more calcium than do most imitation cheese slices (the "imitation superiority" claim).

 CIRCUIT JUDGE FLAUM:

Kraft makes numerous arguments on appeal, but its principal claim is that the FTC erred as a matter of law in not requiring extrinsic evidence of consumer deception. Without such evidence, Kraft claims: (1) that the FTC had no objective basis for determining if its ads actually contained the implied claims alleged, and (2) that the FTC's order chills constitutionally protected commercial speech. Alternatively, Kraft contends that substantial evidence does not support the FTC's finding that the Class Picture ads contain the milk equivalency claim. Finally, Kraft maintains that even if it did make the alleged milk equivalency and imitation superiority claims, substantial evidence does not support the FTC's finding that these claims were material to consumers....

In determining what claims are conveyed by a challenged advertisement, the Commission relies on two sources of information: its own viewing of the ad and extrinsic evidence. Its practice is to view the ad first and, if it is unable on its own to determine with confidence what claims are conveyed in a challenged ad, to turn to extrinsic evidence.... The most convincing extrinsic evidence is a survey "of what consumers thought upon reading the advertisement in question,"...but the Commission also relies on other forms of extrinsic evidence including consumer testimony, expert opinion, and copy tests of ads....

Kraft has no quarrel with this approach when it comes to determining whether an ad conveys express claims, but contends that the FTC should be required, as a matter of law, to rely on extrinsic evidence rather than its own subjective analysis in all cases involving allegedly implied claims. The basis for this argument is that implied claims, by definition, are not self-evident from the face of an ad. This, combined with the fact that consumer perceptions are shaped by a host of external variables—including their social and educational backgrounds, the environment in which they view the ad, and prior experiences with the product advertised...makes review of implied claims by a five-member commission inherently unreliable. The Commissioners, Kraft argues, are simply incapable of determining what implicit messages consumers are likely to perceive in an ad. Making matters worse, Kraft asserts that the Commissioners are predisposed to find implied claims because the claims have been identified in the complaint, rendering it virtually impossible for them to reflect the perceptions of unbiased consumers....

Kraft buttresses its argument by pointing to the use of extrinsic evidence in an analogous context: cases brought under S.43(a) of the Lanham Act.... Courts hearing deceptive advertising claims under that Act, which provides a private right of action for deceptive advertising, generally require extrinsic proof that an advertisement conveys an implied claim.... Were this a Lanham Act case, a reviewing court in all likelihood would have relied on extrinsic evidence of consumer perceptions. While this disparity is sometimes justified on grounds of advertising "expertise"—the FTC presumably possesses more of it than courts ... —Kraft maintains this justification is an illusory one in that the FTC has no special expertise in discerning consumer perceptions.... Indeed, proof of the FTC's inexpertise abounds: false advertising cases makes up a small part of the Commission's workload ..., most commissioners have little prior experience in advertising ..., and the average tenure of commissioners is very brief.... That evidence aside, no amount of expertise in Kraft's view can replace the myriad of external variables affecting consumer perceptions. Here, the Commission found implied claims based solely on its own intuitive reading of the ads (although it did reinforce that conclusion by examining the proffered extrinsic evidence). Had the Commission fully and properly relied on available extrinsic evidence, Kraft argues it would have conclusively found that consumers do not perceive the milk equivalency and imitation superiority claims in the ads.

While Kraft's arguments may have some force as a matter of policy, they are unavailing as a matter of law. Courts, including the Supreme Court, have uniformly rejected imposing such a requirement on the FTC,...and we decline to do so as well. We hold that the Commission may rely on its own reasoned analysis to determine what claims, including implied ones, are conveyed in a challenged advertisement, so long as those claims are reasonably clear from the face of the advertisement....

Our holding does not diminish the force of Kraft's argument as a policy matter, and, indeed, the extensive body of commentary on the subject makes a compelling argument that reliance on extrinsic evidence should be the rule rather than the exception. Along those lines, the Commission would be well-advised to adopt a consistent position on consumer survey methodology—advertisers and the FTC, it appears, go round and round on this issue—so that any uncertainty is reduced to an absolute minimum....

For these reasons, we hold that the specific prohibitions imposed on Kraft in the FTC's cease and desist order are not broader than reasonably necessary to prevent deception and hence not violative of the first amendment. We wish to reemphasize the limits of this order to assuage any fears Kraft might have about compliance. The subject of Kraft's ads (i.e., the milk and calcium content of Singles) is obviously a perfectly legitimate subject of commercial advertising. It is only the manner of presentation that needs rectification. Kraft is free to continue advertising the milk and calcium content in its cheese products, and it can avoid future violations by correcting the misleading elements identified in the FTC's decision. Kraft could, for example, redesign the Skimp and Class Picture ads so that calcium content is accurately presented (i.e., "each Kraft Single contains the calcium equivalent of 3.5 ounces of milk") or it could add prominent, unambiguous disclosures about calcium loss in processing, either of which would put it in full compliance with the order.

As it moved beyond false advertising cases, the FTC's basic difficulty became one of definition. Just what did its statute mean? What exactly are *unfair* methods of competition? To some persons, "all's fair in Love and War"—and Business. The drafters of the statute had clearly left the phrase vague and flexible, so that the FTC would be able to deal with new unfair devices as they were developed. If only specific practices had been prohibited, business firms and their lawyers could quickly circumvent the act by restructuring their operations. Although the uncertainty was intentional, it has nevertheless caused problems.

Unfair methods clearly include violations of the Sherman Act and the Clayton Act (including Robinson-Patman) and incipient Sherman Act violations. The Supreme Court has also held that methods that violate the "basic policy" of the Sherman and Clayton Acts, even though not specifically listed in the acts, can be reached under Section 5. Practices that injure customers can be prosecuted without necessarily showing that any competitor has been injured. All types of behavior that might be classified as "bad business morals" can also be reached under Section 5, including such things as tampering with a competitor's goods, deceptive packaging, and delivering unordered goods. In 1972 the Supreme Court decided that the FTC had general rule-making power; that is, the FTC did not have to proceed on a case-by-case basis but could promulgate rules of behavior, just like the NLRB, the SEC, and other agencies. Since then, the FTC has been quite aggressive in adopting rules for competitive conduct. Most recently, there have been attempts in Congress to curb the FTC's growing power over commercial practices.

Other FTC Jurisdiction. The FTC was also given the responsibility for enforcing a series of labeling acts passed in the 1940s and 1950s; the Wool Products Act (1941), the Fur Products Act (1952), the Textile Fibre Act (1958), and the Flammable Fabrics Act (1954). The enforcement mechanisms include both cease and desist orders and criminal penalties. The FTC also enforces the 1975 Magnuson-Moss Warranty Act, discussed in Chapter 16.

Probably because Congress felt that more specific engineering and technical expertise was needed to deal with the problem, the FTC was not given enforcement responsibility under the 1972 Consumer Product Safety Act. A new Consumer Product Safety Commission (CPSC) and a new Advisory Council were created by the act. The CPSC collects and distributes data on product safety and product-related injuries. Injured consumers can bring suits in the U.S. courts if the alleged damages are $10,000 or more, and the further distribution of the "unsafe" product may be enjoined. The manufacturer may also be fined $2,000 for each violation, but the total fine for a single product cannot exceed $500,000.

PRICE DISCRIMINATION

The Statutory Offense. One of the most difficult antitrust problems occurs when a seller charges different prices to two or more buyers for the same type of goods. As mentioned earlier, this is price discrimination. The original Section 2 of the Clayton Act of 1914 did contain a provision aimed at the seller who cuts prices in competitive locations and maintains higher prices everywhere else. The early cases, however, interpreted this section to prohibit only discrimination between *competing* buyers, and thus there were few prosecutions under it.

By the mid-1930s, grocery store chains had become very powerful buyers and were demanding and getting quantity discounts. As the Supreme Court noted in the *Morton Salt* case, volume discounts of the large chains enabled them to sell Morton Salt at retail for less than the price at which independent wholesalers could sell it to their retail-store customers. In 1936, under intense pressure from small independent retailers and wholesalers, Congress passed the Robinson-Patman Act to amend Section 2 of the Clayton Act. As noted previously, the Robinson-Patman Act is not fully consistent with the idea of free and open competition; it was designed to prevent large buyers from gaining an undue market price advantage, and thus it has the indirect effect of stifling some price competition at the retail level.

The Robinson-Patman Act basically states that it is unlawful for any seller to discriminate in price between different purchasers, if the sale involves goods and not services, if the sales constitute interstate rather than intrastate commerce, if the goods are of like kind and quality, and provided the effect of such discrimination may be to substantially lessen competition or tend to create a monopoly in any line of commerce.

The responsibility for prosecuting Robinson-Patman violations rests with the Federal Trade Commission. As is true with the other antitrust statutes, however, private parties who are injured by illegal price discrimination may bring their own lawsuits for damages.

There are three basic defenses to a charge of price discrimination under the Robinson-Patman Act. They are: (1) the "meeting competition" defense, (2) the "cost justification" defense, and (3) the "obsolete or perishable goods" defense.

In addition to these three statutory defenses, the party accused of price discrimination may also claim that there was no violation of the act to begin with—that is, that one of the statutory elements of the offense cannot be shown. For example, many manufacturers produce a product under their own brand name and also produce a chemically or physically identical product for a volume customer. The secondary product may be sold under the brand name of a large retailer, or may be sold as a generic product (Brand X). Must the manufacturer charge the same prices for these off-brand or generic products? If they are goods of "like grade and quality," the answer is yes. But are they? "Private label" products which are chemically the same were held to be of "like grade and quality" in 1966.

Nonprofit Institutions Exemption.

Only two years after passage of Robinson-Patman, Congress adopted the Nonprofit Institutions Act, as an amendment. The NIA exempts from the application of Robinson-Patman "purchases of their supplies for their own use by schools, . . . hospitals, and charitable institutions not operated for profit." Manufacturers and other suppliers can thus provide special prices to these kinds of nonprofit agencies without violating Robinson-Patman.

Even here there have been definitional problems. The agencies themselves are usually easy enough to categorize. (There may be some question about some of the self-defined "nonprofit" agencies which solicit funds on television and elsewhere.) But there are some tough issues involved in deciding what is an agency's "own use." Can professors get the special discount, as well as the school itself? How about students? How about participants in a one-day seminar at the school? How about librarians at the school? Noninstructional staff? Spouses? "Significant others"? Alumni? Some difficult line-drawing may have to be done when these various groups also demand the special pricing.

The "Meeting Competition" Defense.

Recognizing that in many cases a seller firm must cut its price to meet a lower price quoted by a competitor, Congress specifically provided for such a defense. A seller relying on this defense must be acting in good faith; knowledge that the competitor's lower price is itself illegal would probably prevent a finding of good faith.

The "Cost Justification" Defense.

In an important proviso to Section 2(a), Congress indicated that it did not wish to outlaw price differentials that could be justified by cost savings. If genuine cost savings could be realized on larger orders, a seller ought to be able to pass them along to the buyer. While the theory of this defense is specifically stated in Section 2(a), actual *proof* of the defense has been next to impossible in practice, as *Texaco* discovered in the next case.

TEXACO, INC. v. HASBROUCK
110 S. Ct. 2535 (1990)

FACTS: Texaco is a large integrated oil company. Between 1972 and 1981, it sold gasoline at its retail tank wagon prices to Hasbrouck and eleven other independent Texaco retailers, but gave large discounts to Gull and Dompier. Gull resold the gas under its own name. Dompier resold the gas to retailers as Texaco gas. Both distributors picked up the gasoline from Texaco and delivered it to their retail outlets; neither had any large storage facilities. Texaco also paid Dompier for delivering the gasoline to retailers. Texaco had refused a request by two of the plaintiffs to pick up their own gasoline. The shares of Gull and Dompier in the Spokane market increased dramatically, while the plaintiffs' shares declined. Plaintiffs sued in 1976, alleging violations of the Robinson-Patman Act. Texaco argued that, since Gull and Dompier were performing some wholesaler functions, they could be given a "wholesaler discount." The trial court, after a jury trial, awarded treble damages of $449,900, and the Court of Appeals affirmed.

 JUSTICE STEVENS:

The Robinson-Patman Act contains no express reference to functional discounts. It does contain two affirmative defenses that provide protection for two categories of discounts—those that are justified by savings in the seller's cost of manufacture, delivery, or sale, and those that represent a good faith response to the equally low prices of a competitor.... As the case comes to us, neither of those defenses is available to Texaco....

Texaco's first argument would create a blanket exemption for all functional discounts. Indeed, carried to its logical conclusion, it would exempt all price differentials except those given to competing purchasers. The primary basis for Texaco's argument is the following comment by Congressman Utterback, an active sponsor of the Act: "... [W]here the goods are sold in different markets and the conditions affecting those markets set different price levels for them, the sale to different customers at those different prices would not constitute a discrimination within the meaning of this bill...."

We have previously considered this excerpt from the legislative history, and have refused to draw from it the conclusion which Texaco proposes.... Although the excerpt does support Texaco's argument, we remain persuaded that the argument is foreclosed by the text of the Act itself. In the context of a statute that plainly reveals a concern with competitive consequences at different levels of distribution, and carefully defines specific affirmative defenses, it would be anomalous to assume that the Congress intended the term "discriminate" to have such a limited meaning....

Since we have already decided that a price discrimination within the meaning of § 2(a) "is merely a price difference," we must reject Texaco's first argument....

[A]n injury to competition may be inferred from evidence that some purchasers had to pay their supplier "substantially more for their goods than their competitors had to pay...." Texaco ... argues that this presumption should not apply to differences between prices charged to wholesalers and those charged to retailers.... [T]his argument endorses the position advocated thirty-five years ago in the Report of the Attorney General's National Committee to Study the Antitrust Laws....

The hypothetical predicate for the Committee's entire discussion of functional discounts is a price differential "that merely accords due recognition and reimbursement for actual marketing functions." Such a discount is not illegal. In this case, however, both the District Court and the Court of Appeals concluded that even without viewing the evidence in the light most favorable to [plaintiffs], there was no substantial evidence indicating that the discounts to Gull and Dompier constituted a reasonable reimbursement for their actual marketing functions.... Indeed, Dompier was separately compensated for its hauling function, and neither Gull nor Dompier maintained any significant storage facilities....

The evidence indicates, moreover, that Texaco affirmatively encouraged Dompier to expand its retail business and that Texaco was fully informed about the persistent and marketwide consequences of its own pricing policies. Indeed, its own executives recognized that the dramatic impact on the market was almost entirely attributable to the magnitude of the distributor discount and the hauling allowance.... The special facts of this case thus make it peculiarly difficult for Texaco to claim that it is being held liable for the independent pricing decision of Gull and Dompier.

The "Obsolete or Perishable Goods" Defense. This defense is a rather obvious one. A seller who has obsolete or perishable goods needs to get rid of them for the best price. Also, since the quantity of these goods is limited, they present little likelihood of any substantial lessening of competition in the market.

PREDATORY PRICING

The Robinson-Patman Act also made it illegal "to sell ... goods at unreasonably low prices for the purpose of destroying competition or eliminating a competitor." The courts and commentators have usually referred to this practice as "predatory" price-cutting. Such actions might also be interpreted as an attempt to monopolize, and thus a violation of Section 2 of the Sherman Act. Here again, there are definitional problems. What is an *unreasonably* low price? Isn't price competition to be encouraged, rather than stifled? Don't we want customers to have the benefit of lower prices? As usual, different judges have different ideas about how much price competition to allow.

One indication the courts have used in such cases is evidence that the product is being priced below its cost of production. ("We lose a little bit on each item, but we make it up on the volume.") A big firm may be able to stand such losses on one of many product lines, or in one limited local market; it simply raises prices on those items where it has no competition. The small single-product, or local-area firm cannot absorb such losses indefinitely, but if it does not match the price cuts of its larger rivals, it will lose sales anyway. The small firm is thus driven out of business, and the large firm is then free to charge whatever it wants, since there is no more competition—or so the theory goes.

These cases can involve some fairly sophisticated economic and accounting concepts, and there is disagreement as to what should count as "costs." Traditionally, the courts used a concept of total costs—both variable costs for labor and materials and fixed costs for such things as buildings and research. In 1975, Harvard law professors Phillip Areeda and Donald Turner suggested that the legal test for predatory pricing should be based only on *variable costs*. The fixed costs would be incurred anyway, and a business could very well decide to sell additional units at a price that covered variable costs for perfectly legitimate reasons. The company would probably wish to keep its workers employed and to maintain or increase its market share by making additional sales at a price that covered the variable costs. A number of U.S. Courts of Appeals have adopted the Areeda-Turner analysis. In those circuits it has become more difficult to prove a charge of predatory pricing.

SIGNIFICANCE OF THIS CHAPTER

Pricing decisions are at the heart of the competitive process and are the essence of the free enterprise system. Our national laws nonetheless impose significant restrictions on a business's freedom to make such decisions. Even though the Robinson-Patman Act seems outdated and incompatible with a free marketplace, it lurks in the statute books, waiting to trap the unwary marketer. Persons responsible for pricing and other marketing decisions need to be aware of these basic rules of the game.

Likewise, while the FTC Act does not provide a complete list of "unfair methods of competition," a marketing executive can get a good idea of the outer boundaries by reading some of the landmark cases. This chapter is designed to provide a sensitivity for these legal boundaries on competition.

PROBLEMS FOR DISCUSSION

1. The FTC, after a hearing, ordered Standard to cease and desist from its practice of selling its Red Crown gasoline to four comparatively large "jobber" customers at tank-car prices which were 1½ cents per gallon less than the tank-wagon prices which it charged retail service stations in the Detroit area. The four jobbers were free to resell at retail or wholesale. Each one, at some time, had resold some gasoline at retail; one now did so exclusively. Two of the jobbers had cut prices at the retail level or to their wholesalers. Standard claimed that it had had to reduce jobber prices to keep these customers, since other refiners had offered similar price cuts. The Court of Appeals ordered enforcement of the order after modifying it slightly. Standard requested certiorari.

   How should the Supreme Court rule? Discuss.

2. Utah Pie was a small Utah corporation which made and sold fresh and frozen dessert pies. It started selling frozen pies in 1987, and it built a plant in 1988. It marketed frozen pies under its own name, and it also made pies for grocery stores to sell under their labels. The frozen pie market grew rapidly; Utah's share for 1988 was 66.5 percent, but for the next three years its shares were 34.3 percent, 45.5 percent, and 45.3 percent. Continental and two other large national firms—Pet and Carnation—engaged in local price-cutting on their frozen pies at various times during the four-year period involved in this suit. Utah's pies were usually the lowest in price because Utah's factory was locally situated. Utah's whole-sale prices dropped from $4.15 per dozen to $2.75 per dozen some forty-four months later, when it filed this suit. The jury found for the defendants on the conspiracy charge, but it found for Utah on the price discrimination charge. Judgment was entered for damages and attorney fees. but the Court of Appeals reversed.

   Is there a violation here? Explain.

3. Stiffel secured design and mechanical patents on a pole lamp. Shortly thereafter, Sears began to market a substantially identical lamp. The retail price of the Sears lamp was about the same as the wholesale price of the Stiffel lamp. Stiffel sued in U.S. District Court, alleging: (1) that the Sears copy infringed Stiffel's patents, and (2) that the Sears copy caused confusion in the trade and thereby constituted unfair competition under state (Illinois) law. The District Court declared the Stiffel patents invalid due to lack of invention but it upheld the unfair competition charge and awarded an injunction and damages. The Court of Appeals affirmed, and Sears asked the U.S. Supreme Court for a writ of certiorari.

   What decision, and why?

4. The FTC issued a cease-and-desist order which directed Mary Carter to stop advertising its paint-selling policy as "buy one, get one free." The FTC said that Mary Carter had never sold single cans of paint but had always sold *two* cans for the advertised price, so that the price of a single can was not really the advertised $6.98. Thus Mary Carter had misrepresented the true nature of the transaction by calling one can "free." Mary Carter was not permitted to prove that the quality of its paint was in fact as good as or superior to other paints selling for $6.98 per can. The U.S. Fifth Circuit Court of Appeals set aside the order, and the FTC appealed.

   Is this decision correct? Why or why not?

5. The Borden Company produces and sells evaporated milk under the Borden name. At the same time Borden packs and markets evaporated milk under various private brands owned by its customers. This milk is physically and chemically identical with the milk it distributes under its own brand, but it is sold at both the wholesale and retail level at prices regularly below those obtained for the Borden brand milk. The FTC found the milk sold under the Borden and the private labels to be of like grade and quality as required for the applicability of the Robinson-Patman Act and held the price differential to be discriminatory and to have an adverse effect on commerce. The FTC issued a cease-and-desist order. The Court of Appeals set aside the FTC's order on the ground that the customer label milk was not of the same grade and quality as the milk sold under the Borden brand. The U.S. Supreme Court granted certiorari.

   How will this appeal be decided and why?

Chapter 40
Labor Relations Law

We have already discussed some of the basic legal rules involved in the employer-employee relationship in Chapter 30. We assumed in that discussion that the employer was negotiating with each employee or prospective employee on an individual basis. Many employees, of course, are union members and rely on their unions to negotiate on their behalf for improved wages, hours, and conditions of employment. In order to promote peaceful collective bargaining, the national government regulates this process in some detail. While the states may not enact regulations that conflict with the national labor law system, they are free to regulate collective bargaining by state and local government employees and by any other persons whose activities do not affect interstate commerce.

National and state governments have also enacted a variety of laws which provide benefits and safety standards for employees. Minimum wage laws, the Social Security system, the Employee Retirement Income Security Act, the Occupational Safety and Health Act, and similar laws provide required standards for the employee-employer relationship.

This chapter covers labor relations law and labor standards law. The next chapter will deal with the laws prohibiting discrimination in employment.

SOURCES OF LABOR LAW

Where does the law of employer-employee relationships originate? For many years, the employment contract was treated by the common law in much the same way as other types of contracts; it required offer and acceptance, consideration, and the other elements of a valid contract. It was a two-party contract, with each party having the freedom to accept or to reject the bargain offered by the other and with the parties being pretty much free to agree on any terms they chose. Specific legal rules also developed to cover this "master-servant" relationship, such as the employer's liability for torts committed by his or her servant within the scope of the employment and the employer's responsibility for furnishing a reasonably safe place in which to work. Much of the common law has now been displaced in this area, as both national and state governments have moved in aggressively to redefine this relationship.

Several broad, comprehensive national statutes exist in each of the two major divisions of labor law—*labor relations* and *labor standards*. There is also considerable state regulation of both areas, and the Fourteenth Amendment to the U.S. Constitution may be invoked if the state itself, or one of its agencies or instrumentalities, is directly involved in the relationship as the employer.

In the area of labor relations, the basic piece of national legislation is the National Labor Relations Act of 1935, as amended. The NLRA (also known as the Wagner Act) laid the cornerstone of national labor policy: belief in the process of collective bargaining between the employer and a representative freely chosen by his or her employees. The original act set out a series of forbidden employer "unfair labor practices," so that employers would not interfere with the selection of the bargaining representative and would be required to bargain. The governmental interference here was limited to providing the employees with a freely chosen bargaining representative; it was then up to the union to work out the terms and conditions of employment by bargaining with the employer.

Concern over excessive union power and abuses, coupled with a wave of strikes after World War II, led to the adoption of a series of comprehensive amendments in 1947—the Taft-Hartley Act (or Labor-Management Relations Act). Taft-Hartley set out a series of forbidden *union* unfair labor practices and attempted to ensure certain basic employer and employee rights—such as the employer's right to tell his or her side of the story to the employees and the employee's right to *refrain* from participating in union activity if he or she so chose. These amendments also permitted the several states to prohibit agreements between employer and union which require union membership as a condition of employment (**state right-to-work laws**).

Further disenchantment with union operations and evidence of widespread corruption in the internal management of unions, provided by nationally televised hearings of the McClellan subcommittee, resulted in 1959 in a second substantial revision of the NLRA. The Labor-Management Reporting and Disclosure Act (LMRDA), or Landrum-Griffin Act, again attempted to protect employers, individual employees, and the public from certain union abuses, particularly the abuse of exerting indirect pressure on a recalcitrant employer by involving third parties in the bargaining dispute. The LMRDA also placed certain requirements on the internal management of unions and union funds and provided machinery for dealing with so-called national emergency strikes.

As a result of these two sets of amendments, a good deal of the spirit of the original Wagner Act ("Let the union do it") has been dissipated. The rather considerable limitations contained in Taft-Hartley and Landrum-Griffin are not fully consistent with the free collective bargaining envisaged by the Wagner Act, and the law of labor relations thus becomes susceptible to radically different interpretations at several important points.

Labor standards legislation provides direct regulation of the terms and conditions of employment; in that sense, it limits the freedom of the employer and the union, as well as the individual employee, to set their own terms of association with each other. The Wagner Act represented a basic commitment of national labor policy to the collective bargaining process, but the commitment has never been complete or without qualification. The mandatory "social security" system is itself an important piece of labor standards legislation, since it provides a required arrangement for retirement, disability, and dependent benefits. Social security can be supplemented, but not displaced, through collective bargaining.

The main piece of national **wages and hours legislation** is the Fair Labor Standards Act (FLSA) of 1938, as amended. Once again, it sets boundaries to the parties' freedom of contract by specifying certain minimum wages and required overtime which must be paid (even if there are persons ready and willing to work for less). Also included in this general category are several national statutes requiring the payment of "prevailing minimum wages" in a particular industry, as determined by the secretary of labor. The two such acts with broadest scope are the Walsh-Healy Act, for manufacturers and dealers supplying the national government with supplies valued at $10,000 or more, and the Davis-Bacon Act, covering building contracts with the national government for more than $2,000. Similar provisions have been inserted in national grant-in-aid legislation for the construction of airports, highways, housing for defense personnel, and urban renewal projects.

What is potentially the most far-reaching (and therefore the most costly) piece of "labor standards" legislation ever enacted became law in 1970: the Occupational Safety and Health Act (OSHA). This act is designed to "assure as far as possible every working man and woman in the nation safe and healthful working conditions," by giving the secretary of labor very broad powers to adopt "standards" which will in effect be mandatory health and safety practices. To ensure compliance, the employer's premises are subject to unannounced inspection by "the man from OSHA," either on employee complaint or by random selection. Injunctive relief and criminal penalties are provided for violations.

In 1974, Congress passed another important piece of labor legislation—the Employment Retirement Income Security Act. ERISA establishes a new government agency, financed by contributions from employers with pension plans, to guarantee payment of earned pension benefits. It does not require any employer to establish a pension plan, but when a company does so, the plan must meet certain standards for the funding and management of assets and for the vesting of benefits. ERISA is thus a significant new protection for the more than 30 million workers who are covered by its provisions.

The *Seaman* case applies these ERISA rules.

SEAMAN v. ARVIDA REALTY SALES
985 F.d 543 (11th Cir., 1993)

FACTS: Plaintiff Patricia Seaman sued her former employer, Arvida Realty Sales, Inc., alleging that she was employed as a real estate salesperson and pursuant to her employment contract was entitled to health insurance coverage and participation in a 401(k) pension plan to which she and Arvida contributed. She alleged that she was notified that she and other salespersons would be terminated in order that Arvida could eliminate the cost of providing the health insurance coverage and the employer's contributions to the 401(k) plan, although the health insurance and 401(k) plans were continued in effect. She stated that she and other terminated employees were offered contracts as independent contractors, which did not provide for health insurance or 401(k) participation. She refused to sign the new contracts and was terminated. Arvida acknowledges that Seaman was terminated because she refused to accept the change in status from employee to independent contractor and the concomitant changes in benefits.

Seaman charged that Arvida's conduct violated ERISA. The District Court agreed with Arvida that Seaman's entitlement to health insurance and to future participation in the pension plan were not vested or accrued benefits, therefore elimination of these benefits was not prohibited by ERISA. The court, therefore, dismissed the ERISA claim on the ground that plaintiff's termination did not affect § 510 of ERISA. Seaman appealed.

Section 510 of ERISA provides:

> It shall be unlawful for any person to discharge ... a participant or beneficiary for exercising any right to which he is enticed under the provision of an employee benefit plan ... or for the purpose of interfering with the attainment of any right to which such participant may become entitled under the plan.

 SENIOR CIRCUIT JUDGE GODBOLD:

Arvida relies on *Phillips v. Amoco Oil Co.*, as authority that § 510 does not extend to contingent non-vested benefits. The court of appeals decision in *Phillips* states: "as we noted above, the employer may terminate previously offered contingent non-vested benefits." That statement does not, however, establish that § 510 is never applicable to non-vested benefits. *Phillips* involved a concern that was sold for reasons independent of terminating employee benefits and terminated its pension plan. Amoco sold its propane gas business not for the purpose of interfering with ERISA rights but rather because of legitimate business concerns that stemmed from regulations that limited the price that it could charge for liquid propane. Some employees were terminated in the transaction, but this was "an incidental result of a legitimate business transaction which ERISA was not designed to regulate or prohibit." The district court noted that the purpose of § 510 is to "prohibit ... adverse treatment of a particular employee which amounts to or threatens 'constructive discharge,' and which is carried out for the purpose of interfering with the employee's attainment of future benefits or punishing the employee for the exercise of protected rights."

We agree with the reasoning of the Fourth Circuit in *Conkwright* which held that Congress did not intend to leave employees unprotected once their rights were vested and that § 510 prohibits the employer from discharging an employee for the purpose of preventing the employee from receiving additional vested benefits.

Our holding that an employer may not terminate an employee for the purpose of avoiding payment of plan benefits should not be interpreted to restrict the employer's right to modify a plan.

The combined effect of our holding today is an interpretation of ERISA that prohibits employers from discharging employees to avoid paying benefits but permits employers to reduce or terminate non-vested benefits simply by changing the terms of a plan. This result may appear anomalous, but an examination of ERISA and its legislative history reveals that it is the result intended by Congress. ERISA's legislative history recognizes employers' need for flexibility in the design of benefits plans. ERISA therefore does not require employers to provide a retirement plan at all, or, when an employer chooses to provide benefits, regulate the substantive content of welfare-benefit plans.

If the employer decides to offer benefits, it must allow its employees to take advantage of the plan and must administer the plan in a nondiscriminatory fashion. But the employer can make the initial decision whether to offer any benefits and may even modify or terminate non-vested benefits at any time. Nevertheless, if Seaman's allegations are true Arvida has violated § 510. Arvida did not change the terms of its plan; rather, it threatened to terminate its salespeople unless they agreed to become independent contractors, performing the same job but ineligible to receive the benefits previously offered to them as employees and still offered to Arvida's remaining employees. Plaintiff was, in the exact language of § 510, discharged "for exercising [a] right to which [she was] entitled under the provisions of an employee benefit plan." To excuse this action would prevent § 510 from fulfilling its congressionally intended purpose. That Arvida, by changing the terms of its plan, lawfully could have deprived its salespeople of these benefits does not allow it to offer benefits but prevent its salespeople from taking advantage of those benefits on pain of discharge.

Reversed and remanded.

Labor legislation in a particular state may include all of the above types, plus some additions. Many states now have statutes regulating collective bargaining by public employees, some of which provide for compulsory arbitration of bargaining disputes which the parties are unable to resolve themselves. The states have also enacted workers' compensation laws, which provide a statutory scheme for compensating employees for virtually all job-related injuries. (A similar national statute, the Federal Employees' Compensation Act, covers U.S. government employees.) Finally, workers who have lost their jobs are provided with at least some temporary help through state systems of unemployment compensation.

LABOR RELATIONS LAW—MAJOR PROBLEM AREAS

Selection of a Bargaining Agent. Assuming that a group of employees have indicated a desire for union representation and that they are subject to NLRA jurisdiction, the first step in the procedure for selecting a bargaining agent is to define the extent of the bargaining unit. In some cases, where there is only one business location and where there is a substantial identity of interests among all concerned employees, this is an easy job.

Multiple jobsites create some definitional problems. What if one plant votes "no union" but a majority for all plants operated by the company votes in favor of a union? Do we decide plant by plant or company-wide? The NLRB has generally favored the company-wide approach.

How about employees with substantially different skills, interests, and professional identification? Are they all to be lumped together as an amorphous mass ("one big union"), or are they somehow to be split up (so that some smaller craft unions or even "no union" might have a better chance of winning the separate elections)? Conflicting equities can make it difficult to arrive at a "fair" resolution of these questions. The Board's general approach has been "one big union," meaning that a group of employees wishing to be excluded from the employer-wide unit must have some strong evidence of their "uniqueness."

In addition to determining the appropriate bargaining unit, the Board's pre-election hearing also decides which employees are entitled to vote and which unions will appear on the ballot. The original union petitioning for the election is required to present evidence of 30 percent support, typically by means of signature cards from the requisite number of employees. Any other union wishing to appear on the ballot need only show substantial interest, and the "no union" choice will appear automatically. The election is by secret ballot. The winner need only receive a majority of the votes actually cast. If there is no majority, a runoff election is held between the two choices receiving the highest vote totals. While a secret ballot election is clearly the preferred method and the one normally used, the board does have the power to grant bargaining rights to a union presenting signature cards from a majority, where the cards clearly indicate such an intent, where there has been no union misrepresentation of the purpose of the cards to the individual employees, and where the possibility of holding a fair election is lessened by the employer's serious unfair labor practices.

Section 7 of the NLRA gives employees "the right to self-organization, to form, join or assist labor organizations." Section 8(a)(1) then makes it an unfair labor practice for an employer to "interfere with, restrain or coerce employees in the exercise of the rights guaranteed in Section 7." Labor history contains many cases where unscrupulous employers used puppet unions to forestall genuine representation and to exploit their workers still further. The Board is vigorous and vigilant, therefore, in protecting these important organizing rights, so that the employer's conduct during an organizing campaign must now be circumspect to avoid an unfair labor practice charge. Taft-Hartley guarantees the employer's (and others') right of "free speech," so long as the employer does not make any threat of reprisal or promise any benefit, but the Board has ruled that such conduct may be a basis for invalidating a no-union vote, thus requiring a new election.

The *Lechmere* case discusses the union's right to organize on the employer's premises.

LECHMERE, INC. v. N.L.R.B.
112 S.Ct. 841 (1992)

FACTS: This case stems from the efforts of Local 919 of the United Food and Commercial Workers Union, AFL-CIO, to organize employees at a retail store in Newington, Connecticut, owned and operated by petitioner Lechmere, Inc. The store is located in the Lechmere Shopping Plaza, which occupies a roughly rectangular tract measuring approximately 880 feet from north to south and 740 feet from east to west. Lechmere's store is situated at the Plaza's south end, with the main parking lot to its north. A strip of thirteen smaller "satellite stores" not owned by Lechmere runs along the west side of the Plaza, facing the parking lot. To the Plaza's east (where the main entrance is located) runs the Berlin Turnpike, a four-lane divided highway. The parking lot, however, does not abut the Turnpike; they are separated by a 46-foot-wide grassy strip, broken only by the Plaza's entrance. The parking lot is owned jointly by Lechmere and the developer of the satellite stores. The grassy strip is public property (except for a four-foot-wide band adjoining the parking lot, which belongs to Lechmere).

The union began its campaign to organize the store's 200 employees, none of whom was represented by a union, in June 1987. After a full-page advertisement in a local newspaper drew little response, non-employee union organizers entered Lechmere's parking lot and began placing handbills on the windshields of cars parked in a corner of the lot used mostly by employees. Lechmere's manager immediately confronted the organizers, informed them that Lechmere prohibited solicitation or handbill distribution of any kind on its property, and asked them to leave. They did so, and Lechmere personnel removed the handbills. The union organizers renewed this handbilling effort in the parking lot on several subsequent occasions; each time they were asked to leave and the handbills were removed. The organizers then relocated to the public grassy strip, from where they attempted to pass out handbills to cars entering the lot during hours (before opening and after closing) when the drivers were assumed to be primarily store employees. For one month, the union organizers returned daily to the grassy strip to picket Lechmere; after that, they picketed intermittently for another six months. They also recorded the license plate numbers of cars parked in the employee parking area; with the cooperation of the Connecticut Department of Motor Vehicles, they thus secured the names and addresses of some forty-one nonsupervisory employees (roughly 20% of the store's total). The union sent four mailings to these employees; it also made some attempts to contact them by phone or home visits. These mailings and visits resulted in one signed union authorization card.

Alleging that Lechmere had violated the National Labor Relations Act by barring the non employee organizers from its property, the union filed an unfair labor practice charge with respondent National Labor Relations Board. An administrative law judge ruled in the union's favor.

The Board affirmed the ALJ's judgment and adopted the recommended order.

 JUSTICE THOMAS:

Section 7 of the NLRA provides in relevant part that "'[e]mployees shall have the right to self-organization, to form, join, or assist labor organizations....'" Section 8(a)(1) of the Act, in turn, makes it an unfair labor practice for an employer "to interfere with, restrain, or coerce employees in the exercise of rights guaranteed in [§7]...." By its plain terms, thus, the NLRA confers rights only on *employees* not on unions or their nonemployed organizers. In *NLRB v. Babock & Wilcox Co.* ... however, we recognized that insofar as the employees "right of self-organization depends in some measure on [their] ability ... to learn the advantages of self-organization from others," ... § 7 of the NLRA may, in certain limited circumstances, restrict an employer's right to exclude nonemployed union organizers from his property. It is the nature of those circumstances that we explore today....

In *Babock* ... we held that the Act drew a distinction "of substance," ... between the union activities of employees and nonemployees. In cases involving *employee* activities, we noted with approval, the Board "balanced the conflicting interests of employees to receive information on self-organization on the company's property from fellow employees during non-working time, with the employer's right to control the use of his property...." In cases involving *nonemployed* activities (like those at issue in *Babock* itself), however, the Board was not permitted to engage in the same balancing (and we reversed the Board for having done so). By reversing the Board's interpretation of the statute for failing to distinguish between the organizing activities of employees and nonemployees, we were saying ... that § 7 speaks to the issue of non-employee access to an employer's property, *Babcock's* teaching is straightforward: § 7 simply does not protect nonemployed union organizers except in the rare case where "the inaccessibility of employees makes ineffective the reasonable attempts by nonemployees to communicate with them through the usual channels...." Our reference to "reasonable" attempts was nothing more than a recognition that unions need not engage in extraordinary feats to communicate with inaccessible employees—not an endorsement of the view (which we expressly rejected) that the Act protects "reasonable" trespasses. Where reasonable alternative means of access exist § 7's guarantees do not authorize trespasses by nonemployed organizers, *even* ... under ... reasonable regulations established by the Board....

The threshold inquiry in this case, then, is whether the facts here justify application of *Babcock's* inaccessibility exception. The ALJ below observed that the facts herein convince me that reasonable alternative means [of communicating with Lechmere's employees] *were* available to the Union ... (emphasis added). Reviewing the ALJ's decision, ... however, the Board reached a different conclusion on this point, asserting that there was no reasonable, effective alternative means available for the Union to communicate its message to [Lechmere's] employees)....

We cannot accept the Board's conclusion, because it "rest[s] on erroneous legal foundations...." As we have explained, the exception to *Babcock's* rule is a narrow one. It does not apply wherever nontrespassory access to employees may be cumbersome or less-than-ideally effective, but only where "*the location of a plant and the living quarters of the employees* place the employees *beyond the reach* of reasonable union efforts to communicate with them...." *Babcock's* exception was crafted precisely to protect the § 7 rights of those employees who, by virtue of their employment, are isolated from the ordinary flow of information that characterizes our society. The union's burden of establishing such isolation is, as we have explained, a "heavy one," ... and one not satisfied by mere conjecture or the expression of doubts concerning the effectiveness of nontrespassory means of communication.

The Board's conclusion in this case that the union had no reasonable means short of trespass to make Lechmere's employees aware of its organizational efforts is based on a misunderstanding of the limited scope of this exception. Because the employees do not reside on Lechmere's property, they are presumptively not "beyond the reach" ... of the union's message. Although the employees live in a large metropolitan area (Greater Hartford), that fact does not in itself render them "inaccessible" in the sense contemplated by *Babcock*. Their accessibility is suggested by the union's success in contacting a substantial percentage of them directly, via mailings, phone calls and home visits. Such direct contact, of course, is not a necessary element of "reasonably effective" communication; signs or advertising also may suffice. In this case, the union tried advertising in local newspapers; the Board said that this was not reasonably effective because it was expensive and might not reach the employees.... Whatever the merits of that conclusion, other alternative means of communication were readily available. Thus, signs (displayed, for example, from the public grassy strip adjoining Lechmere's parking lot) would have informed the employees about the union's organizational efforts. (Indeed, union organizers picketed the shopping center's main entrance for months as employees came and went every day.) **Access** to employees, not *success* in winning them over, is the critical issue—although success, or lack thereof, may be relevant in determining whether reasonable access exists. Because the union in this case failed to establish the existence of any "unique obstacles"... that frustrated access to Lechmere's employees, the Board erred in concluding that Lechmere committed an unfair labor practice by barring the nonemployed organizers from its property.

The judgment of the First Circuit is therefore reversed, and enforcement of the Board's order denied.

Union Security and Membership. Once selected as the official bargaining agent, the union is then legally required to bargain for all employees in the unit, union and nonunion alike, as well as to process the grievances of all employees on an equal basis. Violation of this duty of equal and fair representation could lead to decertification of the union by the NLRB or to charges before the EEOC.

Because it is legally required to represent all, the union makes the superficially logical argument that all employees in the unit should be required to become union members in order to keep their jobs. This is the so-called **free rider argument**: No nonunion employee should get a free ride on union-won benefits at the expense of dues-paying fellow employees. The first answer to this argument is that the union not only agreed to accept this status; it aggressively sought it. And second, it should be possible to work up some fair compensation to the union for benefits actually conferred by it on nonunion employees, without forcing them to join and financially support an organization with which they may disagree fundamentally—philosophically, politically, and economically.

From a union's standpoint, the best union-security arrangement is the **closed shop**, where only union members are hired and where employees must remain union members to keep their jobs. The closed shop has been outlawed for nearly all industries, but the legally permitted **union shop** is almost as good. Under a union shop, the employee has an initial period of time after hiring, typically thirty days, to decide whether or not to join the union to keep the job. An employee who decides not to join is fired at the end of the trial period. In addition to the union shop, the union will probably also negotiate a contract provision for automatic payroll deduction of union dues.

Section 14(b) of Taft-Hartley gave the states the authority to ban compulsory unionism if they wished to do so; there are about twenty states with such right-to-work laws. Since Section 14(b) speaks of required "membership" in a union, some of these states permit the **agency shop**, under which an employee is not required to join the union but instead pays it a fee which supposedly represents the value of the union's services to him or her as a member of the bargaining unit. Other states in this group hold that the agency shop is illegal too, and in those states the original open shop prevails. With an **open shop**, each individual employee is legally free to decide whether or not to become, or remain, a union member, and the union leaders are thus responsible to the membership on a continuing basis. Labor's annual drive in Congress to repeal 14(b) has thus far been unsuccessful.

Scope of the Duty to Bargain. Section 8(a)(5) of the NLRA makes it an unfair labor practice for the employer to refuse to bargain collectively with the representative of his or her employees; Section 8(b)(3) contains a similar requirement for the chosen union representative. But the parties are *required* to bargain only as to items which are classified as **mandatory subjects** of collective bargaining. As to those items, not only is it a violation of the NLRA to refuse to bargain, but it is also legally permissible to insist on one's bargaining position as the price of an agreement. That is, where a mandatory subject is involved, either party can use all of the weapons at its command—strike, lockout, picketing, and so on—to enforce the bargaining demand.

What are these mandatory subjects? Generally, they comprise items designated as "wages, hours, and other terms and conditions of employment." Very few bargaining demands would not fall into this category. Pension, profit-sharing, and stock-purchase plans; bonuses and merit raises; seniority and retirement rules; prices for meals and housing furnished by the company; and union security arrangements—all have been ruled mandatory subjects.

Permissive subjects of collective bargaining are those which the parties are free to discuss if they *both* wish to, but which neither can insist on as the price of an agreement. Such insistence and/or the use of bargaining weapons would be a violation of the Section 8 duty to bargain and would subject the wrongdoer to unfair labor practice charges. Nearly all demands held to be merely permissive have related to the mechanics of the bargaining process itself, such as the size of the bargaining teams, or the requirement of a secret employee vote on ratification of the employer's last offer prior to a strike, or a secret ballot vote on ratification of the new contract. Product selection, distribution, and pricing have likewise thus far been held to be **management prerogatives** and thus not mandatory subjects for collective bargaining. But the contracting out of work which was formerly performed by members of the bargaining unit is a mandatory subject, and the NLRB has ordered the resumption of maintenance operations which were so terminated by the company without prior bargaining.

There are a few provisions, such as closed shop and "hot cargo" agreements, which may not be lawfully included in the collective contract even if both parties so desire.

The duty imposed by the NLRA means that the parties must bargain in "good faith." This at least includes meeting with each other, listening to the other side's proposals, and discussing them. In the case of the employer, the duty to bargain also means providing the union with such relevant information as is within its possession and reasonably available. The NLRA does not require any party to agree to a proposal from the other side, or even to make any concession. Despite these clearly stated rules, however, both the NLRB and the U.S. Second Circuit Court of Appeals held that General Electric committed the unfair labor practice of refusing to bargain by making its "last, best offer" at the start of negotiations and indicating to the employees that that was the best it could do.

The following case is a more recent example of these issues.

NATIONAL LABOR RELATIONS BOARD v. UNITED STATES POSTAL SERVICE
8 F.3d 832 (D.C. Circuit, 1993)

FACTS: The APWU is the collective bargaining representative for a nationwide unit of approximately 270,000 full-time and 70,000 part-time clerical, maintenance, motor vehicle, and special delivery messenger Postal Service employees. The events at issue in this case arose under the 1987-1990 collective bargaining agreement between the Postal Service and the Union, and all references to the "CBA" in this opinion are to that agreement.

Article 7 of the CBA provides for a "regular" workforce and a "supplemental" workforce. The supplemental workforce is made up of casual employees, whose numbers are strictly limited by the CBA and none of whom are members of APWU. All employees in the regular workforce are members of the bargaining unit represented by the Union. The regular work force includes full-time employees, who work a fixed schedule and are guaranteed five eight-hour work days per week, and two classes of part-time employees. "Part-time regulars" work a fixed schedule of less than forty hours per week. "Part-time flexibles" ("PTFs"), on the other hand, have no set hours, but work a variable schedule as the Postal Service needs them. Although the CBA guarantees no specific hours to PTFs, the Postal Service and the Union have agreed that PTFs will receive a minimum of either two or four hours of work per pay period, depending on the size of the facility in which they work.

The Postal Service implemented the service reductions at issue in this case in response to the Omnibus Budget Reconciliation Act of 1987 ("OBRA"). OBRA required the Postal Service to reduce its operating costs by $160 million in fiscal 1988 and $270 million in fiscal 1989, and to submit its plan for implementing those cuts to Congress by March 1, 1988. OBRA did not mandate that the Postal Service achieve these savings by any specific means, but did forbid it to borrow funds or to increase postal rates.

The Postal Service began planning cost reductions immediately after OBRA's enactment. On December 23, 1987, Postal Service officials met with representatives from the APWU and informed them that the Postal Service planned to close all of its retail outlets on the Saturdays following Christmas and New Year's Day. On January 14, 1988, the APWU and the Postal Service met again and the Union proposed several areas for potential labor costs savings, none of which were accepted. Neither of the parties claims that this or other meetings constituted bargaining sessions.

On January 20, 1988, the Postal Service announced a $160 million reduction in its operating budget. Two-thirds of these savings were due to cuts in non-labor administrative costs and adjustments to work schedules. The remaining third, an estimated $60 million, was to be saved by reducing service hours. In addition to the two previously announced Saturday closings, the Postal Service planned to adjust Sunday mail processing and collection hours, and to reduce retail window hours by approximately one half day per week. The APWU requested bargaining over the proposed service reductions and met with the Postal Service on two occasions following the January 20th announcement. The Postal Service refused to bargain, however, on the grounds that it had authority pursuant to the CBA to implement the reductions unilaterally. In September 1988, the Postal Service partially restored the retail services it had reduced in response to OBRA. The APWU again requested bargaining and the Postal Service again refused.

The Administrative Law Judge ("ALJ") dismissed the Union's unfair labor practice charge in its entirety on the ground that the service reductions were not mandatory subjects of bargaining because they were implemented in response to a congressional mandate. The NLRB reversed, holding that the service reductions were mandatory subjects, and that the APWU had not waived its right to bargain over them.

CIRCUIT JUDGE EDWARDS:

Sections 8(a)(5) and 8(d) of the NLRA make it an unfair labor practice for an employer to refuse "to bargain collectively" with its employees' representative concerning "wages, hours, and other terms or conditions of employment."... An employer violates sections 8(a)(5) and 8(a)(1) of the Act if it makes a unilateral change in a term or condition of employment—so-called "mandatory subjects"—without first bargaining to impasse....

However, the duty to bargain under the NLRA does not prevent parties from negotiating contract terms that make it unnecessary to bargain over subsequent changes in terms or conditions of employment. "The union may exercise its right to bargain about a particular subject by negotiating for a provision in a collective bargaining contract that fixes the parties' rights and forecloses further mandatory bargaining as to that subject."

A union may also "waive" its right to bargain over a mandatory subject, but the "covered by" and "waiver" inquiries are analytically distinct:

A waiver occurs when a union knowingly and voluntarily relinquishes its right to bargain about a matter; but where the matter is covered by the collective bargaining agreement, the union has exercised its bargaining right and the question of waiver is irrelevant....

[W]hen employer and union bargain about a subject and memorialize that bargain in a collective bargaining agreement, they create a set of rules governing their future relations.... Unless the parties agree otherwise, there is no continuous duty to bargain during the term of an agreement with respect to a matter covered by the contract.... Thus, neither the Board nor the courts may abrogate a lawful agreement merely because one of the bargaining parties is unhappy with a term of the contract and would prefer to negotiate a better arrangement. Quite the contrary, the courts are bound to enforce lawful labor agreements as written, ... and they are even bound to enforce voluntary arbitration awards construing labor agreements.... In short, the courts attempt to interpret collective bargaining contracts so as to respect the agreements reached by the parties who made them. Accordingly, questions of "waiver" normally do not come into play with respect to subjects already covered by a collective bargaining agreement.

In a case such as this one, where the employer acts pursuant to a claim of right under the parties' agreement, the resolution of the refusal to bargain charge rests on an interpretation of the contract at issue.... Indeed, "whether there is a duty to bargain depends solely upon what the contract means."... Normally, under federal labor laws, arbitrators and the courts, rather than the Board, are the primary sources of contract interpretation. The Board, however, has the authority to interpret collective bargaining agreements in order to resolve unfair labor practice cases....

The Board's limited role in interpreting contracts has important implications for our review of its decision in this case, however. Because the courts are charged with developing a uniform federal law of labor contracts under Section 301 of the Labor-Management Relations Act, we accord no deference to the Board's interpretation of labor contracts.... To defer to the Board's contract interpretation would risk the development of conflicting principles for interpreting collective bargaining agreements.... In keeping with the law of this circuit, we interpret the CBA de novo....

In the case before us, it is clear that service reductions are within the compass of Article 3. That provision grants the Postal Service the "exclusive right" "To transfer and assign employees" and "To determine the methods, means and personnel by which [its] operations are to be conducted." Article 3 also gives the Postal Service the more general right "To maintain the efficiency of the operations entrusted to it." These rights surely permit an employer unilaterally to rearrange its employees' work schedules, which the Postal Service contends was the sole result of its service reductions...

There is a crucial distinction between "the waiver of a right and the exercise of a right that extends into the future. To the extent that a bargain resolves any issue, it removes that issue pro tanto from the range of bargaining."... In this case the Board failed even to consider the possibility that the service reductions were covered by the CBA. We conclude that the 1988 service reductions are well within the scope of the powers for which the Postal Service bargained with the APWU. Because the CBA memorializes the terms of that bargain, it covers the dispute before us in this case. The petition for enforcement is therefore denied, and the Board's order is vacated.

Union Tactics and Unfair Labor Practices. The union's main weapons in support of its bargaining demands are the strike, picketing, and the boycott. There are some significant legal limitations (as well as economic ones) on the use of each. In general, both the objectives sought and the tactics used must be lawful.

Both Taft-Hartley and Landrum-Griffin tried to restrict union conduct that had the effect of dragging neutral employers, and their employees, into the primary dispute. The main relevant section of the amended NLRA is Section 8(b)(4). Strikes, refusals to handle or work on certain ("hot") goods, or any other union conduct that threatens, coerces, or restrains any person is illegal if its objective is:

1. To force any employer or self-employed person to enter a labor organization or to enter into a "hot cargo" agreement, illegal under 8(e).

2. To force any person to cease doing business with any other person.

3. To force any employer to bargain with one union where another union has already been certified.

4. To force an employer to assign particular work to one group of employees rather than another.

Section 8(b)(7) further limits the permissible objectives of picketing. Picketing is unlawful where it is done to force an employer to recognize a union or to force his or her employees to accept it as their agent if:

1. Another union has already been recognized and there is no legal question as to its status.

2. A valid election has been held within the past 12 months.

3. Such picketing has been conducted for a reasonable time (not to exceed 30 days) and the union has not filed a petition for an election.

In addition to the above legal restrictions on the purposes for which union collective-action weapons may be used, any such concerted activities must themselves be conducted in a lawful manner. In general, this means that the union's tactics must be "peaceful." Violence or threats of violence directed against the employer, his or her premises, employees who choose to go to work, or customers or others who wish to continue to do business with the "target" employer would clearly be illegal. Access to and egress from the target premises must not be impeded. The laws of libel and slander presumably still apply to picket signs and other information media. And so on.

Illegality of the union's objectives or tactics not only subjects it to unfair labor practice charges; there may also be other consequences. The union itself may be liable for the damages caused and/or subject to an injunction to prohibit the unlawful conduct. Civil rights violations could conceivably be involved in the union's conduct. Employees engaging in an "unprotected" strike are subject to lawful dismissal by the employer, with no right to reinstatement when the strike ends. The 1947 and 1959 amendments, coupled with a more critical public attitude toward unions, now make it reasonably clear that union hooliganism will be punished. However, the public still shows a high tolerance level for illegal, but peaceful, union conduct, such as illegal boycotts and illegal public employee strikes. These issues remain unresolved.

Employer Tactics and Unfair Labor Practices. The employer's arsenal of weapons includes some that are roughly comparable to those used by the union, as well as some for which the union has no real equivalent. The counterpart of the union's denial of services through a strike is the employer's denial of access to the workplace (and therefore wages) by means of a **lockout**. In lieu of picketing, the employer advises employees, customers, and other members of the public of his or her side of the dispute by advertising, typically in a local newspaper. There is no real employer counterpart to the boycott. In addition to the above "corresponding" weapons, the employer also possesses the ultimate sanctions of plant relocation and termination of the business, though the use of either is severely limited by the Board and the courts. Management may also do some forward planning to cushion the effects of a strike, by stockpiling inventories, readjusting contract schedules, or transferring work from one plant to another. The employer may also attempt to restrict the scope of the union's collective action by means of a court injunction.

A lockout designed to prevent unionization or to discourage union membership would be an unfair labor practice, but an employer may use the lockout to protect its own legitimate economic interests. Where there is a bargaining impasse, the employer may lock out in support of its bargaining position. Or, if the union calls or threatens to call a strike, the employer can lock out in retaliation, and also lock out to prevent "economic hardship" to the business.

An employer has an absolute right to go out of business at any time, for any reason, even if the employer's sole reason for doing so its antiunion bias. Where an employer closes only part of an operation, however, the employer's motives must be economic ones and not a desire to "chill unionism" at the company's other locations. In general, the legality of a plant relocation (**runaway shop**) would be tested in the same manner as that of a partial closing.

Throughout most of the early history of unionism, the courts were on the employer's side. The standard operating procedure when confronted with union collective action was to ask for a court injunction to restrict or terminate the union activities. Employers got an unexpected bonanza when the courts applied the Sherman Antitrust Act to union activities, thus further restricting employee collective action.

Congress attempted to limit the use of the courts in labor disputes by including Sections 6 and 20 in the Clayton Act of 1914. Unfortunately, from the union viewpoint, Section 20 said that an injunction could be issued if "necessary to prevent irreparable injury to property, or to a property right," and the courts were very liberal in construing this qualifying phrase. It took the Norris-LaGuardia Act of 1932 to substantially eliminate the labor injunction from the U.S. District Courts. (Many states copied this act.) It is still theoretically possible for an employer to get an injunction in a labor dispute, but the strict jurisdictional requirements make this very unlikely. The one exceptional case where the employer will be granted an injunction is where there is a strike in violation of a no-strike clause in an existing collective agreement. (An employer can also get a specific performance order to enforce an arbitration clause in an existing contract.) In addition, the Board and the Attorney General are not bound by Norris-LaGuardia and can get injunctions issued.

Conflict Resolution. As indicated previously, the government's basic approach to management-union disputes is merely to see to it that the parties meet their obligation to bargain with each other in good faith and then to let the economic chips fall where they may. In 1947, however, Congress opted for additional governmental participation in the bargaining process, with the creation of the Federal Mediation and Conciliation Service (FMCS), an independent administrative agency.

The primary responsibility of bargaining out, and living with, their agreement is still left up to the parties. But the services of the FMCS are available at the request of either party or on its own initiative where the labor dispute involves the public safety and interest or where it threatens to have a substantial adverse impact on interstate commerce. If the parties want to submit their dispute to binding arbitration, the FMCS will also make available to them a list of qualified labor arbitrators from which to select.

Arbitration provides a more civilized method of settling disputes than strikes, lockouts, and the like. It is usually less formal, less complicated, and therefore less time-consuming and less expensive than a court trial. Nearly all arbitration is voluntarily agreed to by the parties, but some states have compulsory arbitration laws for public employees, particularly fire fighters and police officers, and the Taft-Hartley Act contains special procedures for compulsory government action in "national emergency strikes." Today the courts recognize and enforce awards made by third-party arbitrators on matters submitted to them by the parties, and as indicated previously, arbitration clauses in existing contracts are specifically enforceable, despite the Norris-LaGuardia Act.

Internal Union Management; Reporting and Disclosure Requirements. The Landrum-Griffin amendments to the NLRA ushered in a new era in union organization and administration. The Landrum-Griffin Act was passed following the sensational disclosures of the McClellan subcommittee on the extent of corruption and gangster control in the labor movement. The findings received widespread publicity because many of the hearings were televised and because of the popularity of *The Enemy Within*, a book written by subcommittee counsel Robert Kennedy. The result was the passage of the Landrum-Griffin Act, which set out a "bill of rights" for labor union members and imposed substantial reporting and disclosure requirements on unions.

The "bill of rights" is an attempt to provide guarantees of minimum participatory access to the union's decision-making process and to protect the individual member's status within the union. Subject to the union's "reasonable rules," all members are to have equal rights to attend and vote at meetings, to nominate candidates, to vote in elections, and to exercise their freedoms of speech and assembly. Dues increases must be voted by secret ballot at a special membership meeting or by referendum. Except for failure to pay dues, an individual union member cannot be disciplined by his or her union unless served with written, specific charges and given a reasonable time to prepare a defense and a full and fair hearing. If a grievance against the union or its officers or agents is not resolved by internal procedures within four months, the member can bring a civil suit in a U.S. District Court to enforce any rights under the act. The member can demand a copy of any collective contract which affects him or her, and the secretary of labor is directed to bring suit on the member's behalf if a copy is not provided.

The union itself is required to file two major types of reports with the secretary of labor—**procedural** and **financial**. Each union must adopt a constitution and bylaws, and both must be filed. Existing provisions covering such things as membership qualifications, initiation fees, selection and removal of officers, contract ratification, and strike authorization must also be filed if such matters are not covered in the constitution and bylaws. Yearly financial reports must be filed, covering such matters as assets and liabilities; receipts and their sources; salaries, loans, and other payments to officers and employees; and loans to any business. Full, periodic reports must also be filed when the national union places a local under "trusteeship." To try to prevent conflicts of interest, union officers and employees must file personal financial reports covering transactions with companies which the union has organized or is trying to organize.

The Landrum-Griffin Act thus contains important new legal protections for the individual union member and for the public.

The *Buzenius* case deals with employees' rights to *refrain* from participating in union actions.

BUZENIUS v. NATIONAL LABOR RELATIONS BOARD
124 F.3d 788 (Sixth Circuit, 1997)

FACTS: The United Paperworkers International Union, AFL-CIO, CLC, and its Local 1033 are the exclusive collective bargaining representatives of Weyerhaeuser Paper Company's production and maintenance employees. The Union and the Company entered into a collective bargaining agreement ("CBA") containing the following union-security clause:

> It is agreed that all employees who are members of the Union shall remain members of the Union in good standing. All new employees, who after completion of thirty (30) days, shall become and remain members of the Union in good standing as a condition of employment for the term of this Agreement [sic].

The CBA does not define "member in good standing." Additionally, the Union has no procedure to provide employees with information regarding their right to refuse to join the Union or pay full dues, so long as they pay that portion of dues related to the Union's core representational activities.

Petitioner Roland Buzenius works for the Company and was a member of the Union. On April 30, 1993, petitioner informed the Union by letter of his immediate resignation from the Union's membership in accordance with the Supreme Court's decision in *Pattern Makers' League (1985)*. Petitioner also asserted his right under

Communications Workers v. Beck (1988), to object to supporting financially the Union's non-collective bargaining activities. The Union, however, ignored petitioner's letter and continued to deduct dues from petitioner's paycheck in the same amount it had prior to petitioner's resignation. Moreover, in November 1993, the Union mailed petitioner a new Union-membership card.

Petitioner filed a charge against the Union with the National Labor Relations Board. The Board ruled that the Union violated S.8(b)(1)(A) of the National Labor Relations Act by failing to acknowledge petitioner's resignation from the Union; failing to inform petitioner and all other Company employees of their rights under *NLRB v. General Motors* and *Beck*; and collecting and using petitioner's full union-membership fees. The Board issued an order requiring the Union to cease and desist from the unfair labor practices and to undertake a number of remedial actions, including notifying each Company employee in writing of his rights under *General Motors* and *Beck* and that the only required condition of employment under the union-security clause is the payment of any uniform initiation fee and the "financial core" membership service fees. The Board also ordered the Union to post notice at Union business offices and local meeting halls for sixty consecutive days stating that the Union will not restrain and coerce Company employees from exercising their rights. The Board, however, refused to order the Union to expunge or modify the union-security clause. Petitioner timely appealed.

 CIRCUIT JUDGE BATCHELDER:

Petitioner challenges the Board's order to the extent that it allows the union-security clause to remain in the CBA. Petitioner argues that the plain language of the clause patently misleads employees regarding their obligations as defined by the Supreme Court. Therefore, petitioner claims, the clause is facially invalid and the Board abused its discretion in failing to order its expunction from the CBA. We agree....

S.8(a)(3) of the Act explicitly allows union-security clauses that require union "membership" as a condition of employment.... Read literally, this section authorizes an employer and a labor organization to enter into a CBA compelling all employees to join the union and pay full union dues. However, according to the Supreme Court, S.8(a)(3) means no such thing. All that may be required under a union-security clause is the payment of fees and dues related to core representational activities.

The issue in this case is not whether union-security clauses are valid in general, which they clearly are.... Rather, the issue is whether, in light of the language of S.8(a)(3) and the subsequent Supreme Court decisions interpreting that language, a union-security clause that requires "membership in good standing," without concurrent definition of that term in the collective bargaining agreement, is valid. We hold that it is not.

Few federal courts have squarely addressed the facial validity of union-security clauses like the one presented by the instant case. Indeed, our research reveals, and the parties have directed our attention to, decisions from only two federal circuit courts....

We agree with our sister circuits' assertion that the Supreme Court has never explicitly delineated the permissible language of a S.8(a)(3) union-security clause. Indeed, the Court has never squarely faced that issue. We do not agree, however, with the contention that the Supreme Court's silence validates a union-security clause requiring "membership in good standing" without further explanation in the CBA. We believe that in light of the Court's decisions whittling S.8(a)(3) "membership" down to its financial core, such clauses, without concurrent definition in the CBA itself, are facially invalid. To permit the CBA to say what it cannot literally mean does violence both to the Act's policy of voluntary unionism and to principles of contract interpretation.

One of the Act's core policies is that of voluntary unionism.... Although employees subject to a S.8(a)(3) union-security clause are obligated to pay dues and fees related to the union's core representational activities, ... they remain free to join or refuse to join the union.... A union-security clause requiring "membership in good standing" as a condition of employment, however, leaves employees with the distinct impression that they are not free to make that choice. The plain language of such clauses is clear—join the union or be fired. As the Eighth Circuit stated in *Bloom*..., "We fail to see how an employee can discern from such language that he cannot be terminated if he does not wish to become a formal, full-fledged union member burdened with all of the obligations of union membership and subject to the full reach of the union's disciplinary measures." Similarly, though the Board has found union-security clauses of this type to be facially valid, ... it has recognized their deceptive nature....

Allowing a union-security clause requiring union "membership in good standing" to remain unmodified in the CBA turns normal contract interpretation on its head. Under the Board's remedial order, employees must consult extraneous sources and subsequent notices in order to discover that they have a right not to do what the plain language of the clause requires. Because the clause does not mean what it literally says, and because its literal application is unlawful, the clause has no place in the CBA. Subsequent notice of the employees' actual rights under S.8(a)(3), whether by posting temporary notice or providing employees with one-time written notice, will not rectify the situation.... Once Company employees receive their one-time notice, the Board's order provides no other measure to inform employees of their rights and lawful obligations under the union-security clause. However, the union-security clause, which cannot mean what it says and cannot be applied as drafted, remains in the CBA, the on-going contract by which the employees' relationship to the employer is governed. We cannot agree with such a result.

We recognize that Congress, through S.8(a)(3), has sanctioned union-security clauses requiring union "membership" as a condition of employment. We also recognize that a union-security clause requiring "membership in good standing" comports with the literal meaning of S.8(a)(3). However, as previously discussed, S.8(a)(3) does not mean what it literally says. Indeed, as the Seventh Circuit has recently pointed out, the Supreme Court has glossed the statute in a way that virtually inverts the literal meaning.... The Court has not simply carved out exceptions to S.8(a)(3)'s language; it has ruled that the most that may be required under that section is the payment of dues and fees related to core representational activities.... The plain language of S.8(a)(3) and its actual meaning in light of Supreme Court precedent are so dissimilar that "the only realistic explanation for the retention of the statutory language in collective bargaining agreements ... is to mislead employees about their right not to join the union."...

In the present case, the Union has wholly failed to persuade us otherwise. The union has provided no legitimate reasons explaining why it needs to include "membership in good standing" language, without further definition, in the CBA. Nor has the Union explained how requiring that the clause be modified to reflect S.8(a)(3)'s true meaning and employees' true obligations would impose an undue hardship. For these reasons, and because of the clause's misleading nature, the Union may not hide behind S.8(a)(3) to justify this practice....

The union-security clause in the instant case requires employees to become and remain "members of the Union in good standing." Because the express language of this clause is inconsistent with employees' right to refuse to join the Union or pay full dues, so long as they pay that portion of dues related to core representational activities, and because the clause cannot be interpreted without resort to material outside of the CBA, we hold that the clause is facially invalid. We therefore hold that the Board abused its discretion in refusing to order that the clause requiring that employees be "members of the Union in good standing" either be modified to define that requirement or be removed from the CBA. Accordingly, we REVERSE the order of the National Labor Relations Board.

LABOR STANDARDS LEGISLATION

FLSA. Where it applies, the Fair Labor Standards Act places a floor under wage rates; it does *not* place a ceiling on hours of work, either per day or per week. It is almost inconceivable today, but the first national minimum wage so provided was *25 cents* per hour, with the objective of reaching *40 cents* an hour after the act had been in force for seven years. The 1974 Amendments extended coverage to most employees of public agencies and institutions and to "in-home" domestic workers and babysitters, but the U.S. Supreme Court ruled that Congress could not impose such limits on state and local governments.

Subject again to some exceptions, the FLSA also requires the employer to pay overtime at a rate of time and a half for all hours worked in excess of 40 in the employee's normal workweek. There is no provision for daily overtime; the "workweek" is any seven consecutive days. Overtime must be calculated for each successive seven-day period; the employer gets no "credit" if an employee works fewer than forty hours in a given week. An hourly wage must be calculated for each employee, but the employer can exclude such things as gifts, discretionary bonuses, and employer payments to certain qualified savings and profit-sharing plans.

The employer is required to keep records of such wage and hour data for up to three years. For violations of the minimum wage and overtime provisions, the injured employee can bring suit personally or request in writing that the secretary of labor do so on his or her behalf. The secretary can also ask the U.S. District Court for an injunction to prevent further violations and/or for the removal of goods so produced from interstate commerce.

There are also extensive regulations promulgated by the secretary which pertain to the use of child labor; that is, the use of minors under age 18. Generally, the employment of children under age 14 is prohibited; between 14 and 16, some jobs are permitted, subject to strict limits on work hours; between 16 and 18, employment is prohibited only in those industries which the secretary has found to be "hazardous," such as coal and other mining, slaughterhouses and meat-packing plants, building demolition, and roofing and excavation work. Criminal penalties—up to six months in jail, a fine of up to $10,000, or both—and/or injunctions are possible enforcement measures. Goods produced through the use of illegal child labor are subject to removal from the stream of commerce, but innocent purchasers of the goods, for value, are protected against confiscation if they receive a written certificate of compliance stating that the goods were produced in accordance with FLSA standards.

The Equal Pay Act of 1963 and the Age Discrimination in Employment Act passed in 1967 and later amended, were amendments to the FLSA; however, since they are concerned with discrimination in employment they will be discussed in Chapter 41.

Worker Safety. Each state has its own workers' compensation law. Workers' compensation laws are really an example of no-fault liability. Generally speaking, if a worker who is covered by the law is injured by accident while in the scope of employment or if the worker becomes ill as a result of an occupational disease, the worker is entitled to reasonable medical care for the injuries and for compensation for lost wages after a specific waiting period. This period will depend on the particular state law. The amount of compensation is only a percentage of the worker's average weekly wage, and again specific state law will set that percentage figure. There are also minimum and maximum weekly benefits which will be paid. If the worker suffers a permanent impairment, then a settlement based on that impairment will be paid. Most states require employers to carry workers' compensation insurance, or to show evidence of ability to pay if they wish to be considered self-insured. A few states have state-operated plans whereby employers pay a percentage of their payroll to the state, and the state acts as the insurance company.

Many states also have their own Occupational Safety and Health Act (OSHA) laws and commissions and offer their assistance to employers to help employers identify and correct health and safety hazards.

Unemployment Insurance. A national law requiring unemployment compensation insurance was passed in 1935. It provides a tax on employers, with the money being used to pay weekly benefits to certain unemployed workers. Another such area is the Social Security Act, which requires employers to withhold a percentage of the employee's salary and also pay a specific percentage in addition to the amount withheld. This law also provides for benefits for disabled workers under the age of retirement, as well as retirement benefits. The internal revenue laws also impact the employer as the employer must withhold the proper tax from the employee's salary and provide the government with quarterly reports. Other laws regulate plant closings, employee benefits, and family and medical leaves from work.

SIGNIFICANCE OF THIS CHAPTER

The relationship between employer and employee is a significant area of government regulation. Prior to such regulation, we saw blatant discrimination with regard to employees' rights concerning unionism. Every manager needs to have knowledge of at least the major laws that regulate the employer-employee relationship. This chapter gives the manager a basic knowledge of those laws.

PROBLEMS FOR DISCUSSION

1. Yeshiva University is a private (not state supported) university in New York City. The employer-employee relationship between the university and its employees is subject to the provisions of the National Labor Relations Act (NLRA) as amended. Under the NLRA, supervisors and managerial employees may not be a part of the collective bargaining unit. The professors of Yeshiva organized their own union called the Yeshiva University Faculty Association (YUFA). Then the Association requested an election to force the university to recognize them as the certified bargaining unit for all professors. The university objected to the election and alleged all of the professors were managerial employees and as such could not be part of a collective bargaining unit. They alleged the professors acted in an advisory capacity regarding admission of students, setting of teaching loads, curriculum development, and grade distribution.

    You are the Administrative Law Judge, would you consider these professors to be "managerial employees"? Why or why not?

2. Ford provided in-plant cafeteria and vending machine food services. ARA Services, Inc., an independent caterer, managed these services, but Ford had the right to approve the quality, quantity, and prices for the food served. Ford notified the UAW that food prices in its stamping plant at Chicago Heights, Illinois, would be increased by unspecified amounts. UAW Local 588, representing the 3,600 hourly workers at the plant, asked for bargaining on the prices and services and for information relevant to Ford's involvement in the food services operation. Ford refused, and the UAW filed unfair labor practice charges with the NLRB, alleging a refusal to bargain over a mandatory subject. The Board sustained the charges and ordered Ford to bargain. The U.S. Seventh Circuit Court of Appeals upheld the NLRB.

    Is this decision correct? Explain.

3. The regents appealed an order of the state's Court of Industrial Relations which established a collective bargaining unit at the University of Nebraska at Omaha. The regents contended that: (1) the CIR had no jurisdiction over them; (2) the bargaining unit was inappropriate because it included only employees of U/N at Omaha; (3) the bargaining unit was inappropriate because it should not have included department chairpersons, librarians, counselors, assistant instructors, or academic personnel holding special appointments. The U/N-O College of Business Administration Faculty Association also appealed from the dismissal of its petition for intervention, which had asked for the establishment of a separate bargaining unit. Intercollegiate athletic coaches and trainers were excluded from the bargaining unit.

    What is the correct unit?

4. Sam's Maintenance Corp. (SMC) is in the business of providing maintenance crews to companies on a contract basis so the company does not have to hire its own maintenance people. The customers pay the cost of the labor plus a management fee. The employees of SMC are unionized. One of SMC's customers was Greenacres Nursing Home in Brooklyn. Thirty-five of the SMC employees were assigned to work at this nursing home. SMC terminated its contract with Greenacres Nursing Home and then discharged all thirty-five employees who had worked there. The union stated this was a partial closing of the business and that they should have the right to bargain over this partial closing. The union filed an unfair labor practice charge against the company.

   How should the court decide, and why?

5. In the fall of 1997, Levi Strauss' projected production requirements of Dockers pants decreased significantly. As a result of this projected decrease, Levi Strauss decided to close one of its plants. After comparing the costs of producing Dockers pants among the various locations where such clothing was produced, Levi Strauss announced that it planned to close its plant in San Antonio.

   On April 20, 1998, certain employees who were terminated upon the closing of the San Antonio plant filed a class action lawsuit against Levi Strauss. One of the Plaintiffs' ERISA claims charged Levi Strauss with closing the San Antonio plant for the purpose of depriving the Plaintiffs of employment benefits, including pension, severance, and disability benefits, in violation of Section 510 of ERISA.

   Has Levi Strauss violated ERISA? Why or why not?

6. Illinois Coil Spring Company decided to move its assembly operations, formerly conducted at its Milwaukee Division, to its McHenry Division. The labor costs at Milwaukee were $8.00 an hour in wages and $2.00 an hour in fringe benefits; at McHenry, $4.50 in wages and $1.35 in fringes. A labor contract was in force at Milwaukee but not at McHenry. Illinois did bargain with its Milwaukee union about the change, by asking for wage concessions in order to keep the Milwaukee location viable. After the union rejected any concessions, Illinois did begin to relocate its assembly operations to McHenry.

   The union filed unfair labor practice charges. Is there an NLRA violation here? Discuss.

Chapter 41

Employment Discrimination Law

MAJOR STATUTES

Beginning in the early 1960s, the Congress of the United States recognized the need for legislation to eliminate discrimination in employment. Several anti-discrimination laws have been passed by Congress in the past three decades. The first of these laws, the Equal Pay Act of 1963, which was an amendment to the Fair Labor Standards Act of 1938 (FLSA), required equal pay for men and women doing equal work. The next major change was the Civil Rights Act of 1964, which was amended in 1972 and 1991. Title VII of that act forbids discrimination by either an employer or a union against an applicant for employment, an employee, or an applicant for membership and/or benefits in a union if such discrimination is based on race, color, religion, sex, or national origin. Discrimination by an employment agency in the referral of applications is also prohibited. In 1991, after lengthy study and discussion, Congress passed the Civil Rights Act of 1991.

The motivation for this new law was that there had been several recent decisions by the U.S. Supreme Court that were viewed as being too favorable to employers in discrimination cases. In effect, this law reverses and nullifies the effect of the recent cases which have been viewed as being pro-employer. Under the previous civil rights law, victims of discrimination in employment matters were only eligible for back-pay, reinstatement of their job, and injunctive relief if deemed necessary by the court. Under the Civil Rights Act of 1991, victims of intentional discrimination may be eligible for both compensatory damages and punitive damages under certain circumstances. Also, in cases where the employer alleges that the discrimination was unintentional, the burden of proof will be on the employer to prove that the discrimination was unintentional. Also, in these cases, the plaintiff may be awarded attorney fees if he or she prevails in the lawsuit.

In 1967, discrimination on the basis of age was also made illegal by the Age Discrimination in Employment Act of 1967 (ADEA), another amendment to the FLSA. The ADEA was amended in 1978 to prohibit employment discrimination against persons between the ages of 40 and 70. In 1980, Congress again amended the ADEA, declaring that employers may no longer enforce a mandatory retirement age of 65. This new law increased the mandatory retirement age limit from 65 to 70 years of age. In 1986, the Congress amended the 1980 Act, and in effect stated that it is now unlawful to require an individual to retire at any age, and also made it unlawful for employers, labor organizations, and employment agencies covered under this act to discriminate against any individual regarding the hiring, firing, payment of wages, or other terms, conditions, or privileges of employment to that individual because of his or her age. In 1990, the Congress amended the ADEA once again with the enactment of the Older Workers Benefit Protection Act (OWBPA), which forbids age discrimination with regard to employee benefits, and also establishes minimum standards for determining the validity of waivers of rights or claims under the ADEA.

In 1973, the Congress passed the Vocational Rehabilitation Act. This act extends protection to handicapped workers, but it only applies to employees and prospective employees of employers who have federal contracts of $2,500 or more. In 1990, Congress passed the Americans with Disabilities Act of 1990. This act not only amended portions of the 1973 Vocational Rehabilitation Act, but it created new and comprehensive duties for employers with regard to job application procedures, hiring, promotion, discharge, and other terms and conditions of employment. Disability includes both mental and physical impairment. A disabled individual who is a victim of intentional discrimination may sue for and receive both compensatory and punitive damages. In 1974, the Congress passed the Vietnam Veterans Readjustment Act. This law requires certain federal contractors to develop an affirmative action plan to hire Vietnam veterans. In 1978, the Congress passed the Pregnancy Disability Act, which amended Title VII of the Civil Rights Act of 1964. This law prohibits discrimination in employment based on pregnancy or pregnancy-related conditions.

In addition to these laws, Presidential Executive Order 11246 directs the secretary of labor to supervise the various federal contracting agencies to see that there is equal opportunity afforded to employees of certain federal contractors. The secretary of labor created the Office of Federal Contract Compliance Programs (OFCCP) to supervise both the awards of federal contracts and their affirmative action regarding equal employment opportunity.

Equal Pay Act. The Equal Pay Act of 1963 prohibits pay differentials based solely on sex. As indicated previously, it was an amendment to the FLSA and applies only to those employees who are covered by the provisions of the FLSA. Union conduct which causes or attempts to cause such employer discrimination is likewise prohibited.

To show a violation, the government must prove that the jobs in question require equal skill, equal effort, and equal responsibility and are performed under similar working conditions, and that males and females are paid different wages for performing them. If the employer wishes to raise one of the exceptions permitted by the Equal Pay Act as a defense—seniority, merit, quality of production, and any other factor other than sex—the employer then has the burden of proving that the differential is based on the alleged exception. Equal does not mean identical, but minor, insignificant job differences will not justify wage discrimination.

Where a violation is shown to exist, the employer is prohibited from reducing anyone's wages to eliminate the differential; someone's wages must be raised. Aside from this provision, all the standard FLSA enforcement procedures apply to the Equal Pay provisions, including criminal penalties. Originally enforcement of this law was the responsibility of the secretary of labor; however, in 1978, as a result of a Presidential order, the enforcement of this law was transferred to the Equal Employment Opportunity Commission (EEOC).

Civil Rights Act. Title VII of the Civil Rights Act of 1964 forbids discrimination by employers in hiring, promotion, discharge, and with regard to compensation, terms, conditions, and privileges of employment. This law also forbids discrimination by unions with regard to union membership and representation. In addition to the prohibitions against employers and unions, the law also extends its prohibition to discrimination by employment agencies. They must not discriminate in the referral of applicants for employment. Unlawful discrimination under Title VII is discrimination based on a person's race, color, religion, sex, or national origin.

There are, however, several statutory exceptions. Discriminatory hiring on the basis of religion, sex, or national origin is permitted where such limitations can be justified as a **bona fide occupational qualification** which is reasonably necessary to the normal operation of that particular business or enterprise. This is called a BFOQ.

An example of a religious BFOQ would be the requirement that the person hired as a minister for a specific church be a person who has the necessary religious training in the specific faith of that church. Also certain jobs may have a valid BFOQ which would require the employee to be of a specific sex. Other jobs may have a BFOQ requiring a specific national origin. It must be noted however that an employer may not legally use a BFOQ to discriminate against an applicant or employee because of the applicant's race or color.

In the *Johnson Controls* case, the company is arguing that "safety" is a BFOQ.

UNITED AUTO WORKERS v. JOHNSON CONTROLS
111S. Ct. 1196 (1991)

FACTS: Johnson Controls manufactures batteries; lead is a primary ingredient in the process. Lead is a toxic element, especially harmful to the unborn. When eight of its female employees with blood lead levels exceeding the OSHA standard became pregnant, Johnson adopted a policy which prevented fertile women from working on jobs where they would be exposed to lead. The UAW filed a class action in U.S. District Court alleging sex discrimination. The District Court granted summary judgment for Johnson, based on "business necessity," and the Court of Appeals affirmed.

 JUSTICE BLACKMUN:

The bias in Johnson Controls' policy is obvious. Fertile men, but not fertile women, are given a choice as to whether they wish to risk their reproductive health for a particular job.... [Johnson's] fetal-protection policy explicitly discriminates against women on the basis of their sex. The policy excludes women with childbearing capacity from lead-exposed jobs and so creates a facial classification based on gender....

Our conclusion is bolstered by the Pregnancy Discrimination Act of 1978,... in which Congress explicitly provided that, for purposes of Title VII, discrimination "on the basis of sex" includes discrimination "because of or on the basis of pregnancy, childbirth, or related medical conditions." "The Pregnancy Discrimination Act has now made clear that, for all Title VII purposes, discrimination based on a woman's pregnancy is, on its face, discrimination because of her sex...." In its use of the words "capable of bearing children" in the 1982 policy statement as the criteria for exclusion, Johnson Controls explicitly classifies on the basis of potential for pregnancy. Under the PDA, such a classification must be regarded, for Title VII purposes, in the same light as explicit sex discrimination. [Johnson] has chosen to treat all its female employees as potentially pregnant; that choice evinces discrimination on the basis of sex....

[T]he absence of a malevolent motive does not convert a facially discriminatory policy into a neutral policy with a discriminatory effect. Whether an employment practice involves disparate treatment through explicit facial discrimination does not depend on why the employer discriminates but rather on the explicit terms of the discrimination.... The beneficence of an employer's purpose does not undermine the conclusion that an explicit gender-based policy is sex discrimination ... and thus may be defended only as a BFOQ [bona fide occupational qualifaction]....

The wording of the BFOQ defense contains several terms of restriction that indicate the exception reaches only special situations. The statute thus limits the situations in which discrimination is permissible to "certain instances" were sex discrimination is "reasonably necessary" to the "normal operation" of the "particular" business. Each one of these terms—certain, normal, particular—prevents the use of general subjective standards and favors an objective, verifiable requirement. But the most telling term is "occupational;" this indicates that these objective, verifiable, requirements must concern job-related skills and aptitudes....

Johnson Controls argues that its fetal-protection policy falls within the so-called safety exception to the BFOQ. Our cases have stressed that discrimination on the basis of sex because of safety concerns is allowed only in narrow circumstances....

Our case law ... makes clear that the safety exception is limited to instances in which sex or pregnancy actually interferes with the employee's ability to perform the job. This approach is consistent with the language of the BFOQ provision itself, for it suggests that permissible distinctions based on sex must relate to ability to perform the duties of the job. Johnson Controls suggests, however, that we expand the exception to allow fetal protection policies that mandate particular standards for pregnant or fertile women. We decline to do so. Such an expansion contradicts not only the language of the BFOQ and the narrowness of its exception but the plain language and history of the Pregnancy Discrimination Act.

In addition to the BFOQ exception there is a specific exemption for businesses located on or near an Indian reservation; such businesses are permitted to have employment practices that give "preferential treatment" to Indians. Similarly, the U.S. Bureau of Indian Affairs can conduct preferential hiring for Indians.

Not all employers are covered by Title VII provisions. Private sector employers who employ fewer than fifteen employees are exempt from Title VII provisions; however, many states have enacted their own civil rights laws that cover employers with fewer than fifteen employees. Also, not all unions are covered by this law. Unions with fewer than fifteen members are not subject to the provisions of Title VII unless they operate a hiring hall. Unions that operate hiring halls and employment agencies are subject to the provisions of Title VII regardless of the number of members in the union or the number of employees employed by the employment agency or the volume of their referrals. The Civil Rights Act of 1964 also exempted state and local employees; however, the amendments passed by Congress in 1972 extended the coverage of Title VII to most state and local employees.

The Civil Rights Act of 1964 set up the Equal Employment Opportunity Commission (EEOC). The EEOC was granted authority by the 1964 act to investigate and conciliate grievances by individuals who allege discrimination based on race, color, religion, sex, or national origin. The amendments to the Civil Rights Act passed in 1972 gave the EEOC the added authority to not only investigate and conciliate but to file litigation on behalf of the complaining party or parties if they deemed it necessary and proper. If the EEOC investigation reveals that there is reasonable evidence to support the complainant's charge that unlawful discrimination has occurred and further that the party charged is not willing to negotiate and conciliate, then the EEOC attorneys may commence litigation in the U.S. District Court on behalf of the complainant, at the expense of the EEOC. If the EEOC attorneys decide not to litigate the case, the EEOC will issue a "right to sue letter," which authorizes the complainant to file suit, but the suit must be filed at the complainant's expense.

There is a statutory time limit for filing of a complaint by a person who feels he or she has been discriminated against. The complaint (referred to as a charge) must be filed with the EEOC within 180 days after the discriminatory act occurred. If there is a state or local civil rights agency and the local or state law requires that the complaining party file with the state or local agency first before filing with the EEOC, then the time period is extended to 300 days. There is also a time limit for the filing of a lawsuit in U.S. District Court by a complainant in the case where the EEOC decides not to pursue litigation but issues the right to sue letter. The complaining party only has ninety days to file his or her lawsuit after receiving a right to sue letter.

The District Courts that hear these Title VII actions are empowered to issue an injunction to stop an unlawful discriminatory practice if it is a continuing practice, and in certain cases they may also order affirmative action by the guilty party. Also the court may order the hiring or reinstatement of the persons who were discriminated against with or without back pay. The law does, however, limit back pay awards to a period of two years prior to the date the charge was filed.

The 1972 amendments to the Civil Rights Act of 1964 not only gave the EEOC the right to commence litigation on behalf of complainants at the government's expense, the amendments also gave the EEOC a new and very important power to combat discrimination. Prior to the 1972 amendments the EEOC was primarily concerned with individual grievances concerning alleged discrimination. With the passage of the 1972 amendments the EEOC was given the power to bring class actions to litigate allegations of "pattern or practice" of discrimination.

The 1991 Civil Rights Act did not change the persons and entities covered by the act. The primary thrust of this act was to expand the scope of damages which can be awarded to a victim of intentional discrimination and to reverse a trend set by several recent U.S. Supreme Court cases which were viewed as being very pro-employer and thus watering down the effect and purpose of the previous law. This new law has made many changes and additions to the Civil Rights Laws which employers must be aware of, however, space simply does not permit a detailed explanation and review of all of them.

ADEA. In 1967, Congress enacted the Age Discrimination in Employment Act (ADEA). This act was passed as an amendment to the Fair Labor Standards Act of 1938. An amendment to the law enacted in 1974 extended the act's protection to state and local governmental employees. An amendment enacted in 1978 extended the coverage to workers between the ages 40 to 70. An amendment enacted in 1980 prohibited mandatory retirement prior to 70 years of age. In 1986, as previously noted in this chapter, Congress again amended the ADEA making it unlawful for an employer to require an individual to retire at any age. Congress did make an exception regarding the mandatory retirement age for airline pilots, college professors, fire fighters, and law enforcement officers, stating that these types of employees could be required to retire at age 70 until December 31, 1993. Congress amended the ADEA again in 1990 with the passage of the Older Workers Benefit Protection Act (OWBPA) which forbids age discrimination with regard to employee benefits. Also the OWBPA established minimum standards for determining the validity of a waiver which an employee may be requested to sign to waive his or her rights under the ADEA. It is legal for an employer to make an agreement with an employee to retire early; however, since this agreement is a waiver of the employee's rights it must meet the minimum standards of the OWBPA.

The ADEA was originally enforced through FLSA procedures. However, in 1978, under a Presidential Reorganization Plan, the enforcement of this law was transferred from the labor department to the EEOC.

As with religion, sex, and national origin under Title VII, there is a "bona fide occupational qualification" exception to the ADEA. In addition, the employer may differentiate on the basis of **reasonable factors other than age** (RFOTA). For example, a 40-year-old professional football player who was no longer able to run, block, and tackle with the necessary vigor could presumably be fired on the basis of RFOTA even though age as such was not a BFOQ for a position on the team. The employer may also observe the terms of any bona fide seniority system or employee benefit plan, but an employer cannot use the benefit plan as an excuse for refusing to hire an older employee. Of course, an employer can still discharge or discipline an employee for good cause.

The *Britt* case discusses these issues.

BRITT v. THE GROCERS SUPPLY CO., INC.
978 F.2d 1441 (5th Cir., 1992)

FACTS: These two cases were consolidated on appeal, but tried separately. Both suits were brought by groups of former employees of Grocers Supply Company. The Britt plaintiffs appeal the district court's holding that the National Labor Relations Act preempts claims of age discrimination asserted under the Age Discrimination in Employment Act. They also appeal the district court's granting summary judgment on the merits of their age discrimination claims. The Hamilton plaintiffs appeal the district court's granting a directed verdict in favor of the defendants on the plaintiffs' age discrimination claims. They also appeal the district court's granting summary judgment on their claims of breach of contract and intentional infliction of emotional distress and duress.

The underlying facts in both cases are the same. In December 1986, the work force of Grocers Supply Company, a Texas corporation, went on strike after contract negotiations broke down. The work force consisted primarily of employees over forty years old. Grocers Supply immediately hired replacement workers to continue its operations. The replacement workers were told that their positions were temporary; sometime before the end of the strike, however, Grocers offered them permanent positions. Negotiations failed, and in April 1987, the striking workers made an unconditional offer to return to work. The Union explained to the workers that they could return to work only when Grocers needed them. In fact, Grocers and the Union negotiated a "recall" agreement to govern the order of recall as vacancies occurred. The Hamilton plaintiffs contend that this offer to return to work was made in response to a promise by Grocers that if the workers would return unconditionally, they would all be rehired within a few weeks.

Very few of the former workers were ever recalled. Grocers maintains that it simply had few hiring needs during this period due to the low turnover and increased productivity of its new workers. The Plaintiffs assert that the slow rehiring and the undesirability of those jobs offered was purposefully orchestrated to reduce the age of the work force and to encourage older workers to retire and take their retirement benefits.

Two groups of workers sued Grocers as a result of their failure to be recalled. Richard L. Britt and Timothy Jackson, Jr., individually and on behalf of others similarly situated, with 126 additional plaintiffs opting in, assert only an ADEA claim. They contend that their "permanent replacement" was a sham and that they were refused reinstatement because of their age. The district court granted summary judgment on this claim based on two grounds. First, the court held that the ADEA claim was preempted by the NLRA. Second, the district court held that Britt failed to demonstrate a genuine issue of material fact on the discrimination claim sufficient to survive summary judgment.

James E. Hamilton, et al., assert an ADEA claim, a 29 U.S.C. § 301 breach-of-contract claim, and state law claims of intentional infliction of emotional distress and duress. The district court granted summary judgment for Grocers on both the § 301 contract claim and the state law claims. The ADEA claim went to trial, but the district court directed a verdict for Grocers at the close of Hamilton's evidence.

 JUDGE DUHE:

Turning to the question whether this Court has jurisdiction over the age discrimination claims, we hold that this Court does have jurisdiction to hear the claims asserted under the Age Discrimination in Employment Act (ADEA). More specifically, we hold that, to the extent the age discrimination claims encompass conduct that is arguably covered by the National Labor Relations Act, the ADEA governs the prosecution of those claims and not the NLRA....

Because the root of the preemption doctrine lies in the tension between federal and state regulation of labor relations, the analysis of the tension between two conflicting federal statutes is somewhat different. A number of cases reflect this awareness....

[A] decision that the NLRA preempts the ADEA cannot be reconciled with the many cases holding that the ADEA is the exclusive remedy for age discrimination claims.... This has been the holding in cases of both federal employment and nonfederal employment. Additionally, all of these cases hold that the ADEA preempts another federal statute....

In sum, based on: (1) the cases holding that the ADEA is the exclusive remedy for age discrimination claims, (2) the cases holding that traditional preemption analysis does not apply when two federal statutes conflict, and (3) the inapplicability of extending the federal/state policy considerations guiding traditional preemption analysis to conflicts between federal statutes, we conclude that Congress intended the ADEA to be the exclusive remedy for age discrimination claims. Accordingly, we disagree with the district court's holding that the ADEA was preempted by the NLRA, and conclude that this Court has jurisdiction under the ADEA to entertain plaintiffs' age discrimination claims....

Having determined that this Court has jurisdiction over the age discrimination claims, we review both the district court's granting of summary judgment in Grocers' favor on Britt's claims and the district court's directing a verdict in Grocers' favor on Hamilton's claims. After reviewing the merits of the claims, we affirm the respective decisions of the district courts....

When no direct evidence of age discrimination exists, the evidentiary procedure generally adapted to the ADEA context is that announced by the Supreme Court....

Initially, the plaintiff must prove a *prima facie* case of age discrimination. The elements of a *prima facie* case are hotly disputed in these two cases. The elements of a *prima facie* case may be somewhat flexible in an ADEA case according to the facts in issue.... Because we affirm the district courts on an alternative basis, it is unnecessary to resolve the issue of what the proper elements of a *prima facie* case should be.

If the plaintiff proves his *prima facie* case, a presumption of discrimination is established. The burden of production then shifts to the defendant to rebut this resumption by articulating a legitimate nondiscriminatory reason for its disparate treatment of the plaintiff.... Finally, the plaintiff must prove that the defendant's reasons are pretexts for unlawful discrimination either by showing: (1) that a discriminatory reason more likely motivated the defendant, or (2) that the defendant's reason is unworthy of credence.... The plaintiff retains the burden of persuading the fact finder that impermissible discrimination motivated the adverse employment decision....

Because neither plaintiff can show that the defendant's reasons for disparate treatment of the plaintiffs are pretexts for unlawful discrimination, however, we see no need to rummage through the arguments over whether the plaintiffs has established a *prima facie* case. In the context of summary judgment or directed verdict, the question is not whether the plaintiff proves pretext, but rather whether the plaintiff raises a genuine issue of fact regarding pretext....

Contrary to plaintiffs' assertions, Grocers was under no obligation to notify the plaintiffs that they were being replaced. Nor does this lack of notification imply a bias based on age. Hamilton also challenges Grocers' practice of refusing to recall anyone who resigned to obtain his benefits. The theory is that Grocers coerced older workers into resigning to obtain their pension benefits, thereby discriminating against these workers based on age. Nothing in the record supports this claim. Additionally, we do not see how this practice harms older plaintiffs....

In sum, the appellants are left with nothing more than their speculation and be-lief that they were permanently replaced because of age. This type of evidence is insufficient to create a fact issue as to pretext.... Therefore, we uphold the sum-mary judgment in the Britt case and the directed verdict in the Hamilton case.

Vocational Rehabilitation Act. With the passage of the Vocational Rehabilitation Act of 1973 Congress provided protection from private sector discrimination against the handicapped; however, such protection is limited only to the private sector employers making a contract with the U.S. government for $2,500 or more. Even so, coverage extends to most major companies and perhaps half of all the businesses in the country. All such companies must have an affirmative action plan for hiring and promoting qualified handicapped persons at all levels, so in that sense the 1973 act requires more than Title VII of the 1964 act. All departments and agencies of the executive branch of the national government are likewise covered by the 1973 act.

Americans with Disabilities Act. This law is perhaps the most important and comprehensive legislation in the area of employment discrimination since the passage of the original civil rights act in 1964. The Vocational Rehabilitation Act of 1973 only applies to those employers with con-tracts of at least $2,500 with the U.S. Government. The Americans with Disabilities Act of 1990 covers all employers with fifteen or more employees. The title that primarily concerns employ-ment discrimination is Title I. Title I of the Act states that: "No covered entities shall discriminate against a qualified individual with a disability because of the disability of such individual in re-gard to job application procedures, the hiring, advancement or discharge of employees, employee compensations, job training, and other terms, conditions, and privileges of employment." The EEOC is responsible for the enforcement of this law. Disability under the act includes both "physical and mental impairment that substantially limits one or more of the major life activities of such individuals; or being regarded as having such an impairment." This definition is more en-compassing than the handicapped definition under the Vocational Rehabilitation Act of 1973. Under this new law the employer must be concerned not only about the person with an obvious disability such as the blind or hearing impaired or the person with a loss of use of a limb, but also the employer must be concerned with mental disabilities. For example, drug addiction, alcoholism, aids, and various psychological disorders are often not identifiable during the interview of a per-son for employment. The law bans pre-employment medical examinations and prohibits inquiries of job applicants regarding whether or not a disability exists. The employer can require a medical examination, but only after an offer of employment has been made and then subject to several conditions and requirements. If an employee is known to have a disability then the employer has an obligation to make reasonable accommodations to enable the person to perform the tasks re-quired of the person. Reasonable accommodations will no doubt also require physical changes to the employer's buildings, such as wheelchair ramps, restroom availability to handicapped, and the like. Employers must be aware of their duties under this new law.

Vietnam Veterans Readjustment Act. Congress passed the Vietnam Veterans Readjustment Act to give Vietnam veterans a special priority with regard to employment. However, only em-ployers with government contracts of $10,000 or more are required to take affirmative action to employ and advance disabled and qualified veterans of the Vietnam era. No other employers are required by law to give such preference or priority to the veterans of the Vietnam era. All covered employers have an obligation to list all suitable job openings with the appropriate local employment service. Referral priority will then be given to Vietnam era veterans.

Pregnancy Discrimination Act. The most recent major addition to the antidiscrimination laws is the Pregnancy Discrimination Act. This act prohibits discrimination in any aspect of the employment relationship because of a female employee's pregnancy. Health and disability plans for employees, in particular, must provide coverage of pregnancy and childbirth on the same basis as other medical conditions.

State Antidiscrimination Laws. Many states have passed civil rights laws that extend coverage to more employers than the national law. For example, the national Civil Rights Act only covers employers with fifteen or more employees. Some states' civil rights laws cover those employers with six or more employees. Many states also have their own civil rights commissions to enforce these laws.

MAJOR PROBLEM AREAS—CIVIL RIGHTS LAWS

Testing and Education Requirements. Title VII does not prohibit employers from testing applicants or current employees. Tests may be used to measure the applicant's or employee's ability to do the job, provided the test does not discriminate against minorities or women. For example, an employer wants to hire a typist. A typing test would be a legal test if it simply tested the accuracy and speed of typing that could be performed by the applicant. With regard to requiring a certain level of education before a person will be considered for employment, any such requirement must be shown to be job related.

In 1971, the U.S. Supreme Court decided the now famous *Griggs v. Duke Power* case. In that case the employer used preemployment tests and had a job requirement stating that all applicants had to have a high school diploma to be hired. Neither the tests nor the requirement of a high school diploma were found to be job related. In that case both the tests and educational requirement were clearly devices designed to discriminate against blacks.

Generally speaking, employers may use tests and may have educational requirements for certain jobs, but the burden is on the employer to prove that the tests and educational requirements are job related.

Dress and Grooming Requirements. Courts have generally upheld employers' reasonable and uniformly applied standards for employees' appearance. Problems arise, and lawsuits may occur, where a seemingly innocuous and neutral standard adversely impacts a protected class of employees. A requirement that male employees be clean-shaven, for instance, will disqualify Sikhs, whose religion forbids their shaving. Such a rule may also have a statistically disproportionate adverse effect on African-American males, twenty-five percent of whom suffer from a skin condition aggravated by shaving.

Sex discrimination claims may also be raised where grooming policies for men and women are different. Can women be permitted to wear jewelry, while men are prohibited from doing so? Can an employer impose different hair-length standards for men and women? The answers to these and many other similar questions are not absolutely clear. Suffice it to say that an employer needs to think carefully about these issues when establishing such policies. At the very least, employers should be prepared to show the business need for the dress and grooming policies adopted.

The *Harper* case discusses some of these points.

HARPER v. BLOCKBUSTER ENTERTAINMENT
139 F.3d 1385 (Eleventh Circuit, 1998)

FACTS: In May of 1994, Blockbuster implemented a new grooming policy that prohibited men, not women, from wearing long hair. The plaintiffs, four men with long hair, refused to comply with the policy. They protested the policy as discriminatory and communicated their protest to supervisory officials of Blockbuster. Two of the plaintiffs were the subject of media stories concerning their protest of the policy. All of the plaintiffs were subsequently terminated by Blockbuster because they had refused to cut their hair and because they had protested the grooming policy.

The plaintiffs timely filed a charge with the Equal Employment Opportunity Commission ("EEOC"). After the EEOC issued right to sue letters, the plaintiffs filed a four-count complaint alleging: (1) sex discrimination under Title VII, (2) sex discrimination under the Florida Civil Rights Act of 1992, (3) unlawful retaliation under Title VII, and (4) unlawful retaliation under the Florida Civil Rights Act.

Blockbuster moved to dismiss the complaint. The district court granted the motion, and this appeal followed.

 CIRCUIT JUDGE CARNES:

The plaintiffs allege that Blockbuster's grooming policy discriminates on the basis of sex in violation of Title VII. In *Willingham v. Macon Telegraph Pub. Co.*, 507 F.2d 1084, 1092 (5th Cir. 1975) (en banc), our predecessor Court held that differing hair length standards for men and women to not violate Title VII, a holding which squarely forecloses the plaintiffs' discrimination claim.... Accordingly, the district court correctly dismissed Count I....

The Florida courts have held that decisions construing Title VII are applicable when considering claims under the Florida Civil Rights Act, because the Florida act was patterned after Title VII.... No Florida court has interpreted the Florida statute to impose substantive liability where Title VII does not. Therefore, for the same reasons the complaint fails to state a sex discrimination claim under Title VII, it fails to state a sex discrimination claim under the Florida Civil Rights Act. The district court correctly dismissed Count II.

The plaintiffs allege that they were discharged by Blockbuster in retaliation for protesting Blockbuster's grooming policy. To establish a prima facie case of retaliation under Title VII, a plaintiff must demonstrate: (1) that he engaged in statutorily protected activity, (2) that he suffered adverse employment action, and (3) that the adverse employment action was causally related to the protected activity.... A plaintiff engages in "statutorily protected activity" when he or she protests an employer's conduct which is actually lawful, so long as he or she demonstrates "a good faith, reasonable belief that the employer was engaged in unlawful employment practices."... However, it is insufficient for a plaintiff "to allege his belief in this regard was honest and bona fide; the allegations and record must also indicate that the belief, though perhaps mistaken, was objectively reasonable."...

The reasonableness of the plaintiffs' belief in this case is belied by the unanimity with which the courts have declared grooming policies like Blockbuster's non-discriminatory. Every circuit to have considered the issue has reached the same conclusion reached by this Court in the Willingham decision.... The EEOC initially took a contrary position, but in the face of the unanimous position of the courts of appeal that have addressed the issue, it finally "concluded that successful litigation of male hair length cases would be virtually impossible."... Accordingly, the EEOC ran up a white flag on the issue, advising its field offices to administratively close all sex discrimination charges dealing with male hair length....

Nonetheless, the plaintiffs contend that three decisions of the United States Supreme Court, decided after Willingham, made it reasonable to believe that Blockbuster's grooming policy violates the mandate of Title VII. However, ... none of the cases cited by the plaintiffs call into question the continuing validity of Willingham; therefore, the plaintiffs' belief that Blockbuster's grooming policy violated Title VII's prohibition against sex discrimination was not reasonable....

The plaintiffs chose to protest Blockbuster's grooming policy despite the existence of long-standing binding precedent holding that such a policy was not discriminatory. No decision cited by the plaintiffs has supplanted the reasoning or called into question the conclusions set forth in that binding precedent. Therefore, we hold that the plaintiffs could not have had an objectively reasonable belief that Blockbuster's grooming policy discriminated against them on the basis of their sex. Accordingly, the district court correctly dismissed the plaintiffs' Title VII retaliation claim....

The plaintiffs allege that Blockbuster violated the Florida Civil Rights Act by retaliating against them for protesting its grooming policy. As discussed above, decisions construing Title VII guide the analysis of claims under the Florida Civil Rights Act. Accordingly, because the plaintiffs cannot maintain a retaliation claim under Title VII, we conclude that the district court correctly dismissed the plaintiffs' Florida Civil Rights Act retaliation claim....

For the reasons set forth above, we AFFIRM the district court's order dismissing the plaintiffs' complaint.

Sexual Harassment. Section 703 of Title VII has been interpreted as also prohibiting sexual harassment. Sexual harassment has been defined as conduct involving unwelcome sexual advances, requests for sexual favors, and other verbal or physical conduct of a sexual nature.

There is no question but that the person guilty of the sexual harassment, such as a supervisor who requests sexual favors as a condition for hiring an applicant, continued employment, a salary increase, or a promotion is guilty of violating the law. Recently the courts have also held the employer liable for civil damages if it can be shown that the employer knew or should have known of the illegal conduct.

An employer is liable for harassment by its supervisors who are acting within the scope of their authority. The *Harris* case discusses the sort of "injury" that the victimized employee must prove.

HARRIS v. FORKLIFT SYSTEMS, INC.
114 S.Ct. 367 (1993)

FACTS: Teresa Harris worked as a manager at Forklift Systems, Inc., an equipment rental company, from April 1985 until October 1987. Charles Hardy was Forklift's president.

The Magistrate found that, throughout Harris' time at Forklift, Hardy often insulted her because of her gender and often made her the target of unwanted sexual innuendoes. Hardy told Harris on several occasions, in the presence of other employees, "You're a woman, what do you know" and "We need a man as the rental manager"; at least once, he told her she was "a dumb ... woman." Again in front of others, he suggested that the two of them "go to the Holiday Inn to negotiate [Harris'] raise." Hardy occasionally asked Harris and other female employees to get coins from his front pants pocket. He threw objects on the ground in front of Harris and other women, and asked them to pick the objects up. He made sexual innuendoes about Harris' and other women's clothing.

In mid-August 1987, Harris complained to Hardy about his conduct. Hardy said he was surprised that Harris was offended, claimed he was only joking, and apologized. He also promised he would stop, and based on this assurance Harris stayed on the job. But in early September, Hardy began anew: While Harris was arranging a deal with one of Forklift's customers, he asked her, again in front of other employees, "What did you do, promise the guy ... some [sex] Saturday night?" On October 1, Harris collected her paycheck and quit.

Harris then sued Forklift, claiming that Hardy's conduct had created an abusive work environment for her because of her gender. The United States District Court for the Middle District of Tennessee, adopting the report and recommendation of the Magistrate, found this to be "a close case," but held that Hardy's conduct did not create an abusive environment. The court found that some of Hardy's comments "offended [Harris], and would offend the reasonable woman," but that they were not:

> "so severe as to be expected to seriously affect [Harris'] psychological well-being. A reasonable woman manager under like circumstances would have been offended by Hardy, but his conduct would not have risen to the level of interfering with that person's work performance.

> "Neither do I believe that [Harris] was subjectively so offended that she suffered injury.... Although Hardy may at times have genuinely offended [Harris], I do not believe that he created a working environment so poisoned as to be intimidating or abusive to [Harris]."

In focusing on the employee's psychological well-being, the District Court was following Circuit precedent. The U.S. Sixth Circuit affirmed.

JUSTICE O'CONNOR:

Title VII of the Civil Rights Act of 1964 makes it "an unlawful employment practice for an employer ... to discriminate against any individual with respect to his compensation, terms, conditions, or privileges of employment, because of such individual's race, color, religion, sex, or national origin...." As we made clear in *Meritor Savings Bank* ..., this language "is not limited to 'economic' or 'tangible' discrimination. The phrase 'terms, conditions, or privileges of employment' evinces a congressional intent 'to strike at the entire spectrum of disparate treatment of men and women' in employment," which includes requiring people to work in a discriminatorily hostile or abusive environment.... When the workplace is permeated with "discriminatory intimidation, ridicule, and insult," ... that is "sufficiently severe or pervasive to alter the conditions of the victim's employment and create an abusive working environment," ... Title VII is violated.

This standard, which we reaffirm today, takes a middle path between making actionable any conduct that is merely offensive and requiring the conduct to cause a tangible psychological injury. As we pointed out in *Meritor*, "mere utterance of an ... epithet which engenders offensive feelings in a employee," does not sufficiently affect the conditions of employment to implicate Title VII. Conduct that is not severe or pervasive enough to create an objectively hostile or abusive work environment—an environment that a reasonable person would find hostile or abusive—is beyond Title VII's purview. Likewise, if the victim does not subjectively perceive the environment to be abusive, the conduct has not actually altered the conditions of the victim's employment, and there is no Title VII violation.

But Title VII comes into play before the harassing conduct leads to a nervous breakdown. A discriminatorily abusive work environment, even one that does not seriously affect employees' psychological well-being, can and often will detract from employees' job performance, discourage employees from remaining on the job, or keep them from advancing in their careers. Moreover, even without regard to these tangible effects, the very fact that the discriminatory conduct was so severe or pervasive that it created a work environment abusive to employees because of their race, gender, religion, or national origin offends Title VII's broad rule of workplace equality. The appalling conduct alleged in *Meritor*, and the reference in that case to environments "so heavily polluted with discrimination as to destroy completely the emotional and psychological stability of minority group workers," ... merely present some especially egregious examples of harassment. They do not mark the boundary of what is actionable.

We therefore believe the District Court erred in relying on whether the conduct "seriously affect[ed] plaintiff's psychological well-being" or led her to "suffe[r] injury." Such an inquiry may needlessly focus the factfinder's attention on concrete psychological harm, an element Title VII does not require. Certainly Title VII bars conduct that would seriously affect a reasonable person's psychological well-being, but the statute is not limited to such conduct. So long as the environment would reasonably be perceived, and is perceived, as hostile or abusive, ... there is no need for it also to psychologically injurious.

This is not, and by its nature cannot be, a mathematically precise test. We need not answer today all the potential questions it raises, nor specifically address the EEOC's new regulations on this subject.... But we can say that whether an environment is "hostile" or "abusive" can be determined only by looking at all the circumstances. These may include the frequency of the discriminatory conduct; its severity; whether it is physically threatening or humiliating, or a mere offensive utterance; and whether it unreasonably interferes with an employee's work performance. The effect on the employee's psychological well-being is, of course, relevant to determining whether the plaintiff actually found the environment abusive. But while psychological harm, like any other relevant factor, may be taken into account, no single factor is required.

Forklift, while conceding that a requirement that the conduct seriously affect psychological well-being is unfounded, argues that the District Court nonetheless correctly applied the *Meritor* standard. We disagree. Though the District Court did conclude that the work environment was not "intimidating or abusive to [Harris]," ... it did so only after finding that the conduct was not "so severe as to be expected to seriously affect plaintiff's psychological well-being," ... and that Harris was not "subjectively so offended that she suffered injury...." The District Court's application of these incorrect standards may well have influenced its ultimate conclusion, especially given that the court found this to be a "close case...."

We therefore reverse the judgment of the Court of Appeals, and remand the case for further proceedings consistent with this opinion.

Employer Benefit Plans. Most employers provide some type of medical payment plan for employees and their families and some type of retirement plan. These plans can be financed entirely by contributions by the employer, or their cost may be shared between employer and employee. The discrimination problem with regard to these plans has been primarily in the area of sex discrimination. One question that arose was: Does a medical plan have to provide coverage for pregnancy? The Supreme Court of the United States answered that question in the negative in 1976. Then Congress stepped in, and in 1978 enacted the Pregnancy Discrimination Act, which now makes it unlawful for an employer to exclude pregnancy-related disabilities from any medical, hospital, or disability benefits plan, or any company plan or program that allows sick leaves.

In 1983, the U.S. Supreme Court further defined the required "neutrality" in its decision in *Newport News Shipbuilding and Dry Dock Co. v. EEOC*. In that case, the employer gave women employees paid leave time to give birth to a child, and the question was raised as to whether the granting of such benefits to females was discriminatory against males. The Supreme Court held that the employer must also give paid leave time to any male employee whose wife gives birth to a child.

Statistically, women have had a longer life expectancy than men. Pension plans, insurance annuity plans, and other forms of retirement plans have traditionally based contribution rates on life expectancy. That is to say, since women statistically have a longer life expectancy after retirement than men, it can be expected that they will have to be paid more benefits than would be paid to men who have a shorter life expectancy. Insurance companies, to have adequate funding, either increased the contribution to be made by women to offset the fact that they may receive benefits for a longer time, or the companies charged the same contribution rate but then paid the retired woman a lower monthly retirement benefit than the man who had made similar contributions. These practices were based on the contention that the woman would live longer and thus there would be more monthly payments to be made in the case of a retired woman than to a retired man. The Supreme Court has declared both of these practices discriminatory under Title VII.

Thus, after these decisions any contributions by employees to a retirement plan must be "sex-neutral." Any distribution to retired employees from such plans must also be calculated without regard to the sex of the party receiving the distribution benefits.

Comparable Worth Doctrine. We have previously discussed the Equal Pay Act of 1963. As stated, that law requires an employer to pay equal pay for equal work. In order for a claimant to collect back pay under that law it must be shown that one sex (usually the males) is being paid more than the opposite sex, for doing the same job. If the job performed by one sex is not substantially equal to the job performed by the opposite sex, then there is no violation.

Recently the proponents of equal pay for the sexes came up with the concept of "comparable worth." This concept would make the employer not only pay equal pay to both sexes for doing substantially equal work but also for doing jobs which are of comparable worth or value to the company. In 1981 the U.S. Supreme Court, in *County of Washington v. Gunther*, found that women who were not doing substantially the same job as their male counterparts could bring a lawsuit under Title VII for back wages based on alleged intentional sexual discrimination in payment of wages to women.

That case involved complaints by four female prison guards who were being paid less than male prison guards. However, the evidence showed the jobs of the female prison guards and the male prison guards were not substantially the same because the male guards supervised ten times as many prisoners per guard as did the female guards, and also a substantial part of the female guards' job was spent doing clerical work. Thus the jobs were not substantially equal. The Supreme Court found that there was sexual discrimination with regard to the wages paid to the women and remanded the case to provide for payment of back wages, but without basing their decision on the concept of comparable worth. The advocates of comparable worth felt that the case was a first step in the acceptance of the comparable worth doctrine even though the court did not specifically address the comparable worth issue.

The state legislature of Washington was favorably impressed with the fairness of the comparable worth concept and passed a law applying the doctrine of comparable worth to the state employees' jobs, effective in June 1983.

While this doctrine on its face seems to be a fair doctrine and certainly a doctrine that would promote the cause of reducing discrimination against women in the workplace, it has not been widely accepted. The primary reason, of course, is not only the difficulty of deciding comparable worth of the various jobs, but also the bottom line of the dollars and cents cost of making such adjustments. Obviously you could not reduce the pay of one job to the level of the comparative job so it would mean increasing the pay for the lower paying job. Thus the future of comparative worth is still uncertain at this time.

Government Contractors. We have previously referred to the Rehabilitation Act of 1973 and the Vietnam Veterans Readjustment Act of 1974. Both of these acts are legislative enactments that specify that government contractors with contracts exceeding a specific amount must take affirmative action with regard to hiring the persons protected by those laws, namely, the handicapped and Vietnam veterans.

In 1965 President Johnson issued Executive Order No. 11,246 and in 1967 he issued Executive Order No. 11,375. These executive orders set up the Office of Federal Contract Compliance Programs (OFCCP). They also require a contractor who accepts a U.S. government contract of $50,000 or more with fifty employees to file a written Affirmative Action Plan with the OFCCP

This plan involves a complete review of the contractor's workforce and a breakdown of the workforce into categories of race, color, sex, and national origin. The surrounding area from which employees are recruited is then reviewed with regard to the same categories. The contractor is then required to prepare a plan to take affirmative action to increase the numbers of employees in these various categories so that the percentage of persons in the various categories in the workforce of the employer is comparable to the percentage of the available workers in such categories in the recruiting area. Contractors are not required to fire nonminority or male persons or to hire more persons than necessary, nor are they required to hire persons who are not qualified for the job.

In addition to the contractors who accept U.S. contracts of $50,000 or more and who have 50 or more employees, several other groups are affected by executive orders 11,246 and 11,375. Those groups are: (1) contractors or subcontractors that provide the government with more than $10,000 worth of supplies, services or work; (2) contractors or subcontractors that have had more than $10,000 worth of government business in any 12-month period; (3) anyone who has government bills of lading in any amount; (4) any firm that serves as an issuing or paying agent of U.S. savings bonds and notes; (5) any firm that serves as a depository of U.S. funds in any amount; (6) all contractors and subcontractors that hold U.S. assisted contracts in excess of $10,000; (7) any construction contractor's or subcontractor's construction employees who are engaged in on-site construction including those construction employees who work on a nonfederal or non-federally assisted construction site.

The theory of affirmative action is to seek out women and persons from the minority categories to fill new and vacant positions to thus increase the percentage of women and minority persons in the employment of the contractor. OFCCP will periodically review the plan and the progress made. Failure to comply with the plan may cause cancellation of the government contract and disbarment from future government contracts for a period of time.

SIGNIFICANCE OF THIS CHAPTER

Discrimination by employers with regard to selection of employees, wage rates, and promotion have been serious and continuing problems in our economy for some time. Beginning in 1963, Congress began a concerted effort to prevent and correct the problems of discrimination in the hiring process and in the day-to-day work environment. Various national and state laws have been enacted to prohibit current discriminatory practices and to promote affirmative action to correct the effect of past discrimination. Managers should be aware of these laws and urge compliance with them, as violations may have serious consequences. This chapter is designed to give the manager of tomorrow a brief but basic knowledge of the various laws on discrimination which apply to businesses.

PROBLEMS FOR DISCUSSION

1. Mr. Celio Diaz applied for the job of flight cabin attendant (also known as the job of stewardess). Pan Am refused to hire him. Pan Am contended that a BFOQ of the job was that the persons employed in that position must be female. Mr. Diaz filed suit on behalf of himself and all other males as a class being denied access to these jobs, alleging Pan Am had violated the Civil Rights Act of 1964 by refusing to hire him. Pan Am's primary contention was that it was the passengers' preference to be served by females rather than males. The trial court found that being a female was a proper BFOQ for the job. Mr. Diaz appealed.

    How should the appeals court decide, and why?

2. Captain Carl Stotts, a black person employed by the Memphis Tennessee Fire Department, filed a class action in U.S. District Court in Tennessee alleging that the fire department, the local union, and certain city officials of Memphis, Tennessee were engaged in a pattern of discrimination on the basis of race and color. This case was settled by consent of the parties, and a consent decree was entered by the court ordering the Fire Department to remedy the department's hiring and promotion practices with regard to black persons. The consent decree required the city to promote thirteen individuals and to provide back pay to eighty-one employees of the fire department. It also required the city to adopt a long-term goal to increase the amount of minority representation in each job classification. The next year, the city announced a budget cut which would require layoffs throughout city government. Layoffs were to be on the "last hired, first fired" basis. The plaintiff Stotts went back to court and requested an injunction forbidding the layoffs of any black employees.

    Should the injunction be granted? Why or why not?

3. Blackhound Bus Company established a mandatory retirement age for their bus drivers. They required all bus drivers to retire commencing the first day of the year following their 60th birthday. They stated as their reason the fact that the Federal Aviation Administration (FAA) prohibits persons over sixty years of age from being a pilot on a commercial airline. Since bus drivers are also "pilots" of a commercial vehicle and are responsible for the lives and welfare of their passengers, the company felt it would be a good idea to use the same age requirement for bus drivers. This new mandatory retirement age affected thirteen drivers already over age sixty and 129 drivers nearing the age of 60. All of these persons immediately complained to the EEOC alleging a violation of the Age Discrimination in Employment Act.

    Will they be successful? Make arguments pro and con.

4. Midtown Electronics Inc. makes electrical components for radios and televisions sets and their market has been primarily the American manufacturers of radios and TVs. The Department of Defense has offered to give them a contract for a million dollars to produce specially designed electronic parts for a new star wars defense device. Midtown now has eighty-seven employees. They have forty-two women who work in the production line, but they have no blacks and no other minorities. They intend to remodel the present production process, which is heavily people oriented, with robots. They signed the contract, and now they have received a letter from a governmental organization called OFFCP requiring them to file an "Affirmative Action Plan." They come to you for advice.

    What can you tell them with regard to the preparation of an Affirmative Action Plan?

5. Elijah Gottfried applied for a job as a cabdriver for Crakup Cab Company. Due to a congenital birth defect, he had no right hand and his right forearm extended only to about three inches below the elbow. He owned and often wore and used a prosthetic device. He held a valid state driver's license, although it limited him to operating motor vehicles equipped with automatic transmission, self-canceling turn signals, and a wheel spinner. All of Crakup's cabs had automatic transmission and self-canceling turn signals, and Elijah was willing to supply his own wheel spinner, which was simply a small knob that attached easily to the steering wheel and enabled the driver to turn the wheel with one hand. While driving on his own, Elijah had been involved in two minor accidents, neither of which was his fault. Crakup said that it had a company policy against hiring one-handed cab drivers and that this was a valid BFOQ. Elijah says that the company illegally discriminated against him because of his handicap. Does Elijah have a right to file a complaint with the EEOC under the provisions of the 1964 Civil Rights Act as amended?

If not, is there any other law that would allow him to force the cab company to hire him? Explain.

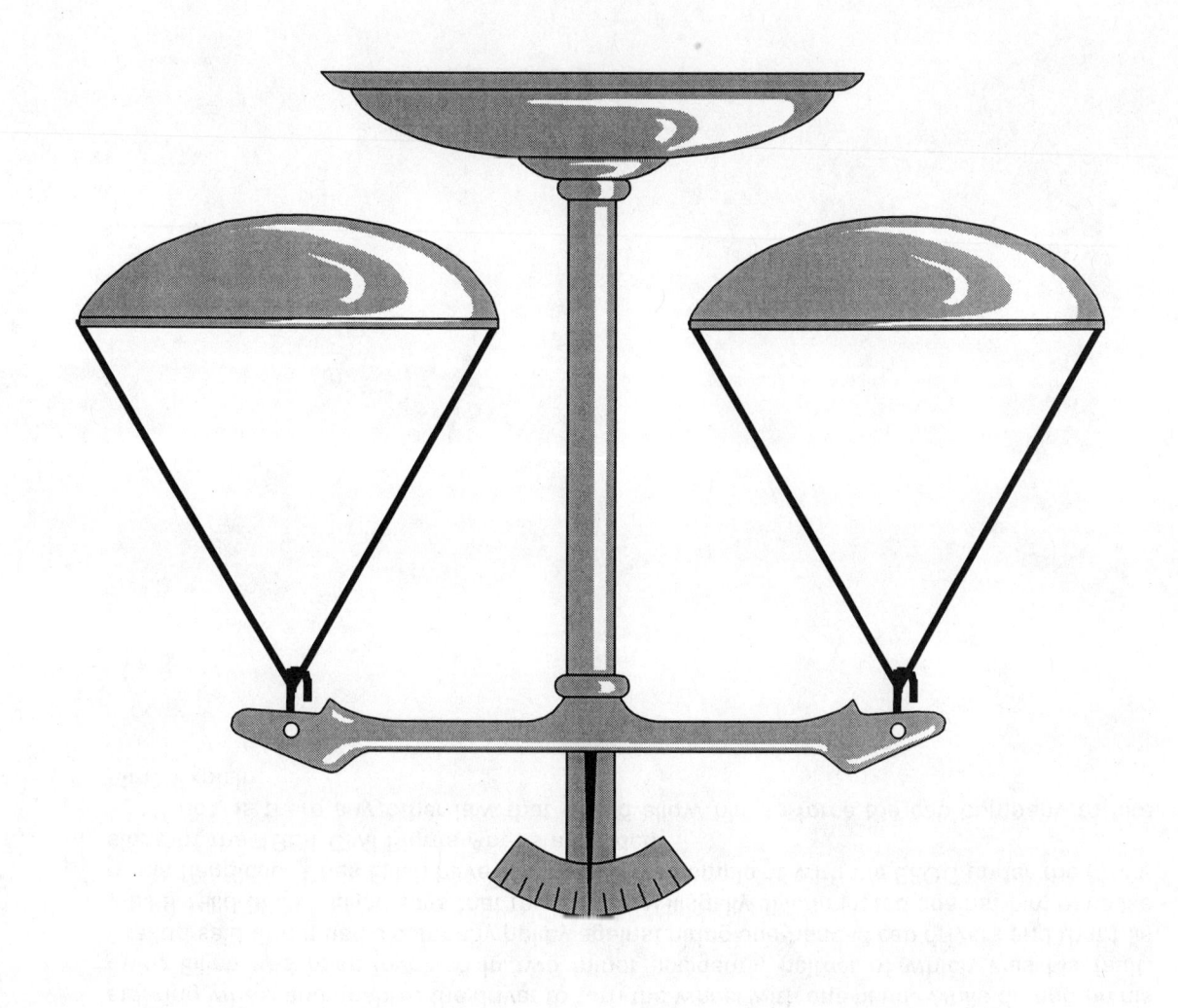

Appendix A
The Constitution of the United States

PREAMBLE

We the People of the United States, in Order to form a more perfect Union, establish Justice, insure domestic Tranquility, provide for the common Defence, promote the general Welfare, and secure the Blessings of Liberty to ourselves and our Posterity, do ordain and establish this Constitution for the United States of America.

ARTICLE 1

Section 1. All legislative Powers herein granted shall be vested in a Congress of the United States, which shall consist of a Senate and House of Representatives.

Section 2. [1] The House of Representatives shall be composed of Members chosen every second Year by the People of the several States, and the Electors in each State shall have the Qualifications requisite for Electors of the most numerous Branch of the State Legislature.

[2] No Person shall be a Representative who shall not have attained to the Age of twenty five Years, and been seven Years a Citizen of the United States, and who shall not, when elected, be an Inhabitant of that State in which he shall be chosen.

[3] Representatives and direct Taxes shall be apportioned among the several States which may be included within this Union, according to their respective Numbers, which shall be determined by adding to the whole Number of free Persons, including those bound to Service for a Term of Years, and excluding Indians not taxed, three fifths of all other Persons The actual Enumeration shall be made within three Years after the first Meeting of the Congress of the United States, and within every subsequent Term of ten Years, in such Manner as they shall by Law direct. The Number of Representatives shall not exceed one for every thirty Thousand, but each State shall have at Least one Representative; and until such enumeration shall be made, the State of New Hampshire shall be entitled to chose three, Massachusetts eight, Rhode Island and Providence Plantations one, Connecticut five, New York six, New Jersey four, Pennsylvania eight, Delaware one, Maryland six,

Virginia ten, North Carolina five, South Carolina five, and Georgia three.

[4] When vacancies happen in the Representation from any State, the Executive Authority thereof shall issue Writs of Election to fill such Vacancies.

[5] The House of Representatives shall chose their Speaker and other Officers; and shall have the sole Power of Impeachment.

Section 3. [1] The Senate of the United States shall be composed of two Senators from each State, chosen by the Legislature thereof, for six Years; and each Senator shall have one Vote.

[2] Immediately after they shall be assembled in Consequence of the first Election, they shall be divided as equally as may be into three Classes. The Seats of the Senators of the first Class shall be vacated at the Expiration of the Second Year, of the second Class at the Expiration of the fourth Year, and of the third Class at the Expiration of the sixth Year, so that one third may be chosen every second Year; and if Vacancies happen by Resignation, or otherwise, during the Recess of the Legislature of any State, the Executive thereof may make temporary Appointments until the next Meeting of the Legislature, which shall then fill such Vacancies.

[3] No Person shall be a Senator who shall not have attained to the Age of thirty Years, and been nine Years a Citizen of the United States, and who shall not, when elected, be an Inhabitant of that State for which he shall be chosen.

[4] The Vice President of the United States shall be President of the Senate, but shall have no Vote, unless they be equally divided.

[5] The Senate shall chose their other Officers, and also a President pro tempore, in the Absence of the Vice President, or when he shall exercise the Office of President of the United States.

[6] The Senate shall have the sole Power to try all Impeachments. When sitting for that Purpose, they shall be on Oath or Affirmation. When the President of the United States is tried, the Chief Justice shall preside: And no Person shall be convicted without the Concurrence of two thirds of the Members present.

[7] Judgment in Cases of Impeachment shall not extend further than to removal from Office, and disqualification to hold and enjoy any Office of Honor, Trust, or Profit under the United States: but the Party convicted shall nevertheless be liable and subject to Indictment, Trial, Judgment, and Punishment, according to Law.

Section 4. [1] The Times, Places and Manner of holding elections for Senators and Representatives, shall be prescribed in each State by the Legislature thereof; but the Congress may at any time by Law make or alter such Regulations, except as to the Places of choosing Senators.

[2] The Congress shall assemble at least once in every Year, and such Meeting shall be on the first Monday in December, unless they shall by Law appoint a different Day.

Section 5. [1] Each House shall be the Judge of the Elections, Returns, and Qualifications of its own Members, and a Majority of each shall constitute a Quorum to do Business; but a smaller Number may adjourn from day to day, and may be authorized to compel the Attendance of absent Members, in such Manner, and under such Penalties as each House may provide.

[2] Each House may determine the Rules of its Proceedings, punish its Members for disorderly Behavior, and, with the Concurrence of two thirds, expel a Member.

[3] Each House shall keep a Journal of its Proceedings, and from time to time publish the same, excepting such Parts as may in their Judgment require Secrecy; and the Yeas and Nays of the Members of either House on any question shall, at the Desire of one fifth of those Present, be entered on the Journal.

[4] Neither House, during the Session of Congress, shall, without the Consent of the other, adjourn for more than three days, nor to any other Place than that in which the two Houses shall be sitting.

Section 6. [1] The Senators and Representatives shall receive a Compensation for their Services, to be ascertained by Law, and paid out of the Treasury of the United States. They shall in all Cases, except Treason, Felony and Breach of the Peace, be privileged from Arrest during their Attendance at the Session of their respective Houses, and in going to and returning from the same; and for any Speech or Debate in either House, they shall not be questioned in any other Place.

[2] No Senator or Representative shall, during the Time for which he was elected, be appointed to any civil Office under the Authority of the United States, which shall have been created, or the Emoluments whereof shall have been increased during such time; and no Person holding any Office under the United States, shall be a Member of either House during his Continuance in Office.

Section 7. [1] All Bills for raising Revenue shall originate in the House of Representatives; but the Senate may propose or concur with Amendments as on other Bills.

[2] Every Bill which shall have passed the House of Representatives and the Senate, shall, before it becomes a Law, be presented to the President of the United States; If he approve he shall sign it, but if not he shall return it, with his Objections to the House in which it shall have originated, who shall enter the Objections at large on their Journal, and proceed to reconsider it. If after such Reconsideration two thirds of that House shall agree to pass the Bill, it shall be sent together with the Objections, to the other House, by which it shall likewise be reconsidered, and if approved by two thirds of that House, it shall become a Law. But in all such Cases the Votes of both Houses shall be determined by yeas and Nays, and the Names of the Persons voting for and against the Bill shall be entered on the Journal of each House respectively. If any Bill shall not be returned by the President within ten Days (Sundays excepted) after it shall have been presented to him, the Same shall be a Law, in like Manner as if he had signed it unless the Congress by their Adjournment prevent its Return in which Case it shall not be a Law.

[3] Every Order, Resolution, or Vote, to Which the Concurrence of the Senate and House of Representatives may be necessary (except on a question of Adjournment) shall be presented to the President of the United States; and before the Same shall take Effect, shall be approved by him, or being disapproved by him, shall be repassed by two thirds of the Senate and House of Representatives, according to the Rules and Limitations prescribed in the Case of a Bill.

Section 8. [1] The Congress shall have Power To lay and collect Taxes, Duties, Imposts and Excises, to pay the Debts and provide for the common Defence and general Welfare of the United States; but all Duties, Imposts and Excises shall be uniform throughout the United States;

[2] To borrow money on the credit of the United States;

[3] To regulate Commerce with foreign Nations, and among the several States, and with the Indian Tribes;

[4] To establish an uniform Rule of Naturalization, and uniform Laws on the subject of Bankruptcies throughout the United States;

[5] To coin Money, regulate the Value thereof, and of foreign Coin, and fix the Standard of Weights and Measures;

[6] To provide for the Punishment of counterfeiting the Securities and current Coin of the United States;

[7] To Establish Post Offices and Post Roads;

[8] To promote the Progress of Science and useful Arts, by securing for limited Times to Authors and Inventors the exclusive Right to their respective Writings and Discoveries;

[9] To constitute Tribunals inferior to the supreme Court;

[10] To define and punish Piracies and Felonies committed on the high Seas, and Offenses against the Law of Nations;

[11] To declare War, grant Letters of Marque and Reprisal, and make Rules concerning Captures on Land and Water;

[12] To raise and support Armies, but no Appropriation of Money to that Use shall be for a longer Term than two Years;

[13] To provide and maintain a Navy;

[14] To make Rules for the Government and Regulation of the land and naval Forces;

[15] To provide for calling forth the Militia to execute the Laws of the Union, suppress Insurrections and repel Invasions;

[16] To provide for organizing, arming, and disciplining, the Militia, and for governing such Part of them as may be employed in the Service of the United States, reserving to the States respectively, the Appointment of the Officers, and the Authority of training the Militia according to the discipline prescribed by Congress;

[17] To exercise exclusive Legislation in all Cases whatsoever, over such District (not exceeding ten Miles square) as may, by Cession of particular States, and the Acceptance of Congress, become the Seat of the Government of the United States, and to exercise like Authority over all Places purchased by the Consent of the Legislature of the State in which the Same shall be, for the Erection of Forts, Magazines, Arsenals, dock-Yards and other needful Buildings;—And

[18] To make all Laws which shall be necessary and proper for carrying into Execution the foregoing Powers, and all other Powers vested by this Constitution in the Government of the United States, or in any Department or Officer thereof.

Section 9. [1] The Migration or Importation of Such Persons as any of the States now existing shall think proper to admit, shall not be prohibited by the Congress prior to the Year one thousand eight hundred and eight, but a Tax or duty may be imposed on such Importation, not exceeding ten dollars for each Person.

[2] The privilege of the Writ of Habeas Corpus shall not be suspended, unless when in Cases of Rebellion or Invasion the public Safety may require it.

[3] No Bill of Attainder or ex post facto Law shall be passed.

[4] No Capitation, or other direct, Tax shall be laid, unless in Proportion to the Census or Enumeration herein before directed to be taken.

[5] No Tax or Duty shall be laid on Articles exported from any State.

[6] No Preference shall be given by any Regulation of Commerce or Revenue to the Ports of one State over those of another: nor shall Vessels bound to, or from, one State be obliged to enter, clear, or pay Duties in another.

[7] No money shall be drawn from the Treasury, but in Consequence of Appropriations made by Law; and a regular Statement and Account of the Receipts and Expenditures of all public Money shall be published from time to time.

[8] No Title of Nobility shall be granted by the United States: And no Person holding any Office of Profit or Trust under them. shall, without the Consent of the Congress, accept of any present, Emolument, Office, or Title, of any kind whatever, from any King, Prince, or foreign State.

Section 10. [1] No State shall enter into any Treaty, Alliance, or Confederation; grant Letters of Marque and Reprisal; coin Money; emit Bills of Credit; make any Thing but gold and silver Coin a Tender in Payment of Debts; pass any Bill of Attainder, ex post facto Law, or Law impairing the Obligation of Contracts, or grant any Title of Nobility.

[2] No State shall, without the Consent of the Congress, lay any Imposts or Duties on Imports or Exports, except what may be absolutely necessary for executing its inspection Laws: and the net Produce of all Duties and Imposts, laid by any State on Imports or Exports, shall be for the Use of the Treasury of the United States; and all such Laws shall be subject to the Revision and Control of the Congress.

[3] No State shall, without the Consent of Congress, lay any Duty of Tonnage, keep Troops, or Ships of War in time of Peace, enter into any Agreement or Compact with another State, or with a foreign Power, or engage in War, unless actually invaded, or in such imminent Danger as will not admit of delay.

ARTICLE II

Section 1. [1] The executive Power shall be vested in a President of the United States of America. He shall hold his Office during the Term of four Years, and, together with the Vice President, chosen for the same Term, be elected, as follows:

[2] Each State shall appoint, in such Manner as the Legislature thereof may direct, a Number of Electors, equal to the whole Number of Senators and Representatives to which the State may be entitled in the Congress; but no Senator or Representative, or Person holding an Office of Trust or Profit under the United States, shall be appointed an Elector.

[3] The Electors shall meet in their respective States,and vote by Ballot for two Persons, of whom one at least shall not be an Inhabitant of the same State with themselves. And they shall make a List of all the Persons voted for, and of the Number of Votes for each; which List they shall sign and certify, and transmit sealed to the Seat of the Government of the United States, directed to the President of the Senate. The President of the Senate shall, in the Presence of the Senate and House of Representatives, open all the Certificates, and the Votes shall then be counted. The Person having the greatest Number of Votes shall be the President, if such Number be a Majority of the whole Number of Electors appointed; and if there be more than one who have such Majority, and have an equal Number of Votes, then the House of Representatives shall immediately chose by Ballot one of them for President; and if no Person have a Majority, then from the five highest on the List the said House shall in like Manner chose the President. But in choosing the President, the Votes shall be taken by States the Representation from each State having one Vote; A quorum for this Purpose shall consist of a Member or Members from two thirds of the States, and a Majority of all the States shall be necessary to a Choice. In every Case, after the Choice of the President, the Person having the greater Number of Votes of the Electors shall be the Vice President. But if there shall remain two or more who have equal Votes, the Senate shall chose from them by Ballot the Vice President.

[4] The Congress may determine the Time of chosing the Electors, and the Day on which they shall give their Votes; which Day shall be the same throughout the United States.

[5] No person except a natural born Citizen, or a Citizen- of the United States, at the time of the Adoption of this Constitution, shall be eligible to the Office of President; neither shall any Person be eligible to that Office who shall not have attained to the Age of thirty-five Years, and been fourteen Years a Resident within the United States.

[6] In case of the removal of the President from Office, or of his Death, Resignation or Inability to discharge the Powers and Duties of the said Office, the Same shall devolve on the Vice President, and the Congress may by Law provide for the Case of Removal, Death, Resignation or Inability, both of the President and Vice President, declaring what Officer shall then act as President, and such Officer shall act accordingly, until the Disability be removed, or a President shall be elected.

[7] The President shall, at stated Times, receive for his Services, a Compensation, which shall neither be increased nor diminished during the Period for which he shall have been elected, and he shall not receive within that Period any other Emolument from the United States, or any of them.

[8] Before he enter on the Execution of his Office, he shall take the following Oath or Affirmation: "I do solemnly swear (or affirm) that I will faithfully execute the Office of President of the United States, and will to the best of my Ability, preserve, protect and defend the Constitution of the United States."

Section 2. [1] The President shall be Commander in Chief of the Army and Navy of the United States, and of the militia of the several States, when called into the actual Service of the United States; he may require the Opinion, in writing, of the principal Officer in each of the Executive Departments, upon any Subject relating to the Duties of their respective Offices, and he shall have Power to grant Reprieves and Pardons for Offenses against the United States, except in Cases of Impeachment.

[2] He shall have Power, by and with the Advice and Consent of the Senate to make Treaties, provided two thirds of the Senators present concur; and he shall nominate, and by and with the Advice and Consent of the Senate, shall appoint Ambassadors, other public Ministers and Consuls, Judges of the supreme Court, and all other Officers of the United

States, whose Appointments are not herein otherwise provided for, and which shall be established by Law; but the Congress may by Law vest the Appointment of such inferior Officers, as they think proper, in the President alone, in the Courts of Law, or in the Heads of Departments.

[3] The President shall have Power to fill up all Vacancies that may happen during the Recess of the Senate, by granting Commissions which shall expire at the End of their next Session.

Section 3. He shall from time to time give to the Congress Information of the State of the Union, and recommend to their Consideration such Measures as he shall judge necessary and expedient; he may, on extraordinary Occasions, convene both Houses, or either of them, and in Case of Disagreement between them, with Respect to the Time of Adjournment, he may adjourn them to such Time as he shall think proper; he shall receive Ambassadors and other public Ministers; he shall take Care that the Laws be faithfully executed, and shall Commission all the Officers of the United States.

Section 4. The President, Vice President and all civil Officers of the United States, shall be removed from Office on Impeachment for, and Conviction of, Treason, Bribery, or other high Crimes and Misdemeanors.

ARTICLE III

Section 1. The judicial Power of the United States, shall be vested in one supreme Court, and in such inferior Courts as the Congress may from time to time ordain and establish. The Judges, both of the supreme and inferior Courts, shall hold their Offices during good Behaviour, and shall, at stated Times, receive for their Services a Compensation, which shall not be diminished during their Continuance in Office.

Section 2. [1] The judicial Power shall extend to all Cases, in Law and Equity, arising under this Constitution, the Laws of the United States, and Treaties made, or which shall be made, under their Authority;—to all Cases

affecting Ambassadors, other public Ministers and Consuls;—to all Cases of admiralty and maritime Jurisdiction;—to Controversies to which the United States shall be a Party;—to Controversies between two or more States;—between a State and Citizens of another State;—between Citizens of different States;—between Citizens of the same State claiming Lands under the Grants of different States, and between a State, or the Citizens thereof, and foreign States, Citizens or Subjects.

[2] In all Cases affecting Ambassadors, other public Ministers and Consuls, and those in which a State shall be a Party, the supreme Court shall have original Jurisdiction. In all the other Cases before mentioned, the supreme Court shall have appellate Jurisdiction, both as to Law and Fact, with such Exceptions, and under such Regulations as the Congress shall make.

[3] The trial of all Crimes, except in Cases of Impeachment, shall be by Jury; and such Trial shall be held in the State where the said Crimes shall have been committed; but when not committed within any State, the Trial shall be at such Place or Places as the Congress may by Law have directed.

Section 3. [1] Treason against the United States, shall consist only in levying War against them, or, in adhering to their Enemies, giving them Aid and Comfort. No Person shall be convicted of Treason unless on the Testimony of two Witnesses to the same overt Act, or on Confession in open Court.

[2] The Congress shall have Power to declare the Punishment of Treason, but no Attainder of Treason shall work Corruption of Blood, or Forfeiture except during the Life of the Person attainted.

ARTICLE IV

Section 1. Full Faith and Credit shall be given in each State to the public Acts, Records, and judicial Proceedings of every other State. And the Congress may by general Laws prescribe the Manner in which such Acts, Records and Proceedings shall be proved, and the Effect thereof.

Section 2. [1] The Citizens of each State shall be entitled to all Privileges and Immunities of Citizens in the several States.

[2] A Person charged in any State with Treason, Felony, or other Crime, who shall flee from Justice, and be found in another State, shall on demand of the executive Authority of the State from which he fled, be delivered up, to be removed to the State having Jurisdiction of the Crime.

[3] No Person held to Service or Labour in one State, under the Laws thereof, escaping into another, shall, in Consequence of any Law or Regulation therein, be discharged from such Service or Labour, but shall be delivered up on Claim of the Party to whom such Service or Labour may be due.

Section 3. [1] New States may be admitted by the Congress into this Union; but no new State shall be formed or erected within the Jurisdiction of any other State; nor any State be formed by the Junction of two or more States, or Parts of States, without the Consent of the Legislatures of the States concerned as well as of the Congress.

[2] The Congress shall have Power to dispose of and make all needful Rules and Regulations respecting the Territory or other Property belonging to the United States; and nothing in this Constitution shall be so construed as to Prejudice any Claims of the United States, or of any particular State.

Section 4. The United States shall guarantee to every State in this Union a Republican Form of Government, and shall protect each of them against Invasion; and on Application of the Legislature, or of the Executive (when the Legislature cannot be convened) against domestic Violence.

ARTICLE V

The Congress, whenever two thirds of both Houses shall deem it necessary, shall propose Amendments to this Constitution, or, on the Application of the Legislatures of two thirds of the several States, shall call a Convention for proposing Amendments, which, in either case, shall be valid to all Intents and Purposes, as part of this Constitution, when ratified by the Legislatures of three fourths of the several States, or by Conventions in three fourths thereof, as the one or the other Mode of Ratification may be proposed by the Congress; Provided that no Amendment which may be made prior to the Year One thousand eight hundred and eight shall in any Manner affect the first and fourth Clauses in the Ninth Section of the first Article; and that no State, without its Consent, shall be deprived of its equal Suffrage in the Senate.

ARTICLE VI

[1] All Debts contracted and Engagements entered into, before the Adoption of this Constitution shall be as valid against the United States under this Constitution, as under the Confederation.

[2] This Constitution, and the Laws of the United States which shall be made in Pursuance thereof; and all Treaties made, or which shall be made, under the Authority of the United States, shall be the supreme Law of the Land; and the Judges in every State shall be bound thereby, any Thing in the Constitution or Laws of any State to the Contrary notwithstanding.

[3] The Senators and Representatives before mentioned, and the Members of the several State Legislatures, and all executive and judicial Officers, both of the United States and of the several States, shall be bound by Oath or Affirmation, to support this Constitution; but no religious Test shall ever be required as a Qualification to any Office or public Trust under the United States.

ARTICLE VII

The Ratification of the Conventions of nine States shall be sufficient for the Establishment of this Constitution between the States so ratifying the Same.

ARTICLES IN ADDITION TO, AND AMENDMENT OF, THE CONSTITUTION OF THE UNITED STATES OF AMERICA, PROPOSED BY CONGRESS, AND RATIFIED BY

THE LEGISLATURES OF THE SEVERAL STATES PURSUANT TO THE FIFTH ARTICLE OF THE ORIGINAL CONSTITUTION.

AMENDMENT I [1791]

Congress shall make no law respecting an establishment of religion, or prohibiting the free exercise thereof; or abridging the freedom of speech, or of the press; or the right of the people peaceably to assemble, and to petition the Government for a redress of grievances.

AMENDMENT II [1791]

A well regulated Militia, being necessary to the security of a free State, the right of the people to keep and bear Arms, shall not be infringed.

AMENDMENT III [1791]

No Soldier shall, in time of peace be quartered in any house, without the consent of the Owner, nor in time of war, but in a manner to be prescribed by law.

AMENDMENT IV [1791]

The right of the people to be secure in their persons, houses, papers, and effects, against unreasonable searches and seizures, shall not be violated, and no Warrants shall issue, but upon probable cause, supported by Oath or affirmation, and particularly describing the place to be searched, and the persons or things to be seized.

AMENDMENT V [1791]

No person shall be held to answer for a capital, or otherwise infamous crime, unless on a presentment or indictment of a Grand Jury, except in cases arising in the land or naval forces, or in the Militia, when in actual service in time of War or public danger; nor shall any person be subject for the same offence to be twice put in jeopardy of life or limb; nor shall be compelled in any criminal case to be a witness against himself, nor be deprived of life, liberty, or property, without due process of law; nor shall private property be taken for public use, without just compensation.

AMENDMENT VI [1791]

In all criminal prosecutions, the accused shall enjoy the right to a speedy and public trial, by an impartial jury of the State and district wherein the crime shall have been committed, which district shall have been previously ascertained by law, and to be informed of the nature and cause of the accusation; to be confronted with the witnesses against him; to have compulsory process for obtaining witnesses in his favor, and to have the Assistance of Counsel for his defence.

AMENDMENT VII [1791]

In Suits at common law, where the value in controversy shall exceed twenty dollars, the right of trial by jury shall be preserved, and no fact tried by jury, shall be otherwise reexamined in any Court of the United States, than according to the rules of common law.

AMENDMENT VIII [1791]

Excessive bail shall not be required, nor excessive fines imposed, nor cruel and unusual punishments inflicted.

AMENDMENT IX [1791]

The enumeration in the Constitution, of certain rights, shall not be construed to deny or disparage others retained by the people.

AMENDMENT X [1791]

The powers not delegated to the United States by the Constitution, nor prohibited by it to the States, are reserved to the States respectively, or to the people.

AMENDMENT XI [1798]

The Judicial power of the United States shall not be construed to extend to any suit in law or equity, commenced or prosecuted against one of the United States by Citizens of another State, or by Citizens or Subjects of any Foreign State.

AMENDMENT XII [1804]

The Electors shall meet in their respective states and vote by ballot for President and Vice President, one of whom, at least, shall not be an inhabitant of the same state with themselves; they shall name in their ballots the person voted for as President, and in distinct ballots the person voted for as Vice-President, and they shall make distinct lists of all persons voted for as-President, and of all persons voted for as Vice President, and of the number of votes for each, which lists they shall sign and certify, and transmit sealed to the seat of the government of the United States, directed to the President of the Senate; The President of the Senate shall, in the presence of the Senate and House of Representatives, open all the certificates and the votes shall then be counted; The person having the greatest number of votes for President, shall be the President, if such number be a majority of the whole number of Electors appointed; and if no person have such majority, then from the persons having the highest numbers not exceeding three on the list of those voted for as President, the House of Representatives shall choose immediately, by ballot, the President. But in choosing the President, the votes shall be taken by states, the representation from each state having one vote; a quorum for this purpose shall consist of a member or members

from two-thirds of the states, and a majority of all states shall be necessary to a choice. And if the House of Representatives shall not choose a President whenever the right of choice shall devolve upon them before the fourth day of March next following, then the Vice-President shall act as President, as in the case of the death or other constitutional disability of the President. The person having the greatest number of votes as Vice-President, shall be the Vice-President, if such number be a majority of the whole number of Electors appointed, and if no person have a majority, then from the two highest numbers on the list, the Senate shall choose the Vice-President; a quorum for the purpose shall consist of two-thirds of the whole number of Senators, and a majority of the whole number shall be necessary to a choice. But no person constitutionally ineligible to the office of President shall be eligible to that of Vice President of the United States.

AMENDMENT XIII [1865]

Section 1. Neither slavery nor involuntary servitude, except as a punishment for crime whereof the party shall have been duly convicted, shall exist within the United States, or any place subject to their jurisdiction.

Section 2. Congress shall have power to enforce this article by appropriate legislation.

AMENDMENT XIV [1868]

Section 1. All persons born or naturalized in the United States, and subject to the jurisdiction thereof, are citizens of the United States and of the State wherein they reside. No State shall make or enforce any law which shall abridge the privileges or immunities of citizens of the United States; nor shall any State deprive any person of life, liberty, or property, without due process of law; nor deny to any person within its jurisdiction the equal protection of the laws.

Section 2. Representatives shall be apportioned among the several States according to their respective numbers, counting the whole number of persons in each State, excluding Indians not taxed. But when the right to vote at any election for the choice of electors for President and Vice President of the United States, Representatives in Congress, the Executive and Judicial officers of a State, or the members of the Legislature thereof, is denied to any of the male inhabitants of such State, being twenty-one years of age, and citizens of the United States, or in any way abridged, except for participation in rebellion, or other crime, the basis of representation therein shall be reduced in the proportion which the number of such male citizens shall bear to the whole number of male citizens twenty-one years of age in such State.

Section 3. No person shall be a Senator or Representative in Congress, or elector of President and Vice President, or hold any office, civil or military, under the United States, or under any State, who having previously taken an oath, as a member of Congress, or as an officer of the United States, or as a member of any State legislature, or as an executive or judicial officer of any State, to support the Constitution of the United States, shall have engaged in insurrection or rebellion against the same, or given aid or comfort to the enemies thereof. But Congress may by a vote of two-thirds of each House, remove such disability.

Section 4. The validity of the public debt of the United States, authorized by law, including debts incurred for payment of pensions and bounties for services in suppressing insurrection or rebellion, shall not be questioned. But neither the United States nor any State shall assume or pay any debt or obligation incurred in aid of insurrection or rebellion against the United States, or any claim for the loss or emancipation of any slave; but all such debts, obligations and claims shall be held illegal and void.

Section 5. The Congress shall have power to enforce, by appropriate legislation, the provisions of this article.

AMENDMENT XV [1870]

Section 1. The right of citizens of the United States to vote shall not be denied or abridged by the United States or by any State on account of race, color, or previous condition of servitude.

Section 2. The Congress shall have power to enforce this article by appropriate legislation.

AMENDMENT XVI [1913]

The Congress shall have power to lay and collect taxes on incomes, from whatever source derived, without apportionment among the several States, and without regard to any census or enumeration.

AMENDMENT XVII [1913]

[1] The Senate of the United States shall be composed of two Senators from each State elected by the people thereof, for six years; and each Senator shall have one vote. The electors in each State shall have the qualifications requisite for electors of the most numerous branch of the State legislatures.

[2] When vacancies happen in the representation of any State in the Senate, the executive authority of such State shall issue writs of election to fill such vacancies: Provided, That the legislature of any State may empower the executive thereof to make temporary appointments until the people fill the vacancies by election as the legislature may direct.

[3] This amendment shall not be so construed as to affect the election or term of any Senator chosen before it becomes valid as part of the Constitution

AMENDMENT XVIII [1919]

Section 1. After one year from the ratification of this article the manufacture, sale, or transportation of intoxicating liquors within, the importation thereof into, or the exportation thereof from the United States and all territory subject to the jurisdiction thereof for beverage purposes is hereby prohibited.

Section 2. The Congress and the several States shall have concurrent power to enforce this article by appropriate legislation.

Section 3. This article shall be inoperative unless it shall have been ratified as an amendment to the Constitution by the legislatures of the several States, as provided in the Constitution, within seven years from the date of the submission hereof to the States by the Congress.

AMENDMENT XIX [1920]

[1] The right of citizens of the United States to vote shall not be denied or abridged by the United States or by any State on account of sex.

[2] Congress shall have power to enforce this article by appropriate legislation.

AMENDMENT XX [1933]

Section 1. the terms of the President and Vice President shall end at noon on the 20th day of January, and the terms of Senators and Representatives at noon on the 3d day of January, of the years in which such terms would have ended if this article had not been ratified; and the terms of their successors shall then begin.

Section 2. The Congress shall assemble at least once in every year, and such meeting shall begin at noon on the 3d day of January, unless they shall by law appoint a different day.

Section 3. If, at the time fixed for the beginning of the term of the President, the President elect shall have died, the Vice President elect shall become President. If the President shall not have been chosen before the time fixed for the beginning of his term, or if the President elect shall have failed to qualify, then the Vice President elect shall act as President until a President shall have qualified; and the Congress may by law provide for the case wherein neither a President elect nor a Vice President elect shall have qualified, declaring who shall then act as President, or the manner in which one who is to act shall be selected, and such person shall act accordingly until a President or Vice President shall have qualified.

Section 4. The Congress may by law provide for the case of the death of any of the persons from whom the House of Representatives may choose a President whenever the right of choice shall have devolved upon them, and for the case of the death of any of the persons from whom the Senate may choose a Vice President whenever the right of choice shall have developed upon them.

Section 5. Sections 1 and 2 shall take effect on the 15th day of October following the ratification of this article.

Section 6. This article shall be inoperative unless it shall have been ratified as an amendment to the Constitution by the legislatures of three-fourths of the several States within seven years from the date of its submission.

AMENDMENT XXI [1933]

Section 1. The eighteenth article of amendment to the Constitution of the United States is hereby repealed.

Section 2. The transportation or importation into any State, Territory, or possession of the United States for delivery or use therein of intoxicating liquors, in violation of the laws thereof, is hereby prohibited.

Section 3. This article shall be inoperative unless it shall have been ratified as an amendment to the Constitution by conventions in the several States, as provided in the Constitution, within seven years from the date of the submission hereof to the States by the Congress.

AMENDMENT XXII [1951]

Section 1. No person shall be elected to the office of the President more than twice, and no person who has held the office of President, or acted as President, for more than two years of a term to which some other person was elected President shall be elected to the office of President more than once. But this Article shall not apply to any person holding the office of President when this Article was proposed by the Congress, and shall not prevent any person who may be holding the office of President, or acting as President, during the term within which this Article becomes operative from holding the office of President or acting as President during the remainder of such term.

Section 2. This article shall be inoperative unless it shall have been ratified as an amendment to the Constitution by the legislatures of three-fourths of the several States within seven years from the date of its submission to the States by the Congress.

AMENDMENT XXIII [1961]

Section 1. The District constituting the seat of Government of the United States shall appoint in such manner as the Congress may direct:

A number of electors of President and Vice President equal to the whole number of Senators and Representatives in Congress to which the District would be entitled if it were a State, but in no event more than the least populous state; they shall be in addition to those appointed by the states, but they shall be considered, for the purposes of the election of President and Vice President, to be electors appointed by a state; and they shall meet in the District and perform such duties as provided by the twelfth article of amendment.

Section 2. The Congress shall have power to enforce this article by appropriate legislation.

AMENDMENT XXIV [1964]

Section 1. The right of citizens of the United States to vote in any primary or other election for President or Vice President, for electors for President or Vice President or for Senator or Representative in Congress, shall not be denied or abridged by the United States, or any State by reason of failure to pay any poll tax or other tax.

Section 2. The Congress shall have power to enforce this article by appropriate legislation.

AMENDMENT XXV [1967]

Section 1. In case of the removal of the President from office or of his death or resignation, the Vice President shall become President.

Section 2. Whenever there is a vacancy in the office of the Vice President, the President shall nominate a Vice President who shall take office upon confirmation by a majority vote of both Houses of Congress.

Section 3. Whenever the President transmits to the President pro tempore of the Senate and the Speaker of the House of Representatives his written declaration that he is unable to discharge the powers and duties of his office, and until he transmits to them a written declaration to the contrary, such powers and duties shall be discharged by the Vice President as Acting President.

Section 4. Whenever the Vice President and a majority of either the principal officers of the executive departments or of such other body as Congress may by law provide, transmit to the President pro tempore of the Senate and the Speaker of the House of Representatives their written declaration that the President is unable to discharge the powers and duties of his office, the Vice President shall immediately assume the powers and duties of the office as Acting President.

Thereafter, when the President transmits to the President pro tempore of the Senate and the Speaker of the House of Representatives his written declaration that no inability exists, he shall resume the powers and duties of his office unless the Vice President and a majority of either the principal officers of the executive department or of such other body as Congress may by law provide, transmit within four days to the President pro tempore of the Senate and the Speaker of the House of Representatives their written declaration and the President is unable to discharge the powers and duties of his office. Thereupon Congress shall decide the issue, assembling within forty-eight hours for that purpose if not in session. If the Congress, within twenty-one days after receipt of the latter written declaration, or, if Congress is not in session, within twenty-one days after Congress is required to assemble, determines by two-thirds vote of both Houses that the President is unable to discharge the powers and duties ties of his office, the Vice President shall continue to discharge the same as Acting President; otherwise, the President shall resume the powers and duties of his office.

AMENDMENT XVI [1971]

Section 1. The right of citizens of the United States, who are eighteen years of age or older, to vote shall not be denied or abridged by the United States or by any State on account of age.

Section 2. The Congress shall have power to enforce this article by appropriate legislation.

Appendix B
Uniform Commercial Code (1994 Text)*

TITLE.

An Act.

To be known as the Uniform Commercial Code, Relating to Certain Commercial Transactions in or regarding Personal Property and Contracts and other Documents concerning them, including Sales, Commercial Paper, Bank Deposits and Collections, Letters of Credit, Bulk Transfers, Warehouse Receipts, Bills of Lading, other Documents of Title, Investment Securities, and Secured Transactions, including certain Sales of Accounts, Chattel Paper, and Contract Rights; Providing for Public Notice to Third Parties in Certain Circumstances; Regulating Procedure, Evidence, and Damages in Certain Court Actions

Involving such Transactions, Contracts or Documents; to Make Uniform the Law with Respect Thereto; and Repealing Inconsistent Legislation.

ARTICLE 1. GENERAL PROVISIONS.

Part 1. Short Title, Construction, Application, and Subject Matter of the Act.

Section 1-101. Short Title.

This Act shall be known and may be cited as Uniform Commercial Code.

Section 1-102. Purposes; Rules of Construction; Variation by Agreement.

(1) This Act shall be liberally construed and applied to promote its underlying purposes and policies.

Authors' note: The texts of some sections have been omitted.

(2) Underlying purposes and policies of this Act are

    (a)   to simplify, clarify, and modernize the law governing commercial transactions;

    (b)   to permit the continued expansion of commercial practices through custom, usage and agreement of the parties;

    (c)   to make uniform the law among the various jurisdictions.

(3) The effect of provisions of this Act may be varied by agreement, except as otherwise provided in this Act and except that the obligations of good faith, diligence, reasonableness and care prescribed by this Act may not be disclaimed by agreement but the parties may by agreement determine the standards by which te performance of such obligations is to be measured if such standards are not manifestly unreasonable.

(4) The presence in certain provisions of this Act of the word "unless otherwise agreed" or words of similar import does not imply that the effect of other provisions may not be varied by agreement under subsection (3).

(5) In this Act unless the context otherwise requires

    (a)   words in the singular number include the plural, and in the plural include the singular;

    (b)   words of the masculine gender ncude the feminine and the neuter, and when the sense so indicates of the neuter gender may refer to any gender.

Section 1-103. Supplementary General Principles of Law Applicable.

Unless displaced by the particular provisions of this Act, the principles of law and equity, including the law merchant and the law relative to capacity to contract, principal and agent, estoppel, fraud, misrepresentation, duress, coercion, mistake, bankruptcy, or other validating or invalidating cause shall supplement its provision.

Section 1-104. Construction Against Implicit Repeal. [Text omitted]

Section 1-105. Territorial Application of the Act; Parties' Power to Choose Applicable Law. [Te4xt omitted]

Section 1-106. Remedies to Be Liberally Administered. [Text omitted]

Section 1-107. Waiver or Renunciation of Claim or Right After Breach.

Any claim or right arising out of an alleged breach can be discharged in whole or in part without consideration by a written waiver or renunciation signed and delivered by the aggrieved party.

Section 1-108. Severability. [Text omitted]

Section 1-109. Section Captions. [Text omitted]

Part 2. General Definitions and Principles of Interpretation.

Section 1-201. General Definitions.

Subject to additional definitions contained in the subsequent Articles of this Act which are applicable to specific Articles or Parts thereof, and unless the context otherwise requires, in this Act:

(1) "Action" in the sense of a judicial proceeding includes recoupment, counterclaim, set-off, suit in equity and any other proceedings in which rights are determined.

(2) "Aggrieved party" means a party entitled to resort to a remedy.

(3) "Agreement" means the bargain of the parties in fact as found in their language or by implication from other circumstances including course of dealing or usage of trade or course of performance as provided in this Act (Sections 1-205 and 2-208). Whether an agreement has legal consequences is determined by the provisions of this Act, if applicable; otherwise

by the law of contracts (Section 1-103). (Compare "Contract.")

(4) "Bank" means any person engaged in the business of banking.

(5) "Bearer" means the person in possession of an instrument, document of title, or certificated security payable to bearer or indorsed in blank.

(6) "Bill of lading" means a document evidencing the receipt of goods for shipment issued by a person engaged in the business of transporting or forwarding goods, and includes an airbill. "Airbill" means a document serving for air transportation as a bill of lading does for marine or rail transportation, and includes an air consignment note or air waybill.

(7) "Branch" includes a separately incorporated foreign branch of a bank.

(8) "Burden of establishing" a fact means the burden of persuading the triers of fact that the existence of the fact is more probable than its non-existence.

(9) "Buyer in ordinary course of business" means a person who in good faith and without knowledge that the sale to him is in violation of the ownership rights or security interest of a third party in the goods buys in ordinary course from a person in the business of selling goods of that kind but does not include a pawnbroker. All persons who sell minerals or the like (including oil and gas) at wellhead or minehead shall be deemed to be persons in the business of selling goods of that kind. "Buying" may be for cash or by exchange of other property or on secured or unsecured credit and includes receiving goods or documents of title under a pre-existing contract for sale but does not include a transfer in bulk or as security for or in total or partial satisfaction of a money debt.

(10) "Conspicuous": A term or clause is conspicuous when it is so written that a reasonable person against whom it is to operate ought to have noticed it. A printed heading in capitals (as: NON-NEGOTIABLE BILL OF LADING) is conspicuous. Language in the body of a form is "conspicuous" if it is in larger or other contrasting type or color. But in a telegram any stated term is "conspicuous." Whether a term or clause is "conspicuous" or not is for decision by the court.

(11) "Contract" means the total legal obligation which results from the parties' agreement as affected by this Act and any other applicable rules of law. (Compare "Agreement.")

(12) "Creditor" includes a general creditor, a secured creditor, a lien creditor and any representative of creditors, including an assignee for the benefit of creditors, a trustee in bankruptcy, a receiver in equity and an executor or administrator of an insolvent debtor's or assignor's estate.

(13) "Defendant" includes a person in the position of defendant in a cross-action or counterclaim.

(14) "Delivery" with respect to instruments, documents of title, chattel paper, or certificated securities means voluntary transfer of possession.

(15) "Document of title" includes bill of lading, dock warrant, dock receipt, warehouse receipt or order for the delivery of goods, and also any other document which in the regular course of business or financing is treated as adequately evidencing that the person in possession of it is entitled to receive, hold and dispose of the document and the goods it covers. To be a document of title a document must purport to be issued by or addressed to a bailee and purport to cover goods in the bailee's possession which are either identified or are fungible portions of an identified mass.

(16) "Fault" means wrongful act, omission or breach.

(17) "Fungible" with respect to goods or securities means goods or securities of which any unit is, by nature or usage of trade, the equivalent of any other like unit. Goods which are not fungible shall be deemed fungible for the purposes of this Act to the extent that under a particular agreement or document unlike units are treated as equivalents.

(18) "Genuine" means free of forgery or counterfeiting.

(19) "Good faith" means honesty in fact in the conduct or transaction concerned.

(20) "Holder," with respect to a negotiable instrument, means the person in possession if the instrument is payable to bearer or, in the

case of an instrument payable to an identified person, if the identified person is in possession. "Holder" with respect to a document of title means the person in possession if the goods are deliverable to bearer or to the order of the person in possession.

(21) To "honor" is to pay or to accept and pay, or where a credit so engages to purchase or discount a draft complying with the terms of the credit.

(22) "Insolvency proceedings" includes any assignment for the benefit of creditors or other proceedings intended to liquidate or rehabilitate the estate of the person involved.

(23) A person is "insolvent" who either has ceased to pay his debts in the ordinary course of business or cannot pay his debts as they become due or is insolvent within the meaning of the federal bankruptcy law.

(24) "Money" means a medium of exchange authorized or adopted by a domestic or foreign government and includes a monetary unit of account established by an intergovernmental organization or by agreement between two or more nations.

(25) A person has "notice" of a fact when

(a)   he has actual knowledge of it; or
(b)   he has received a notice or notification of it; or
(c)   from all the facts and circumstances known to him at the time in question he has reason to know that it exists.

A person "knows" or has "knowledge" of a fact when he has actual knowledge of it. "Discover" or "learn" or a word or phrase of similar import refers to knowledge rather than to reason to know. The time and circumstances under which a notice or notification may cease to be effective are not determined by this Act.

(26) A person "notifies" or "gives" a notice or notification to another by taking such steps as may be reasonably required to inform the other in ordinary course whether or not such other actually comes to know of it. A person "receives" a notice or notification when

(a)   it comes to his attention; or

(b)   it is duly delivered at the place of business through which the contract was made or at any other place held out by him as the place for receipt of such communications.

(27) Notice, knowledge or a notice or notification received by an organization is effective for a particular transaction from the time when it is brought to the attention of the individual conducting that transaction, and in any event from the time when it would have been brought to his attention if the organization had exercised due diligence. An organization exercises due diligence if it maintains reasonable routines for communicating significant information to the person conducting the transaction and there is reasonable compliance with the routines. Due diligence does not require an individual acting for the organization to communicate information unless such communication is part of his regular duties or unless he has reason to know of the transaction and that the transaction would be materially affected by the information.

(28) "Organization" includes a corporation, government or governmental subdivision or agency, business trust, estate, trust, partnership or association, two or more persons having a joint or common interest, or any other legal or commercial entity.

(29) "Party," as distinct from "third party," means a person who has engaged in a transaction or made an agreement within this Act.

(30) "Person" includes an individual or an organization (See Section 1-102).

(31) "Presumption" or "presumed" means that the trier of fact must find the existence of the fact presumed unless and until evidence is introduced which would support a finding of its nonexistence.

(32) "Purchase" includes taking by sale, discount, negotiation, mortgage, pledge, lien, issue or re-issue, gift or any other voluntary transaction creating an interest in property.

(33) "Purchaser" means a person who takes by purchase.

(34) "Remedy" means any remedial right to which an aggrieved party is entitled with or without resort to a tribunal.

(35) "Representative" includes an agent, an officer of a corporation or association, and a trustee, executor or administrator of an estate, or any other person empowered to act for another.

(36) "Rights" includes remedies.

(37) "Security interest" means an interest in personal property or fixtures which secures payment or performance of an obligation. The retention or reservation of title by a seller of goods notwithstanding shipment or delivery to the buyer (Section 2-401) is limited in effect to a reservation of a "security interest." The term also includes any interest of a buyer of accounts or chattel paper which is subject to Article 9. The special property interest of a buyer of goods on identification of those goods to a contract for sale under Section 2-401 is not a "security interest" but a buyer may also acquire a "security interest" by complying with Article 9. Unless a lease or consignment is intended as security, reservation of title thereunder is not a "security interest" but a consignment in any event is subject to the provisions on consignment sales (Section 2-326).

Whether a transaction creates a lease or security interest is determined by the facts of each case; however, a transaction creates a security interest if the consideration the lessee is to pay the lessor for the right to possession and use of the goods is an obligation for the term of the lease not subject to termination by the lessee, and

(a)   the original term of the lease is equal to or greater than the remaining economic life of the goods,

(b)   the lessee is bound to renew the lease for the remaining economic life of the goods or is bound to become the owner of the goods,

(c)   the lessee has an option to renew the lease for the remaining economic life of the goods for no additional consideration or nominal additional consideration upon compliance with the lease agreement, or

(d)   the lessee has an option to become the owner of the goods for no additional consideration or nominal additional consideration upon compliance with the lease agreement.

A transaction does not create a security interest merely because it provides that

(a)   the present value of the consideration the lessee is obligated to pay the lessor for the right to possession and use of the goods is substantially equal to or is greater than the fair market value of the goods at the time the lease is entered into,

(b)   the lessee assumes risk of loss of the goods, or agrees to pay taxes, insurance, filing, recording, or registration fees, or service or maintenance costs with respect to the goods,

(c)   the lessee has an option to renew the lease or to become the owner of the goods,

(d)   the lessee has an option to renew the lease for a fixed rent that is equal to or greater than the reasonably predictable fair market rent for the use of the goods for the term of the renewal at the time the option is to be performed, or

(e)   the lessee has an option to become the owner of the goods for a fixed price that is equal to or greater than the reasonably predictable fair market value of the goods at the time the option is to be performed.

For purposes of this subsection (37):

(x)   Additional consideration is not nominal if (i) when the option to renew the lease is granted to the lessee the rent is stated to be the fair market rent for the use of the goods for the term of the renewal determined at the time the option is to be performed, or (ii) when the option to become the owner of the goods is granted to the lessee the price is stated to be the fair market value of the goods determined at the time the option is to be performed. Additional consideration is nominal if it is less than the lessee's reasonably predictable cost of performing under the lease agreement if the option is not exercised;

(y) "Reasonably predictable" and "remaining economic life of the goods" are to be determined with reference to the facts and circumstances at the time the transaction is entered into; and

(z) "Present value" means the amount as of a date certain of one or more sums payable in the future, discounted to the date certain. The discount is determined by the interest rate specified by the parties if the rate is not manifestly unreasonable at the time the transaction is entered into; otherwise, the discount is determined by a commercially reasonable rate that takes into account the facts and circumstances of each case at the time the transaction was entered into.

(38) "Send" in connection with any writing or notice means to deposit in the mail or deliver for transmission by any other usual means of communication with postage or cost of transmission provided for and properly addressed and in the case of an instrument to an address specified thereon or otherwise agreed, or if there be none to any address reasonable under the circumstances. The receipt of any writing or notice within the time at which it would have arrived if properly sent has the effect of a proper sending.

(39) "Signed" includes any symbol executed or adopted by a party with present intention to authenticate a writing.

(40) "Surety" includes guarantor.

(41) "Telegram" includes a message transmitted by radio, teletype, cable, any mechanical method of transmission, or the like.

(42) "Term" means that portion of an agreement which relates to a particular matter.

(43) "Unauthorized" signature or indorsement means one made without actual, implied or apparent authority and includes a forgery.

(44) "Value." Except as otherwise provided with respect to negotiable instruments and bank collections (Sections 3-303, 4-208 and 4-209) a person gives "value" for rights if he acquires them

(a) in return for a binding commitment to extend credit or for the extension of immediately available credit whether or not drawn upon and whether or not a chargeback is provided for in the event of difficulties in collection; or

(b) as security for or in total or partial satisfaction of a pre-existing claim; or

(c) by accepting delivery pursuant to a preexisting contract purchase; or

(d) generally, in return for any consideration sufficient to support a simple contract.

(45) "Warehouse receipt" means a receipt issued by a person engaged in the business of storing goods for hire.

(46) "Written" or "writing" includes printing, typewriting or any other intentional reduction to tangible form.

Section 1-202. Prima Facie Evidence by Third Party Documents. [Text omitted]

Section 1-203. Obligation of Good Faith.

Every contract or duty within this Act imposes an obligation of good faith in its performance or enforcement.

Section 1-204. Time; Reasonable Time; "Seasonably."

(1) Whenever this Act requires any action to be taken within a reasonable time, any time which is not manifestly unreasonable may be fixed by agreement.

(2) What is a reasonable time for taking any action depends on the nature, purpose and circumstance of such action.

(3) An action is taken "seasonably" when it is taken at or within the time agreed or if no time is agreed at or within a reasonable time.

Section 1-205. Course of Dealing and Usage of Trade.

(1) A course of dealing is a sequence of previous conduct between the parties to a particular transaction which is fairly to be regarded as establishing a common basis of understanding for interpreting their expressions and other conduct.

(2) A usage of trade is any practice or method of dealing having such regularity of observance in a place, vocation or trade as to justify an expectation that it will be observed with respect to the transaction in question. The existence and scope of such a usage are to be proved as facts. If it is established that such a usage is embodied in a written trade code or similar writing the interpretation of the writing is for the court.

(3) A course of dealing between parties and any usage of trade in the vocation or trade in which they are engaged or of which they are or should be aware give particular meaning to and supplement or qualify terms of an agreement.

(4) The express terms of an agreement and an applicable course of dealing or usage of trade shall be construed wherever reasonable as consistent with each other; but when such construction is unreasonable express terms control both course of dealing and usage of trade and course of dealing controls usage of trade.

(5) An applicable usage of trade in the place where any part of performance is to occur shall be used in interpreting the agreement as to that part of the performance.

(6) Evidence of a relevant usage of trade offered by one party is not admissible unless and until he has given the other party such notice as the court finds sufficient to prevent unfair surprise to the latter.

Section 1-206. Statute of Frauds for Kinds of Personal Property Not Otherwise Covered.

(1) Except in the cases described in subsection (2) Of this section a contract for the sale of personal property is not enforceable by way of action or defense beyond five thousand dollars in amount or value of remedy unless there is some writing which indicates that a contract for sale has been made between the parties at a defined or stated price, reasonably identifies the subject matter, and is signed by the party against whom enforcement is sought or by his authorized agent.

(2) Subsection (1) of this section does not apply to contracts for the sale of goods (Section 2-201) nor of securities (Section 8-319) nor to security agreements (Section 9-203).

Section 1-207. Performance or Acceptance Under Reservation of Rights.

A party who with explicit reservation of rights performs or promises performance or assents to performance in a manner demanded or offered by the other party does not thereby prejudice the rights reserved. Such words as "without prejudice," "under protest" or the like are sufficient.

Section 1-208. Option to Accelerate at Will.

A term providing that one party or his successor in interest may accelerate payment or performance or require collateral or additional collate4ral "at will" or "when he deems himself insecure" or in words of similar import shall be construed to mean that he shall have power to do so only if he is good faith believes that the prospect of payment or performance is impaired. The burden of establishing lack of good faith is on the party against whom the power had been exercised.

Section 1-209. Subordinated Obligations.
[Text omitted]

ARTICLE 2. SALES.

Part 1. Short Title, General Construction and Subject Matter.

Section 2-101. Short Title.

This Article shall be known and may be cited as Uniform Commercial Code—Sales.

Section 2-102. Scope; Certain Security and Other Transactions Excluded From This Article.

Unless the context otherwise requires, this Article applies to transactions in goods; it does not apply to any transaction which although in the form of an unconditional contract to sell or present sale is intended to operate only as a security transaction nor does this Article impair or repeal any statute regulating sales to consumers, farmers or other specified classes of buyers.

Section 2-103. Definitions and Index of Definitions.

(1) In this Article unless the context otherwise requires

- (a) "Buyer" means a person who buys or contracts to buy goods.
- (b) "Good faith" in the case of a merchant means honesty in fact and the observance of reasonable commercial standards of fair dealing in the trade.
- (c) "Receipt" of goods means taking physical possession of them.
- (d) "Seller" means a person who sells or contracts to sell goods.

(2) Other definitions applying to this Article or to specific Parts thereof, and the sections in which they appear are:

"Acceptance," Section 2-606.
"Banker's credit, Section 2-325.
"Between merchants, Section 2-104.
"Cancellation," Section 2-106(4).
"Commercial unit, Section 2-105.
"Confirmed credit, Section 2-325.
"Conforming to contract, Section 2-106.
"Contract for sale," Section 2-106.
"Cover," Section 2-712.
"Entrusting, Section 2-403.

"Financing agency, Section 2-104.
"Future goods," Section 2-105.
"Goods," Section 2-105.
"Identification, Section 2-501.
"Installment contract, Section 2-612.
"Letter of Credit," Section 2-325.
"Lot," Section 2-105.
"Merchant, Section 2-104.
"Overseas," Section 2-323.
"Person in position of seller, Section 2-707.
"Present sale, Section 2-106.
"Sale, Section 2-106.
"Sale on approval," Section 2-326.
"Sale or return, Section 2-326.
"Termination," Section 2-106.

(3) The following definitions in other Articles apply to this Article:

"Check," Section 3-104.
"Consignee," Section 7-102.
"Consignor," Section 7-102.
"Consumer goods," Section 9-109.
"Dishonor," Section 3-507.
"Draft," Section 3-104.

(4) In addition Article I contains general definitions and principles of construction and interpretation applicable throughout this Article.

Section 2-104. Definitions: "Merchant;" "Between Merchants;" "Financing Agency."

(1) "Merchant" means a person who deals in goods of the kind or otherwise by his occupation holds himself out as having knowledge or skill peculiar to the practices or goods involved in the transaction or to whom such knowledge or skill may be attributed by his employment of an agent or broker or other intermediary who by his occupation holds himself out as having such knowledge or skill.
(2) "Financing agency" means a bank, finance company or other person who in the ordinary course of business makes advances against goods or documents of title or who by arrangement with either the seller or the buyer intervenes in ordinary course to make or collect payment due or claimed under the contract for sale, as by purchasing or paying

the seller's draft or making advances against it or by merely taking it for collection whether or not documents of title accompany the draft. "Financing agency" includes also a bank or other person who similarly intervenes between persons who are in the position of seller and buyer in respect to the goods (Section 2-707).

(3) "Between merchants" means in any transaction with respect to which both parties are chargeable with the knowledge or skill of merchants.

Section 2-105. Definitions: Transferability; "Goods;" "Future" Goods; "Lot;" "Commercial Unit."

(1) "Goods" means all things (including specially manufactured goods) which are movable at the time of identification to the contract for sale other than the money in which the price is to be paid, investment securities (Article 8) and things in action. "Goods" also includes the unborn young of animals and growing crops and other identified things attached to realty as described in the section on goods to be severed from realty (Section 2-107).

(2) Goods must be both existing and identified before any interest in them can pass. Goods which are not both existing and identified are "future" goods. A purported present sale of future goods or of any interest therein operates as a contract to sell.

(3) There may be a sale of a part interest in existing identified goods.

(4) An undivided share in an identified bulk of fungible goods is sufficiently identified to be sold although the quantity of the bulk is not determined. Any agreed proportion of such a bulk or any quantity thereof agreed upon by number, weight or other measure may to the extent of the seller's interest in the bulk be sold to the buyer who then becomes an owner in common.

(5) "Lot" means a parcel or a single article which is the subject matter of a separate sale or delivery, whether or not it is sufficient to perform the contract.

(6) "Commercial unit" means such a unit of goods as by commercial usage is a single whole for purposes of sale and division of

which materially impairs its character or value on the market or in use. A commercial unit may be a single article (as a machine) or a set of articles (as a suite of furniture or an assortment of sizes) or a quantity (as a bale, gross, or carload) or any other unit treated in use or in the relevant market as a single whole.

Section 2-106. Definitions: "Contract;" "Agreement;" "Contract for Sale;" "Sale;" "Present Sale;" "Conforming to Contract;" "Termination;" "Cancellation."

(1) In this Article unless the context otherwise requires "contract" and "agreement" are limited to those relating to the present or future sale of goods. "Contract for sale" includes both a present sale of goods and a contract to sell goods at a future time. A "sale" consists in the passing of title from the seller to the buyer for a price (Section 2-401). A "present sale" means a sale which is accomplished by the making of the contract.

(2) Goods or conduct including any part of a performance are "conforming" or conform to the contract when they are in accordance with the obligations under the contract.

(3) "Termination" occurs when either party pursuant to a power created by agreement or law puts an end to the contract otherwise than for its breach. On "termination" all obligations which are still executory on both sides are discharged but any right based on prior breach or performance survives.

(4) "Cancellation" occurs when either party puts an end to the contract for breach by the other and its effect is the same as that of "termination" except that the cancelling party also retains any remedy for breach of the whole contract or any unperformed balance.

Section 2-107. Goods to Be Severed From Realty: Recording.

(1) A contract for the sale of minerals or the like (including oil and gas) or a structure or its materials to be removed from realty is a contract for the sale of goods within this Article if they are to be severed by the seller but until severance a purported present sale thereof

which is not effective as a transfer of an interest in land is effective only as a contract to sell.

(2) A contract for the sale apart from the land of growing crops or other things attached to realty and capable of severance without material harm thereto but not described in subsection (1) or of timber to be cut is a contract for the sale of goods within this Article whether the subject matter is to be severed by the buyer or by the seller even though it forms part of the realty at the time of contracting, and the parties can by identification effect a present sale before severance.

(3) The provisions of this section are subject to any third party rights provided by the law relating to realty records, and the contract for sale may be executed and recorded as a document transferring an interest in land and shall then constitute notice to third parties of the buyer's rights under the contract for sale.

Part 2. Form, Formation and Readjustment of Contract.

Section 2-201. Formal Requirements; Statute of Frauds.

(1) Except as otherwise provided in this section a contract for the sale of goods for the price of $500 or more is not enforceable by way of action or defense unless there is some writing sufficient to indicate that a contract for sale has been made between the parties and signed by the party against whom enforcement is sought or by his authorized agent or broker. A writing is not insufficient because it omits or incorrectly states a term agreed upon but the contract is not enforceable under this paragraph beyond the quantity of goods shown in such writing.

(2) Between merchants if within a reasonable time a writing in confirmation of the contract and sufficient against the sender is received and the party receiving it has reason to know its contents, it satisfies the requirements of subsection (1) against such party unless written notice of objection to its contents is given within 10 days after it is received.

(3) A contract which does not satisfy the requirements of subsection (1) but which is valid in other respects is enforceable

(a) if the goods are to be specially manufactured for the buyer and are not suitable for sale to others in the ordinary course of the seller's business and the seller, before notice of repudiation is received and under circumstances which reasonably indicate that the goods are for the buyer, has made either a substantial beginning of their manufacture or commitments for their procurement; or

(b) if the party against whom enforcement is sought admits in his pleading, testimony or otherwise in court that a contract for sale was made, but the contract is not enforceable under this provision beyond the quantity of goods admitted; or

(c) with respect to goods for which payment has been made and accepted or which have been received and accepted (Section 2-606).

Section 2-202. Final Written Expression: Parol or Extrinsic Evidence

Terms with respect to which the confirmatory memoranda of the parties agree or which are otherwise set forth in a writing intended by the parties as a final expression of their agreement with respect to such terms as are included therein may not be contradicted by evidence of any prior agreement or of a contemporaneous oral agreement but may be explained or supplemented

(a) by course of dealing or usage of trade (Section 1-205) or by course of performance (Section 2-208); and

(b) by evidence of consistent additional terms unless the court finds the writing to have been intended also as a complete and exclusive statement of the terms of the agreement.

Section 2-203. Seals Inoperative.

The affixing of a seal to a writing evidencing a contract for sale or an offer to buy or sell goods does not constitute the writing a sealed instrument and the law with respect to sealed instruments does not apply to such a contract or offer.

Section 2-204. Formation in General.

(1) A contract for sale of goods may be made in any manner sufficient to show agreement, including conduct by both parties which recognizes the existence of such a contract.

(2) An agreement sufficient to constitute a contract for sale may be found even though the moment of its making is undetermined.

(3) Even though one or more terms are left open a contract for sale does not fail for indefiniteness if the parties have intended to make a contract and there is a reasonably certain basis for giving an appropriate remedy.

Section 2-205. Firm Offers.

An offer by a merchant to buy or sell goods in a signed writing which by its terms give assurance that it will be held open is not revocable, for lack of consideration, during the time stated or if no time is stated for a reasonable time, but in no event may such period of irrevocability exceed three months; but any such term of assurance on a form supplied by the offeree must be separately signed by the offeror.

Section 2-206. Offer and Acceptance in Formation of Contract.

(1) Unless otherwise unambiguously indicated by the language or circumstances

    (a)   an offer to make a contract shall be construed as inviting acceptance in any manner and by any medium reasonable in the circumstances;

    (b)   an order or other offer to buy goods for prompt or current shipment shall be construed as inviting acceptance either by a prompt promise to ship or by the prompt or current shipment of conforming or nonconforming goods, but such a shipment of nonconforming goods does not constitute an acceptance if the seller seasonably notifies the buyer that the shipment is offered only as an accommodation to the buyer.

(2) Where the beginning of a requested performance is a reasonable mode of acceptance an offeror who is not notified of acceptance within a reasonable time may treat the offer as having lapsed before acceptance.

Section 2-207. Additional Terms in Acceptance or Confirmation.

(1) A definite and seasonable expression of acceptance or a written confirmation which is sent within a reasonable time operates as an acceptance even though it states terms additional to or different from those offered or agreed upon, unless acceptance is expressly made conditional on assent to the additional or different terms.

(2) The additional terms are to be construed as proposals for addition to the contract. Between merchants such terms become part of the contract unless:

    (a)   the offer expressly limits acceptance to the terms of the offer;

    (b)   they materially alter it; or

    (c)   notification of objection to them has already been given or is given within a reasonable time after notice of them is received.

(3) Conduct by both parties which recognizes the existence of a contract is sufficient to establish a contract for sale although the writings of the parties do not otherwise establish a contract. In such case the terms of the particular contract consist of those terms on which the writings of the parties agree, together with any supplementary terms incorporated under any other provisions of this Act.

Section 2-208. Course of Performance or Practical Construction.

(1) Where the contract for sale involves repeated occasions for performance by either party with knowledge of the nature of the performance and opportunity for objection to it by the other, any course of performance accepted or acquiesced in without objection shall be relevant to determine the meaning of the agreement.

(2) The express terms of the agreement and any such course of performance, as well as any course of dealing and usage of trade, shall be construed whenever reasonable as consistent with each other, but when such construction is unreasonable, express terms shall control course of performance and course of performance shall control both course of dealing and usage of trade (Section 1-205).

(3) Subject to the provisions of the next section on modification and waiver, such course of performance shall be relevant to show a waiver or modification of any term inconsistent with such course of performance.

Section 2-209. Modification, Rescission and Waiver.

(1) An agreement modifying a contract within this Article needs no consideration to be binding.

(2) A signed agreement which excludes modification or rescission except by a signed writing cannot be otherwise modified or rescinded, but except as between merchants such a requirement on a form supplied by the merchant must be separately signed by the other party.

(3) The requirements of the statute of frauds section of this Article (Section 2-201) must be satisfied if the contract as modified is within its provisions.

(4) Although an attempt at modification or rescission does not satisfy the requirements of subsection (2) or (3) it can operate as a waiver.

(5) A party who has made a waiver affecting an executory portion of the contract may retract the waiver by reasonable notification received by the other party that strict performance will be required of any term waived, unless the retraction would be unjust in view of a material change of position in reliance on the waiver.

Section 2-210. Delegation of Performance; Assignment of Rights.

(1) A party may perform his duty through a delegate unless otherwise agreed or unless the other party has a substantial interest in having his original promisor perform or control the acts required by the contract. No delegation of performance relieves the party delegating of any duty to perform or any liability for breach.

(2) Unless otherwise agreed all rights of either seller or buyer can be assigned except where the assignment would materially change the duty of the other party, or increase materially the burden or risk imposed on him by his contract, or impair materially his chance of obtaining return performance. A right to damages for breach of the whole contract or a right arising out of the assignor's due performance of his entire obligation can be assigned despite agreement otherwise.

(3) Unless the circumstances indicate the contrary a prohibition of assignment of "the contract" is to be construed as barring only the delegation to the assignee of the assignor's performance.

(4) An assignment of "the contract" or of "all my rights under the contract" or an assignment in similar general terms is an assignment of rights and unless the language or the circumstances (as in an assignment for security) indicate the contrary, it is a delegation of performance of the duties of the assignor and its acceptance by the assignee constitutes a promise by him to perform those duties. This promise is enforceable by either the assignor or the other party to the original contract.

(5) The other party may treat any assignment which delegates performance as creating reasonable grounds for insecurity and may without prejudice to his rights against the assignor demand assurances from the assignee (Section 2-609).

Part 3. General Obligations and Construction of Contract.

Section 2-301. General Obligations of Parties.

The obligation of the seller is to transfer and deliver and that of the buyer is to accept and pay in accordance with the contract.

Section 2-302. Unconscionable Contract or Clause.

(1) If the court as a matter of law finds the contract or any clause of the contract to have been unconscionable at the time it was made the court may refuse to enforce the contract, or it may enforce the remainder of the contract without the unconscionable clause, or it may so limit the application of any unconscionable clause as to avoid any unconscionable result.
(2) When it is claimed or appears to the court that the contract or any clause thereof may be unconscionable the parties shall be afforded a reasonable opportunity to present evidence as to its commercial setting, purpose and effect to aid the court in making the determination.

Section 2-303. Allocation or Division of Risks.

Where this Article allocates a risk or a burden as between the parties "unless otherwise agreed," the agreement may not only shift the allocation but may also divide the risk or burden.

Section 2-304. Price Payable in Money, Goods, Realty, or Otherwise.

(1) The price can be made payable in money or otherwise. If it is payable in whole or in part in goods each party is a seller of the goods which he is to transfer.
(2) Even though all or part of the price is payable in an interest in realty the transfer of the goods and the seller's obligations with reference to them are subject to this Article, but not the transfer of the interest in realty or the transferor's obligations in connection therewith.

Section 2-305. Open Price Term.

(1) The parties if they so intend can conclude a contract for sale even though the price is not settled. In such a case the price is a reasonable price at the time for delivery if

(a) nothing is said as to price; or
(b) the price is left to be agreed by the parties and they fail to agree; or
(c) the price is to be fixed in terms of some agreed market or other standard as set or recorded by a third person or agency and it is not so set or recorded.

(2) A price to be fixed by the seller or by the buyer means a price for him to fix in good faith.
(3) When a price left to be fixed otherwise than by agreement of the parties fails to be fixed through fault of one party the other may at his option treat the contract as cancelled or himself fix a reasonable price.
(4) Where, however, the parties intend not to be bound unless the price be fixed or agreed and it is not fixed or agreed there is no contract. In such a case the buyer must return any goods already received or if unable so to do must pay their reasonable value at the time of delivery and the seller must return any portion of the price paid on account.

Section 2-306. Output, Requirements and Exclusive Dealings.

(1) A term which measures the quantity by the output of the seller or the requirements of the buyer means such actual output or requirements as may occur in good faith, except that no quantity unreasonably disproportionate to any stated estimate or in the absence of a stated estimate to any normal or otherwise comparable prior output or requirements may be tendered or demanded.
(2) A lawful agreement by either the seller or the buyer for exclusive dealing in the kind of goods concerned imposes unless otherwise agreed an obligation by the seller to use best

efforts to supply the goods and by the buyer to use best efforts to promote their sale.

Section 2-307. Delivery in Single Lot or Several Lots.

Unless otherwise agreed all goods called for by a contract for sale must be tendered in a single delivery and payment is due only on such tender but where the circumstances give either party the right to make or demand delivery in lots the price if it can be apportioned may be demanded for each lot.

Section 2-308. Absence of Specified Place for Delivery.

Unless otherwise agreed

(a) the place for delivery of goods is the seller's place of business or if he has none his residence; but

(b) in a contract for sale of identified goods which to the knowledge of the parties at the time of contracting are in some other place, that place is the place for their delivery; and

(c) documents of title may be delivered through customary banking channels.

Section 2-309. Absence of Specific Time Provisions; Notice of Termination.

(1) The time for shipment or delivery or any other action under a contract if not provided in this Article or agreed upon shall be a reasonable time.

(2) Where the contract provides for successive performances but is indefinite in duration it is valid for a reasonable time but unless otherwise agreed may be terminated at any time by either Party.

(3) Termination of a contract by one party except on the happening of an agreed event requires that reasonable notification be received by the other party and an agreement dispensing with notification is invalid if its operation would be unconscionable.

Section 2-310. Open Time for Payment or Running of Credit: Authority to Ship Under Reservation.

Unless otherwise agreed

(a) payment is due at the time and place at which the buyer is to receive the goods even though the place of shipment is the place of delivery; and

(b) if the seller is authorized to send the goods he may ship them under reservation, and may tender the documents of title, but the buyer may inspect the goods after their arrival before payment is due unless such inspection is inconsistent with the terms of the contract (Section 2-513); and

(c) if delivery is authorized and made by way of documents of title otherwise than by subsection (b) then payment is due at the time and place at which the buyer is to receive the documents regardless of where the goods are to be received; and

(d) where the seller is required or authorized to ship the goods on credit the credit period runs from the time of shipment but postdating the invoice or delaying its dispatch will correspondingly delay the starting of the credit period.

Section 2-311. Options and Cooperation Respecting Performance.

(1) An agreement for sale which is otherwise sufficiently definite (subsection (3) of Section 2-204) to be a contract is not made invalid by the fact that it leaves particulars of performance to be specified by one of the parties. Any such specification must be made in good faith and within limits set by commercial reasonableness.

(2) Unless otherwise agreed specifications relating to assortment of the goods are at the buyer's option and except as otherwise provided in subsections (1) (c) and (3) of Section 2-319 specifications or arrangements relating to shipment are at the seller's option.

(3) Where such specification would materially affect the other party's performance but is not seasonably made or where one party's cooperation is necessary to the agreed performance of the other but is not seasonably forthcoming, the other party in addition to all other remedies

(a)   is excused for any resulting delay in his own performance; and

(b)   may also either proceed to perform in any reasonable manner or after the time for a material part of his own performance treat the failure to specify or to cooperate as a breach by failure to deliver or accept the goods.

Section 2-312. Warranty of Title and Against Infringement; Buyer's Obligation Against Infringement.

(1) Subject to subsection (2) there is in a contract for sale a warranty by the seller that

(a)   the title conveyed shall be good, and its transfer rightful; and

(b)   the goods shall be delivered free from any security interest or other lien or encumbrance of which the buyer at the time of contracting has no knowledge.

(2) A warranty under subsection (1) will be excluded or modified only by specific language or by circumstances which give the buyer reason to know that the person selling does not claim title in himself or that he is purporting to sell only such right or title as he or a third person may have.

(3) Unless otherwise agreed a seller who is a merchant regularly dealing in goods of the kind warrants that the goods shall be delivered free of the rightful claim of any third person by way of infringement or the like but a buyer who furnishes specifications to the seller must hold the seller harmless against any such claim which arises out of compliance with the specifications.

Section 2-313. Express Warranties by Affirmation, Promise, Description, Sample.

(1) Express warranties by the seller are created as follows:

(a)   Any affirmation of fact or promise made by the seller to the buyer which relates to the goods and becomes part of the basis of the bargain creates an express warranty that the goods shall conform to the affirmation or promise.

(b)   Any description of the goods which is made part of the basis of the bargain creates an express warranty that the goods shall conform to the description.

(c)   Any sample or model which is made part of the basis of the bargain creates an express warranty that the whole of the goods shall conform to the sample or model.

(2) It is not necessary to the creation of an express warranty that the seller use formal words such as "warrant" or "guarantee" or that he have a specific intention to make a warranty, but an affirmation merely of the value of the goods or a statement purporting to be merely the seller's opinion or commendation of the goods does not create a warranty.

Section 2-314. Implied Warranty: Merchantability; Usage of Trade.

(1) Unless excluded or modified (Section 2-316), a warranty that the goods shall be merchantable is implied in a contract for their sale if the seller is a merchant with respect to goods of that kind. Under this section the serving for value of food or drink to be consumed either on the premises or elsewhere is a sale.

(2) Goods to be merchantable must be at least such as

(a)   pass without objection in the trade under the contract description; and

(b) in the case of fungible goods, are of fair, average quality within the description; and

(c) are fit for the ordinary purposes for which such goods are used; and

(d) run, within the variations permitted by the agreement, of even kind, quality and quantity within each unit and among all units involved; and

(e) are adequately contained, packaged, and labeled as the agreement may require; and

(f) conform to the promises or affirmations of fact made on the container or label if any.

(3) Unless excluded or modified (Section 2-316) other implied warranties may arise from course of dealing or usage of trade.

Section 2-315. Implied Warranty: Fitness for Particular Purpose.

Where the seller at the time of contracting has reason to know any particular purpose for which the goods are required and that the buyer is relying on the seller's skill or judgment to select or furnish suitable goods, there is unless excluded or modified under the next section an implied warranty that the goods shall be fit for such purpose.

Section 2-316. Exclusion or Modification of Warranties.

(1) Words or conduct relevant to the creation of an express warranty and words or conduct tending to negate or limit warranty shall be construed wherever reasonable as consistent with each other; but subject to the provisions of this Article on parol or extrinsic evidence (Section 2-202) negation or limitation is inoperative to the extent that such construction is unreasonable.

(2) Subject to subsection (3), to exclude or modify the implied warranty or merchantability or any part of it the language must mention merchantability and in case of a writing must be conspicuous, and to exclude or modify any implied warranty of fitness the exclusion must be by a writing and conspicuous. Language to exclude all implied warranties of fitness is sufficient if it states, for example, that "There are no warranties which extend beyond the description on the face hereof."

(3) Notwithstanding subsection (2)

(a) unless the circumstances indicate otherwise, all implied warranties are excluded by expressions like "as is," "with all faults" or other language which in common understanding calls the buyer's attention to the exclusion of warranties and makes plain that there is no implied warranty; and

(b) when the buyer before entering into the contract has examined the goods or the sample or model as fully as he desired or has refused to examine the goods there is no implied warranty with regard to defects which an examination ought in the circumstances to have revealed to him; and

(c) implied warranty can also be excluded or modified by course of dealing or course of performance or usage of trade.

(4) Remedies for breach of warranty can be limited in accordance with the provisions of this Article on liquidation or limitation of damages and on contractual modification of remedy (Sections 2-718 and 2-719).

Section 2-317. Cumulation and Conflict of Warranties Express or Implied.

Warranties whether express or implied shall be construed as consistent with each other and as cumulative, but if such construction is unreasonable the intention of the parties shall determine which warranty is dominant. In ascertaining that intention the following rules apply:

(a) Exact or technical specifications displace an inconsistent sample or model or general language of description.

(b) A sample from an existing bulk displaces inconsistent general language of description.

(c) Express warranties displace inconsistent implied warranties other than an implied warranty of fitness for a particular purpose.

Section 2-318. Third Party Beneficiaries of Warranties Express or Implied.

Note: *If this Act is introduced in the Congress of the United States this section should be omitted. (States to select one alternative.)*

Alternative A

A seller's warranty whether express or implied extends to any natural person who is in the family or household of his buyer or who is a guest in his home if it is reasonable to expect that such person may use, consume or be affected by the goods and who is injured in person by breach of the warranty. A seller may not exclude or limit the operation of this section.

Alternative B

A seller's warranty whether express or implied extends to any natural person who may reasonably be expected to use, consume or be affected by the goods and who is injured in person by breach of the warranty. A seller may not exclude or limit the operation of this section.

Alternative C

A seller's warranty whether express or implied extends to any person who may reasonably be expected to use, consume or be affected by the goods and who is injured by breach of the warranty. A seller may not exclude or limit the operation of this section with respect to injury to the person of an individual to whom the warranty extends.

Section 2-319. F.O.B. AND F.A.S. Terms.

(1) Unless otherwise agreed the term F.O.B. (which means "free on board") at a named place, even though used only in connection with the stated price, is a delivery term under which

(a) when the term is F.O.B. the place of shipment, the seller must at that place ship the goods in the manner provided in this Article (Section 2-504) and bear the expense and risk of putting them into the possession of the carrier; or

(b) when the term is F.O.B. the place of destination, the seller must at his own expense and risk transport the goods to that place and there tender delivery of them in the manner provided in this Article (Section 2-503);

(c) when under either (a) or (b) the term is also F.O.B. vessel, car or other vehicle, the seller must in addition at his own expense and risk load the goods on board. If the term is F.O.B. vessel the buyer must name the vessel and in an appropriate case the seller must comply with the provisions of this Article on the form of bill of lading (Section 2-323).

(2) Unless otherwise agreed the term F.A.S. vessel (which means "free alongside") at a named port, even though used only in connection with the stated price, is a delivery term under which the seller must

(a) at his own expense and risk deliver the goods alongside the vessel in the manner usual in that port or on a dock designated and provided by the buyer; and

(b) obtain and tender a receipt for the goods in exchange for which the carrier is under a duty to issue a bill of lading.

(3) Unless otherwise agreed in any case falling within subsection (1) (a) or (c) or subsection (2)

the buyer must seasonally give any needed instructions for making delivery, including when the term is F.A.S. or F.O.B. the loading berth of the vessel and in an appropriate case its name and sailing date. The seller may treat the failure of needed instructions as a failure of cooperation under this Article (Section 2-311). He may also at his option move the goods in any reasonable manner preparatory to delivery or shipment.

(4) Under the term F.O.B. vessel or F.A.S. unless otherwise agreed the buyer must make payment against tender of the required documents and the seller may not tender nor the buyer demand delivery of the goods in substitution for the documents.

Section 2-320. C.I.F. AND C. & F. Terms.

(1) The term C.I.F. means that the price includes in a lump sum the cost of the goods and the insurance and freight to the named destination. The term C. & F. or C.F. means that the price so includes cost and freight to the named destination.

(2) Unless otherwise agreed and even though used only in connection with the stated price and destination, the term C.I.F. destination or its equivalent requires the seller at his own expense and risk to

(a)   put the goods into the possession of a carrier at the port for shipment and obtain a negotiable bill or bills of lading covering the entire transportation to the named destination; and

(b)   load the goods and obtain a receipt from the carrier (which may be contained in the bill of lading) showing that the freight has been paid or provided for; and

(c)   obtain a policy or certificate of insurance, including any war risk insurance, of a kind and on terms then current at the port of shipment in the usual amount, in the currency of the contract, shown to cover the same goods covered by the bill of lading and providing for payment of loss to the order of the buyer or for the ac-

count of whom it may concern; but the seller may add to the price the amount of the premium for any such war risk insurance; and

(d)   prepare an invoice of the goods and procure any other documents required to effect shipment or to comply with the contract; and

(e)   forward and tender with commercial promptness all the documents in due form and with any indorsement necessary to perfect the buyer's rights.

(3) Unless otherwise agreed the term C. & F. or its equivalent has the same effect and imposes upon the seller the same obligations and risks as a C.I.F. term except the obligation as to insurance.

(4) Under the term C.I.F. or C. & F. unless otherwise agreed the buyer must make payment against tender of the required documents and the seller may not tender nor the buyer demand delivery of the goods in substitution for the documents.

Section 2-321. C.I.F. or C. & F.: "Net Landed Weights;" "Payment on Arrival;" Warranty of Condition on Arrival.

Under a contract containing a term C.I.F. or C. & F.

(1) Where the price is based on or is to be adjusted according to "net landed weights," "delivered weights," "out turn" quantity or quality or the like, unless otherwise agreed the seller must reasonably estimate the price. The payment due on tender of the documents called for by the contract is the amount so estimated, but after final adjustment of the price a settlement must be made with commercial promptness.

(2) An agreement described in subsection (1) or any warranty of quality or condition of the goods on arrival places upon the seller the risk of ordinary deterioration, shrinkage and the like in transportation but has no effect on the place or time of identification to the contract for sale or delivery or on the passing of the risk of loss.

(3) Unless otherwise agreed where the contract provides for payment on or after arrival of the goods the seller must before payment allow such preliminary inspection as is feasible; but if the goods are lost delivery of the documents and payment are due when the goods should have arrived.

Section 2-322. Delivery "Ex-Ship."

(1) Unless otherwise agreed a term for delivery of goods "ex-ship" (which means from the carrying vessel) or in equivalent language is not restricted to a particular ship and requires delivery from a ship which has reached a place at the named port of destination where goods of the kind are usually discharged.
(2) Under such a term unless otherwise agreed

- (a) the seller must discharge all liens arising out of the carriage and furnish the buyer with a direction which puts the carrier under a duty to deliver the goods; and
- (b) the risk of loss does not pass to the buyer until the goods leave the ship's tackle or are otherwise properly unloaded.

Section 2-323. Form of Bill of Lading Required in Overseas Shipment; "Overseas."

(1) Where the contract contemplates overseas shipment and contains a term C.I.F. or C. & F. or F.O.B. vessel, the seller unless otherwise agreed must obtain a negotiable bill of lading stating that the goods have been loaded on board or, in the case of a term C.I.F. or C. & F., received for shipment.
(2) Where in a case within subsection (1) a bill of lading has been issued in a set of parts, unless otherwise agreed if the documents are not to be sent from aboard the buyer may demand tender of the full set; otherwise only one part of the bill of lading need be tendered. Even if the agreement expressly requires a full set

- (a) due tender of a single part is acceptable within the provisions of this Arti-

cle on cure of improper delivery (subsection (1) of Section 2-508); and
- (b) even though the full set is demanded, if the documents are sent from abroad the person tendering an incomplete set may nevertheless require payment upon furnishing an indemnity which the buyer in good faith deems adequate.

(3) A shipment by water or by air or a contract contemplating such shipment "overseas" insofar as by usage of trade or agreement it is subject to the commercial, financing or shipping practices characteristic of international deep water commerce.

Section 2-324. "No Arrival, No Sale" Term.

Under a term "no arrival, no sale" or terms of like meaning, unless otherwise agreed,

- (a) the seller must properly ship conforming goods and if they arrive by any means he must tender them on arrival but he assumes no obligation that the goods will arrive unless he has caused the nonarrival; and
- (b) where without fault of the seller the goods are in part lost or have so deteriorated as no longer to conform to the contract or arrive after the contract time, the buyer may proceed as if there had been casualty to identified goods (Section 2-613).

Section 2-325. "Letter of Credit" Term; "Confirmed Credit."

(1) Failure of the buyer seasonably to furnish an agreed letter of credit is a breach of the contract for sale.
(2) The delivery to seller of a proper letter of credit suspends the buyer's obligation to pay. If the letter of credit is dishonored, the seller may on seasonable notification to the buyer require payment directly from him.
(3) Unless otherwise agreed the term "letter of credit" or "banker's credit" in a contract for sale means an irrevocable credit issued by a

financing agency of good repute and, where the shipment is overseas, of good international repute. The term "confirmed credit" means that the credit must also carry the direct obligation of such an agency which does business in the seller's financial market.

Section 2-326. Sale on Approval and Sale or Return; Consignment Sales and Rights of Creditors.

(1) Unless otherwise agreed, if delivered goods may be returned by the buyer even though they conform to the contract, the transaction is

(a) a "sale on approval" if the goods are delivered primarily for use, and

(b) a "sale or return" if the goods are delivered primarily for resale.

(2) Except as provided in subsection (3), goods held on approval are not subject to the claims of the buyer's creditors until acceptance; goods held on sale or return are subject to such claims while in the buyer's possession.

(3) Where goods are delivered to a person for sale and such person maintains a place of business at which he deals in goods of the kind involved, under a name other than the name of the person making delivery, then with respect to claims of creditors of the person conducting the business the goods are deemed to be on sale or return. The provisions of this subsection are applicable even though an agreement purports to reserve title to the person making delivery until payment or resale or uses such words as "on consignment" or "on memorandum." However, this subsection is not applicable if the person making delivery

(a) complies with an applicable law providing for a consignor's interest or the like to be evidenced by a sign, or

(b) establishes that the person conducting the business is generally known by his creditors to be substantially engaged in selling the goods of others, or

(c) complies with the filing provisions of the Article on Secured Transactions (Article 9).

(4) Any "or return" term of a contract for sale is to be treated as a separate contract for sale within the statute of frauds section of this Article (Section 2-201) and as contradicting the sale aspect of the contract within the provisions of this Article on parol or extrinsic evidence (Section 2-202).

Section 2-327. Special Incidents of Sale on Approval and Sale or Return.

(1) Under a sale on approval unless otherwise agreed

(a) although the goods are identified to the contract the risk of loss and the title do not pass to the buyer until acceptance; and

(b) use of the goods consistent with the purpose of trial is not acceptance but failure seasonably to notify the seller of election to return the goods is acceptance, and if the goods conform to the contract acceptance of any part is acceptance of the whole; and

(c) after due notification of election to return, the return is at the seller's risk and expense but a merchant buyer must follow any reasonable instructions.

(2) Under a sale or return unless otherwise agreed

(a) the option to return extends to the whole or any commercial unit of the goods while in substantially their original condition, but must be exercised seasonably; and

(b) the return is at the buyer's risk and expense.

Section 2-328. Sale by Auction.

(1) In a sale by auction if goods are put up in lots each lot is the subject of a separate sale.

(2) A sale by auction is complete when the auctioneer so announces by the fall of the hammer or in other customary manner. Where a bid is made while the hammer is falling in

971 Uniform Commercial Code

acceptance of a prior bid the auctioneer may in his discretion reopen the bidding or declare the goods sold under the bid on which the hammer was falling.

(3) Such a sale is with reserve unless the goods are in explicit terms put up without reserve. In an auction with reserve the auctioneer may withdraw the goods at any time until he announces completion of the sale. In an auction without reserve, after the auctioneer calls for bids on an article or lot, that article or lot cannot be withdrawn unless no bid is made within a reasonable time. In either case a bidder may retract his bid until the auctioneer's announcement of completion of sale, but a bidder's retraction does not revive any previous bid.

(4) If the auctioneer knowingly receives a bid on the seller's behalf or the seller makes or procures such a bid, and notice has not been given that liberty for such bidding is reserved, the buyer may at his option avoid the sale or take the goods at the price of the last good faith bid prior to the completion of the sale. This subsection shall not apply to any bid at a forced sale.

Part 4. Title, Creditors and Good Faith Purchasers.

Section 2-401. Passing of Title; Reservation for Security; Limited Application of This Section.

Each provision of this Article with regard to the rights, obligations and remedies of the seller, the buyer, purchasers or other third parties applies irrespective of title to the goods except where the provision refers to such title. Insofar as situations are not covered by the other provisions of this Article and matters concerning title become material the following rules apply:

(1) Title to goods cannot pass under a contract for sale prior to their identification to the contract (Section 2-501), and unless otherwise explicitly agreed the buyer acquires by their identification a special property as limited by

this Act. Any retention or reservation by the seller of the title (property) in goods shipped or delivered to the buyer is limited in effect to a reservation of a security interest. Subject to these provisions and to the provisions of the Article on Secured Transactions (Article 9), title to goods passes from the seller to the buyer in any manner and on any conditions explicitly agreed on by the parties.

(2) Unless otherwise explicitly agreed title passes to the buyer at the time and place at which the seller completes his performance with reference to the physical delivery of the goods, despite any reservation of a security interest and even though a document of title is to be delivered at a different time or place; and in particular and despite any reservation of a security interest by the bill of lading

    (a) if the contract requires or authorizes the seller to send the goods to the buyer but does not require him to deliver them at destination, title passes to the buyer at the time and place of shipment; but

    (b) if the contract requires delivery at destination, title passes on tender there.

(3) Unless otherwise explicitly agreed where delivery is to be made without moving the goods.

    (a) if the seller is to deliver a document of title, title passes at the time when and the place where he delivers such documents; or

    (b) if the goods are at the time of contracting already identified and no documents are to be delivered, title passes at the time and place of contracting.

(4) A rejection or other refusal by the buyer to receive or retain the goods, whether or not justified, or a justified revocation of acceptance revests title to the goods in the seller. Such revesting occurs by operation of law and is not a "sale."

Section 2-402. Rights of Seller's Creditors Against Sold Goods.

(1) Except as provided in subsections (2) and (3), rights of unsecured creditors of the seller with respect to goods which have been identified to a contract for sale are subject to the buyer's rights to recover the goods under this Article (Sections 2-502 and 2-716).

(2) A creditor of the seller may treat a sale or an identification of goods to a contract for sale as void if as against him a retention of possession by the seller is fraudulent under any rule of law of the state where the goods are situated, except that retention of possession in good faith and current course of trade by a merchant-seller for a commercially reasonable time after a sale or identification is not fraudulent.

(3) Nothing in this Article shall be deemed to impair the rights of creditors of the seller

(a) under the provision of the Article on Secured Transactions (Article 9); or

(b) where identification to the contract or delivery is made not in current course of trade but in satisfaction of or as security for a pre-existing claim for money, security or the like and is made under circumstances which under any rule of law of the state where the goods are situated would apart from this Article constitute the transaction a fraudulent transfer or voidable preference.

Section 2-403. Power to Transfer; Good Faith Purchase of Goods: "Entrusting."

(1) A purchaser of goods acquires all title which his transferor had or had power to transfer except that a purchaser of a limited interest acquires rights only to the extent of the interest purchased. A person with voidable title has power to transfer a good title to a good faith purchaser for value. When goods have been delivered under a transaction of purchase the purchaser has such power even though

(a) the transferor was deceived as to the identity of the purchaser, or

(b) the delivery was in exchange for a check which is later dishonored, or

(c) it was agreed that the transaction was to be a "cash sale," or

(d) the delivery was procured through fraud punishable as larcenous under the criminal law.

(2) Any entrusting of possession of goods to a merchant who deals in goods of that kind gives him power to transfer all rights of the entruster to a buyer in ordinary course of business.

(3) "Entrusting" includes any delivery and any acquiescence in retention of possession regardless of any condition expressed between the parties to the delivery or acquiescence and regardless of whether the procurement of the entrusting or the possessor's disposition of the goods have been such as to be larcenous under the criminal law.

(4) The rights of other purchasers of goods and of lien creditors are governed by the Articles on Secured Transactions (Article 9), Bulk Transfers (Article 6) and Documents of Title (Article 7).

Part 5. Performance.

Section 2-501. Insurable Interest in Goods; Manner of Identification of Goods.

(1) The buyer obtains a special property and an insurable interest in goods by identification of existing goods as goods to which the contract refers even though the goods so identified are nonconforming and he has an option to return or reject them. Such identification can be made at any time and in any manner explicitly agreed to by the parties. In the absence of explicit agreement identification occurs

(a) when the contract is made if it is for the sale of goods already existing and identified;

(b) if the contract is for the sale of future goods other than those described in paragraph (c), when goods are shipped, marked or otherwise designated by the seller as goods to which the contract refers;

(c) when the crops are planted or otherwise become growing crops or the young are conceived if the contract is for the sale of unborn young to be born within twelve months after contracting or for the sale of crops to be harvested within twelve months or the next normal harvest season after contracting whichever is longer.

(2) The seller retains an insurable interest in goods so long as title to or any security interest in the goods remains in him and where the identification is by the seller alone he may until default or insolvency or notification to the buyer that the identification is final substitute other goods for those identified.

(3) Nothing in this section impairs any insurable interest recognized under any other statute or rule of law.

Section 2-502. Buyer's Right to Goods on Seller's Insolvency.

(1) Subject to subsection (2) and even though the goods have not been shipped a buyer who has paid a part or all of the price of goods in which he has a special property under the provisions of the immediately preceding section may on making and keeping good a tender of any unpaid portion of their price recover them from the seller if the seller becomes insolvent within ten days after receipt of the first installment on their price.

(2) If the identification creating his special property has been made by the buyer he acquires the right to recover the goods only if they conform to the contract for sale.

Section 2-503. Manner of Seller's Tender of Delivery.

(1) Tender of delivery requires that the seller put and hold conforming goods at the buyer's disposition and give the buyer any notification reasonably necessary to enable him to take de-

livery. The manner, time and place for tender are determined by the agreement and this Article, and in particular

(a) tender must be at a reasonable hour, and if it is of goods they must be kept available for the period reasonably necessary to enable the buyer to take possession; but

(b) unless otherwise agreed the buyer must furnish facilities reasonably suited to the receipt of the goods.

(2) Where the case is within the next section respecting shipment tender requires that the seller comply with its provisions.

(3) Where the seller is required to deliver at a particular destination tender requires that he comply with subsection (1) and also in any appropriate case tender documents as described in subsections (4) and (5) of this section.

(4) Where goods are in the possession of a bailee and are to be delivered without being moved

(a) tender requires that the seller either tender a negotiable document of title covering such goods or procure acknowledgement by the bailee of the buyer's right to possession of the goods; but

(b) tender to the buyer of a non-negotiable document of title or of a written direction to the bailee to deliver is sufficient tender unless the buyer seasonably objects, and receipt by the bailee of notification of the buyer's rights fixes those rights as against the bailee and all third persons; but risk of loss of the goods and of any failure by the bailee to honor the non-negotiable document of title or to obey the direction remains on the seller until the buyer has had a reasonable time to present the document or direction, and a refusal by the bailee to honor the document or to obey the direction defeats the tender.

(5) Where the contract requires the seller to deliver documents

    (a)   he must tender all such documents in correct form, except as provided in this Article with respect to bills of lading in a set (subsection (2) of Section 2-323); and

    (b)   tender through customary banking channels is sufficient and dishonor of a draft accompanying the documents constitutes nonacceptance or rejection.

Section 2-504. Shipment by Seller.

Where the seller is required or authorized to send the goods to the buyer and the contract does not require him to deliver them at a particular destination, then unless otherwise agreed he must

    (a)   put the goods in the possession of such a carrier and make such a contract for their transportation as may be reasonable having regard to the nature of the goods and other circumstances of the case; and

    (b)   obtain and promptly deliver or tender in due form any document necessary to enable the buyer to obtain possession of the goods or otherwise required by the agreement or by usage of trade; and

    (c)   promptly notify the buyer of the shipment.

Failure to notify the buyer under paragraph (c) or to make a proper contract under paragraph (a) is a ground for rejection only if material delay or loss ensues.

Section 2-505. Seller's Shipment Under Reservation.

(1) Where the seller has identified goods to the contract by or before shipment:

    (a)   his procurement of a negotiable bill of lading to his own order or otherwise reserves in him a security interest in the goods. His procurement of the bill to the order of a financing agency or of the buyer indicates in addition only the seller's expectation of transferring that interest to the person named.

    (b)   a non-negotiable bill of lading to himself or his nominee reserves possession of the goods as security but except in a case of conditional delivery (subsection (2) of Section 2-507) a non-negotiable bill of lading naming the buyer as consignee reserves no security interest even though the seller retains possession of the bill of lading.

(2) When shipment by the seller with reservation of a security interest is in violation of the contract for sale it constitutes an improper contract for transportation within the preceding section but impairs neither the rights given to the buyer by shipment and identification of the goods to the contract nor the seller's powers as a holder of a negotiable document.

Section 2-506. Rights of Financing Agency.

(1) A financing agency by paying or purchasing for value a draft which relates to a shipment of goods acquires to the extent of the payment or purchase and in addition to its own rights under the draft and any document of title securing it any rights of the shipper in the goods including the right to stop delivery and the shipper's right to have the draft honored by the buyer.

(2) The right to reimbursement of a financing agency which has in good faith honored or purchased the draft under commitment to or authority from the buyer is not impaired by subsequent discovery of defects with reference to any relevant document which was apparently regular on its face.

Section 2-507. Effect of Seller's Tender; Delivery on Condition.

(1) Tender of delivery is a condition to the buyer's duty to accept the goods and, unless otherwise agreed, to his duty to pay for them.

Tender entitles the seller to acceptance of the goods and to payment according to the contract.

(2) Where payment is due and demanded on the delivery to the buyer of goods or documents of title, his right as against the seller to retain or dispose of them is conditional upon his making the payment due.

Section 2-508. Cure by Seller of Improper Tender or Delivery; Replacement.

(1) Where any tender or delivery by the seller is rejected because non-conforming and the time for performance has not yet expired, the seller may seasonably notify the buyer of his intention to cure and may then within the contract time make a conforming delivery.

(2) Where the buyer rejects a non-conforming tender which the seller had reasonable grounds to believe would be acceptable with or without money allowance the seller may if he seasonably notifies the buyer have a further reasonable time to substitute a conforming tender.

Section 2-509. Risk of Loss in the Absence of Breach.

(1) Where the contract requires or authorizes the seller to ship the goods by carrier

(a)   if it does not require him to deliver them at a particular destination, the risk of loss passes to the buyer when the goods are duly delivered to the carrier even though the shipment is under reservation (Section 2-505); but

(b)   if it does require him to deliver them at a particular destination and the goods are there duly tendered while in the possession of the carrier, the risk of loss passes to the buyer when the goods are there duly so tendered as to enable the buyer to take delivery.

(2) Where the goods are held by a bailee to be delivered without being moved, the risk of loss passes to the buyer

(a)   on his receipt of a negotiable document of title covering the goods; or

(b)   on acknowledgment by the bailee of the buyer's right to possession of the goods; or

(c)   after his receipt of a non-negotiable document of title or other written direction to deliver, as provided in subsection (4) (b) of Section 2-503.

(3) In any case not within subsection (1) or (2), the risk of loss passes to the buyer on his receipt of the goods if the seller is a merchant; otherwise the risk passes to the buyer on tender of delivery.

(4) The provisions of this section are subject to contrary agreement of the parties and to the provisions of this Article on sale on approval (Section 2-327) and on effect of breach on risk of loss (Section 2-510).

Section 2-510. Effect of Breach on Risk of Loss.

(1) Where a tender or delivery of goods so fails to conform to the contract as to give a right of rejection the risk of their loss remains on the seller until cure or acceptance.

(2) Where the buyer rightfully revokes acceptance he may to the extent of any deficiency in his effective insurance coverage treat the risk of loss as having rested on the seller from the beginning.

(3) Where the buyer as to conforming goods already identified to the contract for sale repudiates or is otherwise in breach before risk of their loss has passed to him, the seller may to the extent of any deficiency in his effective insurance coverage treat the risk of loss as resting on the buyer for a commercially reasonable time.

Section 2-511. Tender of Payment by Buyer; Payment of Check.

(1) Unless otherwise agreed tender of payment is a condition to the seller's duty to tender and complete any delivery.

(2) Tender of payment is sufficient when made by any means or in any manner current in the

ordinary course of business unless the seller demands payment in legal tender and gives any extension of time reasonably necessary to procure it.

(3) Subject to the provisions of this Act on the effect of an instrument on an obligation (Section 3-802), payment by check is conditional and is defeated as between the parties by dishonor of the check on due presentment.

Section 2-512. Payment by Buyer Before Inspection.

(1) Where the contract requires payment before inspection non-conformity of the goods does not excuse the buyer from so making payment unless

    (a)   the non-conformity appears without inspection; or

    (b)   despite tender of the required documents the circumstances would justify injunction against honor under the provisions of this Act (Section 5-114).

(2) Payment pursuant to subsection (1) does not constitute an acceptance of goods or impair the buyer's right to inspect or any of his remedies.

Section 2-513. Buyer's Right to Inspection of Goods.

(1) Unless otherwise agreed and subject to subsection (3), where goods are tendered or delivered or identified to the contract for sale, the buyer has a right before payment or acceptance to inspect them at any reasonable place and time and in any reasonable manner. When the seller is required or authorized to send the goods to the buyer, the inspection may be after their arrival.

(2) Expenses of inspection must be borne by the buyer but may be recovered from the seller if the goods do not conform and are rejected.

(3) Unless otherwise agreed and subject to the provisions of this Article on C.I.F. contracts (subsection (3) of Section 2-321), the buyer is not entitled to inspect the goods before payment of the price when the contract provides

    (a)   for delivery "C.O.D." or on other like terms; or

    (b)   for payment against documents of title, except where such payment is due only after the goods are to become available for inspection.

(4) A place or method of inspection fixed by the parties is presumed to be exclusive but unless otherwise expressly agreed it does not postpone identification or shift the place for delivery or for passing the risk of loss. If compliance becomes impossible, inspection shall be as provided in this section unless the place or method fixed was clearly intended as an indispensable condition failure of which avoids the contract.

Section 2-514. When Documents Deliverable on Acceptance; When on Payment.

Unless otherwise agreed documents against which a draft is drawn are to be delivered to the drawee on acceptance of the draft if it is payable more than three days after presentment; otherwise, only on payment.

Section 2-515. Preserving Evidence of Goods in Dispute.

In furtherance of the adjustment of any claim or dispute

    (a)   either party on reasonable notification to the other and for the purpose of ascertaining the facts and preserving evidence has the right to inspect, test and sample the goods including such of them as may be in the possession or control of the other; and

    (b)   the parties may agree to a third party inspection or survey to determine the conformity or condition of the goods and may agree that the findings shall be binding upon them in any subsequent litigation or adjustment.

Part 6. Breach, Repudiation, and Excuse.

Section 2-601. Buyer's Rights on Improper Delivery.

Subject to the provisions of this Article on breach in installment contracts (Section 2-612) and unless otherwise agreed under the sections on contractual limitations of remedy (Sections 2-718 and 2-719), if the goods or the tender of delivery fail in any respect to conform to the contract, the buyer may

    (a)   reject the whole; or
    (b)   accept the whole; or
    (c)   accept any commercial unit or units and reject the rest.

Section 2-602. Manner and Effect of Rightful Rejection.

(1) Rejection of goods must be within a reasonable time after their delivery or tender. It is ineffective unless the buyer seasonably notifies the seller.

(2) Subject to the provisions of the two following sections on rejected goods (Sections 2-603 and 2-604).

    (a)   after rejection any exercise of ownership by the buyer with respect to any commercial unit is wrongful as against the seller; and
    (b)   if the buyer has before rejection taken physical possession of goods in which he does not have a security interest under the provisions of this Article (subsection (3) of Section 2-711), he is under a duty after rejection to hold them with reasonable care at the seller's disposition for a time sufficient to permit the seller to remove them; but
    (c)   the buyer has no further obligations with regard to goods rightfully rejected.

(3) The seller's rights with respect to goods wrongfully rejected are governed by the provisions of this Article on Seller's remedies in general (Section 2-703).

Section 2-603. Merchant Buyer's Duties as to Rightfully Rejected Goods.

(1) Subject to any security interest in the buyer (subsection (3) of Section 2-711), when the seller has no agent or place of business at the market of rejection a merchant buyer is under a duty after rejection of goods in his possession or control to follow any reasonable instructions received from the seller with respect to the goods and in the absence of such instructions to make reasonable efforts to sell them for the seller's account if they are perishable or threaten to decline in value speedily. Instructions are not reasonable if on demand indemnity for expenses is not forthcoming.

(2) When the buyer sells goods under subsection (1), he is entitled to reimbursement from the seller or out of the proceeds for reasonable expenses of caring for and selling them, and if the expenses include no selling commission then to such commission as is usual in the trade or if there is none to a reasonable sum not exceeding ten per cent on the gross proceeds.

(3) In complying with this section the buyer is held only to good faith and good faith conduct hereunder is neither acceptance nor conversion nor the basis of an action for damages.

Section 2-604. Buyer's Options as to Salvage of Rightfully Rejected Goods.

Subject to the provisions of the immediately preceding section on perishables if the seller gives no instructions within a reasonable time after notification of rejection the buyer may store the rejected goods for the seller's account or reship them to him or resell them for the seller's account with reimbursement as provided in the preceding section. Such action is not acceptance or conversion.

Section 2-605. Waiver of Buyer's Objections by Failure to Particularize.

(1) The buyer's failure to state in connection with rejection a particular defect which is ascertainable by reasonable inspection precludes

him from relying on the unstated defect to justify rejection or to establish breach

    (a)   where the seller could have cured it if stated seasonally; or

    (b)   between merchants when the seller has after rejection made a request in writing for a full and final written statement of all defects on which the buyer proposes to rely.

(2) Payment against documents made without reservation of rights precludes recovery of the payment for defects apparent on the face of the documents.

Section 2-606. What Constitutes Acceptance of Goods.

(1) Acceptance of goods occurs when the buyer

    (a)   after a reasonable opportunity to inspect the goods signifies to the seller that the goods are conforming or that he will take or retain them in spite of their non-conformity; or

    (b)   fails to make an effective rejection (subsection (1) of Section 2-602), but such acceptance does not occur until the buyer has had a reasonable opportunity to inspect them; or

    (c)   does any act inconsistent with the seller's ownership; but if such act is wrongful as against the seller it is an acceptance only if ratified by him.

(2) Acceptance of a part of any commercial unit is acceptance of that entire unit.

Section 2-607. Effect of Acceptance; Notice of Breach; Burden of Establishing Breach After Acceptance; Notice of Claim or Litigation to Person Answerable Over.

(1) The buyer must pay at the contract rate for any goods accepted.
(2) Acceptance of goods by the buyer precludes rejection of the goods accepted and if made with knowledge of a non-conformity cannot be revoked because of it unless the acceptance was on the reasonable assumption that the non-conformity would be seasonably cured but acceptance does not of itself impair any other remedy provided by this Article for nonconformity.
(3) Where a tender has been accepted

    (a)   the buyer must within a reasonable time after he discovers or should have discovered any breach notify the seller of breach or be barred from any remedy; and

    (b)   if the claim is one for infringement or the like (subsection (3) of Section 2-312) and the buyer is sued as a result of such a breach he must so notify the seller within a reasonable time after he receives notice of the litigation or be barred from any remedy over for liability established by the litigation.

(4) The burden is on the buyer to establish any breach with respect to the goods accepted.
(5) Where the buyer is sued for breach of a warranty or other obligation for which his seller is answerable over

    (a)   he may give his seller written notice of the litigation. If the notice states that the seller may come in and defend and that if the seller does not do so he will be bound in any action against him by his buyer by any determination of fact common to the two litigations, then unless the seller after seasonable receipt of the notice does come in and defend he is so bound.

    (b)   if the claim is one for infringement or the like (subsection (3) of Section 2-312) the original seller may demand in writing that his buyer turn over to him control of the litigation including settlement or else be barred from any remedy over and if he also agrees to bear all expense and to satisfy any adverse judgment, then unless the buyer after seasonable receipt of the demand does turn over control the buyer is so barred.

(6) The provisions of subsections (3), (4) and (5) apply to any obligation of a buyer to hold the seller harmless against infringement or the like (subsection (3) of Section 2-312).

Section 2-608. Revocation of Acceptance in Whole or in Part.

(1) The buyer may revoke his acceptance of a lot or commercial unit whose nonconformity substantially impairs its value to him if he has accepted it

   (a)   on the reasonable assumption that its nonconformity would be cured and it has not been seasonably cured; or
   (b)   without discovery of such nonconformity if his acceptance was reasonably induced either by the difficulty of discovery before acceptance or by the seller's assurances.

(2) Revocation of acceptance must occur within a reasonable time after the buyer discovers or should have discovered the ground for it and before any substantial change in conditions of the goods which is not caused by their own defects. It is not effective until the buyer notifies the seller of it.
(3) A buyer who so revokes has the same rights and duties with regard to the goods involved as if he had rejected them.

Section 2-609. Right to Adequate Assurance of Performance.

(1) A contract for sale imposes an obligation on each party that the other's expectation of receiving due performance will not be impaired. When reasonable grounds for insecurity arise with respect to the performance of either party the other may in writing demand adequate assurance of due performance and until he receives such assurance may if commercially reasonable suspend any performance for which he has not already received the agreed return.

(2) Between merchants the reasonableness of grounds for insecurity and the adequacy of any assurance offered shall be determined according to commercial standards.
(3) Acceptance of any improper delivery or payment does not prejudice the aggrieved party's right to demand adequate assurance of future performance.
(4) After receipt of a justified demand failure to provide within a reasonable time not exceeding thirty days such assurance of due performance as is adequate under the circumstances of the particular case is a repudiation of the contract.

Section 2-610. Anticipatory Repudiation.

When either party repudiates the contract with respect to a performance not yet due the loss of which will substantially impair the value of the contract to the other, the aggrieved party may

   (a)   for a commercially reasonable time await performance by the repudiating party; or
   (b)   resort to any remedy for breach (Section 2-703 or Section 2-711), even though he has notified the repudiating party that he would await the latter's performance and has urged retraction; and
   (c)   in either case suspend his own performance or proceed in accordance with the provisions of this Article on the seller's right to identify goods to the contract notwithstanding breach or to salvage unfinished goods (Section 2-704).

Section 2-611. Retraction of Anticipatory Repudiation.

(1) Until the repudiating party's next performance is due he can retract his repudiation unless the aggrieved party has since the repudiation cancelled or materially changed his position or otherwise indicated that he considers the repudiation final.

(2) Retraction may be by any method which clearly indicates to the aggrieved party that the repudiating party intends to perform, but must include any assurance justifiably demanded under the provisions of this Article (Section 2-609).

(3) Retraction reinstates the repudiating party's rights under the contract with due excuse and allowance to the aggrieved party for any delay occasioned by the repudiation.

Section 2-612. "Installment Contract;" Breach.

(1) An "installment contract" is one which requires or authorizes the delivery of goods in separate lots to be separately accepted, even though the contract contains a clause "each delivery is a separate contract" or its equivalent.

(2) The buyer may reject any installment which is non-conforming if the non-conformity substantially impairs the value of that installment and cannot be cured or if the non-conformity is a defect in the required documents; but if the non-conformity does not fall within subsection (3) and the seller gives adequate assurance of its cure the buyer must accept that installment.

(3) Whenever non-conformity or default with respect to one or more installments substantially impairs the value of the whole contract there is a breach of the whole. But the aggrieved party reinstates the contract if he accepts a non-conforming installment without seasonably notifying of cancellation or if he brings an action with respect only to past installments or demands performance as to future installments.

Section 2-613. Casualty to Identified Goods.

Where the contract requires for its performance goods identified when the contract is made, and the goods suffer casualty without fault of either party before the risk of loss passes to the buyer, or in a proper case under a "no arrival, no sale" term (Section 2-324) then

(a) if the loss is total the contract is avoided; and

(b) if the loss is partial or the goods have so deteriorated as no longer to conform to the contract the buyer may nevertheless demand inspection and at his option either treat the contract as avoided or accept the goods with due allowance from the contract price for the deterioration or the deficiency in quantity but without further right against the seller.

Section 2-614. Substituted Performance.

(1) Where without fault of either party the agreed berthing, loading, or unloading facilities fail or an agreed type of carrier becomes unavailable or the agreed manner of delivery otherwise becomes commercially impracticable but a commercially reasonable substitute is available, such substitute performance must be tendered and accepted.

(2) If the agreed means or manner of payment fails because of domestic or foreign governmental regulation, the seller may withhold or stop delivery unless the buyer provides a means or manner of payment which is commercially a substantial equivalent. If delivery has already been taken, payment by the means or in the manner provided by the regulation discharges the buyer's obligation unless the regulation is discriminatory, oppressive or predatory.

Section 2-615. Excuse by Failure of Presupposed Conditions.

Except so far as a seller may have assumed a greater obligation and subject to the preceding section on substitute performance:

(a) Delay in delivery or non-delivery in whole or in part by a seller who complies with paragraphs (b) and (c) is not a breach of his duty under a contract for sale if performance as agreed has been made impracticable by the occurrence of a contingency the nonoccurrence of which was a basic assumption on which the contract was made or by compliance in good faith with any applicable foreign or domestic governmental regulation or order whether or not it later proves to be invalid.

(b) Where the causes mentioned in paragraph (a) affect only a part of the seller's capacity to perform, he must allocate production and deliveries among his customers but may at his option include regular customers not then under contract as well as his own requirements for further manufacture. He may so allocate in any manner which is fair and reasonable.

(c) The seller must notify the buyer seasonably that there will be delay or non-delivery and, when allocation is required under paragraph (b), of the estimated quota thus made available for the buyer.

Section 2-616. Procedure on Notice Claiming Excuse.

(1) Where the buyer receives notification of a material or indefinite delay or an allocation justified under the preceding section he may by written notification to the seller as to any delivery concerned, and where the prospective deficiency substantially impairs the value of the whole contract under the provisions of this Article relating to breach of installment contracts (Section 2-612), then also as to the whole,

(a) terminate and thereby discharge any unexecuted portion of the contract; or
(b) modify the contract by agreeing to take his available quota in substitution.

(2) If after receipt of such notification from the seller the buyer fails so to modify the contract within a reasonable time not exceeding thirty days the contract lapses with respect to any deliveries affected.

(3) The provisions of this section may not be negated by agreement except in so far as the seller has assumed a greater obligation under the preceding section.

Part 7. Remedies.

Section 2-701. Remedies for Breach of Collateral Contracts Not Impaired.

Remedies for breach of any obligation or promise collateral or ancillary to a contract for sale are not impaired by the provisions of this Article.

Section 2-702. Seller's Remedies on Discovery of Buyer's Insolvency.

(1) Where the seller discovers the buyer to be insolvent he may refuse delivery except for cash including payment for all goods theretofore delivered under the contract, and stop delivery under this Article (Section 2-705).

(2) Where the seller discovers that the buyer has received goods on credit while insolvent he may reclaim the goods upon demand made within ten days after the receipt, but if misrepresentation of solvency has been made to the particular seller in writing within three months before delivery the ten day limitation does not apply. Except as provided in this subsection the seller may not base a right to reclaim goods on the buyer's fraudulent or innocent misrepresentation of solvency or of intent to pay.

(3) The seller's right to reclaim under subsection (2) is subject to the rights of a buyer in ordinary course or other good faith purchaser under this Article (Section 2-403). Successful reclamation of goods excludes all other remedies with respect to them.

Section 2-703. Seller's Remedies in General.

Where the buyer wrongfully rejects or revokes acceptance of goods or fails to make a payment due on or before delivery or repudiates with respect to a part or the whole, then with respect to any goods directly affected and, if the breach is of the whole contract (Section

2-612), then also with respect to the whole undelivered balance, the aggrieved seller may

(a) withhold delivery of such goods;

(b) stop delivery by any bailee as hereafter provided (Section 2-705);

(c) proceed under the next section respecting goods still unidentified to the contract;

(d) resell and recover damages as hereafter provided (Section 2-706);

(e) recover damages for non-acceptance (Section 2-708) or in a proper case the price (Section 2-709);

(f) cancel.

Section 2-704. Seller's Right to Identify Goods to the Contract Notwithstanding Breach or to Salvage Unfinished Goods.

(1) An aggrieved seller under the preceding section may

(a) identify to the contract conforming goods not already identified if at the time he learned of the breach they are in his possession or control;

(b) treat as the subject of resale goods which have demonstrably been intended for the particular contract even though those goods are unfinished.

(2) Where the goods are unfinished an aggrieved seller may in the exercise of reasonable commercial judgment for the purposes of avoiding loss and of effective realization either complete the manufacture and wholly identify the goods to the contract or cease manufacture and resell for scrap or salvage value or proceed in any other reasonable manner.

Section 2-705. Seller's Stoppage of Delivery in Transit or Otherwise.

(1) The seller may stop delivery of goods in the possession of a carrier or other bailee when he discovers the buyer to be insolvent (Section 2-702) and may stop delivery of carload, truckload, planeload or larger shipments of express or freight when the buyer

repudiates or fails to make a payment due before delivery or if for any other reason the seller has a right to withhold or reclaim the goods.

(2) As against such buyer the seller may stop delivery until

(a) receipt of the goods by the buyer; or

(b) acknowledgment to the buyer by any bailee of the goods except a carrier that the bailee holds the goods for the buyer; or

(c) such acknowledgment to the buyer by a carrier by reshipment or as warehouseman; or

(d) negotiation to the buyer of any negotiable document of title covering the goods.

(3) (a) To stop delivery the seller must so notify as to enable the bailee by reasonable diligence to prevent delivery of the goods.

(b) After such notification the bailee must hold and deliver the goods according to the directions of the seller but the seller is liable to the bailee for any ensuing charges or damages.

(c) If a negotiable document of title has been issued for goods the bailee is not obliged to obey a notification to stop until surrender of the document.

(d) A carrier who has issued a nonnegotiable bill of lading is not obliged to obey a notification to stop received from a person other than the consignor.

Section 2-706. Seller's Resale Including Contract for Resale.

(1) Under the conditions stated in Section 2-703 on seller's remedies, the seller may resell the goods concerned or the undelivered balance thereof. Where the resale is made in good faith and in a commercially reasonable manner the seller may recover the difference between the resale price and the contract price together with any incidental damages allowed under the provisions of this Article (Section 2-

710), but less expenses saved in consequence of the buyer's breach.

(2) Except as otherwise provided in subsection (3) or unless otherwise agreed resale may be at public or private sale including sale by way of one or more contracts to sell or of identification to an existing contract of the seller. Sale may be as a unit or in parcels and at any time and place and on any terms but every aspect of the sale including the method, manner, time, place and terms must be commercially reasonable. The resale must be reasonably identified as referring to the broken contract, but it is not necessary that the goods be in existence or that any or all of them have been identified to the contract before the breach.

(3) Where the resale is at private sale the seller must give the buyer reasonable notification of his intention to resell.

(4) Where the resale is at public sale

(a) only identified goods can be sold except where there is a recognized market for a public sale of futures in goods of the kind; and

(b) it must be made at a usual place or market for public sale if one is reasonably available and except in the case of goods which are perishable or threaten to decline in value speedily the seller must give the buyer reasonable notice of the time and place of the resale; and

(c) if the goods are not to be within the view of those attending the sale the notification of sale must state the place where the goods are located and provide for their reasonable inspection by prospective bidders; and

(d) the seller may buy.

(5) A purchaser who buys in good faith at a resale take the goods free of any rights of the original buyer even though the seller fails to comply with one or more of the requirements of this section.

(6) The seller is not accountable to the buyer for any profit made on any resale. A person in the position of a seller (Section 2-707) or a buyer who has rightfully rejected or justifiably

revoked acceptance must account for any excess over the amount of his security interest, as hereinafter defined (subsection (3) of Section 2-711).

Section 2-707. "Person in the Position of a Seller."

(1) A "person in the position of a seller" includes as against a principal an agent who has paid or become responsible for the price of goods on behalf of his principal or anyone who otherwise holds a security interest or other right in goods similar to that of a seller.

(2) A person in the position of a seller may as provided in this Article withhold or stop delivery (Section 2-705) and resell (Section 2-706) and recover incidental damages (Section 2-710).

Section 2-708. Seller's Damages for Non-acceptance or Repudiation.

(1) Subject to subsection (2) and to the provisions of this Article with respect to proof of market price (Section 2-723), the measure of damages for non-acceptance or repudiation by the buyer is the difference between the market price at the time and place for tender and the unpaid contract price together with any incidental damages provided in this Article (Section 2-710), but less expenses saved in consequence of the buyer's breach.

(2) If the measure of damages provided in subsection (1) is inadequate to put the seller in as good a position as performance would have done then the measure of damages is the profit (including reasonable overhead) which the seller would have made from full performance by the buyer, together with any incidental damages provided in this Article (Section 2-710), due allowance for costs reasonably incurred and due credit for payments or proceeds of resale.

Section 2-709. Action for the Price.

(1) When the buyer fails to pay the price as it becomes due the seller may recover, together

with any incidental damages under the next section, the price

(a) of goods accepted or of conforming goods lost or damaged within a commercially reasonable time after risk of their loss has passed to the buyer; and

(b) of goods identified to the contract if the seller is unable after reasonable effort to resell them at a reasonable price or the circumstances reasonably indicate that such effort will be unavailing.

(2) Where the seller sues for the price he must hold for the buyer any goods which have been identified to the contract and are still in his control except that if resale becomes possible he may resell them at any time prior to the collection of the judgment. The net proceeds of any such resale must be credited to the buyer and payment of the judgment entitles him to any goods not resold.

(3) After the buyer has wrongfully rejected or revoked acceptance of the goods or has failed to make a payment due or has repudiated (Section 2-610), a seller who is held not entitled to the price under this section shall nevertheless be awarded damages for non-acceptance under the preceding section.

Section 2-710. Seller's Incidental Damages.

Incidental damages to an aggrieved seller include any commercially reasonable charges, expenses or commissions incurred in stopping delivery, in the transportation, care and custody of goods after the buyer's breach, in connection with return or resale of the goods or otherwise resulting from the breach.

Section 2-711. Buyer's Remedies in General; Buyer's Security Interest in Rejected Goods.

(1) Where the seller fails to make delivery or repudiates or the buyer rightfully rejects or justifiably revokes acceptance then with respect to any goods involved, and with respect to the whole if the breach goes to the whole contract (Section 2-612), the buyer may cancel

and whether or not he has done so may in addition to recovering so much of the price as has been paid

(a) "cover" and have damages under the next section as to all the goods affected whether or not they have been identified to the contract; or

(b) recover damages for non-delivery as provided in this Article (Section 2-713).

(2) Where the seller fails to deliver or repudiates the buyer may also

(a) if the goods have been identified recover them as provided in this Article (Section 2-502); or

(b) in a proper case obtain specific performance or replevy the goods as provided in this Article (Section 2-716).

(3) On rightful rejection or justifiable revocation of acceptance a buyer has a security interest in goods in his possession or control for any payments made on their price and any expenses reasonably incurred in their inspection, receipt, transportation, care and custody and may hold such goods and resell them in like manner as an aggrieved seller (Section 2-706).

Section 2-712. "Cover;" Buyer's Procurement of Substitute Goods.

(1) After a breach within the preceding section the buyer may "cover" by making in good faith and without unreasonable delay any reasonable purchase of or contract to purchase goods in substitution for those due from the seller.

(2) The buyer may recover from the seller as damages the difference between the cost of cover and the contract price together with any incidental or consequential damages as hereinafter defined (Section 2-715), but less expenses saved in consequence of the seller's breach.

(3) Failure of the buyer to effect cover within this section does not bar him from any other remedy.

Section 2-713. Buyer's Damages for Non-Delivery or Repudiation.

(1) Subject to the provisions of this Article with respect to proof of market price (Section 2-723), the measure of damages for nondelivery or repudiation by the seller is the difference between the market price at the time when the buyer learned of the breach and the contract price together with any incidental and consequential damages provided in this Article (Section 2-715), but less expenses saved in consequence of the seller's breach.
(2) Market price is to be determined as of the place for tender or, in cases of rejection after arrival or revocation of acceptance, as of the place of arrival.

Section 2-714. Buyer's Damages for Breach in Regard to Accepted Goods.

(1) Where the buyer has accepted goods and given notification (subsection (3) of Section 2-607) he may recover as damages for any nonconformity of tender the loss resulting in the ordinary course of events from the seller's breach as determined in any manner which is reasonable.
(2) The measure of damages for breach of warranty is the difference at the time and place of acceptance between the value of the goods accepted and the value they would have had if they had been as warranted, unless special circumstances show proximate damages of a different amount
(3) In a proper case any incidental and consequential damages under the next section may also be recovered.

Section 2-715. Buyer's Incidental and Consequential Damages.

(1) Incidental damages resulting from the seller's breach include expenses reasonably incurred in inspection, receipt, transportation and care and custody of goods rightfully rejected, any commercially reasonable charges, expenses or commissions in connection with effecting cover and any other reasonable expense incident to the delay or other breach.

(2) Consequential damages resulting from the seller's breach include

(a) any loss resulting from general or particular requirements and needs of which the seller at the time of contracting had reason to know and which could not reasonably be prevented by cover or otherwise; and
(b) injury to person or property proximately resulting from any breach of warranty.

Section 2-716. Buyer's Right to Specific Performance or Replevin.

(1) Specific performance may be decreed where the goods are unique or in other proper circumstances.
(2) The decree for specific performance may include such terms and conditions as to payment of the price, damages, or other relief as the court may deem just.
(3) The buyer has a right of replevin for goods identified to the contract if after reasonable effort he is unable to effect cover for such goods or the circumstances reasonably indicate that such effort will be unavailing or if the goods have been shipped under reservation and satisfaction of the security interest in them has been made or tendered.

Section 2-717. Deduction of Damages From the Price.

The buyer on notifying the seller of his intention to do so may deduct all or any part of the damages resulting from any breach of the contract from any part of the price still due under the same contract.

Section 2-718. Liquidation or Limitation of Damages; Deposits.

(1) Damages for breach by either party may be liquidated in the agreement but only at an amount which is reasonable in the light of the anticipated or actual harm caused by the breach, the difficulties of proof of loss, and the inconvenience or nonfeasibility of otherwise

obtaining an adequate remedy. A term fixing unreasonably large liquidated damages is void as a penalty.

(2) Where the seller justifiably withholds delivery of goods because of the buyer's breach, the buyer is entitled to restitution of any amount by which the sum of his payments exceeds

    (a) the amount to which the seller is entitled by virtue of terms liquidating the seller's damages in accordance with subsection (1), or

    (b) in the absence of such terms, twenty percent of the value of the total performance for which the buyer is obligated under the contract or $500, whichever is smaller.

(3) The buyer's right to restitution under subsection (2) is subject to offset to the extent that the seller establishes

    (a) a right to recover damages under the provisions of this Article other than subsection (1), and

    (b) the amount or value of any benefits received by the buyer directly or indirectly by reason of the contract.

(4) Where a seller has received payment in goods their reasonable value or the proceeds of their resale shall be treated as payments for the purposes of subsection (2); but if the seller has notice of the buyer's breach before reselling goods received in part performance, his resale is subject to the conditions laid down in this Article on resale by an aggrieved seller (Section 2-706).

Section 2-719. Contractual Modification or Limitation of Remedy.

(1) Subject to the provisions of subsections (2) and (3) of this section and of the preceding section on liquidation and limitation of damages,

    (a) the agreement may provide for remedies in addition to or in substitution for those provided in this Article and may limit or alter the measure of damages recoverable under this Article, as by limiting the buyer's remedies to return of the goods and repayment of the price or to repair and replacement of nonconforming goods or parts; and

    (b) resort to a remedy as provided is optional unless the remedy is expressly agreed to be exclusive, in which case it is the sole remedy.

(2) Where circumstances cause an exclusive or limited remedy to fail of its essential purpose, remedy may be had as provided in this Act.

(3) Consequential damages may be limited or excluded unless the limitation or exclusion is unconscionable. Limitation of consequential damages for injury to the person in the case of consumer goods is prima facie unconscionable but limitation of damages where the loss is commercial is not.

Section 2-720. Effect of "Cancellation" or "Rescission" on Claims for Antecedent Breach.

Unless the contrary intention clearly appears, expressions of "cancellation" or "rescission" of the contract or the like shall not be construed as a renunciation or discharge or any claim in damages for an antecedent breach.

Section 2-721. Remedies for Fraud.

Remedies for material misrepresentation or fraud include all remedies available under this Article for non-fraudulent breach. Neither rescission or a claim for rescission of the contract for sale nor rejection or return of the goods shall bar or be deemed inconsistent with a claim for damages or other remedy.

Section 2-722. Who Can Sue Third Parties for Injury to Goods.

Where a third party so deals with goods which have been identified to a contract for sale as to cause actionable injury to a party to that contract

(a) a right of action against the third party is in either party to the contract for sale who has title to or a security interest or a special property or an insurable interest in the goods; and if the goods have been destroyed or converted a right of action is also in the party who either bore the risk of loss under the contract for sale or has since the injury assumed that risk as against the other;

(b) if at the time of the injury the party plaintiff did not bear the risk of loss as against the other party to the contract for sale and there is no arrangement between them for disposition of the recovery, his suit or settlement is, subject to his own interest, as a fiduciary for the other party to the contract;

(c) either party may with the consent of the other sue for the benefit of whom it may concern.

Section 2-723. Proof of Market Price: Time and Place.

(1) If an action based on anticipatory repudiation comes to trial before the time for performance with respect to some or all of the goods, any damages based on market price (Section 2-708 or Section 2-713) shall be determined according to the price of such goods prevailing at the time when the aggrieved party learned of the repudiation.

(2) If evidence of a price prevailing at the times or places described in this Article is not readily available the price prevailing within any reasonable time before or after the time described or at any other place which in commercial judgment or under usage of trade would serve as a reasonable substitute for the one described may be used, making any proper allowance for the cost of transporting the goods to or from such other place.

(3) Evidence of a relevant price prevailing at a time or place other than the one described in this Article offered by one party is not admissible unless and until he has given the other party such notice as the court finds sufficient to prevent unfair surprise.

Section 2-724. Admissibility of Market Quotations.

Whenever the prevailing price or value of any goods regularly bought and sold in any established commodity market is in issue, reports in official publications or trade journals or in newspapers or periodicals of general circulation published as the reports of such market shall be admissible in evidence. The circumstances of the preparation of such a report maybe shown to affect its weight but not its admissibility.

Section 2-725. Statute of Limitations in Contracts for Sale.

(1) An action for breach of any contract for sale must be commenced within four years after the cause of action has accrued. By the original agreement the parties may reduce the period of limitation to not less than one year but may not extend it.

(2) A cause of action accrues when the breach occurs, regardless of the aggrieved party's lack of knowledge of the breach. A breach of warranty occurs when tender of delivery is made, except that where a warranty explicitly extends to future performance of the goods and discovery of the breach must await the time of such performance the cause of action accrues when the breach is or should have been discovered.

(3) Where an action commenced within the time limited by subsection (1) is so terminated as to leave available a remedy by another action for the same breach such other action may be commenced after the expiration of the time limited and within six months after the termination of the first action unless the termination resulted from voluntary discontinuance or from dismissal for failure or neglect to prosecute.

(4) This section does not alter the law on tolling of the statute of limitations nor does it apply to causes of action which have accrued before this Act becomes effective.

ARTICLE 2A. LEASES.

Authors' note: *Article 2A has been omitted as unnecessary for the purposes of this text.*

ARTICLE 3. NEGOTIABLE INSTRUMENTS. [Revised]

Part 1. General Provisions and Definitions.

Section 3-101. Short Title.

This Article may be cited as Uniform Commercial Code—Negotiable Instruments.

Section 3-102. Subject Matter.

(a) This Article applies to negotiable instruments. It does not apply to money, to payment orders governed by Article 4A, or to securities governed by Article 8.

(b) If there is conflict between this Article and Article 4 or 9, Articles 4 and 9 govern.

(c) Regulations of the Board of Governors of the Federal Reserve System and operating circulars of the Federal Reserve Banks supersede any inconsistent provision of this Article to the extent of the inconsistency.

Section 3-103. Definitions.

(a) In this Article:

(1) "Acceptor" means a drawee who has accepted a draft.

(2) "Drawee" means a person ordered in a draft to make payment.

(3) "Drawer" means a person who signs or is identified in a draft as a person ordering payment.

(4) "Good faith" means honesty in fact and the observance of reasonable commercial standards of fair dealing.

(5) "Maker" means a person who signs or is identified in a note as a person undertaking to pay.

(6) "Order" means a written instruction to pay money signed by the person giving the instruction. The instruction may be addressed to any person, including the person giving the instruction, or to one or more persons jointly or in the alternative but not in succession. An authorization to pay is not an order unless the person authorized to pay is also instructed to pay.

(7) "Ordinary care" in the case of a person engaged in business means observance of reasonable commercial standards, prevailing in the area in which the person is located, with respect to the business in which the person is engaged. In the case of a bank that takes an instrument for processing for collection or payment by automated means, reasonable commercial standards do not require the bank to examine the instrument if the failure to examine does not violate the bank's prescribed procedures and the bank's procedures do not vary unreasonably from general banking usage not disapproved by this Article or Article 4.

(8) "Party" means a party to an instrument.

(9) "Promise" means a written undertaking to pay money signed by the person undertaking to pay. An acknowledgment of an obligation by the obligor is not a promise unless the obligor also undertakes to pay the obligation.

(10) "Prove" with respect to a fact means to meet the burden of establishing the fact (Section 1-201(8)).

(11) "Remitter" means a person who purchases an instrument from its issuer if the instrument is payable to an identified person other than the purchaser.

(b) Other definitions applying to this Article and the sections which they appear are:

"Acceptance," Section 3-409.
"Accommodated party," Section 3-419.
"Accommodation party," Section 3-419.
"Alteration," Section 3-407.

"Anomalous indorsement," Section 3-205.
"Blank indorsement," Section 3-205.
"Cashier's check," Section 3-104.
"Certificate of deposit," Section 3-104.
"Certified check," Section 3-409.
"Check," Section 3-104.
"Consideration," Section 3-303.
"Draft," Section 3-104.
"Holder in due course," Section 3-302.
"Incomplete instrument," Section 3-115.
"Indorsement," Section 3-204.
"Indorser," Section 3-204.
"Instrument," Section 3-104.
"Issue," Section 3-105.
"Issuer," Section 3-105.
"Negotiable instrument," Section 3-104.
"Negotiation," Section 3-201.
"Note," Section 3-104.
"Payable at a definite time," Section 3-108.
"Payable on demand," Section 3-108.
"Payable to bearer," Section 3-109.
"Payable to order," Section 3-109.
"Payment," Section 3-602.
"Person entitled to enforce," Section 3-301.
"Presentment," Section 3-501.
"Reacquisition," Section 3-207.
"Special indorsement," Section 3-205.
"Teller's check," Section 3-104.
"Transfer of instrument," Section 3-203.
"Traveler's check," Section 3-104.
"Value," Section 3-303.

(c) The following definitions in other Articles apply to this Article:

"Bank," Section 4-105.
"Banking day," Section 4-104.
"Clearing house," Section 4-104.
"Collecting bank," Section 4-105.
"Depositary bank," Section 4-105.
"Documentary draft," Section 4-104.
"Intermediary bank," Section 4-105.
"Item," Section 4-104.
"Payor bank," Section 4-105.
"Suspends payments," Section 4-104.

(d) In addition, Article 1 contains general definitions and principles of construction and interpretation applicable throughout this Article.

Section 3-104. Negotiable Instrument.

(a) Except as provided in subsections (c) and (d), "negotiable instrument" means an unconditional promise or order to pay a fixed amount of money, with or without interest or other charges described In the promise or order, if it:

(1) is payable to bearer or to order at the time it is issued or first comes into possession of a holder;

(2) is payable on demand or at a definite time; and

(3) does not state any other undertaking or instruction by the person promising or ordering payment to do any act in addition to the payment of money, but the promise or order may contain (i) an undertaking or power to give, maintain, or protect collateral to secure payment, (ii) an authorization or power to the holder to confess judgment or realize on or dispose of collateral, or (iii) a waiver of the benefit of any law intended for the advantage or protection of an obligor.

(b) "Instrument" means a negotiable instrument.

(c) An order that meets all of the requirements of subsection (a), except paragraph (1), and otherwise falls within the definition of "check" in subsection (f) is a negotiable instrument and a check.

(d) A promise or order other than a check is not an instrument if, at the time it is issued or first comes into possession of a holder, it contains a conspicuous statement, however expressed, to the effect that the promise or order is not negotiable or is not an instrument governed by this Article.

(e) An instrument is a "note" if it is a promise and is a "draft" if it is an order. If an instrument falls within the definition of both "note" and "draft," a person entitled to enforce the instrument may treat it as either.

(f)"Check" means (I) a draft, other than a documentary draft, payable on demand and drawn on a bank or (ii) a cashier's check or teller's check. An instrument may be a check even though it is described on its face by another term, such as "money order."

(g)"Cashier's check" means a draft with respect to which the drawer and drawee are the same bank or branches of the same bank.

(h) "Teller's check" means a draft drawn by a bank (i) on another bank, or (ii) payable at or through a bank.

(i) "Traveler's check" means an instrument that (i) is payable on demand, (ii) is drawn on or payable at or through a bank, (iii) is designated by the term "traveler's check" or by a substantially similar term, and (iv) requires, as a condition to payment, a countersignature by a person whose specimen signature appears on the instrument.

(j) "Certificate of deposit" means an instrument containing an acknowledgment by a bank that a sum of money has been received by the bank and a promise by the bank to repay the sum of money. A certificate of deposit is a note of the bank.

Section 3-105. Issue of Instrument.

(a) "Issue" means the first delivery of an instrument by the maker or drawer, whether to a holder or non-holder, for the purpose of giving rights on the instrument to any person.

(b) An unissued instrument, or an unissued incomplete instrument that is completed, is binding on the maker or drawer, but nonissuance is a defense. An instrument that is conditionally issued or is issued for a special purpose is binding on the maker or drawer, but failure of the condition or special purpose to be fulfilled is a defense.

(c) "Issuer" applies to issued and unissued instruments and means a maker or drawer of an instrument.

Section 3-106. Unconditional Promise or Order.

(a) Except as provided in this section, for the purposes of Section 3-104(a), a promise or order is unconditional unless it states (i) an express condition to payment, (ii) that the promise or order is subject to or governed by another writing, or (iii) that rights or obligations with respect to the promise or order are stated in another writing. A reference to another writing does not of itself make the promise or order conditional.

(b) A promise or order is not made conditional (i) by a reference to another writing for a statement of rights with respect to collateral, or acceleration, or (ii) because payment is limited to resort to a particular fund or source.

(c) If a promise or order requires, as a condition to payment, a countersignature by a person whose specimen signature appears on the promise or order, the condition does not make the promise or order conditional for the purposes of Section 3-104(a). If the person whose specimen signature appears on an instrument fails to countersign the instrument, the failure to countersign is a defense to the obligation of the issuer, but the failure does not prevent a transferee of the instrument from becoming a holder of the instrument.

(d) If a promise or order at the time it is issued or first comes into possession of a holder contains a statement, required by applicable statutory or administrative law, to the effect that the rights of a holder or transferee are subject to claims or defenses that the issuer could assert against the original payee, the promise or order is not thereby made conditional for the purposes of Section 3-104(a); but if the promise or order is an instrument, there cannot be a holder in due course of the instrument.

Section 3-107. Instrument Payable in Foreign Money.

Unless the instrument otherwise provides, an instrument that states the amount payable in foreign money may be paid in the foreign money or in an equivalent amount in dollars calculated by using the current bank-offered spot rate at the place of payment for the purchase of dollars on the day on which the instrument is paid.

Section 3-108. Payable on Demand or at Definite Time.

(a) A promise or order is "payable on demand" if it (i) states that it is payable on demand or at sight, or otherwise indicates that it is payable at the will of the holder, or (ii) does not state any time of payment.

(b) A promise or order is "payable at a definite time" if it is payable on elapse of a definite period of time after sight or acceptance or at a fixed date or dates or at a time or times readily ascertainable at the time the promise or order is issued, subject to rights of (i) prepayment, (ii) acceleration, (iii) extension at the option of the holder or (iv) extension to a further definite time at the option of the maker or acceptor or automatically upon or after a specified act or event.

(c) If an instrument, payable at a fixed date, is also payable upon demand made before the fixed date, the instrument is payable on demand until the fixed date and, if demand for payment is not made before that date, becomes payable at a definite time on the fixed date.

Section 3-109. Payable to Bearer or to Order.

(a) A promise or order is payable to bearer if it:

    (1)   states that it is payable to bearer or to the order of bearer or otherwise indicates that the person in possession of the promise or order is entitled to payment;

    (2)   does not state a payee; or

    (3)   states that it is payable to or to the order of cash or otherwise indicates that it is not payable to an identified person.

(b) A promise or order that is not payable to bearer is payable to order if it is payable (i) to the order of an identified person or (ii) to an identified person or order. A promise or order that is payable to order is payable to the identified person.

(c) An instrument payable to bearer may become payable to an identified person if it is specially indorsed pursuant to Section 3-205(a). An instrument payable to an identified person may become payable to bearer if

it is indorsed in blank pursuant to Section 3-205(b).

Section 3-110. Identification of Person to whom Instrument Is Payable.

(a) The person to whom an instrument is initially payable is determined by the intent of the person, whether or not authorized, signing as, or in the name or behalf of, the issuer of the instrument. The instrument is payable to the person intended by the signer even if that person is identified in the instrument by a name or other identification that is not that of the intended person. If more than one person signs in the name or behalf of the issuer of an instrument and all the signers do not intend the same person as payee, the instrument is payable to any person intended by one or more of the signers.

(b) If the signature of the issuer of an instrument is made by automated means, such as a check-writing machine, the payee of the instrument is determined by the intent of the person who supplied the name or identification of the payee, whether or not authorized to do so.

(c) A person to whom an instrument is payable may be identified in any way, including by name, identifying number, office, or account number. For the purpose of determining the holder of an instrument, the following rules apply:

    (1)   If an instrument is payable to an account and the account is identified only by number, the instrument is payable to the person to whom the account is payable. If an instrument is payable to an account identified by number and by the name of a person, the instrument is payable to the named person, whether or not that person is the owner of the account identified by number.

    (2)   If an instrument is payable to:

        (I) a trust, an estate, or a person described as trustee or representative of a trust or estate, the instrument is payable to the trustee, the representative, or a successor of either, whether or not the beneficiary or estate is also named;

(ii) a person described as agent or similar representative of a named or identified person, the instrument is payable to the represented person, the representative, or a successor of the representative;

(iii) a fund or organization that is not a legal entity, the instrument is payable to a representative of the members of the fund or organization: or

(iv) an office or to a person described as holding an office the instrument is payable to the named person, the incumbent of the office, or a successor to the incumbent.

(d) If an instrument is payable to two or more persons alternatively, it is payable to any of them and may be negotiated, discharged, or enforced by any or all of them in possession of the instrument If an instrument is payable to two or more persons not alternatively, it is payable to all of them and may be negotiated, discharged, or enforced only by all of them. If an instrument payable to two or more persons is ambiguous as to whether it is payable to the persons alternatively, the instrument is payable to the persons alternatively.

Section 3-111. Place of Payment.

Except as otherwise provided for items in Article 4, an instrument is payable at the place of payment stated in the instrument. If no place of payment is stated, an instrument is payable at the address of the drawee or maker stated in the instrument. If no address is stated, the place of payment is the place of business of the drawee or maker. If a drawee or maker has more than one place of business, the place of payment is any place of business of the drawee or maker chosen by the person entitled to enforce the instrument. If the drawee or maker has no place of business, the place of payment is the residence of the drawee or maker.

Section 3-112. Interest.

(a) Unless otherwise provided in the instrument, (i) an instrument is not payable with interest, and (ii) interest on an interest-bearing instrument is payable from the date of the instrument.

(b) Interest may be stated in an instrument as a fixed or variable amount of money or it may be expressed as a fixed or variable rate or rates. The amount or rate of interest may be stated or described in the instrument in any manner and may require reference to information not contained in the instrument. If an instrument provides for interest, but the amount of interest payable cannot be ascertained from the description, interest is payable at the judgment rate in effect at the place of payment of the instrument and at the time interest first accrues.

Section 3-113. Date of Instrument.

(a) An instrument may be antedated or postdated. The date stated determines the time of payment if the instrument is payable at a fixed period after date. Except as provided in Section 4-401(c), an instrument payable on demand is not payable before the date of the instrument.

(b) If an instrument is undated, its date is the date of its issue or, in the case of an unissued instrument, the date it first comes into possession of a holder.

Section 3-114. Contradictory Terms of Instrument.

If an instrument contains contradictory terms, typewritten terms prevail over printed terms, handwritten terms prevail over both, and words prevail over numbers.

Section 3-115. Incomplete Instrument.

(a) "Incomplete instrument" means a signed writing, whether or not issued by the signer, the contents of which show at the time of signing that it is incomplete but that the signer intended it to be completed by the addition of words or numbers.

(b) Subject to subsection (c), if an incomplete instrument is an instrument under Section 3-104, it may be enforced according to its terms if it is not completed, or according to its terms as augmented by completion. If an incomplete instrument is not an instrument under Section 3-104, but, after completion, the requirements of Section 3-104 are met, the instrument may be enforced according to its terms as augmented by completion.

(c) If words or numbers are added to an incomplete instrument without authority of the signer, there is an alteration of the incomplete instrument under Section 3 407.

(d) The burden of establishing that words or numbers were added to an incomplete instrument without authority of the signer is on the person asserting the lack of authority.

Section 3-116. Joint and Several Liability; Contribution.

(a) Except as otherwise provided in the instrument, two or more persons who have the same liability on an instrument as makers, drawers, acceptors, indorsers who indorse as joint payees, or anomalous indorsers are jointly and severally liable in the capacity in which they .

(b) Except as provided in Section 3-419(e) or by agreement of the affected parties, a party having joint and several liability who pays the instrument is entitled to receive from any party having the same joint and several liability contribution in accordance with applicable law.

(c) Discharge of one party having joint and several liability by a person entitled to enforce the instrument does not affect the right under subsection (b) of a party having the same joint and several liability to receive contribution from the party discharged.

Section 3-117. Other Agreements Affecting Instrument.

Subject to applicable law regarding exclusion of proof of contemporaneous or previous agreements, the obligation of a party to an instrument to pay the instrument may be modified, supplemented, or nullified by a separate agreement of the obligor and a person entitled to enforce the instrument, if the instrument is issued or the obligation is incurred in reliance on the agreement or as part of the same transaction giving rise to the agreement. To the extent an obligation is modified, supplemented, or nullified by an agreement under this section, the agreement is a defense to the obligation.

Section 3-118. Statute of Limitations.

(a) Except as provided in subsection (e), an action to enforce the obligation of a party to pay a note payable at a definite time must be commenced within six years after the due date or dates stated in the note or, if a due date is accelerated, within six years after the accelerated due date.

(b) Except as provided in subsection (d) or (e), if demand for payment is made to the maker of a note payable on demand, an action to enforce the obligation of a party to pay the note must be commenced within six years after the demand. If no demand for payment is made to the maker, an action to enforce the note is barred if neither principal nor interest on the note has been paid for a continuous period of 10 years.

(c) Except as provided in subsection (d), an action to enforce the obligation of a party to an unaccepted draft to pay the draft must be commenced within three years after dishonor of the draft or 10 years after the date of the draft, whichever period expires first.

(d) An action to enforce the obligation of the acceptor of a certified check or the issuer of a teller's check, cashier's check, or traveler's check must be commenced within three years after demand for payment is made to the acceptor or issuer, as the case may be.

(e) An action to enforce the obligation of a party to a certificate of deposit to pay the instrument must be commenced within six years after demand for payment is made to the maker, but if the instrument states a due date and the maker is not required to pay before that date, the six-year period begins when a demand for payment is in effect and the due date has passed.

(f) An action to enforce the obligation of a party to pay an accepted draft, other than a certified check, must be commenced (i) within six years after the due date or dates stated in the draft or acceptance if the obligation of the acceptor is payable at a definite time, or (ii) within six years after the date of the acceptance if the obligation of the acceptor is payable on demand.

(g) Unless governed by other law regarding claims for indemnity or contribution, an action (i) for conversion of an instrument, for money had and received, or like action based on conversion, (ii) for breach of warranty, or (iii) to enforce an obligation, duty, or right arising under this Article and not governed by this section must be commenced within three years after the [cause of action] accrues.

Section 3-119. Notice of Right to Defend Action.

In an action for breach of an obligation for which a third person is answerable over pursuant to this Article or Article 4, the defendant may give the third person written notice of the litigation, and the person notified may then give similar notice to any other person who is answerable over. If the notice states (i) that the person notified may come in and defend and (ii) that failure to do so will bind the person notified in an action later brought by the person giving the notice as to any determination of fact common to the two litigations, the person notified is so bound unless after seasonable receipt of the notice the person notified does come in and defend.

Part 2. Negotiation, Transfer, and Indorsement.

Section 3-201. Negotiation.

(a) "Negotiation" means a transfer of possession, whether voluntary or involuntary, of an instrument by a person other than the issuer to a person who thereby becomes its holder.

(b) Except for negotiation by a remitter, if an instrument is payable to an identified person, negotiation requires transfer of possession of the instrument and its indorsement by the holder. If an instrument is payable to bearer, it may be negotiated by transfer of possession alone.

Section 3-202. Negotiation Subject to Rescission.

(a) Negotiation is effective even if-obtained (i) from an infant, a corporation exceeding its powers, or a person without capacity, (ii) by fraud, duress, or mistake, or (iii) in breach of duty or as part of an illegal transaction.

(b) To the extent permitted by other law, negotiation may be rescinded or may be subject to other remedies, but those remedies may not be asserted against a subsequent holder in due course or a person paying the instrument in good faith and without knowledge of facts that are a basis for rescission or other remedy.

Section 3-203. Transfer of Instrument; Rights Acquired by Transfer.

(a) An instrument is transferred when it is delivered by a person other than its issuer for the purpose of giving to the person receiving delivery the right to enforce the instrument.

(b) Transfer of an instrument, whether or not the transfer is a negotiation, vests in the transferee any right of the transferor to enforce the instrument, including any right as a holder in due course, but the transferee cannot acquire rights of a holder in due course by a transfer, directly or indirectly, from a holder in due course if the transferee engaged in fraud or ille-gality affecting the instrument.

(c) Unless otherwise agreed, if an instrument is transferred for value and the transferee does not become a holder because of lack of indorsement by the transferor, the transferee has a specifically enforceable right to the unqualified indorsement of the transferor, but negotiation of the instrument does not occur until the indorsement is made.

(d) If a transferor purports to transfer less than the entire instrument, negotiation of the instrument does not occur. The transferee obtains no rights under this Article and has only the rights of a partial assignee.

Section 3-204. Indorsement.

(a) "Indorsement" means a signature, other than that of a signer as maker, drawer, or acceptor, that alone or accompanied by other words is made on an instrument for the purpose of (i) negotiating the instrument, (ii) restricting payment of the instrument, or (iii) incurring indorser's liability on the instrument, but regardless of the intent of the signer, a signature and its accompanying words is an indorsement unless the accompanying words, terms of the instrument, place of the signature, or other circumstances unambiguously indicate that the signature was made for a purpose other than indorsement. For the purpose of determining whether a signature is made on an instrument, a paper affixed to the instrument is a part of the instrument.

(b) "Indorser" means a person who makes an indorsement.

(c) For the purpose of determining whether the transferee of an instrument is a holder, an indorsement that transfers a security interest in the instrument is effective as an unqualified indorsement of the instrument.

(d) If an instrument is payable to a holder under a name that is not the name of the holder, indorsement may be made by the holder in the name stated in the instrument or in the holder's name or both, but signature in both names may be required by a person paying or taking the instrument for value or collection.

Section 3-205. Special Indorsement; Blank Indorsement; Anomalous Indorsement.

(a) If an indorsement is made by the holder of an instrument, whether payable to an identified person or payable to bearer, and the indorsement identifies a person to whom it makes the instrument payable, it is a "special indorsement." When specially indorsed, an instrument becomes payable to the identified person and may be negotiated only by the indorsement of that person. The principles

stated in Section 3-110 apply to special indorsements.

(b) If an indorsement is made by the holder of an instrument and it is not a special indorsement, it is a "blank indorsement." When indorsed in blank, an instrument becomes payable to bearer and may be negotiated by transfer of pos-session alone until specially indorsed.

(c) The holder may convert a blank indorsement that consists only of a signature into a special indorsement by writing, above the signature of the indorser, words identifying the person to whom the instrument is made payable.

(d) "Anomalous indorsement" means an indorsement made by a person who is not the holder of the instrument. An anomalous indorsement does not affect the manner in which the instrument may be negotiated.

Section 3-206. Restrictive Indorsement.

(a) An indorsement limiting payment to a particular person or otherwise prohibiting further transfer or negotiation of the instrument is not effective to prevent further transfer or negotiation of the instrument.

(b) An indorsement stating a condition to the right of the indorsee to receive payment does not affect the right of the indorsee to enforce the instrument. A person paying the instrument or taking it for value or collection may disregard the condition, and the rights and liabilities of that person are not affected by whether the condition has been fulfilled.

(c) If an instrument bears an indorsement (i) described in Section 4-201(b), or (ii) in blank or to a particular bank using the words "for deposit," "for collection," or other words indicating a purpose of having the instrument collected by a bank for the indorser or for a particular account, the following rules apply:

(1) A person, other than a bank, who purchases the instrument when so indorsed converts the instrument unless the amount paid for the instrument is received by the indorser or applied consistently with the indorsement.

(2) A depositary bank that purchases the instrument or takes it for collection when so indorsed converts the instrument unless the amount paid by the bank with respect to the instrument Is received by the indorser or applied consistently with the indorsement.

(3) A payor bank that is also the depositary bank or that takes the instrument for immediate payment over the counter from a person other than a collecting bank converts the instrument unless the proceeds of the instrument are received by the indorser or applied consistently with the indorsement.

(4) Except as otherwise provided in paragraph (3), a payor bank or intermediary bank may disregard the indorsement and is not liable if the proceeds of the instrument are not received by the indorser or applied consistently with the indorsement.

(d) Except for an indorsement covered by subsection (c), if an instrument bears an indorsement using words to the effect that payment is to be made to the indorsee as agent, trustee, or other fiduciary for the benefit of the indorser or another person, the following rules apply:

(1) Unless there is notice of breach of fiduciary duty as provided in Section 3-307, a person who purchases the instrument from the indorsee or takes the instrument from the indorsee for collection or payment may pay the proceeds of payment or the value given for the instrument to the indorsee without regard to whether the indorsee violates a fiduciary duty to the indorser.

(2) A subsequent transferee of the instrument or person who pays the instrument is neither given notice nor otherwise affected by the restriction in the indorsement unless the transferee or payor knows that the fiduciary dealt with the instrument or its proceeds in breach of fiduciary duty.

(e) The presence on an instrument of an indorsement to which this section applies does not prevent a purchaser of the instrument from becoming a holder in due course of the instrument unless the purchaser is a converter under subsection (c) or has notice or knowledge of breach of fiduciary duty as stated in subsection (d).

(f) In an action to enforce the obligation of a party to pay the instrument, the obligor has a defense if payment would violate an indorsement to which this section applies and the payment is not permitted by this section.

Section 3-207. Reacquisition.

Reacquisition of an instrument occurs if it is transferred to a former holder, by negotiation or otherwise. A former holder who reacquires the instrument may cancel indorsements made after the reacquirer first became a holder of the instrument. If the cancellation causes the instrument to be payable to the reacquirer or to bearer, the reacquirer may negotiate the instrument. An indorser whose indorsement is cancelled is discharged, and the discharge is effective against any subsequent holder.

Part 3. Enforcement of Instruments.

Section 3-301. Person Entitled to Enforce Instrument.

"Person entitled to enforce" an instrument means (i) the holder of the instrument, (ii) a nonholder in possession of the instrument who has the rights of a holder, or (iii) a person not in possession of the instrument who is entitled to enforce the instrument pursuant to Section 3-309 or 3-418(d). A person may be a person entitled to enforce the instrument even though the person is not the owner of the instrument or is in wrongful possession of the instrument.

Section 3-302. Holder in Due Course.

(a) Subject to subsection (c) and Section 3-106 (d), "holder in due course" means the holder of an instrument if:

    (1)   the instrument when issued or negotiated to the holder does not bear such apparent evidence of forgery or alteration or is not otherwise so irregular or incomplete as to call into question its authenticity; and

    (2)   the holder took the instrument (i) for value, (ii) in good faith, (iii) without notice that the instrument is overdue or has been dishonored or that there is an uncured default with respect to payment of another instrument issued as part of the same series, (iv) without notice that the instrument contains an unauthorized signature or has been altered, (v) without notice of any claim to the instrument described in Section 3-306, and (vi) without notice that any party has a defense or claim in recoupment described in Section 3-305-(a).

(b) Notice of discharge of a party, other than discharge in an insolvency proceeding, is not notice of a defense under subsection (a), but discharge is effective against a person who became a holder in due course with notice of the discharge. Public filing or recording of a document does not of itself constitute notice of a defense, claim in recoupment, or claim to the instrument.

(c) Except to the extent a transferor or predecessor in interest has rights as a holder in due course, a person does not acquire rights of a holder in due course of an instrument taken (i) by legal process or by purchase in an execution, bankruptcy, or creditor's sale or similar proceeding, (ii) by purchase as part of a bulk transaction not in ordinary course of business of the transferor, or (iii) as the successor in interest to an estate or other organization.

(d) If, under Section 3-303(a)(1), the promise of performance that is the consideration for an instrument has been partially performed, the holder may assert rights as a holder in due course of the instrument only to the fraction of the amount payable under the instrument equal to the value of the partial performance divided by the value of the promised performance.

(e) If (i) the person entitled to enforce an instrument has only a security interest in the instrument and (ii) the person obliged to pay the instrument has a defense, claim in recoupment, or claim to the instrument that may be asserted against the person who granted the security interest, the person entitled to enforce the instrument may assert rights as a holder in due course only to an amount payable under the instrument which, at the time of enforcement of the instrument, does not exceed the amount of the unpaid obligation secured.

(f) To be effective, notice must be received at a time and in a manner that gives a reasonable opportunity to act on it.

(g) This section is subject to any law limiting status as a holder in due course in particular classes of transactions.

Section 3-303. Value and Consideration.

(a) An instrument is issued or transferred for value if:

    (1)   the instrument is issued or transferred for a promise of performance, to the extent the promise has been performed;

    (2)   the transferee acquires a security interest or other lien in the instrument other than a lien obtained by judicial proceeding;

    (3)   the instrument is issued or transferred as payment of, or as security for, an antecedent claim against any person, whether or not the claim is due;

    (4)   the instrument is issued or transferred in exchange for a negotiable instrument; or

    (5)   the instrument is issued or transferred in exchange for the incurring of an irrevocable obligation to a third party by the person taking the instrument.

(b) "Consideration" means any consideration sufficient to support a simple contract. The drawer or maker of an instrument has a defense if the instrument is issued without consideration. If an instrument is issued for a promise of performance, the issuer has a defense to the extent performance of the promise is due and the promise has not been performed. If an instrument is issued for value as stated in subsection (a). the instrument is also issued for consideration.

Section 3-304. Overdue Instrument.

(a) An instrument payable on demand becomes overdue at the earliest of the following times:

(1) on the day after the day demand for payment is duly made;
(2) if the instrument is a check, 90 days after its date; or
(3) if the instrument is not a check, when the instrument has been outstanding for a period of time after its date which is unreasonably long under the circumstances of the particular case in light of the nature of the instrument and usage of the trade.

(b) With respect to an instrument payable at a definite time the following rules apply:

(1) If the principal is payable in installments and a due date has not been accelerated, the instrument becomes overdue upon default under the instrument for nonpayment of an installment, and the instrument remains over due until the default is cured.
(2) If the principal is not payable in installments and the due date has not been accelerated, the instrument becomes overdue on the day after the due date.
(3) If a due date with respect to principal has been accelerated, the instrument becomes overdue on the day after the accelerated due date.

(c) Unless the due date of principal has been accelerated, an instrument does not become overdue if there is default in payment of interest but no default in payment of principal.

Section 3-305. Defenses and Claims in Recoupment.

(a) Except as stated in subsection (b), the right to enforce the obligation of a party to pay an instrument is subject to the following:

(1) a defense of the obligor based on (i) infancy of the obligor to the extent it is a defense to a simple contract. (ii) duress, lack of legal capacity, or illegality of the transaction which, under other law, nullifies the obligation of the obligor, (iii) fraud that induced the obligor to sign the instrument with neither knowledge nor reasonable opportunity to learn of its character or its essential terms, or (iv) discharge of the obligor in insolvency proceedings;
(2) a defense of the obligor stated in another section of this Article or a defense of the obligor that would be available if the person entitled to enforce the instrument were enforcing a right to payment under a simple contract; and
(3) a claim in recoupment of the obligor against the original payee of the instrument if the claim arose from the transaction that gave rise to the instrument; but the claim of the obligor may be asserted against a transferee of the instrument only to reduce the amount owing on the instrument at the time the action is brought.

(b) The right of a holder in due course to enforce the obligation of a party to pay the instrument is subject to defenses of the obligor stated in subsection (a)(1), but is not subject to defenses of the obligor stated in subsection (a)(2) or claims in recoupment stated in subsection (a)(3) against a person other than the holder.

(c) Except as stated in subsection (d), in an action to enforce the obligation of a party to pay the instrument, the obligor may not assert against the person entitled to enforce the instrument a defense, claim in recoupment, or claim to the instrument (Section 3-306) of another person, but the other person's claim to the instrument may be asserted by the obligor if the other person is joined in the action and personally asserts the claim against the person entitled to enforce the instrument. An obligor is not obliged to pay the instrument if the person seeking enforcement of the instrument does not have rights of a holder in due course and the obligor proves that the instrument is a lost or stolen instrument.

(d) In an action to enforce the obligation of an accommodation party to pay an instrument, the accommodation party may assert against the person entitled to enforce the instrument any defense or claim in recoupment under subsection (a) that the accommodated party could assert against the person entitled to enforce the instrument, except the defenses of discharge in insolvency proceedings, infancy, and of legal capacity.

Section 3-306. Claims to an Instrument.

A person taking an instrument, other than a person having rights of a holder in due course, is subject to a claim of a property or possessory right in the instrument or its proceeds, including a claim to rescind a negotiation and to recover the instrument or its proceeds. A person having rights of a holder in due course takes free of the claim to the instrument.

Section 3-307. Notice of Breach of Fiduciary Duty.

(a) In this section:

(1) "Fiduciary" means an agent, trustee, partner, corporate officer or director, or other representative owing a fiduciary duty with respect to an instrument.

(2) "Represented person" means the principal, beneficiary, partnership, corporation, or other person to whom the duty stated in paragraph (1) is owed.

(b) If (i) an instrument is taken from a fiduciary for payment or collection or for value, (ii) the taker has knowledge of the fiduciary status of the fiduciary, and (iii) the represented person makes a claim to the instrument or its proceeds on the basis that the transaction of the fiduciary is a breach of fiduciary duty, the following rules apply:

(1) Notice of breach of fiduciary duty by the fiduciary is notice of the claim of the represented person.

(2) In the case of an instrument payable to the represented person or the fiduciary as such, the taker has notice of the breach of fiduciary duty if the instrument is (i) taken in payment of or as security for a debt known by the taker to be the personal debt of the fiduciary, (ii) taken in a transaction known by the taker to be for the personal benefit of the fiduciary, or (iii) deposited to an account other than an account of the fiduciary, as such, or an account of the represented person.

(3) If an instrument is issued by the represented person or the fiduciary as such, and made payable to the fiduciary person-ally, the taker does not have notice of the breach of fiduciary duty unless the taker knows of the breach of fiduciary duty.

(4) If an instrument is issued by the represented person or the fiduciary as such, to the taker as payee, the taker has notice of the breach of fiduciary duty if the instrument is (i) taken in payment of or as security for a debt known by the taker to be the personal debt of the fiduciary, (ii) taken in a transaction known by the taker to be for the personal benefit of the fiduciary, or (iii) deposited to an account of the represented person.

Section 3-308. Proof of Signatures and Status as Holder in Due Course.

(a) In an action with respect to an instrument, the authenticity of, and authority to make, each signature on the instrument is admitted unless specifically denied in the pleadings. If the validity of a signature is denied in the pleadings, the burden of establishing validity is on the person claiming validity, but the signature is presumed to be authentic and authorized unless the action is to enforce the liability of the purported signer and the signer is dead or incompetent at the time of trial of the issue of validity of the signature. If an action to enforce the instrument is brought against a person as the undisclosed principal of a person who signed the instrument as a party to the instrument, the plaintiff has the burden of establishing that the defendant is liable on the instrument as a represented person under Section 3-402(a)

(b) If the validity of signatures is admitted or proved and there is compliance with subsection (a), a plaintiff producing the instrument is entitled to payment if the plaintiff proves entitlement to enforce the instrument under Section 3-301, unless the defendant proves a defense or claim in recoupment. If a defense or claim in recoupment is proved, the right to payment of the plaintiff is subject to the defense or claim, except to the extent the plaintiff proves that the plaintiff has rights of a holder in due course which are not subject to the defense or claim.

Section 3-309. Enforcement of Lost, Destroyed, or Stolen Instrument.

(a) A person not in possession of an instrument is entitled to enforce the instrument if (i) the person was in possession of the instrument and entitled to enforce it when loss of possession occurred, (ii) the loss of possession was not the result of a transfer by the person or a lawful seizure, and (iii) the person cannot reasonably obtain possession of the instrument because the instrument was destroyed, its whereabouts cannot be determined, or it is in the wrongful possession of an unknown person or a person that cannot be found or is not amenable to service of process.

(b) A person seeking enforcement of an instrument under subsection (a) must prove the terms of the instrument and the person's right to enforce the instrument. If that proof is made, Section 3-308 applies to the case as if the person seeking enforcement had produced the instrument. The court may not enter judgment in favor of the person seeking enforcement unless it finds that the person required to pay the instrument is adequately protected against loss that might occur by reason of a claim by another person to enforce the instrument. Adequate protection may be provided by any reasonable means.

Section 3-310. Effect of Instrument on Obligation for Which Taken.

(a) Unless otherwise agreed, if a certified check, cashier's check, or teller's check is taken for an obligation, the obligation is discharged to the same extent discharge would result if an amount of money equal to the amount of the instrument were taken in payment of the obligation. Discharge of the obligation does not affect any liability that the obligor may have as an indorser of the instrument.

(b) Unless otherwise agreed and except as provided in subsection (a) if a note or an uncertified check is taken for an obligation, the obligation is suspended to the same extent the obligation would be discharged if an amount of money equal to the amount of the instrument were taken, and the following rules apply:

(1) In the case of an uncertified check, suspension of the obligation continues until dishonor of the check or until it is paid or certified. Payment or certification of the check results in discharge of the obligation to the extent of the amount of the check.

(2) In the case of a note, suspension of the obligation continues until dishonor of the note or until it is paid. Payment of the note results in discharge

of the obligation to the extent of the payment.

(3)   Except as provided in paragraph (4), if the check or note is dishonored and the obligee of the obligation for which the instrument was taken is the person entitled to enforce the instrument, the obligee may enforce either the instrument or the obligation. In the case of an instrument of a third person which is negotiated to the obligee by the obligor, discharge of the obligor on the instrument also discharges the obligation.

(4)   If the person entitled to enforce the instrument taken for an obligation is a person other than the obligee, the obligee may not enforce the obligation to the extent the obligation is suspended. If the obligee is the person entitled to enforce the instrument but no longer has possession of it because it was lost, stolen, or destroyed, the obligation may not be enforced to the extent of the amount payable on the instrument, and to that extent the obligee's rights against the obligor are limited to enforcement of the instrument.

(c) If an instrument other than one described in subsection (a) or (b) is taken for an obligation, the effect is (i) that stated in subsection (a) if the instrument is one on which a bank is liable as maker or acceptor, or (ii) that stated in subsection (b) in any other case.

Section 3-311. Accord and Satisfaction by Use of Instrument.

(a) If a person against whom a claim is asserted proves that (i) that person in good faith tendered an instrument to the claimant as full satisfaction of the claim, (ii) the amount of the claim was unliquidated or subject to a bona fide dispute, and (iii) the claimant obtained payment of the instrument, the following subsections apply.

(b) Unless subsection (c) applies, the claim is discharged if the person against whom the claim is asserted proves that the instrument or an accompanying written communication contained a conspicuous statement to the effect that the instrument was tendered as full satisfaction of the claim.

(c) Subject to subsection (d), a claim is not discharged under subsection (b) if either of the following applies:

(1)   The claimant, if an organization, proves that (i) within a reasonable time before the tender, the claimant sent a conspicuous statement to the person against whom the claim is asserted that communications concerning disputed debts, including an instrument tendered as full satisfaction of a debt, are to be sent to a designated person, office, or place, and (ii) the instrument or accompanying communication was not received by that designated person, office, or place.

(2)   The claimant, whether or not an organization, proves that within 90 days after payment of the instrument, the claimant tendered repayment of the amount of the instrument to the person against whom the claim is asserted. This paragraph does not apply if the claimant is an organization that sent a statement complying with paragraph (1)(i).

(d) A claim is discharged if the person against whom the claim is asserted proves that within a reasonable time before collection of the instrument was initiated, the claimant, or an agent of the claimant having direct responsibility with respect to the disputed obligation, knew that the instrument was tendered in full satisfaction of the claim.

Part 4. Liability of Parties.

Section 3-401. Signature.

(a) A person is not liable on an instrument unless (i) the person signed the instrument, or (ii) the person is represented by an agent or representative who signed the instrument and the signature is binding on the represented person under Section 3-402.

(b) A signature may be made (i) manually or by means of a device or machine, and (ii) by the use of any name, including a trade or assumed name, or by a word, mark, or symbol executed or adopted by a person with present intention to authenticate a writing.

Section 3-402. Signature by Representative.

(a) If a person acting, or purporting to act, as a representative signs an instrument by signing either the name of the represented person or the name of the signer, the represented person is bound by the signature to the same extent the represented person would be bound if the signature were on a simple contract. If the represented person is bound, the signature of the representative is the "authorized signature of the represented person" and the represented person is liable on the instrument, whether or not identified in the instrument.

(b) If a representative signs the name of the representative to an instrument and the signature is an authorized signature of the represented person, the following rules apply:

(1) If the form of the signature shows unambiguously that the signature is made on behalf of the represented person who is identified in the instrument, the representative is not liable on the instrument.

(2) Subject to subsection (c), if (i) the form of the signature does not show unambiguously that the signature is made in a representative capacity or (ii) the represented person is not identified in the instrument, the representative is liable on the instrument to a holder in due course that took the instrument without notice that the representative was not intended to be liable on the instrument. With respect to any other person, the representative is liable on the instrument unless the representative proves that the original parties did not intend the representative to be liable on the instrument.

(c) If a representative signs the name of the representative as drawer of a check without indication of the representative status and the check is payable from an account of the represented person who is on the check, the signer is not liable on the check if the signature is an authorized signature of the represented person.

Section 3-403. Unauthorized Signature.

(a) Unless otherwise provided in this Article or Article 4, an unauthorized signature is ineffective except as the signature of the unauthorized signer in favor of a person who in good faith pays the or takes it for value. An unauthorized signature may be ratified for all purposes of this Article.

(b) If the signature of more than one person is required to constitute the authorized signature of an organization, the signature of the organization is unauthorized if one of the required signatures is lacking

(c) The civil or criminal liability of a person who makes an unauthorized signature is not affected by any provision of this Article which makes the unauthorized signature effective for the purposes of this Article.

Section 3-404 Impostors; Fictitious Payees.

(a) If an impostor, by use of the mails or otherwise, induces the issuer of an instrument to issue the instrument to the impostor, or to a person acting in concert with the impostor, by impersonating the payee of the instrument or a person authorized to act for the payee, an indorsement of the instrument by any person in the name of the payee is effective as the indorsement of the payee in favor of a person who, in good faith, pays the instrument or takes it for value or for collection.

(b) If (i) a person whose intent determines to whom an instrument is payable (Section 3-110(a) or (b)) does not intend the person identified as payee to have any interest in the instrument, or (ii) the person identified as payee of an instrument is a fictitious person, the following rules apply until the instrument is negotiated by special indorsement:

(1) Any person in possession of the instrument is its holder.

(2) An indorsement by any person in the name of the payee stated in the instrument is effective as the indorsement of the payee in favor of a person who, in good faith, pays the instrument or takes it for value or for collection.

(c) Under subsection (a) or (b), an indorsement is made in the name of a payee if (i) it is made in a name substantially similar to that of the payee or (ii) the instrument, whether or not indorsed, is deposited in a depositary bank to an account in a name substantially similar to that of the payee.

(d) With respect to an instrument to which subsection (a) or (b) applies, if a person paying the instrument or taking it for value or for collection fails to exercise ordinary care in paying or taking the instrument and that failure substantially contributes to loss resulting from payment of the instrument, the person bearing the loss may recover from the person failing to exercise ordinary care to the extent the failure to exercise ordinary care contributed to the loss.

Section 3-405. Employer's Responsibility for Fraudulent Indorsement by Employee.

(a) In this section:

(1) "Employee" includes an independent contractor and employee of an independent contractor retained by the employer.

(2) "Fraudulent indorsement" means (i) in the case of an instrument payable to the employer, a forged indorsement purporting to be that of the employer, or (ii) in the case of an instrument with respect to which the employer is the issuer, a forged indorsement purporting to be that of the person identified as payee.

(3) "Responsibility" with respect to instruments means authority (i) to sign or indorse instruments on behalf of the employer, (ii) to process instruments received by the employer for book-keeping purposes, for deposit to an account, or for other disposition, (iii) to prepare or process instruments for issue in the name of the employer, (iv) to supply information determining the names or addresses of payees of instruments to be issued in the name of the employer, (v) to control the disposition of instruments to be issued in the name of the employer, or (vi) to act otherwise with respect to instruments in a responsible capacity. "Responsibility" does not include authority that merely allows an employee to have access to instruments or blank or incomplete instrument forms that are being stored or transported or are part of incoming or outgoing mail, or similar access.

(b) For the purpose of determining the rights and liabilities of a person who, in good faith, pays an instrument or takes it for value or for collection, if an employer entrusted an employee with responsibility with respect to the instrument and the employee or a person acting in concert with the employee makes a fraudulent indorsement of the instrument, the indorsement is effective as the indorsement of the person to whom the instrument is payable if it is made in the name of that person. If the person paying the instrument or taking it for value or for collection fails to exercise ordinary care in paying or taking the instrument and that failure substantially contributes to loss resulting from the fraud, the person bearing the loss may recover from the person failing to exercise ordinary care to the extent the failure to exercise ordinary care contributed to the loss.

(c) Under subsection (b), an indorsement is made in the name of the person to whom an instrument is payable if (i) it is made in a name substantially similar to the name of that person or (ii) the instrument, whether or not indorsed, is deposited in a depositary bank to an account in a name substantially similar to the name of that person.

Section 3-406. Negligence Contributing to Forged Signature or Alteration of Instrument.

(a) A person whose failure to exercise ordinary care substantially contributes to an alteration of an instrument or to the making of a forged signature on an instrument is precluded from asserting the alteration or the forgery against a person who, in good faith, pays the instrument or takes it for value or for collection.

(b) Under subsection (a), if the person asserting the preclusion fails to exercise ordinary care in paying or taking the instrument and that failure substantially contributes to loss, the loss is allocated between the person precluded and the person asserting the preclusion according to the extent to which the failure of each to exercise ordinary care contributed to the loss.

(c) Under subsection (a), the burden of proving failure to exercise ordinary care is on the person asserting the preclusion. Under subsection (b), the burden of proving failure to exercise ordinary care is on the person precluded.

Section 3-407. Alteration.

(a) "Alteration" means (i) an unauthorized change in an instrument that purports to modify in any respect the obligation of a party, or (ii) an unauthorized addition of words or numbers or other change to an incomplete instrument relating to the obligation of a party.

(b) Except as provided in subsection (c), an alteration fraudulently made discharges a party whose obligation is affected by the alteration unless that party assents or is precluded from asserting the alteration. No other alteration discharges a party, and the instrument may be enforced according to its original terms.

(c) A payor bank or drawee paying a fraudulently altered instrument or a person taking it for value, in good faith and without notice of the alteration, may enforce rights with respect to the instrument (i) according to its original terms, or (ii) in the case of an incomplete instrument altered by unauthorized completion, according to its terms as completed.

Section 3-408. Drawee Not Liable on Unaccepted Draft.

A check or other draft does not of itself operate as an assignment of funds in the hands of the drawee available for its payment, and the drawee is not liable on the instrument until the drawee accepts it.

Section 3-409. Acceptance of Draft Certified Check.

(a) "Acceptance" means the drawee's signed agreement to pay a draft as presented. It must be written on the draft and may consist of the drawee's signature alone. Acceptance may be made at any time and becomes effective when notification pursuant to instructions is given or the accepted draft is delivered for the purpose of giving rights on the acceptance to any person.

(b) A draft may be accepted although it has not been signed by the drawer, is otherwise incomplete, is overdue, or has been dishonored.

(c) If a draft is payable at a fixed period after sight and the acceptor fails to date the acceptance, the holder may complete the acceptance by supplying a date in good faith.

(d) "Certified check" means a check accepted by the bank on which it is drawn. Acceptance may be made as stated in subsection (a) or by a writing on the check which indicates that the check is certified. The drawee of a check has no obligation to certify the check, and refusal to certify is not dishonor of the check.

Section 3-410. Acceptance Varying Draft.

(a) If the terms of a drawee's acceptance vary from the terms of the draft as presented, the holder may refuse the acceptance and treat the draft as dishonored. In that case, the drawee may cancel the acceptance.

(b) The terms of a draft are not varied by an acceptance to pay at a particular bank or place in the United States, unless the acceptance states that the draft is to be paid only at that bank or place.

(c) If the holder assents to an acceptance varying the terms of a draft, the obligation of each drawer and indorser that does not expressly assent to the acceptance is discharged.

Section 3-411. Refusal to Pay Cashier's Checks, Teller's Checks, and Certified Checks.

(a) In this section, "obligated bank" means the acceptor of a certified check or the issuer of a cashier's check or teller's check bought from the issuer.

(b) If the obligated bank wrongfully (i) refuses to pay a cashier's check or certified check, (ii) stops payment of a teller's check, or (iii) refuses to pay a dishonored teller's check, the person asserting the right to enforce the check is entitled to compensation for expenses and loss of interest resulting from the nonpayment and may recover consequential damages if the obligated bank refuses to pay after receiving notice of particular circumstances giving rise to the damages.

(c) Expenses or consequential damages under subsection (b) are not recoverable if the refusal of the obligated bank to pay occurs because (i) the bank suspends payments, (ii) the obligated bank asserts a claim or defense of the bank that it has reasonable grounds to believe is available against the person entitled to enforce the instrument, (iii) the obligated bank has a reasonable doubt whether the person demanding payment is the person entitled to enforce the instrument, or (iv) payment is prohibited by law.

Section 3-412. Obligation of Issuer of Note or Cashiers Check.

The issuer of a note or cashier's check or other draft drawn on the drawer is obliged to pay the instrument (i) according to its terms at the time it was issued or, if not issued, at the time it first came into possession of a holder, or (ii) if the issuer signed an incomplete instrument, according to its terms when completed, to the extent stated in Sections 3-115 and 3-407. The obligation is owed to a person entitled to enforce the instrument or to an indorser who paid the instrument under Section 3-415.

Section 3-413. Obligation of Acceptor.

(a) The acceptor of a draft is obliged to pay the draft (i) according to its terms at the time it was accepted, even though the acceptance states that the draft is payable "as originally drawn" or equivalent terms, (ii) if the acceptance varies the terms of the draft, according to the terms of the draft as varied, or (iii) if the acceptance is of a draft that is an incomplete instrument, according to its terms when completed, to the extent stated in Sections 3-115 and 3-407. The obligation is owed to a person entitled to enforce the draft or to the drawer or an indorser who paid the draft under Section 3-414 or 3-415.

(b) If the certification of a check or other acceptance of a draft states the amount certified or accepted, the obligation of the acceptor is that amount. If (i) the certification or acceptance does not state an amount, (ii) the amount of the instrument is subsequently raised, and (iii) the instrument is then negotiated to a holder in due course, the obligation of the acceptor is the amount of the instrument at the time it was taken by the holder in due course.

Section 3-414. Obligation of Drawer.

(a) This section does not apply to cashier's checks or other drafts drawn on the drawer.

(b) If an unaccepted draft is dishonored, the drawer is obliged to pay the draft (i) according to its terms at the time it was issued or, if not issued, at the time it first came into possession of a holder, or (ii) if the drawer signed an incomplete instrument, according to its terms when completed, to the extent stated in Sections 3-115 and 3-407. The obligation is owed to a person entitled to enforce the draft or to an indorser who paid the draft under Section 3-415.

(c) If a draft is accepted by a bank, the drawer is discharged, regardless of when or by whom acceptance was obtained.

(d) If a draft is accepted and the acceptor is not a bank, the obligation of the drawer to pay the draft if the draft is dishonored by the acceptor is the same as the obligation of an indorser under Section 3-415(a) and (c).

(e) If a draft states that it is drawn "without recourse" or otherwise disclaims liability of the drawer to pay the draft, the drawer is not liable under subsection (b) to pay the draft if the draft is not a check. A disclaimer of the liability stated in subsection (b) is not effective if the draft is a check.

(f) If (i) a check is not presented for payment or given to a depository bank for collection within 30 days after its date, (ii) the drawee suspends payments after expiration of the 30-day period without paying the check, and (iii) because of the suspension of payments, the drawer is deprived of funds maintained with the drawee to cover payment of the check, the drawer to the extent deprived of funds may discharge its obligation to pay the check by assigning to the person entitled to enforce the check the rights of the drawer against the drawee with respect to the funds.

Section 3-415. Obligation of Indorser.

(a) Subject to subsections (b), (c), and (d) and to Section 3-419(d), if an instrument is dishonored, an indorser is obliged to pay the amount due on the instrument (i) according to the terms of the instrument at the time it was indorsed, or (ii) if the indorser indorsed an incomplete instrument, according to its terms when completed, to the extent stated in Sections 3-115 and 3-407. The obligation of the indorser is owed to a person entitled to enforce the instrument or to a subsequent indorser who paid the instrument under this section.

(b) If an indorsement states that it is made "without recourse" or otherwise disclaims liability of the indorser, the indorser is not liable under subsection (a) to pay the instrument.

(c) If notice of dishonor of an instrument is required by Section 3-503 and notice of dishonor complying with that section is not given to an indorser, the liability of the indorser under subsection (a) is discharged.

(d) If a draft is accepted by a bank after an indorsement is made, the liability of the indorser under subsection (a) is discharged.

(e) If an indorser of a check is liable under subsection (a) and the check is not presented for payment, or given to a depository bank for collection, within 30 days after the day the indorsement was made, the liability of the indorser under subsection (a) is discharged.

Section 3-416. Transfer Warranties.

(a) A person who transfers an instrument for consideration warrants to the transferee and, if the transfer is by indorsement, to any subsequent transferee that:

(1) the warrantor is a person entitled to enforce the instrument;

(2) all signatures on the instrument are authentic and authorized;

(3) the instrument has not been altered;

(4) the instrument is not subject to a defense or claim in recoupment of any party which can be asserted against the warrantor; and

(5) the warrantor has no knowledge of any insolvency proceeding commenced with respect to the maker or acceptor or, in the case of an unaccepted draft, the drawer.

(b) A person to whom the warranties under subsection (a) are made and who took the instrument in good faith may recover from the warrantor as damages for breach of warranty an amount equal to the loss suffered as a result of the breach, but not more than the amount of the instrument plus expenses and loss of interest incurred as a result of the breach.

(c) The warranties stated in subsection (a) cannot be disclaimed with respect to checks. Unless notice of a claim for breach of warranty is given to the warrantor within 30 days after the claimant has reason to know of the breach and the identity of the warrantor, the liability of the warrantor under subsection (b) is discharged to the extent of any loss caused by the delay in giving notice of the claim.

(d) A [cause of action] for breach of warranty under this section accrues when the claimant has reason to know of the breach.

Section 3-417. Presentment Warranties.

(a) If an unaccepted draft is presented to the drawee for payment or acceptance and the drawee pays or accepts the draft, (i) the person obtaining payment or acceptance, at the time of presentment, and (ii) a previous transferor of the draft, at the time of transfer, warrant to the drawee making payment or accepting the draft in good faith that:

  (1)   the warrantor is, or was, at the time the warrantor transferred the draft, a person entitled to enforce the draft or authorized to obtain payment or acceptance of the draft on behalf of a person entitled to enforce the draft;
  (2)   the draft has not been altered; and
  (3)   the warrantor has no knowledge that the signature of the drawer of the draft is unauthorized.

(b) A drawee making payment may recover from any warrantor damages for breach of warranty equal to the amount paid by the drawee less the amount the drawee received or is entitled to receive from the drawer because of the payment. In addition, the drawee is entitled to compensation for expenses and loss of interest resulting from the breach. The right of the drawee to recover damages under this subsection is not affected by any failure of the drawee to exercise ordinary care in making payment. If the drawee accepts the draft, breach of warranty is a defense to the obligation of the acceptor. If the acceptor makes payment with respect to the draft, the acceptor is entitled to recover from any warrantor for breach of warranty the amounts stated in this subsection

(c) If a drawee asserts a claim for breach of warranty under subsection (a) based on an unauthorized indorsement of the draft or an alteration of the draft, the warrantor may defend by proving that the indorsement is effective under Section 3-404 or 3-405 or the drawer is precluded under Section 3-406 or 4-406 from asserting against the drawee the unauthorized indorsement or alteration.

(d) If (i) a dishonored draft is presented for payment to the drawer or an indorser or (ii) any other instrument is presented for payment to a party obliged to pay the instrument, and (iii) payment is received, the following rules apply:

  (1)   The person obtaining payment and a prior transferor of the instrument warrant to the person making payment in good faith that the warrantor is, or was, at the time the warrantor transferred the instrument, a person entitled to enforce the instrument or authorized to obtain payment on behalf of a person entitled to enforce the instrument.
  (2)   The person making payment may recover from any warrantor for breach of warranty an amount equal to the amount paid plus expenses and loss of interest resulting from the breach.

(e) The warranties stated in subsections (a) and (d) cannot be disclaimed with respect to checks. Unless notice of a claim for breach of warranty is given to the warrantor within 30 days after the claimant has reason to know of the breach and the identity of the warrantor, the liability of the warrantor under subsection (b) or (d) is discharged to the extent of any loss caused by the delay in giving notice of the claim.

(f) A [cause of action] for breach of warranty under this section accrues when the claimant has reason to know of the breach.

Section 3-418. Payment or Acceptance by Mistake.

(a) Except as provided in subsection (c), if the drawee of a draft pays or accepts the draft and the drawee acted on the mistaken belief that (i) payment of the draft had not been stopped pursuant to Section 4-403 or (ii) the signature of the drawer of the draft was authorized, the drawee may recover the amount of the draft from the person to whom or for whose benefit payment was made or, in the case of acceptance, may revoke the acceptance. Rights of the drawee under this subsection are not affected by failure of the drawee to exercise ordinary care in paying or accepting the draft.

(b) Except as provided in subsection (c), if an instrument has been paid or accepted by mistake and the case is not covered by subsection (a), the person paying or accepting may, to the extent permitted by the law governing mistake and restitution, (i) recover the payment from the person to whom or for whose benefit payment was made or (ii) in the case of acceptance, may revoke the acceptance.

(c) The remedies provided by subsection (a) or (b) may not be asserted against a person who took the instrument in good faith and for value or who in good faith changed position in reliance on the payment or acceptance. This subsection does not limit remedies provided by Section 3-417 or 4-407.

(d) Notwithstanding Section 4-215, if an instrument is paid or accepted by mistake and the payor or acceptor recovers payment or revokes acceptance under subsection (a) or (b), the instrument is deemed not to have been paid or accepted and is treated as dishonored, and the person from whom payment is recovered has rights as a person entitled to enforce the dishonored instrument

Section 3-419. Instruments Signed for Accommodation.

(a) If an instrument is issued for value given for the benefit of a party to the instrument ("accommodated party") and another party to the instrument ("accommodation party") signs the instrument for the purpose of incurring liability on the instrument without being a direct beneficiary of the value given for the instrument, the instrument is signed by the accommodation party "for accommodation."

(b) An accommodation party may sign the instrument as maker, drawer, acceptor, or indorser and, subject to subsection (d), is obliged to the instrument in the capacity in which the accommodation party signs. The obligation of an accommodation party may be enforced notwithstanding any statute of frauds and whether or not the accommodation party receives consideration for the accommodation.

(c) A person signing an instrument is presumed to be an accommodation party and there is notice that the instrument is signed for accommodation if the signature is an anomalous indorsement or is accompanied by words indicating that the signer is acting as surety or guarantor with respect to the obligation of another party to the instrument. Except as provided in Section 3-605, the obligation of an accommodation party to pay the instrument is not affected by the fact that the person enforcing the obligation had notice when the instrument was taken by that person that the accommodation party signed the instrument for accommodation.

(d) If the signature of a party to an instrument is accompanied by words indicating unambiguously that the party is guaranteeing collection rather than payment of the obligation of another party to the instrument, the signer is obliged to pay the amount due on the instrument to a person entitled to enforce the instrument only if (i) execution of judgment against the other party has been returned unsatisfied, (ii) the other party is insolvent or in an insolvency proceeding, (iii) the other party cannot be served with process, or (iv) it is otherwise apparent that payment cannot be obtained from the other party.

(e) An accommodation party who pays the instrument is entitled to reimbursement from the accommodated party and is entitled to enforce the instrument against the accommodated party. An accommodated party who pays the instrument has no right of recourse against, and is not entitled to contribution from, an accommodation party.

Section 3-420. Conversion of Instrument.

(a) The law applicable to conversion of personal property applies to instruments. An instrument is also converted if it is taken by transfer, other than a negotiation, from a person not entitled to enforce the instrument or a bank makes or obtains payment with respect to the instrument for a person not entitled to enforce the instrument or receive payment. An action for conversion of an instrument may not be brought by (i) the issuer or acceptor of the instrument or (ii) a payee or indorsee who did not receive delivery of the instrument either directly or through delivery to an agent or a co-payee.

(b) In an action under subsection (a), the measure of liability is presumed to be the amount payable on the instrument, but recovery may not exceed the amount of the plaintiff's interest in the instrument.

(c) A representative, other than a depositary bank, who has in good faith dealt with an instrument or its proceeds on behalf of one who was not the person entitled to enforce the instrument is not liable in conversion to that person beyond the amount of any proceeds that it has not paid out.

Part 5. Dishonor.

3-501. Presentment.

(a) "Presentment" means a demand made by or on behalf of a person entitled to enforce an instrument (i) to pay the instrument made to the drawee or a party obliged to pay the instrument or, in the case of a note or accepted draft payable at a bank, to the bank, or (ii) to accept a draft made to the drawee.

(b) The following rules are subject to Article 4, agreement of the parties, and clearinghouse rules and the like:

(1) Presentment may be made at the place of payment of the instrument and must be made at the place of payment if the instrument is payable at a bank in the United States; may be made by any commercially reasonable means, including an oral, written, or electronic communication; is effective when the demand for payment or acceptance is received by the person to whom presentment is made; and is effective if made to any one of two or more makers, acceptors, drawees, or other payors.

(2) Upon demand of the person to whom presentment is made, the person making presentment must (i) exhibit the instrument, (ii) give reasonable identification and, if presentment is made on behalf of another person, reasonable evidence of authority to do so, and (. . .) sign a receipt on the instrument for any payment made or surrender the instrument if full payment is made.

(3) Without dishonoring the instrument, the party to whom presentment is made may (i) return the instrument for lack of a necessary indorsement, or (ii) refuse payment or for failure of the presentment to comply with the terms of the instrument, an agreement of the parties, or other applicable law or rule.

(4) The party to whom presentment is made may treat presentment as occurring on the next business day after the day of presentment if the party to whom presentment is made has established a cut-off hour not earlier than 2 p.m. for the receipt and processing of instruments presented for payment or acceptance and presentment is made after the cutoff hour.

Section 3-502. Dishonor.

(a) Dishonor of a note is governed by the following rules:

(1) If the note is payable on demand, the note is dishonored if presentment is duly made to the maker and the note is not paid on the day of presentment.

(2) If the note is not payable on demand and is payable at or through a bank or the terms of the note require presentment, the note is dishonored if presentment is duly made and the note is not paid on the day it becomes payable or the day of presentment, whichever is later.

(3) If the note is not payable on demand and paragraph (2) does not apply, the note is dishonored if it is not paid on the day it becomes payable.

(b) Dishonor of an unaccepted draft other than a documentary draft is governed by the following rules:

(1) If a check is duly presented for payment to the payor bank otherwise than for immediate payment over the counter, the check is dishonored if the payor bank makes timely return of the check or sends timely notice of dishonor or nonpayment under Section 4-301 or 4-302, or becomes accountable for the amount of the check under Section 4-302.

(2) If a draft is payable on demand and paragraph (1) does not apply, the draft is dishonored if presentment for payment is duly made to the drawee and the draft is not paid on the day of presentment.

(3) If a draft is payable on a date stated in the draft, the draft is dishonored if (i) presentment for payment is duly made to the drawee and payment is not made on the day the draft becomes payable or the day of presentment, whichever is later, or (ii) presentment for acceptance is duly made before the day the draft becomes payable and the draft is not accepted on the day of presentment.

(4) If a draft is payable on elapse of a period of time after sight or acceptance, the draft is dishonored if presentment for acceptance is duly made and the draft is not accepted on the day of presentment.

(c) Dishonor of an unaccepted documentary draft occurs according to the rules stated in subsection (b)(2), (3), and (4), except that payment or acceptance may be delayed without dishonor until no later than the close of the third business day of the drawee following the day on which payment or acceptance is required by those paragraphs.

(d) Dishonor of an accepted draft is governed by the following rules:

(1) If the draft is payable on demand, the draft is dishonored if presentment for payment is duly made to the acceptor and the draft is not paid on the day of presentment.

(2) If the draft is not payable on demand, the draft is dishonored if presentment for payment is duly made to the acceptor and payment is not made on the day it becomes payable or the day of presentment, whichever is later.

(e) In any case in which presentment is otherwise required for dishonor under this section and presentment is excused under Section 3-504, dishonor occurs without presentment if the instrument is not duly accepted or paid.

(f) If a draft is dishonored because timely acceptance of the draft was not made and the person entitled to demand acceptance consents to a late acceptance, from the time of acceptance the draft is treated as never having been dishonored.

Section 3-503 Notice of Dishonor.

(a) The obligation of an indorser stated in Section 3-415(a) and the obligation of a drawer stated in Section 3-414(d) may not be enforced unless (i) the indorser or drawer is given notice of dishonor of the instrument complying with this section or (ii) notice of dishonor is excused under Section 3-504(b).

(b) Notice of dishonor may be given by any person; may be given by any commercially reasonable means, including an oral, written, or electronic communication; and is sufficient if it reasonably identifies the instrument and indicates that the instrument has been dishonored or has not been paid or accepted. Return of an instrument given to a bank for collection is sufficient notice of dishonor.

(c) Subject to Section 3-504(c), with respect to an instrument taken for collection by a collecting bank, notice of dishonor must be given (i) by the bank before midnight of the next banking day following the banking day on which the bank receives notice of dishonor of the instrument, or (ii) by any other person within 30 days following the day on which the person receives notice of dishonor. With respect to any other instrument, notice of dishonor must be given within 30 days following the day on which dishonor occurs.

Section 3-504. Excused Presentment and Notice of Dishonor.

(a) Presentment for payment or acceptance of an instrument is excused if (i) the person entitled to present the instrument cannot with reasonable diligence make presentment, (ii) the maker or acceptor has repudiated an obligation to pay the instrument or is dead or in insolvency proceedings, (iii) by the terms of the instrument presentment is not necessary to enforce the obligation of indorsers or the drawer, (iv) the drawer or indorser whose obligation is being enforced has waived presentment or otherwise has no reason to expect or right to require that the instrument be paid or accepted, or (v) the drawer instructed the drawee not to pay or accept the draft or the drawee was not obligated to the drawer to pay the draft.

(b) Notice of dishonor is excused if (i) by the term of the instrument notice of dishonor is not necessary to enforce the obligation of a party to pay the instrument, or (ii) the party whose obligation is being enforced waived notice of dishonor. A waiver of presentment is also a waiver of notice of dishonor.

(c) Delay in giving notice of dishonor is excused if the delay was caused by circumstances beyond the control of the person giving the notice and the person giving the notice exercised reasonable diligence after the cause of the delay ceased to operate.

Section 3-505. Evidence of Dishonor.

(a) The following are admissible as evidence and create a presumption of dishonor and of any notice of dishonor stated:

   (1)   a document regular in form as provided in subsection (b) which purports to be a protest;

   (2)   a purported stamp or writing of the drawee, payor bank, or presenting

bank on or accompanying the instrument stating that acceptance or payment has been refused unless reasons for the refusal are stated and the reasons are not consistent with dishonor;

   (3)   a book or record of the drawee, payor bank, or collecting bank, kept in the usual course of business which shows dishonor, even if there is no evidence of who made the entry.

(b) A protest is a certificate of dishonor made by a United States consul or vice consul, or a notary public or other person authorized to administer oaths by the law of the place where dishonor occurs. It may be made upon information satisfactory to that person. The protest must identify the instrument and certify either that presentment has been made or, if not made, the reason why it was not made, and that the instrument has been dishonored by nonacceptance or nonpayment. The protest may also certify that notice of dishonor has been given to some or all parties.

Part 6. Discharge and Payment.

Section 3-601. Discharge and Effect of Discharge.

(a) The obligation of a party to pay the instrument is discharged as stated in this Article or by an act or agreement with the party which would discharge an obligation to pay money under a simple contract.

(b) Discharge of the obligation of a party is not effective against a person acquiring rights of a holder in due course of the instrument without notice of the discharge.

Section 3-602. Payment.

(a) Subject to subsection (b), an instrument is paid to the extent payment is made (i) by or on behalf of a party obliged to pay the instrument, and (ii) to a person entitled to enforce the instrument. To the extent of the payment, the obligation of the party obliged to pay the instrument is discharged even though payment is made with knowledge of a claim to the instrument under Section 3-306 by another person.

(b) The obligation of a party to pay the instrument is not discharged under subsection (a) if:

> (1) a claim to the instrument under Section 3-306 is enforceable against the party receiving payment and (i) payment is made with knowledge by the payor that payment is prohibited by injunction or similar process of a court of competent jurisdiction, or (ii) in the case of an instrument other than a cashier's check, teller's check, or certified check, the party making payment accepted, from the person having a claim to the instrument, indemnity against loss resulting from refusal to pay the person entitled to enforce the instrument; or
>
> (2) the person making payment knows that the instrument is a stolen instrument and pays a person it knows is in wrongful possession of the instrument.

Section 3-603. Tender of Payment.

(a) If tender of payment of an obligation to pay an instrument is made to a person entitled to enforce the instrument, the effect of tender is governed by principles of law applicable to tender of payment under a simple contract.

(b) If tender of payment of an obligation to pay an instrument is made to a person entitled to enforce the instrument and the tender is refused, there is discharge, to the extent of the amount of the tender, of the obligation of an indorser or accommodation party having a right of recourse with respect to the obligation to which the tender relates.

(c) If tender of payment of an amount due on an instrument is made to a person entitled to enforce the instrument, the obligation of the obligor to pay interest after the due date on the amount tendered is discharged. If presentment is required with respect to an instrument and the obligor is able and ready to pay on the due date at every place of payment stated in the instrument, the obligor is deemed to have made tender of payment on the due date to the person entitled to enforce the instrument.

Section 3-604. Discharge by Cancellation or Renunciation.

(a) A person entitled to enforce an instrument, with or without consideration, may discharge the obligation of a party to pay the instrument (i) by an intentional voluntary act, such as surrender of the instrument to the party, destruction, mutilation, or cancellation of the instrument, cancellation or striking out of the party's signature, or the addition of words to the instrument indicating discharge, or (ii) by agreeing not to sue or otherwise renouncing rights against the party by a signed writing.

(b) Cancellation or striking out of an indorsement pursuant to subsection (a) does not affect the status and rights of a party derived from the indorsement.

Section 3-605. Discharge of Indorsers and Accommodation Parties.

(a) In this section, the term "indorser" includes a drawer having the obligation described in Section 3-414(d).

(b) Discharge, under Section 3-604, of the obligation of a party to pay an instrument does not discharge the obligation of an indorser or accommodation party having a right of recourse against the discharged party.

(c) If a person entitled to enforce an instrument agrees, with or without consideration, to an extension of the due date of the obligation of a party to pay the instrument, the extension discharges an indorser or accommodation party having a right of recourse against the party whose obligation is extended to the extent the indorser or accommodation party proves that the extension caused loss to the indorser or accommodation party with respect to the right of recourse.

(d) If a person entitled to enforce an instrument agrees, with or without consideration, to a material modification of the obligation of a party other than an extension of the due date, the modification discharges the obligation of an indorser or accommodation party having a right of recourse against the person whose obligation is modified to the extent the modification causes loss to the indorser or accommodation party with respect to the right of recourse. The loss suffered by the indorser or accommodation party as a result of the modification is equal to the amount of the right of recourse unless the person enforcing the instrument proves that no loss was caused by the modification or that the loss caused by the modification was an amount less than the amount of the right of recourse.

(e) If the obligation of a party to pay an instrument is secured by an interest in collateral and a person entitled to enforce the instrument impairs the value of the interest in collateral, the obligation of an indorser or accommodation party having a right of recourse against the obligor is discharged to the extent of the impairment. The value of an interest in collateral is impaired to the extent (i) the value of the interest is reduced to an amount less than the amount of the right of recourse of the party asserting discharge, or (ii) the reduction in value of the interest causes an increase in the amount by which the amount of the right of recourse exceeds the value of the interest. The burden of proving impairment is on the party asserting discharge.

(f) If the obligation of a party is secured by an interest in collateral not provided by an accommodation party and a person entitled to enforce the instrument impairs the value of the interest in collateral, the obligation of any party who is jointly and severally liable with respect to the secured obligation is discharged to the extent the impairment causes the party asserting discharge to pay more than that party would have been obliged to pay, taking into account rights of contribution, if impairment had not occurred. If the party asserting discharge is an accommodation party not entitled to discharge under subsection (e), the party is deemed to have a right to contribution based on joint and several liability rather than a right to reimbursement. The burden of proving impairment is on the party asserting discharge.

(g) Under subsection (e) or (f), impairing value of an interest in collateral includes (i) failure to obtain or maintain perfection or recordation of the interest in collateral, (ii) release of collateral without substitution of collateral of equal value, (iii) failure to perform a duty to preserve the value of collateral owed, under Article 9 or other law, to a debtor or surety or other person secondarily liable, or (iv) failure to comply with applicable law in disposing of collateral.

(h) An accommodation party is not discharged under subsection (c), (d), or (e) unless the person entitled to enforce the instrument knows of the accommodation or has notice under Section 3-419(c) that the instrument was signed for accommodation.

(i) A party is not discharged under this section if (i) the party asserting discharge consents to the event or conduct that is the basis of the discharge, or (ii) the instrument or a separate agreement of the party provides for waiver of discharge under this section either specifically or by general language indicating that parties waive defenses based on suretyship or impairment of collateral.

ARTICLE 4. BANK DEPOSITS AND COLLECTIONS.

Part I. General Provisions and Definitions.

Section 4-l0l. Short Title.

This Article shall be known and may be cited as Uniform Commercial Code—Bank Deposits and Collections.

Section 4-102. Applicability.

(a) To the extent that items within this Article are also within Articles 3 and 8, they are subject to those Articles. If there is conflict, this Article governs Article 3, but Article 8 governs this Article.

(b) The liability of a bank for action or nonaction with respect to an item handled by it for purposes of presentment, payment, or collection is governed by the law of the place where the bank is located. In the case of action or non-action by or at a branch or separate office of a bank, its liability is governed by the law of the place where the branch or separate office is located.

Section 4-103. Variation by Agreement; Measure of Damages; Action Constituting Ordinary Care.

(a) The effect of the provisions of this Article may be varied by agreement, but the parties to the agreement cannot disclaim a bank's responsibility for its lack of good faith or failure to exercise ordinary care or limit the measure of damages for the lack or failure. However, the parties may determine by agreement the standards by which the bank's responsibility is to be measured if those standards are not manifestly unreasonable.
(b) Federal Reserve regulations and operating circulars, clearinghouse rules, and the like have the effect of agreements under subsection (a), whether or not specifically assented to by all parties interested in items handled.
(c) Action or non-action approved by this Article or pursuant to Federal Reserve regulations or operating circulars is the exercise of ordinary care and, in the absence of special instructions, action or nonaction consistent with clearinghouse rules and the like or with a general banking usage not disapproved by this Article, is prima facie the exercise of ordinary care.
(d) The specification or approval of certain procedures by this Article is not disapproval of other procedures that may be reasonable under the circumstances.
(e) The measure of damages for failure to exercise ordinary care in handling an item is the amount of the item reduced by an amount that could not have been realized by the exercise of ordinary care. If there is also bad faith it includes any other damages the party suffered as a proximate consequence.

Section 4-104. Definitions and Index of Definitions.

(a) In this Article, unless the context otherwise requires

(1) "Account" means any deposit or credit account with a bank, including a demand, time, savings, passbook, share draft, or like account, other than an account evidenced by a certificate of deposit;
(2) "Afternoon" means the period of a day between noon and midnight;
(3) "Banking day" means the part of a day on which a bank is open to the public for carrying on substantially all of its banking functions;
(4) "Clearing house" means an association of banks or other payors regularly clearing items;
(5) "Customer" means a person having an account with a bank or for whom a bank has agreed to collect items, including a bank that maintains an account at another bank:
(6) "Documentary draft" means a draft to be presented for acceptance or payment if specified documents, certificated securities (Section 8-102) or instructions for uncertificated securities (Section 8-308), or other certificates, statements, or the like are to be received by the drawee or other payor before acceptance or payment of the draft;
(7) "Draft" means a draft as defined in Section 3-l04 or an item, other than an instrument, that is an order.
(8) "Drawee" means a person ordered in a draft to make payment.
(9) "Item" means an instrument or a promise or order to pay money handled by a bank for collection or payment. The term does not include a payment order governed by Article 4A or a credit or debit card slip;
(10) "Midnight deadline" with respect to a bank is midnight on its next banking day following the banking day on which it receives the relevant item or notice or from which the time for taking action commences to run, whichever is later;

(11) "Settle" means to pay in cash, by clearinghouse settlement, in a charge or credit or by remittance, or otherwise as agreed. A settlement may be either provisional or final.

(12) "Suspends payments" with respect to a bank means that it has been closed by order of the supervisory authorities, that a public officer has been appointed to take it over, or that it ceases or refuses to make payments in the ordinary course of business.

(b) Other definitions applying to this Article and the sections in which they appear are:

"Agreement for electronic presentment,"
  Section 4-110.
"Bank," Section 4-105.
"Collecting bank," Section 4-105.
"Depositary bank," Section 4-105.
"Intermediary bank," Section 4-105.
"Payor bank," Section 4-105.
"Presenting bank," Section 4-105.
"Presentment notice," Section 4-110.

(c) The following definitions in other Articles apply to this Article:

"Acceptance," Section 3-409.
"Alteration," Section 3-407.
"Cashier's check," Section 3-104.
"Certificate of deposit," Section 3-104.
"Certified check," Section 3-409.
"Check," Section 3-104.
"Good faith," Section 3-103.
"Holder in due course," Section 3-302.
"Instrument," Section 3-104.
"Notice of dishonor," Section 3-503.
"Order," Section 3-103.
"Ordinary care," Section 3-103.
"Person entitled to enforce," Section 3-301.
"Presentment," Section 3-501.
"Promise," Section 3-103.
"Prove," Section 3-103.
"Teller's check," Section 3-104.
"Unauthorized signature," Section 3-403.

(d) In addition, Article 1 contains general definitions and principles of construction and interpretation applicable throughout this Article.

Section 4-105. "Bank"; "Depositary Bank"; "Payor Bank;" "Intermediary Bank;" "Collecting Bank;" "Presenting Bank."

In this Article:

(1) "Bank" means a person engaged in the business of banking, including a savings bank, savings and loan association, credit union, or trust company.

(2) "Depositary bank" means the first bank to take an item even though it is also the payor bank, unless the item is presented for immediate payment over the counter;

(3) "Payor bank" means a bank that is the drawee of a draft;

(4) "Intermediary bank" means a bank to which an item is transferred in course of collection except the depositary or payor bank ;

(5) "Collecting bank" means a bank handling an item for collection except the payor bank;

(6) "Presenting bank" means a bank presenting an item except a payor bank.

Section 4-106. Payable Through or Payable at Bank Collecting.

(a) If an item states that it is "payable through" a bank identified in the item, (i) the item designates the bank as a collecting bank and does not by itself authorize the bank to pay the item, and (ii) the item may be presented for payment only by or through the bank.

Alternative A

(b) If an item states that it is "payable at" a bank identified in the item. the item is equivalent to a draft drawn on the bank.

Alternative B

(b) If an item states that it is "payable at" a bank identified in the item, (i) the item designates the bank as a collecting bank and does not by itself authorize the bank to pay the item, and (ii) the item may be presented for payment only by or through the bank.

(c) If a draft names a nonbank drawee and it is unclear whether a bank named in the draft is a codrawee or a collecting bank, the bank is a collecting bank.

Section 4-107. Separate Office of Bank.

A branch or separate office of a bank is a separate bank for the purpose of computing the time with-in which and determining the place at or to which action may be taken or notices or orders shall be given under this Article and under Article 3.

Section 4-108. Time of Receipt of Items.

(a) For the purpose of allowing time to process items, prove balances, and make the necessary entries on its books to determine its position for the day, a bank may fix an afternoon hour of 2 P.M. or later as a cutoff hour for the handling of money and items and the making of entries on its books.

(b) An item or deposit of money received on any day after a cutoff hour so fixed or after the close of the banking day may be treated as being received at the opening of the next banking day.

Section 4-109. Delays.

(a) Unless otherwise instructed, a collecting bank in a good faith effort to secure payment of a specific item drawn on a payor other than a bank, and with or without the approval of any person involved, may waive, modify, or extend time limits imposed or permitted by this [Act] for a period not exceeding two additional banking days without discharge of drawers or indorsers or liability to its transferor or a prior party.

(b) Delay by a collecting bank or payor bank beyond time limits prescribed or permitted by this [Act] or by instructions is excused if (i) the delay is caused by interruption of communication or computer facilities, suspension of payments by another bank, war, emergency conditions, failure of equipment, or other circumstances beyond the control of the bank, and (ii) the bank exercises such diligence as the circumstances require.

Section 4-110. Electronic Presentment.

(a) "Agreement for electronic presentment" means an agreement, clearing-house rule, or Federal Reserve regulation or operating circular, providing that presentment of an item may be made by transmission of an image of an item or information describing the item ("presentment notice") rather than delivery of the item it self. The agreement may provide for procedures governing retention, presentment, payment, dishonor, and other matters concerning items subject to the agreement.

(b) Presentment of an item pursuant to an agreement for presentment is made when the presentment notice is received.

(c) If presentment is made by presentment notice, a reference to "item" or "check" in this Article means the presentment notice unless the context otherwise indicates.

Section 4-111. Statute of Limitations.

An action to enforce an obligation, duty, or right arising under this Article must be commenced within three years after the [cause of action] accrues.

Part 2. Collection of Items: Depository and Collecting Banks.

Section 4-201. Status of Collecting Bank as Agent and Provisional Status of Credits; Applicability of Article; Item Indorsed "Pay Any Bank."

(a) Unless a contrary intent clearly appears and before the time that a settlement given by a collecting bank for an item is or becomes final, the bank, with respect to an item, is an agent or sub-agent of the owner of the item and any settlement given for the item is provisional. This provision applies regardless of the form of indorsement or lack of indorsement and even though credit given for the item is subject to immediate withdrawal as of right or is in fact withdrawn; but the continuance of ownership of an item by its owner and any rights of the owner to proceeds of the item are subject to rights of a collecting bank, such as those resulting from outstanding advances on the item and rights of recoupment or setoff. If an item is handled by banks for purposes of presentment, payment, collection, or return, the relevant provisions of this Article apply even though action of the parties clearly establishes that a particular bank has purchased the item and is the owner of it.

(b) After an item has been indorsed with the words "pay any bank" or the like, only a bank may acquire the rights of a holder until the item has been:

(1)   returned to the customer initiating collection; or
(2)   specially indorsed by a bank to a person who is not a bank.

Section 4-202. Responsibility for Collection or Return; When Action Timely.

(a) A collecting bank must exercise ordinary care in:

(1)   presenting an item or sending it for presentment;
(2)   sending notice of dishonor or nonpayment or returning an item other than a documentary draft to the bank's transferor after learning that the item has not been paid or accepted, as the case may be;
(3)   settling for an item when the bank receives final settlement; and
(4)   notifying its transferor of any loss or delay in transit within a reasonable time after discovery thereof.

(b) A collecting bank exercises ordinary care under subsection (a) by taking proper action before its midnight deadline following receipt of an item, notice, or settlement. Taking proper action within a reasonably longer time may constitute the exercise of ordinary care, but the bank has the burden of establishing timeliness.

(c) Subject to subsection (a)(1), a bank is not liable for the insolvency, neglect, misconduct, mistake, or default of another bank or person or for loss or destruction of an item in the possession of others or in transit.

Section 4-203. Effect of Instructions.

Subject to Article 3 concerning conversion of instruments (Section 3-420) and restrictive indorsements (Section 3-206), only a collecting bank's transferor can give instructions that affect the bank or constitute notice to it, and a collecting bank is not liable to prior parties for any action taken pursuant to the instructions or in accordance with any agreement with its transferor.

Section 4-204. Methods of Sending and Presenting; Sending Directly to Payor Bank.

(a) A collecting bank shall send items by a reasonably prompt method, taking into consideration relevant instructions, the nature of the item, the number of those items on hand, the cost of collection involved, and the method generally used by it or others to present those items.

(b) A collecting bank may send:

(1)   an item directly to the payor bank;
(2)   an item to a nonbank payor if authorized by its transferor; and
(3)   an item other than documentary drafts to a nonbank payor, if authorized by Federal Reserve regulation or operating circular, clearinghouse rule, or the like.

(c) Presentment may be made by a presenting bank at a place where the payor bank or other payor has requested that presentment be made.

Section 4-205. Depositary Bank Holder of Unindorsed Item.

If a customer delivers an item to a depositary bank for collection:

(1) the depositary bank becomes a holder of the item at the time it receives the item for collection if the customer at the time of delivery was a holder of the item, whether or not the customer indorses the item, and, if the bank satisfies the other requirements of Section 3-302, it is a holder in due course; and

(2) the depositary bank warrants to collecting banks, the payor bank or other payor, and the drawer that the amount of the item was paid to the customer or deposited to the customer's account.

Section 4-206. Transfer Between Banks.

Any agreed method that identifies the transferor bank is sufficient for the item's further transfer to another bank

Section 4-207. Transfer Warranties.

(a) A customer or collecting bank that transfers an item and receives a settlement or other consideration warrants to the transferee and to any subsequent collecting bank that:

(1) the warrantor is a person entitled to enforce the item;

(2) all signatures on the item are authentic and authorized;

(3) the item has not been altered;

(4) the item is not subject to a defense or claim in recoupment (Section 3-305(a)) of any party that can be asserted against the warrantor; and

(5) the warrantor has no knowledge of any insolvency proceeding commenced with respect to the maker or acceptor or, in the case of an unaccepted draft, the drawer.

(b) If an item is dishonored, a customer or collecting bank transferring the item and receiving settlement or other consideration is obliged to pay the amount due on the item (i) according to the terms of the item at the time it was transferred, or (ii) if the transfer was of an incomplete item, according to its terms when completed as stated in Sections 3-115 and 3-407. The obligation of a transferor is owed to the transferee and to any subsequent collecting bank that takes the item in good faith. A transferor cannot disclaim its obligation under this subsection by an indorsement stating that it is made "without recourse" or otherwise disclaiming liability.

(c) A person to whom the warranties under subsection (a) are made and who took the item in good faith may recover from the warrantor as damages for breach of warranty an amount equal to the loss suffered as a result of the breach, but not more than the amount of the item plus expenses and loss of interest incurred as a result of the breach.

(d) The warranties stated in subsection (a) cannot be disclaimed with respect to checks. Unless notice of a claim for breach of warranty is given to the warrantor within 30 days after the claimant has reason to know of the breach and the identity of the warrantor, the warrantor is discharged to the extent of any loss caused by the delay in giving notice of the claim.

(e) A cause of action for breach of warranty under this section accrues when the claimant has reason to know of the breach.

Section 4-208. Presentment Warranties.

(a) If an unaccepted draft is presented to the drawee for payment or acceptance and the drawee pays or accepts the draft, (i) the person obtaining payment or acceptance, at the time of presentment, and (ii) a previous transferor of the draft, at the time of transfer, warrant to the drawee that pays or accepts the draft in good faith that:

(1) the warrantor is, or was, at the time the warrantor transferred the draft, a person entitled to enforce the draft or authorized to obtain payment or ac-

ceptance of the draft on behalf of a person entitled to enforce the draft;

(2) the draft has not been altered; and

(3) the warrantor has no knowledge that the signature of the purported drawer of the draft is unauthorized.

(b) A drawee making payment may recover from a warrantor damages for breach of warranty equal to the amount paid by the drawee less the amount the drawee received or is entitled to receive from the drawer because of the payment. In addition, the drawee is entitled to compensation for expenses and loss of interest resulting from the breach. The right of the drawee to recover damages under this subsection is not affected by any failure of the drawee to exercise ordinary care in making payment. If the drawee accepts the draft (i) breach of warranty is a defense to the obligation of the acceptor, and (ii) if the acceptor makes payment with respect to the draft, the acceptor is entitled to recover from a warrantor for breach of warranty the amounts stated in this subsection.

(c) If a drawee asserts a claim for breach of warranty under subsection (a) based on an unauthorized indorsement of the draft or an alteration of the draft, the warrantor may defend by proving that the indorsement is effective under Section 3-404 or 3-405 or the drawer is precluded under Section 3-406 or 4-406 from asserting against the drawee the unauthorized indorsement or alteration.

(d) If (i) a dishonored draft is presented for payment to the drawer or an indorser or (ii) any other item is presented for payment to a party obliged to pay the item, and the item is paid, the person obtaining payment and a prior transferor of the item warrant to the person making payment in good faith that the warrantor is, or was, at the time the warrantor transferred the item, a person entitled to enforce the item or authorized to obtain payment on behalf of a person entitled to enforce the item. The person making payment may recover from any warrantor for breach of warranty an amount equal to the amount paid plus expenses and loss of interest resulting from the breach.

(e) The warranties stated in subsections (a) and (d) cannot be disclaimed with respect to checks. Unless notice of a claim for breach of warranty is given to the warrantor within 30 days after the claimant has reason to know of the breach and the identity of the warrantor, the warrantor is discharged to the extent of any loss caused by the delay in giving notice of the claim.

(f) A cause of action for breach of warranty under this section accrues when the claimant has reason to know of the breach.

Section 4-209. Encoding and Retention Warranties.

(a) A person who encodes information on or with respect to an item after issue warrants to any subsequent collecting bank and to the payor bank or other payor that the information is correctly encoded. If the customer of a depositary bank encodes, that bank also makes the warranty.

(b) A person who undertakes to retain an item pursuant to an agreement for electronic presentment warrants to any subsequent collecting bank and to the payor bank or other payor that retention and presentment of the item comply with the agreement. If a customer of a depositary bank undertakes to retain an item, that bank also makes this warranty.

(c) A person to whom warranties are made under this section and who took the item in good faith may recover from the warrantor as damages for breach of warranty an amount equal to the loss suffered as a result of the breach, plus expenses and loss of interest incurred as a result of the breach.

Section 4-210. Security Interest of Collecting Bank in Items, Accompanying Documents, and Proceeds.

(a) A collecting bank has a security interest in an item and any accompanying documents or the proceeds of either:

(1) in case of an item deposited in an account, to the extent to which credit

given for the item has been withdrawn or applied;

(2) in case of an item for which it has given credit available for withdrawal as of right, to the extent of the credit given, whether or not the credit is drawn upon or there is a right of chargeback; or

(3) if it makes an advance on or against the item.

(b) If credit given for several items received at one time or pursuant to a single agreement is withdrawn or applied in part, the security interest remains upon all the items, any accompanying documents or the proceeds of either. For the purpose of this section, credits first given are first withdrawn.

(c) Receipt by a collecting bank of a final settlement for an item is a realization on its security interest in the item, accompanying documents, and proceeds. So long as the bank does not receive final settlement for the item or give up possession of the item or accompanying documents for purposes other than collection, the security interest continues to that extent and is subject to Article 9, but.

(1) no security agreement is necessary to make the security interest enforceable (Section 9-203(1)(a));

(2) no filing is required to perfect the security interest; and

(3) the security interest has priority over conflicting perfected security interests in the item, accompanying documents or proceeds.

Section 4-211. When Bank Gives Value for Purposes of Holder in Due Course.

For purposes of determining its status as a holder in due course, a bank has given value to the extent it has a security interest in an item if the bank otherwise complies with the requirements of Section 3-302 on what constitutes a holder in due course.

Section 4-212. Presentment by Notice of Item Not Payable by, Through, or at Bank; Liability of Drawer or Indorser.

(a) Unless otherwise instructed, a collecting bank may present an item not payable by, through, or at a bank by sending to the party to accept or pay a written notice that the bank holds the item for acceptance or payment. The notice must be sent in time to be received on or before the day when presentment is due and the bank must meet any requirement of the party to accept or pay under Section 3-501 by the close of the bank's next banking day after it knows of the requirement (b) If presentment is made by notice and payment, acceptance, or request for compliance with a requirement under Section 3-501 is not received by the close of business on the day after maturity or, in the case of demand items, by the close of business on the third banking day after notice was sent, the presenting bank may treat the item as dishonored and charge any drawer or indorser by sending it notice of the facts.

Section 4-213. Medium and Time of Settlement by Bank.

(a) With respect to settlement by a bank, the medium and time of settlement may be prescribed by Federal Reserve regulations or circulars, clearing-house rules, and the like, or agreement. In the absence of such prescription:

(1) the medium of settlement is cash or credit to an account in a Federal Reserve bank of or specified by the person to receive settlement; and

(2) the time of settlement, is:

(i) with respect to tender of settlement by cash, a cashier's check, or teller's check, when the cash or check is sent or delivered;

(ii) with respect to tender of settlement by credit in an account in a Federal Reserve Bank, when the credit is made;

(iii) with respect to tender of settlement by a credit or debit to an account in a bank, when the credit or debit is made or, in the case of tender of settlement by authority to charge an account, when the authority is sent or delivered; or

(iv) with respect to tender of settlement by a funds transfer, when payment is made pursuant to Section 4A-406(a) to the person receiving settlement.

(b) If the tender of settlement is not by a medium authorized by subsection (a) or the time of settlement is not fixed by subsection (a), no settlement occurs until the tender of settlement is accepted by the person receiving settlement.

(c) If settlement for an item is made by cashier's check or teller's check and the person receiving settlement, before its midnight deadline:

(1) presents or forwards the check for collection, settlement is when the check is finally paid; or

(2) fails to present or forward the check for collection, settlement is final at the midnight deadline of the person receiving settlement.

(d) If settlement for an item is made by giving authority to charge the account of the bank giving settlement in the bank receiving settlement, settlement is final when the charge is made by the bank receiving settlement if there are funds available in the account for the amount of the item.

Section 4-214. Right of Charge-Back or Refund; Liability of Collecting Bank: Return of Item.

(a) If a collecting bank has made provisional settlement with its customer for an item and fails by reason of dishonor, suspension of payments by a bank, or otherwise to receive settlement for the item which is or becomes final, the bank may revoke the settlement given by it, charge back the amount of any credit given for the item to its customer's account, or obtain refund from its customer, whether or not it is able to return the item, if by its midnight deadline or within a longer reasonable time after it learns the facts it returns the item or sends notification of the facts. If the return or notice is delayed beyond the bank's midnight deadline or a longer reasonable time after it learns the facts, the bank may revoke the settlement, charge back the credit, or obtain refund from its customer, but it is liable for any loss resulting from the delay. These rights to revoke, charge back, and obtain refund terminate if and when a settlement for the item received by the bank is or becomes final.

(b) A collecting bank returns an item when it is sent or delivered to the bank's customer or transferor or pursuant to its instructions.

(c) A depositary bank that is also the payor may charge back the amount of an item to its customer's account or obtain refund in accordance with the section governing return of an item received by a payor bank for credit on its books (Section 4-301).

(d) The right to charge back is not affected by

(1) previous use of a credit given for the item; or

(2) failure by any bank to exercise ordinary care with respect to the item, but a bank so failing remains liable.

(e) A failure to charge back or claim refund does not affect other rights of the bank against the customer or any other party.

(f) If credit is given in dollars as the equivalent of the value of an item payable in foreign money, the dollar amount of any charge-back or refund must be calculated on the basis of the bank-offered spot rate for the foreign money prevailing on the day when the person entitled to the charge-back or refund learns that it will not receive payment in ordinary course.

Section 4-215. Final Payment of Item by Payor Bank; When Professional Debits and Credits Become Final; When Certain Credits Become Available for Withdrawal.

(a) An item is finally paid by a payor bank when the bank has first done any of the following:

    (1)   paid the item in cash;

    (2)   settled for the item without having a right to revoke the settlement under statute, clearinghouse rule, or agreement; or

    (3)   made a provisional settlement for the item and failed to revoke the settlement in the time and manner permitted by statute, clearinghouse rule, or agreement.

(b) If provisional settlement for an item does not become final, the item is not finally paid.

(c) If provisional settlement for an item between the presenting and payor banks is made through a clearing house or by debits or credits in an account between them, then to the extent that provisional debits or credits for the item are entered in accounts between the presenting and payor banks or between the presenting and successive prior collecting banks seriatim, they become final upon final payment of the item by the payor bank.

(d) If a collecting bank receives a settlement for an item which is or becomes final, the bank is accountable to its customer for the amount of the item and any provisional credit given for the item in an account with its customer becomes final.

(e) Subject to (i) applicable law stating a time for availability of funds and (ii) any right of the bank to apply the credit to an obligation of the customer, credit given by a bank for an item in a customer's account becomes available for withdrawal as of right:

    (1)   if the bank has received a provisional settlement for the item, when the settlement becomes final and the bank has had a reasonable time to receive return of the item and the item has not been received within that time;

    (2)   if the bank is both the depositary bank and the payor bank, and the item is fin-ally paid, at the opening of the bank's second banking day following receipt of the item.

(f) Subject to applicable law stating a time for availability of funds and any right of a bank to apply a deposit to an obligation of the depositor, a deposit of money becomes available for withdrawal as of right at the opening of the bank's next banking day after receipt of the deposit.

Section 4-216. Insolvency and Preference.

(a) If an item is in or comes into the possession of a payor or collecting bank that suspends payment and the item has not been finally paid, the item must be returned by the receiver, trustee, or agent in charge of the closed bank to the presenting bank or the closed bank's customer.

(b) If a payor bank finally pays an item and suspends payments without making a settlement for the item with its customer or the presenting bank which settlement is or becomes final, the owner of the item has a preferred claim against the payor bank.

(c) If a payor bank gives or a collecting bank gives or receives a provisional settlement for an item and thereafter suspends payments, the suspension does not prevent or interfere with the settlement's becoming final if the finality occurs automatically upon the lapse of certain time or the happening of certain events.

(d) If a collecting bank receives from subsequent parties settlement for an item, which settlement is or becomes final and the bank suspends payments without making a settlement for the item with its customer which settlement is or becomes final, the owner of the item has a preferred claim against the collecting bank.

Part 3. Collection of Items: Payor Banks.

Section 4-301. Deferred Posting; Recovery of Payment by Return of Items; Time of Dishonor, Return of Items by Payor Bank.

(a) If a payor bank settles for a demand item other than a documentary draft presented otherwise than for immediate payment over the counter before midnight of the banking day of receipt, the payor bank may revoke the settlement and recover the settlement if, before it has made final payment and before its midnight deadline, it

(1) returns the item; or
(2) sends written notice of dishonor or nonpayment if the item is unavailable for return.

(b) If a demand item is received by a payor bank for credit on its books, it may return the item or send notice of dishonor and may revoke any credit given or recover the amount thereof withdrawn by its customer, if it acts within the time limit and in the manner specified in subsection (a).

(c) Unless previous notice of dishonor has been sent, an item is dishonored at the time when for purposes of dishonor it is returned or notice sent in accordance with this section.

(d) An item is returned:

(1) as to an item presented through a clearing house, when it is delivered to the presenting or last collecting bank or to the clearing house or is sent or delivered in accordance with clearing-house rules; or
(2) in all other cases, when it is sent or delivered to the bank's customer or transferor or pursuant to instructions.

Section 4-302. Payor Bank's Responsibility for Late Return of Item.

(a) If an item is presented to and received by a payor bank, the bank is accountable for the amount of:

(1) a demand item, other than a documentary draft, whether properly payable or not, if the bank, in any case in which it is not also the depositary bank, retains the item beyond midnight of the banking day of receipt without settling for it or, whether or not it is also the depositary bank, does not pay or return the item or send notice of dishonor until after its midnight deadline; or
(2) any other properly payable item unless, within the time allowed for acceptance or payment of that item, the bank either accepts or pays the item or returns it and accompanying documents.

(b) The liability of a payor bank to pay an item pursuant to subsection (a) is subject to defenses based on breach of a presentment warranty (Section 4-208) or proof that the person seeking enforcement of the liability presented or transferred the item for the purpose of defrauding the payor bank.

Section 4-303. When Items Subject to Notice, Stop Payment Order, Legal Process, or Setoff; Order in Which Items May Be Charged or Certified.

(a) Any knowledge, notice, or stop-payment order received by, legal process served upon, or setoff exercised by a payor bank comes too late to terminate, suspend, or modify the bank's right or duty to pay an item or to charge its customer's account for the item if the knowledge, notice, stop-payment order, or legal process is received or served and a reasonable time for the bank to act thereon expires or the setoff is exercised after the earliest of the following:

(1) the bank accepts or certifies the item;
(2) the bank pays the item in cash;
(3) the bank settles for the item without having a right to revoke the settlement under statute, clearing-house rule, or agreement;

(4) the bank becomes accountable for the amount of the item under Section 4-302 dealing with the payor bank's responsibility for late return of items; or

(5) with respect to checks, a cutoff hour no earlier than one hour after the opening of the next banking day after the banking day on which the bank received the check and no later than the close of that next banking day or, if no cutoff hour is fixed, the close of the next banking day after the banking day on which the bank received the check.

(b) Subject to subsection (a), items may be accepted, paid, certified, or charged to the indicated account of its customer in any order.

Part 4. Relationship Between Payor Bank and its Customer.

Section 4-401. When Bank May Charge Customer's Account.

(a) A bank may charge against the account of a customer an item that is properly payable from the account even though the charge creates an overdraft. An item is properly payable if it is authorized by the customer and is in accordance with any agreement between the customer and bank.

(b) A customer is not liable for the amount of an overdraft if the customer neither signed the item nor benefitted from the proceeds of the item.

(c) A bank may charge against the account of a customer a check that is otherwise properly payable from the account, even though payment was made before the date of the check, unless the customer has given notice to the bank of the postdating describing the check with reasonable certainty. The notice is effective for the period stated in Section 4-403(b) for stop-payment orders, and must be received at such time and in such manner as to afford the bank a reasonable opportunity to act on it before the bank takes any action with respect to the check described in Section 4-303. If a bank charges against the account of a customer a check before the date stated in the notice of postdating, the bank is liable for damages for the loss resulting from its act. The loss may include damages for dishonor of subsequent items under Section 4-402.

(d) A bank that in good faith makes payment to a holder may charge the indicated account of its customer according to:

(1) the original terms of the altered item; or

(2) the terms of the completed item, even though the bank knows the item has been completed unless the bank has notice that the completion was improper.

Section 4-402. Bank's Liability to Customer for Wrongful Dishonor; Time of Determining Insufficiency of Account.

(a) Except as otherwise provided in this Article, a payor bank wrongfully dishonors an item if it dishonors an item that is properly payable, but a bank may dishonor an item that would create an overdraft unless it has agreed to pay the overdraft.

(b) A payor bank is liable to its customer for damages proximately caused by the wrongful dishonor of an item. Liability is limited to actual damages proved and may include damages for an arrest or prosecution of the customer or other consequential damages. Whether any consequential damages are proximately caused by the wrongful dishonor is a question of fact to be determined in each case.

(c) A payor bank's determination of the customer's account balance on which a decision to dishonor for insufficiency of available funds is based may be made at any time between the time the item is received by the payor bank and the time that the payor bank returns the item or gives notice in lieu of return, and no more than one determination need be made. If, at the election of the payor bank, a subsequent balance determination is made for the purpose of reevaluating the bank's decision to dishonor the item, the account balance at that time is determinative of whether a dishonor for insufficiency of available funds is wrongful.

Section 4-403. Customer's Right to Stop Payment; Burden of Proof.

(a) A customer or any person authorized to draw on the account if there is more than one person may stop payment of any item drawn on the customer's account or close the account by an order to the bank describing the item or account with reasonable certainty received at a time and in a manner that affords the bank a reasonable opportunity to act on it before any action by the bank with respect to the item described in Section 4-303. If the signature of more than one person is required to draw on an account, any of these persons may stop payment or close the account.
(b) A stop-payment order is effective for six months, but it lapses after 14 calendar days if the original order was oral and was not in writing within that period. A stop-payment order may be renewed for additional six-month periods by a writing given to the bank within a period during which the stop-payment order is effective.
(c) The burden of establishing the fact and amount of loss resulting from the payment of an item contrary to a stop-payment order or order to close an account is on the customer. The loss from payment of an item contrary to a stop-payment order may include damages for dishonor of subsequent items under Section 4-402.

Section 4-404. Bank Not Obliged to Pay Check More Than Six Months Old.

A bank is under no obligation to a customer having a checking account to pay a check, other than a certified check, which is presented more than six months after its date, but it may charge its customer's account for a payment made thereafter in good faith.

Section 4-405. Death or Incompetence of Customer.

(a) A payor or collecting bank's authority to accept, pay, or collect an item or to account for proceeds of its collection, if otherwise effective, is not rendered ineffective by incompetence of a customer of either bank existing at the time the item is issued or its collection is undertaken if the bank does not know of an adjudication of incompetence. Neither death nor incompetence of a customer revokes the authority to accept, pay, collect, or account until the bank knows of the fact of death or of an adjudication of incompetence and has reasonable opportunity to act on it.
(b) Even with knowledge, a bank may for 10 days after the date of death pay or certify checks drawn on or before that date unless ordered to stop payment by a person claiming an interest in the account.

Section 4-406. Customer's Duty to Discover and Report Unauthorized Signature or Alteration.

(a) A bank that sends or makes available to a customer a statement of account showing payment of items for the account shall either return or make available to the customer the items paid or provide information in the statement of account sufficient to allow the customer reasonably to identify the items paid. The statement of account provides sufficient information if the item is described by item number, amount, and date of payment.
(b) If the items are not returned to the customer, the person retaining the items shall either retain the items or, if the items are destroyed, maintain the capacity to furnish legible copies of the items until the expiration of seven years after receipt of the items. A customer may request an item from the bank that paid the item, and that bank must provide in a reasonable time either the item or, if the item has been destroyed or is not otherwise obtainable, a legible copy of the item.
(c) If a bank sends or makes available a statement of account or items pursuant to subsection (a), the customer must exercise reasonable

promptness in examining the statement or the items to determine whether any payment was not authorized because of an alteration of an item or because a purported signature by or on behalf of the customer was not authorized. If, based on the statement or items provided, the customer should reasonably have discovered the unauthorized payment, the customer must promptly notify the bank of the relevant facts.

(d) If the bank proves that the customer failed, with respect to an item, to comply with the duties imposed on the customer by subsection (c), the customer is precluded from asserting against the bank:

(1) the customer's unauthorized signature or any alteration on the item, if the bank also proves that it suffered a loss by reason of the failure; and

(2) the customer's unauthorized signature or alteration by the same wrongdoer on any other item paid in good faith by the bank if the payment was made before the bank received notice from the customer of the unauthorized signature or alteration and after the customer had been afforded a reasonable period of time, not exceeding 30 days, in which to examine the item or statement of account and notify the bank.

(e) If subsection (d) applies and the customer proves that the bank failed to exercise ordinary care in paying the item and that the failure substantially contributed to loss, the loss is allocated between the customer precluded and the bank asserting the preclusion according to the extent to which the failure of the customer to comply with subsection (c) and the failure of the bank to exercise ordinary care contributed to the loss. If the customer proves that the bank did not pay the item in good faith, the preclusion under subsection (d) does not apply.

(f) Without regard to care or lack of care of either the customer or the bank, a customer who does not within one year after the statement or items are made available to the customer (subsection (a)) discover and report the customer's unauthorized signature on or any alteration on the item is precluded from asserting against the bank the unauthorized signature or alteration. If there is a preclusion under this subsection, the payor bank may not recover for breach or warranty under Section 4-208 with respect to the unauthorized signature or alteration to which the preclusion applies.

Section 4-407. Payor Bank's Right to Subrogation on Improper.

If a payor bank has paid an item over the order of the drawer or maker to stop payment, or after an account has been closed, or otherwise under circumstances giving a basis for objection by the drawer or maker, to prevent unjust enrichment and only to the extent necessary to prevent loss to the bank by reason of its payment of the item, the payor bank is subrogated to the rights

(1) of any holder in due course on the item against the drawer or maker;

(2) of the payee or any other holder of the item against the drawer or maker either on the item or under the transaction out of which the item arose; and

(3) of the drawer or maker against the payee or any other holder of the item with respect to the transaction out of which the item arose.

Part 5. Collection of Documentary Drafts.

Section 4-501. Handling of Documentary Drafts; Duty to Send for Presentment and to Notify Customer of Dishonor.

A bank that takes. a documentary draft for collection shall present or send the draft and accompanying documents for presentment and, upon learning that the draft has not been paid or accepted in due course, shall seasonably notify its customer of the fact even though it may have discounted or bought the draft or extended credit available for withdrawal as of right.

Section 4-502. Presentment of "On Arrival" Drafts.

If a draft or the relevant instructions require presentment "on arrival", "when goods arrive" or the like, the collecting bank need not present until in its judgment a reasonable time for arrival of the goods has expired. Refusal to pay or accept because the goods have not arrived is not dishonor; the bank must notify its transferor of the refusal but need not present the draft again until it is instructed to do so or learns of the arrival of the goods.

Section 4-503. Responsibility of Presenting Bank for Documents and Goods; Report of Reasons for Dishonor; Referee in Case of Need.

Unless otherwise instructed and except as provided in Article 5, a bank presenting a documentary draft:

(1) must deliver the documents to the drawee on acceptance of the draft if it is payable more than three days after presentment; otherwise, only on payment; and

(2) upon dishonor, either in the case of presentment for acceptance or presentment for payment, may seek and follow instructions from any referee in case of need designated in the draft or, if the presenting bank does not choose to utilize the referee's services, it must use diligence and good faith to ascertain the reason for dishonor, must notify its transferor of the dishonor and of the results of its effort to ascertain the reasons therefore, and must request instructions. However, the presenting bank is under no obligation with respect to goods represented by the documents except to follow any reasonable instructions seasonably received; it has a right to reimbursement for any expense in-

curred in following instructions and to prepayment of or indemnity for those expenses.

Section 4-504. Privilege of Presenting Bank to Deal With Goods; Security Interest for Expenses.

(a) A presenting bank that, following the dishonor of a documentary draft has seasonably requested instructions but does not receive them within a reasonable time may store, sell or otherwise deal with the goods in any reasonable manner.

(b) For its reasonable expenses incurred by action under subsection (a) the presenting bank has a lien upon the goods or their proceeds, which may be foreclosed in the same manner as an unpaid seller's lien.

Authors' note: *Articles 4A, 5, 6, 7, and 8 have been omitted as unnecessary for the purposes of this text.*

ARTICLE 9. SECURED TRANSACTIONS; SALES OF ACCOUNTS AND CHATTEL PAPER.

Part 1. Short Title, Applicability and Definitions.

Section 9-101. Short Title.

This Article shall be known and may be cited as Uniform Commercial Code—Secured Transactions.

Section 9-102. Policy and Subject Matter of Article.

(1) Except as otherwise provided in Section 104 on excluded transactions, this Article applies

(a) to any transaction (regardless of its form) which is intended to create a security interest in personal property or fixtures including goods, documents, instruments, general intangibles, chattel paper or accounts; and also

(b) to any sale of accounts or chattel paper.

(2) This Article applies to security interests created by contract including pledge, assignment, chattel mortgage, chattel trust, trust deed, factor's lien, equipment trust, conditional sale, trust receipt, other lien or title retention contract and lease or consignment intended as security. This Article does not apply to statutory liens except as provided in Section 9-310.

(3) The application of this Article to a security interest in a secured obligation is not affected by the fact that the obligation is itself secured by a transaction or interest to which this Article does not apply. **Note:** The adoption of this Article should be accompanied by the repeal of existing statutes dealing with conditional sales, trust receipts, factor's liens where the factor is given a nonpossessory lien, chattel mortgages, crop mortgages, mortgages on railroad equipment, assignment of accounts and generally statutes regulating security interests in personal property Where the state has a retail installment selling act or small loan act, that legislation should be carefully examined to determine what changes in those acts, are needed to conform them to this Article. This Article primarily sets out rules defining rights of a secured party against persons dealing with the debtor; it does not prescribe regulations and controls which may be necessary to curb abuses arising in the small loan business or in the financing of consumer purchases on credit. Accordingly there is no intention to repeal existing regulatory acts in those fields by enactment or reenactment of Article 9. See Section 9-203(4) and the Note thereto.

Section 9-103. Perfection of Security Interest in Multiple State Transactions.

(1) Documents, instruments and ordinary goods.

(a) This subsection applies to documents and instruments and to goods other than those covered by a certificate of title described in subsection (2), mobile goods described in subsection (3), and minerals described in subsection (5).

(b) Except as otherwise provided in this subsection, perfection and the effect of perfection or non-perfection of a security interest in collateral are governed by the law of the jurisdiction where the collateral is when the last event occurs on which is based the assertion that the security interest is perfected or unperfected.

(c) If the parties to a transaction creating a purchase money security interest in goods in one jurisdiction understand at the time that the security interest attaches that the goods will be kept in another jurisdiction, then the law of the other jurisdiction governs the perfection and the effect of perfection or non-perfection of the security interest from the time it attaches until thirty days after the debtor receives possession of the goods and thereafter if the goods are taken to the other jurisdiction before the end of the thirty-day period.

(d) When collateral is brought into and kept in this state while subject to a security interest perfected under the law of the jurisdiction from which the collateral was removed, the security interest remains perfected, but if action is required by Part 3 of this Article to perfect the security interest, (i) if the action is not taken before the expiration of the period of perfection in the other jurisdiction or the end of four months after the collateral is brought into this state, whichever period first expires, the security interest becomes unperfected at the end of that period and is thereafter deemed to have been unperfected as against a person who became a purchaser after removal; (ii) if the action is taken before the expiration of the period specified in subparagraph (i), the security interest continues perfected thereafter; (iii) for the purpose of priority over a buyer of consumer goods (subsection (2) of Section 9-307), the period of the effectiveness of a filing in the jurisdiction from which the collateral is removed is governed by the rules with respect to perfection in subparagraphs (i) and (ii).

(2) Certificate of title.

    (a)   This subsection applies to goods covered by a certificate of title issued under a statute of this state or of another jurisdiction under the law of which indication of a security interest on the certificate is required as a condition of perfection.

    (b)   Except as otherwise provided in this subsection, perfection and the effect of perfection or non-perfection of the security interest are governed by the law (including the conflict of law rules) of the jurisdiction issuing the certificate until four months after the goods are removed from that jurisdiction and thereafter until the goods are registered in another jurisdiction, but in any event not beyond surrender of the certificate. After the expiration of that period, the goods are not covered by the certificate of title within the meaning of this section.

    (c)   Except with respect to the rights of a buyer described in the next paragraph, a security interest, perfected in another jurisdiction otherwise than by notation on a certificate of title, in goods brought into this state and thereafter covered by a certificate of title issued by this state is subject to the rules stated in paragraph (d) of subsection (1).

    (d)   If goods are brought into this state while a security interest therein is perfected in any manner under the law of the jurisdiction from which the goods are removed and a certificate of title is issued by this state and the certificate does not show that the goods are subject to the security interest or that they may be subject to security interests not shown on the certificate, the security interest is subordinate to the rights of a buyer of the goods who is not in the business of selling goods of that kind to the extent that he gives value and receives delivery of the goods after issuance of the certificate and without knowledge of the security interest.

(3) Accounts, general intangibles and mobile goods.

    (a)   This subsection applies to accounts (other than an account described in subsection (5) on minerals) and general intangibles (other than uncertificated securities) and to goods which are mobile and which are of a type normally used in more than one jurisdiction, such as motor vehicles, trailers, rolling stock, airplanes, shipping containers road building and construction machinery and commercial harvesting machinery and the like, if the goods are equipment or are inventory leased or held for lease by the debtor to others, and are not covered by a certificate of title described in subsection (2).

    (b)   The law (including the conflict of laws rules) of the jurisdiction in which the debtor is located governs the perfection and the effect of perfection or nonperfection of the security interest.

    (c)   If, however, the debtor is located in a jurisdiction which is not a part of the United States, and which does not provide for perfection of the security interest by filing or recording in that jurisdiction, the law of the jurisdiction In the United States in which the debtor has its major executive office governs the perfection and the effect of perfection or non-perfection of the security interest through filing. In the alternative, if the debtor is located in a jurisdiction which is not a part of the United States or Canada and the collateral is accounts or general intangibles for money due or to become due, the security interest may be perfected by notification to the account debtor. As used in this paragraph, "United States" includes its territories and possessions and the Commonwealth of Puerto Rico.

(d) A debtor shall be deemed located at his place of business if he has one, at his chief executive office if he has more than one place of business, otherwise at his residence. If however, the debtor is a foreign air carrier under the Federal Aviation Act of 1958, as amended, it shall be deemed located at the designated office of the agent upon whom service of process may be made on behalf of the foreign air carrier.

(e) A security interest perfected under the law of the jurisdiction of the location of the debtor is perfected until the expiration of four months after a change of the debtor's location to another jurisdiction, or until perfection would have ceased by the law of the first jurisdiction, whichever period first expires. Unless perfected in the new jurisdiction before the end of that period, it becomes unperfected thereafter and is deemed to have been unperfected as against a person who became a purchaser after the change.

(4) Chattel paper. The rules stated for goods in subsection (1) apply to a possessory security interest in chattel paper. The rules stated for accounts in subsection (3) apply to a nonpossessory security interest in chattel paper, but the security interest may not be perfected by notification to the account debtor.

(5) Minerals. Perfection and the effect of perfection or non-perfection of a security interest which is created by a debtor who has an interest in minerals or the like (including oil and gas) before extraction and which attaches thereto as extracted, or which attaches to an account resulting from the sale thereof at the wellhead or minehead are governed by the law (including the conflict of laws rules) of the jurisdiction wherein the wellhead or minehead is located.

(6) Uncertificated securities. The law (including the conflict of laws rules) of the jurisdiction of organization of the issuer governs the perfection and the effect of perfection or nonperfection a security interest in uncertificated securities.

Section 9-104. Transactions Excluded From Article.

This Article does not apply

(a) to a security interest subject to any statute of the United States, to the extent that such statute governs the rights of parties to and third parties affected by transactions in particular types of property; or

(b) to a landlord's lien; or

(c) to a lien given by statute or other rule of law for services or materials except as provided in Section 9-310 on priority of such liens; or

(d) to a transfer of a claim for wages, salary or other compensation of an employee; or

(e) to a transfer by a government or governmental subdivision or agency; or

(f) to a sale of accounts or chattel paper as part of a sale of the business out of which they arose, or an assignment of accounts or chattel paper which is for the purpose of collection only, or a transfer of a right to payment under a contract to an assignee who is also to do the performance under the contract or a transfer of a single account to an assignee in whole or partial satisfaction of a preexisting indebtedness; or

(g) to a transfer of an interest in or claim in or under any policy of insurance, except as provided with respect to proceeds (Section 9-306) and priorities in proceeds (Section 9-312); or

(h) to a right represented by a judgment (other than a judgment taken on a right to payment which was collateral); or

(i) to any right of set-off; or

(j) except to the extent that provision is made for fixtures in Section 9-313, to the creation or transfer of an interest in or lien on real estate, including a lease or rents thereunder; or

(k) to a transfer in whole or in part of any claim arising out of tort; or

(l) to a transfer of an interest in any deposit account (subsection (1) of Section 9-105), except as provided with respect to proceeds (Section 9-306) and priorities in proceeds (Section 9-312).

Section 9-105. Definitions and Index of Definitions.

(1) In this Article unless the context otherwise requires:

(a) "Account debtor" means the person who is obligated on an account, chattel paper or general intangible;

(b) "Chattel paper" means a writing or writings which evidence both a monetary obligation and a security interest in or a lease of specific goods, but a charter or other contract involving the use or hire of a vessel is not chattel paper. When a transaction is evidenced both by such a security agreement or a lease and by an instrument or a series of instruments, the group of writings taken together constitutes chattel paper;

(c) "Collateral" means the property subject to a security interest, and includes accounts and chattel paper which have been sold;

(d) "Debtor" means the person who owes payment or other performance of the obligation secured, whether or not he owns or has rights in the collateral,

and includes the seller of accounts on chattel paper. Where the debtor and the owner of the collateral are not the same person, the term "debtor" means the owner of the collateral in any provision of the Article dealing with the collateral, the obligor in any provision dealing with the obligation, and may include both where the context so requires;

(e) "Deposit account" means a demand, time, savings, passbook or like account maintained with a bank, savings and loan association, credit union or like organization, other than an account evidenced by a certificate of deposit;

(f) "Document" means document of title as defined in the general definitions of Article 1 (Section 1-201), and a receipt of the kind described in subsection (2) of Section 7-201;

(g) "Encumbrance" includes real estate mortgages and other liens on real estate and all other rights in real estate that are not ownership interests;

(h) "Goods" includes all things which are movable at the time the security interest attaches or which are fixtures (Section 9-313), but does not include money, documents, instruments, accounts, chattel paper, general intangibles, or minerals or the like (including oil and gas) before extraction. "Goods" also includes standing timber which is to be cut and removed under a conveyance or contract for sale, the unborn young of animals, and growing crops;

(i) "Instrument" means a negotiable instrument (defined in Section 3-104), or a certificated security (defined in Section 8-102) or any other writing which evidences a right to the payment of money and is not itself a security agreement or lease and is of a type which is in ordinary course of business transferred by delivery with any necessary indorsement or assignment;

(j) "Mortgage" means a consensual interest created by a real estate mortgage, a trust deed on real estate, or the like;

(k) An advance is made "pursuant to commitment" if the secured party has bound himself to make it, whether or not a subsequent event of default or other event not within his control has relieved or may relieve him from his obligation;

(l) "Security agreement" means an agreement which creates or provides for a security interest;

(m) "Secured party" means a lender, seller or other person in whose favor there is a security interest, including a person to whom accounts or chattel paper have been sold. When the holders of obligations issued under an indenture of trust, equipment trust agreement or the like are represented by a trustee or other person, the representative is the secured party;

(n) "Transmitting utility" means any person primarily engaged in the railroad, street railway or trolley bus business, the electric or electronics communications transmission business, the transmission of goods by pipeline, or the transmission or the production and transmission of electricity, steam, gas or water, or the provision of sewer service.

(2) Other definitions applying to this Article and the sections in which they appear are:

"Account," Section 9-106.
"Attach," Section 9-203.
"Construction mortgage," Section 9-313 (1).
"Consumer goods, Section 9-109 (1).
"Equipment," Section 9-109 (2).
"Farm products," Section 9-109 (3).
"Fixture," Section 9-313 (1).
"Fixture filing," Section 9-313 (1).
"General intangibles," Section 9-106.
"Inventory," Section 9-109 (4).
"Lien creditor," Section 9-301(3).
"Proceeds," Section 9-306 (1).

"Purchase money security interest," Section 9-107.
"United States," Section 9-103.

(3) The following definitions in other Articles apply to this Article:

"Check," Section 3-104.
"Contract for sale," Section 2-106.
"Holder in due course," Section 3-302.
"Note," Section 3-104.
"Sale," Section 2-106.

(4) In addition Article 1 contains general definitions and principles of construction and interpretation applicable throughout this Article.

Section 9-106. Definitions: "Account"; "General Intangibles."

"Account" means any right to payment for goods sold or leased or for services rendered which is not evidenced by an instrument or chattel paper, whether or not it has been earned by performance. "General intangibles" means any personal property (including things in action) other than goods, accounts, chattel paper, documents, instruments, and money. All rights to payment earned or unearned under a charter or other contract involving the use or hire of a vessel and all rights incident to the chart or contract are accounts.

Section 9-107. Definitions: "Purchase Money Security Interest."

A security interest is a "purchase money security interest" to the extent that it is

(a) taken or retained by the seller of the collateral to secure all or part of its price; or

(b) taken by a person who by making advances or incurring an obligation gives value to enable the debtor to acquire rights in or the use of collateral if such value is in fact so used.

Section 9-108. When After-Acquired Collateral Not Security for Antecedent Debt.

Where a secured party makes an advance, incurs an obligation, releases a perfected security interest, or otherwise gives new value which is to be secured in whole or in part by after-acquired collateral shall be deemed to be taken for new value and not as security for an antecedent debt if the debtor acquires his rights in such collateral either in the ordinary course of his business or under a contract of purchase made pursuant to the security agreement within a reasonable time after new value is given.

Section 9-109. Classification of Goods: "Consumer Goods;" "Equipment"; "Farm Products;" "Inventory."

Goods are

(1) "consumer goods" if they are used or bought for use primarily for personal, family or household purposes;
(2) "equipment" if they are used or bought for use primarily in business (including farming or a profession) or by a debtor who is a nonprofit organization or a governmental subdivision or agency or if the goods are not included in the definitions of inventory, farm products or consumer goods;
(3) "farm products" if they are crops or livestock or supplies used or produced in farming operations or if they are products of crops or livestock in their unmanufactured states (such as ginned cotton, wool-clip, maple syrup, milk and eggs), and if they are in the possession of a debtor engaged in raising, fattening, grazing or other farming operations. If goods are farm products they are neither equipment nor inventory;
(4) "inventory" if they are held by a person who holds them for sale or lease or to be furnished under contracts of service or if he has so furnished them, or if they are raw materials, work in process or materials used or consumed in a business. Inventory of a person is not to be classified as his equipment.

Section 9-110. Sufficiency of Description.

For the purposes of this Article any description of personal property or real estate is sufficient whether or not it is specific if it reasonably identifies what is described.

Section 9-111. Applicability of Bulk Transfer Laws.

The creation of a security interest is not a bulk transfer under Article 6 (see Section 6-103).

Section 9-112. Where Collateral Is Not Owned by Debtor.

Unless otherwise agreed, when a secured party knows that collateral is owned by a person who is not the debtor, the owner of the collateral is entitled to receive from the secured party any surplus under Section 9-502(2) or under Section 9-504(1), and is not liable for the debt or for any deficiency after resale, and he has the same right as the debtor

(a) to receive statements under Section 9-208;
(b) to receive notice of and to object to a secured party's proposal to retain the collateral in satisfaction of the indebtedness under Section 9-505;
(c) to redeem the collateral under Section 9-506;
(d) to obtain injunctive or other relief under Section 9-507(1); and
(e) to recover losses caused to him under Section 9-208(2).

Section 9-113. Security Interests Arising Under Article on Sales or Under Article on Leases.

A security interest arising solely under the Article on Sales (Article 2) or the Article on Leases (Article 2A) is subject to the provisions of this Article except that to the extent that and so long as the debtor does not have or does not lawfully obtain possession of the goods

(a) no security agreement is necessary to make the security interest enforceable and

(b) no filing is required to perfect the security interest; and

(c) the rights of the secured party on default by the debtor are governed (i) by the Article on Sales (Article 2) in the case of a security interest arising solely under such Article or (ii) by the Article on Leases In the case of a security interest arising solely under such Article.

Section 9-114. Consignment.

(1) A person who delivers goods under a consignment which is not a security interest and who would be required to file under this Article by paragraph (3) (c) of Section 2-326 has priority over a secured party who is or becomes a creditor of the consignee and who would have a perfected security interest in the goods if they were the property of the consignee, and also has priority with respect to identifiable cash proceeds received on or before delivery of the goods to a buyer, if

(a) the consignor complies with the filing provision of the Article on Sales with respect to consignments (paragraph(3) (c) of Section 2-326) before the consignee receives possession of the goods; and

(b) the consignor gives notification in writing to the holder of the security interest if the holder has filed a financing statement covering the same types of goods before the date of the filing made by the consignor; and

(c) the holder of the security interest receives the notification within five years before the consignee receives possession of the goods; and

(d) the notification states that the consignor expects to deliver goods on consignment to the consignee, describing the goods by item or type.

(2) In the case of a consignment which is not a security interest and in which the requirements of the preceding subsection have not been met, a person who delivers goods to another is subordinate to a person who would have a perfected security interest in the goods if they were the property of the debtor.

Part 2. Validity of Security Agreement and Rights of Parties Thereto.

Section 9-201. General Validity of Security Agreement.

Except as otherwise provided by this Act a security agreement is effective according to its terms between the parties, against purchasers of the collateral and against creditors. Nothing in this Article validates any charge or practice illegal under any statute or regulation thereunder governing usury, small loans, retail installment sales, or the like, or extends the application of any such statute or regulation to any transaction not otherwise subject thereto.

Section 9-202. Title to Collateral Immaterial.

Each provision of this Article with regard to rights, obligations and remedies applies whether title to collateral is in the secured party or, in the debtor.

Section 9-203. Attachment and Enforceability of Security Interest; Proceeds; Formal Requisites.

(1) Subject to the provisions of Section 4-208 on the security interest of a collecting bank, Section 8-321 on security interests in securities and Section 9-113 on a security interest arising under the Article on Sales, a security interest is not enforceable against the debtor or third parties with respect to the collateral and does not attach unless:

(a) the collateral is in the possession of the secured party pursuant to agreement, or the debtor has signed a security agreement which contains a description of the collateral and in addition, when the security interest covers crops growing or to be grown or timber to be cut, a description of the land concerned;

(b) value has been given; and

(c) the debtor has rights in the collateral.

(2) A security interest attaches when it becomes enforceable against the debtor with respect to the collateral. Attachment occurs as soon as all of the events specified in subsection (1) have taken place unless explicit agreement postpones the time of attaching.

(3) Unless otherwise agreed a security agreement gives the secured party the rights to proceeds provided by Section 9-306.

(4) A transaction, although subject to this Article, is also subject to . .*, and in the case of conflict between the provisions of this Article and any such statute, the provisions of such statute control. Failure to comply with any applicable statute has only the effect which is specified therein.

Note: *At * is subsection (4) insert reference to any local statute regulating small loans, retail installment sales and the like.*

For foregoing subsection (4) is designed to make it clear that certain transactions, although subject to this Article, must also comply with other applicable legislation.

This Article is designed to regulate all the "security" aspects of transactions within its scope. There is, however, much regulatory legislation, particularly in the consumer field, which supplements this Article and should not be repealed by its enactment. Examples are small loan acts, retail installment selling acts and the like. Such acts may provide for licensing and rate regulation and may prescribe particular forms of contract. Such provisions should remain in force despite the enactment of this Article. On the other hand if a retail installment selling act contains provisions on filing, rights on default, etc., such provisions should be repealed as inconsistent with this Article except that inconsistent provisions as to deficiencies, penalties, etc., in the Uniform Consumer Credit Code and other recent relat-

ed legislation should remain because those statutes were drafted after the substantial enactment of the Article and with the intention of modifying certain provisions of this Article as to consumer credit.

Section 9-204. After-Acquired Property; Future Advances.

(1) Except as provided in subsection (2), a security agreement may provide that any or all obligations covered by the security agreement are to be secured by after-acquired collateral.

(2) No security interest attaches under an after-acquired property clause to consumer goods other than accessions (Section 9-314) when given as additional security unless the debtor acquires rights in them within ten days after the secured party gives value.

(3) Obligations covered by a security agreement may include future advances or other value whether or not the advances or value are given pursuant to commitment (subsection (1) of Section 9-105).

Section 9-205. Use or Disposition of Collateral Without Accounting Permissible.

A security interest is not invalid or fraudulent against creditors by reason of liberty in the debtor to use, commingle or dispose of all or part of the collateral (including returned or repos goods) or to collect or compromise accounts or chattel paper, or to accept the return of goods or make repossessions, or to use, commingle or dispose of proceeds, or by reason of the failure of the secured party to require the debtor to account for proceeds or replace collateral. This section does not relax the requirements of possession where perfection of a security interest depends upon possession of the collateral by the secured party or by a bailee.

Section 9-206. Agreement Not to Assert Defenses Against Assignee; Modification of Sales Warranties Where Security Agreement Exists.

(1) Subject to any statute or decision which establishes a different rule for buyers or lessees

of consumer goods, an agreement by a buyer or lessee that he will not assert against an assignee any claim or defense which he may have against the seller or lessor is enforceable by an assignee who takes his assignment for value, in good faith and without notice of a claim or defense, except as to defenses of a type which may be asserted against a holder in due course of a negotiable instrument under the Article on Commercial Paper (Article 3). A buyer who as part of one transaction signs both a negotiable instrument and a security agreement makes such an agreement.

(2) When a seller retains a purchase money security interest in goods the Article on Sales (Article 2) governs the sale and any disclaimer, limitation or modification of the seller's warranties.

Section 9-207. Rights and Duties When Collateral Is in Secured Party's Possession.

(1) A secured party must use reasonable care in the custody and preservation of collateral in his possession. In the case of a instrument or chattel paper reasonable care includes taking necessary steps to preserve rights against prior parties unless otherwise agreed.

(2) Unless otherwise agreed, when collateral is in the secured party's possession

- (a) reasonable expenses (including the cost of any insurance and payment of taxes or other charges) incurred in the custody, preservation, use or operation of the collateral are chargeable to the debtor and are secured by the collateral;
- (b) the risk of accidental loss or damage is on the debtor to the extent of any deficiency in any effective insurance coverage;
- (c) the secured party may hold as additional security any increase or profits (except money) received from the collateral, but money so received, unless remitted to the debtor, shall be applied in reduction of the secured obligation;

- (d) the secured party must keep the collateral identifiable but fungible collateral may be commingled;
- (e) the secured party may repledge the collateral upon terms which do not impair the debtor's right to redeem it.

(3) A secured party is liable for any loss caused by his failure to meet any obligation imposed by the preceding subsections but does not lose his security interest.

(4) A secured party may use or operate the collateral for the purpose of preserving the collateral or its value or pursuant to the order of a court of appropriate jurisdiction or, except in the case of consumer goods, in the manner and to the extent provided in the security agreement.

Section 9-208. Request for Statement of Account or List of Collateral.

(1) A debtor may sign a statement indicating what he believes to be the aggregate amount of unpaid indebtedness as of a specified date and may send it to the secured party with a request that the statement be approved or corrected and returned to the debtor. When the security agreement or any other record kept by the secured party identifies the collateral a debtor may similarly request the secured party to approve or correct a list of the collateral.

(2) The secured party must comply with such a request within two weeks after receipt by sending a written correction or approval. If the secured party claims a security interest in all of a particular type of collateral owned by the debtor he may indicate that fact in his reply and need not approve or correct an itemized list of such collateral. If the secured party without reasonable excuse fails to comply he is liable for any loss caused to the debtor thereby; and if the debtor has properly included in his request a good faith statement of the obligation or a list of the collateral or both the secured party may claim a security interest only as shown in the statement against persons misled by his failure to comply. If he no longer has an interest in the obligation or

collateral at the time the request is received he must disclose the name and address of any successor in interest known to him and he is liable for any loss caused to the debtor as a result of failure to disclose. A successor in interest is not subject to this section until a request is received by him.

(3) A debtor is entitled to such a statement once every six months without charge. The secured party may require payment of a charge not exceeding $10 for each additional statement furnished.

Part 3. Rights of Third Parties; Perfected and Unperfected Security Interests; Rules of Priority.

Section 9-301. Persons Who Take Priority Over Unperfected Security Interests; Rights of "Lien Creditor".

(1) Except as otherwise provided in subsection (2), an unperfected security interest is subordinate to the rights of

- (a) persons entitled to priority under Section 9-312;
- (b) a person who becomes a lien creditor before the security interest is perfected;
- (c) in the case of goods, instruments, documents and chattel paper, a person who is not a secured party and who is a transferee in bulk or other buyer not in ordinary course of business or is a buyer of farm products in ordinary course of business, to the extent that he gives value and receives delivery of the collateral without knowledge of the security interest and before it is perfected;
- (d) in the case of accounts and general intangibles, a person who is not a secured party and who is a transferee to the extent that he gives value without knowledge of the security interest and before it is perfected.

(2) If the secured party files with respect to a purchase money security interest before or within ten days after the debtor receives possession of the collateral, he takes priority over the rights of a transferee in bulk or of a lien creditor which arise between the time the security interest attaches and the time of filing.

(3) A "lien creditor" means a creditor who has acquired a lien on the property involved by attachment, levy or the like and includes an assignee for benefit of creditors from the time of assignment, and a trustee in bankruptcy from the date of the filing of the petition or a receiver in equity from the time of appointment.

(4) A person who becomes a lien creditor while a security interest is perfected takes subject to the security interest only to the extent that it secures advances made before he becomes a lien creditor or within 45 days thereafter or made without knowledge of the lien or pursuant to a commitment entered into without knowledge of the lien.

Section 9-302. When Filing is Required to Perfect Security Interest; Security Interests to Which Filing Provisions of this Article Do Not Apply.

(1) A financing statement must be filed to perfect all security interests except the following:

- (a) a security interest in collateral in possession of the secured party under Section 9-305;
- (b) a security interest temporarily perfected in instruments or documents without delivery under Section 9-304 or in proceeds for a 10 day period under Section 9-306;
- (c) a security interest created by an assignment of a beneficial interest in a trust or a decedent's estate;
- (d) a purchase money security interest in consumer goods; but filing is required for a motor vehicle required to be registered; and fixture filing is required for priority over conflicting interests in fixtures to the extent provided in Section 9-313;

(e) an assignment of accounts which does not alone or in conjunction with other assignments to the same assignee transfer a significant part of the outstanding accounts of the assignor;

(f) a security interest of a collecting bank (Section 4-208) or in securities (Section 8-321) or arising under the Article on Sales (see Section 9-113) or covered in subsection (3) of this section;

(g) an assignment for the benefit of all the creditors of the transferor, and subsequent transfers by the assignee thereunder.

(2) If a secured party assigns a perfected security interest, no filing under this Article is required in order to continue the perfected status of the security interest against creditors of the transferees from the original debtor.

(3) The filing of a financing statement otherwise required by this Article is not necessary or effective to perfect a security interest in property subject to

(a) a statute or treaty of the United States which provides for a national or international registration or a national or international certificate of title or which specifies a place of filing different from that specified in this Article for filing of the security interest; or

(b) the following statutes of this state: [list any certificate of title statute covering automobiles, trailers, mobile homes, boats, farm tractors, or the like, and any central filing statute.*]; but during any period in which collateral is inventory held for sale by a person who is in the business of selling goods of that kind, the filing provisions of this Article (Part 4) apply to a security interest in that collateral created by him as debtor; or

(c) a certificate of title statute of another jurisdiction under the law of which indication of a security interest on the certificate is required as a condition of

perfection (subsection (2) of Section 9-103).

(4) Compliance with a statute or treaty described in subsection (3) is equivalent to the filing of a financing statement under this Article, and a security interest in property subject to the statute or treaty can be perfected only by compliance therewith except as provided in Section 9-103 on multiple state transactions. Duration and renewal of perfection of a security interest perfected by compliance with the statute or treaty are governed by the provisions of the statute or treaty; in other respects the security interest is subject to this Article.

*Note: *It is recommended that the provisions of certificate of title acts for perfection of security interests by notation on the certificates should be amended to exclude coverage of inventory held for sale.*

Section 9-303. When Security Interest Is Perfected: Continuity of Perfection

(1) A security interest is perfected when it has attached and when all of the applicable steps required for perfection have been taken. Such steps are specified in Sections 9-302, 9-304, 9-305 and 9-306. If such steps are taken before the security interest attaches, it is perfected at the time when it attaches.

(2) If a security interest is originally perfected in any way permitted under this Article and is subsequently perfected in some other way under this Article, without an intermediate period when it was unperfected, the security interest shall be deemed to be perfected continuously for the purposes of this Article.

Section 9-304. Perfection of Security Interest in Instruments, Documents, and Goods Covered by Documents; Perfection by Permissive Filing; Temporary Perfection Without Filing or Transfer of Possession.

(1) A security interest in chattel paper or negotiable documents may be perfected by filing. A security interest in money or instruments (other than certificated securities or instruments

which constitute part of chattel paper) can be perfected only by the secured party's taking possession, except as provided in subsections (4) and (5) of this section and subsections (2) and (3) of Section 9-306 on proceeds.

(2) During the period that goods are in the possession of the issuer of a negotiable document therefor, a security interest in the goods is perfected by perfecting a security interest in the document, and any security interest in the goods otherwise perfected during such period is subject thereto.

(3) A security interest in goods in the possession of a bailee other than one who has issued a negotiable document therefor is perfected by issuance of a document in the name of the secured party or by the bailee's receipt of notification of the secured party's interest or by filing as to the goods.

(4) A security interest in instruments (other than certificated securities) or negotiable documents is perfected without filing or the taking of possession for a period of 21 days from the time it attaches to the extent that it arises from new value given under a written security agreement.

(5) A security interest remains perfected for a period of 21 days without filing where a secured party having a perfected security interest in an instrument (other than a certificated security), a negotiable document or goods in possession of a bailee other than one who has issued a negotiable document therefor

   (a) makes available to the debtor the goods or documents representing the goods for the purpose of ultimate sale or exchange or for the purpose of loading, unloading, storing, shipping, transshipping, manufacturing, processing or otherwise dealing with them in a manner preliminary to their sale or exchange, but priority between conflicting security interests in the goods is subject to subsection (3) of Section 9-312; or

   (b) delivers the instrument to the debtor for the purpose of ultimate sale or exchange or of presentation, collection, renewal or registration of transfer.

(6) After the 21-day period in subsections (4) and (5) perfection depends upon compliance with applicable provisions of this Article.

Section 9-305. When Possession by Secured Party Perfects Security Interest Without Filing.

A security interest in letters of credit and advices of credit (subsection (2) (a) of Section 5-116), goods, instruments (other than certificated securities), money, negotiable documents, or chattel paper may be perfected by the secured party's taking possession of the collateral. If such collateral other than goods covered by a negotiable document is held by a bailee, the secured party is deemed to have possession from the time the bailee receives notification of the secured party's interest. A security interest is perfected by possession from the time possession is taken without a relation back and continues only so long as possession is retained, unless otherwise specified in this Article. The security interest may be otherwise perfected as provided in this Article before or after the period of possession by the secured party.

Section 9-306. "Proceeds"; Secured Party's Rights on Disposition of Collateral.

(1) "Proceeds" includes whatever is received upon the sale, exchange, color other disposition of collateral or proceeds. Insurance payable by reason of loss or damage to the collateral is proceeds, except to the extent that it is payable to a person other than a party to the security agreement. Money, checks, deposit accounts, and the like are "cash proceeds." All other proceeds are "non-cash" proceeds."

(2) Except where this Article otherwise provides, a security interest continues in collateral notwithstanding sale, exchange or other disposition thereof unless the disposition was authorized by the secured party in the security agreement or otherwise, and also continues in any identifiable proceeds including collections received by the debtor.

(3) The security interest in proceeds is a continuously perfected security interest if the inter-

est in the original collateral was perfected but it ceases to be a perfected security interest and becomes unperfected ten days after receipt of the proceeds by the debtor unless

(a) a filed financing statement covers the original collateral and the proceeds are collateral in which a security interest may be perfected by filing in the office or offices where the financing statement has been filed and, if the proceeds are acquired with cash proceeds, the description of collateral in the financing statement indicates the types of property constituting the proceeds; or

(b) a filed financing statement covers the original collateral and the proceeds are identifiable cash proceeds; or

(c) the security interest in the proceeds is perfected before the expiration of the ten-day period.

Except as provided in this section, a security interest in proceeds can be perfected only by the methods or under the circumstances permitted in this Article for original collateral of the same type.

(4) In the event of insolvency proceedings instituted by or against a debtor, a secured party with a perfected security interest in proceeds has a perfected security interest only in the following proceeds:

(a) in identifiable non-cash proceeds and in separate deposit accounts containing only proceeds;

(b) in identifiable cash proceeds in the form of money which is neither commingled with other money nor deposited in a deposit account prior to the insolvency proceedings;

(c) in identifiable cash proceeds in the form of checks and the like which are not deposited in a deposit account prior to the insolvency proceedings; and

(d) in all cash and deposit accounts of the debtor in which proceeds have been commingled with other funds, but the perfected security interest under this paragraph (d) is

(i) subject to any right to setoff; and

(ii) limited to an amount not greater than the amount of any cash proceeds received by the debtor within ten days before the institution of the insolvency proceedings less than sum of (I) the payments to the secured party on account of cash proceeds received by the debtor during such period and (II) the cash proceeds received by the debtor during such period to which the secured party is entitled under paragraphs (a) through (c) of this subsection (4).

(5) If a sale of goods results in an account or chattel paper which is transferred by the seller to a secured party, and if the goods are returned to or are repossessed by the seller or the secured party, the following rules determine priorities:

(a) If the goods were collateral at the time of sale, for an indebtedness of the seller which is still unpaid, the original security interest attaches again to the goods and continues as a perfected security interest if it was perfected at the time when the goods were sold. If the security interest was originally perfected by a filing which is still effective, nothing further is required to continue the perfected status; in any other case, the secured party must take possession of the returned or repossessed goods-or must file.

(b) An unpaid transferee of the chattel paper has a security interest in the goods against the transferor. Such security interest is prior to a security interest asserted under paragraph (a) to the extent that the transferee of the chattel paper was entitled to priority under Section 9-308.

(c) An unpaid transferee of the account has a security interest in the goods against the transferor. Such security interest is subordinate to a security interest asserted under paragraph (a).

(d) A security interest of an unpaid transferee asserted under paragraph (b) or (c) must be perfected for protection against creditors of the transferor and purchasers of the returned or repossessed goods.

Section 9-307. Protection of Buyers of Goods.

(1) A buyer in ordinary course of business (subsection (9) of Section 1-201) other than a person buying farm products from a person engaged in farming operations takes free of a security interest created by his seller even though the security interest is perfected and even though the buyer knows of its existence.
(2) In the case of consumer goods, a buyer takes free of a security interest even though perfected if he buys without knowledge of the security interest, for value and for his own personal, family or household purposes unless prior to the purchase the secured party has filed a financing statement covering such goods.
(3) A buyer other than a buyer in ordinary course of business (subsection (1) of this section) takes free of a security interest to the extent that it secures future advances made after the secured party acquires knowledge of the purchase, or more than 45 days after the purchase, whichever first occurs, unless made pursuant to a commitment entered into without knowledge of the purchase and before the expiration of the 45-day period.

Section 9-308. Purchase of Chattel Paper and Instruments.

A purchaser of chattel paper or an instrument who gives new value and takes possession of it in the ordinary course of his business has priority over a security interest in the chattel paper or instrument

(a) which is perfected under Section 9-304 (permissive filing and temporary perfection) or under Section 9-306 (perfection as to proceeds) if he acts without knowledge that the specific paper or instrument is subject to a security interest; or

(b) which is claimed merely as proceeds of inventory subject to a security interest (Section 9-306) even though he knows that the specific paper or instrument is subject to the security interest.

Section 9-309. Protection of Purchasers of Instruments, Documents and Securities.

Nothing in this Article limits the rights of a holder in due course of a negotiable instrument (Section 3-302) or a holder to whom a negotiable document of title has been duly negotiated (Section 7-501) or a bona fide purchaser of a security (Section 8-302) and the holders or purchasers take priority over an earlier security interest even though perfected. Filing under this Article does not constitute notice of the security interest to such holders or purchasers.

Section 9-310. Priority of Certain Liens Arising by Operation of Law.

When a person in the ordinary course of his business furnishes services or materials with respect to goods subject to a security interest, a lien upon goods in the possession of such person given by statute or rule of law for such materials or services takes priority over a perfected security interest unless the lien is statutory and the statute expressly provides otherwise.

Section 9-311. Alienability of Debtor's Rights: Judicial Process.

The debtor's rights in collateral may be voluntarily or involuntarily transferred (by way of sale, creation of a security interest, attachment, levy, garnishment or other judicial process) notwithstanding a provision in the security agreement prohibiting any transfer or making the transfer constitute a default.

Section 9-312. Priorities Among Conflicting Security Interests in the Same Collateral.

(1) The rules of priority stated in other sections of this Part and in the following sections shall govern when applicable: Section 4-208 with respect to the security interests of collecting banks in items being collected, accompanying documents and proceeds; Section 9-103 on security interests related to other jurisdictions; Section 9-114 on consignments.

(2) A perfected security interest in crops for new value given to enable the debtor to produce the crops during the production season and given not more than three months before the crops become growing crops by planting or otherwise takes priority over an earlier perfected security interest to the extent that such earlier interest secures obligations due more than six months before the crops become growing crops by planting or otherwise, even though the person giving new value had knowledge of the earlier security interest.

(3) A perfected purchase money security interest in inventory has priority over a conflicting security interest in the same inventory and also has priority in identifiable cash proceeds received on or before the delivery of the inventory to a buyer if

  (a) the purchase money security interest is perfected at the time the debtor receives possession of the inventory; and

  (b) the purchase money secured party gives notification in writing to the holder of the conflicting security interest if the holder had filed a financing statement covering the same types of inventory (i) before the date of the filing made by the purchase money secured party, or (ii) before the beginning of the 21-day period where the purchase money security interest is temporarily perfected without filing or possession (subsection (5) of Section 9-304); and

  (c) the holder of the conflicting security inter-est receives the notification within five years before the debtor receives possession of the inventory; and

  (d) the notification states that the person giving the notice has or expects to acquire a purchase money security interest in inventory of the debtor, describing such inventory by item or type.

(4) A purchase money security interest in collateral other than inventory has priority over a conflicting security interest in the same collateral or its proceeds if the purchase money security interest is perfected at the time the debtor receives possession of the collateral or within ten days thereafter.

(5) In all cases not governed by other rules stated in this section (including cases of purchase money security interests which do not qualify for the special priorities set forth in subsections (3) and (4) of this section), priority between conflicting security interests in the same col-lateral shall be determined according to the following rules:

  (a) Conflicting security interests rank according to priority in time of filing or per-fection. Priority dates from the time a filing is first made covering the collateral or the time the security inter-est is first perfected, whichever is earlier, provided that there is no period thereafter when there is neither filing nor perfection.

  (b) So long as conflicting security interests are unperfected, the first to attach has priority.

(6) For the purposes of subsection (5) a date of filing or perfection as to collateral is also a date of filing or perfection as to proceeds.

(7) If future advances are made while a security interest is perfected by filing, the taking of possession, or under Section 8-321 on securities, the security interest has the same priority for the purposes of subsection (5) with respect to the future advances as it does with respect to the first advance. If a commitment is made

before or while the security interest is so perfected, the security interest has the same priority with respect to advances made pursuant thereto. In other cases a perfected security interest has priority from the date the advance is made.

Section 9-313. Priority of Security Interests in Fixtures.

(1) In this section and in the provisions of Part 4 of this Article referring to fixture filing, unless the context otherwise requires

(a) goods are "fixtures" when they become so related to particular real estate that an interest in them arises under real estate law.

(b) a "fixture filing" is the filing in the office where a mortgage on the real estate would be filed or recorded of a financing statement covering goods which are or are to become fixtures and conforming to the requirements of subsection (5) of Section 9-402.

(c) a mortgage is a "construction mortgage" to the extent that it secures an obligation incurred for the construction of an improvement on land including the acquisition cost of the land, if the recorded writing so indicates.

(2) A security interest under this Article may be created in goods which are fixtures or may continue in goods which become fixtures, but no security interest exists under this Article in ordinary building materials incorporated into an improvement on land.

(3) This Article does not prevent creation of an encumbrance upon fixtures pursuant to real estate law.

(4) A perfected security interest in fixtures has priority over the conflicting interest of an encumbrancer or owner of the real estate where

(a) the security interest is a purchase money security interest, the interest of the encumbrancer or owner arises before the goods become fixtures, the

security interest is perfected by a fixture filing before the goods become fixtures or within ten days thereafter, and the debtor has an interest of record in the real estate or is in possession of the real estate; or

(b) the security interest is perfected by a fixture filing before the interest of the encumbrancer or owner is of record, the security interest has priority over any conflicting interest of a predecessor in title of the encumbrancer of owner, and the debtor has an interest of record in the real estate or is in possession of the real estate; or

(c) the fixtures are readily removable factory or office machines or readily removable replacements of domestic appliances which are consumer goods, and before the goods become fixtures the security interest is perfected by any method permitted by this Article; or

(d) the conflicting interest is a lien on the real estate obtained by legal or equitable proceedings after the security interest was perfected by any method permitted by this Article.

(5) A security interest in fixtures, whether or not perfected, has priority over the conflicting interest of an encumbrancer or owner of the real estate where

(a) the encumbrancer or owner has consented in writing to the security interest or has disclaimed an interest in the goods as fixtures; or

(b) the debtor has a right to remove the goods as against the encumbrancer or owner. If the debtor's right terminates, the priority of the security interest continues for a reasonable time.

(6) Notwithstanding paragraph (a) of subsection (4) but otherwise subject to subsections (4) and (5), a security interest in fixtures is subordinate to a construction mortgage recorded before the goods become fixtures if the goods become fixtures before the completion of the

construction. To (the) extent that it is given to refinance a construction mortgage, a mortgage has this priority to the same extent as the construction mortgage.

(7) In cases not within the preceding subsections, a security interest in fixtures is subordinate to the conflicting interest of an encumbrancer or owner of the related real estate who is not the debtor.

(8) When the secured party has priority over all owners and encumbrances of the real estate, he may, on default, subject to the provisions of Part 5, remove his collateral from the real estate but he must reimburse any encumbrancer or owner of the real estate who is not the debtor and who has not otherwise agreed for the cost of repair of any physical injury, but not for any diminution in value of the real estate caused by the absence of the goods removed or by any necessity of replacing them. A person entitled to reimbursement may refuse permission to remove until the secured party gives adequate security for the performance of this obligation.

Section 9-314. Accessions.

(1) A security interest in goods which attaches be-fore they are installed in or affixed to other goods takes priority as to the goods installed or affixed (called in this section "accessions") over the claims of all persons to the whole except as stated in subsection (3) and subject to Section 9-315(1).

(2) A security interest which attaches to goods after they become part of a whole is valid against all persons subsequently acquiring interests in the whole except as stated in subsection (3) but is invalid against any person with an interest in the whole at the time the security interest attaches to the goods who has not in writing consented to the security interest or disclaimed an interest in the goods as part of the whole.

(3) The security interests described in subsection (1) and (2) do not take priority over

(a) a subsequent purchaser for value of any interest in the whole; or

(b) a creditor with a lien on the whole subsequently obtained by judicial proceedings; or

(c) a creditor with a prior perfected security interest in the whole to the extent that he makes subsequent advances if the subsequent purchase is made, the lien by judicial proceedings obtained or the subsequent advance under the prior perfected security interest is made or contracted for without knowledge of the security interest and before it is perfected. A purchaser of the whole at a foreclosure sale other than the holder of a perfected security interest purchasing at his own foreclosure sale is a subsequent purchaser within this section.

(4) When under subsections (1) and (2) and (3) a secured party has an interest in accessions which has priority over the claims of all persons who have interests in the whole, he may on default subject to the provisions of Part 5 remove his collateral from the whole but he must reimburse any encumbrancer or owner of the whole who is not the debtor and who has not otherwise agreed for the cost of repair of any physical injury but not for any diminution in value of the whole caused by the absence of the goods removed or by any necessity for replacing them. A per-son entitled to reim-bursement may refuse per-mission to remove until the secured party gives adequate security for the performance of this obligation.

Section 9-315. Priority When Goods Are Commingled or Processed.

(1) If a security interest in goods was perfected and subsequently the goods or a part thereof have become part of a product or mass, the security interest continues in the product or mass if

(a) the goods are so manufactured, processed, assembled or commingled that their identity is lost in the product or mass; or

(b) a financing statement covering the original goods also covers the product into which the goods have been manufactured, processed or assembled.

In a case to which paragraph (b) applies, no separate security interest in that part of the original goods which have been manufactured, processed or assembled into the product may be claimed under Section 9-314.

(2) When under subsection (1) more than one security interest attaches to the product or mass, they rank equally according to the ratio that the cost of the goods to which each interest originally attached bears to the cost of the total product or mass.

Section 9-316. Priority Subject to Subordination.

Nothing in this Article prevents subordination by agreement by any person entitled to priority.

Section 9-317. Secured Party Not Obligated on Contract of Debtor.

The mere existence of a security interest or authority given to the debtor to dispose of or use collateral does not impose contract or tort liability upon the secured part for the debtor's acts or omissions.

Section 9-318. Defenses Against Assignee; Modification of Contract After Notification of Assignment; Term Prohibiting Assignment Ineffective; Identification and Proof of Assignment.

(1) Unless an account debtor has made an enforceable agreement not to assert defenses or claims arising out of a sale as provided in Section 9-206 the rights of an assignee are subject to

(a) all the terms of the contract between the account debtor and assignor and any defense or claim arising therefrom; and

(b) any other defense or claim of the account debtor against the assignor which accrues before the account debtor receives notification of the assignment.

(2) So far as the right to payment or a part thereof under an assigned contract has not been fully earned by performance, and notwithstanding notification of the assignment, any modification of or substitution for the contract made in good faith and in accordance with reasonable commercial standards is effective against an assignee unless the account debtor has otherwise agreed but the assignee acquires corresponding rights under the modified or substituted contract. The assignment may provide that such modification or substitution is a breach by the assignor.

(3) The account debtor is authorized to pay the assignor until the account debtor receives notification that the amount due or to become due has been assigned and that payment is to be made to the assignee. A notification which does not reasonably identify the rights assigned is ineffective. If requested by the account debtor, the assignee must seasonably furnish reasonable proof that the assignment has been made and unless he does so the account debtor may pay the assignor.

(4) A term in any contract between an account debtor and an assignor is ineffective if it prohibits assignment of an account or prohibits creation of a security interest in a general intangible for money due or to become due or requires the account debtor's consent to such assignment or security interest.

Part 4. Filing.

Section 9-401. Place of Filing; Erroneous Filing; Removal of Collateral.

First Alternative Subsection (1)

(1) The proper place to file in order to perfect a security interest is as follows:

(a) when the collateral is timber to be cut or is minerals or the like (including oil and gas) or accounts subject to subsection (5) of Section 9-103, or when the financing statement is filed as a fixture filing (Section 9-313) and the collateral is goods which are or are to become fixtures, then in the office where a mortgage on the real estate would be filed or recorded;

(b) in all other cases, in the office of the [Secretary of State].

Second Alternative Subsection (l)

(1) The proper place to file in order to perfect a security interest is as follows:

(a) when the collateral is equipment used in farming operations, or farm products, or accounts or general intangibles arising from or relating to the sale of farm products by a farmer, or consumer goods, then in the office of the ____ in the county of the debtor's residence or if the debtor is not a resident of this state then in the office of the ____ in the county where the goods are kept, and in addition when the collateral is crops growing or to be grown in the office of the ____ in the county where the land is located;

(b) when the collateral is timber to be cut or is minerals or the like (including oil and gas) or accounts subject to subsection (5) of Section 9-103, or when the financing statement is filed as a fixture filing (Section 9-313) and the collateral is goods which are or are to become fixtures, then in the office where a mortgage on the real estate would be filed or recorded;

(c) in all other cases, in the office of the [Secretary of State].

Third Alternative Subsection (l)

(1) The proper place to file in order to perfect a security interest is as follows:

(a) when the collateral is equipment used in farming operations, or farm products, or accounts or general intangibles arising from or relating to the sale of farm products by a farmer, or consumer goods, then in the office of the _____ in the county of the debtor's residence or if the debtor is not a resident of this state then in the office of the _____ in the county where the goods are kept, and in addition when the collateral is crops growing or to be grown in the office of the ____ in the county where the land is located;

(b) when the collateral is timber to be cut or is minerals or the like (including oil and gas) or accounts subject to subsection (5) of Section 9-103, or when the financing statement is filed as a fixture filing (Section 9-313) and the collateral is goods which are or are to become fixtures, then in the office where a mortgage on the real estate would be filed or recorded:

(c) in all other cases, in the office of the [Secretary of State] and in addition, if the debtor has a place of business in only one county of this state, also in the office of ____ of such county, or, if the debtor has no place of business in this state, but resides in the state, also in the office of _____ of the county in which he resides.

Note: *One of the three alternatives should be selected as subsection (1).*

(2) A filing which is made in good faith in an improper place or not in all of the places required by this section is nevertheless effective with regard to any collateral as to which the filing complied with the requirements of this Article and is also effective with regard to collateral covered by the financing statement against any person who has knowledge of the contents of such financing statement.

(3) A filing which is made in the proper place in this state continues effective even though the debtor's residence or place of business or

the location of the collateral or its use, which-ever controlled the original filing, is thereafter changed.

Alternative Subsection (3)

(3) A filing which is made in the proper coun-ty continues effective for four months after a change to another county of the debtor's resi-dence or place of business or the location of the collateral, whichever controlled the origi-nal filing. It becomes ineffective thereafter unless a copy of the financing statement signed by the secured party is filed in the new county within said period. The security interest may also be perfected in the new county after the expiration of the four-month period; in such case perfection dates from the time of perfection in the new county. A change in the use of the collateral does not impair the effec-tiveness of the original filing.]
(4) The rules stated in Section 9-103 determine whether filing is necessary in this state.
(5) Notwithstanding the preceding subsections, and subject to subsection (3) of Section 9-302, the proper place to file in order to perfect a se-curity interest in collateral, including
fixtures, of a transmitting utility is the office of the [Secretary of State]. This filing constitutes a fixture filing (Section 9-313) as to the collateral described therein which is or is to become fix-tures.
(6) For the purposes of this section, the resi-dence of an organization is its place of busi-ness if it has one or its chief executive office if it has more than one place of business.

Note: *Subsection (6) should be used only if the state chooses the Second or Third Alterna-tive Subsection (1).*

Section 9-402. Formal Requisites of Financing Statement; Amendments; Mortgage as Financ-ing Statement.

(1) A financing statement is sufficient if it gives the names of the debtor and the secured party, is signed by the debtor, gives an address of the secured party from which information concern-ing the security interest may be obtained, gives a mailing address of the debtor and contains a statement indicating the types, or describing the items, of collateral. A financing statement may be filed before a security agreement is made or a security interest otherwise attaches. When the financing statement covers crops growing or to be grown, the statement must also contain a description of the real estate concerned. When the financing statement covers timber to be cut or covers minerals or the like (including oil and gas) or accounts subject to subsection (5) of Section 9-103, or when the financing statement is filed as a fixture filing (Section 9-313) and the collateral is goods which are or are to become fixtures, the statement must also comply with subsec-tion (5). A copy of the security agreement is sufficient as a financing statement if it contains the above information and is signed by the debtor. A carbon, photographic or other repro-duction of a security agreement or a financing statement is sufficient as a financing statement if the security agreement so provides or if the original has been filed in this state.
(2) A financing statement which otherwise complies with subsection (1) is sufficient when it is signed by the secured party instead of the debtor if it is filed to perfect a security interest in

(a) collateral already subject to a security interest in another jurisdiction when it is brought into this state, or when the debtor's location is changed to this state. Such a financing statement must state that the collateral was brought into his state or that the debtor's loca-tion was changed to this state under such circumstances; or

(b) proceeds under Section 9-306 if the security interest in the original collat-eral was perfected. Such a financing statement must describe the original collateral; or

(c) collateral as to which the filing has lapsed; or

(d) collateral acquired after a change of name, identity or corporate structure of the debtor (subsection (7)).

(3) A form substantially as follows is sufficient to comply with subsection (1):

Name of debtor (or assignor)

Address

Name of secured party (or assignee)

Address

1. This financing statement covers the following types (or type) of property:
(Describe)
2. (If collateral is crops) The above described crops are growing or are to be grown on:
(Describe Real Estate)
3. (If applicable) The above goods are to become fixtures on*
(Describe Real Estate) and this financing statement is to be filed [for record] in the real estate records. (If the debtor does not have an interest of record) The name of a record owner is

Where appropriate substitute either "The above timber is standing on . . .." or "The above minerals or the like (including oil and gas) or accounts will be financed at the wellhead or minehead of the well or mine located on...."

4. (If products of collateral are claimed) Products of the collateral are also covered.

(use whichever is applicable) Signature of Debtor (or Assignor) Signature of Secured Party (or Assignee)

(4) A financing statement may be amended by filing a writing signed by both the debtor and the secured party. An amendment does not extend the period of effectiveness of a financing statement. If any amendment adds collateral, it is effective as to the added collateral only from the filing date of the amendment. In this Article, unless the context otherwise requires, the term "financing statement" means the original financing statement and any amendments.

(5) A financing statement covering timber to be cut or covering minerals or the like (including oil and gas) or accounts subject to subsection (5) of Section 9-103, or a financing statement filed as a fixture filing (Section 9313) where the debtor is not a transmitting utility, must show that it covers this type of collateral, must recite that it is to be filed [for record] in the real estate records, and the financing statement must contain a description of the real estate [sufficient if it were contained in a mortgage of the real estate to give constructive notice of the mortgage under the law of this state]. If the debtor does not have an interest of record in the real estate, the financing statement must show the name of a record owner.
(6) A mortgage is effective as a financing statement filed as a fixture filing from the date of its recording if

(a) the goods are described in the mortgage by item or type; and
(b) the goods are or are to become fixtures related to the real estate described in the mortgage; and
(c) the mortgage complies with the requirements for a financing statement in this section other than a recital that it is to be filed in the real estate records; and
(d) the mortgage is duly recorded.

No fee with reference to the financing statement is required other than the regular recording and satisfaction fees with respect to the mortgage.

(7) A financing statement sufficiently shows the name of the debtor if it gives the individual, partnership or corporate name of the debtor, whether or not it adds other trade names or names of partners. Where the debtor so changes his name or in the case of an organization its name, identity or corporate structure that a filed financing statement becomes seriously misleading, the filing is not effective to perfect a security interest in collateral acquired by the debtor more than four months after the change, unless a new appropriate financing statement is filed before the expiration of that

time. A filed financing statement remains effective with respect to collateral transferred by the debtor even though the secured party knows of or consents to the transfer.

(8) A financing statement substantially complying with the requirements of this section is effective even though it contains minor errors which are not seriously misleading.

Note: *Language in brackets is optional.*

Note: *Where the state has any special recording system for real estate other than the usual grantor-grantee index (as, for instance, a tract system or a title registration or Torrens system) local adaptations of subsection (5) and Section 9-403(7) may be necessary. See Mass. Gen. Laws Chapter 106, Section 9-409.*

Section 9-403. What Constitutes Filing; Duration of Filing; Effect of Lapsed Filing; Duties of Filing Officer.

(1) Presentation for filing of a financing statement and tender of the filing fee or acceptance of the statement by the filing officer constitutes filing under this Article.

(2) Except as provided in subsection (6) a filed financing statement is effective for a period of five years from the date of filing. The effectiveness of a filed financing statement lapses on the expiration of the five-year period unless a continuation statement is filed prior to the lapse. If a security interest perfected by filing exists at the time insolvency proceedings are commenced by or against the debtor, the security interest remains perfected until termination of the insolvency proceedings and thereafter for a period of sixty days or until expiration of the five-year period, whichever occurs later. Upon lapse the security interest becomes unperfected, unless it is perfected without filing. If the security interest becomes unperfected upon lapse, it is deemed to have been unperfected as against a person who became a purchaser or lien creditor before lapse.

(3) A continuation statement may be filed by the secured party within six months prior to the expiration of the five-year period specified in subsection (2). Any such continuation state-

ment must be signed by the secured party, identify the original statement by file number and state that the original statement is still effective. A continuation statement signed by a person other than the secured party of record must be accompanied by a separate written statement of assignment signed by the secured party of record and complying with subsection (2) of Section 9-105, including payment of the required fee. Upon timely filing of the continuation statement, the effectiveness of the original statement is continued for five years after the last date to which the filing was effective whereupon it lapses in the same manner as provided in subsection (2) unless another continuation statement is filed prior to such lapse. Succeeding continuation statements may be filed in the same manner to continue the effectiveness of the original statement. Unless a statute on disposition of public records provides otherwise, the filing officer may remove a lapsed statement from the files and destroy it immediately if he has retained a microfilm or other photographic record, or in other cases after one year after the lapse. The filing officer shall so arrange matters by physical annexation of financing statements to continuation statements or other related filings, or by other means, that if he physically destroys the financing statements of a period more than five years past, those which have been continued by a continuation statement or which are still effective under subsection (6) shall be retained.

(4) Except as provided in subsection (7) a filing officer shall mark each statement with a file number and with the date and hour of filing and shall hold the statement or a microfilm or other photographic copy thereof for public inspection. In addition the filing officer shall index the statement according to the name of the debtor and shall note in the index the file number and the address of the debtor given in the statement.

(5) The uniform fee for filing and indexing and for stamping a copy furnished by the secured party to show the date and place of filing for an original financing statement or for a continuation statement shall be $_____ if the statement is in the standard form prescribed by the [Secretary of State] and otherwise shall be

$_____$, plus in each case, if the financing statement is subject to subsection (5) of Section 9-402, $\_\_\_\_\_$. The uniform fee for each name more than one required to be indexed shall be $\_\_\_\_\_$. The secured party may at his option show a trade name for any person and an extra uniform indexing fee of $\_\_\_\_\_$ shall be paid with respect thereto.

(6) If the debtor is a transmitting utility (subsection (5) of Section 9-401) and a filed financing statement 80 states, it is effective until a termination statement is filed. A real estate mortgage which is effective as a fixture filing under subsection (6) of Section 9-402 remains effective as a fixture filing until the mortgage is released or satisfied of record or its effectiveness otherwise terminates as to the real estate.

(7) When a financing statement covers timber to be cut or covers minerals or the like (including oil and gas) or accounts subject to subsection (5) of Section 9-103, or is filed as a fixture filing, [it shall be filed for record and] the filing officer shall index it under the names of the debtor and any owner of record shown on the financing statement in the same fashion as if they were the mortgagors in a mortgage of the real estate described, and, to the extent that the law of this state provides for the indexing of mortgages under the name of the mortgagee, under the name of the secured party as if he were the mortgagee thereunder, or where indexing is by description in the same fashion as if the financing statement were a mortgage of the real estate described.

Note: *In states in which writings will not appear in the real estate records and indices unless actually recorded the bracketed language in subsection (7) should be used.*

Section 9-404. Termination Statement.

(1) If a financing statement covering consumer goods is filed on or after, then within one month or within ten days following written demand by the debtor after there is no outstanding secured obligation and no commitment to make advances, incur obligations or otherwise give value, the secured party must file with each filing officer with whom the financing statement was filed, a termination statement to the effect that he no longer claims a security interest under the financing statement, which shall be identified by file number. In other cases whenever there is no outstanding secured obligation and no commitment to make advances, incur obligations or otherwise give value, the secured party must on written demand by the debtor send the debtor, for each filing officer with whom the financing statement was filed, a termination statement to the effect that he no longer claims a security interest under the financing statement, which shall be identified by file number. A termination statement signed by a person other than the secured party of record must be accompanied by a separate written statement of assignment signed by the secured party of record complying with subsection (2) of Section 9 105, including payment of the required fee. If the affected secured party fails to file such a termination statement as required by this subsection, or to send such a termination statement within ten days after proper demand therefor, he shall be liable to the debtor for one hundred dollars, and in addition for any loss caused to the debtor by such failure.

(2) On presentation to the filing officer of such a termination statement he must note it in the index. If he has received the termination statement in duplicate, he shall return one copy of the termination statement to the secured party stamped to show the time of receipt thereof. If the filing officer has a microfilm or other photographic record of the financing statement, and of any related continuation statement, statement of assignment and statement of release, he may remove the originals from the files at anytime after receipt of the termination statement, or if he has no such record, he may remove them from the files at any time after one year after receipt of the termination statement.

(3) If the termination statement is in the standard form prescribed by the [Secretary of State], the uniform fee for filing and indexing the termination statement shall be $\_\_\_\_\_$ and otherwise shall be $\_\_\_\_\_$, plus in each case an additional fee of $\_\_\_\_\_$ for each name

more than one against which the termination statement is required to be indexed.

Note: *The date to be inserted should be the effective date of the revised Article 9.*

Section 9-405. Assignment of Security Interest; Duties of Filing Officer; Fees.

(1) A financing statement may disclose an assignment of a security interest in the collateral described in the financing statement by indication in the financing statement of the name and address of the assignee or by an assignment itself or a copy thereof on the face or back of the statement. On presentation to the filing officer of such a financing statement the filing officer shall mark the same as provided in Section 9-403(4). The uniform fee for filing, indexing and furnishing filing date for a financing statement so indicating as assignment shall be $_____ if the statement is in the standard form prescribed by the [Secretary of State] and otherwise shall be $_____, plus in each case an additional fee of $_____ for each name more than one against which the financing statement is required to be indexed.

(2) A secured party may assign of record all or part of his rights under a financing statement by the filing in the place where the original financing statement was filed of a separate written statement of assignment signed by the secured party of record and setting forth the name of the secured party of record and the debtor, the file number and the date of filing of the financing statement and the name and address of the assignee and containing a description of the collateral as copy of the assignment is sufficient as a separate statement if it complies with the preceding sentence. On presentation to the filing officer of such a separate statement, the filing officer shall mark such separate statement with the date and hour of the filing. He shall note the assignment on the index of the financing statement, or in the case of a fixture filing, or a filing covering timber to be cut, or covering minerals or the like (including oil and gas) or accounts subject to subsection (5) of Section 9-103, he shall index the assignment under the name of the assignor as

grantor and, to the extent that the law of this state provides for indexing the assignment of a mortgage under the name of the assignee, he shall index the assignment of the financing statement under the name of the assignee. The uniform fee for filing, indexing and furnishing filing data about such a separate statement of assignment shall be $_____ if the statement is in the standard form prescribed by the [Secretary of State] and otherwise shall be $_____, plus in each case an additional fee of $_____ for each name more than one against which the statement of assignment is required to be indexed. Notwithstanding the provisions of this subsection, an assignment of record of a security interest in a fixture contained in a mortgage effective as a fixture filing (subsection (6) of Section 9-402) may be made only by an assignment of the mortgage in the manner provided by the law of this state other than this Act.

(3) After the disclosure or filing of an assignment under this section, the assignee is the secured party of record.

Section 9-406. Release of Collateral; Duties of Filing Officer; Fees.

A secured party of record may by his signed statement release all or a part of any collateral described in a filed financing statement. The statement of release is sufficient if it contains a description of the collateral being released, the name and address of the debtor, the name and address of the secured party, and the file number of the financing statement. A statement of release signed by a person other than the secured party of record must be accompanied by a separate written statement of assignment signed by the secured party of record and complying with subsection (2) of Section 9-405, including payment of the required fee. Upon presentation of such a statement of release to the filing officer he shall mark the statement with the hour and date of filing and shall note the same upon the margin of the index of the filing of the financing statement. The uniform fee for filing and noting such a statement of release shall be $..if the statement is in the standard form prescribed by the [Sec-

retary of State] and otherwise shall be $____,
plus in each case an additional fee of $____
for each name more than one against which
the statement of release is required to be indexed.

Section 9-407. Information From Filing Officer.

(1) If the person filing any financing statement,
termination statement, statement of assignment, or statement of release, furnishes the
filing officer a copy thereof, the filing officer
shall upon request note upon the copy the file
number and date and hour of the filing of the
original and deliver or send the copy to such
person.

(2) Upon request of any person, the filing officer shall issue his certificate showing whether
there is on file on the date and hour stated
therein, any presently effective financing statement naming a particular debtor and any statement of assignment thereof and if there is,
giving the date and hour of filing of each such
statement and the names and addresses of
each secured party therein. The uniform fee for
such a certificate shall be $____ if the request
for the certificates in the standard form prescribed by the Secretary of State] and otherwise shall be $____ Upon request the filing
officer shall furnish a copy of any filed financing statement or statement of assignment for a
uniform fee of $____ per page.

Note: *This section is proposed as an optional
provision to require filing officers to furnish
certificates. Local law and practices should be
consulted with regard to the advisability of
adoption.*

Section 9-408. Financing Statements Covering Consigned or Leased Goods.

A consignor or lessor of goods may file a financing statement using the terms "consignor,"
"consignee," "lessor," "lessee" or the like instead of the terms specified in Section 9-402.
The provisions of this Part shall apply as
appropriate to such a financing statement but
its filing shall not of itself be a factor in deter-

mining whether or not the consignment or
lease is intended as security (Section 1-
201(37)). However, if it is determined for other
reasons that the consignment or lease is so
intended, a security interest of the consignor
or lessor which attaches to the consigned or
leased goods is perfected by such filing.

Part 5. Default.

Section 9-501. Default; Procedure When Security Agreement Covers Both Real and Personal Property.

(1) When a debtor is in default under a security agreement, a secured party has the rights
and remedies provided in this Part and except
as limited by subsection (3) those provided in
the security agreement. He may reduce his
claim to judgment, foreclose or otherwise
enforce the security interest by an available
judicial procedure. If the collateral is documents the secured party may proceed either as
to the documents or as to the goods covered
thereby.

A secured party in possession has the rights,
remedies and duties provided in Section
9-207. The rights and remedies referred to in
this subsection are cumulative.

(2) After default, the debtor has the rights and
remedies provided in this Part, those provided
in the security agreement and those provided
in Section 9-207.

(3) To the extent that they give rights to the
debtor and impose duties on the secured
party, the rules stated in the subsections referred to below may not be waived or varied
except as provided with respect to compulsory
disposition of collateral (subsection (3) of
Section 9-504 and Section 9-505) and with
respect to redemption of collateral (Section
9-506) but the parties may by agreement determine the standards by which the fulfillment of
these rights and duties is to be measured if
such standards are not manifestly unreasonable:

(a) subsection (2) of Section 9-502 and subsection (2) of Section 9-504 insofar as they require accounting for surplus proceeds of collateral;

(b) subsection (3) of Section 9-504 and subsection (1) of Section 9-505 which deal with disposition of collateral;

(c) subsection (2) of Section 9-505 which deals with acceptance of collateral as discharge of obligation;

(d) Section 9-506 which deals with redemption of collateral; and

(e) subsection (1) of Section 9-507 which deals with the secured party's liability for failure to comply with this Part.

(4) If the security agreement covers both real and personal property, the secured party may proceed under this Part as to the personal property or he may proceed as to both the real and the personal property in accordance with his rights and remedies in respect of the real property in which case the provisions of this Part do not apply.

(5) When a secured party has reduced his claim to judgment the lien of any levy which may be made upon his collateral by virtue of any execution based upon the judgment shall relate back to the date of the perfection of the security interest in such collateral. A judicial sale, pursuant to such execution, is a foreclosure of the security interest by judicial procedure within the meaning of this section, and the secured party may purchase at the sale and thereafter hold the collateral free of any other requirements of this Article.

Section 9-502. Collection Rights of Secured Party.

(1) When so agreed and in any event on default the secured party is entitled to notify an account debtor or the obligor on an instrument to make payment to him whether or not the assignor was theretofore making collections on the collateral, and also to take control of any proceeds to which he is entitled under Section 9-306.

(2) A secured party who by agreement is entitled to charge back uncollected collateral or

otherwise to full or limited recourse against the debtor and who undertakes to collect from the account debtors or obligors must proceed in a commercially reasonable manner and may deduct his reasonable expenses of realization from the collections. If the security agreement secures an indebtedness, the secured party must account to the debtor for any surplus, and unless otherwise agreed, the debtor is liable for any deficiency. But, if the underlying transaction was a sale of accounts or chattel paper, the debtor is entitled to any surplus or is liable for any deficiency only if the security agreement so provides.

Section 9-503. Secured Party's Right to Take Possession After Default.

Unless otherwise agreed a secured party has on default the right to take possession of the collateral. In taking possession a secured party may proceed without judicial process if this can be done without breach of the peace or may proceed by action. If the security agreement so provides the secured party may require the debtor to assemble the collateral and make it available to the secured party at a place to be designated by the secured party which is reasonably convenient to both parties.

Without removal a secured party may render equipment unusable, and may dispose of collateral on the debtor's premises under Section 9504

Section 9-504. Secured Party's Right to Dispose of Collateral After Default; Effect of Disposition.

(1) A secured party after default may sell, or lease or otherwise dispose of any or all of the collateral in its then condition or following any commercially reasonable preparation or processing. Any sale of goods is subject to the Article on Sales (Article 2). The proceeds of disposition shall be applied in the order following to

(a) the reasonable expenses of retaking, holding, preparing for sale or lease, selling, leasing and the like and, to the extent provided for in the agreement and not prohibited by law, the reasonable attorney's fees and legal expenses incurred by the secured party;

(b) the satisfaction of indebtedness secured by the security interest under which the disposition is made;

(c) the satisfaction of indebtedness secured by any subordinate security interest in the collateral if written notification of demand therefor is received before distribution of the proceeds is completed. If requested by the secured party, the holder of a subordinate security interest must seasonably furnish reasonable proof of his interest, and unless he does so, the secured party need not comply with his demand.

(2) If the security interest secures an indebtedness, the secured party must account to the debtor for any surplus, and, unless otherwise agreed, the debtor is liable for any deficiency. But if the underlying transaction was a sale of accounts or chattel paper, the debtor is entitled to any surplus or is liable for any deficiency only if the security agreement so provides.

(3) Disposition of the collateral may be by public or private proceedings and may be made by way of one or more contracts. Sale or other disposition may be as a unit or in parcels and at any time and place and on any terms but every aspect of the disposition including the method, manner, time, place and terms must be commercially reasonable. Unless collateral is perishable or threatens to decline speedily in value or is of a type customarily sold on a recognized market, reasonable notification of the time and place of any public sale or reasonable notification of the time after which any private sale or other intended disposition is to be made shall be sent by the secured party to the debtor, if he has not signed after default a statement renouncing or modifying his right to notification of sale. In

the case of consumer goods no other notification need be sent. In other cases notification shall be sent to any other secured party from whom the secured party has received (before sending his notification to the debtor or before the debtor's renunciation of his rights) written notice of a claim of an interest in the collateral. The secured party may buy at any public sale and if the collateral is of a type customarily sold in a recognized market or is of a type which is the subject of widely distributed standard price quotations he may buy at private sale.

(4) When collateral is disposed of by a secured party after default, the disposition transfers to a purchaser for value all of the debtor's rights therein, discharges the security interest under which it is made and any security interest or lien subordinate thereto. The purchaser takes free of all such rights and interests even though the secured party fails to comply with the requirements of this Part or of any judicial proceedings

(a) in the case of a public sale, if the purchaser has no knowledge of any defects in the sale and if he does not buy in collusion with the secured party, other bidders or the person conducting the sale; or

(b) in any other case, if the purchaser acts in good faith.

(5) A person who is liable to a secured party under a guaranty, indorsement, repurchase agreement or the like and who receives a transfer of collateral from the secured party or is subrogated to his rights has thereafter the rights and duties of the secured party. Such a transfer of collateral is not a sale or disposition of the collateral under this Article.

Section 9-505. Compulsory Disposition of Collateral; Acceptance of the Collateral as Discharge of Obligation.

(1) If the debtor has paid sixty per cent of the cash price in the case of a purchase money security interest in consumer goods or sixty per cent of the loan in the case of another security interest in consumer goods, and has not signed

after default a statement renouncing or modifying his rights under this Part a secured party who has taken possession of collateral must dispose of it under Section 9-504 and if he fails to do so within ninety days after he takes possession the debtor at his option may recover in conversion or under Section 9-507(1) on secured party's liability.

(2) In any other case involving consumer goods or any other collateral a secured party in possession may, after default, propose to retain the collateral in satisfaction of the obligation. Written notice of such proposal shall be sent to the debtor if he has not signed after default a statement renouncing or modifying his rights under this subsection. In the case of consumer goods no other notice need be given. In other cases notice shall be sent to any other secured party from whom the secured party has received (before sending his notice to the debtor or before the debtor's renunciation of his rights) written notice of a claim of an interest in the collateral. If the secured party receives objection in writing from a person entitled to receive notification within twenty-one days after the notice was sent, the secured party must dispose of the collateral under Section 9-504. In the absence of such written objection the secured party may retain the collateral in satisfaction of the debtor's obligation.

Section 9-506. Debtor's Right to Redeem Collateral.

At any time before the secured party has disposed of collateral or entered into a contract for its disposition under Section 9-504 or before the obligation has been discharged under Section 9-505(2) the debtor or any other secured party may unless otherwise agreed in writing after default redeem the collateral by tendering fulfillment of all obligations secured by the collateral as well as the expenses reasonably incurred by the secured party in retaking, holding and preparing the collateral for disposition, in arranging for the sale, and to the extent provided in the agreement and not prohibited by law, his reasonable attorney's fees and legal expenses.

Section 9-507. Secured Party's Liability for Failure to Comply with this Part.

(1) If it is established that the secured party is not proceeding in accordance with the provisions of this Part disposition may be ordered or restrained on appropriate terms and conditions. If the disposition has occurred the debtor or any person entitled to notification or whose security interest has been made known to the secured party prior to the disposition has a right to recover from the secured party any loss caused by a failure to comply with the provisions of this Part. If the collateral is consumer goods, the debtor has a right to recover in any event an amount not less than the credit service charge plus ten per cent of the principal amount of the debt or the time price differential plus 10 per cent of the cash price.

(2) The fact that a better price could have been obtained by a sale at a different time or in a different method from that selected by the secured party is not of itself sufficient to establish that the sale was not made in a commercially reasonable manner. If the secured party either sells the collateral in the usual manner in any recognized market therefor or if he sells at the price current in such market at the time of his sale or if he has otherwise sold in conformity with reasonable commercial practices among dealers in the type of property sold he has sold in a commercially reasonable manner. The principles stated in the two preceding sentences with respect to sales also apply as may be appropriate to other types of disposition. A disposition which has been approved in any judicial proceeding or by any bona fide creditors' committee or representative of creditors shall conclusively be deemed to be commercially reasonable, but this sentence does not indicate that any such approval must be obtained in any case nor does it indicate that any disposition not so approved is not commercially reasonable.

Authors' note: *Articles 10 and 11 have been omitted as unnecessary for the purposes of this text.*

Appendix C

Glossary

—A—

Ab initio. From the beginning.

Abandonment. An owner's voluntary relinquishment of the possession of an item of personal property, with the owner exercising no further interest or control.

Acceleration clause. Provision in a contract that shortens the time for the performance of that contract.

Adverse possession. Gaining legal ownership of real property by openly, exclusively, and continuously occupying the land for a required amount of time.

Abstract of title. A historical record of the title to a parcel of land, including all changes in the chain of title and all liens and encumbrances recorded against the parcel.

Acceptance. An offeree's manifestation of assent to the terms of an offer made to him or her by an offeror. The acceptance is the act, the oral or written assent, or in certain instances the silence that creates contractual liabilities for both the offeror and the offeree.

Accession. The acquisition of title to something because it has been added to the property one owns. For example, a tenant plants shrubs and trees on the owner's land, and the owner thus acquires title by accession.

Accommodation party. A cosigner to a credit transaction who signs without receiving any payment or value therefore, merely to help a person get credit.

Accord. A new contract which replaces another contract.

Accord and satisfaction. Two persons agree that one of them has a right of action against the other, but they accept a substitute or different act or value as performance.

Account. Any right to payment for goods sold, leased, or delivered or for services performed. Also referred to as an account receivable.

Accretion. Adding to the boundaries of property naturally by gradual deposits of silt, sand, or other solid material. For example, a river deposits sand and silt and builds up the land on its sides.

Acknowledgment. A formally signed statement (usually before a notary public) denoting the execution of a particular legal document.

Act of God. In civil law, an unforeseen accident or casualty caused strictly by the forces of nature, such as flood, drought, and hurricane.

Action. Something that is done; conduct; behavior; in legal terms, a court proceeding for the enforcement of rights.

Ad valorem. According to value.

Adjudication. The pronouncement of a judgment or a decree; a final court determination. (In bankruptcy cases, the proclaiming that a debtor is a bankrupt.)

Affiant. A person who subscribes to or makes an affidavit.

Affidavit. A printed or written statement or declaration made under oath before an authorized public official, usually a notary public.

Agency. A relationship whereby the principal authorizes another (the agent) to act for and on behalf of the principal and to bind the principal in contract.

Air rights, airspace. Ascertainment of the ownership of the airspace (sky) above one's land.

Alien. Born in one country and residing in another country without being admitted to citizenship in that country.

Alimony. An allowance granted from the husband or wife to his or her spouse, who is living separately or legally divorced. (Laws regarding alimony differ among the states.)

Allegation. The statement or declaration made in a pleading in which a party points out the facts that the party intends to prove.

Amicus curiae. A Latin phrase which means "a friend of the court." An amicus curiae would be a person with a strong interest in the case and the legal principles involved who requests permission to file a legal brief giving his or her views to the court.

Amnesty. In international law, the act of absolution for past offensive acts ("burying the hatchet").

Answer. The defendant's response to plaintiffs petition or complaint.

Anticipatory breach. Before the performance time on a contract is due, one party announces that he or she will not perform his or her part of the contract, thus giving the non breaching party an opportunity to seek a remedy in the courts.

Apparent authority. The assumed authority or permission, not actually granted, which a principal knowingly permits an agent to possess when dealing with a third person.

Appellant. The party appealing to a higher court to overrule a decision made by a lower court.

Appellee. The party against whom an appeal is made; the respondent.

Arbitration. To settle a dispute, an appointed arbitrator (third person) comes in to help the parties make an out-of-court decision. This saves the time and expense of litigation.

Arbitrator. A third person chosen to decide a dispute between two other persons.

Articles of incorporation. A legal document submitted to a designated officer of the state for permission to commence business as a corporation. The articles of incorporation or the corporate charter state the purpose, rights, and duties of the corporation and must comply with state corporation laws.

Articles of partnership. An agreement drawn up to govern a business to be operated by a partnership. The agreement need not be filed with any state official.

Artisan's lien. A possessory claim levied on goods owned by another because of improvements made or work done thereon by the artisan. An artisan is a skilled trades person, such as a carpenter or a plumber.

Assignee. The person to whom an assignment is made.

Assignment. A transfer of rights (usually contract rights) from an assignor to an assignee.

Assignor. The person who makes an assignment.

Attachment. The seizure through legal process by proper legal authority, usually the sheriff, of nonexempt property of the defendant, pending a lawsuit for the collection of a debt owed by the defendant to a creditor.

Attestation. The act of witnessing the signing of a legal document.

Attractive nuisance. Any dangerous object or condition on real property which is inviting to young children and tempts them to trespass.

Auction with reserve. A sale whereby the goods sold may be withdrawn before the actual bid is accepted by the owner.

Auction without reserve. An auction sale wherein goods are sold to the highest bidder with no chance of withdrawal by the owner after the goods are placed on the auction block.

—B—

Bailee. A person who receives personal property under contract of bailment.

Bailment. The temporary transfer of possession of personal property without a change of ownership for a specific purpose and with the intent that possession will revert to the owner at a later date. *Example:* Owner gives his or her car to a mechanic for repairs; owner will get the car back when it has been repaired.

Bailor. A person who entrusts or bails personal property to another under a bailment arrangement.

Bankrupt. An insolvent person, one who has been declared by the court to have more debts than assets.

Bankruptcy. When a person is bankrupt, the court proceeds to have that person's nonexempt assets distributed to his or her creditors and releases him or her from further payment of past debts.

Bearer. A person in possession of a security, instrument, or document of title payable to the bearer or indorsed in blank.

Beneficiary. A person receiving proceeds from a will, insurance policy, trust, or third-party beneficiary contract.

Bilateral contract. A contract formed by the mutual exchange of promises between an offeror and an offeree.

Bilateral mistake. Both parties to a contract are in error as to the terms of the contract or the performance expected.

Bill of exchange. A written command ordering the addressee to pay on demand or at a predetermined time, a certain sum of money to the holder of the bill.

Bill of lading. A formal document issued by a carrier of goods to a shipper of goods. This document identifies the goods and states the terms of the shipping agreement.

Bill of sale. A written statement by which a seller acknowledges transfer of personal property to another.

Blue-sky laws. State regulatory and supervisory laws governing investment companies to avoid fraudulent sales to investors in get-rich-quick schemes.

Board of directors. A specific number of persons elected by a corporation's stockholders to manage and govern the corporation on their behalf.

Bona fide. With good faith or in good faith.

Bond. With regard to corporate financing, a legal instrument which is evidence of a corporation's debt to the bondholder. The instrument obligates the corporation to pay the bondholder a fixed rate of interest on the principal amount and to pay the principal to the bondholder at a fixed maturity date.

Broker. In real property law, a person who acts as an agent and representative of others to negotiate the purchase and sale of real estate.

Bulk transfer. A sale or transfer of all or the major portion of the total inventory of materials, supplies, or merchandise or other inventory not in the ordinary course of the transferor's business.

—C—

C&F. Cost plus freight.

Cause of action. The legal grounds needed to successfully pursue a lawsuit in court.

Caveat emptor. A Latin phrase which means "let the buyer beware."

Certiorari. A Latin term which means "to be informed of." It is a writ or certification by which an appellate court orders a review of a case from a lower court. The lower court must then send a certified record of the case to the appellate court.

Chancellor. The name given in some states to the presiding judge of a court of chancery (also called a court of equity).

Chancery court. A court of equity.

Charter. A grant or certification from a state to a corporation granting the corporation the right to operate its business. In maritime law, the leasing or hiring of a vessel.

Chattel. A term used to describe tangible and movable personal property.

Chattel mortgage. A mortgage showing that another person besides the title holder has an interest (lien) on the personal property.

Chattel paper. A writing which shows that there is both a monetary obligation and a security interest in specific goods.

Check. A signed document by which a depositor to a bank orders payment of a certain sum of money to a named payee.

Chose in action. A right to personal things of which the owner does not have possession but the owner does have a right of action for their possession.

CIF. Cost, insurance, and freight.

COD. Cash on delivery.

Collateral. Something of value, either real or personal property, which a creditor can convert into cash to pay off a debt if the debtor fails to pay the debt. For example, you borrow money from a bank, and the bank has you pledge your household furniture as collateral.

Common carrier. A carrier which holds itself out as being for hire to the general public for the transportation of goods and passengers for compensation.

Common law. Written or unwritten laws which have evolved through custom and usage (from English common law) without written legislation.

Common stock. A class of corporate stock which is usually the voting stock in a corporation. Common stockholders have a right to dividends and assets upon dissolution second only to that of preferred stockholders, if any.

Composition agreement. An agreement whereby an insolvent debtor pays each of the creditors a portion of what he or she owes them in return for a release from them for the whole debt.

Condition. A qualifying or limiting provision or clause in a contract which must be taken into consideration by all of the parties involved.

Conditional sales contract. A contract which covers the sale of goods or real estate wherein the seller retains title until the buyer makes the payment in full; however, the buyer has possession and use while he or she makes the payments.

Consignment. The transfer of personal property from one person to another for the purpose of transportation or sale. The owner retains ownership of the property.

Consumer goods. Products primarily purchased for home or private and family use.

Consumer Product Safety Act. This act established the Consumer Product Safety Commission, which oversees the safety of consumer-oriented products.

Contract carrier. A private carrier which transports goods for an individual but not for the general public.

Conveyance. A written instrument which transfers an interest in real property, ordinarily by the execution and delivery of a deed. Personal property can also be conveyed, and this is ordinarily done by a bill of sale.

Corporate express powers. Powers specifically set out in the corporation's articles of incorporation and in statutes.

Corporate implied powers. Those powers reasonable and necessary to carry out the corporation's express powers.

Corporation. A legal entity created by authority of statutory law upon application to a proper state authority. This legal entity is an artificial person with the right to sue or be sued in its own name and to purchase, own, and sell property, real and personal, tangible and intangible.

Counterclaim. In a civil suit, the claim the defendant makes in opposition to the plaintiffs claim.

Counteroffer. A counterproposal different from an offer which an offeree makes in response to the offer. In making a counteroffer, the offeree rejects the previous offer

Course of dealing. When two parties have previously been involved in a contract matter, their past performance may be used as a basis for interpreting ambiguities, if any, in the present contract.

Covenant. A contractual promise contained in a deed, mortgage, lease, or contract.

Creditor. A person to whom money or performance is owed.

—D—

D/b/a. Doing business as.

Damages. Monetary harm or monetary loss caused by wrongdoing that the injured person may recover in court.

De facto. A Latin phrase which means "in fact." A de facto corporation has not "in fact" complied with the laws of a state, and therefore its existence can be challenged by the state.

De jure corporation. A de jure corporation is one which has been rightfully formed in full compliance with the laws of a state.

De novo. (Latin) Starting anew.

Debtor. One who owes payment or performance.

Deceit. Fraudulent misrepresentation of facts intended to mislead or trick another, which in turn causes financial loss or harm.

Deed. A legal instrument which transfers property ownership.

Defamation. The act of intentionally injuring the character or reputation of another person.

Default. The failure to perform a legal obligation or duty.

Defendant. The person who is being sued in a legal action.

Deficiency judgment. A personal judgment against a debtor in default, where the value of the secured property was not equal to the amount of the indebtedness.

Demurrer. This is a pleading which disputes the legal sufficiency of the other party's pleading. It is also referred to as a motion to dismiss for the failure to state a legal cause of action.

Deposition. Testimony which is taken under oath and subject to cross-examination in order to discover what the witness is going to say and to ensure the preservation of the witness's testimony should the witness die or disappear or forget before the trial.

Derivative suit. An action filed by one or more stockholders of a corporation under the corporation name to enforce a corporate cause of action.

Devise. To give a gift of property by will.

Directed verdict. A verdict that the jury returns as directed by the judge.

Discharge. The termination of a contractual obligation regarding the payment of money or the performance of an act.

Disclaimer. A repudiation or denial of a claim or obligation.

Dissolution. The process by which a corporation or partnership terminates its existence.

Dividend. The portion of corporate profits which is distributed periodically to stockholders.

Document of title. A warehouse receipt, a bill of lading, or any other paper which is evidence of the holder's right to have the goods it covers.

Domestic corporation. A corporation doing business in the state where its incorporation took place.

Donee. A person who receives a gift.

Donor. A person who gives a gift.

Draft. A legal instrument wherein one person orders another person to pay a third party a sum of money.

Duress. Coercion, threat, or force which causes a person to do something he or she would not have done otherwise.

—E—

Earnest money. Money advanced on a contract by a buyer to bind a seller to his or her obligations. This money is given as an indication of good faith by the buyer and usually will be forfeited if the buyer does not perform.

Easement. The right to use the land of another for a special purpose (such as an easement to lay power lines) .

Emancipation. Setting free; release. This term is used with reference to the release of a child from the care and custody of his or her parents before the child reaches the age of majority.

Eminent domain. The government's right to take over private property for public use with just compensation.

Equity. This was a court system separate from the common-law system, originating in England. Fairness and justice in the particular case were the concern of the law and the court.

Estoppel. This is a rule of law which bars, prevents, and precludes a party from alleging or denying certain facts because of a previous allegation or denial or because of his or her previous conduct or admission.

Eviction. The legal process of removing a tenant from a landlord's property.

Ex contractu. A Latin phrase which means a right arising out of a contract.

Ex delicto. A Latin phrase which refers to a right arising out of a tort.

Ex post facto law. A law passed to punish wrongdoers, which is alleged to apply to acts committed before its passage. Such laws are unconstitutional. Criminal law may only apply to acts committed after their passage.

Express authority. The authority which a principal gives to an agent either in writing or orally.

—F—

Factor. A person or a legal entity that is employed as an agent to sell goods for a principal. Usually the factor is given possession of the goods for sale and sells them in his or her own name. The factor then receives a commission on the sale.

Fair market value. The price that a willing buyer is willing to pay and that a willing seller will accept for real or personal property.

FAS. An abbreviation of the phrase "free alongside" (a boat).

Fee simple. Absolute ownership of a specific tract of real estate. This gives the owner the unconditional power to dispose of the property during his or her lifetime and to pass the absolute ownership on to his or her heirs at death.

Felony. A statutory criminal offense which is more serious than a misdemeanor. Felonies are punishable by fine or imprisonment or both, and in some situations, by death.

Fiduciary. A person who handles another person's money or property in a capacity that involves a confidence or trust. Examples of fiduciaries are executors or guardians of the estates of minors or deceased persons.

Fixture. An article of personal property which has been affixed to real property with the intent that it become a permanent part of the real property.

FOB. An abbreviation of the phrase "free on board." This phrase means that the seller or consignor of goods will place them on board a carrier such as a train or truck at a designated place with instructions to ship them through to a designated destination. The expense of the shipping and insurance for the trip are to be paid by the buyer or consignee, and thus the shipping and insurance are free to the seller or consignor.

Foreclosure. The legal process used to enforce the payment of a debt secured by a mortgage whereby the secured property is sold to satisfy the debt.

Foreign corporation. A corporation doing business in a state other than the state in which it was incorporated. *Foreign* does not mean from outside the country, only from outside the particular state.

Forensic medicine. Medical jurisprudence; the science of applying medical knowledge to the law.

Forgery. Falsely making or materially altering with criminal intent a legal document such as a check, power of attorney, or deed.

Franchise. In the public sector, a franchise is a right to operate a certain essential business which a city, county, state, or national authority grants to a private entity. For example, a city grants a bus company a franchise to be the sole bus company that can operate within the city, or it grants an electric company a franchise to be the exclusive supplier of electricity to the city. In the private sector, a franchise is a means by which one person can grant another person the right to use his or her name and business expertise on a contract basis. Examples include the various fast-food franchises.

Fraud. An intentional concealment or misrepresentation of a material fact with the intent to deceive another person, which concealment or misrepresentation causes damage to the deceived person. Such deceived persons may then sue for their damages, provided they can show that they justifiably relied upon such misrepresentation or concealment and that such reliance caused the damage.

Fungible goods. Goods that if mixed cannot be individually identified, one unit of which is equivalent to any other unit. For example, the milk from five dairy farms is pumped into a storage tank. Each farmer owns the number of gallons taken from him or her but cannot identify the specific milk that he or she contributed once it is mixed with the rest.

Future advances clause. A clause found in security agreements which permits the collateral of the debtor, if sufficiently valuable, to be used to secure future loans.

—G—

Garnishment. A legal proceeding whereby a creditor can secure the payment of a judgment against a debtor by securing a court order which requires an employer or other person having funds belonging to the debtor to pay such funds directly to the creditor.

Gift causa mortis. (Latin) A gift which is given in contemplation of death, usually with the understanding that the gift will be returned if the donor survives.

Gift inter vivos. (Latin) An irrevocable gift which is given during the donor's lifetime.

Grantee. The person to whom a conveyance of real property is made.

Grantor. The person by whom a conveyance of real property is made.

Guaranty. A promise by one person to pay some or all of the debts of another person or to answer for the performance of some act or acts by another person.

—H—

Holder in due course. As defined by the Uniform Commercial Code, a holder who takes the instrument for value, in good faith and without notice that it is overdue or has been dishonored or of any defense against or any claim to it.

—I—

Illusory. Like an illusion; something that seems to be so but really isn't so. An illusory promise appears to be a binding promise but actually promises nothing, as the choice of performance or nonperformance is really left up to the promiser.

Independent contractor. A person who contracts to do a specific piece of work under his own direction and control for an employer.

Indictment. A formal accusation of a crime by a grand jury.

Indorsement. The signing of one's name on a negotiable instrument such as a check or draft for the purpose of passing title to the instrument to another person. Usually the endorsement is on the back of the instrument.

Infant. A person who has not reached the legal age of majority.

Injunction. An order of a court of equity that tells a person to do or refrain from doing some act or acts.

In pari delicto. Equally at fault, equally guilty.

In re. A Latin phrase which means "in the matter of." The phrase precedes the name of the party involved in estate and guardian's matters and other non adversary judicial proceedings. For example: In re Estate of John Jones, Deceased.

In rem. A Latin phrase which means "against the thing."

Insolvency. A party's inability to pay his debts as they come due.

Inter alia. A Latin phrase which means "among other things."

Ipso facto. A Latin phrase which means "by the fact itself."

—J—

Joint tenancy. An estate owned by two or more persons recognizing the right of survivorship.

Judgment. The final determination of a court in an action or proceeding instituted in that court.

Judgment n.o.v. Judgment notwithstanding the verdict.

Jurisdiction. The power of a specific court to hear and decide certain cases.

—L—

Lease. A contract whereby an owner of real property, the landlord, agrees to give possession to the tenant, the person requesting possession, for a specific period of time in return for the payment of money or service.

Legacy. A gift made by will.

Legal entity. Also referred to as an artificial person. Legal entities include corporations, which exist by legal creation and have the right to contract and the right to own and dispose of property as well as other rights and duties of natural persons.

Levy. To seize, assess, or collect property or money.

Libel. Written or visual defamation intentionally made to injure the reputation of another.

License. Formal personal authorization to perform some act.

Lien. A claim against property. A lien can be agreed upon under contract, or it can be imposed by law. A carpenter who works on your home will have a right to a lien on your home if you do not pay the reasonable cost of his or her services.

Life estate. An interest in property only for the duration of someone's life, not transferable to an heir.

Liquidated damages. The amount of money which, according to the contract, is to be forfeited or paid as a remedy for breach of the contract.

Long arm statute. A state enactment allowing service of process on out-of-state residents who own property in the state, had an automobile accident in the state, or do business in the state.

—M—

Malpractice. Failure of a professional person such as an accountant, physician, or lawyer, to provide reasonably competent services.

Mandamus. A Latin term which means "we command." A mandamus is an order commanding that some specific act be done which a court can issue to an inferior court, a person, or a corporation.

Mechanic's lien. A workman's claim by law against property (including the land upon which a building rests) until services and materials provided are paid for.

Mens rea. Guilty mind or wrongful intent.

Minor. A person who has not yet reached the age of majority. The common-law age of majority was 21. Most states now set the age of majority for contracts at 18 but still make 21 the age of majority with regard to the drinking of intoxicating beverages.

Misdemeanors. Minor criminal offenses that usually encompass all crimes not classified as felonies or treason.

Mortgage. An interest in property, given to another as security for payment of a debt.

—N—

Necessaries. This term refers to the needs of minors, such as food, reasonable clothing, reasonable lodging, and medical attention. The reasonableness of such items as food, clothing, and lodging depends on the minor's earning level and the mode of living of the minor's parents.

Negligence. The failure to exercise reasonable care, thereby causing harm to another or to property.

No-par stock. Corporate stock to which no "par" value is assigned. Before stock is issued, the directors fix a sale price per share, but that price is not stated on the stock certificate.

Nominal damages. An award given to a party whose rights have been violated but where no actual loss or damages have occurred.

Non obstante veredicto. A Latin phrase which means "notwithstanding the verdict." It is used to indicate that the court has entered a judgment contrary to the verdict of the jury. In essence, the judge has vetoed the jury's verdict.

Notary public. An appointed public officer who has the authority to administer oaths; to attest to and certify certain legal documents; and to take and certify acknowledgments of deeds, mortgages, and other such legal documents. A notary public is limited in jurisdiction to the state where he or she is appointed and in some instances to the county where he or she resides.

Novation. The substitution of a new obligation for a previous one with the understanding that the previous obligation has been discharged and terminated.

Nuisance. Any activity or use of land which is offensive, obstructs use of property, or is harmful to others.

—O—

Obiter dictum. Remarks by the court said in passing that are unrelated to the decision of that case.

Obligee. A person to whom an obligor owes an obligation.

Obligor. A person who owes an obligation to an obligee.

Offer. A proposal to make a contract. It is made orally, in writing, or by other conduct, and it must contain the terms legally necessary to create a contract. Acceptance of the proposal creates the contract.

Offeree. A person to whom an offer is made.

Offeror. person who makes an offer.

Option contract. A contract to hold open an offer to buy or sell something for a certain price within a specified period of time.

Ordinances. The term used to identify the legislative enactments of a city or municipality.

—P—

Par stock. Shares of corporate stock that have been assigned a fixed "par value" by the articles of incorporation. The par value of one share is printed on each stock certificate.

Pari delicto. A Latin term which means "the parties are equally at fault."

Patent. A title of land given to an individual by the government, or an exclusive right given to an inventor to manufacture and sell an invention for a certain period of time.

Pawn. To pledge tangible personal property as a guarantee for payment of a debt within a certain period of time or the property will be sold.

Pecuniary. Relating to money or financial matters.

Penal damages. A monetary penalty agreed upon in a contractual clause not as compensation for actual losses but as punishment for possible nonperformance or late performance. If in fact the agreed damage amount is a penalty and not a reasonable compensation for loss, the court will not enforce the clause.

Per curiam. A Latin term which means "by the court." The entire court wrote the opinion, not just one justice.

Per se. A Latin term which means "in itself; taken alone; unconnected with other matters."

Plaintiff. A person who files a lawsuit in court.

Pledge. Pawning or giving up the possession of an item of personal property as security for a loan. You borrow $100 from the pawnshop and leave your gold pocket watch as security.

Possession. Occupancy or control of personal property, land, or buildings.

Power of attorney. A writing whereby one person appoints and authorizes another person to act on his or her behalf. This power can be limited or unlimited and can be for a specified time or for life.

Preferred stock. A class of corporate stock, usually nonvoting stock, that has rights to dividends superior to those of common stock and in case of dissolution also has rights to the assets of the corporation superior to those of common stock.

Prima facie. A Latin phrase which means "on the face of it." For example, a valid driver's license in your possession is prima facie evidence that you have a valid right to drive; however, this evidence could be disproved by evidence that there was a court judgment to pick up and suspend your license which had not yet been served upon you.

Principal. A person who has given an agent authority to do some act or acts for him or her.

Privity. A close mutual relationship, such as that between parties to a contract.

Pro rata. A Latin phrase which means "proportionately." In other words, to share equally.

Pro tem. A Latin phrase which means "temporarily." For example, a judge pro tem might be a judge who is sitting in temporarily for the regular judge while the regular judge is on vacation.

Probate. The term describing the legal procedure followed in the administration of the estate of deceased persons and persons under guardianship.

Promise. A person to whom a contractual promise
is made.

Promisor. A person who makes a contractual promise.

Promissory estoppel. A rule of law which is often called justifiable reliance. When the promisor makes a promise and the promise justifiably relies on that promise to his or her detriment, the promisor is estopped from denying liability on the promise.

Promoters. Person or persons who form and organize a corporation.

Proximate cause. The act or omission to act which, in a natural and continuous sequence, unbroken by an intervening cause, produces damage or injury.

Proxy. A document which authorizes another to vote for you. Stockholders who will be absent from stockholders' meetings often give their proxy to persons who will attend the meetings.

Punitive damages. Damages awarded against a person to punish him or her. These damages are in addition to compensatory damages, which pay the plaintiff for his or her actual losses. Punitive damages are often also referred to as exemplary damages because they are awarded not only to punish but to set an example for similar wrongdoers.

—Q—

Qualified acceptance. A conditional acceptance that modifies the terms of an offer; it is usually a counteroffer.

Quantum meruit. "As much as he deserved." When seeking compensation under common law for services rendered, this term will be used; it also can be interpreted as meaning the reasonable value of the services rendered.

Quasi contract. The word quasi means resembling or somewhat like; thus a quasi contract is not a true contract. It resembles a contract but does not possess all the elements of a legally binding contract. The law does not allow unjust enrichment, and it provides a restitutory remedy (quasi contract) that allows the person with a claim for damages to recover the reasonable value of the goods or services which he or she provided to the other party. Quasi contract is often referred to as a contract implied in law.

Quit claim deed. A deed which is intended to pass any title or interest which the grantor has in a certain tract of real estate, but does not warrant, profess, or guarantee that the grantor had any title or interest in the real estate or that his or her title was free and clear of liens.

Quo warranto. A Latin phrase which means "by what authority." It is a legal action which a government may commence to remove a person from a public office or to dissolve a corporation.

Quorum. Both incorporated and unincorporated organizations have a governing body, and a quorum is the minimum number of persons in the governing body that have to be present at a meeting to lawfully conduct the business of an organization. The usual requirement for a quorum is a majority of the persons who are eligible to vote, but a lesser number may be agreed upon in the organization's charter or bylaws.

—R—

Ratification. The present confirmation of a previous promise or act. In the case of a former minor, ratification is the confirmation by that person once he or she has reached the age of majority of the intention to be bound by a contract which he or she had entered into as a minor. In agency law, ratification is the confirmation by a principal of a promise or act made by his or her agent which was unauthorized at the time it was made. The ratification legalizes the previously unauthorized promise or act and creates a binding contract.

Receiver. A person or a bank or other fiduciary institution appointed by the court to receive and preserve property or funds in litigation. The receiver must have no interest in the litigation and will simply hold and manage the property or funds until directed to hand them over to whomever the court awards them.

Redemption. The repurchasing or buying back of property legally taken from a person and sold. In a mortgage foreclosure, a person's land is taken and sold by the sheriff to secure money to pay the person's debt. After the sale the owner has a limited time during which he or she can redeem the property.

Referee. In bankruptcy, this is the person who is in charge of the administration of the bankrupt's estate until the bankrupt has been discharged and the estate has been distributed among the bankrupt's creditors.

Reformation. The rewriting of a contract by the court to correct ambiguities and errors so that the contract reflects the agreement of the parties.

Release. The voluntary giving up of a claim for money or property from another person, usually for consideration.

Remedy. Action taken to enforce a right or to compensate a violation of rights.

Replevin. A legal action whereby the owner of goods can legally recover them from someone who is holding them unlawfully.

Res. A Latin word which means "the thing."

Res ipsa loquitur. A Latin phrase which means "the thing speaks for itself." For example, an airplane may explode in midair. In tort law, the heirs of the deceased passengers would normally have the burden of proving negligence on the defendant. However, it is obvious that planes do not explode unless there was negligence on someone's part. Thus the plaintiff sues and pleads res ipsa loquitur, and the defendants must prove that they were not negligent.

Res judicata. A Latin phrase which means "the thing is settled"; that is, the case is finished.

Respondeat superior. A Latin phrase which means "let the master answer." In other words, let the employer be liable for the acts of his or her employees for damages that the employees have caused to others.

Riparian. A term which refers to the bank of a river. A riparian owner is a person who owns land on the bank of a river.

—S—

Scienter. The knowledge of a person making a representation that the representation he or she is making is false. In a tort action for deceit, scienter must be proved.

Security agreement. An agreement which gives a security interest in certain property to a creditor. Such an agreement must be in writing to be enforced.

Security interest. An interest in a specific item of personal property which a creditor retains to secure the payment of a debt.

Seal. Under common law, an identification mark impressed in wax. Today the letters "l.s." or the word "seal" itself are used and accepted.

Setoff. A claim which a defendant has against a plaintiff; similar to a counterclaim. For example, if the plaintiff sued the defendant for $100 but owed the defendant $50, the plaintiff's $50 debt to the defendant would be a set off and the balance owed by the defendant to the plaintiff would be only $50.

Severable contract. A contract divisible into separate parts; a default of one section does not invalidate the whole contract.

Shareholder. A person who owns a portion of the capital stock of a corporation. The shareholder's interest in the corporation is evidenced by a stock certificate.

Shop right. The employer's right to use, without paying royalties, any invention which an employee developed while, using the employer's facilities or any invention which the employee conceived in the course of the employee's employment with the employer. An employee who is hired to do research and development agrees by contract that the employer will own the employee's inventions and discoveries as that is what such an employee would be getting paid for.

Situs. The location of a thing. All tangible property has a situs.

Slander. Defamatory statements orally made by one person which injure the reputation of another person.

Specific performance. A remedy by which a court of equity orders a person to perform in accordance with the terms of his or her contract.

Stare decisis. A Latin phrase which means "to abide by." This phrase is also defined as "let the decision stand." Once a case has set a precedent, courts will follow that precedent wherever it is feasible to do so. However, law must change as technology and mores change; thus no precedent is cast in concrete.

Status quo. A Latin phrase which means "the state of things at any given time."

Statute of limitations. A statute which sets limits to the time in which a lawsuit may be filed in certain causes of action. For example, a tort lawsuit must be filed within two years from the day the wrongful act was committed, and if it was not filed by that time, the action is forever barred.

Subpoena. A legal process from a court ordering a witness to appear and testify or ordering a witness to produce certain documents for the court's inspection.

Subrogation. The act of substituting one person for another to prosecute a lawful claim. In insurance, the insurance company pays the collision loss to your automobile, and you give the company subrogation rights to sue and collect from the person who negligently damaged your automobile.

Substantive law. The law that is concerned with the rights and duties of the parties, as contrasted with procedural law, which is concerned with the procedure to be followed in the litigation.

Sui generis. One of a kind, unique.

Summons. A writ to appear in court in defense of a civil action.

Surety. A person who binds himself or herself with another person, called the principal, for the payment of money or the performance of some obligation. However, the principal is already bound to that payment or obligation and the surety serves as a backup person who is available in case the principal does not pay or perform properly.

—T—

Tangible property. Property which can be touched a tract of land, a chair, a table, etc. Intangible property, on the other hand, is property which cannot be touched, such as the ownership of a patent right or of corporate stock and other such ownerships of rights, not things.

Tenancy. The leasing or renting of land or property, giving certain ownership rights to the tenant.

Tender. An offer to settle or perform an obligation in contract. If a party offers to perform his or her obligation under a contract, such an offer is called a tender. If the other party unjustifiably refuses to accept the performance offered, that party would be guilty of breach of contract.

Testimony. Witnesses' answers given under oath as evidence.

Third-party beneficiary. A person who was not a party to a contract but a party to whom the contracting parties intended benefits to be given.

Torrens system. A system of land registration which was developed by Sir Robert Torrens in Australia in 1858. This system has been adopted in some jurisdictions in the United States.

Tort. A civil wrong for which civil damages may be awarded, as contrasted with a criminal wrong for which punishment may be given. A wrongful act may be both a tort and a crime.

Trade fixtures. Personal property which has been attached to land or a building and is necessary for conducting a trade.

Trade name. A name under which a particular business operates.

Trademark. A distinctive mark or emblem which a manufacturer prints on or affixes to goods so that consumers can identify the manufacturer's goods in the marketplace.

Trespass. Although most commonly used to refer to a person's unauthorized entry onto another person's real property, in its broadest sense this term refers to any intentional injury or damage caused by force to either the person or the property of another.

Trust. A transfer of property or money to one party to be held for the benefit of another.

—U—

Ultra vires. A Latin phrase which means "beyond the powers of," or beyond the scope of authority. An ultra vires act is an act which is not within the powers of the person who does it.

Unconscionability. Conduct by a party to a contract which cannot be shown to be fraud and is not duress but is unjust and unfair and because of which the court will not enforce performance of the contract.

Undue influence. A condition which results from the use of unfair persuasion by one person in order to overcome the free will of another person and to influence that person to act in the manner in which he or she is directed to act.

Usury. The charging of an unlawful rate of interest.

—V—

Valid. Legally sufficient and binding.

Vest. To take effect. To vest a right is to give a right to a present or future benefit. The term *vest* is used in pension law. One's rights in a pension plan will be vested after certain minimum requirements have been met.

Verdict. A jury's decision given to the court.

Void. No legal effect; not binding. If an agreement is void, it is legally unenforceable.

Voidable. A term which means that a contract is not void but can be avoided by one or both of the parties at their will. A contract between a minor and an adult is voidable by the minor only; a contract between two minors can be avoided by either minor.

—W—

Waiver. The voluntary relinquishment by a person of a right which he or she has.

Warehouse receipt. A written acknowledgment of the receipt of goods by a person engaged in the business of storing goods for hire.

Warranty. In the sale of goods, a promise or guarantee by the seller that goods have certain qualities or that the seller has title to the goods. A warranty may be offered by the seller as a contractual term, or a warranty not stated in the contract may be imposed by law. The warranties imposed by law are the warranty of merchantability and the warranty of fitness for purpose. The warranty of merchantability warrants that the goods are of at least fair or average quality. The warranty of fitness for purpose warrants that the goods are fit for the particular purpose of the buyer.

Watered stock. Par value stock which is issued by a corporation as fully paid-up stock when in fact the whole amount of the par value has not been paid in.

Writ. A written document issued by a court, directed to a sheriff or some other officer of the law, and ordering that person to carry out a command of the court. For example, a writ of attachment orders a sheriff to attach certain property and hold it for disposition by the court.

—Z—

Zoning. The process of separating the areas of a city or county by confining them to particular uses, such as residential use, industrial use, or business use.

Appendix D
Index of Cases

—T—

—U—

—V—

—W—

—XYZ—

Index

—B—

—C—

—E—

—F—

—N—

—O—

—P—

—Q—

—R—

—V—

—W—

—XYZ—